Literature Criticism from 1400 to 1800

Guide to Gale Literary Criticism Series

When you need to review criticism of literary works, these are the Gale series to use:

If the author's death date is:	You should turn to:

After Dec. 31, 1959 (or author is still living)

Contemporary Literary Criticism

for example: Jorge Luis Borges, Anthony Burgess, William Faulkner, Mary Gordon, Ernest Hemingway, Iris Murdoch

1900 through 1959

Twentieth-Century Literary Criticism

for example: Willa Cather, F. Scott Fitzgerald, Henry James, Mark Twain, Virginia Woolf

1800 through 1899

Nineteenth-Century Literature Criticism

for example: Fedor Dostoevski, Nathaniel Hawthorne, George Sand, William Wordsworth

1400 through 1799

Literature Criticism From 1400 to 1800 (excluding Shakespeare)

for example: Anne Bradstreet, Daniel Defoe, Alexander Pope, Francois Rabelais, Jonathan Swift, Phillis Wheatley

Shakespearean Criticism

Shakespeare's plays and poetry

Antiquity through 1399

Classical and Medieval Literature Criticism

for example: Dante, Homer, Plato, Sophocles, Vergil, the Beowulf Poet

---

Gale also publishes related criticism series:

Children's Literature Review

This series covers authors of all eras who have written for the preschool through high school audience.

Short Story Criticism

This series covers the major short fiction writers of all nationalities and periods of literary history.

ISSN 0740-2880

Volume 14

Literature Criticism from 1400 to 1800

Excerpts from Criticism of the Works
of Fifteenth-, Sixteenth-, Seventeenth-, and
Eighteenth-Century Novelists, Poets, Playwrights,
Philosophers, and Other Creative Writers,
from the First Published Critical Appraisals
to Current Evaluations

James P. Draper
James E. Person, Jr.
Editors

 **Gale Research Inc.** · *DETROIT* · *NEW YORK* · *LONDON*

STAFF

James P. Draper, James E. Person, Jr., *Editors*

Shannon J. Young, *Associate Editor*

John P. Daniel, Allyson J. Wylie, *Assistant Editors*

Jeanne A. Gough, *Permissions and Production Manager*

Linda M. Pugliese, *Production Supervisor*
Suzanne Powers, Maureen A. Puhl, Jennifer VanSickle, *Editorial Associates*
Donna Craft, Lorna Mabunda, James G. Wittenbach, *Editorial Assistants*

Victoria B. Cariappa, *Research Manager*
H. Nelson Fields, Judy L. Gale, Maureen Richards, *Editorial Associates*
Paula Cutcher, Alan Heblad, Jill M. Ohorodnik, *Editorial Assistants*

Sandra C. Davis, *Text Permissions Supervisor*
Josephine M. Keene, Denise Singleton, Kimberly F. Smilay, *Permissions Associates*
Maria L. Franklin, Michele M. Lonoconus, Camille P. Robinson,
Shalice Shah, Rebecca A. Stanko, *Permissions Assistants*

Patricia A. Seefelt, *Permissions Supervisor (Pictures)*
Margaret A. Chamberlain, *Permissions Associate*
Pamela A. Hayes, Lillian Quickley, *Permissions Assistants*

Mary Beth Trimper, *Production Manager*
Shanna G. Philpott, *External Production Assistant*

Arthur Chartow, *Art Director*
C. J. Jonik, *Keyliner*

Laura Bryant, *Production Supervisor*
Louise Gagné, *Internal Production Associate*
Yolanda Y. Latham, *Internal Production Assistant*

The paper used in this publication meets the minimum requirements
of American National Standard for Information Sciences—Permanence
Paper for Printed Library Materials, ANSI Z39.48-1984. ∞™

Copyright © 1991
Gale Research Inc.
835 Penobscot Bldg.
Detroit, MI 48226-4094

Library of Congress Catalog Card Number 84-643570
ISBN 0-8103-6113-2
ISSN 0740-2880

Printed in the United States of America

Published simultaneously in the United Kingdom
by Gale Research International
(An affiliated company of Gale Research Inc.)

10 9 8 7 6 5 4 3

Contents

Preface   vii

Acknowledgments   xi

Authors to Appear in Future Volumes   xv

Preface

*L*iterature Criticism from 1400 to 1800 (LC) presents criticism of world authors of the fifteenth through eighteenth centuries. The literature of this period reflects a turbulent time of radical change that saw the rise of drama equal in stature to that of classical Greece, the birth of the novel and personal essay forms, the emergence of newspapers and periodicals, and major achievements in poetry and philosophy. Much of modern literature reflects the influence of these centuries. Thus the literature treated in *LC* provides insight into the universal nature of human experience, as well as into the life and thought of the past.

Scope of the Series

LC is designed to serve as an introduction to authors of the fifteenth through eighteenth centuries and to the most significant interpretations of these authors' works. The great poets, dramatists, novelists, essayists, and philosophers of this period are considered classics in every secondary school and college or university curriculum. Because criticism of this literature spans nearly six hundred years, an overwhelming amount of critical material confronts the student. *LC* therefore organizes and reprints the most noteworthy published criticism of authors of these centuries. Readers should note that there is a separate Gale reference series devoted to Shakespearean studies. For though belonging properly to the period covered in *LC,* William Shakespeare has inspired such a tremendous and ever-growing corpus of secondary material that the editors have deemed it best to give his works extensive coverage in a separate series, *Shakespearean Criticism.*

Each author entry in *LC* attempts to present a historical survey of critical response to the author's works. Early criticism is offered to indicate initial responses, later selections document any rise or decline in literary reputations, and retrospective analyses provide students with modern views. The size of each author entry is intended to reflect the author's critical reception in English or foreign criticism in translation. Articles and books that have not been translated into English are therefore excluded. Every attempt has been made to identify and include the seminal essays on each author's work and to include recent commentary providing modern perspectives.

The need for *LC* among students and teachers of literature was suggested by the proven usefulness of Gale's *Contemporary Literary Criticism (CLC), Twentieth-Century Literary Criticism (TCLC),* and *Nineteenth-Century Literature Criticism (NCLC),* which excerpt criticism of works by nineteenth- and twentieth- century authors. Because of the different time periods covered, there is no duplication of authors or critical material in any of these literary criticism series. An author may appear more than once in the series because of the great quantity of critical material available and because of the aesthetic demands of the series's *thematic organization.*

Thematic Approach

Beginning with Volume 12, roughly half the authors in each volume of *LC* are organized in a thematic scheme. Such themes include literary movements, literary reaction to political and historical events, significant eras in literary history, and the literature of cultures often overlooked by English-speaking readers. The present volume, for example, focuses upon the literary accomplishments and philosophical significance of writers of the French Enlightenment. Future volumes of *LC* will devote substantial space to authors of the Age of Samuel Johnson, the English Metaphysical poets, and the Spanish Golden Age, among many others. The rest of each volume will be devoted to criticism of the works of authors not aligned with the selected thematic authors and chosen from a variety of nationalities.

Organization of the Book

Each entry consists of the following elements: author or thematic heading, introduction, list of principal works (in author entries only), annotated works of criticism (each followed by a bibliographical citation), and a bibliography of further reading. Also, most author entries contain author portraits and other illustrations.

- The **author heading** consists of the author's full name, followed by birth and death dates. If an author wrote consistently under a pseudonym, the pseudonym is used in the author heading, with the real name given in parentheses on the first line of the biographical and critical introduction. Also located here are any name variations under which an author wrote, including transliterated forms for authors whose native languages use nonroman alphabets. Uncertain birth or death dates are indicated by question marks. The **thematic heading** simply states the subject of the entry.

- The **biographical and critical introduction** contains background information designed to introduce the reader to an author and to critical discussion of his or her work. Parenthetical material following many of the introductions provides references to biographical and critical reference series published by Gale in which additional material about the author may be found. The **thematic introduction** briefly defines the subject of the entry and provides social and historical background important to understanding the criticism.

- Most *LC* author entries include **portraits** of the author. Many entries also contain illustrations of materials pertinent to an author's career, including author holographs, title pages, letters, or representations of important people, places, and events in an author's life.

- The **list of principal works** is chronological by date of first book publication and identifies the genre of each work. In the case of foreign authors whose works have been translated into English, the title and date of the first English-language edition are given in brackets beneath the foreign-language listing. Unless otherwise indicated, dramas are dated by first performance, not first publication.

- **Criticism** is arranged chronologically in each author entry to provide a useful perspective on changes in critical evaluation over the years. For the purpose of easy identification, the critic's name and the composition or publication date of the critical work are given at the beginning of each piece of criticism. Unsigned criticism is preceded by the title of the source in which it appeared. All titles by the author featured in the critical entry are printed in boldface type. Publication information (such as publisher names and book prices) and parenthetical numerical references (such as footnotes or page and line references to specific editions of works) have been deleted at the editors' discretion to provide smoother reading of the text.

- Critical essays are prefaced by **annotations** as an additional aid to students using *LC*. These explanatory notes may provide several types of useful information, including: the reputation of a critic, the importance of a work of criticism, the commentator's individual approach to literary criticism, the intent of the criticism, and the growth of critical controversy or changes in critical trends regarding an author's work. In some cases, these notes cross-reference the work of critics within the entry who agree or disagree with each other.

- A complete **bibliographical citation** of the original essay or book follows each piece of criticism.

- An annotated bibliography of **further reading** appears at the end of each entry and suggests resources for additional study of authors and themes. It also includes essays for which the editors could not obtain reprint rights.

Cumulative Indexes

Each volume of *LC* includes a cumulative **author index** listing all the authors that have appeared in *Contemporary Literary Criticism, Twentieth-Century Literary Criticism, Nineteenth-Century Literature Criticism, Literature Criticism from 1400 to 1800,* and *Classical and Medieval Literature Criticism,* along with cross-references to the Gale series *Short Story Criticism, Children's Literature Review, Authors in the News, Contemporary Authors, Contemporary Authors Autobiography Series, Contemporary Authors Bibliographical Series, Dictionary of Literary Biography, Concise Dictionary of Literary Biography, Something about the Author, Something about the Author Autobiography Series,* and *Yesterday's Authors of Books for Children.* Readers will welcome this cumulative author index as a useful tool for locating an author within the various series. The index, which includes authors' birth and death dates, is particularly valuable for those authors who are identified with a certain period but whose death dates cause them to be placed in another, or for those authors whose careers span two periods. For example, F. Scott Fitzgerald is found in *TCLC,* yet a writer often associated with him, Ernest Hemingway, is found in *CLC.*

Beginning with Volume 12, *LC* includes a cumulative **topic index** that lists all literary themes and topics treated in *LC, NCLC* Topics volumes, *TCLC* Topics volumes, and the *CLC* Yearbook. Each volume of *LC* also includes a cumulative **nationality index** in which authors' names are arranged alphabetically under their respective nationalities and followed by the numbers of the volumes in which they appear.

Each volume of *LC* also includes a cumulative **title index**, an alphabetical listing of the literary works discussed in the series since its inception. Each title listing includes the corresponding volume and page numbers where criticism may be located. Foreign-language titles that have been translated are followed by the titles of the translations—for example, *El ingenioso hidalgo Don Quixote de la Mancha (Don Quixote).* Page numbers following these translated titles refer to all pages on which any form of the titles, either foreign-language or translated, appear. Titles of novels, dramas, nonfiction books, and poetry, short story, or essay collections are printed in italics, while individual poems, short stories, and essays are printed in roman type within quotation marks.

A Note to the Reader

When writing papers, students who quote directly from any volume in the Literary Criticism Series may use the following general forms to footnote reprinted criticism. The first example pertains to material drawn from periodicals, the second to material reprinted from books.

T. S. Eliot, "John Donne," *The Nation and the Athenaeum,* 33 (9 June 1923), 321-32; excerpted and reprinted in *Literature Criticism from 1400 to 1800,* Vol. 10, ed. James E. Person, Jr. (Detroit: Gale Research, 1989), pp. 28-9.

Clara G. Stillman, *Samuel Butler: A Mid-Victorian Modern* (Viking Press, 1932); excerpted and reprinted in *Twentieth-Century Literary Criticism,* Vol. 33, ed. Paula Kepos (Detroit: Gale Research, 1989), pp. 43-5.

Suggestions Are Welcome

In response to various suggestions, several features have been added to *LC* since the series began, including a nationality index, a Literary Criticism Series topic index, a continuously revised list of authors to appear in future volumes, thematic entries, a descriptive table of contents, and more extensive illustrations.

Readers who wish to suggest new features, themes, or authors to appear in future volumes, or who have other suggestions, are cordially invited to write to the editors.

Acknowledgements

The editors wish to thank the copyright holders of the excerpted criticism included in this volume, the permissions managers of many book and magazine publishing companies for assisting us in securing reprint rights, and Anthony Bogucki for assistance with copyright research. We are also grateful to the staffs of the Detroit Public Library, Wayne State University Purdy/Kresge Library Complex, and the University of Michigan Libraries for making their resources available to us. Following is a list of the copyright holders who have granted us permission to reprint material in this volume of *LC*. Every effort has been made to trace copyright, but if ommissions have been made, please let us know.

COPYRIGHTED EXCERPTS IN *LC,* VOLUME 14, WERE REPRINTED FROM THE FOLLOWING PERIODICALS:

Essays by Divers Hands, n.s. v. XLIII, 1984 for "J. J. Rousseau and the Birth of Romanticism" by Maurice Cranston. © the author 1984. Reprinted by permission of the Peters Fraser & Dunlop Group Ltd.—*History,* n. 3, 1960 for "The Unity of the French Enlightenment" by Peter Gay. © 1990 by the Helen Dwight Reid Educational Foundation. Renewed 1988 by Peter Gay. Reprinted by permission of the author.—*Journal of the History of Ideas,* v. X, January, 1949. Copyright 1949, renewed 1976 by Journal of the History of Ideas, Inc. Reprinted by permission of the publisher./ v. XXIII, 1962. Copyright 1962, Journal of the History of Ideas, Inc. Reprinted by permission of the publisher.—*Representations,* n. 13, Winter, 1986. © 1986 by The Regents of the University of California. Reprinted by permission of the publisher.—*Studies on Voltaire and the Eighteenth Century,* v.VII, 1964. © Theodore Besterman 1964. Reprinted by permission of the publisher.

COPYRIGHTED EXCERPTS IN *LC,* VOLUME 14, WERE REPRINTED FROM THE FOLLOWING BOOKS:

Aldridge, A. Owen. From *Voltaire and the Century of Light.* Princeton University Press, 1975. Copyright © 1975 by Princeton University Press. All rights reserved. Reprinted with permission of the publisher.—Ayer, A. J. From *Voltaire.* Weidenfeld and Nicolson, 1986. © 1986 A. J. Ayer. All rights reserved. Reprinted by permission of the publisher.—Barthes, Roland. From *Critical Essays.* Translated by Richard Howard. Northwestern University Press, 1972. Copyright © 1972 by Northwestern University Press. All rights reserved. Reprinted by permission of the publisher.—Becker, Carl L. From *The Heavenly City of the Eighteenth-Century Philosophers.* Yale University Press, 1932. Copyright 1932 by Yale University Press. Renewed 1960 by Carl L. Becker. All rights reserved. Reprinted by permission of the publisher.—Besterman, Theodore. From *Voltaire.* Revised edition. Basil Blackwell, 1976. © Theodore Besterman 1969, 1976. All rights reserved. Reprinted by permission of Basil Blackwell Limited.—Bloom, Allan. From "Rousseau on the Equality of the Sexes," in *Justice and Equality Here and Now.* Edited by Frank S. Lucash. Cornell University Press, 1986. Copyright © 1986 by Cornell University. All rights reserved. Used by permission of the publisher, Cornell University Press.—Cairns, Huntington, Allen Tate, and Mark Van Doren. From *Invitation to Learning.* Random House, 1941. Copyright, 1941, by The Columbia Broadcasting System, Inc. Renewed 1968 by Huntington Cairns. Reprinted by permission of the Literary Estates of Allen Tate and Mark Van Doren.—Cassirer, Ernst. From *The Philosophy of the Elightenment.* Translated by Fritz C. A. Koelln and James P. Pettegrove. Princeton University Press, 1951. Copyright 1951 by Princeton University Press. Renewed 1979 by James P. Pettegrove and Fritz C. A. Koelln.—Claydon, Leslie F. From "Introduction: The Man and His Work," in *Rousseau on Education.* Edited by Leslie F. Claydon. Collier-Macmillan Limited, 1969. Copyright © Macmillan Publishing Company. All rights reserved. Reprinted with permission of the publisher.—Cranston, Maurice. From *Philosophers and Pamphleteers: Political Theorists of the Enlightenment.* Oxford Universtiy Press, Oxford, 1986. © Maurice Cranston 1986. All rights reserved. Reprinted by permission of Oxford University Press.—Deanne, Seamus. From *The French Revolution and Enlightenment in England: 1789-1832.* Cambridge, Mass.: Harvard University Press, 1988. Copyright © 1988 by the President and Fellows of Harvard College. All rights reserved. Excerpted by permission of the publishers and the author.—di Prima, Diane. From "Paracelsus: An Appreciaton," in *The Hermetic and Alchemical Writings of Aureolus Philippus Theophrastus Bombast, of Hohenheim, Called Paracelsus the Great: Hermetic Chemistry, Vol. I.* By Paracelsus, edited by Arthur Edward Waite. University Books, Inc., 1967. Copyright © 1967 by University Books Inc. Published by arrangement with Carol Publishing Group.—Gaxotte, Pierre. From *Frederick the Great.* Translated by R. A. Bell. Yale University Press, 1942. Copyright, 1942, by Yale University Press. Renewed 1970 by Richard Allen Bell. All rights renewed. Reprinted by permission of the publisher.—Gay, Peter. From an introduction to *Basic Political Writings.* Edited and translated by Donald A. Cress. Hackett Publishing Company, 1987. Copyright © 1987 by Hackett Publishing Company. All rights reserved. Reprinted by permission of the pubisher.—Gay, Peter. From *The Party of Humanity: Essays in the French Enlightenment.* Knopf, 1964. Copyright © 1963 by Peter Gay. All rights reserved. Reprinted by permission of Alfred A. Knopf, Inc.—Gay, Peter. From *Voltaire's Politics: The Poet as Realist.* Princeton University Press, 1959. Copyright © 1959 by Princeton University Press. Renewed 1987 by Peter Gay. All rights reserved. Reprinted with permission of the author.—Gundulf, Friedrich. From "Frederick's Essay on German Literature,"

PHOTOGRAPHS AND ILLUSTRATIONS APPEARING IN *LC,* VOLUME 14, WERE RECEIVED FROM THE FOLLOWING SOURCES:

Authors to Appear in Future Volumes

Abravenel, Isaac 1437-1508
Abravenel, Judah 1460-1535
Addison, Joseph 1672-1719
Agricola, Johannes 1494?-1566
Agrippa, Cornelius
    Heinrich 1486?-1535
Akenside, Mark 1721-1770
Alabaster, William 1567-1640
Alarcón y Mendoza, Juan Rúiz
    1581-1634
Alberti, Leon
Battista 1404-1472
Alembert, Jean Le Rond d'
    1717-1783
Amory, Thomas 1691?-1788
Anton Ulrich, Duke of
    Brunswick 1633-1714
Ascham, Roger 1515-1568
Ashmole, Elias 1617-1692
Aubigne, Théodore Agrippa d'
    1552-1630
Aubrey, John 1620-1697
Bâbur 1483-1530
Bacon, Sir Francis 1561-1626
Bale, John 1495-1563
Barber, Mary 1690-1757
Baretti, Giuseppi 1719-1789
Barker, Jane 1652-1727?
Bartas, Guillaume de Salluste du
    1544-1590
Baxter, Richard 1615-1691
Bayle, Pierre 1647-1706
Beaumarchais, Pierre-Augustin
    Caron de 1732-1799
Beaumont, Francis 1584-1616
Belleau, Rémy 1528-1577
Berkeley, George 1685-1753
Bessarion, Johannes 1403-1472
Bijns, Anna 1493-1575
Bisticci, Vespasiano da
    1421-1498
Blackmore, Sir Richard
    1650-1729
Boccalini, Traiano 1556-1613
Bodin, Jean 1530-1596
Bolingbroke, Henry St. John
    1678-1751

Boyle, Roger 1621-1679
Bradford, William 1590-1657
Brant, Sebastian 1457-1521
Bredero, Gerbrand
    Adriaanszoon 1585-1618
Breitinger, Johann
    Jakob 1701-1776
Breton, Nicholas 1545-1626
Broome, William 1689-1745
Brown, Thomas 1663-1704
Browne, Sir Thomas 1605-1682
Bruni, Leonardo 1370-1444
Bruno, Giordano 1548-1600
Buffon, George-Louis Leclerc,
    Comte de 1707-1788
Burgoyne, John 1722-1792
Burnet, Gilbert 1643-1715
Burnett, James 1714-1799
Burton, Robert 1577-1640
Butler, Samuel 1612-1680
Byrd, William, II 1674-1744
Byrom, John 1692-1763
Calderón de la Barca,
    Pedro 1600-1681
Calvin, John 1509-1564
Camden, William 1551-1623
Campion, Thomas 1567-1620
Cantemir, Antioch
    Dmitrievich 1708-1744
Capgrave, John 1393-1464
Carew, Richard 1555-1620
Carver, Jonathan 1710-1780
Castillejo, Cristobalde
    1492-1550
Cavendish, William 1592-1676
Caxton, William 1421?-1491
Centlivre, Susanna 1667?-1723
Chapman, George 1560-1634
Chartier, Alain 1390-1440
Chaucer, Geoffrey 1340?-1400
Cibber, Colley 1671-1757
Cleveland, John 1613-1658
Collyer, Mary 1716?-1763?
Colonna, Vittoria 1490-1547
Commynes, Philippe de
    1445-1511
Condillac, Etienne Bonnot,

    Abbé de 1714?-1780
Cook, James 1728-1779
Corneille, Pierre 1606-1684
Cortés, Hernán 1485-1547
Cotton, John 1584-1652
Courtilz de Sandras, Gatiende
    1644-1712
Cowley, Abraham 1618-1667
Cranmer, Thomas 1489-1556
Crashaw, Richard 1612-1649
Crébillon, Prosper Jolyot de
    1674-1762
Cruden, Alexander 1701-1770
Curll, Edmund 1675-1747
D'Alembert, Jean le Rond
    1717-1783
Dampier, William 1653-1715
Dancourt, Florent Carton
    1661-1725
Daniel, Samuel 1562-1619
Davidson, John 1549?-1603
Day, John 1574-1640
Dekker, Thomas 1572-1632
Denham, Sir John 1615-1669
Deloney, Thomas 1543?-1600?
Descartes, René 1596-1650
Desfontaines, Pierre François
    Guyot, Abbé 1685-1745
Diaz del Castillo, Bernal
    1492?-1584
Diderot, Denis 1713-1784
Douglas, Gavin 1475?-1522
Drummond, William 1585-1649
Du Guillet, Pernette 1520?-1545
Dunbar, William 1460?-1520?
Edwards, Richard 1523?-1566
Emin, Fedor ?-1770
Erasmus, Desiderius 1466-1536
Etherege, Sir George 1635-1691
Eusden, Laurence 1688-1730
Evelyn, John 1620-1706
Fabyan, Robert ?-1513
Fairfax, Thomas 1621-1671
Fanshawe, Sir Richard
    1608-1666
Farquhar, George 1678-1707
Fénelon, François 1651-1715

Fergusson, Robert 1750-1774
Fletcher, John 1579-1625
Florian, Jean Pierre Claris de 1755-1794
Florio, John 1553?-1625
Fontaine, Charles 1514-1565
Fontenelle, Bernard Le Bovier de 1657-1757
Fonvizin, Denis Ivanovich 1745-1792
Ford, John 1586-1640
Franklin, Benjamin 1706-1790
Froissart, Jean 1337-1404?
Fuller, Thomas 1608-1661
Galilei, Galileo 1564-1642
Garrick, David 1717-1779
Gascoigne, George 1530?-1577
Gay, John 1685-1732
Gibbon, Edward 1737-1794
Gildon, Charles 1665-1724
Glanvill, Joseph 1636-1680
Góngora y Argote, Luis de 1561-1627
Gosson, Stephen 1554-1624
Gottsched, Johann Christoph 1700-1766
Gower, John 1330?-1408
Gracian y Morales, Baltasar 1601-1658
Graham, Dougal 1724-1779
Greene, Robert 1558?-1592
Griffith, Elizabeth 1727?-1793
Guarini, Giambattista 1538-1612
Guicciardini, Francesco 1483-1540
Hakluyt, Richard 1553-1616
Hall, Edward 1498-1547
Harrington, James 1611-1677
Hartley, David 1705-1757
Helvetius, Claude Arien 1715-1771
Henry, Patrick 1736-1799
Henryson, Robert 1430?-1506
Henslowe, Philip ?-1616
Herbert, George 1593-1633
Herbert of Cherbury 1583-1648
Heywood, Thomas 1574-1641
Hobbes, Thomas 1588-1679
Hoccleve, Thomas 1370?-1450
Hogarth, William 1697-1764
Holinshed, Raphael ?-1582?

Hooker, Richard 1544-1600
Hooker, Thomas 1586-1647
Hopkinson, Francis 1737-1791
Howard, Henry, Earl of Surrey 1517-1547
Hung Sheng 1646-1704
Hutcheson, Francis 1694-1746
Ibn Khaldun, Abd al-Rahman ibn Muhammad 1332-1406
Iriarte, Tomas de 1750-1791
Isla y Rojo, José Francisco de 1703-1781
Ivan IV 1533-1584
James I, King of Scotland 1394-1437
Johnson, Samuel 1709-1784
King, William 1662-1712
Knox, John 1514?-1572
Kyd, Thomas 1558-1594
La Bruyére, Jean de 1645-1696
La Fontaine, Jean de 1621-1695
Langland, William 1330?-1400
La Rochefoucauld, Francois de 1613-1680
Law, William 1686-1761
L'Estrange, Sir Roger 1616-1704
Let-we Thon-dara 1752-1783
Lilly, William 1602-1681
Lipsius, Justus 1547-1606
Littleton, Sir Thomas 1422-1481
Lodge, Thomas 1558-1625
Lomonosov, Mikhail Vasilevich 1711-1765
Lope de Vega 1562-1635
Lopez de Ayala, Pero 1332-1407?
Louis XIV 1638-1715
Lovelace, Richard 1618-1657
Loyola, Ignacio de 1491-1556
Lydgate, John 1370?-1452
Lyly, John 1554-1606
Lyndsay, Sir David 1490?-1555
MacDomhnaill, Sean Clarach 1691-1754
Macpherson, James 1736-1796
Maitland, Sir Richard 1496-1586
Mandeville, Bernard de 1670-1733
Marlowe, Christopher

1564-1593
Marston, John 1576-1634
Massinger, Philip 1583-1640
Mather, Cotton 1663-1728
Mather, Increase 1639-1723
Medwall, Henry 1462?-?
Mendelssohn, Moses 1729-1786
Metastasio, Pietro 1698-1782
Middleton, Thomas 1580-1627
Montfort, Hugo von 1357-1423
Moore, Francis 1657-1714
Morton, Thomas 1575-1647
Muret, Marc-Antoine de 1526-1585
Nashe, Thomas 1567-1601
Nawa i 1441-1501
Newton, Sir Isaac 1642-1727
North, Sir Thomas 1535?-1601?
Norton, Thomas 1532-1584
Nostradamus 1503-1566
Oldham, John 1653-1683
Orleans, Charles, duc d' 1391?-1465
Otway, Thomas 1652-1685
Pade-tha-ya-za 1684-1754
Painter, William 1540?-1594
Parr, Catharine 1512-1548
Pascal, Blaise 1623-1662
Pasek, Jan Chryzostom 1636-1701
Peele, George 1556-1596
Pembroke, Mary Sidney, Countess of 1561-1621
Penn, William 1644-1718
Pico della Mirandola, Giovanni 1463-1494
Poliziano, Angelo 1454-1494
Prokopovich, Feofan 1681-1736
Quarles, Francis 1592-1644
Quevedo y Villegas, Francisco Gomez de 1580-1645
Racine, Jean 1639-1699
Raleigh, Sir Walter 1552-1618
Rapin, René 1621-1687
Raynal, Guillaume 1713-1796
Regnard, Jean François 1655-1709
Reuter, Christian 1665-1712
Revius, Jacobus 1586-1658
Reynolds, Sir Joshua 1723-1792
Robertson, William 1721-1793
Rochester, John Wilmot, Earl of

1648-1680
Rojas, Fernando de 1475?-1538
Rojas Zorilla, Francisco
  de 1607-1648
Rowe, Elizabeth 1674-1737
Rutherford, Samuel 1600?-1661
Sackville, Thomas 1536-1608
Saint-Simon, Louis de Rouvroy
  1675-1755
Santeuil, Jean Baptiste de
  1630-1697
Savage, Richard 1696-1742
Savonarola, Girolamo
  1452-1498
Scarron, Paul 1610-1660
Scott, Sarah 1723-1795
Selden, John 1584-1654
Sewall, Samuel 1652-1730
Shadwell, Thomas 1642-1692
Shaftesbury, Anthony Ashley
  Cooper, Earl of 1671-1713
Shenstone, William 1714-1763
Shirley, James 1596-1666
Sidney, Sir Philip 1554-1586
Skelton, John 1464?-1529
Smith, Adam 1723-1790
Sorsky, Nil 1433-1508
Spee, Friedrich von 1591-1635
Sprat, Thomas 1635-1713
Stanhope, Philip 1694-1773

Steele, Sir Richard 1672-1729
Suckling, Sir John 1609-1642
Sumarokov, Aleksandr
  Petrovich 1718-1777
Swedenborg, Emanuel
  1688-1772
Takeda Izumo 1690-1756
Tasso, Bernardo 1494-1569
Taylor, Jeremy 1613-1667
Temple, Sir William 1629-1699
Tencin, Madame de 1682-1749
Teresa de Jesús 1515-1582
Testi, Fulvio 1593-1646
Thomson, James 1700-1748
Tourneur, Cyril 1570-1626
Traherne, Thomas 1637-1674
Trai, Nguyen 1380-1442
Trediakovski, Vasili
  Kirilovich 1703-1769
Tristan 1601-1655
Turgot, Anne Robert
  Jacques 1727-1781
Tyndale, William 1494?-1536
Udall, Nicholas 1505-1556
Urquhart, Sir Thomas
  1611-1660
Ussher, James 1581-1656
Vanbrugh, Sir John 1664?-1707
Vasari, Giorgio 1511-1574
Vaughan, Henry 1621-1695

Vaughan, Thomas 1622-1666
Vico, Giambattista 1668-1744
Villiers, George 1628-1687
Villon, François 1431-1463
Waller, Edmund 1606-1687
Walton, Izaak 1593-1683
Warburton, William 1698-1779
Warner, William 1558-1609
Warton, Thomas 1728-1790
Washington, George 1732-1799
Webster, John 1580-1638
Weise, Christian 1642-1708
Wesley, Charles 1701?-1788
Wesley, John 1703-1791
Wesley, Samuel 1662?-1735
Whetstone, George 1544?-1587?
White, Gilbert 1720-1793
Wigglesworth, Michael
  1631-1705
Williams, Roger 1603-1683
Winckelman, Johann Joachim
  1717-1768
Winthrop, John 1588-1649
Wyatt, Sir Thomas 1503-1542
Yuan Mei 1716-1797
Zólkiewski, Stanislaw
  1547-1620
Zrinyi, Miklos 1620-1664
Zwingli, Ulrich 1484-1531

Readers are cordially invited to suggest additional authors to the editors.

John Foxe
1516?-1587

English martyrologist, historian, sermonist, essayist, editor, translator, and dramatist.

Foxe is recognized as one of the most controversial and influential writers of the English Renaissance and Reformation. His monumental ecclesiastical history, *Rerum in Ecclesia gestarum* (*Actes and Monuments of these latter and perillous dayes*), had an enormous impact on the development of Anglicanism and Protestant theology in Europe. This work, which was considered second only to the Bible as a primary scriptural authority of the Established Church, was consulted by Anglicans of virtually every social strata for over two centuries. Today, though the popularity of Foxe's work has declined, its lasting influence is still widely apparent in Anglican perceptions of Christianity and Roman Catholicism.

Foxe devoted his life to defending his religious convictions. He was born in Boston, Lincolnshire to a middle class family. Little is known of his childhood except that even as a youth he was deeply interested in theology. In 1534 he entered Brasenose College, Oxford, where he earned a Bachelor of Arts degree in 1537. Less than two years later he was honored with a fellowship at Magdalen College, Oxford. He received a Master of Arts degree in 1543. Foxe studied Greek, Latin, and Hebrew extensively at Oxford, concentrating upon religious doctrines and contemporary theological issues. During this time he also completed *Titus et Gesippus,* a Latin academic drama. A fellow and lecturer for seven years, he resigned in 1545 to protest Magdalen's requirement that all fellows be ordained and take a vow of celibacy. Despite having been raised as a Roman Catholic, he converted to Protestantism after years of ecclesiastical study and deliberation. Foxe married Agnes Randall in 1547. He secured a position in London as tutor to the grandchildren of the then-imprisoned duke of Norfolk. Although the duke was Roman Catholic, his sister, the duchess of Richmond, was Protestant and concurred with Foxe's views. During the six years the children were in her charge, Foxe instructed them both academically and scripturally. He was well liked and formed particularly close ties with Thomas Howard, the future successor of the imprisoned duke. Howard proved a lifelong friend and valuable connection, aiding his teacher financially and opening his home to him on several occasions.

In London Foxe became known as an outspoken defender of the Reformed Church. In 1548, he began publishing propagandist tracts and translating the sermons of leading anti-Catholic theologians Martin Luther and Johannes Oecolampadius. He cultivated friendships with well-known Anglican figures, notably Nicolas Ridley, Hugh Latimer, John Bale, and Edmund Grindal, and in 1550 was ordained deacon by Bishop Ridley. Upon the accession of Mary in 1553, Protestantism officially fell out of favor. This made Foxe's religious beliefs and practices dangerously unpopular. To avoid imprisonment, he went into hiding and then secretly fled to Antwerp. From there

he journeyed to Rotterdam and Frankfurt, finally settling with Protestant refugees in Strasbourg, where he continued to write and speak in defense of the Protestant cause. In 1554 he hastily completed the first edition of an ecclesiastical history, *Commentarii rerum in ecclesia gestarum.* Citing the example of John Wycliffe and the English Lollards, Foxe countered the derisive assertion made by Roman Catholics that Protestantism was a new religion. The following year he traveled to Basel where he worked as a proofreader for the printer John Oporinus. Although exhausted from overwork, Foxe continued to write fervently. Among his publications of this time are *Christus Triumphans,* a Renaissance academic comedy; a book of commonplaces, *Locorum Communium tituli & ordines centum quinquaginta;* and, most notably, *Ad inclytos ac præpotentes Angliæ proceres,* an address entreating the English aristocracy to help the Protestant cause.

Upon the accession of Elizabeth I in 1558, Foxe was free to return to England. He remained in Basel for over a year, however, completing the second edition of his martyrology, *Rerum in Ecclesia gestarum,* an expanded text that traces Protestant history from the Lollards to the 1556 execution of Thomas Cranmer. In 1564, at the behest of several prominent Anglicans, he published *Actes and Monu-*

ments, the first English-language edition of his Protestant history. This text, which is almost 1800 pages long, contains numerous firsthand descriptions of Protestant martyrdoms and is illustrated by over fifty graphic woodcuts. An extremely effective piece of propaganda, *Actes and Monuments* reinforced Anglican fear of the perceived Roman Antichrist and of the dire consequences of Roman Catholic rule. Foxe's vivid portrayal, particularly of the Marian terrors, gained him instant recognition. He became known as Father Foxe and was raised almost to the level of sainthood by his followers. Frequently consulted for his interpretation of scripture, he was called upon by cleric, nobleman, and commoner alike to assist in the healing of the sick through divine intervention. Despite his fame, Foxe lived much of his remaining life in desperate poverty. Although he fell ill more than once from malnutrition and exhaustion, he gave away much of his money and refused to take respite from his scholarly pursuits. Before his death in 1587, he completed three more editions of his martyrology, published religious and political works on a variety of contemporary issues, and participated actively in the church. Foxe was buried in St. Giles, Cripplegate, his death greatly mourned by Protestants throughout England.

Virtually all of Foxe's important work treats contemporary theological issues. He was interested chiefly in the interpretation and application of church doctrine and expressed his concerns in numerous sermons and tracts. He wrote to the monarchy, aristocracy, and clergy, calling for stricter adherence to scripture yet also pleading for an end to the putting to death of those convicted of committing religious infractions. Foxe also addressed the general populace in such discourses as *A Sermon of Christ Crucified* and *A Sermon at the christening of a certaine Jew,* in which he explained Christian atonement and emphasized contrasts between Roman Catholic and Protestant theology. He spoke most ardently and at greatest length on Protestant and Catholic disputes in *Actes and Monuments.* The text, expanded from a 200-page chronicle of the English Lollards to a 2100-page history of Protestantism, traces the growth of the Christian church from its inception to the time of Elizabeth I. Foxe divided his history into five books, relying heavily upon secondary sources for the majority of the pre-Wycliffite period. For ancient history he was indebted to Eusebius of Caesarea and Hermias Sozomen. For the Dark and Middle Ages as well as the Reformation, he relied upon Bede, Matthew Paris, Johannes Sleidanus, and Francisco de Enzinas. The text covering the transition from the English Renaissance to the Reformation is almost entirely original, however. Foxe consulted parish records and public registers, often quoting them verbatim. In addition, he interviewed numerous eyewitnesses, collected secondhand testimonies, and whenever possible, printed autobiographical material written by the martyrs. The resulting text is a compendium of Protestant history written by Foxe and illustrated with episodes by the martyrs and witnesses themselves.

Because of the controversial nature of Foxe's work, criticism of *Actes and Monuments* has often been based primarily upon the religious persuasion of the critic. Few pre-twentieth-century scholars objectively addressed the controversies treated in the text, assessed its value as an historical document, or discussed its literary merits. Instead, the majority either praised or condemned the work whole-sale, depending upon whether the critic was Protestant or Roman Catholic. During Foxe's lifetime, supporters of the work included some of the most important religious figures in England. Such defenders, for the most part, considered *Actes and Monuments* a work of genius and of paramount importance as an ecclesiastical authority. As early as 1571, the convocation of Canterbury ordered copies of Foxe's work installed in all cathedral churches and in the homes of Protestant clerics. Indeed, during the sixteenth and seventeenth centuries, copies of *Actes and Monuments* were literally chained together with the Bible, Desiderius Erasmus's *Paraphrases of the New Testament* (translated in 1548), and John Jewel's *An apologie or aunswer in defence of the Church of England* (1562) for public use in many Anglican churches. For as many Protestant critics who deemed *Actes and Monuments* a work of divine inspiration, however, an equal number of Catholic critics concurred with Thomas Harding's judgment that Foxe had knowingly "infarced lies more in number and notabler for vanity than ever were raked together into any one heap or book." Among the most vituperative detractors were Harding, Nicholas Harpsfield, and Robert Parsons. Parsons's criticism was particularly damaging to Foxe's reputation. In a lengthy three-volume tract he attempted to discredit *Actes and Monuments,* questioning Foxe's integrity and sanity. The ultimate success of Parson's refutation is evidenced by the extensive use of his disparaging arguments by later commentators.

Critical interest in Foxe's work waned somewhat during the latter half of the eighteenth century, and it was not until the publication of a new edition of *Actes and Monuments* in 1837 that the controversy was revived. English historian S. R. Maitland adamantly opposed the reintroduction of such an anti-Catholic text and thus, in a series of essays and books written over a ten-year period, systematically attacked Foxe, *Actes and Monuments,* and edition editor Stephen R. Cattley. In much the same manner as Parsons and Harding, Maitland queried the historical accuracy of the martyrologist's work, pointing to numerous factual mistakes as evidence of willful misrepresentation of history. The critic questioned whether Foxe's " 'never-mind' school of history should be allowed to cut its way through matters of fact, with reckless slaughter of names, and places, and dates, and with any translation or mistranslation of documents, in order to establish any point of faith, or practice, or opinion which it may see fit to select." Despite efforts by Cattley and biographer George Townsend to refute such negative criticism, even Foxe's supporters began questioning the accuracy of the text. In addition, the perceived value of *Actes and Monuments* was further lessened as many eighteenth- and nineteenth-century Protestant editors abridged the text, reducing it to little more than a catalog of horrific tortures and executions and renaming it *The Book of Martyrs.* Warren W. Wooden best summarizes the contradictory use of Foxe's work: "On the one hand, Foxe's book was chopped, shaped, and presented to function as a tool of Protestant propaganda whose veracity was automatically assumed among its target audience; and on the other hand, in the academy, the *Actes and Monuments* was often regarded as a work of dubious authority written in the heat of passion by a careless, biased, and intemperate chronicler."

During the twentieth century, though some criticism has been based upon religious convictions, most scholars have approached *Actes and Monuments* from a more secular perspective. Commentators have addressed a variety of topics including Foxe's portrayal of women, the impact of his work upon young audiences, and his ultimate influence upon the development of Protestant thought. Interest in *Actes and Monuments* was sparked by the 1940 publication of J. F. Mozley's critical biography. Mozley's well-documented study resulted in a reversal of the predominantly negative assessments of Foxe as an individual, historian, and literary figure. To assertions that he purposely falsified documents, scholars now counter that while *Actes and Monuments* contains many factual errors, it is unlikely that its author knowingly lied. Indeed, some critics consider his handling of such a massive amount of information admirable. Mozley asserts: "We are overwhelmed by the sheer bulk of his achievement. . . . This colossal labour disposes us to think well of Foxe." As an historical work, *Actes and Monuments* is valued for its firsthand recounting of contemporary events rather than for Foxe's reiteration of church history before his own lifetime. Most critics concur that earlier historians better portrayed their subjects. Scholars have recently begun treating the purely literary aspects of the martyrologist's work as well. Because Foxe employed various translators, often quoted verbatim from sources, and incorporated stories written by his subjects, objective evaluation of his skill as a writer has proven difficult. Critics have reached widely differing conclusions concerning his literary talent. Some deem his narrative laborious to read and totally uninspired, while others concur with Helen C. White, who praised his ability as "a storyteller of quite remarkable power, one of the greatest in a great age." In general, despite the recent resurgence of critical interest and assessments by such critics as V. Norskov Olsen and William Haller, scholars have yet to touch upon many literary and historical aspects of *Actes and Monuments*. In addition, few critics have examined the other works in Foxe's canon.

Today, while scholars continue to debate the historical and literary merits of Foxe's work, most concur that it had a lasting impact on the development of Protestantism in England. *Actes and Monuments* played a vital role in uniting Protestants. William Lamont affirms that *Actes and Monuments* "conditioned generations of English Protestants to a belief in the historic mission of their role." Further, the popularity of Foxe's work both during his lifetime and in subsequent centuries is affirmed by numerous editions and reprints. Olsen concludes that the complexity of Foxe's personality and his ultimate contribution to Protestantism cannot be underestimated: "Foxe's life and work had many facets: he was Foxe, the Historiographer, the Martyrologist, the Humanist, the Erasmian, the Puritan, the Anglican, the Elizabethan Eusebius, the Gospeller, the Ecclesiologist, the Erastian, the precursor of Elizabethan nationalism, the Lutheran, and so on. . . . John Foxe towers above all the Englishmen who contributed to shaping English history into a Protestant mold."

PRINCIPAL WORKS

Titus et Gesippus (drama) 1545?
  [*Titus et Gesippus,* 1973]
*Commentarii rerum in ecclesia gestarum, maximarum-que, per totam Europam, persecutionum, à Vuiclevi temporibus ad hanc usque ætatem descriptio (prose)

1554; also published as *Rerum in Ecclesia gestarum, quæ postremis et periculosis his temporibus evenerunt, maximarumque; per Europam persecutionum, ac sanctorum Dei martyrum, cæterarumque; rerum si quae insignoris exempli sunt, digesti per regna et nationes commentarii. Pars prima. In qua primum de rebus per Angliam et Scotiam gestis, atque in primis de horrenda, sub Maria nuper Regina, persecutione, narratio continetur* [revised edition], 1559; also published as *Chronicon Ecclesiæ, continens historiam rerum gestarum, maximarumque per totam Europam persecutionum à Vuiclevi temporibus usque ad nostram ætatem* [revised edition], 1564
  [*Actes and Monuments of these latter and perillous dayes, touching matters of the Church, wherein ar comprehended and described the great persecutions and horrible troubles, that have bene wrought and practised by the Romanishe prelates, speciallye in this Realme of England and Scotlande, from the yeare of our Lorde, a thousande, unto the tyme nowe present. Gathered and collected according to the true copies and wrytinges certificatorie, as wel of the parties them selves that suffered, as also out of the Bishops Registers which wer the doers therof,* 1563; revised edition, 1583; also published as *The Ecclesiasticall History, Contayning the Actes and Monuments of thynges passed in every kynges tyme in this realme, especially in the Church of England principally to be noted . . . from the primitive tyme till the reigne of K. Henry VIII* [revised edition], 1570]
Christus triumphans, comoedia Apocalyptica (drama) 1556
  [*Christ Jesus Triumphant,* 1579; also published as *Christus triumphans,* 1973]
Ad inclytos ac præpotentes Angliæ proceres, ordines et status, totamque ejus gentis nobilitatem, pro afflictis fratribus supplicatio (essay) 1557
Locorum Communium tituli & ordines centum quinquaginta, ad seriem prædicamentorum decem descripti: in quos . . . quæcumque sunt usquam ex autoribus colligenda lectores congerant (essay) 1557; also published as *Pandectæ locorum communium,* 1585
A Sermon of, Christ Crucified [*on 2 Cor. v. 20, 21*] *preached at Paules Crosse, the Friday before Easter, commonly called Good Fryday. A. D. 1570. Written and dedicated to all such as labour and be heavy laden in conscience, to be read for their spiritual comfort* (sermon) 1570
A Sermon at the christening of a certaine Jew [*Nathanael*] *at London. . . . Conteining an exposition of the XI. Chapter of S. Paul to the Romanes* (sermon) 1578
The Book of Martyrs, containing an Account of the Sufferings and Death of the Protestants in the Reign of Queen Mary the First [abridged edition] (prose) 1761

---

*This work is commonly known as *Actes and Monuments.* It is known in an abridged version as *Foxe's Book of Martyrs.*

Edmund Grindal   (letter date 1557)

[*Grindal was a sixteenth-century English cleric who shared Foxe's religious convictions as well as his interest in documenting the events surrounding the Marian persecutions. He contributed greatly to Foxe's work, providing information from his own collection of "the writings and stories of the learned and pious sufferers in England" and channeling numerous documents from a variety of sources to the martyrologist. In the following excerpt from a letter written in 1557, he counsels Foxe on translating* Commentarii rerum in ecclesia gestarum *into English.*]

As to variety of opinions, you need not be much concerned. Good men will speak well of you, bad men ill. It is enough to be praised by men of reputation; to please all men falls to the lot of none. As to the mode of translating, no one is more competent to judge than yourself; for you well know the licence which is allowed to a faithful translator. Those who would require you to translate word for word would instantly betray their want of judgment. It has always been the approved mode to render the sense, provided the translator manifestly express his author's mind, and not his own. In all these matters, as also in most others, it will be safer to hold a middle course. My judgment is the same with regard to style. For neither is the ecclesiastical style to be fastidiously rejected, as it is by some, especially when the heads of controversies cannot sometimes be perspicuously explained without it; nor, on the other hand, is it to be so superstitiously followed, as to prevent us sometimes from sprinkling it with the ornaments of language. A remarkable illustration of this is presented to us by Master Calvin, whom for honour's sake I mention, who has not neglected the grace of style, and yet frequently adopts ecclesiastical forms of speech, as if naturalized. As to the inversion of books, which the bishop of Winchester practises, this is my judgment; that he should be allowed to follow his own discretion and order, and that you should transpose nothing. There are two reasons which principally prevail with me. First, the adversaries will cry out, that the arguments are moved out of their position with a fraudulent intention. For as in battles commanders do not always commence the engagement in the same order, but sometimes attack the front, at other times assail the wings; they make the first charge upon the enemy sometimes with cavalry, frequently also with light-armed skirmishers, (for it would be a most unreasonable thing to be dictated to by the enemy as to the order of commencing the conflict;) so also they will complain of you, if the forces of the bishop of Winchester are drawn up in array after any other plan than that according to which he himself has arranged them. Again, this method seems to me to tend to the exhibition of the author's character. For it is but meet, that one who all his life long has been, so to speak, the most preposterous inverter of all things human and divine, should shew himself to be preposterous also in writing, and, as the saying is, *Joannes ad oppositum.*

This is my opinion; you in your candid judgment may come to a different conclusion. As to the title of the book, none will give a more fitting one than the translator, who has considered not only every sentence, but almost the very words and points. (pp. 234-35)

Consider these things to be so written by me, as that I wish, notwithstanding, every thing to be done according to your own judgment. I merely put these thoughts of my own mind before you, my friend and brother, more candidly perhaps than wisely. Salute Bale and the rest of my friends. Fare you right well in the Lord. (p. 236)

Edmund Grindal, in a letter to John Foxe on December 28, 1557, in his The Remains of Edmund Grindal, *edited by Rev. William Nicholson, The Parker Society, 1843, pp. 234-36.*

John Foxe   (essay date 1563)

[*In the following preface to the first English edition of* Actes and Monuments, *published in 1563, Foxe defends himself against charges made by his Catholic opponents.*]

It is dangerous (he says) to publish anything now; the most circumspect writer is sure to be calumniated. Happy are they that can look on in dignified ease. But I have scarce ever tasted the delights of leisure; constant labour, trouble and contention have been my lot. True, I despise fortune, nor do I mind labours if only they profit others as much as they vex me. But I am unhappy enough to labour on a work which beside the mournful theme, beside the irksomeness of the language, beside the difficulty of treatment, compels me to choose between narrating history falsely, and speaking the truth at the price of winning the hatred of many. I write of things of our own age and of men yet living. "I ask, what else must I look for than when I have in vain by my exertions worn out my health, impaired my eyes, hastened the coming of old age, and exhausted my body, after all this to expose myself to the hatred, hissings, envy and calumny of many men." God alone can protect me here; and to God I commend my cause.

I am sure to have trouble; I must expect bites, hissings, and the poison of tongues. "One will say that the story is untrue; another that the book lacks art, carefulness or judgment. A third maybe will be displeased by its bulk, or by its departure from exact chronological order. . . . Nay, already I hear the mutterings of some who say they have been waiting a very long time for the publication of this our golden legend, as they call it." But let these critics remember the proverb: Hasten slowly. We have done our best, and more than our health would stand. We have worked quicker than a trifler could, quicker indeed than was befitting in a work of this moment and size, which demanded a longer time and a greater care; whereas "to us scarce eighteen months was given for preparing the material, collecting the facts, comparing the copies, reading the manuscripts, rewriting documents written by hand, correcting the print, ordering and arranging the history. Those can bear me out who were witnesses; who knew the time I spent on it, and were partakers in the labour."

Golden legend! They call it so, without even waiting for the publication. Clearly they are ashamed of their own Golden Legend, with which they have mocked the world. They judge others by themselves. Are we to have no solid ecclesiastical history in these times? As to my book, I make known to all that I have taken pains to put in nothing that is fabulous, or in any way like their golden (say rather leaden) legend. My story is compiled from the archives and registers of the bishops, and partly from the letters of the martyrs themselves. I say not that all is an oracle, but we have come as near as possible to the old law, to avoid the two pests of history, fear and flattery, saying too much or saying too little. Yet of this it is fairer that men should judge by the work itself rather than by my commendation. "For truth has its own simple and natural face", which can soon be recognised. I wish this history were *not* so true as it is, were really like their golden legend and their other lying stories. These miseries were inflicted by you, not feigned by me; we have more witness to them than we would choose.

I come now to the second accusation, that concerning the kalendar. I hear that some of the papists not merely think, but say openly, that it is wrong of me to thrust out of the kalendar the saints and martyrs of the old church, and bring in new martyrs and confessors in their place. But I am not belittling the old saints, nor do I make new saints by putting these names into my kalendar. I am no Gregory IX; I prescribe no new law of feast days nor new cult of saints. We have too many saints-days as it is. Would that we could keep only the Lord's sabbath worthily! Let the papists keep their kalendar, provided that they fill it with true saints, and do not worship them. Jerome said that some saints are in hell. What would he say to the official kalendar of these days? My kalendar is but an index, giving the month and year of each martyr. The cause, not the punishment, makes the martyr; one Cranmer is worth six hundred Beckets. I hurt the memory of no good man, nor do I intend my kalendar to be set up in churches.

But to return to you, learned reader, I know that in this vast compilation you will find many things to merit your disapproval. In a work so hastily composed (*in tanta operis praecipitatione*) everything could not be done perfectly. The writer may sleep from weariness, or may omit something through carelessness or haste. I ask your pardon rather than your censure. And if I gain your favour, I shall care less for the opinions of others, mindful of the Greek proverb: It is easier to blame than to imitate. (pp. 132-34)

> *John Foxe, in an extract in* John Foxe and His Book *by J. F. Mozley, Society for Promoting Christian Knowledge, 1940, pp. 132-34.*

Thomas Harding   (essay date 1565)

[*A sixteenth-century English Roman Catholic cleric and essayist, Harding was one of Foxe's earliest adversaries. In a series of written exchanges with the Protestant bishop of Salisbury, John Jewel, Harding defended Catholicism, censuring Jewel's written defense of the reformed church,* Apologia ecclesiae englicanae *(1562;* An apologie or aunswer in defence of the Church of England, *1562). Although Harding chiefly attacked Jewel's work, he also opposed* Actes and Monuments, *chastising Foxe in* A Confutation of a Booke Intituled "An Apologie of the Church of England" *(1565) and* A Reioindre to M. Iewels Replie Against the Sacrifice of the Masse *(1567). In the following excerpt from the former work, he claims that Foxe distorted facts in his martyrology concerning the execution of Protestants for heresy.*]

There haue not so many thousandes of your brethren ben burnt for heresie in these last twenty yeres, as ye pretend.

But when ye come to boasting, then haue ye a great grace in vsing the figure *Hyperbole*. Then scores be hundreds, hundreds be thousands, thousands be millions. Neither haue those brethren of yours by their due punishment of burning borne witnes vnto the truth, but shewed their desperat obstinacie against the truth. But what wisedome or reason is it to make their burning an argument of the truth of your syde? were all they that haue ben burnt by commaundement of Christen Magistrates in those your later twenty yeres your brethren? Verely then haue ye a holy brotherhed. Was Michael Seruetus the Arian, who was burnt at Geneua by procurement of Caluine, a brother of yours? Dauid George that tooke vpon him to be Christ, who was taken vp after he was buried and burnt at Basile, whas he your brother? to come neare home, Ioan of Kent that filth, who tooke forth a lesson further then ye taught her (I trowe) or yet preach, was she a syster of yours? So many Adamites, so many Zwenckfeldians, so many hundreds of Anabaptistes and libertines, as haue within your twenty yeres ben ridde out of their liues by fyre, sword, and water in sundry partes of christendome, were they all of your blessed brotherhed? If ye forswere their companie, and saye they were none of your congregation: why make ye the burning of brethren an argument of the truth of your gospell, whereof the professours of those other sectes haue as great aduantage as your owne sect? yet is this the greatest argument wherewith ye bleare the eyes of the ignorant people. And this is the chiefe argument ye make in in all that huge dongehill of your stinking martyrs, which ye haue intituled ***Actes and monumentes.*** But we tell you. It is not death that iustifieth the cause of dying. But it is the cause of dying that iustifieth the death. He that dieth for maintenance of a good cause, is blessed. He that dieth for an euil dede, suffereth his deserued punishment. He that dieth in defence of your or any other heresres, beginneth his hell here, and from the smoke of temporall fyre leapeth into the flame of euerlasting fyre. (p. 14)

> *Thomas Harding, in an excerpt in his* A Confutation of a Booke Intituled "An Apologie of the Church of England," *Ihon Laet, 1565, 351 p.*

Thomas Harding   (essay date 1567)

[*In the following excerpt from one of his final attacks upon Jewel,* A Reioindre to M. Iewels Replie against the Sacrifice of the Masse *(1567), Harding queries Foxe's definition and use of the term martyr.*]

Whereas as you wil nedes haue [the Protestant martyrs] to be called Martyrs, and now be canonizate a Gods name by M. Foxe, and set in a solemne Calender, that holy daies and hye feastes be kept for them, who can otherwise do, but laugh at you? . . . It is not the paine, that maketh a Martyr, but the cause, saith S. Augustine. Remember you not, what he writeth of such companions? It may serue very fitly, for to be said vnto you. . . . The whole question is, whether ye doo not euil, whom the worlde chargeth with the mischeuous crime of so great schisme, the due diseussion of which question ye leaue, and speake voide and vaine wordes. And whereas ye liue as Theeues, ye bragge that ye dye, as Martyrs.

In an other place likewise faith he to such heretiques, as

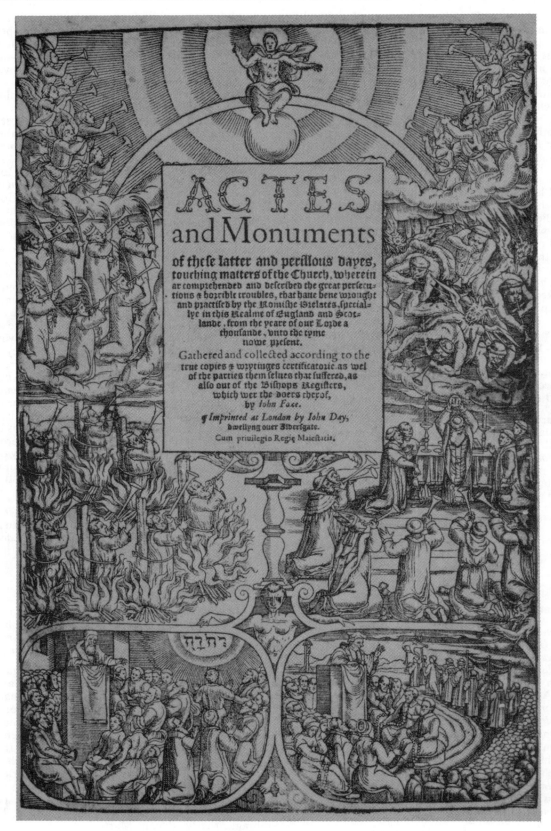

Title page of the 1563 edition of Foxe's Actes and Monuments.

being persecuted for their desert, chalenged vnto them the glorie of Martyrdom, as you and your companions do, *Rectè ist a dicerentur à vobis quarentibus Martyrum gloriam, si Martyrum cansam haberetis.* These thinges were wel said of you seeking for the glorie of Martyrs, in case ye had the cause of Martyrs.

According to his teaching there be true Martyrs, and false Martyrs. That voice in the Psalme, he vnderstandeth to be the voice of true Martyrs, being desirous to be discerned from false Martyrs. *Iudica me Deus . Iudge me ô God, and discerne my cause from the people that is vnholy.* He said not (faith S. Augustine) . . . discerne my paine, but discerne my cause.

And as there be true and false Martyrs, so he saith, there be two sortes of persecutions. *There is* (saith he) *an vnits persecution, whiche the wicked make against the Churche of Christe, and there is a iust persecution, whiche the Churches of Christ make against the wicked. The Church is blessed, that suffereth persecution for righteousnes, they be miserable, that suffer persecution for vnrighteousnes.*

Now if ye can iuscifie your cause no better, then ye haue done hitherto, crake, and bragge no more of your Martyrdomes: Let M. Foxe make no Martyrs. Or if ye wil needes allow him for a Martyrmaker stil, let him be warned to vse a more discretion, then heretofore he hath vsed, els his huge booke of ***Actes and Monumentes*** can not long kepe credit. For what wil wisemen thinke, euen they of your owne side, when they shal consider, what persons he hath canonizate, and registred for Martyrs? As Robert King of Dednam, Robert Debnam of Elfbergholt, Nicolaus Marsh of Dednam, who were hanged for Felonie: William Cowbridge burnt at Oxford, who as it is openly knowen, could not abide the name of Christe, but said it was a fowle name, and that Christe is not the redemer of the worlde, and helde many other blasphemous heresies: Peter the Germaine, who besides that he was a Sacramentarie, helde opinion, that our Lorde tooke not flesne of the blessed virgin Marie his Mother: Dicke Adames hanged at Bristow for felonie, and William Flower, that drew forth his hanger, and strake the Priest in S. Margaretes Churche in Westminster, as he was ministring the blessed Sacrament to the people. Al these, and many others of like qualities, murderers, theeues, Churcherobbers, rebelles, and Traitours, and by your owne confession detestable heresiques, haue ye made Martyrs. I speake not of Sir Iohn Oldecastel, and Sir Roger Acton, put to death for high treason, whom neuerthelesse Foxe hath canonizate for holy Martyrs: Neither of Dame Eleonor Cobham, bannished for conspiring the death of King Henry the sixth by wytchecrafte, who in Foxes great booke is regestred for a worthy Confessour. Whereby it seemeth that he hath a commission (from whens I knowe not) to make, not onely Martyrs, but also Confessours. As for Virgins, I trowe these men canonizate none, for their sprite brooketh not very wel, that holy srate of lyse.

Whereas he is about to set foorth his *famous **Actes and Monumentes*** againe, as I heare, if he had a desire to increase his number, and wil take the paines to come ouer into the Low countrie: He shal finde stoare of new mater, yea of as good Martyrs, as he hath made any yet, ten, twelue, sixteen in a Clustre hanging vpon one bough by the waiesside in sundry places. Their hues, and Faithes were so notable, their hartes so sroute and constant in contempt of the holy Sacramentes and al godly thinges: that I dare say, if he had the Registres and instrumentes made of their examinations, answeres, bolde and hardy deedes in burning liberaries, and religious Howses, in robbing and spoiling of Churches, and Abbaies, in doing villanie to holy Nonnes by diuers waies, and in rebelling openly against their lawful Prince: he could not find in his harte for the Gospels sake, to let them passe not rewarded with the renome of his Canonization. (pp. 180-82)

• • • • •

Yea, but *a poore Innocent Babe falling from the mothers wombe, was taken, and throwen cruelly into the Fier.* What if it were denied you, that euer any such thing was done? Let vs heare, how you are hable to prooue it. O say you, it must needes be true. For we finde it so written by M. Iohn Foxe in his great booke of ***Actes and Monumentes.*** Why Sir dare you so constantly auouche this facte onely vppon the reporte of Foxe? As though he had not tolde vs in his false Martyrologe, a thousand mo lyes then this? I pitie you M. Iewel, that craking so muche of antiquitie, and appealing continually to the Fathers of the six hundred yeres, you are now driuen to stay your credite vppon Foxe, who hath into that Huge volume infarced lyes, moe in number, and notabler for vanitie, then euer were raked together into any one heape, or booke. Wel, if al were false, that here you tel, then haue you loste a ioily tale. Foxe him selfe reporteth, when Commissioners in London vpon a complaint examined the mater, that it was founde but probable. And probable he meaneth in the iudgement of them, who gladly finde fault with al that was done touching the punishment of heresie in Queene Maries reigne. Now the thing (if any such thing were done at al) being so Notorious, so openly executed, so fewe yeresthen past since it was doone, so many men ye lyuing, that would haue ben present at the examination in case they had bene commaunded, the charges of the iourney from Garnesey (where it is said to haue bene done) to London being borne, and could haue brought true witnesse, neuerthelesse to be founde but probable: I weene, it wil not to any wise man appeare very probable.

How be it let the Fable be a Storie, and the same be taken for true, according as Foxe doth describe it to the aduantage, and as you M. Iewel report it: That in Garnesey three wemen, that is, the mother, and her twoo daughters were burnt, and that one of the Daughters was with childe, and the childe issued from her wombe being riued with the fier, and was consumed together with the fier. What of al this? In whom was the faulte, in the officer, that tooke not the childe out of the fier, or in the vnnatural mother, that brought it into the fier? In the Storie there is mention made of a childe, and of the mother, but of the childes Father, there is no woorde spoken. It appeareth very credible, that the historiographer was a shamed to name the childes Father, least so he should haue defaced the glorie of the mothers Martyrdom. For I would faine know who was the husband to the daughter. M. Fox doth not expresse it.

But you wil say, how so euer the childe was begotten, the mother being in that case should haue bene by no Law, iustice, or reason committed vnto the fier. True it is, a woman in that case may for once claime the benefite of her belly. Mary I haue heard Lawiers say, that if whiles she is in prison, she play the strompet againe, by Lawe the judge may denie her the benefite of her belly, and geue sentence of death vpon her. But as for your pratteling parrat Paratine (for so was her name as M. Fox registreth her) it was not knowen to the Iudge, that she was with childe. Had it bene knowen, doubtelesse her death had bene differred vntil she had ben brought on bed. But the honest woman, bicause she would not shame the Gospel, keping it priuy from the Magistrates, claimed not the benefite of the Lawe, and so now not only like an harlot or Heretique, but like a Murtherer went desperatly to the fier, and murdered bothe her selfe, and her childe conceiued within her. So farre the Deuil carrieth them, whom he possesseth, and leadeth at his wil. This abominable facte God by his most iust iudgement reueled, to the condemnation bothe of her, and of the cause for which she dyed, by suffering the childe to fal from her wombe, in the sight of al that stoode by.

Iudge now discrete Reader, to whom redoundeth the blame of the crime, whether to the Ministers of Iustice, who not knowing the thing, executed the Lawe: or to the woman, that for auoiding a worldly shame, conceeling her owne turpitude, became a murtherer of her owne babe, before it came to perfection. So that she died gilty of three heinous crimes, of heresie, lecherie, and murther. And to these theste may be added for the fourth. For it appeareth by the tale, that Foxe him selfe to her best estimation telleth of her, that she was a thefe, as being accessorie to the honest woman Vincent Gosset, that stole a siluer gobblet. If the mater were wel examined, I doubte not she would be tried an honest woman, and a fitte vessel to receiue the glorie of these newe inuented Martyrdomes.

Here I appeale vnto your owne wisedome M. Iewel, and demaunde of you, what you could, or would haue done for that vnperfite and dead childe in that case, better, then was done. If they had taken it out of the fyer, what should that haue auailed? Life it had none, and therfore was it not to be baptized. Sense it had none: and therfore had it not ben holpen by sauing it from burning. As for burial, sith it was neither Christened, nor come to be perfite man: it was afwel burnt, and buried in earth, yea in some respecte better, bicause being burnt with the wicked mother, besides the more detestation of the horrible crime to the example of others, it was a testimonie against the mothers vnnaturalnes. Neither in deede truly to speake, was it *a poore innocent Babe,* as to aggrauate the facte, more rhetorically, then truly you reporte. For being a dead thing, as it could not be riche, or hurtful, so neither properly ought it to be called, *poore,* or *innocent.* This much considered, you haue gotten litle honestie to your Gospel M. Iewel, by rehersal of casting this *poore innocent Babe* into the fyer: And the mother your Syster in the Lorde, is fownd but a meane Martyr, and witnesse of the truth. Of the fruite of such Martyrdome, the famous Tree of Tybourne bringeth forth good stoare. (pp. 184-86)

> *Thomas Harding, in an excerpt, in his* A Rejoindre to M. Jewels Replie against the Sacrifice of the Masse, *Lovanii, 1567, pp. 180-86.*

John Lowth   (letter date 1579)

[*Lowth (or, alternatively, Louth) was a sixteenth-century English cleric. In the following excerpt from a letter written in 1579, he encourages Foxe to continue his work, offering additional information on certain contemporaries who appeared in* Actes and Monuments.]

Salutem in Christo Jhesu.

The love that I beare to the churche of Chryste constraynythe me to gyve yow thankes for the happy and dayly paynes yow take in settynge forthe the worthy actes of those late martyres of Chryste in Englande. That worke servythe to the glory of Chryste, the comforte of his members lyvyng, and godly memory of them which are departed; to the overthrow of Antichryste and eternall shame of all antichrysteanes; and I doghte not but that booke wyll brynge to repentance the rable of the reste bloody butcheres yet lyvynge, so many at lest as are not gyvyne up into a reprochfull mynde, who have shutt up theyre eyes that thei may not see, &c. Of these sorte are they that cry dayly, "Lyes, lyes! more lies founde in the booke of *Actes and Monumentes of Martyres!"* Wherwith yow owght not to be discowraged (as I truste yow are not), but rather encowraged to go forwarde in the same. *Tu solus hanc Spartam nactus es, hanc adorna.* Rejoyce that yow are lyke to them same martyres that so were rayled apon, yea lyke to Jeremy, crying: *Cur fecisti me virum rixæ? hominem objurgiorum!* When ye reade of these Romyshe raylynges, ye may have greate joye and cawse to thanke God that in this poynte ye are resembled to his owne sonne the lorde Jhesus Chryste. The dyvyles cryed against hym; but they most rored when thei sawe thei muste come forth of the man, and lose theyre kyngdome and power. Therfore wryght styll, cease not, seyng the booke dothe so muche good in Chrystes churche, yt wyll doe more good after your dethe then lyff. The memory of mr. John Philpott, ons my compaygnion in Wynthone, Oxforde, and London, wyll never dye. The same may be sayd of the other sanctes and martyres, and *god a mercy* to yow, and your booke. God wyll not forgett your labores and paynes, that hathe cawsed his sainctes, his servantes, and his enymies to be in perpetuall memory. Yt ys he that gyvyth yow the wytt, the lernyng, the wyll, the philopony, and infrangyble diligens. Els your helthe wolde be a lett, these peynes wold weary yow, these tawntes wold dismay yow, wych dayly come forthe of those lyyng lypps that crye, "Lyes, lyes; so many lynes so many lies!" Yet they perceave not that are of that religyone, how that the father of lies and murder hathe devysed by ther helpe to deface the heavenly doctryne of our Savioure Jhesus Chryste, by whome comythe all trewth and grace, beynge hymselfe the lyght to lyghten the gentyles, and to be the glory of hys people Israel. You are weak and to weake of yourself to doo this noble acte; but he hathe enabled yow therto, that sayd to Pawle, *Virtus mea in infirmitate perficitur.*

Admitte that a Lovanyone luske, [Alan Cope] lyinge longe in waygt with so many felows, hath fownd in yowr great volume some smalle unthroths (untruths), muste he therfor cry owt lyke a dyvylle agaynst the whole booke, for a letter, a syllable, a man's name, a towne, or suche tryfle? *In multis peccavimus omnes.* The poettes can suffer theyr good Homere sometyme to slomber and sleepe, and the papistes theyr erthly God the Pope; they can full smothly solve in horryble sores of lyffe, doctrine, relygione, and conscience. An historiographer ys excusable, not when he maketh a lye, but when he of an other's informatione setteth down an untrothe. Then wee and the papistes must neades alow the commun rule: *Sit fides penes aucthorem: imo sit culpa penes eundem.* In some thynges that yow wryght, I can shew that yow have not putt in wrytyng very muche that wolde dawnte the adversares, honor God, comforte his churche, and sett owt the mighty power of God. As here folowing I wyll doo yow understand.

Now to yow pestilent papistes: I myght more justely falle owt with my brother John Foxe then yow, I (aye), for that [he] hathe not wrytten these thynges so necessary as ys declared. But he hathe one answere for us bothe: "The fawlte was not in me, but in the informatione gyven, or not gyven; truly gyven, or not truly gyven." But this I say, yf mr. Foxe wer as swhyfte a scrybe as Esras, yet he shoulde not be able to wryght all your abhominable lyffes and doctrines, yowr cruell tormentyng and manaclyng of Chrystes saynctes in this lyff, and (lyke divyles) ye labore so muche as any fynde of hell can do to bereave them, by yowr doctrine, of lyff everlastyng. Then what lye can he or any man wryght of yow, but yt shalbe fownde trew, ether in your detestable crueltee, fylthy sodomy, or divyllyshe doctrine: he as muche offendythe that thus termythe yow, as he that should call yowr father the divill knave, by whose suggesyons yow fullfylle the measure of your fathers in all manner of crueltee and butchery of godly men. Theyr blood with Abel's cry owt for vengans agaynst yow. Yowr forfathers could not murder all God's chyldren, for some escaped theyr handes, and some were not then borne as yet to fulfyll the number of their bretheren by martyrdome; but those that to yow were left by them, how butcherly have yow slayne! Ye are the chyldren of your murdryng fathers, havyng the same hate that they to Gode [and] godlynes, the same tyranny, all laws caste behynde yow, the same doctrine, the same syar the devyll, and therfor the same murderyng hartes as perteynyth to suche a race, to make havoke (O cruell wolves!) of Chrystes flocke. God forgive yow; God open yowr eyes; God, thorow repentance, make yow meeke Pawles, wych have ben so ragyng Sawles, thretnyng blasphemously wrath and slawghter to innocent lambes of Chrystes flocke!

Now, mr. Foxe, thoghe your booke ys paste the prynte, yet I wyll sett downe truly here (God ys wytnes) what I have creably herd of some of the martyres more then yowr booke reportyth, in the wych I beleeve I shall nether make lye, nor tell lye. The aucthores therof ar so lawfull, I myght saye authentycke. Of whom I may say with the poett: *Quorum pars magna fuere.* I know not whyther ye may be occasyoned to use any of these additionall historyes wych I have sent yow, as a taste of many more I have wrytten, *a Martyrio Jó. Frythi.* I pray yow encreace yowr booke, for I hope it wyll be adbrydged, and also enlarged, when yow shalbe gon to Chryste. (pp. 15-18)

John Lowth, "The Reminiscences of John Louth: Introductory Letter Addressed to John Foxe," in Narratives of the Days of the Reformation: Chiefly from the Manuscripts of John Foxe the Martyrologist, *edited by John Gough Nichols, The Camden Society, 1859, pp. 15-18.*

Robert Parsons   (essay date 1604)

[*Parsons was an English Jesuit and essayist. He is remembered as one of the severest and most outspoken detractors of* Actes and Monuments. *In a biting three-volume work.* A Treatise of Three Conversions of England, *he repeatedly questioned Foxe's veracity and methodology, seeking to destroy the martyrologist's credibility by inferring that he was little more than a madman who had concocted a book of lies. This early work long remained one of the most damaging to Foxe's reputation. In the following excerpt from the third part of* A Treatise of Three Conversions, *Parsons points to Foxe's perceived unstable character and lack of judgment and understanding as principal reasons for his perpetrating "divers falshoods, falsifications, deceyts and shifts."*]

Notwithstandinge that throughout the whole course of this our Treatise against *John Fox,* and his **Acts and Monuments,** we haue often had occasion to giue our opinion as well of the man, as of his wrytings; yet now drawinge towards the end of that we designed to wryte in this behalfe; yt shall not be amisse perhapps, to repeate heere briefly that, which els where dispersedly hath byn vttered about this point, to the end that the discreet Reader may see more cleerly in what accoumpt both the wryter and his wrytinges are iustly to be held.

And first then to say nothing of the mans person, he being now dead, nor of the notorious infirmityes commonly related of him, as that he imagined himselfe sometymes to be an vrinall of glasse; sometymes a crowinge cocke, & other like fancyes which might fall vnto him eyther by weaknes of brayne, or by other disturbance of his senses through ouermuch study, phrensy of heresy, or other like causes; These personall thinges (I say) that might happen vnto him without his default, and consequently are rather to be pittyed in him, then any way exprobrated vnto him; I shall wholy lay aside, and treate in this place only of some points that must needs be presumed to haue proceeded from his free-will and iudgement, and thereby the more reprehensible, they being eyther false or wicked, and not iustifiable in themselues. Albeit in this kind againe, I must needs help to excuse him also in diuers things, which I ascribe rather to his lacke of vnderstandinge and iudgment, then to meere malice, as are those vvhich make more against him then for him, or are so impertinent, as no man of learninge & iudgement would haue alleaged, or noted in that fashion which he doth.

To which head or branch I do reduce all those large discourses, vvhich he maketh of our Church in many ages against himselfe; his relations also and prolix narrations of the Waldensians, Albigensians, Wickliffians, Hussits and the Lutherans affayres, vvhich conteyne a great part of his volume, and haue infinite things in them against Fox his sect of Sacramentaryes: In like manner his coopling togeather of so different and repugnant sectaryes, as Saints of one Calendar and Church, can be excused by no other meanes then by this, that the good man vnderstood not or considered not, how farre his narrations made for his cause or against yt, so they might seeme to sound somwhat against the Roman Church or Religion. And for that the greatest part of his whole volume may be comprehended vnder this branch, I will not stand heere in discussing the particulars, but referre the Reader to the first and second parts of this Treatise, that do runne ouer the whole worke, & make the matter cleere to the said Readers eye, in euery age from the Apostles.

4. Now then those things remoued, we shall only call into consideration for the present, such other points, as concerne his falshood & lacke of conscience, or rather (to mitigate the matter also in this point somewhat) his error of conscience, whereby it seemeth that he came to persuade

himselfe in conscience, that supposinge (as he did) that the Protestant or Puritan profession of England was the only true Religion, he might say or wryte any thinge in furderance thereof, without scruple of conscience, whether it were in deed true or false. And that this was his persuasion I am induced to beleeue rather (as I haue said) for his excuse then commendation: For that otherwise, yf he had not had that opinion, I can hardly thinke so euill of any man Christened, as that he would recoumpt so many false thinges, as Fox doth against his owne conscience. For truly to speake as I thinke, after I had read ouer the whole worke with some attention, and to speake without all exaggeration or passion, as one that doth hartily pitty the mans case, and must follow him out of this world ere yt be longe (though I hope to another place) I do not thinke there be many storyes in this whole volume (though so huge & vast as yow see) but that one way or other, yf they belonge to matters of controuersie, he corrupteth or falsifyeth some part therof, eyther in the beginninge, endinge, entrance, goinge forth, matter, manner of handlinge, or some other kind of adulteration; and yet doth he vse euery where such holy protestations of piety, as neuer perhapps other author before or after him, addinge alwayes whersoeuer he promiseth any thinge, or speaketh of the tyme to come, these deuout phrases, *the Lords holy spiritt assistinge me therin; The Lords diuine grace gewinge me leaue: yf* Iesvs *shall lend me his helpinge hand: by the Lords good leaue and pleasure;* and other like most sainctlike phrases, repeated & iterated aboue a thousand tymes throughout this worke; And for that comonly soone after these godly protestations, yow shall find him in diuers falshoods, falsifications, deceyts and shifts, I am rather induced to thinke that he esteemeth this manner of dealinge lawfull in so good a cause, as he presumed his owne to be, then that he did yt expressely against his conscience and iudgement.

5. The particular proofes, examples and demonstrations of this kind of dealinge in him, were ouer longe and tedious to prosecute in this place, and yow haue had store of them before, both in this third part, as also in the former two, and in the Warn-word, where it shalbe sufficient to referre the Reader to the word (*Fox*) in the table of each booke; and the next ensuinge Chapter shall giue a fuller tast, of his manner of proceedinge in this behalfe, though it be not the hundreth part of the false and deceytfull dealinge, which is to be noted out of these his lyinge **Acts and Monuments;** a booke composed wholy to deceyue, and by iudgement of many men, hath done more hurt alone to simple soules in our countrey, by infectinge and poysoninge them vnwares, vnder the bayte of pleasant historyes, fayre pictures and painted pageants, then many other the most pestilent bookes togeather.

6. For first as I haue said, the variety of the history it selfe, draweth many to read yt: then the foresaid spectacle and representation of martyrdomes (as they are called) delighteth many to gaze on, who cannot read; thirdly the hypocrisy of the wryter, makinge those protestations which before haue byn mentioned, and otherwise, gayninge opinion of piety with the common people, by a certayne affected simplicity of life: Fourthly certayne tender speaches attributed by him to sectaryes at their deathes, with his owne sanctifying & canonizing them for Saints: these things I say, & other circumstances togeather, with the very greatnes of the booke yt selfe, obtruded to be read in very many

parish Churches, and other publike places, haue byn causes of infinite spirituall hurt, to many thousand soules of our countrey, for which this miserable man, and his abetters haue, no doubt, to yield a straite and heauy accoumpt to their redeemer, at the most dreadfull accoumpting day.

7. And to the end yow may the better perceaue the deadly hurt, which this most poysened Fox-den hath brought forth, & wought not in simple soules only, but in many of iudgement and some learning also, yow must consider, that from the beginninge to the end of this whole volume, he commonly setteth downe nothinge affirmatiue or positiue of his owne in matters of Religion, nor any certaine rule what to beleeue, but only carpeth, or scoffeth at that which was in vse before: so as the Reader is brought only into vnbeleefe, distrust and contempt of that, which was accoumpted piety and Religion by his forefathers, and nothinge certayne taught him in place therof, but only negatiue or scornefull taunts, the proper meanes to make Atheists &c. infidells. For proofe wherof yow may please to consider, that yf yow begin (for examples sake) with the first planting of Christian faith in the English nation by *S. Gregory & S. Austen,* and other English Apostles, Iohn Fox and his fellowes do iest euery where at them, and at the Religion brought in by them, so as these our first Fathers in Religion, as also our predecessors & ancestors in bloud, that were conuerted from paganisme to Christian Religion by them, being proued now by these later Doctors, to haue byn no true Christians in deed but only in name, as these men hold, what good doth the Reader receaue by this doctrine, but only remaine in mistrust of all, and to thinke that the whole history of the English Church for a thousand yeares togeather, is a meere fable?

8. Againe, when Fox his history commeth downe for 600 yeares togeather after this our first conuersion, to witt, beneath the conquest, iesting still and scoffing at most things that passed in that Church and time, and after that beginneth to recoumpt the Acts & Gests of diuers new-fangled people, condemned for heresie, as the Acts of Saints & holy men, sent especially from God, & illuminated particularly by his holy spiritt, as the *Waldensians, Albigersians, Lollards, VVickliffians, Husitts, Thaboritts Lutherans,* and in all these or the most of them he is forced to acknowledge many hereticall opinions, which himselfe and his Church (yf he haue any at all) condemneth, and yet, as I said, setteth them forth for great Saints and men of perfection, without reprouinge their false opinions; how is yt possible but that the Readers mynd must remayne heere poysoned, and coinquinated with these dregges sett before him by Iohn Fox, seing that no cleere rule is put downe for discerninge the same, but only referringe ouer each man and woman to the examination of scriptures, which both these heretiks, & all other alleage most aboundantly for themselues, and the interpretation standeth in each ones particular iudgement to allow or follow?

9. Thus then the mynds of English Christians standinge firme and fixed in one Religion, before the readinge of Iohn Fox his booke, for more then a thousand yeares togeather, and attendinge only to the exercises of piety and godly life prescribed by that Religion; now by readinge this booke, they are all put out of ioint; and being brought into doubt & contempt of their said old Religion, which had endured from their first conuersion; they are now to

chuse new opinions what each man liketh best, eyther of the *VValdensian, Albigensian, Wickliffian, Lutheran, Caluinian,* and other such opinions or sects, and vpon these they are to rest their soules, & to receaue the authors of these opinions into their Ecclesiasticall Calendar, in steed of the old Saints, that were there before, and for that, where such choyce of Religion is giuen, yt is hard for simple men and weomen, as also for the learned to determyne vvhat they like best, or whereon they will lay hand in so great a matter, as concerneth their eternall saluation or condemnation; we must imagine that infinite people remayne in suspence, & doubtfull in our countrey at this day, and haue not yet determined, what certayne sect to be of; but only to doubt or contradict the Catholike, and for the rest to hould of this or that sect what euery one liketh best, when they shall resolue to determine of any; which is the most miserable estate that can be imagined; for that it is indeed to haue no Religion at all. And this is the very principall effect of Fox his booke or history.

10. For better confirmation wherof, do yow read with attention but any one of the historyes before mentioned, as for example of *Iohn Husse,* or *Iohn Wickliffe,* and albeit I know yow will be weary before you come to the end, yet do marke with diligence, what yow can gather, or what Fox doth gather out of all that history for your profitt, but only their contradiction against the Catholike Church (which he might gather also out of all ould heretiks:) but for the rest yow shall see, that sometymes he will tell yow matters indifferent of them, sometymes others that seeme to sound towards his Religion, sometymes other that make flatt against him, & not seldome others that are opposite to vs both, to witt, Catholiks and Caluinists: and yet are the men auouched by him to be good and holy, but no particular conclusion is made about their whole Religion; whether yt were good or badd. And what then can the Reader gather out of these discourses, but only doubtfullnes and breakinge of his owne braine, for that most tymes Fox concludeth thus, after he hath rehearsed both good and badd of these new Saints, that haleaueth all to the Reader, both men and matters, to iudge thereof as he shall thinke best, and therby to take and leaue what he listeth or liketh best: so as in very truth he hath no certainty at all, nor sure direction how to find yt. Wherby a man may pronounce of this Fox-den booke more fitly, then one did of another in old tyme: *Hic liber ex stultis insanos facit,* this booke is fitt to make madd men of fooles, to witt heretiks of ignorant people. And this is another principall effect of Fox his booke.

11. Wherfore not to proceede any further vpon this subiect, my counsell should be vnto my Countrymen, not to leese any more time in reading ouer so vaft and vayne a heape of vntruthes laid togeather, as this worke of Fox conteyneth, wherin there is neyther certainty of truth in the narration, nor good order in the method, nor any exact distinction of tymes obserued,. . . . (pp. 396-405)

> *Robert Parsons, "A Brief Censure of John Fox and His Writings," in his* A Treatise of Three Conversions of England from Paganisme to Christian Religion, *n.p., 1604, pp. 396-412.*

Gilbert Burnet   (essay date 1681)

[*Burnet was a prominent seventeenth- and eighteenth-century ecclesiastic, historian, biographer, and sermonist. A prolific author, he wrote biographies on several of his contemporaries. In the following excerpt from* The History of the Reformation of the Church of England, *he briefly assesses Foxe as an historian.*]

I intend not to write a pompous martyrology, and therefore hereafter I shall only name the persons that suffered, with the reasons for which they were condemned: but, except in a very few instances, I shall not enlarge on the manner of their trial and sufferings; which being so copiously done by Fox, there is nothing left for any that comes after him. In some private passages which were brought to him upon flying reports, he made a few mistakes, being too credulous; but in the account he gives from records, or papers, he is a most exact and faithful writer; so that I could never find him in any prevarication, or so much as a designed concealment. He tells the good and the bad, the weakness and passion, as well as the constancy and patience of those good men who sealed their faith with their blood; who were not all equal in parts nor in discretion: but the weaker any of them were, it argued the more cruelty in their persecutors to proceed so severely against such inconsiderable persons.

> *Gilbert Burnet, in an excerpt, in his* The History of the Reformation of the Church of England, Vol. II, *edited by Nicholas Pocock, 1865. Reprint by Gregg International Publishers Limited, 1969, p. 492.*

Rev. John Milner   (essay date 1798)

[*An eighteenth- and nineteenth-century Roman Catholic priest and historian, Milner objected strongly to Foxe's interpretation and portrayal of sixteenth-century religious controversies in England. He therefore attempted to discredit Foxe by revealing factual inaccuracies in* Actes and Monuments. *Milner attacked Foxe and defended Catholicism in three works:* The History Civil and Ecclesiastical, and Survey of the Antiquities, of Winchester *(1798),* Letters to a Prebendary *(1800), and* The End of Religious Controversy *(1818). All three contain arguments against Foxe in the tradition of Nicholas Harpsfield and Robert Parsons. In the following excerpt from* Survey of Winchester, *he reproaches Foxe for knowingly writing a book filled with "falsehood, misrepresentation, and absurdity."*]

[The] huge history of these persecutions, written by John Fox, which has been the store-house for all succeeding writers on the same subject, has been demonstrated to be one tissue of falsehood, misrepresentation, and absurdity. Some of his pretended martyrs were alive at the time when he was describing the circumstances of their death; many of them were executed for rebellion, assassination, theft, or other crimes; not a few of them died in the open profession of the Catholic, doctrine, or only differed in certain points of no great consequence to the main subjects of controversy; whilst the greater part either differed from the received doctrines of the established church, or differed from each other in some of the points at least, on which they were arraigned and condemned. (pp. 357-58)

> *Rev. John Milner, in an excerpt in his* The History Civil and Ecclesiastical, & Survey of the

Antiquities, of Winchester, Vol. I, *J. Robbins, 1798, pp. 357-58.*

George Townsend (letter date 1841)

[*Townsend was a nineteenth-century English clergyman, editor, poet, historian, and essayist. In the following excerpt from an 1841 letter published in the January 1842 edition of the* British Magazine and Monthly Register, *he defends himself, editor Stephen R. Cattley, and Foxe himself against a scathing attack by S. R. Maitland upon a recent edition of* Actes and Monuments *(see Further Reading).*]

SIR,—I perceive, in your Number for the present month, some observations, from the pen of Mr. Maitland, on the new edition of the **Acts and Monuments** of John Foxe. Mr. Maitland has advertised, also, *Notes on the Contributions of Mr. Townsend to this Edition.* He has republished, too, the last Six Letters of a series of twelve, animadverting upon the same work, which were originally given to the world in the years 1837 and 1838, in the pages of your Magazine. Will you oblige me, as an original subscriber to, and as a constant reader of, your lucubrations, by inserting the very brief replies which I shall think it my duty to make to any observations which Mr. Maitland may submit to the public through this channel; and permit me, that I may more effectually clear the way for my answers to his letters in the Magazine, first to notice his advertisement in the several newspapers, and also his *Six more Letters.* I will then, as shortly, yet as fully, as his several attacks may demand, reply to them all, beginning with that in the Number for December [see Further Reading].

With respect to his advertisement, *Notes on Mr. Townsend's Contributions to the New Edition of John Foxe,* I can only inform Mr. Maitland that I shall be most happy to read them; and he may be assured that I shall be no less happy to improve my mind and increase my knowledge by his criticisms—

> *If some more sober critic comes abroad,*
> *If right, I smile; if wrong, I kiss the rod.*

Mr. Maitland also will be no less happy to be benefited by me; and thus our mutual remarks may be considered as a mutual effort to improve each other. I will inform him, as we proceed in the discussion, of the benefit which I may derive from his efforts. It will, I trust, be greater than that which I can remember to have followed from my study of his previous labours.

The next point on which I would speak is the *Six more Letters.*

Very sorry was I, in these days of apostasy and treason, when the dry rot of indifference to the progress of the ancient superstitions, which neither our fathers nor ourselves were able to hear, is corrupting the beams of our tabernacle in the wilderness, to read many of his observations. Your pages are too valuable to permit me to examine them in detail. I will therefore merely mention the subject of each letter, and condense my replies in the smallest possible space.

The first letter contains remarks on Foxe's account of Francis of Assissi, the founder of the Franciscan order.

John Foxe derides him. Mr. Maitland considers his derision as most absurd. My answer shall be derived from Mr. Maitland's own comparison in p. 76:—"The false enemies and foolish friends have daubed the originators of the mendicant orders with alternate coats of dirty slander and childish praise, till they become in the predicament of some of the figures in our churches, where, between the Iconoclast rebel and the whitewashing churchwarden, the features can scarcely be traced."

This is a pretty comparison. John Foxe is the Iconoclast, and Mr. Maitland the churchwarden; and I wish him joy of the self-assumed office. He confesses that he "cannot decide whether Francis actually pierced his hands and feet with nails." John Foxe believes the common story that he did so.

Foxe expresses the disbelief of the saintship of Francis in no drawing-room language, but in the bold and coarse style which shocks the present day. Mr. Maitland calls his language "trash." He demands, "what good can be done by reprinting it? and whether the church of England has no resource against Rome but railing and calling names?" Our resources, I answer, against Rome, are derived from the holy Scriptures, from antiquity, from the Fathers, from sound learning, scholarlike criticism, and every feeling which the love of truth and liberty can engender in the human heart; and all controversy ought to be discussed in the most calm and unimpassioned manner. But Foxe lived in a day when men were burnt to death for not believing doctrines which were supported by the false legends and detestable frauds of such impositions as the stigmata of St. Francis; and indignation against cruelty made him no less severe with the impositions by which they were upheld. The strong language of that indignation deserves to be described by other epithets than "trash and railing."

The second letter contains further remarks on the language of Foxe, some of which is defensible, some indefensible. I shall only notice that which Mr. Maitland calls "sad stuff, in point of taste and religion."

In the high and palmy state of the church of Rome, one of its bitter opponents wrote a paper against its bishops and clergy, which purported to be a letter from Lucifer, Prince of Darkness, to the princes of the church, to thank them for "the manner in which their influence crowded his dominions." Mr. Maitland expresses his profound contempt for this brochure. I have already, in a former publication, called it a severe and bitter libel. Our ancestors used more uncourteous language, as well as more fiery arguments, on both sides, than their silky sons; but I tell Mr. Maitland, in all soberness of feeling, that if it be indeed true, as he believes, and as I believe, that moral and spiritual evil was introduced, and is continued in the world, by a fallen and powerful spirit, who rejoices to destroy the effects of Christ's redemption; that the devil in his hell is to be congratulated when the clergy of Christ's church poison the waters of life, and instead of healing souls, increase their diseases, and thus thrust them down from heaven to hell. In vain do they worship God, teaching for doctrines the commandments of men. This may seem strong language; but stronger language must be used before we can expel from our church the poison which is beginning once more to pervade it.

The third letter abuses Wycliffe and some of his friends,

who are defended by Foxe, for asserting that the temporalities of the church are resumable at the pleasure of the princes and great men who were their donors.

Is not the assertion in one sense true? The property of the church was given at the first, and the same property is secured by the state in perpetuity, on condition that true Christianity is taught to the people. If the clergy of the present day, from Archbishop Howley to the poorest incumbent of the church, were to conspire together to teach submission to a foreign power, treason to the state, unitarianism, or popery, would not the state be justified in withdrawing its protection from that property, and in punishing conspiracy by confiscation? The clergy are not the church. The church is the congregation of faithful men, the family of Christ, of whom the clergy are the servants, as well as the fathers and instructors. The clergy have once taught the people erroneously and served them treacherously, and they may do so again. If so, the congregation must punish them.

The fourth letter treats with just contempt the story that six thousand children's heads were found in a fish pond. Mr. Maitland, with much humour and most amusing sarcasm, proves Foxe to be credulous, and his editor to be unwise. (pp. 23-5)

The last letter condemns the martyrologist for his general abuse of the prelates and bishops of the church. Arundel, the Archbishop of Canterbury, had put some churches under an interdict; that is, he had prohibited the worship of God on the Lord's-day because the bells were not rung as he passed. Foxe condemns this conduct in his usual unsparing language. Mr. Maitland calls this language "low radical mockery at all ecclesiastical authority." He asks whether any one of the admirers of Foxe will come forward and say that this was written in the style and with the feelings of a Christian?

I answer, that I approve most of the language which Foxe has used. With respect to the affirmation that the circulation of such remarks on bishops and prelates will injure the cause of the church and its higher magistrates in the present day, I can only say it produces more surprise than conviction. No reader of the pages of John Foxe can possibly imagine that the language which the martyrologist applies to Arundel and the martyr-burning bishops, who exerted themselves to reduce England to the yoke of Rome, can be applied to the mild and gentle virtues of Howley and his brethren. It might have been supposed that Mr. Maitland would have paused before he imagined the possibility of such an identity. He may be assured of this, that if he and his brethren, who are beginning to palliate the follies, defend the conduct, explain away the doctrines, and endeavour to reconcile the people and church of England to the yoke of Rome, shall persevere much longer in their wickedness and folly, they will provoke a reaction against them, which shall elicit from the people much severer language than John Foxe has used. I tell him, too, that if our Howleys, Blomfields, and Sumners, imitate the conduct of Arundel, they will deserve the same contempt which Foxe heaped on Arundel. If they behave like Laud, they will deserve, not to lose their heads, but to be deposed from their high office by a national synod, amidst the universal execration of the people. Mr. Maitland may be certain that the people love the clergy of their church; but they love more, far more than they love their clergy, the

truth of Christ's gospel, and the constitutional liberty, both of which Rome opposed and hated. (p. 26)

I have much higher, nobler, worthier objects claiming and receiving my attention than this controversy; and that I earnestly recommend him to employ his undoubted talents, in imitation of my example, on matters which he may reflect upon with greater pleasure at the last, than in winning the approbation of the papist and the tractarian, and obtaining the contempt and disgust of the protestant, yet catholic churchman. I have the honour to be, Sir, your obedient servant. (p. 28)

George Townsend, "Foxe's Martyrology," in The British Magazine and Monthly Register, *Vol. XXI, January 1, 1842, pp. 23-9.*

John Gough Nichols   (essay date 1859)

[*Nichols was a nineteenth-century English essayist and antiquarian who continued the work of his father and grandfather as an editor of the* Gentleman's Magazine *from 1828 to 1856. In the following excerpt from* Narratives of the Days of the Reformation, Chiefly from the Manuscripts of John Foxe the Martyrologist, *he deems Foxe an honest but careless writer.*]

Foxe, though a very laborious, was never a careful author. He admits this himself in the reply which he made to Alan Cope with respect to the story of Sir John Oldcastle lord Cobham: "I heare what you will saie, I should have taken more leisure, and done it better. I graunt and confesse my fault; such is my vice, I cannot sit all the daie (M. Cope,) fining and minsing my letters, and combing my head, and smoothing myself all the daie at the glasse of Cicero. Yet notwithstanding, doing what I can, and doing my good will, me thinkes I should not be reprehended."

The contents of the present volume certainly prove that Foxe, though always busy, was not fond of revising his writings. Several of the papers preserved among his Manuscripts were, like that of Horne, communicated to him for the express purpose of correcting his great work, were preserved by him for that purpose, and yet were never brought to their destined use.

I deem it perfectly unnecessary, however, to attempt any formal defence of Foxe's honesty and veracity. I believe him to have been truth-seeking, but liable to mistakes in an age of difficult communication, and perhaps occasionally subjected to intentional misinformation. The violence of his invective too often overshoots its object, and the coarseness of his abuse is necessarily offensive in the ears of a more refined age. In that respect he too much resembles his friend and associate Bale, who may very probably have been the author of some of the comments, particularly in the sidenotes, of the **Book of Martyrs,** that are so much in his style. It must also be admitted that in his remarks on the conduct and sufferings of those from whom he differed in matters of faith and discipline, Foxe too constantly discovers a merciless and unsympathising spirit, as well as a jocularity towards holy things which is both ill-timed and profane.

The Rev. Dr. Maitland, in his various essays on Foxe's great work [see Further Reading], has not only taken just exception to the tone and spirit in which its author wrote, but has shown some instances of what must be condemned as culpable carelessness in the treatment of historical evidence, and imperfect skill in learning and scholarship. All this Dr. Maitland has demonstrated with such minuteness and perseverance as might have been deemed unnecessary, or excessive, had not the advocates of the martyrologist, in a spirit of blind and injudicious partisanship, assumed undue weight for his historical authority. The proposition of the Convocation of 1571, that the *Monuments of the Martyrs* should be placed for public perusal in the houses of bishops, deans, and dignitaries, and in cathedral churches—which last expression has been grossly exaggerated into "all parish churches,"—in company with the Holy Bible and other like books pertaining to religion, seems to have exalted the *Actes and Monuments* of John Foxe, in the estimation of his over-zealous admirers, to a rank scarcely inferior to that of the Acts of the Apostles.

It can now no longer be disputed that as a general history of the Church, in its earlier ages, Foxe's work has been shown to be partial and prejudiced in spirit, imperfect and inaccurate in execution; but it is when approaching his own times—if allowance be still made for the prejudices and partiality which of course continue—that the book becomes most valuable as a record of the doings and sufferings, a mirror of the opinions, passions, and manners of the people of England. For the early annals of the Church

there are other authors to be preferred, both of antecedent and of subsequent date; but for familiar pictures of public and private struggles for conscience sake, it is probably unequalled in any country or language. It is the Chronicle of the days of the Reformation, the *Book of Martyrs* upon which the intense interest of their own and many subsequent generations was concentrated.

John Foxe had set himself the task of writing a History of the Church in Latin, and he thought it derogatory to his character as a scholar to appear in any other language. It was the demand of the English public—or, if there was then no literary public in England, of John Day his London publisher, supported, no doubt, by Bishop Grindal and other influential persons,—that, even against the author's will, produced the English edition, and it was the zeal and enthusiasm of a Protestant people that made it so successful. Foxe had given his work in its original language the title of *Commentarii,* and in its English form that of *The Actes and Monuments of the Church;* it was the English people themselves that called it *The Book of Martyrs.* This popular title in itself shows that the portions of the work which really fastened themselves upon the public mind, were not its early historical details, whether faithfully or partially related, but its heart-stirring narratives of events of more recent occurrence, which came home to the sympathies and the passions of

"The rack." From a nineteenth-century English edition of The Book of Martyrs.

those who had shared or witnessed their transaction and their effects.

For a similar reason the autograph Narratives of some of the sufferers still appeal to us with a more than ordinary degree of interest. Nor are they altogether merely the details of private doings and sufferings. They are connected, indirectly, with many of the most important national events. . . . (pp. xxi-xxv)

> *John Gough Nichols, in a preface to* Narratives of the Days of the Reformation: Chiefly from the Manuscripts of John Foxe the Martyrologist, *edited by John Gough Nichols, The Camden Society, 1859, pp. xi-xxviii.*

Richard Watson Dixon   (essay date 1900?)

[*A nineteenth-century English cleric, poet, historian, and essayist, Dixon is best known for his involvement in the Pre-Raphaelite movement. In the following excerpt from his* History of the Church of England—*a multivolume work completed shortly before his death in 1900—he assesses Foxe's writing in terms of the nature and bias of the author.*]

A greater work than even the *Apologia* of Jewel stepped at the same moment from the Latin into the English vesture, when the ***Acts and Monuments*** of John Fox issued from the press of John Day. Those now neglected researches, on their first appearance, awoke an emotion in the country which cannot be conceived. The families, the relations, the friends and neighbours of the hundreds who had been done to death by fire in the late persecution, read with mingled grief and pride the narratives of the trials of their lost ones, their boldness, constancy, and acuteness under examination, their sufferings and death. The story of divinely strengthened fortitude and of baffled and mistaken cruelty was carried through the land. A vast collection of originals, of acts and processes, of minutes of examinations taken down by notaries, of the recollections of eye-witnesses, records of every kind, brought again before the eyes which had beheld the terrible scenes which had scarcely ceased to be enacted; and renewed in certainty the power of reality. The labours of the historian in gathering matter had been prodigious: no place or person had escaped him: he had been largely aided during his exile by collectors in England, as Grindal; but the mass was his own, moulded by him, bearing his stamp. "The toils, anxieties, vigils, and miseries that I have endured in bringing this work to completion," said he, "might have killed an ass, yea, the best among them that bear fardels." The form which he invented for his work, half biographical, half historical, was the fittest for his purpose. The history of a great and critical epoch was never presented to the world with so little delay. Whatever be said, one thing is certain, that, if it had not been for Fox, England would never have known so much as the names of scores of her own martyrs: he is not without a claim on the gratitude of his country. No other country, save France, neither Spain nor the Netherlands, possesses a martyrology. No writer has been more severely treated: for he has been assailed both by rage and contempt. He was vehemently attacked by the great party, which he exposed, as soon as his book appeared. "No English papist almost in all the realm thought himself a perfect Catholic," said he, "until he had cast out

some word or other to give that book a blow." But the charges of falsification, suppression, alteration of documents, which have been laid against him, amount to little, most often to nothing. His adversaries of this kind usually know nothing beyond what they find in him, and all that they do is that they try to turn his own words against him. For the first part of the present age he has suffered much from sham editions and inefficient editors, the castigation of whom by critics has greatly involved their author. Irritated by the partiality and prejudice which are manifest in him, the critics have denounced him for dishonesty. He was indeed prejudiced. In the least valuable part of his book he has set the persecutions of the emperors against the persecutions of the Popes, the persecutions "sought and wrought by heathen emperors, as well as now lately practised by Romish prelates," as if both had proceeded from the same motives. He was one of the first Latinists of the age; his Latin style is fine; but when he puts it into English, there is at times a flatness and meanness of expression which is due to prejudice. (pp. 326-29)

> *Richard Watson Dixon, "A.D. 1560-1562," in his* History of the Church of England from the Abolition of the Roman Jurisdiction: Elizabeth.—A.D. 1558-1563, *Vol. V, Oxford at the Clarendon Press, 1902, pp. 275-367.*

James Gairdner   (essay date 1908)

[*Gairdner was a Scottish essayist, biographer, historian, and editor who contributed over seventy-five articles to the* Dictionary of National Biography. *In the following excerpt from his four-volume* Lollardy and the Reformation in England: An Historical Survey *(1908-13), he explores the spirit in which Foxe composed* Actes and Monuments.]

After amassing documents and exploring episcopal registers with unwearied industry, [John Foxe] gave to the world in 1563 the results of his labours in an enormous folio volume entitled ***Actes and Monuments of these latter perillous dayes touching matters of the Church.*** That is not the whole title, but the reader may as well pause to take breath before reading the rest. The words which follow are significant of the spirit and purport of the book: ***wherein are comprehended and described the great persecutions and horrible troubles that have been wrought and practised by the Romishe Prelates, speciallye in this Realme of England and Scotlande, from the yeare of our Lorde a thousande, unto the tyme nowe present.***

Under what special favour and encouragement so large and expensive a work was produced we do not distinctly know. It was printed by his friend John Daye, and illustrated by an abundance of wood-cuts vividly representing not only the burnings of martyrs, but numerous other forms of torture always inflicted, as the reader was led to understand, on men who were constant to the true Gospel in opposition to the authorities. Of the effect of its publication Dr. Dixon informs us that it "awoke an emotion in the country which cannot be conceived":—

> The families, the relations, the friends and neighbours of the hundreds who had been done to death by fire in the late persecution, read with mingled grief and pride the narratives of the trials of their lost ones, their boldness, constancy, and acuteness

under examination, their sufferings and death. The story of divinely strengthened fortitude and of baffled and mistaken cruelty was carried through the land. A vast collection of originals of acts and processes, of minutes of examinations taken down by notaries, of the recollections of eye-witnesses, records of every kind, brought again before the eyes which had beheld [them] the terrible scenes which had scarcely ceased to be enacted; and renewed in certainty the power of reality.

Notwithstanding some criticisms passed upon it by friends and foes even on its first publication, the book certainly attained a wonderful popularity. It was three times reprinted during Foxe's own life, and a fifth edition appeared before the end of the century. In 1571 it was ordered by Convocation that every bishop should have a copy of it in his house, along with a large edition of the Bible and other religious works. It was chained to desks in parish churches as an edifying and godly book. Probably it rose in public favour after the papal excommunication of Queen Elizabeth, which was fulminated in the year just before the order of Convocation. Under any circumstances, the impression which it made was deep and lasting, and has continued down to our own day. But the time has surely come when history may dispassionately weigh its merits and do something to counteract the partisanship of the judgments that have been passed on it by writers of opposite schools. Complete freedom from bias may not even yet, of course, be attainable; but time itself has abated many prejudices, and modern facilities for research ought to favour clearness of view. I accordingly venture to hope that the following comments will assist in the formation of something like a reasonable estimate of a work which the Church historian of England can in no case allow himself to overlook.

It was the distinct purpose of Foxe in this work to invest the martyrs of his own day with the same halo of sanctity as that with which pious tradition had illuminated those of the primitive Church. "If martyrs are to be compared with martyrs," he writes, "I see no cause why the martyrs of our time deserve any less commendation than the others in the primitive Church, which assuredly are inferior unto them in no point of praise, whether we view the number of them that suffered, or greatness of their torments, or their constancy in dying, or also consider the fruit that they brought to the amendment of posterity and increase of the Gospel. *They* did water with their blood the truth that was newly springing up; so these by their deaths restored it again, being sore decayed and fallen down." Inspired by this idea he had set himself to write a great book which should rival the legends of saints and displace a good many of them in the popular estimation. And in this he succeeded. But in planning his work he determined to follow precedent to some extent, and prefixed to it a "Kalender" of the twelve months of the year, in which, while Christmas Day, Lady Day, and most of the Apostles' days were retained in their old places, almost all the other days were consecrated to the memory of very modern martyrs, chiefly of Mary's reign. Here the result was somewhat extraordinary; for it can hardly be said, however much we sympathise with their sufferings, that the names of a host of fervid artisans who gave their lives to testify their faith in a simple gospel have been embalmed in our memories by Foxe's "Kalender." There, indeed, we find, conspicuous with red-letter honours, the names of

Wycliffe, Hus, Luther, Cranmer, Tyndale, and various other famous reformers; but the great majority of the names call up no very vivid associations. Indeed, there are cases in which the bewildered martyrologist himself, unable to obtain the names of the sufferers, fills up the line as he does on the 18th May: "a blind boy and another with him," or, as on the 4th December, "an old man of Buckinghamshire."

Nor was the "Kalender," after all, by any means accurate as to facts. Some of those called martyrs met with no violent death; among others, Wycliffe, who, moreover, has the 2nd January assigned to him, when the day of his death was the 31st December. But in several cases the names in the "Kalender" are names only, the persons named are quite unknown, and nothing is said in the history itself to enable us to identify them. Putting such cases aside, when we go over the list of known martyrs, it certainly is a strange medley, considering the object for which the work was written. The truth which dispelled the errors of Romanism one might have expected to be harmonious in itself; but Lollards and Lutherans, and Zwinglians and Calvinists, are here glorified as if witnesses to a common faith against the corruptions of Popery. Men who strongly upheld and men who strongly denied the Real Presence in the sacrament are here found in the same holy company; to which are also admitted some who were only charged with sorcery and witchcraft, such as Roger Onley (or Bolingbroke), dignified as a red-letter martyr, and Eleanor Cobham, the mistress (or wife) of Humphrey, Duke of Gloucester, who, as she only suffered public penance, is designated, not a martyr, but a "confessor." The fact that she was condemned for something by the Church of Rome seems to have been sufficient in Foxe's eyes to give her a place in the "Kalender." Leaving out, however, the less reputable in the list, the new saints were undoubtedly characterised by discrepancies in their belief which Foxe himself was most anxious to conceal; and we shall see that the heretics of Mary's time were anxious to conceal them also.

Foxe's aim, then, was to discredit what he called "the Pope's Church" by glorifying all who had suffered for their opposition to it during the two centuries before he wrote. Opposition to Rome was to him almost a proof of sanctity; and whoever had suffered for his antagonism to the Pope or the Romish clergy was for that very reason exalted to the dignity of saint or martyr. Nay more, a man might be guilty of simple felony and hanged as a felon by civil law; yet if his object had been only by some outrage to attack superstition he was sure of a good place in Foxe's narrative. (pp. 334-38)

We thus perceive the spirit in which Foxe wrote: the lawlessness of a deed was nothing to him if the doer was animated by a just hatred of what he called idolatry. To violate law as a protest against idolatry was the act of a saint "moved by the Spirit of God," and to be hanged for it was martyrdom.

But how far does this vehement bigotry in the historian affect his view of facts? Does it not injure his credibility throughout? I certainly think we ought to be on our guard against the bias of a writer capable of taking such distorted views. At the same time there is one thing to be said, viz. that bigotry like this may be taken as very sincere; and an author who was at such pains to gather information, though he may have relied on doubtful authorities at times, ought not to be lightly suspected of wilfully perverting facts. Roman Catholic writers of his own and a later generation have openly accused him of lying, and the Jesuit Parsons, who was most incensed at him, made what he calls "A note of more than a hundred and twenty lies uttered by John Fox in less than three leaves of his *Acts and Monuments.*" But the severity of that "Note" is considerably modified by the words immediately subjoined, although they are added with the view of strengthening the indictment still further. For the effect is this: "more than a hundred and twenty lies . . . and this in one kind only of perfidious dealing, in falsifying the opinions of Catholics touching divers chief points of their religion." The "Note," in fact, denounces a number of statements as false concerning the theological positions of Romanists, which it may be conceded that a mind like Foxe's was pretty sure to misinterpret. But it would be quite unprofitable to follow up this investigation, for we are not concerned here with theology of any school, and, if we were, we should be slow to reiterate the charge of lying on account of misstatements due to bias.

On the other hand, we are very much concerned to inquire how this bias of the martyrologist affected his view of the facts themselves, and how far his credulity was ready to accept stories that could not possibly have been true. I think there is no doubt that there were such cases. Take the following touching the poor sufferer, John Nicholson, otherwise called Lambert, who was burnt in Smithfield in the time of Henry VIII, after a trial before the King himself, and sentence pronounced upon him by Thomas Cromwell:—

> Upon the day that was appointed for this holy martyr of God to suffer, he was brought out of the prison at eight o'clock in the morning unto the house of the lord Cromwell, and so carried into his inward chamber, where, it is reported of many, that Cromwell desired of him forgiveness for what he had done. There, at the last, Lambert, being admonished that the hour of his death was at hand, was greatly comforted and cheered; and being brought out of the chamber into the hall, he saluted the gentlemen, and sat down to breakfast with them, showing no manner of sadness or fear. When the breakfast was ended, he was carried straightway to the place of execution, where he should offer himself unto the Lord, a sacrifice of sweet savour, who is blessed in his saints, for ever and ever. Amen.

This is very touching, and of course adds lustre to the halo round the head of this patient and magnanimous martyr. He forgave the Lord Cromwell; he was cheered by the intimation that the hour of his death was at hand, and sat down to breakfast with the gentlemen in Cromwell's hall, showing no manner of fear. But how came this condemned heretic, solemnly judged to death by authority of the King himself, to be conveyed to the house, and even into the inner chamber of the King's great minister, just before he suffered? It could only have been done by Cromwell's own direction; and if Cromwell, the ever busy tool of Henry VIII., occupied from morning till night with State affairs, actually caused him to be sent for that he might beg his pardon, he showed himself a wonderfully different person from that callous Cromwell who wrote down in his memoranda at what places the abbots of Glastonbury and Read-

ing should be executed before they were even tried! But even if he had felt a touch of compassion for this particular victim (who indeed had been encouraged in his heresies by Cromwell's revolutionary Church policy), how could Cromwell, the judge who actually pronounced sentence on him, have ever thought of asking his pardon for doing so? Such an action would have been a reflection upon the King himself and the justice of the whole proceedings; and it would have given a handle to Cromwell's enemies to say that he was in sympathy with sacramentaries and Anabaptists.

Another instance of Foxe's credulity is really not a little ludicrous. At the end of his work he relates some examples "of the Lord's judgment and severity practised upon the cruel persecutors of His people," of which the following is undoubtedly the most remarkable. A good man of the name of Cooper was executed, according to Foxe, on a false charge of having uttered treasonable words, and one of the perjured witnesses against him was a certain Grimwood of Hitcham in Suffolk. What befell this Grimwood let Foxe tell in his own words:—

> In the harvest after, the said Grimwood of Hitcham . . . as he was in his labor stacking up a goff of corn, having his health, and fearing no peril, suddenly his bowels fell out of his body, and immediately most miserably he died. Such was the terrible judgment of God, etc.

This is the most extraordinary end ever made by a human being, and surely ought to have been verified by an inquest, for doctors of later times have heard of nothing like it. But an inquest there could hardly have been, for the story had a very curious sequel. About a quarter of a century later, when Foxe's book, having been commended by Convocation, was frequently placed for popular use in churches, and supplied parsons at times with matter for their discourses, a parson named Prit, newly instituted to the cure of Hitcham, was preaching against perjury, of which he gave the story from Foxe as a terrible example. But it so happened that Grimwood, who, in fact, was not dead even then, was among the parson's hearers, and, indignant at being thus slandered, he brought an action against the clergyman for calling him a perjured person. But the case being tried at assizes, the Chief Justice directed the jury to acquit the parson, as he had only reported a story without malice.

Thus it appears that Foxe had credulously accepted and embodied in his history a tale which was not only false in itself, but accompanied by details which were absolutely against common sense; and yet the facts, as he related them, conveyed unjust imputations upon living men. (pp. 340-44)

Briefly, however, let us sum up those facts which are past contradiction. Foxe stated in his book that Grimwood, and another named White, had sworn away the life of an honest man named Cooper, and that Grimwood had afterwards met with a horrible (and quite impossible) kind of death in the fields. Immediately after the book was published he was informed by more than one friend that these statements were erroneous: that Cooper was not an honest man, but a felon; that White had sworn truly against him, not falsely; and that Grimwood, who had really not sworn against him at all, had certainly not come to any such sudden or violent end as Foxe had written. On this Foxe applied to his original informant Punt, who had circulated the statements some time before, and he applied to *his* original informants, two young men who are not named, and the young men stood to what they had said; but it is evident from Rushbroke's letter at the time that Punt was expected to try and make out a case in favour of his own credibility. Finally, more than twenty years later, Grimwood himself, in his own parish church, hearing this story from Foxe delivered from the pulpit by a new parson, protested not only that he was alive, but that he was grossly slandered by what was said of him. Yet Foxe had meanwhile gone on printing edition after edition, and actually four editions of the work had appeared before this final refutation of the story of Grimwood's fate. The fifth edition of the book was published after Foxe's death, and retained the story, of course, as every edition has done since.

After this, we probably know how to estimate a few other things of the like kind, as when we are told that "Morgan, Bishop of St. David's, sitting upon the condemnation of the blessed martyr, Bishop Ferrar, and unjustly usurping his room, not long after was stricken by God's hand after such a strange sort that his meat would not go down, but rise and pick up again, sometimes at his mouth, sometimes blown out at his nose, most horrible to behold; and so he continued till his death. Where note, moreover, that when Master Leyson, being then sheriff at Bishop Ferrar's burning, had fet away the cattle of the said bishop from his servant's house called Matthew Harbottle, into his own custody, the cattle coming into the sheriff's ground, divers of them would never eat meat, but lay bellowing and roaring, and so died." A fair collection of stories like these will be found in illustration of what the reader is expected to regard as God's judgments upon popish persecutors. As to Bishop Morgan, he died at Wolvercote, not far from Oxford; but Anthony Wood could hear of no tradition of the misery of his latter days.

Foxe, indeed, perhaps from overstudy, became the victim of delusions even about himself; and after his death we find it related of him as notorious "that he imagined himself sometimes to be an urinal of glass, sometimes a crowing cock, and other like fancies." For such things he deserves our sincere compassion; but we must take them certainly as evidence of a mind not very well fitted to grasp the immense subject that he had taken in hand, or to prove by accurate and impartial narration how from about A.D. 1000, from which he dates "the loosing out of Satan," and a four hundred years' reign of Antichrist, the Church was overwhelmed with corruptions which almost completely extinguished "both doctrine and sincerity of life," till at last a Reformation began which had been contantly growing till his day, "about the space of two hundred and fourscore years." Such was the theme that he had proposed to himself, and of the manner of its execution as a whole it would be superfluous to speak. No one, I believe, is prepared to vindicate his account of the Albigenses or of the Waldenses, or any other part of the bulky history, before he comes to relate the separate stories of a multitude of different sufferers in his own day. And, however touching may be these detailed and particular anecdotes, he certainly fails entirely to show what it was his object all along to set forth,—that professors of a pure gospel, with an unvarying standard of doctrine, had been consistently fighting for nearly two centuries against the errors and corruptions of Rome. (pp. 355-57)

[Having] said so much about Foxe's defects, I should be sorry to end this chapter without a word or two more about his real merits. I should have greatly preferred to begin with them, but it was absolutely necessary, in the first place, to consider the aim and object of the writer, and consequently to discuss his bias. It would be unjust to say, however, that the work did not possess very real merits, to which its extraordinary success was largely due. That its authority has been strangely over-estimated for a period of three centuries and more—that its influence has coloured and prejudiced the views which we have taken of the Reformation, even to the present day—are all the more reasons for recognising what was really praiseworthy in the author's zeal and industry. There is no doubt that he was perfectly sincere. Driven, as he might be, after publication, into corners from which he tried to escape in irregular and unworthy fashions, he certainly had addressed himself to the task in the first instance with sincere enthusiasm and a full intention to state nothing that was not true. Among the numerous documents in his book there may, possibly, be one or two that are spurious; but it is not to be supposed that he connived at forgery. Where the originals are attainable it does not appear that he ever tampered with the text of one of them; indeed, one might say that he is generally a very careful editor. Where he only gives, or professes to give, the substance of documents in his own words, he is, undoubtedly, less to be trusted; but there is no reason for imputing his misrepresentations to anything but carelessness. Parsons, writing abroad, was altogether wrong in his surmise that Foxe had destroyed many documents upon which his statements are founded. The episcopal registers from which so much of the story was drawn are to this day available for consultation, and sometimes furnish valuable corrections of particular incidents. But no doubt a good many original documents are lost; and it is all the more important, where we cannot go to the fountain-head for our information, that we should study this indispensable historian with a due appreciation alike of his merits and of his weaknesses. For the most part, when we take account of his bias he is tolerably clear and intelligible. (pp. 364-65)

James Gairdner, "How the Past Was Viewed Under Queen Elizabeth," in his Lollardy and the Reformation in England: An Historical Survey, Vol. I, *Macmillan and Co., Limited, 1908, pp. 328-65.*

Charles Whibley   (essay date 1909)

[*Whibley was an English literary critic and journalist. In the following excerpt from his article "Chroniclers and Antiquaries" in* The Cambridge History of English Literature, *he judges the historical influence and current value of* Actes and Monuments.]

An encyclopaedic method claims for John Foxe, the martyrologist, a place among the chroniclers. Not that his aim and purpose resembled theirs. It was not for him to exalt his country, or to celebrate the triumphs of her past. His was the gloomier task of recounting the torments suffered by the martyrs of all ages, and he performed it with so keen a zest that it was not his fault if one single victim escaped his purview. In other words, he was content only with universality, and how well he succeeded let Fuller tell: 'In good earnest, as to the particular subject of our English martyrs, Mr Foxe hath done everything, leaving posterity nothing to work upon.' And so he goes back to the beginning, describing the martyrdoms of the early church, and of those who suffered in England under king Lucius. As he passes by, he pours contempt upon Becket, proving that he, at least, was no true martyr, being the open and avowed friend of the pope. But it is when he arrives within measurable distance of his own time that he finds the best food for his eloquence. The prowess of Henry VIII, the exploits of Thomas Cromwell, his prime hero, the magnanimity of Anne Boleyn, 'who, without controversy, was a special comforter and aider of all the professors of Christ's gospel,' tempt him to enthusiasm, and he rises to the highest pitch of his frenzy when he recounts the tortures of those who suffered death in the reign of queen Mary. He is no sifter of authorities; he is as credulous as the simplest chronicler; he gathers his facts where Grafton and Stow gathered theirs, and he makes no attempt to test their accuracy. His sin is the greater because he is not writing to amuse or to enlighten his readers, but to prove a point in controversy. He is, in brief, a violent partisan. His book is the longest pamphlet ever composed by the hand of man. It is said to be twice as long as Gibbon's *Decline and Fall,* and never for one moment does it waver from its purpose, which is to expose the wickedness of 'the persecutors of God's truth, commonly called Papists.' It is idle, therefore, to expect accuracy or a quiet statement from Foxe. If anyone belong to the other side, Foxe can credit him neither with honesty nor with intelligence. Those only are martyrs who die for the protestant cause. The spilt blood of such men as Fisher and More does not distress him. For the author of *Utopia,* indeed, he has a profound contempt. He summarily dismisses him as 'a bitter persecutor of good men, and a wretched enemy against the truth of the gospel.' It follows, therefore, that Foxe's mind also was enchained. It was not liberty of opinion which seemed good in his eyes, but the vanquishing of the other side. Though he interceded for certain anabaptists condemned by queen Elizabeth, it was his object to rescue them not from punishment but from the flames, which was, he thought, in accord with a Roman rather than with a Christian custom. However, the success of his *Actes and Monuments* was immediate. It was universally read, it aroused a storm of argument, it was ordered to be chained in churches for the general edification of the people. The temper in which it is written, the inflexible judgment which, throughout, distorts the truth with the best motive, have rendered the book less valuable in modern than in contemporary eyes. If we read it to-day, we read it not for its matter or for its good counsel, but for its design. As a mere performance, the *Actes and Monuments* is without parallel. Foxe was an astounding virtuoso, whose movement and energy never flag. With a fever of excitement he sustains his own interest (and sometimes yours) in his strange medley of gossip, document and exhortation. The mere style of the work—homely, quick and appropriate—is sufficient to account for its favour. The dramatic turn which Foxe gives to his dialogues, the vitality of the innumerable men and women, tortured and torturers, who throng his pages—these are qualities which do not fade with years. Even the spirit of bitter raillery which breathes through his pages amazes, while it exasperates, the reader. From the point of view of presentation, the work's worst fault is monotony. Page after page, the mar-

tyrologist revels in the terms of suffering. He spares you nothing, neither the creeping flames, nor the chained limb, until you begin to believe that he himself had a love of blood and fire.

The man was just such a one as you would expect from his book. Born in 1517, to parents 'reputed of good estate,' sent to Oxford, in 1533, by friends who approved his 'good inclination and towardness to learning,' and elected fellow of Magdalen College, he was presently accused of heresy and expelled from Oxford. He was of those who can neither brook opposition nor accept argument. Henceforth, though he never stood at the stake, he suffered the martyrdom of penury and distress. Now tutor in a gentleman's house, now in flight for the sake of his opinions, he passed some years at Basel reading for the press, and, in 1559, he published at Strassburg the first edition of his masterpiece, in Latin. In 1563, it was printed in English by John Day, with the title *Actes and Monuments of these latter and perilous times touching matters of the Church.* With characteristic ingenuity, he composed four dedications: to Jesus Christ, to the queen, to the learned reader and to the persecutors of God's truth, commonly called papists. The last is a fine example of savage abuse, and, as Foxe wrote in safety and under the protection of a protestant queen, its purpose is not evident. No more can be said than that rage and fury are in his heart and on his tongue, that he possessed a genius of indignation which he had neither wish nor power to check and that he bequeathed to us a larger mass of invective than any writer in any age has been able to achieve. (pp. 331-34)

> *Charles Whibley, "Chroniclers and Antiquaries," in* The Cambridge History of English Literature: Renascence and Reformation, Vol. III, *edited by A. W. Ward and A. R. Waller, Cambridge at the University Press, 1909, pp. 313-38.*

Hugh Massingham   (essay date 1935)

[*Massingham was an English editor and essayist. In the following excerpt, he examines Foxe's use of language, assessing the historical and propagandist content of* Actes and Monuments.]

Foxe is famous as the author of *The Book of Martyrs,* once a work to be found in every good Protestant home, but now even more neglected than the Bible. There are, indeed, few things more striking in the history of literature than the popularity Foxe enjoyed in his lifetime and long afterwards, and the neglect with which he is treated to-day. It is not only that he devotes a great deal of space to nice theological points that are no longer of fashionable or popular interest. On the top of his theology, his naïvety, his verboseness, his pages of unimaginative prose, he uses a violence of language that shocks an age which prides itself upon its scientific and accurate interpretation of facts. Foxe is partisan and violently partisan. He is a fighter and not a refined observer looking at a riot from the safety of the drawing-room window.

In the sixteenth-century they were not so squeamish. Protestants were neither shocked by Foxe's prejudiced and vigorous way of saying things, nor bored by his long theological discussions. On the contrary, they enjoyed both. They admired his frankness, and found in his theology arguments to answer the contentions of their enemies. Foxe, indeed, stands to the Protestant movement as Tom Paine stands to the American Revolution. He was the great Protestant journalist of the Tudor period; and in a sense he is the first great journalist in English history. Because he wrote books and not for newspapers is no reason why we should hesitate to say that he was a journalist. Like all the great editors of the nineteenth century Foxe thought of himself as a preacher first, a propagandist, and as a literary man second, if he ever thought of himself as a literary man at all. He was in many ways like W. T. Stead. He had Stead's sensationalism, Stead's passion for the truth, Stead's furious intention to hit the bull's-eye; and like Stead, he sometimes hit the bull's-eye first time, and he sometimes missed it, not by a yard, but by a mile.

He could not have been the great journalist that he was had he been born rich and a nobleman. Foxe was not born with a silver spoon in his mouth, and all his life he was forced to fight against extreme poverty. He started therefore with the great advantage of knowing what the ordinary man had to contend with. He understood perfectly the fear of poverty and the shadow of unemployment. He did not see these things imaginatively, as something distant and intriguing; he had experienced them himself.

He was, of course, a Protestant. But he was far more than just intellectually sympathetic to the new movement. Although Foxe died in his bed, and although his life seems almost tranquil when compared with the terrible deaths he describes in the ***Book of Martyrs,*** he suffered for his religion socially as most Protestants did during the Tudor period. (pp. 379-80)

Foxe, of course, wrote up his history, and had he stopped at putting magnificent language into the mouths of people incapable of saying the things that he records, his critics would not have found it so easy to attack him. Foxe, however, sometimes juggled with facts, and both during his life and since he has been charged with being inaccurate and falsifying his evidence. His most famous critic is . . . [S. R.] Maitland, who accused Foxe of being biased, copying manuscripts hastily and inaccurately, muddling his dates, borrowing without acknowledgment, being vague in his references, magnifying trivial incidents into events of the utmost importance, and including among his martyrs people condemned for secular offences [see Further Reading]. Maitland is by far the ablest and most scholarly of the critics, but before Maitland and in Foxe's lifetime, people severely criticised the accuracy of the work. Foxe himself seems to have been greatly irritated by the charge that it was "as full of lies as lines," and he made some effort to correct mistakes after Mary was dead and he was back again in England. The effort was not very thorough, and Maitland points out one glaring instance where Foxe does not correct a statement even after he found it to be untrue. Maitland's list of mistakes is a long one, but considering the difficulty under which Foxe wrote and the colossal scope of the work, it is surprising that there were not more inaccuracies. Foxe was certainly slapdash (he even forgets the date of the act of the Six Articles), and we have a right to ask a higher standard of scholarship from a man who proudly quoted Cicero's remark that "Historie is the witnesse of truth, the glasse of times."

At the same time Maitland goes too far when he tries to suggest that Foxe is valueless as an historian. He was a most industrious worker, collecting a greater number of original documents from the bishops' registers, and preserving the stories of men who had actually seen the burnings which he describes. The pity is that he was not able to sift evidence and to reject stories that were mere malicious gossip. Foxe had not a historical mind. He had none of the objectivity of the unimaginative historian who feels that all facts are equal in the sight of God and sees events almost as if they were a row of Chinamen, alike in size, feature, and colour. He was a man of imagination; but his imagination was untrained, and he was unable, like the great historians, to use it in order to project his mind into the being of somebody whose views he might detest. Foxe was aware of his failings:

> I heare what you will saie," he wrote to a Mr. Cope who had taxed him with inaccuracy, "I should have taken more leisure, and done it better. I graunt and confesse my fault; such is my vice, I cannot sit all the daie (Mr. Cope) fining and mincing my letters and combing my head, and smoothing myself all the daie at the glasse of Cicero. Yet notwithstanding, doing what I can, and doing my good will, me thinkes I should not be reprehended.

Maitland goes much farther than saying that Foxe was a bad historian. He attacks the whole tone of Foxe's writing, and gives as an instance of bad taste this description of St. Francis. . . . (pp. 384-85)

There are plenty of instances of this offensive language in the ***Book of Martyrs,*** and it is not all written by Foxe. The martyrs themselves are sometimes even more vigorous. For instance, a man called Filmer, who was charged with heresy, said that if the sacrament were no more than a sign, then he had eaten twenty gods in his lifetime. Another attacked a priest who was holding the chalice and struck him on the head with a wood knife. A third wrote to Bishop Bonner, who was not the bloody tyrant that Foxe makes him out to be, telling him that—

> You are the common cut-throat and general slaughterslave of all the bishops of England; and therefore it is wisdom, for we and all other simple sheep of the Lord, to keep us out of your butcher's stall as long as we can.

These remarks, together with Foxe's description of St. Francis, should not be judged without reference to the age in which they were spoken. Men naturally expressed themselves more vituperously in the sixteenth century than they do now. The present generation is more scientific, and we are so self-conscious in our empirical attitude to life, that we have lost the power to believe in any particular case passionately. We are like the cautious professor who, when asked if a certain sheep were white, replied, "It is white on this side." We feel easier with a footnote to support every statement. At the same time our passion for objectivity has really given us an understanding of the other man's case, and therefore we instinctively dislike hearing anyone abused. No modern person can read Foxe without immediately reacting against his consistent unfairness, and without feeling that there is a case for the Church which Foxe has not put. Indeed, the reports of the trials that Foxe gives show how humane the judges were, how anxious to save the accused. We do not have to know the Catholic Bishop Bonner was not the monster that Foxe says to prove that the ***Book of Martyrs*** gives only one side of the picture.

Foxe had every reason to feel strongly about the Catholics. He not only hated the Church intellectually. He felt that it had prevented people from understanding what Christianity really was, as revealed in the Bible. He hated it because of what it had done to himself and his friends. Foxe had gone in fear of his life. He had been forced to live in exile. His friends had been burnt at the stake. He had no certainty that the Church might not yet be triumphant, that the same scenes might not be re-enacted, and that he himself might not be one of the victims. Foxe felt about the Catholics as we feel about Hitlerism, and a man filled with forebodings, who was a participant in the struggle, and not an aloof spectator of it, could not be expected to take up such a commendable attitude of objectivity as the tolerant and comfortable Protestants and atheists of the twentieth century.

The offensiveness of some of the accused during their trials was not solely because they were uneducated men who would naturally express themselves more outspokenly than Foxe. The reports suggest that their most objectionable phrases were spoken, partly out of defiance, partly out of contempt for what they considered the sophistry of their opponents; but sometimes the heretics seem to have been deliberately insolent in order to break a kind of net that they felt the Catholics were drawing round them. Foxe calls the Catholic judges "subtle," and they were certainly subtle in the sense that they supported their case by reference to a wealth of knowledge that the accused lacked. It is no reflection on the sincere humanity of the judges to say that their reluctance to condemn heretics was not disinterested; their great object was to win them back to Catholicism, and the accused being well aware of this intention, saw in this kindness only a Machiavellian method of seduction. The offensiveness of a man like Filmer is a kind of defence and a way to avoid being drawn, step by step, into an intellectual position where a denial of his faith was inevitable. The accused purposely insulted their judges so that they could cut short their trials and avoid long intellectual argument in which they might have to acknowledge with their minds what their hearts told them was false. Hence the brutality of their language and their relief at seeing the stake.

If Foxe was a bad historian, he had great qualities as a propagandist, and he did more than he is given credit for in bringing the people of England out of the old churches and into the new. He was a single-hearted creature. He loved few things and he loved them passionately. He wrote at all times about the things that afflicted men's hearts, and he wrote of them in a language that everybody could understand. But he did more than write simply. Foxe wrote about simple people for simple people. Kings, bishops, prelates, and aristocrats move indeed through his pages, and the records of their sins or achievements take up much of his space. But in the main, the ***Book of Martyrs*** is the story of how the ordinary man defied his oppressors, revealed unsuspected heroic qualities, and eventually won immortality. The butcher, the baker, the labourer, the carpenter, these are the heroes of the ***Book of Martyrs,*** just as they are the important characters in the gospels. No one who read Foxe felt out of his depth. No one could feel that he was reading about unreal people who moved in an orbit

infinitely remote from the reader's. No one could feel that his stories were just romances. Everybody knew Foxe's martyrs. They were not like the remote St. Cecilie, whom Chaucer describes as "hevenes lilie," "of noble kinde," and on whose behalf heaven intervened at the moment of trial. They were simply the people that the reader met every day of his life, and angels never intervened to save them from the torment of the stake. They were reassuringly earthy. Just as everybody can understand St. Peter and very few people can sympathise with Herod, so the man that read the ***Book of Martyrs*** felt instantly that he knew all about the characters who are the heroes of Foxe's narrative. They were actually his father and his mother, his brother and his sister, his friends and his beloved.

There are other reasons why the ***Book of Martyrs*** became so popular. Like Bunyan, indeed, like a great deal of the teaching of Jesus, the book appealed both to men's sense of excitement and drama as well as to their religious nature. The ***Book of Martyrs*** is a wonderful book, not only because it is the record of man's suffering and a picture of his nobility in the moment of passion and trial, but because it also contains stories just as dramatic as the stories chosen by a novelist. Foxe was a born story-teller. He was verbose, ribald, and cantankerous in his argumentative passages, but when he came to description he wrote with great power, and great simplicity. Take, for instance, this well-known and moving description of the death of Dr. Taylor, the Vicar of Hadleigh. . . . (pp. 386-89)

No one can read this simple account of Dr. Taylor's martyrdom without being profoundly moved, and there are a thousand Dr. Taylors in Foxe's pages. The reading of these stories, most of them showing the spotless virtue of Protestants and the monstrous villainy of Roman Catholics, inevitably inflamed men's passions, increased the hatred of Protestants for the Church, and thus helped to delay the coming of religious toleration. At the same time they taught men something about Protestantism that was not to be found in more learned and profound treatises. They taught him the power of the spirit to redeem man. Unlike Calvin, who wanted to take men out of one ecclesiastical pen only to shepherd them into another ruled by himself, Foxe instinctively knew that Protestantism is an affair of the spirit, and nothing but an affair of the spirit. It is simply what George Santayana calls in another connection the "weather of the soul." Other beliefs have their dogmas and their creeds, landmarks by the aid of which the spiritual traveller can find his way; Protestants have nothing but the word of the Bible, and the promptings of their conscience. This inner light needed to be nourished, not only by constant meditation and prayer, but also by the study of the lives of the saints, and the early Protestants found in the records of the innumerable martyrs in Foxe's pages a source both of inspiration and comfort. They were amazed afresh by the immense power of spiritual passion, they longed to be given a similar opportunity of "witnessing to the truth," and as they read of the sufferings of the martyrs they determined to endure the persecution that they themselves had to contend with.

Constant study of the Bible led them to believe that they had discovered the real intention of God, and in consequence they arrogated to themselves an infallibility that they denied to the Pope. There are plenty of instances of arrogance in Foxe's work, for the ***Book of Martyrs*** records the faults as well as the virtues of Protestantism. But if a conviction that we must live as our hearts tell us to live led some Protestants to fall into spiritual arrogance, it also gave them the most amazing fortitude and transformed ordinary men into heroes and saints. (pp. 389-90)

The *Book of Martyrs* is essentially the story of how "the life rose over it all" to refresh men's faith in their own goodness. Foxe, of course, is not primarily concerned with the gentler side of Protestantism, and he makes no particular effort to bring it out in his narrative. He is concerned with the way Protestants behaved when given the choice of death or the renunciation of their convictions; he uses all his power to bring out the tremendous heroism they showed in the supreme trial of their lives. Foxe is perfectly right to stress the sterner side, for had Protestantism not been a militant force it could never have triumphed, Charles I would not have lost his head, and the subsequent history of England would have been very different. But Protestants did not—as we might think after reading Foxe—spend all their time in being martyrs, in defying bishops, and in thinking of their souls. They thought of the goodness of God as well as of the punishment of being "secluded eternally, eternally, eternally from the sight of God." Read again, both for the beauty of the language and the calm assurance of its spirit, the conversation Ridley wrote shortly before he died and which Foxe quotes. It is remarkable first of all for his scrupulous fairness to the Catholic point of view. It is remarkable for the warmth and moderation of his language. And finally it is remarkable for a humility and tenderness that comes out most forcibly at the end in the moving words of Latimer:

> Pardon me, and pray for me, I say. For I am sometimes so fearful that I would creep into a mousehole; sometimes God doth visit me again with his comfort. So he cometh and goeth, to teach me to feel and know my infirmity, to the intent to give thanks to him that is worthy, lest I should rob him of his due, as many do, and almost the whole world. Fare ye well.

These are the passages that suddenly illuminate Foxe's pages. The *Book of Martyrs* is in many ways an ugly book with its story of intolerance and cruelty. But it is also an invigorating one. Read it again for the light it throws upon the feeling of his time. But read it above all for the unforgettable picture it gives of the fortitude of man. Because of this it is more than an interesting historical document; it is a book for all ages and conditions of men. And it may perhaps have more to say to this generation than we imagine. (pp. 391-92)

> *Hugh Massingham, "John Foxe," in* The Great Tudors, *edited by Katharine Garvin, E. P. Dutton and Co. Inc., 1935, pp. 377-93.*

J. F. Mozley   (essay date 1940)

[*In the following excerpt from his critical biography of Foxe, Mozley examines the martyrologist's methodology, or lack thereof, in compiling* Actes and Monuments.]

What are we to say of the result [of the *Book of Martyrs*]? The first impression left on our minds is that of size; we are overwhelmed by the sheer bulk of his achievement.

Two or three gigantic folio volumes in the old editions, or in the modern editions eight volumes of big octavo size, close printed and in small type, containing seven or eight hundred pages apiece—this is what is offered to us. We are even more staggered to think of the enormous number of books and documents that lies behind this work, many of them cited by name. This colossal labour disposes us to think well of Foxe. A man like that, with little or no reward of money, chooses to spend a dozen years of his life on such a task, must at least (one might think) have had earnestness and principle, and an overmastering belief in the justice of his cause.

But this very size makes it hard for us to estimate the book. Who can follow the author through the many centuries of history, tracing the documents on which he relies, and comparing his use of them with the original texts, weighing up the inherent probability of this and that narrative? To do this properly would take the better part of a lifetime. Happily, however, we can reduce our task by nearly one half. From our point of view his stories of the pre-Wycliffe ages and of the continental reformers of the sixteenth century count for little or nothing. They have no first-hand value; they are simply based on previous writers whose works are open to us. Eusebius, Socrates, Sozomen in antiquity; Bede, Matthew Paris, Walsingham, Aeneas Silvius for the dark and middle ages; Sleidan, Crespin, Enzinas in the reformation period—these and scores of other writers provide him with his ammunition. Many of them were not accessible to the English of the Elizabethan age, and so Foxe thought it worth while to put them into his book, but we have no such need. For us the worth of his book begins with the English Lollards and attains its height in the Tudor period, and above all in the Marian period. Here Foxe writes upon his own land, moves amid scenes with which he is familiar; he has access to documents many of which have since perished, while some still repose in obscurity in episcopal registers. Above all, for the Tudor period he has the power to call documents into being; for he is in touch with eye-witnesses, and can persuade them to commit their memories to paper, and so to hand them down to posterity through his agency. This is the heart of his book; here is his citadel. On this ground he must be attacked and overthrown, if his authority is to be discredited.

This is no new discovery; it has always been felt by Foxe's readers. He himself first planned the book as a history of the English martyrs, and his readers welcomed it on that basis. It was not because it told of Constantine or Barbarossa or Hildebrand that four editions were sold out in a quarter of a century, that copies were set up in churches, and plain men and women pored over its pages. It was because it told of Tyndale, Latimer, Anne Askew, Cranmer and many a humble victim—parent, maybe, or brother, or friend of the reader—undergoing sufferings which the readers counted themselves lucky to have escaped, but which might easily be revived in England should Elizabeth die. When therefore Maitland shows, as he easily does, errors, mistranslations, carelessness in the earlier part, he is doing little; he wins a skirmish on the wings of the field, but he leaves Foxe secure in his stronghold.

To judge Foxe fairly we must understand his method, or want of method, as some might term it. He is not properly a historian at all, rather he is a compiler on a gigantic scale. His book is a colossal storehouse of material gathered from many quarters and of differing merit. This material he uses in a casual and unsystematic way. Sometimes he is the mere archivist, giving his document verbatim, or nearly so. Sometimes he shortens it or boils it down, but otherwise lets it stand in its own right. Sometimes he rewrites it in his own words, and tries to combine it—rather clumsily, it may be—with information taken from another source. But even when he rewrites and combines, he is never the complete historian, master of all his material, rounding off the rough edges of his authorities, taking equal responsibility for all parts of his narrative. His arrangement leaves much to be desired. The book is a history of martyrs rather than a history of persecutions, and each victim is described under his year of death; but many things are intruded into this scheme, and have to be fitted in as best they can. The same subjects come up in different parts of the book, and if Foxe is following different authors, the accounts given may disagree. Frequently his dates do not tally. In a word, the reader of Foxe must be prepared to meet plenty of small errors and inconsistencies, which could easily have been amended with a little trouble, nay, which are resolved by a comparison of one part of the book with another. It may be added too that not a few misprints crept by little and little into the later editions.

This casual method springs partly out of the haste with which he worked. He himself regretted this and complains of it more than once. His Latin book was written "at breakneck speed", his English was "so hastily rashed up at that present," and his second edition was not much better. He was pressed forward by a burning desire to bring his book before the people of England, that his countrymen might know the glorious story of their martyrs. Meanwhile fresh information rained in upon him, the mass of documents became more and more unmanageable; even while the book was in printing, valuable manuscripts came to hand: for Foxe rightly considered it more important to get new material than to perfect the old. And when once the book had attained its full form, the fruit of a dozen years' labour, fit to break down the author, a more systematic mind than Foxe's might quail before the task of a full revision.

But haste apart, Foxe is temperamentally incapable of writing what is now called a scientific history: he is no dry delver into documents, no dispassionate arranger of his discoveries, no follower of minute accuracy. He has too warm a heart for this, and he lacks the patience. Of his own disposition he was well aware, and he makes an interesting confession of it in a controversy with Harpsfield.

> I grant that in a laboured story, such as you seem to require, containing such infinite variety of matter as this doth, much more time would be required: but such time as I had, that I did bestow; if not so laboriously as others could, yet as diligently as I might. But here partly I hear what you will say—I should have taken more leisure and done it better. I grant and confess my fault. Such is my vice, I cannot sit all the day, master Cope, fining and mincing my letters, and combing my head, and smoothing myself all the day at the glass of Cicero; yet notwithstanding, doing what I can, and doing my good will, methinks I should not be reprehended, at least not so much be railed on at master Cope's hand: who if he be so pregnant in finding fault with other men's labours, which is an easy thing to do, it were to be wished that he had enterprised himself upon the matter; and so should he have proved what faults might have been found in him. Not that I herein do utterly excuse myself, yea, rather am ready to accuse myself, but yet notwithstanding think myself ungently dealt withal at master Cope's hand.

Foxe is no mere archivist, though there is much archivism in his book. He wishes at all costs to get on with his story, to put the substance of the matter before his readers, and he recks little of small errors, disorders or obscurities. Let the main trend only be true and sound, and he is satisfied. Considering his warm and ardent feelings, it is surprising that he submitted to the enormous drudgery which his task imposed on him. He could not possibly have endured, had he not been carried forward by a great and ardent belief in the justice of his cause, had he not been a thoroughgoing partizan of the protestant side.

Now at the very word partizan scientific historians begin always to look uncomfortable. The partizan hardly plays the game of history as they understand it. Not that they are hard men or severe in their judgments: far from it. They can forgive much: they can bear with any amount of dulness, particularly when buttressed by terrific arrays of footnotes; ignorance even does not distress them, they are glad to hold out a helping hand, hoping to lead a man up to better things. But partizanship—to have strong feelings and opinions, especially on religious matters, and to show them—this comes near to putting a man outside the pale; a shadow rests on all his operations; he stands under a cloud.

But here I make bold to say that partizanship is a quite natural and proper thing in a historian, provided that it is open and provided that it is honest, that is to say, if he is careful not to misstate facts. An open partizanship is at least a less dangerous thing than that veiled or negative partizanship which rules in some of our modern scholars, who are considered to be models of scientific accuracy. It is also at least as noble a thing as that timid prudence which makes a scholar sit on the fence, pronouncing no opinion of his own, while issues are in question that are decisive for the future history of the world. Is the historian not made of flesh and blood? Why should we demand of him a soulless calm?

Foxe at all events has no use for such "impartiality". He has passed through the fire, and learnt to dread it. He has seen his friends perish, and fears that again they may come into danger. He writes with a purpose; he is no mere transcriber of old documents. He must honour the dead victims, and warn and encourage the living. His book is a stout blow in the battle against cruelty: and Foxe hated cruelty with all his heart. Had he not felt as he did, he could never have written the book. He might have toyed with his subject, he could never have treated it so thoroughly; his partizanship bore him forward.

Of course this partizanship affects his choice of material and his treatment of events. He must make his readers see how urgent was the need of reform, and that even in earlier days there were forerunners of protestantism. He paints the scandals of medievalism in the blackest colours, and it is not his business to seek for excuses, or to bring out the nobler side of things. A striking instance is provided by his treatment of Dominic and Francis of Assisi, both of whom he dismisses with a few scornful words: for they were the founders of the friars, those swarms of idlers, whose degeneracy the Tudor age knew only too well. He classes them with their degenerate posterity, and will not stop to ask whether their foundations did not at first render good service to the world. But such onesidedness of selection or treatment is not the same thing as dishonesty; a historian becomes dishonest only if it can be shown that he knowingly misstates the facts to suit his own ends.

From these passionate feelings spring the trenchant and bitter words which have given offence to some modern readers. Many of these take the form of side-notes or glosses. Foxe makes comments of his own on the story of the text, and sometimes his comments are cutting. . . . (pp. 152-57)

Foxe's fierceness is but a following of the fashion of his age, and he had more reason for it than some. The strong feelings of the combatants issued easily in strength of language, and the modern reader should take this in his stride. If he cannot, he would do well to keep away from the study of the reformation altogether. We should judge these ancient warriors not by the vehemence of their words, but by the truthfulness of their story, and the sincerity and honesty of their lives.

But we can say more for Foxe than that. His fierceness is a matter of words only and not of deeds; his bark is always worse than his bite. Here he stands far in advance of his age. Foxe wished to send no man to the stake or to the gallows; and he pleaded passionately for those in danger of such a fate. The same cannot be said of More nor even of Cranmer, both of whom have gained a reputation for gentleness and width of sympathy. Indeed, it can be said of very few in the sixteenth century: but it can be said of Foxe.

But Foxe is not only himself a partizan; he lives in a world peopled with partizans. Much of his evidence came from men that had seen brother, father, wife or friend perish at the stake, and so had the best of reasons for hating the papal system. The stories in the book are often coloured by the indignant feelings of the narrators, and where they are reported only at second hand or at a distance of time, there may be legendary accretions. That there are some fables in the **Book of Martyrs** is undeniable, but there is no reason to question Foxe's good faith in the matter. He was honestly misled; he believed what he was told. Some writers have even suggested that the friends of the pope invented these fables, and had them communicated to Foxe, in order to bring discredit upon his book: but such deep-laid guile seems very unlikely. The fierce passions of the protestants are quite enough to account for the growth and ready acceptance of a number of fables.

Yet it is a mistake to say, as some do, that Foxe accepted uncritically everything that was told him, and made no attempt to divide between truth and falsehood. He took great pains to discover the facts, and when he was informed that a story printed by him was untrue, he set further inquiries afoot, so that he might make any necessary corrections in a new edition. There are scores of cases where he amends his matter or even cuts out whole incidents, in order to bring his narrative into better harmony with the facts. Thus, when he learnt (the letter still survives) that his story of the imprisonment of John Boulton in Reading was open to very serious cavil, he cuts out the whole from his second edition. In the same edition he drops the tale of the death by foul play of his wife's kinsman, John Randall, at Cambridge. (pp. 158-59)

In an age of strong passions it was not easy to arrive at the truth. Modern writers too readily assume that any protest made at the time against Foxe's stories is a serious blow to his credit. They forget that his enemies were quite as strong party men as his friends. If his friends had cause to hate the Marian persecution, his enemies had every cause to conceal or minimize their share of it, living as they now were in a reign where the whole thing was anathema. When we consider how much hard lying goes on in the law courts to-day for the purpose of upholding a man's credit with his neighbours or even of financial gain, we cannot doubt that some of the men held up to opprobrium in the book would be ready to swear that black was white, if so they might clear their name. If Foxe had been softhearted enough to cut out of his book everything to which objection was taken by some interested party, many true things would have been sacrificed. (p. 161)

In dealing with ancient history Foxe was of course hampered by the uncritical standards of his age. Knowledge was indeed spreading, ancient documents were being recovered, and solid methods of scholarship being slowly built up, but this process was not as yet gone very far, and much legendary matter was generally believed on the authority of old chroniclers and historians. Thus Foxe tells us of the description of Christ sent by Pilate to the emperor Tiberius, of the letter to king Lucius of England from Eleutherius bishop of Rome, of the female pope Joan and her child, of the poisoning of king John by a monk, though in the last case he also gives two or three other versions of the king's death. All these things we now know to be fables, and yet they are to be found in Eusebius or Bede or other writers of respectable credit.

Nor does Foxe escape the snare of credulity when he comes down to the events of his own time. The men of his age believed fervently in miracles and in the constant and direct intervention of God in human affairs by way of reward and punishment. Any misfortune that befell a man, ill health, accident, loss of repute or money, and above all, death, might be interpreted by his enemies as a judgment from heaven. From this it is but a short step to embellishing the misfortune with strange and lurid details in order to give it more the guise of a judgment; and it is not a very long step to inventing a misfortune that never occurred: for when men feel and say that this or that piece of cruelty or evil doing invites and will receive punishment, the belief easily spreads that the punishment has been inflicted. The old church historians have a gruesome tale of Arius' bowels falling out of his body: and these ideas descended into the reformation period. Thomas More tells how Miles Forrest, one of the murderers of the little princes, "piecemeal rotted away", and how Richard III's preacher, Dr. Shaw, was so struck to the heart for the shame of his sermon, that "within few days after he withered and consumed away." The religious controversialists on both sides are full of judgment stories, and Foxe is not behind hand in retailing them. When he finds them in the printed books of the continental historians or in the manuscripts of his English informants, he swallows them without difficulty, and duly hands them on to his readers. These judgment stories are the weakest part of his book. Most of them are suspicious in one way or another. At the best we scent embellishment, while in a few cases the alleged disaster seems to be a fable from beginning to end. (pp. 163-64)

When he comes down to the English martyrs, Foxe keeps matters more in his own hand. This was the heart of the book; this was the part that specially moved him. The narratives have to be created; they do not exist ready made, awaiting only the labour of a translator. But even here he depended, as we have seen, greatly upon copyists. He could not consult all the registers himself, still less could he commit their contents to paper. The transcripts that survive among the Foxian manuscripts are in many different hands, and though they are trustworthy in the main, it is not to be supposed that they contain no errors or that all transcribers were equally careful. If therefore a discrepancy should be found between a register and Foxe's text, this may not always be his own doing. (p. 165)

Foxe's standard of honesty in quoting his authorities is a high one. In many cases he gives his document verbatim; indeed, considering that his book was intended for the general reader, he devotes a surprising amount of space to archivism of this kind. Sometimes however he will shorten it or condense it in one way or another; and this he does honestly, though not always in a way that would approve itself to the scientific historian of to-day. In a very few cases he indulges in a little adaptation which has exposed him to attack from his ill-wishers; but there is no ground for questioning his good faith, whatever may be thought of his wisdom. The matter will come before us later; meanwhile it is enough to give the verdict of so strong an anti-Foxian as Gairdner, that when he quotes verbatim, he is "generally a very careful editor."

Such then is Foxe's book. It is not perfect; he would have been the last to claim that it was. He worked in haste, he was casual by temperament, a partizan by conviction, and not averse to violent language; he wrote for a somewhat credulous age, whose standards of exactitude are not ours: but these are but spots on the sun. Such errors count for little against the solid mass of historical fact that is the strength of his book. First-hand documents jostle one another, that would never have been preserved but for his zeal, documents written by simple folk straight from the heart, giving us the most lifelike and vivid pictures of the manners and feelings of the day, full of details that could never have been invented by a forger. And his method of using them proclaims the honest man, the sincere seeker after truth. On this last point it may be well to quote his own words in answer to the attack of Harpsfield.

> And first, where he layeth against me whole heaps and cart-loads, I cannot tell how many, of lies and falsities: I here briefly answer Master Cope again, or what English Harpsfield else soever lieth covered under this English 'Cope,' that if a lie be, after the definition of St. Augustine, whatsoever thing is pronounced with the intent to deceive another; then I protest to you, Master Cope! and to all the world, there is never a lie in all my book. What the intent and custom is of the papists to do, I cannot tell: for mine own I will say, although many other vices I have, yet from this one I have always of nature abhorred, wittingly to deceive any man or child, so near as I could, much less the church of God,

> whom I with all my heart do reverence, and with fear obey.

Is it possible to believe that these words spring out of a feigning heart? Such a man may be misled by his easy nature or warm feelings, but he will not sin against the light. (pp. 167-69)

Foxe's account of Tyndale is an excellent specimen of his methods. We see him advancing from small beginnings, seeking information from many quarters, gathering documents of first class value, slowly building up his story to greater perfection. We observe that sometimes he names his authorities, sometimes he does not: but those whom he does not name (*e.g.* "Webb" and Coverdale) are quite as likely to be good as those (*e.g.* Poyntz) whom he does. We observe too that most of the story is drawn from the memories of living persons, and not from registers and other official documents; and these memories are of events that happened at least a quarter of a century ago, and in some cases forty years ago: nevertheless they are accurate and trustworthy. Thus it would be a great mistake to draw a hard and fast line, as some have tried to do, between Foxe depending on registers and Foxe depending on personal information. If this were done, not only would vast masses of true history be thrown under suspicion, but the narratives of the persecution would lose nearly all their vividness and power.

On the other hand, Foxe often uses his material in a loose and clumsy way. His arrangement is faulty; he is casual about details, and is not worried if his documents clash. Thus in describing the foundation of Cardinal college at Oxford, he says that Tyndale was one of the scholars invited by Wolsey to man it, though his own narrative elsewhere shows that Tyndale was in Germany at the time. Again, in narrating Monmouth's story, he states that the bishop of London who rejected Tyndale was Stokesley, whereas in his main section on Tyndale he had correctly named him as Tonstall. He is also loose in his marks of time, and gives no clear date even for so important an event as the printing of the first New Testament. In his main narrative he dates this about 1527, but elsewhere, when he is following Halle, he dates it about 1529; the true date was 1526, as he might have gathered from Tonstall's injunction which he prints. Again, he does not notice that Coverdale's story of the visit to Hamburg (which is correct) does not tally in its details with Halle's narrative of Tonstall buying up testaments at Antwerp for burning. All these errors and disagreements are cleared up and resolved by the *Acts and Monuments* itself. Good as Foxe's book is, it might have been made even better, had he had the time and the patience to do the necessary editing.

But what are these small blemishes compared to the solid merit of his work? That we know to-day what manner of man Tyndale was, is due far more to Foxe than to anybody else. And the service which he renders to Tyndale, he has rendered to many other martyrs, and indeed to some who were not martyrs at all. His book abounds in first class material, preserved to us by his pains and industry. Everywhere we find the same slow building up, the same search for fresh documents, the same advance upon the past. Other men stood to watch, his friends to applaud, his foes to scoff and to pick holes; but he did the work. He hewed the gold out of the rock—not always pure gold, may be, but still gold. None can compare with him here; this is his glory; his book stands and will stand. (pp. 172-74)

J. F. Mozley, in his John Foxe and His Book, *Society for Promoting Christian Knowledge, 1940, 254 p.*

C. S. Lewis (essay date 1954)

[*Lewis is considered one of the foremost mythopoeic authors of the twentieth century. He is regarded as a formidable Christian polemicist, a perceptive literary critic, and—perhaps most highly—as a writer of fantasy literature. Also a noted academic and scholar, Lewis held posts at Oxford and Cambridge, where he was an acknowledged authority on medieval and Renaissance literature. In the following excerpt from* English Literature in the Sixteenth Century, Excluding Drama *(1954), he defends Foxe against critics who debate the sixteenth-century historian's integrity and impartiality.*]

The good fame of John Foxe (1517-87) has had many vicissitudes. In his own time he was, naturally, attacked from the Roman side by . . . Harding in 1565 [see excerpt dated 1565] and by Harpsfield under the pseudonym of Alan Cope in his *Sex Dialogi* (1566). Among Protestants he soon acquired and long retained almost scriptural authority, but in 1837 the work of S. R. Maitland [see Further Reading] ushered in a violent reaction. Maitland had many successors and the nineteenth-century tradition represents Foxe as an unscrupulous propagandist who records what he knows to be false, suppresses what he knows to be true, and claims to have seen documents he has not seen. In 1940, however, Mr. J. F. Mozley reopened the whole question and defended Foxe's integrity, as it seems to me, with complete success [see excerpt dated 1940]. From his examination Foxe emerges, not indeed as a great historian, but as an honest man. For early Church history he relies on the obvious authorities and is of very mediocre value. For the Marian persecution his sources are usually the narratives of eyewitnesses. Such narratives, whispered in secret during a Terror and emulously proclaimed as soon as the Terror is over, are liable to distortion. Men who have seen their friends die in torture are not always inspired by that coolly scientific spirit which the academic researcher so properly demands. But there seems no evidence that Foxe ever accepted what he did not himself believe or ever refused to correct what he had written in the light of fresh evidence. The most horrible of all his stories, the Guernsey martyrdoms, was never refuted, though violently assailed; in some ways the defence may be thought scarcely less damaging than the charge. And in one respect—in his hatred of cruelty—Foxe was impartial to a degree hardly parelleled in that age. His earliest original work, the *De Non Plectendis Morte Adulteris* (1548) is a plea for mercy; he confesses that he could never pass a slaughter-house without discomposure; and when his own party was on top he interceded (vainly, of course) to save Anabaptists from the stake in 1575 and Jesuits from the gallows in 1581.

Foxe's enormous influence is curiously out of proportion to his actual status as an English man of letters. Latin was the medium he preferred. The first form taken by his Martyrology was the *Commentarii* published at Strassburg in 1554, which dealt mainly with the Lollards. This was enlarged to include the Marian persecution and published as *Rerum in Ecclesia Gestarum . . . Commentarii* at Basel in 1559. The *Acts and Monuments* of 1563 contains a translation (not by Foxe) of the *Rerum* and adds masses of new material which had poured in on him since his return to England. The narratives of others are sometimes reproduced *verbatim*, sometimes abridged, sometimes conflated. The *Ecclesiastical History* (1570) extends the story back to Apostolic times and abridges (not always judiciously) the later periods. It will be seen, therefore, that it is only in the earlier portions of the 1570 text that we have long stretches of pure Foxian English composition as distinct from Foxe translated by others or Foxe working with scissors and paste. This section is in every way the least valuable part of his work and his English style has no high merits. The sentences have not energy to support their great length. In the Marian parts, as in Malory, we find plenty of good reading without being able to trace our pleasure confidently to any single author's skill. But the composite result is by no means to be neglected. Many excellent scenes recur to the mind: Jullins Palmer talking to his mother, Mrs. Wardall's lodger coming to the window to explain that she is a stranger in these parts and is afraid of spirits walking by night, Mr. Lewes making a sumner eat his citation. Better than all is the moment at which Elizabeth Folkes, stripping for the fire and prevented by the police from giving her petticoat to her mother, flings it away with the words, 'Farewell all the world! Farewell Faith, farewell Hope, welcome Love!' (pp. 299-301)

C. S. Lewis, "Drab and Transitional Prose," in his English Literature in the Sixteenth Century, Excluding Drama, *Oxford at the Clarendon Press, 1954, pp. 272-317.*

Philip Hughes (essay date 1954)

[*In the following excerpt from* The Reformation in England, Volume II: Religio Depopulata, *Hughes questions the reliability of* Actes and Monuments *as an historical account of the Marian campaign against heresy.*]

Whoever writes on the repression of heresy in the reign of Mary must, at the outset, take account of John Foxe; for the work popularly known as Foxe's *Book of Martyrs* is the historian's sole available source for much of the story. It is very far from being a really satisfactory source. In the first place, while what Foxe has to tell runs to 1,889 pages of close print, nearly a third of this vast space has nothing to do with the lives of his heroes; it is given up to reprints of such various matters as the debates at Oxford between the Protestant bishops and the Catholic theologians, to anti-Catholic tracts, and to other matter of the kind we now call propaganda. Next we find that a wholly disproportionate space is given to the lives of the more celebrated of the victims. Out of 1,302 pages, which is the total given to the "lives", nearly two-thirds—832 pages in all—goes to describe 17 only of the 273 victims of Foxe's list. And what of Foxe's reliability? Is he careful and exacting in his attitude towards the testimony on which he is relying? Is he critical or credulous as the stories come in out of which he is to build his narrative? And is he a truthful writer? Not only must we ask, Does he invent? but, Does he tell all? Or does he "arrange" his matter with a view to some purpose other than the exact recording of what took place? Has he any other purpose in view than to make such an exact record? Is there any important matter that he suppresses? Does he suppress it habitually? Foxe's **Book of Martyrs,** it has been seriously said, by one generally acknowledged as a leading authority, was almost a second Bible to the England of the late sixteenth and seventeenth centuries. What, actually, is it worth, as fact? Few questions are more important to the historians. For centuries they have used Foxe as a quarry, increasingly with reservations, each writer with his own particular grumble at the faults and flaws. But no writer, in all that time, has set himself to make a critical study of these forbidding tomes, only too well described, in recent years, as "primeval forest, closely packed, richly various, and untamed". (pp. 255-56)

The **Book of Martyrs** has all the qualities that will delight the partisan, and that must torment the historian. There is, for example, Foxe's purpose. Why did he write the lives of Queen Mary's victims? Very simply, as a might piece of anti-Catholic propaganda. "If anything could make England protestant for ever, it would be the memory of the Marian terror; and [Foxe] desired to burn his dreadful history into the minds of his countrymen, both high and low." Then, too, the liveliest parts of the narrative, the interchanges between the judges and the prisoners, for example—in which the prisoners are invariably victorious—are presented as being the prisoners' own accounts: it is the trial, and the judge, described from the condemned cell. And it is the prisoners' own account, unchecked, uncorroborated, that is also very often the sole authority for the story of the minor horrors inflicted on them. And where it is not the prisoner's account (or what is alleged to be the prisoner's account) it is, very often, the hearsay account of some eye-witness who remains anonymous. Here, then, there must enter, very powerfully, into consideration the kind of mind Foxe had. Foxe's story, it is not surprising, was very promptly called in question, and by critics who had themselves been active in the persecution—by Nicholas Harpsfield, for example, Archdeacon of Canterbury from 1554 to 1559, whose book appeared just three years after Foxe's first English edition. Such early critics made no bones about calling Foxe a liar. But while no one, nowadays, suggests that Foxe deliberately invented incidents, no one denies that he had not the mentality of a historian, or that he was credulous to a degree, and ready to accept any anti-Catholic tale on its face value. "A compiler on a gigantic scale", says one critic, "neither scrupulous nor scholarly", adding that Foxe had "loose notions of literary morality".

Foxe's imaginative and credulous book is, it would seem, the equivalent, in this first dawn of Protestant England, of those wonder-stories about apocryphal saints on which the grandfathers of these Protestants had nourished their piety in the last days of Catholic England. The instinct that demands a Golden Legend is still active and, all unconsciously, Foxe is supplying the need. All the vices of the old hagiography are here—the ordinary related as though miraculous, when it occurs in the life of the hero, the wonderful being needed at every stage since it is the occurrence of the wonderful that is the test and proof of sanctity. And horror is piled on horror, as in the apocryphal legends of the early martyrs. We are told, for example, how Bonner personally scourged his victims, and how

he held their hands in the flame of a candle. We read how "the faces of some were scratched and torn with the nails of bishops, and their beards half pulled off ", and how another bishop (unnamed) who had an obstinate heretic in his prison, "made him privily to be snarled, and his flesh to be plucked and torn away with a pair of pincers, and bringing him before the people said the rats had eaten him". And when the fate of Hunne is recalled, constructive imagination adds to the horrors; he is now the man whom Bonner's predecessor "caused to be thrust in at the nose with burning needles, and then to be hanged".

The most serious charge brought against Foxe, however, is not that he will swallow any tale that will tell against Catholicism, nor that "his coarse ribalry . . . exceeds all literary licence", but that when the evidence before him tells against his purpose he is capable of suppressions. The one element in the vast compilation to which historians have continuously turned with confidence—trusting in Foxe as an honest man, however strong his prejudices—is the series of translated extracts from the episcopal records of the heresy trials, where we are given the questions put to the accused and their answers, the actual sentences passed upon them, with the official statement of the heretical belief for which they were sentenced. These transcripts have always been taken as substantially reliable. Here is

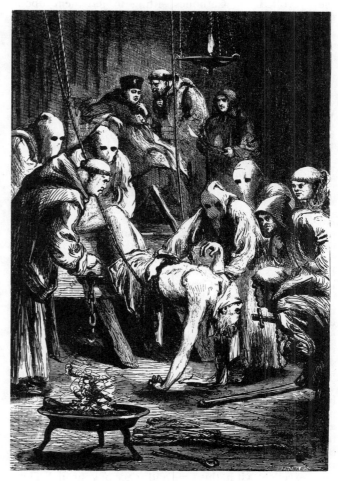

"The first time of torturing." From a nineteenth-century English edition of The Book of Martyrs.

almost the only part of Foxe's story that we are in a position to check by testimony that is independent; and we are now told, by one who has made the experiment, "One has to remember that his summaries are trustworthy only up to a certain point: he does not insert what is not in the original, but he often omits particulars there given, especially charges accusing the heretics of opinions he did not share". (pp. 257-59)

Foxe's account has been used [herein] as though it were substantially true—it is taken as fact that the men and women he names were really put to death for the offence of heresy at the times and places he records, after trials such as he describes: that these events did so happen, no one doubts. As to Foxe's own comments, and the alleged comments of the actors in the tragedy, that is another matter. Even though we take it for granted that the accounts are authentic—are really the work of those presented by Foxe as their authors—we cannot also take for granted that they are either accurate (e.g. complete) or fair. In the present state of our knowledge, looking on all this, if we are able, "with the coolness of an unconcerned spectator", our judgment must be held in suspense. And what if Foxe has the habit of suppressing the sufferer's beliefs where these are not orthodox Protestantism? where these are such as would revolt orthodox Protestants as surely as they revolted the Catholics sitting in judgment upon them? (p. 259)

> *Philip Hughes, "A Catholic Queen, 1553-1558: The Fate of Heretics," in his* The Reformation in England: Religio Depopulata, Vol. II, *The Macmillan Company, 1954, pp. 254-304.*

William Haller   (essay date 1963)

[*Haller was an essayist and historian. His 1963 study* John Foxe and the Elect Nation *is considered a major examination of the martyrologist's work. In the following excerpt from this work, he examines Foxe's attempt to demonstrate to Elizabeth I her role in the "elect nation."*]

Actes and Monuments in 1563 was the most elaborate expression of the apocalyptical expectancy with which the returned exiles and their party greeted Elizabeth at her accession. Naturally, therefore, the book was dedicated to her, and hers was the crowning story in its pages. The dedication likened her to Constantine bringing healing peace to the Church after an era of hatred and persecution, and the author to Eusebius begging only for the privilege of writing the history of the sufferings of the saints which she had brought to an end. A little later in the same year, having received a copy of Elizabeth's recent speech to the scholars at Cambridge, Foxe addressed a letter to her asking leave to transmit her words to posterity along with 'other monuments of historical matters'. It was a grief to him that 'when I am preparing a full account of you . . . many things are wanting which are yet unknown to me and cannot be known but by your majesty'. And, he continued, if he were permitted to make them known, they could not 'be described better by any than by your own commentary, which I wish might be obtained by your most excellent wit in this time and space of your life'. This was nothing less than an invitation to Elizabeth to add her own story to those of the other victims of persecution in

the late reign. Fuller tells us that she called him Father Foxe, but we are left only to imagine what a story she might have told if she had risen to the lure of her indefatigable collector of monuments of historical matters.

But he could not on that account leave her out of his book. He never wrote the promised history of her reign, but from information which probably came to him from Roger Ascham, Mistress Ashley and other members of her household, he rounded out his Book of Martyrs with an account of the person he regarded as the most illustrious victim of them all. In the elaborately conceited style in which Elizabeth's subjects and Elizabeth herself liked to wrap up their thoughts on formal occasions, Foxe opens his account of her experiences before she came to the throne by playing again on the theme of the godly prince, the part that Edward had not lived to act out and that the Lady Jane had not been permitted to bring off.

> For what man reputing with himself the singular ornaments and noble graces given of God to this so princely a Lady and puissant princess, the mildness of her nature, the clemency of her royal estate and majesty, the peaceableness of her reign, who a virgin so mildly ruleth men, governeth her subjects, keepeth all things in order, quieteth foreign nations, recovereth towns, enlargeth her kingdom, nourisheth and [re]concileth amity, uniteth hearts and love with foreign enemies, helpeth neighbours, reformeth religion, quencheth persecution, redresseth dross, frameth the things out of joint, so feared with such love, and so loved with such fear.

This was, of course, a way of instructing his royal mistress in the way she should conduct her affairs by praising her for already having done so. But fortunately the writer soon lays aside the style of courtship. Lest it should happen to her as it had happened to her brother to be extolled while living but soon forgotten when dead—she had just nearly died after reigning fewer years than he had done—Foxe undertakes to write her history up to the present. It is a story which the responsible biographer should be chary of crediting in every detail, but a well-told story for all that.

It is the kind of tale which people at all times love to be told about royalty, though no such tale about a reigning monarch as Foxe now told about Elizabeth had ever before been told in English print. He begins by glancing back at the account he had given earlier in the book of her birth and baptism with Cranmer for godfather. He pictures her modest, studious girlhood as Ascham was to picture it again in *The Scholemaster*. He goes on to tell of the trials she had had to endure under her hard-hearted sister's rule—how she was rudely summoned to Westminster and accused of complicity in Wyatt's rebellion, sent to the Tower, nearly drowned at the shooting of the bridge, landed at the Traitors' Gate and held under false suspicion of treason, then dispatched to Woodstock under a boorish jailer, next brought back to Hampton Court to be examined by Gardiner and the privy council in the hope of getting her to incriminate herself, summoned in the night to a last audience with the queen in the royal bedchamber, Mary grim, suspicious and withdrawn, her husband listening 'behind a cloth and not seen'. Finally, of course, we have Elizabeth coming to the throne at Mary's death amid the rejoicing of the people.

All this is told with seeming artlessness, but with great skill in the handling of action and dialogue and the depiction of character, and with effective touches of sentiment and humour. A little boy in the Tower garden brings the princess flowers at the risk of a whipping. Villagers on the road to Woodstock ring the bells at her passing and are put in the stocks for their devotion. A merry conceited fellow, in order to amuse her and annoy her keeper, picks up the goat pastured in the enclosure where she takes her recreation and brings the creature to Bedingfield her keeper, saying 'what talk they have had I cannot tell. For I understand him not, but he should seem to me some stranger, and I think verily a Welshman.'

There is above all Elizabeth herself, princely and gracious with her friends and the people, steadfast and self-possessed in the presence of her enemies. 'This that I have said,' Foxe reports her to have told Gardiner, 'I will stand to. For I will never belie myself.' (Her portraits bore the legend *Semper eadem*.) 'Well,' we are told that Queen Mary said in that last interview at Hampton Court, 'you stiffly still persevere in your truth. Belike you will not confess but that you have been wrongfully punished?' and Elizabeth replies, 'I must not say so, if it please your majesty, to you.' 'Why then,' says the queen, 'belike you will to other[s],' and the princess, guarding every utterance, 'No, if it please your majesty . . . I have borne the burden and must bear it.' Probably by 1563 there were others who had analyzed Elizabeth's qualities as shrewdly as Foxe, but had anyone else depicted so convincingly the character which legend was to fix upon her? Or had any monarch ever been so served by a writer with such a sense of what people would delight to hear concerning their ruler?

The conclusion Foxe intended his readers to draw from the story was unmistakable. If Elizabeth was not herself actually one of the martyrs, it was only because providence in its care for the English nation had intervened to save her. (pp. 124-27)

While the Catholic rebellion was coming to a head in the north, author and publisher of **Actes and Monuments** were making ready to issue a new and greatly enlarged edition of their book. Their labours were drawing to a conclusion as the uprising was being suppressed, and the book appeared towards the close of 1570 as the queen was being constrained by the public outcry against the Queen of Scots and the rebellious earls to summon another parliament.

The edition of 1570 fixed the Book of Martyrs in the form which was to remain substantially unchanged through six subsequent editions down to the eighteenth century. Of the two large folio volumes the first was entitled *The First Volume of the Ecclesiasticall history contaynying the Actes and Monuments of thynges passed in every kynges tyme in this Realme . . . from the primitive tyme till the reigne of K. Henry VIII*. The second volume was described as going on *from the tyme of K. Henry VIII to Queene Elizabeth our gratious Lady now reignyng.* The two volumes taken together showed how much author and publisher had learned about suiting a work of such a character, scope and size to the needs of their public. (pp. 128-29)

In the text of the work Foxe now made some revisions, corrections and additions in his accounts of the Marian martyrs, rearranged the order of presentation here and there, translated or summarized Latin documents, but otherwise left this part of the work substantially the same as before. Where, however, he had formerly taken at most a hundred pages to relate the history of the Church and the nation before Wyclif, he now took five hundred, and where he had formerly taken something less than eight hundred pages to get from Wyclif to Mary, he now took over a thousand, the type-pages being at least a third larger. That is, he now led up to his account of Mary's reign and the stories of the Marian martyrs with a much extended account of the whole course of the history of Church and nation from the very beginning to the crisis in which the queen and her people now found themselves. Most important, he thus set before the Elizabethan public the current Protestant version of the traditional Christian conception of the meaning of history, its application to England, and the lessons to be deduced from it for the instruction of the queen no less than her subjects.

No one, of course, would now think of turning to Foxe for information concerning the history of the Christian Church or the English nation before his own time. Every part of his book is deeply coloured by the passions and prejudices of the man and his age. But all writing of history is a rewriting of history nearer to the historian's own notion of what must have happened, and the question here is not, did Foxe tell the truth as we would have it told, but what did he take the truth to be and induce so many of his countrymen in so critical a moment to accept as such.

In dedicating his first English edition to the queen he had likened Elizabeth to Constantine and himself to Eusebius. The comparison was appropriate, since it was no new thing in the history of Christianity for an upsurge of the religious spirit to find expression in a rewriting of history. History was what Christianity was about. What Christian teachers had to tell mankind that was different from the teachings of rival cults was a story of mankind's past and what it portended for the future. The telling and retelling of that story had been the occupation of Christians in every age of active faith.

For the essence of that faith was the conviction, the certain knowledge as they supposed, that at a particular moment in time a particular event had occurred which was both the consummation of everything that had occurred before and the revelation of everything that it behoved men to know of what was still to come in so much of time as still remained. To seek escape from history like the millenarians, or to think of it like the pagans as an endless succession of revolving circumstance, was to reject Christianity. To hold faithfully to the idea of history thus conceived was to be of that true Church which had come down in the process of time from the prime witnesses of the unique event which gives history its meaning and reveals its purpose. Meaning and purpose were always the same. History had always the same story to tell of men condemned for disobedience to God's command and of men saved from time to time by God's grace from the consequences of their fall, of grace manifested in the faithfulness of the elect under temptation and affliction. This story, of which the Scriptures were the prime authentic record, it was the historian's business to relate to the conditions of men in his own time.

But as the history of mankind was the subject of Christian

faith, so the history of the Church was the subject which preoccupied Christian historians, and the effect of the Reformation was merely to give the subject a new turn and a fresh relevance. Catholics, regarding the visible Church as the appointed vehicle for the transmission of truth revealed in scripture and history, demanded of Protestant reformers, where was your Church before Luther? Protestant reformers, denying the identification of a fallible priesthood with the Church, turned to the supposedly infallible record of the Scriptures. The whole history of the Church must be reviewed and rewritten according to the Word as set down in the book, the one book of unique authority, though in the even that turned out to mean not only that book but a multitude of others now being put into men's hands by the printing-press and the book-trade.

The uniqueness claimed for scriptural authority lay in this, that in the Scriptures the record of accomplished fact and the revelation of universal truth authenticated one another. The future which the prophets foretold had either become the past which the chroniclers had recorded, or was on its way to becoming so. Nothing that had ever happened had in truth been unforeseen; nothing that was still to happen had been unforetold. History and prophecy were in effect one continuing revelation of divine providence working upon the life of mankind. Thus in the Scriptures historians were provided with a key to the authentication and interpretation of all other records of the past and all tradition of whatever origin. Not the least important effect of the Reformation, aside from its effect upon religious life as such, was to make the art and science of historiography of momentous concern.

From this point of view the ancient classical notion that time and the universe run on for ever, and that the course of events is determined by chance for ever repeating itself, was untenable. Granted a creator, creation must have a beginning and an end, a principle and a purpose revealed in the record of things past and foretold, which it is for the historian to elucidate and demonstrate. For though the life of mankind does not go round and round with fortune's wheel, it does move in successive waves to break finally upon a predestined shore. It moves from age to age and so on to a concluding age, always more or less imminent. As to the exact chronological limits of these ages of the world's history, there might be some variation of opinion, but there could be no doubt as to the fact of their procession one after the other in a definite order through time towards an inevitable conclusion.

The history of mankind in general followed the same order as the history of man in particular. In every age of the world some man or men, however obscure or few, love God and obey him in innocence of heart. In every age as it proceeds men fall into disobedience and corruption from which there would be no escape did not God from time to time again interpose His grace in the lives of men chosen by Him to that end. In every age of the world, out of the generality of fallen men, some are called to believe, obey, and be saved and to show the way of salvation to others—some one man it might be, some one family, some one people, Noah, Abraham, the children of Israel, the tribe of Judah, the house of David, the apostles and Church of Christ. Thus mankind was believed to have been moving from the beginning through alternating lapses and recoveries, from crisis to crisis, always towards one greater crisis still to come, in which the whole process of history was to reach its final consummation in accordance with the foreordained scheme of things revealed in prophecy and the record of things past.

The Christian historian did not think of this process as one of development or progress from one stage to another, from lower to higher, primitive to advanced, simple to complex. He did not concern himself with the evolution and effect of laws and institutions. These things were works of creation, not products of growth. They became corrupt through disobedience, and they were renewed as men were renewed by the grace of God, but they did not evolve or progress. Through grace men regain their lost knowledge of truth and their power to obey it, but such knowledge and power come as new and original acts of creation or revelation, the will of God making itself felt as a spontaneous, authentic experience in the consciousness of one man at a time, not as the cumulative result of the experience of one man following and building upon another. The prime factor in historical causation was not human determination or conditioning circumstance. There was no such thing as accident, only providence, no learning by trial and error, only the creative will of God working in this man or that, this people or that.

The historian must centre his attention, therefore, first and last on the experience of individual souls, beginning with his own, on their reawakening one by one to knowledge of truth and their adhering to truth through the compulsion of what they know. The significant facts of history, report of which he was bound to credit and transmit, were the facts of spiritual experience presented as nearly as possible in the testimony of the individuals concerned or as reported by those nearest to them. And since the essence of spiritual experience in this life is a kind or measure of martyrdom, the history of the elect, which is to say of the Church, is a story of martyrdom.

Here was the basic conception of history which Foxe found in Christian historians from Eusebius and Augustine to Bale and Flacius. Adapting it in his own way to his own purposes in the circumstances of his own time, he transmitted it to the generations who pored over his famous book or had it retailed to them through one channel or another. To object to his lack of originality or to his misrepresentation of facts is beside the point. The primary enterprise of writers and publishers of books in his age was to get the literature and accumulated knowledge of past ages transposed into English and put into print. His accomplishment was to transpose the traditional Christian conception of history into terms that would be comprehensible to his own people in his own time. This meant to rewrite the history of the Church from an English Protestant point of view fitted to present circumstances. His people must be made to understand the whole pattern of events from the beginning to the present in order that they should realize their own place as a nation in that process, their immediate responsibility, the destiny to which they were called. Only thus could they rightly grasp the meaning of the current struggle with alien powers threatening their destruction and the necessity of supporting the queen and her government.

That the grounds for such a view of England's place in history were to be looked for first in scripture was, of course, beyond dispute. The will of God had made itself known directly to the people of Israel as to no people before or since. It followed that the record of Israel's experience was the most authentic and authoritative record of God's will that ever was, and that the history of every other people, notably now the English people, was to be understood only by the light of the record of that chosen nation as brought to fulfilment in Christ and His church.

This meant that the whole body of prophecy and chronicle in scripture was relevant to the whole course of events to the end of time, and the summation of the whole, foreshadowing the whole history of Christ's people clear through to their ultimate triumph with Christ over Antichrist, was the Apocalypse of St John. Bale had advanced this idea in his *Image of Both Churches*. Bullinger had expounded it at length to the English and other exiles at Zürich. Day had published Bullinger's exposition shortly after resuming business at Elizabeth's accession, and the translator had assured his readers that the book of Revelation thus expounded was 'as it were an ecclesiastical history of the troubles and persecutions of the church, especially from the apostles' time until the last day, wherein Christ . . . shall come a righteous judge to condemn Antichrist and all antichristian hypocrites and bloody persecutors, but to receive his elect people and to crown them with glory.'

Thus in his new and extended version of the Book of Martyrs Foxe endeavoured to place the stories of the recent victims of Catholic persecution in England in the perspective of history as conceived by Christian historians all the way back to Eusebius and Augustine. It is a conception which sees history, as he explains at the very start, occupied throughout by conflict between the world and the kingdom of Christ, the world consisting of 'all such as be without or against Christ', the kingdom of Christ consisting of 'all them which belong to the faith of Christ, and here take his part in this world against the world'. Two sorts of people made up the Church as we know it in this world, 'such as be of outward profession only' and 'such as by election inwardly are joined to Christ'. The first are of the visible Church only, partaking of the sacraments but not of Christ's inward blessing. The others are of 'the invisible church . . . partaking not only of the sacraments, but also the heavenly blessings and grace of Christ'. And 'as between the world and the kingdom of Christ there is a continual repugnance, so between the two parts of this visible church aforesaid groweth great variance and mortal persecution, insomuch that sometimes the true church of Christ hath no greater enemies than those of their own profession and company.

So it was in the time of Christ Himself and His apostles; so it has been ever since; so it is in these latter days. The history of the Church, like the history of mankind in general and of man in particular, has always to do with the contention of Christ and Antichrist for possession of man's soul. Hence the pattern to be looked for in the record of events is always one of lapse and recovery, of falling away due to the weakness and wickedness of men and of recovery due to renewal of divine grace, of Antichrist breaking out again and again and of Christ intervening to redeem His own and cast the devil out. History was the process by which God sifted out the souls of His elect through trial and conflict, made endurable for them by the inner assurance that, God's purpose fulfilled, they would

see a new heaven and a new earth. But God's purpose within the limits of time was not to bring forth a state of things that had never existed before—Foxe was no John of Münster—but to recover and keep what had been lost and might be lost again.

His intention, he tells his readers, is to show that the Church as now established in England was 'not the beginning of any new church of our own' but 'the renewing of the old ancient church of Christ'. The reformed Church had not swerved from Rome; Rome had swerved from itself. Following the pattern revealed in scripture, the Church in its history had passed first through a time of trial and martyrdom, next a time of flourishing and growth, next a time of backsliding and declining, next a time of oppression and persecution renewed, and finally a time of reformation continuing to the present and pointing forward to a day of perfect restoration and triumph, after which time would be no more. (pp. 129-36)

[Foxe] does not omit the lessons which this history has to teach the English people and their ruler at the moment of writing. 'Thus have we,' he says, 'the unquiet and miserable state of the emperors of Rome until the time of the Christian Constantine, with the examples . . . of God's severe justice upon them.' And in like manner, he continues, 'to come more near home . . . I could infer [the same lessons] of this our country of England.' Gildas had preached repentance to the ancient Britons and they had laughed him to scorn. 'What followed? God sent in their enemies on every side and destroyed them and gave the land to other nations.' Wyclif had exhorted the people to amend their lives and forsake idolatry and papistry, and they had despised him and after his death burned his bones and his books. 'What followed? They slew their right king and set up three wrong kings on a row, under whom all the noble blood was slain up and half the commons thereto.'

Foxe next looks ahead to the treatment which had been accorded to Tyndale, Bilney, Frith, and Barnes when they too preached repentance to their countrymen, but this was indeed coming close to home, and he breaks off simply with an exhortation to the godly wise to judge for themselves whether or not the nation has since had to suffer for its offences. 'Neither is it here any need to speak of these our lower and latter days.' Enough to say 'that God yet once again is come on visitation to this church of England, yea and that more lovingly and beneficially than ever he did afore. For in this his visitation he hath redressed many abuses and cleansed his church of much ungodliness and superstition and made it a glorious church, if it be compared to the old form and state'.

'If it be compared to the old form and state.' Foxe was not losing sight of what was for him the main issue. He was all for determined action in support of the national faith, and he hoped for a still more perfect reformation. But he perceived that the probable effect of the proposals put forth by Cartwright in this critical year of 1570 would be to jeopardize everything that had been gained so far in the war of the two Churches by stirring up unnecessary internal strife and weakening the power of the queen. For in his judgment the accomplishment of the more perfect reformation in the face of Catholic opposition depended everywhere on the security and success of the regime then established under Elizabeth in England. Consequently he would take no part in the Puritan attempt to force Elizabeth's hand at this time, and he designed his book in its extended form to set forth the lessons which history, especially English history, had to teach both queen and people concerning their mutual obligations under the law of God. (pp. 138-39)

> *William Haller, in his* Foxe's "Book of Martyrs" and the Elect Nation, *Jonathan Cape, 1963, 258 p.*

Helen C. White   (essay date 1963)

[*An American novelist, essayist, and academic, White is especially known for her scholarly studies of English history. In the following excerpt from her 1963 study* Tudor Books of Saints and Martyrs, *she examines Foxe's perceived propagandist intent in writing a contemporary ecclesiastical history.*]

[Although] **Actes and Monuments** has now for almost four hundred years held a quite unique position as the English book of martyrs par excellence, it is in fact a good deal more than that. Foxe clearly meant it to be. For, as we have seen from his address to Queen Elizabeth, he never intended to be considered a successor to the author of the despised *Golden Legend*, but rather to the first great historian of the Church, Eusebius Pamphili, the early fourth-century Bishop of Caesarea. (p. 169)

Foxe takes a very different approach, of course, from Eusebius or Jacobus, for clearly his main interest is the growth of corruption. His basic principle of historical criticism he gives almost at the beginning of his vast book: "In summe, to geve thee one generall rule for all, this thou shalt observe, the higher thou goest upwarde to the Apostles time, the purer thou shalt finde the churche: the lower thou doest descend, ever the more drosse and dregges thou shalt perceyve in the bottome, and especiallye within this laste 500 yeares, according to the trew sayinge of Tertullian: quod primum, id rectum est, that which is the first, is right etc." Then, as so often, Foxe returns to his own time, which is never long out of his mind: "Therfore as that was the firste, and golden age: so I may well call this the olde, or brasen age of the churche." Foxe relies on Eusebius for his account of the apostolic age, but he underscores his own points. There is no claiming of superiority by the apostles, including Peter, he insists; humbleness of mind was the characteristic of this first age. And then after it came the second age, when the "word of God" was preached everywhere, not just in Jewry. This was, indeed, the "florishing age of the churche," when every church had its appointed honor. As for the duration of this primitive period, it may be said to end with the beginning of the middle age of the Church, which was when Polychronius, the Bishop of Jerusalem, about 440 began to claim the supremacy of his see of Jerusalem. Then came "The middle age of the Churche," in which the Church wrestled with sects and schisms, especially such as contended for supremacy. Somewhere about eight or nine hundred years after Christ, the Church began to decay. This deterioration Foxe attributed to the fact that "through the great sufferance of princes" she had subdued not only all cathedral churches but all dispossessing princes. Popes and prelates, thus exalted by princes and emperors, began to forget themselves. The result is that the third age of the

Church saw its strength begin to fail, "opprest with cold humors of worldly pompe, avarice, and tirrany." But the degeneration became most apparent when the thousand years were complete, and Sylvester II held the see of Rome. Foxe carried this account of the third age down to 1374, about the time Master John Wycliffe became reader of divinity at Oxford. The end of the first part of Foxe's history would seem to finish this discussion of the decay of the Middle Ages.

But when he began the second part of his history, with the marginal date of 1371, he nevertheless went back to pick up some of those who before Wycliffe had wrestled in the same cause. Then Foxe began what is really his fourth age, with John Wycliffe. . . . This was for Foxe really the beginning of the Reformation. He did, of course, pay tribute to other controversies of the period, including the work of a couple of Councils, and to the martyrs of the Bohemian and other foreign churches. Then he returned to England, with a note to the reader, assuring him of the faithfulness of the present settlement to the real Christian tradition. The very plan of the book shows that Foxe belonged to that group of Protestant apologists who were most sensitive to the charges of heresy and innovation that their Catholic adversaries cast at them. In his preface to "the gentle Reader" before this third part of his ecclesiastical history, Foxe quite explicitly attacked the notion which he found widespread among the common people, "that this religion nowe generally used, hathe sprong up and risen but of late and few yeres, even by the space, (as many do think) of XX. or XXX. yeres," and assured his reader "that not only the actes and monuments heretofore passed, but also the histories here after following, shal manifest and declare that thys professyon of Christes religion hath bene spread abrode in Englande, by the space almost of CC. yeres, yea and before that time, and hath oftentimes sparkled although the flames thereof have never so perfectly burst out, as it hath done within these C. yeres and more." And he proceeded to document that claim, beginning with William Taylor, "a favourer of Wickleffe," burned at Smithfield in 1422, and going on to the end of the reign of Henry VIII. The fourth part of the book treats of "the milde and Alcion days of king Edward the sixte," the fifth of "the horrible and bloudye tyme of Queene Marye," and the sixth of "the most florishing reigne of Queen Elizabeth." So Foxe's history ends with the personal victory of Queen Elizabeth and the triumph of her religious settlement. As he said in the beginning of his great undertaking, Foxe wrote his book in order that his countrymen, instructed as to what they had escaped from and come into, might "therfore power oute more aboundant thanks to the Lord for this his so swete and mercifull reformacion." It is really the victory of the Lord that Foxe is celebrating.

Actes and Monuments tells an exciting story of a great struggle and a great victory in the triumphs of the martyrs, but it does a good deal more than that. It gives the religious history of England from the beginning to the present in ever-increasing detail. It sets that history of the breaking of the light, and the struggle of the light with darkness, in its larger world context in the history of Christianity, presenting the ancient pedigree of the martyrs, as we have seen, and accompanying the story of the breaking English Reformation with that of the Continent. The result is that the local struggle is given dignity by its relation to the world struggle, and, on the other hand, the larger struggle is brought home to the English reader in homely local terms.

It is quite clear, too, from even the bare outline of Foxe's history, what he conceived to be most central to the whole history of Christianity, and that was the question of what should be the central organizing institution of Christian society. By and large, the question of whether the Church was international or national did not bother Foxe because the issue he was interested in was the supremacy of the king. Consequently, though the basis of the discussion of the relations of the national and the international Church that was so much to interest later controversialists is to be seen in his challenge to the primacy of the Roman see as an usurpation and an aggression with regard to other sees, he is much more interested in building up the case against the Papacy as a threat to royal authority, and documenting that menace from past history. No ultramontane ever took the importance of the Papacy to the continuing order of the Catholic Church more seriously than Foxe. (pp. 170-73)

On this issue Foxe developed his attack along historic lines. The Church never knew any such papal supremacy in the religious sense until Boniface I called himself universal bishop six hundred years after Christ. Indeed, the claims to papal supremacy were not known in the Primitive Church, which followed the injunction of Paul in the Thirteenth Epistle to the Romans that every soul should be subject to the superior power, the power which bears the sword, not the spiritual but the temporal. That was to be the great foundation of the prince's power for the sixteenth-century Protestant, and that was, Foxe believed, the mind of the apostles for the Primitive Church, to which he looked back for his model. Indeed, Foxe quotes Niccolò Machiavelli, "the secretary of the cytie of Florence," in what must be one of his most respectable Elizabethan appearances, to the effect that "before Theodoricke kyng of Lombardes, that is, before the yeare of our Lorde 500. in all pollitike affayres the Byshoppe of Rome ever obeyed the Emperours and kynges." It was only in the third age of the Church, about the year 1000, that "the supremacy of Rome raged in his ruffe, which being once established in consciences of men, the power of all other princes christian did quake and decay, for dread of the popes interdict, suspense, and excommunication, which they feared no lesse, then Christe his owne sentence from heaven."

Foxe went on to document that thesis abundantly. Hildebrand was, of course, a notable villain in that story, and the episode of Canossa was presented in full detail with colorful comments in the margin. The famous waiting of the Emperor at the gates of the castle of Canossa is described marginally as "A wonderous submissyon of a valiant Emperour to a vyle pope." Against his account of the terms of the promise by which Henry bound himself not to exercise his imperial functions until a council should have passed on his conduct, Foxe wrote: "Here the beast of the Apocalipse appeareth in hys couloures." When Hildebrand refused to excommunicate Rudolf for his rebellious invasion of the empire until he should have a hearing, Foxe not only accused the Pope of using the law for a pretext, but labeled the whole transaction marginally, "The pope traitor to themperor." And rifling the gossip of an

age which might give even his own models in the art of denigration, Foxe drew a character of Hildebrand commensurate with what he judged his historic role. Hildebrand was, so almost all writers testify, "a sorcerer most notable, and a Necromansier." The Countess Matilda was the Pope's paramour; the Pope set in motion a device for murdering the King. While Henry was presented as a model of kingly virtue that would have doubtless astounded Henry himself, Hildebrand was depicted as "the first author, and patrone of all misrule that followed in Popes," a verdict which Foxe justified by explaining that "here came firste the subjection of the temporall regiment, under the spirituall jurisdiction. And Emperours which before were theyr masters, now are made their underlings."

With such a reading of history it is not surprising that for Foxe Thomas à Becket was "that olde Romish traytor." True, the version which he gave of the death of Thomas is more like the traditional one than like that which was reprinted among "Certain Injunctions" published by royal authority in 1539, in which the false martyrdom was explained as having "happened uppon a reskue by him made," but Foxe's opinion was no higher than Henry's of the character of the traitor. (pp. 173-75)

Foxe was in a difficult position when he faced the record of Henry VIII. For . . . Henry had to a preëminent degree the virtue of having resisted the Pope. Indeed, in that category of excellence he had no peer. It was hard to believe that such a man could have been so misguided on the subject of the Sacrament of the Altar as he clearly was. For it was one of the basic premises of Foxe's position that the king as an institution could be trusted to maintain religion—that is, a Scripture-devoted king. According to the theory of the Supremacy, the king was the final court of appeal for the maintenance of the establishment of religion. He undeniably had the sword and the right to use the sword. He used it to good effect against traitors who refused his supremacy, and Foxe approved. But he used it also against Sacramentarians who refused to acknowledge the Real Presence and who preached and who agitated for the abolition of what they and Foxe himself regarded as idolatry. At that point Foxe was in trouble. (p. 176)

It was never easy for Foxe to grasp the notion of development of religious positions, any more than it was easy for most of his contemporaries. Indeed, much of his power lay in the very fact that he habitually dealt in black-and-white wholes, not in complex or intertwining strands of various shades between. (p. 177)

If the possession of a central theme be one of the prerequisites for a great view of human history, then it cannot be denied that Foxe has it. He goes through past history, garnering up every rebel against Rome that he can find whose position can be reasonably interpreted as involving a return to the position of the Primitive Church, and out of these figures and movements of the past he establishes what he regards as a continuing tradition of striving for the restoration of the Church to the purity of its first days.

But even if one grant Foxe his ambition to be considered a sober historian, his history is a good deal more than a history. It is, also, an encyclopedia of the Reformation in England. All the main issues of the English Reformation are fought out before one's eyes, in résumés of books and pamphlets, sometimes in the reprinting of a substantial portion of a pamphlet, like Simon Fish's *The Supplication of Beggars,* in full reports of councils and conferences, in oftentimes verbatim accounts of debates and disputes and inquiries, in official memoranda and definitions and articles and ordinances, in letters, personal and public. Certain issues are debated again and again, with the result that the most casual reader cannot help becoming familiar with the points in dispute. And if at any point his memory fails him, he has only to turn to the index which Foxe has very thoughtfully provided at the end of the volume: "A diligent index or table, of the most notable things, matters, and wordes contained in this whole worke." This is, in fact, an extensive analytical index of argument as well as topic and name and place, covering thirty-eight and a half three-columned folio pages. For example, the crucial word "Image" (or "Images") is repeated thirty-two times, sometimes with subheadings and multiple page references, and the entries beginning with "Pope" or "Popes" cover more than two columns. The result is that the layman eager to keep abreast of the controversies of the time is here provided with easy and convenient access to a whole encyclopedia not only of historic information but of apologetics.

And the great thing about this apologetics is that it substantially represents the position which a large section of the English Church had reached at that period, as was realized plainly by those who used the book in the churches of the time. It is always hazardous to attempt to sum up anything so complex in its nature, and so diverse in its components and its possibilities, as the English Church of the year 1563. But it will be illuminating to take one example, particularly since it is at once central to the over-all situation and central to our inquiry, as we have seen, and that is the revolt against supernaturalism, to use a very rough term for a phenomenon that ranges from the crusade against superstition in which, say, a Thomas More or an Erasmus could take an active and convinced part, to the attack on sacramentalism that was to disturb the English Church for a good many years to come.

When Foxe says that Britain, of all nations, was the most superstitious in the old days, one wonders what has happened to his staunch patriotism. But it turns out that this is just another way of saying that in the old days Britain was exceptionally generous in its support of the monasteries. For Foxe the monasteries were the great centers of the superstition of the time, but they were not the only offenders. There were the pilgrimages, which had long been the target of criticism on various social grounds, but which Foxe attacked for being sources of support for idolatry. There were the shrines, which invited superstitious devotion, the offering of candles and, doubtless, of treasure for which the opponents of superstition could easily envisage a better use. But, above all, there were the idols and the images. For this is, as we have seen above, one of the great ages of iconoclasm. Foxe was clearly one of those many men of the sixteenth century who seem to have been sincerely incapable of envisaging any use of the visual arts for religion that would not be idolatrous. The result is a genuine iconoclastic passion, not a negative reaction of rejection or neglect, but a positive, crusading fervor that was by no means satisfied by its own refusal to participate in idolatry but could not suffer anybody else to indulge in it. Here one may see already in Foxe's pages the first stirrings of the tender conscience that is to play so conspicuous a

part in the Puritan assault upon the Established Church. For the iconoclast cannot understand how anyone can deny him relief from the horror he feels at the sight of an idol, the sheer compulsion of destruction. That there should be any sentiment of outraged reverence on the part of the idolater is only fresh fuel to his righteous indignation. Foxe's account of the hanging of three men for the burning of the "Idoll" or Rood of Dovercourt is a case in point. That the punishment was excessive, that the image of God in the least of his creatures is more precious than any image in wood, was not the burden of his argument. Rather it was that these men had been punished for a deed for which any but blind and ignorant men would have applauded them.

This attitude is apparent, also, in Foxe's handling of the sacramental disturbances which played so conspicuous a part in the iconoclastic activities of the time. (pp. 179-81)

Foxe entered into all these sacramental disputations with great sympathy and at great length. Once at least he suggested that it would be well if men agreed on the presence of Christ in the Sacrament, leaving the question of the how of the mystery alone. But it is hard to reconcile with that position, so suggestive of the "comprehensive" position of a later day, the sympathy with which Foxe recounted in great detail a series of sacramental episodes, difficult to understand in terms of any belief in the sacred character of the Sacrament. (pp. 181-82)

For Foxe, of course, any notion of development of religious rite or practice was a confession of corruption or of artificiality. His final comment, after he had reprinted, with appropriate marginal comments and interlinear explanations, Coverdale's English translation of the canon from the Mass book of Salisbury Use, was on the way it had grown with time: "And thus have ye in some the gatherynges of the masse, with the canon and all the appurtenances of the same, which, not much unlike the crow of Esope being patched with the feathers of so many birdes, was so longe a getheryng, that the temple of Salomon was not so long in building, as the popes masse was in making."

The seriousness with which Foxe took this charge of the idolatry of the Mass is shown in his discussion of the case of Master Hales, whose drowning of himself raised the old awkward problem of suicide for religious reasons. Foxe discussed with great sympathy the possibility that Master Hales killed himself to escape the defilement of hearing Mass, like those early Christian virgins who killed themselves to save their virginity from pagan spoilers. He did not feel justified in including him among the martyrs, but neither did he give him up for damned. Again, the popular version of the issue was cruder and more dramatic. Young Rose Allen, who carried on the ancient tradition of the sharp-tongued virgin, declared that the Mass stank in the face of God. There is no question that these Sacramentarians would agree with the later Recusants as to the central importance of the Mass, cosmically as they would disagree as to the character of that importance.

Such iconoclastic episodes must have caused a good deal of shock and even some social disturbance. Earlier Foxe had made it clear that if heresay disturbed the peace of the commonwealth, the severity of magistrates was justified, and he had found himself unable to believe that a man with such sound evangelical ideas as John Ball could be mixed up in so un-Gospel-like a proceeding as the rising in Kent of 1382. But in the case of the sacramental episodes Foxe clearly agreed with William Gardiner that the true cause of the social disturbance was not the curative violence but the initial idolatry that had challenged such drastic action. And this conclusion is confirmed by the exception which he made to what he defined as the chief of the good works which declare the faith of a Christian man, and that was to be obedient to the magistrates, unless they command idolatry. That seemed so self-evident to Foxe that he did not bother to argue it, but in the event it was as grave a potential threat to the state Church as the ancient tenet of refusal of obedience to an heretical prince, which was to make the Catholics so feared, and in the hands of the Puritans it was to prove an even graver actuality as the conflict with the Established Church drew to the Civil War. But here again Foxe seems to have felt confident that his own stoutly Protestant position would hold the field, and, of course, in this he reflects the confidence of his point of view in this still pre-Hooker period in the development of the Established Church.

But it would be a mistake to take Foxe simply as the voice of certain elements in the life of his time, or even of certain movements gathering force for the life of succeeding generations. And it would be an injustice. For Foxe is very much more than the voice of his time. He is a propagandist of deep conviction and of deliberate and sustained purpose. There is nothing of the speculative philosopher or of the academically objective and impersonal reporter about him. He is always an advocate, even a champion, reporting every round of the struggle with the energy and delight of the devoted partisan. The result is to be seen not only in the judicious selection of material, but in the careful underscoring of the main lines of the evidence, in the frankly debating summary of the results, in the careful repetition and reinforcement of the lessons to be drawn, in the ardently interested and often highly emotional commentary on the whole transaction. There is in Foxe nothing of the modern, or even of the Shakespearean, sense of tragedy, nothing of the mystery of human fortune in which the greatest are brought low, and the best of human nature is spent seemingly for nothing. Any suggestion of that sort of tragic view of the world would have seemed desperate to Foxe, something not to be pitied but despised. For victory, and that in the fairly short run (at least as regards the Henrician and Marian martyrs), was to him not simply the reward of effort, but the vindication of the cause itself. For Foxe, to alter a little the definition of Milton's archangel, to be weak was to be miserable indeed, but to be beaten was to be proved wrong.

It is this conviction not only of the rightness of his cause but of its vindication in human history that gives such power to Foxe's passionate and unremitting partisanship, that enables him to sweep through the vicissitudes of the history he chronicles and deliver his verdicts as to their significance with so much confidence. For it is of something larger than anything man could do that he is speaking, and as he reports it, insensibly he assumes the large surety of omniscience. (pp. 182-85)

It is significant, too, that though Foxe mentions the fact of the division of opinion at the accession of Elizabeth, he does not enter into the details of the struggle. He is content to record the victory without giving any information as to instruments or methods. The effect is, of course, immensely impressive. This is the victory of the Lord. The work of men may be criticized, may be impugned. It is vitiated by the passions of struggle and the moral imperfection of means. But the work of the Lord has an ease and a purity not possible to human effort. (p. 185)

Not the least of Foxe's sources of strength is his complete incapacity to understand how anyone can fail to see the significance of this verdict of history. That is the source of the constant insinuation, which, operating on the known incapacity of most men to grasp how different the familiar world might look to another point of view from their own, impugns the basic integrity of his opponents, and makes them, as it were, witnesses against themselves in his cause. Perhaps the best example of this is to be found in the preface "To the Persecutors of Gods truth, commonlye called Papistes" at the beginning of the book, where having assured his adversaries that they are beaten and should give up so hopeless a cause, he goes on to suggest that those who still hold out in such circumstances must in their consciences know they are wrong. . . . (p. 186)

It would be a mistake, however, to impute any undue naïveté about the rationale of propaganda to Foxe. It is at the end of this same appeal to the erstwhile persecutors, that he shows that he very well appreciates the foundations of an effective revolution, especially the importance of the proper education of youth. For he goes on: "Moreover, Universities and schooles in al quarters be set up againste you, and youthe so trayned in the same, that you shal never be able to matche them. To conclude, in Countries, kingdomes, Cities, Townes, and Churches reformed, your errours and superstitious vanities bee so blotted out within the space of these forty yeares in the harts of men, that their children and youth being so long nouseled in the sound doctrine of Christ, like as they never heard of your ridiculous trumpery, so they wyl never be brought to the same." (pp. 186-87)

But Foxe was not merely a master of the techniques of propaganda. He was also a master of those arts of emotional appeal that can alone give the mechanics of technique the vitality of inspired creation. Indeed, it is the sureness of his appeal to the basic human emotions that is the great strength of both Foxe's storytelling method and his incidental or implied apologetics. A good example of both is the story of the preacher Laurence Saunders and his infant son. (p. 188)

Conversely, Foxe is no less expert in the techniques of denigration. He is a master of the emotional adjective, the label that can be counted upon to call forth the proper response. "Horrible" is a favorite adjective of his, as we have seen from the very title of the book. Where his Protestants are "symple" and "seely," his Papists are likely to be "craftie." The epithet "franticke Francis" helps to dispose of the claims to serious attention of the founder of one body of the hated friars, in a fashion that anticipates the seventeenth-century attack on "enthusiasm." What he can do in this important genre is brilliantly illustrated in that passage in his account of the education of the young Cranmer in which he describes the condition of the universities at the turn of the century. . . . (pp. 188-89)

The attack on the Mass was, as we have seen, one of the central strategies of the movement to which Foxe devoted his very great talents. There was nothing frivolous in the purpose of this exuberant mockery, and nothing careless in the spray of its needling contempt. Foxe had, as we have seen, thoroughly appreciated the enormous advantage that his side had enjoyed in the popular appeal of the cheaper printed books in the vernacular which had brought religious controversy with all its heady excitements to the unlearned and the unprofessional. It was for that public that he wrote, and to that public that he shrewdly addressed all his remarkable powers of popular appeal. He understood that public, too, as few men of his time did, except for the great dramatists, with whom he has so much in common. He appreciated the passion of the time for history, particularly its own history, and he set out to satisfy it with what seemed to him, and to most of his contemporaries of a serious mind, the most important aspect of the recent national history, the religious settlement. He saw, too, the importance of having that history viewed in what he conceived to be its true light by the great mass of his countrymen. And he saw that to have that view of history accepted was the strongest guarantee possible of the defense of that settlement against the only adversaries he or most Anglicans of his time feared, the Catholics.

Foxe was quite aware of the national preoccupations of his age, especially of the passion for affairs of state which so many observers of the time, both harassed representatives of the government and disinterested visitors, noted as characteristic of the English of that period. He knew, too, how much that public enjoyed being taken behind the scenes, and he took them there. And this was true not only of the actions on the main stage but also of the major decisions and definitions behind them. Foxe admitted the humblest subject who could read, or be read to, to the disputes of convocations and the debates of kings and lords.

To a lesser degree the *Golden Legend* had already done that, and presently Shakespeare was to do something like it in his histories, but there is something quite different from either in *Actes and Monuments.* There are kings and popes and cardinals and great ones aplenty in the book, but the popes and cardinals are almost always seen at a disadvantage, and sometimes even the kings. And the infirmities of the great are in the last analysis overcome by the virtues of the humble. Foxe gives a gallery it would be hard to rival for the time, of men, and even women, of humble life who took the spotlight in at least one scene of their lives and acquitted themselves with the best for courage and resolution and often, from Foxe's point of view, intelligence and wisdom. Many of the familiar figures of the next century, the theological weaver, the Scripture-expounding and exhorting housewife, the disputing artisan and tradesman, appear in the roster of the martyrs. (pp. 190-91)

So viewed, this material must have been extraordinarily exciting to the braced wills of a class that was growing conscious of its strength and coming out of the shadows of an obscure past into a growing influence. This moral excitement is not to be overemphasized; it was more often beneath the surface than expressed, but it was there, and none the less operative because its triumph was still in the future. In this respect, Foxe must have contributed to the growing power of popular Puritanism at least as much as any man of his time. The reprinting of his book in the crucial year of 1641 is, as the great historian of the Puritan movement, William Haller, has pointed out, evidence that the seventeenth-century leaders of that movement were aware of the fact.

But that is in the future. What Foxe did for the men of his own time, for whom *Actes and Monuments* was first written, was quite enough. He knew that most of his readers would not have the background to understand many of the things he discussed, and he gave it to them, both historically and theologically. And in giving what he considered the true history of the Christian Church, he built up the intellectual world he wanted his public to possess.

This great tome is not only a martyrology and a history and an encyclopedia all in one, but it is even more a whole library in a single volume, presenting the vast panorama of a centuries-old crusade and an epoch-making revolution. The whole history of a great and historic change is here unfolded in almost every species of literary record. There are accounts of personal experience from at home and abroad, histories of nations, trifling anecdotes and passions of valiant leaders, articles of arraignment and processes of examination, interrogatories and investigations, private debates and echoes of village arguments, and public disputations between protagonists of learning and power; there are manifestoes and petitions, supplications and protests, appeals and complaints of grievances, articles of religion, injunctions, decrees, proclamations, acts and processes of counsels and parliaments, judicial sentences, measures for the organization of church life, lists of books prohibited and commended, apologias, declarations of faith, testimonials, wills and testaments, letters, obituaries, accounts of ceremonies from the degrading of a bishop to the baptism of a princess, translations of liturgies (with careful annotations of a highly controversial character), orations, sermons, summaries and précis of books, and even at times whole pamphlets. There can have been few books in the world like it, few that would give an innocent reader such a sense of being in the know, past, present, and future, that would give a simple man so complete a picture of the world in which he found himself and how it came to be so; few books that would so completely furnish forth an untutored mind with a whole intellectual world, so perfectly suited to its tastes and adapted to its powers, so completely to arm it against the challenges and pressures of an age of unprecedented moral and mental aggression. The ordinary reader who worked conscientiously through the disputations and the reports of hearings and investigations must have been often at a loss to understand some of the issues that have challenged some of the finest metaphysical minds of the race. Here Foxe explained, and defined, and interpolated, and summarized. The result, on the whole, was lacking in subtlety of discrimination or breadth of imagination, but it was clear with the kind of simplicity and surety that will stand by a man in a fight.

But Foxe did something more; he dramatized all this in individual episodes, in stories. Whether his matter be horrible or merry, Foxe is a first-rate storyteller. He certainly needed all his gifts to keep his reader going through the enormous masses of controversial discussion, much of it of a very specialized and even technical character, with which he stuffed his book. But he has the born storyteller's sensitiveness to the limits of his reader's endurance, the dramatist's instinct for comic relief even to tragedy, and he does not scorn to yield to the necessities of the popular entertainer. Nor need he, for he knows how to turn even the comic interlude to the driving purpose of the main plot. . . . (pp. 191-93)

This power of style in Foxe's work is important for two reasons. First of all, it is illuminating for the period. The pungent dialogue of the Elizabethan dramatists seems less of a miracle after one has read page after page of dialogue and dramatic narrative as brilliant as anything written for the stage. If this was pretty close to the most popular reading of the serious-minded public of those days, one is not so surprised at the color and verve of the literature of the less serious-minded. But it is even more important for the aid it gave to Foxe in the accomplishment of his propagandist purpose. The material he offered was as emotionally exciting as any romantic material of the time. It presented heroes of authentic proportions and villains of proper dye. It called forth all those emotions, of partisanship, of competition, of admiration, of hate, of horror, of pride, that not even the sober-minded have ever been able long to live without. And it offered them to edification and to salvation. The graves of men could have a very good time with a very good conscience.

The age loved stories, even though that sober-minded public, the newly literate as distinguished from the cultivated and the learned, had been given grounds enough for having qualms about the works of the imagination, and suspicions of the adornments of art. What Foxe offered he offered as sober, even sacred, fact, and he offered it with a devotion to the matter in hand, a simplicity and directness, that suggest that he had caught the first undertow of that insistence on plain writing and talking that was to play so large a part in the history of Puritan preaching in the next century. But this material has another element of popular appeal. These stories abound in homely detail of every day life, developed with often amazing precision. The result must have been an immeasurable heightening of confidence in the author who got so many of the things that could be checked so right. And this confidence made it possible for Foxe to do for his fellow countrymen what he had set out to do, perhaps more than he could ever have dreamed of doing, for there is usually in works of genius like his something that transcends intention.

In a time of great confusion, when most of his fellow countrymen had seen so many of the familiar landmarks of their lives swept away, Foxe gave them not only an explanation of what had happened but a rationalization and a justification. He gave them answers not only for the questions they were asking but for those they had probably never thought of asking. But more than that, for the view of the world by which they had lived for the most part tacitly and traditionally, and which they were now assured they had been mistaken to accept so long, he offered them a substitute view of the world and of human history, past and present, that not only made it easy for them to accept the new order but persuaded them that it was their plain duty to do so. And, as we have seen, he did it with such power that he made acceptance of the new order seem an entrance into an heroic heritage that was in a very real sense the distinctive possession of the loyal and the up-to-

date Englishman. In so doing, he gave to his countrymen a view of the world to live by, as Haller has again said, "a conception of universal history and of England's place in history, a conception which continued to prevail in the English mind long after the book had gone out of fashion though not out of use and memory." Of course, the element of propaganda was in the martyr story from the beginning, but Foxe's ecclesiastical history must be pretty nearly in a class by itself, not only ogreatest but one of the most effective examples of the literature of propaganda on record. (pp. 194-95)

> *Helen C. White, "Foxe's Ecclesiastical History," in her* Tudor Books of Saints and Martyrs, *The University of Wisconsin Press, 1963, pp. 169-95.*

V. Norskov Olsen (essay date 1973)

[*Olsen is a Danish clergyman, academic, and essayist. In the following excerpt, he examines Foxe's view of the nature and role of the universal church in sixteenth-century England.*]

The church is a divine society built upon Christ and preserved by Him. Commenting upon the apostle Peter's confession, "Thou art the Christ, the Son of the living God," and Christ's words, ". . . upon this rock I will build my church," Foxe stresses three points: "First, that Christ will have a church in this world. Secondly, that the same church should mightily be impugned, not only by the world, but also by the uttermost strength and powers of all hell. And, thirdly, that the same church, notwithstanding the uttermost of the devil and all his malice, should continue."

Concerning the concept of the church there are, according to Foxe, two particulars which are "most requisite and necessary for every christian man to observe and to note, for his own experience and profit." The first is "the disposition and nature of this world" and the second, "the nature and condition of the kingdom of Christ." Foxe compares the two by referring to "the unprosperous and unquiet state of the one, ruled by man's violence and wisdom, and the happy success of the other, ever ruled by God's blessing and providence; the wrath and revenging hand of God on the one, and his mercy on the other." The people in "the world" are defined as those who are "without or against Christ, either by ignorance not knowing him, or by heathenish life not following him, or by violence resisting him." On the other hand the kingdom of Christ is composed of "all them which belong to the faith of Christ, and here take his part in this world against the world; the number of whom although it be much smaller than the other, and always, lightly, is hated and molested of the world, yet it is the number which the Lord peculiarly doth bless and prosper, and ever will." It should be observed that "this number of Christ's subjects is it, which we call the visible church here in earth."

It is also significant to notice that in defining the nature of the church Foxe laid down another basic principle. As mankind belongs either to the kingdom of the world or the kingdom of Christ, so the visible church is divided into two parts, or composed of two kinds of people, where "the one standeth of such as be of outward profession only, the other of such as by election inwardly are joined to Christ: the first in words and lips seem to honour Christ, and are in the visible church only, but not in the church invisible, and partake the outward sacraments of Christ, but not the inward blessings of Christ."

When Foxe describes the relationship between the two parts of the visible church he points out another axiom, so fundamental to his concept of the church. Between the two sections there is often "great variance and mortal persecution, insomuch that sometimes the true church of Christ hath no greater enemies than those of their own profession and company." This has been true since the time of Christ, "but especially in these latter days of the church under the persecution of Antichrist and his retinue." Apparently one of the major objectives of the **Acts and Monuments** is to illustrate this point. Having noticed Foxe's basic definitions regarding the nature of the church, it will be profitable to turn to his idea of predestination before a further inquiry is made into his view of the visible and invisible church.

Theologically, the question of election and predestination has a central place in Foxe's concept of the church, true also of other Elizabethan Divines. In some notes upon the matter of election and faith, Foxe explains "what God's election is, and what is the cause thereof." He first defines the difference between predestination and election: "predestination is as well to the reprobate, as to the elect; election pertaineth only to them that be saved." For the rejected, predestination is called reprobation, while for the saved it is called election. Furthermore, "predestination is the eternal decreement of God, proposed before in himself, what shall befall on all men, either to salvation or damnation." Election, on the other hand, "is the free mercy and grace of God in his own will, through faith in Christ his Son, choosing and preferring to life such as pleaseth him."

Foxe himself points out four important factors in this definition. First, "the mercy and grace of God . . . excluded all the works of the law, and merits of deserving, whether they go before faith, or come after." Second, this mercy is "free," and "thereby is to be noted the proceeding and working of God not to be bounded to any ordinary place, or to any succession of chair, nor to state and dignity of person, nor to worthiness of blood, etc.; but all goeth by the mere will of his own purpose." Third, this mercy is "in his own will." Foxe comments, "by this falleth down the free will and purpose of man, with all his actions, counsels, and strength of nature. . . . Furthermore, as all then goeth by the will of God only, and not by the will of man: so again here is to be noted, that this will of God never goeth without faith in Christ Jesus his Son." This leads to the last point in defining election. Foxe writes: "Whosoever will be certain of election in God, let him first begin with his faith in Christ; which if he find in him to stand firm, he may be sure, and nothing doubt, but that he is one of the number of God's elect."

The concept of election theologically gives the assurance that all God's eschatological promises to the church will be fulfilled. It is therefore also interesting to notice that when Foxe speaks about the church in relationship to some distressing events, he is referring to the church of the elect, which valiantly will survive and in which God's eternal plans will be realized. Those belonging to "the church of the elect are clearly immune from the plagues, which are destined to be inflicted on the reprobates." When in 1586 Foxe refers to the time period of 294 years, which in his opinion began in A.D. 1300, he writes: "The Lord knows whether [the period] will be shortened for the sake of the elect."

"Christ is the one Head of His church, and in a more specific sense, He is the sole Head of the elect from the beginning." When Christ at the time of His resurrection founded the church "he shewed not himselfe to the world, but onely to his elect which were but few. The same Church after that encreased and multiplyed mightely among the Jewes, yet had not the Jewes eyes to see Gods Church, but did persecute it, till at length all their whole nation was destroyed."

Faith in Christ and true Christian doctrines are attributes of the elect. The true worshipers are those who are united to Christ "by the grace of election" and thus "adore Him in spirit and truth," while "through the true faith and preaching they observe the proper worship of God." Foxe mentions a third characteristic, godly living. The church of the elect, as opposed to the apostate church, is known by Christian living worthy of the true spiritual church or kingdom of Christ. The "elect of Christ . . . possess integrity of life." Foxe explains how godly living is a visible fruitage of election and as such a sign of the true church. As a good tree bears good fruits, "so with the elect who are true members of the church; they are indeed known from their fruit, not made elect by their fruit." Foxe thus defines the church with the Reformers and the Anglican Fathers "in relation to grace and faith, not to institutional continuity." For them as for Foxe "the Church, in the deepest sense, was the community of the elect or those who have saving faith in Christ." Hooper, Whitaker, and Hooker make use of the word invisible, thinking of "the Church as composed of sanctified individuals." Foxe speaks about "the blameless church of Christ."

If the elect should turn away from God and profane His worship with idolatry, neither attending His word nor following His counsels, then they would be punished in order to bring them to their senses and to their repentance. Foxe writes: "As the Israelites, being brought out of Egypt, when they sinned against God, were punished in the desert, and yet the promise of the plentiful land nevertheless still went forward—even so the elect members of Christ's church, after their deliverance, when they sin against God by fragility of weak flesh, their sins are punished with temporal scourges in this world, but yet the truth of God's everlasting favour standeth for ever, to all them that repent by faith." Foxe expected that the Reformation would bring the elect back to God and thus restore the church of the elect or the true church of Christ.

The church at the time of the eschatological fulfillment is characterized by Foxe as the church of the elect. Thus when the church is glorified the song of victory is sung by the elect: "In brief, this mystic song of praise none but the elect understands." In the same connection the elect are described as "the true church, which is a congregation of men redeemed from the earth by the precious blood of the immaculate Lamb."

When Foxe defines the church in its absolute and purest sense, then he has in mind only the elect. Thus he speaks about "the true Church of Christ" to be composed of "Gods elect." (pp. 101-05)

Reference has been made to Foxe's division of the church into two groups of people, the one having "outward profession only," the other "by election inwardly joined to Christ." The first are in only the visible church, but "the other are both in the visible, and also in the invisible church of Christ, which not in words only and outward profession, but also in heart do truly serve and honour Christ, partaking not only the sacraments, but also the heavenly blessings and grace of Christ." Here Foxe defines the visible and invisible church not as two churches but as one; the one church composed of "two sorts of people, so is it to be divided into two parts." This means that the visible church is composed of a mixed group of people, mixed in regard to sincerity of worship and godly living. This point is further illustrated in Foxe's letter "To the True and Faithfull Congregation of Christes Vniuersall Church, with all and singular the members thereof, wheresoeuer congregated or dispersed through the Realme of England." The title of this letter is most interesting in that it speaks of the true and faithful congregation as a part of the universal church of Christ. Furthermore, Foxe writes to those members who are congregated and dispersed through the realm of England. In his introduction Foxe expresses the desire that God would bless the *Acts and Monuments* to the advancement of His glory and profit of the church just as He had answered Solomon's prayer for the blessing of the Lord's temple. (pp. 106-07)

In his discussion with the Catholics, Foxe insists that to acknowledge a visible church is not to prove the Catholic Church the church of Christ. He writes: "I know that there is never a church which is not visible in the earth. But it does not follow because a church is visible that on that account it is the church of Christ; what it does should be the criterion." Foxe addresses four questions "To All the Professed Frendes And Folowers Of The Popes Proceedinges." In the close of this letter he takes up the problem: "That forsomuch as Christ must nedes haue a catholique Church euer continuyng here in earth, which all men may see and whereunto all men ought to resort: and seyng no other Church hath endured continually from the Apostles, visible here in earth, but onely the Church of Rome: they conclude therefore the Church onely of Rome to be the right catholicke Church of Christ. (p. 107)

In the opinion of Foxe the visible hierarchical organization of Rome does not represent the church of Christ. Therefore, when addressing the followers of the pope he emphasizes that the religion of Christ is spiritual, not corporal; his statement about the visible and invisible church was made with this in mind. (p. 108)

The church is maintained by the gifts of the Holy Spirit, the active force within it. Christ has no need of the pope as vicar, for the Holy Spirit is Christ's vicar. Foxe states that Christ's rule is distinguished from that of the world by the fact that he "sustains, fosters and governs the affairs of His church through the Holy Spirit, through whom He sanctifies the minds of his people, giving peace and instilling patience." Elsewhere Foxe writes that "the spiritual church of God" has "the real worship," characterized by "the genuine knowledge and faith of Christ, the true invocation, the gracious favour of the Godhead, the preaching of sacred doctrine, the charismata of the divine spirit." The gift of the Holy Spirit to the church is also described as follows: "I know that there are both many and eminent vertues, wherewith the Spirit of Christ always adorns his Church." He adds that "the church of God must be measured, not by external splendour or amplitude, but by genuine gifts of the spiritual good." Speaking about the work of the Reformation, Foxe writes: "The temple which must be repaired, I mean, is the spiritual church of Christ." Foxe places great emphasis upon the spiritual aspect of the church, noticeable also in his dealing with the Christian ministry.

In defining the church, Foxe makes rich use of the expression "the kingdom of Christ," which he takes "to be all them which belong to the faith of Christ." This "kingdom of Christ first began upon the cross," and whatever may happen Christ "cannot, and will not totally and finally forsake his church, which is his kingdom." When Foxe refers to the church as the kingdom, he is usually speaking of either the present spiritual values of the Gospel or the eternal or eschatological aspects of the church. Foxe clearly states: "The church is the spiritual kingdom;" and he speaks about "the kingdom of the gospel." He comments about the remission of sins by faith: "So that to them that be repenting sinners, and be in Christ Jesus, there is no law to condemn them, though they have deserved condemnation: but they are under a perpetual kingdom, and a heaven, full of grace and remission to cover their sins, and not to impute their iniquities, through the promise of God in Christ Jesus our Lord."

In another connection Foxe quotes Paul: "For ye see your calling, brethren, how that not many wise men after the flesh, nor many mighty, nor many noble, are called," then comments: "In this way, I perceive the wonderful way in which God chooses those who are to be saints, by His peculiar favour, in the kingdom of His Son." In the great drama between the church and the world, the church is also described as the kingdom. Having referred to the kingdom of Satan with its great power and external magnificence, Foxe emphasizes that "none the less Christ has His kingdom, His church and the sons of His Church in the midst of these forces." The eschatological aspect of the churchly kingdom is mentioned: "Christ has His kingdom and eternal riches and good things stored in heaven, which He promised to His own." The church is depicted in the book of Revelation under the symbol of a beautiful woman, greatly adorned. The details of her ornaments "typify the exceeding glory of the church of God, if not in this world, yet certainly it has and will always have, in the kingdom of Christ.

In considering the application Foxe makes of the expression "the universal church," or "the church universally," it would be profitable to examine his interpretation of the "temple, court and city" of Revelation 11. Here he elaborates further upon the question of the church, visible and invisible. The Revelator's picture of the measuring of the temple refers, according to Foxe, to the restoration or spiritual reformation of the church after A.D. 1300. It is not generally understood, says Foxe, that the restoration of the church applies only to those parts of the church that God has chosen to show forth His glory. Those nations that God had permitted to be overrun by the Turks He had rejected. Foxe would no doubt agree with Hooker "that Saracens, Jews and Infidels are excluded out of the bounds of the Church."

In his interpretation of "the city" Foxe states that it "signifies the universal church of Christians" which although suppressed by the Gentiles "will emerge victorious from this inundation, in no part extinct." This will be accomplished because "God always has his remnants, in the midst of the lost. The church therefore is never totally overthrown." The true church of Christ is here characterized as the city. When Foxe calls the church a city, which in spite of difficulties within and persecution without will emerge triumphant, he has no doubt been influenced by Saint Augustine's concept of the church as the city of God. Discussing the persecution of the church he writes: "Antichrist with his church of the wicked has throughout the centuries persecuted the beloved city of God," but they do not know that their final and fatal judgment is near.

In the temple building, symbolizing the Reformation, Foxe describes two groups of worshipers. He first states that "God will not build into his temple all those who are contained within the ambit of the church as part of the congregation." Foxe describes one group of worshipers as "those who are united to Him by election of divine grace, whether they are pastors or people, who adore Him in spirit and truth, who by sincere faith and preaching observe and promote the true worship of God." Connected with the temple are the inner and outer courts. According to Foxe true followers of Christ worship in the inner court, while the others worship in the outer one. The two groups here described are not merely a mixed group of worshipers within the one visible church, even though there is some overlapping, but represent a true and a false church. Foxe clearly states that those in the inner court "signify the true church of God" but the others in the outer court "are ordered to be cut off."

The "true church" is clearly related to the "invisible church," as she is the true church in its absolute and full sense. Thus Cranmer and Hooper apply the expression only to the invisible church. On the other hand, Foxe, like Hooker, Covell, Field, and Philpot, would "refuse to make a rigid division between visible and invisible and to admit that the visible Church is not the true Church." Foxe uses the expression "the true church" to distinguish, theologically and historically, between the true visible church and the apostate church. Regarding this point he writes: "There has been up to the present much controversy among the theologians about the true and false church. No one denies that there is one certain church of Christ on earth. But there is no agreement as to which is the true church, where it is to be sought, by what marks and signs it is to be measured." The false church is composed of "those who profess themselves Catholics, who hold that incontestably the true Christian church is at Rome and so has ever been." The members of the true church are those "whose profession is nearer to the gospel, who all the more reject this Roman church. . . . Having left Rome, they cling to Christ rather than to the Pontiff."

In the opinion of Foxe "the true Church of God" is not alone "but is accompanied with some other Church or Chappell of the deuill to deface and maligne the same." The same was true in the time of Christ, for "who would have thought, but the congregation and councels of the Pharisies had bene the right Church: and yet had Christ an other Church in earth besides that, which albeit, it was not so manifest in the sight of the world, yet was it the onely true Church in the sight of God." In the opinion of Foxe the Pharisees represent Rome, whose church is designated as the synagogue of Satan. (pp. 109-13)

Foxe illuminates the question of the true and false church with historical references. With Constantine liberty came to the church, but as the years went by there was much deterioration in evangelical doctrine. However, up to the time of Gregory VII and Innocent III, the church remained, "albeit not without some repugnance and difficultie, yet in some meane state of truth and veritie," and it was called "the true Church of Christ." After Innocent III things were altogether "turned vpside downe." Furthermore, "the clere sunne shine of Gods word was ouershadowed with mistes and darknes," and "the true visible Church began now to shrinke." From Foxe's comparison between the ancient church of Rome and the Roman church of his own time, the following words are taken: ". . . this latter pretended church of Rome hath utterly sequestred itself from the image and nature of the ancient and true church of Rome, and they have erected to themselves a new church of their own making."

If Rome ceased to be the true church from the time of Gregory VIII, yet God always has His true church on earth, then where was the true church of Christ from that time until the Reformation? Foxe answers: "Duryng which space, the true Church of Christ, although it durst not openly appeare in the face of the world, oppressed by tyranny; yet neither was it so inuisible or vnknowen, but by the prouidence of the Lord, some remnaunt alwayes remayned, from tyme to tyme, which not onely shewed secret good affection to sincere doctrine, but also stode in open defence of truth agaynst the disordered Church of Rome."

Beginning with Joachim and the Waldenses and enumerating a great number of preachers down to Wycliffe, Huss, Luther, and Zwingli, Foxe describes how the true church continued in the midst of her enemies by "faithfull witnesses of the truth, not teachyng any new doctrines contrary to the determination of holy Church: but rather shall finde that Church to be vnholy, which they preached agaynst, teachyng rather it selfe hereticall opinions contrary both to antiquitie, and verity of Christes true Catholicke Church." In this connection the following words should be noticed: "What shal nede then any more witnes to proue this matter, when you see so many yeares ago, whole armies and multitudes, thus standyng agaynst the Pope? who though they be termed here for heretickes and schismatickes: yet in that, which they call heresy, serued they the liuyng Lord, within the Arke of his true spirituall, and visible Church." The reformed church of the sixteenth century is thus shown by Foxe to be the true spiritual and visible church, and as such is not a new church. Arguing against the opinion of Rome, "that neuer was any other Church demonstrable here in earth for men to follow" than Rome, Foxe writes: ". . . when as we haue sufficiently proued before by the continual descent of the Church till this present time, that the sayd Church, after the doctrine which is now reformed, is no newbegun matter, but euen the old continued Church, by the prouidence and promise of Christ still standyng." Resistance against the Pope should not therefore be considered a "new thing in these days in the church of Christ." (pp. 113-15)

In Foxe's discussion of the pope's church and the true church of Christ, the question of apostolicity and catholicity has a prominent place. With the Protestant Reformers at large Foxe asserts that the church had been apostolic and catholic before Rome developed into the papacy; accordingly the church could be catholic without the papacy. The Reformers contended that they adhered to catholicity while Rome had forgotten its catholicity. Thus Luther, in his invective against the Catholic Duke Henry of Brunswick, said: "I shall prove that we have remained with the true, ancient church, yea, that we are the true, ancient church. But you have fallen from us, that is, from the ancient church, and set up a new church opposition to the old."

Foxe's lengthy comparison between the primitive and latter churches of Rome purposes to disprove the apostolicity and catholicity of Rome but to prove the same regarding the church reformed. Foxe says that the early doctors, "speaking of the church of Rome which then was, said not untruly, calling it catholic and apostolical; for that the same church took not only their ordinary succession of bishops but also their ordinary doctrine and institution from the apostles. But speaking of the church of Rome which now is, we say the said places of the doctors are not true, neither do appertain to the same; all which doctors neither knew the church of Rome that now is, nor, if they had, would ever have judged any thing therein worthy such commendation." He expresses the same thought in this way: ". . . the church of Rome, as it is now governed with this manner of title, jurisdiction, life and institution of doctrine, never descended from the primitive age of the apostles, or from their succession." When therefore Rome boasts of the name Catholic, it is a "false Name." Referring to the reformed church Foxe states: ". . . our church was, when this church of theirs was not yet hatched out of the shell, nor did yet ever see any light: that is, in the time of the apostles, in the primitive age, in the time of Gregory I, and the old Roman church." Thus "we have sufficient matter for us to show that the same form, usage and institution of this our present reformed church, are not the beginning of any new church of our own, but the renewing of the old ancient church of Christ."

In the opinion of Foxe Rome has broken away from and disrupted the unity of the universal church; accordingly, he accuses Rome of having her own sect of religion. Referring to her life, practices, and doctrines he exclaims: ". . . into what diuision of sectes they cut the vnitie of Christian Religion," elsewhere explaining, "This is the reason of that unhappy division among Christians, which has for so long disturbed the church, and is still disturbing it so lamentably." Foxe was most anxious to restore the unity of the church. Discussing the "great defection from faith in so many churches" by the conquests of the Turks, Foxe comments that their horrible persecutions are "the scourge of God" for "sins, and corrupt doctrine." He further states: "The consideration of this horrible persecution of the Turks rising chiefly by our discord and dissension among ourselves, may reduce us again from our domestical wars, in killing and burning one another, to join together in christian patience and concord." Foxe expresses sorrow at these divisions which penetrated even into the

ranks of the Protestants in his well-known sermon at Saint Paul's Cross: "Such dissension and hostility Satan hath set amongst us, that Turks are not more enemies to christians, than christians to christians, papists to protestants; yea, protestants with protestants do not agree, but fall out for trifles. So that the poor little flock of thy church, distressed on every side, hath neither rest without, nor peace within."

Foxe sincerely hoped that the Reformation would restore the unity of the church: "This hope I have, and do believe, that when the church of Christ, with the sacraments thereof, shall be so reformed, that Christ alone shall be received to be our justifier, all other religions, merits, traditions, images, patrons, and advocates set apart, the sword of the Christians, with the strength of Christ, shall soon vanquish the Turks' pride and fury." In his sermon at the baptism of a converted Jew, he expresses the hope that the Jews and Gentiles might someday embrace Christ in whom the unity of the church and mankind has its center. He writes: "So that at the length, all nations, as well Jews and Gentiles, embracing the faith and sacraments of Christ Jesus, acknowledging one Shepherd, uniting together in one sheepfold, may, with one voice, one soul, and one general agreement, glorify the only begotten Son, our Saviour Jesus Christ." Surprisingly Foxe, who through the *Acts and Monuments* created and nourished anti-Roman feelings, sought in a most kind and hearty way to appeal to the Roman Catholics. . . . In his sermon preached on Good Friday, A.D. 1570, Foxe closes his message with an appeal to Roman Catholics. The same is true in the last pages of his commentary on the book of Revelation, where Foxe says that he writes especially to "the honest men of the catholic persuasion." He calls them "beloved friends and brothers in Christ." (pp. 115-18)

While Foxe labels Rome as Antichrist and a false church, he would admit with many Anglican Divines of the sixteenth century that she retained some parts of truth and was still to some degree a part of the visible church. She was an apostate church, yet her baptism was still valid. Foxe makes the point clear when he states: "Nor indeed do we deny to Rome any share in the communion of the Church, neither that it has any part when joined to the body of Christ. We know of so many who have been born and baptised as infants in Rome, whom we do not necessarily judge to be damned because they are Romans." The word "almost" in the following statement makes it a comprehensive expression of Foxe's modified view of Rome. He writes: ". . . ye haue lost the favor both of God and men, the safety of your soules, and almost the kingdome of the Lorde, except you take the better heede." The Rome of the Middle Ages was not denied the name "church," but was called "the disordered Church."

In the name of the universal church Foxe asserts that the reformed church has not departed from the visible church: "We therefore do reproue certen assertions and opinions in some false teachers, from whom we sequester our selues of very necessitie; yet in such wise as we depart not at al from the visible church, in the which we have our being and reliancie as well as they." He further states that the Protestants were "enforced to depart from them rather by violence, and plaine thrusting out, then of any our volunary willingnesse: so that to set down the matter in plaine termes, it may be saide more properly that we do disagree

and dissent from them rather than depart from them."
(pp. 119-20)

In defining and illustrating the nature of the church, Foxe
uses expressions other than those already mentioned. The
relationship between the church and Christ is compared
to that between bride and bridegroom, or husband and
wife. This relationship is further illustrated by other titles
given to Christ. He is identified as "Our Shepherd . . . our
Head, our Husband, our Bishop, our Pastor, our Prince
and King." Reference is made to "the Arke of his true
spirituall, and visible Church," and to the church as "the
ship," which "by the hidden guidance of God, after a
stormy voyage, will be safely guided into the harbour."
Christ is "the Prince and Author of the Church," and He
is asked to manifest grace to "his whole beloued church."
The true churches are called "devout churches, a chaste
virgin in Christ," and "thy poor church militant." The
church is referred to as a commonwealth, the republic of
Christ, or a Christian society, especially where the state
is under Christian kings. Within the universal church are
particular churches and within them, congregations. Foxe
does not make use of the phrase "the mystical body of
Christ" as some writers do; and when he uses the word
"body" as a metaphor for the church, it is generally with
reference to Christ as the head of the universal church:
"Truly, Christ is the one Head of the universal church, fitting, principal, and vital, from whom as Chief, derive the
vital energies for the rest of the body." In the headship of
Christ rests the organic unity of the universal church; and
through the Holy Spirit the living Christ Himself infuses
grace into all the members of the body, thus creating a true
spiritual and visible church.

Summarizing Foxe's concept of the nature of the church,
we stress the following main features: Christ will always
have a church in this world, and its unity and preservation
are found in Him. The visible church is the universal
church. During certain historical periods it is less easily
discerned than in others. The visible church is composed
of two groups of people, those by outward profession only
and those by election. The latter group make up the invisible church called the church of the elect. In the latter days
are found a false and a true church. The former is Antichrist, the Synagogue of Satan; and the latter is Christ's
true spiritual church, His bride. However, Foxe does not
go so far as to say that there is no element of the true
church in Rome. Christ is the head of the universal
church, but in a more specific sense He is the Head of the
church of the elect. When the church is referred to as "the
kingdom," it is generally in connection with present spiritual values of the Gospel or the eternal or eschatological
aspects of the church. Foxe's favorite designation for the
church is "the church of Christ." It is used for the church
universal, but especially for the true church as opposed to
the false. The true church of Christ is apostolic and catholic and in Foxe's own time visible in the church reformed.
Foxe emphasizes the continuity and unity of the church,
and believes the church to be one, holy, apostolic, and
catholic. (pp. 121-22)

V. Norskov Olsen, in his John Foxe and the
Elizabethan Church, *University of California
Press, 1973, 264 p.*

John Hazel Smith   (essay date 1973)

[*Smith is an American essayist, translator, and academic. In the following excerpt from the introduction to his
1973 edition and study* Two Latin Comedies by John
Foxe the Martyrologist: "Titus et Aesippus," "Christus Triumphans," *he closely examines Foxe's version of*
Titus et Gesippus.]

Whether acted or not, the writing of **Titus et Gesippus** at
Oxford in 1544-1545 is noteworthy, for this is a romantic
comedy with important Terentian additions. It is thus an
epitome of English Renaissance comedy, but quite an
early specimen. The immediate source was English, but
the play is only one step removed from the well-spring of
all the sixteenth-century versions of the Titus-Gesippus
story, the eighth tale of the tenth day of Boccaccio's *Decamerone*. We may be forced, then, to modify Boas' statement that the "first University play with a plot of undoubted Italian origin" was *Hymenaeus* in 1579. Mary A.
Scott counted thirty-three Elizabethan plays with Boccac-
cion plots, but those plays were written considerably later
than **Titus et Gesippus;** as F. P. Wilson wrote, "England
did not become Italianate until Elizabeth's reign was well
undder way," but **Titus et Gesippus** was written while
Henry VIII sat on the throne. (p. 9)

Perhaps as surprising as anything else about this romantic

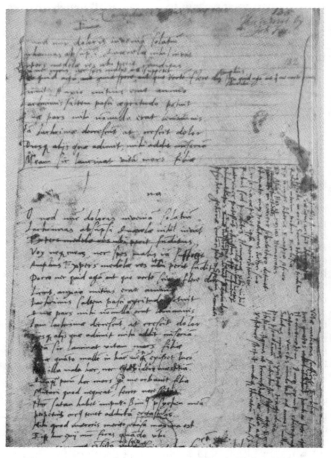

The opening page of the manuscript of Foxe's Christus Triumphans.

comedy is that it was written by John Foxe the martyrologist. Although very few people today have read the entire **Book of Martyrs,** everyone recognizes it as a work which can be called comic only in some specialized sense, if at all, and Foxe is so completely identified with that work that his name is seldom mentioned without the distinctive title "martyrologist." Few other men are so thoroughly identified with a genre in which they wrote.

None of Foxe's previously known works could be called imaginative literature; for instance, his pieces published before his exile in 1554 include translations from the German of sermons by Luther and Oecolampadius and of a tract on Christian faith by Urbanus Regius, an original tract opposing the death penalty, and a few other controversialist pieces. Some years after writing **Titus et Gesippus,** Foxe himself described his writing as "literary labours on behalf of the Christian republic." Even his one previously known comedy, **Christus Triumphans,** is not so recognizably comic by later standards, or so different in spirit from the **Book of Martyrs,** that anyone would have thought of Foxe as a comedian. So pervasive is Foxe's reputation as a religious controversialist that the only two scholars I know of who have referred to **Titus et Gesippus** both assumed that it belonged to the same class of comedy as **Christus Triumphans.** Josiah Pratt, in his note to Foxe's letter, cited earlier, which names the play, stated where the "said Comedy, or rather Sacred Drama," could be found; and J. F. Mozley, also citing the location of the play, identified it as one of the "Latin plays on religious subjects" which Foxe wrote at Oxford.

Though Pratt and Mozley must both have looked at the play, perhaps they may be forgiven their misjudgment. Like most other scholars who have worked on Foxe's papers, they were looking for biographical or historical information, not literary works. Perhaps, too, they were misled by several pages of the **Titus et Gesippus** manuscript which are headed by prayerful crosses and, in one instance, by the name *Jesus.* Even the old biography supposed to be by Foxe's son failed to distinguish more than one kind of comedy. . . . (pp. 10-11)

[**Titus et Gesippus**] is not a play of which a man with Foxe's moral proclivities would need to feel ashamed, for it is informed with ethical principles which were perfectly orthodox in the Renaissance. Unlike **Christus Triumphans,** it does not have a prologue, but, if it did, Foxe might very well have included a statement of the Horatian principle echoed by the prologue of the later play: "Placere actores omnibus; / Prodesse poeta, nocere studet nemini." In Boccaccio, the tale fulfills the requirement of the tenth day for stories about generosity in love, and after telling the story Fiammetta comments on its theme of sacred friendship; we hear, moreover, that a common social game in Italy was to debate whether Titus or Gesippus (to use Foxe's forms of their names) had shown the greater generosity. And Sir Thomas Elyot's version is frankly told as a "goodly example" to "minister to the readers singular pleasure and also incredible comfort to practise amity." No doubt Foxe (or perhaps his mentor at Oxford) chose the story for the same reason and, having written his version, Foxe then used it to demonstrate his competence as a teacher of the young. (pp. 12-13)

Foxe used Elyot's exemplum [*The Boke Named the Governour* (1531)] as his principal, and probably his only,

source. In a number of ways Elyot had altered the story so that his version is fundamentally different from all other known versions: in consequence, we cannot be certain about Elyot's source, though no one except perhaps Mills has radically disputed Wolff's conclusion that Elyot used Boccaccio or Beroaldo or both. In any case, for our present purposes we may conveniently classify the versions available to Foxe into two types: Elyot's and (essentially including all others) Boccaccio's. Foxe did not follow Elyot in all details, including one or two very important ones; in a few places we find parallels between Foxe and Boccaccio; in many more places we see unprecedented innovations in Foxe. Yet the number and quality of the parallels between Foxe and Elyot, as shown in the accompanying chart, make it virtually certain that Foxe knew Elyot. (pp. 14-15)

On this evidence I see no reason to believe that Foxe knew any Boccaccian version. Although he was an avid reader, his reading, from what we know of it, was not in works like the *Decamerone;* Terence, whom he had certainly read, was a school text, and Boccaccio was not. The departures from Elyot are best explained as Foxe's inventions which happen to coincide with Boccaccio. For one thing, they are like Boccaccio only in a general way; in each case the specific details are different. We can see, moreover, why a man treating the story dramatically would alter Elyot's nondramatic exemplum in precisely these ways. The introduction of the bride's father, Simo, for instance, like the inclusion of Chremes (who dies in all other versions), permits Foxe to show us some Terentian fathers—men worried about their social and financial status, gleeful over their successes, peevish when thwarted by their juniors. Raising the question of the bride's response to the situation corrects a serious flaw in Elyot from a dramatic viewpoint, though in his treatise it would perhaps be irrelevant. The invention which is easiest of all to explain is the finding of a bride for Gesippus: comedies, after all, are supposed to end in marriage. Elyot elected to show the vindication of the true friend politically, for in his version (like Boccaccio's) politics is important: Gisippus is exiled from Athens by political enemies whose hand is strengthened by resentment of the Athenian's giving up his bride to a Roman. Foxe, however, eliminated all references to tension between Athens and Rome and included no political elements except one or two speeches by Fulvius about the need for a public figure to ignore private considerations: in the play, Gesippus must leave Athens because his father disowns him. The true friend must be vindicated, of course, but it is no denial of the virtues of friendship to have the friend succeed in love as well. Indeed, Foxe invented a situation to make Gesippus' love-interest ironically parallel that of Titus: Pamphila, whom Gesippus finally marries, is a former sweetheart of Titus whom Gesippus would have wooed long ago but for the hurt it would have caused his friend.

Probably the best argument for calling these departures from Elyot inventions rather than borrowings is the number of other variations that Foxe could not have found in any known source. Some are trivial, some crucial. Foxe's Gesippus, for instance, falls asleep in a public road (near Titus' house, apparently) rather than in a barn (as in Elyot) or in a cave (as in Boccaccio); and his heroine is called Sempronia rather than Sophronia. These alterations are not so readily explained as some of the other inventions. The decision, for instance, to keep the victim of Martius' robbery alive is what we would expect in a comedy—though we would hope for a more artful revelation of his survival than Foxe achieves. The omission of the political elements that are so important in Elyot tightens up the play's unity. So do several other omissions, including those of details preceding Gesippus' proposed wedding day: the reasons for Titus' being in Athens, the length of his stay, Gesippus' courtship of Sempronia, and the meeting of Titus and Sempronia. A strict neoclassicist would presumably have striven for even tighter unity by setting the whole action at Rome, thus avoiding the serious disunity of time and place of which Foxe's play is guilty. From the technical terms which Foxe uses in these plays we can be certain that he had been exposed to critical works which discussed such questions, but he (and the presumed tutor for whom he may have written this play) obviously did not believe that plays must observe the minor unities. (pp. 17-18)

Some of Foxe's most significant alterations are in the characters. He supplied names for several characters who are nameless in the sources: Martius, the cutthroat; Cratinus, a member of the Roman posse which arrests Gesippus; and Simo, father of the bride. And he adds several new characters: Crito, who travels to Rome with a message for Gesippus; Stylpho and his daughter Phrygia, who are involved in a plan for a marriage with Gesippus; Trebatius, a messenger from Rome; and a number of comic characters: Dromo, Midas, Stephanio, and Pythias, all slaves; and Marsias and Misenus, musicians. Most of these names seem to have been chosen for some relevant association: Martius suggests Mars, the fighting god; Marsias, the piper, was presumably named for Marsyas, the satyr who challenged Apollo on the flute; the name of Misenus, another musician, recalls that of Aeneas' trumpeter, the son of Aeolus; and Trebatius, who performs the quasi-legal function of informing Titus of his father's death, may have been suggested by the name of a lawyer friend of Cicero. All the other names listed are Terentian: Stephanio looks after the kitchen in both *Adelphoi* and ***Titus et Gesippus;*** Simo is an old man in Foxe and in the *Andria;* Dromo and Syrus are slaves in Foxe and Terence; and Sophrona, the old mother in our play, is an old nurse in several Terentian plays.

The most important Terentian addition by Foxe was Phormio, who functions here as he does in Terence: there he is a scheming adventurer; here he is the clever slave who manipulates affairs on behalf of his master. For a time in ***Titus et Gesippus,*** Phormio is the dominant figure. Foxe clearly was aiming not only at making his play Terentian, but also at improving its effectiveness, and Phormio was his way around a dilemma inherent in his story.

If one accepts the orthodox Renaissance (and Platonic) view that friendship is a nobler relationship than heterosexual love, Gesippus' sacrifice of his bride almost at the altar is both noble and understandable; Elyot tried to emphasize this attitude by making Gisippus woo Sophronia in secret at first, as though his romantic interest were a betrayal of his friendship for Titus. But if one accepts the theory, Titus' longing for the girl like a medieval courtly lover is more than a social flaw: it is a gross violation of a most fundamental principle of morality. On the other hand, if one does not accept the theory, Gesippus' gesture,

though noble, becomes psychologically incomprehensible. In the former case, one protagonist loses moral stature in a way which is difficult to overcome; in the latter, the other protagonist suffers even more serious loss of intellectual stature. To describe such a dilemma is not to deny the facts of the Renaissance philosophy, but to assert the conflict between humanist theory and human thought. (pp. 18-19)

Foxe did not want to eliminate this conflict, and his philosophic bias is apparently orthodox. Yet he did want to make his characters' behavior credible, and the Titus-Gesippus story is one of the very few that call for the friend to sacrifice his love interest so completely. That Foxe was aware of a problem is shown by a soliloquy which he gives to Gesippus during the off-stage union of Titus and Sempronia: Gesippus expresses the orthodox theory, but only after he has voiced his fear that people will think him a stupid weakling for surrendering his bride. Judging from his father's reaction to the sacrifice, Gesippus' fear is well founded, but Foxe tried to keep the audience from such a reaction. Early in the play we see Gesippus impatiently hurrying along the wedding preparations: he is clearly eager to marry Sempronia, whose beauty he rapturously praises. But even before he knows of Titus' love for Sempronia, we also hear him confess that he has a strong interest in another girl, whom he would have carried off as Paris did Helen if she were not (as he thinks) Titus' sweetheart. This device cleverly maintains the nobility of Gesippus' sacrifice even as it makes that sacrifice more understandable. Even more important in serving this end is Phormio. As Phormio becomes the dominant figure for a time, and thus gives the comedy a properly Terentian tone, he also assumes much of the onus of guilt. He overhears Gesippus' confession of interest in Pamphila, and it encourages his efforts on behalf of Titus. It is Phormio who describes the deadly nature of Titus' disease, Phormio who allows Gesippus to uncover its cause, Phormio who subtly implants the idea of Gesippus' sacrifice, and Phormio who devises the scheme to make it work.

The effect of Phormio's machinations on Titus is even more marked. Titus does not have to confess to Gesippus the nature of his illness (Gesippus' visit to his sick friend occurs offstage). More importantly, Titus does not even know what Phormio is doing. In the opening scene, Titus admits his problem to Phormio and asks for help; but the help he specifies is for Phormio to kill him or to arrange a postponement of Gesippus' wedding so that Titus can leave town, and it is entirely Phormio's idea to promote the substitution while telling Titus that nothing can be done. The go-between, who comically emphasizes the importance of his function in a hyperbolic soliloquy, thus assumes most of the moral guilt that adheres to Titus in other versions. Not all of it, however, for Foxe deliberately includes certain details that make Titus appear insensitive: though Titus does not know that Gesippus is listening to his exultation after the consummation of the union with the girl whom Gesippus was to have married (II.2.1ff), yet the juxtaposition of this scene with Gesippus' unhappy soliloquy in II. in II.I. adversely affects Titus' impression on the audience. So does his precipitous departure from Athens, which we hear about from Gesippus, who is fearful of its consequences: Titus' departure, we realize from Trebatius' news, is motivated by a desire to collect an inheritance, and we sense the unfairness of fortune's workings. In the end, Titus proves his worth as a friend, but before then he fails one more time: his failure to recognize Gesippus is perhaps dramatically justified, since Gesippus is in rags and at first does not speak and since, at the trial, Titus is convinced that the man before him has committed an act of which Gesippus is incapable; yet Titus' instinctive coldness toward a less fortunate mortal (a difference in fortune which is emphasized by Titus' rich appearance and his materialistic conversation with Sempronia) seems a character flaw, and by contrast Phormio recognizes Gesippus the instant he sees him.

By this time in the play, the protagonists have come to dominate the action. Phormio is still active in Rome, but nothing comes of most of his activity. He is sent to see Gesippus in prison and confirm Titus' fears about the Athenian's identity, but the confirmation comes before Phormio returns when Crito arrives from Athens. After Titus and Gesippus are both confined for the murder, Phormio runs to tell Sempronia what has happened, but it is Martius' confession that resolves the difficulty. The one useful purpose which Phormio serves in Rome is to promote the wedding of Pamphila and Gesippus. In an effective scene, Phormio finds Pamphila somewhat testily resentful of Titus for abandoning her and apparently of Gesippus for helping him to do so. But Phormio cleverly persuades her to entertain the idea of marrying Gesippus by noting his resemblance to Titus and by alluding to her as a spinster. Otherwise, Phormio's continuing presence in the play after the action moves to Rome is dramatically useless.

Though Phormio is not consistently useful, on the whole Foxe has improved his play by adding him. Foxe's general conception, moreover, and the broad structural outlines of his play are effective. But there are structural flaws. When Foxe first introduced the idea that Titus had once loved Pamphila, it prepared for Gesippus' sacrifice of Sempronia and, as we have seen, set up an ironic parallel to the Titus-Sempronia-Gesippus triangle. That parallel could not be carried on after Gesippus learned that Titus loved Sempronia rather than Pamphila, but at least the matter was brought to fruition in the final arrangement between Gesippus and Pamphila. The addition was a happy one, moreover, if only for the opportunity it gave to Foxe to create an impressive vignette of Pamphila. Not all of his additions worked out so neatly. Most glaring is the unresolved situation in Athens. There, Chremes and Simo become reconciled and actually arrange a new marriage for Gesippus, to Simo's niece Phrygia. Phrygia is brought onstage and Gesippus is sent for. But of course he does not come (though the Argument indicates that he will), for he finds a Roman bride; we do not learn Chremes' response to this, and we may wonder why Foxe included Phrygia at all.

Foxe's handling of Sempronia also raises questions. Her role in the play is larger than in the sources, but her only real contribution to the dramatic action is to send Phormio for Pamphila in order to help Gesippus' romantic cause. Her appeal to Fulvius to spare Gesippus is the sort of scene which was later used to good effect by Shakespeare in *Measure for Measure* and *Coriolanus,* but in this play it comes to naught and carries little emotional weight. After her first appearance in III.8, she says all the right things but is not a little vapid; this is especially true in her

first scene as she answers Titus' questions about her feelings. It is a little surprising that she does not appear earlier in the play, since all of the action in the first two acts revolves around the question of whom she will marry. On the other hand, Foxe avoided showing the two friends together throughout the first two acts, too, even though the theme of the play concerns friendship. I have attempted to explain the latter omission by noting the dramatic importance of Phormio in those acts. Perhaps the failure to show Sempronia has a similar explanation. By raising the question of how Sempronia had reacted to the substitution of Titus for Gesippus, Foxe showed a concern for the feelings of the bride which Elyot had not shown at all. Boccaccio had deliberately emphasized the bride's feelings in his version by having her become furious and complain to her family about the deception, but Foxe did not want to complicate an already difficult problem by suggesting that both Titus and Gesippus were acting inhumanely in ignoring the wishes of the girl. He may have consciously decided, then, that if the audience did not see Sempronia until late in the play, until he had allowed time for the fully developed love marriage which it sees in III.8, it would not think of the possible harm to the bride's sensitivities. Conceivably he could have shown a scene in which Titus and Sempronia fall in love with each other, but such scenes do not seem to appear until some time later in English drama. For instance, in Gascoigne's *Supposes* (1566), taken from Ariosto's *Suppositi,* there are no Polynesta-Erostrato

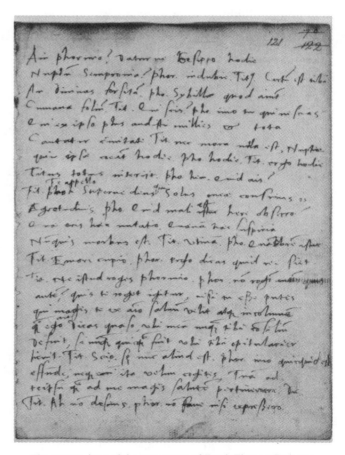

The opening lines of the manuscript of Foxe's Titus et Gesippus.

scenes, and we do not even see Polynesta between the first scene and the last.

Most of the structural flaws in *Titus et Gesippus* are in the middle of the play. As I have attempted to show, the beginning is effectively structured. The ending is reasonably effective also. The thrust of the action in Rome is toward the discovery of Gesippus' identity. Here too Foxe was burdened with a difficult fundamental problem: Gesippus' initial decision, not really comprehensible, to conceal his identity. Given that inherent defect, Foxe invents details which effectively bring on the gradual discovery: the ironic mistaking of Gesippus for a vagabond and Gesippus' refusal to answer Titus in the first trial scene are the most notable. The innovation of suspending the trial so that Titus can investigate the case, and later of postponing sentencing so that Fulvius can go on a fruitless trip to consult the Senate, allows time for Martius' guilt to develop and make his confession somewhat less surprising than in the sources. But far too many key decisions are revealed in soliloquies. Much of the dialogue of the play, especially in comic scenes, is very good, but the piling up of soliloquies . . . shows an inconsistent concern for developing naturalistic dialogue and an occasionally expedient decision.

A significant nonstructural addition by Foxe is the comic business. Two scenes involving musicians are largely irrelevant, though there is some irony in their preparation for an expected wedding which will not occur. The first of these scenes, with its long discussion of musical modes, is too long, but the tricking of Syrus into thinking that the music of the spheres is being played is a nice comic bit, at least for a (possible) university audience. In the other scene, the comic by-play between Pythias, who wants to go on dancing, and the musicians who are ready to leave is a homely and sophisticated touch. One joke in this scene requires comment. As Misenus emerges from a doorway, he utters a Terentian appeal to Juno Lucina and claims that the house is giving birth to him; Marsias answers by parodying Horace's dictum, "A mountain in labor produces a ridiculous mouse (*mus*)": "A house in labor produces a ridiculous man (*mas*)." No doubt the Magdalen audience thought that funny, and it anticipates some of the courtly wit found in later comedy: one thinks, for instance, of the *mas-mass-Mars* and *as-ass-ars* trick which Dares and Samias play on Sir Tophas in *Endymion*. Equally esoteric is the humor when Phormio appeals to a large group of beings for help in his difficult task: beginning simply enough with the names of some gods, he moves through practitioners of mythological magic to end with references to Plato, Aristotle, and Pythagoras. Far more effective, I think, is the humor resulting from Chremes' and Crito's rage at being outwitted by Gesippus, for this is germane to the play and comes from the naturalistic conversation of two silly old men.

When we consider the nature of the material with which Foxe burdened himself and the status of the comic art when he was writing, we must conclude that Foxe wrote a more than creditable play. If it has flaws, it also has positive virtues. It is clearly a better play than *Christus Triumphans.* Perhaps, if we had Foxe's final revision, we would find some of the flaws eliminated, for we must remember that we are dealing with a draft play. On the other hand, the completely revised state of *Christus Triumphans* does

not indicate that Foxe's revisions necessarily removed all faults, and it is perhaps best not to speculate on the quality of a revision which we cannot now see. (pp. 20-5)

> *John Hazel Smith, in an introduction to* Two Latin Comedies by John Foxe the Martyrologist: "Titus et Gesippus," "Christus Triumphans," *edited and translated by John Hazel Smith, Cornell University Press, 1973, pp. 1-49.*

Warren W. Wooden   (essay date 1983)

[*In the following excerpt from his 1983 critical biography of Foxe, Wooden examines the mixture of classical, medieval, and renaissance elements in* Titus et Gesippus *and* Christus Triumphans.]

While Foxe's great book [*Acts and Monuments*] overshadowed, in his own day as for posterity, his other literary productions, several other areas of his literary endeavor produced work of both historical interest and literary merit. Much of his writing and translating was service work: introductions and translations of the works of continental Reformers, for example, and various polemical contributions to the literature of Reformation controversy, often commissioned by members of the Anglican hierarchy. For the most part, these service and polemical works are of interest only to students of Reformation history. As an academic dramatist, a popular preacher, and an author of pastoral rather than theological tracts, however, Foxe composed a body of work which would have secured him a modest niche in the literary history of the English Renaissance even had he not written the *Acts and Monuments.*

Foxe's son Simeon spoke in his memoir of "divers *Latine* Comedies yet to be seen" written by his father while a fellow at Magdalen College in the 1540s. Only two of Foxe's Latin comedies survive, and one of these appears to date not from his Oxford years but from a decade later when he was in exile abroad. Although the two plays are both academic Latin comedies laced with characters, devices, and verbal echoes of Plautus and Terence, they are actually quite dissimilar productions. Brought together in a modern edition and translation by John Hazel Smith, paradoxically these two plays are today the most accessible works in the Foxe canon—and the only ones available in a modern scholarly edition.

Titus et Gesippus is the sole survivor of Foxe's Oxford comedies. . . . Foxe sent copies of the play to two friends, apparently as a demonstration of his competence to teach Latin, in early 1545 when he had determined to leave Oxford and seek a tutorial post. In his letters accompanying the copies, Foxe notes that he wrote the play during the previous autumn and hopes to revise it; these presentation copies are lost and the surviving manuscript is presumably an early version. The play was not published until Smith's modern edition, and although there was a good deal of dramatic activity at Magdalen during the 1540s, there is no evidence to indicate whether or not the play was acted there or elsewhere. Nevertheless, the very existence of a romantic comedy from the pen of Foxe, even if written as an academic exercise, suggests another facet of his character, one at odds with the modern perception of him as a sober moralist and ecclesiastical historian.

The plot of *Titus et Gesippus,* the story of two exemplary friends, ultimately derives from one of the tales in Boccaccio's *Decameron,* although Foxe seems to have followed a version found in Sir Thomas Elyot's *Book of the Governour.* Foxe's play is one of the earliest English dramatic treatments of a favorite Renaissance theme, the conflict between Friendship and Love, the subject a generation later of Lyly's *Euphues,* Shakespeare's *Two Gentlemen of Verona,* and a host of other literary works. (pp. 77-8)

Even in the rough state preserved in the Lansdowne manuscript, the play is an interesting example of Renaissance academic comedy; Smith calls it "an epitome of English Renaissance comedy, but quite an early specimen." Foxe has some problems providing convincing motivation for Gesippus's initial grand gesture; he relies very heavily on coincidence to make the plot function; and he reveals a penchant for crowding key decisions into soliloquies rather than allowing them to develop out of the natural interchange of dialogue between characters. Still, some of the dialogue is quite lively, and in the addition of the Terentian witty slave Phormio, who manipulates much of the early action in particular, Foxe gave a new cast to the story he found in Elyot. In presenting a popular moral exemplum on the ideal of friendship in a lively neoclassical comic mode, Foxe's dramatic experiment in *Titus et Gesippus* is on balance a success.

Closer in spirit to Foxe's nondramatic works is his "apocalyptic comedy" *Christus Triumphans.* This play was printed in Basel in March, 1556, by Oporinus, for whom Foxe was working as a proofreader. Foxe dedicated the work to several English merchants living in Frankfort, apparently hoping both to patch up some of the still festering problems in the congregation there and also to secure some financial support for himself. (pp. 79-80)

Christus Triumphans is not, as one might expect from the title, a Resurrection play. Instead it is a fascinating mix of elements drawn from chronicle, mystery, morality, and classical dramatic traditions. In his prologue, Foxe writes that "Our matter is totally sacred and totally apocalyptic, what has been heard of by many but never seen before." In the admixture of dramatic traditions, conventions, and characters (they range from the historical, like Peter and Paul, to the typical, like Hierologus the preacher, to the allegorical, like Pseudamnus the false lamb), Foxe's play does resemble several earlier Latin plays in the "Christian Terence" tradition, such as Thomas Kirchmeyer's *Pammachius* (1536) to which Foxe's play may be indebted. Structurally, *Christus Triumphans* is a great sprawling play, only loosely divided into acts; Foxe does not even get around to introducing his apparent central character, Ecclesia (the true church), until the third act. As his prologue promises, the plot is rooted in scenes from the book of Revelation, dramatizing the war between the angelic host and the dragon who is cast into hell by the Lamb. Satan retaliates with his creatures the beast and the false lamb persecuting Ecclesia and her children. The Whore of Babylon appears to fornicate with the kings of the earth, and the play ends with the fall of Babylon, the capture of the beast, and the expectation of the imminent Marriage of the Lamb. However, Foxe also includes incidents from the Gospels and Acts as well as a capsule historical sweep

through the history of the church from apostolic times to the Reformation similar to that he would work out in detail in the 1570 edition of the *Acts and Monuments.* (pp. 80-1)

Artistically, *Christus Triumphans* is less successful than *Titus et Gesippus;* even J. H. Smith, the play's editor and principal modern apologist, admits the play is "seriously flawed." Foxe attempts too much, his plan is too vast for his dramatic skills, and consequently there are numerous problems of execution. There is a surplus of characters, most of them flat and colorless, and, more disturbing, allegorical equivalents are not always firmly fixed, as in the case of Ecclesia, Pornapolis, and some other central characters whose precise identification seems to shift from scene to scene. The Latin verse is generally undistinguished, and the sudden shifts and grand sweep of the action require a heavy dependence upon messengers to report the doings of off-stage characters.

As a specimen of the development of academic comedy in the sixteenth century, on the other hand, the play is most interesting. Marvin T. Herrick considers it in his discussion of the Christian Terence, the body of Biblical drama incorporating classical principles written especially for the instruction of students, and Ruth H. Blackburn relates it to the tradition of Latin humanist drama exemplified by the plays of Kirchmeyer and John Bale. But it is the very ambitiousness of Foxe's attempt in *Christus Triumphans* that distinguishes it from earlier plays of a similar type. In particular, Foxe's extremely eclectic borrowings from earlier dramatic traditions make *Christus Triumphans* more interesting to historians of Renaissance drama than *Titus et Gesippus.* Along with his indebtedness to the semiallegorical propaganda plays of Kirchmeyer and Bale, Foxe's portrayal of Ecclesia seduced, buffeted, and comforted by various good and evil characters, along with the allegorical characters and inset nondramatic theological discussions, points to the influence of the medieval morality play. In its free amplification of biblical materials and, as J. H. Smith suggests, especially in the radical telescoping of time, *Christus Triumphans* betrays an indebtedness to the medieval mystery plays. The attempt to dramatize the events of a 1,500-year period, complete with the appearance of selected historical characters, suggests like Foxe's prologue that the dramatist aimed at a kind of chronicle play. And in the five-act division, the extensive use of a messenger to report off-stage action, and the employment of the language of Roman comedy throughout, Foxe's debt to the classical tradition is manifest. In sum, then, *Christus Triumphans* is a fascinating, although admittedly flawed, amalgam of divergent dramatic traditions brought together by Foxe as an experiment in academic comedy. The record of its printings in the sixteenth century and its revival as a school text in the seventeenth century indicate that Foxe's experiment was not altogether unappreciated during the Renaissance. (pp. 82-3)

Warren W. Wooden, in his John Foxe, *Twayne Publishers, 1983, 144 p.*

Barbara Rosen   (essay date 1986)

[*In the following excerpt, Rosen explicates and defends the sixteenth- and seventeenth-century English practice of using* Actes and Monuments *to instruct children.*]

It is hard for us, as modern parents, to imagine that in 1563 the first books we bought for our children might have been the Bible and *The Acts and Monuments of John Foxe* (most frequently known as Foxe's *Book of Martyrs*); and that we might then have regarded the child's reading needs as filled for several years to come. Many of us would, if pressed, subscribe to Penelope Lively's statement that "We do actually believe now that children's books need to be fun and nothing else", yet even in the Romantic era such a statement would have been regarded as a monumental evasion of responsibility and an extraordinary begging of the question. If we are to understand what prescriptive reading of Foxe or the Bible might have meant to children of the past, it is necessary to divest ourselves of many current notions about children and reading.

The first printed books came out of a monastic tradition of slow and painstaking production, slow mastery, and long-continued use. The educational system associated with them at all levels depended upon authorities accepted for centuries, upon endless repetition of exercises, translation, and retranslation, learning by heart. It was the common understanding that this was what books were for. In England, the first printed book that most ordinary people had wanted to read was the Bible in their own tongue; in 1538 Thomas Cromwell urged bishops to place it in their churches and began the process of licensing cheap editions. The very high value set on literacy by Puritans and Renaissance theorists confirms our sense that reading in the sixteenth and seventeenth centuries meant rereading and reflection on serious material as much as the mere ability to recognize words.

Even for those who were not Puritans, the *Book of Martyrs* stood beside the Bible near the beginning of every path to literacy. (p. 223)

There is no question that in many families "real reading" of Foxe or the Bible was the medium through which admiration, family affection, and feelings of self-worth were mediated. Adam Martindale records his gleeful discovery of literacy about 1628, when he was five, when his mother let him have an "ABC" given by a relative, and he begged lessons from his siblings and his sister's suitor:

> Then of mine owne accord I fell to reading the bible and any other English booke, and such greate delight I tooke in it, and the praises I got by it from my parents, which preferred my reading before any other in the family, that I think I could almost have read a day together without play or meat, if breath and strength would have held out, and thus it continued to the end of the first seven yeares of my life.

Notice that reading for Adam means reading aloud, often in competition with siblings. Thus when Edward Harvey, according to his mother "begins now to delight in reading" and "would not let me be in peace, till I promised him to send for [a Bible]," he is looking forward to a rite of passage into full family membership. When family unity is demonstrated in a religious context (family prayers, family reading, grace before meals) children absorb religious rhetoric as love and security; when one can actively join the magic circle by serious reading, then the content of one's reading becomes material for growth, for play, and for imitation. (Many of Janeway's little saints held services for their siblings, preached sermons, and lectured them on salvation; today we should recognize this as imi-

tative play.) What, particularly, might children have found valuable for their own growth in the content of Foxe's *Book of Martyrs?*

This vast compilation is one of the classics it is easier to be witty about than to read, and much of what is said of it betrays slight acquaintance with its actual contents. Foxe was by temperament and training a scholar as much as a polemicist. In recording the histories of the Marian martyrs and their predecessors he works by overkill; he traveled widely, questioned ceaselessly, consulted mountains of documents. Subsequent discoveries have, as Mozley suggests, tended to make him seem more rather than less reliable. He includes transcripts of Latin and even Anglo-Saxon documents; he gives accounts of lengthy disputes on theological cruces; he prints letters by queens, acts of Parliament, and legal interpretations. In his quest for completeness he prints altogether too much. Yet he is showing us history in the making—the laws, the political pressures which caused them to be made, the people who applied them, the means by which people were entrapped in conversation and brought to trial, the ways in which the courts worked for or against the accused, the reasons for their bias. A child puzzling and skipping his way through must often have been completely bewildered. The complexity of the world and the vast consequences of small actions are on view all at once.

Yet in the midst of this are trenchant, brilliantly dramatic scenes of interrogation or execution, where Foxe's exacerbated sensibilities express their outrage through the selection of telling detail, the contrast between power and helplessness, the pathos of the ignorant caught up in matters beyond their understanding. We think of the death of Cranmer, finally holding steady in the flame the hand that had signed his recantations or the farewell of Dr. Rowland Taylor, his wife and son. Foxe records the ambiguities and unsolved questions which lead the reader away from doctrine to raw experience; when on the same day three Protestants were burned for religion and three Catholics hanged for denying the supremacy of Henry VIII, a foreigner exclaimed, "Deus bone! quomodo hic vivunt gentes?" (colloquial translation: "Good God! what sort of people are these?") and the sight "brought the people into a marvelous admiration and doubt of their religion, which part to follow and take." The sheer drama of the set scenes quite often obscures the narrow theological points at issue, and the variety of literary modes presents a reader with changing conventions and genres. The effect is one of multiplicity rather than unity, of a human panorama rather than a sermon. Compared with Janeway's grim single message that children "are not too Little to go to Hell," Foxe frees rather than constrains the spirit.

Much has been made of the horrifying nature of the illustrations in the larger editions of Foxe, and of the clinical descriptions of torture and elaborated execution. Few of the woodcuts are as graphic as the picture of William Gardiner hung over a slow fire, his hands amputated, or Lambert propped up by pikes in the flames; yet even the formalized cuts of flames and faggots would give some children scope for imagination and nightmares. The descriptions are another matter; the obsessive and pitiless clarity of their physical detail is sometimes hard to bear. It is more understandable when we learn that Foxe pleaded with Elizabeth for the lives of Anabaptists and Catholic priests and, above all, for the abolishment of burning as a form of execution. As he says despairingly "Nor do I favour the lives of *men* alone: would that I could succour the very beasts too. For such is my disposition (I will say this of myself, foolishly perhaps, but yet truly) that I can scarce pass the shambles where beasts are slaughtered but that my mind secretly recoils with a feeling of pain." That pain is reproduced, over and over, in the book, in grief and horror that men could do such things to each other.

Foxe was unusual; the child of the sixteenth or seventeenth century was faced with the sort of direct horror which today is confronted only by the very poor of the Third World. Bodies of felons hung rotting in chains, heads were set over city gates. Traitors were hanged, drawn and quartered in the public streets; children were flogged and animals tormented. Vagrants, sick or crazy, wandered the land or lay dying in ditches outside homes. More than we can easily recognize, the world of Foxe and of the children who read him was a world shaped by expectation of pain; we are separated from it by our own good health. Most of our brothers and sisters survive; we are not used to our mothers and daughters dying in childbirth, without anesthetic (Alice Thornton's autobiographical record of bizarre gynecological disasters is probably not atypical). When children have scarlet fever or pneumonia today, the disease may be cut short by antibiotics. Three hundred years ago such illnesses had to run their prolonged and painful course, with the ensuing complications and relapses. The child of this era had in fact only one all-consuming task, and that was to grow up; the two qualities required for this were obedience and endurance. (pp. 224-26)

In Foxe's book a child would have read about people who were recognizably fallible, able to be confused in talk or forced into humiliating abjuration by fear of the fire. Foxe's sympathy extends to those who were "molested and vexed and, at last, compelled to abjure." The child would have found situations of bondage, imprisonment, and arbitrary pain which, to a few, provided opportunities for heroism. He or she would have seen that a high proportion of those executed were women or young people—even children—who, by bearing what had to be borne, became heroic. The virtues demanded were not those of the Crusades or the warlike saints, but those of Milton's Adam, who performs no active deed—he simply makes moral choices and endures their consequences.

These were virtues peculiarly apt to women and children of the time, for they turned upon the uttering of words, the giving or withholding of oaths, the ability to maintain a sense of self under the threat or reality of pain, the endurance of exhausting conditions and attrition by humiliation. In the stories told by Foxe, children could find models for making inward choices in situations of apparent helplessness; if they must suffer, then they could suffer uncomplainingly, like Charles Bridgman, on the pattern of the great martyrs; if they were treated unjustly or misunderstood then they became part of a silent army of sufferers. Within submission, there could still be an assertion of moral choice; without control of circumstances, there could still be self-control of response. It is easy to see something societally imposed in the picture of a child praying to be good, trying to borrow the courage of the martyrs to endure the pains and trials of his own existence,

yet patterning one's life after a model of courageous endurance may be a positive means of self-creation when no other is possible. And some few would perceive the avenue of escape later depicted in Samuel Richardson's *Clarissa*: religious conviction alone offered strength to an adult to defy family or social norms without guilt.

If, finally, we turn back to consider Foxe's book as material for children—as, in our own terms, "fun"—we recall that it was written for adults. Yet it was so long recommended as fare for children that we must consider it at least as part of a background which adults and children shared for two centuries or so. And this brings us to the sharpest distinction of attitude between the shared cultural background then and now.

Death in Foxe is never unimportant; it is not dignified, and he does not show it so, yet he suggests that its grotesqueries do not exist merely in their own right, as sources of curiosity or amusement when skillfully captured on screen, stage, or cartoon. The way in which a man or woman meets death—or even the fact that, however shrinkingly, that person chose to meet it—is seen in the light of eternal destiny. Yet Foxe's eye for character and human foible ensures that we also see the particular nature of a person's death as an extension of a human self, a growth and development. It is shocking to realize how often in films seen by children our only interest in a dying man might be in the pattern his body makes as it falls from a roof, or in the witty verisimilitude with which that body leaks ketchup. Violence and death in Foxe are not transmuted into entertainment or sermon; they are traversed in the service of human courage and ultimate meaning.

What do we suggest about our view of human nature when, for fun on Saturday mornings, we shut up children in an endless loop of cartoons with an obsessively repeated pattern of quarrel-chase-act of violence; or feed them "cop shows" where the good guys endlessly mow down the bad with gunfire, often to cheers and laughter? In Foxe's book, the reader is aligned, not with those who inflict suffering, but with those who bear it; and those who suffer are less guilty than those who execute. Is it necessary to entertain our children with the notion that the hero is always the man with a smoking gun in his hand? Is there finally no room in our concept of children's reading and viewing for stories that show a triumph of the human spirit over violence through endurance? For many victims of racism or colonialism, that is the story of their friends and families.

No one today would see it as feasible to turn back the clock and present six-year-olds with the Bible and the **Book of Martyrs** and nothing else. Yet, by projecting our sympathies backwards, we may see what was positive for the child readers in Foxe, a source of empowerment in a world that was harsh and difficult for them. We may ask whether the reading and viewing we allow our children equally prepares them in strength and compassion for the world that we have made, in which they may feel—and be—equally powerless. And we may be reminded that to find nourishment for growth in unlikely places—to wrench honey from the lion's carcass—as so many children did, is in itself one more proof of the unquenchable vitality and versatility of the human spirit. (pp. 227-29)

Barbara Rosen, "John Foxe's 'Book of Martyrs' and Its Value as a Book for Children," in

Triumphs of the Spirit in Children's Literature, *edited by Francelia Butler and Richard
Rotert, Library Professional Publications,
1986, pp. 223-29.*

Carole Levin   (essay date 1986)

[*Levin is an American essayist and academic. In the following excerpt, she explores Foxe's portrayal in* Actes
and Monuments *of powerful women in his attempt to
demonstrate to Elizabeth I "the nature of her true
duty."*]

In his *Acts and Monuments* John Foxe played a critical
role in shaping perceptions of history in Elizabethan England. First published in 1563, the book was republished
and greatly expanded in 1570 and went through three
more editions in the sixteenth century. Though much of
the interest in Foxe's book centered on his account of the
Protestant martyrs, *Acts and Monuments* is far more than
a recitation of the trials of the godly; it is also a history
of England written from the perspective of the true reformed Church. Foxe expanded his book to include this
history for a purpose. He wanted to instruct both the
Queen and the people about their mutual duties and obligations. Dedicating his work to Elizabeth, Foxe was both
praising her and warning her of the need to establish the
true Church. Foxe wrote, then, both to "honour the dead
victims, and [to] warn and encourage the living." A humanist whose earlier work was published in Latin, Foxe
chose to present *Acts and Monuments* in the less prestigious vernacular, seeking to inform the British people of
what had happened and could happen again without a
godly ruler. Above all, the person Foxe wanted to warn
and encourage was his Queen.

Like many of the other returned Marian exiles, Foxe was
unsatisfied with the Anglican Church settlement, which
he considered incomplete and inadequate. Coming out of
the tradition of William Tyndale and John Bale, he believed in an active God who directly intervenes in the
human world. In *Acts and Monuments* he presented the
history of the Church of England from the Lutheran perspective of the operation of Providence: God had saved
Elizabeth from the perils of her sister's reign to rule the
nation He had chosen to usher in the new age of faith.
Elizabeth had a duty to defend the true Church against the
Church of Rome and to insist upon a complete reformation. When apprising Elizabeth of her duty, Foxe did not
want to attack her openly; he was all too aware of the dangers that could come to Protestant England if the Queen's
position were weakened. Instead he sought to demonstrate
to Elizabeth the nature of her true duty by presenting examples from earlier times of rulers and their fates.

Among rulers Elizabeth was special, of course, since she
was not only a monarch, but a woman. As a result, Foxe's
representation of earlier powerful women became crucial
as a message to the reigning Queen. This essay will examine Foxe's portrayal of medieval queens, such as Matilda,
Eleanor of Aquitaine, Isabel, wife of Edward II, and Margaret of Anjou, as well as such Tudor queens as Anne Boleyn, Catherine Parr, and Lady Jane Grey. Such an exploration not only reveals Foxe's important view of Elizabeth
in particular; it also illuminates the influential role played
by *Acts and Monuments* in the ardent debate about

women's capacities as rulers that had been going on
throughout the sixteenth century.

In both his work and his life, Foxe exhibited an ambiguity
and subtlety that give his work a depth and significance
in adding to our understanding of Elizabethan England.
While Foxe's sense of complexity is not confined to his attitude toward women, it is discernible in the ambivalence
he expressed about female rule. His ambivalence arises directly from the conflict he perceived between a woman's
power and her femininity. If a queen were to demonstrate
the strong attributes of kingship, she would not be acting
in a womanly manner; yet, approved womanly behavior
would ill-fit her for the rigors of rule. This was a problem
with which both Mary and Elizabeth had to come to
terms. One solution, of course, was for the queen to marry.
Though Mary's marriage to Philip of Spain had been a disaster, many people hoped Elizabeth would also relieve
herself of responsibility in just that manner. Elizabeth's refusal made the concern over women's rule all the more significant. (pp. 113-15)

[Despite] his celebration of Elizabeth, Foxe's descriptions
of earlier powerful women betray some of the ambivalence
that he felt about the concept of a woman ruler. Although
he praised Elizabeth's rule as God's plan, he also showed
God's role in punishing other strong women rulers. Examining the depictions of earlier queens in *Acts and Monuments* is useful in gaining an understanding of Foxe's expectations for Elizabeth and in demonstrating how unique
he thought she was as a woman who was also God's instrument. A number of the powerful women Foxe discusses are queen consorts. Though Elizabeth was queen reg-
nant, Foxe clearly saw these examples as useful guides for
her. The English very much hoped that Elizabeth would
marry, and examples of married women became appropriate models as well. Indeed, since she was a woman ruler,
these examples were considered more appropriate than
those of kings.

Foxe's presentation of queens fits into his broader perspective on women's behavior in general. Didactic literature
of the sixteenth century advised women to be models of
chaste, passive obedience. Pearl Hogrefe and Ruth Kelso
both suggest that the ideals for women of the Renaissance
were the passive Christian virtues. Sermons and courtesy
books emphasized such qualities as modesty, humility,
sweetness, and piety. Yet it is the more active Christian
virtues, such as learning, proficiency at arms, ability to
command, and provision of justice that would be most
suitable for a ruler; these latter were seen as the traditional
kingly virtues. Foxe, in his examples of women rulers,
both reinforces and modifies the concern for appropriate
feminine behavior.

Some of the presentations Foxe makes of women rulers are
simply negligible. Other historians of the period have
made much more of their activities. For example, in the
case of Henry I's daughter Matilda, Foxe points out that
barons and churchmen swore to uphold her claim, but
they foreswore themselves and supported her cousin Stephen. Foxe, whose view of history contains an active God
who punishes wrongdoing, demonstrates the horrors that
befell those who broke their just oath. Yet, though Foxe
refers to Matilda making "strong war" on her cousin Stephen, and Stephen's wrongs are clearly enunciated, Matilda herself plays a rather small role in the proceedings,

mostly making sure of the claim of her son Henry II, whom Foxe treats at great length when he comes to Henry's reign.

Foxe also pays rather less attention than his contemporaries to Henry's wife, Eleanor of Aquitaine. For the most part, Eleanor's reputation was a very bad one in sixteenth-century history and drama. Foxe, however, drew only minimally on this tradition. He mentions the problems between Eleanor and Henry that lead to Eleanor's imprisonment, but he is careful about ascribing a cause. Henry imprisoned Eleanor "as some think, for the love of Rosamund." Foxe does not, however, refer to the oft-cited legend that Eleanor murdered her rival. Rather, he uses Henry's imprisonment of Eleanor as a reason for God to stir their sons to rebel against Henry. Despite the rebellion, Foxe reports inaccurately that Eleanor was soon reconciled with Henry. In fact, except for brief ceremonial visits, Henry kept Eleanor in prison for the rest of his reign.

Perhaps Foxe is less interested in Eleanor because of his greater interest in Henry. His concerns about the king, for the most part, center on two conflicts. The first is with Becket; not surprisingly, Foxe treats Henry sympathetically and does all he can to strip away from Becket the saint's and martyr's image. He presents Becket as a rebel against his king and a supporter of the corrupt Catholic Church. The other conflict Foxe describes is that between Henry and his sons. Foxe is more ambivalent about this latter conflict. He cites actions on Henry's part, such as the imprisonment of Eleanor, that would lead to God's punishment. But though Henry may deserve the rebellion as a punishment for his unjust acts, his sons are still wrong to rebel against him, and Foxe also emphasizes their culpability. In depicting this complex web of relationships and retribution, Foxe pays little attention to Eleanor.

When recounting the reign of Eleanor's son Richard, Foxe makes other comments about her that are brief but positive. He pictures Eleanor bringing Berengaria to be espoused to Richard and then journeying on to Rome in search of preferment for her other son Geoffrey. Here again Foxe was inaccurate historically. The Geoffrey who was consecrated Archbishop of York was *not* Eleanor's son Geoffrey, but rather Henry's illegitimate son, who had the same name. Though Eleanor did go to Rome at Richard's request to convince Pope Celestine to elect Geoffrey as Archbishop, the reason was to remove any possibility of his reaching for the crown. With this action Eleanor moves out of the narrative, never to return.

We can see in his treatment of Matilda and Eleanor that Foxe is not hostile, but neither is he devoting much space to presenting them as examples of powerful female rulers. Isabel of France and Margaret of Anjou receive much more attention from Foxe, and both came to far more tragic, if also, according to Foxe, well-deserved ends.

For most of his account of her, Foxe presents Edward II's wife Isabel in a fairly sympathetic manner. It is only at the end, when her actions have transgressed conceptions of appropriate behavior that Foxe condemns her. Part of his sympathy is occasioned by his attitude toward her husband Edward and his homosexual relationship with Piers Gaveston, who "brought the king, by means of his wanton conditions, to manifold vices, as adultery, and the like . . .

so much was the king's heart infatuated by this wicked person." Edward's passion for Gaveston was so intense that he impoverished his wife's estate by giving Gaveston her possessions. Isabel's problems with Edward allied her interests with those of the kingdom. "If [Gaveston] were still suffered . . . the queen could not enjoy the love of the king, neither could there be any quietness in the realm." (pp. 117-19)

Because of Edward's tyranny, Parliament proclaimed him deposed. His son Edward was crowned in his place. Had Isabel allowed her young son to rule at that point, she might well have been described as a good example of a woman who acts only when there is need and then returns to her accustomed subordinate position. But Isabel did not do that. No longer considered as powerful herself, she handed her power to her lover Mortimer, who used it corruptly.

The next year Sir Roger Mortimer ordered the deposed Edward II to be murdered. Even worse, Mortimer used his position with Isabel to convince the young Edward that his uncle, the Earl of Kent, was trying to have him poisoned. Because of this false information, the innocent Earl was executed. "But the just judgement of God," Foxe proclaims, does not permit "such odious crimes to be unpunished or undetected." Soon Mortimer was destroyed, and Isabel with him. The fall of Mortimer began when Isabel was found to be carrying his child. When the young king received word of this, he also began an investigation into Mortimer's role in the deaths of Edward II and the Earl of Kent. In Foxe's world, sexual misconduct for women is always severely condemned. It indicates total ethical lapse. Mortimer was executed, but Isabel was also punished, being "restrained of her liberty." Foxe does not mention whatever became of the child that proclaimed her guilt, and, in fact, there is no such record of pregnancy for Isabel at that time. But to demonstrate Foxe's vision of the world, the tale of Isabel's pregnancy worked well.

Foxe is not the only Elizabethan to equate sexual impropriety with female immorality in general. As Lawrence Stone points out, Early Modern English society stressed honor but had very different conceptions of what constituted male and female honor. While male honor depended on the integrity of one's word and courage, sexual chastity was the sole determinant of female honor. One of the ways in which people denigrated Elizabeth as queen was to accuse her of illicit sexual behavior and to suggest that she had illegitimate children. For example, in 1563 Edmund Baxter stated "that Lord Robert [Dudley] kept her Majesty, and that she was a naughty woman, and could not rule her realm, and that justice was not being administered." His wife added that when she saw the Queen at Ipswich, "she looks like one lately come out of child-bed." For Elizabeth, one way she could continue to command the love and respect of her people was *not* to engage in inappropriate sexual behavior, and, even when she did not, the rumors continued.

In much the same manner, Foxe portrays Isabel as both powerful and good until she becomes involved with Mortimer. Once that happens she becomes powerless; we do not hear of anything else she herself accomplishes. And for her transgressions she is punished. Yet both Isabel's crimes and the just punishment that follows are mild compared to those that befall another powerful queen, Margaret of Anjou, wife of Henry VI.

Foxe's portrayal of Margaret is hostile from the beginning. The marriage arranged between her and Henry VI was, Foxe states, "unprofitable and unhonourable." In narrating Henry VI's reign, he portrays Humphrey, Duke of Gloucester, as one of the heroes of the period. Margaret is presented in contrast as a "sore enemy and mortal plague to this duke."

Foxe described Margaret as "being of haughty stomach, and all set upon glory, of wit and wiliness lacking nothing, and perceiving her husband to be of simple wit, and easy to be ruled, took upon her to rule and govern both the king and his kingdom." In Isabel's situation, her husband was depraved, and at a crucial moment she was the best person to rescue England from his tyranny. With Margaret, her husband is not evil but only simple, and there are more appropriate people than she to help him rule.

In an observation characteristic of sixteenth-century accounts of powerful women, Foxe refers to Margaret as this "manly woman and courageous queen." The word "manly" others also used at times to praise women's brave deeds. For example, an Italian residing in England during Mary's reign described Lady Jane Grey at her death as "submitting the neck to the axe with more than manly courage." Given Foxe's condemnation of Margaret's treatment of Gloucester, however, one suspects that in Foxe's view, for a woman to be manly and courageous is immoral. (pp. 120-22)

What Foxe condemns most in Margaret is her blindness in not realizing how her own actions led to the destruction of her hopes. When Edward IV triumphed over the Lancastrians, she "was so dismayed, disquieted, and pierced with sorrow . . . that she feared and took on with herself . . . crying out of fortune, as though blind fortune were she that governeth times and tides . . . and not the secret power and terrible justice of Almighty God." Margaret finishes her role in Foxe's history by once again going to battle. Captured when she was "almost dead for sorrow," she was eventually ransomed by her father. By this time both her husband and her son were dead.

For the most part, Foxe's view of medieval queens who exercise power is negative. Matilda and Eleanor do not come to terrible ends, but neither does Foxe give them much attention. Isabel, and even more, Margaret, show courage and resolution but are destroyed, one through her inappropriate sexual behavior, the other because of her ambition. In his depiction of medieval queens, Foxe does not really present Elizabeth with appropriate models, though he is certainly providing cautionary tales on the misuse of power.

This perspective partially shifts when Foxe discusses Protestant queens in the sixteenth century. In these cases religion seems to be a more significant determinant than gender. Anne Boleyn, Catherine Parr, and Lady Jane Grey are all queens who are virtuous women concerned with fostering the true Church. Yet even here the model is not completely positive, since two of these women died at the executioner's hand, and the third, Catherine Parr, only narrowly escaped this fate.

Following Foxe's treatment of earlier queens, Anne Boleyn's life appears well-suited to embody the laws of his moral universe. Rising to become queen of England, Anne died on the executioner's block, a fate she shared with the men accused of being her lovers. How much more of an object lesson Anne's fate could have provided than either Isabel's or Margaret's! Foxe, however, had certain problems in presenting Anne Boleyn, since he was writing about the ruling sovereign's mother, who had been executed on the order of Elizabeth's father. Though Foxe discusses Anne's death, he is vague about the cause; he simply states that she was sent to the Tower with her brother and certain others and was beheaded a few weeks later. Foxe begins his commentary on Anne Boleyn's character by calling her "godly." He does admit that this description may cause some objections, but he then goes on to demolish them.

Although historians may question the veracity of Foxe's portrait of Anne Boleyn, his emphases in it suggest the values that he believes comprise a positive model for queenly behavior. Given Foxe's concerns, it is not surprising that he first praises Anne's "sincere faith and trust in Christ"; he is also impressed with "her quiet modesty . . . [the] gentleness, modesty, and pity toward all men . . . the quiet moderation of her mild nature." As queen, according to Foxe, Anne Boleyn kept her ladies occupied sewing garments for the poor. Of course Anne was the mother of the reigning Queen Elizabeth, and, for Foxe, this fact is the best proof of her virtue: "Furthermore, to all other sinister judgements and opinions, whatsoever can be conceived of man against that virtuous queen, I object and oppose again (as instead of answer) the evident demonstration of God's favour, in maintaining, preserving, and advancing the offspring of her body, the lady Elizabeth, now queen." Gentleness, modesty, piety, and moderation, then, are obviously characteristics Foxe approved of in a woman ruler. Yet none of these qualities was sufficient to preserve Anne so that she might continue her support of the true Church.

Unlike Anne Boleyn, Henry's last queen, Catherine Parr, did manage to survive during her husband's reign. Foxe's description of her is useful in the lessons it suggests for the survival of an intelligent, forceful woman who is also virtuous and pious. (pp. 122-24)

Although Catherine Parr survived, she did so by hiding her intelligence, posing as a "silly, poor woman," and manipulating Henry. Elizabeth as queen also learned to be manipulative, to give "answerless answers" when asked by Parliament or her advisors to do what she wished to avoid. Yet one wonders if Foxe perceived this evasiveness as the best method of behavior for his queen, however much he might admire it in Catherine Parr. Elizabeth also used the technique of manipulation in her dealings with Parliament to avoid further reformation of the Church.

Both Catherine Parr and Anne Boleyn, as well as the medieval queens Eleanor, Isabel, and Margaret, were queens by virtue of the fact that they were married to kings. Foxe presents one sixteenth-century example of a woman whose reign would have perpetuated the true Church had she been allowed to rule, and that was Lady Jane Grey, queen for only nine days. Foxe has great admiration for Lady Jane Grey, and yet he depicts her position as ambiguous, since she was the center of a plot that, had it succeeded, would have eliminated not only Mary's succession but also Elizabeth's.

Foxe solves this problem by presenting Jane Grey's virtue as a Protestant, while, accurately enough, demonstrating that she had no volition in the conspiracy. He calls her and her husband Guilford "two innocents in comparison of them that sat upon them. For they did but ignorantly accept that which the others had willingly devised." But while Lady Jane Grey was an innocent pawn in the conspiracy, she was an ardent and steadfast Protestant whose faith did not waver even in the face of death.

In portraying Jane Grey as a Protestant heroine, Foxe describes two incidents that occurred late in Edward VI's reign. These events emphasize not only her piety, but her willingness to speak out for her beliefs. Both incidents involved her cousin the Lady Mary, the future queen. One occurred when she was visiting Mary. In defiance of the law, Mary had mass said in her household. While passing the chapel, Lady Jane saw Anne Wharton make a low curtsy to the sacrament on the altar. Jane asked Lady Wharton why she had curtsied. Was the Lady Mary in there? Lady Wharton replied no, "that she made her curtsy to Him that made us all." "Why. . . . how can He be there, that made us all, and the baker make him?" Mary was insulted when this conversation was reported to her and she "did never love Jane after," Foxe reports. Lady Jane demonstrated the same want of tact in another confrontation with Mary, this time over the issue of simple dress. Mary had sent her cousin a richly elaborate dress as a gift. Jane refused to wear it: "Nay, that were a shame to follow my Lady Mary against God's word, and leave my Lady Elizabeth which followed God's word." (Ironically, given her later performance, Elizabeth dressed with great simplicity during her brother's reign.) Hester Chapman suggests that while today people might censure Jane Grey's behavior for its rudeness, in her own time, Protestants used such remarks as examples of her high principles and courage in speaking out for her beliefs.

Examples of high education and steadfast religion are in general the lessons John Foxe taught when writing about Lady Jane Grey. He praises her as being "in learning and knowledge of the tongues" superior to her cousin Edward. She used her learning to defend her religious beliefs. Foxe gives a full transcript of the religious debate between Lady Jane and Master Feckham, whom Queen Mary had sent to attempt to convert Jane before her death. Naturally Foxe presents their discussion so that Lady Jane Grey appears not only able to best Feckham at theological argument, but also to do so with tranquillity, even as she approaches her own death.

Foxe describes in great detail Lady Jane's behavior on the scaffold. Her serene courage especially impresses him. To the very last minutes of her life she stayed true to the Protestant precepts which had brought her such comfort: "I pray you all, good christian people, to bear me witness that I die a true christian woman, and that I do look to be saved by no other means, but only by the mercy of God, in the blood of his only Son Jesus Christ." Since, as a Protestant, she did not believe in purgatory and thus saw only blasphemy in prayers for the dead, she asked the people to pray for her only while she lived: "And now, good people, while I am alive, I pray you assist me with your prayers."

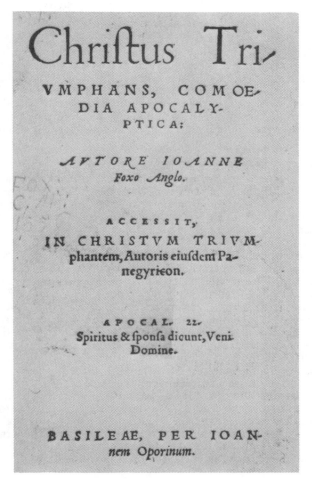

Title page of the first edition of Foxe's Christus Triumphans *(1556).*

To this decorous, probably well-rehearsed speech, Foxe adds a description of Lady Jane Grey's last moments. After requesting the executioner to "dispatch me quickly," she tied a handkerchief around her eyes. She misjudged the space, however, and could not then find the block, saying, "What shall I do? Where is it? Where is it?" Finally one of the standersby guided her. She "laid her head down upon the block . . . and said, 'Lord into thy hands I commend my spirit,' and finished her life."

Lady Jane Grey did not survive to ensure a godly reformation, and Mary I's reign was a tragedy for England. . . . Foxe was convinced that Elizabeth survived her sister's reign through God's direct intervention: "We have to consider again . . . how strangely, or rather miraculously, she was delivered from danger, what favour and grace she found with the Almighty; who, when all help of man and hope of delivery was past, stretched out his mighty protection." God had his plan for England, and this plan was embodied in Elizabeth. It was her duty to bring to England the godly reformation the country needed. Yet though Foxe was convinced that Elizabeth was part of God's plan, one can still sense his ambivalence about women's rule from his treatment of earlier queens, and this treatment demonstrates the unresolved contradictions in his advice.

Elizabeth was as well aware of the contradictions between being a woman and being a ruler as anyone. Much of her reign was spent as a balancing act: "I know I have the body of a weak and feeble woman, but I have the heart and stomach of a king," she proclaimed at a moment of national crisis. But Elizabeth's solutions to the problems of her reign were far different from those suggested by John Foxe.

One can see how different their approaches were when one examines the actions for which Foxe celebrated his queen. Several times in the *Acts and Monuments,* Foxe's praises of Elizabeth have an ironic overtone; he is acclaiming her for actions that he wishes she would take, rather than deeds she has actually done. The use of praise to effect change in a prince is a typical rhetorical device of the Renaissance, and Foxe was following Erasmus' advice in employing it. But we can feel the disparity between Foxe's desires and Elizabeth's behavior when, for example, Foxe commends Elizabeth who, during her sister's reign, took "little delight in . . . gay apparel, rich attire, and precious jewels." At the time Foxe was writing this passage, Elizabeth, to the dismay of some Protestants, was dressing with regal splendor. Similarly, in his dedication Foxe praises Elizabeth for her "provident zeal, full of solicitude, you have, minding (speedily I trust) to furnish all quarters and countries of this your realm with the voice of Christ's gospel and faithful preaching of his word." But, as noted earlier, many of the returned Marian exiles (including Foxe) were not satisfied with the Anglican Settlement, although it was already more Protestant in doctrine than Elizabeth had originally wanted. And once the Acts of Supremacy and Uniformity and the Thirty-Nine Articles were in place, Elizabeth considered the matter closed. There would be no further discussion of reforming the Church. As the reign progressed, the Puritans became more and more vociferous in their arguments, and Elizabeth responded by pushing them out of the established Church. This struggle between ruler and Puritans was eventually to lead to armed conflict in the seventeenth century.

Unlike the Puritans, Foxe was never openly willing to criticize his queen. Instead, he hoped that examples of ecclesiastical history would urge Elizabeth to further the reformation. Foxe's own ambivalence, however, in some ways blunted the message he was attempting to promote. Lyndsay, Becon, Goodman, and Knox had all condemned women's rule. Vives, despite his encouragement of women's education, condemned it also. The discomfort implicit in Vives' attitude toward women's capabilities is very much evident in the writings of those, such as Elyot and Aylmer, who favored women's participation in public affairs. By the middle of the sixteenth century, queenship was no longer a theoretical issue. Women were ruling as regents or queen regnants in much of Europe. Like the others who wrote on queenship in the sixteenth century, Foxe was never able to reconcile completely the conflict over how a female ruler could act in both a womanly and a regal fashion. The qualities needed for strong rule were antithetical to the expectations of appropriate female behavior. If a queen followed the expectations, she could be condemned for not ruling well, but if she ignored the expectations, she was perceived as unwomanly. Though this paradox was one Foxe was never able completely to reconcile, his perception of Elizabeth as God's chosen instrument was the best method available to him.

John Foxe's *Acts and Monuments* is in some sense circular; dedicated to Elizabeth, it ends with praising her at the beginning of her reign for what her rule will mean to England. The examples of earlier women rulers show how perilous Foxe considered Elizabeth's situation to be. Isabel and Margaret had been destroyed by lust and ambition. The examples of Anne Boleyn, Catherine Parr, and Lady Jane Grey demonstrated that even the godly were not exempt from the dangers of the world. The reform of the church had been left to Elizabeth. Foxe's lessons of earlier queens worked both as cautionary tales and as celebrations of godly acts. Elizabeth had survived to become queen for a purpose. Foxe gave her these examples in the hope that she would carry that purpose forward. (pp. 125-29)

Carole Levin, "John Foxe and the Responsibilities of Queenship," in Women in the Middle Ages and the Renaissance: Literary and Historical Perspectives, *edited by Mary Beth Rose, Syracuse University Press, 1986, pp. 113-33.*

FURTHER READING

Bainton, Roland H. "John Foxe and the Ladies." In *The Social History of the Reformation,* edited by Lawrence P. Buck and Jonathan W. Zophy, pp. 208-22. Columbus: Ohio State University Press, 1972.
> Explores Foxe's portrayal of women in *Actes and Monuments.*

Dickens, A. G. "Heresy and the Origins of English Protestantism." In *Britain and the Netherlands,* edited by J. S. Bromley and E. H. Kossmann, Volume II, pp. 47-66. Groningen: J. B. Wolters, 1964.
> Assesses Foxe's treatment of the Lollards in his literary works.

Haller, William. "John Foxe and the Puritan Revolution." In *The Seventeenth Century: Studies in the History of English Thought and Literature from Bacon to Pope,* by Richard Foster Jones and others, pp. 209-24. Stanford: Stanford University Press, 1951.
> Examines the nature of Foxe's skill as an historian, emphasizing his attempt to provide his countrymen with a "conception of universal history and of England's place in history."

Hargrave, O. T. "Bloody Mary's Victims: The Iconography of John Foxe's 'Book of Martyrs'." *Historical Magazine of the Protestant Episcopal Church* LI, No. 1 (March 1982): 7-21.
> Considers the impact of the woodcuts in *Actes and Monuments* upon both literate and illiterate users of the book.

King, John N. "Continuities: Foxe, Spenser, and Milton." In his *English Reformation Literature: The Tudor Origins of the*

Protestant Tradition, pp. 407-56. Princeton: Princeton University Press, 1982.

Provides a broad historical setting for the works of Foxe, Spenser, and Milton, concentrating particularly upon the portrayal of the Marian persecutions and Elizabethan reforms in *Actes and Monuments.*

Lamont, William M. *Godly Rule, Politics and Religion: 1603-60.* London: Macmillan, 1969, 200 p.

Includes a discussion of the impact of *Actes and Monuments* upon religious controversies of the seventeenth century.

Levin, Carole. "Women in 'The Book of Martyrs' as Models of Behavior in Tudor England." *International Journal of Women's Studies* 4, No. 2 (March-April 1981): 196-207.

Considers the manner in which Foxe portrayed women in *Actes and Monuments.*

Levy, F. J. *Tudor Historical Thought.* San Marino, Calif.: Huntington Library, 1967, 305 p.

Contains an assessment of the influence of *Actes and Monuments* upon Renaissance historiography.

McNeill, John T. "John Foxe: Historiographer, Disciplinarian, Tolerationist." *Church History* 43, No. 2 (June 1974): 216-29.

Explicates Foxe's theological perspective in the light of major issues of the English Renaissance.

Maitland, Rev. S. R. "Remarks on the New Edition of Fox's Work, and on the Work Itself" and "Fox's Acts and Monuments." *British Magazine and Monthly Register* XI-XIII (June 1837-June 1838).

Scathing twelve-part review of a new edition of *Actes and Monuments,* faulting virtually every aspect of the text and questioning the reliability and integrity of Foxe himself.

Murphy, Michael. "John Foxe, Martyrologist and 'Editor' of Old English." *English Studies* XLIX, Nos. 1-6 (1968); 516-23.

Questions whether Foxe edited the works of the Old English writer Ælfric for inclusion in *Actes and Monuments.*

Rechtien, John G. "John Foxe's 'Comprehensive Collection of Commonplaces': A Renaissance Memory System for Students and Theologians." *The Sixteenth Century Journal* IX, No. 1 (1978): 83-89.

Technical discussion of the function of commonplaces, focusing upon *Pandectae locorum communium.*

Williams, Neville. *John Foxe the Martyrologist: His Life and Times.* London: Dr. Williams's Trust, 1975, 24 p.

Lecture on Foxe's life, personality, and contribution to Tudor historical and ecclesiastical literature.

Wooden, Warren W. "John Foxe's 'Book of Martyrs' and the Child Reader." In his *Children's Literature of the English Renaissance,* pp. 73-78. Lexington: University Press of Kentucky, 1986.

Assesses Foxe's tailoring of certain aspects of *Actes and Monuments* for an audience of young children.

Yates, Frances. "Foxe as Propagandist." *Encounter* XXVII, No. 4 (October 1966): 78-86.

Argues that an "imperial theme" is repeated throughout *Actes and Monuments,* historically justifying sixteenth-century Tudor monarchical reforms.

Frederick the Great

1712-1786

(Born and acceded to the throne as Frederick II) Prussian monarch, essayist, and poet.

Often viewed as a militaristic dictator who inspired a cult of German aggression that lasted from his day through the mid-twentieth century, Frederick the Great is also recognized as one of the most influential eighteenth-century cultivators of literature and the sciences. Dedicated to the pursuit of academic and literary excellence, he revived the Academy of Sciences and Letters upon his accession to the throne of Prussia by inviting eminent scholars of the time to reside in Berlin as members of this intellectual society. Hailed as the long-awaited "philosopher king" by Voltaire and other philosophes, he sought to implement the principles of enlightened despotism, which resulted in the separation of the monarchy from the church. This gave him the freedom as king to institute widespread reforms of the Prussian legal system and consequently liberalize the laws regarding censorship and torture. Toleration of previously persecuted religious groups reached a new peak. According to Pierre Gaxotte, "Frederick abstracted the idea of monarchy from its religious background. He deprived it of its character as a divine institution: this was the intellectual revolution, this was the revolution of principle which enraptured the philosophers who devoted both life and talents to a struggle against 'the Beast'."

Eldest son of Frederick William I of Prussia and Princess Sophie Dorothea of Hanover, Frederick was born on 12 January 1712. The history of his childhood and youth is painfully intriguing. Frederick William was a firm-willed leader and strict disciplinarian whose two great passions were ensuring the strength of the Hohenzollern line and building an army of exceptionally tall troops. When young Frederick evidenced an enthusiasm for literature and music, shunning all military displays and administrative duties, conflict erupted between father and son. Frederick William was physically and emotionally abusive to every member of his family, but Frederick suffered the cruelest treatment. On several recorded occasions the king nearly killed his heir during fits of rage. The friction between the two was brought to a head in 1730 when the heir apparent attempted to escape to England with his friend, Jean Hermann von Katte. The plan was thwarted, however, and the two were arrested and imprisoned. There is conflicting information regarding the trial and punishment of the pair, but many historians claim that eventually, through a series of threats, Frederick William ensured a death sentence for Katte and also declared that the prince was to be executed. According to some historians, it was only the intervention of Charles VI of Austria that prevented the beheading of Frederick. On the morning of 5 November 1730, the prince was made to watch from his cell window as Katte was beheaded before his eyes. This act appeared to have broken Frederick's independent streak; he applied himself to learning administrative procedure and military strategy under a strict regimen at the fortress at Cüstrin. After satisfying Frederick William that he was a capable

leader, Frederick was appointed commander of an infantry regiment in 1732.

The following year, Frederick married Elisabeth Christine of Brunswick-Bevern, according to his father's wishes. While the marriage was fairly cordial, most historians agree that it was never close; even when living in the same palace each followed his own interests, and after Frederick William's death Elisabeth Christine remained in Berlin while the new king chose to divide his time between Potsdam and Ruppin. The couple had no children, so Frederick named his nephew, Frederick William, as his successor.

Frederick William I died on 31 May 1740, and Frederick II acceded to the throne of Prussia. In October of the same year, Charles VI of Austria, last male heir of the Hapsburgs, died, giving the Prussian monarch his first opportunity to test his military and political strength. Prussia had already accepted the Pragmatic Sanction, created by Charles to ensure that his daughter, Maria Theresa, should succeed him to the throne of Austria. Frederick decided that he needed more territory full of resources to consolidate the scattered Prussian lands in order to protect his people from a Russian invasion. Frederick also believed that he held inherited rights to the region of Silesia, a province rich in farmland, minerals, and numerous cloth mills. Ignoring the pledge to honor the Pragmatic Sanction, Frederick invaded Silesia, beginning the War of the Austrian Succession. When this conflict ended in 1748, Silesia was in Prussian hands. This gross breach of promise established Frederick's status as a military leader, but also rendered his diplomatic word untrustworthy among the other powers of Europe.

Concerned that Austria would attempt to regain Silesia, Frederick grew alarmed when, in 1756, France joined Austria, Russia, and Saxony to form a quadruple diplomatic and military alliance. Believing his nation in danger, Frederick attacked Austria, which he considered the weakest of the powers surrounding him. This effectively brought all of Europe into the Seven Years' War. The war dragged on, and by 1762 the Prussian army was exhausted and state bankruptcy was imminent. But Frederick's fortunes were restored when the insane Peter III took the Russian throne following the death of Empress Elizabeth in 1762; an ardent admirer of Frederick, he drew Russia out of the war, giving Frederick the opportunity to end hostilities with Austria under the Treaty of Hubertusberg, signed in 1763. For the remainder of his reign, Frederick concentrated on the reformation of the Prussian legal system, supporting literature and music, and continuing the production of his own writings. He died on 17 August 1786, at his beloved Sans-Souci, the palace that he had designed himself.

Throughout his life, Frederick was a lover of literature. He wrote poems on all occasions, and it was his wish to have a French mentor of supreme intellect and reputation. Enter Voltaire, recognized as one of the most important writers of the period. Frederick began corresponding with the celebrated author in 1736, thus beginning a turbulent relationship that lasted over 40 years. The early years were marked by profuse flattery; Frederick desired educated criticism of his works, and Voltaire wanted royal protection (when needed) and patronage. Accordingly, Voltaire reveals in his *Memoirs* (1759) that "I gave him [Frederick] all my reasons in writing, and thus composed a manual of rhetoric and poetry for his use; he made good use of it, and his genius served him even better than my lessons." In 1739, Frederick wrote to Voltaire that he was planning a refutation of Niccolò Machiavelli's *The Prince*. In this piece the king would argue against the maxims set down in the 1513 treatise, claiming that its doctrines opposed the humanitarian ideals of the Enlightenment. Voltaire agreed to write an introduction to and edit the work, and it was published anonymously in 1740 under the title *L'Anti-Macchiavel.* Frederick was displeased with this first edition, claiming that Voltaire had been too liberal with his editing duties and had deleted passages integral to understanding of the work. This marked the beginning of the near-constant feuding between the two men that was to dominate the later years of their long relationship. As Gaxotte relates: "[Voltaire] was supposed to have said of the King, with a sneer, 'That man is Caesar and a Grub Street hack.' Another time when a raw poet was proffering him his works, a second pile of verses was handed to him: 'There,' said he, 'the King has sent me his dirty linen to wash, yours must wait.' Frederick, referring to his guest, was supposed to have calmed his impatient followers with these words: 'Let be, I need him for another year at the outside; first squeeze the orange, then throw away the

peel.' " The mock-friendship of the two reached its low point in 1753, when Frederick had Voltaire imprisoned for a time; yet it continued until Voltaire's death in 1778. According to historians, Frederick's behavior following the publication of *L'Anti-Macchiavel* initiated the decay of the formerly enthusiastic friendship. Voltaire was incredulous that Frederick could hypocritically adopt a set of ideals in his writings and then act in direct opposition to them: denouncing Machiavelli's theories and then, shortly afterward, ignoring a treaty and invading Silesia. A great deal of later criticism of this work focused on its historical relevance to Frederick's career, paying particular attention to this discrepancy.

Another of Frederick's published works was a long overview of the first five years of his reign, *Histoire de mon temps.* This effort focuses specifically on political and military issues and was not published until after Frederick's death. As Robert Asprey comments, it was "neither memoir nor commentary. . . . It was an ambitious project that did not altogether match its author's pretensions, but it offers valuable insights into his thinking." While *Histoire de mon temps* had dealt with a portion of Frederick's own time as ruler of Prussia, his next work was a study of the reigns of several of his predecessors. Published in 1751, *Mémoires pour servir à l'histoire de la maison de Brandebourg* reveals a mature Frederick who understood the intricacies and responsibilities of his position and wanted fervently to meet all expectations. Some critics feel that this work suffers because of a lack of immediacy and intimacy, but most agree that, when read in conjunction with *Histoire de mon temps,* it offers a more complete understanding of Frederick, monarch and man. Due in large part to their comprehensive nature, these three works are generally considered by literary scholars and critics to be the most significant of Frederick's enormous quantity of writings.

Frederick the Great is one of the most recognizable names in world history, and this fact lends interest to his works. Most commonly known as a military aggressor, and occasionally as an ideological forefather of Adolph Hitler, Frederick the writer is often neglected. An uneven collection of poetry and essays on political and military matters, Frederick's writings offer the reader the opportunity to perceive the beliefs behind the man; the genteel, lettered aspect of a despot.

PRINCIPAL WORKS

*L'Anti-Macchiavel (essay) 1740
   [*An Examination of Machiavel's 'Prince,'* 1741]
Les principes généraux de la guerre (essay) 1748
Mémoirs pour servir à l'histoire de la maison de Brandebourg (history) 1750
   [*Memoirs of the House of Brandenburg,* 1751]
"*L'Art de la Guerre*" (poetry) 1751
   ["The Art of War," 1816]
Œuvres du Philosophe de Sans-souci. 4 vols. (prose) 1750-62
De la Littérature allemande, des défauts qu'on peut lui reprocher, quelles en son les causes, et par quels moyens on peut les corriger (essay) 1780
†Histoire de mon temps (memoirs) 1788

Oeuvres de Frédéric le Grand. 31 vols. (essays, poetry, prose) 1846-57

*This work is also known as *Réfutation du Prince de Machiavel.*

†This work was written from 1742 to 1746 and published posthumously.

Voltaire   (letter date 1750)

[*Voltaire was a major figure of the French Enlightenment. His philosophical writings gained him the attention of Frederick the Great, who invited Voltaire to Potsdam. In the following excerpt from a 1750 letter to the Count d'Argental, Voltaire offers criticism of the king's writing style.*]

He has more imagination than I, but I have more method. I profit by the confidence he has in me by telling him the truth more boldly than I would tell it to Marmontel, to d'Arnaud, or to my niece. He does not send me to the mines because I criticize his verses; he thanks me, he corrects them, and always with improvement. He has wrote some which are admirable. His prose equals his verse, at least; but here he goes too quickly. There were some good courtiers who told him that all was perfect; but what is perfect, is that he believes me rather than his flatterers—he loves, he perceives the truth. We must not say *Caesar est supra grammaticam.* Caesar wrote as he fought. Frederick plays upon the flute like *Blavet;* why should he not write like our best authours? This occupation is worth more than gaming or hunting. His ***History of Brandenburg*** will be a masterpiece when he has revised it with care; but has a king the time for such cares? a king who, alone, governs a vast monarchy?—aye; 'tis this confounds me; I am in a perpetual surprize. And you must know, moreover, that he is the best of men—or I am the most foolish. Philosophy has made his character even more perfect. He has corrected himself, as he corrects his works. (pp. 202-03)

> *Voltaire, in an excerpt from a letter to the Count d'Argental in 1750, in* Voltaire *by C. E. Vulliamy, Dodd, Mead & Company, 1930, pp. 202-03.*

Thomas Babington Macaulay   (essay date 1842)

[*Macaulay was an English statesman and historian. In the following excerpt, originally published in the April 1842 issue of the* Edinburgh Review, *he finds fault with the writing style of Frederick and comments on the stormy relationship between the King of Prussia and Voltaire.*]

As the highest human compositions to which [Frederic the Great] had access were those of the French writers, it is not strange that his admiration for those writers should have been unbounded. His ambitious and eager temper early prompted him to imitate what he admired. The wish, perhaps, dearest to his heart was, that he might rank among the masters of French rhetoric and poetry. He wrote prose and verse as indefatigibly as if he had been a starving hack of Cave or Osborn; but Nature, which had bestowed on him, in a large measure, the talents of a cap-

tain and of an administrator, had withheld from him those higher and rarer gifts, without which industry labours in vain to produce immortal eloquence and song. And, indeed, had he been blessed with more imagination, wit, and fertility of thought, than he appears to have had, he would still have been subject to one great disadvantage, which would, in all probability, have forever prevented him from taking a high place among men of letters. He had not the full command of any language. There was no machine of thought which he could employ with perfect ease, confidence, and freedom. He had German enough to scold his servants, or to give the word of command to his grenadiers; but his grammar and pronunciation were extremely bad. He found it difficult to make out the meaning even of the simplest German poetry. On one occasion a version of Racine's *Iphigénie* was read to him. He held the French original in his hand; but was forced to own that, even with such help, he could not understand the translation. Yet, though he had neglected his mother tongue in order to bestow all his attention on French, his French was, after all, the French of a foreigner. It was necessary for him to have always at his beck some men of letters from Paris to point out the solecisms and false rhymes of which, to the last, he was frequently guilty. Even had he possessed the poetic faculty, of which, as far as we can judge, he was utterly destitute, the want of a language would have prevented him from being a great poet. No noble work of imagination, as far as we recollect, was ever composed by any man, except in a dialect which he had learned without remembering how or when, and which he had spoken with perfect ease before he had every analysed its structure. Romans of great abilities wrote Greek verses; but how many of those verses have deserved to live? Many men of eminent genius have, in modern times, written Latin poems; but, as far as we are aware, none of those poems, not even Milton's, can be ranked in the first class of art, or even very high in the second. It is not strange, therefore, that, in the French verses of Frederic, we can find nothing beyond the reach of any man of good parts and industry, nothing above the level of Newdigate and Seatonian poetry. His best pieces may perhaps rank with the worst in Dodsley's collection. In history, he succeeded better. We do not, indeed, find, in any of his voluminous ***Memoirs,*** either deep reflection or vivid painting. But the narrative is distinguished by clearness, conciseness, good sense, and a certain air of truth and simplicity, which is singularly graceful in a man who, having done great things, sits down to relate them. On the whole, however, none of his writings are so agreeable to us as his ***Letters,*** particularly those which are written with earnestness, and are not embroidered with verses.

It is not strange that a young man devoted to literature, and acquainted only with the literature of France, should have looked with profound veneration on the genius of Voltaire. "A man who has never seen the sun," says Calderon, in one of his charming comedies, "cannot be blamed for thinking that no glory can exceed that of the moon. A man who has seen neither moon nor sun, cannot be blamed for talking of the unrivalled brightness of the morning star." Had Frederick been able to read Homer and Milton or even Virgil and Tasso, his admiration of the *Henriade* would prove that he was utterly destitute of the power of discerning what is excellent in art. Had he been familiar with Sophocles or Shakspere, we should have expected him to appreciate *Zaire* most justly. Had he been able to study Thucydides and Tacitus in the original Greek and Latin, he would have known that there were heights in the eloquence of history far beyond the reach of the author of the *Life of Charles the Twelfth.* But the finest heroic poem, several of the most powerful tragedies, and the most brilliant and picturesque historical work that Frederick had ever read, were Voltaire's. Such high and various excellence moved the young Prince almost to adoration. The opinions of Voltaire on religious and philosophical questions had not yet been fully exhibited to the public. At a later period, when an exile from his country, and at open war with the Church, he spoke out. But when Frederic was at Rheinsberg, Voltaire was still a courtier; and, though he could not always curb his petulant wit, he had as yet published nothing that could exclude him from Versailles, and little that a divine of the mild and generous school of Grotius and Tillotson might not read with pleasure. In the *Henriade,* in *Zaire,* and in *Alzire,* Christian piety is exhibited in the most amiable form; and, some years after the period of which we are writing, a Pope condescended to accept the dedication of *Mahomet.* The real sentiments of the poet, however, might be clearly perceived by a keen eye through the decent disguise with which he veiled them, and could not escape the sagacity of Frederic, who held similar opinions, and had been accustomed to practise similar dissimulation.

The Prince wrote to his idol in the style of a worshipper; and Voltaire replied with exquisite grace and address. A correspondence followed, which may be studied with advantage by those who wish to become proficient in the ignoble art of flattery. No man ever paid compliments better than Voltaire. His sweetest confectionery had always a delicate, yet stimulating flavour, which was delightful to palates wearied by the coarse preparations of inferior artists. It was only from his hand that so much sugar could be swallowed without making the swallower sick. Copies of verses, writing-desks, trinkets of amber, were exchanged between the friends. Frederick confided his writings to Voltaire; and Voltaire applauded, as if Frederic had been Racine and Bossuet in one. One of his Royal Highness's performances was a refutation of Machiavelli. Voltaire undertook to convey it to the press. It was entitled the **Anti-Machiavel,** and was an edifying homily against rapacity, perfidy, arbitrary government, unjust war, in short, against almost everything for which its author is now remembered among men. (pp. 892-94)

But we should very imperfectly describe the state of Frederic's mind, if we left out of view the laughable peculiarities which contrasted so singularly with the gravity, energy, and harshness of his character. . . . In the midst of all the great King's calamities, his passion for writing indifferent poetry grew stronger and stronger. Enemies all round him, despair in his heart, pills of corrosive sublimate hidden in his clothes, he poured forth hundreds upon hundreds of lines, hateful to gods and men, the insipid dregs of Voltaire's Hippocrene, the faint echo of the lyre of Chaulieu. It is amusing to compare what he did during the last months of 1757, with what he wrote during the same time. It may be doubted whether any equal portion of the life of Hannibal, of Cæsar, or of Napoleon, will bear a comparison with that short period, the most brilliant in the history of Prussia and of Frederic. Yet at this very time the scanty leisure of the illustrious warrior was employed in producing odes and epistles, a little better than Cibber's,

and a little worse than Hayley's. Here and there a manly sentiment which deserves to be in prose makes its appearance in company with Prometheus and Orpheus, Elysium and Acheron, the Plaintive Philomel, the poppies of Morpheus, and all the other frippery which, like a robe tossed by a proud beauty to her waiting woman, has long been contemptuously abandoned by genius to mediocrity. We hardly know any instance of the strength and weakness of human nature so striking, and so grotesque, as the character of this haughty, vigilant, resolute, sagacious blue-stocking, half Mithridates and half Trissotin, bearing up against a world in arms, with an ounce of poison in one pocket and a quire of bad verses in the other.

Frederic had some time before made advances towards a reconciliation with Voltaire; and some civil letters had passed between them. After the battle of Kolin their epistolary intercourse became, at least in seeming, friendly and confidential. We do not know any collection of Letters which throws so much light on the darkest and most intricate parts of human nature, as the correspondence of these strange beings after they had exchanged forgiveness. Both felt that the quarrel had lowered them in the public estimation. They admired each other. They stood in need of each other. The great King wished to be handed down to posterity by the great Writer. The great Writer felt himself exalted by the homage of the great King. Yet the wounds which they had inflicted on each other were too deep to be effaced, or even perfectly healed. Not only did the scars remain; the sore places often festered and bled afresh. The letters consisted for the most part of compliments, thanks, offers of service, assurances of attachment. But if anything brought back to Frederic's recollection the cunning and mischievous pranks by which Voltaire had provoked him, some expression of contempt and displeasure broke forth in the midst of eulogy. It was much worse when anything recalled to the mind of Voltaire the outrages which he and his kinswoman had suffered at Frankfort. All at once his flowing panegyric was turned into invective. "Remember how you behaved to me. For your sake I have lost the favour of my native King. For your sake I am an exile from my country. I loved you. I trusted myself to you. I had no wish but to end my life in your service. And what was my reward? Stripped of all that you had bestowed on me, the key, the order, the pension, I was forced to fly from your territories. I was haunted as if I had been a deserter from your grenadiers. I was arrested, insulted, plundered. My niece was dragged through the mud of Frankfort by your soldiers, as if she had been some wretched follower of your camp. You have great talents. You have good qualities. But you have one odious vice. You delight in the abasement of your fellow-creatures. You have brought disgrace on the name of philosopher. You have given some colour to the slanders of the bigots, who say that no confidence can be placed in the justice or humanity of those who reject the Christian faith." Then the King answers, with less heat but equal severity—"You know that you behaved shamefully in Prussia. It was well for you that you had to deal with a man so indulgent to the infirmities of genius as I am. You richly deserved to see the inside of a dungeon. Your talents are not more widely known than your faithlessness and your malevolence. The grave itself is no asylum from your spite. Maupertuis is dead; but you still go on calumniating and deriding him, as if you had not made him miserable enough while he was living. Let us have no more of this. And, above all, let me hear no more of your niece. I am sick to death of her name. I can bear with your faults for the sake of your merits; but she has not written *Mahomet* or *Merope*."

An explosion of this kind, it might be supposed, would necessarily put an end to all amicable communication. But it was not so. After every outbreak of ill humour this extraordinary pair became more loving than before, and exchanged compliments and assurances of mutual regard with a wonderful air of sincerity. (pp. 928-30)

> *Thomas Babington Macaulay, "Frederick the Great," in* Great Short Biographies of the World: A Collection of Short Biographies, Literary Portraits, and Memoirs Chosen from the Literatures of the Ancient and Modern World, *edited by Barrett H. Clark, Robert M. McBride & Company, 1929, pp. 886-942.*

Charles Whibley   (essay date 1917)

[*Whibley was an English historian and literary critic. In the excerpt below, he comments on Frederick's distorted view of his own literary abilities and the friendship between the king and Voltaire.*]

Despite all his professions of modesty, Frederick was one who could brook neither criticism nor contradiction. Unwilling to meet anybody on terms of equality, the victim always of a sudden caprice, he would set a slight arrogance against the fidelity of a lifetime, and dismiss the oldest of his servants for some paltry, inadequate reason. He lived and died friendless, because he did not understand that friendship meant giving as well as taking, and he was content, for the most part, to be surrounded by sycophants, whom he was free to insult either in speech or in the practical jokes of a rare brutality. His passion to be thought a poet made the task of conciliation far more difficult. He allowed himself the freedom of criticism; he allowed it to no other, and the unfortunate Catt was compelled to hear more bad verse and to praise it than ever before had fallen to the lot of man to hear and praise. Nor was Frederick ever tired of repeating such scraps of flattery as Voltaire had thrown to him. With an ingenuous pride he declared that Voltaire had commended the doggerel in which he describes a trip to Strasburg. 'You see from this approbation,' said he, 'that I am not such a bad poet as you might believe.' One day, as a concession of kindness, he read to Catt some passages of his poem on war. 'Nothing is so difficult,' said he by way of comment, 'as to make interesting the precepts of an art, whatever it is. Voltaire assured me that I had succeeded.' And of course there was no more to be said. Nor did he understand that any higher reward could be given to those who served him than a few verses from the royal hand. These verses were to Frederick what the iron cross is to William II. They were distributed so lavishly, that they were very soon cheapened. He even paid his bets at times in the same currency. When the Empress Elizabeth was lying ill, he made a wager with Catt about her death. The winner was to pay at his discretion. 'I shall make you a present if I lose,' said the King, 'and you what you please if I win.' The Empress died, and all that the wretched Catt got for his present was an epitaph in verse! He owned to himself that 'this was getting off rather lightly for an affair of this importance,' but he was too full of joy to hint, even in jest, that the discretion was

very slight. After all, had he not shown a proper admiration of the King's poetry, his tenure of office would have been brief indeed. And who would withhold praise when Voltaire had given it—Voltaire who, in the King's esteem, was a poet who never flattered, and who was very severe in this matter?

So Frederick, by a double error, was sure that, as he had the poet's virtues, *teste* Voltaire, so he had not the poet's vices. 'Do not think,' he adjured the innocent Catt, 'that I attach any great value to what I do! Not at all; if I have the passion for authorship, I have assuredly not its arrogance.' Thus he deceived himself always. If ever there was a man who believed that he, the King, could do no wrong, it was Frederick. He drank in praise with all the eagerness of a thirsty soul. He knew that his verses were masterpieces all, because he had written them. He insisted fiercely upon having his own opinion supported. He was, indeed, an actor, who acted even to himself. He lived as on parade, though none were present save Catt. The slovenliness of his person, the squalor of his dress, were mere versions of his pride. He was, so to say, a dandy upside down, who knew that the Spanish snuff which besmirched his face would call attention to him more loudly than delicately perfumed ruffles. But his own verses apart, he seems to have been honest in his love of letters. Though he had but a smattering of Latin, though he made childish mistakes in spelling, though he had all the faults of the late-learner, he surrendered himself whole-heartedly to poetry and eloquence. 'With them,' he said, 'I am never bored, and I can do without anybody.' It gave him a manifest pleasure to read aloud—a pleasure which explains the necessity of the listening Catt. He adored declamation, both for its own sake and as a proper accompaniment of kingship. 'Why should I not declaim,' he asks, 'when all Nature declaims?' Thus he deceived himself, not seeing that Nature has never declaimed, except in the eighteenth century, when she was neatly clipped and barbered out of herself after the fashion of Potsdam.

Nevertheless, he carried such baggage on his campaigns as no other soldier has carried. Wherever he went, in the field or at winter quarters, a library went with him. 'Lucretius,' he boasted, 'is my breviary.' Bacon, Cæsar, Tacitus, Plutarch, Cicero—these are some of the authors who never left him, and from whom he drew the lessons of his life and trade. Overcome by grief at the death of his sister, the Margravine of Baireuth, he turned for consolation to the funeral orations of Bossuet and Fléchier, and as he was always intent to imitate what he read, to play 'the sedulous ape,' in fact, he produced himself a funeral oration upon Matthew Reinhart, master shoemaker, and presented it with pomp and circumstance to Catt. 'That, my dear sir,' said he, 'is the fruit of the readings which astonished you. Bossuet and Fléchier made funeral orations to celebrate the life and death of illustrious men. As for me, not worthy to untie the latchet of the shoes of these great preachers, I have written the funeral praise of a poor shoemaker, who by his abilities, his virtues, and his piety, was more deserving than kings and princes to pass to the most distant posterity.' There in a few phrases you have the real Frederick, a monarch histrionic and insincere, with a rare talent for the trite and a constant love for copybook headings. Fresh from the study of the masterpieces of literature, he could yet murmur in the ear of Catt such maxims as these: 'Mortals, employ your time,' or 'The fate of a king is very sad'; and then perplex his hearer by putting the question: 'Do you know any prince who is as much of a pedagogue as I am?'

But he cherished one admiration always, which was sincere and complete—an admiration of Racine. The works of that great poet could never leave him, because they were stored in his brain. Not only did he know his plays by heart; he showed at times a clear appreciation of their qualities. Indeed, it was Racine, not Lucretius, who was his true breviary. In *Athalie* or *Britannicus* or *Mithridate* he sought pleasure in his happiest, encouragement in his darkest, moments. 'To rest ourselves,' says he one day, 'let us read the tragedy of *Britannicus;* and read it he did, with a pinch of snuff at the end of every act, until his reading was interrupted by the tears which flowed easily at the royal command. He looked even upon defeat through the words of Racine, which were for him at once a consolation and a commentary. After the disaster which befell him at Hochkirchen, Catt faced him 'in a state of extreme emotion.' He need not have yielded to his excitement. The King came up to him 'with a rather open air,' and in a quiet voice repeated these lines from *Mithridate:*

> Enfin, après un an, tu me revois, Arbate;
> Non plus, comme autrefois, cet heureux Mithridate
> Qui, de *Vienne* toujours balançant le destin,
> Tenais entr'elle et moi l'univers incertain:
> Je suis vaincu. *Daunus* a saisi l'avantage
> D'une nuit qui laissait peu de place au courage.

Did ever a beaten soldier accept disaster in so strange a spirit of literary detachment? Frederick was, as he said, 'a poor, conquered man,' and he fell to declaiming the lines of Racine, like the consummate actor that he was. So eager was he to speak and to recite that he left the poor Catt no chance of saying a word; and presently, in forgetfulness of literature, undid his collar, and pulled out the famous box of gold, containing eighteen opium pills, which he deemed 'sufficient to take him to that dark bourne whence we do not return.' But he was soon back at Racine, invoking God in the words of the poet:

> Daigne, daigne, mon Dieu, sur *Kaunitz* et sur elle
> Répandre cet esprit d'imprudence et d'erreur,
> De la chute des rois funeste avant-coureur.

And truly it was not upon the golden box but upon the golden-tongued poet that he relied for help and succour.

But there was one poet who exerted a deeper influence upon Frederick even than Racine, and that poet was Voltaire. Voltaire, indeed, was his constant obsession. In whatever he did or wrote his first thought was: What will Voltaire think of it? A word of praise thrown to him by the great writer was as precious to him as victory itself. He treasured piously the poor little verses of his own composing, upon which Voltaire had smiled approval. Before the great man's name he abased himself—to others. 'Voltaire has a genius for verse,' he told Catt; 'and I haven't. I am only a poor dilettante, who has great need of indulgence.' Had another dared to hint so much, he would have chased him from his presence with insult. 'By heavens! a letter from Voltaire,' he exclaims one day, 'what a lucky day!' And when he had read the letter, 'you must acknowledge, my dear sir,' he insisted to Catt, 'that this Voltaire writes like the angels.' And thereafter he expresses his gratitude, like the humblest of mortals. 'This Voltaire is

admirable,' he confesses, 'to think of me, and with his letters and works to feed my mind, which has great need of good nourishment.' When he was in high spirits he would brag that he had acted the part of critic to the great man himself. 'How many times,' he recalls with rapture, 'have I not corrected Voltaire himself, yes, Voltaire.' But while he admitted Voltaire's genius, he never ceased to revile Voltaire the man. His royal vanity had been wounded too deeply for forgetfulness, though his royal taste sternly refused to be perverted. He was never tired of talking about Voltaire's 'diabolical character.' 'When you see him quiet,' says he, 'be assured that he is meditating some wickedness. His great pleasure is to set people at loggerheads, and, when he has succeeded, he roars with laughter, jumps and skips about. "The scamps," he says, with the laugh of a satyr, "the scamps; that is the way to treat them."'

At Catt's first appearance, Frederick had summed up for his profit the opinion which he held of Voltaire. 'The world has produced no finer genius than Voltaire,' he admitted; 'but I despise him supremely, because he is not upright. If he had been, what a superiority he would have had over everything that exists!' That Frederick should reproach Voltaire on a matter of conduct is supremely ridiculous, and the reproach puts in question once more the relationship which existed between the poet and the King. Truly the poet has the better of it in morals as in genius. It is Voltaire who is cast for the *beau rôle* in the tragicomedy enacted at Potsdam and elsewhere. Manifestly superior in wit and intellect, Voltaire was superior also in the justice of his cause. The friendship which linked the two men together was a friendship of hostility. They thought that they could not live apart from one another, and they knew that they could not live together amicably. And it was Voltaire who gave far more than he received, who had every claim to regard himself as the victim of autocratic impertinence. In the poor little squabble with Maupertuis, Voltaire was in the right of it, and he covered his assailant with the ridicule which he deserved. Though Frederick desired ardently to be thought a poet, he could not enjoy the equal company of poets, because he never forgot that he was crowned. The friendship which he offered Voltaire was tainted at its source. Here is Voltaire's 'little dictionary as used by kings':

> My *friend* means my *slave.*
> My *dear friend* means *I am more than indifferent to you.*
> For *I will make you happy,* read *I will endure you as long as I have use for you.*
> *Sup with me to-night* means *I will mock at you this evening.*

It is clear, then, that Voltaire had no illusions, even though pride had blinded the eyes of Frederick. As he said himself, if he had no sceptre he had a pen, which he proceeded to use, dipped in gall. And then came the supreme insult of Frankfort, where Voltaire was arrested and imprisoned. Never did a 'crowned philosopher' so wickedly forget his dignity as when Frederick ordered a clumsy clown called Freytag to maltreat the poet, who had been his guest. That Voltaire should never have forgiven the affront was right and proper. That he gave too violent expression to his malice is perhaps true. But for the King to shed tears over the moral delinquency of a great man, whom he thought he could use as he presently used Catt, and whom he exposed to the insolence of a petty official, was a sublime act of hypocrisy. After all, the tragi-comedy could have but one ending. There is even a kind of pathos in the King's lifelong submission to the poet, whose presence he wished for and could not endure. And Voltaire may surely be forgiven if he laughed at the memory of the poor verses and poorer philosophy, upon which he had once smiled with interested benignity. (pp. 111-20)

> Charles Whibley, "The Crowned Philosopher," in his Political Portraits, Macmillan and Co., Limited, 1917, pp. 107-29.

Wyndham Lewis   (essay date 1927)

[*Lewis was an English novelist who, with T. S. Eliot, Ezra Pound, and T. E. Hulme, was instrumental in establishing the anti-Romantic movement in literature during the first decades of the twentieth century. In the excerpt below, he comments upon Frederick's Anti-Machiavel and reign as king.*]

In the evolution of the machiavellian type under modern conditions Frederick the Great furnishes in a sense the furthest perfection that the type has yet attained. And he started most characteristically by writing a book against Machiavelli, in which he expressed his unlimited disgust and horror at this poisonous tract shamelessly extolling "rapacity, perfidy, arbitrary government, unjust wars." These are the things, of course, for which subsequently Frederick became famous: for his greatness rests on the fact that he was warlike, treacherous, tyrannic, and extremely stingy at the same time as extremely ostentatious; building a palace, but refusing to have any ministers because he did not wish to have to pay their salaries, and conducting all the work of government himself with the help of a groom, who read all his letters in the small hours of the morning, and brought what he considered it necessary Frederick should see at seven o'clock in a big bundle under his arm.

There is no more curious fact in history than this warlike despot beginning his career with such a book as his **Anti-Machiavel.** Voltaire expressed the belief at a later date that it was written in good faith, that Frederick was not intelligent enough for it to have been otherwise. In his *Memoirs* we read as follows:

> The King of Prussia, some time before the death of his father, took it into his head to write a book against the principles of Machiavelli. If Machiavelli had had a prince for disciple, the first thing he would have recommended him to do would have been to write a book against machiavellism!

This is such an extremely obvious truth that, seeing what Frederick's subsequent career was like, it is very difficult to believe that his book against Machiavelli did not indeed prove that he had become perhaps that philosopher's most brilliant disciple. Macaulay also draws attention to this very obvious conclusion, that at least it was strange that this king should have written a refutation of Machiavelli while he was himself an illustrious practitioner of all the machiavellisms he inveighed against. (pp. 102-03)

> Wyndham Lewis, "Frederick the Great," in his The Lion and the Fox: The Role of the Hero in the Plays of Shakespeare, 1927. Reprint by Methuen & Co. Ltd., 1955, pp. 98-105.

Pierre Gaxotte   (essay date 1942)

[*Gaxotte was a French journalist and historian who wrote extensively on the age of the Enlightenment and Frederick II. In the excerpt below, he comments on the literary style of Frederick and his Aristotle/Alexander type of relationship with Voltaire.*]

Frederick was a man of letters and a Frenchman. All his life he was tormented by an itch for writing; all his life he overcame his nervousness by versifying. He was ambitious to bestow upon posterity some great poetical work in the style of Voltaire, a tragedy like *Œdipe* or an epic poem like the *Henriade*. In 1738 he started a three-act play in verse, the plot of which was drawn from the *Aeneid* and was to show "the tender and constant friendship of Nisus and Euryalus"; but he did not feel sure of his powers and abandoned it for a refutation of Machiavelli. With the utmost politeness he repeated that it was impossible to imitate Voltaire without actually being Voltaire himself; he begged pardon that he, "the humble frog of the sacred vale," should dare to croak in the presence of the god. But he did not only ask for French lessons from the Apollo of Cirey, he also tried to extract from him some of the secrets of his art and a spark of his genius. It was true he had Jordan as corrector in chief at Rheinsberg:

> Jordan, my critic-secretary,
> You who pursue, with nose as wary
> As bloodhound's, those mistakes of mine,
> For pity's sake deign to refine,
> Erase, efface, correct, transcribe. . . .

However, he wanted more than a Jordan. In nearly all his letters to Voltaire he asked for criticism and advice. Voltaire would have much preferred to confine himself to compliments, for he was more interested in the Prince than in the scholar. Why not admit once and for all that Frederick's nurse had been Madame de Sévigné and his tutor Bossuet, that he spoke French excellently, and that he did their language a great honor by making use of it? But the Prince was insistent, and from time to time the master complied: "I find no mistakes of language in the 'Epistle to Pesne' and it breathes with good taste throughout. It is the painter of Reason writing to the common painter. I can assure you, Sire, that the last six lines, for example, are a masterpiece:

> Oh, be a traitor to designs of haloed saints,
> And subjects more polite portray now with thy paints;
> Sketch us the simple graces Amaryllis had,
> The forest with its nymphs, the Graces three half-clad;
> Keep always in thy mind that 'tis by love alone
> That thy art so divine saw the light and has grown.

That is how Despréaux would have written them. You will take all this for flattery. You are quite capable, Sire, of not knowing your own worth."

"The **'Epistle to Monsieur Duhan'** is indeed worthy of you; it comes from a sublime spirit and a grateful heart. . . . On reading all that you have deigned to send me I perceive that there is not a single false thought in it. I find from time to time some small mistakes of language, which it is hardly possible to avoid; now, for example, how could you have guessed that 'nourricier' is a word of three syllables and not one of four? That 'aient' has one syllable and not two? The Epistle that you have deigned to address to me, Sire, is a fine justification of poetry and a great encouragement to me. . . . Should I dare to scrutinize this Epistle (and I must as I owe you the truth), I would tell you, Sire, that 'trompette' does not rhyme with 'tête,' because 'tête' has a long vowel sound and 'pette' a short one, and rhyme should please the ear and not the eye. 'Défaites' for the same reason does not rhyme with 'Conquêtes'; 'quê'tes' is long, 'faites' is short. If anyone saw my letters he would say, 'There is a complete pedant who goes and talks of long and short vowels to a prince full of genius.' But the Prince deigns to descend to every detail. When this Prince reviews his regiment, he examines the equipment of the individual soldier. The great man neglects nothing, he will win battles when he has a chance, he will confirm the happiness of his subjects with the same hand with which he turns eternal truth into rhymes." Could a lesson be given more gracefully?

To encourage Frederick to condense his style his teacher found a charming phrase, "this gold filigree will have greater weight and brilliance if made more compact." To teach him what a poetic image was he amused himself by transposing a phrase of simple prose into verse, and once again it was a compliment, "There is in the world a young and virtuous prince who is full of talents and loathes envy and fanaticism." Another time he rewrote one of the odes he had been sent, following the ideas closely but expressing them in different ways.

In spite of all this trouble Frederick was never satisfied. He compared himself to those folk who are dependent on charity and always ask for more. What Voltaire did not tell him he determined to discover on his own by making a careful study of the great writers. He learned Boileau and Racine by heart; when a new edition of the *Henriade* came out he compared the two texts and tried to discover the reason for each change. At last he ventured to put before his master some reflections of his own on the aptness of certain words, and the master replied that he had taken his advice in correcting the fourth and fifth acts of *Mérope*. What a triumph!

Before getting to know Voltaire Frederick wrote a cumbrous, slow, unpolished French. The refugees who surrounded him had brought with them the language of a certain date—deprived as it was of continuous impetus from daily life, this language preserved ways of speech which had fallen into disuse, and on the other hand it lacked those which had been brought in imperceptibly by common usage and were the most typical expressions of the spirit of the language. Finally by dint of preaching before mixed audiences pastors had weighed it down with Germanisms which went against its natural development and marked the sect, the conventicle. By hard work Frederick learned the French of France and the French of his own times, mobile, subtle, precise, admirably suitable for analysis and for the play of ideas. Frederick's verses were not good, it is true; some of them were even execrable. Anyhow, the thing they were most lacking in was poetry. But his prose was excellent and the moment soon came when he grasped and handled it in such a way that he could really hold his own against Voltaire. And then, in the long run, he ended by rhyming pretty well. Great lyrical effusions were never to be in his line. He tried to be witty and was merely insipid, to be gallant and was coarse. But he also had some lucky finds, verses which stick in the memory quite apart from the rest. The didactic poem, the paro-

dy, the elegant display of rhetoric, the chaffing letter—such were the styles which suited his talents. Alas, "there is nothing that can restrain a poet in his rage!" Sometimes he was ashamed of sending so many bloated alexandrines to Cirey. "It is the invasion of the Goths!" cried he in mock dismay. Then he sighed a little sadly on rereading his verses:

> The good are those which are hard for me,
> As for the bad they cost me naught.

> (pp. 141-44)

Pierre Gaxotte, in his Frederick the Great, *translated by R. A. Bell, Yale University Press, 1942, 420 p.*

Friedrich Gundolf   (essay date 1947)

[*Gundolf was a German translator and literary historian. In the excerpt below, he examines the literary influences on and style of* De la Litterature allemande *and Frederick's dissatisfaction with the cultural life of Prussia.*]

Among the European rulers who were really rulers (rather than schoolmasters, such as James I of England, or bluestockings, such as Christina of Sweden) Frederick remains a miracle of true thoughtfulness—which goes hand in hand with his prodigious activity—by the number, variety, and keenness of his contemplative writings. (I purposely wish to exclude here the political and historical documents, such as inscriptions, decrees, and memorabilia, which great men of action have used since classical times to further their purposes and immortalize their actions.) In classical history Frederick found a model for his contemplative bent in Marcus Aurelius, and he was more than pleased to be compared to this saintly and energetic stoic; probably even secretly proud that, all things considered, he had achieved even more in word and deed. (In the East, we know of at least one sage, in the true sense of the word, who was an absolute prince: the grand mogul Akbar, a genuine philosopher-king, who made that proverbial glory come true.) By contrast to the Latins or the Anglo-Saxons, whose thinking was almost always propelled or carried along by will power, the Germans—especially since Luther—permitted almost all their values, including the very core of politics, to be shaped by teachers rather than by men of action—a vexation or an embarrassment to the few geniuses of power to appear among them. For this reason, even an intelligent and aware prince of Prussia found it easier to focus the still unformed, unstructured, and vacillating fantasies of his imagination upon an intellectual rather than a warlike ideal. His horrible childhood, in which he was so often constricted by the demands of the state, as well as the only happy period of his life, the leisure of Rheinsberg where he basked in the rays of that European universal genius, Voltaire (and Voltaire, for all his restlessness, was a contemplative mind, and as such the most persuasive master of the word since Petrarch, or at least Erasmus, for cosmopolitan amateurs of culture), were bound to make the reputation of a *bel esprit* appear in a rather more seductive light than the bloodstained and dirty toil of a conqueror. Like every true man of action, Frederick realized his strength and, above all, his true vocation only when called upon to act. Unable to remain idle, he filled his period of waiting communing with the Muses who were to teach him, the disciple of Voltaire and of the Enlightenment, how to be a king when the time came, or else with accumulating and choosing useful and agreeable knowledge whose eventual application he could not know, but only dimly foresee. But crown prince and pupil of the Muses, "effeminate fellow" and secretly demonic spirit—the fact is that in the decisive period of his coming to maturity in a barbaric land with a veneer of French civilization, as he and Voltaire saw it, Frederick found no other outlet for his supple intelligence than writing. Even in those dreams where he saw himself as Alexander or Caesar, he knew that it would be incumbent upon him to bring the civilization of Pericles, of the Medici, and of the Sun-King to the presumptive field of his future activity by means of the humanities. The talent—part blessing and part curse—of his entire life, which made him the very personification of the enlightened despot, namely, the will to do everything himself, even the things that cannot be done but must be allowed to happen, his own creativity, and the school of Voltaire, misled him into writing his French book about German literature soon after he had accomplished his first successful acts of statesmanship. His twin motive was the literary pretension of a German outsider and the desire of a presumably expert lord and master to chart the course of his cultural policies. This book remains a monument to his all-encompassing paternalism even where he was stricken with blindness; it is also a warning that even the most talented minds have little of value to contribute outside the sphere of their expertise. Napoleon's judgment of Shakespeare and Bismarck's rather average taste in novels do not debase these eminent men, both of whom had a certain literary culture—any more than Plato's *Laws* taint the vision of the state of this seer of ideas. But where complete faith in authority exists or a hero-worship that swallows everything emanating from the revered authority, it is only proper to speak of such folly. The greatest men are not those who err least, but those who, without impairing their stature, may, indeed must, commit the greatest errors.

The essay on German literature in its published form is a work of Frederick's old age, published by the splenetic, sick, and world-famous king, who, as a conscientious administrator, felt duty-bound to give his attention not only to welfare institutions, military security, and armaments for his state, but also to cultural matters; and who did so with almost inhuman single-mindedness, with his customary ponderous swiftness and spasmodic buoyancy. It has been thought that the contents of this book date back a generation, and that they were originally meant as a reply of the young king to a book by a Baron Bielfield, *Über die Fortschritte der Deutschen in Künsten und schönen Wissenschaften* (1752). Bielfeld was a French-educated nobleman who had the patriotic ambition of showing that from the time of Opitz to Gottsched the dominant influence of various foreign powers had brought about a flourishing of the German language, and his book is interspersed with proud or wistful references to the foreign models that were supposedly surpassed. Frederick the Great had already attempted an outline of European intellectual history in the **Histoire de mon temps** (1746), a work he revised stylistically and completed or amended in 1775. From the Rheinsberg period until his death his general conception of world history remained virtually unchanged, though the fundamental ideas he had formed in conversation with Voltaire were justly strengthened and

clarified by Voltaire's great study, the *Essai sur les moeurs* (1756). What did change was the *mood* in which Frederick later expounded the ideas he had formed early in life. (Development, becoming, metamorphosis of inner resources, complete change of form, as we understand and conceive them since Herder, especially through the example of Goethe's entire life and work—these are things that no author of the Enlightenment of the seventeenth and eighteenth century has experienced—"experienced" to be taken in the double sense of "lived" and "perceived." In this area as in others, Lessing, with his *Erziehung des Menschengeschlechts,* surpassed the Enlightenment, binding though its tenets still were for him. Beyond English and French aims and ends [beyond the *Esprit des lois* and the *Essai sur les moeurs,* beyond Bossuet's *Discours sur l'histoire universelle* and the Church Fathers upon whom the latter was based, and who felt that the course of history is fixed by a divine *telos,* a guiding Providence] Lessing believed in the possibility of perfecting the human race by virtue of an unexplained, unrevealed, but ultimately explicable *sense* of existence.) As for Frederick, it is true that he amplified and clarified his thinking over the years and placed the emphasis differently, but he did not develop it, as a bud becomes fruit. For the understanding of his books as intellectual, rather than diplomatic documents, it is highly important to know in which decade they appeared. The unquestioning enthusiasm of this sensitive and impetuous crown prince and victorious conqueror who shared the faith in progress of the Enlightenment—despite the Voltairean pretense of doubt and scorn and despite the profound knowledge of human nature of this man of action—had yielded after the Seven Years' War to disappointment, disgust, and misanthropy. Yet his fundamental commitment to action, to service to the state, to power, the mainspring of all his activities, was salvaged from his youth and remained unbroken. He clung almost desperately to the principles he had learned, because he considered them the imperatives of his existence, hardened as he was in defiant fatalism, in ascetic terror, as if he were to lose the meaning of his life if he were to demur against the dictates of fate. What had been deeply pleasurable to him in his youth now congealed into joyless duty, hollow-eyed defiance in the face of all odds, and the sublime obstinancy of a man possessed who has become impervious to any soothing illusion. Napoleon once called himself the slave of implacable necessity, of the nature of things, comparing himself to the menace of divine scourges, to the horsemen of the Apocalypse, or to the makers of a new age. *Der alte Fritz* was filled with a similar grating arrogance, but his arrogance lacked this swelling pride, this love of adventure, this sense of awe; and rather than enjoying his own exuberance—in the joyful or in the sinister sense of the word—he delighted in the severity of the inescapable servitude of which he would be both victim and creator. In later years, he incorporated even his pleasures into that servitude; what he had cultivated in his youth because it had challenged the surplus of his imperious powers he later pressed into the routine of the wise tyrant. The *bel esprit* of Rheinsberg is to the philosopher of Sans Souci what the horseman is to the animal trainer, what the strong man is to the prize fighter: in his calling he possesses, uses, and enjoys the same skills he once practiced for pleasure, and replaces his lost cheerfulness with the dignity of responsibility. Not that Frederick lost all cheerfulness, any more than his wit and humor. But all the subsidiary powers of his genius were now made to serve his main endeavor, to which he devoted himself without the heedless gaiety of youthful self-sufficiency. His very fame now became prestige; it was no longer a brilliant image, but a menacing means of power.

If the reply to Bielfeld about German literature was probably an act of patronizing benevolence, an equally important ingredient of the publication of 1780 was without doubt the despot's irritation with the increasing noisiness of the awakening German literature. Its best-known passages about Goethe's Götz von Berlichingen and about Shakespeare's aberrations were only outbursts of a vexation that gives a sour tone to the entire book; but this vexation almost certainly had not disfigured the earlier version, any more than the outbursts. Even in Frederick's conversations with Gottsched and Gellert during the Seven Years' War we sense a certain good-natured condescension of a soldier for these more or less respectable schoolmasters, we see the mocking but friendly smile of one who deals with the cultural concerns of these advocates of the Muses amidst the thunder of great events; but we also sense that, for all his blindness, he still is willing to listen and to understand. If Gottsched bored him, if Gellert elicited only a lukewarm response, they did not anger him as the unfolding of the mysteriously budding creativity of

Lieutenant Hans Hermann von Katte—Frederick's confidant and friend as a young man.

great German poetry angered him. Under his eyes in Berlin, Doebbelin's German actors had performed *Romeo and Juliet, Othello, Macbeth, Hamlet,* and *King Lear* between 1768 and 1778. They had used Schröder's questionable prose-versions, and while these gave no idea of Shakespeare the poet, that magician of the word and interpreter of the heart, they made a great deal of noise on the stage. Of all this, the king heard no more than the noise, and all the things that spoke, indeed screamed, against his classicistic attitudes and desires; in short, the barbaric ranting of a mob. That his taste was violated in this fashion, in his own capital, in his very presence, made him angry, because he was in charge but obviously not in control of literature. He did not even take the trouble to distinguish between Goethe's *Götz,* a German innovation, and Schröder's Shakespeare-libretti. For him it was sufficient that these fellows neglected the three unities and talked some noisy gibberish unfit for polite society. For it was the transgression of the law that struck the giver and servant of the law; and, being an old man, he did not listen to the source of the transgression.

As enlightened ruler he renounced the use of political terror and assumed the attitude of the scornful but magnanimous misanthropist who ordered hostile pamphlets to be posted lower so that they could be easily read, and permitted shoemakers' apprentices to laugh at him. Authoritarian suppression would have been beneath the dignity of a crowned sage. This is why his royal displeasure in cultural matters was incorporated into his essay *De la Littérature allemande.* As a patron and founder, he did not want to censor, but hoped to improve. As an adherent of the Enlightenment he had faith—as a matter of duty rather than of joyful optimism—in the healing power of the right teaching and, possibly even more than thirty years before, in the impression of his public admonitions. But by now, these were much less attuned to the situation, and therefore much less effective, than they would have been in 1750. At that time, German literature—despite Luther's and Hutten's use of language, despite the church hymns, despite Grimmelshausen, Gryphius, Fleming, and others—could not compete with the universality of the rest of European literature. Even Klopstock's Odes and his *Messias* promised, rather than produced, a flourishing of literature. But when Frederick actually launched his broadside, he laid hands on two creative geniuses—one dead and one living—who made the whole classicistic splendor look pale: Shakespeare and Goethe. Now he looked foolish not because he lacked a sense of the future, but because of the backwardness of old age. But his book, by its very wrongheadedness, which was part and parcel of Frederick's powerful mind, is emblematic of the tragic struggle of the greatest German king against the powers of the German spirit. Let us briefly interpret it as the scene of the battle between the old Enlightenment and the new feeling for Nature.

Even the genre of Frederick's manifesto is part of an intellectual tradition that—at least since the days of Romanticism, and that means since Herder's revelations about individual creativity, about the Bible, Shakespeare, Homer—is as alien to us as the belief that the citing of a Biblical passage, a verse of Virgil, or a sentence of Aristotle constitutes conclusive proof. Our reverence for Dante's works is in no way impaired by the fact that his rationalistic apparatus no longer has any power over us; his visions will endure because he was the first to receive them, and receive them in this form. Frederick's political, military, and autobiographical writings affect us in a similar way, because his extraordinary personality still pervades them beyond their specific concern and beyond their message. Ever since Plato (who was the first to attempt the intellectual fixation of the visions of the mind, that is, who wanted to make them binding by way of proofs, and tried to change insight into knowledge by arranging and ordering it) all ages have considered certain intellectual operations as leading to conclusive proof and have attempted to press their indispensable values, needs, dreams, and ideals—whatever their origin—upon their respective audiences by supposedly conclusive chains of reasoning. For Plato, mathematics was already a temptation, and his great new system of proofs, dialectics, was mathematics in a different guise applied to a different intellectual field. The age of science to which Frederick's teacher, Voltaire, felt indebted for his entire intellectual formation—an age that had freed itself of the absolute rule of scholasticism, of the magic hold of the Bible, and of the Aristotelian straitjacket—this age of experiment, of eager receptivity, of Kepler, Galileo, Newton, Leibniz, and Descartes, had also attempted to "prove" the universe mathematically, i.e., to apprehend it through its laws. To subordinate God's commands, as they are given by theology, to mathematics, or to replace them by mathematically controllable proofs, as Spinoza did, was the main endeavor of the European thinkers in whose milieu Voltaire ripened to his mission. The quasi-superstitious reverence of his acute mind for everything that can withstand the scrutiny of mathematics, the pious belief that everything that can be understood can be proven, the distrust for mystery and the unprovable forces of change, the determination to transform cognition into processes of reasoning, the desire to shape even taste, pleasure, and enjoyment by teachable precedents, namely rules and models—all of these questionable virtues of the cleverest of Frenchmen, Frederick had learned to admire, love, and practice. But since he had less leisure for cultural endeavors than Voltaire, since his conscience as a ruler was a heavier responsibility, and since he had found (or created) a more severe master in the Prussian state than Voltaire had found in the French-European society of cultural amateurs, he expressed his cultural opinions, wherever they seemed binding to him, in much stricter rules and regulations than Voltaire needed to do in his pliable and adaptable curiosity for everything. Constantly standing at the periphery of dangerous activity, Frederick's imperious mind could never afford the leisure or the mood of enchanting play, whether it be for studying or for applying what he had learned. And he never placed delight above usefulness, power, and effectiveness.

Although he was no schoolmaster, the lack of vivacity, of playfulness and lightness makes even his treatise on taste very different from Voltaire's scholarly essays. The king did not feel that delight with his own intelligence, his own capability, his own knowledge, which not only excuses but positively glorifies Voltaire's famous vanity. If he sometimes displayed unnecessary bits of information, he did not wear them, as Voltaire did, like so many alluring ornaments, but rather used them as imposing uniform accessories, as parts of his professional attire. Witness his passing stab at the German pedants who, when discussing the customary law of Osnabrück, brought in the Egyptian system of law, or his scathing remarks about the genealogists and

chronologists. Such sallies expressed genuine scorn, but they also implied: I know about such esoteric matters. He was rather like a general who dutifully wears his decorations at a parade, but at times also displays them on social occasions in order to show that he has earned such honors. Frederick had derived almost all of his factual knowledge, all of his value-judgments and his entire outlook in matters of cultural history and natural philosophy from Voltaire's works. Once they were formed, he used them either summarily, like a commanding officer who is perpetually pressed for time, or else in a humorously clumsy way like an old soldier who is making light conversation with the ladies and brings in some civilian knowledge as if he did not really care about it. This was the case when he discussed Spinoza's system or the barbaric dialect of the Italians at the time of Charlemagne. They were meant as perfectly serious disciplinary hints to the German intellectuals, but they were also an authoritarian, yet somewhat bashful, display of knowledge. These discrepancies were aggravated not only by Frederick's character—for he had taken up writing from inclination and from a sense of duty and was determined to achieve victory and influence in this domain as in all others, and as soon as possible—but also by his lack of intimacy with the language in which he was writing, despite his artistic use of it, and despite the fact that he was Voltaire's pupil. Unlike Voltaire himself, he had not assimilated the treasures of learning with natural facility, but had appropriated them. He marshaled knowledge as possessor, not as an inventor or even a finder. In cultural matters a comparison with Voltaire makes him look like a good pupil next to an authoritative teacher—powerful master though he was in all matters of war and statecraft, even where he was mistaken. His French didactic prose is devoid of that mystery which gives such a vibrant quality to the language of Voltaire and Diderot, and in Germany to Lessing's didactic works. Frederick's French prose not only lacks all the qualitites of warmth and intimacy but even—and this is difficult to prove but can be sensed—the tension between its German content and the foreign medium of expression. I am thinking of passages like the following:

> As I said before: The first step is to perfect the language. It must be planed and polished, must be shaped by skillful hands. Clarity is the first rule for all those who want to write or speak, since they must illustrate their thoughts and express their ideas in words.

This passage has neither Gallic charm nor Germanic force; it is neither witty small talk nor imperious bidding, but a limp juxtaposition of occasional thoughts and professional concern in which the author's power falters, even though he thinks correctly and writes clearly. This discordance becomes even more obvious if we read similar passages in the writings of Prince de Ligne. Ligne was not nearly as great a man as Frederick, but he was more gifted because he felt the awakening of his language while his spirit was still slumbering and because he had been awakened in it and by it, never completely leaving the depths from which it came to him. Frederick the Great tried in vain to escape from his all too Prussian youth by entering into the spirit of the French-European language. He faltered in his flight whenever he strayed too far from his German deeds and from his French diversions, and especially when he tried to legislate German acts of the spirit with French words and the earnestness of a Prussian king.

Just as Frederick the Great wrote treatises containing operational and tactical rules in order to instruct his generals and make his presence felt even in their planning, so his essay on German literature was first of all meant to convey a few orders to some of his more independent subjects whom he could not reach directly. In this case, he had to state the reasons for his orders more explicitly than in his own specialty, for in literature his will was not as binding as on the battlefield. Here, it was not a matter of citing a few specific cases to which the writer could promptly apply prescribed rules, but of creating a fixed frame of mind capable of accommodating the constantly evolving demands of history and of the future. He therefore prefaced the main body of the essay, concerning the teaching of the various kinds of writing, with a historical survey of the important European literatures, or rather with an exposé of the universally recognized ideals and models of literature. In his enumeration of the four Golden Ages—that of Pericles and Alexander, that of Cicero and Augustus, that of the Medici, and that of Louis XIV—he adopted the order given by Voltaire in the introduction to the *Siècle de Louis XIV*. This book had established the first progressive sequence in the history of civilizations other than divine scripture, and had gone beyond the annals, chronicles, memoirs, and collections of documents that had hitherto satisfied the historian. Frederick did not actually copy Voltaire, but he owed the very direction of his endeavors, his views of what is important and what is not, and his perspective of time to the man whose words had first taught him to see the mind as a historical phenomenon. It is true that he praised the Greeks for their harmonious language, which he considered an essential advantage and one of the reasons for the beauty of their literature. This observation did not come from Voltaire but from his own struggle with his unwieldy native language. Later too, in the prescriptive part of his essay, he placed special emphasis on enhancing the harmony of the German language and proposed summary remedies, such as vocalic endings. This is a child's rationalistic belief that anything that has been observed can be reproduced. In a similar vein Napoleon on St. Helena expressed regret that he had not promulgated an edict abolishing all exceptions to the rules of the French language. (Frederick's endeavors in this direction were later to elicit many angry and sarcastic comments from Klopstock, who felt prompted to exalt the German language above the Greek.) One of Frederick's Voltairean—i.e., antitheological and antimetaphysical—statements stressed the fact that Greek literature was created by poets; and poets, he said, are professional experts in *tours heureux* and *expressions pittoresques,* so that their followers learned to express themselves with *grâce, politesse,* and *décence.* The Romans, he continued, had long been occupied with war and had been more concerned with force than with style. Having come to *lettres* only after the fall of Carthage at the time of Scipio, they reached the maturity of their language and style only with Cicero and Augustus. Basing his judgment on Cicero's treatises and example books, *De claris oratoribus* and *De oratore* (probably in the translation of Bourgoin de Villefore) and on his rhetoric, *Ad Herennium,* Frederick accepted a few good orators between Scipio and Augustus—the Gracchi, Antonius, and Crassus. For Frederick, Greek and Latin were either naturally harmonious or refined by their poetic origins, and he

contrasted them with the unharmonious sounds of northern Europe and its civilization. Without prejudice but in favor of his nation and his region, he had to admit that the language of Germany was still half-barbaric, split into many dialects, disorganized, and rough. He pointed out that the languages of classical antiquity were unified since earliest times and very widely used, so that their expressions, sanctioned by great artists, could by tacit agreement become universal conventions and consequently binding, unquestioned, and appealing. Here is the concept of classicism in two aspects: positively, as a choice of rules and models that must be followed; negatively, as the despot's desire to eliminate any particularities of language, speech, or expression which might obstruct or confuse his long-range planning. It shows the same tyrannical mentality that was betrayed by Napoleon's misgivings about exceptions, or by Caesar's advice to writers to avoid obsolete or unusual expressions, as a ship's captain avoids shoals.

In Frederick's case, this attitude was expressed by the statement that in German the meaning of the sentence is drowned in irrelevant bombast. The lack of measure, of directness, of tautness—in short, of classical order, irritated him, and he sought to justify his irritation by a survey of German literature where he looked in vain for a German Homer, Virgil, Anacreon, Horace, Demosthenes, Cicero, Thucydides, or Livy. It may be significant that he did not include Aeschylus and Pindar, but it may also be that he would have thought it pedantic to enumerate the entire canon. He also mentioned Catullus, Tibullus, and Propertius, and placed them above Gessner's much-praised idylls. Phaedrus and Aesop he compared to Gellert, the only German to have done well in the minor genre of the fable. He considered Canitz a weak imitator of Horace—no doubt he knew him better as a councilor of his royal grandfather. But he did say that some of the German philosophers can be placed side by side with the famous ancients—perhaps even above them. He was thinking of Leibniz and Wolff, but as mathematicians rather than as stylists. In his opinion German historians hardly existed; such as they were, Mascov was probably the most thorough. He considered Quandt of Königsberg, the court preacher, as the only German to have shown his compatriots what harmonious language was; but since no one responded, he had abandoned his efforts. The praise was a personal gesture of the royal patron; it hardly constitutes the canonization of a German classic. Frederick also praised Christian Ewald von Kleist's anonymously published *Frühling* for achieving harmonious sound by using a mixture of dactylics and spondaics. Here, too, there is an element of royal patronage for an officer whose cultural endeavors did not escape the perceptive attention of this keen administrator. In a later section of the essay, where he made his literary survey, Frederick no longer remembered the name of Kleist. But he probably felt that the absence of rhyme made German poetry sound classical and that this form should be imitated. Klopstock, the restorer of the soaring verse of antiquity, was altogether rejected, because Frederick did not like his theological subject matter. He also condemned the entire German theater as stilted, vulgar, and contrary to the rules. The only exception was Ayrenhoff's *Postzug* (1769), which he considered a good exposition of mores.

After this interlude—sitting in judgment of contemporary German literature, and allowing for extenuating, that is, outside circumstances—Frederick returned to the development of harmonious sound and comprehension and looked to other countries that could furnish models and rules—France and Italy. His guiding idea was the "Renaissance" of the arts and sciences after the dark Middle Ages. Here, too, he tried to find models and to establish their recognizable preconditions as well as their teachable rules. The House of Este, Lorenzo de' Medici, and Leo X, he said, had become patrons of the arts and sciences in Italy, while Germany was rent asunder as the theologians set man against man, and while France was kept from cultivating the arts by the Wars of the League, until Richelieu renewed the cultural plans of Francis I and Louis XIV brought them to fruition.

In content and style the next section of Frederick's essay is the most original. Here the author, out of the full measure of his own experiences and insights, evokes the suffering of Germany during the wars that were fought while France was recovering and flourishing. Here the elegant disquisitions of the *bel esprit* almost yield to a prophetic rumble, and the horrors he has seen in the Seven Years' War vibrate in his lament about the Thirty Years' War. The pupil of Voltaire cries out against the famous French cardinal and the glorious monarch who had been so highly exalted by his teacher, and, almost despite himself, the isolated German breaks out of the sociable European. Here is the same intense anger that had exploded at the triumph of Rossbach and Zorndorf, groaned at the defeats of Kunersdorf and Colin. Here the bitter wit of a man who suffers with the world and hates mankind comes through in passages that are reminiscent of Shakespeare's *Timon* rather than of Voltaire's *Candide.*

> While the Turks besieged Vienna and Melac laid waste to the Palatinate, while houses and towns burned to ashes, while undisciplined mercenaries desecrated even the preserve of death and tore dead emperors from their tombs to rob them of their miserable coverings, while desperate mothers fled with their starving children from the ruins of their country—were sonnets to be composed and epigrams wrought in Vienna or Mannheim?

In this act of accusation Frederick justified German barbarism not only as a king who years for a Golden Age of his own, but also as a German patriot whose heart is filled with the terrible fate of his people and as a victim of the foreign language which keeps him from expressing his deepest feelings. Beneath the glittering surface of such sentences with their vain figures of speech, there is a dark undertone reaching down to the ancient depths that have yielded Walter's warning calls, Hutten's curses, Grimmelshausen's apocalyptic sighs, Lessing's heart-sick wit, and even the resigned muttering of Goethe's old age—all the desperate or pleading responses of full hearts to the empty quarreling of the Germans, all the sorrow of these fertile minds in the face of the madness of our fellow men. The encompassing pity for the misery of the world, a feeling every deep person will at some time experience so sharply that he must weep at his own role in that foolish comedy, came to this great German when he looked at his state. He did not wish to serve it in blind submission and knew that he must remain a free and watchful individual; as a victorious ruler he wondered for whom he had gained his victories.

From this involuntary outburst Frederick returned to his arbitrary prescriptions or palliatives, not without propagandistic pride in his own achievements for the state and praise for his wise ancestors. They, he wrote, have cultivated the fields, rebuilt the devastated homes, replenished a new generation, cleared the wilderness.

> Population growth has stimulated manufacture, and the luxury trade—ruinous to a small state, but beneficial for the circulation of money in a large state—is growing apace. . . . Germany is rich in flourishing towns and cities, and the ancient Hyrcanian forest is covered with extraordinary edifices. . . . German manliness has not only repaired old damages, but is preparing for new growth. . . . No longer is the citizen languishing in misery. . . . Parents are able to educate their children without sinking into debt. . . . Generous competition is springing up everywhere. . . . Losses and missed opportunities are being compensated by hard work. . . . Indigenous style is aspiring to national glory.

In this paragraph, Frederick is more than a *bel esprit.* He is speaking as a political economist and theorist, as a progressive master of reality who, like blind old Faust, deadens his ever-present anxiety by unrelenting activity. And because of this activity, we must honor his anxiety, just as the dramatist shows Faust's end and his ultimate endeavors only as a parable, as an emblem for the flight of a driven mind from endless, futile brooding into useful work in the necessarily limited Here and Now.

After these digressions of a proud or despairing statesman, Frederick, the literary amateur, devoted his attention to the improvement of the German language. With good common sense, he advanced perfectly plausible rules—which were invalidated only by the fact that they were unnecessary. For Frederick knew German literature no better than the citizens of Schilda knew the nature and properties of the crab, of light, and of salt; and he gave advice without the slightest knowledge of the case. Here are some of his suggestions: the German language should be planed and polished, but its unwieldiness should not be replaced with shallowness. The great ancients, who sharpen the sense of language and promote clarity of thinking and knowledge, should be studied in the text, but in a critical fashion, without blind idolatry—especially since the highly praised neighboring nations were already beginning to rest on their laurels. Teachers should be made to give up their stiff, schoolmasterly attitude and their bombast (some samples are included) and brought to simple logic through mathematics. The German language should be tightened, clarified, and strengthened by translations of the best classics, such as Thucydides, Xenophon, the *Poetics* of Aristotle, Demosthenes, Epictetus, Marcus Aurelius, Caesar, Sallust, Tacitus, and the *Ars Poetica* of Horace; among the French, La Rochefoucauld's *Réflexions ou sentences et maximes morales,* Montesquieu's *Lettres persanes* and his *Esprit des lois.* The German language should take on vocalic endings, vulgar expressions should be expunged, clear logic should be taught to teachers and students from the works of Christian Wolff or from Bayle. Being a contemporary of Lessing and sharing his views on this point, Frederick denied the possibility of creating geniuses, but like Lessing, he wanted to train already existing talents and to rectify current abuses by models and rules. As models for the writing of history—its style, not its content—he once again recommended Livy, Sallust,

Tacitus, as well as Bossuet, Vertot, and Robertson's *Charles V.* Thus he made a rapid survey of all areas of literature, pointing to this and that with his cane; but I shall pass over the details.

The truly remarkable thing in all of this is Frederick's imperious attitude. He found time to catalogue all the intellectual treasures of the world with a view to what he considered their proper use for civilization. Even when acting as a literary critic, he could not help treating autonomous intellectual creations as he would treat matters of high policy. This is reminiscent of Napoleon, who once ordered a French scholar to report to him, by the day after next, what Kant's teaching was all about. Frederick's straightforwardness was disturbed, more than Napoleon's, by the pretension of a *bel esprit* which he could not quite suppress, and by the smug attitude of a patron and connoisseur of the arts. Yet in the end the imperious ruler reappears beneath the rustling of paper, the resigned and pessimistic sage beneath the commanding tone. It is as the prophet of a German Golden Age which he was not to experience that Frederick sadly takes leave, a Moses who sees the Promised Land without entering it. And as we put aside this depressing essay we see him in the same awesome light that envelops his entire life, cold and clear, sallow as the evening—the German outsider who asks his tormented "why" and holds fast to his obstinate "nevertheless." (pp. 200-17)

> *Friedrich Gundolf, "Frederick's Essay on German Literature," translated by Elborg Forster, in* Frederick the Great: A Profile, *edited by Peter Paret, Hill and Wang, 1972, pp. 199-217.*

G. P. Gooch   (essay date 1947)

[*Gooch was an English historian. In the following excerpt he discusses Frederick's historical writings, concentrating on* Histoire de Brandebourg *and* Histoire de mon temps, *outlining much of their content. Occasional commentary is also given on the writing style of the works and their reliability as historical documents.*]

Frederick's political and military achievements loom so large that his place among German historians is often overlooked. He is the only modern sovereign to have written detailed accounts of all his campaigns and to have discussed with considerable candor the most controversial features of his policy. His historical writings are much more than an elaborate apologia or a colorless record of events. No one can doubt his inner truthfulness, declares Koser, the oracle of Frederician studies. Impartial he was not, for no maker of history can be impersonal and detached in dealing with his own performances; but he was franker than Cæsar or Napoleon. His books are full of factual errors, for he complained of a bad memory; he trusted too much to his bulletins from the seat of war, often written at top speed and compiled with a purpose, and to the dispatches of his diplomatists, frequently based on imperfect knowledge. Yet no student of his character would care to exchange the portraits, personal touches, and reflections for a more accurate and lifeless survey.

His first historical venture, ***Mémoires pour servir à l'histoire de la Maison de Brandebourg***, published in 1751, embodies material from the archives, and the later chapters are of great interest. After the First Silesian War he compiled a narrative of the struggle, nearly all of which has disappeared. After the second he revised the work, added a long Introduction, and called the whole work ***Histoire de Brandebourg.*** Only the former was given to the public, "for the use of our youth," after portions had been read to the Academy of Sciences as they were completed. The voluminous ***Histoire de mon temps,*** written at long intervals and covering the whole reign, was not intended for publication during his life. The purpose of the history of the Hohenzollerns is explained in three preliminary dissertations. The Dedicatory Letter to his brother and heir August Wilhelm declares that he has concealed nothing. "I have shown the princes of your house as they were. The same brush that has painted the civil and military virtues of the Great Elector has indicated the failings of the first King of Prussia. I have risen above all prejudice. I have regarded princes, kings, relatives as ordinary men. Far from being led astray by my position, far from idolizing my ancestors, I have boldly censured their vices, for vice should find no refuge on the throne. I have praised virtue wherever I found it, guarding myself against the enthusiasm it inspires so that truth pure and simple may prevail." After this parade of impartiality it is curious to find an extravagant eulogy of the mediocre heir. His brother, he declares, was worthy of his rank. He had coolly exposed his life in battle and subordinated all private interest to the welfare of the state. The gentleness and humanity of his character were the pledges of the happiness of his future subjects. The Preface and the Preliminary Discourse explain that, despite the multitude of historical works on the market, the story of Brandenburg had never been told. Having discovered this vacuum, he had endeavored to fill it. He had utilized the royal archives and had tried to tell the truth. The study of history was as useful to subjects as to princes. He had dealt very briefly with the early rulers, for the story only became important with John Sigismund, in whose reign East Prussia and Cleves were added to the state. The Thirty Years' War could not be ignored by any German or Prussian, for it continued to color affairs. The design of the house of Austria to establish despotism in the Empire had failed, and the Peace of Westphalia had restored the equilibrium between the ambition of the emperors and the Electoral College.

After a few arid pages on the first two centuries of Hohenzollern rule the historian begins his detailed narrative with George William, whose reign he describes as the darkest chapter in the annals of the dynasty. "His territories were desolated during the Thirty Years' War, the deep traces of which are visible to this day. All the plagues in the world broke over this ill-fated Electorate—a prince incapable of governing, a traitor for his Minister, a war or rather a universal cataclysm, invasion by both friendly and enemy troops equally thievish and barbarous like waves driven by a tempest, and finally pestilence that completed the desolation." The sack of Magdeburg, vividly described, was merely the worst of many horrors. "Though George William cannot be held responsible for all the misfortunes which befell his territories, his mistakes were numerous and costly. He trusted Schwartzenberg, who betrayed him. An army of 20,000 men, which he could well afford, might have defended the country against violations of its neutrality. It would have secured him consideration from the Emperor, and he could have chosen whether to become the ally or the enemy of the Swedes instead of being the slave of the first comer. His weakness only left him a choice of errors. He had to choose between the imperialists and the Swedes, and his allies were always his masters. Sometimes, outraged by the harshness of Ferdinand II, he threw himself in despair into the arms of Gustavus Adolphus; at other times, exasperated by the projects of Oxenstierna, he sought aid from the court of Vienna. Powerless and in continual uncertainty, he always changed over to the strongest side; but he could offer too little to his allies to secure their protection against their common enemies." The sorry plight of his great-great-grandfather, faithfully described except in the presentation of Schwartzenberg as a traitor, confirmed the author's conviction that his country must be strong if it was not once again to be trampled underfoot.

Frederick William I, deservedly known as the Great Elector, is acclaimed in terms of rapturous enthusiasm. "Heaven had fashioned him expressly to establish order in a state that the misrule of the preceding reign had thrown into total confusion, to be the defender and restorer of his country, the honor and glory of his nation. The merit of a great King was mated to the humble fortune of an Elector. Rising above his rank, he displayed the virtues of a steadfast soul and a superior genius, sometimes tempering his heroism with prudence, sometimes giving rein to that noble enthusiasm which compels admiration. He restored his old possessions by his wisdom and secured new ones by his policy. He formed his projects and carried them out himself. His good faith enabled him to aid his allies, his valor to defend his peoples. He confronted unexpected emergencies with improvised resources. In little things and important affairs he always appeared equally great. The rout of the Swedes at Fehrbellin was the crowning triumph of the reign. He was praised by his enemies and blessed by his subjects, and his posterity dates the rise of the house of Brandenburg from this memorable day."

The defender of his peoples in time of war was inspired by the noble ambition to be their father in the years of peace. "He succored the families ruined by the enemy; he rebuilt the ruined villages; deserts were transformed into cultivated fields; forests gave place to villages; settlers pastured their flocks in places that the ravages of war had made the lair of wild beasts; agriculture was encouraged; every day witnessed fresh initiatives. He was even greater in his goodness and devotion to the public weal than in his military prowess. His skillful policy led him to do everything at the right moment and in the way essential to success. Valor makes great heroes, humanity good princes." The virtues of "the oracle of Germany" were recognized far and wide. "His fine qualities earned the confidence of his neighbors. His sense of equity made him a sort of supreme tribunal beyond his frontiers, whence he judged or reconciled sovereigns and kings." His welcome to twenty thousand industrious Huguenots was among the wisest of his acts; religious toleration became one of the principles of the state.

The chapter closes with a burst of trumpets. "He had all the qualities that make great men, and providence furnished him with occasions to display them. He was prudent when youth is usually sowing its wild oats. He fought only to defend his country and to succor his allies. He was cautious and wise, which made him a great statesman; laborious and humane, which made him a good prince. Insensible to the seductions of love, his only weakness was for his wife. If he loved wine and company, he set limits to his indulgence. His warm temper sometimes led to a loss of self-control; but if he failed to repress the first emotion, he always mastered the second, and his heart fully repaired the mistakes of his hot blood. Prosperity could not intoxicate him nor misfortune break his spirit. Magnanimous, polite, generous, humane, he never belied his character. He became the restorer and defender of his country, the founder of the power of Brandenburg, the arbiter of his equals, the honor of his nation. In a word, his life is his eulogy." He surpassed Louis XIV, not in power or splendor, but in merit, for he had no Richelieu to smooth his path, no Condé to win him victories, no Colbert or Louvois to aid his efforts. Thus, while the greatness of the one was the work of his ministers and generals, the heroism of the other was entirely his own. His supreme merit was that he never despaired of his country. Both broke treaties, the one from ambition, the other by necessity. "Powerful princes escape from bondage to their word by their own free will; weak ones fail in their engagements because they are often overpowered by circumstances. Both met death stoically, ruling till the end, directing their last thoughts to their people, whom they confided to their successors with paternal tenderness." Here is something more than a chapter in the history of the author's country: it is his ideal of statecraft. In these glowing pages we sense his desire that history would offer a similar tribute to himself.

Everything, we are expected to realize, depends on the character and capacity of the ruler. The chronicler finds little to admire in Frederick, the first King, least of all his subservience to the house of Austria. His Francophobia was nourished by Vienna with the legend of universal monarchy in which half of Europe was persuaded to believe. "Germany was often impressed by this puerile trick and plunged into wars that did not concern her. Yet, as the best blades become blunt, these arguments insensibly lost their hold, and the German princes realized that, if despotism threatened, it was not that of Louis XIV. Caring more for show than for realities, more for ceremonial than for business, more for flattery than for truth, he coveted the royal title won by the Elector of Saxony in Poland and the Prince of Orange in England. Yet the crown, desired for reasons of vanity, turned out to be a political master-stroke, which rescued the house of Brandenburg from the yoke imposed by Austria on all the German princes. I have acquired a title, he seemed to say to his successors; show yourselves worthy of it. I have laid the foundations of your greatness; it is for you to complete the work." To secure the prize he employed every kind of intrigue and was prepared for almost any sacrifice. The support of the Emperor, which was essential, was bought by the return of the Circle of Schwiebus and by the provision of troops in the conflict with France. His promotion found many critics within and beyond his frontiers, and cost the lives of thirty thousand soldiers. "He desired the dignity so eagerly merely to satisfy his taste for ceremonial as an excuse for his extravagance. The crowd applauds the magnificence of princes, but a sovereign should remember that he is the first servant and the first magistrate of the state. He trampled on the poor in order to pander to the rich. His favorites received large pensions while his people were in misery. His stables were of Asiatic magnificence. He was great in little things and small in great issues." The only virtues allowed him by his contemptuous grandson were a good heart and fidelity to his wives. Voltaire, whose task it was to revise the work before publication, suggested that the attack was pressed too far, but his protests were in vain.

The closing chapter was the most difficult to write, for the torments of his youth were fresh in the author's memory, but he skates over thin ice with skill and writes with filial piety. "Frederick William I combined an instinct for work with a robust body. No man ever had such capacity for details. He busied himself with the smallest affairs because he felt that they add up to great totals. He related every aspect of his work to his general policy so that the perfection of each part should produce the rounded whole. His example of austerity and frugality were worthy of the early days of the Roman Republic." The object of his domestic reforms and economies was to render himself formidable to his neighbors by the possession of a large army. The fate of George William had taught him the peril of a prince unable to defend himself, and the traces of his wisdom would remain as long as Prussia was a nation.

The most striking feature of the chapter on his father is the author's detestation of Austria. The evil genius of the reign was her agent Seckendorf, of whom he speaks with anger and contempt. Lying was so ingrained in him that he had lost the habit of truth. The soul of a usurer was embodied sometimes in the soldier, sometimes in the diplomatist. He argued that the Emperor was a better ally than the King of England, and promised support for the succession of Berg. He gained possession of the King's mind so skillfully that he persuaded him to sign the Treaty of Wusterhausen, and it was his ambition to govern the whole court. The King, who was as honorable in politics as in his private life, was no match for this unscrupulous intriguer. "His example showed that good faith and virtue, being alien to the corruption of the century, cannot prosper." The scales fell from his eyes when the promises concerning Berg were unfulfilled. A visit to the Emperor at Prague ended the friendship of the two courts, for the King was incensed by the bad faith and the arrogance that he met. Despite this disillusion he married his eldest son to a niece of the Empress out of complaisance for Vienna. He kept out of war, and his grave illness in 1734 increased his dislike of risks. In his last years he was only kept alive by the care of his doctors; and he met death with the firmness of a philosopher and the resignation of a Christian. "His policy was rooted in justice. Armed always for defense, never for the detriment of Europe, he preferred the useful to the agreeable. Building lavishly for his subjects and only spending the minimum for his own accommodation, cautious in his engagements, faithful to his promises, austere in his habits and rigorous in regard to others, insistent on military discipline, governing his state on the same principles as his army, he thought so well of humanity that he assumed his subjects were stoics like himself. He left an army of 66,000 men, his finances improved, the treasury full, and marvelous order in all his affairs. The whole world will agree that the laborious life and wise measures of this prince embody the principles of prosperity that his house has enjoyed since his death." The dark shadows of the reign are indicated in a single tactful sentence. "We have passed over in silence the domestic vexations of this

great prince; one should have some indulgence for children's faults in favor of the virtues of such a father."

Frederick's largest and most important historical work, *Histoire de mon temps,* which opens with his accession, was begun after the close of the First Silesian War; revised and continued after the second, again revised and continued in the evening of his life. "My works are scarcely worth reading," he wrote to his brother in 1746. "I write partly for my amusement, partly to show posterity my actions and motives. I ask neither praise nor blame. I only desire to escape self-reproach. We all know that it is impossible to satisfy everyone." Like Cæsar, he writes throughout in the third person. The Preface of 1746 denounces the performances of others and makes high claim for his own impartiality. Many have written history, he declares, but very few have told the truth. Some have reported anecdotes at second hand or invented them; others have merely collected materials, rumors, and popular superstitions; still others have published insipid and diffuse journals of campaigns. In these romances the principal facts are scarcely to be recognized. The heroes think, speak, and act as the author directs. We are offered his dreams, not their actions. Such books are unworthy to survive, yet Europe is swamped with them, and people are foolish enough to believe what they tell. Except for the sage de Thou, Rapin, and a few others, we have only feeble historians, who must be read with particularly critical eyes. Truth of fact is important, but it is not enough. The historian must be objective, must write with discernment, and above all must consider things with a philosophic eye.

Frederick's object is to record the experiences and reflections of an actor in the scenes he describes. "It is to you, posterity, that I dedicate this work, in which I try to sketch the affairs of other powers and less briefly those of Prussia directly concerning my house, which may regard the acquisition of Silesia as the beginning of its growth." The fragment of history he proposed to write was particularly attractive since it was filled with outstanding events. "Indeed, I venture to suggest that since the fall of the Roman Empire there has been no epoch more deserving of study than that of the death of the Emperor Charles VI, the last male of the Hapsburg line, which led to that famous league or rather conspiracy of so many kings pledged to the ruin of the house of Austria." Nothing would be stated without proofs from the archives and the testimony of reliable witnesses; the account of the campaigns would record the immortal glory of the officers and would serve as an expression of the author's gratitude. He would try to compare the present with the past, to survey Europe as a whole, to include the little details that led to the greatest events. Writing only for posterity, he would be fettered by no thought of the public response. "I shall say out loud what many persons think secretly, painting princes as they are, without prejudice against my enemies or predilection for my allies. I shall only speak of myself when I must; no one is worthy of the attention of future centuries. During his lifetime a king is the idol of his court; the great burn incense, the poets sing his praises, the people fear him or love him tepidly. When he is dead the truth appears, often revenging itself to excess for insipid flattery. Posterity will judge us after our death and we must judge ourselves during our life. When our intentions are pure, when we love virtue, when our heart is not the accomplice

Sans-Souci Palace. Designed by Frederick II, it served as his home in Potsdam for 40 years.

of the errors of our mind, when we feel we have done our peoples all the good we can, that should be enough for us."

Frederick proceeds to explain the most controversial incident in his career. "Here you will find treaties made and broken. I must point out that we are conditioned by our resources and capacities, and when our interests change we must change with them. Our task is to watch over the happiness of our peoples. When we find they are endangered by an alliance, it is our duty to break it, the sovereign thereby sacrificing himself for their welfare. History is full of such examples and indeed there is no alternative. The stern critics who condemn this conduct are people who regard a pledge as something sacred. They are right and as a private person I agree, for honor is above interest. But a prince who makes engagements exposes his state to a thousand mishaps; thus it is better that the sovereign should break his word than that the people should perish. What should we say of a ridiculously scrupulous surgeon who declined to cut off a gangrened arm in order to save life? Acts should be judged good or bad according to circumstances and results. Yet how few judge from knowledge of causes! Human beings are like sheep following their shepherd. What a clever man says a thousand fools repeat."

The discursive Preface closes with reflections inspired by the events described. Princes who fight too far beyond their frontiers are always unfortunate, since they cannot supply or rescue the exposed troops. Nations are more courageous when they fight for their homes than when they attack their neighbors. "The war that started in Silesia is becoming epidemic and grows in malignity as it spreads. Fortune is inconstant. No power enjoys uninterrupted success. The worst feature is the horrible effusion of blood. Europe is like a slaughter-house, bloody battles everywhere. One would think the kings had resolved to depopulate the world. The complexity of events has changed the causes of wars. The effects continue when the motive changes. I seem to behold gamblers who, in the heat of the game, keep on till they have lost everything or ruined their adversaries. The history of cupidity is the school of virtue." The Preface of 1775 reiterates and expands the arguments and reflections of 1746 without adding anything of interest.

The long Introduction contains a vivid and valuable survey of the resources, rulers, and culture of the chief European states when the author ascended the throne. In Prussia the chief weakness was the lack of industries. The prestige of Austria had waxed with the victories of Prince Eugene and waned on his death, for the Emperor Charles VI was a well-meaning mediocrity—a good linguist, a good father, a good husband, but bigoted and superstitious like all the princes of his house. Under the wise, thrifty, and pacific guidance of Cardinal Fleury, France had largely recovered from the disasters of the closing years of Louis XIV. Yet "the arbiter of Europe" suffered from serious weaknesses. The people were poor, though the luxury of Paris recalled the Rome of Lucullus. The moral standard was low, and the French, above all the Parisians, were enervated by their pleasures. Spain, with a moody King and an ambitious Queen, was on the down grade. Her population was too small to cultivate the soil, and superstition ranged her with half-barbarian nations. The portrait of George II, the author's uncle, is painted in a few vigorous strokes of the brush. He had virtues and talent, but his passions were too strong. "Firm in his resolutions, avaricious rather than economical, capable of work but not of patience, violent, brave, governing England in the interests of Hanover, he was too little master of himself to direct a nation idolizing its liberty." Peter the Great had made Russia the arbiter of the north; the failure of Charles XII had proved that nothing was to be gained and everything might be lost by attacking such a colossus.

The verdict on Poland is particularly severe. "This kingdom is in a state of perpetual anarchy. The great families are at loggerheads. They prefer their interests to the public welfare, and agree only in their harshness towards their dependents, whom they treat less as human beings than as beasts of burden. The Poles are vain, arrogant in good fortune, broken in adversity; capable of the greatest infamies in amassing money, which they hasten to waste; frivolous, without judgment, capable of forming and abandoning plans without cause and of ruining themselves by their inconsequence. Laws exist, but for lack of sanctions they are ignored. The King sells posts. A single member of the Diet can veto its decisions. The women intrigue and decide everything, while their husbands get drunk." Saxony, a country with a richer soil, was ruled by Brühl, the extravagant and contemptible favorite. "He understood nothing but the finesses and ruses that constitute the policy of princelets; he was double-dealing, false, and capable of the basest actions to keep his power. No man of his century had so many clothes, watches, belts, shoes, and slippers or so much lace. Only with a prince like Augustus III could a man of this type play the part of Prime Minister." Bavaria, the most fertile part of Germany, had the smallest brains—an earthly paradise inhabited by animals.

The description of the Empire is unflattering but not unjust. Judged by the number of kings, electors, and princes, it was powerful; owing to the clash of interests it was weak. The Diet at Regensburg was a ghost, a gathering of publicists caring more for forms than realities. If a question of war arose, the Imperial court cleverly identified its quarrel with the interests of the Empire in order to use German strength for its own ambitions. The different Churches continued to exist, but their zeal had diminished. Many politicians were surprised that such a singular system could survive so long, and they attributed it to the national indifference. That was not the reason. The emperors were elective, and since the extinction of the Carolingians different families had been raised to the throne. Quarrels with their neighbors and the popes prevented the establishment of despotism in the Empire. The electors, certain princes and bishops were strong enough

if united to oppose the ambition of the emperors, but not to change the form of government. Since the Imperial crown had been worn by the house of Austria the danger of despotism became more apparent. Charles V could have made himself sovereign after the Battle of Mühlberg, but he missed his chance. When Ferdinand II and III attempted the enterprise, the jealousy of the French and Swedes frustrated their plan. The princes, for their part, were kept from aggrandizement by mutual jealousies.

After all this acid criticism of the states and statesmen of Europe it is refreshing to find a little praise. Since the time of Cæsar, Switzerland had preserved her liberty except for a short period when she was subdued by the Hapsburgs; subsequent attempts to reimpose their yoke failed. "The love of liberty and the mountains were their bulwarks against the ambition of their neighbors." Despite the differences of race, language, and religion, the people had never swerved from the principles of moderation and had reaped their reward. The barbarous custom of selling their sons as mercenaries was their only fault. A contemptuous reference to the Papacy concludes the panorama of the European stage. By 1740 the Pope was merely the first bishop of Christendom. The sphere of faith was left to him, but his political influence had waned. The Renaissance and the Reformation had struck a mortal blow at superstition. A saint was canonized from time to time so as to keep up the tradition, but a pope who tried to preach a crusade in the eighteenth century would not have collected a score of rascals. He was reduced to exercising his priestly functions and to making the fortunes of his nephews.

The author turns with relief from "the imbeciles and charlatans" on the political stage to the solid triumphs of the human spirit in science and philosophy, literature and the arts. Writing as a grateful child of the *Aufklärung,* he salutes the English sage who made experience his only guide. Locke tore away the bandage of error that the skeptic Bayle, his precursor, had partially detached. Fontenelle and Voltaire appeared in France, Thomasius in Germany, Hobbes, Collins, Shaftesbury, and Bolingbroke in England. "These great men and their disciples struck a mortal blow at religion. Men began to examine what they had stupidly adored; reason overthrew superstition; people became disgusted with the fables they had believed and turned away in horror from the blasphemies they had piously accepted. Deism, the simple cult of the Supreme Being, gained many followers. With this sensible religion, toleration came in and ideological differences no longer bred hostility. Epicureanism destroyed pagan idolatry, and deism was not less fatal to the Judaic visions adopted by our ancestors." (pp. 312-23)

> *G. P. Gooch, in his* Frederick the Great: The Ruler, the Writer, The Man, *Alfred A. Knopf, 1947, pp. 312-42.*

Harold Nicolson   (essay date 1960)

[*Nicolson was an English journalist, biographer, and literary critic. In the excerpt below, he discusses Frederick's penchant for the French language and succinctly refutes the idea of Frederick as a "philosopher king."*]

Nationalism, which in the nineteenth and twentieth centuries has proved so disruptive a ferment, was born with the American Revolution. Until 1775 the emotion of patriotism—although often, as Dr. Johnson observed, exploited for unworthy motives—was associated with pride, glory, and honor, and closely identified with the conceptions of loyalty and obedience. It was only in the last two decades of the century that patriotism became blurred by nationalism and acquired for itself such novel ideas as liberty, equality, emancipation, and even rebellion.

During the first two thirds of the eighteenth century culture was more international or cosmopolitan than it had ever been since the Middle Ages. Writers, artists, and thinkers did not regard themselves as natives of any particular country: they looked upon themselves as citizens of what they called "the Republic of Letters," and we must remember that in those days the word "Republic" was no commonplace term. Educated Englishmen, such as Lord Chesterfield or Horace Walpole, felt themselves equally at home in the salons of Paris and the drawing rooms of Mayfair. Although it was as true then as now that very few French people thought it necessary or interesting to learn English, no European could claim to be a man of the world unless he possessed a thorough knowledge of the language, literature, and art of France. The eighteenth century, it must again and again be emphasized, was intellectually dominated by French culture, even as French culture was in itself dominated, guided, and disciplined by Paris. Newton may well have been lauded as a god and Locke and Hume venerated as major prophets; but it was by the *philosophes* and Encyclopédistes that the thought and taste of the civilized world were formed; the whole of Europe thought in French. It must be repeated that the term "philosophy" during the eighteenth century was employed to designate, not merely the study of abstract ideas, but also scientific knowledge and technology. Benjamin Franklin was hailed as a typical "philosopher," not because of his ideas on ethics and metaphysics, but because of his experiments in electricity. We should thus bear in mind, when using the term "philosopher" or *"philosophe,"* that in the eighteenth century it was applied to describe such aptitudes or professions as would today be classified under such names as "scientist," "biologist," "economist," "inventor," or even "research worker." "Philosophy" was used as an equivalent for "advanced knowledge."

Frederick the Great furnishes the classic example of a man who, although he regarded himself as a passionate patriot, had no conception even of the meaning of nationalism. He is rightly lauded by the Germans as the genius who rendered Prussia a great power and as the architect from whose designs the mighty German Empire eventually arose. But in fact Frederick had little or no conception of a German nation: his unflinching ambition was to widen and fortify the dominions of the House of Brandenburg, to enhance the glory of the Hohenzollerns, and to enlarge what he regarded as his family estate. With this in mind he ran inconceivable risks and displayed superhuman endurance and prowess: but the conception of a greater Germany hardly entered his mind.

Intellectually he was wholly French. French was his natural language; he wrote in French, he spoke in French, he thought in French. His knowledge of the German language was rudimentary; he spoke it, when obliged to do

so, "like a coachman"; he could not spell it at all. He regarded his native tongue as some savage Teutonic dialect, so crude and rough that it could never give birth to any literature at all. And this at a date when Lessing had already published his *Laokoon,* and when the whole of Europe was shedding tears over the sorrows of Werther. To the young Goethe, Frederick the Great was a national hero; he forgave him his preference for French language and literature and even, in his delightful autobiography, *Dichtung und Wahrheit,* argues that Frederick's contempt acted as a stimulus to German letters, impelling the younger generation to storm the bastions of the Republic of Letters.

Frederick was hailed by Voltaire and the Encyclopédistes as the philosopher king whose coming had been dreamed of by Plato and who was now incarnated in the person of the autocrat of Prussia. Yet his conduct was neither philosophical nor progressive. In the most rapacious manner he plunged Europe into a sequence of terrible wars. He tore up the treaties which he had signed, violated the pledges that he had given, destroyed such elements as then existed of the law of nations, committed the signal crime of partitioning Poland, and proved to the world that the only principle that he respected was the principle of force. Seldom has there existed a monarch whose ambition was so cynical and egoistic: he possessed no principles and few ideas beyond those of self-aggrandizement and *Realpolitik.* Compared to him, Napoleon was cautious and high-principled. He found Prussia a feudal state and, in spite of his loudly proclaimed liberalism, he left it even more feudal than it had been before. His gospel of "success through strength" did permanent damage to the character of his countrymen. He was an utterly unscrupulous man, who may have gained great benefits for the Hohenzollerns but who imposed much suffering upon his own country, upon Germany, and upon the world.

The extraordinary thing about Frederick the Great is that he was not a complete hypocrite. There were moments when he believed sincerely in the lofty ideals in which he rhetorically indulged. He really did believe that he was nothing but the "first servant (*domestique*) of his people" and he did really strive in many cases to see that justice was done. Even more extraordinary is the fact that, even after the Silesian and the Seven Years' wars, even after the partition of Poland, the *philosophes* of Paris continued to regard him as a benevolent despot, as the champion of enlightenment. One of the two most startling aberrations in which the Age of Reason indulged was to take as its hero and heroine two tyrants who, to our minds, violated all the principles by which reason should be judged and applauded. If we are to grasp how utterly unreasonable the Age of Reason really was, it is useful to examine what was felt at the time about their strange heroines and heroes. It is merely curious that they should have been taken in by such obvious charlatans as Saint Germain, Cagliostro, and Casanova. What is to our minds almost incredible is that they should have continued to admire and applaud a feckless courtesan such as Madame de Pompadour, a murderess and adulteress such as Catherine II, and a bloodstained aggressor such as Frederick the Great. (pp. 108-11)

Harold Nicolson, "Philosopher King (Frederick the Great, 1712-1786)," in his The Age of Reason: The Eighteenth Century, *1960. Re-*

print by Doubleday and Company, Inc., 1961, pp. 108-27.

Ludwig Reiners (essay date 1960)

[*In the following excerpt, Reiners explores the extent to which Frederick allowed Enlightenment ideals to pervade his thoughts and actions.*]

No ruler in world history has written as much as Frederick. As he himself confessed: "As soon as I have a spare moment, the itch to write seizes me; I cannot resist this frivolous pleasure; it amuses me, distracts me and puts me in a better frame of mind for the work which I have to do afterwards." He composed thousands of verses, one or two comedies, several epic poems, half a dozen major historical works, two long political testaments, memoranda, treaties and essays on political questions, numerous literary dialogues, satires and parodies, military treatises and a rhyming dictionary. His private correspondence fills sixty volumes; his official political letters have been published in forty-four volumes, but there are more to come. From the first word to the last all this vast output was written in French.

Frederick was also an insatiable reader. "I have read more than all the Benedictine friars put together. . . . Without my books I would have gone mad." Frederick liked to call himself a thinker rather than a man of action. When his deeds made him famous, he felt like a philosopher "who has marvellously strayed from his sphere." During the siege of Schweidnitz he read Cardinal Fleury's thirty-six-volume history of the Church, extracted long passages and had them printed separately for his personal use. Five sets of his basic library consisting of two or three dozen books uniformly bound in bright red morocco were distributed between Sanssouci, Potsdam, Berlin and Breslau, with the fifth set reserved for use in the field. The library included French translations of the masterpieces of Greek and Latin literature, the works of Corneille, Racine, Boileau, Voltaire, Montesquieu, Bossuet, Pascal, Locke and other philosophers and also a number of historical works. Frederick was steeped in classical French literature; in a letter home, d'Alembert wrote that he could quote no major passage with which the King was not conservant. But the library contained no German books; the King could understand the spoken but not the written language.

Frederick was a child of the Enlightenment. He believed in the supremacy of rational thought, he detested everything that reason could not penetrate. We are inclined nowadays to deride the logic-chopping rationalistic outlook, but we should not forget that the dawning of independent thought held much of the effulgence that belongs to youth in every sphere. Rejoicing in its new-won freedom from the fetters of superstition and prejudice, the intellect felt entitled in those days to claim sovereign powers over life. No one doubted that the task of literature was to set up firm principles for action and cure humanity's ills and that the task could be fulfilled. Enjoying life, confident of penetrating its secrets and believing in progress, men chose to ignore what Reason failed to explain. Gaiety was their key-note, for they were sure of themselves, sure of their ability to create the best of all possible worlds. So at night, when the flute trilled in the blue, silk-lined rooms of Rheinsberg or Sanssouci and the company danced, chatted, or watched theatricals, the very statues and temples in the moonlit park seemed infused with a cool and airy optimism. Certainly, it filled the heart of the brilliant, handsome young man who was heir to a throne and felt he had already inherited paradise. Longing to embrace the whole of creation, he rhymed:

If my soul like Thebes had a hundred doors
I would bid joys enter in tens and scores

—and if tiresome learned allusion was one of these joys, that did not make him the less sincere.

But if Frederick was a child of the Enlightenment, this only applied to his cast of mind and limitations of intellect. His personality was too complex to be labelled, as Dilthey has suggested in an excellent essay, *Friedrich und die deutsche Aufklärung*. Those, he writes, who were able to study Frederick at close quarters were at once attracted and repelled, fascinated and baffled by his fluid, contradictory character. Sometimes the discordant elements seemed to fuse, at others to predominate singly in rapid succession: "the disposition to enjoy life in cheerful company, conversation, music, reading or in literary creation—and the awareness that the ruler must sacrifice himself to the State; the ambitious military commander in pursuit of fame—and the philosopher-king anxious to contribute to the welfare of his people and the progress of mankind; the king who cultivated friendship and treated men of letters as his equals—and the authoritarian despot; self-surrender, abandonment, almost, to the impressions of the moment—and a heroism in confronting fate unequalled since the days of ancient Rome."

Frederick faced public and private tribulation without the comforts of religious faith. But he rejected atheism, perhaps from a sense of monarchic solidarity. "As we have to penetrate the labyrinth, I will be guided only by the thread of reason. Reason compels me to assume that an Intelligence rules over this world and keeps the machine working as a whole. I imagine this Intelligence as the original source of life and movement." But he repeatedly stressed that the supreme Intelligence was not concerned with the fates of individual men, though at the end of his *Histoire de Mon Temps* he did recommend Prussia to the care of Providence, "if human misery is not beneath her attention." On the other hand he was too much the master of his own fate to accept the popular argument that suffering was incompatible with the existence of a benevolent deity.

As regards free will, Frederick held different opinions in youth and maturity. As Crown Prince he had written to Voltaire: "You act according to a principle, according to sublime reason, and therefore according to necessity." But as King he was obliged to believe in some measure of free will, as he explained in a letter to d'Alembert: "Whence have all human beings a feeling of freedom, how do they come to love it? Would this be possible if freedom did not exist? I dare to surmise that there is a contradiction somewhere in the system of fatalism; for if one accepts it, one must also consider laws, education, punishments and rewards as superfluous and pointless. If all is necessary, then nothing can be changed. But my experience proves to me that education can do a great deal for men, that they can be improved and given an incentive."

His answer to the question of immortality was much less

ambiguous. The capacity for thought, considered Frederick, derived from our physical organisation and both would perish together. The mind was like a flame. Both needed nourishment. When the wood had burnt to ashes the flame was extinguished. In his testament Frederick wrote with lofty detachment: "Without regret I return the breath of life which has inspired me to beneficent Nature which lent it to me, and my body to the elements of which it is composed." In this testament he also expresses the essence of his philosophy: "Our life is a hurried transition from birth to death; in this short interval the task of man is to work for the welfare of the society of whose body he is a member." But Frederick had always been wary of metaphysical problems because he considered the human intellect incapable of solving them. Ethics seemed to him more important because of their practical application. He was concerned, not to know why he was alive or what happened to him after he was dead, but being alive to discover how he should act. He did not believe in the innate goodness of human nature. To a correspondent who had extolled it he replied: "You do not know the accursed race to which we belong." But he did believe that men could be changed for the better by the use of reason: "I could wish that the motive force of egoism could be directed by proving to men that it is to their own advantage to be good citizens, good fathers and good friends, in short, to practise all the moral virtues. And as it is indeed so, it ought not to be difficult to convince them." So, in old age, he reached a gentle and realistic humanitarianism: "Those who consider all men to be devils and rage cruelly against them are seeing them through the eyes of a fanatical misanthrope. Whoever thinks they are angels and leaves them to their own devices is dreaming like a feeble-minded Capuchin. But he who believes that men are neither all good nor all evil, who rewards good actions above their deserts and punishes bad ones more lightly than is due, who shows consideration to the weak and humanity to every man, that person is acting as a reasonable man should." But one should beware of imagining that these admirable though somewhat trite principles of Frederick the philosopher were consistently applied by Frederick the King. In 1776 the British Ambassador, Sir James Harris, wrote: "Although as an individual he often appears and really is humane, benevolent and friendly, yet the instant he acts in his royal capacity these attributes forsake him and he carries with him desolation, misery and persecution wherever he goes." The contrast is overdrawn, nevertheless it reflects the existence in Frederick of two almost separate beings: the affectionate, sensitive, contemplative idealist who was always ready to believe that his opinions might be mistaken, and the ruthless, cynically realistic man of action, the despot who never doubted that he held a monopoly of wisdom and who shaped Prussia to his will, ferociously indifferent to the hardships and sufferings he caused. Yet in some curious way these two beings were not psychologically antagonistic. Each refreshed the other. A friendly, almost tender literary conversation on the eve of a great battle—and next morning the commander would awake with courage renewed, mind cleared and heart rearmoured against adversity. Frederick to Voltaire: "You came into the world that I might know happiness." The King: "If I wanted to punish a province, I would have it ruled by men of letters."

In old age, Frederick's interests narrowed and his prejudices deepened. Mathematics and the natural sciences were dismissed as mere playthings, astronomy and geometry as valueless to navigation. In agriculture, the practice was everything, theory was irrelevant. Electricity? A pastime for the curious. Sublime Reason's earthly interpreters, the Encyclopædists, he mostly disliked—Diderot for his arrogance, Rousseau for his politics, Holbach for his aggressive atheism. D'Alembert, on the other hand, seemed "a very nice fellow" and Frederick corresponded with him for twenty years. But here again, though no trace of personal rancour or petulance marked their letters, the King did not always see eye to eye with the philosopher—on Church questions, for instance. Frederick declined to offend the pious after Voltaire's death by installing his bust in a place of worship. Voltaire, he told d'Alembert courteously, would certainly feel bored there. He also refused to build a Temple of Reason in Potsdam. Apart from the fact that experience had undermined his confidence in the ultimate triumph of reason, he had no intention of being accused of blasphemy by his subjects.

Frederick's personal attitude to Christianity was of the "nothing but" kind. Voltaire's mockeries had laid bare the distinction between religious faith and historical fact, and the contrast between his father's pious words and his mad and fumbling cruelties had filled Frederick with revulsion for organised religious worship. To him personally, the Church was based on superstition and it bred hypocrisy. His reaction was to interpret Christianity by the light of primitive reason: "Like all forces in the world, Christianity had modest beginnings. The hero of this sect is a Jew from the scum of the people, of dubious origin who weaves some good moral doctrines into the insipidities of the ancient Hebrew prophesies. Miracles are ascribed to him and at the end he is condemned to a shameful death. Twelve enthusiasts spread his teaching from the East as far as Italy, win adherents by the pure and saintly morality which they preach and—apart from some miracles which excite people of fervid imagination—teach nothing but Deism. . . . "

But in his public capacity Frederick saw the danger of mocking established and venerated institutions and he held too low an opinion of average human intelligence to believe with d'Alembert and others that once superstition had been derided out of existence cold reason could take its place. When Voltaire told him of a young Frenchman who had been condemned to death for damaging a religious statue and failing to take his hat off to his village priest when the latter was carrying the Host, the King's attitude reflected the experience of the ruler: "Remember what Fontenelle said: 'If I had a fistful of truths I would think twice before opening it.' The mass of people do not deserve to be enlightened. If you ask me whether I would have passed so severe a sentence, my answer is: No. I would have suited the punishment to the crime. I would have said: You broke the statue, so you must repair it. You failed to remove your hat to the priest when he was carrying the well-known object, so for fourteen days you must appear in church without a hat. You have read the works of Voltaire, so you must study the *Summa* of St. Thomas under the parson's supervision. The dizzy fellow would have been much more severely punished in this way than he was by his judges, for boredom lasts a century, but death only a moment. Toleration must allow every citizen the freedom to believe what he will. But it should not extend to condoning the insolent rowdyism of young hotheads who grossly insult objects venerated by the people. That is my view. It is consistent with the measures necessary to ensure freedom of thought and the public peace—and that is the prime object of all legislation." And elsewhere: "Believe me, if philosophers founded a system of government, within fifty years the people would have created some new superstition, have set up other idols—would be praying at the grave of the founders or calling on the sun. Some aberration or other would thrust out the pure and simple cult of the Supreme Being."

Frederick even recommended that Voltaire should not give his history of Louis XIV to the general public, stating roundly: "Nothing is more absurd than the desire to root out superstition. Prejudices are the people's reason. And does this stupid people deserve to be enlightened?" King Frederick's tolerance was largely one of contempt and political expediency.

Though Frederick once told the poet Gottsched that he had never read a book in German and that he spoke the language *"comme un cocher,"* he freely expressed views on German literature and devoted a thorough discussion to it in his treatise *De la Littérature Allemande,* which was published in 1780, but for the most part had been written twenty years before. Seldom can a writer have been so profoundly ignorant of his subject. With one exception, Goethe's drama *Götz von Berlichingen,* which he thought "detestable," Frederick had read nothing of Lessing, Klopstock, Wieland, Herder, Kant, Winckelmann or of Goethe himself. But it was enough that they were Germans, ignorant of the French language and the wonders it could perform, for Frederick to know that they were men hopelessly adrift on the turbid waters of the barbaric German tongue without even a star, a standard of excellence, to guide them to the harbour of literary merit. And if proof were needed, the fact that they imitated the bad, base and boring plays of the Englishman Shakespeare showed that they were heading for the rocks or, rather, the rocky mountains of Canada, whose savages, said Frederick, might find Shakespeare's "abominable pieces" to their taste. Yet the literary future was not without hope. German culture had been retarded by the Thirty Years War. German literature might yet astonish Europe if a concerted effort were made to reform the language and improve prose style. At present, "it is physically impossible even for the most brilliant writer to master this harsh language." Frederick found it cumbersome, particularly the syntax which placed the verb on which the whole meaning of a sentence depended at the very end. It was also ugly; the verbs *to give, to take* and *to say,* for instance: *geben, nehmen* and *sagen.* The last syllable was mute in each case. "Let an *a* be added to these endings, so that they become *gebena, nehmena, sagena*—this sound is pleasant to the ear." Frederick, in other words, missed the even stress given to syllables in French. Finally, a German ruler was wanted with a real interest in literature who would patronise the best writers and bring them to the fore. This ruler could not be Frederick. The great days of German literature were yet to come—but come they would: "Like Moses I discern the Promised Land from afar." The King believed that with this treatise he had made a solid contribution to the furtherance of German culture. "You may laugh," he wrote to d'Alembert, "at the trouble I have taken to convey some small idea of good taste and Attic spice to a people who hitherto have known only how to

eat, drink, fight and make love. But it is human to want to make oneself useful, and often a word falls on good soil and brings forth unexpected fruit. . . . " Attic spice, or an understanding of the Greek spirit, was indeed needed to wean German literature away from imitations of French classicism and so enable it to achieve independence, but the teacher was Lessing, not Frederick, though the fruits were ultimately to be that same calm humanitarianism that glowed in the ageing King when the fires of Rationalism were spent.

And what of Frederick's own creative talent, both literary and musical? His verses are diligently rhymed prose. His comedies and epic poems are paltry. His prose style, on the other hand, is splendidly clear and fluid. But his verse lacks feeling and sincerity. Both qualities are found in his musical compositions. Frederick was a passionate flute-player. Until his teeth began to fall out in old age, he practised assiduously, often for several hours a day. He composed over a hundred sonatas and concertos, all of them consisting of intricate elaborations on some simple main theme which he embroidered with elegant and cheerful figurations, runs, trills and cadenzas. Here, too, of course, he was a rationalist: "It always pleases me when I find that music provides scope for intelligence. I enjoy a learned-sounding piece of music as much as clever conversation at table." In his music he succeeded sometimes in giving expression to deep feelings. At a competition held in 1869 one of his marches was chosen as the Spanish national anthem. It was retained until 1922. His musical taste did not develop beyond the preferences of his youth. Anticipating a fashionable word, he rejected Haydn and Mozart as "degenerate." In music his overburdened spirit found relaxation and a refuge and his innate sensibility an outlet. (pp. 271-79)

> *Ludwig Reiners, in his* Frederick the Great: A Biography, *translated by Lawrence P. R. Wilson, G. P. Putnam's Sons, 1960, pp. 271-79.*

Paul Sonnino   (essay date 1981)

[*Sonnino translated an English edition of Frederick's* Anti-Machiavel. *In the following excerpt from the introduction to that work, he explores the thoughts behind the refutation of Machiavelli's famous treatise.*]

The Refutation of Machiavelli's Prince purports to be a thoroughgoing rejection of cruelty, duplicity, and superstition in favor of a new way of life in which humanity, forthrightness, and reason rule the day. It is more accurately the outpouring of an enthusiastic young man who seems unable to choose between optimism and pessimism, between liberty and determinism, between the vision of the "Enlightenment" which he professes without believing and the world of Machiavelli which he despises without understanding. Frederick almost expects to overwhelm his readers with a torrent of rhetoric, showing little regard for their patience and even less for their intelligence. He borrows here from the world as it should be and there from the world as it is, without making the slightest distinction between the two. In the process, the crown prince falls into considerably greater contradictions than those he claims to find in his *bête noire,* and utterly misses the glaring similarities between Machiavelli and himself.

Frederick has certainly contemplated the new vision of man, the reasonable, virtuous man à la Locke or Fénelon, who seeks only "to preserve his wealth and to increase it in legitimate ways." All men love liberty, and "it is this spirit of pride and independence which has produced so many great men in the world." Men may have passions, but "a reasonable being" will struggle against them for "his own good and the advantage of society." This sanguine view of enlightened self-interest, however, is hardly consonant with the crown prince's assessment of the passions themselves. Man is their slave. He may have conceptions and combine ideas, but "few persons are rational," and "intemperate as we are, we want to conquer everything as if our life had no end." Man's reason cannot sustain liberty for long. Much stronger, bewails the anti-clerical Frederick, "is the power of superstition upon idiots and of fanaticism on the human mind." There would seem to be no remedy, for our passions depend on the "arrangement of certain organs in our body" and other such physiological causes. Machiavelli would have had to ask his royal antagonist to think again.

It is the reasonable, virtuous man of the "Enlightenment" who is also at the heart of the crown prince's official theory of the state. Ignorant of the *Discourses* and critical of Machiavelli's pragmatic approach to this matter in the *Prince*, Frederick decides to be more philosophical in the **Anti-Machiavel.** He describes a kind of social contract in which men, out of enlightened self-interest, choose the most qualified and just among themselves to govern and protect them. Echoing Montesquieu's parable of the Troglodytes, the crown prince asserts that "there is no security for men without virtue." Everyone must respect the laws,

Frederick II as a young man.

for without a rule of law each political unit would become "an empire of wolves." Frederick has a special place in his heart for republics, like the Roman of old or the Dutch of his own time, although he concedes that in the long run the character of most men is best geared to a legitimate hereditary monarchy, sustained by a devoted nobility. Still, there is a cocky assurance in all this that government is a purely utilitarian arrangement that stands upon the services that it performs and needs no additional supernatural sanction. Yet the crown prince's simultaneous belief that the varieties in men's customs are caused by differences in climate, diets, and upbringing tears to shreds his political ideal, for he finds that the characteristic of men that makes them venerate the peculiarities of their environment is their stupidity. The stolid Chinese, the frivolous French, the passionate Italians all live under the regimes they deserve and blindly obey rulers who are fortunate enough to profit from the public ignorance. No rulers take better advantage of this human credulity than the priestly ones, for "religion is an old machine that will never wear out." Machiavelli, who wants the lawgiver to draw virtue out of the worst passions of men, might have hoped that his critic was beginning to see the point.

Frederick is never so demanding as in his expectations of the sovereign. He wants him to be a paragon of virtue and justice, or in the phrase that he launched into the slogan of "Enlightened Despotism", the "first servant of his people". The sovereign is to be guided in his fervor to uphold the laws by the same enlightened self-interest that inspires his people to obey him, a peculiar imperative since the crown prince is never so misanthropic as in his evaluation of sovereigns. He readily admits that "since the seduction of the throne is very powerful, it takes an uncommon virtue to resist it." The only admirable princes that he can dredge up from antiquity are three Roman emperors, and neither the middle ages nor his own time seem to provide him with anything more worthy of praise than the beneficence of an obscure Duke of Lorraine. It is hard to escape the conclusion that Frederick ultimately believes that the only sovereign with the requisite virtues will be himself. But Machiavelli, too, did not think that Cesare Borgias were born every day.

The crown prince's ideal sovereign would not only be an example to his people, he would also participate in that happy diplomatic invention of modern times, "the balance of Europe, which establishes the alliance of some important princes in order to oppose the ambitious." But the impression very definitely emerges in the course of the **Refutation** that this balance did not always function smoothly. Somehow, those incompetent sovereigns who occupied so many European thrones were also ambitious and dangerous. Frederick accuses the French monarchy of following Machiavellian principles and the emperor of acting imperiously in the Empire. It was a dangerous game, this balance of Europe, and so the crown prince, while roundly castigating Machiavelli for preaching faithlessness, admits "that there are some disturbing necessities when a prince cannot avoid breaking his treaties and alliances. He must, however, do it properly, by warning his allies in time and not unless the welfare of his people and extreme necessity oblige him." But when did Machiavelli ever advise princes to violate treaties unnecessarily?

Frederick's indignant tirades against Machiavelli might

well have turned to abject submission had it not been for the great weapons that the "Enlightenment" had placed at his disposal: its theory of history and its theory of progress; for the crown prince had joyously sensed what the introduction to Voltaire's *Age of Louis XIV* had so neatly confirmed; the world had changed. History, save for a few centuries of Greek and Roman grandeur, was indeed a dismal record of ignorance and of superstition in which men were the blind instruments of priestly obscurantism. The fifteenth century, both Voltaire and Frederick agreed, had seen a limited revival of the arts, but it was the modern era which had discovered the laws of motion along with all sorts of technological innovations. It was the modern era which had discovered the advantages to society of intellectual freedom and the costs of religious persecution. It was the modern era which cherished the thought that its discoveries held the key to the continued happiness and progress of mankind. To Voltaire's indices of advancement, however, the crown prince added a few criteria of his own. The uniform, the rifle, the standing army, all the instruments of eighteenth century warfare seem to have been as important to him as the laws of universal gravitation and of morality in conducting modern man toward virtue and duty. These are the foundations of his new utilitarianism that render the old divine right sanctions obsolete. These are the reasons that he considers any popular revolt against the French, Prussian, or most other contemporary monarchies out of the question. Add to the military forces the balance of power diplomacy that inspired even princes to be moderate, and we see why Frederick believes that "all these things have produced such a general change that they render most of Machiavelli's maxims inapplicable." (pp. 14-18)

> *Paul Sonnino, in an introduction to* The Refutation of Machiavelli's "Prince" or Anti-Machiavel *by Frederick of Prussia, edited and translated by Paul Sonnino, Ohio University Press, 1981, pp. 1-22.*

FURTHER READING

Ages, Arnold. "Voltaire and Frederick: The Image of the Old Testament in Their Correspondence." *Revue de Litterature Comparee* 40 (1966): 81-90.
    Studies recurrent allusions to Old Testament scripture in the letters between Frederick and Voltaire.

Aldington, Richard. Introduction to *Letters of Voltaire and Frederick the Great*, edited by Richard Aldington, pp. 1-16. New York: Brentano's, 1927.
    Concise biographical sketch of Frederick's life to the time at which he contacted Voltaire for literary advice. Aldington then discusses the friendship and ensuing correspondence between Frederick and Voltaire.

Asprey, Robert B. *Frederick the Great: The Magnificent Enigma.* New York: Ticknor and Fields, 1986, 715 p.
    Examines the childhood, training, and reign of Frederick. Asprey discusses the literary and diplomatic influ-

ences upon him and territorial gains as a monarch, with emphasis on the political turmoil of the time.

Broglie, Duc de. *Frederick the Great and Maria Theresa: From Hitherto Unpublished Documents, 1740-1742.* 2 vols. Translated by Cashel Hoey and John Lillie. London: Sampson Low, Marston, Searle, and Rivington, 1883.
    Exhaustive treatment of the reigns of both monarchs and their conflicts with each other.

Carlyle, Thomas. *History of Friedrich II of Prussia, Called Frederick the Great.* Edited by John Clive. Chicago: University of Chicago Press, 1969, 479 p.
    Focuses on the childhood and training of Frederick to be king, with an examination of the friendship between Frederick and Voltaire.

Catt, Henri de. *Frederick the Great: The Memoirs of His Reader, Henri de Catt.* 2 vols. Translated by F. S. Flint. London: Constable and Co., 1916.
    Chronicles the thoughts and actions of the Prussian king during approximately three of the years Catt served Frederick (1758-62).

Durant, Will and Durant, Ariel. "Frederick the Great and Maria Theresa." In their *The Age of Voltaire: A History of Civilization in Western Europe from 1715 to 1756, with Special Emphasis on the Conflict between Religion and Philosophy*, pp. 431-71. The Story of Civilization: Part IX. New York: Simon and Schuster, 1965.
    Explores the childhood and reign of Frederick II, focusing on his relationships with his father and sister, and upon the diplomatic relations between he and Maria Theresa of Austria.

Goldsmith, Margaret. *Frederick the Great.* New York: Charles Boni, 1929, 218 p.
    Biographical work focusing on Frederick's actions as king and his personal reactions to political situations.

Hubatsch, Walther. *Frederick the Great of Prussia: Absolutism and Administration.* Translated by Patrick Doran. London: Thames and Hudson, 1975, 303 p.
    Examines the administration of Frederick William and Frederick II's subsequent reforms. Hubatsch also discusses Frederick's armed conflicts over European provinces and their eventual occupation by Prussian forces.

Johnson, Hubert C. *Frederick the Great and His Officials.* New Haven: Yale University Press, 1975, 318 p.
    Discusses the political structure of Frederick II's court, focusing on Frederick's reforms of political offices.

Lavisse, Ernest. *The Youth of Frederick the Great.* Translated by Stephen Louis Simeon. London: Richard Bentley and Son, 1891, 471 p.
    Traces the history of the Hohenzollerns from Frederick I through his grandson, Frederick II. Lavisse provides an indepth look at the treatment of Frederick II by his father, Frederick William, and examines the escape attempt by Frederick and its consequences.

Paret, Peter. "The King's View of the World." In *Frederick the Great: A Historical Profile*, by Gerhard Ritter, translated by Peter Paret, pp. 44-60. Berkeley and Los Angeles: University of California Press, 1968.
    Discusses the poetry of Frederick the Great and questions of French imitation and German influence raised by the poems. Paret also examines the role of the mon-

arch in promoting the arts and Frederick's Enlighten-
ment-influenced religious philosophy.

Strachey, Lytton. "Voltaire and Frederick the Great." In his
Books and Characters: French and English, pp. 137-62. London: Chatto and Windus, 1928.
    Examination of the mutually parasitic relationship be-
    tween Frederick and Voltaire.

Thaddeus, Victor. *Frederick the Great: The Philosopher King.*
New York: Brentano's Publishers, 1930, 330 p.
    Treats the life of Frederick the Great, with an examina-
    tion of his personal and diplomatic relationships with
    various European powers, especially Maria Theresa of
    Austria.

French Enlightenment

INTRODUCTION

The French Enlightenment was an eighteenth century movement that fervently proclaimed the merits of reason and the scientific method while rejecting traditional social, religious, and political ideas. In the words of Immanuel Kant, enlightenment is "man's release from his self-incurred tutelage." The major proponents of Enlightenment thought were the philosophes, a group of deistic or materialistic thinkers and writers mainly centered in Paris. The philosophes adopted as their rallying cry the motto *sapere aude,* challenging society to "dare to know." To most scholars the French Revolution represents the terminus of the Enlightenment era, but many dispute the date of its inception—some place it at 1685, others at 1660 or as early as 1600. However, the majority of commentators concede that the siècle des lumières—"the century of lights"—encompassed the years between 1715 and 1789. The latter part of the period flourished with intellectual activity and witnessed the publication of the *Encyclopédie,* a work that has been viewed as the embodiment of Enlightenment spirit.

Scholars are divided about whether the Enlightenment was primarily a philosophic, political, social, religious or literary movement, but most concur that the visionary quality of the age generated revolutionary views of society and culture. Norman Hampson wryly remarked: "Within limits, the Enlightenment was what one thinks it was." Indeed, the eighteenth century observed the full flowering of ideas first suggested in the previous century. The philosophes extolled reason and the scientific method, embracing the systems of thought promulgated by seventeenth-century English philosophers Francis Bacon, Isaac Newton, and John Locke. Particularly influential upon the thought of Enlightenment figures Voltaire, Jean-Jacques Rousseau, and Paul Henri d'Holbach was the Lockean theory of sensationalism. This body of beliefs held that knowledge is solely derived through sensation and perception. The eighteenth-century notion of rationalism established reason as the fundamental criterion for the acquisition of knowledge, superior to and independent of sense perception. With this maxim in mind, the philosophes argued for the irrefutable existence of discoverable and universally valid principles governing human beings, nature, and society. Ferdinand Vial, in the *Dictionary of French Literature* (1958), observed: "From sensationalism to materialism, to theism and atheism, to rationalism and religious tolerance, the road was now open and the French 'philosophes' trod it with alacrity."

Out of this consciousness developed what has come to be known as the Enlightenment theory of progress. Therein the philosophes propounded humanity's ability to perfect itself and society and named the state the proper instrument of that progress. The philosophes deplored the social conditions of contemporary France, but they remained confident that humanity was capable of attaining happiness and that society could improve its living standards. A burgeoning theory of naturism, which asserted the fundamental goodness of man, fueled their hopeful expectations as did the reports from the Americas that fostered the idea of the "noble savage"—a happy individual living in an idyllic state, unburdened by formalized religion and social organization. Armed with these concepts and fortified by science and reason, the philosophes attacked Christian tradition and dogma, denouncing religious persecution and propagating the idea of religious tolerance. The ascendency of deism—an ethos favoring natural religion and emphasizing morality, while denying the supernatural significance of events—complemented the philosophe's revolt against long-standing and unquestioned social restraints. Most scholars recognize that enlightened intellectuals of the time examined nearly every facet of eighteenth-century European culture. According to Hampson: "The Enlightenment was an attitude of mind rather than a course in science and philosophy."

Critics acknowledge that open expression of enlightened thought in eighteenth-century France was regularly curtailed by a stringent, but often capricious, censorship. Literary works were published only with permission of the Director of Publications, but even when granted, books could be suppressed by the clergy, the Parlement of Paris, the Sorbonne, the Châtelet, or, more commonly, by a royal *lettre de cachet.* In 1754 a royal decree ordered the death penalty for "all those who shall be convicted of having composed, or caused to be composed and printed, writings intended to attack religion, to assail our authority, or to disturb the ordered tranquility of our realm." Despite its threatening tone, enforcement of the measure was often arbitrary. The *Encyclopédie,* for example, was published with royal sanction yet championed nearly all the radical doctrines of the century. Nevertheless, the philosophes conveyed their views through sophisticated subterfuge, enduring daily anxiety and uncertainty about whether they would be subpoenaed or imprisoned. Usually without compromising their individual writing styles, they often devised novel and ingenious ways to circumvent the censors. Innuendo and hyperbolic praise frequently were exploited to conceal subversive ideas. One of the most popular methods of disguise entailed the creation of a literary character unacquainted with French customs and imbued with a sense of false naiveté. These characters expressly criticized society—a most effective technique because the authors vigilantly distanced themselves from the extremist views of their literary creations.

Of related interest is the role played by salons in the propagation of Enlightenment thought. If the philosophes had to dissemble their views to evade the censors, they had also to consider their reception in the salons. The women of the salons of the eighteenth century dictated the standards of taste and exerted considerable influence in matters of fame and fortune. According to Whittaker Chambers: "Their world held for them one terror, ennui, and only one horror, a lapse of taste." Among the more prominent salons were those of Mademoiselle de Lespinasse and Mesdames Geoffrin, de Tecin, and du Deffand, but reputedly the very best was that of d'Holbach, who hosted internationally renowned dinner parties in his Paris townhouse, nicknamed the "Café de l'Europe." Nearly all of the philosophes depended on the salons for the success of their literary ventures. According to Kingsley Martin: "The future of a book was largely determined by its reception in the leading drawing-rooms where the cultured aristocracy of Europe forgathered to discuss, to applaud or condemn." The philosophes necessarily maneuvered for the social patronage of the more esteemed salons because most of the hostesses also possessed influence in the dispensation of academic chairs. Intrigue and intense rivalry therefore characterized much of the restrictive, elitist society of the salons. In such an atmosphere a highly developed sense of wit, both in conversation and in writing, was one's sole saving grace and commonly ensured one's success. Denis Diderot, principal editor of the *Encyclopédie,* commented: "Women accustom us to discuss with charm and clarity the driest and thorniest subjects. We talk to them unceasingly; we wish them to listen; we are afraid of tiring or boring them; hence we develop a particular method of explaining ourselves easily, and this passes from conversation into style."

The dawning of the Age of Enlightenment heralded the appearance of the modern era in the history of ideas, its thought drastically altering the ways humans viewed their world. Out of the intellectual foment of the Enlightenment emerged the French Revolution; it also helped influence the spirit of the American Revolution and contributed to the philosophic premise of two fundamental documents of the United States, the Declaration of Independence and the Constitution. On a more literary level, some scholars have connected Enlightenment ideology with the rise of the novel and the development of literary realism. Romanticism was in part a reaction against Enlightenment philosophy, as was the German *Sturm und Drang* literary movement. According to Chambers: "The vision of the Enlightenment was freedom—freedom from superstition, freedom from intolerance, freedom to know (for knowledge was held to be the ultimate power), freedom from the arbitrary authority of church or state, freedom to trade or work without vestigial feudal restrictions. . . . [The] Enlightenment finally reversed the whole trend of European culture."

THE QUESTION OF DEFINITION

Immanuel Kant

[*A highly influential German philosopher, Kant propounded a system in which knowledge is derived from the senses and the reasoning processes of the mind. He elaborated his theories in his* Critique of Pure Reason *(1781) and in other works. In the following essay, originally published in the* Berlinische Monatsschrift *in 1784, he interprets the meaning of the term "Enlighten-*ment," *defining it as "man's release from his self-incurred tutelage."*]

Enlightenment is man's release from his self-incurred tutelage. Tutelage is man's inability to make use of his understanding without direction from another. Self-incurred is this tutelage when its cause lies not in lack of reason but in lack of resolution and courage to use it without direction from another. *Sapere aude!* "Have courage to use your own reason!"—that is the motto of enlightenment.

Laziness and cowardice are the reasons why so great a portion of mankind, after nature has long since discharged them from external direction (*naturaliter maiorennes*), nevertheless remains under lifelong tutelage, and why it is so easy for others to set themselves up as their guardians. It is so easy not to be of age. If I have a book which understands for me, a pastor who has a conscience for me, a physician who decides my diet, and so forth, I need not trouble myself. I need not think, if I can only pay—others will readily undertake the irksome work for me.

That the step to competence is held to be very dangerous by the far greater portion of mankind (and by the entire fair sex)—quite apart from its being arduous—is seen to by those guardians who have so kindly assumed superintendence over them. After the guardians have first made their domestic cattle dumb and have made sure that these placid creatures will not dare take a single step without the harness of the cart to which they are confined, the guardians then show them the danger which threatens if they try to go alone. Actually, however, this danger is not so great, for by falling a few times they would finally learn to walk alone. But an example of this failure makes them timid and ordinarily frightens them away from all further trials.

For any single individual to work himself out of the life under tutelage which has become almost his nature is very difficult. He has come to be fond of this state, and he is for the present really incapable of making use of his reason, for no one has ever let him try it out. Statutes and formulas, those mechanical tools of the rational employment or rather misemployment of his natural gifts, are the fetters of an everlasting tutelage. Whoever throws them off makes only an uncertain leap over the narrowest ditch because he is not accustomed to that kind of free motion. Therefore, there are only few who have succeeded by their own exercise of mind both in freeing themselves from incompetence and in achieving a steady pace.

But that the public should enlighten itself is more possible; indeed, if only freedom is granted, enlightenment is almost sure to follow. For there will always be some independent thinkers, even among the established guardians of the great masses, who, after throwing off the yoke of tutelage from their own shoulders, will disseminate the spirit of the rational appreciation of both their own worth and every man's vocation for thinking for himself. But be it noted that the public, which has first been brought under this yoke by their guardians, forces the guardians themselves to remain bound when it is incited to do so by some of the guardians who are themselves capable of some enlightenment—so harmful is it to implant prejudices, for they later take vengeance on their cultivators or on their descendants. Thus the public can only slowly attain enlightenment. Perhaps a fall of personal despotism or of avaricious or tyrannical oppression may be accomplished by revolution, but never a true reform in ways of thinking. Rather, new prejudices will serve as well as old ones to harness the great unthinking masses.

For this enlightenment, however, nothing is required but freedom, and indeed the most harmless freedom of all, which alone should be called by this name. It is the freedom to make public use of one's reason at every point. But I hear on all sides, "Do not argue!" The officer says: "Do not argue but drill!" The tax-collector: "Do not argue but pay!" The cleric: "Do not argue but believe!" Only one prince in the world says, "Argue as much as you will, and about what you will, but obey!" Everywhere there is restriction on freedom.

Which restriction is an obstacle to enlightenment, and which is not an obstacle but a promoter of it? I answer: The public use of one's reason must always be free, and it alone can bring about enlightenment among men. The private use of reason, on the other hand, may often be very narrowly restricted without particularly hindering the progress of enlightenment. By the public use of one's reason I understand the use which a person makes of it as a scholar before the reading public. Private use I call that which one may make of it in a particular civil post or office which is intrusted to him. Many affairs which are conducted in the interest of the community require a certain mechanism through which some members of the community must passively conduct themselves with an artificial unanimity, so that the government may direct them to public ends, or at least prevent them from destroying those ends. Here argument is certainly not allowed—one must obey. But so far as a part of the mechanism regards himself at the same time as a member of the whole community or of a society of world citizens, and thus in the role of a scholar who addresses the public (in the proper sense of the word) through his writings, he certainly can argue without hurting the affairs for which he is in part responsible as a passive member. Thus it would be ruinous for an officer in service to debate about the suitability or utility of a command given to him by his superior; he must obey. But the right to make remarks on errors in the military service and to lay them before the public for judgment cannot equitably be refused him as a scholar. The citizen cannot refuse to pay the taxes imposed on him; indeed, an impudent complaint at those levied on him can be punished as a scandal (as it could occasion general refractoriness). But the same person nevertheless does not act contrary to his duty as a citizen when, as a scholar, he publicly expresses his thoughts on the inappropriateness or even the injustice of these levies. Similarly a clergyman is obligated to make his sermon to his pupils in catechism and his congregation conform to the symbol of the church which he serves, for he has been accepted on this condition. But as a scholar he has complete freedom, even the calling, to communicate to the public all his carefully tested and well-meaning thoughts on that which is erroneous in the symbol and to make suggestions for the better organization of the religious body and church. In doing this, there is nothing that could be laid as a burden on his conscience. For what he teaches as a consequence of his office as a representative of the church, this he considers something about which he has no freedom to teach according to his own lights; it is something which he is appointed to propound at the dictation of and in the name of another. He will say, "Our

church teaches this or that; those are the proofs which it adduces." He thus extracts all practical uses for his congregation from statutes to which he himself would not subscribe with full conviction but to the enunciation of which he can very well pledge himself because it is not impossible that truth lies hidden in them, and, in any case, there is at least nothing in them contradictory to inner religion. For if he believed he had found such in them, he could not conscientiously discharge the duties of his office; he would have to give it up. The use, therefore, which an appointed teacher makes of his reason before his congregation is merely private, because this congregation is only a domestic one (even if it be a large gathering); with respect to it, as a priest, he is not free, nor can he be free, because he carries out the orders of another. But as a scholar, whose writings speak to his public, the world, the clergyman in the public use of his reason enjoys an unlimited freedom to use his own reason and to speak in his own person. That the guardians of the people (in spiritual things) should themselves be incompetent is an absurdity which amounts to the eternalization of absurdities.

But would not a society of clergymen, perhaps a church conference or a venerable classis (as they call themselves among the Dutch), be justified in obligating itself by oath to a certain unchangeable symbol in order to enjoy an unceasing guardianship over each of its members and thereby over the people as a whole, and even to make it eternal? I answer that this is altogether impossible. Such a contract, made to shut off all further enlightenment from the human race, is absolutely null and void even if confirmed by the supreme power, by parliaments, and by the most ceremonious of peace treaties. An age cannot bind itself and ordain to put the succeeding one into such a condition that it cannot extend its (at best very occasional) knowledge, purify itself of errors, and progress in general enlightenment. That would be a crime against human nature, the proper destination of which lies precisely in this progress; and the descendants would be fully justified in rejecting those decrees as having been made in an unwarranted and malicious manner.

The touchstone of everything that can be concluded as a law for a people lies in the question whether the people could have imposed such a law on itself. Now such a religious compact might be possible for a short and definitely limited time, as it were, in expectation of a better. One might let every citizen, and especially the clergyman, in the role of scholar, make his comments freely and publicly, i.e., through writing, on the erroneous aspects of the present institution. The newly introduced order might last until insight into the nature of these things had become so general and widely approved that through uniting their voices (even if not unanimously) they could bring a proposal to the throne to take those congregations under protection which had united into a changed religious organization according to their better ideas, without, however, hindering others who wish to remain in the order. But to unite in a permanent religious institution which is not to be subject to doubt before the public even in the lifetime of one man, and thereby to make a period of time fruitless in the progress of mankind toward improvement, thus working to the disadvantage of posterity—that is absolutely forbidden. For himself (and only for a short time) a man can postpone enlightenment in what he ought to know, but to renounce it for himself and even more to renounce it for posterity is to injure and trample on the rights of mankind.

And what a people may not decree for itself can even less be decreed for them by a monarch, for his lawgiving authority rests on his uniting the general public will in his own. If he only sees to it that all true or alleged improvement stands together with civil order, he can leave it to his subjects to do what they find necessary for their spiritual welfare. This is not his concern, though it is incumbent on him to prevent one of them from violently hindering another in determining and promoting this welfare to the best of his ability. To meddle in these matters lowers his own majesty, since by the writings in which his subjects seek to present their views he may evaluate his own governance. He can do this when, with deepest understanding, he lays upon himself the reproach, *Caesar non est supra grammaticos.* Far more does he injure his own majesty when he degrades his supreme power by supporting the ecclesiastical despotism of some tyrants in his state over his other subjects.

If we are asked, "Do we now live in an *enlightened age?*" the answer is, "No," but we do live in an *age of enlightenment.* As things now stand, much is lacking which prevents men from being, or easily becoming, capable of correctly using their own reason in religious matters with assurance and free from outside direction. But, on the other hand, we have clear indications that the field has now been opened wherein men may freely deal with these things and that the obstacles to general enlightenment or the release from self-imposed tutelage are gradually being reduced. In this respect, this is the age of enlightenment, or the century of Frederick.

A prince who does not find it unworthy of himself to say that he holds it to be his duty to prescribe nothing to men in religious matters but to give them complete freedom while renouncing the haughty name of *tolerance,* is himself enlightened and deserves to be esteemed by the grateful world and posterity as the first, at least from the side of government, who divested the human race of its tutelage and left each man free to make use of his reason in matters of conscience. Under him venerable ecclesiastics are allowed, in the role of scholars, and without infringing on their official duties, freely to submit for public testing their judgments and views which here and there diverge from the established symbol. And an even greater freedom is enjoyed by those who are restricted by no official duties. This spirit of freedom spreads beyond this land, even to those in which it must struggle with external obstacles erected by a government which misunderstands its own interest. For an example gives evidence to such a government that in freedom there is not the least cause for concern about public peace and the stability of the community. Men work themselves gradually out of barbarity if only intentional artifices are not made to hold them in it.

I have placed the main point of enlightenment—the escape of men from their self-incurred tutelage—chiefly in matters of religion because our rulers have no interest in playing the guardian with respect to the arts and sciences and also because religious incompetence is not only the most harmful but also the most degrading of all. But the manner of thinking of the head of a state who favors religious enlightenment goes further, and he sees that there is no danger to his lawgiving in allowing his subjects to make public use of their reason and to publish their thoughts on a better formulation of his legislation and even their open-minded criticisms of the laws already made. Of this we have a shining example wherein no monarch is superior to him whom we honor.

But only one who is himself enlightened, is not afraid of shadows, and has a numerous and well-disciplined army to assure public peace can say: "Argue as much as you will, and about what you will, only obey!" A republic could not dare say such a thing. Here is shown a strange and unexpected trend in human affairs in which almost everything, looked at in the large, is paradoxical. A greater degree of civil freedom appears advantageous to the freedom of mind of the people, and yet it places inescapable limitations upon it; a lower degree of civil freedom, on the contrary, provides the mind with room for each man to extend himself to his full capacity. As nature has uncovered from under this hard shell the seed for which she most tenderly cares—the propensity and vocation to free thinking—this gradually works back upon the character of the people, who thereby gradually become capable of managing freedom; finally, it affects the principles of government, which finds it to its advantage to treat men, who are now more than machines, in accordance with their dignity. (pp. 286-92)

> *Immanuel Kant, "What Is Enlightenment?" in his* Critique of Practical Reason and Other Writings in Moral Philosophy, *edited and translated by Lewis White Beck, The University of Chicago Press, 1949, pp. 286-92.*

Ira O. Wade

[*Wade was an American educator and author who wrote extensively on the French Enlightenment and its major personalities, particularly Voltaire. His works include* The Clandestine Organization and Diffusion of Philosophic Ideas in France from 1700 to 1750 *(1938),* The Intellectual Development of Voltaire *(1969), and* The Intellectual Origins of the French Enlightenment *(1971). In the following excerpt from the last-named work, Wade defines the chronology and essential characteristics of the Enlightenment.*]

If the events which led to the Revolution are difficult to assess in the developing conditions of the Enlightenment, the causes of the Enlightenment are equally confused. Indeed, the question as to what constitutes the Enlightenment time span has in the past sixty years been given various answers. At the end of the nineteenth century, for instance, it was looked upon as a period of transition which extended between a declining classicism and a nascent romanticism, and spanning a relatively short period of time, from the middle of the eighteenth century to the French Revolution. The emphasis was placed not upon the literary and artistic production, but upon the thought of a few writers, particularly Montesquieu, Voltaire, and Rousseau. The scholars of the time were mainly preoccupied with the responsibility which the thinkers of the Enlightenment must accept for the excesses of the Revolution. In general this view stressed the non-literary, non-artistic aspect of the movement, emphasizing the development of destructive, unorthodox ideas leading to a political, social, and intellectual explosion. It was conditioned by the particular interests of the scholars. Literary scholars felt that the Enlightenment, being an age of transition, was less inviting, in an organic way, than the Classical Period which preceded it or the Romantic which followed. Neoclassicism was judged less worthy than classicism, and pre-romanticism less attractive than romanticism. Literary critics were therefore tempted to direct their efforts to two or three outstanding writers who dominated the period. Historians directed all their attention to the effects of the movement: What interested them, as we have seen, was the Revolution, not any inherent personality in the Enlightenment itself. Philosophers found even less appeal in the development, limiting themselves to Locke, or Hume, or Kant, and leaving the impression that what was not important was the work of the "Philosophes." Only the historian of ideas continued his search in the field, doing what he could to combine the activity of the literary critic with that of the historian and the philosopher.

The original view of the Enlightenment reinforced the belief that the century extended from 1715 to 1789. The second part, 1750 to 1789, was the active period; the earlier period, 1715 to 1750, was a time of preparation. In due time, however, a number of scholars (Brunetière, Lanson, Hazard) came to feel that the death of Louis XIV did not mark a change in the direction of thought, or even an intensification. The ideas which were developed between 1715 and 1750 were found to have existed in the period between 1685 and 1715. The studies of Lanson and his students gave great impetus to this opinion. For them, the important thing in the Enlightenment was no longer the way in which it produced the Revolution; it was rather the way in which the "esprit philosophique," organized during the period, prepared modern times.

This view was naturally susceptible to great expansion. Once "esprit philosophique" had been identified with rationalism, once the belief was adopted that there is a correlation between thought and action, and an identification between rationalism, "esprit philosophique," and science, the limits of the Enlightenment became suddenly extended. The date 1685 no longer marked the beginning of the movement, particularly if one is inclined to accept Kant's definition. With Hazard, the important period became 1680 to 1715; with Lenoble, the crisis period extended from 1630 to 1660; with Pintard, the author of *Le Libertinage érudit,* from 1600 to 1660. With his three books on *Le Rationalisme en France,* Busson has carried the movement back to the early years of the Renaissance in Italy and followed its growth from the formation of Italian free-thinking to the opening years of the eighteenth century. Thus the trend of Enlightenment scholarship has been to expand the period of its origins backward, and at the same time to bring down toward the twentieth century its consequences. There is also the tendency to identify the Enlightenment with "l'esprit philosophique," with the growth of rationalism, with the development of free-thinking, with skepticism, with unbelief, particularly religious disbelief, and with the movement in science. In its consequences, the Enlightenment has been thought to tend toward irrationalism rather than toward a refined rationalism.

Seen in this perspective, the central problem of Enlightenment would be to grasp the way in which rationalism, having set out to become aware of its possibilities, has encountered hidden forces within itself which have made it con-

scious of its impossibilities. Simply stated, it is the story how the human mind came to know and to turn into realities its inner powers, but how, in doing so it discovered not only their ultimate unreality, but their uselessness in achieving human satisfactions. To study how this realization was brought about would make an interesting footnote on the hopelessness of our present condition, but we cannot promise so important a diagnosis, nor a lucid demonstration of the ways whereby we have become the heirs, or the victims, of the movement. It is our task here merely to record its origins.

The difficulties of establishing the correct time span were paralleled by obstacles in marking out its locale. Practically everyone would agree that the center of the movement is in France, but the historians would immediately insist that the preponderant influence in the eighteenth century as far as Europe is concerned is that of England. The general view now held would be that the English influence is very important, especially upon France who introduced it throughout Europe. It is thought, however, that in doing this, France enhanced her own importance. What made this expansion possible was the widespread use of the French language in Europe so eloquently exemplified by the subject proposed by the Berlin Academy when Rivarol took the prize with his *Discours sur l'universalité de la langue française* in 1784. But as early as 1685, in the *Nouvelles de la république des lettres,* Bayle had remarked (I, 3) that the French language was already the common medium of communication of the peoples of Europe. As a matter of fact, it was more widely used in Germany and the central European countries than in England and the Latin countries. Voltaire noted its use in Germany and commented that it had made more extensive conquests than Charlemagne. In reality, it was the language of an international European *élite,* and was propagated in the salons controlled by women. French literature followed the vogue of the language, either in translation or in the original. Germany, especially, assimilated both French thought and French art and re-exported them into the countries to the north and to the east. Foremost among the writers and thinkers who were thus adopted throughout Europe via Germany was Voltaire, but Rousseau's influence became stronger and stronger, and the popularity of the *Encyclopédie* also grew in time. Rousseau was more and more appreciated because he united French reason with that "sentiment," which appealed so deeply to the German genius. After literature came art, which also deeply penetrated German culture. In England, there was a strong opposition to the influence of France as early as 1738, when some journalist remarked that the ridiculous imitation of things French—clothes, furnishings, even food—had become an epidemic disease. In 1762, someone asserted that the English passion for things French was as nothing compared to the French passion for things English. Actually, there was a broad merging of the manners and customs of the two countries, as we shall see.

Some of the causes which underlay the merging are easily perceived, such as the dominant position held by Louis XIV in European affairs. French émigrés, like Saint-Evremond and the Duchesse de Mazarin, enhanced the prestige of France in England. The constant flow of travelers between the two countries was very important to the merging process. After the *Revocation,* the Protestant refugees, who could operate only in a social atmosphere which subordinated the notion of fatherland to the concept of humanity, were a very effective force in bringing together the civilization of Europe. The cosmopolitan spirit prevailed, particularly among the European *élite,* but the qualities of the French so appreciated throughout Europe—clarity of thought, sociability, a talent for making conversation, respect for authority of reason—rendered the position of Louis XV's kingdom almost paramount in the culture of Europe.

There were even definite indications of a widespread interest in an integrated Europe, a feeling that more important than the superiority of England or Italy was the superiority of Europe. Indeed, many now proclaimed that Europe surpassed the other parts of the world; it had a common legal system, a common religion, and although the national states had different types of government—some monarchies, some republics, some mixed—the same religion, the same principles of public and political law united them all (see Voltaire's *Siècle de Louis XIV,* chapter II). Europe itself was often regarded as a kind of grand republic: the Europeans more than any other peoples were distinguished by their insatiable curiosity, their science, their arts, their culture, their intellectual supremacy. Indeed, there were those who remarked upon the rapid advance which the Europe of the eighteenth century had made when compared with previous centuries: the Europeans not only surpassed the inhabitants of other continents; those of the eighteenth century were deemed superior to those of the preceding centuries. This primacy had been assured by the facility of travel, the circulation of newspapers and reviews, and the publication of large, all-embracing compendia, dictionaries and encyclopedias. Into this concept of a united, intellectual Europe, France, the geographical center, with its political and economic ascendancy, its widespread artistic and intellectual activities, and its language widely accepted as the medium of international communication, took on the role of leader of European life, storehouse of European thought, and distributor of European aspirations. Voltaire, whose criticism of eighteenth-century France was certainly not disingenuous, celebrated both her position of primacy and Europe's mission in the making of civilization. (pp. 15-19)

Nevertheless, for a Europe focused upon France, for a European *élite* attracted by French language, customs, and intellectual activities, there was another Europe in which each country was already solidly committed to its own national traits, acknowledging its superiorities and stressing the defects of the others. It was at this point that one country—England—arose to challenge the supremacy of France. Having given to Europe outstanding scientists, moralists, and philosophers, it now claimed the right to impose its literature, its manners, and its arts. France, the leader of Europe, was impressed with the qualities of its rival to the point of widely adopting English costumes, gardens, thought, and manners. Indeed, recent studies have indicated that it was France and its infatuation with things English which was largely responsible for the widespread English influence throughout Europe. There was nonetheless built into this new orientation a tendency toward separate nationalities which contradicted the urge toward integration. The drive toward nationalism, which was to characterize the nineteenth century, had already begun. It became all the more acute since two countries, Prussia and Russia, were demanding their place in the

The Paris Opéra during the ancien régime.

family of European nations. Thereby entered into the mind of Europe the diversity which has also become one of its characteristics; not a Europe of one religion, but of several; not one political or economic union, but several; not a Europe directed by one intellectual and artistic activity, but by several; coalitions will be blocs, and there will be wars, revolutions, and ultimately each country will have its own Enlightenment. (pp. 19-20)

In his article entitled "What is Enlightenment?", Kant best described its psychological foundations [see essay above]. To the question proposed, he responded that the Enlightenment is "man's leaving his self-caused immaturity." Immaturity he defined as the incapacity to use one's mind without another's guidance. Such immaturity is self-caused if it is brought about not by lack of intelligence, but of determination and courage to use one's own reason. Instead of this abdication, Kant proposed the slogan, which long before had been adopted from Horace by Gassendi: "Sapere aude!"

Kant, however, admits that, once we leave to others the guidance of our lives, it is not easy to abandon the state of immaturity. Indeed, so accustomed has everyone become to his condition that it appears almost natural. However, this state of affairs does not have to continue; the public can enlighten itself, if it is given its freedom. But it cannot do so rapidly; the process of acquiring liberty from the guardians of the public is necessarily slow and awkward, since they who exercise this right of maturity are sometimes loath to relinquish it to the public in general, thus fostering what Kant called "prejudices." Any attempt to abolish them in a revolutionary way may lead to oppression. To avoid these consequences, Kant insists, man must have freedom for the public use of his reason, which is "the sacred right of mankind." This is particularly the case, he adds, in matters of religion.

Thus nature has fostered within itself the need and the inclination for free thought: "This free thought gradually works upon the minds of the people and they become more capable of acting in freedom. Eventually, the government is also influenced by this free thought and thereby it treats man, who is now more than a machine, according to his dignity." For Kant, as for Voltaire, the Enlightenment is identified with the growth of knowledge which leads to the assertion of maturity, the avoidance of prejudices, and the search for freedom. Freedom thus becomes the source of free thought which liberates man and assures him of his dignity.

Cassirer, accepting Kant's definition as the one which best characterizes the intellectual tendencies of Enlightenment philosophy, stressed that the period rejected the view of the world which derived its strength from a belief in divine revelation, and substituted in its place a view established on the powers of human understanding. Those who adopted this latter view are convinced that reason can, by its own power, and without any assistance from any supernatural force, comprehend the system of the world and find means of using it to advantage. The Enlightenment was thus always moving from a system of the universe in which all the important decisions in life were made outside of man to a system where it became the responsibility of man to care for them himself. The instrument which he believed devised for this undertaking was the human understanding, which though called by various vague names—"esprit, pensée, raison, conscience, savoir," etc.—was reduced to the term reason. Since the phenomena first attacked by reason were in the realm of nature, all other phenomena gradually gravitated around the concept of nature, and in that way, the central problem became the relationship of reason and nature.

The Enlightenment thus started with the realm of nature and that of mind, understanding its task to be the penetration of nature's reality by an intellectual awareness of that reality. What the age wanted to do was to collect the largest body of impressions in nature from which to deduce the greatest number of principles which would contribute to maximum human activity and happiness.

Nature, to the thinkers of the Enlightenment, is a closed system of causes and effects, of reasons and implications; there is nothing accidental or arbitrary therein. Everything is subjected to universal laws which can be known by conceptual analysis rather than by experience or observation. The method practiced was to reduce the natural event to mathematical statement. The principle, once established in natural phenomena, was introduced likewise in the area of social and historical fact. The being of man can be explained by the same universal laws which govern the being of nature, since no distinction can be made between nature and human nature. Man's world being no longer separate from nature's world, he has no exceptional place in the scheme of things.

The Enlightenment was concerned not only with the penetration of nature, that is total organic nature, by reason, it wanted also to devise an absolute identity between the natural and the reasonable. Natural law is right reason working in the field of human and natural relationships. Natural religion is the working of right reason in the field of religion. Finally, natural morality is right reason working in the field of ethics. The just, the true, and the good are both reasonable and natural. They transcend both time and space, and they have a universal validity because they stand at the origin of positive laws, religions, and moralities. The Enlightenment was fascinated with those laws which are not of "yesterday," and the thinkers inquired diligently into the origin of things as a means of comprehending their meaning for man.

The Enlightenment did not attempt to develop a new body of teachings, though, nor did it seek a new dogma. Anxious to discover new facts, it insisted upon their dissemination among the widest number of people. It was by nature encyclopedic and propagandistic. Convinced that in the corps of facts lay an infinite number of inner formative forces, it conceived as its task to seek out the structures which, treated properly, could transform a world of contradiction and chaos into an organic unity. It recommended an effort to sift, clarify, arrange, and organize the ideas which it already possessed. It was confident, too, that the inner formative forces which derived from its corps of facts could create a whole new spirit. This conviction, indeed, led to a totally new kind of philosophical thought, based upon systematic analysis. Cassirer explains that "instead of tying philosophy to definite, immutable axioms and deductions from them, the Enlightenment wants it to move freely and in this immanent activity to discover the fundamental form of reality." No longer a special field of knowledge, philosophy is rather the all-comprehensive medium in which the principles of all knowledge are free to develop. No longer mere thought, it wants to enter into the activity of the spirit. Its task is not to reflect but to shape life. Hence, the Enlightenment's inquiry concerned first the competence of thought. The problem was naturally derived from Locke's *Essay,* but the solution differed from Locke's conception in that it involved both the limits of thought and its capabilities as a dynamic force. Thought became the center of all activity, regarded not only as the unifying element, but also as the immutable factor in all life. In addition to being a collection of knowledge, of truths, and of principles, it was conceived as a dynamic process, an energy, which can be grasped only in its activity. It is a *manner of thinking,* devoted to constant analysis, to separation into component parts, to the reconstruction of those parts into a whole, and to the expression of this whole in terms of laws. It functions in every enterprise in which the human being is engaged, and by its *manner of thinking,* it aims to change the *common way of thinking and doing.* Thus Enlightenment thought carries within itself powers of destruction as well as powers of construction. Finally, knowledge of the world does not stop with knowledge of external objects; it is the means whereby one sees reflected the possibilities of his inner reality. Since the cosmos is limitless both in time and space, knowledge tends to become a never-ending series of relationships between the self and the phenomena of life, in which the correlation between the universe and the self guarantees the validity of thought and the legality of the external world. Knowledge thus involves both thinking and feeling, sensibility and thought, experience and rational awareness.

Being and knowing are consequently two poles of the same ontological phenomenon, present both in nature and in all the creations of human nature: history, morality, the state, religion, and aesthetics.

Thus the eighteenth century gave a priority to nature, in which were incorporated all the phenomena of man. The real achievement of natural science did not lie in the all-embracing content, but rather in the possibility which this content offered to the human mind for self-realization. The limitless expansion of natural science increased the mind's awareness of a new force within itself. It is not in its infinity, however, that nature informs man of his real intensity. His deepest meaning lies in the mind's maintaining itself against the infinite universe. Thus there is a double tendency seen in nature: toward the particular, the concrete, the factual, and contrariwise to the absolutely universal. It is this duality which shifts the importance of nature from the realm of the created to that of the creative process. Nature participates in the divine essence, and eventually identifies herself with God. Contained within herself is the whole plan of the cosmos waiting for the human mind to recognize and express it, and when this occurs, the operation carries with it both identity and autonomy. With one stroke, is brought out the self-sufficiency of nature and mind, the one perfectly accessible to the other.

The Enlightenment accepted, though, that certain changes must be effected. The sciences must be organized in a unified way; and the bond between theology and physics must be severed. Nature must incorporate within herself all the intellectual sciences, even laws, society, politics, and poetry; she can be grasped only by that method which begins with facts and attempts to reach to principles. In theory, however, one should never expect to venture beyond description of natural phenomena, since there is no way whereby we can explain the mechanism of the universe or see into the essence of things. We possess no knowledge of first principles, and consequently no final criterion of the truth of phenomena, only a "moral certainty," which is not logical, but rather biological. Indeed, there is a definite shift, recorded by Diderot in the *Pensées sur l'interprétation de la nature,* from mathematics and mathematical physics to biology and physiology, exhibiting a strong tendency to materialism.

For the Enlightenment the basic science became psychology, despite the fact that the word itself became current only late in the century. Thought cannot turn to the objects of external nature without at the same time reverting to itself. The truth which it perceives in nature becomes in a way the truth in itself. Hence the two questions which are constantly propounded in the eighteenth century concern the reality of the objects of nature and the capacity of the mind to penetrate that reality. Involved in those two problems are two larger issues: the limits of the understanding and the nature of the things understood. The question constantly posed is: what kind of object is commensurate with, and determinable by, our knowledge? No legitimate answer, however, can be given to this question until an exact insight into the specific character of the human understanding is achieved by examining the extent of its activity and the course of its development. Thus psy-chology became the foundation of epistemology. The capacities of knowledge are known only by tracing the processes of thought: the critical analysis of the instrument discloses the extent of its possibilities.

Fundamentally, what the Enlightenment wanted to ascertain was how one can know, and the connection between knowledge and action. It was faced with the necessity of seeking the agreement between concepts and objects, expressed by the simple question: What is the relationship between knowledge and reality? The Enlightenment's answer to this question was that every idea in our minds is based on a previous impression. This belief resulted in the reassertion of the Stoic statement that "nihil est in intellectu quod non antea fuerit in sensu." But there was no proof of this statement.

There were in fact three explanations for ideas in the Enlightenment. Locke stuck to the senses as their source, but he retained in his explanation of the operations of the understanding such innate factors as comparing, reflection, judging, and willing. Leibniz for his part thought ideas took their origin in the active energy of the mind. Condillac saw the senses as the source, but he eliminated all such innate notions as reflection, comparing, etc.

In these explanations there was some ground for agreement: the insistence upon the dominance of the passions, the stress laid upon the concept of effort, the drive toward the active energy. In fact, though only Leibniz stated so categorically, the century tended to insist that the mind is not a composite of faculties, mechanically organized, but a composite of formative forces. The task of philosophy henceforth is to elucidate those forces in their structure and to understand their reciprocal relations. In this way there was opened up a new approach to the spontaneity of the ego, and new paths for progress in epistemology, aesthetics, and morality.

Since the initial shift of the Enlightenment was from a system dominated by a religious order to one in which the individual accepted responsibility for making his world, it was inevitable that the institution of religion should be put in question. Usually this attitude was interpreted as an attack which the writers and thinkers of the Enlightenment made against established religion. A thorough-going review of the proofs of the divinity of Christianity—miracles, prophecies, the continuity of Christian history from the old to the new dispensation, its morality, and its martyrs—was made. Many works investigating these proofs circulated in France and England. Many analyzed the *Bible* in an effort to point out the inaccuracies of a historical, scientific, moral, even of a computational, order. The conclusion drawn was that a work so filled with errors could not be accorded universal religious significance. Practically all these works affirmed the validity of natural religion, natural morality, and natural law, basing them upon a divinely inspired reason, and stressing that this reason was the source of love of God, justice toward one's fellowmen, and social and political morality.

These ideas were propagated by the deists who in a negative way denied the need for dogma, rites and ceremonies, religious organization and a priesthood, but who in a positive way reasserted their belief in the existence of God and in the necessity for a reasonable, natural morality. As a religious movement, deism was very widespread in the eighteenth century. It drew its strength from its pretense to universality, having been the religion of all the wise men of the past. But it was also the religion of all men everywhere, since it was the voice of God-given reason in the hearts of all men. It had its weaknesses, however, the foremost being its instability. Deists found it difficult to explain how every man with God-given reason acted so terribly unreasonably at times, more difficult still to explain how the divine sense of justice seldom led to just acts. The whole realm of evil—natural evil; positive, moral evil; metaphysical evil—became an inexplicable phenomenon in a universe filled with wonders which declared the glory of God, while pain, suffering, and sin declared at least that something had gone awry. It was not consoling to realize that everything lived in this world at the expense of everything else. Since the deist affirmed the wisdom, the goodness, and the all-powerfulness of the Deity, evil could not be explained by reason without putting into question at least one of these qualities. And any rejection of these qualities reduced the concept of the Deity to Nature, and left the way open to atheism, naturalism, determinism, materialism. Pascal had long before seen the deist dilemma and had reaffirmed the doctrine of original sin and the necessity for the Atonement. He experienced difficulty in making salvation universal, however, but the Enlightenment did succeed in making it universal, though not without involving the all-powerfulness of the Deity, and even His mode of existence.

Cassirer explains that this impossible situation merely indicates that the period was not ripe for the creation of a theodicy, and consequently, the Enlightenment sought replacements for the deficiency, one of which was the doctrine of tolerance. Since there is no metaphysical imperative in any formal religion, there is no absolute validity in any religious sect. Therefore the only reasonable way of approaching a sect is respect for its beliefs and the elimination of all forms of persecution. The Enlightenment was prepared to proclaim that even heresy was the natural state of man and was entitled to the respect of everybody. Indeed, in accordance with the formula expressed by Spinoza in the *Tractatus,* the century maintained that every man was entitled to the freedom of his beliefs, which the State should protect. The doctrine of tolerance, accordingly, became grounded upon the brotherhood of man and the right to err. In a way this was a social theodicy which justified the ways of God to man, but it was strictly limited to this world and to this life. It led straight to the suggestion of two other replacements for the old theodicy: with Shaftesbury and down to Diderot, the highest form of spiritual expression was not theological but aesthetic; with Rousseau, its highest form was moral and above all political. For the Enlightenment as a whole, however, all of these replacements merely put great emphasis upon the moral category and attributed a preponderant importance to the inner energy of man and his right to express that energy in any manifestation of human creation. (pp. 20-7)

Ira O. Wade, in his The Intellectual Origins of the French Enlightenment, *Princeton University Press, 1971, 678 p.*

LE SIÈCLE DES LUMIÈRES

Peter Gay

[*A German-born American, Gay is a social historian who has written numerous essays and books on the Enlightenment, nineteenth-century middle-class culture, and the arts and politics of Imperial and Weimar Germany. In the following excerpt, he claims that the intellectual incongruities evident among the individual philosophes "merely [dramatize] the richness and the unity of the French Enlightenment."*]

The *philosophes* were not optimists: Voltaire proclaimed life to be a shipwreck and lamented the decline of taste in his century; Holbach insisted on the viciousness and Helvétius on the selfishness of the human animal; even Rousseau, the champion of a just Providence, defended his optimism in the most anxious and lugubrious of tones. Yet they were too active, too energetic, too deeply opposed to the Christian doctrine of man's depravity, to lapse into pessimism or pious resignation. The *philosophes* were not rationalists: Condillac, d'Alembert, and Voltaire attacked the rationalists' construction of metaphysical systems, and insisted on the limits of reason, the ignorance of humanity, and the futility of seeking certainty. Yet they despised and combated anti-rationalist theories of knowledge and dwelled admiringly on the achievements of scientific method. The *philosophes* battled for toleration and the humane treatment of society's victims—their humanitarian activities have withstood the scrutiny of the most hardheaded critic. Yet in their personal lives they were often intolerant and inhumane: Voltaire hounded his literary and political adversaries; d'Alembert, the enemy of censorship, peevishly asked the censors to suppress the pamphlets of his critics. The *philosophes* prided themselves on their knowledge of science: Maupertuis brilliantly confirmed and Voltaire brilliantly popularized Newton's cosmology; Diderot anticipated many discoveries in psychology and biology; the *Encyclopédie* was a massive tribute to technology and the scientific method. Yet the alert reader detects undertones of philistine aversion to scientific speculation, sometimes in the heart of the scientific camp, as in Diderot's hostility to mathematics. Perhaps the safest generality about the *philosophes* (certainly the most popular) has been that they were "cold" rationalists, contemptuous of the power of emotion, and existed in a universe stripped of love and color, devoid of any passion but sex. But for all its plausibility, this generality also dissolves under scrutiny. It would hold only if we disregarded the *philosophes'* defense of imagination, their pioneering analysis of passion, their bold creation of literary forms, and their almost unanimous infatuation with Richardson's sensibility. And we would have to rob the French Enlightenment of Rousseau and Diderot by calling them pre-Romantics—a larcenous and unjust, although widely practiced, proceeding.

I could go on listing divergences among the *philosophes:* deists against atheists, aristocrats against democrats, believers in free will against determinists. Close inspection even ruins the harmonious portrait of a friendly debate within the philosophic family—or clique, as frightened enemies called it. Voltaire collaborated with an *Encyclopédie* in which he never really believed and to whose chief editor he gave reserved and uncomprehending respect; Diderot, in return, offered reluctant tributes to the literary dictator whom he admired and distrusted as a brilliant but unstable child; Rousseau, at first welcomed by all came to reject, and to be rejected, by all. The *philosophes* moved in a highly charged atmosphere in which quarrels were bitter, reconciliations fervent, conversations intense, interests sometimes exalted but often trivial—an energetic atmosphere in which, despite all distractions, everyone worked, all the time.

It is this almost obsessive dedication to work that provides us with our escape from nominalism. For the *philosophes,* work was pleasure, obligation, consolation, fulfillment. For obvious reasons I shall resist the temptation of saying that it was salvation.

The environment in which work is performed imposes tasks, suggests styles, draws limits, and is in turn transformed by work done. Now, the *philosophes'* world (and I mean more than the censorship or the salons, I mean their total experience, including their experience of themselves) defined their task. Let me put their situation into a formula: as men of letters at home in a world that was losing its Christian vocation, the *philosophes* felt this critical loss as a deep problem and solved it by reinterpreting and transforming their civilization. They made themselves the spokesmen for a revolutionary age in search of an interpreter.

The *philosophes* were men of letters. This is more than a phrase. It defines their vantage point, and eliminates the stale debate over their status as philosophers. As men of letters who took their craft seriously, they devoted to their writing an incessant care which is one of the secrets of their style. Their output was enormous, and they sent less to the printer than they threw away. They knew the pleasure of self-criticism, and the sweeter pleasure of criticizing others. Grimm corrected Diderot, Diderot corrected Voltaire, and Voltaire corrected everybody. Rousseau, far from tossing off his masterpieces in a fit of feverish inspiration, struggled with them for years; Voltaire rewrote untiringly, and treated first editions as drafts to be recast in the next printing; Diderot poured early versions of articles into his letters to Sophie Volland. While there is no single Enlightenment style, all *philosophes had* style.

This devotion to the art of writing gave the *philosophes* the strength that comes from membership in a respectable guild; it gave them, for all their quarrels, common interests and a common vision. No matter how varied their concerns, they were men with a single career. To attribute two careers to Voltaire—the irresponsible *littérateur* before the Calas case, the grim reformer after—is to misunderstand the unity of his life. Of course, the *philosophes'* versatility opens them to the charge of dilettantism, and it is true that they sometimes tried to teach what they had not learned—as writers will. But the range of their knowledge was extraordinary. Diderot translated works on medicine and ethics; wrote articles on crafts, industry, philosophy, theology, history, politics, classical and modern literature; rode editorial herd on a stable of willful encyclopedists; broke new paths in the bourgeois drama, in dramatic and art criticism, the novel and the dialogue. Voltaire took an informed and passionate interest in all the countries of Europe and all the countries of the mind.

Yet the *philosophes* were never so deeply engaged in politics to neglect literature, and they were never so deeply engaged in literature to neglect the society in which they lived. While they were literary men, they were neither bohemians nor alienated artists. While their view of their world was critical, and especially in religion, disruptive, they knew and loved the world they wished to change. Rousseau in some moods rejected it altogether, and asked for man's total regeneration, but it is significant that his fellow *philosophes* treated him as a madman long before his clinical symptoms became obvious. When they denounced civilization, they did so urbanely.

The *philosophes,* then, much as they wished to change it, were at home in their world. To divide the century into two sharply defined forces—the subversive *philosophes* against the orthodox—may be convenient and dramatic, but it is also much too simple. There were moments of crisis when two parties crystallized and Catholics squared off against unbelievers, but subtler and more pervasive than hostility were the ties that bound the *philosophes* to their society. They edited respectable magazines, flattered royal mistresses, wrote unexceptionable entertainments, and held responsible posts.

Nor was their attachment to the existing order based solely on calculation: they shared with literate Christians a religious education, a love for the classics of Roman and French literature, and an affection for the pleasures of cultivated leisure. Seeking to distinguish themselves, they did not wish to abolish all distinctions. When they participated in politics, they often supported one orthodox party against another: Montesquieu, the *parlements* against the king; Voltaire, the king against the *parlements.* While they helped to prepare the way for the Jacobins, they were not Jacobins themselves.

Their attachment was strengthened by their association with a spectrum of would-be *philosophes,* half-*philosophes,* or Christians liberal enough to tolerate, or even to enjoy, men whose doctrines they rejected. Hangers-on, who basked in borrowed glory or second-hand notoriety, smuggled *philosophes'* letters, arranged for theatrical claques, and offered true friendship in a quarrelsome world. Strategically placed officials stood between *philosophes* and the severities of the law, and good Christians who dabbled in higher criticism or polite anticlericalism spread philosophic doctrines in respectable circles. In brief, the *philosophes* were deeply embedded in the texture of their society.

Yet this did not prevent them from being at war with it at the same time. The *philosophes* never developed a coherent political program or even a consistent line of political tactics, but their polemics called for a France profoundly different from the country in which they lived—France after, not before, 1791. The regime could make concessions: boredom, a lost sense of purpose, could make many a bourgeois, priest, or aristocrat receptive to subversive propaganda. But aggressive deism or materialism, doctrines of the rule of law, complete toleration, and subordination of church to state—these tenets could not be assimilated by the old order. To neglect either side of their dual situation is to make the *philosophes* more revolutionary or more conservative than in fact they were.

This tension, which is yet not alienation, places not only

the *philosophes* in their century, it places the century itself. To say that the eighteenth century was an age of contradictions, is to say nothing: all ages have this characteristic in common. We must be specific: eighteenth-century France was a Christian culture that was rapidly losing its Christian vocation without being fully aware of it.

"One day," writes Paul Hazard [in *La Crise de la conscience Européenne* (1935)], "the French people, almost to a man, were thinking like Bossuet. The day after, they were thinking like Voltaire." This is doubly wrong. The *philosophes* had much opposition among the educated and the powerful. While the writings of Montesquieu, Voltaire, and Diderot have survived, those of their adversaries have not, but survival is an unreliable guide to the intellectual map of the past: in the age of Louis XV Christianity had many a persuasive and intelligent defender. Moreover, we cannot properly speak of a "French people" in the eighteenth century. Most Frenchmen were wholly untouched by the Enlightenment and lived, as it were, in an earlier century. They believed in witches, applied spells, used home remedies long condemned by physicians, displayed a trust in authority long discarded by the educated, lived and died happily ignorant of the battles between Cartesians and Newtonians.

Yet for men sensitive or educated enough to be aware of intellectual currents, the eighteenth century was a time of turmoil. A whole complex of ideas and experiences, usually lumped together in the slippery word "secularization," came together in the reign of Louis XV to haunt thinking men. The literature of travel offered the spectacle of happy and civilized non-Christian cultures; the demands of international politics forged secular rather than sectarian alliances; the growth of the European economy stimulated the desire for worldly goods; the great discoveries of science suggested the appalling possibility of a universe without God.

Secularization did not mean the death of religion. Eight Frenchmen out of ten—perhaps nine—were uncontaminated by skepticism. Even the businessman or artisan, who greatly benefited from advances in technology, rarely allowed them to affect his faith. Still, what Troeltsch has called the "Church-directed civilization" was crumbling. Christians lived by the image of hierarchy: as God, his angels, and his creatures were arranged in an order of rank, so by analogy the skies, the family, law, society, the Church, were naturally hierarchical. Now, as natural scientists demonstrated that the hierarchies of terrestrial and celestial motion, or the spheres of the heavens, were absurd, other revolutionaries were exposing the absurdity of other hierarchies.

Philippe d'Orléans, regent of France from 1715 to 1723, and his nephew Louis XV.

In this time of trouble the two great hierarchical institutions, the Church and the nobility, did little to counteract this exposure. It is easy to exaggerate the worldliness of the eighteenth-century cleric or the uselessness of the eighteenth-century nobleman. Too much has been written about the atheist abbé and the idle marquis. There were many aristocrats who served their country ably, and who rose above the interests of their order to advocate truly national policies. Yet as the history of eighteenth-century France demonstrates, the French aristocracy was on the whole unwilling to make the sacrifices necessary to integrate it into a state that required some centralization of power and some revision of the tax structure. Born in an age that had given it a social function, the aristocratic caste was losing its vocation, as embittered renegades like the marquis D'Argenson did not fail to point out.

A similar loss of vocation threatened the Church. Thousands of priests fulfilled their offices with devotion; even some bishops believed in God. But in a time when natural philosophers were offering alternative explanations of the origins of man, the nature of evil, and the purpose of life, the Church needed a firmness of character, adroitness, and above all a unity that it could not muster. Many a young man of talent went into the opposition, and used the dialectical skill and classical learning imparted by his priestly instructors for their destruction.

Still, for all the impiety of the age, religion survived, and one reason for its survival was that the famous war between science and theology did not take place in the simple form familiar to us from the Whig Interpretation. The warfare began not between theology and science, but theology and some philosophical consequences drawn from science. It was not necessary to accept d'Alembert's positivism to be a good mathematician; or to be driven by Voltaire's anticlerical spleen to be a good Newtonian. Science, travel, politics, wealth, the great secularizing forces, did their work by indirection, as it were, behind the century's back.

Still they did their work, and they did it in the eighteenth century. In a celebrated book Paul Hazard has expended much learning to establish a crisis in the European conscience before 1715. It is true that practically all the most aggressive ideas of eighteenth-century propagandists had a prehistory, but they did not touch a significant number of people until well after Newton's death in 1727. The typical seventeenth-century scientist was a good Christian: he was a Pascal, not a Hobbes. By separating theology from natural philosophy, or by ingeniously arguing that natural philosophy *supported* theology, seventeenth-century scientists concealed from themselves, as much as from others, the revolutionary implications of their work. It is a commonplace, but one all too often forgotten, that the geniuses from Galileo to Newton lived comfortably with convictions that eighteenth-century *philosophes* would stigmatize as incompatible. John Donne's famous and too much quoted lament that "new philosophy calls all in doubt," was the exceptional response of an exceptional man. In general, the imagination of the seventeenth century was unaffected, or generously expanded, by the new universe glimpsed in the new instruments. For Newton, God was active in the universe, occasionally correcting the irregularities of the solar system. The Newtonian heavens proclaimed God's glory.

This happy marriage of theism and science was not dissolved until the eighteenth century, when the discoveries of the age of genius were pushed to their logical conclusion. "Once the foundation of a revolution has been laid down," d'Alembert wrote in the *Encyclopédie*, "it is almost always in the next generation that the revolution is accomplished." Several brilliant French mathematicians, d'Alembert among them, generalized Newton's laws of gravitation far beyond Newton's wishes. By the last quarter of the century, Lagrange and Laplace had established, in elegant equations, the stability of the solar system. The goal of eighteenth-century science had become evident: Newton's physics without Newton's God.

The crisis of secularization, then, was slower and subtler than we have been led to believe. It was also more pervasive. It was not confined to educated Christians, tormented by the startling conclusions of physicists. It was a problem for the *philosophes* themselves. It is not surprising that their anguish has received little attention—they covered it well with urbanity and noisy anticlericalism.

But anguish there was. The *philosophes* had two enemies: the institutions of Christianity and the idea of hierarchy. And they had two problems: God and the masses. Both the enemies and the problems were related and woven into the single task of rethinking their world. The old questions that Christianity had answered so fully for so many men and so many centuries, had to be asked anew: What—as Kant put it—what can I know? What ought I to do? What may I hope?

Science itself did not answer these questions. It only suggested—ever more insistently as the century went on—that the old answers were wrong. Now, the *philosophes* were products of Christian homes and Christian schools. If they became enemies of Christianity, they did so not from indifference or ignorance: they knew their Bible, their catechism, their Church Fathers, their apologetics. And they knew, because it had been drummed into them early, the fate that awaits heretics or atheists in the world to come. Their anticlerical humor therefore has the bitter intimacy of the family joke; to embrace materialism was an act of rejection.

The struggle of the *philosophes* was a struggle for freedom. They did not fully understand it, but to the extent that they did understand it, they knew their situation to be filled with terror and delight. They felt the anxiety and exhilaration of the explorer who stands before the unknown.

To use such existentialist language may seem like a rather portentous way of describing men noted for their sociability and frivolity. It is of course true that the *philosophes* did not suffer alone: they had the comforting company of elegant salons and of respectable philosophical forebears.

Yet even the supple Voltaire, who had been initiated into unbelief by fashionable teachers, was not free from the symptoms of this struggle. Much of his mockery was a weapon in a grim fight, and a device to keep up his own morale. Much of his philosophical rumination on free will reveals the persistence of a troublesome inner conflict.

It may not be fair to call to witness Rousseau, whose malaise was perpetual. But the shape of his suffering mirrors the suffering of his century. Nothing is more pathetic than Rousseau's attempt to rescue at least some comforting aspects of his universe from the icy blasts of Voltaire's cosmic pessimism. "All the subtleties of metaphysics," he wrote Voltaire, seeking to answer the poem on the Lisbon earthquake, "will not make me doubt for a moment the immortality of the soul or a beneficent Providence. I feel it, I believe it, I want it, I hope for it, and I shall defend it to my last breath." But the edifice of Rousseau's faith was flimsily built on illogical hope: the immortality of the soul and a beneficent Providence are articles of faith to which a Christian happily subscribes, but to which the deist, nourished on scientific skepticism, has no right.

Diderot, the most ebullient of *philosophes,* the freest and most inventive of spirits, was driven from position to position and haunted by doubts. Born into a family richly endowed with priests, of pious parents and with a fanatical brother, long toying with entering the priesthood, Diderot moved from Catholicism to theism, from theism to deism, from deism to skepticism, and from skepticism to atheism. But atheism, with its cold determinism, repelled him even though he accepted it as true; while Catholicism, with its colorful ceremony, moved him even though he rejected it as false. Writing to his mistress, Sophie Volland, he cursed the philosophy—his own—that reduced their love to a blind encounter of atoms. "I am furious at being entangled in a confounded philosophy which my mind cannot refrain from approving and my heart from denying."

The materialists of course claimed to be defiantly happy at being cosmic orphans. But the question—If God is dead, what is permitted?—was not a question calculated to make men sleep easy.

I am not simply arguing that the *philosophes* were less cheerful than they appeared in their social roles—most of us are. Nor that they suffered personal crises— philosophers, especially young philosophers, often do. I am arguing that the *philosophes'* anguish was related to the crisis in their Christian civilization; that (to use different language) whatever childhood experiences made them psychologically vulnerable in adult life, their obsessions, their self-questionings, their anxieties, were poured into their religious, moral, and political speculation.

But the *philosophes'* crisis was not only a crisis felt, it was also a crisis conquered. And this brings me back to the idea of work, and to the philosophy of energy.

There are several ways of dealing with a sense of helplessness. The *philosophes* might have given way to panic, despair, or paralyzing skepticism; they might have escaped from the terrifying spectacle of an empty universe by a doctrine of art for art's sake. Instead they overcame their anxiety by work. They escaped not from, but into reality.

The philosophy of energy was not a technical philosophical position, but a style of life. Whatever its form, it was confidence in the rational will, a humanist's pride in man's possibilities tempered by an empiricist's humility before man's limitations. Men, Voltaire said, must dare to do more than they have done. "We do not want enough," he warned, and late in life he wrote to a friend, "We must battle nature and fortune until the last moment, and never despair of anything until we are good and dead."

Sometimes work was an escape. The drudgery of reading proofs on an *Encyclopédie* or of correcting a king's verses were bulwarks against uncertainty, loneliness, and *Welt-*

schmerz. "If I were by your side, I'd complain and you would comfort me; but you are absent, and work is the only means I have of diverting my thoughts from my sufferings." Thus Diderot, depressed and alone in Paris, to his best friend Grimm. "To work and think of you, that's my life." Thus Voltaire, after his disastrous stay at the Prussian court, to his niece and mistress Madame Denis. Love and work: an energetic program to make an unpalatable world less unpalatable.

But work as consolation is only the most primitive level of the philosophy of energy. Its most familiar expression, which pervaded the *philosophes'* writings through the century, was the drive to assert man's power over his environment. Even the materialists, for all their determinism, taught the virtue of rational activity and the possibility of modifying nature.

Power over nature was more than a cliché: the *philosophes* knew precisely what they meant by it. They had learned it, partly from Bacon, partly (although rather less) from Descartes, and above all from the needs and possibilities of their time. Medieval man had not abjectly resigned himself to misery or pathetic dependence on divine intervention in his behalf. Yet even sympathetic historians have conceded that the Middle Ages were an age of precarious and violent existence. Men aged young and died young; those fortunate enough to survive infancy, epidemics, or famines, were likely victims of bandits, pirates, sudden war, or brutal migrations. "Beneath all social life," Marc Bloch writes [in *La Société féodale: La formation des liens de dépendance* (1939)], "there was a soil of primitivism, of submission to ungovernable powers."

To remedy this—to prolong life, clear the roads of assassins, keep men from starving, and give them hope of enjoying the fruits of their labors—required more than a stable political organization. It required a spiritual revolution, and the culmination of that revolution was the philosophy of the *philosophes.*

But words alone did not eliminate illness, starvation, or insecurity, scourges that continued to haunt the world of Bacon and even the world of Voltaire. French civilization of the eighteenth century still wore a half-finished look. Polish was bright, because it was new; the decline of religious fervor did not prevent occasional terrifying outbursts of hysteria, the advances of education did not eliminate brutal games, sadistic sports, or destructive riots.

The survival of coarseness was related to the continuing ravages of diseases and the pressures of hunger: the uncertainty of life did not allow the generous grace of conduct that comes with true ease. The fate of the royal family— the death in rapid succession of the only son and two of the grandsons of Louis XIV—dramatically underlined the general precariousness. At the age of forty-six, Diderot, on a visit to his native town, found most of his schoolmates gone, and mused darkly on the brevity of life.

Yet the *philosophes'* attitude to the blows of fate was one of defiance, not resignation. While deists continued to protest that the Lord gave, they saw no reason why they might not enjoy what he had given, and why they might not try to keep it as long as possible. In the Middle Ages, the accidents of nature had dominated man; in the eighteenth century, to use Diderot's phrase, men were seizing nature and tormenting her. Scientists were beginning to force from her reluctant lips the secrets of her operations.

Evidence for this sense of mastery is everywhere. It is in medicine, which had a place of honor among the *philosophes*. Some of them were physicians, others took an abiding interest in what La Mettrie, himself a doctor, praised as the supreme art of healing. It is, too, in Diderot's *Encyclopédie*. Its alphabetical arrangement vividly emphasizes its single-minded purpose. The anticlerical articles are not just bait to make the reader tolerate dull pieces on crafts; the articles on crafts are not just padding for daring heresies. Both have a single purpose: to reinterpret the world and by reinterpreting it, to change it. In a phrase which has become too familiar to have retained its original vigor, Diderot said that he wanted his *Encyclopédie* to "change the general way of thinking."

The *philosophes,* men with a single career which took a variety of forms, also had a single task which took a variety of expressions. The philosophy of energy is the glass that collects all their activities in a single focus. Diderot spoke for them all: "Everything belongs together in the human understanding; the obscurity of one idea spreads over those that surround it. An error throws shadows over neighboring truths, and if it happens that there should be in society men interested in forming, as it were, centers of shadow, soon the people will find itself plunged into a profound darkness." The spreading of light operates by the same Keynesian multiplier: the *philosophes'* propaganda campaign, from the bulky *Encyclopédie* to the sprightly *Dictionnaire philosophique,* is a series of lamps from which others will find illumination and spread the light in their turn.

The *philosophes'* task cannot therefore be contained in the word *humanitarianism.* It was greater than that: the campaign to abolish torture cannot be divorced from the campaign to abolish Jesuits or to spread technological knowledge—all are part of the struggle to impose man's rational will on the environment. Nor was it simply the acquisition of knowledge. As good Baconians, the *philosophes* preached that knowledge is power, but few of them were naïve enough to believe that knowledge automatically creates virtue: their writings are filled with warnings against the misuse of intelligence or the brutalizing of learning. They did argue that since knowledge is power, ignorance is impotence. It followed that the men who wanted to keep others in ignorance were enemies of humanity. What does one do with monsters who want to castrate mankind? All—or almost all—methods are fair against them.

The philosophers of energy face to face with their enemies: this confrontation leads us back to the beginning, for it helps to solve the puzzling contradictions that beset the interpreter of the Enlightenment. The French Enlightenment had its own history, and that history mirrors, and helped to shape, the history of the century. Something happened in Europe in the 1760's. It was the beginning of industrial society; the beginning of modern politics and the great democratic revolt against aristocratic regimes. It was a time of turmoil within the Christian world itself: witness the suppression of the Jesuits, and the outbursts of hysterical prosecutions of Huguenots and blasphemers.

In this time of trouble, the *philosophes* added to their sense

of power over the environment a sense of mission. The moderate anticlericalism of a Montesquieu gave way to the belligerent cry, *Écrasez L'infâme;* democratic political ideas found a favorable hearing even from the skeptic Voltaire. The *philosophes* grew more radical, more combative, more convinced than ever that they were the prophets of a new age that would rise on the ruins of the old.

As they became more violently partisan, the contradictions in their views became more obvious. As a historian, Voltaire delighted in the past for its own sake; as an aesthetician, Diderot delighted in the play of light and shade on canvas. But as prophets, both found it necessary to import moral lessons into their writings. If the old civilization must give way to the new, if men must learn to dare and to rely on themselves, if even the uneducated are to find their place in this revolution, then *philosophes* must teach, and teach again, and teach everywhere. Cultivated men possessed by a sense of mission temper their cultivation for the sake of their mission. This will lead to inconsistencies. But these inconsistencies do not destroy, they merely dramatize, the richness and the unity of the French Enlightenment. (pp. 114-32)

> *Peter Gay, "The Unity of the French Enlightenment," in his* The Party of Humanity: Essays in the French Enlightenment, *Alfred A. Knopf, 1964, 290 p.*

WOMEN AND THE SALONS

David Williams

[*In the following excerpt, Williams discusses the rise and decline of feminist activity in eighteenth-century France, remarking on its character as "unprecedented in its volume and intensity."*]

Nearly four decades have passed since Mornet conducted his inquiry into the intellectual origins of the French Revolution. Subsequent research into public attitudes during the revolutionary period towards the great charismatic names of Enlightenment thinking has tended to blur rather than clarify the rather precise relationships delineated by Mornet between ideological stimulus and historical phenomena. The general proposition is still an open issue of course, but the debate around the nature and status of women in eighteenth-century France, engendering a formidable corpus of dissident literature, does highlight an example of conspicuous hiatus between the movement of ideas and the movement of events. The feminist dilemma from this point of view underscores the tenuous nature of certain assumptions that are still occasionally put forward with regard to historical processes as well as to the contemporary impact of eighteenth-century liberalism.

Ideals of sexual egalitarianism, voiced in a multiplicity of literary, philosophical and political contexts, seemed on the surface to be a potentially rewarding direction in which to channel reformist energies. The eighteenth century saw feminism emerge from its shadowy status as a mi-

Theatrical tribute to Voltaire at the Théâtre Français in March 1778.

nority aberration from the Aristotelian-based consensus of opinion into an apparently viable movement. In England and France the ideology of feminism was well orchestrated, and it imparted a distinctive colour to the broader fabric of the period's political thought, not to mention its literary conventions. No longer could the issue of women's rights be kept safely refrigerated within the centuries-long traditional abstractions of theological and metaphysical nicety.

Ever since Aristotle had countered Plato's development of the principle of equality—such as it was in the dialogue between Glaucon and Socrates in the fifth book of the *Republic,* and reaffirmed in the first book of the *Politics* the legitimacy of the state of subordination in which one sex lived in relation to the other, it was clear that much more than a technical collision of philosophical viewpoints was at stake. Any challenge to the rationale of inequality would necessarily represent a challenge to the interpretation of natural law from which society's institutions drew part of their ultimate authority.

A renewed awareness of the radical political element inherent in the problem quickened the pulse of eighteenth-century feminism, and brought into focus the more dazzling corollary: the ephemeral nature of social structures *per se.* What d'Alembert was to describe as "l'esclavage et l'espèce d'avilissement où nous avons mis les femmes" came to be seen as a contingent consequence of positive law and no longer as a necessary fact of natural law. In itself this was nothing new, but the degree to which it permeated the general movement of ideas in eighteenth-century France was new. Scale and momentum gives to eighteenth-century feminism, and indeed to the whole intellectual superstructure of the Enlightenment, much of its characteristic flavour.

Previously liberal trends in this area had made little impact on the view sanctified by that formidable trinity Aristotelian precept, Roman law and Christian ethic, which, together, envisaged the servitude of women as an unalterable and perfectly justifiable part of the nature of things in this world and most probably in the next. The revival of Platonic attitudes during the Renaissance had certainly marked a faint resurgence of respect for the notion of a rationally based egalitarianism. Generally speaking however, dissent on this issue remained the prerogative of eccentrics who could be ridiculed, or of the occasional woman who could be ignored.

It is largely because of their rarity rather than their merit that certain premature luminaries stand out so sharply against the darker conservative firmament of the pre-Enlightenment period. Despite the disappointingly ano-dyne nature of his arguments, one should perhaps mention Henri-Cornelius Agrippa, who as early as 1509 could publish a work with a title as perverse as *La Supériorité du sexe féminin*. A gradual and inexorable build-up of pressure around feminist preoccupations was however taking place inside and outside literary circles. If the indignant testimony of the jesuit Jean Cordier can be accepted, this coincided in France with a growing expertise on the part of upper and middle class women with the arts of contraception. Statistical evidence indicates, moreover, a decline in population growth during this period, and a correlation has been suggested, at least in part, between this and the increasing concern of women to free themselves from the disadvantages of their biological function. Writing well over a century after Cordier, Auget de Montyon could report in 1778 that the use of birth control techniques had percolated down even to peasant women. Between 1771 and 1820 the birth rate in France fell by slightly more than .7%.

As far as the documentation of the earlier period is concerned, overt feminist protest still remained spasmodic rather than continuous and cumulative. An early radical note had certainly been sounded by Marie le Jars de Gournay, author of two very avant-garde essays: *Egalité des hommes et des femmes* (1622) and *Les Griefs des dames* (1626), both of which were extended and republished in 1634 and again in 1641. An element which was to feature in eighteenth-century feminism was also present in the embryonic feminist world of seventeenth-century France—namely the sympathy that such aspirations and protests found with certain ecclesiastical writers. Jacques Du Bosc's *L'Honneste Femme* (1632) is a well known example, as is François Poulain de la Barre's highly unorthodox *De l'Egalité des deux sexes* (1673), whose circulation benefited a great deal from the scandalous publicity of the author's public renunciation of celibacy, and his abandonment of the priesthood for marriage in a Genevan church. The views expressed by such writers still lacked broad support, but distinguishable patterns of protest were slowly emerging and gaining cogency. This is particularly noticeable in works dealing with questions of education and social training—issues which with birth control and constitutional rights were to become the anchor themes of the feminist polemic as it was to develop in the Enlightenment. However, the need for serious, sustained feminist argument failed to attract the services of a really great name until Fénélon objected to the harmful social and psychological effects of the conditioning given to women through current educational practices. Even with Féné-lon, only a small section of his 1687 essay, *Traité de l'éducation des filles,* is devoted specifically to women, in spite of the title. The Age of the Sun King tended, not surprisingly, to circumscribe its analysis of the society-male-female relationship, and to avoid the more explosive social and political implications.

Those scattered fragments of pre-Enlightenment protest that can be identified however, began to come together in the following century in the work of novelists, playwrights, essayists, *philosophes,* and of course of the women themselves, the new *femmes-hommes* or "hyenas in petticoats" as Walpole called them. Sentimental appeals to the public conscience were now to be supplemented by "hard"

argument and research around woman's *condition,* and the legal-political realities which defined and reinforced that condition. The result was that by the 1780's feminism had become well integrated into the broader movements for social change.

In the key areas of jurisprudence and judicial philosophy the work of an Orléans counsellor and respected jurist, Robert Joseph Pothier, remains perhaps the most authoritative and forbidding statement of the position of women before the law. In the defensive elaboration of the situation in his *Traité de la puissance du mari sur la personne et les biens de la femme et des donations entre mari et femme* (1770) Pothier declared the powers of the husband over his wife to consist by natural law in the inalienable right to demand from her all the duties of submission which are due from an inferior to a superior. This in effect was a reiteration of article nine of the *Ordonnance des donations,* passed by the Paris Parlement in 1731, which had virtually deprived women in France of equality before the law, and marked a high water mark in the history of repressive legislation. Pothier, after listing the duties of wives, was still able to reaffirm the justification for submission based on natural law arguments nearly half a century after Montesquieu had re-opened the doubts about the legitimacy of this principle in the thirty-eighth letter of the *Lettres persanes.* The *arrêt* of the Paris Parlement (February 12, 1731) measures the distance between liberal philosophies and official policies, and it exemplifies the ferocity of the legislation affecting women in a variety of circumstances irrespective of class or economic status. Poverty was, of course, an added disadvantage. Middle class women were reasonably well shielded from the worst indignities, such as those imposed by the laws relating to pregnancy. Pothier's formulations concerning the inviolable rights of men over women were moreover to reappear in the 1804 civil code—a further pointer to the ironic fate that awaited French feminism in the immediate post-revolutionary period.

The edifice of legalised prejudice, together with a public opinion still conditioned to a "tout est au mieux" philosophy of Panglossian proportions, did little however to discourage the upsurge of reformist energy and confidence. This was based, partly at least, upon that endearing faith of the Enlightenment on man's potential ability to rationalize his environment. It was this new found confidence that separated eighteenth-century feminism, in tone at least, from the sporadic outbursts of activity that had preceded it.

Voltaire, in most respects the most influential propagandist of the period, is somewhat ambivalent on the issue. The article *Femme* in the *Dictionnaire philosophique,* for example, has an anthropological rather than sociological emphasis, and contains little trace of feminist sympathies. In the article *Homme* Voltaire saw positive moral advantages accruing to women as a result of their physical and social inferiority. The sympathetic approach to women's position in the section *Mémoire pour les femmes* in *Adultère* is more than balanced by his comments on female infidelity in the first part of that article. There are Platonic comments on the political potential of women, at present wasted, in the section dealing with Salic law in the *Essai sur les moeurs,* and in the *Dictionnaire* article: *Loi Salique.* A spirited defence of the rights of women to an intellectual life is to be found in the *épitre* to Mme du Châtelet prefacing *Alzire*—in which the case for intellectual parity is not quite stated. Many of Voltaire's comments direct attention to the vulnerability of women in society as a result of their physical disadvantages, and he seems to run close to a regretful acceptance of natural law arguments for the *status quo.* The correspondence, moreover, is very reticent on the point. However, Voltaire, by virtue of his position, gave the whole debate plenty of valuable publicity, even if he added little that was at all original or even sympathetic.

The main political thrust in the second half of the century was to come from Diderot, Holbach and Condorcet. They were supported by a dynamic, now largely forgotten undercurrent of writing. Feminist literature was acquiring status as a modish genre. Even in the rather academic form of essays and treatises, feminist publications were beginning to meet with a remarkable response. A little essay like that of Pierre-Joseph Boudier de Villemert's *L'Ami des femmes, ou la philosophie du beau sexe,* originally published in 1758, could run to six editions within twelve months of publication, and went through three more reprintings in expanded form by 1788. Villemert, another of those strange beasts the clerical feminists, advanced a theory of the complementary nature of the sexes in terms very close to those used by the Saint-Simonians. Equally prominent among those writers who do not occupy centre stage, but whose works were at the time important familiar currency, was Jacques-Philippe de Varennes. Varennes published a robust defence of the egalitarian principle in his 1727 essay *Les Hommes,* insisting somewhat heretically on the equality of perfection in the souls of men and women, and explicitly rejecting the traditional confirmations of women's inferiority with regard to natural law and the will of God. Another jesuit Philippe Joseph Caffiaux devoted four *tomes* to the *Défenses du beau sexe,* including, most usefully, a bibliography of contemporary feminist literature. In addition to such tracts, there was a fast growing corpus of works of an ostensibly historical or lexicographical nature with strong feminist undertones.

Then there were the more overtly militant brochures from essayists such as Cerfvol, Puisieux, and of course from the women themselves who were far from silent on the issue. Mme Galien's *Apologie des dames appuyée sur l'histoire* (1737), Mme Gacon-Dufour's *Mémoire pour le sexe féminin contre le sexe masculin* (1787) and Mme de Coicy's *Les Femmes comme il convient de les voir* (1787) were in their time all reputable essays on the nature of women, marriage and the role of women in society. They effectively supplemented the more celebrated novels and tracts of such writers as Mme de Lambert, Mme de Graffigny, Mme de Robert, Mme de Roland and Mme d'Argenson and of course Mme de Staël. Between 1734-1736 the aggressive journalism of Mlle Archembault made its mark on the *Mercure de France,* and Mme de Maisonneuve did much to publicise female claims to intellectual respectability in her monthly magazine, the *Journal des Dames* which first appeared in 1764.

In the novel and the theatre writers continued the exploration of the love relationship, but the theme expanded to take in the victimisation of the female, not simply by men, but by a male-oriented social structure. The psychology of love began to assume in the world of prose fiction and drama uneasy social and political connotations. The novelist, in particular, will present now a picture of empty, fragile relationships in which the female is trapped, vulnerable, an undeserving prisoner of the male and of the system. The literary pattern is exemplified in such works as Crébillon's *Les Egarements du coeur et de l'esprit* (1736-38), and *Lettres Athéniennes* (1771), Duclos's *Les Confessions du Comte de XXX* (1741), Diderot's *La Religieuse* (1760, publ. 1798), and *Supplément au voyage du Bougainville* (1772, publ. 1796). Powerful in impact and implication Laclos's *Les Liaisons dangereuses* (1782) captured in the portrayal of its *héroïne malfaisante* the essence of the period's literary treatment of female victimisation and the dehumanising effects of the social game. In an essay written in 1783, a short time after the publication of the *Liaisons,* throwing incidentally an interesting light on the themes of that work, Laclos asserted that there could be no improvement in the position of women until they themselves took the initiative against their male oppressors. . . . (pp. 333-41)

In the Republic of Letters at least France seemed to be poised for reformative action during the decade prior to 1789. The mounting tensions were reflected in the work of three writers in particular: Diderot, Holbach and Condorcet. In 1772 Mme Geoffrin's protégé Antoine Léonard Thomas presented a paper to the Académie entitled *Sur Le Caractère, les moeurs et l'esprit des femmes dans les différents siècles.* The blandness of Thomas's comments provoked a sharp review from Diderot, who considered that Thomas "a beaucoup pensé, mais . . . n'a pas assez senti." The review in question became a compact, impassioned treatise: *Sur les Femmes.*

Criticising Thomas for his vagueness and lack of radical bite, Diderot moved in, without preamble, on the central, tangible issue of legal prejudice, and deplored a situation in which society was able legally to exploit and perpetuate female subservience through the development of its peculiar social and political institutions. . . . (p. 342)

Translating issues raised in much of the period's feminist fiction into a commentary on the real situation, Diderot explored the interplay between political structures, social customs and the psychological and physiological nature of women. Again a natural law element begins to intrude, but in Diderot's case it is not allowed to compromise the argument. Diderot is particularly concerned with the damaging propagandist effects of traditional notions of love and *galanterie,* which send women, like the men in Rousseau's state of nature, running to meet their chains. . . . The deceptions inherent in western notions of love, the harsh legal implications of marriage, the burdens of motherhood and the cruel neglect of old age feature prominently in Diderot's analysis of women's fate in society. . . . (p. 343)

The year 1773 saw the appearance of another key feminist document of the decade: Holbach's essay *Des Femmes,* published in the third volume of his *Système social.* Expanding several of the themes discussed briefly in Diderot's essay, Holbach advanced the feminist case at several vital levels. His thesis deployed legal, sociological, moral and psychological comments and data in a pattern of argument that illuminates sharply the political nature of the factors contributing to the subjugation of women and which conditioned them at an early stage to acceptance of that subjugation. . . . Holbach proceeded to compare the open tyranny practised in so-called uncivilised societies with the equally uncompromising, but camouflaged, tyranny inherent in the European systems. In France, in particular, political and social organisation impelled women, through education, marriage, religious training, sexual convention and legal restraint, to accept passively their secondary role. . . . Current educational philosophies were for Holbach simply the mirror-image of society's prejudiced view of women's role. If a girl received an education at all, other than that of a "vain and criminally negligent mother," it would probably be in a convent which would send her out into the world armed only with a knowledge of music, dance, posture, the cosmetic arts and of course faith. If she did not belong to a class fortunate enough to receive even that training, then the situation was worse. Holbach was particularly concerned in his treatise with a phenomenon that had become something of a common-place in English feminist writing of the period, namely prostitution with specific reference to the plight of the working-class girl in an urban environment. With the social effects of industrialisation becoming only too obvious in England, the whole question of class exploitation and economic principles will from now on add another dimension to the feminist problem.

Setting his argument within a broad, but quite specific, political framework, Holbach analyses the processes of moral corruption to which women are purposefully made vulnerable. At one end of the scale the working-class prostitute is a sacrificial victim to "le vice oppulent." There are no laws to protect her, only pressures to mould her to her role. "Galanterie" has for Holbach aspects which are symptomatic of the malaise of society's institutions: "Quelle idée peut-on former des loix qui laissent sans châtiment des séducteurs aussi cruels que les assassins les plus déterminés?" At the other end of the scale, in "respectable" society, marriage itself has contributed, through its inflexibility, to the atmosphere of moral decadence in which infidelity has become the norm, "traitée de bagatelle," and adultery and debauchery prevalent. Here Holbach argued the case for divorce as a remedy to the situation: "Une législation assez sensée pour permettre le divorce remédierait en grande partie à la corruption publique". Once more the legal situation stands behind the abuse. As with Diderot the feminist viewpoint is becoming closely linked with wider issues. The social system, with its legal, moral, political, religious and psychological apparatus has succeeded in poisoning at source the citizen's happiness. . . . Holbach, in terms ironically reminiscent of those used by Rousseau in a slightly different context, singled out the arts, in particular the theatre and the novel, as sources of psychological pressure more potent in their conditioning effect than any of the prohibitive legislation still militating against women's freedom.

An English tea—thé à l'anglaise—hosted by the Princess de Conti, by Michel Barthélemy Ollivier.

Emotionally the theatre has a "funeste effet" on women by appealing to harmful passions; even the plays of France's greatest dramatists conspire to seduce, soften and corrupt the heart and the mind. . . . Like Laclos, Holbach ends his treatise with an exhortation to action.

That feminism during the years immediately before the Revolution was turning into a Trojan horse behind which proposals aiming at the radical political transformation of society could be advanced received further confirmation from the writings of Voltaire's disciple Condorcet. Condorcet's essay, *Sur l'Admission des femmes aux droits de cité* (1790), is a well-known demand on behalf of women for the implementation of full constitutional rights, closely anticipating the appearance in England of what is perhaps the most celebrated feminist document of the period—Mary Wollstonecraft's *A Vindication of the Rights of Women*. As far as France is concerned Condorcet's *Admission* can be seen quite legitimately as the climactic point of feminist polemics, marking the final convergence of the movement with the mainstream of the period's political iconoclasm. Condorcet pointed up the irony which had allowed France to have a revolution in the name of equality "en faveur de trois ou quatre cents hommes qu'un préjugé absurde en avait privés," but to forget, through the paralyzing effects of traditional habits of thought, the rights of twelve million women. To perpetuate a situation in which women continue to be deprived of their constitutional rights, observed Condorcet, it would have to be clearly demonstrated that women were incapable of exercising those rights competently. Condorcet then proceeded in the rest of the *Admission* to dismantle point by point the main anti-feminist positions justifying the exclusion of women from political affairs. Prejudice was reducible to one issue: the public interest ("l'utilité publique"). This, Condorcet insisted, was merely an argument of convenience, a principle fabricated to justify not only woman's continuing subservience to man, but also tyranny in most of its contemporary guises. It was in the name of "utilité" that French commerce and industry were groaning in chains, that the African Negro was enslaved, that the Bastille was full, that books were censored, that torture and secret trials were accepted.

The feminist cause with Condorcet was made in effect to encompass the most flagrant aspects of contemporary injustice and cruelty, and as a result the political temperature of the issue rose even higher than with Diderot and Holbach. Answering the "utilité" argument, Condorcet went on to assert that a transformation in women's civil status would not work against the public interest. Women would not necessarily be torn from their domestic duties; on the contrary the fabric of family life would be strengthened once the sense of injustice which women felt had been removed. Thus with Condorcet's *Admission* an argument going back at least to Plato comes full circle.

Two years before the publication of the *Admission,* Condorcet had raised the issue of admitting women to full citizenship in the *Lettres d'un bourgeois de Newhaven à un citoyen de Virginie* (1788). In the second of these *Lettres* Condorcet elaborated the general principle which was to preface the more specific proposals of the *Admission.* . . . The principle was reiterated in the 1788 *Essai sur la Constitution et les fonctions des assemblées provinciales.*

For Condorcet female equality implied an entirely new order of things affecting the full range of society's institutions. It was no longer primarily a moral issue, but a wider constitutional problem relating to the sources of legislative and executive power in the state. Justice for women would involve a basic reappraisal of the mechanics of government administration to enable both sexes to play an active part in political life. Condorcet managed in fact to weld together many of the more explosive ideas of his contemporaries and predecessors into a relatively coherent and practical programme for social change.

Moreover, it was Condorcet who, apart from clarifying the radical political meaning behind the feminist phenomenon, also touched upon the other fundamental principle: the maternal role and the right and necessity to regulate pregnancies. The "maternal role" argument was one of the major weapons in the armoury of the anti-feminists, permitting the invocation of natural law to confirm *de facto* female dependence and the impracticality of egalitarian principles. Most of the eighteenth-century feminists in France conceded the point, but attempt to argue around it—sometimes with considerable intellectual discomfort. Condorcet faced the problem squarely and made some attempt to think through the logical conclusion of the arguments advanced by the opposing group. The issue was mentioned, with differing emphases in both the *Admission* and the *Lettres d'un bourgeois.* In his last and greatest work, the *Esquisse d'un tableau historique des progrès de l'esprit humain* (1795), however, what had appeared to be exclusively a feminine problem and feminist issue was illuminated with a startlingly modern perspective, which took Condorcet well beyond the horizons of his age. (pp. 343-48)

Such visionary warnings, however, were to have little effect. In the event the efforts of the philosopher-reformers to create an issue of public conscience out of the unhappy position of women were abortive. A climate of opinion sympathetic to the political, social and moral implications of a revolution in the relationship between the sexes, was not really produced. The politics of feminism, in the light of events, turned out to be yet another of those promising little flowers, cultivated carefully in all the best philosophic gardens, which bloomed only to wither in the hostile climate of public opinion. If in France, as Cobban has suggested, the Revolution tended to betray rather than fulfil the aspirations of eighteenth-century liberalism, the betrayal was particularly acute within the melancholy context of women's rights.

After a decade of particularly intense propaganda in favour of equal rights, many thought that with the events of 1789 the cause would be publicly acclaimed. The deputations, petitions and proclamations that went before the Revolutionary Convention from female political organisations and clubs testify to the vigour and confidence with which the feminist viewpoint was now advanced. In 1788 Olympe de Gouges, declared in her *Remarques patriotiques* that her sex was "prêt à secouer le joug d'un esclavage honteux." Together with Théroigne de Méricourt and Etta Palm d'Aelders she went on to found in 1793 the Club des Citoyennes Républicaines Révolutionnaires. In 1791 she issued her *Déclaration des droits de la femme et de la citoyenne,* a fiery brochure of seventeen *articles*. The tenth *article* of that work is an exhortation to the women of Paris to end once and for all the imbalance between the sexes in the sphere of civil rights, and to crown the political revolution with an equally effective moral one: "La femme a le droit de monter sur l'échafaud, elle doit avoir également celui de monter à la tribune." Of the two rights claimed, Olympe was allowed to enjoy only the former. By 1793 the Convention clearly felt that a legion of New Amazons was arising in the streets of Paris. By the end of 1793 the Revolutionary government was moving against the "républicaines révolutionnaires." In October 1793 a deputation of red-bonneted women headed by Claire Lacombe was addressed by Pierre-Gaspard Chaumette, *Procureur de la Commune.* Chaumette, a disciple of Rousseau, was even more uncompromising in his anti-feminism than either Robespierre or Fabre d'Eglantine. Admonishing the demonstration Chaumette pronounced the epitaph upon eighteenth-century feminism in France: "Rappelez-vous l'impudente Olympe de Gouges qui, la première, institua des sociétés de femmes, qui abandonna les soins de son ménage pour se mêler de la République et dont la tête est tombée sous le fer vengeur des lois." Possibly a blueprint for revolution had been established. For the immediate future, however, not only had poor Olympe's head fallen beneath the "venging blade of the law," but also the hopes and aspirations of a century of feminist activity that had been unprecedented in its volume and intensity: a classic case of Nature refusing to imitate Art. (pp. 349-51)

David Williams, "The Politics of Feminism in the French Enlightenment," in The Varied Pattern: Studies in the 18th Century, *edited by Peter Hughes and David Williams, A. M. Hakkert, Ltd., 1971.*

Marius Roustan

[*In the following excerpt from a work originally published in French in 1906, Roustan considers the role of the salons in the propagation of philosophic ideas during the eighteenth-century.*]

Up to this time men of letters devoted to study and living in retirement thought only of the judgment of posterity although they were working for their contemporaries. The directness and simplicity of their manners was alien from the great world; and polite society, less educated than it is to-day, admired their work (or rather the names of the authors), but hardly thought of associating with them. It was respect more than dislike that was the motive for this aloofness.

The taste for literature, science and the arts has grown insensibly, and has reached the point that those who have no such taste affect it. Those who cultivated these things were drawn into society more and more as the pleasure found in associating with them increased.

Both parties gained by the association. Society people cultivated their minds, formed their tastes, and found fresh entertainment. The men of letters found some advantages too. They were treated with consideration; they perfected their taste, polished their wit, softened their manners, and in several directions gained the knowledge unobtainable from books.

These are the opening words of Chapter II.—"On Men of Letters"—of Duclos' *Considérations sur les Mœurs,* and it

must be acknowledged that they give a good idea of the social standing of men of letters in the present and the past. The *rapprochement* between authors and men of the world took place at the beginning of the eighteenth century, and the movement has continued since that date. It was much more true in 1750 than at the end of the seventeenth century that a man of letters was "of as little account as a post at the corner of the market-place." In 1750 he spends less time in the solitude of his study, and if Clitophon desires his services he has not to mount to a garret on the fifth floor. He will find the *philosophe* either in the *café* or in the *salon,* wherever there is conversation or the interchange of ideas. La Bruyère lived still more remote from the world than those men of letters of whom Duclos spoke. The eighteenth-century *philosophe* had more intimate connection with contemporary society; the author could no longer avoid being captured by society. Henceforth, and contrary to the dictum of Clitiphon's friend, "He may be of great importance, and he means to be."

Duclos indicates clearly enough the advantages derived by society from this intercourse; we need not return to them again, as many critics have noted them since. But I should like to define the certain advantages derived by philosophy from the *salons,* and to show how the innovators met in polite society valuable auxiliaries who helped them more or less directly, more or less efficaciously, with more or less good will, but who did definitely collaborate in the triumph of revolutionary ideas by extending their patronage to those who defended them.

I shall speak, first of all, of the material support given by the *salons* to authors. To be "launched" by a *salon* constituted, at that time, the surest avenue to success; the *salon* was to new and even assured reputations what the Press is to-day; it was there that publicity was to be obtained. Did a man wish to draw attention to himself, to have a chance of obtaining the academic chair soon to be vacant? If a prize for poetry or rhetoric was in question, talent would not suffice, perhaps not even genius; ask a Thomas, a Delille, a La Harpe, an Abbé Maury, a Chamfort; the essential thing was to be recommended by a *salon.* Was a man a candidate for the coveted chair in the Academy? Were he even a Montesquieu or a Voltaire, it was indispensable to have the support of women. That is how things were done from the beginning of the century, and d'Argenson declares that Madame de Lambert created "half the academicians of that day." Hostesses—I mean hostesses who were not content with dinners and cardparties—conducted the elections sometimes with marvellous tact, sometimes with wild passion; all, from the Queen and her favourites and the princesses of the blood-royal downwards, took a hand in the game—down to the Duchesse de Chaulnes, who, as the climax of her escapades, created a scandal by procuring the nomination of her lover. "The Abbé de Boismont, chaplain and lover of the Duchesse de Chaulnes," writes d'Argenson, "was elected to succeed the Bishop of Mirepoix. By the disgraceful acquiescence of the Academy in this shameful intrigue that body completed its own disrepute." And certainly a few more elections of this kind would have destroyed the reputation of the Forty-Five. Years before, Madame de Boufflers, who had become Maréchale de Luxembourg, had secured the nomination of M. de Bissy, whose sole distinction was the eccentricity of his spelling. Commenting on this, Collé, Comte de Montboissier, commanding a regiment of *Mous-*

quetaires, declared that in future he would receive only Masters of Arts, maintaining that he would "have them all created Immortals since it had been possible to make M. de Bissy of the company."

But, for a handful of Bissys and de Boismonts launched by certain aristocratic *salons,* how many men of talent were advanced by the *salons* which the *philosophes* frequented! Madame de Lambert secured the election of Montesquieu, Madame de Tencin of Marivaux, Madame du Deffand of d'Alembert; Madame Geoffrin created three Immortals in a single year—Watelet, Saurin and the Abbé de Rohan; two years later she backed Marmontel successfully, in spite of the active efforts of the enemies of the *philosophes,* then Arnaud, then Suard. The Duc de Duras, Boisgelin de Cicé, La Harpe and Chastellux were nominated by Mademoiselle de Lespinasse, who was all-powerful after d'Alembert had succeeded Duclos as permanent secretary. And did not Duclos himself present the unheard-of-spectacle of a young man received into the Academy of Inscriptions before having published anything, solely on his society reputation? Did he not enter the French Academy, thanks to the patronage of the *salon* of the Brancas? The correspondence exchanged on this subject between the Comtesse de Rochefort and M. de Forcalquier shows what eighteenth-century ladies were capable of when they sought to advance an author: eulogy of the candidate, subtle intrigue and diplomacy, fervid appeals to their partisans, epithets more than coarse for their opponents, all are there. They only stopped short of overturning the ballot-boxes. Duclos was beaten, and the Comtesse de Rochefort received the following letter: "I am incensed, but don't tell anyone, though I am none the less furious. It is nevertheless probable that Duclos will be received on the first vacancy." The Abbé Mongault in fact died very opportunely, and the prediction was realised. "Such were," said Villenave, in relating the story in his *Notice* on Duclos, "the keys which opened and shut the doors of the Academy at this period. Since that day a new kind of activity has come into fashion; and the public can decide whether elections by knife and fork to-day are more honourable than those secured in former days by aristocratic intrigue." Innocent malice of a scholar who had not read *L'Immortel!* In any case it is clear that constant support was given by society to men of letters; I hasten to say that these are not the best services rendered to them.

The *salons* in fact gave men of letters the opportunity of rising to their full stature. We must take into account that with rare exceptions eighteenth-century authors shone more by their conversation even than by their works. Villemain was able to define the literature of the eighteenth century as conversation rather than published work, and the following statement of Marivaux is true of this epoch: "I think that men are much superior to the books they write." I will not go so far as to pretend that Voltaire and Montesqueu were more brilliant in their conversation than in their writing, but there is plenty of testimony that they were at least as brilliant. I might affirm in any case that neither the *Mémoires* nor the *Correspondances* convey any idea of the fiery and imaginative conversation of a Diderot. There are two authors clearly superior to anything they have left behind. If we knew nothing of d'Alembert except his works he would appear to us a "pontiff" of philosophy, stiff, stilted, a sort of Mentor, but more ponderous and tiresome; he was in reality one of the wittiest

members of the *salons* of his day, with a reputation for his caustic epigrams, not disdaining, in order to divert his audience, to condescend to mimic people and give humorous caricatures of them; doubtless he had less dignity on these occasions, but it helps to explain the influence that he exercised.

Duclos supplies the most striking example of the man of letters; feared for his disposition, of commanding intelligence, who, thanks to his conversation, secured a most envied position, one which Chamfort alone aspired to fill after his death. Duclos was a man who spent all his resources in society; he was so prodigal of his epigrams and his wit in the *salons* that more than one critic, who had known the man before becoming acquainted with his writings, experienced a real disillusion when he came to read them. "He was," said Sainte-Beuve, "one of those bold and daring conversationalists who pass their life in society, make their mark there in the first instance, maintain their footing there, but dissipate their energies in this way, and leave behind them no work equal to their reputation or perhaps to their real worth. Duclos exhausted his talent in conversation." How many witticisms launched by Duclos were carried by his associates into *salons* which he himself did not frequent! Some of them are harsh, even violent; they scarify their victim. "He is such a rogue," said the philosopher of the Abbé d'Olivet, "that, in spite of all the insults with which I overwhelm him, he does not hate me more than another." He was on his way to the Tuileries when he was told that Calonne had just given his *rapport* against La Chalotais. "Would you believe," he was asked, "that here, in the Tuileries, in broad daylight, this abominable *rapport* is for sale?" "Like the judge," interrupted Duclos. Other epigrams, less harsh, have the same vigour: "So-and-so is a fool. I say it, but he proves it." Yet others have a finer edge. The Solicitor-General Séguier came to ask for his vote, in the ordinary course, for the Academy. "To whom have I the honour of speaking?" "I am Séguier." "You have a name, Sir, which needs no honour, and an honour which needs no name." Others are simple puns. De l'Averdy nominated one of his creatures, L'Anglais, as Intendant of Finance, although he was a man in bad repute, or, as the eighteenth-century phrase ran, *une espèce.* "Excellent!" cried Duclos; "a Controller-General ought to be able to turn *les espèces* to account."

There are other droll, unexpected sallies. In 1771 all Paris rushed to see an elephant whose prowess is described in memoirs of the time. A popular rhyme suggested that the famous beast was a candidate for the Academy—

> Cet éléphant, sorti d'Asie,
> Vient-il amuser nos badauds?
> Non; il vient avec ses rivaux
> Concourir àl'Académie.

At that juncture the *philosophe* had a grudge against the Government. Duclos arrived one day at the Academy, where imprudent remarks about Ministers were being made. "Gentlemen," he cried, "let us speak of the elephant; it is the only beast worth any consideration about which it is safe to speak at the moment." Duclos and his fellow men of letters were continually striking off this coin of wit, with its own stamp of originality, which the *salons* put into circulation; at the same time the *salons* supplied men of letters with a field for the display of their powers of conversation. In this way the *salons* made the fame of writers who were esteemed the more because they were most distinguished in the peculiarly French art of conversation.

It would have been difficult for the authors when they returned to their desks to maintain the pedantry of their predecessors; society did them the real service of compelling them to express themselves agreeably and clearly. The *précieuses* of the Hôtel Rambouillet and of the *levée* had long ago taught the authors to shave and to make their toilet before appearing in the dim light of the *salon* or the broad daylight of publicity. The *salons* of the eighteenth century had a similar influence; nor do I see why what held good in the days of Madame de Vivonne and Mademoiselle de Scudéry should not do so in the days of Madame de Lambert and Madame de Tencin, nor do I see why M. Brunetière, so enthusiastic in his praise of the benefits conferred on literature by the *salons* of the seventeenth century, should find such bitter words to decry those of the eighteenth. It is true that the ladies of the eighteenth-century *salons* had lovers, while those of the seventeenth "esteemed" men who were not their husbands; I see much more difference in the form than in the reality. It is true that the ladies of the seventeenth century neither housed nor fed the men of letters who had not had, like the marquises, the good fortune to be born in opulence or, like others, the faculty of making dupes. But every impartial mind should recognise that, throughout literary history, the aristocratic spirit has exercised on authors an almost identical influence, and if there was less decorum in the *salon* of Madame Geoffrin than at the Hôtel Rambouillet, I console myself with thinking that there was less ridiculous prudery and tiresome fuss in presence of a vulgar word.

"The men of letters," wrote Duclos, "have perfected their style, polished their wit"; that is true. "There were no books," wrote Taine, "save those which were written for society and even for *les femmes du monde.*" That is true of the greatest: *L'Esprit des Lois, L'Essai sur les Mœurs, Émile, Le Traité des Sensations.* We will consult Marmontel as to the advantage he thought he had derived from the intercourse in the *salon* in which he spent his life. He says in his *Mémoires:*

> The conversation there was a school for me, not less useful than agreeable, and I profited by their lessons as much as possible. He who only wishes to write with precision, energy and vigour, may mix with men only; but he who wishes to have a style which is supple, pleasant, attractive, and with what is called "charm," will do well, I believe, to live among women. When I read that Pericles sacrificed all his mornings to the Graces, I interpret it as meaning that he lunched every morning with Aspasia.

Marmontel lunched often with Aspasia; he had the perfect digestion required, and, if it is objected that he was far from the stature of Pericles, we will reply that if he acquired a certain graceful facility, if he has left us a series of sketches of personalities which a contemporary critic has called "illustrations to the *Encyclopédie,*" we have to thank the good company of his time for them.

We may go farther, and say that the service rendered from this point of view by society was still more valuable in the seventeenth than in the eighteenth century. Well, it is agreed that the seventeenth century in everything concerned with psychology had an incommensurable depth, a delicacy of analysis unparalleled in any other time and place; and if to interpret its intimate discoveries to our innermost mind the seventeenth century found a language clear, simple and capable of conveying the finest shades, society had a great deal to do with it. But certain of these qualities were even more indispensable in the next century; it now became necessary to convey ideas which the preceding century would have thought to lie rather outside the boundaries of literature, and with which it was little concerned; I venture to say that style is less artistic than in the preceding century, but also that it is less bookish, that it is more intellectual, in fact more serviceable. The style of the period is transformed after La Bruyère; it is brisk and clear-cut, the style of true conversation, a style which the bookmaker at the corner of the street may pride himself on understanding, yet so elegant and witty as to be attractive and lively reading. *Vive l'esprit* is the watchword passed on from one writer to another, from Le Sage to Voltaire, from Voltaire to Beaumarchais. We may now understand what Marmontel meant, and why Montesquieu and Voltaire had, from the point of view of style, much more to gain from contact with society than had Pascal and La Rochefoucauld.

I have kept until the end the most important of the services rendered by the *salons,* which was to win over to the new ideas people of good breeding and high social standing. We have made this observation about the nobility; it should be extended to all those whose position left them a little leisure. The *habitués* of the *salons* of the seventeenth century had become psychologists; those of the eighteenth became philosophers—I do not add "without knowing it," for it was with them a point of honour to profess great and generous theories, however disquieting they might be for the existing regime or menacing to their own privileges. The infiltration of the new ideas took place not only among those of noble birth, but among all those who would be overthrown the moment that those ideas were converted into precise and energetic action. I shall show one day the same infiltration among the regular and the secular clergy. Is an irrefutable proof desired? Read the list of subscribers to the *Encyclopédie;* beside the great names of France, you will find noble names of all ranks—abbés, magistrates, intendants, placemen, financiers. This is what society gave in return to the men of letters, and the exchange took place in the *salons.* The idea of underrating this last service will not occur to anyone; in France especially, where the code of manners and conduct is always gibed at, but always scrupulously obeyed, *la philosophie* was sure of success when it had once gained the support of society.

> This first epoch of our Revolution [says the Vicomtesse de Noailles] was one of great injustice to our upper classes. They are represented even to-day with characteristics which they no longer had, and they are calumniated in spite of the evidence of the facts. Philosophy had no *apostles more benevolent than the great aristocrats.* Horror of abuses, scorn of hereditary distinctions, all the sentiments which lower classes made use of in their own interests, owed their first impulse to the enthusiasm of the aristocrats, *and the most ardent and most active pupils of Rousseau were courtiers rather than men of letters.* Exaltation with some of them reached the

point of blindness. Finally, like the astrologer in the fable, they fell into a well while looking at the stars.

We know what the great lords did when they emerged from the well; they crossed the frontier, persuaded that it would be easy to cross it afresh at the head of the enemies of the nation. But a great number of them were won over before the catastrophe and it is hard to maintain that the work of the *philosophes* was not facilitated by the *salons,* which brought them into contact with rank and fortune. This is one more reason for leaving to Voltaire, to d'Alembert, and all those who fought for the same cause, the merit of having prepared the Revolution of 1789.

Is that to say that we need not consider the drawbacks as well as the advantages? These drawbacks must be accorded a large place; some, at least, of the writers of the eighteenth century perceived them, men who, like others, had profited by intercourse with the great world. I am far from denying these drawbacks, but I ask myself whether they did not already exist in the seventeenth century, whether they ought not to be considered as a general part of the price to be paid for the advantages which we have indicated.

I am not concerned with the *salons* which were not literary. There were, it is clear, in the eighteenth century an infinite number of *salons* which were negligible. In *Le Cercle ou la Soirée à la Mode,* a comedy played at the Théâtre Français in 1764, Poinsinet paints for us the interior of one of these *salons:*

"Ismène and Cydalise, weary of *tri* [a fashionable card game], and not knowing what to talk slander about, look round for an occupation. Araminte is finishing a flower in her tapestry; Cydalise picks up some gold thread; she has an embroidery frame beside her arm-chair, and with a yawn she begins to embroider a strip for a dress, while Ismène, at full length on the sofa, works at a flounce." The footman announces the Marquis, who, having complimented the ladies in carefully turned phrases, approaches. "He draws from his pocket a case, selects a golden needle, takes a piece of silk, and begins to work at the tapestry. The ladies watch and admire. But this is only the beginning. He leaves Araminte and her work, crosses over to Cydalise, takes her embroidery frame, and in a moment his quick fingers complete the outline of the flower. Then he dashes to the sofa, seizes a piece of the flounce, working all the quicker in his desire to be near the charming Ismène." This Marquis probably belonged to the army of Soubise. Abbés, colonels and fine gentlemen then occupied themselves with embroidery, tapestry, drawn-thread work, cutting out, pulling the strings of little mechanical puppets, according to the fashion of the day. A man would arrive in a *salon,* carrying his work-bag, afterwards nicknamed his "ridicule," which contained his sewing materials, pastilles, scents, bonbons and snuff. Naturally the fine gentlemen of the period could not devote themselves to these occupations without the accompaniment of tearing to pieces their neighbours' reputations; the *salon* was a field for the exercise of that persiflage which Duclos has attacked with his angry sarcasms. Evidently in speaking seriously of the *salons* one must eliminate all of this kind. They existed in the seventeenth as in the eighteenth. In any case I must admit that the gallants were better employed in parties which were frivolous and of no importance but yet well-mannered than in the cabarets where

they got drunk, or in the streets where they were all for ever flourishing their swords. Let us leave on one side all the *salons* which were not literary, and let us take care not to be too severe on the eighteenth century, but to measure it by the standards of the seventeenth or the twentieth. "How many agreeable things, how many useful reflexions do you not hear on the season's dresses, ribbons, coiffures and the art of dressing." So speaks the Abbé Coyer in a *Lettre à une Dame Anglaise.* We will not say that the remark smacks of to-day, for fear of offending someone; but let us admit that it seems to smack of yesterday.

We may take it that Duclos' reproaches are addressed only to society of this kind. He says: "Every important question, every sensible opinion, is excluded from these brilliant parties of *le bon ton.*" And he defines *le bon ton:* "It consists of those people who display the most wit in saying agreeable nothings, and in not permitting the smallest reasonable remark unless it justifies itself by the grace of its expression." It would be a mistake to take this too seriously, for this is how he describes, in the *Confessions du Comte,* the *salon* of Madame de Tencin, frequented by the *philosophes:*

> I really found much of what is called intelligence in Madame de Tonins and some members of her little court, that is to say much facility of expression, brilliance and lightness of touch, but it seemed to me that this last quality was abused. The conversation which I had interrupted was a sort of metaphysical dissertation. To enliven the matter of it Madame de Tonins and her friends were careful to

Salon-goers disport at whist. According to Whittaker Chambers, "Their world held for them one terror, ennui, and only one horror, a lapse of taste."

include in their learned conversation a great many quips, epigrams, and, unfortunately, some rather trivial witticisms.

Let us recognise that we have here a part of the truth (to have the real opinion of Duclos on Madame de Tencin's wit we must go to the *Mémoires Secrets,* and we shall see that that opinion is much more favourable); it is evident that society had its code, and imposed on authors tiresome obligations, among which the first was to display wit, to treat the most serious subjects like a gentleman—that is, pleasantly; the second was only to deal with subjects which were of interest to polite society—that is to say, too often to eliminate large questions and serious problems. It may be believed that where the second condition was observed the first was comparatively easy. Godeau, Bishop of Venice, in declaring himself in prose and verse "Julie's dwarf," and Montausier, in describing himself as dying for love of her, were scarcely in danger of tackling problems too recondite or of dealing heavy-handed with subjects in which the code demanded the equivocal and pretty fancies of Marini and Gongors, excellent French names, to figure as patterns in a Parisian *salon*!

After all this it is easy for M. Brunetière to reproach the *salons* of the eighteenth century: "We owe to them the custom of treating serious questions in an amusing manner—that is to say, wrongly; for how can we treat amusingly the question of poverty or the advancement of science, or how treat trifles seriously?" M. Brunetière is right. But would he prefer the *salon* over which Julie, already mature in years and vowed to St Catherine till the age of forty, reigned, to enjoy the gentle pleasure of hearing stout rhymers dying in metaphor, celebrating her charms and complaining of her cruelty? Assuredly not, and the critic who has so happily defined French literature as a "social" literature ought certainly to realise that a great deal of time was wasted in teaching Julie the language of flowers. We agree that the question of poverty or the advancement of science ought not to be treated as opportunities for the display of wit; but in my opinion it is much more serious not to treat of them at all, to suppress them, not even to know that they exist, and to have no suspicion that beside this garden in which the rose, the heliotrope, the lily and the narcissus are made to express such tawdry gallantries, there is a desolate countryside where the starving peasant lies on his stomach to browse on the grass which the beasts have refused; to imagine that humanity needed nothing but the sonnets, the madrigals, the polite casuistry and the *carte du tendre,* that we are compelled to live artificially in a hot-house atmosphere; that we have all been created and sent into the world to serve the purpose of Chinese vases in a *salon,* and not to go out in the sunlight on the great roads along which the peoples under the guidance of science are marching forward towards a better future which comes nearer with every step forward, material or moral. (pp. 177-88)

I venture to say that even when they hindered independence of thought the *salons* of the eighteenth century rendered a service to philosophy. This is no paradox; on the contrary. Doubtless more than one hothead found it difficult to endure the yoke of Madame Geoffrin, this *sœur du Pot de la philosophie,* as M. de Lescure, author of the *Femmes Philosophes,* who did not love her, called her. Paciaudi

called her the *Czarine de Paris;* the painter Greuze, to whom, as to so many others, she had been rude, said of her: "*Mort Dieu,* if she annoys me again, let her beware; I will paint her." According to some, Greuze added: "I will paint her with a ferule." Grimm in his turn wrote:

> Mother Geoffrin informs us that she will renew the prohibitions and the prohibitive laws of former years, and that it will not be permissible to speak in her *salon* of home or foreign affairs; nor of the affairs of the Court and the town, nor of the affairs of the North and the South, etc. etc. etc.. . . . nor, in general, of anything at all.

But who can fail to see the services she rendered, perhaps in spite of herself, not only to the doctrines of the *philosophes,* which she prevented from becoming a bugbear to the timorous, whose name is legion, but to the men of letters whom she prevented from terrifying the great nobles and society? She told Marmontel, who had been censured by the Academy, that she could dispense with his presence, but at the same time discreetly subscribed *200,000 livres* to the *Encyclopédie;* she did not even like her *philosophes* to die without a priest; she sent to them, as unobtrusively as possible, an ecclesiastic who would absolve them from their irreligion; that was the proper thing to do. Some were impatient, and I can well understand it; but the men who were annoyed by this discipline could take their revenge at the "Tuesdays" of Helvetius and at the "Thursdays" or the "Sundays" of d'Holbach. Marmontel himself behaved like a schoolboy on these occasions; he literally romped, quoting Virgil the while. But if they had had only their philosophical synagogues the miscreants would have made far fewer disciples. "They said things," says Morellet, "which would have brought thunderbolts on the house, if thunderbolts ever fell for that reason." There were still plenty of people who believed in thunderbolts and who would have stayed at home.

Thus Madame du Deffand, in her *salon* of yellow moiré, with flame-coloured ribbons, where the learned were one day to be found insipid, and to be banished almost completely, helped the triumph of the new ideas; it was she who placed d'Alembert in the Academy, and who put Marmontel, Rousseau, La Harpe and Grimm in touch with the Mirepoix, the Forcalquiers, the Brancas, the Luxembourgs, the Maurepas, the Choiseuls, the Broglies and the Beauvaus. . . . That was even worth some concession in the interest of the success of *la philosophie.* Let us add, for the rest, that no concession, or hardly any, was demanded in the *salons* of Madame de Lambert, Madame de Tencin, above all, in that of Mademoiselle de Lespinasse, whose motto was: "Moderation in tone and great energy in action." None was required even in the *salon* of Madame de Necker, so pious, so frank in the expression of her religious convictions, so that (a feature too seldom noted) the most impious *philosophes* were the readier to make the most concessions.

It remains to note one point on which I can be more definite. I shall not hesitate to pronounce the influence of the *salons* of the eighteenth century as more fortunate than that of the *salons* of the seventeenth century when I consider the point that, thanks to the first, our influence in Europe and in the world was increased. I will not return to the dangers threatened to French taste by the imitation of the Spaniards and the Italians in the seventeenth century, nor speak of the service which Molière and Boileau rendered in compelling this literature to recross the Alps and the Pyrenees. From that time it is to England that our writers turned, but they were to return to England and the civilised nations a hundredfold more than they borrowed. The answer to those who accuse the *philosophes* of lack of patriotism is this. It is enough to recall that when our arms suffered an eclipse the literary glory of France shone with a light so dazzling that her popularity was never more complete; never was her genius more admired, never was she more queen of the world. Now the *salons* had much to do with the conquest of this hegemony of which we have the right to be proud. "Paris is the café of Europe," says Galiani, the tiny abbé from Naples; "foreigners ask, as soon as they arrive, to be taken to Madame de Tencin; there you may rub shoulders with Bolingbroke, Chesterfield, the Comte de Guasco, or with Tronchin from Geneva. Grimm recapitulates in his *Correspondance Littéraire* all the news which he learned in the *salons* where he occupied the place of honour and in others. Creutz, Gleichen, Lord Stormont, the Marquis de Fuentes are brought by Grimm to Madame d'Epinay's; when Madame Geoffrin went to Poland to visit her young friend Stanislas, all the sovereigns, princes and ministers of the countries through which she passed came to pay their respects to her; the petulant—the too petulant—Abbé Galiani is one of the faithful circle of 'Sister Necker.' " . . . If all Europe went to school with us let us not forget it was in the *salons* of the day that they took their lessons, and let us be proud of having given those lessons, for it is one of our best titles to the admiration of men of all times and all countries.

First of all I conclude that the influence of the *salons* of the eighteenth century had its good and its bad points, but that the good predominated. Secondly, that it is unjust to attribute to the *salons* of the eighteenth century alone the disadvantages which are true of all *salons*. We must either condemn the one and the other, or absolve both at the same time. Proudhon was not more logical. "When," he said, "in a society, or in a literature, the feminine element comes to dominate or even to balance the masculine element, there is a pause in the advance of that society or that literature, and presently decadence." I do not see why, according to him, the decadence of our literature should begin with Rousseau, *"ce femmelin de l'intelligence."* It would have begun much earlier, at the beginning of the seventeenth century. Our judgment is quite different; we recognise that women—that is to say, polite society—have rendered signal services to our literature, and we render honour to those of the eighteenth century for having rendered services more numerous and more important than their predecessors, because they were the auxiliaries of the ideas which form the patrimony of our nation—the ideas of liberty and humanity. (pp. 193-96)

Marius Roustan, "The 'Philosophes' and the 'Salons'," in his *The Pioneers of the French Revolution, translated by Frederic Whyte, Little, Brown and Company, 1926, pp. 177-96.*

CENSORSHIP

Robert Shackleton

[*Shackleton was an English editor and essayist. In the following excerpt from a lecture delivered in 1975, he details the censorship practices of eighteenth-century French authorities, especially those of the state and the church.*]

I use the words "censure" and "censorship" to represent two different forms of interference with free publication. "Censorship" is the examination of a text before publication, by someone in authority, with a view to ascertaining its fitness to appear. "Censure" is the examination of a text, after publication, with a view to deciding whether it had been fit to appear. In either case the examination envisages the possibility of action by the examining body: the granting or the withholding of leave to publish, in the case of censorship; and in the case of censure, the withdrawing of such leave and the imposition of penalties. The French language does not possess two separate words which can make this discrimination, and compels us to talk of *censure préventive* and *censure répressive*. The first of these, the preventive censure, though it must by its nature precede publication, may come either before or after printing, particularly when the complete process was of necessity rapid. (pp. 10-11)

In medieval France the responsibility for censorship prior to works being placed in circulation was not clearly defined and was claimed both by the University, as custodian of theological orthodoxy, and by the Parlements, as custodians of the law. The importance of this censorship was increased immensely at the end of the Middle Ages by the invention of printing, which transformed the mode and the speed of circulation of ideas, and by the Reformation, which generated new and dangerous ideas; and the development of the concept of legal property was a further argument for the creation of firm rules for approval and licensing.

Three separate pieces of legislation established the basis for the control of censorship in the eighteenth century. The first was the ordinance of Moulins of 1566, for which the Chancellor Michel de L'Hospital was largely responsible. This laid down that no person might print or cause to be printed any book or treatise without leave of the king and letters of privilege sealed with the great seal, and the printer was ordered to insert in the book or treatise his name and town, along with the text of the privilege. The requirement that the great seal should be affixed placed the responsibility in the hands of the Chancellor of France, the highest official of the central power, and removed it from the University and the Parlement. These bodies, however, were not easily dispossessed, and the absence of any special organisation under the Chancellor meant that the royal authority was not effectively asserted, and the old rivalries continued.

The Code Michaud of 1629 laid down the procedure to be followed: two copies of the manuscript text were to be presented to the Chancellor, who would nominate a censor to examine the work; the censor was to write his attestation on one of the manuscripts. The Chancellor thereupon would decide, in the light of the censor's judgment, whether a privilege was to be given. The endorsed manuscript, if the judgment was favourable, was returned to the author, while the other was kept as a check. Further, the Code forbade anonymous publication. In this respect it was soon a wholly dead letter.

The censors, nevertheless, were usually chosen by the Chancellor from the doctors of the Sorbonne, save that it appears that authors were often able, from the same category, to nominate censors of their own choice. This continued subservience to the Sorbonne the great Séguier, for many years Chancellor, sought to remedy by establishing a group of royal censors nominated by himself. The administrative pattern in force throughout the eighteenth century was now set.

It was consolidated by the *Code de la librairie of 1723, which formalized the procedure, prescribed the rules for legal deposit, and defined the copyright which resulted from the privilege. The conditions for an era of struggles, delays, and evasions were consolidated.*

Delays were often lamented, and decisions inscrutable. As early as 1685, Pierre Bayle, writing in his journal the *Nouvelles de la république des lettres* about an artificially prolonged theological controversy involving the Jansenist Arnauld, spoke of delays of four or five years imposed by the censor. He likened the poor authors hoping for their privilege to the souls of the dead waiting for Charon to row them across the Styx, and quotes Virgil's *Aeneid* on their plight:

> Craving the far shore stood the suppliant band,
> Seeking first passage, each with outstretched hand;
> But the sad sailor takes now these, now those,
> The rest repels, abandoned, as he goes.

Sixty-seven years later Diderot, in his article CENSEURS in the *Encyclopédie,* quotes the same passage from the *Aeneid* on authors hungry for their privilege: so constant were the law's delays and the charm of Virgil, so strong the repute of Bayle. (pp. 11-12)

At the end of the century Isaac d'Israeli comments on the French censors. His *Domestic Anecdotes of the French Nation* of 1795 is an unusual work worthy of attention for its comments on literary activity in France. The author writes:

> The Censors of books, in France, were a kind of literary inquisitors, which have long been unknown in England. . . . The original institution of these censors was merely designed as a guard of those publications which might be injurious to society. Their laws were simple, and their approbation, at first, was drawn up in this concise manner. They declared that they found nothing in the work contrary to religion, government, and morals. They had not even a right to judge of its intrinsic merit. It was not long, indeed, before this system was corrupted. To gratify a faction or a friend, these censors assumed the liberty of loading their approbations with high eulogisms and impertinent criticisms.

This is true. The basic formula is simply "I have read by order of the Chancellor a book entitled . . . , and have found in it nothing which should impede its being printed." Often this simple attestation is added to. The censor of the 1713 edition of the *Odes* of Houdard de La Motte

cannot content himself, in his *approbation,* with the minimum, but adds that he has found in the work two things which rarely go together, solidity of reasoning and great poetic beauty. He was a nobody called Burette and La Motte was a famous man and an academician. Another censor, worthy but insignificant, Moreau de Mautour, piles generous praise on the *Réflexions critiques sur la poésie et la peinture* of Dubos when a new edition was being prepared in 1732. The author held the influential post of Perpetual Secretary of the Academy. The *approbation* for the 1708 edition of the *Poésies pastorales* of Fontenelle describes the book as one of the small number of original works which will do honour to the age. The certificate is signed 24 July 1707; earlier in the year the censor, Saurin, had been elected to the Academy of Sciences, which was dominated by Fontenelle. In a new edition, appearing in 1755, of Montesquieu's *Considérations sur les Romains* the censor writes that he has found in it nothing unworthy of the reputation of the book and of the author; but the censor of his earlier, mildly erotic, *Temple de Gnide,* the only work of Montesquieu the first edition of which appeared openly, with privilege, would not commit himself even to the normal *nil obstat* formula. A frigid, non-committal admission "I have read the book" was all that he would sign. The *Bibliographie instructive* of De Bure receives in 1764 the most whole-hearted eulogy from its censor. The book, he says, was lacking in our literature; it will be of the greatest use to men of letters and bibliophiles, and the author must continue without flinching in a career in which he alone can walk with confident steps. The censor was Caperonnier who dated his approval from the Bibliothèque du Roi; a librarian, then as now, could not but give the highest tribute to the finest bibliography of his age.

Who then were the censors? From 1742 onwards their names appear in the *Almanach royal,* and Lottin, in the list of booksellers and printers which he published in 1789, enumerates them with their dates of activity. They were appointed, on a part-time basis and with no immediate remuneration though with some prospect of it, and were assigned to specific subjects. In 1758—an important year, we shall see, in the history of censorship—there were ten censors for theology, all naturally in holy orders, almost all college professors or doctors of the Sorbonne. As censors these were the most active but the most obscure. The best known is Ladvocat, librarian of the Sorbonne and author of a biographical dictionary. The names of three of the others were faintly remembered through their hostile involvement in the publication of the *Encyclopédie,* and the rest are no more than shadows. For jurisprudence there were fourteen censors, all of them obscure. Of the eighteen scientists ten were, either then or later, members of the Academy of Sciences and thus enjoyed some eminence. There were three surgeons and ten mathematicians. Belles-lettres and history required no fewer than fifty-two, and the list is closed with one censor for geography and navigation, and one—who was the artist Cochin—for prints. The fifty-two literary censors include some of reputation: the elder Crébillon and a number of other Academicians, one of whom was Du Resnel whose French translation of Pope's *Essay on Man* was one of the controversial landmarks of the Enlightenment. Another was Condillac, an outstanding man and the most philosophical of the *philosophes.* The most striking fact, however, is that the list of censors in 1758 includes no fewer than thirteen of Diderot's collaborators in the *Encyclopédie.* Some of them, indeed, were continuous and major contributors, fully committed to that powerful and, in the eyes of the government, subversive enterprise. It is wrong to think of the censors and the whole apparatus of censorship as basically and unanimously opposed to the new ways of thought, or even as essentially repressive. There were too many amiable complicities for this to be true.

In cases when the censors were bound to be hostile, moreover, it was sometimes possible to harass or bully them. The fact of the publication in 1758, with *approbation* and *privilège,* of one of the century's most advanced and controversial works, *De l'esprit,* by Helvétius, is well known. . . . When Helvétius had completed his materialist treatise, responsibility for its publication was handed to a friend, Charles-Georges Leroy, a minor *philosophe* with a vigorous and combative mind, and a contributor to the *Encyclopédie.* Leroy himself selected a censor from the panel, an overworked Foreign Office official called Tercier, and obtained official ratification of the choice. He fed the manuscript to Tercier in small sections, thirty pages at a time, never allowing him to see to it as a whole; he made him read it under heavy pressure; he tenaciously disputed all the censor's changes, and wrung a final signature out of him by a trick. Leroy's activity was in fact counterproductive. The fierce retaliation by the government was a set-back to the progress of the philosophical movement in France. If instead of seeking to show that the machinery of censorship could be manipulated Helvétius had discreetly published abroad or in some other semi-legal way, he might have secured a personal triumph. As it was, he had to publish a recantation in terms so humiliating, said Grimm, that one would not be surprised if a man chose rather to take flight to the land of the Hottentots.

There were indeed alternative methods of publication of which the most important was by tacit permission. There are of course various imaginable degrees of tacitness, and the term has been frequently misunderstood. A *permission tacite* was a quite specific authorisation, and it has been described by no one more precisely than by the great liberal functionary who was *directeur de la librairie* during the most crucial years of book production in France of the *ancien régime.* This was Malesherbes, one of the most enlightened figures of the age of the Enlightenment. His father was Chancellor of France, and the son was appointed to take charge of the affairs of publication and book-production which fell under the Chancellor's authority. His posthumously published *Mémoires sur la librairie* give invaluable information about the rules governing publication. In particular they clarify the whole situation of the *permissions tacites.* However much, he says, some people may object to these apparent infractions of the law, in practice it is quite impossible to dispense with them. They are not simply acts of tolerance or connivance. They are formal decisions which, though not printed in the book in respect of which they are given, are recorded in a register of which copies are given to the professional organisation of booksellers and publishers, the *Chambre syndicale de la librairie* and to the Lieutenant of Police. The first of these copies, he adds, is anomalously entitled "List of works printed in foreign countries, the sale of which is permitted in France."

This is true, and this register along with others similar is now to be found in the Bibliothèque Nationale. The head-

ing is not in fact completely misleading, since the *permission tacite* related both to books published abroad which it was desired to introduce into France, and to unpublished works for which leave to publish in France was sought. Ostensibly, moreover, the categories were difficult to distinguish because a publisher who received a *permission tacite* was expected to use a false imprint and to give the impression that the book in question was published abroad. I will give one example from this register of the grant of a *permission tacite* which shows how the public interest might inspire a government department. In 1765 the *chambre syndicale* requested a permission for the publication of a quarto edition of Montesquieu's works. The request was for the renewal of previous permission. The decision is recorded:

> Leave is granted to the Paris *librairies* on condition that they make a fine quarto edition, with fine characters and on fine paper, and sell it at a reasonable price. Promise given to allow the entry of no foreign edition of the same format and inferior to the Paris edition.

Only two quarto editions of the collected works of Montesquieu appeared before 1770. This permission must relate to that of 1767, bearing the imprint *Londres, chez Nourse.* Since the permission is a renewal, it must also have related to the 1758 edition, with the imprint *A Amsterdam & à Leipsick, chez Arkstée & Merkus.* So from the register we learn what was not otherwise known, that the two quarto editions of Montesquieu, of which the second is clearly based on the first, were not produced abroad, but in Paris with *permission tacite.* Montesquieu was not always so well thought of by the government. The preceding volume of the register records a request for tacit permission for the introduction into France of the *Lettres persanes,* published in Holland. "Absolutely rejected," was the judgment: *"absolument réprouvé."*

A large number of books appeared in France with *permission tacite;* perhaps a larger number appeared outside French frontiers, in countries where French-speaking Protestant exiles lived—England, Holland, Switzerland— and also in small, independent territories, enclaves sometimes, where the writ of the French king did not run: Bouillon with its duke, Liège with its prince-bishop, Trévoux with its sovereign prince, Avignon with its legate. The eighteenth century moreover was the age of the imaginary imprint: Cosmopolis, Ratopolis, At the expense of the Society of Jesus (in the case of irreligious works), Cologne, chez Pierre Marteau—this last being doubtless the only non-existent man to be the subject of a bibliography. And if all else failed, the age of printing had not wholly abolished the art of writing, and many outspoken works in the first half of the century circulated clandestinely in manuscript.

The various loopholes associated with the system of censorship and licensing by the Chancellor gave a great degree of importance to censure after publication, particularly at times when advanced ideas were being expressed. The *censure répressive* was exercised by a number of different bodies, both ecclesiastical and lay. The ecclesiastical authority concerned on the international level was the Holy See; in France, the bishops, either separately or collectively in the general assembly of the clergy, and the University were included. A bishop could discipline his clergy by suspension; he could adjure the laity in his diocese to abstain from reading or possessing a book which he had denounced, and he could excommunicate the refractory. The Sorbonne could issue condemnation of a book. But in eighteenth-century France there was no inquisition. There was no ecclesiastical tribunal which could impose sentences of imprisonment or banishment, or levy fines. The Church had no automatically responsive secular arm. For ecclesiastical condemnation to have punitive effect, it was necessary for the civil power to act. The Crown might impose exile or imprisonment by *lettre de cachet* without legal process. The civil courts which dealt with matters of publication were the Conseil d'Etat, the Châtelet, the Grand Conseil, and above all the Parlement. It was usual in serious cases for a condemned book to be burned by the public hangman, as well as for penalties to be imposed on the author. A list of books condemned by the civil power from 1715 to 1789 was drawn up, in the last century, by Félix Rocquain. Here, along with a great number of controversial theological writings, are enrolled many of the most influential and celebrated works of the French Enlightenment: Voltaire's *Lettres philosophiques,* burnt in 1734, Diderot's *Pensées philosophiques,* burnt in 1746, *Les Moeurs* of Toussaint, burnt in 1748, *De l'esprit* of Helvétius, burnt in 1759, Rousseau's *Emile,* burnt in 1762, the *Dictionnaire philosophique* of Voltaire, burnt in 1765, D'Holbach's *Système de la nature,* burnt in 1770, the *Histoire philosophique et politique des deux Indes* by Raynal, burnt in 1782, the *Encyclopédie,* condemned in 1759 but not sentenced to burning because of the amount of capital invested in the enterprise. The Parlement was in each case the court which pronounced judgement, and in each case the renown and influence of the book were increased by its condemnation.

Towards the middle of the eighteenth century hostility to the new ways of thinking reached its peak, and censure was at its most active. The General Assembly of the Clergy, meeting in May 1750, began to discuss the works of the *philosophes,* with a view to requesting action against them by the King. Montesquieu's *L'Esprit des lois* was one of the works under consideration. After a month's study of the problem, the Assembly's President reported that the task was too great, and that they would do better to restrict their attention to a single work. The book chosen was by one Daniel Bargeton, *Ne repugnate vestro bono*—do not resist what is good for you—which was a plea for ending the clergy's immunity from taxation.

More energetic was the Sorbonne, or more precisely the Faculty of Theology of the University of Paris, for in strict terminology the Sorbonne was a college within that Faculty. We have seen that within the seventeenth century the traditional responsibility of the University for censorship was effectively terminated though the Chancellor still selected theological censors from its body. The Faculty remained ready, however, to engage in criticism and censure of published works which were suspect, a task much less tedious than the laborious reading of innumerable manuscripts submitted before publication, and indeed potentially exciting, since a denunciation by the University might result in legal action by the courts. The Sorbonne became particularly busy in 1750 and the story of these activities has never been fully told, but is there to be read in contemporary records, printed and manuscript. On 1 August 1750, the Faculty of Theology, perturbed by the great outpouring of irreligious works, appointed a committee to investigate them. It began by arming itself for documentation with a copy of the leading Jansenist journal of the time, the *Nouvelles ecclésiastiques,* which had conscientiously listed and denounced undesirable publications. The major items for consideration were Buffon's *Histoire naturelle,* Montesquieu's *L'Esprit des lois,* and two French translations of Pope's *Essay on Man.* It was decided to approach those responsible with the suggestion that they should retract. They responded in different ways. The translators of Pope made no difficulties; Buffon, liking to be left in peace, retracted likewise; Montesquieu was obstinate, wished to resist, and was able to move the Archbishop of Paris to intervene in his behalf.

While this was pending, however, and while the Sorbonne was glorying in its role of custodian of catholic orthodoxy, an unforeseen event occurred. A young ecclesiastic, the Abbé de Prades, submitted a thesis for the degree of licentiate in theology. Some of his friends were exponents of the new ideas and these had penetrated into his thesis. Passages from Voltaire and D'Alembert had been incorporated into his academic Latin, and he baldly advances heterodox statements: religion is no more than a further development of natural law; all religions, including Christianity, display their miracles too boastfully; the cures effected by Christ and related in the scriptures are no more than equivocal miracles.

Had a layman publicly expressed such ideas, he would have been in trouble. Now an ecclesiastic was putting them forward in a theological thesis presented to the Sorbonne. To make matters worse, the thesis had been approved by the examiners before its content was noticed. The Faculty of Theology, involved in vindicating religious orthodoxy in the outer world, had set the seal of its approval, within its own walls, on dangerous and apparently anti-Christian doctrines.

This was indeed a moment of crisis. Talk of the thesis of the Abbé de Prades dominated Parisian life, and the salons spoke only of miracles and prophecies. The Sorbonne, after an inquiry into the nature of the thesis and the behaviour of the examiners, issued its censure, now famous. The Holy Faculty declared itself aghast at the work of darkness completed by one of its own bachelors, and fortified with the signatures of three of its own masters. Ten propositions from the thesis were condemned as false, temerarious, injurious to catholic theologians, scandalous, evilly sounding, offensive to pious ears, erroneous, blasphemous, heretical, favouring materialism, pernicious to society and public tranquility. The Abbé was stripped of his degrees, his diocesan, the Bishop of Montauban, issued a furious *mandement* against him, the Parlement ordered his arrest, and the government despatched a *lettre de cachet.* The Abbé fled from Paris and took refuge in Prussia, where he was given the not very onerous duties of chaplain to Frederick the Great.

We have seen that the prior censorship of literary works in France was governed by fixed rules, and that even if the rules were flexible, the flexibility itself was ordered. The censure of works already published, however, was sporadic and irregular, and the procedures were developed *ad hoc.* This was not the case with the activities of the Holy See which, though unarmed with punitive powers, at least in France, enjoyed great influence and prestige.

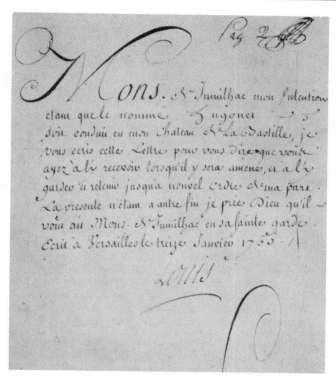

A royal lettre de cachet, signed by Louis XV.

The activity of the Holy See, in relation to censure, took more than one form. First, a condemnation might emanate from the Pope himself. For example, when the Paris nuncio, Durini, sent to the Holy Office a copy of the thesis of the Abbé de Prades, Benedict XIV saw it, read it, disapproved, and himself issued a brief of condemnation. Nor was this simply a repetition of the condemnation by the Sorbonne, since the Pope disagreed in one point with the university authorities. He did not see, among the multiple reproaches which could be made against the thesis, the taint of Socinianism, and therefore excluded this from his censure. For this personal censure Benedict cited a precedent, which was that of Clement XI: not a parallel he would have favoured in his relatively pro-Jansenist days as a cardinal, since Clement XI, as the Pope responsible for the anti-Jansenist Bull *Unigenitus,* was the author of a century of discord within the Church.

Apart from the Pontifical condemnation, the Holy See had other procedures for the censure of books. These go back to the Council of Trent, where the Church's disciplinary provisions were intensified. The rigour of the mentality of some of the Council is shown by the pronouncement of Becatelli, Archbishop of Ragusa, reported by the not untendentious pen of Fra Paolo Sarpi:

> There is no need of books, the world hath too many already, especially since printing was invented; and it is better to forbid a thousand books without cause, than permit one that deserveth prohibition.

The sixteenth century saw established in the Church the Congregation of the Holy Office and the Congregation of the Index. The former, known also as the Congregation of the Inquisition, was an organic continuation of the me-

dieval Inquisition; but the medieval coercive power survived only in Spain and Portugal, where regalist doctrines made it as much a national as an ultramontane body, and in the Papal States. The Congregation of the Index was charged with the maintenance of the Index of Prohibited Books, to which the Holy Office also might add books. The relations between these two Congregations were the subject of legislation by Benedict XIV in 1753. The Congregation of the Index was in 1917 merged in the Congregation of the Holy Office, which was itself remodelled in 1965 and redesignated the Congregation of the Doctrine of the Faith. The Archives of these two Congregations are not governed by the generous rule which permits access to the Vatican's archives in general, but are closed to the scholar. What can be discovered of the mode of operation of these bodies?

In the municipal library of Bologna there exists an eighteenth-century letterbook of the Inquisitor of Bologna (then in the Papal States), giving copies of his missives to the Holy Office. He received a complaint from Rome that prohibited books were on sale in the shops of Bologna. His reply, which I translate from the Italian, throws what must be a characteristic light on the illegal circulation of banned books. It is dated 14 March 1764.

> I would not venture to assert that none are ever sold. That could happen all too easily here, where various booksellers have ample privileges, deemed necessary in a famous university city like this and granted either by His Holiness the late Pope or by the Sacred Supreme Congregation of the Holy Office. In virtue of the said privileges they may keep and sell prohibited books of any sort on the sole condition of not putting them on view and not selling them except to those who can produce legal license to read and possess them.

He asks what he can do. Contravenors would not be easy to find. He could summon all booksellers and make them submit their up-dated lists of prohibited books, but illegal sales, in a city like Bologna, could never be stamped out.

Another letter, dated 28 March 1753, discloses the Inquisitor's mode of handling one individual problem, which happens to be a case of a priori censorship. A duodecimo volume had been submitted to him with a request for leave for its reprinting at Bologna. It is *The Oeconomy of Human Life,* drawn (he seems to think literally) from the Indian manuscript of an ancient Brahmin. It first appeared at London, was then reprinted successively at Edinburgh, at Berlin (twice), and at Milan, here with the approbation of the Milanese branch of the Holy Office. The moral maxims it advances seem really to be those of an honest man. Nevertheless (he continues)

> since the earlier editions appeared in suspect countries, since the author's name is suppressed, and since it apparently seeks to restrict happiness in the present life and the pursuit of eternal felicity to the practice of natural moral precepts, I have thought it necessary, before conceding leave to print a book so esteemed in suspect countries, to seek the oracular counsel of Your Eminences.

The Cardinals of the Holy Office were apparently satisfied, for he writes to them again on 26 April to say that he has authorised the publication on the usual conditions, *servatis servandis,* and *The Oeconomy of Human Life,* whether by

Chesterfield or Dodsley, escaped the censure of the Papal Court.

The Holy Office was informed of dubious books also by the Papal nuncios at foreign courts. We have seen that the Paris Nuncio Durini sent a copy of the thesis of the Abbé de Prades to the Holy Office. On 31 January 1752 he had written to the Secretary of State about the first two volumes of the *Encyclopédie,* which he heartily deplores at some length. He adds however that he has not sent a copy for the Holy Office since it is large and costly, but that he will despatch one if the Holy Office will provide for the expense. There are other examples of the Nuncio reporting books to the Holy Office through his hierarchical superior the Secretary of State.

When seized of the case of a dubious book, the Holy Office might handle the question itself, or might refer it to the Congregation of the Index. The Congregation of the Holy Office was more august, since its prefect was the Pope himself, and it met frequently, sometimes as often as three times a week, so that its procedure could be less prolonged. Some editions of the *Index* differentiate between condemnations emanating from the Holy Office and those of the Congregation of the Index. Particularly flagrant cases or cases requiring early decision appear to have been retained by the Holy Office for its own decision. Such are the *Istoria civile del regno di Napoli* by Giannone, published in March 1723 and condemned by the Holy Office on 1 July of the same year, Rousseau's *Emile,* condemned, though with greater delay, on 9 September 1762, and the *Système de la nature* of D'Holbach, published in February 1770 though not circulating widely until later in the year, and condemned on 9 November 1770.

The Congregation of the Holy Office had many duties, but the Congregation of the Index was concerned only with the *Index librorum prohibitorum.* Many editions of the *Index* have appeared, both at Rome and elsewhere, from the first in the sixteenth century to the last, in 1948. The early editions present some difficulty in use, since they have followed such odd bibliographical practices as listing authors under their first names, not their surnames. I cannot forebear to mention one edition which is assuredly the most unusual. Its author was a firm, not to say intolerant, Protestant. He was Thomas James, the first person to hold the office of Bodley's Librarian, having been appointed by Sir Thomas Bodley himself. His work, entitled *Index generalis librorum prohibitorum a Pontificibus,* was published at Oxford in 1627 and was dedicated to the Curators of the Bodleian Library who, in that day as in this, were the Library Committee. The *Index* was viewed by James quite simply and avowedly as a desiderata list. The books were good ones, he said, and the library should aim at acquiring them all.

The official editions of the *Index* list together the works originally proscribed by the Council of Trent, along with those subsequently condemned by the Popes, the Holy Office, and the Congregation of the Index. Supplements were published at intervals during the eighteenth century and were followed in due course by conflated editions. Typographically and bibliographically the best edition of the century was that authorized, towards the end of his Pontificate, by Benedict XIV, and published in 1758. It is a handsome quarto with an engraved title page showing men throwing books on to the flames and bearing the legend from the Acts of the Apostles, 'Many of them also which used curious arts brought their books together and burned them before all men' (XIX,19).

Though inaccessibility of archives stands between us and knowledge of the procedures by which a book reached the pages of the *Index,* a parallel documentation is sometimes afforded. Such documentation is particularly full in the case of Montesquieu, the condemnation of whose *L'Esprit des lois* was one of the century's major events in the history of the Congregation. Montesquieu's own correspondence and that of his Italian friends, notably of members of the Corsini family, enable the story to be almost completed. I am not now going to recount the events, having done so elsewhere. Suffice it to say that his work was denounced to the Congregation of the Index early in 1750, some eighteen months after its publication, that the French Ambassador to the Holy See intervened incessantly in Montesquieu's behalf, that the two successive *rapporteurs* of the Congregation were both great admirers of the work, that three powerful cardinals were markedly favourable to him, that the Pope himself, again the enlightened Benedict XIV, was well disposed, but that nevertheless on 29 November 1751, the Congregation pronounced sentence and *L'Esprit des lois* was placed on the *Index.*

It was undoubtedly as a result of this controversy that Benedict XIV was impelled to carry the reform of the procedure of censure that he had envisaged from the start of his reign. So far as documents of censure can be, his Constitution *Sollicita ac provida* of 1753 is a liberal document. It tentatively suggests that some cases in the curial tribunals may have been decided rashly and perfunctorily; it insists that fixed rules might be laid down and lays them down; it provides notably that an accused author, otherwise in good odour with the Church, should have the right to be heard in his own defence.

This attitude of the Pope, along with the high-placed resistances to the condemnation of Montesquieu, indicates a suppleness, even a subtlety, on the part of ecclesiastical authority which at the first glance are unexpected, and which are analogous to the official complicities we have seen in Paris. Both Benedict XIV and Malesherbes were tinged with the new ideas. Neither the Papal Court nor the Chancellor's department in Paris was monolithic in its composition and outlook, for the forces responsible for censure were by no means unanimous. Bishops might be in disagreement. Cardinals might be opposed to their Congregations. The Crown and the Sorbonne might be divided. The Parlement, most of all, was unpredictable, and ready to censure the pronouncements of other disciplinary bodies. We must reject the idea that there was an agreement of all who were in power in Church and State to curb free publication.

Too carefully to avoid over-simplification can however be itself an error. Perhaps the machines which the Pope and the *directeur de la librairie* were operating involved intellectual presuppositions and commitments different from the liberal leanings of Benedict and Malesherbes. Perhaps, within their framework of belief, the hard-liners on both sides were right and where they proclaimed incompatibility, incompatibility existed. Certainly as the century advanced the *philosophes* and their enemies became more rigidly opposed. Not for nothing did D'Argenson, in the atmosphere of crisis of February 1752, write with dismay that the Inquisition was gaining ground in France. Malesherbes was in the end to perish on the guillotine.

Let the case of Montesquieu, finally, be called in evidence. He was stricken with grief, reduced to despair, when his work was placed on the *Index.* Did he have a justified complaint, did his grief have intellectual basis? In the very work condemned he had written of the Inquisition:

> This tribunal is insupportable in all governments. In monarchies, it only makes informers and traitors; in republics, it only forms dishonest men; in a despotic State, it is as destructive as the government itself.

Could the Congregations of the Index and of the Holy Office have let that pass? Not unless they disbelieved in their own mission. (pp. 13-26)

> *Robert Shackleton, in his* Censure and Censorship: Impediment to Free Publication in the Age of Enlightenment, *Humanities Research Center, The University of Texas at Austin, 1975, 26 p.*

Kingsley Martin

> [*Martin was an English editor and author. During his thirty-year editorship of the* New Statesman, *he also contributed numerous articles to* Punch, *the* Atlantic Monthly, *and the* New Republic, *among others. In the following excerpt from a 1954 revision of his* French Liberal Thought in the Eighteenth Century: A Study of Political Ideas from Bayle to Condorcet, *Martin discusses the effects of censorship upon philosophic thought in eighteenth-century France.*]

Louis XIV. was a grand and tyrannous figure, an overpowering myth who subdued criticism even when he did not convince reason. At his death it was as though a spring were released and the first effect of that release was laughter. And laughter, at first a trivial gaiety in the social life of the Regency, made way for thought. The hushed circulation of sceptical comment was followed by open raillery, raillery by considered criticism, and out of criticism came visions of a better social order. In 1721 Montesquieu published the *Persian Letters.* Almost for the first time since Rabelais a book had appeared in which nothing was sacred. The attack upon French society contained in the letters of Usbec and Rica is barely disguised, though, to be sure, Persian travellers, commenting on the morals and manners prevalent in Europe, can make remarks which would be unseemly from a Frenchman, but which may nevertheless be true. The reader is imperceptibly led to the conclusion that the institutions he has revered, and the authorities he has obeyed, are perhaps unworthy of his reverence and obedience. The King, these observant Persians notice, is "a magician," who persuades men to kill one another though they have no quarrel. What else but magic could make them so irrational? Again self-constituted legislators pretend "their own wills are the laws of nature." Judges condemn "by the light within, without concerning themselves with useless knowledge." The highest aristocrat they visited was a little man who lost no "opportunity of making all who came near him sensible of his superiority, who took snuff with so much dignity, blew his nose so unmercifully, spat with so much phlegm, and caressed his

dog in a manner so offensive to the company that I could not but wonder at him. Ah! I said to myself, if when I was at the Court of Persia I had behaved so I should have been considered a great fool." The religious authorities were not treated with more respect. If the King was a magician, hypnotizing men into obedience, what was the Pope himself but "an old idol"? As for the Spanish Inquisitors, they were a "cheery species of dervishes" who burnt those who differed from them about obscure trivialities. And what reason was there for believing that Christianity embodied the final truth, when there were so many religions, each claiming universal validity? It was grievous for a kindly Persian to have to entertain the idea that all these Christians who had never worshipped in a mosque would end miserably in hell. Surely, he thinks, we can all agree about certain moral principles, and leave doubtful questions of dogma to the varying judgments of the sects? It is man who has made God in his own image, and if triangles had to construct a God, the new deity would certainly consist of three sides rather than three persons. In these circumstances, was not Louis XIV. unwise in thinking to "increase the number of the faithful by diminishing the number of his subjects"? Questions, hints and criticisms of this kind are everywhere spread among the one hundred and sixty *Persian Letters.* But the correspondence of Usbec and Rica is not solely concerned with philosophy or politics, for Usbec, in seeking wisdom abroad, has abandoned the joys of a well-stocked harem from which he receives a constant stream of letters dealing with love, hatred, strife and death. Even this side of the correspondence has a certain philosophical bearing. It provides an example of the revenge of outraged nature which can be denied no more in the seraglio than in the convent. The chief object of these passages however was to please the ladies who frequented Madame de Tencin's *salon,* where Montesquieu was a constant visitor. His friends there were only likely to listen to appeals for toleration or social reform when spiced with more appetizing ingredients; social criticism is, therefore, intermingled with descriptions of the sufferings of beautiful women and the pathos of thwarted desire in the eunuchs who assisted at their more intimate adornment.

These two characteristics, the trivial libertinism and the thin disguise of an indirect satire, were used throughout eighteenth-century literature to cover the most savage and subversive attacks. They reflect the two main conditions under which the *philosophes* wrote. It was essential to please a *salon* audience, which could enjoy an artistic and ironical attack upon social evils, but had no notion of practical and inconvenient remedies. It was also necessary to circumvent a censorship which would not permit any direct criticism of the political or religious authorities. Eighteenth-century *philosophes* made no pretence of being detached seekers after truth, and had the greatest contempt for most of what is usually called philosophy. The *philosophes* were humanists and journalists with a common object of propaganda. They wanted publicity and, unlike their Renaissance predecessors, they sought not for immortality in the praise of posterity, but for tangible and immediate influence. "Our philosopher," wrote Diderot, "does not count himself an exile in the world; he does not suppose himself in the enemy's country, he would fain find pleasure with others, and to find it he must give it; he is a worthy man who wishes to please and to make himself useful. The ordinary philosophers, who meditate too much, or rather who meditate to wrong purpose, are as surly and arrogant to all the world as great people are to those whom they do not think their equals; they flee men, and men avoid them. But our philosopher who knows how to divide himself between retreat and the commerce of men is full of humanity. Civil society is, so to say, a divinity for him on the earth; he honours it by his probity, by an exact attention to his duties, and by a sincere desire not to be a useless or an embarrassing member of it. The sage has the leaven of order and rule; he is full of ideas connected with the good of civil society. What experience shows us every day is that the more reason and light people have, the better fitted they are and the more to be relied on for the common intercourse of life."

Men who regarded civil society as a divinity on earth, and wished to enlist its support in practical reforms, were likely to busy themselves with metaphysical problems only in so far as their free treatment would cause amusement by annoying the ecclesiastical authorities. In any case, all systems of philosophy seemed remote and scholastic to a generation which believed that science could build a new heaven and a new earth. Almost all the *philosophes* began by studying some branch of science. Voltaire talked of devoting his life to the study of chemistry and worked with enthusiasm both to understand and expound Newtonian physics. D'Alembert was a physicist as well as a mathematician. Montesquieu's first publications were scientific. Diderot dabbled in all the sciences, and even Rousseau wrote a botanical dictionary. In spite of all their differences the party of the *philosophes* was united by their faith in science, their acceptance of Locke and Newton, and their hatred of the Catholic Church.

Writing in 1765, Horace Walpole asked: "Do you know who the *philosophes* are or what the term means here? In the first place it comprehends almost everybody, and, in the next, means men who are avowing war against Popery and aim, many of them, at the subversion of religion." A few years later, Bachaumont noted in his journal that there had been in France for some years "a sect of bold philosophers who seemed to have had a deliberate plan of carrying a fatal clarity into men's minds, of disturbing all belief, of upsetting religion and sapping her very foundations. Some of these, the light troops of the party, armed with sarcasm and irony, began by using transparent allegories and ingenious fictions as a method of covering with ineffaceable ridicule her liturgy and even her code of morals; others, profound speculative thinkers, armed with learning and bristling with metaphysics, stood out openly attacking her by force. . . . These, being unable to find worthy opponents, have unhappily retained the mastery of the battlefield. To-day, when these unbelievers consider their work to be well advanced . . . they are attacking their adversaries in their last strongholds. They claim to prove that politics has not the least need of religion for the maintenance and government of States."

In the sixties Walpole and Bachaumont could write of the *philosophes* as a united party, engaged in a combined assault on the Church. This unity among the critics of orthodoxy dated only from the middle of the century. During the twenty-seven years which elapsed between the *Persian Letters* and *The Spirit of the Laws* only Voltaire's *Letters on the English,* published in 1734, was comparable with Montesquieu's work in ability, or in audacity. The other

political books of the period—Utopias, for instance, like Morelly's metrical *Basiliade,* or the ceaseless imitations of *Télémaque* by the Abbé Ramsay—were not the kind of books which disturb administrations. Fleury was indeed surprisingly successful in maintaining the relationship of silence between monarch and subject, and even forbade the private meetings of the Entresol club where Saint-Pierre and his friends discussed political principles. In 1748 both Church and State seemed as secure as they had been fifty years earlier; the King was still popular after a successful war, the Jansenists and the *Parlements* were at the ebb of their fortunes in their long struggle with Jesuitism, and the *philosophes* and *libertins* were still disunited, individual critics, apparently as impotent as their predecessors under Louis XIV.

This was the last respite permitted to the champions of the *ancien régime. The Spirit of the Laws* appeared in 1748 and the first volumes of the *Encyclopœdia* in 1751. The *Encyclopœdia,* at first approved by the authorities as a mere bookseller's project, became in the hands of Diderot a central arsenal from which all the apostles of enlightenment could borrow weapons for their combined attack. Against the united forces of the *philosophes* the official attempts to preserve silence were turned to ridicule, and before the death of Louis XV. the Encyclopædic literature had penetrated into all educated sections of society.

The regulations of the publishing trade remained substantially as Francis I. had laid them down in the sixteenth century. No work could be legally published without the permission of the Director of Publications, and all books were supposed to be submitted to him for examination. In practice, however, the authorities rarely took notice of uncensored books unless they caused offence to someone of importance at Court or among the clergy. In such a case the book would be suppressed, a raid carried out upon the *colporteurs,* and the author imprisoned. If, on the other hand, the author obeyed the law and secured permission to publish, his security was scarcely greater. The Director's permission might always be reversed even after the expense of publication had been incurred, if the clergy or the *Parlement* of Paris or the Sorbonne or the *Châtelet* cared to demand the book's suppression. Finally, it was no uncommon thing for a royal *lettre de cachet* to intervene at the last moment, and condemn an author to the Bastille and his book to the flames. Indeed, remarks Figaro, "Provided I did not write about the Government, religion, politics, morality, officials, or anyone who has any claim to anything, I was at liberty to print what I chose—under the inspection of two or three censors."

In these circumstances most of the bolder books were published under pseudonyms and printed abroad, usually in Holland, and an elaborate secret organization grew up for the distribution of banned or illegally published works. Thus the publishing trade became a game in which the whole of literary France joined. The object of the game was to ensure the circulation of the books of your party, and though hundreds of books were censored all the important Philosophic publications found an excellent market. This constant struggle with authority had two immediate effects upon the Philosophic writing of the century. In the first place the Encyclopædists became a clique. They lost the capacity to laugh at themselves, and were enraged beyond measure or reason when a satirical attack like Moreau's *Les Cacouacs* or a feeble lampoon like Palissot's *Les Philosophe* passed the censorship. They learned to regard every critic as an accomplice of the powers of darkness. In their quarrel with Rousseau, Grimm, Madame D'Epinay and the rest pursued him with the venom of a secret society against a deserter. They lied about his work and his character; they forged documents to discredit him with posterity. Their inventions were the more remarkable since the truth about Rousseau offered the most bitter opponent ample scope for detraction. The Church itself could scarcely have shown more intolerance or waged more unscrupulous warfare than the *philosophes*. In their long battle with Fréron they treated *L'Année litéraire* and its editor with a contempt and bitterness which often seem quite undeserved. Fréron's defence of the *ancien régime* was based on principles which were implicit in Montesquieu; and the same principles in Burke's *Reflections on the French Revolution* afterwards proved the most powerful challenge to the Liberalism of the *philosophes*. "Ancient abuses," Fréron wrote, "in the process of growth have become implicated in so many small matters, and are so bound up with the course of affairs, and their roots, in brief, are now so deep and so extensive that to touch them would provoke a serious upheaval. An observer often thinks only of the benefits of the remedy he imagines already applied: and he does not foresee the inconveniences attending their application at the time." "Is not the fanaticism of your irreligion," he asked, "more absurd and more dangerous than the fanaticism of superstition? Begin by tolerating the faith of your fathers. You talk of nothing but tolerance and never was a sect more intolerant." The *philosophes* usually replied by calling him a scoundrel and a bigot. There was a certain dignity in his declaration: "Pour moi, je ne tiens à aucune cabale de belesprit, à aucun parti, si n'est à celui de la religion, des mœurs et de l'honnêteté." Unfortunately, he added, no such party existed in his day.

Turgot, perhaps the very greatest of the *philosophes*, contributed to the *Encyclopædia* and did more to advance the ideas of economic Liberalism than Quesnay himself. But he complained that the *Encyclopædia* was "the book of a sect," and always refused to call himself a Physiocrat because he disliked cliques and party labels. There were others, such as d'Alembert, who sought to be above the battle. D'Alembert's desertion from the joint editorship of the *Encyclopædia*, which left Diderot alone to cope with contributors, publishers and authorities, was not due to fear of the Bastille, but to the shrinking of a timid and thoughtful man from a struggle in which science was confounded with politics and personal and party rancour seemed as likely to interfere with truth as religious intolerance itself.

The censorship had a second no less disastrous effect: the *philosophes* were forced to adopt subterfuges harmful both to the reader and to the writer. Outward conformity to a despised creed is not in the long run compatible with clear thought and intellectual integrity, however conscious the inward reservations. When Voltaire criticized the *Encyclopædia*, d'Alembert replied: "No doubt we have bad articles in theology and metaphysics, but since we publish by favour, and have theologians for censors, I defy you to make them any better. There are other articles that are less exposed to the daylight, and in them all is repaired. Time will enable people to distinguish what we have thought from what we have said."

Voltaire's own recipe for evading the censorship was one which he was certainly incapable of following himself. He thought it wise to live on the borders of Switzerland, and amused his friends and annoyed his enemies by attending Mass in his village church. He might publish anonymously or under a false name, but the authorship of his books was always apparent however sturdy his lies. He did not disguise his style. Every new subterfuge only brought more laughter and more readers, since no one else could have written *Candide* or the *Histoire du Docteur Akakia*. Nevertheless it was Voltaire who wrote to d'Alembert to try "if you can, to weaken your style, write dully, certainly no one will then guess your identity. One can say good things in a heavy way. You will have the pleasure of enlightening the world without compromising yourself; that would be a fine action and you would be an apostle without being a martyr."

The method of disguise adopted in the *Persian Letters* remained one of the most popular. To describe a foreign country possessing all the freedom and good government which France lacked involved no weakening of style and was compatible with the highest literary standards. Sometimes the *philosophes* described the happier conditions of primitive people, who presumably obeyed the laws of nature by instinct or natural reason, unimpeded by the artifices and barriers erected by priests and kings. Sometimes they talked of China, where a benevolent monarch was supposed to rule in the full light of philosophic knowledge; or, again, of a Utopia, where everything suited everybody, including Plato and Sir Thomas More; more often still, the sober freedom of English constitutional government provided a satisfactory foil to the arbitrary ignorance of Louis' ministers.

There were other methods of baffling and teasing the authorities. Ever since the later Middle Ages, men who wished to avoid making up their minds, who disliked committing themselves or who feared punishment, had adopted the doctrine of "double truth." If reason, science and historical evidence came to one conclusion and the unchallengeable authority of Scripture to another, it was safest, and also most effective as propaganda, not to attempt a reconciliation. Bayle had been fond of explaining in a footnote how unlikely the Bible story would have appeared had not we known that with God all things, even contradictions and absurdities, are possible. So an article in the *Encyclopædia* proves with some ease that the cubical capacity of the Ark was insufficient to contain the full bulk of the enumerated inhabitants—another case in which reason would lead astray without the help of revelation. The New Testament story is treated in much the same way. The evidence for the Resurrection is such that it carries proof of the truth of Christianity "to a geometrical demonstration." Similarly Voltaire adds, after a solemn examination of contemporary evidence of the life and death of Christ, that the reason why none but Biblical authorities record that the world was plunged into darkness for the space of three hours, or that the innocents were massacred by the orders of Herod, is no doubt that "God did not desire divine things to be written by profane hands."

Buffon attempted to escape censorship by the same device in his *Histoire naturelle*. The inadequacy of the biological theory, hitherto accepted on the authority of Genesis, by which each species of animals was created in its original and eternal form at one stroke without relation to any other, became increasingly obvious to him. After a consideration of evidence which led him to formulate an early evolutionary hypothesis, he wrote: "if we regard the matter thus, not only the ass and the horse but even man himself, the apes, the quadrupeds, and all animals might be regarded as forming members of one and the same family . . . if we once admit that there are families of plants and animals, so that the ass may be of the family of the horse, and that one might only differ from another by degeneration from a common ancestor (even as the ass and the horse differ), we might be driven to admit that the ape is of the family of man, that he is but a degenerate man, and that he and man have had a common ancestor, even as the ass and horse have had. . . . The naturalists who are so ready to establish families among animals and vegetables do not seem sufficiently to have considered the consequences which should follow from their premises, for that would limit direct creation to as small a number of forms as anyone should think fit. For . . . if the point were once gained that among animals and vegetables there had been, I do not say several species, but even a single one, which had been produced in the course of direct descent from another species—if for instance it could be once shown that the ass was but a degeneration from the horse—then there is no further limit to be set to the power of Nature, and we should not be wrong in supposing that with sufficient time she could have evolved all other organic forms from one primordial type. But no! It is certain from divine revelation that all animals have alike been favoured with the grace of an act of direct creation, and that the first pair of every species issued full-formed from the hands of the creator."

It was not surprising that the Sorbonne condemned fourteen subversive propositions in the *Histoire naturelle*. Buffon, who was botanist to the King, and anxious not to lose his position nor to have the result of many years' labour destroyed, promptly renounced everything in his book "that might be contrary to the narrative of Moses."

In 1750 Malesherbes was appointed Director of the publishing trade, with the delicate task of steering a course among these conflicting forces. He was himself the most moderate of men and shared many of the sceptical views of the *philosophes*. They overwhelmed him with requests for support. For thirteen years he struggled amid philosophic pique, legal bigotry, court arrogance and religious intolerance. His best efforts did not prevent an extraordinary confusion and constant fluctuations of policy. Savage, and necessarily inoperative, decrees were frequently issued. In 1754, when the attempt on Louis' life by Damiens had frightened the Government, blame was thrown first on the Jesuits, then upon the Jansenists and their supporters in the *Parlements*, and finally upon the *philosophes*. Many arrests were made, and a royal decree was passed announcing that death was the penalty for "all those who shall be convicted of having composed, or caused to be composed and printed, writings intended to attack religion, to assail our authority, or to disturb the ordered tranquillity of our realm." Not only were authors and publishers threatened with execution but also "all those who print the aforesaid works, all book-sellers, *colporteurs,* and other persons who shall circulate them among the public."

A decree of this kind was calculated to rouse only laughter, except among a number of obscure men and women who were sent to the galleys for selling books "contrary to good manners and religion." The *Encyclopædia*, which contained all the subversive doctrines of the century, was at that very moment being published under royal sanction. Arbitrary and uncertain persecution had its usual effect in rendering authority ridiculous and criticism both more subtle in its methods and more effective in its attacks. The propagandist is most blessed when ineffectively persecuted.

Though this was at times realized by the *philosophes* themselves, they bitterly resented their position. They lived in an atmosphere of constant anxiety, and were never certain from day to day whether they would be courted or imprisoned. Rousseau's *Emile*, which was largely devoted to an exposition of an educational method and which was the most genuinely religious book of the century, was censored by the Archbishop of Paris and burnt by the *Parlement* of Paris. The case of Marmontel, who was at best but a second-rate writer and comparatively orthodox in his views, provides an instructive example of the uncertainty of literary life. Having succeeded with great difficulty in piloting his *Belisarius* through the censorship, nine thousand copies were quickly circulated before the Sorbonne discovered that it advocated the theory of toleration and questioned "the right of the sword to exterminate heresy, irreligion and impiety, and to bring the whole world under the yoke of the true faith." "The thing for me," he remarked while the Sorbonne was considering its verdict, "was to appear neither timid nor rebellious, and to gain time till the editions of my book were multiplied and spread over Europe." In spite of his caution, Marmontel found himself confined in the Bastille. His imprisonment lasted only eleven days. The governor was extremely polite and supplied him with an excellent dinner from his own table. Marmontel gained an adventure with which to amuse the more advanced among his hostesses and friends, but lost both the editorship of the official *Mercure* and his bride, who preferred to marry a man who had not incurred the King's displeasure.

Prison archives show that most of the Philosophic party spent short periods in the Bastille, and the poorer among them may have found it less comfortable than did Marmontel. Diderot had been imprisoned after the publication of his *Letters on the Blind*, which contained a phrase derogatory to a Minister's mistress. During his editorship of the *Encyclopædia* he was never free from the interference of the Government and the Jesuits, and never knew how long he would be at liberty. When the significance of the first volumes of the *Encyclopædia* was appreciated the Jesuits succeeded in obtaining an order for their suppression. It was typical of the régime, however, that no order was issued forbidding its circulation, and that Diderot was requested by the Government to continue the editorship. The Jesuits indeed confiscated his papers, notes and plates, but, being, as he remarked, unable to confiscate his brains at the same time, they waited for the appearance of the next volumes before again interfering. In 1757, when the struggle between the *Parlements* and Jesuits was at its

A special assembly conducted by Louis XVI at the Palais de Justice in November 1787.

height, d'Alembert's article on Geneva, indirectly critical of the lives and dogmas of Catholic priests, roused once more a furious opposition. The publication of Helvétius' *De l'Esprit,* in the next year, led to the suppression by the Council of State of numerous Philosophic works, and the sale of past numbers of the *Encyclopædia* was prohibited. No steps however were taken to prevent their circulation, which continued without the least interruption.

On the whole it may be said that during the ascendancy of Madame de Pompadour the royal policy, in spite of many fluctuations, tended rather to flirt with philosophy than to oppose it. Voltaire described the Pompadour as "one of us," and though she was not a very faithful devotee at the shrine of reason, and though her opposition to Jesuitism may have been due rather to personal than to philosophical causes, the Encyclopædists had reason to be grateful to her. After the banishment of the Jesuits the *Parlements* emulated their zeal in banning and burning the work of the *philosophes;* but in the later years of Louis' reign an official ban was most effective as an advertisement. (pp. 90-102)

> *Kingsley Martin, "Philosophy and Propaganda," in his* French Liberal Thought in the Eighteenth Century: A Study of Political Ideas from Bayle to Condorcet, *edited by J. P. Mayer, revised edition, Turnstile Press Ltd., 1954, pp. 90-116.*

THE PHILOSOPHY OF REASON

Ernst Cassirer

[*Cassirer was a German-born philosopher and historian who is recognized as one of the foremost philosophical interpreters of human civilization. His study of the history of epistemology,* The Problem of Knowledge *(1950), is esteemed for its comprehensive scope and is considered a standard work on the history of human thought. In the following excerpt from a 1951 translation of his* Die Philosophie der Aufklärung *(1932), he studies the "method of reason" that was applied to eighteenth-century natural science, psychology, politics and sociology, contrasting it with that of the seventeenth century.*]

D'Alembert begins his essay on the *Elements of Philosophy* with a general portrait of the mind of the mid-eighteenth century. He prefaces his portrait with the observation that in the intellectual life of the last three hundred years the mid-century mark has consistently been an important turning-point. The Renaissance commences in the middle of the fifteenth century; the Reformation reaches its climax in the middle of the sixteenth century; and in the middle of the seventeenth century the Cartesian philosophy triumphantly alters the entire world picture. Can an analogous movement be observed in the eighteenth century? If so, how can its direction and general tendency be characterized? Pursuing this thought further, d'Alembert writes:

> If one examines carefully the mid-point of the century in which we live, the events which excite us or at any rate occupy our minds, our customs, our achievements, and even our diversions, it is difficult not to see that in some respects a very remarkable change in our ideas is taking place, a change whose rapidity seems to promise an even greater transformation to come. Time alone will tell what will be the goal, the nature, and the limits of this revolution whose shortcomings and merits will be better known to posterity than to us. . . . Our century is called, accordingly, the century of philosophy par excellence. . . . If one considers without bias the present state of our knowledge, one cannot deny that philosophy among us has shown progress. Natural science from day to day accumulates new riches. Geometry, by extending its limits, has borne its torch into the regions of physical science which lay nearest at hand. The true system of the world has been recognized, developed, and perfected. . . . In short, from the earth to Saturn, from the history of the heavens to that of insects, natural philosophy has been revolutionized; and nearly all other fields of knowledge have assumed new forms. . . .
>
> The study of nature seems in itself to be cold and dull because the satisfaction derived from it consists in a uniform, continued, and uninterrupted feeling, and its pleasures, to be intense, must be intermittent and spasmodic. . . . Nevertheless, the discovery and application of a new method of philosophizing, the kind of enthusiasm which accompanies discoveries, a certain exaltation of ideas which the spectacle of the universe produces in us—all these causes have brought about a lively fermentation of minds. Spreading through nature in all directions like a river which has burst its dams, this fermentation has swept with a sort of violence everything along with it which stood in its way. . . . Thus, from the principles of the secular sciences to the foundations of religious revelation, from metaphysics to matters of taste, from music to morals, from the scholastic disputes of theologians to matters of trade, from the laws of princes to those of peoples, from natural law to the arbitrary laws of nations . . . everything has been discussed and analyzed, or at least mentioned. The fruit or sequel of this general effervescence of minds has been to cast new light on some matters and new shadows on others, just as the effect of the ebb and flow of the tides is to leave some things on the shore and to wash others away.

These are the words of one of the most important scholars of the age and of one of its intellectual spokesmen. Hence they represent a direct expression of the nature and trend of contemporary intellectual life. The age of d'Alembert feels itself impelled by a mighty movement, but it refuses to abandon itself to this force. It wants to know the whence and whither, the origin and the goal, of its impulsion. For this age, knowledge of its own activity, intellectual self-examination, and foresight are the proper function and essential task of thought. Thought not only seeks new, hitherto unknown goals but it wants to know where it is going and to determine for itself the direction of its journey. It encounters the world with fresh joy and the courage of discovery, daily expecting new revelations. Yet its thirst for knowledge and intellectual curiosity are directed not only toward the external world; the thought of this age is even more passionately impelled by that other question of the nature and potentiality of thought itself. Time and again thought returns to its point of departure from its various journeys of exploration intended to broaden the horizon of objective reality. Pope gave brief and pregnant expression to this deep-seated feeling of the age in the line: "The proper study of mankind is man." The age senses that a new force is at work within it; but it is even more fascinated by the activity of this force than by the creations brought forth by that activity. It rejoices not only in results, but it inquires into, and attempts to explain, the form of the process leading to these results. The problem of intellectual "progress" throughout the eighteenth century appears in this light. Perhaps no other century is so completely permeated by the idea of intellectual progress as that of the Enlightenment. But we mistake the essence of this conception, if we understand it merely in a quantitative sense as an extension of knowledge indefinitely. A qualitative determination always accompanies quantitative expansion; and an increasingly pronounced return to the characteristic center of knowledge corresponds to the extension of inquiry beyond the periphery of knowledge. One seeks multiplicity in order to be sure of unity; one accepts the breadth of knowledge in the sure anticipation that this breadth does not impede the intellect, but that, on the contrary, it leads the intellect back to, and concentrates it in, itself. For we see again and again that the divergence of the paths followed by the intellect in its attempt to encompass all of reality is merely apparent. If these paths viewed objectively seem to diverge, their divergence is, nevertheless, no mere dispersion. All the various energies of the mind are, rather, held together in a common center of force. Variety and diversity of shapes are simply the full unfolding of an essentially homogeneous formative power. When the eighteenth century wants to characterize this power in a single word, it calls it "reason." "Reason" becomes the unifying and central point of this century, expressing all that it longs and strives for, and all that it achieves. But the historian of the eighteenth century would be guilty of error and hasty judgment if he were satisfied with this characterization and thought it a safe point of departure. For where the century itself sees an end, the historian finds merely a starting-point for his investigation; where the century seems to find an answer, the historian sees his real problem. The eighteenth century is imbued with a belief in the unity and immutability of reason. Reason is the same for all thinking subjects, all nations, all epochs, and all cultures. From the changeability of religious creeds, of moral maxims and convictions, of theoretical opinions and judgments, a firm and lasting element can be extracted which is permanent in itself, and which in this identity and permanence expresses the real essence of reason. For us the word "reason" has long since lost its unequivocal simplicity even if we are in essential agreement with the basic aims of the philosophy of the Enlightenment. We can scarcely use this word any longer without being conscious of its history; and time and again we see how great a change of meaning the term has undergone. This circumstance constantly reminds us how little meaning the terms "reason" and "rationalism" still retain, even in the sense of purely historical characteristics. The general concept is vague, and it becomes clear and distinct only when the right "differentia specifica" is added. Where are we to look for this specific difference in the eighteenth century? If it liked to call itself a "century of reason," a "philosophic century," wherein lies the characteristic and distinguishing feature of this designation? In what sense is the word "philosophy" used here? What are its special tasks, and what means are at its disposal for accomplishing these tasks in order to place the doctrines of the world and of man on a firm foundation?

If we compare the answers of the eighteenth century to these questions with the answers prevailing at the time when that century began its intellectual labors, we arrive at a negative distinction. The seventeenth century had seen the real task of philosophy in the construction of the philosophical "system." Truly "philosophical" knowledge had seemed attainable only when thought, starting from a highest being and from a highest, intuitively grasped certainty, succeeded in spreading the light of this certainty over all derived being and all derived knowledge. This was done by the method of proof and rigorous inference, which added other propositions to the first original certainty and in this way pieced out and linked together the whole chain of possible knowledge. No link of this chain could be removed from the whole; none was explicable by itself. The only real explanation possible consisted in its "derivation," in the strict, systematic deduction by which any link might be traced back to the source of being and certainty, by which its distance from this source might be determined, and by which the number of intermediate links separating a given link from this source might be specified. The eighteenth century abandons this kind of deduction and proof. It no longer vies with Descartes and Malebranche, with Leibniz and Spinoza for the prize of systematic rigor and completeness. It seeks another concept of truth and philosophy whose function is to extend the boundaries of both and make them more elastic, concrete, and vital. The Enlightenment does not take the ideal of this mode of thinking from the philosophical doctrines of the past; on the contrary, it constructs its ideal according to the model and pattern of contemporary natural science.

The attempt to solve the central problem of philosophic method involves recourse to Newton's "Rules of Philosophizing" rather than to Descartes' *Discourse on Method,* with the result that philosophy presently takes an entirely new direction. For Newton's method is not that of pure deduction, but that of analysis. He does not begin by setting up certain principles, certain general concepts and axioms, in order, by virtue of abstract inferences, to pave the way to the knowledge of the particular, the "factual." Newton's approach moves in just the opposite direction. His phenomena are the data of experience; his principles are the goal of his investigation. If the latter are first according to nature ($\pi\rho o\tau\epsilon\rho o\nu\ \tau\eta\ \phi\upsilon\sigma\epsilon\iota$), then the former must always be first to us ($\pi\rho\tau\epsilon\rho o\nu\ \pi\rho\delta\ \eta\mu\alpha\delta$). Hence the true method of physics can never consist in proceeding from any arbitrary *a priori* starting-point, from a hypothesis, and in completely developing the logical conclusions implicit in it. For such hypotheses can be invented and modified as desired; logically, any one of them is as valid as any other. We can progress from this logical indifference to the truth and precision of physical science only by applying the measuring stick elsewhere. A scientific abstraction or "definition" cannot serve as a really unambiguous starting-point, for such a starting-point can only be obtained from experience and observation. This does not mean that Newton and his disciples and followers saw a cleavage between experience and thinking, that is, between the realm of bare fact and that of pure thought. No such conflicting modes of validity, no such dualism between "relations of ideas" and "matters of fact" as we find in Hume's *Enquiry concerning Human Understanding,* is to be found among the Newtonian thinkers. For the goal and basic presupposition of Newtonian research is universal order and law in the material world. Such regularity means that facts as such are not mere matter, they are not a jumble of discrete elements; on the contrary, facts exhibit an all-pervasive form. This form appears in mathematical determinations and in arrangements according to measure and number. But such arrangements cannot be foreseen in the mere concept; they must rather be shown to exist in the facts themselves. The procedure is thus not from concepts and axioms to phenomena, but vice versa. Observation produces the datum of science; the principle and law are the object of the investigation.

This new methodological order characterizes all eighteenth century thought. The value of system, the *"espirit systématique,"* is neither underestimated nor neglected; but it is sharply distinguished from the love of system for its own sake, the *"esprit de systéme."* The whole theory of knowledge of the eighteenth century strives to confirm this distinction. D'Alembert in his "Preliminary Discourse" to the French *Encyclopedia* makes this distinction the central point of his argument, and Condillac in his *Treatise on Systems* gives it explicit form and justification. Condillac tries to subject the great systems of the seventeenth century to the test of historical criticism. He tries to show that each of them failed because, instead of sticking to the facts and developing its concepts from them, it raised some individual concept to the status of a dogma. In opposition to the "spirit of systems" a new alliance is now called for between the "positive" and the "rational" spirit. The positive and the rational are never in conflict, but their true synthesis can only be achieved by the right sort of medication. One should not seek order, law, and "reason" as a rule that may be grasped and expressed prior to the phenomena, as their *a priori;* one should rather discover such regularity in the phenomena themselves, as the form of their immanent connection. Nor should one attempt to anticipate from the outset such "reason" in the form of a closed system; one should rather permit this reason to unfold gradually, with ever increasing clarity and perfection, as knowledge of the facts progresses. The new logic that is now sought in the conviction that it is everywhere present on the path of knowledge is neither the logic of the scholastic nor of the purely mathematical concept; it is rather the "logic of facts." The mind must abandon itself to the abundance of phenomena and gauge itself constantly by them. For it may be sure that it will not get lost, but that instead it will find here its own real truth and standard. Only in this way can the genuine correlation of subject and object, of truth and reality, be achieved; only so can the correspondence between these concepts, which is the condition of all scientific knowledge, be brought about.

From the actual course of scientific thinking since its revival in modern times the Enlightenment derives its concrete, self-evident proof that this synthesis of the "positive" and the "rational" is not a mere postulate, but that the goal set up is attainable and the ideal fully realizable. In the progress of natural science and the various phases it has gone through, the philosophy of the Enlightenment believes it can, as it were, tangibly grasp its ideal. For here it can follow step by step the triumphal march of the modern analytical spirit. It had been this spirit that in the course of barely a century and a half had conquered all reality, and that now seemed finally to have accomplished its great task of reducing the multiplicity of natural phenomena to a single universal rule. And this cosmological formula, as contained in Newton's general law of attraction, was not found by accident, nor as the result of sporadic experimentation; its discovery shows the rigorous application of scientific method. Newton finished what Kepler and Galileo had begun. All three names signify not only great scientific personalities, but they have also become symbols and milestones of scientific knowledge and thought. Kepler pushes the observation of celestial phenomena to a degree of precision never achieved before his time. By indefatigable toil he arrived at the laws which describe the form of the planetary orbits and determine the relation between the revolution periods of the individual planets and their respective distances from the sun. But this factual insight is only a first step. Galileo envisages a more general problem: his doctrine of motion marks an advance to a broader and deeper stratum of the logic of scientific concepts. It is no longer a question of describing a field of natural phenomena, however broad and important; a general foundation of dynamics, of the theory of nature as such, has now to be evolved. And Galileo is aware that direct observation of nature cannot accomplish this task, and that other cognitive means must be invoked. The phenomena of nature present themselves to perception as uniform events, as undivided wholes. Perception grasps only the surface of these events, it can describe them in broad outline and in the manner of their taking place; but this form of description is not sufficient for a real explanation. For the explanation of a natural event is not merely the realization of its existence thus and so; such an explanation consists rather in specifying the conditions of the event, and in recognizing exactly how it depends on these conditions. This demand can only be satisfied by an analysis of the uniform presentation of the event as given in perception and direct observation, and by its resolution into its constitutive elements. This analytical process, according to Galileo, is the presupposition of all exact knowledge of nature. The method of formulation of scientific concepts is both analytical and synthetic. It is only by splitting an apparently simple event into its elements and by reconstructing it from these that we can arrive at an understanding of it. . . . Taking the three laws of Kepler as its point of departure, Newton's theory is not content merely to interpret them as expressing the factual results of observation. It seeks to derive these results from their presuppositions and to show that they are the necessary effect of the concurrence of various conditions. Each of these sets of conditions must be investigated by itself and its function known. Thus the phenomenon of planetary motion, which Kepler had regarded as a simple entity, is proved to be a complex structure. It is reduced to two fundamental forms of natural law: to the laws of freely falling bodies and to the laws of centrifugal force. Both forms of law had been investigated independently by Galileo and Huygens and precisely determined; now it was a question of reducing these discoveries to one comprehensive princi-

ple. Newton's great achievement lay in this reduction; it was not so much the discovery of hitherto unknown facts or the acquisition of new material but rather the intellectual transformation of empirical material which Newton achieved. The structure of the cosmos is no longer merely to be looked at, but to be penetrated. It yields to this approach only when mathematics is applied and it is subjected to the mathematical form of analysis. In as much as Newton's theory of fluxions and Leibniz's infinitesimal calculus provide a universal instrument for this procedure, the comprehensibility of nature seems for the first time to be strictly demonstrated. The path of natural science traverses indefinite distances; but its direction remains constant, for its point of departure and its goal are not exclusively determined by the nature of the objective world but by the nature and powers of reason as well.

The philosophy of the eighteenth century takes up this particular case, the methodological pattern of Newton's physics, though it immediately begins to generalize. It is not content to look upon analysis as the great intellectual tool of mathematico-physical knowledge; eighteenth century thought sees analysis rather as the necessary and indispensable instrument of all thinking in general. This view triumphs in the middle of the century. However much individual thinkers and schools differ in their results, they agree in this epistemological premise. Voltaire's *Treatise on Metaphysics,* d'Alembert's *Preliminary Discourse,* and Kant's *Inquiry concerning the Principles of Natural Theology and Morality* all concur on this point. All these works represent the true method of metaphysics as in fundamental agreement with the method which Newton, with such fruitful results, introduced into natural science. Voltaire says that man, if he presumes to see into the life of things and know them as they really are in themselves, immediately becomes aware of the limits of his faculties; he finds himself in the position of a blind man who must judge the nature of color. But analysis is the staff which a benevolent nature has placed in the blind man's hands. Equipped with this instrument he can feel his way forward among appearances, discovering their sequence and arrangement; and this is all he needs for his intellectual orientation to life and knowledge. "We must never make hypotheses; we must never say: Let us begin by inventing principles according to which we attempt to explain everything. We should say rather: Let us make an exact analysis of things. . . . When we cannot utilize the compass of mathematics or the torch of experience and physics, it is certain that we cannot take a single step forward." But provided with such instruments as these, we can and should venture upon the high seas of knowledge. We must, of course, abandon all hope of ever wresting from things their ultimate mystery, of ever penetrating to the absolute being of matter or of the human soul. If, however, we refer to empirical law and order, the "inner core of nature" proves by no means inaccessible. In this realm we can establish ourselves and proceed in every direction. The power of reason does not consist in enabling us to transcend the empirical world but rather in teaching us to feel at home in it. Here again is evident a characteristic change of meaning in the concept of reason as compared with seventeenth century usage. In the great metaphysical systems of that century—those of Descartes and Malebranche, of Spinoza and Leibniz—reason is the realm of the "eternal verities," of those truths held in common by the human and the divine mind. What we know through reason, we therefore behold "in God." Every act of reason means participation in the divine nature; it gives access to the intelligible world. The eighteenth century takes reason in a different and more modest sense. It is no longer the sum total of "innate ideas" given prior to all experience, which reveal the absolute essence of things. Reason is now looked upon rather as an acquisition than as a heritage. It is not the treasury of the mind in which the truth like a minted coin lies stored; it is rather the original intellectual force which guides the discovery and determination of truth. This determination is the seed and the indispensable presupposition of all real certainty. The whole eighteenth century understands reason in this sense; not as a sound body of knowledge, principles, and truths, but as a kind of energy, a force which is fully comprehensible only in its agency and effects. What reason is, and what it can do, can never be known by its results but only by its function. And its most important function consists in its power to bind and to dissolve. It dissolves everything merely factual, all simple data of experience, and everything believed on the evidence of revelation, tradition and authority; and it does not rest content until it has analyzed all these things into their simplest component parts and into their last elements of belief and opinion. Following this work of dissolution begins the work of construction. Reason cannot stop with the dispersed parts; it has to build from them a new structure, a true whole. But since reason creates this whole and fits the parts together according to its own rule, it gains complete knowledge of the structure of its product. Reason understands this structure because it can reproduce it in its totality and in the ordered sequence of its individual elements. Only in this twofold intellectual movement can the concept of reason be fully characterized, namely, as a concept of agency, not of being.

This conviction gains a foothold in the most varied fields of eighteenth century culture. Lessing's famous saying that the real power of reason is to be found not in the possession but in the acquisition of truth has its parallels everywhere in the intellectual history of the eighteenth century. Montesquieu attempts to give a theoretical justification for the presence in the human soul of an innate thirst for knowledge, an insatiable intellectual curiosity, which never allows us to be satisfied with any conception we have arrived at, but drives us on from idea to idea. "Our soul is made for thinking, that is, for perceiving," said Montesquieu; "but such a being must have curiosity, for just as all things form a chain in which every idea precedes one idea and follows another, so one cannot want to see the one without desiring to see the other." The lust for knowledge, the *libido sciendi*, which theological dogmatism had outlawed and branded as intellectual pride, is now called a necessary quality of the soul as such and restored to its original rights. The defense, reinforcement, and consolidation of this way of thinking is the cardinal aim of eighteenth century culture; and in this mode of thinking, not in the mere acquisition and extension of specific information, the century sees its major task. This fundamental tendency can also be traced unambiguously in the *Encyclopedia,* which became the arsenal of all such information. Diderot himself, originator of the *Encyclopedia,* states that its purpose is not only to supply a certain body of knowledge but also to bring about a change in the mode of thinking—*pour changer la façon commune de penser.* Consciousness of this task affects all the minds of the age and gives rise to a new sense of inner tension. Even the calmest

and most discreet thinkers, the real "scientists," are swayed by this movement. They do not dare as yet to specify its final aim; but they cannot escape its force, and they think they feel in this trend the rise of a new future for mankind. "I do not think that I have too good an idea of my century," writes Duclos in his *Thoughts on the Customs of this Century,* "but it seems to me there is a certain universal fermentation whose progress one could direct or hasten by the proper education." For one does not want simply to catch the contagion of the time and to be driven blindly on by whatever forces it may contain. One wants to understand these forces and control them in the light of such understanding. One does not care merely to dive into the eddies and whirlpools of the new thoughts; one prefers to seize the helm of the intellect and to guide its course toward definite goals.

The first step which the eighteenth century took in this direction was to seek a clear line of demarcation between the mathematical and the philosophical spirit. Here was a difficult and intrinsically dialectic task, for two different and apparently contradictory claims were to be equally satisfied. The bond between mathematics and philosophy could not be severed, or even loosened, for mathematics was the "pride of human reason," its touchstone and real guarantee. Yet it became increasingly clear that there was also a certain limitation inherent in this self-contained power of mathematics; that mathematics to be sure formed the prototype of reason, and yet it could not with respect to content completely survey and exhaust reason. A strange process of thinking now develops which seems to be motivated by diametrically opposed forces. Philosophical thinking tries at the same time to separate itself from, and to hold fast to, mathematics; it seeks to free itself from the authority of mathematics, and yet in so doing not to contest or violate this authority but rather to justify it from a new angle. In both its efforts it is successful; for pure analysis is recognized in its essential meaning as the basis for mathematical thinking in the modern era; and yet at the same time, precisely because of its universal function, such analysis is extended beyond the limits of the purely mathematical, beyond quantity and number. The beginnings of this trend are already discernible in the seventeenth century. Pascal's work *Of the Geometric Spirit* seriously attempts to draw a clear and distinct line between mathematical science and philosophy. He contrasts the "geometric spirit" with the "subtle spirit" (*esprit fin*) and tries to show how they differ both in structure and in function. But this sharp line of demarcation is soon obliterated. "The geometric spirit," says, for instance, Fontenelle in the preface to his work *On the Usefulness of Mathematics and Physics,* "is not so exclusively bound to geometry that it could not be separated from it and applied to other fields. A work on ethics, politics, criticism, or even eloquence, other things being equal, is merely so much more beautiful and perfect if it is written in the geometric spirit." The eighteenth century grapples with this problem and decides that, as long as it is understood as the spirit of pure analysis, the "geometric spirit" is absolutely unlimited in its application and by no means bound to any particular field of knowledge.

Proof of this thesis is sought in two different directions. Analysis, whose force had hitherto been tried only in the realm of number and quantity, is now applied, on the one hand, to psychological and, on the other, to sociological

The slave trade in Martinique. The Enlightenment idea of the "noble savage" is said to have been sparked by the exploration and exploitation of the New World.

problems. In both cases it is a matter of showing that here too new vistas open up, and that a new field of knowledge of the highest importance becomes accessible to reason as soon as reason learns to subject this field to its special method of analytic dissection and synthetic reconstruction. But psychological reality, concretely given and immediately experienced, seems to elude any such attempt. It appears to us in unlimited abundance and infinite variety; no element, no form, of psychological experience is like any other, and no content ever recurs in the same way. In the flux of psychological events no two waves exhibit the same form; each wave emerges, as it were, out of nothingness, and threatens to disappear into nothingness again. Yet, according to the prevailing view of psychology in the eighteenth century, this complete diversity, this heterogeneity and fluidity, of psychological content is illusory. Closer inspection reveals the solid ground and the permanent elements underlying the almost unlimited mutability of psychological phenomena. It is the task of science to discover those elements which escape immediate experience, and to present them clearly and individually. In psychological events there is no diversity and no heterogeneity which cannot be reduced to a sum of individual parts; there is no becoming which is not founded in cons-

tant being. If we trace psychological forms to their sources and origins, we always find such unity and relative simplicity. In this conviction eighteenth century psychology goes one step beyond its guide and master, Locke. Locke had been content to indicate two major sources of psychological phenomena; in addition to "sensation" Locke recognizes "reflection" as an independent and irreducible form of psychological experience. But his pupils and followers attempt in various ways to eliminate this dualism and to arrive at a strictly monistic foundation of psychology. Berkeley and Hume combine "sensation" and "reflection" in the expression "perception," and they try to show that this expression exhausts both our internal and external experience, the data of nature and those of our own mind. Condillac considers his real merit and his advance beyond Locke to be that, while retaining Locke's general method, he extended it into a new field of psychological facts. Locke's analytical art is effective in the dissection of ideas, but it goes no farther. It shows how every idea, be it ever so complex, is composed of the materials of sensation or reflection, and how these materials must be fitted together in order to produce the various forms of psychological phenomena. But, as Condillac points out, Locke stops with his analysis of psychological forms. He limits his investigation to these forms but does not extend it to the whole realm of psychological events and activity, or to their origin. Here then is a province for research hitherto scarcely touched and of untold riches. In Locke the different classes of psychological activity were left alone, as original and irreducible wholes like the simple data of sense, the data of sight, hearing, touch, motion, taste, and smell. Observing, comparing, distinguishing, combining, desiring, and willing are looked upon by Locke as individual independent acts existing only in immediate experience and not reducible to anything else. But this view robs the whole method of derivation of its real fruits. For psychological being remains an irreducible manifold which can be described in its particular forms but can no longer be explained and derived from simple original qualities. If such derivation is to be taken seriously, then the maxim which Locke applied to the realm of ideas must be applied to all operations of the mind. It must also be shown that the apparent immediacy of these ideas is an illusion which does not withstand scientific analysis. Individual acts of the mind, when analyzed, are in no sense original, but rather derivative and mediate. In order to understand their structure and true nature, one must examine their genesis; one must observe how, from the simple sense data which it receives, the mind gradually acquires the capacity to focus its attention on them, to compare and distinguish, to separate and combine them. Such is the task of Condillac's *Treatise on Sensation*. Here the analytical method seems to celebrate a new triumph in the scientific explanation of the corporeal world, a triumph not inferior to its performances in the realm of natural science. The material and mental spheres are now, as it were, reduced to a common denominator; they are composed of the same elements and are combined according to the same laws.

But in addition to these two spheres of reality there is a third which, similarly, must not be accepted as consisting of simple sense data, but which must be traced to its origins. For we can only succeed in reducing this reality to the rule of law and reason by an inquiry into its sources. The third sphere of reality is that which we find in the structure of the state and of society. Man is born into this world; he neither creates nor shapes it, but finds it ready-made about him; and he is expected to adapt himself to the existing order. But here too passive acceptance and obedience have their limits. As soon as the power of thought awakens in man, it advances irresistibly against this form of reality, summoning it before the tribunal of thought and challenging its legal titles to truth and validity. And society must submit to being treated like physical reality under investigation. Analysis into component parts begins once more, and the general will of the state is treated as if it were composed of the wills of individuals and had come into being as a result of the union of these wills. Only by virtue of this basic supposition can we make a "body" of the state and subject it to that method which had proved its fruitfulness in the discovery of universal law in the physical world. Hobbes had already done this. The fundamental principle of his political theory, that the state is a "body," means just this: that the same process of thought which guides us to an exact insight into the nature of physical body is also applicable without reservation to the state. Hobbes's assertion that thinking in general is "calculation" and that all calculation is either addition or subtraction also holds for all political thinking. Such thinking too must sever the bond which unites the individual wills, in order to join them again by virtue of its own special method. Thus Hobbes resolves the "civic state" into the "natural state"; and in thought he dissolves all bonds of individual wills only to find their complete antagonism, the "war of all against all," remaining. But from this very negation is derived the positive content of the law of the land in its unconditional and unlimited validity. The emergence of the will of the state from the form of the covenant is set forth because this will can only be known by, and founded in, the covenant. Here is the bond which connects Hobbes's doctrine of nature with his doctrine of state. These doctrines are different applications of Hobbes's logical basic assumption, according to which the human mind really only understands that which it can construct from the original elements. Every true formulation of a concept, every complete definition, must therefore start from this point; it can only be a "causal" definition. Philosophy as a whole is understood as the sum total of such causal definitions; it is simply the complete knowledge of effects from their causes, of derivative results from the totality of their antecedents and conditions.

The eighteenth century doctrine of the state and society only rarely accepted without reservations the content of Hobbes's teaching, but the form in which Hobbes embodied this content exerted a powerful and lasting influence. Eighteenth century political thought is based on that theory of the contract whose underlying assumptions are derived from ancient and medieval thought, but it develops and transforms these assumptions in a manner characteristic of the influence exerted by the modern scientific view of the world. In this field too the analytic and synthetic method is henceforth victorious. Sociology is modeled on physics and analytical psychology. Its method, states Condillac in his *Treatise on Systems,* consists in teaching us to recognize in society an "artificial body" composed of parts exerting a reciprocal influence on one another. This body as a whole must be so shaped that no individual class of citizens by their special prerogatives shall disturb the equilibrium and harmony of the whole, that on the contrary all special interests shall contribute and be subordinated to the welfare of the whole. This for-

mulation in a certain sense transforms the problem of sociology and politics into a problem in statics. Montesquieu's *Spirit of the Laws* looks upon this same transformation as its highest task. The aim of Montesquieu's work is not simply to describe the forms and types of state constitutions—despotism, constitutional monarchy, and the republican constitution—and to present them empirically, it is also to construct them from the forces of which they are composed. Knowledge of these forces is necessary if they are to be put to their proper use, if we are to show how they can be employed in the making of a state constitution which realizes the demand of the greatest possible freedom. Such freedom, as Montesquieu tries to show, is possible only when every individual force is limited and restrained by a counterforce. Montesquieu's famous doctrine of the "division of powers" is nothing but the consistent development and the concrete application of this basic principle. It seeks to transform that unstable equilibrium which exists in, and is characteristic of, imperfect forms of the state into a static equilibrium; it attempts further to show what ties must exist between individual forces in order that none shall gain the ascendancy over any other, but that all, by counterbalancing one another, shall permit the widest possible margin for freedom. The ideal which Montesquieu portrays in his theory of the state is thus the ideal of a "mixed government," in which, as a safeguard against a relapse into despotism, the form of the mixture is so wisely and cautiously selected that the exertion of a force in one direction immediately releases a counterforce, and hence automatically restores the desired equilibrium. By this approach Montesquieu believes he can fit the great variety and diversity of the existing forms of the state into one sound intellectual structure within which they can be controlled. Such a basic arrangement and foundation is Montesquieu's primary aim. "I have established principles," he points out in the preface to the *Spirit of the Laws,* "and I have observed how individual cases, as if by themselves, yielded to these principles, and I have seen that the histories of all nations are but sequences, and that each individual law is connected with another law or depends on a more general law."

The method of reason is thus exactly the same in this branch of knowledge as it is in natural science and psychology. It consists in starting with solid facts based on observation, but not in remaining within the bounds of bare facts. The mere togetherness of the facts must be transformed into a conjuncture; the initial mere co-existence of the data must upon closer inspection reveal an interdependence; and the form of an aggregate must become that of a system. To be sure, the facts cannot simply be coerced into a system; such form must arise from the facts themselves. The principles, which are to be sought everywhere, and without which no sound knowledge is possible in any field, are not arbitrarily chosen points of departure in thinking, applied by force to concrete experience which is so altered as to suit them; they are rather the general conditions to which a complete analysis of the given facts themselves must lead. The path of thought then, in physics as in psychology and politics, leads from the particular to the general; but not even this progression would be possible unless every particular as such were already subordinated to a universal rule, unless from the first the general were contained, so to speak embodied, in the particular. The concept of the "principle" in itself excludes that absolute character which it asserted in the great metaphysical systems of the seventeenth century. It resigns itself to a relative validity; it now pretends only to mark a provisional farthest point at which the progress of thought has arrived—with the reservation that thought can also abandon and supersede it. According to this relativity, the scientific principle is dependent on the status and form of knowledge, so that one and the same proposition can appear in one science as a principle and in another as a deduced corollary. "Hence we conclude that the point at which the investigation of the principles of a science must stop is determined by the nature of the science itself, that is to say, by the point of view from which the particular science approaches its object. . . . I admit that in this case the principles from which we proceed are themselves perhaps scarcely more than very remote derivations from the true principles which are unknown to us, and that, accordingly, they would perhaps merit rather the name of conclusions than that of principles. But it is not necessary that these conclusions be principles in themselves; it suffices that they be such for us." Such a relativity does not imply any skeptical perils in itself; it is, on the contrary, merely the expression of the fact that reason in its steady progress knows no hard and fast barriers, but that every apparent goal attained by reason is but a fresh starting-point.

Thus it is evident that, if we compare the thought of the eighteenth century with that of the seventeenth, there is no real chasm anywhere separating the two periods. The new ideal of knowledge develops steadily and consistently from the presuppositions which the logic and theory of knowledge of the seventeenth century—especially in the works of Descartes and Leibniz—had established. The difference in the mode of thinking does not mean a radical transformation; it amounts merely to a shifting of emphasis. This emphasis is constantly moving from the general to the particular, from principles to phenomena. But the basic assumption remains; that is the assumption that between the two realms of thought there is no opposition, but rather complete correlation—except for Hume's skepticism which offers an entirely different approach. The self-confidence of reason is nowhere shaken. The rationalistic postulate of unity dominates the minds of this age. The concept of unity and that of science are mutually dependent. "All sciences put together," says d'Alembert repeating the opening sentences of Descartes' *Rules for the Conduct of the Understanding,* "are nothing but human intelligence, which always remains one and the same, and is always identical with itself, however different the objects may be to which it is applied." The seventeenth century owed its inner solidarity, particularly as exemplified in French classical culture, to the consistency and rigor with which it clung to this postulate of unity and extended its application to all the spheres of knowledge and living. This postulate prevailed not only in science, but in religion, politics and literature as well. "One king, one law, one faith"—such was the motto of the epoch. With the advent of the eighteenth century the absolutism of the unity principle seems to lose its grip and to accept some limitations and concessions. But these modifications do not touch the core of the thought itself. For the function of unification continues to be recognized as the basic role of reason. Rational order and control of the data of experience are not possible without strict unification. To "know" a manifold of experience is to place its component parts in such a relationship to one another that, starting

from a given point, we can run through them according to a constant and general rule. This form of discursive understanding had been established by Descartes as the fundamental norm of mathematical knowledge. Every mathematical operation, according to Descartes, aims in the last analysis to determine the proportion between an unknown quantity and other known quantities. And this proportion can only be strictly determined when the unknown and the known participate in a "common nature." Both elements, the unknown and the known, must be reducible to quantity and as such they must be derivable from the repetition of one and the same numerical unit. Thus the discursive form of knowledge always resembles a reduction; it proceeds from the complex to the simple, from apparent diversity to its basic identity. Eighteenth century thought holds firmly to this fundamental method, and attempts to apply it to broader and broader fields of knowledge. The very concept of "calculus" thus loses its exclusively mathematical meaning. It is not merely applicable to quantities and numbers; from the realm of quantities it invades the realm of pure qualities. For qualities too may be placed in such a relationship to one another that they are derivable from one another in a strict order. Whenever this is possible, the determination of the general laws of this order enables us to gain a clear view of the whole field of their validity. The concept of "calculus," therefore, is co-extensive with that of science itself; and it is applicable wherever the conditions of a manifold of experience can be reduced to certain fundamental relations and thus completely determined. Condillac, who first clearly formulated this general scientific concept in his essay *The Language of Calculus,* attempted in his psychology to give a characteristic sample and a fruitful application of the concept. For Condillac, who supports the Cartesian concept of the immateriality and spirituality of the soul, there can be no doubt that a direct mathematical treatment of psychological experience is impossible. For such a direct application of the concepts of quantity is valid only where the object itself consists of parts and can be constructed from these parts; and this can take place only in the realm of corporeal substance, which is defined as pure extension, but not in the realm of thinking "indivisible" substance. However, this fundamental and unalterable opposition between body and soul is no insurmountable barrier for the pure function of analytical knowledge. This function ignores material differences for, by virtue of the purity of its form and the formal nature of its operation, it is bound by no presuppositions regarding content. Even if psychological experience cannot like corporeal experience be divided into parts, yet in thought it can be analyzed into its constitutive elements. To this end it is only necessary that the apparent diversity of such experience be resolved by showing that it is a continuous development from a common source of all psychological phenomena. As proof, Condillac introduces the famous illustration which he places at the center of his psychology. Assuming a marble statue, he describes how it progressively comes to life and acquires an increasingly rich spiritual content because the individual senses engrave their special qualities on the marble. Condillac tries to show that the continuous series of "impressions" and the temporal order in which they are produced are sufficient to build up the totality of psychological experience and to produce it in all its wealth and subtle shadings. If we succeed in producing psychological experience in this manner, we have at the same time reduced it to the quantitative concept. Now everything that we call psychological reality and that we experience as such proves to be fundamentally a mere repetition and transformation of a certain basic quality which is contained in the simplest sense perception. Sense perception forms the borderline between the marble as dead matter and a living being endowed with a soul. But once this borderline has been passed, there is no need of any further assumptions or of any essentially new creations. What we commonly regard as the "higher" powers of the mind, contrasting these powers with sensation, is in reality only a transformation of the basic element of sense perception. All thinking and judging, all desiring and willing, all powers of the imagination and all artistic creation, qualitatively considered, add nothing new, nothing essentially different to this fundamental element. The mind neither creates nor invents; it repeats and constructs. But in this repetition it can exhibit almost inexhaustible powers. It extends the visible universe beyond all bounds; it traverses the infinity of space and time; and yet it is unceasingly engaged in the production of ever new shapes within itself. But throughout its activities the mind is concerned only with itself and its "simple ideas." These constitute the solid ground on which the entire edifice constructed by the mind, both in its "external" and in its "internal" aspects, rests—and from which the mind can never depart.

Condillac's attempt to show that all psychological reality is a transformation, a metamorphosis, of simple sense perception is continued by Helvetius in his book *On the Mind* (*De l'Esprit*). The influence which this weak and unoriginal work exerted on the philosophical literature of the eighteenth century is explicable in that the epoch found here a basic element of its thought expressed with pregnant clarity, and indeed with an exaggeration which parodies this thought. In Helvetius's exaggeration the methodological limitation and danger of this mode of thinking is clearly presented. The limitation consists in a leveling process which threatens to deny the living wealth of human consciousness and to look upon it merely as a disguise. Analytical thinking removes this disguise from pshchological phenomena; it exposes them, and in so doing reveals their naked sameness rather than their apparent diversity and inner differentiation. Differences in form as well as in value vanish and prove to be delusions. As a result, there is no longer a "top" and "bottom" or a "higher" and a "lower" in the realm of psychological phenomena. Everything is on the same plane—equal in value and in validity. Helvetius develops this line of thought especially in the field of ethics. His main intention was to sweep away all those artificial differentiations which convention had erected and was trying hard to maintain. Wherever traditional ethics spoke of a special class of "moral" sensations, wherever it thought it found in man an original "feeling of sympathy" which rules over and restrains his sensual and egotistical appetites, Helvetius tries to show how poorly such a hypothesis corresponds to the simple reality of human feeling and action. Whoever approaches this reality without prejudice will find none of that apparent dualism. He will find everywhere and always the same absolutely uniform motivation. He will see that all those qualities which we refer to as unselfishness, magnanimity, and self-sacrifice are different only in name, not in reality, from the elementary impulses of human nature, from the "lower" appetites and passions. No moral greatness rises above this plane. For no matter how high

the aims of the will may be, no matter what supernatural values and supersensible goals it may imagine, it remains nonetheless confined within the narrow circle of egotism, ambition, and vanity. Society does not achieve the suppression of these elemental impulses, but only their sublimation; and in so far as society understands its own function, this is all it can ever expect or ask of the individual. Consideration of the theoretical world should be guided by the same viewpoint. According to Helvetius there are neither fundamental gradations in the scale of ethical values nor radical gradations of theoretical form. On the contrary, all such distinctions boil down to the same undifferentiated mass of sensation. The so-called faculties of judgment and cognition, imagination and memory, and understanding and reason, are by no means specific original powers of the soul. Here again we have been subject to the same delusion. We think we have transcended the sphere of sense perception when we have only slightly modified its appearance. The criticism which explains away this modifications also applies to theoretical distinctions. All operations of the mind can be reduced to judgment, and judgment consists only in grasping similarities and differences between individual ideas. But the recognition of similarity and difference presupposes an original act of awareness which is analogous to, or indeed identical with, the perception of a sense quality. "I judge or I perceive that of two objects the one I call 'fathom' makes a different impression on me from the one I call 'foot,' and that the color I call 'red' affects my eyes differently from the color I call 'yellow.' Hence I conclude that in such a case to judge is simply to perceive." Here, as one sees, both the edifice of ethical values and the logically graded structure of knowledge are demolished. Both structures are, as it were, razed to the ground because it is thought that the only unshakable foundation of knowledge lies in sensation.

It would be erroneous to consider the fundamental viewpoint represented by Helvetius as typical of the content of the philosophy of the Enlightenment, as has often been done; and it is equally erroneous to regard it as typical of the thought of the French Encyclopaedists. For the sharpest criticism of Helvetius's work was exercised by precisely this school of thought; and this criticism originated among the best minds in French philosophical literature, as, for instance, Turgot and Diderot. But one thing is undeniable, namely, that in Helvetius as well as in Condillac a certain methodology appears, a methodology characteristic of and decisive for the entire eighteenth century. Here was a form of thinking whose positive achievement and immanent limitations, whose triumphs and defeats, were so to speak predetermined. (pp. 3-27)

Ernst Cassirer, in his The Philosophy of the Enlightenment, *translated by Fritz C. A. Koelln and James P. Pettegrove, Princeton University Press, 1951, 366.*

Carl L. Becker

[*Becker was a distinguished American scholar and educator whose historical writings are esteemed for their literary merit and theoretical content. Perhaps his best-known work is* The Heavenly City of the Eighteenth-Century Philosophers (1932). *In this work he offers an innovative perspective on Enlightenment philosophers, maintaining that their "rationalist" thought was based as much on religious faith as on reason. In the following excerpt from this work, Becker expounds on the "pervasive power" of eighteenth-century conceptions of nature and natural law upon philosophical thought.*]

When we think of the *Philosophes* we think first of all, and quite rightly, of certain French names so much written about that they are familiar to all the world—Montesquieu and Voltaire and Rousseau, Diderot and Helvétius and Baron d'Holbach, Turgot and Quesnay and Condorcet, to mention only the best known. If we were interested in the Enlightenment as a prelude to the Revolution we also might conveniently forget, as most writers do, that France was not the only country blessed (or cursed, if you like) with Philosophers; but since we are concerned less with the consequences than with the preconceptions of the Enlightenment we will do well to note that it is not a peculiarly French but an international climate of opinion that is in question. Leibnitz and Lessing and Herder, the young Goethe even (in some of his varying moods); Locke and Hume and Bolingbroke, Ferguson and Adam Smith, Price and Priestley; and in the new world Jefferson, whose sensitized mind picked up and transmitted every novel vibration in the intellectual air, and Franklin of Philadelphia, printer and friend of the human race—these also, whatever national or individual characteristics they may have exhibited, were true children of the Enlightenment. The philosophical empire was an international domain of which France was but the mother country and Paris the capital. Go where you like—England, Holland, Italy, Spain, America—everywhere you meet them, Philosophers speaking the same language, sustained by the same climate of opinion. They are of all countries and of none, having openly declared their allegiance to mankind, desiring nothing so much as to be counted "among the small number of those who by their intelligence and their works have merited well of humanity." They are citizens of the world, the emancipated ones, looking out upon a universe seemingly brand new because so freshly flooded with light, a universe in which everything worth attending to is visible, and everything visible is seen to be unblurred and wonderfully simple after all, and evidently intelligible to the human mind—the mind of Philosophers.

There is one not unimportant point about the Philosophers that ought, in simple fairness to them, to be noted in passing, especially since few writers take the trouble to mention it: the Philosophers were not philosophers. I mean to say they were not professors of philosophy whose business it was to publish, every so often, systematic and stillborn treatises on epistemology and the like subjects. Exceptions there were no doubt. Leibnitz and Locke and Hume, Adam Smith perhaps, and maybe Helvétius will be found catalogued under philosophy and mentioned in formal histories of that subject. But for the most part the Philosophers were men of letters, writers of books intended to be read and designed to spread abroad new ideas or to shed new light on old ones. I need only mention that Voltaire wrote plays, histories, tales, and an *A B C* of Newtonian physics for ladies and gentlemen unblessed with a knowledge of mathematics; that Franklin was a scientist, inventor, politician, diplomat, political economist, moralist, and the first and most successful of American "columnists"; that Diderot, besides being the literary editor and promoter of the *Encyclopédie,* was a journalist who wrote

on everything that struck his lively fancy—on art salons, the social implications of a mechanistic theory of the universe, the baneful effect of emotional repression on nuns; that Rousseau, in defense of the thesis that art is injurious to mankind, employed a high degree of art in the writing of political propaganda and didactic romances; that Mably wrote a long history to prove that France once possessed, but had somehow mislaid, a most admirable political constitution.

But if the Philosophers were not philosophers they had, like their modern counterparts, a philosophical message to deliver: they were the eager bearers of good tidings to mankind. Disinterested? Objectively detached? By no means. Do not look for these high virtues in the Philosophers, least of all when they make a point of them. No doubt the objective attitude may sometimes be found—in the scientific expositions of Newton and his confrères, in some of the writings of Franklin perhaps, or those of Hume. But to be amused and detached observers of the human scene was not characteristic of them. It is true you will find plenty of cynical wit—in Voltaire above all, as everyone knows. But the wit is too superficially cynical to be more than a counterirritant. There is more fundamental pessimism to be found in the seventeenth than in the eighteenth century, in the *Libertins* than in the *Philosophes.* The disillusionment of Hume and Franklin was deep enough, but it found easy release in a genial irony that disturbed no one, least of all themselves. The cynicism of Voltaire was not bred in the bone as the great Frederick's was; nor was it, like that of La Rochefoucauld, the cold-blooded systematization of a grand seignior's indifference; still less, like that of Pascal, a fatal spiritual malady troubling the heart. It was all on the surface, signifying nothing but the play of a supple and irrepressible mind, or the sharp impatience of an exasperated idealist. In spite of *Candide* and all the rest of it, Voltaire was an optimist, although not a naïve one. He was the defender of causes, and not of lost causes either—a crusader pledged to recover the holy places of the true faith, the religion of humanity. Voltaire, skeptic—strange misconception! On the contrary, a man of faith, an apostle who fought the good fight, tireless to the end, writing seventy volumes to convey the truth that was to make us free.

At this point I ought perhaps to mention the well-worn word "enthusiasm." Do not the writers of the eighteenth century, the early eighteenth century, commonly insist on the just measure, the virtue of keeping cool and not straying beyond the call of common sense? Do they not even become a little heated and scornful when confronted with examples of "enthusiasm"? They do indeed, and there's the rub. To be scornful is not to be detached. The aversion of the Philosophers to enthusiasm did not carry them to the high ground of indifference. Their aversion to enthusiasm was itself an enthusiasm, a mark of their resolute rejection of all that was not evident to the senses, of their commendable passion for opening up and disinfecting all the musty, shuttered closets of the mind. (pp. 33-7)

[The eighteenth century's] characteristic note is not a disillusioned indifference, but the eager didactic impulse to set things right. *Bienfaisance, humanité*—the very words, we are told, are new, coined by the Philosophers to express in secular terms the Christian ideal of service. In this connection one is reminded of that earnest and amiable and

The construction of a mountain road, by Joseph Vernet. This work is recognized as a major visual representation of the Enlightenment concept of progress.

rather futile Abbé de Saint-Pierre, the man "at whom every one laughs, and who is alone serious and without laughter." How industriously this priest labored in the secular vineyard of the Lord! How many "projects" he wrote, helpful hints for the improvement of mankind— "Project for Making Roads Passable in Winter," "Project for the Reform of Begging," "Project for Making Dukes and Peers Useful." And then one day, quite suddenly, so he tells us, "there came into my mind a project which by its great beauty struck me with astonishment. It has occupied all my attention for fifteen days." The result we know: *A Project for Making Peace Perpetual in Europe!*

Well, let us join the others and laugh at the Abbé, but does not his *penchant* for projects remind us of Jefferson, does not his passion for improvement recall Poor Richard? Let us laugh at him, by all means, but be well assured that when we do we are laughing at the eighteenth century, at its preoccupation with human welfare, at its *penchant* for projects. Who, indeed, was not, in this bright springtime of the modern world, making or dreaming of projects? What were most of the scientific academies in France doing but discussing, quarreling about, and having a jolly time over the framing of projects? What was the *Encyclopédie,* what was the Revolution itself? Grand projects, surely. What, indeed (the question stares us in the face), was this enlightened eighteenth century doing, what significance had it in the world anyway if not just this: that with earnest purpose, with endless argument and impassioned propaganda and a few not unhappy tears shed in anticipation of posterity's gratitude, it devoted all its ener-

gies to sketching the most naïvely simple project ever seen for making dukes and peers useful, for opening all roads available to the pursuit of happiness, for securing the blessings of liberty, equality, and fraternity to all mankind? Maybe this project was less futile than those of the Abbé de Saint-Pierre, maybe it only seems so; but it was at all events inspired by the same ideal—the Christian ideal of service, the humanitarian impulse to set things right.

I do not forget that during the course of the century there is to be noted a change in the outward expression of this didactic impulse to set things right. Sometime about 1750, men of sense became men of sentiment, and presently men of sentiment began to weep. The tears of the later century have often been attributed to the influence of Rousseau, wrongly I think. It is certain that Diderot shed tears before he knew Rousseau, and continued to do so after he quarreled with him. As early as 1760, the practice was so common that the little Abbé Galiani shocked Diderot one day by confessing that *he* had never shed a tear in his life; and some years before the statement of Fontenelle that he had "relegated sentiment to the *églogue*" aroused in the cold and upright Grimm a feeling very near aversion. Too much may easily be made of this change in manners. The reserve of a Fontenelle or the expansiveness of a Diderot were but outward characteristics—the outward evidence of an inward grace; an inward grace, they would have you know, far more efficacious than that of the religious. But the Philosophers were more akin to the religious than they knew. They were the secular bearers of the Protestant and the Jansenist tradition. Their aversion to enthusiasm was in truth but the measure of their irritation. It irritated them, the enlightened ones, to think that mankind had been so long deluded by priests and medicine men who had played their game, and still played it, by keeping the minds of the vulgar loosely wrapped in a warm, emotional fog. "It has taken centuries," exclaimed Grimm, "to subdue the human race to the tyrannical yoke of the priests; it will take centuries and a series of efforts and successes to secure its freedom." We need not be deceived. In spite of their persiflage and wit, in spite of their correct manner and restrained prose, we can still hear, in the very accents of the saints, the despairing cry, "How long, O Lord, how long!"

Not so long, at that, if the Philosophers could have their way. And they were bent on having it. They were out for the cold facts, out to spoil the game of the mystery-mongers. That species of enthusiasm was indeed to be banned; but only to be replaced by an enthusiasm, however well concealed beneath an outward calm, for the simple truth of things. Knowing beforehand that the truth would make them free, they were on the lookout for a special brand of truth, a truth that would be on their side, a truth they could make use of in their business. Some sure instinct warned them that it would be dangerous to know too much, that "to comprehend all is to pardon all." They were too recently emancipated from errors to regard error with detachment, too eager to spread the light to enjoy the indolent luxury of the suspended judgment. Emancipated themselves, they were conscious of a mission to perform, a message to deliver to mankind; and to this messianic enterprise they brought an extraordinary amount of earnest conviction, of devotion, of enthusiasm. We can watch this enthusiasm, this passion for liberty and justice, for truth and humanity, rise and rise throughout the century until it becomes a delirium, until it culminates, in some symbolical sense, in that half admirable, half pathetic spectacle of June 8, 1794, when Citizen Robespierre, with a bouquet in one hand and a torch in the other, inaugurated the new religion of humanity by lighting the conflagration that was to purge the world of ignorance, vice, and folly.

Too much has been made of the negations of these crusaders of the age of reason: too much by the nineteenth century because it had no liking for the enlightened ones; too much by our own century because we have no liking for the Victorians. Their negations more often than not were mere surface cynicisms, and there is less in these surface cynicisms than we are apt to think. Take one of Voltaire's swift shining shafts of wit: "History is after all only a pack of tricks we play on the dead." Ah, yes, how true it is, we say; and we are astonished that Voltaire could have been so profound. Then we realize that he did not really mean it. To him it was a witticism intended to brand dishonest historians, whereas we perceive that it formulated, in the neatest possible way, a profound truth—the truth that all historical writing, even the most honest, is unconsciously subjective, since every age is bound, in spite of itself, to make the dead perform whatever tricks it finds necessary for its own peace of mind. And this leads us to reconsider another of his sayings: "Nothing is more annoying than to be obscurely hanged." And we wonder whether he understood all the implications of this pregnant saying as well as we do; whether he understood as well as we do, or think we do, that he and his brother *Philosophes* must have

fed their enthusiasm for liberty and justice not a little on the satisfaction they found in being conspicuously hanged (if only in effigy) for their brave little blasphemies.

But, if we have understood their negations too well, we have accepted their affirmations, their professions of faith, rather too much as a matter of course. Let Voltaire define natural religion: "I understand by natural religion the principles of morality common to the human race." If it does not bore us too much we ask a perfunctory question, What is morality? and pause not for an answer. If by chance we really attend to these affirmations they puzzle us. Over against the Angelic Doctor's definition of natural law, set that of Volney:

> The regular and constant order of facts by which God rules the universe; the order which his wisdom presents to the sense and reason of men, to serve them as an equal and common rule of conduct, and to guide them, without distinction of race or sect, towards perfection and happiness.

The language is familiar, but the idea, once we examine it critically, is as remote as that of Thomas Aquinas. Important if true, we say; but how comes it, we ask, that you are so well acquainted with God and his purposes? Who told you, skeptic as we have been led to suppose, that there is a regular and constant order of nature? And this animal man (that "damned race" as the great Frederick defined it), how can you be so sure that he knows what perfection is, or would be happy if he had it?

Indeed, it is all too simple, this dogmatic affirmation. It assumes everything that most needs to be proved, and begs every question we could think of asking. These skeptics who eagerly assent to so much strike our sophisticated minds as overcredulous. We feel that they are too easily persuaded, that they are naïve souls after all, duped by their humane sympathies, on every occasion hastening to the gate to meet and welcome platitudes and thin panaceas. And so our jaded and somewhat morbid modern curiosity is at last aroused. We wish to know the reason for all this fragile optimism. We wish to know what it is that sustains this childlike faith, what unexamined prepossessions enable the Philosophers to see the tangled wilderness of the world in this symmetrical, this obvious and uncomplicated pattern. Have they perhaps had some recent revelation authorizing them to speak in the very accents of the voice of God? Across the decades we hear the timid vagabond from Geneva, in passion-laden tones, thunder his arrogant challenge in the teeth of an archbishop: "Is it simple, is it natural that God should go in search of Moses to speak to Jean Jacques Rousseau?" Well, frankly, we do not know. But it seems obvious that Rousseau has up his sleeve some good answer to his own question, some answer that all the *Philosophes* will surely regard as conclusive. There must be, we begin to be aware, some private passageway to the heavenly throne, some secret backstairs entry that all the *Philosophes* know of, some door, closed to us, that will open to them when they give it a certain understood succession of raps. We should like to enter this door. We should really like to discover what it is that Jean Jacques Rousseau goes in search of when he wishes to know what God has said to him.

If we would discover the little backstairs door that for any age serves as the secret entranceway to knowledge, we will do well to look for certain unobtrusive words with uncertain meanings that are permitted to slip off the tongue or the pen without fear and without research; words which, having from constant repetition lost their metaphorical significance, are unconsciously mistaken for objective realities. In the thirteenth century the key words would no doubt be God, sin, grace, salvation, heaven, and the like; in the nineteenth century, matter, fact, matter-of-fact, evolution, progress; in the twentieth century, relativity, process, adjustment, function, complex. In the eighteenth century the words without which no enlightened person could reach a restful conclusion were nature, natural law, first cause, reason, sentiment, humanity, perfectibility (these last three being necessary only for the more tender-minded, perhaps).

In each age these magic words have their entrances and their exits. And how unobtrusively they come in and go out! We should scarcely be aware either of their approach or their departure, except for a slight feeling of discomfort, a shy self-consciousness in the use of them. The word "progress" has long been in good standing, but just now we are beginning to feel, in introducing it into the highest circles, the need of easing it in with quotation marks, that conventional apology that will save all our faces. Words of more ancient lineage trouble us more. Did not President Wilson, during the war, embarrass us not a little by appearing in public on such familiar terms with "humanity," by the frank avowal of his love for "mankind"? As for God, sin, grace, salvation—the introduction of these ghosts from the dead past we regard as inexcusable, so completely do their unfamiliar presences put us out of countenance, so effectively do they, even under the most favorable circumstances, cramp our style.

In the eighteenth century these grand magisterial words, although still to be seen, were already going out of fashion, at least in high intellectual society. It is true that theologians still made much of them, but even they felt called upon to offer a rational apology for doing so. Bishop Butler's famous *Analogy of Religion, Natural and Revealed* (1737) was only one, although one of the most elaborate and painstaking, of many exercises of this kind. But for the sophisticated, men of letters and men of the world, these masterful words were regarded with distaste. Unable to pronounce them without discomfort, enlightened "men of parts" commonly employed substitutes or euphemisms with less explicit, less compromising implications. The picture of salvation in the Heavenly City they toned down to a vague impressionistic image of a "future state," "immortality of the soul," or a more generalized earthly and social *félicité* or *perfectibilité du genre humain*. Grace was translated into virtue, virtue with a certain classical implication in the meaning—*ce fonds de rectitude et de bonté morale, qui est la base de la vertu,* as Marmontel defined it. To be esteemed a "man of virtue" was both sufficient and efficacious, and likely to give one, without any painful searchings of the heart, the assurance of being in a state of social justification, or even, if the esteem were general enough, of complete sanctification. I suppose that Hume and Franklin, when they were in France, for example, must have had this assurance as fully as any saint of the church ever did.

With the Heavenly City thus shifted to earthly foundations, and the business of justification transferred from divine to human hands, it was inevitable that God should be differently conceived and more indifferently felt. Not that he could be (except by a few unnaturally hardened souls) dispensed with altogether. Most eighteenth-century minds were too accustomed to a stable society with fixed ranks, too habituated to an orderly code of manners and a highly conventionalized art, to be at all happy in a disordered universe. It seemed safer, therefore, even for the enlightened ones, to retain God, or some plausible substitute, as a kind of dialectical guaranty that all was well in the most comfortable of commonsense worlds. But, obviously, the Creator as a mere first premise no longer needed those rich and all too human qualities of God the Father. Having performed his essential function of creation, it was proper for him to withdraw from the affairs of men into the shadowy places where absolute being dwells. Thus withdrawn, he ceased to be personal and inconvenient. No longer demanding propitiatory sacrifices, he could be regarded merely as that Omniscience or Beneficence which men of sense could serenely contemplate with respect untempered with fear or adoration. Yet, even men of sense needed some word for this necessary thing, some suitable substitute for God the Father. Supreme Being? Author of the Universe? Great Contriver? Prime Mover? First Cause? Surely, any of these would serve. We know at least, to our great discomfort, that all of them were freely used.

It would have been impossible, would it not, for the *Philosophes* to have thus complacently permitted God the Father to fade away into the thin abstraction of a First Cause unless they were prepared to dispense with his revelation to men—the revelation through Holy Writ and Holy Church. This was, indeed, the whole point of their high, offensive gesture. Renunciation of the traditional revelation was the very condition of being truly enlightened; for to be truly enlightened was to see the light in all its fulness, and the light in its fulness revealed two very simple and obvious facts. One of these contained the sum of those negations which we understand so well—the fact that the supposed revelation of God's purposes through Holy Writ and Holy Church was a fraud, or at best an illusion born of ignorance, perpetrated, or at least maintained, by the priests in order to accentuate the fears of mankind, and so hold it in subjection. The other fact contained the sum of those affirmations which we understand less easily—that God had revealed his purpose to men in a far more simple and natural, a far less mysterious and recondite way, through his works. To be enlightened was to understand this double truth, that it was not in Holy Writ, but in the great book of nature, open for all mankind to read, that the laws of God had been recorded. This is the new revelation, and thus at last we enter the secret door to knowledge. This open book of nature was what Jean Jacques Rousseau and his philosophical colleagues went in search of when they wished to know what God had said to them.

Nature and natural law—what magic these words held for the philosophical century! Enter that country by any door you like, you are at once aware of its pervasive power. I have but just quoted, in another connection, extracts from the writings of Hume, Voltaire, Rousseau, Volney: in each of them nature takes without question the position customarily reserved for the guest of honor. To find a proper title for this lecture I had only to think of the Declaration of Independence—"to assume, among the powers of the earth, the separate and equal station, to which the laws of nature and of nature's God entitle them." Turn to the

French counterpart of the Declaration, and you will find that "the aim of every political association is the preservation of the natural and imprescriptible rights of man." Search the writings of the new economists and you will find them demanding the abolition of artificial restrictions on trade and industry in order that men may be free to follow the natural law of self-interest. Look into the wilderness of forgotten books and pamphlets dealing with religion and morality: interminable arguments, clashing opinions, different and seemingly irreconcilable conclusion you will find, and yet strangely enough controversialists of every party unite in calling upon nature as the sovereign arbiter of all their quarrels. The Christian Bishop Butler affirms with confidence that "the whole analogy of nature . . . most fully shews that there is nothing incredible in the general [Christian] doctrine of religion, that God will reward and punish men for their actions hereafter." The deist Voltaire, rejecting the Christian doctrine of religion, asserts with equal dogmatism that "natural law . . . which nature teaches all men" is that "upon which all religion is founded." The atheist Holbach, rejecting all religion, nevertheless holds that "the morality suitable to man should be founded on the nature of man." Christian, deist, atheist—all acknowledge the authority of the book of nature; if they differ it is only as to the scope of its authority, as to whether it merely confirms or entirely supplants the authority of the old revelation. In the eighteenth-century climate of opinion, whatever question you seek to answer, nature is the test, the standard: the ideas, the customs, the institutions of men, if ever they are to attain perfection, must obviously be in accord with those laws which "nature reveals at all times, to all men." (pp. 39-53)

Not the exclusive possession of the eighteenth century, this "ideal image" of nature; no, but after all a different, a more substantial image arises to charm that century. In earlier centuries the ideal image of nature was, as one may say, too ghostly ever to be mistaken for nature herself. Nature herself had hitherto seemed to common sense intractable, even mysterious and dangerous, at best inharmonious to man. Men therefore desired some authoritative assurance that there was no need to be apprehensive; and this assurance came from theologians and philosophers who argued that, since God is goodness and reason, his creation must somehow be, even if not evidently so to finite minds, good and reasonable. Design in nature was thus derived *a priori* from the character which the Creator was assumed to have; and natural law, so far from being associated with the observed behavior of physical phenomena, was no more than a conceptual universe above and outside the real one, a logical construction dwelling in the mind of God and dimly reflected in the minds of philosophers.

Once safely within the eighteenth century we cease to be haunted by this ghostly ideal image. The ideal image is still with us, but it has taken on a more familiar and substantial body. No one ever looked more attentively at the eighteenth-century image of nature than Hume, who knew better than anyone else that it was an illusion; and for that very reason there is no better description of it than that which he put into the mouth of Cleanthes, one of the characters in his *Dialogues Concerning Natural Religion*. In defense of natural religion, Cleanthes says:

Look around the world: contemplate the whole and

every part of it: You will find it to be nothing but one great machine, subdivided into an infinite number of lesser machines, which again admit of subdivisions, to a degree beyond what human senses and faculties can trace and explain. All these various machines, and even their most minute parts, are adjusted to each other with an accuracy, which ravishes into admiration all men, who have ever contemplated them. The curious adapting of means to ends, throughout all nature, resembles exactly, though it much exceeds, the productions of human . . . intelligence. Since therefore the effects resemble each other, we are led to infer . . . that the causes also resemble; and that the Author of Nature is somewhat similar to the mind of man; though possessed of much larger faculties, proportioned to the grandeur of the work, which he has executed.

The passage is significant in two respects. We note at once that the logical process has been reversed. Cleanthes does not conclude that nature *must* be rational because God *is* eternal reason; he concludes that God *must* be an engineer because nature *is* a machine. From this reversal of the logical process it follows that natural law is identified with the actual behavior of nature. What ravishes Cleanthes into admiration is not the exceeding beauty of a logical concept of the world, but the exceeding intricacy and delicate adjustment of the world itself. For him nature is not a logical concept, but a substantial reality; and natural law, instead of being a construction of deductive logic, is the observed harmonious behavior of material objects.

This transformation of the ideal image of nature was the result, as everyone knows, of the scientific discoveries of the seventeenth century. Galileo observed that the pendulum behaved in a certain manner, and then formulated the law of the pendulum in terms of mathematics. Newton did not doubt that the heavens declare the glory of God; but he was concerned to find out, by looking through a telescope and doing a sum in mathematics, precisely how they managed it. He discovered that every particle of matter, whether in the heavens or elsewhere, behaved as if it attracted every other particle with a force proportional to the product of the masses and inversely proportional to the square of the distance. This was a new kind of "law of nature." Formerly, as the editor of the second edition of the *Principia* tells us, philosophers were "employed in giving names to things, and not in searching into things themselves." Newton himself noted the difference by saying: "These Principles I consider not as occult Qualities, supposed to result from the specific Forms of Things, but as general Laws of Nature, by which the Things themselves are form'd." This was the new way to knowledge opened up by "natural philosophy": to "search into Things themselves," and then to formulate the "general Laws of Nature by which the Things themselves are form'd."

Certainly, this new philosophy ravished the eighteenth century into admiration; and not the least astonishing thing about it was the commonplace methods employed to discover such marvelous truths. That Newton discovered the nature of light seemed even less significant to his contemporaries than that he did so by playing with a prism. It was as if nature had for the first time been brought close to men, close enough to be tangible and clearly visible in all its wonderful details. Nature, it seemed, was, after all, just the common things that common men observed and handled every day, and natural law only the uniform way these things behaved. Steam bubbling from the spout of a kettle, smoke whisking up a chimney, morning mist lifting from meadows—here was nature all about, moving in ways not mysterious her wonders to perform; and revealing, to the eyes of common men, no less than to the learned, those laws that imposed on all things their reasonable and beneficent, even if curious and intricate, commands.

When philosophy became a matter of handling test tubes instead of dialectics everyone could be, in the measure of his intelligence and interest, a philosopher. As Goethe tells us:

> Many a one became convinced that nature had endowed him with as great a portion of good and straight-forward sense as, perchance, he required to form such a clear notion of objects that he could manage them and turn them to his own profit, and that of others, without laboriously troubling himself about the most universal problems. . . . Men made the trial, opened their eyes, looked straight before them, observant, industrious, active. . . .
>
> . . . every one was now entitled, not only to philosophize, but also by degrees to consider himself a philosopher. Philosophy, therefore, was more or less sound and practised common sense, which ventured to enter upon the universal, and to decide upon inner and outer experiences. . . . and thus at last philosophers were found in all the faculties, nay, in all classes and trades.

"Until philosophers become kings, . . . cities will not cease from ill," said Plato; but philosophy is perhaps in an even better way to exert influence (whether for good or ill) when common men become philosophers. The reason is that common men take up philosophy, if at all, not as an exercise in dialectic, but as something that holds for them the assurance of a better way of life. They are apt, therefore, to associate any philosophy that interests them with the name of some great man, whom they can love or hate for having given the world a new idea; and they are sure to invest the new idea with some meaning that it did not originally have. We are familiar with this procedure, having noted, during the last fifty years, the association of the "evolutionary philosophy" with the name of Darwin, and the transformation of "Darwinism" into "monkeyism" or the "white man's burden" as the case may be—into something at all events which Darwin, simple man, would be astonished to hear of. The same thing happened in the eighteenth century. Common men associated the new philosophy with the name of Newton because it appeared that Newton, more than any other man, had banished mystery from the world by discovering a "universal law of nature," thus demonstrating, what others had only asserted, that the universe was rational and intelligible through and through, and capable, therefore, of being subdued to the uses of men.

The "Newtonian philosophy" was, accordingly, as familiar to common men in the middle eighteenth century as the "Darwinian philosophy" is in our day. "Very few people read Newton," Voltaire explained, "because it is necessary to be learned to understand him. But *everybody talks about him.*" Why, indeed, should ordinary men read Newton? They were not greatly interested in the proposition

that "reaction is always equal and opposite to action." They were interested in the Newtonian philosophy, a very different thing. No need to open the *Principia* to find out what the Newtonian philosophy was—much better not, in fact. Leave that to the popularizers, who could find in the *Principia* more philosophy than common men could, very often more, I must say, than Newton himself ever did. (pp. 54-61)

[Common] men could find the Newtonian philosophy, a philosophy which was of interest to them, not so much for the scientific discoveries it set forth as for the bearing of those discoveries upon the most fundamental of human problems—that is to say, the relation of man to nature and of both to God. What those relations were, or were taken to be, is admirably stated by Colin Maclaurin, Professor of Mathematics in the University of Edinburgh, in his book, *An Account of Sir Isaac Newton's Philosophical Discoveries,* perhaps the ablest of the popular expositions in English.

> To describe the *phenomena* of nature, to explain their causes . . . and to inquire into the whole constitution of the universe, is the business of natural philosophy. A strong curiosity has prompted men in all times to study nature; every useful art has some connexion with this science; and the inexhausted beauty and variety of things makes it every agreeable, new, and surprising.
>
> But natural philosophy is subservient to purposes of a higher kind, and is chiefly to be valued as it lays a sure foundation for natural religion and moral philosophy; by leading us, in a satisfactory manner, to the knowledge of the Author and Governor of the universe. . . .
>
> We are, from his works, to seek to know God, and not to pretend to mark out the scheme of his conduct, in nature, from the very deficient ideas we are able to form of that great mysterious Being. . . .
>
> Our views of Nature, however imperfect, serve to represent to us, in the most sensible manner, that mighty power which prevails throughout, acting with a force and efficacy that appears to suffer no diminution from the greatest distances of space or intervals of time; and that wisdom which we see equally displayed in the exquisite structure and just motions of the greatest and subtilest parts. These, with perfect goodness, by which they are evidently directed, constitute the supreme object of the speculations of a philosopher; who, while he contemplates and admires so excellent a system, cannot but be himself *excited and animated to correspond with the general harmony of nature.*

The closing words of this passage may well be taken as a just expression of the prevailing state of mind about the middle of the eighteenth century. Obviously the disciples of the Newtonian philosophy had not ceased to worship. They had only given another form and a new name to the object of worship: having denatured God, they deified nature. They could, therefore, without self-consciousness, and with only a slight emendation in the sacred text, repeat the cry of the psalmist: "I will lift up mine eyes to Nature from whence cometh my help!" With eyes uplifted, contemplating and admiring so excellent a system, they were excited and animated to correspond with the general harmony.

The desire to correspond with the general harmony springs perennial in the human breast. Saints of all ages have aspired to become one with whatever gods there be. In medieval times the approved method, in Europe, was thought to be fasting and prayer, denial of the flesh, the renunciation of the natural man. "Who shall deliver me from the body of this death!" The physical dwelling place of the spirit was thought to be a disharmony, a soiled and cloying vesture of decay closing in and blinding the spirit so that, during its earthly pilgrimage, it could only with difficulty, if at all, enter into the harmony that was God. But the enlightened ones knew that it was not so. From this darkness also they had emerged into the light which enabled them to see that the natural and the spiritual man were but different manifestations of one harmonious whole.

The rationalization of this will to believe was provided by John Locke in his epoch-making book, *An Essay Concerning Human Understanding,* which became the psychological gospel of the eighteenth century. Its great service to the men of that time was to demonstrate that the mind owed nothing to inheritance, to "innate ideas"; everything to environment, to the sensations that flowed in upon it from the outer world. A modern critic assures us that the theory of innate ideas which Locke demolished was "so crude that it is difficult to suppose that any serious thinker ever held it." That may well be. Maybe serious thinkers are few, and maybe the world is ruled by crude ideas. What Locke aimed at no doubt, what the eighteenth century acclaimed him for having demolished, was the Christian doctrine of total depravity, a black, spreading cloud which for centuries had depressed the human spirit. For if, as Locke maintained, the mind at birth was devoid of implanted and ineradicable ideas and dispositions, was in fact no more than a blank white sheet of paper upon which the outer world of nature and human association was to write whatever of good or ill repute might be found recorded there, why, then, the mind of man was a record made by that outer world: jazzed and discordant now that the outer world was so; a satisfying and ordered symphony when that outer world should become, as it might, what men had conceived it ought to be. This was Locke's great title to glory, that he made it possible for the eighteenth century to believe with a clear conscience what it wanted to believe, namely, that since man and the mind of man were shaped by that nature which God had created, it was possible for men, "barely by the use of their natural faculties," to bring their ideas and their conduct, and hence the institutions by which they lived, into harmony with the universal natural order. With what simple faith the age of enlightenment welcomed this doctrine! With what sublime courage it embraced the offered opportunity to refashion the outward world of human institutions according to the laws of nature and of nature's God!

I need not say that the difficulties were great: endless difficulties in the realm of practice; one fundamental difficulty in the realm of theory. Hidden away in the elaborate structure of Locke's *Essay* was a most disconcerting corollary. It was this: if nature be the work of God, and man the product of nature, then all that man does and thinks, all that he has ever done or thought, must be natural, too, and in accord with the laws of nature and of nature's God. Pascal had long since asked the fundamental question: "Why is custom not natural?" Why, indeed! But if all is natural,

then how could man and his customs ever be *out of harmony* with nature? No doubt the difficulty could be avoided by declaring that there was no disharmony.

> All are but parts of one stupendous whole,
> Whose body nature is, and God the soul;
>
> . . . . .
>
> All discord, harmony not understood;
> All partial evil, universal good:
> And, spite of pride, in erring reason's spite,
> One truth is clear, *Whatever is, is right.*

But this, addressed to the intelligence, was not an answer; it was merely an avoidance, a dishonest begging of the question. To assert that all that is, is right, was to beat all meaning out of the word "right," unless indeed one were willing to hood one's eyes once more in the cloak of Christian faith. For Pope was merely repeating St. Thomas, who had written twenty volumes to reassure a world on the verge of doubt—twenty volumes to say that it was really right that things should be wrong, God only knows why.

A poet in search of peace and epigrams might be permitted to repeat the ancient theologians, but the Philosophers could not do so unless they were willing to renounce their premises or deny the evidence of common sense. The very foundation of the new philosophy was that the existence of God, if there was one, and his goodness, if goodness he could claim, must be inferred from the observable behavior of the world. Following Newton, the Philosophers had all insisted on this to the point of pedantry, and so, even, had the enlightened Christian theologians in their desperate effort to find arguments to convince doubting Thomases. How then could Philosophers say that all was somehow good in God's sight unless they could also say that there was no evil to be observed in the world of nature and man? Yet to say that there was no evil in the world—a world where Lisbon earthquakes occurred, where Bastilles functioned, where crowds still gathered to gloat over the lingering agony of men broken on the wheel—was an insult to common sense. No, whatever Locke may have done, he had done nothing to solve, even if for the unwary he had done much to obscure, the problem of evil in the world.

Before the middle of the century Hume had taken up this world-old problem, had looked at it straight, had examined it attentively round and round about; and then, in his *Dialogues Concerning Natural Religion,* with all the dialectical resources of the new philosophy, with a penetrating insight matched only by the serene urbanity with which he displayed it, had remorselessly exposed the futility of reason to establish either the existence or the goodness of God. "Epicurus's old questions are yet unanswered. Is he [God] willing to prevent evil, but not able? Then he is impotent. Is he able, but not willing? Then he is malevolent. Is he both able and willing? Whence then is evil?" In the end Hume manages to chevy Christian mystics and atheists into the same camp, since they obviously agree on the main point, that reason is totally incompetent to answer ultimate questions; and so he concludes with that masterpiece of irony: "To be a philosophical Sceptic is, in a man of letters, the first and most essential step towards being a sound, believing Christian." To read Hume's *Dialogues* after having read, with sympathetic understanding, the earnest deists and optimistic philosophers of the early century, is to experience a slight chill, a feeling of apprehension. It is as if, at high noon of the Enlightenment, at the hour of the siesta when everything seems so quiet and secure all about, one were suddenly aware of a short, sharp slipping of the foundations, a faint far-off tremor running underneath the solid ground of common sense.

There it was then—the ugly dilemma, emerging from the beautiful premises of the new philosophy: if nature is good, then there is no evil in the world; if there is evil in the world, then nature is so far not good. How will they meet it, the enlightened ones who with so much assurance and complacent wit have set out with the rule of reason to rebuild an unlovely universe according to nature's design? Will they, closing their eyes to the brute facts, maintain that there is no evil in the world? In that case there is nothing for them to set right. Or will they, keeping their eyes open, admit that there is evil in the world? In that case nature fails to provide them with any standard for setting things right. They have followed reason faithfully. Will they follow her to the end? She is pointing in two directions: back toward Christian faith; forward toward atheism. Which way will they choose? It does not really matter much, since in either case she will vanish at last, leaving them to face existence with no other support than hope, or indifference, or despair.

Well, we know what the Philosophers did in this emergency. They found, as we all find when sufficiently hard pressed, that reason is amenable to treatment. They therefore tempered reason with sentiment, reasons of the heart that reason knows not of; or held it in leash by experience, the universal judgment of mankind; or induced it to delay its pronouncements in view of the possibility (which in a pinch might be taken as a fact) that the world was after all neither a completed drama nor a perfected machine, but rather something as yet unfinished, something still in the making. (pp. 61-70)

> Carl L. Becker, *"The Laws of Nature and of Nature's God," in his* The Heavenly City of the Eighteenth-Century Philosophers, *Yale University Press, 1932, pp. 33-70.*

INFLUENCE AND LEGACY

Henri Peyre

[*A French-born American, Peyre was one of the foremost critics of French literature in the United States. He wrote extensively on modern French literature, most notably* French Novelists of Today *(rev. ed. 1967). In the following excerpt from another work, he traces the evolutionary history of the philosophes's ideas, showing how they "prepared the way for the Revolution."*]

The problem of the effect of the philosophy of Enlightenment on the French Revolution is one of the most important problems that confront the pure historian as well as

the historian of thought and of literature. It is without doubt the most complex of the thousand aspects involved in the study of the Revolution, that is to say the origins of the modern world. Together with investigation of the origins of Christianity and the end of the ancient world, this study concerns one of the two most important upheavals that the philosophically minded historian can conceive: Taine and Renan, as well as Michelet and Tocqueville, the four most important French historians of the past century, quite rightly realized its magnitude. This problem is inevitable for every teacher of literature who lectures on Voltaire and Rousseau to his students, for every historian of the years 1789-1799 in France, and likewise for every historian of those same years and of the beginning of the nineteenth century in Germany, England, the United States, and Latin America. It presents itself to every voter who reflects even a little about the things in his country's past that he would like to maintain and those that he desires to reform.

But because it presents itself so insistently to everyone, this problem has often been met with solutions that are crude or at the very least lacking in necessary overtones; because it closely parallels our present-day preoccupations, it has aroused the partisan spirit; because it concerns not only facts but ideas, it has favored excessively dogmatic generalizations on the one hand and, on the other, the voluntary blind timidity of chroniclers who have chosen to see in the events of the Revolution nothing but a series of improvisations and haphazard movements.

There is for one thing a long and devious current of ideas which, first springing forth as a swift and turgid torrent in the sixteenth century, becoming a more or less tenuous water course in the great period of the reign of Louis XIV, and finally like a river encircling the most obdurate islets of resistance within its multiple arms, seems to have engulfed the eighteenth century in the years 1750-1765. More and more clearly, those who set forth and develop these ideas take it upon themselves to influence the existing facts, to change man by education, to free him from outmoded superstitions, to increase his political liberty and his well-being. In no way do they dream of a general cataclysm, and several of them are not insensitive to the refined amenity of the life that surrounds them or to the exquisite blend of intellectual boldness and voluptuous refinement that characterizes their era.

Suddenly, this pleasant eighteenth-century security, "table d'un long festin qu'un échafaud termine," as Hugo's beautiful image calls it, crumbles. The Revolution breaks out, and within a few years, rushes through peaceful reforms, produces a profusion of constitutions, sweeps aside the old regime, devours men, and causes heads to fall. This great movement is certainly confused, turbulent, and irrational like everything that men accomplish by collective action. However, lawyers, officers, priests, and journalists play a part in it that is often important. These men had grown up in an intellectual climate that had been established by Montesquieu, Voltaire, Rousseau, Raynal, and Mably. May we accurately reach a conclusion of "post hoc, ergo propter hoc"? (pp. 63-4)

[Let us] differ with those who claim a priori that the Revolution sprang from the teachings of the "philosophes" only in order to justify their condemnation of both the Revolution and the teaching. But in opposition to this

Portrait of Louis XVI, by Joseph Sifrède Duplessis.

hostility of parliaments that had been alienated by encroachments upon their prerogatives, etc. Perhaps in doing so they are choosing the easiest way. Their history does grasp the events, the things that change, that is, the things that would be presented in today's newspapers as facts or news—a tax measure, a famine, the dismissal of a minister, a change in the price of bread, or a treaty. But it often fails to apprehend the slow subterranean movements which minds inclined to be too matter-of-fact find intangible, until they one day make their appearance as acts that make news or usher in a historical era. Now there are cases in which they never appear as acts; and orthodox history gives scant consideration to abortive movements or history's side roads into which the past has ventured briefly only to turn back.

The history of ideas has the advantage of being able to give leisurely consideration to elements of history that changed only slowly and did not necessarily express themselves in events which demand attention by virtue of their suddenness. It would gladly declare that ideas rule the world. This would doubtless be an over-optimistic creed, if one did not add immediately that these ideas often turn into those truths wrapped in the gilt paper of falsehood that our contemporaries call in France "mystiques," or that they crystallize into a few fetish-words which imprison or falsify them. The history of the idea of progress has been sketched, although insufficiently in our opinion, by J. Delvaille and the English writer J. M. Bury. History itself would owe much to the man who would attempt to write the story of the idea of evolution, or the idea of revolution, the idea of comfort, or the idea of efficiency and the myth of success in the United States, among many others. On occasion he would have to go beyond the texts or interpret them, but this should not be forbidden provided that it is done with intellectual honesty. One must also remember the fact that the history of ideas is not simply the exposition of theoretical views expressed in philosophical writings, but at the same time the history of the deformations undergone by those ideas when other men adopt them, and also the history of the half-conscious beliefs into which ideas first clearly conceived by the few promptly transform themselves. In his lectures published in Buenos Aires in 1940 under the title *Ideas y creencias* the Spanish philosopher Ortega y Gasset has rightly claimed for these half-formulated "beliefs" a position in historical works on a par with that of ideas.

The difficulties presented by such a history of ideas when they become beliefs, articles of faith, or emotional drives and impel men to action are enormous: they should, by this very fact, challenge research men. Up to now, sociology has failed to make over the study of literature to any considerable degree because histories of the prevailing taste and the environment in which a writer lived and of the social and economic conditions in which he was placed while conceiving his work have little bearing on the creation and even the content of the original work. But a knowledge of the public that greeted a literary work or of the work's subsequent career might on the contrary prove extremely fruitful. Such knowledge requires painstaking inquiry into the work's success, based on a great number of facts; it also demands a qualitative interpretation of history and statistics and the occasional intervention of that much feared "queen of the world" called imagination. For the most read book is not the one that exerts the greatest

group, the admirers of the "philosophes" and even more the admirers of Rousseau, who was not exactly one of the "philosophes," have taken up the cudgels in an attempt to deny the responsibility or even the guilt of the eighteenth-century political writers in the upheaval that ensued. Particularly notable among these efforts is Edme Champion's abstruse but well-informed book, *Rousseau et la Révolution française* (Colin, 1909). Bringing the concept of retroactive responsibility into these matters is a questionable method. "My God!" Karl Marx is said to have exclaimed on one of the rare occasions when he seems to have called upon heaven, "preserve me from the Marxists!" Rousseau has accused himself of enough sins without our taxing his memory with the errors of his followers. Without inquiring whether the Revolution was good or bad, which would be entirely too naïve in this day, may we not be able to show how and in what way it absorbed, reflected, or brought to fruition the ideas of thinkers who had prepared it without wishing for it?

Professional historians generally tend to limit the part played by ideas in world events: the best of them devote, apparently for the sake of form, one or two chapters to the literature, painting, and music of the periods studied by their manuals. But the history of civilization and culture is still very clumsily related to general history. Historians prefer to emphasize the purely historical causes of the Revolution: financial disorder, ministerial blunders, or the influence. A hundred thousand passive or half-attentive readers who bought and even leafed through the *Encyclopédie,* for example, count for less than five hundred passionate admirers of the *Contrat Social* if among the latter may be counted Robespierre, Saint-Just or Babeuf. A schoolmaster or a lecturer heard with interest may pass on Marx or Nietzsche to generations of barely literate people who will never guess the source of a thought that has modified their whole lives. It is not even necessary to have understood a book or even to have read it through in order to be profoundly influenced by it. An isolated phrase quoted in some article or a page reproduced at some time in an anthology may have done more to spread some of the opinions of Montesquieu, Proudhon, or Gobineau that thirty re-editions of their writings bought by private libraries and commented upon by ten provincial academies. (pp. 67-70)

The special quality of the French Revolution, compared with other revolutionary movements in France or other countries, obviously lies not only in the titanic proportions of this upheaval but also in an ardent passion for thought, for embodying ideas in deeds, and for proposing universal laws. This accounts for the unparalleled worldwide influence of the work of destruction and construction which was accomplished between 1789 and 1795. An abstract passion for justice and liberty, the latter being sometimes conceived in strange fashion, inspired the men who made the Revolution and those who prepared it. The original tone that characterizes the Revolution and the verve that enlivens it, which are fundamental things although they elude the grasp of facts and figures, are due in part to the movement of thought and sensibility which goes from Montesquieu to Rousseau and from Bayle to the abbé Raynal.

If there is really one almost undisputed conclusion on the origins of the Revolution reached by historical studies coming from radically opposite factions, it is that pure historical materialism does not explain the Revolution. Certainly riots due to hunger were numerous in the eighteenth century and Mornet draws up the list of them; there was discontent and agitation among the masses. But such had also been the case under Louis XIV, such was the case under Louis-Philippe, and deep discontent existed in France in 1920 and 1927 and 1934 without ending in revolution. No great event in history has been due to causes chiefly economic in nature and certainly not the French Revolution. France was not happy in 1788, but she was happier than the other countries of Europe and enjoyed veritable economic prosperity. Her population had increased from nineteen to twenty-six or twenty-eight million since the beginning of the century and was the most numerous in Europe. French roads and bridges were a source of admiration to foreigners. Her industries such as ship-fitting at Bordeaux, the silk industry at Lyons, and the textile industry at Rouen, Sedan, and Amiens were active, while Dietrich's blast furnaces and the Creusot were beginning to develop modern techniques in metallurgy. The peasants were little by little coming to be owners of the land. Foreign trade reached the sum of 1,153 million francs in 1787, a figure not to be attained again until 1825. The traffic in colonial spices and San Domingo sugar was a source of wealth. Banks were being founded and France owned half the specie existing in Europe. So misery in France was no more than relative. But truly wretched peoples such as the Egyptian fellah, the pariah of India, or even the Balkan or Polish peasant or Bolivian miners, for example, rarely bring about revolutions. In order to revolt against one's lot, one must be aware of his wretched condition, which presupposes a certain intellectual and cultural level; one must have a clear conception of certain reforms that one would like to adopt; in short, one must be convinced (and it was on this point that the books of the eighteenth century produced their effect) that things are not going well, that they might be better, and that they will be better if the measures proposed by the reformist thinkers are put into practice.

Eighteenth-century philosophy taught the Frenchman to find his condition wretched, or in any case, unjust and illogical, and made him disinclined to the patient resignation to his troubles that had long characterized his ancestors. It had never called for a revolution or desired a change of regime; it had never been republican, and Camille Desmouslins was not wrong in stating: "In all France there were not ten of us who were republicans before 1789." Furthermore he himself was not one of those ten. But only an oversimplified conception of influence would indulge in the notion that political upheaval completely embodies in reality the theoretical design drawn up by some thinker. Even the Russian revolution, imbued as it was with Marxian dialectic, did not make a coherent application of Marxism, or quickly found it inapplicable when tried. The reforms of limited scope advocated by *L'Esprit des Lois, L'Homme aux quarante écus, L'Encyclopédie,* and the more moderate writings of Rousseau struck none the less deeply at the foundations of the ancien régime, for they accustomed the Frenchman of the Third Estate to declaring privileges unjust, to finding the crying differences between the provinces illogical and finding famines outrageous. The propaganda of the "philosophes" perhaps more than any other factor accounted for the fulfillment of the preliminary condition of the French Revolution, namely, discontent with the existing state of things.

In short, without enlarging upon what is already rather well known, we may say that eighteenth-century writers prepared the way for the Revolution, without wishing for it, because:

(a) They weakened the traditional religion, winning over to their side a great number of clerics, and taught disrespect for an institution which had been the ally of the monarchy for hundreds of years. At the same time they had increased the impatience of the non-privileged groups by uprooting from many minds the faith in a future life which had formerly made bearable the sojourn in this vale of tears that constituted life for many people of low estate. They wished to enjoy real advantages here on earth and without delay. The concept of well-being and then that of comfort slowly penetrated among them.

(b) They taught a secular code of ethics, divorced from religious belief, independent of dogma, and made the ideal of conduct consist of observation of this system of ethics, which was presented as varying in accordance with climate and environment. Furthermore they gave first importance in this ethical code to the love of humanity, altruism, and service due society or our fellow men. The ideas of humanity, already present in the teaching of Christ, in

Seneca and Montaigne, but often dormant, suddenly exerted fresh influence over people's minds.

(c) They developed the critical spirit and the spirit of analysis and taught many men not to believe, or to suspend judgment rather than accept routine traditions. In D'Argenson, Chamfort, Morelly, Diderot, Voltaire of course, D'Holbach, Condillac, and many others, and even in Laclos and Sade, we will find the effort to think courageously without regard for convention or tradition that will henceforth characterize the French intellectual attitude. From this time on, inequality with respect to taxation, the tithe paid to the Church, and banishment or persecution for subversive opinions will shock profoundly the sense of logic and critical spirit of the readers of the "philosophes."

(d) Lastly, these very thinkers who have often been depicted as builders of utopias are the creators of history or the historical sense, or almost so. Montesquieu studiously examined the origins of law and constitutions and saw men "conditioned" by soil and climate in contrast to the absolute rationalists, who were foreign jurists and not Frenchmen. Boulainvilliers and many others of lesser fame studied France's past. Voltaire's masterpiece is probably his work on general history. The result of this curiosity about history was twofold: it encouraged faith in progress and convinced numbers of Frenchmen that it was their task to fulfill humanity's law, to endeavor to increase the sum of liberty, relative equality, "enlightenment," and happiness in the world; it also proved to many men of the law who examined old documents and the titles of nobility and property that the privileges of nobility were based on a flimsy foundation. The respect that these bourgeois or sons of the people might have felt for the aristocrats was accordingly diminished, at the very moment when the bourgeois saw the nobles not only accept with admiration but take under their protection destructive writings produced by the pens of commoners: sons of tailors (Marmontel), vine growers (Restif), cutlers (Diderot) and watchmakers (Rousseau). And the history of the origins of royal sovereignty itself seemed to them scarcely more edifying than that of the feudal privileges.

As for the means of dissemination of those ideas or new beliefs that the "philosophes" were spreading between the years 1715 and 1770 or 1789, it will suffice to enumerate them rapidly, for numerous studies have examined them: they were the salons, although very few of the future revolutionaries frequented society gatherings; the clubs that more and more called for tolerance, preached deism, demanded the abolition of slavery (Société des Amis des Noirs) and dreamed of imitating the American Revolution (Club Américain); books or tracts which made their appearance as works of small format, easily carried or hidden, lively and sharp in style and prone to surprise and arouse the reader; periodicals; the theatre, especially after the coming of the "drame bourgeois" and the "comédie larmoyante," and then with Beaumarchais; and the education given in the secondary schools. Mornet's book sums up the essential material on the subject that can be found in documents. The other means of spreading new ideas, such as conversation, which is doubtless the most effective means man has always used to borrow and pass on new views, elude documentary research. (pp. 71-5)

Montesquieu and Rousseau are certainly the two great

names worthy of consideration in some detail. The presiding judge of the High Court of Bordeaux obviously did not want the Revolution; had he lived to see it, he would not have approved of its reorganization of the judiciary, or its audacity in reform, or the Declaration of the Rights of Man, or even the interpretation of certain principles he himself had enunciated. Still he is one of the spiritual fathers of the first two revolutionary assemblies. Like so many other men who have made history, he influenced the fateful years of 1789-1792 by what he did say almost involuntarily, by the thoughts other men read into his sentences and by the tone even more than by the content of his writings. His great work breathes a veritable hatred of despotism founded on fear; it shows no moral respect for monarchy, and so helped to alienate the most reasonable minds from it. The great principle of the separation of powers presumes the right to seize from the king the united powers that he believed he held as a whole by divine right. Finally, Montesquieu, however elevated his position as a citizen or as a magistrate may have been, uttered words which will assume a mystic authority in later times on the subject of the people's inherent good qualities and their ability to select their leaders: "The common people are admirable in choosing those to whom they must delegate some part of their authority" (II, ii), or "When the common people once have sound principles, they adhere to them longer than those we are wont to call respectable people. Rarely does corruption have its beginning among the people" (V, ii).

Finally, in his admirable XIth book, Montesquieu had defined liberty in terms that were to remain etched in people's memories: this liberty required stable laws, which alone could establish and protect it. Those laws were also to correct economic inequality. Certainly its historical examples adduced in great profusion, highly technical juridical considerations, certain generalizations that had been too cleverly made symmetrical, and its lack of order made this voluminous treatise hard to read. But Montesquieu's influence was not one of those that can be gauged by the number of readers: it expressed itself in action thanks to a few thoughtful minds who found in it a sufficiently coherent over-all plan capable of replacing the old order, which obviously was crumbling. Montesquieu's influence inspired a more important group of revolutionaries who were familiar with only a few chapters of his work, but these chapters were filled with the love of freedom and the great feeling for humanity that condemned slavery and the iniquitous exploitation of some men by others.

Montesquieu's influence on the French Revolution began to decline at the time when Rousseau's was coming to the fore. Many studies have been devoted to the subject of Rousseau and the French Revolution; and the subject deserves still further study, for perhaps no more notable case of the effect of thought on life exists in the whole history of ideas and of dynamic ideas in particular. But this broad subject has too often been narrowed down by the most well-meaning historians. So many dogmatic and partisan statements had portrayed Rousseau as the great malefactor who was guilty of the excesses committed by the Terrorists and as the father of collectivism that, as a reaction, the best-disposed scholars set about proving by facts and texts that the author of the *Contrat Social* was guiltless of so many misdeeds. As a result they have belittled his influence. But there is some narrowness and naïveté in these scholarly arguments. (pp. 75-7)

It is quite true (D. Mornet has proved this once again) that the influence of the *Contrat Social* was very weak between the years 1762 and 1789; the book caused so little disturbance that Rousseau was not even molested; and it is probable that Rousseau would have been frightened by certain inferences that were later drawn from his ideas. What he wrote in 1765 in no way justifies an assertion on our part that he would still have written the same thing in 1793, and so it is quite as conceivable that Rousseau might have violently changed his point of view and espoused the cause of the revolutionaries, had he lived long enough to receive their acclaim. And above all, without having consciously wanted the Revolution, Rousseau did a great deal, if not to cause it, at least to give it direction when it had broken out. The success of Rousseau's works and the reception accorded them in his lifetime have been investigated in sufficient detail. From now on, groups of research men might well give their attention to the enormous influence Rousseau exerted on the men of the Convention and on those of the Empire or the Restoration or on the romantics. Granted that Rousseau was neither a republican nor a revolutionary, he was in revolt, and that is no less important. A. Aulard, who was not inclined to overestimate the influence of the intellectuals on the French Revolution, nevertheless accurately described the paradoxical result of any fairly broad study of this subject: "All these men in revolt want to keep the monarchy and all of them blindly deal it mortal blows. The French, monarchists to a man, take on republicanism without their knowledge."

Not one of the men of the Revolution adopted Rousseau's philosophical system outright in order to put it into practice; that is only too plain. Not one of them understood Rousseau's thought in its subtleties, its contradictions, and its alterations as the scholar of the present day can understand it with the aid of much posthumous documentation: this is scarcely less obvious. Whatever chagrin it may cause minds devoted to strict methods, the unparalleled effect produced on the imagination of posterity by Montaigne, Rousseau, or Nietzsche can be credited to quotations drawn from their contexts and probably perverted from their original sense. This influence is not so much an influence of ideas as it is an influence of "idées-forces," to use Fouillée's expression, and exerts its power more by setting men's sensibilities aflame than by convincing their minds. (pp. 79-80)

But the way in which Rousseau's influence profoundly modified the men and women of the revolutionary and imperial eras, and then the romantics great and small, and the continuators of the Revolution, in and out of France, in the nineteenth and twentieth centuries—these are the questions that intellectual history seems to have been reluctant to investigate.

Its timidity is regrettable and our knowledge of the past suffers twice over because of it: first, because history that devotes itself too exclusively to what we call material facts such as a military victory, the fall of a ministry or the opening up of a railroad track, seriously falsifies our perspective of what took place. The development of the Napoleonic legend, the quietly working influence of Rousseau or Voltaire, the growth of anti-clericalism, and the elaboration of socialist myths are phenomena which are partly literary or sentimental in nature, but are second to no other order of phenomena in importance and in the effects they had on the course of human affairs. Our knowledge of the past suffers additionally because historians, by turning aside from the history of ideas and sentiments with their vigorous influence on the lives of men, abandon these research subjects to men less well trained than themselves in exact methods of study; the latter are disposed to write with the sole intent of finding in the past arguments to support their political views or their partisan claims. Meanwhile youth is tempted to reject history as it is officially presented—as an endless series of wars, diplomatic ruses, crimes, examples of intense selfishness and the impotent efforts of men to bring more reason into the world. It refuses to lend credence to those who advise it that man has remained a religious and ideological animal even more than an economic creature. Youth's awakening, when it is suddenly placed face to face with the terrible power of ideas, myths, and fanaticisms in the world, is sometimes a rude shock, as we have seen in our time.

The Frenchmen in particular who have thought fit in the past few years to deny their eighteenth-century thinkers as traitors to the classic and monarchical tradition of France have only to open their eyes in order to ascertain that no French tradition is more alive than that of the Century of Enlightenment. Pascal and Descartes are doubtless greater; Montaigne has more charm and Saint Thomas more logical power: but it is Voltaire and Rousseau, and sometimes Montesquieu and Condorcet, that one finds almost always behind the living influence of France on the masses and the ideologies of South America, of the United States itself, of Central and Eastern Europe, and that one will find tomorrow in Africa and Asia. The world of today expects from post-war France, and France herself expects from her political thinkers who lost the habit of expressing themselves in universal terms during the last fifty years, a renewal and a modernization of her liberal ideas of the eighteenth century, boldly adapted to the social and economic problems of today, but still inspired by the same faith in man and his possibilities. (pp. 81-6)

> *Henri Peyre, "The Influence of Eighteenth-Century Ideas on the French Revolution," in his* Historical and Critical Essays, *University of Nebraska Press, 1968, pp. 62-87.*

Alfred Cobban

[Esteemed as an authority on French history and the history of political thought, Cobban was an English historian, educator, editor, and author. In the following excerpt from In Search of Humanity: The Role of the Enlightenment in Modern History *(1960), he examines the ethical implications of Enlightenment thought in twentieth-century society.]*

To attribute prime importance . . . to theoretical trends mainly apparent in philosophy, science and literature, will seem to some a distortion of the true proportions of history; and it would be wrong to suggest that there were no other factors involved both in the rise and decline of the Enlightenment. A movement so completely initiated and fashioned by an intellectual élite is hardly conceivable in a society of feudal barons and serfs, for example, or in the absence of a class with sufficient leisure to devote itself to disinterested inquiry. The mutual influence of different States or nations, with differing policies, social patterns, religious and ideals, was a fructifying force which could not have operated in a closed civilization lacking such varieties of behaviour and belief. The subsequent rise of the sovereignty of the State was facilitated, if not made unavoidable, by the pressure of economic problems resulting from the colossal and unprecedented growth of population, beginning in Western Europe, which may well be considered the basic fact in modern history. The ideas of sovereignty and of the nation state became immensely more menacing when they were applied not to the comparatively small, unpopulous, and by modern standards rudimentarily governed, States of the eighteenth century, but to the leviathans of the modern world. It is in these, and above all in the social and political patterns characteristic of Fascist, Nazi and Communist totalitarianisms, that are to be seen the most patent manifestation of the problem of inhumanity, with which this inquiry began.

But these patterns are intimately associated with changes in ideas. To say that they have justified the pessimism which was such a marked trend in nineteenth-century thought, in striking contrast to that of the previous century, would be true; and it would also be fair to observe that the new ideas of the nineteenth century played an important part in bringing about this very justification of their own pessimism. The new trend of ideas, and new social forces arising at the end of the eighteenth century, together swept Western society into a harsher climate, in which the ideals of the Enlightenment could not but wither.

To speak of the strength of the forces which opposed the Enlightenment is, however, to imply the existence of weaknesses and limitations in the Enlightenment itself, and the picture would be incomplete if no mention were made of these. The most obvious is its geographical limitation. The theory of sovereignty may have developed in Western Europe and flowered in the Bourbon monarchy of Louis XIV, but it was never unqualified or unchallenged even there. Farther east, under Habsburg, Hohenzollern and Romanov, uninfluenced, or only superficially influenced, by the moderating tendencies in Western society, more ruthless despotisms prevailed, which remained fundamentally unaffected by such stray beams of enlightened thought as penetrated their darkness. The Enlightenment of the seventeenth and eighteenth centuries, as we have described it, was confined to France, the Low Countries, some of the Swiss cantons, Great Britain and its American colonies, and to a certain extent Scandinavia, with a minor influence on a small educated class in Spain, Italy and Germany. It never really crossed the *limes Germanici* or became translated into German. The Slav world remained almost untouched and the extra-European world completely immune.

On the other hand, within strict geographical limits, and if we judge the Enlightenment by something more modest than worldwide success, we must admit that where it took root its influence was lasting. Its tolerant, liberal, scientific, reforming ideals have survived in those nations of Western Europe, and their overseas extensions, where they first became influential; and the great totalitarian dictatorships which shortly dominated the world now seem

less the portentous anticipation of the future than the last monstrous survivals of an earlier age.

Within a limited geographical environment the Enlightenment has been justified of its children. The progress of scientific knowledge and technological invention has vindicated the methods of those who founded modern science and carried discovery far beyond their highest hopes; and as the realm of science has expanded so that of superstition has contracted. Toleration of religious, and even of irreligious, opinion is now an accepted principle, and religion itself has been purged of many of its grosser elements. The zeal for persecuting and burning those of a different faith, if still latent, is not allowed to take practical form. Freedom of thought and expression is subject to increasingly few restrictions. Liberal political ideals are widely accepted and the arbitrary element in government has been greatly reduced. The law is now directed much more to the protection than to the suppression of the individual. It is almost universally accepted that the object of government is utilitarian, to promote the welfare of all members of society. An hereditary system of privilege is much less dominant in society, and what Burke called 'that unbought grace of life' is no longer the monopoly of a caste. Jeremy Bentham, if he could see his country a century and a quarter after his death could take pride in the achievement of his disciples. Voltaire would find the struggle against cruelty an unending one, but the victories of humanitarianism notable. Locke and Rousseau would see education still regarded as the key to a good society.

If this seems an idealized picture, it will be more impressive if we compare it with the realities of the age in which the men of the Enlightenment worked. Yet we must admit that it does not quite carry conviction. The pessimistic spirit still prevails in contemporary society, and not only because of the fact of war and the menace of nuclear destruction. Plague was an equally ever-present menace to an earlier generation, and with the further knowledge that if no human choice could let it loose on society, none could restrain it; but it did not inhibit a basic optimism. The Enlightenment, it may be said, was a greater age than ours, because it was making the effort to create, with great hopes and without overriding fears, the civilization that we seem to be trying to destroy. This is a reason for pessimism. Another explanation offered for the decline of the optimistic spirit is that the ideals developed by an intellectual élite look rather different when they have become the heritage of the masses. But enlightened Europe, even if it despised the canaille, believed in the universal validity of its ideas, and therefore could not have consistently accepted this explanation. It would, I believe, have been pleased to find how many of its aspirations could be adopted by the majority of the population.

The real explanation of the contemporary malaise, I suggest, is none of these. Nor is it a mere survival of Wagnerian gloom. Even the cult of irrationality is not quite adequate to account for it. An explanation of the conflict between enlightened hopes and the realities of practical politics has been offered by the American theologian, Reinhold Niebuhr, which should be considered at this point, since it is one of the few serious and influential discussions of the problem of ethics in our time, and it also offers, I believe, an explanation of the pessimistic spirit. For Niebuhr the conflict between actual political behaviour and the moral consciousness, of which we are uneasily aware, exemplifies that deeper conflict between 'moral man' and 'immoral society' in which, according to him, lies the universal and tragic dilemma of mankind. To use his own words:

> The inevitable hypocrisy, which is associated with all of the collective activities of the human race, springs chiefly from this source: that individuals have a moral code which makes the action of collective man an outrage to their conscience.

The tragedy of the human spirit, he believes, is 'its inability to conform its collective life to its individual ideals': 'Our contemporary culture, he writes, 'fails to realize the power, extent and persistence of group egoism in human relations.'

What Niebuhr argues is that there are three different levels of moral behaviour: the standards we recognize in our relations as individual to individual are attenuated in collective actions within our society, and vanish in relations between societies. He takes this conflict of ethical standards to be—to use current jargon—a universal human predicament, and one from which there is no escape. If his position is a valid one, no other explanation for contemporary pessimism need be sought, and there can be no solution to a universal and insoluble problem.

The first point to be noticed, however, is that it is not universal. There seems no reason to doubt that in tribal society individual morality is normally satisfied by conformity with the social code of the tribe and is conscious of no obligations outside it. If this is so, the conflict of standards between individual and social morality must be an historically conditioned and not a universal phenomenon. It can only appear when the individual, on moral grounds and as more than an isolated event, challenges the validity of the social code.

Ancient Greece provides—at least in the history of the Western world—the first recorded major revolt of the individual against the moral code of society. It is associated with the name of Socrates, but the rise of the sophists and the decline of accepted religious ideas had earlier prepared the way for him. Like others later, he was unjustly condemned as a cause of the attack on religious orthodoxy, when he was merely a result. Along with the speculations of the sophists, the development of Greek scientific thought also played its part in undermining the foundations of Olympus. The result was to expose social customs to rational discussion, and out of this came the Socratic appeal to the individual conscience.

A further development followed from the decay of city states and the rise of universal empire. Stoic thought enlarged the ethical community to include all humanity, and replaced local tribal law with the idea of a universal Natural Law. The scientific conception of nature was extended to include the idea of uniformities in the ethical as well as the physical realm. These ethical norms were called Natural Laws, and they were regarded as consistent with, and capable of being discovered by, reason. The ethical content of Natural Law, incorporated in and expanded by way of the Roman *jus gentium* and Christianity, passed on to the medieval peoples without experiencing any further development until the early modern period. There then ensued a renewed wave of ethical discussion. The emer-gence of the modern State may have been the factor which led to a concentration of attention at this time on the rights of the individual, but it would be mistaken to suppose that this was essentially new, though the specific emphasis may have been. As Gierke wrote: 'A fugitive glance at Medieval Doctrine suffices to perceive how throughout it all . . . runs the thought of the absolute and imperishable value of the Individual.'

It is not difficult to identify the new ethical contributions of the Enlightenment. . . . Slowly and hesitantly the principle of religious toleration came to be affirmed; torture, taken for granted from time immemorial as a necessary adjunct to civil and religious society, was discredited; war was no longer regarded as a necessary evil; the rule of law was asserted and arbitrary police powers condemned; slavery was denounced; utilitarianism proclaimed that the object of government was the greatest happiness of the greatest number. Such ideas—and the list could be extended—have become the commonly accepted norms of Western civilization. They are the essential ingredients in the 'moral man' of whom Niebuhr speaks.

The social forces which are regarded as 'immoral' are also not difficult to place, for basically there is nothing new about them. They arise out of the survival or re-creation of earlier ethical conceptions. Some nations almost completely, as has already been suggested, and some sections in almost all nations, escaped the influence of the ethical revolution of the eighteenth century; and even where it seemed to have triumphed there has since been a partial withdrawal. The consequent conflict of ethical standards is, I suggest, the real source of what seems to Niebuhr to be a conflict between moral man and immoral society. It appears as such only because the broader ethical norms of the Enlightenment are those that are associated with the idea of an ethical standard applicable to all men; while the narrower morality is a new kind of tribalism, for which the social unity or State is an ethical end in itself, and which excludes from the obligations of ethics all who are outside it. In a sense, therefore, the Enlightenment is correctly identified as the source of the current conflict in ethical values and the consequent pessimism; for without it most of what seems to those still under its influence immoral in the behaviour patterns of the contemporary world would simply be taken for granted.

One solution to this conflict, of course, might be to abandon the ethics of the Enlightenment in toto, and this is what Nazi Germany did. But it is not really a solution, or at least it cannot stop at that, for the Enlightenment is all of a piece and cannot be accepted or rejected in parts. Along with its ethics we must be prepared to jettison its science, utilitarianism and the whole rationality of social life. This is what happened in Nazi Germany and for a time in Stalinist Russia, only the loss of science was concealed by the progress of technology. It is still too early to say that it may not be happening, more slowly and more insidiously, elsewhere. (pp. 223-28)

Alfred Cobban, "The Moral Crisis of the Twentieth Century," in his In Search of Humanity: The Role of the Enlightenment in Modern History, *Jonathan Cape, 1960, pp. 223-38.*

Peter Gay

[In the following excerpt, Gay refutes prevalent twenti-eth-century interpretations of the significance and influ-ence of the French Enlightenment.]

In its career as the target of polemical attack, the Enlight-enment has been assailed for ideas it did not hold, and for consequences it did not intend and did not produce. Over the years, it has acquired a reputation that covers its mo-bile face like a rigid mask. Yet the accepted view of the Enlightenment does not reflect the work of the specialists: I can think of no area of historical study in which the gap between the scholar and the general public is as wide, and as fateful, as it is with the Enlightenment. And in speaking of the "general public" I am speaking of the consumers of textbooks, and, I am afraid, all too often their producers as well. We have at our command a rich supply of authori-tative monographs which demonstrate in detail that the *philosophes* were often pessimists, usually empiricists, gen-erally responsible hard-headed political men, with sensible programs, limited expectations, and a firm grasp of histo-ry. Yet everybody seems to be sure that the men of the En-lightenment were naïve optimists, cold rationalists, ab-stract literary men, with a Utopian vision of the world and (worst of all) no sense of ambiguity or tragedy whatever. The *Shorter Oxford English Dictionary,* presumably a seri-ous and objective authority, defines the Enlightenment as "shallow and pretentious intellectualism, unreasonable contempt for authority and tradition," thus collecting most current prejudices in one convenient spot.

The origins of such stubborn misreadings are not hard to discover. Many of the criticisms later leveled against the Enlightenment were first leveled by the *philosophes* them-selves: as I have suggested elsewhere, they were a quarrel-some family who liked criticizing each other almost as much (but not quite) as the Church. Some of the most per-sistent clichés about the *philosophes* can be traced back to the Enlightenment: Voltaire was among the first to spread the canard about Rousseau's primitivism, a canard echoed by other *philosophes* and later given its final vulgar form by Napoleon: "I am especially disgusted with Rousseau," he said in 1803, "since I have seen the Orient. Savage man is a dog." No amount of documented refutation has ever been able to destroy the supposed ideal of Rousseau, the "noble savage." In return, by an act of poetical injustice, the reputation of Voltaire the irresponsible, flighty poet was, if not established, at least propagated by such *philo-sophes* as David Hume. The game of criticism was enliv-ened by caustic British visitors like Horace Walpole, who shared many of the Enlightenment's ideas while disliking its most articulate spokesmen. "The *philosophes,*" wrote Walpole in 1765, "are insupportable, superficial, overbear-ing, and fanatic: they preach incessantly." And at the same time in the German states, *Aufklärer* like Lessing es-tablished their identity as German literary men by noisily freeing themselves from their French models.

All this mutual denunciation was the vigorous rough and tumble of a healthy family. In the face of a threat from church or state the squabbling brethren united in a solid and formidable army. The really damaging criticism came from other sources. In the 1770's the enthusiasts of the *Sturm und Drang* vehemently objected to what they called the deadly materialism of the Enlightenment: in a famous passage of his autobiography, Goethe pictures himself and

his youthful friends shuddering at Holbach's *Système de la nature:* "it seemed to us so grey, so Cimmerian, so deathlike, that it was hard for us to stand its presence." But the *Sturm und Drang* faded, and Goethe developed a sympathetic understanding of the Enlightenment as a whole. He translated Voltaire and Diderot, studied Rous-seau and Kant. It was, of course, the so-called French Revolution—a world-wide revolution that took its most spectacular form in France—that made criticism of the Enlightenment into a really serious business. A king de-capitated, thousands executed, a whole army of aristocrats driven into exile, church property secularized, Jews and actors enfranchised, schools and hospitals put under pub-lic secular authority, an irresistible army officered by com-moners and manned by conscripts—this was the fruit of a century of philosophic criticism!

As usual, to be sure, the critics did not agree just which aspects of the Enlightenment had been most lethal: some of the German Romantics separated Rousseau from the rest of the *philosophes,* and exalted him as the prophet of true feeling, while French counterrevolutionaries treated Rousseau as the most extreme, and hence most despicable product of the Age of Reason. Voltaire, too, was some-times pictured as a malicious wrecker, and sometimes as a brilliant writer, the pride of French letters despite it all, who had merely gone too far and been too clever. But these divergences mattered little: uncertain allies though they were, the critics created an image of the Enlighten-ment which still haunts us today. In fact, we do not see the Enlightenment directly but through the eyes of the Romantic period.

The ingredients of the Romantic interpretation of the En-lightenment, whether favorable or unfavorable, are few but powerful: the Enlightenment was not serious, it was abstract and literary, impious and superficial. Even Byron, a *philosophe* out of his time, saw his much-admired Vol-taire as a Protean talent, as

>   fire and fickleness, a child
> Most mutable in wishes;

while Blake, who had much sympathy for radical humani-tarian ideas, fiercely repudiated the form they had taken in the Enlightenment:

> Mock on, mock on, Voltaire, Rousseau;
> Mock on, mock on, 'tis all in vain!
> You throw the sand against the wind,
> And the wind blows it back again.

The scholar who knows the history of the Enlightenment's reputation reads these lines with a shock of recognition: they anticipate more than a century of conservative French criticism, from Chateaubriand to Taine, from Ta-uine to Faguet and Brunetière, and from Faguet and Bru-netière to most of the textbooks now in use. Nor do these lines anticipate merely the conterrevolutionary views of Frenchmen who hated the Third Republic as the irreli-gious offspring of the First. Friendly critics, too, were cap-tured by the Romantic vision: Alfred North Whitehead, who had high regard for the *philosophes'* clarity of intellect and humanity of purpose summed up the case against them in 1925, in a celebrated phrase: *"les philosophes,"* he wrote, "were not philosophers."

Once the Romantic interpretation was fixed, little was

The Petit Trianon, Versailles.

done through the nineteenth century to change it. In fact, it was buttressed by two of the most influential writers on the eighteenth century that the nineteenth century produced: Tocqueville and Morley. There is no need for me to dwell on the merits of a man who is more worshiped than analyzed today: Tocqueville was an unmatched observer and prescient social philosopher. But he was also, I think, a much overrated historian. In his book on the Old Regime, he argued that the *philosophes* treated political questions "casually, even, one might say, toyed with them." Their "kind of abstract, literary politics found its way, in varying proportions, into all the writings of the day." They worshiped reason and intellect—their own: the ideal society, as they envisioned it, would be based on "simple, elementary rules deriving from the exercise of the human reason and natural law." This secular Utopianism was, in a sense, not their fault, it was their fate, the only political vision available to them: "living as they did, quite out of touch with practical politics, they lacked the experience which might have tempered their enthusiasms." This is persuasive, especially because it is offered without reproach, and with the large sense of human destiny that marks Tocqueville's work: the *philosophes* are not to be blamed for their irresponsibility; they were as much the victims of their society as their society was to become *their* victim. And yet, Tocqueville's analysis does grave injus-

tice to the *philosophes:* it concentrates on the trivial side effects rather than on the central purposes of Enlightenment speculation.

From a different perspective, John Morley's biographies of the *philosophes,* sympathetic and intelligent as they were, perpetuated the misconceptions and gave weight to the kind of criticism they were designed to eradicate. Morley was an agnostic, an anticlerical, an articulate supporter of the philosophy of the Enlightenment, and in the 1860's and 1870's he wrote some lucid lives of Voltaire, Rousseau, and Diderot that embodied his radicalism. They are well informed, energetically argued, and sensitively aware of the lesser lights that surrounded these central luminaries: in separate essays, or chapters in the large biographies, Morley gave favorable accounts of Vauvenargues, Turgot, Condorcet, and others. Yet the burden of his judgment is that the *philosophes* were Utopians, addicted to "socialistic sophisms" and a certain immoral "looseness of opinion"; they were the victims of "confident exultation." Morley was too much in agreement with Voltaire's anticlericalism or Diderot's political radicalism to turn his books into just another condemnation of the Enlightenment, and he was too widely read to pronounce his criticisms without reservations: if the *philosophes* in general despised the Middle Ages, Turgot at least appreciated them; if the *philosophes* in general had an unreasonable faith in reason, Vauvenargues at least valued the passions. Yet Morley's very sympathy for the Enlightenment, and his very qualifications, strengthened the case against the *philosophes:* if a sympathizer could call the Enlightenment impractical and immoral, why should an opponent not feel free to do the same? And, as the literature shows, the opponents did feel free.

This consensus of criticism did not, of course, go unchallenged. Quite early, Kant defended Rousseau against the common imputation that he was an advocate of a return to the savage state; while Goethe, a faithful reader of Rousseau, attributed the foolish and fashionable primitivism of his time to "misunderstood suggestions of Rousseau." In more recent times there was even an influential textbook by Gustave Lanson, which did the *philosophes* justice—especially in the later editions written after Lanson had read the eighteenth-century writers with some care. There were even specialized works, like the little book by Georges Pellissier, which accorded Voltaire the status of a philosopher.

But works such as these had about as much impact on the governing interpretation as peas shot from a pea-shooter have on the hide of an elephant. The monographs multiply, and they are duly listed in the bibliographies of our texts, but their message does not register. The specialist continues to write for other specialists who are already convinced, and on occasion he feels a little like Matthew Arnold's Byron, "a beautiful and ineffectual angel, beating in the void his luminous wings in vain"—as ineffectual, in any event, even if rather less beautiful.

This is poetic and sad. Let me be prosy and specific, and list the criticisms of the Enlightenment that are generally accepted today. First, it is argued that the *philosophes* had an unmeasured faith in reason, rigid mechanical reason. Reason, writes one recent historian of political thought, was "regarded as a panacea for all human ills." And the same writer adds, presumably to lend specific gravity to his charge, "To Diderot reason was everything." This is popular stuff and sounds unimpeachable, but it is nonsense. Diderot was at once the receptive medium and the revolutionary theoretician of sensibility, while his fellow *philosophes* were, on the whole, wary of treating reason as any kind of panacea at all. The *philosophes* ridiculed the rationalism of seventeenth-century philosophers as "metaphysics"; Kant spent most of his philosophical career trying to determine the limits of reason; Condillac developed a thoroughgoing empiricist psychology hostile to all rationalism; Hume made the remark that reason is, and ought to be, the slave of the passions, and constructed a theory of social behavior in which habit dominates and reason plays a subordinate part; Voltaire and d'Alembert treated reason with cautious reserve. The brilliant anticipations of modern psychology that pervade the *philosophes'* writings sprang from their appreciation of the passions. Diderot formulated the Oedipus complex one hundred and fifty years before Freud; Hume's analysis of habit was modern enough to serve John Dewey as the starting point for his social psychology; Montesquieu and Gibbon made important contributions to political sociology by analyzing the nature of ideology and the devices of mass-manipulation. Sigmund Freud, the thinker who above all others is supposed to have destroyed the foundations of Enlightenment

rationalism, was the greatest child of the Enlightenment our century has known. In short, the Enlightenment was not an Age of Reason, but a Revolt against Rationalism.

The *philosophes,* then, may be called rationalists only if the epithet is defined in a special way. They argued that knowledge is superior to ignorance; that social problems can be solved only through reasonable action based on research and analysis rather than through prayer, renunciation, reliance on all-wise authority, or patient waiting for God; that discussion is superior to fanaticism; and that barriers to inquiry, whether barriers of religion, tradition, or philosophical dogmatism, are all pernicious barriers to understanding.

The second criticism is closely related to the first—the Enlightenment, we are told, preached the inevitability of progress: the theory of progress, "was one of the dominant ideas of the Age of Enlightenment." This notion has the status of an established truth, and yet it is a myth. Locke, Montesquieu, Hume, Diderot had no theory of progress; Rousseau's thought stressed the fact of man's retrogression and the hope for man's regeneration; Voltaire saw human history as a long string of miseries broken by four happy ages. Only Kant, with his speculative world history, Turgot with his three stages, and Condorcet with his ten epochs, may be said to have held a theory of progress, and these three thinkers stood not at the center but at the bright end of the spectrum of Enlightenment thought.

Indeed, the *philosophes* looked upon their world with sturdy, Stoic courage. They did not deny that progress is possible—some of them maintained that humanity had in fact lightened the burden of its existence through the centuries, while others were impelled by the moderate confidence that if *their* proposals were adopted, the world *would* progress. But the empirical observation that progress has occurred, or the rational opinion that progress will result from specified policies, cannot be called a theory of progress. That grandiose phrase should be reserved for the metaphysical claim that progress is an inevitable process immanent in history, and it is this claim which has been imputed to the *philosophes* with great frequency and little justice.

No doubt, some of the *philosophes'* confidence was misplaced—confidence is often misplaced. But a careful reading of eighteenth-century writings will reveal the gloomier side of philosophic speculation. Long before the Lisbon earthquake ruined even the remnants of Voltaire's cosmic optimism, Voltaire had inveighed against the doctrine that palpable evils are really hidden goods, and that all is for the best in the best of all possible worlds. In *Candide* his savage assault on optimism was not a capricious expression of low spirits, but a reasoned philosophical position. Similarly, Diderot's savage criticisms of political institutions, Holbach's pessimism about human nature, Gibbon's cynicism, or Hume's skepticism cannot be called fatuous optimism—they were neither fatuous nor optimistic. Even Condorcet, whose paean to progress is more often denounced than read, did not overlook the cruelty, the fanaticism, and the misery of men. He hoped for relief in the future, in the Tenth Epoch, but even in the present, Ninth Epoch, the most enlightened mankind had yet achieved, Condorcet saw little to cheer him: "civilization occupies only a small part of the globe," and the "number of those who are really civilized disappears before the mass of men delivered over to prejudice and ignorance. We see vast countries groaning in slavery; in one place we see nations degraded by the vices of a civilization whose corruption impedes progress; in another, nations still vegetating in the infancy of its first epochs. We see that the labors of these last ages have done much for the human spirit, little for the perfection of the human species; much for the glory of man, something for his liberty, but as yet almost nothing for his happiness. In several places our eyes are struck by a dazzling light; but dark shadows still cover an immense horizon. The mind of the philosopher rests with satisfaction on a small number of objects; but the spectacle of stupidity, slavery, extravagance, barbarity, afflicts him still more often; and the friend of humanity can enjoy unmixed pleasure only by surrendering to the sweet hopes of the future." Whatever our views of Condorcet's categorical division of mankind into enlightened and superstitious, we will recognize this paragraph as a depressing catalogue. And, as the last sentence of the quotation shows, Condorcet's optimism is a form of therapy: he hopes that he may not despair.

Condorcet's hope was to escape from the past, and in this he was representative of the Enlightenment, which was committed to the future. This brings me to the third criticism: the *philosophes*, it is said, had no sense of history. In the light of the conclusive refutations with which this myth has been confronted, in the light of the sheer bulk of excellence in historical writings (in the light, that is, of Voltaire's *Essai sur les mœurs,* Gibbon's *Decline and Fall of the Roman Empire,* and Hume's *History of England*), this charge looks a little tarnished now. But it is not dead. As recently as 1953, a historian of political theory observed that the eighteenth century "was a time when the historical spirit was lacking and when men had little reverence for the past," and there are many today who would agree with him.

Admittedly, the rise of modern conceptions of history was slow and tortuous; and the moralizing, relatively static histories written in the eighteenth century cannot be called unmitigated triumphs of the historical mentality. All too often, the *philosophes* turned history into propaganda— sometimes on purpose, more often unwittingly, through their very conception of the past as a struggle between rational and irrational forces. Ranke's celebrated dictum that all epochs are equally close to God, with which the modern craft of history attained maturity, was beyond the horizon of the Enlightenment. But there are many ways of expressing a sense of history. The *philosophes* were the first to treat whole cultures as a unit of historical study, and greatly improved the critical stance of historians toward their subject matter. It is true that they wanted to escape from the worship of the past because, as they rightly believed, it was used all too often as an ideological prop for reactionary policies. "At best," said Locke shrewdly, "an argument from what has been, to what should of right be, has no great force." But the *philosophes* were also convinced that the only way to escape from the past was to know it.

What was the future to be like? This brings up the fourth criticism—that the *philosophes* hoped to realize the perfect society of their dreams by means of the enlightened despot. At least one respected book I know calls Napoleon's Caesaristic despotism the logical fulfillment of the *philo-*

sophes' program, and it is common property that the political theory of the Enlightenment consisted largely of d'Alembert flattering Frederick the Great, Diderot flattering Catherine the Great, and Voltaire flattering both. Obviously, the *philosophes* enjoyed their proximity to power, partly because it soothed their vanity, partly because it provided them with audiences and customers, partly because it protected them from the harassment of censors. It is equally true that the close, and often informal, association of these bourgeois men of letters with royalty created intermittent fantasies. There were occasions when some of the *philosophes* dramatized themselves as modern Aristotles guiding modern Alexanders. But to take such private delusions and social aspirations for a reasoned political theory, to call Voltaire "by conviction and temperament an enthusiast of enlightened despotism," is to mistake accident for essence. In fact, the physiocrats alone advocated what they called *legal despotism.* But, in the first place, they hedged this idea with qualifications, treating this despotism as a transitional expedient to be supervised, at all times, by an alert public opinion. And, in the second place, the other *philosophes* disliked this despotism heartily. Rousseau denounced it in a violent letter to the elder Mirabeau; Turgot told Du Pont that "this devil 'despotism' will forever stand in the way of the propagation of your doctrine"; while Diderot asserted that "the arbitrary government of a just and enlightened prince is always bad." Other *philosophes,* like Holbach, were profoundly skeptical of the benefits conferred by an omnipotent ruler, no matter how benevolent. Voltaire is more complicated, but far from being a consistent admirer of enlightened despotism, he was a thoroughgoing relativist.

The political theory of the Enlightenment has not yet been completely explored. In the absence of such a systematic study, nothing has seemed more plausible than the picturesque scene of the all-wise, all-powerful prince laying down rational laws and dealing out rational justice with a *philosophe* by his side. The *philosophes* certainly did their part in propagating this image of themselves, and posterity has revenged itself upon them by accepting their self-portrait and not reading their writings. And yet, the notion that "enlightened despotism" was the *philosophes'* favorite form of government is simply still another myth. Few of the *philosophes* were full-fledged political theorists: generally they treated politics as though it were no more than a set of concrete controversies. This had the disadvantage of preventing them from seeing all the consequences of their positions. But it also demands that we see these positions in the context in which they were developed. When the *philosophes* favored absolutism, they did so because they were opposed to the alternative—the traditional government by a powerful aristocracy. In their eyes, absolutism was not a rationalistic scheme but a political party in the real world. They could see the virtues of British constitutionalism, or of the kind of moderate aristocracy advocated by leading Dutch or Genevan political figures. And in any event, their long-range program envisaged a government responsible to a wide public, and expressive of the autonomy of the citizen.

For the *philosophes,* the question of forms of government always involved the question of the masses: should ordinary men, nearly always illiterate and almost definitely unfit for self-government, be allowed a share in political life? Should they be told the truth about religion and be trusted to exercise moral self-restraint? Or should they be kept in check by politic lies, by a *religion civile?* There were few matters the *philosophes* debated more intensively and more inconclusively than this. The balance of opinion was in favor of telling the truth, not in favor of organized deceit. Even Voltaire came to place considerable trust in the rationality of the poor, as he grew older, more mellow, and more politically experienced. Montesquieu had said in 1748, in the Preface to his *Esprit des lois,* "It is not a matter of indifference that the minds of the people be enlightened." And, in the second half of the eighteenth century, more and more *philosophes* could see the advantages, and were willing to take the risks, of universal enlightenment.

Behind the four criticisms I have listed, there stands a fifth which usually accompanies them: that the Enlightenment was the work of lightheaded wits who glittered in salons and invented irresponsible Utopias. A splendid recent instance, which exhibits all five of these charges together is Sir Harold Nicolson's portrait gallery of the eighteenth century, characteristically but unhappily entitled *The Age of Reason.* To Sir Harold, the *philosophes* were all rationalists, except of course Rousseau, who, he tells us, felt "distrust for and incapacity for all rational thought." They created an age of optimism and expected to solve all problems with a handful of rules. Sir Harold says nothing about historical writing in the eighteenth century, but this very omission from his crowded panorama suggests that he did not find the historical achievements of a Gibbon or a Voltaire worth mentioning. And, of course, the *philosophes* favored enlightened despotism. Sir Harold says many generous things about Voltaire's fight for freedom and humanitarianism, but he concludes that while "Rousseau desired the dictatorship of the proletariat, Voltaire desired the dictatorship of kings," which is to make two major errors in one sentence. I need hardly add that Sir Harold's light hand, and his talent for biography by anecdote leaves untouched the accepted picture of the philosophes—they remain, in his book, earnest but not serious, impractical, witty, and shocking. The monographs grind on, telling the truth to the few who already know it. If anyone wants a refutation of the theory of progress, let him compare the popular treatment of the Enlightenment two centuries ago and today.

While scholars have valiantly directed their fire against this battery of misinterpretations, they have recently been fired upon from a new direction. I said at the beginning that the Enlightenment has been assailed for consequences it neither intended nor produced. This new attack has often been made on mutually exclusive grounds, but that has not slowed down the critics. It is becoming increasingly fashionable to criticize the Enlightenment for producing what is called "the crisis of our time." Some critics charge the *philosophes* with subverting stable Christian values and throwing man into the flux of relativism. Others charge them with professing Utopian goals with such grim single-mindedness that they produced the totalitarian mentality which makes our age a hell on earth. Some agile logicians have, in fact, charged the Enlightenment with both crimes at once: with one hand the infidel crew destroyed a secure religious basis for morality, and with the other it fostered a messianic attitude toward politics. The *philosophes,* in short, are widely accused today of having been cynics and fanatics at the same time.

I do not wish to minimize the horrors of our time, or to ridicule the search for their causes. The *philosophes,* great advocates of pragmatic history, would have been the first to defend the utility of such a search. I think too, that these new critics of the Enlightenment are confronting serious issues: they are trying to discard the now outworn political categories of "right" and "left," and to understand the psychological and social strains that a civilization undergoes when it secularizes its world view. I am taking issue with these critics here not because I disagree with their goals or deprecate their questions, but because I think their answers are wrong. (pp. 262-79)

No modern historian can afford to neglect the intellectual formulations that incite men to action. Even if they are rationalizations of underlying psychological pressures or economic institutions, they become autonomous historical forces. But neither the Terror in the French Revolution, nor the totalitarian regimes of our time, are merely the products of certain ideas, the "ultimate result" of speculations by eighteenth-century writers who were thinking of something else and hoped for a far different future. The pressure of events, the heritage of institutions often quite at variance with intellectual formulations, technological developments in industry or in mass-communications, changes in weaponry or developments in economics—all these brought certain ideas into prominence and, ultimately, to victory. Germany did not go Fascist because of Nietzsche, but Germans ready to go Fascist selected and distorted some of Nietzsche's teachings to suit their purposes. And what happened, in this same country, to the humane, cosmopolitan classicism of a Goethe, whom every German read and professed to worship? These are considerations so obvious that they require restatement only because they are being forgotten by the latest critics of the Enlightenment.

The flaws that vitiate Talmon's analysis of the Enlightenment as a source of totalitarianism, vitiate the criticism of writers who treat the Enlightenment as a source of modern nihilism. Lester G. Crocker's ambitious and erudite *Age of Crisis,* the first volume in a proposed trilogy on ethical thought in eighteenth-century France, treats the exceptional as typical, and the relation of ideas to facts with blithe disregard for historical realities. Crocker's thesis is announced in his dramatic title: the decline of the Christian "metaphysic" caught eighteenth-century thinkers "in the conflicts of an age of profound cultural crisis." They were compelled to seek other foundations for conduct—natural law, and, increasingly as the century progressed, social utility. This breakdown of old standards caused, or at least revealed, a pervasive breakdown of moral and political decency, which resulted in the extreme philosophy of the marquis de Sade and of the Terror in the French Revolution, and which foreshadowed modern totalitarianism. History shows that "the rationalistic solutions of the middle ground have not succeeded, and have lost their formerly powerful appeal. We are impelled to extremes—to those of Sade, of Morelly, of Kant, or of the Grand Inquisitor—towards absolutes of some kind." Sade is, if not Crocker's hero, certainly Crocker's protagonist: he appears in the book with strategic regularity, and is stressed because he has "an important place in the thought of his age," and has been "shamefully neglected." Sade is important because he draws the "ultimate conclusions" from the "radical philosophies developed earlier in the century."

These radical philosophies include the right to suicide, which opens the way to Ivan Karamazov, and the "positions of Montesquieu and Hume," which obviously contain "the seed of moral nihilism." Thus the Enlightenment moves on, toward nihilism, toward the Terror, toward the Crisis of our Time.

This view has its uses, if largely as a corrective. The eighteenth century was not an age of crisis—no span of a hundred years could sustain an atmosphere of perpetual emergency with any degree of cheerfulness or productivity—but it was an age of readjustment in which the decline of Christian modes of thought produced a variety of naturalistic philosophies designed to replace the dying world view. Moreover, Crocker's reminder that the *philosophes* were not always easy with themselves is of value. But it was precisely the character of the Enlightenment *not* to be "impelled to extremes." As sturdy disciples of classical antiquity (of Cicero, Seneca, and Horace) the *philosophes* took extreme care to avoid extremes. The philosophy of practical paganism—reasonable pride, moderate reform, sensible expectations—was good enough for them. It is ironic that the *philosophes* should be taken as the fathers of fanatical ideologies when they both fought fanaticism and sought to avoid fanaticism in their own thinking. It was one of their most attractive virtues that they did not draw the kind of ultimate conclusions that would subvert the humanism of their purpose. Holbach was an atheist, but did not extol crime, and did not argue that if God is dead, all is permitted. Helvétius was a utilitarian, but his psychological account of man's nature tried to lay the foundation of reasonable social policies. Diderot celebrated sexual freedom, but his ideal was the genital personality and not polymorphous perversion. Even if we concede that there were seeds of ethical nihilism in Hume and Montesquieu, it is precisely the point of the Enlightenment that these seeds were not allowed to ripen.

When they did ripen, as with Sade, they turned into a vicious parody of the Enlightenment: Sade was not an heir but a caricature of the *philosophes*. Sade, as even some discriminating admirers will admit, was a turgid and disorganized writer, and there is little point in turning a tedious voluptuary into an archetypical thinker. The philosophical disquisitions with which Sade interrupts his adolescent sexual fantasies are little more than exclamations, borrowed from the *philosophes* without being in any way philosophical themselves. (pp. 282-85)

The Terror was neither the culmination of the Revolution nor the ultimate consequence of the Enlightenment. And to argue, even by implication, that the very movement that devoted its vast energies and stores of wit to fight censorship, nonsense, slavery, torture, intolerance, cruelty, and war, was responsible for these horrors in our time is to stand logic on its head. Every large cluster of ideas contains within itself intimations of its own opposite—that is inevitable. But to concentrate on these intimations at the expense of the ideas themselves is to substitute fancy for history—and where history is dead, all is permitted.

There has long been a debate, started in large measure by the *philosophes'* aggressive rhetoric, over whether the Enlightenment was destructive or constructive. The *philosophes* themselves had a ready answer: demolition and construction were two aspects of the same activity. Voltaire, thinking of his gardens at Ferney, spoke for the En-

lightenment as a whole when he told a correspondent in 1759 that he destroyed only in order to build. It is just as true, I think, that before we can appreciate the real virtues of the Enlightenment, we must dispose of its imagined vices. That is why I have spent so much space on criticizing its critics.

Obviously, the Enlightenment is not beyond criticism, and I have offered some criticisms in this [discussion]. But the faults of the movement were built, I think, into their situation. The *philosophes* were pragmatic, playful, and polemical. This attitude was necessary, considering the people they wished to persuade and the authorities they had to flatter and evade. But this necessity also had some unfortunate results. The *philosophes'* fetish of practicality, their horror of speculation for its own sake, drove them close to a philistine disregard for ideas, and blinded them to the possibilities of some of the most adventurous notions produced in their own ranks. In their own devotion to literature and the arts, they avoided the separation of sensibility and energy, beauty and experience, that has haunted bourgeois culture since their days, but their cult of practicality may be in part responsible for that later divorce. In addition, their moral pssion, Roman in its earnestness, drove them to find moral lessons in all things, even in the universe, so that the *philosophes,* champions of science, were on the whole unappreciative of its real methods. Voltaire, d'Alembert, and Buffon were the most distinguished exceptions: the others did not fully grasp the amoral, mathematical nature of the natural sciences.

At the same time, seeking to popularize new and daring ideas, and struggling against a determined opposition, the *philosophes* were both playful and polemical. The world view they held and wished to propagate was perfectly serious, but they clothed it in dialogues, stories, didactic plays so that the charge of their irresponsibility, although unjustified, is easy to understand.

The interpreter of the Enlightenment who tries to characterize the movement after he has disposed of the myths that surround it finds the *philosophes'* style of philosophizing at once regrettable and tantalizing. For implicit in all their belligerent arguments and witty formulations there is a philosophy of real seriousness and enduring relevance. I shall do no more here than to name that philosophy, in a series of paradoxes. I have made them paradoxes because it is precisely the vision of ambiguity that has been denied the *philosophes.* Yet they had it, even if they did not clothe it in the vocabulary that is fashionable in our age.

The Enlightenment, then, was an aristocratic liberalism. In politics, as in other matters, the range of *philosophe* opinions was wide, but at the center was a program for government responsible to its citizens, governing by laws rather than arbitrary enactments, protecting the rights of civil and religious minorities. At the same time, while there were democrats among the *philosophes,* even these democrats cherished an élite of civilized men and women, who knew the classics both of ancient and modern times, loved and practiced the arts, cared for conversation, and participated in a kind of timeless assembly of the happy few.

In ethics, the Enlightenment professed an Epicurean Stoicism. The *philosophes* preached courage before death without fear of hell or hope of heaven, and those among them who knew that death was coming, like David Hume, practiced in that supreme moment what they had preached all their lives. They believed in public service—but also in pleasure. They enjoyed advising legislators, but they also enjoyed the dazzle of wit, and the play of humor in the face of grim realities.

On a deeper level, the *philosophes* glimpsed a general view of the world that I should like to call a passionate rationalism. Their rationalism, as I have said before, was not an abstract devotion to reason or a naïve trust in its omnicompetence. It was, rather, a devotion to the critical spirit that treats all positions as tentative—including their own. The *philosophes* were the enemies of myth, and the myths to which they themselves were victims were nothing more than limitations which all mortals share. Their rationalism was, one might say, programmatic: it called for debate of all issues, examination of all propositions, and penetration of all sacred precincts. But I cannot repeat often enough that this critical, scientific view of life was anything but frigid. The *philosophes* at once studied and rehabilitated the passions, tried to integrate the sexual urge into civilized life, and laid the foundation for a philosophy that would attempt to reconcile man's highest thinking with his deepest feeling.

Yet the Enlightenment did not advocate an easy, superficial reconciliation between emotion and rationality, desire and self-control. The tension between them pervades their thought and gives it the touch of tragic resignation that is so often overlooked. For—and I know that this characterization seems least credible of all—the *philosophes* professed a tragic humanism. The word humanism is rich in overtones, but the *philosophes* could claim to be humanists in all senses of that word: they believed in the cultivation of the classics, they were active in humanitarian causes, and in the widest philosophical sense, they placed man in the center of their moral universe. Yet, this humanism was also tragic. The *philosophes* were poignantly conscious of the limitations of human effort, the brevity of human life, the pervasiveness of human suffering, men's disappointed hopes, wasted lives, and undeserved misfortunes. Hence their reformist writings are a mixture of activism and acceptance: man must cultivate his garden. (pp. 286-90)

> *Peter Gay, in his* The Party of Humanity: Essays in the French Enlightenment, *Alfred A. Knopf, 1964, 290 p.*

FURTHER READING

Barber, W. H.; Brumfitt, J. H.; Leigh, R. A.; Shackleton, R.; and Taylor, S. S. B., eds. *The Age of Enlightenment: Studies Presented to Theodore Besterman.* Edinburgh: Oliver and Boyd, 1967, 468 p.
Collection of essays detailing several aspects of the Enlightenment.

Bredvold, Louis I. *The Brave New World of the Enlightenment.* Ann Arbor: University of Michigan Press, 1961, 164 p.
Examines Enlightenment conceptions of natural law and nature and their social relevance.

Brown, S. C., ed. *Philosophers of the Enlightenment.* Royal Institute of Philosophy Lectures, Vol. XII. Atlantic Highlands, N.J.: Humanities Press, 1979, 265 p.
Essay collection offering interdisciplinary perspectives on eighteenth-century European philosophy.

Brumfitt, J. H. *The French Enlightenment.* London: Macmillan Press, 1972, 176 p.
General survey of the Enlightenment. Includes historical and social background and offers commentary on the thought of major figures of the period.

Chambers, Whittaker. "The Age of Enlightenment." In his *Ghosts on the Roof: Selected Journalism of Whittaker Chambers, 1931-1959,* edited by Terry Teachout, pp. 212-22. Washington, D.C.: Regnery Gateway, 1989.
Sketches the vicissitudes of culture and the human spirit during the Enlightenment.

Coleman, Patrick. "Writing the Political." In *A New History of French Literature,* edited by Denis Hollier, pp. 496-500. Cambridge: Harvard University Press, 1989.
Discusses the main targets of political writing in the French Enlightenment: "abuse of authority based on sectarian prejudice and intellectual complacency."

Crocker, Lester G. *An Age of Crisis: Man and World in Eighteenth Century French Thought.* Baltimore: Johns Hopkins Press, 1959, 496 p.
Studies the scientific and philosophic revolutions of the eighteenth century, focusing on human nature and motivation and the psychological conditions of ethical theory.

——. *Nature and Culture: Ethical Thought in the French Enlightenment.* Baltimore: Johns Hopkins Press, 1963, 540 p.
Surveys eighteenth-century commentary on the ethical questions of the "origin of moral judgments" and the "object of moral approbation."

Frankel, Charles. *The Faith of Reason: The Idea of Progress in the French Enlightenment.* New York: Octagon Books, 1969, 165 p.
Discusses the relationship of science to society and morals in eighteenth-century France, noting its consequences in concepts of progress.

Gay, Peter. *The Enlightenment: An Interpretation,* Vol. I: *The Rise of Modern Paganism.* New York: Alfred A. Knopf, 1966, 555 p.
Treats the philosophes' "rebellion against their Christian world and their appeal to classical pagan thought."

——. *The Enlightenment: An Interpretation,* Vol. II: *The Science of Freedom.* New York: Alfred A. Knopf, 1969, 705 p.
Analyzes the philosophes' social environment and agenda, including their views on progress, science, art, society, and politics.

Goodman, Dena. *Criticism in Action: Enlightenment Experiments in Political Writing.* Ithaca: Cornell University Press, 1989, 244 p.
Explores the question of "how writers might change the world through the writing of texts," focusing on Montesquieu's *Lettres persanes,* Rousseau's *Discours sur l'inegalite,* and Diderot's *Supplement au Voyage de Bougainville.*

Gossman, Lionel. *French Society and Culture: Background*

for 18th Century Literature. Englewood Cliffs, N.J.: Prentice-Hall, 1972, 149 p.
> Structuralist interpretation of the Enlightenment, offering an "image of the society in and for which the literature of eighteenth century France was produced."

Green, F. C. *Minuet: A Critical Survey of French and English Literary Ideas in the Eighteenth Century.* New York: E. P. Dutton & Co., 1935, 489 p.
> Explores literary conventions of the eighteenth century. Includes critical appendices on specific works of the period.

Grimsley, Ronald. *From Montesquieu to Laclos: Studies of the French Enlightenment.* Geneva: Librairie Droz, 1974, 159 p.
> Collection of essays covering various philosophes' treatments of the question of human nature.

Hampson, Norman. *The Enlightenment.* Harmondsworth, England: Penguin Books, 1968, 304 p.
> Examines attitudes and ideas of the French Enlightenment.

Havens, George Remington. *The Age of Ideas: From Reaction to Revolution in Eighteenth-Century France.* New York: Henry Holt and Co., 1955, 474 p.
> Proposes to "tell the story of [eighteenth-century French] ideas in terms of the varied and colorful men who gave them expression."

Kleinbaum, Abby R. "Women in the Age of Light." In *Becoming Visible: Women in European History,* edited by Renate Bridenthal and Claudia Koonz, pp. 217-35. Boston: Houghton Mifflin Co., 1977.
> Surveys Enlightenment attitudes towards women in society.

La Fontainerie, F. de. *French Liberalism and Education in the Eighteenth Century: The Writings of La Chalotais, Turgot. Diderot, and Condorcet on National Education.* Edited and translated by F. de la Fontainerie. New York: McGraw-Hill Book Co., 1932, 385 p.
> Collection of the educational writings of Louis René La Chalotais, Anne Robert Jacques Turgot, Denis Diderot, and Jean Antoine Nicholas Condorcet, with introductory commentaries by the editor.

Lough, John. *An Introduction to Eighteenth Century France.* New York: Longmans, Green and Co., 1960, 349 p.
> Sketches the economic, social, and political history of eighteenth-century France. Includes commentary on the principal literary issues of the period.

Nicolson, Harold. *The Age of Reason: The Eighteenth Century.* Garden City, N. Y.: Doubleday & Co., 1961, 433 p.
> Examines, through biographical sketches of prominent individuals, the transition from scepticism to sensibility in eighteenth-century European thought.

Nitze, William A., and Dargan, E. Preston. "The Eighteenth Century: History and Society." In their *A History of French Literature: From the Earliest Times to the Present,* pp. 361-72. New York: Henry Holt and Co., 1922.
> Provides general background on the historical and social features of the ancien régime, including detailed examination of the salons.

Palmer, Robert Roswell. *Catholics and Unbelievers in Eighteenth Century France.* Princeton: Princeton University Press, 1939, 236 p.
> Analyzes eighteenth-century Jesuit and Jansenist thought in France.

Palmer, Robert Roswell, and Colton, Joel. "The Age of Enlightenment." In their *A History of the Modern World,* pp. 295-340. New York: Alfred A. Knopf, 1978.
> Discusses the influence of the French Enlightenment upon other European nations, noting as well the role it assumed in the American Revolution.

Payne, Harry C. *The Philosphes and the People.* New Haven: Yale University Press, 1976, 214 p.
> Investigates the "legend" of the French philosophes "who believed in the perfectibility and reasonableness of Man but who scorned and despised the masses."

Rex, Walter E. *The Attraction of the Contrary: Essays on the Literature of the French Enlightenment.* Cambridge: Cambridge University Press, 1987, 251 p.
> Analyzes the "transformation from latency to manifestation, and from symbol to reality," of eighteenth-century French literature.

Sampson, Ronald Victor. *Progress in the Age of Reason: The Seventeenth Century to the Present Day.* London: Heinemann, 1956, 259 p.
> Examines the Enlightenment concept of progress.

Smith, Preserved. "The Propaganda of the Enlightenment." In his *A History of Modern Culture,* Vol. II: *The Enlightenment: 1687-1776,* pp 355-401. New York: Henry Holt and Co., 1934.
> Examines the collective influence of the philosophes both inside and outside France.

Spencer, Samia I., ed. *French Women and the Age of Enlightenment.* Bloomington: Indiana University Press, 1984, 429 p.
> Anthology of essays focusing on the political, social, cultural, and scientific accomplishments of eighteenth-century French women.

Talmon, Jacob Leib. *The Rise of Totalitarian Democracy.* Boston: Beacon Press, 1952, 366 p.
> Explores the role of Enlightenment thought in the development of modern totalitarianism.

Toepfer, Karl. "Orgy Salon: Aristocracy and Pornographic Theatre in Pre-Revolutionary Paris." *Performing Arts Journal* XII, No. 2: 110-36.
> Examines the motives and social attitudes that produced the "clandestine" theatre subculture of eighteenth-century Paris.

Vyverberg, Henry. *Human Nature, Cultural Diversity, and the French Enlightenment.* New York: Oxford University Press, 1989, 223 p.
> Treats the French philosophes' conceptions of human nature and the diversity of history and cultures by reconsidering their "presumed complete blindness" to the former and their "consequent utter failure to understand" the latter.

Wade, Ira O. *The Structure and Form of the French Enlightenment,* Vol. I: *Esprit Philosophique.* Princeton: Princeton University Press, 1977, 690 p.
> Identifies and discusses the "ideas and movements which shaped the Enlightenment's intellectual destiny."

——. *The Structure and Form of the French Enlightenment,* Vol. II: *Esprit Revolutionnaire.* Princeton: Princeton University Press, 1977, 456 p.
> Considers the "organic unity" of the Enlightenment, focusing on the evolution of an "esprit revolutionnaire" among its leading personalities.

Paul Henri Thiry, Baron d'Holbach

1723-1789

(Born Paul Heinrich Dietrich; also wrote under the pseudonyms Nicolas Boulanger, John Trenchard, An Epicurean of Sceaux, Cesar Chesneau Dumarsais, and J. B. Mirabeau) French encyclopedist, philosopher, and essayist.

An eminent eighteenth-century proponent of atheism and materialism, d'Holbach was also a generous friend and benefactor of some of the most famous men of his day. Denis Diderot was an intimate acquaintance, and such men as David Garrick, Jean-Jacques Rousseau, and Benjamin Franklin were sometimes guests at d'Holbach's Thursday and Sunday philosophical dinners. D'Holbach's thought was not original, however; skepticism of religion and its beliefs existed long before the baron wrote on the subject. Nevertheless, considering the probable persecution he faced if discovered, d'Holbach's perseverence in publishing his works is recognized as a daring novelty that made him one of the most important antireligious and political propagandists of the Enlightenment.

There is much conflicting information regarding the early life of d'Holbach. He was born in 1723 in Edesheim in the Palatinate, and little is known of his boyhood. His father took twelve-year old Paul Heinrich to Paris to live with an ennobled and wealthy uncle, Franciscus Adam d'Holbach. This afforded the boy social and educational opportunities not available to him in the Palatinate. Young Dietrich adopted Paris as his home and d'Holbach as his new surname. He attended the University of Leiden, where he studied English empiricist philosophy and natural sciences such as metallurgy and mineralogy. He also cultivated a life-long friendship with the future British political reformer John Wilkes. Upon the death of Franciscus in 1753, d'Holbach inherited the title of baron and much of the family fortune. In 1753, he married Basile Genevieve Suzanne d'Aine, daughter of a wealthy landowner outside Paris, and incidentally his second cousin. Following the death of Madame d'Holbach in August 1754, the baron received a special dispensation from the pope to marry his deceased wife's sister, Charlotte Suzanne d'Aine, in 1755. Dividing their time between their Paris home in the rue Royale and their country estate, Grandval, the two lived together happily for the rest of their lives and raised several children.

D'Holbach was a wealthy and exceptionally unselfish man, and he cultivated an extreme generosity toward those less fortunate than himself. The annual income from an estate he owned in Westphalia totalled 60,000 livres, and the baron used this money to support and encourage writers and artists who showed promise. When the French Jesuits began to be persecuted in earnest, the atheist d'Holbach opened Grandval to them, believing that such repression was abhorrent. Repayment of d'Holbach's loans was neither demanded nor expected. According to William H. Wickwar, the baron's philanthropy was heartfelt. "Don't say anything about this to anybody," d'Holbach asked of a poor family in the Vosges after rescuing them from devastation. "Any one would say that I

am trying to play the rich benefactor and the good-natured philosopher. I am neither benefactor nor philosopher, but just a human being, and my charities are the pleasantest expense I have on these journeys."

Perhaps the best-known display of d'Holbach's wealth and genrosity is seen in his willingness to house and feed friends for prolonged periods of time. For nearly half a century, d'Holbach hosted dinners on Thursdays and Sundays for a large group of friends. The character of the group gradually transformed into what was dubbed "the café of Europe." While the Sunday dinners were more socially oriented, Thursday became "the day of the synagogue," and philosophizing and intellectual entertainment ruled the day. Some of the most important figures of the eighteenth century were guests at these meetings: Wilkes, Laurence Sterne, Garrick, Horace Walpole, Claude Adrien Helvétius, and David Hume. The more permanent inhabitants of the rue Royale and Grandval included Diderot, Friedrich Melchior von Grimm, Rousseau (until his well-publicized defection from the "coterie holbachique—the group surrounding d'Holbach), and Jean d'Alembert. It was at one of these meals (or so Diderot claimed) that Hume stated that he had never met an atheist. D'Holbach replied: "Then you have been unlucky; here you are at table with seventeen." Many of the regular guests were contributors to Diderot's *Encyclopédie*. The baron himself began writing for the *Encyclopédie* in the early 1750s. His articles were primarily on scientific matters—metallurgy, mineralogy, chemistry, and physics—though he also wrote on travel and political and linguistic issues. Eventually, well over 350 entries (and possibly more than 400) were attributed to d'Holbach.

During the last decade of his life, d'Holbach did little writing. Suffering from gout, he fulfilled his social obligations by sending his oldest son on a grand tour and later purchasing him a commission in the army. Most of his close friends were dead, among them Helvétius and Diderot. The philosophy of the day was moving away from atheism and materialism and towards faith and optimism, concepts the baron still did not accept. On 21 January 1789, d'Holbach died at his home in Paris.

While d'Holbach translated many scientific papers and works of English deism into French, he is not readily remembered for these efforts. It is chiefly for his atheistic and materialistic works that the baron is recognized. Most of these polemical pieces were produced between 1760 and 1770. Following the death of Nicolas Boulanger in 1759, d'Holbach acted as his friend's literary executor and published Boulanger's *Recherches sur l'origine du despotisme oriental* in 1761. This gave the baron the idea of publishing his own works under the names of recently deceased men of letters in order to avoid governmental persecution. It was in this way that his first major piece, *Christianisme dévoilé* (*Christianity Unveiled*), was released in 1761 under Boulanger's name. In like fashion, his 1768 *Contagion sacrée* was attributed to John Trenchard, his 1768 *Lettres à Eugénie* (*Letters to Eugenia*) to an Epicurean of Sceaux, and his 1769 *Essai sur les préjugés* to Cesar Chesneau Dumarsais. His most famous work, the 1770 *Système de la Nature* (*The System of Nature*), was put down as the work of J. B. Mirabeau.

The decade of 1760-1770 was remarkable for the sheer volume of antireligious works published in French, a great many of which were produced either by d'Holbach and his friends or by Voltaire. As Diderot wrote: "It is raining bombs on the house of the Lord. I go in fear and trembling lest one of these terrible bombers gets into difficulties." Virgil Topazio claimed: "[The] concerted drive by d'Holbach . . . in the printing, publishing and dissemination of anti-religious pamphlets and books coincided with Voltaire's great propaganda effort that emanated from Ferney, once this master of light mockery, satire, and irony realized the uselessness of attempting to compromise with so uncompromising a monster as superstition. The full force of Voltaire's rapier thrusts at religion were often blunted, however, by his reiterated affirmation of a belief in a deistic God. D'Holbach's attacks, on the other hand, although they produced nothing new, produced a more shocking effect because of the rigid absoluteness with which he presented his polemical views."

D'Holbach believed that religion, with its ultimate goal of heaven, demeans human life. He held that this is especially true of Christianity. According to the baron, one should strive to live a moral life in order to achieve happiness and security on earth, acting out of personal choice rather than basing actions on clerical superstitions about heaven, purgatory, and the fear of hell. According to d'Holbach, it is best to choose to live morally by rationally determining that to do so will result in peace and fulfillment. This is preferable to acting out of fear of divine retribution, which may cause resentment and anger. Moreover, d'Holbach believed that when the clergy emphasizes the impossibility of living up to God's expectations, people resign themselves to defeatist, mediocre attitudes and efforts. He saw the government and the church as two powers fighting for control of society's morals. Government, he perceived, theoretically strove to pull diverse groups of people together to work for the common good, while the Church claimed to want her followers to love one another yet promoted separation of culturally disparate people by claiming superiority over other religious groups. This is one of the main themes of d'Holbach's writings: that religion is harmful to society.

Although widely read, d'Holbach's works were harshly criticized due to their extreme claims. The clergy predictably denounced the writings as heretical, thereby convincing members of the Parlement that the works should be banned. Many of them were therefore outlawed or burned. Objective critical review at the time of their publication was not possible in the learned journals; the works were viewed as evil and as a threat to the church and could not therefore be studied as pieces of literature. If the identity of the author had been known at the time, severe punishment might have been meted out, with execution a real possibility. However, d'Holbach's identity remained a secret until his death, when it was safe to reveal his part in the "bombings on the house of the Lord." Later criticism focused on d'Holbach's theories on atheism and political ethics, his place as the head of a leading eighteenth-century intellectual circle, and possible influences upon his writings by other scholars of the day.

Baron d'Holbach was one of the most important French authors of the eighteenth century. His actions were not spurred by hopes of recognition or fame but by a desire to change the world into a happier, more rational place. In this world, he hoped, enlightened people would work to help others help themselves rather than coerce them with fear of eternal punishment or, even worse, turn them against one another. D'Holbach was a generous and influential man; perhaps Maurice Cranston best summarized his importance and the diversity of his roles: "Of all the leading philosophers of the French Enlightenment, Baron d'Holbach remains the least well known. . . . Yet his name is familiar enough; in almost every history of the intellectual life of France Holbach is mentioned, either as the most systematic eighteenth-century exponent of materialism, or as the leader of intellectual society, the richest of the Encyclopedists, the one in whose house the others met and dined, the host to foreign philosophers on their visits to Paris, and the benefactor of any friend who found himself in need."

PRINCIPAL WORKS

*Le Christianisme dévoilé, ou Examen des principes et des effets de la religion chrétienne, par feu M. Boulanger (prose) 1761
  [*Christianity Unveiled; being an examination of the principles and effects of the Christian Religion, from the*

French of Boulanger, Author of Researches into the Origin of Oriental Despotism, 1795]

La Contagion sacrée, ou Histoire naturelle de la superstition, ouvrage traduit de l'anglais de Jean Trenchard (prose) 1768; revised edition, 1797

Lettres à Eugénia, ou Préservatif contre les préjugés (letters) 1768

[*Letters to Eugenia on the absurd, contradictory and demoralizing Dogmas and Mysteries of the Christian Religion,* 1819]

Lettres philosophiques, sur l'origine des Préjugés, du Dogme de l'Immortalité de l'Ame, de l'Idolatrie et de la Superstition; sur le Système de Spinosa et sur l'origine du mouvement dans la matière. (letters) 1768

Théologie portative, ou Dictionnaire Abrégé de la Religion Chrétienne. (prose) 1768; revised edition, 1776

Essai sur les préjugés, ou, De l'influence des opinions sur les moeurs et sur le bonheur des hommes. Ouvrage contenant l'apologie de la philosphie par Mr. D. M. (essay) 1770

Histoire critique de Jésus-Christ, ou Analyse raisonné des Evangiles. Ecce Homo (prose) 1770

[*Ecce Homo! or, A Critical Inquiry into the History of Jesus of Nazareth: Being a Rational Analysis of the Gospels,* 1827]

L'Esprit du Judaïsme, ou Examen raisonné de la Loi de Moyse, et de son influence sur la Religion Chrétienne (prose) 1770

Système de la Nature, our Des Loix du Monde Physique et du Monde Moral. (prose) 1770; revised editions, 1780, 1781

[*The System of Nature* 1797]

†*Le Bon-sens ou idées naturelles opposées aux idées surnaturelles, par l'auteur du 'Système de la Nature'* (prose) 1772

[*Common Sense; or, Natural ideas opposed to supernatural,* 1795]

La politique naturelle, ou, Discours sur les vrais principes du Governement. (prose) 1773

Système Social, ou principes naturels de la moral et de la politique, avec un examen de l'influence du gouvernement sur les moeurs (prose) 1773

Ethocratie ou le gouvernement fondé sur la morale (prose) 1776

La Morale universelle, ou les Devoirs de l'homme fondés sur la nature (prose) 1776

*The publication date of this work is disputed.

†This is an abridged popular edition of *The System of Nature.*

Paul Henri Thiry, Baron d'Holbach (essay date 1770?)

[*In the following excerpt from the introduction to his* Histoire critique de Jesus-Christ *(1770?), d'Holbach prophesies that the work will be badly received and misunderstood and defends himself against detractors*].

The author does himself the justice to believe, that he has written enough [in *Ecce Homo! or, A Critical Inquiry into the History of Jesus of Nazareth; Being a Rational Analysis of the Gospels*] to be attacked by a host of writers,

obliged, by situation to repel his blows, and to defend, right or wrong, a cause wherein they are so deeply interested. He calculates that, on his death, his book will be caluminated, as well as his reputation, and his arguments misrepresented, or multilated. He expects to be treated as impious—a blasphemer—an atheist, and to be loaded with all the epithets which the pious are in use to lavish on those who disquiet them. He will not, however, sleep the less tranquil for that; but as his sleep may prevent him from replying, he thinks it his duty to inform his antagonists before hand, that *injuries are not reasons.* He does more—he bequeaths them charitable advice, to which the defenders of religion do not usually pay sufficient attention. They are then apprised, that if, in their learned refutations, they do not resolve completely *all* the objections brought against them, they will have done nothing for their cause. The defenders of a religion, in which it is affirmed that every thing is divinely inspired, are bound not to leave a single argument behind, and ought to be convinced that answering to an argument is not always refuting it.

> *Paul Henri Thiry, Baron d'Holbach, in his* Ecce Homo! or A Critical Inquiry into the History of Jesus of Nazareth, *revised edition, 1827. Reprint by Gordon Press, 1977, 212 p.*

William H. Wickwar (lecture date 1928-29)

[*In the following excerpt, Wickwar discusses d'Holbach's theories on materialism, atheism, and political ethics*].

Had Helvétius any use for the Christian religion? Was he a partisan of enlightened despotism, or of Parliamentarism? Had he any use for other social groupings in between the individual and the State? Did he think that society was held together simply by laws and legislation? To questions such as these his books return no straightforward answer.

Far different was the dogmatism of Holbach. He began by developing the distinction drawn by Helvétius between religious and civic conceptions of morality. He opened his first book with the axiom: "A reasonable being ought to set before himself, in all his actions, his own happiness and that of his fellows." And he proceeded to judge and condemn all the religions of the world because they did not contribute appreciably to human happiness. Of course, he admitted that religion can in some cases minister to the satisfaction of this or that individual; but what he maintained was that this satisfaction was either useless or harmful to society. Instead of preaching the duties of man to man as something dictated by nature and by common sense, it made them part of the duties of man to God, with the result that many a man on becoming a disbeliever became at the same time a libertine. The most important duties of man to God consisted in prayer and praise, fasts and feasts, confession and communion—all of them socially useless. Add to these the ceremonies that accompany all the turning-points of life—baptism, marriage, extreme unction, and burial—and it was clear that in Christianity everything, sins included, contributed to the existence and turned to the profit of the priesthood. There thus existed in Christian countries two powers, miscalled the spiritual and the temporal, and in the long run priestcraft always proved stronger than statecraft. Scriptures were contradictory, tradition was doubtful, religious disputes were for ever arising, and, instead of getting on with their proper work, governments felt themselves bound to intervene in these frivolous discussions and to decide which opinions and which practices were most in accordance with the Divine Will. Rulers were thus able to gain to their side the spiritual power, and if they attended well enough to divine service they were able to save themselves the trouble of attending to the social services by which alone their existence was morally justified. They became intolerant, because how could they tolerate what they believed to be an abomination in the eyes of God? They would not allow their subjects to serve their country as soldiers or magistrates unless they could satisfy some test of orthodoxy, and they tried to force them all into an artificial unity of belief. The result was always disunion: the Habsburgs had failed to crush the Lutherans of Germany, and the Dutch Calvinists had shaken off their rule; one of the Stuarts had lost his head for trying to force his subjects into conformity with the Church of England; his son had lost his throne for trying to make them conform to the Church of Rome; and the French Huguenots had been driven into the hands of the enemies of France. But of course kings did not always obey the dictates of religion, and they sometimes became obstacles in the way of their people's salvation; so the Jesuits had preached tyrannicide, and Henry IV, the best of French kings, had been murdered. Thus government was reduced to a nullity, while religion was like an epidemic rampant. Compare the civil commotion it has caused with the good conduct it has inspired in men who would have been good in any case, and it was obvious to Holbach that the ill it has done is vast as the ocean, and the good as small as a drop of water.

This influence of religion on human society was no miracle; it could easily be explained by the two chief principles of contemporary psychology. According to one principle—the principle of sensation and association—the beliefs that govern human conduct are not innate ideas implanted in us by God or nature, but are, on the contrary, the product of education, confirmed by habit; governments can reform education and transform the habits of people, but they are not likely to do so, as rulers are themselves the victims of an education that prevents them from thinking for themselves, gives them no clear idea of their duties, and makes them attach supreme importance to things that do not matter. The other principle—the principle of utility—was that man seeks always his own happiness, and always tries to avoid misfortune; finding himself subject to the forces of nature, he has pictured nature as a divinity liable to human emotions, and has tried to appease it and gain its goodwill by human means; but modern science gives men other ideas of nature and suggests other means of attaining happiness.

The universe consists of matter and movement, the different forms of matter being essentially different forms of movement. Everything that exists is composed of smaller units of matter, which tend constantly to fall apart and regroup themselves; but, for a while at least, they tend also to hang together, and science had recently given names to this tendency. In the physical world it was gravitation, molecular attraction, *vis inertiæ*. In the moral world, in the human body, it was called self-preservation or interest, and it was no doubt this same electromagnetic tendency that accounted for sexual attraction and friendship, and for the union of individuals in families and states.

Man is a material being who acts according to ineluctable laws; but, like every other material being, he has a way of acting that is all his own. What is more, men differ also among themselves, and this brings us to a second explanation of society; for diversity produces a natural division of labour, and puts us in a position of mutual dependence. Diversity means inequality; men are born unequal; society is founded on inequality; and Rousseau and Helvétius were both wrong. The elements on which this all-important inequality depends are essentially physiological; men differ in their bodily makeup, in their humours, in their energy, in the functioning of their brains and their nerves; and these natural differences are enhanced by differences of environment, food, drink, and clothing. Herein lies the possibility of progress—that is, of the material improvement of the human race. It is for medical science to show the way to bodily well-being; it is for kings and rulers to become the doctors of their people. The soul of man is a function of his body; look after his body, and *ipso facto* his *moral* will improve.

There is also, according to Holbach, a certain way of acting that distinguishes mankind as a whole from other animals or machines. Thanks to the modifications effected in our brains by the movement of our nerves we know by experience that like causes produce like effects; and man is a reasonable animal in so far as he thinks and acts in accordance with this experience, in seeking to live and to live happily. Ethics and politics are sciences like any others; they are founded on the experience that man cannot live alone, that he has need of other people, and that others have need of him. It is in his interest to be sociable. Nature thus imposes on him many duties, many social obligations; he is naturally bound by a social contract, pact, or covenant. But it often happens that his experience is not great enough, or that his reason works too slowly for him to act in a way that is really and durably useful to his fellows. This is where political science comes in; it must enlighten men on their true interests, and make them work together for the good of the social whole; in other words, the pact must be enforced by the sanctions of the law. A government is justified in making the law only in so far as it interprets the general will. Sovereigns are the representatives and servants of the people, and they reign only on condition that they facilitate and do not thwart the natural desire to live and be happy. The people have the right to change the form of government, and rulers who do more harm than good lose the right to be obeyed. The law ought to restrain the passions of the sovereign at the same time as those of the people; it ought to limit and define his powers; it ought to be, according to Montesquieu's definition, the embodiment of reason.

> It ought to aim at the general interest of society—that is to say, it ought to assure to the greatest number of citizens the advantages for which they are leagued together in society. These advantages are liberty, property, and security. Liberty means the possibility of doing for one's own happiness everything that does not militate against the happiness of one's fellows; for, in entering into a league, each individual has agreed not to exercise the part of his own natural freedom that might be prejudicial to that of others. Property means the possibility of enjoying the advantages which labour has procured to each member of society. Security means the certainty of being protected by the laws in the enjoy-

ment of one's person and of one's property in so far as one observes faithfully one's engagements with society.

Nothing could show more clearly the source of Holbach's inspiration. Locke and the English Whigs were his masters in social theory, just as surely as Hobbes was his master in psychology. He rejected Rousseau's vision of direct democracy, sanctified intolerance, and the sovereignty of the people. He rejected Rousseau's hypothesis that all men are born good, as surely as he rejected the Pauline hypothesis that all men are born wicked. He reverted to his friend Seneca's common-sense point of view, that nature has made man neither good nor bad. He is simply an animal or a machine—there is no difference—because, as Descartes said, an animal is a machine—an animal or a machine driven in the pursuit of happiness by various passions which are all equally natural. The justification of virtue is not that it is implanted in us all by nature, or that it is given to the elect among us by divine grace, but that experience shows all reasonable men that it is really and permanently useful to mankind.

This distinction made clear, Holbach shows himself as the most moral man under the sun. Far be it from him to say with Mandeville that vice is sometimes virtue, or with Helvétius that there is no such thing as vice for the loyal servant of the State. Virtue is always virtue, and vice vice. The only thing is that vice is perfectly natural, and virtue useless or suicidal, if society is so corrupt that virtue goes unhonoured and unrewarded, while vice leads to comparative happiness and well-being. Now that was the very thing that had happened, because governments did not do their duty. The Courts were the centres of the corruption of the peoples; they encouraged man's passion for dangerous futilities, and attached dishonour to useful occupations; they were deaf to the voice of experience, and prejudiced against the use of the reason; they regarded truth as dangerous, and falsehood and error as necessary to man's welfare both here and hereafter. In short, they discouraged virtue and encouraged vice. On moral grounds Holbach therefore launched out into as severe a criticism of the State as of the Church.

Religion, he contended, was worse than useless, because primitive man had fallen in the fundamental error of personifying the forces of nature. Similarly governments had become a menace to moral and material well-being because they had failed to put limits on the passion for wealth, and because this passion was becoming increasingly dangerous with the rapid exploration and exploitation of the East and West Indies, or, as we should now say, with the development of commercial capitalism.

The evil was not beyond remedy, if only man looked the facts in the face. One fundamental fact, brought home to eighteenth-century thinkers by Turgot and the French 'rural philosophers,' and enhanced in importance by the impossibility of foreseeing the imminence of the Industrial Revolution, was that the land was the material foundation of all society. Another fact, and a momentous one in the history of European thought—one which Locke, with his half-blind insight, was the first to enunciate—was that in the original state of nature property was justified in so far as it was the fruit of labour, and *only* to that extent.

Labour was the law of life, the chief of our duties towards our fellows, and the only way of justifying our existence. The work of all for the well-being of all was the essence of the social contract. But work was a painful duty from which men naturally shrank; they tried to appropriate to themselves the fruit of the labour of others; property was thus incessantly violated; and the unity of society and all social justice were destroyed by the struggle between a minority of rich 'never-sweats' and the immense majority of workers. Differences of wealth and rank would be justified if they were proportioned to differences in social usefulness; but hereditary distinctions were a pernicious abuse, an encouragement to idleness.

Justice is the supreme virtue, and is, like utility, a balance in which all social institutions should be weighed. It is a disposition to maintain men in the enjoyment of their rights, and to do for them all that we would that they should do for us. The rights of man consist in such use of liberty as is in conformity with justice; and, as liberty means freedom to work out our own happiness and well-being, a just State will allow the utmost possible liberty to its members. It will not tax their property without their own consent. It will not concern itself with their beliefs. It will leave them free to write what they like about the government, since government exists only for their good. The juster the government, the freer the people, the stronger the country. The nation would be happy, for the majority of the people would be able to satisfy their needs without overwork, and enlightened self-interest would encourage their public spirit and patriotism.

A man is free when he obeys just laws. He is a slave when he obeys the will or the whim of another man. Judged by this standard, the kings of France are debonair despots, and the people are slaves, even though their chains are gilded. Nothing but the consent of the people can make them legitimate sovereigns, and such consent is given only in return for services rendered—in return for the fulfilment of the fundamental laws of the constitution, or, if such laws have never been framed, of the title-deeds which nature has engraved for ever in the heart of man. The nation has the right and the power to rise against its despots, to limit their powers, and, if need be, to dethrone them. But this resistance must come from the nation, and not from odd individuals; private citizens have the right to leave the country as *émigrés,* but not to plunge the country into disorder and oppose passion to passion, so that the last state is worse than the first. A revolution might be perfectly justified and exceedingly useful, but only if it was carried out as constitutionally as possible, with perfect cool-headedness, and under the guidance of virtuous and enlightened leaders.

In a well-governed country the government would devote itself, above all, to the condition of the common people—of the greatest number—for it is on *their* labour that society depends. It would allow them to enjoy the fruit of their labour. It would educate them, so as to prevent them from becoming the playthings of ambition and fanaticism. It would not expect them to rule themselves, but would allow them to make their wishes known by the voice of their representatives; for every class of useful citizens ought to be able to make itself heard. *How,* exactly? Holbach is not clear. He recognises the advantages of mixed monarchy; but he recognises also the corruption of English Parliamentarism. France too has had her *parlements,* until 1770, and Holbach is less averse from them than his friend Turgot; for in these "intermediary bodies," as Montesquieu had called them, the people had representatives of a kind, non-elected it was true, but none the less popular, as they alone stood between the people and the menace of Oriental despotism. It would be under the leadership of such organs as these that the people would be justified in forcing their will on the government.

The internal constitution of a country is only one of the conditions on which its happiness depends. Its attitude towards foreign countries is another. Experience shows that the reasonable way of looking at foreign relations is to regard all the nations as members of "the great world-society," seeking their own well-being, but respecting the interests of each other at the same time. In fact, they might well codify their mutual obligations, and submit their disputes to a world-court. Instead of that, they live in a so-called state of nature, which is thoroughly unnatural because it is unsocial, unjust, and worse than useless. Governments neglect their own people in order to give all their attention to foreign affairs; they oppress their own people in order to oppress their neighbours and increase the number of their misruled subjects. In such a state of anarchy 'good faith' is a suicidal superstition, and an enlightened government often does well to break its word, when that means breaking an unjust treaty that has been forced upon it as the result of an unjust war. For nearly a century all the wars undertaken by Christian countries had been undertaken for the sake of commerce; the national debts accumulated as a result made the burden of taxation as heavy in peace-time as in time of war, while it gave rise to a new class of *rentiers* who lived without doing any useful work; finally, and in France more than in any other country, kings who could not raise revenue by other means farmed out the right to tax their subjects, in return for ready money; the great financiers set the tone for the whole society, and the people set out to imitate them and find a way of getting rich without working. Almost the whole society was thus demoralised. The taste for luxury was spreading. The nation was becoming dependent on a foreign trade in which thousands of useful lives were lost every year. The natives of non-Christian countries were being enslaved. The colonists who went out to the New World were themselves being exploited so unjustly that they would undoubtedly be driven to assert their freedom. And all the time, while the world was becoming a prey to the passion for money-getting, the moral and material welfare of the people was being neglected.

But nature had set limits to commerce, and this passion would destroy itself. Merchant-ridden States like Britain and Holland would go the way of Venice, Carthage, and Tyre, because they were too dependent on foreign countries. The wisest attitude a government could adopt towards commerce would be to leave it severely alone— *laissez-faire*—and above all not to give monopolies to East India Companies. Bitter experience would drive men back to the land. Each country would produce as much as it could. The countries that were most industrious would export the most, and would thus force less industrious countries into dependence on them. Their wealth would increase, and would be spread equitably among the whole working population. By a moderate amount of work it would be possible to satisfy all the real needs of life. France would become an earthly paradise, a paradise of

peasants, like the Italy of Virgil's dreams. Men would no longer regret the size of their families; home life would be a joy to the greatest number; the population would increase, helped by the building of hospitals and the improvement of sanitation; and, when it outgrew the productive power of the homeland, overseas colonisation would be justifiable, the colonists continuing to be citizens of the mother-country and retaining the same rights and the same duties as their fellow-citizens who remained at home.

Holbach was no Condorcet; he did not believe that progress was a straight line that ran from eighteenth-century France to infinity. He knew only too well that the moral world, like the material, is for ever in movement. No social order, just or unjust, could possibly be permanent. Everything that existed was marching steadily towards inevitable dissolution. No nation would ever enjoy perpetual bliss. But that universal tendency would not prevent man, in some countries, and for a while at least, from enjoying a period of well-being—because men have in them a longing for happiness and self-preservation. It was that possibility, sometimes faint, yet always real—for it is rooted in the nature of man—that ought to occupy the thoughts of statesmen and of all thinking citizens and well-wishers of the commonweal.

Holbach was living and writing in a period of great uncertainty. Taught by Montesquieu and by other writers who had lived through the days of Law's bubble, to attach supreme moral importance to the development of luxury, he saw well enough that capitalism had reached one of the turning-points of its development, and he is hardly to blame for the nonrealisation of his prophecy. The main lines of subsequent social evolution may have been necessary and inevitable; but it is easier for us to see the inevitability from our end of the long chain of cause and effect than it was for him at his end to foresee it. Commercial exploitation was making possible the long-drawn-out industrial revolution in which we happen to be living, and this totally new turn given to human progress has made it impossible for any but a simpleton to see the world through Holbach's eyes. It has taken the bottom out of his economic theories, by making the nations of the world inextricably interdependent. It has provided an answer to his religious *impasse,* by creating conditions of life and death in which social preoccupations have inevitably triumphed over religious disputes as the dominant subject-matter of politics.

Holbach is dead, and his works are dead, but they have played their part in the intellectual and constitutional history of Christendom. Lord Shelburne went to Paris, and his librarian, Joseph Priestley, with him. They were welcomed by the Encyclopædists, and on their return to England Priestley, proud to have been told that he was the first intelligent Christian that had been seen in Paris for a long while, did his best to popularise their materialist psychology and ethics, but in as Christianised—or at least as unitarianised—a form as possible. Through this medium their thoughts filtered into English radicalism. But the French originals were not unknown; another *habitué* of Shelburne's house, young Bentham, undoubtedly knew Helvétius's work directly; and when Horne Tooke received presentation copies of Priestley's works he developed the habit of filling the margins with extracts from the far more logical *System of Nature.* It was the *System of Nature,* Helvétius, and Rousseau, who together, and in that order, led Godwin to start on the search for political justice. When Shelley had tried to convince Oxford of the necessity of atheism he set to work to translates that same *System of Nature.* But it was too late; it had already been translated. And an edition published in 1821, at the same time as an English version of Helvétius's *Mind,* by a Radical bookseller who had been imprisoned for the part he played in the agitation of 1819, made Holbach's influence a serious rival to that of Paine, while others of his works, less definitely atheistic in tone, were brought out by Paine's leading disciple—a man who nevertheless enjoyed the support of Place and Bentham and the Mills—Richard Carlile. Thus Holbach, like Helvétius, played his part in the hundred years' struggle of the British Radicals against the dominant conceptions of government and religion.

In France itself the history of sober thought is clouded by the passions and personalities of the war and the Revolution. These men were not forgotten, but their ideas lost their clarity and distinction, and mingled all in a common stream. The Babouvists, in their last desperate attempt to effect a social and not merely a political revolution, were as incapable as Rousseau himself of distinguishing clearly between the communism of Morelly and Mably and the egalitarianism of Helvétius—both were equally revolutionary, and that was all that mattered. One of Holbach's books was reissued in the heat of '93, for the sake of its strict, stern conception of civic virtue; and another, when the Concordat was looming ahead, as a reminder of the dangers of priestcraft, dangers brought home to many a reformer and patriot by the recent religious civil war. After the deist despotism of Robespierre Naigeon republished all the philosophical articles of the *Encyclopædia;* he set Diderot and Helvétius in their place in world-thought, but let the anonymous Holbach fall into oblivion, probably for the sake of his widow and children. A catholic revival followed; but it bore in all its social thinking the marks of the Encyclopædist movement. The first generation tried to justify the Church and the Papacy on the ground of their social utility, an argument that Holbach had met in advance; and the second generation of neo-Catholics, fed on Rousseauism and accepting by implication the arguments of Rousseau's enemies, abandoned the standpoint of St Thomas, set the heart above the head, and gave up the attempt to harmonise their beliefs with the dictates of reason and science. At the same time Saint-Simon was proclaiming the social duties of industrialists; he saw things that the Encyclopædists had lived too soon to see, but they were the masters who taught him the importance of labour, the relations between science and industry, and the co-operative nature of human society.

In Germany, in Masonic and philosophic circles, the first impulse was away from materialist conceptions of life; but in the eighteen-forties Arnold Ruge tried to bring together the new humanism of Feuerbach and Marx and the philosophy of the Encyclopædists; though how far Marx owed his materialist conception of life to Holbach and Helvétius, and his economics to Turgot, is one of the riddles of history. Ideas that had been new and strange in the eighteenth century had become common property in the nineteenth.

Man differs from other animals in the greater complexity

of his social life, and in his greater self-consciousness. Political and social thought is his way of expressing his consciousness of the increasing complication of the conditions of his existence. As the conditions of life change, and as science pushes back the frontiers of knowledge and opens up new unknowns, our social and political ideas must also necessarily change. But through all these changes the thought of the Encyclopædists, Helvétius and Holbach, always retains its significance; for they were the founders of a tradition of which we are heirs; they were the forerunners of all of us who try to envisage social experience in a scientific though not unenthusiastic spirit, and to make our age not of blind passion, but of ordered progress enlightened by reason and experience. (pp. 203-15)

William H. Wickwar, "Helvétius and Holbach," in The Social & Political Ideas of Some Great French Thinkers of the Age of Reason, *edited by F. J. C. Hearnshaw, 1930. Reprint by Dawsons of Pall Mall, 1967, pp. 195-216.*

Virgil W. Topazio   (essay date 1954)

[*Topazio has written extensively on d'Holbach. In the excerpt below, he addresses the issue of Denis Diderot's possible contributions to the baron's religious pieces, concluding that Diderot had very little influence, if any, on these works*].

We are confronted today with a persistent tradition, whose veracity has been less questioned with the passing years, that Diderot not only contributed extensively to the thought and style, but also wrote many of the pages, of D'Holbach's works. (p. 173)

The judgments of critics fall into two general patterns: Diderot's contribution was limited to the influence of his personality and ideas, and to the stylistic changes he suggested after having read D'Holbach's manuscripts; and Diderot not only read and edited the manuscripts, but also inserted many pages and even chapters of his own. In general, the attempt is made, principally on the word of Meister and Bachaumont, to show a far-reaching collaboration especially in the *Système de la nature* of 1770.

D'Holbach's literary production can be conveniently divided into three parts: first, the scientific period, roughly to 1760, during which he translated hundreds of scientific articles from German into French, principally for the *Encyclopédie,* and wrote three articles on the history of religion . . . second, the anti-religious crusade or destructive period, from approximately 1760 to 1770, during which decade his translations of English deistical and polemical literature were interspersed with his own violent attacks on Church and religion: the *Christianisme dévoilé,* the *Théologie portative,* the *Contagion sacrée,* and the *Essai sur les préjugés,* and third, the constructive period, from 1770 to his death, which set forth a positive program, a new moral code in opposition to that of the Church, in the following works: the *Système de la nature,* the *Bon-Sens,* the *Système social,* the *Politique naturelle, Ethocratie,* and the *Morale universelle.*

No problem presents itself with respect to D'Holbach's scientific writings. His superiority in this field, his invaluable contribution to the dissemination of scientific knowledge in France were and still are universally acknowledged. No one seriously contends that Diderot collaborated in the preparation of the some four hundred articles for the *Encyclopédie* or the scientific books, even though some proof does exist that Diderot helped D'Holbach to get some of the latter published.

On the other hand, it is difficult to ascertain whether Diderot had any specific knowledge of the operations of D'Holbach's "fabrique d'écrits impies." From Diderot's own report to Sophie Volland, in a letter of 24 September 1767, we learn that he had read only one of six books in the publication of which D'Holbach figured prominently as editor, translator, or author. Had Diderot been aware of his friend's major role in the publication of these books, he would scarcely have referred to the one he did read as "un assez bon nombre de bonnes plaisanteries noyées dans un beaucoup plus grand nombre de mauvaises."

Grimm's unfavorable reviews in the *Correspondance littéraire* of D'Holbach's publications strengthen our conviction that neither Diderot nor Grimm definitely associated D'Holbach with "la manufacture établie à Amsterdam dans la boutique du libraire Marc-Michel Rey." Grimm, who took the Baron on a three months' tour to distract him after the loss of his first wife, would hardly have knowingly belittled the efforts of so close a friend. (pp. 173-75)

On the other hand, if Diderot had known D'Holbach to be the author or had he collaborated in the *Christianisme dévoilé,* as some propose, it is fairly safe to assume that he would have communicated such knowledge to Grimm, his closest friend, or to his mistress, Sophie Volland. Yet, despite Diderot's avowed intention to keep her posted on everything he did, and Babelon assures us that "Sur le même ton qu'à Sophie Volland, Diderot raconte à Grimm toute sa vie," his letters make no mention of this knowledge. Instead, we find Diderot, as late as July 1767, asking Falconet who, in his opinion, had written the *Dévoilé.*

Two letters to Sophie Volland in the fall of 1760 furnish additional proof that Diderot was not assisting D'Holbach with the preparation of the *Christianisme dévoilé.* The letter of 30 September describes the leisure he enjoyed at Grandval during the months when the Baron was presumably preparing his first original manuscript for publication. About a month later, in the letter of 28 October, Diderot notified Sophie that the Baron chided him for wasting his time working for others. . . . Would D'Holbach have condemned others for monopolizing Diderot's time if he himself had been equally guilty? It does not seem likely. Furthermore, in relating the Glénat incident to Sophie on 19 September 1762, Diderot said: "N'est-ce pas le plus heureux hasard que je n'aie rien écrit de hardi depuis un temps infini!"

As a matter of fact, the very episode of the copyist, Glénat, whom Diderot befriended from 1758 to 1762, reveals ignorance of the Baron's systematic program to undermine religion. Here in brief is what happened. Favorably impressed by Glénat's ability and moved by his poverty, Diderot solicited his friends to employ Glénat as a copyist. One day he sent him to Damilaville, who later reported that the manuscript entrusted to Glénat had mysteriously come into the hands of the police. Much to his dismay, Diderot discovered that Glénat was a spy working for the police. What horrified him, he confided to Sophie, was that

he had been on the verge of sending him to Grimm. Yet in the years during which Diderot was helping Glénat find work as a copyist, D'Holbach wrote among other things the *Christianisme dévoilé.* The possibility existed therefore, if Diderot was really fully cognizant of D'Holbach's literary endeavors, that he might have subjected the Baron to far greater danger than any to which Grimm could have been exposed. Yet Diderot expressed no relief at the thought of the possible danger which D'Holbach had escaped.

D'Holbach's next original manuscript was the *Théologie portative* in 1767. This is the one work Diderot reported having read in the letter of 24 September 1767. But as we recall, in this same letter he listed five other works from D'Holbach's "fabrique d'écrits impies": the *Esprit du clergé;* the *Prêtres démasqués;* the *Militaire philosophe;* the *Imposture sacerdotale;* and the *Doutes sur la religion.* It is difficult to see how Diderot could have either known of D'Holbach's authorship of the *Théologie portative* or cooperated in its writing in view of his professed ignorance of these five other works. What logical reason would have led the Baron to seek Diderot's help in one work and at the same time conceal from him his important part in the publication of the other five?

Yet oddly enough, many critics present three quotations from this letter of 24 September 1767 as the first tangible proof that Diderot was spending considerable time reading D'Holbach's manuscripts. The quotations follow, transcribed from the Babelon edition of the letters (a study of a microfilm copy of the original letters reveals Babelon's reading to be substantially correct): "Je lis ses ouvrages. Je le promène, je le secoue, il va bien . . ."; "Je me hâte d'expédier le reste des manuscrits du Baron pour me mettre à l'ouvrage de Grimm . . ."; and "Tout à travers la besogne du Baron, j'ai clandestinement entamé la mienne . . .".

To assume on the basis of these quotations that Diderot spent a great deal of his time working on D'Holbach's manuscripts is unwarranted inasmuch as Diderot professed unfamiliarity with the Baron's other recent translations and publications. Further justification of the untenability of such an assumption can be found in a letter written to Sophie Volland only four days later (28 Sept. 1767). In this letter Diderot gives a detailed description of how he spent his time at Grandval:

> Un peu de travail le matin, une partie de billiard, ou un peu de causerie au coin du feu en attendant le dîner; un dîner qui ne finit point; et puis des promenades qui m'auroient conduit à Isle et par-delà, si, depuis huit ou neuf jours que je suis ici, elles avoient été mises l'une au bout de l'autre.
>
> (pp. 175-77)

One could argue that even though D'Holbach had excluded Diderot from his anti-religious endeavors up to that time, he then asked his assistance in the preparation of one or more of the following manuscripts: the *Contagion sacrée,* D'Holbach's only original work of 1768; the *Lettres à Eugénie; David, ou l'Histoire de l'homme selon le cœur de Dieu;* the *Examen des prophéties;* and the *Lettres philosophiques.* These in addition to three less significant translations exhaust D'Holbach's efforts for the year 1768. The acceptance of this theory, however, presents some difficulties. All of the above-mentioned publications, with the exception of the *Examen des prophéties,* were published by August. Yet, in a letter of 22 November 1768, Diderot seemed to be as ignorant of the authorship of these as he had been of the preceding publications listed in his letter of 24 September 1767. To argue that Diderot concealed the Baron's and his own share in these manuscripts for security reasons is untenable, for Sophie was certainly to be trusted, and the letters were sent, for the most part, through his very close friend, Damilaville, who was able to frank them with the "cachet du contrôleur général des finances." In 1769, D'Holbach published two original works, the *Esprit du judaïsme* and the *Essai sur les préjugés.* Diderot may have been proofreading these, but this seems unlikely for two reasons. First, neither Grimm nor Diderot ever mentioned them and, secondly, considering the speed with which D'Holbach wrote, it would have been most unusual for him to have been working on these relatively short manuscripts two years before they were published.

Another factor invalidating the claim of collaboration in the anti-religious publications of D'Holbach is Diderot's promise to his brother, Didier-Pierre. After the father's death in 1759, Diderot visited Langres and at that emotionally charged moment effected a reconciliation with his bigoted, intransigent brother, the Canon, by promising not to write anything offensive to the Church. The promise was motivated to a large extent by Diderot's desire to bring greater harmony between his sister, Denise, and his jealous brother.

This uneasy peace between the brothers lasted only until the end of 1760. Years of respectful hostility once more ensued before Diderot learned in 1770 from his sister and Caroillon, his future son-in-law, that another reconciliation had been broached by the brother. In a letter of 24 May 1770 Diderot expressed his happiness at the prospect and stoutly maintained he had kept his word. . . . (pp. 177-78)

Admittedly the genuineness of this highly emotional protestation of innocence, repeated in another letter of 20 August 1770, should be appraised in the light of Diderot's emotional nature and his literary output, which included a number of anti-Catholic articles written for the *Encyclopédie* during the sixties. But though the latter would scarcely have incurred the blessing of the Church, Diderot did not share D'Holbach's monomaniac desire to destroy religion. For example, he was quick to point out to Sophie Volland that his *Rêve de d'Alembert* contained "pas un mot de religion." The fact remains, however, that he compromised with the truth. Yet, granted this distortion of the truth, it nevertheless seems inconceivable that Diderot could have made such inflexible statements to his brother only a short time after having presumably participated in the writing of the *Système de la nature,* a work so destructive of the very idea of God and of the efficacy of religion as a moral force that even some Encyclopedists, including Voltaire and D'Alembert, felt constrained to align themselves against it. To see Diderot capable of such behavior would be not only to negate completely his well-known dislike of broken promises, but also to destroy the universally accepted picture of Diderot as a man of great moral rectitude.

Yet the most telling quotation, taken from the letter to Sophie Volland of 2 November 1769, which reads "tout mon tems au Grandval s'en va à blanchir les chifons salles du Baron," has been and still is repeatedly used to prove that Diderot was at that time proofreading, revising, and, as some assert, adding pages to D'Holbach's *Système de la nature.* More specifically, some critics considered Diderot the author of the concluding "Abrégé du code de la nature," wherein a dogmatic atheism was espoused. Had he been, the letters to his brother would have betrayed a casuistic cleverness most unworthy of the integrity normally associated with Diderot. The necessity in the eighteenth century to cloak oneself with anonymity or pseudonymity in order to escape persecution is universally recognized and condoned today, but Diderot's hiding behind the twofold shield of D'Holbach and Mirabaud simply to deceive his brother presents a moral problem of a different stamp.

With the *Système de la nature,* the most important phase of the collaboration controversy is entered upon. The quotations antedating the letter of 2 November 1769 merely refer to Diderot's reading the works of the Baron. But Diderot's statement, "tout mon tems au Grandval s'en va à blanchir les chifons salles du Baron," does seem to imply something more than a simple reading of what obviously must have been the manuscript of the *Système de la nature.* The best refutation of this generally accepted interpretation, however, can be found in this same letter. For example, Diderot told Sophie: "J'ai donc passé dix jours au Grandval; comme on les y passe: dans la plus grande liberté, et la plus grande chère." And on the next page he said, referring to a proposed return to Grandval: "Je me débarrasserois là d'une multitude de besognes importantes qui me rendroient honneur et profit, et qui me conduiroient jusqu'à la fin de ma carrière." How could Diderot have spent all his time "à blanchir les chifons salles du Baron," when in this letter, as in others, he himself said that he enjoyed complete liberty there? How could he have been tied down by the Baron's selfish demands on his time, when it was at Grandval that he was able to clear up the importunate demands of his other friends and acquaintances?

The final letter of Diderot to be studied was written to Grimm on 10 November 1770; it contains this overworked sentence: "Mais il m'apporte le soir ses chiffons; le matin il vient voir si je m'en suis occupé; nous en causons et d'autres choses." The acceptance of these words at their face value produces certain difficulties. To begin with, the *Système de la nature* had already been published, early in 1770. The next work of D'Holbach was the *Bon-Sens* of 1772; this was nothing more than a condensation of the *Système de la nature.* It is unlikely that the Baron would have needed Diderot's assistance for this task. During the same year, D'Holbach translated Hobbes's *Human Nature, or the Fundamental Elements of Policy.* However, the fact that Diderot called this translation a desecration of Hobbes's sublime work is incontestable proof that he had no hand in the translation.

Next came the *Système social* and the *Politique naturelle* in 1773. Working against the association of the 10 November quotation with these works is Naigeon's statement, "la plupart des ouvrages qu'il a composés ou traduits ne lui ont guères coûté que le temps et la peine de les écrire." Furthermore, just a week before the 10 November 1770 letter, Diderot wrote to Grimm from Grandval: "On épie mes veillées à la diminution de ma bougie, et l'on m'en fait des querelles très-sérieuses." This certainly nullifies the impression that Diderot spent his nights reading and correcting D'Holbach's "scribblings" in order to be in a position to discuss them with the Baron in the morning.

The implausibility of Diderot's having given any time to the preparation of the *Système social* and the *Politique naturelle* becomes more apparent from a study of how Diderot spent his time during the years 1772 and 1773. There is an interruption in the letters to Sophie from December 1770 to 18 June 1773. Fortunately, however, twenty-six letters to Grimm have been preserved, and they are spaced rather conveniently, for our purpose, from March through December of 1772. It is quite evident from these letters that Diderot remained in Paris throughout the year, visiting D'Holbach briefly only once in October along with Morellet, Delormes, and Grimm. Another trip to Grandval had been planned in June in conjunction with the Chevalier de Chastelux, Naigeon, and another unidentified person, but Diderot was indisposed and yielded his place in the carriage to Grimm. His ill health plus the necessary arrangements for the wedding of his only child, Angélique, on 9 September contrived to keep him close to home. After the wedding he had more reason not to separate himself from the new *ménage.* Mme Diderot's terrible disposition and her dislike for the son-in-law kept Diderot in constant fear she would bring disharmony to the new household. Moreover, we learn from Diderot's letter of 14 October that Angélique had a miscarriage which left her dangerously weak. To disturb Diderot's peace of mind even more, Caroillon simultaneously came down with a fever. He was so sick that the excitable Diderot "le tenoit pour mort."

In addition to all these complications, a major event was looming on the horizon. Diderot had, at least as early as 7 October 1772, decided to make the trip to Russia in order to thank Catherine II for the many favors shown him. Consequently, all his affairs in Paris had to be settled before the departure on 10 May 1773. Meister must have been cognizant of these facts. But unfortunately, traditional opinion had already made it difficult for unprejudiced minds and virtually impossible for the biased ones like Meister's to dissociate Diderot from D'Holbach's work. As a result, in spite of the obvious difficulties inherent in the acceptance of an actual Diderot collaboration with the Baron on any works during 1772 and 1773, Meister came forth with this weak generality in defense of the Diderot partisans: "Il a eu beaucoup moins de part au Système social et à la *Morale universelle* . . .".

As for the *Morale universelle,* Diderot's recommendation of it in the *Plan d'une université pour le gouvernement de Russie* does reveal a knowledge of its impending publication in 1776, and his reference to it as "un ouvrage où je suis sûr qu'il y aura d'excellentes choses" leaves little doubt that he must have read it. From this evidence alone, one authority inferred that "sa plume dut bien y laisser quelque trace," and went further astray in concluding that Diderot's mention of this work in the *Plan d'une université* "nous montre que Diderot dut revoir à Amsterdam, chez Rey, les épreuves de la *Morale universelle,* qui parut en effet en 1776." And this, notwithstanding the well-known fact that Diderot returned from the Hague in September 1774. (pp. 178-81)

Having read all of D'Holbach's works in the space of a few weeks, and having reread the *Système de la nature,* the

Système social, and the *Morale universelle* with the question of style in mind, we failed completely to notice any jarring notes, any pages or sections which were not typically D'Holbachian. The sameness of style and the oneness of content, indeed the constant recurrence of the same ideas, sometimes in almost the identical words, make it impossible for anyone who has read a great deal of D'Holbach to mistake his style or ideas. The various books, especially starting with the *Système de la nature,* represent, as Henri Lion so aptly phrased it, "les ailes, les dépendances, de l'édifice principal," the "édifice principal" being the *Système de la nature.* In addition to the logical development of eighteenth-century deistic and materialistic ideas, this "edifice" contains all the themes, social, political, and ethical, which are systematically developed in greater detail in the *Système social,* the *Politique naturelle, Ethocratie,* and the *Morale universelle.*

The methodicalness employed by D'Holbach would have been abhorrent to Diderot; the repetition and monotony discernible throughout would have shocked him, as it shocked Voltaire. Diderot's predilection for discursiveness is well known, but he never would have been guilty of or tolerated the matter-of-fact presentation of ideas and the obvious disregard for stylistic expression which characterized all of D'Holbach's work. If Diderot did spend as much time as is thought working over the *Système de la nature,* why did he not "d'un trait de plume" correct these faults? In criticizing Helvétius' *De l'Esprit,* he implied that one of his genius could have done as much for that work.

Unlike Diderot, D'Holbach laid no claim upon the attention of posterity, either as a philosopher or as a writer. His goal was to propagandize his ideas on religion, government, and ethics, to erect a natural system of "philosophie" by appealing to reason. He had no mind for the "rhythm of a champion's sentences or the turn of his periods." . . . Perhaps he had no style worth polishing, as has been suggested, but we are certain that this realization would not have disturbed him in the least. His books were meant to be the weapons with which to destroy a powerful enemy. He was intent not upon style, but upon the iterative stroke of his battering ram.

Diderot's name is not the only one proposed as a contributor to the style of D'Holbach. The importance of Naigeon has long been recognized. In the opinion of Wickwar, an opinion with which we are more inclined to agree, "Naigeon certainly did more than any other single man to prepare d'Holbach's manuscripts for publication." As great a claim has been made in Suard's behalf. . . . The only thing that has prevented these . . . claims of stylistic contribution from becoming substantial contributions of pages and even chapters is that neither Naigeon nor Suard has attained the literary stature nor commanded the attention of Diderot. Judging D'Holbach's works from their style, one can only conclude that all the "leçons" of Suard and the revisions of Naigeon and Diderot were to no avail. The reading of any two of D'Holbach's works, the *Système de la nature* included, would convince the reader of this fact, as it would convince him that there are no outstanding pages indicative of literary genius.

An additional word about the *Système de la nature,* since the controversy generally revolves around this work. Everyone has agreed that the ideas presented in this "Bible of scientific materialism and dogmatic atheism" were consonant with the philosophy of the Baron, although some have maintained that D'Holbach must have received many of these ideas from listening to the inspired Diderot. On this score, it is interesting to note that Morellet, and many others of the inner circle, including Saint-Lambert, Suard, the chevalier de Chastellux, Roux, Darcet, Raynal, and Helvétius, recognized in the *Système de la nature* "les principes et la conversation" of D'Holbach. (pp. 181-86)

The concluding chapter of the *Système de la nature,* the "Abrégé du code de la nature," was the only specific part of D'Holbach's works tentatively attributed to Diderot. This attribution was made on the somewhat nebulous assumption that its exhortations and final apostrophe to Nature denoted a greater eloquence than had been demonstrated in the other parts of the book. In a letter to his brother, Diderot disclaimed the authorship of the "Code de la nature" and argued that he would not have been so foolish as to sacrifice his friends, family, and happiness by an "étourderie" of that kind. Some doubt, it is true, does exist as to whether Diderot was referring to the "Abrégé du code de la nature" or to Morelly's "Code de la nature" of 1755. But because the brothers had made their peace late in 1759, many years after Morelly's "Code de la nature," thus making the recurrence as late as 1770 of the identical bone of contention most improbable, the likelihood is that the brothers were referring to the last chapter of the *Système de la nature.* Even so, if Diderot could persuasively argue that it was impossible for him to have written Morelly's "Code de la nature," it would have been even more impossible for him to have authored the last chapter of D'Holbach's book. For there was no more audacious bid to eradicate religion than that found in such passages as: "La morale de la nature est la seule religion que l'interprete de la nature offre à ses concitoyens, aux nations, au genre humain, aux races futures, revenues des préjugés qui oni si souvent troublé la félicité de leurs ancêtres"; and "Il [the apostle of nature] sçait que ce n'est qu'en extirpant jusqu'aux racines l'arbre empoisonné qui depuis tant de siecles obombre l'univers, que les yeux des habitans du monde appercevront la lumiere propre à les éclairer, à les guider, à réchauffer leurs ames."

As for the eloquence of the apostrophe to Nature, the works of D'Holbach are so strewn with similar apostrophes that there is no need to cite examples. One can not read many pages of any of his works without encountering numerous apostrophes which convey D'Holbach's sincerity and conviction to the reader. Moreover, no one has singled out the passages from the "Abrégé du code de la nature" which are completely in accord with the principles of D'Holbach, the exemplar of conjugal fidelity and happiness, but which would sound at the very least somewhat hypocritical coming from Diderot. Consider for example the following: " . . . que l'estime d'une compagne chérie te fassent oublier les peines de la vie; sois fidele à sa tendresse, qu'elle soit fidelle à la tienne; que sous les yeux de parents unis & vertueux tes enfants apprennent la vertu," or, "Vois la division & la haine régner entre ces Epoux adulteres," and a direct admonition like "sois Epoux fidele" (II, 404). Could the virtuous Diderot have written these lines at the very time when he was beginning an amorous liaison with yet another woman, Mme de Maux? In our estimation, this final chapter differs not at all from the rest

of the *Système de la nature* or any other of D'Holbach's works.

The following conclusions can therefore be drawn from this study: first, in agreement with almost every authority, we feel there is little if any evidence to justify the belief that Diderot had any part in the writing and translating of D'Holbach's scientific articles and books, which occupied him until about 1760; secondly, in opposition to the unsupported claims of some critics and the indecisive position of those who after a cursory obeisance to critical objectivity invariably acquiesced, some rather reluctantly, to traditional criticism, we believe that Diderot not only did not collaborate with D'Holbach, but that it is unlikely he was even conscious of the scope of the Baron's antireligious undertaking of the sixties; and lastly, we find that his major philosophical, political, and ethical works: the *Système de la nature,* the *Bon-Sens,* the *Système social,* the *Politique naturelle, Ethocratie,* and the *Morale universelle* were as much the thought and work of D'Holbach alone, as any work could have been the product of any member of that eighteenth-century society of "Encyclopédistes" distinguished for its interplay of ideas.

D'Holbach is, in fact, noted for an unusual consistency of thought. (Diderot himself admired this quality in the Baron.) This uniformity is apparent to anyone who reads more than one of D'Holbach's books. To read all of them is like listening to the same piece of music played in different keys, or with emphasis on different chords. His style—if we can refer to that flat, repetitious, humorless, and monotonous method of writing as style—is as consistent as the thought content. Diderot, Naigeon, Suard, and others may have read and commented on various portions of D'Holbach's manuscripts before they were published, but the works themselves and the evidence available irrefutably point to D'Holbach as the one and only author.

Though D'Holbach would probably be the last to complain, so little did he seek honors during his lifetime, it nevertheless seems most unjust, and Diderot would be the first to agree, to perpetuate the idea that Diderot was the author or inspirer of all the pages in which some indefinable kernel of genius can be detected. (pp. 186-88)

Virgil W. Topazio, "Diderot's Supposed Contribution to D'Holbach's Works," in PMLA, *Vol. LXIX, No. 1, March, 1954, pp. 173-88.*

Virgil W. Topazio   (essay date 1956)

[*In the following excerpt, Topazio discusses the influences upon and development of d'Holbach's atheistic philosophy*].

Unlike his French contemporaries, most of whom were content to remain within the confines of a philosophical skepticism or deism from which they could hurl their ironic or satiric darts with some degree of security, d'Holbach presented from the outset a dogmatic materialism worthy of Epicurus and an atheistic zeal which even exceeded his materialism. He was successful in forging a consistent philosophy by realistically incorporating the necessary complementary elements from the various philosophies of Hobbes, Locke, the English critical deists, and the early French deists.

The principal English influences upon d'Holbach were the materialistic hedonism of Hobbes and the sensationalistic epistemology of Locke. But d'Holbach drew his main atheistic inspiration from the disciples of Hobbes and Locke, whose greater temerity and firmer convictions more closely paralleled the radical thinking of d'Holbach. For example, he quickly accepted Toland's idea that motion was an essential property of matter—a cardinal tenet of materialism. In the works of Anthony Collins, whose attacks upon literal prophecy were made possible by the absence of religious inhibitions which had handicapped Locke, d'Holbach found more fully developed the conclusion that all men's actions were necessarily determined by pleasure and pain. The negative and vitriolic content of Woolston's "Six Discourses" also had a particular appeal to the anti-religious d'Holbach, because of the uninhibited nature of their attacks upon the miracles. Peter Annet's assertion that Christians were not only deceived but also immoral found a sympathetic reader in d'Holbach. He was also impressed by Annet's severe criterion for judging historical evidence, a criterion which caused him to reject as pure fable much of the historical foundation of Christianity. D'Holbach was likewise in complete agreement with Tindal's recognition of rewards and punishment as inseparable attendants of virtuous and vicious actions, a philosophy that rendered the existence of God as a rewarder and punisher unnecessary and forced those whose logic controlled their fears to travel the road leading directly toward atheism. (p. 252)

According to d'Holbach, every religion, every doctrine, that imprisoned the mind of man represented a threat to his welfare and happiness. Consequently, his works "aimed at the total destruction, not only of Catholicism, but of all religions." His sincerity was accompanied by such an impressive array of arguments that Damiron was compelled to state: "If the reader is not able to control himself in reading d'Holbach, he will run the risk, on many a point, of succumbing to d'Holbach's arguments, and he would thereby lose himself by abandoning more than one religious belief." D'Holbach's anticlerical attacks, taking up the cudgels where the English deists had, to his way of thinking, prematurely abandoned them, ruthlessly exposed the selfishness of priests. He pictured them as money-grabbing, power-seeking fanatics, ready to promise eternal salvation to the most flagrant offender, if it were sufficiently profitable to them.

The origin of priests was traced by d'Holbach to the first leaders or chieftains, who gained power by explaining the calamities of nature as the handiwork of some Superior Power and urged their followers to assuage that Power responsible for these disruptions. In the beginning, nature itself was adored. Later, anthropomorphic symbols were adopted in order to exercise greater control over man. The people's ignorance fostered the idea of God; the priests' imposture gave Him form and rendered Him forbidding. The result was that "the common man, conceiving his celestial monarch as a formidable creature, did not dare to approach Him directly; he was afraid to gaze upon Him with his own eyes . . . and therefore commissioned his ministers, whom he considered the favorites of God, to act as mediators."

The priests thus consolidated their power by conjuring up a cruel, terrible, and vindictive God who continually had to be appeased. They spoke in allegories and riddles to confuse the multitude and to inspire awe. It became a simple matter to impress the idea of religion upon the minds of men, because "when the brain is disturbed, one believes all and no longer examines anything." The theologians pictured God as infinite, omniscient, and omnipotent, but continually underscored man's inability to comprehend Him. So well did they dissuade the people from scrutinizing their religion that even intelligent and otherwise reasonable people refused to bring in a verdict against religion, when their reason found it wanting.

D'Holbach asked how men could reasonably be called upon to imitate, worship, and respect someone whom they could not understand. "If God is infinite," argued d'Holbach, "no finite being can have any common bond or intercourse with Him" (*Bon Sens*). The priests, recognizing the appeal of mysteries to the vivid imagination born of credulity and nourished by ignorance, enshrouded God with an impenetrable haze. They managed thus to keep man in a constant state of fear that rendered him docile and pliant. The seeds of superstition were sown in this fertile ground, and a harvest of social evils was reaped. D'Holbach denied the contention of religious zealots that the catastrophes and bloodshed of the past had resulted from the abuse of religion. "It is in the principles of religion itself, in the God who serves as its base, in the fatal ideas that humanity formed of them, that one must look for the source of the evils which were and always shall be the necessary results of such beliefs" (*Contagion sacrée*).

D'Holbach attempted to prove that "Religion is the result of habit and custom. . . . Chance alone decides one's religion: the French today would be as good Mohammedans as they are Christians if their ancestors had not previously repulsed the Saracens" (*Bon Sens*). If the idea of God were inmate, reasoned d'Holbach, how could the different conceptions of God be explained? Why would some conceive Him in the form of a serpent, some as an elephant, others as a spirit, and still others as a man? Unfortunately, d'Holbach discovered, people were reluctant to apply their reasoning powers to religious problems: "where religion is concerned, people seem to glory in remaining perpetually in a state of infancy and barbarity" (*Christianisme dévoilé*).

Just as religion in its beginning had been the product of ignorance and fear, Christianity was the result of ignorance and hope. D'Holbach found delight in pointing out that the first to embrace Christianity were the lowest elements of society, those eager to grasp at the hope for a better fate in the afterlife to compensate for their suffering and misfortunes on earth (see *Christianisme dévoilé*). To be sure, they claimed Christianity was the true religion of God. But, countered d'Holbach, every religion made the same claim, so how could one be sure.

In discussing Christian miracles and the resurrection, d'Holbach firmly held that the facts of Christ had not been sufficiently corroborated to warrant their acceptance as historical facts. And because miracles were contrary to the laws of nature, he sought confirmation by impartial and intelligent witnesses. He found none. Neither Suetonius nor Tacitus nor any of the contemporary writers of that period of great intellectual ferment and literary production mentioned the miracles supposedly performed by Christ. Indeed, they seemed to have been totally unaware of His importance. All the reports available came from Christians who were, as they themselves admitted, ignorant, and as d'Holbach insisted, most partial. Miracles, d'Holbach accordingly concluded, were nothing more than the inventions of priests "to prove to the satisfaction of men those things which they otherwise would have found impossible to believe" (*Christianisme dévoilé*). "From the very foundation of the Church, there were men who doubted the death and therefore the resurrection of Jesus Christ, and we are asked to believe it today."

The doctrine of the Trinity d'Holbach dismissed as the figment of someone's imagination, possibly based upon the "rêveries" of Plato, who along with Pythagoras, Socrates, and Xenophon, had produced beautifully worded ideas, but nothing upon which to build a real morality. Baptism was shown to be ineffectual, since men still died even though it had been designed to save man from the original sin of Adam and Eve, the punishment of which had been death. The Old and New Testaments were rejected as artistically and historically unworthy of any God, because of the inconsistencies and errors contained therein. D'Holbach agreed with Toland and Collins in refusing to accept a literal interpretation of the scriptural passages when to do so would offend one's reason and even quoted St. Augustine to justify his position (*Christianisme dévoilé*). But d'Holbach went on to attack Christ himself; he cavalierly dismissed Him with the statement that "the only marvel of which He was incapable was to convince the Jews, who, far from being impressed by His good deeds, made Him suffer a death of ignominious torture." His criticism of confession was equally bitter. Instead of acting as a brake on the passions, he found that it encouraged the commission of sins because of the ease with which one could expiate them. In addition, confession encouraged the stupid practice of asking forgiveness not of the injured party, but rather of God (*Système de la nature*).

Unlike the majority of the English deists and most of his contemporaries, d'Holbach was not content to refute isolated points of dogma and to highlight the abuses of the clergy and the Church. His goal was to destroy the whole foundation of religion by exposing it as a hoax perpetrated on the people and by proving it incapable of promoting a better way of life. Hence, one of his main attacks was leveled at the existence of God. "Ask anyone if he believes in God," suggested d'Holbach. "He will be surprised that you can doubt it. Then ask him what he means by the word God; you will place him in the greatest embarrassment; you will notice immediately that he is unable to attach any concrete idea to the word which he repeats continuously" (*Bon Sens*). This was a positive and robust atheism seldom proposed by his fellow philosophes.

Even Diderto, who in the consensus of many scholars had arrived at a full-blown atheism with the writing of the *Lettre sur les aveugles* in 1749, would have been uncomfortable within the uncompromising confines of d'Holbach's beliefs. Diderot's brilliant, fermentative mind, which never ceased exploring all the intellectual possibilities inherent in any problem, made it impossible for him to expound as coherent and systematized a doctrine of materialism and atheism as that to be found in the works of d'Holbach.

Other deistic thinkers, like Voltaire, who could have derived nothing but joy from the avalanche of d'Holbach's anticlerical propaganda, recoiled before the logical development of the ideas which had formed the backbone of the attacks upon the Church. In the *Système de la nature* Voltaire saw the first audacious attempt to supply a substitute for God and became alarmed at the thought of a people left without His support. He did think it presumptuous of man to try to explain God and His actions, but he considered it even bolder to deny His existence (see *Œuvres*, XXXVII). Some sixteen years later, in denying the authorship of the *Christianisme dévoilé*, Voltaire reaffirmed his unalterable opposition to atheism: "The *Christianisme dévoilé*, is entirely opposed to my principles. This book leads to an atheistic philosophy abhorrent to me" (*Œuvres*, XLIV, 534). Teleologically and cosmologically, Voltaire argued for the existence of a Superior Intelligence, even while doing his utmost to discredit the Church and its clergy. D'Holbach, on the other hand, wished to destroy the very idea of God and His identification with nature. As Lange asserted: "It is precisely the mystical tendency in man's nature that he [d'Holbach] regards as the disease that causes the greatest evils that afflict humanity." And throughout d'Holbach's life, his constant concern was the construction of a workable secular system of ethics the primary objective of which would be the betterment of man's lot within his social milieu.

Like Hume, d'Holbach enumerated the dilemmas which arose once God was accepted as the priests had presented Him through the Scriptures. God performed miracles which theologians admitted were opposed to the laws of nature, but within His power. But who devised the laws of nature? God. Therefore, He violated His own laws. Why? The clergy answered that God employed these supernatural means to convince the people who might otherwise have doubted His divinity. Yet history had proved how dangerous it was to accept as miracles the workings of nature which at the time were beyond the comprehension of man. Had no innumerable so-called miracles later been shown to be the result of natural causes? An equally perplexing dilemma presented itself with respect to reason. In one breath the theologians declared reason to be the gift of God, and in the next, they contended it should not be used to examine religion. But, maintained d'Holbach, to say that "reason is an untrustworthy guide and that our senses deceive us is to say that our errors are necessary and that our ignorance is invincible" (*Bon Sens*).

A grave danger presented by religion, d'Holbach was convinced, was that it sought to dominate the minds of kings and legislators. Religion encouraged tyranny in two ways. First, it inspired a lust for power in the monarch, especially when the form of despotism encouraged would grant more power to the clergy, and second, it accustomed the people to accept meekly the yoke of bondage by blinding them to the true dignity of man (*Contagion sacrée,*). Consequently, it became apparent to d'Holbach that the success of his ethical doctrine depended upon his ability to "undeceive mankind of the religious false beliefs which have so marked an effect in politics."

Religion exercised a deleterious effect upon the workings of government and laws in two other respects. It had long since usurped the responsibility of establishing a moral code. This traditional association of ethics with religion deterred the legislative powers from assuming their rightful responsibility and thereby retarded any possibility of progress toward the enactment of a workable morality based upon human nature. This linking of religion and ethics was particularly baneful, though d'Holbach, for one of the most important tenets of his ethical philosophy held that "Morality and politics are interdependent; their interests cannot be separated nor can they stop helping each other without incurring great risks." Religion posed another serious threat to government by encouraging its members to obey ecclesiastical dogmas and laws whenever they conflicted with the civil laws of the land. "Surely, if religion is more important than anything else, it is clear that a Christian must obey every command of his spiritual head and that ecclesiastical authority must always triumph over civil authority." The acceptance of this position, concluded d'Holbach, could and would undermine the very authority of the government.

In the **Contagion sacrée,** d'Holbach presented a detailed study of the gradual rift between Church and State and underlined the desire of the ecclesiastics to recapture the temporal power which they had been forced to relinquish to the stronger arm of the monarchs. A double role was played by the higher clergy in this quest for power, summarized by d'Holbach in these words: "The Christian religion favors the tyranny of sovereigns when they are willing to defer to it; it directs their subjects to fanatical rebellion whenever these sovereigns show no disposition to please religion" (**Christianisme dévoilé**). The devout or impotent ruler who became a tool of the religious leaders invariably menaced the prosperity and happiness of the nation. The people were reduced to helpless pawns in the ecclesiastics' bid for power. The ignorance of the people, combined with a superstitious trembling before invisible and incomprehensible powers, made them easy prey for any tyrannically minded despot and produced suitable subjects for tyrants (see **Christianisme dévoilé**). Conniving and ambitious priests were rendered powerless only when confronted by enlightened rulers, who by precept and example encouraged their citizens to be useful and virtuous.

D'Holbach wanted man to see himself as he really was, the product of nature, whose actions were irrevocably determined by the laws of nature. On the question of the origin of man, he quite frankly admitted his ignorance, but insisted that the metaphysicians and theologians knew no more than he did on the subject. He rejected the idea that a divine spark differentiated man from beast. All creatures were manifestations of nature. Physical man was the work of nature; moral man was the same physical man judged by and according to his social environment (see **Système de la nature**). Like Toland and Diderot, d'Holbach believed that "With the aid of movement, an exchange, transformation, or continual circulation of the molecules of matter takes place. These molecules dissolve to combine into new forms of matter." There could be only natural causes and effects in nature. What appeared to be supernatural was only an effect whose cause was unknown due to an insufficient knowledge of nature. And inasmuch as motion was determined by the basic characteristics or properties of that object, "one must conclude . . . that each being of nature, restricted by its inherent characteristics and circumstances as it is, cannot act otherwise."

To understand d'Holbach's position, the proper value should be attributed to the words "restricted by its inherent characteristics and circumstances." They meant that every effect or action was the inevitable result of a certain cause or combination of causes which existed at the particular moment of the action. Given a set of circumstances or conditions, the action or effect would necessarily be determined. Every living organism had to act in accordance with its nature and the existing conditions. With respect to man, this deterministic outlook, when transferred from the purely philosophic to the moral sphere, did not present a hopeless fatalism. As d'Holbach had shown, these "circumstances" and "inherent characteristics" could be changed to conform with the type of actions deemed more desirable. In a word, the world was eternal, and matter was undergoing continual transformation due to the new combinations constantly being formed. Even death was just the passage from one stage to another in the over-all picture, the decay of one body contributing to the creation of some other production of nature (**Système de la nature**).

The culmination of d'Holbach's antireligious campaign, the goal of which was to awaken man to the inconsistencies between the religious conception of man and the true nature of man, was reached with the publication of the **Système de la nature** in 1770. This was a systematic presentation of the whole concept of materialism and a stanch denial of religion. It was, according to Henri Lion, "a great effort toward the logical construction of a rigorous system and represented the ambitious claim of bringing all under a single, vast synthesis," and for this very reason, "it remained until about the second quarter of the twentieth century—the most important demonstration of materialism and atheism, and consequently, the center of attacks by both 'philosophes' and theologians."

D'Holbach tried to prove that religion was the handiwork of men intent upon subjugating their fellow men. He wanted the people to examine more critically the ethical doctrine founded upon religion, certain that such an examination would reveal how inimical it really was to the best interest of mankind. In his unrelenting attacks upon religion and its dogmas, he incorporated the best arguments of the English and French deists of the seventeenth and eighteenth centuries and carried these ideas to their ultimate and logical conclusions: to an atheism which denied not only the very concept of God, but also the practicality of the idea of God, and to a morality entirely dependent upon reasoned experience. (pp. 253-60)

Virgil W. Topazio, "D'Holbach, Apostle of Atheism," in Modern Language Quarterly, *Vol. 17, No. 3, September, 1956, pp. 252-60.*

Everett C. Ladd, Jr.   (essay date 1962)

[*In the excerpt below, Ladd examines the relationship between Helvétius's* De l'esprit *and d'Holbach's* Système de la Nature, *focusing on theories of utilitarianism, enlightened monarchy, and social freedom*].

Helvétius' *De l'esprit* and d'Holbach's **Système de la nature** were in XVIIIth-century Europe two of the best known, most widely discussed and perhaps most influential works. Today, Claude-Adrien Helvétius and Paul Thirty, Baron d'Holbach, are remembered chiefly for them, and for the most notable element of each: *De l'esprit* and its systematic statement of a utilitarian ethics; the **Système** and its most thorough-going and uncompromising materialism. The political thought of Helvétius and d'Holbach, developed principally in their later works, has received, however, little attention. Writing in 1922, Henri Lion commented that d'Holbach the political and social philosopher had been left completely in the shadows by the emphasis on d'Holbach the debunker of religion. This observation regrettably is still valid, despite Lion's efforts. His "Essai sur les oeuvres politiques et morales du Baron d'Holbach," published in six parts between 1922 and 1924 in *Annales révolutionnaires,* and unfortunately never reprinted in book form, remains the best and most comprehensive examination of the Baron's political thought. Though three commendable, fairly recent studies of d'Holbach have been published, each is devoted primarily to an examination of his materialism, and to his attempt to propound a clearly defined secular ethic in the light of what he considered to be the inadequacy of religion as a moral force. None of the works in which d'Holbach's political thought is developed has been translated into English; no editions of the **Politique naturelle** or the **Ethocratie** have appeared since 1776; and we do not have an edition of the *Oeuvres complètes*. Helvétius has fared somewhat better. Still, the only satisfactory study of his political thought is to be found in Albert Keim's excellent volume, *Helvétius: sa vie et son oeuvre.* The recent and highly readable book by Ian Cumming is primarily an effort to give Helvétius what the author considers to be a deservedly high place in the growth of educational thought.

The political thought of Helvétius and d'Holbach merits a more careful and extensive consideration, and it is hoped that this essay will make a contribution to this end. More specifically, however, the thesis that Helvétius and d'Holbach were in essential agreement in the broad outlines of their political thought will be developed. Certain similarities have of course been noted by other writers. There has not been, however, any attempt to examine carefully the extent and depth of their agreement on social and political questions. Our philosophes started from the same basic premises, were agreed on the means for reform, gave essentially the same criticism of existing institutions and practices, and shared much the same vision of the good society. The close parallel exists despite marked differences in style and emphasis. Helvétius, for example, paid little attention to the theological disputes of the day with which d'Holbach was so intimately concerned. Helvétius' writings are oriented around the question of motivation; d'Holbach's approach is always that of the moralist. Helvétius filled the pages of *De l'esprit* with anecdotal illustrations which are amusing if not very illustrative. D'Holbach had no time for this; his works are tedious and repetitive, yet bold and systematic. His tone is always harsh and strident, while Helvétius at times gives the impression that he is enjoying a dilettantish romp. Nor are their differences confined to matters of style and emphasis. Areas in which the assumptions of our philosophes differed sharply will be noted throughout this essay. Still, following their own paths, they pursued the same goal; in d'Holbach's words, *"la moralisation de la politique."* This was, paradoxically, the source of their greatest weaknesses, and their most profound insight.

Helvétius and d'Holbach started from essentially similar analyses of the nature of man, of the standard by which his actions should be evaluated, and of the "vehicles for reform," that is, the means of attaining the good society. They accepted a mechanistic psychology, believed that men are motivated only in their own self-interest, rigorously applied a utilitarian standard to all actions, and were optimistic about the possibilities of social engineering, about the efficacy of legislation and education.

Our philosophes adopted Locke's sensationalist theory of knowledge, and acknowledged their indebtedness to him. Man's physical organization, d'Holbach argued in **La Morale universelle,** enables him to receive impressions from objects with which his senses come into contact. These sensations give birth to ideas. The ability to consider ideas even when the objects which produced them are no longer present we call memory. Here more consistent than Locke, our philosophes refused to admit any innate ideas. Anything not accessible to man's physical senses simply is not subject to his understanding. D'Holbach went beyond Helvétius in the extent of, and in the temerity with which he proclaimed his materialism. He insisted that a materialistic metaphysics is logically implied by a mechanistic psychology. Helvétius never took this step, and largely ignored questions of metaphysics, referring occasionally to a deistic god. Of much greater importance for the development of their political thought, Helvétius and d'Holbach were in disagreement on whether, given the proper environment, any man could become a d'Holbach; Helvétius insisted that all men have the same capabilities. Still, the materialism of our philosophes played essentially the same rôle in their systems. If man is to a large extent "all education," meaning by education the sum-total of environmental influences, then their demands for reform become particularly compelling. Put men in reasonable social situations, coordinate the interests of each individual with those of society, and virtue will appear of its own accord, as surely as a stone is drawn to earth by the force of gravity.

Our philosophes maintained that self-love is a necessary result of physical sensibility, and hence is common to all men. They were agreed that "hope of a good or fear of an evil" is the only motive for human action. Helvétius in particular took delight in the brashness of his attack on the conventional virtues:

> If a hermit or monk imposes on himself the law of silence, flogs himself every night, lives on pulse and water, sleeps on straw, offers to God his nastiness and ignorance, he thinks by virtue of emaciation to make a fortune in heaven.

Their intention was not, however, to justify individual self-seeking, not even to reconstruct morality on the firm foundation of enlightened self-interest. We would be unfair to these philosophes if we did not see them primarily as reformers, seeking to bring about changes in a society which they believed was not rational, humane or just; and who found in self-interest psychology an excellent vehicle for their program. For if all men at all times seek to achieve their own happiness, how imperative the need to educate men as to the true demands of that happiness. And how pernicious a society which makes it in man's self-inteest to cheat, deceive, and oppress his fellows. Through education and a proper organization of society, individual self-seeking could be guided to—in fact, transformed into—activity benefiting the whole society.

Here, then, is the "is" for our philosophes: Man, his consciousness determined by his physical environment, compelled by his very nature to seek his own happiness constantly. The "ought" was defined in terms of the utility principle—that actions should be considered good or bad depending on their effect on happiness. Helvétius was the first to give this an extended and explicit application in *De l'esprit.* He maintained that

> it is . . . on the uniformity of the legislator's views, and the dependence of these laws on each other, that their excellence consists. But in order to establish this dependence, it would be necessary to refer them all to one simple principle, such as that of the public utility; or to that of the greatest number of men subject to the same form of government; a principle more extensive and more fruitful than imagination can conceive; a principle that includes all morality and all legislations, of which many men discourse without understanding them, and of which the legislators themselves have yet but a very superficial idea, at least if we may judge from the unhappiness of almost all the nations upon earth.

He was the founder of doctrinal utilitarianism. D'Holbach accepted Helvétius' statement of utility, and rigorously applied the principle in all his later works. The object of society, our philosophes agreed, is to allow man to enjoy more securely those advantages which his mental and physical capacities permit him. D'Holbach maintained that each individual contracts in almost these terms with society:

> Help me . . . and I will help you with all my talents . . . work for my happiness, if you want me to concern myself with yours. . . . Secure for me advantages great enough to persuade me to give up to you a part of those which I possess.

While Helvétius did not refer explicitly to a contract, he conceived the relationship of man to the State as similarly utilitarian. Our philosphes sought, then, to substitute for Locke's self-evident rights a single standard of value—the greatest happiness for the greatest number. In this they were not wholly successful. Not surprisingly, the demands of utility closely resemble at many points the demands of Locke's manifest truths. Utility and natural right did not logically lead to similar practical conclusions, but the arguments were kept together by a broad basic agreement on the goals which society should attain. And, as Sabine has observed, utilitarian ethics when actually worked out contained assumptions that were in no way justified by the principle of utility, but which were accepted as self-evident. Why, for example, should the State promote the happiness of the greatest number? Our philosophes presumed that one man's happiness should be given the same value as another's—in fact, a belief in natural equality.

To get from the "is" (Man, the pleasure-seeking receptacle and organizer of environmental stimuli) to the "ought" (Man, achieving his happiness through actions which maximize the happiness of the whole society), Helvétius and d'Holbach relied upon a program of education and legislation. Helvétius argued that a major cause of man's anti-social acts is the inadequacy of his education. D'Holbach agreed. What, he asked, prevents the different classes from working together for the end of life in society, that is, for their mutual happiness? It is in part their inability to see that their interests are essentially harmonious,

not conflicting. Our philosophes did not believe, however, that enlightenment would be enough. Of what use is it, Helvétius asked, that I teach my son to be virtuous, if all around him he sees virtue punished? Men must be freed from the unnatural and pernicious demands which society had placed on their actions. Their conception of the rôle of legislation did not stop with this negative, "freeing from" function. Positive legislation was necessary to force men through their feeling of self-love, to act in the best interests of society. The science of legislation involved the use of rewards and penalties to unite the individual with the general interest; and in fairly precise terms Helvétius and d'Holbach outlined the kind of program which Bentham was later to develop. (pp. 221-25)

The science of politics, Helvétius and d'Holbach agreed, "consists in exciting, directing and regulating the passions of men so as to lead them to work for their mutual happiness."

There were, then, these close parallels in the basic premises from which our philosophes approached the problem of government and the good society. We can now examine in some detail their understanding of a properly constituted government, and of the functions which such a govern-

---

THE

SYSTEM OF NATURE;

OR,

THE LAWS

OF THE

MORAL AND PHYSICAL WORLD.

TRANSLATED

FROM THE ORIGINAL FRENCH OF

M. DE MIRABAUD.

VOL. I.

IN THREE VOLUMES.

LONDON:

PRINTED AND PUBLISHED BY THOMAS DAVISON,

Duke Street, West Smithfield;

AND SOLD BY ALL OTHER BOOKSELLERS.

1820.

Title page of Volume I of an English edition of The System of Nature, *published by d'Holbach under the name of the lately deceased M. de Mirabaud.*

ment must perform and the specific values which it must secure in order to realize the good society.

There has been considerable disagreement concerning the form of government to which Helvétius and d'Holbach were committed. They have been described most frequently as champions of "enlightened" monarchy. Dissents from this position, however, have been numerous. Kingsley Martin, for example, has argued that within limits Helvétius was a democrat. Wickwar placed Helvétius among the most ardent defenders of enlightened despotism, but thought that d'Holbach took a more liberal position, somewhere between Helvétius and Rousseau, as an advocate of a constitutionally limited monarchy. Naville concurred in this judgment. Keim observed that at times Helvétius seemed to hope for the establishment of a federated republic, while at other times he moved very close to Voltaire's position on the possibility of an intelligent, philosophic monarch. That this confusion has occurred is attributable in part to the presence of passages in the writings of our philosophes supporting each of these positions. In fact, certain of these positions are clearly wrong, and none of them can stand alone as an adequate description of the essential orientation of our philosophes. Neither Helvétius or d'Holbach were democrats, though there were democratic elements in their political doctrine. Neither favored enlightened despotism, if one understands by the term a form of government which emphasizes reform at the expense of freedom. And though both placed their hopes primarily on enlightened, limited monarchy, this position must be understood much less as a commitment to a particular system of government, than as a product of (1) their reluctance and inability to explore seriously the question of what form of government would be required to realize the objectives which they set up; (2) their faith in the process of enlightenment; (3) their skepticism about the possibility of any form of government other than monarchy at the time; and (4) their interpretation of the preceding three centuries of French history in which French kings had struggled to dominate the feudal nobility and clergy, both objects of their most violent opposition. Before considering each of these, we must first describe in more detail the position taken by our philosophes on the form of government best suited to maximize the happiness of society.

D'Holbach undertook in a number of his works to examine systematically each of the three classical forms of government, to determine the strengths and weaknesses of each. The dangers of monarchy were all too evident: public welfare frequently had been sacrificed to the ambition and greed of the king and his court. And even if one succeeded in "enlightening" a monarch, there were no assurances that his successor would not be a tyrant. Yet if monarchy could be bad, the alternatives could be far worse. Aristocratic government elicited his strongest disapproval; the nobility was self-seeking and self-centered, willing to sacrifice the common good on the altar of self-interest, inanely jealous of undeserved privileges. Society would be reduced to a morass of plots, intrigue and civil war by the struggle for power among the aristocratic elite. In the end, a few families would become masters of the state, sharing the spoils. Instead of just one tyrant, the people would have many; and while one man may have his moments of charity, group interests are always reduced to their lowest

common denominator. His condemnation of democracy, however, was as categorical:

> The authority is without power, because it is too divided. It is not respected because each individual, thinking himself its agent, acts as though he had acquired the right to abuse it. . . . A sovereign people, flattered by demagogues, becomes their slaves and the instrument of their wicked designs. Turbulent citizens divide into factions . . . civil wars tear to pieces a society which, blind in its attachments and its hates, often elevates its most cruel enemies. . . . Finally, worn out by its own excesses, the people delivers itself to slavery . . . and thinks itself fortunate to have exchanged license for chains.

It "escapes from freedom." He rejected out of hand all possibility of popular government. The uneducated and those without property would not be allowed to exercise political power. Even the merchants and manufacturers, though entitled to the full protection of the State, were not true members of it, and could not be until they had acquired landed property: "It is the soil . . . which makes the citizen. . . . The land is the physical and political base of the State."

D'Holbach did not preclude, however, all possibility of representative government. He referred favorably to a "mixed" government in which intermediate political bodies—assemblies—would function as instruments of resistance to despotism. He developed the idea of a monarchy limited by a representative power in the *Politique naturelle,* in a discussion of the advantages which a form of federal arrangement might bring to the large state. In such states, he observed, the population is widely scattered; local restraints tend to break down, and a more elaborate governmental machine is needed. There is a greater tendency for these states to fall under despotic government. It would be advantageous, then, to divide such states into provinces with certain powers of self-government, uniting these under a monarch and a general assembly. This representative body would be composed of deputies chosen by elected provincial assemblies. Suffrage would be limited to those who possessed landed wealth. It seems doubtful, however, that d'Holbach saw these assemblies as anything more than consultative bodies, and he gave no indication of how they would have any effective power. He spoke of their activity in very vague terms: The people would "speak" to the monarch through these assemblies, "making known" its needs and grievances. As Naville has observed, d'Holbach's assembly "would act as a kind of permanent session of the Estates General."

D'Holbach, then, favored limited monarchy. At times he demonstrated full awareness that it was not enough merely to enlighten the monarch, to open his eyes to the coincidence of his interests with those of his subjects. Like Helvétius, he had developed a quite sophisticated conception of interests; and he did not believe that men would always determine their actions by a somewhat questionable ultimate harmony of the individual with the general interest. It is for this reason that he emphasized the importance of legislation. And this is why he referred to a system of representation noted above, to the threat of revolution, and to pluralism of a sort. The representative body, however, was to be only consultative; his conception of pluralism was vague to say the least; and the threat of revolution was a theoretical and hardly reliable sanction. D'Holbach maintained that fear is the only obstacle which society can effectively raise against the passions of its leaders; that society must set boundaries to its confidence, must limit the power that it delegates to the ruling elite, and should reserve for itself enough authority to prevent corruption and abuse by that elite; that the record of history testifies to the fact that man is continually tempted to abuse power. He never developed his argument, however, beyond this promising statement of principles. (pp. 226-29)

Our philosophes removed all trappings from the monarch. They brought him down to earth, a man, no more virtuous or talented than his fellows. They required him to rule in the best interests of all members of the society on pain of losing his right to rule. For the rest, they left him his throne. Their willingness to rely on the monarchy for reform, despite the anti-monarchical implications of their thought, must be understood in terms of the several factors noted above. First, Helvétius and d'Holbach shared the limited but still substantial confidence of their fellow philosophes in the process of enlightenment. The assumption, after all, of the possibility of a more rational man in a more rational society was central to their attack on the "irrationality" of the old order. We must take care, however, that we do not give undue emphasis to this point; for their optimism was tempered by a self-interest psychology and a concomitant theory of interests, and a full awareness that in the sweep of history monarchical abuses had rarely been deterred by a recognition of the ultimate harmony of interests. Much more important was their inability to conceive of an alternative to limited monarchy which would be both practical and desirable. D'Holbach questioned the practicality and desirability of any other form of government; Helvétius only the former. Helvétius did not seriously expect any change from the monarchical structure of the governments of Europe. Certain reforms were palpably necessary, and he wanted immediate action. The king was there, and he considered it to be immediately practical to look to him. Neither philosophe constructed a defense of monarchy, but instead accepted it on pragmatic considerations.

Still another factor in the willingness of our philosophes to place their hopes on the monarchy is their conditioning by the French political experience. By the time opposition to royal power developed in England in the XVIIth century, Parliament had been securely established as the major contender in the struggle for power, and was able to serve as the effective alternative around which opponents of the monarchy could rally. Such a situation was impossible in France. There, the lines of battle were drawn between the royal and aristocratic parties. Opposition to royal absolutism failed in large part because it was in alliance with a medieval particularism which was in no way compatible with strong, centralized national government. In their struggle against the clergy and the firmly entrenched feudal nobility, and the privileges which these interests defended, our philosophes looked to a strong monarchy. Peter Gay's description of Voltaire's royalism as "the result not of detachment from practical affairs and addiction to geometrical speculation, but of involvement in French politics and an intimate knowledge of French history," could as well have been applied to Helvétius or d'Holbach.

One final factor of particular significance in understanding

their positions should be noted: Our philosophes had little interest in seriously exploring the question of what institutional structure would be required to secure the values which they had postulated. Helvétius expressed this most succinctly when he wrote: "There are, therefore, only two forms of government, the one good, the other bad. . . ." Any government which maximizes the happiness of all members of the society is good government; any which does not is bad. This is, of course, far too facile. That good government must be defined in terms of good actions is not in question; it is no less true, however, that it must in addition be defined in terms of institutional structure; and that the former cannot be securely realized without the latter. Helvétius and d'Holbach sought *"la moralisation de la politique"* and were really unwilling and unable to go far in building an adequate constitutional structure. Our criticism should not be too harsh, for there are mitigating circumstances. Still, our philosophes must answer for the fact that they ultimately offered nothing beyond pious wishes to make certain that the monarch would work for the greatest happiness of all members of society.

One of the tasks initially set for this essay remains: To describe with some precision the nature of the good society of our philosophes. More specifically, what functions must government perform, and what values must it realize to promote the establishment of such a society?

With Hobbes and Locke, the presumption that individual self-interest is clear and compelling, while the public or community interest is derivative, came of age. To be sure, there was also the presumption that once liberated from external impediments, men would be able to create the good life; and that the pursuit of enlightened self-interest does in fact promote the greatest good for society. But the emphasis was clearly on the individual, not the community. Writing in the latter half of the XVIIIth century, our philosophes were in this tradition. Neither Helvétius nor d'Holbach, however, wholeheartedly espoused the main currents of the growing individualism. Their reservations, it should be noted, were not at all the same, and arose from significantly different expectations. For the most part, for example in the vigor and temerity with which he developed his philosophic materialism, in his frontal assault on the Church, in his rejection of the *thèse nobiliaire* and in his application of the utilitarian standard, d'Holbach without question stood in the vanguard of the intellectual community in which he moved. There was another d'Holbach, however, so much the man of the XVIIIth century; there was an element in his thought which constituted a defense of the status quo against certain ideas and forces effecting change. He harked back to the feudal idea of harmony in maintaining that the inequality which nature had provided, far from causing unhappiness, is the true basis of the happiness and well-being of society. Each has a task and each task is essential. And in his argument that government must promote the happiness of all citizens, there is blended with the idea of individual rights preventing any interference with liberty and property, the older notion of law enjoining the common good of society. This aspect of d'Holbach's thought can be seen clearly in his opposition to certain economic trends, particularly to the expansion of trade and commerce. Helvétius, on the other hand, tempered individualism with an analysis which, though rudimentary in form, was an anticipation of the need to regulate individual profit-seeking in the interest of social justice. His thought was egalitarian, and he had great confidence in the possibilities of social engineering. His demand for governmental intervention in the economic life of the nation was predicated on the quite modern assumption that the state should assure all its citizens a minimum standard of living. Neither this difference in the basis of their reservations, or the reservations themselves should be overemphasized. Helvétius and d'Holbach were in essential agreement, and were spokesmen for those men of ability who found the special privileges, restrictions, and oppression of the *ancien régime* intolerable. Their dissents nonetheless must be recognized as we consider their conceptions of the rôle of government, and the values to be realized in the good society.

"The love of liberty," d'Holbach maintained, "is the strongest of man's passions; it is rooted in the drive for self-preservation, and in the desire to use his talents without restraint in order to achieve a happy life." The good society must be a free society. Like their fellow philosophes, d'Holbach and Helvétius had been victims of the restrictions on freedom of expression, and it is in defense of these basic civil liberties that they offered some of their most impassioned argument. Good government, they insisted, far from fearing full freedom of expression, profits from it, knowing that extreme or silly ideas will be ridiculed, rejected, and soon forgotten. Our philosophes asserted the high value of truth. To ask if one owes men the truth is to ask if they are to be permitted to be virtuous and to do good.

Full religious freedom was also essential. Helvétius and d'Holbach were bitterly critical of the Church and its record. And they were agreed on the remedy: the laws of the State should carefully restrict the political power of the Church, and the State must in the last resort be superior. At the same time, the Church should have an entirely free hand in questions of dogma. Each man is strongly attached to his own religious beliefs, and these beliefs inevitably vary. It would be both useless and pernicious, then, to try to change them, to attempt to impose a uniformity of belief, or of disbelief. There must be complete toleration of all expression of religious thought. A multiplicity of sects is never dangerous; what must be prevented is the arrogation by any one sect of the right to persecute or oppress others. D'Holbach and Helvétius considered complete separation of Church and State to be necessary. The State must assure equal rights to all sects; and standing above them, must maintain a just balance, never allowing any to oppress the others or to upset the general tranquility.

Economic rights, as well as civil liberties, were prominent in our philosophes' definition of the good society. They defended the "right" to private property on the basis of utility. Since it is impossible for man to be happy unless he can enjoy exclusively the things which he procures through his work, the State must secure private property. Some inequality in the distribution of private property is unavoidable and even desirable. To be happy, men do not require equal pieces of the economic pie. But Helvétius and d'Holbach were agreed that the existing gross inequality would not do, for three fourths of the population had nothing, while a few were wallowing in superfluity. The right of a few, enjoying special privileges, to exploit the labor of the vast majority had to be brought to an end;

D'Holbach pointedly observed that when a few control the economic structure, they control the State. He recognized that the existing caste system had a profound psychological impact, as well as the more readily observable material effects; and the student of social psychology finds important insight in his statement of the problem. He maintained that the self-esteem of the individual sunk in poverty is shattered. Such an individual comes to despise himself, because he sees himself as an object of universal scorn. He hates authority which he considers to be only oppressive. Both Helvétius and d'Holbach anticipated the Marxian argument that the poor have no country, that the boundaries of the State are only barriers to the oppressed poor:

> There is no native land for the unfortunate who have nothing. Have the poor really a country? Does the man without property owe anything to the country where he possesses nothing?

Our philosophes urged as remedial action that each individual be given a stake in society—the possession of something of his own. Property, particularly landed property, would give him a feeling of self-worth. It was the responsibility of the State to "enrich its subjects as equally as possible." "The well-being of a nation does not demand," d'Holbach insisted, "that a handful of citizens enrich themselves and revel in over-abundance, but rather that the greatest number enjoy the comforts and conveniences of life, or at minimum, have the necessities."

Helvétius was more explicit. He suggested that the large concentrations of landed property should be broken up by making the taxes on excessive acreage higher than the revenue which the owner received. And, "what can hinder a people from declaring themselves the heirs of the whole nation; and in that case, on the decease of a very rich individual, dividing among several a property that would be too considerable for a single person?" The goal for Helvétius was to give each man property, and the opportunity to provide for his and his family's wants in seven or eight hours labor a day. If not the first, he was certainly one of the earliest advocates of the eight-hour day. This having been achieved, he thought, society would have done all it could in the economic sphere to make men happy.

Helvétius and d'Holbach were committed by their self-interest psychology and their utilitarianism to support governmental activity in the economic sphere in order to achieve a more equitable distribution of wealth. They were concerned not only with the effects of such redistribution on individual happiness, however, but with the necessity of redistribution if a stable, vigorous and ordered society was to be achieved. "Have the poor really a country?" they asked. Given a stake in society, the individual would become a better citizen. Such considerations were particularly important to d'Holbach. The alternatives, he thought, were as clear as the need to act wisely was crucial: either a more equitable distribution of wealth producing a more patriotic citizen and a more vigorous polity; or a continuation of the existing gross inequality with "indolence, despondency, sterile envy and crime." Reference was made above to certain significantly different expectations about the nature of the good society held by our philosophes—in brief, the distinct feudal overtones in d'Holbach's thought in contrast to the larger element of modernity in Helvétius'. This is in evidence here. Both men were concerned with securing order in society, just as they sought to maximize individual happiness. D'Holbach, however, differed from Helvétius in his desire to preserve a stratified society; and he was acutely conscious of the problem of maintaining order and stability in such a society as it became more severely challenged.

For the most part, our philosophes shared the physiocratic view that legal and customary restraints on agriculture and trade should be removed. The government, d'Holbach wrote, "could do nothing for the merchant except leave him alone." He referred to commerce as the "child of liberty," and insisted that it could not prosper in a tyrannous state. "In a country where chance, intrigue and favor determine everything . . . what encouragement is there for commercial activity scorned by the upper classes, oppressed, limited, circumscribed by the government, exposed to extortion by its financiers?"

Their argument to a point was profoundly sympathetic to mercantile and commercial interests. Still, our philosophes could not accept the theory of the natural harmony of economic interests held by the Physiocrats, or the latter's assumption that the unimpeded search for wealth was synonymous with happiness. Universal *laissez-faire* was not yet considered to be an unmixed blessing. Particularly interesting here are their positions in the debate on luxury, positions which reflect the different expectations which, we have noted, lay at the heart of their objections to a growing individualism. There exists in any society in transition a tension between the old and the new. D'Holbach in part reflected this tension in his thought, and in this sense showed himself to be so much a man of the XVIIIth century. With Montesquieu and d'Argenson, he warned that there was a danger that commercial prosperity, which was being promoted by the abolition of privilege, monopoly, and other restraints on commerce, would swamp true happiness which depended on other than economic considerations. Luxury, he argued, is the product of a society in which love of money has become the principle passion. In such a society, real needs are sacrificed; specious needs created. Public virtue is discouraged: the citizen is taught that nothing is substantial but money, nothing desirable but pleasure. Money buys decisions in courts of law, rank in the army, and salvation in the Church. The man of letters is no longer motivated by that disinterested enthusiasm which is at the essence of genius, but instead seeks to enrich himself. He leaves his study for the salon. All classes are corrupted, even the poor. For although they suffer economically, luxury is all about them, creating imaginary needs, and breeding dissatisfaction with the good, simple country life. Finally, luxury produces the ultimate corruption of individual and societal morality, expressed in the maxim: "Man must live for himself. . . . Thus, luxury . . . makes men unfeeling, cruel, breaking even those sacred bonds on which their domestic happiness depends."

Helvétius could not accept the main thrust of this attack, that commercial prosperity and its concomitant, individual profit seeking, played leading rôles in the corruption of man. He thought that these "vague panegyrics" of moralists directed against riches fell short of the mark. They had confused effect with cause: "Luxury . . . is in most countries the immediate and necessary effect of despotism. It is therefore despotism that the enemies of luxury should

oppose. To suppress an effect, we should destroy the cause." (pp. 230-36)

The argument against luxury in the XVIIIth century, as it is found in d'Holbach, was in fact a secular statement of the older claim of religious austerity. Helvétius avoided these overtones and had a much clearer conception of the requirements for economic justice in the kind of society which was emerging. But it was d'Holbach who, in summing up the attack on the new economic order from the viewpoint of the old, offered the most eloquent, and in some ways the most incisive critique:

> Entire nations are the dupes of the avarice of hungry businessmen who beguile them with the hope of wealth, the fruit of which they gather only for themselves. States are depopulated, taxation greatly increased, and nations impoverished in order to satisfy the avarice of a small group of citizens. . . . Wealth has become the signal for war between Powers. . . . If one might read in the future the effects on this unbridled passion for trade which now divides the nations, one would see, perhaps, that when they had destroyed each other under this pretext, the peoples would severally end by confining themselves to farming their own land, engaging only in that trade which proved essential for each. Governments more humane, just and sensible will perceive that money does not create the true happiness of society any more than of individuals. They will get to dislike sending armies of citizens to perish annually in scorching climates, in fighting and on the seas. At last, perhaps, the day will come when Indians, having learned the art of war from Europeans, will hunt them from their shores, where their greed has inevitably made them odious.

There is, we have argued, a close parallel in the political thought of Helvétius and d'Holbach, this despite great differences in emphasis, and areas of important substantive disagreement. In psychology, they went beyond Locke's sensationalism; of particular importance here is their clear recognition of the significance of a sensationalist psychology for ethics, legislation and social organization, as well as for education. Both believed that they had discovered in the concept of utility a simple, positive principle on which men would be able to agree in reforming society. Both tried to found what they considered to be the "art" of ethics and legislation on an objective science of behavior. The individual and society were seen as clean slates on which almost anything could be written. This assumption led to their emphasis on positive government, pursued by Helvétius to the amusing conclusion that since it is desirable that all men be healthy, "every wise government . . . [should] establish gymnastic exercises." It was the government's responsibility to "excite the citizens to work, to employ them according to their talents, to stop them from being idle, or from profiting without doing any of the work of society. . . ." Income should be redistributed. The State, in short, should undertake any activity necessary to secure the happiness of the individual, and to lead him by his self-love to conduct benefiting the whole society. It was not enough for either d'Holbach or Helvétius that the corruption and restraints of the old order be removed. The good society of our philosophes was to be created only through positive action, and the task cut out for the State was a most ambitious one. But it was precisely at this point that our philosophes became silent. In failing to seriously examine the question of implementation, they failed to take that step which could have transformed exhortations into a meaningful and consistent theory. They were enlightened men. Their social concern was real, and their criticism of the wrongs of the existing society had a power, and at times a vehemence which has rarely been equaled. Yet however penetrating their analysis, however far-reaching the implications of their argument, they could offer in effect only a pious wish that the monarchy, with its long history of bad government, would suddenly through enlightenment become the instrument of the will of the people, the guarantor of its happiness. (pp. 237-38)

> Everett C. Ladd, Jr., "Helvétius and D'Holbach: 'La moralisation de la politique',' " in Journal of the History of Ideas, *Vol. XXIII,* 1962, pp. 221-38.

Jim Herrick   (essay date 1985)

[*In the excerpt below, Herrick examines the development of d'Holbach's atheism through the baron's published works*].

'It is raining bombs on the house of the Lord. I go in fear and trembling lest one of these terrible bombers gets into difficulties.' When Diderot wrote these words in 1768, his close friend d'Holbach was secretly leading the bombing raid. Between 1760 and 1770 d'Holbach masterminded the publication of some twenty or thirty pamphlets, edited, translated and partly written by himself. Their theme was clearly stated in the title of the first of the batch, **Christianity Unveiled,** attributed posthumously to Nicolas Boulanger. D'Holbach wrote in **Christianity Unveiled:**

> Many men without morals have attacked religion because it was contrary to their inclinations. Many wise men have despised it because it seemed to them ridiculous. Many persons have regarded it with indifference, because they have never felt its true disadvantages. But it is as a citizen that I attack it, because it seems to me harmful to the happiness of the state, hostile to the march of the mind of man, and contrary to sound morality, from which the interests of state policy can never be separated.

D'Holbach was probably the first avowedly atheist writer. His emphasis on attack, his vigorous pamphleteering efforts, his hammering of the record of Christianity, and the most thorough-going materialism of his position, gave him a unique and underestimated place in the history of the Enlightenment. He was also a key figure in binding together the *philosophes* and ensuring, as host at Grandval and in Paris, that their ideas were constantly shared and their writings at times almost a communal effort. (p. 85)

After he was established in Paris, d'Holbach quickly became friendly with Diderot and other *philosophes*. Abbé Morellet, writing in what must have seemed a different age, after the French Revolution and the rise and fall of Napoleon, gave a vivid picture of d'Holbach's *salon:*

> The Baron d'Holbach held two dinner-parties regularly each week, on Sundays and Thursdays, where—without prejudice to the other days of the week—ten, twelve, or even fifteen or twenty, men

of letters, men of the world, or foreigners, who loved and cultivated the things of the mind were wont to meet together. There was plenty of food, and good food too; excellent wine, excellent coffee; plenty of discussion and never a quarrell; the simple manners that are suited to intelligent and educated men, yet do not degenerate into ill-breeding; gaiety without folly; and so much charm in the company there that although we arrived at two o'clock, as was then the custom, we were often nearly all still there at seven or eight in the evening. . . .

> And it was there too—one must admit it—that Diderot, Dr Roux, and the good Baron himself, used dogmatically to argue the cause of absolute atheism—as in the **System of Nature**—with persuasiveness, a good faith, and a probity that was edifying even for those who, like myself, did not share their beliefs. For it must not be thought that these ultra-liberal opinions were held by all the members of this society—*philosophique* though it was, in the unfavourable sense sometimes given to that word. A goodly number of us were theists—and not ashamed of it—and we defended ourselves vigorously against atheists, though we loved them for being such good company.

D'Holbach's social occasions were noticeable for the liveliness and intellectual daring of the participants and also for their cosmopolitan company. Morellet cites a list which included 'Hume, Wilkes, Sterne, Galiani, Beccaria, Caraccioli, Lord Shelburne, Count Creutze, Veri, Frizi, Garrick, the Crown Prince of Brunswick, Franklin, Priestley, Colonel Barré. . . .' D'Holbach was not himself much of a traveller—the world came to his doorstep—but he stayed with the actor Garrick on a visit to England in 1765. His English contacts were to be a useful source of pamphlets and a useful route for the devious publication and distribution of his own writings.

Amongst the salon *philosophes* Diderot was d'Holbach's closest friend and collaborator. Their relationship was enduring, but uneasy. Diderot found d'Holbach's moodiness difficult and vividly depicted d'Holbach's temperament in a letter to Sophie Volland:

> Can you imagine, my friend, how someone who has an excellent heart, good spirit, whom one could not with justice deny any of the essential human qualities and whose goodness and generosity on important occasions are notable, can contrive deliberately to make disagreeable the lives of his mother-in-law, wife, friends, domestics, and all who surround him? How can he so alternate between the delicate and the churlish? . . .

> The Baron would destroy himself by reading history which only serves to injure his spirit and incense his heart. He only looks at the atrocities of man and his nature. More and more he comes to hate his fellows. Will an encounter with some black pages make him tremble? He takes secret delight in regaling me with the details. He is sure that if life resembles what he has shown me, he cannot go on.

> On such days he seems touched: first with pleasure, then with pain. It is impossible to be on good terms with this wretched man. You can only care for him and pity him. He is the first victim of his faults.

The peevish side of his personality was revealed mainly to his close friends: the cosmopolitan visitors saw only a man of charm and generosity. His friends were loyal however, and Diderot, despite some disagreements and periods of distance, remained close to him until his death. D'Holbach's bitterness and anger certainly showed itself in the harshness of his attacks on Christianity.

One of the fruits of Diderot and d'Holbach's friendship was d'Holbach's articles for the *Encyclopédie*. D'Holbach's translation from German of treatises on mining, the formation of metals, stratification, and other aspects of mineralogy and physics brought him membership of academies in Berlin, Petersburg and Mannheim and were a useful contribution to the dissemination of scientific knowledge. Although not a practising scientist, his interest in science was enduring and he kept a cabinet of scientific specimens at Grandval. He contributed some four hundred articles to the *Encyclopédie* between 1751 and 1765. Many were very short factual items, but there were long essays on fossils, glaciers, the sea, volcanoes and mines and also pieces on the constitution of the Holy Roman Empire.

D'Holbach may well have been influenced by the thorough-going materialism and lurid description of man's religious history to be found in *De l'Esprit* by Helvétius; but the condemnation of the book and Helvétius's narrow escape from imprisonment may have been a further reason for his decision to publish clandestinely when he embarked upon his own attack on Christianity. (pp. 86-8)

D'Holbach began his programme to educate the public about atheism with the publication of *Christianity Unveiled* in 1761. At what point his anti-clericalism turned into atheism is unclear. An anecdote recounts d'Holbach's conversion from deism to atheism by Diderot, but the evidence is of a steady progress from science to scepticism, from the ardent pantheism of Akenside's poem 'Pleasures of the Imagination' to anti-clerical distaste for Christianity, and finally to avowed atheism.

Christianity Unveiled was attributed to Nicolas Boulanger who had died two years before its publication. Boulanger was a civil engineer engaged in the construction of main roads; he developed an interest in geology, the early history of man, and the history of religion and folklore as a response to disturbances of nature. His frequent appearance at d'Holbach's house gave it the soubriquet 'la grande boulangerie'. D'Hollbach appointed himself Boulanger's literary executor and posthumously published his *Oriental Despotism* (1761), the indirect message of which did not escape contemporary Western despots. D'Holbach's position as literary executor gave plausibility to Boulanger's alleged lauthorship of *Christianity Unveiled,* and he was carrying out Boulanger's suggested programme of presenting a picture of the errors of history. The sub-title of *Christianity Unveiled* was 'An Examination of the principles and effects of the Christian religion'. D'Holbach depicted Christianity as a combination of Judaism and Eastern mythologies which dominated by playing upon the fears and passions of humanity and by blinding reason with a series of fantastic dogmas and rites. This *mélange* produced conflict within states and wars between nations. He thought that freedom of thought would cause superstition to 'fall away by itself'. 'Tolerance and freedom of thought are the veritable antidotes to religious fanaticism.'

He was not prepared to risk imprisonment, but he doubt-less thought that superstition would fall away if enough people read enough of the right pamphlets. After 1765, an avalanche of polemical works poured from d'Holbach's house. They were translations, collaborations and original works: he continued his policy of attributing them to dead or imaginary authors. This has created a nightmare for bibliographers, for it was not until after his death in 1789 that d'Holbach's authorship was openly divulged, although it was certainly already known to friends.

D'Holbach was assisted in his campaign by the brothers Naigeon. Jacques-André Naigeon lived with d'Holbach as his secretary from about 1765 onwards and, in his own words, enjoyed 'his full confidence and his most intimate, most tender, and most constant friendship'. He was a pedant with an interest solely in classics without the usual range of interests of the Enlightenment. He did much to edit, 'correct' and tidy up d'Holbach's careless writing. According to Diderot, with Naigeon anti-clericalism became a kind of nervous *tic*. Naigeon had a high opinion of his own contribution to d'Holbach's writings, and in his obituary article and later writings about him provided the primary source for knowledge of his life. Naigeon's brother assisted by copying manuscripts and transporting them to Amsterdam for printing. There were indirect routes by which they then circulated back to France: on one occasion d'Holbach received copies with a batch of new English novels.

The book and pamphlet trade was dangerous. Hawking forbidden books might bring profit or the galleys. Diderot wrote of an incident in which a pedlar sold copies of *Christianity Unveiled* to a grocer's apprentice, who sold one to his master. After an argument the grocer reported the apprentice to the police for dealing in forbidden books. The pedlar, his wife and the apprentice were condemned to three days in the pillory; then the boy was branded and sent for nine years in the galleys, the pedlar similarly was branded and given five years' galley service, while his wife was imprisoned for five years.

D'Holbach's pamphlets are repetitive and authorship is very uncertain some cases. They fall roughly into three groups: existing manuscripts, reprinted with amendments and additions by d'Holbach and Naigeon; translations; original works by Naigeon and d'Holbach, with the division of work not being easy to distinguish.

Works known to have been in existence in manuscript for some time were *Letter from Thrasybulus to Leucippus,* which claimed to be translated from the Greek or written by a philosopher to dissuade his sister from taking the veil, *Critical Examination of the Apologists of the Christian Religion,* known to have been already in existence and *The Military Philosopher, or Difficulties of Religion,* written during the final years of Louis XIV's reign and subsequently reprinted with additions by d'Holbach. Straightforward translations were principally from the English deists. Among the best-known works are Peter Annet's piece about David, *History of the Man after God's own Heart,* Anthony Collins' *Examination of the Prophets who founded the Christian Religion,* John Toland's *Letters to Serena,* and Thomas Woolston's *Discourse on Miracles.* A curiosity was a translation of the seventeenth-century English pamphlet *Of the Torments of Hell: the foundations and pillars thereof discovered, searched, shaken, removed*

(London, 1658). Such works were important in the move towards a critical approach to the Bible.

Original works by d'Holbach, with the collaboration of Naigeon, include *Sacred Contagion, or the natural History of Superstition, Essay on the prejudices and the Influence of opinions on customs and the happiness of mankind, Letters to Eugénie or Preservative against prejudice. The Critical History of Jesus Christ, or reasoned Analysis of the Gospels* was the first (rather primitive) attempt to write a life of Jesus from a purely human viewpoint. D'Holbach's pamphleteering has been criticized as weak in scholarship and limited in understanding of the psychological appeal of religion, but he was indefatigable and strongly influenced subsequent criticism of religion and the clergy.

Eventually d'Holbach inflated all his ideas into a long two-volume work entitled *System of Nature.* It was published in 1770 and attributed to J. B. Mirabaud, a long-deceased secretary of the French Academy. In *System of Nature* the materialist basis of all life is emphasized. D'Holbach affirmed that the universe was given unity by its material basis. He had a monist vision of the oneness of the universe, and saw man as a part of the entirety of nature. He thought the idea of a metaphysical component of the universe was mere prejudice and error fostered by the clergy. He could become quite lyrical, if not literal, in his comparison between religion and nature:

> O Nature, sovereign of all beings, and your adorable daughters, virtue, reason, truth! be for ever our sole divinities; it is to you that the incense and homage of the earth are due. Show us, then, O Nature, what man must do to obtain the happiness which you have made him desire. . . . Inspire the intelligent being with courage; give him energy, that he can eventually love himself, esteem himself, feel his dignity; that he dares free himself, that he is happy and free, that he will never be a slave to your laws; that he perfects his fate; that he cherishes his fellow-beings; that he makes himself happy, that he makes others happy.

But it was d'Holbach's harangue against gods and priests which brought notoriety and condemnation from Parlement to the *System of Nature.* Voltaire thought it was dangerous and sorely tested the principle of tolerance, while Frederick the Great prepared a criticism of it, so that, as Voltaire wryly observed, 'God had on his side the two least superstitious men in all Europe—which ought to have pleased him immensely.' D'Alembert considered the *System of Nature* long-winded and 'too rigid and dogmatic'.

The criticism of long-windedness was met when two years later d'Holbach produced an abridged version called *Le Bons Sens (Good Sense).* It became a favourite with nineteenth-century freethinkers and is clear, sharp and forthright. The concluding paragraph gives the tone:

> Religion has ever filled the mind of man with darkness, and kept him in ignorance of his real duties and true interest. It is only by dispelling the clouds and phantoms of Religion, that we shall discover Truth, Reason, and Morality. Religion diverts us from the causes of evils, and from the remedies which nature prescribes; far from curing, it only aggravates, multiplies, and perpetuates them. Let us observe with the celebrated Lord Bolingbroke, that

> 'theology is the box of Pandora; and if it is impossible to shut it, it is at least useful to inform men that this fatal box is open.'

D'Holbach also addressed himself to the question which had blunted the pen of many nascent atheists: 'The vulgar, it is repeatedly said, must have a Religion. If enlightened persons have no need of the restraint of opinions, it is at least necessary to rule men, whose reason is uncultivated by education.' D'Holbach was unimpressed by the power of religion to act as a restraint on the 'vulgar'. 'Do we see, that this religion preserves them from intemperance, drunkenness, brutality, violence, fraud, and every kind of excess?' However, he advocated caution in preaching atheism to the masses: 'It would be madness to write for the vulgar, or to attempt to cure prejudices all at once. We write for those only, who read and reason; the multitudes read but little, and reason still less. Calm and rational persons will require new ideas, and knowledge will be gradually diffused.' *Good Sense* had more impact upon men of action and campaigners against injustice than upon intellectuals, but Godwin was an admirer of d'Holbach and Shelley refers to him in his notes to *Queen Mab,* having once contemplated making his own translation of *Système de la Nature.* Another example of an English freethinker influenced by d'Holbach was Matthew Turner (*d.* 1788?) to whom is attributed An Answer to Dr Priestley's *Letters to a Philosophical Unbeliever.*

In the 1770s d'Holbach turned to moral and political questions, writing works which were moderate, liberal and based on a utilitarian morality: they caused much less stir than his attacks on religion, but were admired by his friends. Diderot praised the three-volume *Morale Universelle* (1776) and suggested that 'fathers and mothers recommend it to their children for their daily reading'.

D'Holbach and Diderot continued to collaborate in publishing the works of Seneca, but Diderot's health was declining and d'Holbach's force seems to have been spent. D'Holbach's final decade before his death in 1789 passed quietly: he outlived the *philosophes* whose host he had been. His intellectual curiosity was not dead and he was visited by Mesmer in 1780—all his experiments failed before d'Holbach's sceptical eye. Among younger writers he knew Volney, an orientalist who studied comparative religion and visited the Near East. (Volney developed a passionate hatred of despotism and devout faith in progress and his *Ruins of Empire* became a freethought classic.)

In January 1789, only a few months before the start of a revolution whose development would have fascinated him, he died at the age of sixty-six. According to Naigeon he is said to have told a fellow-patient at a spa in Vosges, where he had been saving a peasant family from misery: 'Don't say anything about this to anybody. Any one would say that I am trying to play the good-natured philosopher. I am neither benefactor nor philosopher, but just a human being, and my charities are the pleasantest expense I have on these journeys.' He was buried a Catholic, as he had always, to outward appearances, remained.

Immediately after his death writers began to attribute authorship of his writings correctly and to comment upon his work. An example was Condorcet who published an analysis of a later work, *Politique Naturelle.* During the French Revolution religion became a matter of public policy as well as of intellectual debate: there was a hard battle to secularize society. There were numerous reprints of d'Holbach's works during the period of attempted Church reform known as 'the civil constitution of the clergy' and the religious rising in the Vendée. Later, following the Terror and then the Directorate, copies of **Contagion Sacrée** were sent by the Minister of the Interior to all prefects of departments to discourage a Roman Catholic revival.

The *philosophes* have been made scapegoats responsible for the excesses of the Terror. In fact, a reverse perspective shows that the period of panic, fear and war produced a reaction that did much to prevent the spread of the ideas of the Enlightenment. Although the complex series of events known as the French Revolution were bound to be influenced by the reformist ideas of some of the *philosophes,* the deification of the state and worship of the Goddess of Reason would have been anathema to the spirit of toleration, scepticism and open-mindedness that are part of the Epicurean-humanist-Enlightenment tradition. A hymn sung at the fête for the restoration of the Supreme Being proclaimed:

Où sont-ils ceux qui t'osaient menacer?
Quis sous le manteau de civisme,
Vils professeurs de l'athéisme,
Du coeur de l'homme espéraient t'éffacer!

(Where are those who dared to threaten you? who under the cloak of civism, vile teachers of atheism, have hoped to remove you from the heart of man!)

(pp. 89-94)

Jim Herrick, "D'Holbach: 'Raining Bombs on the House of the Lord'," in his *Against the Faith: Essays in Deists, Skeptics and Atheists, Prometheus Books, 1985, pp. 85-95.*

Maurice Cranston   (essay date 1986)

[*In the following excerpt, Cranston discusses d'Holbach's ethical writings, focusing on fatalism, determinism, and political radicalism*].

Of all the leading philosophers of the French Enlightenment, Baron d'Holbach remains the least well known. His numerous works have seldom been reprinted and are difficult to find except in specialized libraries. Yet his name is familiar enough; in almost every history of the intellectual life of France Holbach is mentioned, either as the most systematic eighteenth-century exponent of materialism, or as the leader of intellectual society, the richest of the *encyclopédistes,* the one in whose house the others met and dined, the host to foreign philosophers on their visits to Paris, and the benefactor of any friend who found himself in need.

With the characteristic tendency of intellectuals to bite the hand that feeds them, the *philosophes* often spoke ungraciously about Holbach. Rousseau accused him of leading a hostile conspiracy; Voltaire and Buffon condemned him as a man without judgement. Even Diderot, his closest friend, said of Holbach, 'He has benevolence only in his head; his idea of doing good to others is to engage in an argument; he has no heart.'

And yet Diderot perhaps more than anyone else had rea-

son to be grateful to Holbach, for Holbach was no ordinary contributor to the *Encyclopédie,* but the author of over four hundred of the most important articles, notably those on applied science and technology; he was a loyal supporter of Diderot when the authorities threatened action against the *Encyclopédie* and other contributors withdrew from the enterprise.

Holbach's **Système de la nature** is a remarkably modern book, more sophisticated than other expositions of eighteenth-century materialism, such as Helvétius on *l'Esprit* or La Mettrie on *L'Homme machine;* it adumbrates much that is nowadays known as 'logical positivism' or 'behaviourism' and foreshadows ideas developed in our time by such philosophers as Gilbert Ryle and B. F. Skinner. Holbach is a clear and robust stylist, and he does not mince his words on sensitive matters as most of his contemporaries felt it necessary to do. Considering the provocative nature of his writings, it may seem surprising that he was never imprisoned, like Voltaire and Diderot, or exiled like Rousseau, or reduced, like Helvétius, to silence; but Holbach had a simple way of protecting himself: he brought out his books under the names of respectable authors recently deceased. His **Système de la nature,** for example, was published as the work of the late Monsieur de Mirabeau of the Academie Française. Since Holbach had no belief in life after death, he had no fear of meeting in another world writers whose names he had so shamelessly filched.

In his works on ethics, Holbach suggests that prosperity is the reward of virtue, but his own material advantages owed more to good luck and the French system of inheritance. He lived to the age of 66 in uninterrupted opulence, and died in the comfort of his own bed just before the outbreak of the Revolution which was inspired in part by his ideas and which destroyed the world in which he flourished. (pp. 121-22)

Holbach is sometimes spoken of as being very 'German' in his temperament, partly by reason of his industry and thoroughness—for he is known to have written at least thirty-five books besides the four hundred articles he produced for the *Encyclopédie* and partly because of his tendency to push things to extremes. He was certainly among the most radical of the philosophers, in his atheism and his materialism if less so in his politics. He detested anything that savoured of compromise. And yet in many ways Holbach, with his passion for systems, for clear and distinct ideas, and his impatience with irregularity and unbridled imagination, was the model French rationalist, just as Diderot, with his aesthetic fantasies, his dialectical thinking, and his love of the extraordinary, was close to the ideal type of a German romantic. If they were both 'Baconians', Holbach no more than Diderot can be fairly described as a champion of enlightened despotism. Holbach's political ideas may come as a surprise to the reader who knows only his writings on metaphysics and morals, for his attachment to the Baconian gospel of salvation through science might prompt one to assume, with several historians, that he also subscribed to Bacon's ideas on politics; but this was not the case.

Holbach's radicalism expressed itself in taking ideas which he shared with other *encyclopédistes* and pushing them to extremes. His atheism might seem a shade obsessive as well as excessive. More than half the books he wrote are directed against Christianity; even his master-piece, *Le Système de la nature,* is one volume of philosophy and another, slightly larger, volume of atheist polemics. Holbach considered that his views on religion were more logical than those of his fellow philosophers. He did not seek like Voltaire to replace the God of the Christian tradition with a Supreme Being of his own invention; he felt that every argument against orthodox religion was equally an argument against so-called 'natural religion'. Nor did Holbach propose like Rousseau to initiate a civil religion with a simple set of dogmas to sustain civic virtue. He had no patience with the view held by so many philosophers that it was necessary for ordinary people to believe in God as a means of upholding morality. He came closer to the opinion of Marx that religion was an influence the popular classes would be better off without, only he did not call it an 'opiate' but a stimulant, an 'eau de vie' which excited the people's lust for sensations and made them feast on the thrills of burning heretics, persecuting dissenters, and torturing prisoners.

Even so, Holbach did not advocate the actual suppression of religious institutions. Acknowledging that religious faith was more precious to some people than their physical property, he felt it would be wrong to rob them of it. All religious cults, he argued, should be tolerated until such time as people could be weaned away from them, and such re-education could not be expected to take effect overnight. What Holbach found hard to stomach were arguments such as Pascal's, that there was nothing to be lost by betting on the unverifiable claims of Christianity being true.

Holbach had an equally uncompromising attitude in philosophy. It was the general view of the philosophers of the Enlightenment from Montesquieu onwards that one must look to science for knowledge; Holbach pushed this policy to extremes: all so-called knowledge which is not scientific, he suggests, is meaningless. He proclaimed himself, as did most of the *encyclopédistes,* a follower of Locke, but in his *Système de la nature* he offers a positivist's criticism of Locke: 'How has it come about', he asks,

> that the profound Locke . . . and all those who, like him, have recognized the absurdity of the theory of innate ideas, have not drawn out the immediate, the necessary consequences? . . . Why have they not had the courage to apply this clear principle to all the chimeras with which the human mind has so long and so vainly occupied itself?

This is a characteristic demand of Holbach's: why have they not drawn out the necessary consequences? The consequences he saw as necessary included the total banishment of metaphysics—something less harmful than religion, but just as unscientific. What had been called the queen of the sciences, Holbach condemned as a mere system of words.

In this chapter on the soul, he protests against the bifurcation of man into mind and matter, and he attributes this to the influence of Descartes. What is called the soul, he suggests, is simply a way of considering the body in relation to some of its functions. We have no experience of disembodied souls, and Holbach claims that neither the ancient philosophers nor the earliest doctors of the Church 'had any thought of the soul being immaterial.'

He suggests that our peculiar capacity for thinking, feeling, and behaving in certain distinctively 'human' ways prompts us to talk of mens' souls or minds; but that such words should be understood as a sort of shorthand, not implying the existence of what Holbach—anticipating Gilbert Ryle—calls an 'occult power'. Because the words 'mind' and 'soul' mislead people, Holbach proposes to dispense with them; 'they convey no sense that is accessible either to us or to those who invented them, and therefore cannot be of the slightest use for science or for ethics'.

Holbach admits a distinction between what he calls 'the physical man' and 'the moral man', but maintains that the distinction is not based on any division within man himself; it simply expresses our different ways of understanding man. The physical man is the man we see jumping when he is burned; he is the man whose actions are the effects of causes we can observe. The moral man is the man whose actions are the effect of causes we cannot observe, and which we attribute in our ignorance to the occult power called the mind. For example, we see a man running away from a battlefield, and we judge him to be animated by fear—we cannot see what is motivating him so we attribute it to a 'cowardly soul' within him.

This common way of thinking, Holbach continues, breeds even more extravagant fantasies, such as the idea that the soul can survive the body, which, he protests, is just like believing that a clock could continue to chime after its works have been destroyed. The belief in the freedom of the will is in Holbach's eyes another popular illusion that needs to be demolished. How does it originate?

When we go back to the sources of our actions, he argues, we find that they are always the necessary results of our desires and wishes, over which we have no control. People have believed that we are free because we have a will, and the power to choose, but 'they have not paid attention to the fact that our wishes and desires are necessarily caused by objects or factors which are entirely independent of us'.

Diderot was evidently shocked by Holbach's idea that determinism meant the total elimination of moral responsibility. In a letter he quoted with dismay Holbach's assertion that 'a human being who injures me acts no more freely than a tile which falls from the roof and hits me on the head and is therefore no more to be blamed'. Diderot suggested that Holbach was in effect a fatalist, and some of Holbach's remarks seem to confirm this judgement. For example, we find him writing: 'O vain and feeble Man! You claim to be free. You do not see the chains that bind you. Do you think your weak will can force nature to stop her eternal march, or change her course?'

But fatalism was a charge that Holbach would not accept. He claimed that the elimination of free will did not remove the possibility of altering the future. If all actions are caused, then the intervention of new causes can modify men's actions; if every choice is conditioned, different conditions will generate different choices. According to Holbach, it was the sceptics, such as Montaigne and David Hume, who were the true fatalists; for these were philosophers who could find no solid basis for challenging the imperfections of existing institutions, and so resigned themselves to accepting and even supporting whatever habit, custom, and tradition had established. A perpetually open mind, Holbach thought, was useless; the sceptics, resting their heads 'on the pillow of doubt', appeared to him to be the most rigid of conservatives.

Holbach, for his part, was a believer: an ardent believer in nature. But nature has more than one meaning in Holbach's philosophy. First of all, nature is everything that is. All the movements we observe in the world, including those movements we speak of as human actions, are movements governed by the laws of nature; this is why there can be a science of human behaviour as well as a science of astronomy.

Secondly, nature appears in Holbach's writings as a sort of Supreme Ruler. At the end of his ***Système de la nature,*** he gives nature a voice and makes it—or her—speak to the human race in these words:

> O Man, in following the impulse I have implanted in you to strive every instant of your life for happiness, do not resist my sovereign law. Labour to your own felicity . . . You will find the means clearly written in your own heart . . . Dare to liberate yourselves from the yoke of religion, my supreme rival . . . It is in my empire that freedom reigns . . . Come back, wandering child, come back to nature. She will console you. She will banish cares from your heart. O man, be happy!

There are more passages in Holbach's ethical writings of a similar kind, pleas which would seem to make sense only if man is assumed to have the freedom to obey—or disobey—the supreme ruler, nature. For there can be no doubt that Holbach is saying that it is open to man either to obey the laws of nature and flourish, or disobey the laws of nature and suffer. Nature, in other words, enacts the role in Holbach's system which God performs in religious systems. Nature is the fountain of all that is good. Truth, reason, and virtue he describes in a poetic phrase as the 'three daughters of nature'; and he goes on to suggest that nature upholds morality by punishing vice with diseases and death and rewarding virtue with happiness.

There is, however, a third sense of 'nature' as it appears in Holbach's theory. This is sometimes distinguished as 'undeveloped nature' or 'brutish nature' and sometimes as 'corrupted nature'; it is responsible for those impulses which turn men away from virtue. Moreover, Holbach was more alive to the power of such evil impulses than were most philosophers of the Enlightenment. Despite his opulent style of living, he was a puritan; and he drew between happiness and pleasure a sharp distinction which puts him at odds with the utilitarians, with Helvétius and other moralists of the Enlightenment for whom happiness was to be measured by the felicific calculus, or the predominance of pleasure over pain.

Holbach simply could not believe the stories of Bougainville and Diderot which suggested that the natives of Tahiti were both happy and sexually promiscuous. Since such practices were immoral, Holbach reasoned that the Tahitians *must* be unhappy as well as ignorant. 'There are countries', he wrote, 'where public opinion attaches merit to the most abominable conduct . . . From this we conclude that human reason has not yet been sufficiently developed in many countries for the people to distinguish what is really good from what merely appears to be good.'

The cult of nature for Holbach is manifestly not a policy of liberation, of freeing men from constraints which hin-

der natural enjoyment. The enthronement of good nature requires a constant struggle against bad nature. He calls the system of government that is needed to procure this end ethocracy, or the rule of morality. This is a regime which fits into no taxonomy of constitutions familiar to political science, either that of Aristotle or that of Montesquieu; but it has striking resemblance to the theocracies of Savonarola and Calvin. It is ironical that so impassioned an atheist as Holbach should be placed in the same category as those fervent Christian reformers, but they were his direct forerunners as champions of a political order ruled by morality, albeit in their case of a morality conceived as divinely ordained.

The extremes, we are often told, meet; ethocracy is puritan politics without puritan theology. Holbach's determinism poses analogous problems to those posed by Calvin's predestination; and the places of God and the Devil in Calvin's scheme are taken by good nature and bad nature in Holbach's. For both, morality can become supreme in earthly societies only as a result of a continuous struggle against immorality; and the two theorists have curiously similar ideas about the institutional arrangements that are needed to ensure the rule of morality.

Most philosophers of the French Enlightenment admired the English political system as much as they admired English philosophy—at any rate, until the North American wars of the 1770s diminished their Anglomania, they tended to follow the lead of Montesquieu and Voltaire in considering the English constitution 'the mirror of liberty'. If they did not all have the same conception of liberty, or the same notion of how the English system worked, nearly all of them considered England the best governed country in Europe. Holbach thought differently. He received a highly critical account of English politics from his radical friend of Leiden University days, John Wilkes, and when he went to see England for himself for six months in 1756 he formed a most unfavourable opinion of both the government and the people. The inequality between rich and poor appeared to him to be even more shocking and gross than it was in France; English politicians seemed to him to be wholly unprincipled and Parliament, corrupt. Reversing the judgement of Voltaire, he said that the King of England was free to do harm but had his hands tied when he wanted to do good. Holbach complained that English universities paid no attention to science and scant attention to any other branch of scholarship. The English people did not know the difference between freedom and licence, and far from being a 'mirror of liberty', the whole kingdom was a 'mirror of anarchy'. The standards by which Holbach judged England were not those of liberalism, but of ethocracy: and the criteria he invoked were probity, purity, and equity.

The one lesson that Holbach proposed to derive from English experience was the need to subordinate freedom to discipline, law, and virtue. He disagreed with Montesquieu's view that virtue was not compatible with royal government, and suggested that both in republics and in monarchies 'virtue and honour should be inseparable'. Since Holbach was writing mainly for French readers, one can understand why his book concentrates on monarchies, and discusses ways in which virtue can be made to prevail under the sovereignty of a king.

The first essential, he suggests, is that the king himself

should be virtuous. How is that to be assured? To begin with, the state should take the education of heirs to the throne out of the hands of the royal family, and give the princes a civil upbringing to fit them for their high office. Next, the king himself should be shielded from the corrupting influence of courtiers and flatterers.

Since all are agreed that a king must be loved, the state must ensure that he deserves to be loved. And just as princes must be educated for kingship, so must the people be educated for citizenship. Like Calvin, once again, Holbach proposed a system of free and compulsory public instruction, on the grounds that 'the happiest state is that which contains the greatest number of enlightened people'. The aim of all education should be the improvement of morals at the same time as the enlargement of knowledge. The teaching of history, for example, should be designed to show pupils how *virtue* has contributed in the past to the glory and prosperity of nations, and how *vice* has brought about their decay. The teaching of sciences should be directed to awakening the pupil's awareness of the usefulness of science as distinct from the purely academic content. There should be no wasting of time, Holbach suggests, on dead languages; but there should be daily teaching of a 'moral catechism' and a 'moral code', so as to prepare children for a life of virtue. Moreover, this education should be provided for girls as well as boys, for the 'experience of Sparta', Holbach writes, 'demonstrates that women can acquire a patriotism, a greatness of soul and wisdom of which men themselves are incapable in corrupt and enslaved nations'.

Despite the stress he put on education, Holbach did not agree with Helvétius that education could do almost anything in shaping a child's character. He rejected Helvétius' claim that inherited factors were nothing and environmental factors everything, so that, given the right training, any child could be made to do whatever the teacher designed he should do. Holbach agreed that education was necessary to produce good citizens, but argued that it was not enough to prevent some from backsliding into vice. Legislation was also needed, together with the continued direction of society by the state to ensure that the people were kept in the path of virtue.

Holbach was a good enough Lockian to proclaim every man's rights to life, liberty, and property, but he added a warning: 'liberty is a dangerous weapon in the hands of a corrupt people'. How, then, can liberty and virtue be kept alive in tandem?

First, Holbach recommends sumptuary laws. These must begin at the top: 'it is not with ostentatious palaces that a prince should impress his subjects, but by the wisdom of his administration'. The frugality of the monarch should match that of his people, and, what is even more important, his chastity should be exemplary: 'the royal palace should be a sanctuary into which nothing impure can enter'.

There is a place for nobility in Holbach's model kingdom, but not for the kind of landed aristocracy that dates from medieval feudalism. 'Feudalism', he wrote, 'was nothing but a massive brigandage, and a nobility of blood based on ancient or Gothic lineage is worthless.' Nobility as it is known in eighteenth-century France is a 'frivolous and empty distinction', and the ethos of the *noblesse de race*

which exalts 'idleness, military prowess, luxury, gambling, and gallantry' is no good for anyone. An aristocrat is useful only in his capacity as landowner, and members of that class, Holbach suggests, should be made to apply themselves to managing and improving their estates, organizing farms, developing industries, and transforming the countryside into a source of social wealth. Their class would then become a genuine aristocracy with a wholly new set of values: work, production, service.

Holbach did not carry his enthusiasm for this idea to the point of removing himself to his own very large estates in Germany in order to manage and improve them, any more than he imposed sumptuary laws on the life-style of his château and his *hôtel particulier* in Paris; his perception of his own function was within the aristocracy of the mind, as a hard-working philosopher who was also a convenor of meetings of other philosophers, the head of an invisible college. He made no attempt, as did Voltaire, to defend the privileges of the rich. Indeed, he suggested that great fortunes were generally the fruit of injustice, and he argued that it was one of the duties of the state, in a society where there were great disparities of wealth, to subdue the rich and take care of the poor. He stopped short of the proposals of such contemporaries as the Abbé de Mably that the state should actually redistribute wealth. He was strongly critical of Helvétius' doctrine of human equality. His only contribution to the birth of socialism was to question the right of the rich to own the wealth they held. He considered belief in democracy to be absurdly Utopian.

Holbach accepted Locke's theory that the right to property was originally derived from the intermixing of a man's labour with the produce of nature. 'Property', he wrote, 'has as its basis a necessary relation established between a man and the fruit of his labour. The field watered with the sweat of his brow becomes, as it were, a part of himself. The fruits it brings forth belong to him . . . because were it not for his labour these fruits would either not exist at all or at least in a different form'.

Where Holbach differs from Locke is that he does not modify the labour theory by adding a doctrine of tacit consent to the use of money, which serves in the end for Locke to justify property based on rent and inheritance as distinct from labour; Holbach sticks to labour as the one source of entitlement, adding to it only a utilitarian justification of differences in wealth: 'society reduces men to mutual dependence; the great have need of the small and the small of the great'. Elsewhere he suggests: 'An enlightened policy ought to work in such a way that the greatest number of citizens may possess some property of their own . . . when a small number of men absorb all the property and wealth of a state, they become its masters, and thereafter it is only with the very greatest difficulty that it can take from them the fortune they have amassed.'

Holbach singled out two sorts of large fortune for condemnation; first there were those, like that of Helvétius, derived from tax-farming, a form of revenue-raising which Holbach described as suited only to a despot, since it led to taxes paid by the king's subjects being doubled, one part serving to finance the state and the other going to enrich extortioners. Secondly, Holbach condemned fortunes derived from rent or interest by idle landowners, who were corrupted by their own exemption from labour; 'every man who does not work becomes a bad citizen, a vicious libertine'. Holbach himself could never be accused of idleness. He wrote books which brought him no income; and the unearned income he derived from rents and investments gave him the freedom to do so. Hence his strictures on 'idle landowners' could not apply to himself, since he was the most industrious of men.

As for fortunes derived from commerce, Holbach's attitude was much more critical. He was mistrustful of trade. He believed that the happiest nation was one with a predominantly pastoral economy. He was not at all in favour of industrialization. In this respect he was far closer to Rousseau, whom he disliked, than to Diderot, whom he loved. 'A nation . . . will be sufficiently rich', said Holbach, 'when, without excessive labour, its soil provides the products necessary to its existence.' An unbridled passion for trade had, he suggested, been the chief cause of the corruption of England. And far from sharing the progressive opinion that commerce was conducive to peace, he suggested that most of the wars which afflicted Europe in his time were essentially commercial wars. The age of dynastic wars was over. The only reason why the French and the English were still fighting each other in the eighteenth century was that the two kingdoms had collided in their colonial and commercial adventures in the New World and in India.

As an early critic of what is now called 'imperialism' Holbach was really closer to Lenin than was Diderot, who is often claimed as a forerunner of Lenin. For Holbach ascribes the empire-building of his time to specifically capitalist motives, contrasting it with the Roman endeavour to build an empire for the sake of power and the Spanish endeavour to build an empire in order to propagate religion. The new imperialists—French, English, Dutch—he alleged were scrambling for markets, profits, and gold, to such an extent that rivalry between them was the greatest single cause of war. He seems to have considered the English the most culpable in this activity. In one of his more purple passages, he implores the people of England—'O Albion' is the form of address—to turn away from their worship of money and rediscover virtue in the cultivation of their own soil.

To some extent Holbach was simply reflecting a changed attitude in French public opinion towards the English after the defeat of French armies in Canada; but his chief objections to the English were peculiarly his own. Indeed, he disliked and disapproved of the English for features of their character which other French intellectuals admired, and his hostility to English politics and English philosophy extended to English economics. He had no belief in Adam Smith and his theory of an invisible hand reconciling the individual's pursuit of his own good with the realization of the common good. Holbach said that the common good could be realized only if everyone sought directly to promote the common good; hence the necessity of virtue, understood by Holbach, as by Montesquieu, as the disposition in the citizen always to put the public interest before his private interest.

And yet there is a kind of 'invisible hand' in Holbach's own scheme, and that is the hand exercised by nature—in the sense of Mother Nature. The workings of this force help to explain how Holbach could be at the same time a puritan and a utilitarian. The end he points out to man is happiness. Nature impels everyone to seek happiness, but it does not instruct everyone how to achieve happiness. The wise man alone knows that the happiness of each is only to be found in the happiness of all, since Mother Nature has arranged things so that unselfish actions are rewarded and selfish actions punished, with the result that the individual whose actions are directed towards the realization of universal happiness will experience enduring personal happiness, while the individual who pursues only personal gratification is doomed to disappointment. Admittedly brutish nature impels many men to seek such short-term satisfaction, but in the long run Mother Nature will deny them real happiness.

Since the word 'pleasure' is commonly associated with the kind of instant gratification that Holbach warns against, 'pleasure' cannot serve in his type of utilitarian ethics, as it does in that of Helvétius and Jeremy Bentham, as a measure of the good. Happiness, as Holbach understands it, is often achieved only at the expense of pleasure. Happiness is the reward of virtue; and virtue is as often as not a matter of self-denial. Theorists like Adam Smith and Voltaire seemed to Holbach to be suggesting that one could have one's cake and eat it; think of yourself and the invisible hand will ensure that everyone is thought of. Holbach's Mother Nature is altogether less indulgent to her children. She will reward efforts and abstinence; but she has nothing but misery to offer the self-indulgent, the lazy, and the licentious.

On the subject of luxury, so much debated in the Enlightenment, Holbach is with Diderot and Rousseau and against Voltaire and Hume. He argues that there is no substance in the claim that luxury benefits the poor by providing employment for their skills as artisans. He maintains that luxury is injurious to the working classes in diverting their skills from the production of useful to the production of useless goods. As for the middle and upper classes, they derive no real advantages from luxury; for the middle classes are forced to spend more than they can afford in order to make themselves look richer than they really are, while the upper classes are led to seek satisfaction in the empty pleasures and frivolous refinements of life instead of pursuing true happiness by doing their duty and cultivating pure joys, which are the most intense that human beings can experience. In a society where luxury dominates, Holbach concludes, wealth itself comes to be thought of as honourable and poverty disgraceful.

Such is the reasoning behind Holbach's pleas for the abolition of conspicuous consumption. He suggests that this should be accomplished partly by means of sumptuary laws, and partly by heavy taxation on palaces, carriages, liveried servants, ornamental gardens, jewellery, and finery. Gambling and prostitution he would have suppressed by law. He quotes Hesiod's remark that 'The gods gave men work in order to preserve virtue'; and these words hold the key to Holbach's scheme. Work is productive from the point of view of the economy, and redemptive from that of morals. The 'work ethic' is yet another feature of his thinking which he shares with Calvin. Indeed Holbach's whole programme of social reform recalls that devised by Calvin for Geneva in the sixteenth century. Holbach never mentions Geneva. His references are always to the more glamorous republics of Sparta and Rome, although he singles out for praise those institutions of the ancient world which Calvin copied. Holbach evokes, for example, the censorial tribunals of Rome, which served 'as a powerful barrier against luxury and vice'. By the surveillance of private morals they helped individuals to resist temptation. 'Men, all too often lacking in experience and reason, are nothing but children perpetually driven by vices, passions, and tastes that a solicitous government should carefully correct.' In practice this means that the state, in doing its duty to overcome 'brutish nature', must put a stop to all activities on which brutish nature feeds: not only gambling and prostitution, but balls, public festivities, feasts, entertainments, comedies, operas, and indeed all drama except serious tragedies which convey a moral. The state, as Holbach saw it, would not be diminishing happiness by taking away so many pleasures: it would simply be removing impediments to a life of virtue, which is the path of true happiness.

Since Holbach advocates such radical changes in the organization of society, the question is bound to be asked: is Holbach a revolutionary? In a certain sense he is. In another sense he is not. His situation has much in common with that of Rousseau, another theorist close to Calvin, and understandably so as a native of Calvin's Geneva. When Rousseau considered what a society would be like in which men were both free and ruled, he outlined the republic we find in his *Social Contract,* an idealized fusion of Geneva and Sparta. When Holbach came to describe a society in which men could recover both happiness and morality, he envisaged an ideal kingdom where a virtuous monarch ruled over virtuous subjects, with much the same laws as those of Rousseau's city-state. There is, however, one great difference between Rousseau's model republic and Holbach's model kingdom; Rousseau demands absolute and undivided sovereignty for the people; Holbach refuses to allow absolute and undivided sovereignty to the king. Here we meet another side of Holbach's thinking, one which has echoes of Locke and Montesquieu.

The sovereignty which reposes in the king, Holbach argues, must derive from the consent of the people; and he adds that constitutional or fundamental laws are needed to prevent a monarch from slipping into despotism. Even an enlightened monarch is intolerable if he becomes despotic: 'No man can acquire the right to rule a nation against its will. The most legitimate, wise, and virtuous of sovereigns would be no better than a tyrant if he governed in the teeth of his people's wishes.' A nation therefore has the right 'to force its monarchs to be just and reasonable, and failing that to depose them from the throne'. In another context Holbach wrote: 'It is impossible to repeat too often that the rights of nations are prior to those of the kings they have chosen to put at their head. They have never lost the right to limit, alter, circumscribe, and revoke the powers they have given, whenever they recognize that they have been abused.' The word 'nation' is crucial here, because Holbach does not confer on the population in general the right to rebel against their king. Revolutions which are manifestations of popular rage are likely to lead to anarchy. Tyrannicide is wrong; persecuted minorities should simply emigrate. The people must never take the law into their own hands: 'it is only the nation as a whole, through its representatives, that has the right to resist, to enforce obligations and to punish its oppressors'.

When Holbach asserted the right of a society to overthrow its sovereign by force, he may have been thinking of the kind of revolution which happened in England in 1689 when the national magistrates had placed a new king on the throne of a monarch who had fled; but when he spoke of society acting through a 'corps of representatives', he did not have in mind an elected assembly on the lines of the English Parliament; he refers to that body of citizens who are 'the most upright, the most enlightened and the most devoted to the public interest'. In a word, an aristocracy is here envisaged as the authentic representative body of the nation. Furthermore, Holbach suggested that this corps should be institutionalized, with a right to meet without being convoked by the monarch. Hence, although he speaks approvingly in dedicating his book *Éthocratie* to Louis XVI of that king's 'absolute power', the constitution he sketches out in the text is plainly one where the monarch's sovereignty is *not* absolute, but limited by the right of the 'corps of representatives' to have a share in that sovereignty, and to function as an autonomous institution in the state.

If there are similarities between Holbach's 'ethocracy' and Calvin's 'theocracy', one must not overlook one great difference. Calvin's theory made provision for its translation from the world of intellectual speculation to that of practical politics, as indeed it needed to, since Calvin was called upon by the burghers of Geneva to redraft the constitution for their city-state. No one gave such a commission to Holbach, and his *Éthocratie* offers little indication of how its programme might be actualized in the France of the 1770s. His book calls for a king who is educated from infancy in the paths of austere virtue. But Louis XVI was 60 years old in 1770, and far removed from any Spartan ethic; his heir was already 16. France would have to wait a long time for a prince who could be educated on entirely new lines. Holbach also calls for the institution of a 'censorial tribunal' to preserve the people's virtue by means of surveillance and sanctions. Calvin provided such a body, under the control of his Church, and it proved to be very active for several generations in upholding puritan morality in Geneva. But Holbach, as an atheist, could have no church from which to recruit a similar censorial tribunal. Then again, Holbach calls for the institution of a *corps of representatives,* composed of the most virtuous and enlightened persons in the kingdom. But how was such an aristocracy of morals to be recognized?

In the event, as Holbach lifted his eyes from his books to survey the real world of French politics outside, he saw no corps of 'the most virtuous and most enlightened men in the kingdom', but only a body which fancied itself to be composed of such men, namely the *noblesse de robe* as assembled in the *parlements.* Thus he found himself in a position where, to the horror of Voltaire, he felt it necessary to accept the self-image of the *parlements;* and to come out in the 1770s as a champion of those *parlements* when they were suppressed by the King. Finding no other point of contact between his abstract schemes of reform and the concrete exigencies of his situation, he passed from his argument that an aristocracy of virtue was necessary to a good monarchy to the conclusion that the restoration of the powers of the *noblesse de robe* was necessary to the regeneration of France.

It would be a vulgar error to suggest that Holbach came down from the clouds of revolutionary speculation to end up as yet another ideologue of his class; a *baron* at last, alarmed at the suppression of a privileged order. He was not, after all, a member, like Montesquieu, of the *noblesse de robe;* he derived his nobility from the regime of Louis XIV, who made a point of giving titles to tradesmen. Holbach owed his rank to unencumbered royal absolutism, which made it all the harder for Voltaire to understand how Holbach could go over to the other side.

But it seems that Holbach felt forced into this position by the lack of any alternatives; better a defective corps of representatives than no corps of representatives at all. Besides, he could not fail to listen to the arguments of Diderot, who had come to be more than ever opposed to royal absolutism after his experience with the Empress Catherine. Diderot helped to persuade him that the *parlements* were essential to maintain what little was left of liberty.

Holbach and Diderot had stood together before against Voltaire and the *voltairiens.* They had been for atheism against deism; for the state management of the economy against *laissez-faire;* for the poor against the rich. In 1770 they found themselves together once more.

From the perspective of Voltaire, the *parlements* were the judicial murderers of Calas and Lally and la Barre, the burners of books, the defenders of feudal privilege; so that when Louis XV banished them and replaced them with royal salaried magistrates Voltaire felt that his cry of 'écrasez l'infâme!' had at last been heard at Versailles. He saw the suppression of the *noblesse de robe* as the removal of the chief obstacle to reform in France. But Holbach shared with Diderot the fear that what was being removed was rather the last obstacle to tyranny in France. So Holbach pleaded for the restoration of the *parlements,* and attacked the centralizing policy of Versailles. He did not want enlightened government if royal despotism was the price of it. He preferred the haphazard oppression of familiar, confused, and divided authorities, a situation in which a clever man could find freedom in the interstices, and make blueprints of a better world. (pp. 123-39)

> Maurice Cranston, "Holbach," in his *Philosophers and Pamphleteers: Political Theorists of the Enlightenment,* Oxford University Press, Oxford, 1986, pp. 121-39.

Seamus Deane (essay date 1988)

[*Deane is an Irish poet and literary scholar. He claims that "in scholarship, I have been influenced by the writings of the French Enlightenment." In the excerpt below, he explores d'Holbach's theories on crime and punishment, emphasizing the relationship between conscience, natural law, and punishment*].

The Abbé Bergier, Holbach's most formidable contemporary critic, accused him of destroying morality by reducing all things to the level of the physical and the useful: "It is evident that the confounding of the moral with the useful, virtue with physical well-being, duty with desire, moral obligation with the forever renewed wishes of our hearts, leads to the destruction, not the establishment of a moral system; to do this is to form a code for brute-animals, not for men." In one sense this is true; but then Holbach's terminology and that of the Abbé were based on entirely different assumptions about the nature of man and the world. No one was more ardent or hectoring in

his desire to create a new ethical system based on exclusively materialist premises than was Holbach.

The remorseless aggression of his writing gives his work the appearance of consistency; yet despite the uniformity of its expression, his thought is a tissue of contradictions. Nevertheless, his works had a profound influence in nineteenth-century England, and Godwin was attracted to one of their most striking anomalies—Holbach's concept of conscience. This embraced precisely those relationships between honor, reputation, self-respect, and the guilt of secret crime which Helvétius had failed to develop.

According to Holbach, disorder results when some person or thing acts in contradiction to its nature. Chance or accident is only apparent; knowledge would reveal the interaction of cause and effect. All is linked in the great chain of necessity: "There is nothing accidental or fortuitous in nature." In this tightly constructed world, man seems to have little possible margin of error. He is nothing more than a transient combination of particles of matter who must adapt to his environment or perish. His intellectual and moral life is rooted in the physical and, like it, is part of the inescapably determined and determining system of the universe. Freedom is out of the question: "Man is no more free to think than to act."

The Helvétian reciprocity between private and public good takes its place quite naturally in this system: the good is what is socially useful, evil what is socially harmful. But Holbach, unlike Helvétius, also paid attention to the internal harmony of the personality. His *Système de la nature* acknowledges the Helvétian system of external harmony and determinism; but *Système social* and *La Morale universelle* both concentrate on the psychology of the individual who acts in a moral manner and, more interestingly in the present case, on the individual who acts immorally toward his environment and his fellows. Good and evil are not measured in this internal world by beneficial and harmful effects. Order in the internal world, like order in the adjacent world outside, is dependent on each person's abiding by the principles of his nature; good and evil are then defined in those terms: "The Good is that which is in conformity with our nature; Evil is anything contrary to it."

Just as enlightened reason reveals the source of disorder in the external world, conscience examines the shortcomings of the internal universe. The perceptions of conscience seem, according to Holbach, to be limited to a privileged elite:

> The voice of conscience is heard only by those who are introspective, who reason about their actions and in whom a sound education has nurtured the wish to please and the habitual fear of being despised or hated. A person formed in this manner becomes capable of judging himself; he reproaches himself when he commits an action which he knows might alter the feelings which he wants constantly to arouse in those whose esteem and affection are necessary to his happiness. Every time he behaves badly, he feels shame, remorse, repentance; he examines his behaviour, he corrects himself, out of fear of undergoing again the painful recognitions which often force him to hate himself, because at such times he sees himself as he is seen by others.

The conscience-striken man is acutely conscious of the

loss of his reputation in the eyes of those whom he has injured; and this loss disturbs his own well-being. Holbach was obviously trying to build up an internal world of reciprocal relationships to balance the deterministic external system which he had adopted from Helvétius and others.

Conscience, then, is the internal faculty by which man becomes aware of any contravention of his own nature. Similarly, it alone can impart that feeling of satisfaction which a good reputation, an unblemished honor, deserves. Holbach was careful to distinguish this from the traditional aristocratic honor, with all its military and religious connotations. True honor consists in a balance between self-respect and the respect of others: "No force on earth can deprive the good man of that true honour which belongs to him alone." The possession or loss of reputation becomes a barometer of the moral climate in which man lives. As long as a man follows his nature and acts morally, he will feel at peace with himself and is at home everywhere. He is integrated into his milieu and is part of the great natural process of life. If society at large has become vicious, the virtuous man, like Godwin's St. Leon, retreats to the bosom of his family. In this as in many other details of Holbach's philosophy a religious shadow is visible; Holbach tends to think of his virtuous men of conscience as a persecuted elite or sect. This contrasts sharply with Helvétius's idea of the great man rising above the praise of particular societies to bask in the esteem of the general public. Both writers have in common a preoccupation with the issues of self-esteem and public reputation and the need to make these congruent with each other. The emphasis is different in each case, largely because Holbach confronts the problem of secret crime which Helvétius ignores. As a consequence he is much more involved with the dilemma of the private conscience and its system of internal censorship and punishment.

To put it bluntly—as Holbach does—the issue of the undetected crime is resolved by the claim that the criminal punishes himself with a severity which society could not equal. "Laws can only punish visible crimes and public misdemeanours; they cannot deal with hidden faults and unknown crimes. Nevertheless, these do not remain unpunished on that account. Man's very nature punishes him for them. The wrongdoer is always in a state of fear, while the good man, even in the midst of misfortune and despite human injustice, enjoys the respect of men of good will, and savours the sweetness of a clear conscience." The good man enjoys the respect of his comrades in belief and the pleasure of his own clear conscience in the midst of a hostile and corrupt world.

Just as the good man enjoys reputation and status wherever he goes, the criminal, conversely, becomes an outcast throughout the civilized world. Having lost the esteem of others, he loses self-esteem; these are interdependent. The predictable result is that he learns to despise himself. Trapped in this unequal struggle against society and against his own nature, the criminal becomes a social outcast: "Only the good man is a truly social being. The criminal is always anti-social . . . Wickedness is a constant struggle of one man against all and against his own happiness." The criminal is guilty not of sin but of social immorality. Yet this itself is nothing more than a new version of what had been called sinfulness, with reputation, public opinion, and the fear of dislike acting as the deterrents instead of wild superstitions; and as deterrents they are, in Holbach's view, much more effective than the vague terrors of religion. Yet the tortures of the criminal are as vividly portrayed and as excruciating as those provided by conventional religion:

> Nature's law decrees that the criminal can never know a pure happiness in this world. His wealth, his power do not save him from his own nature. In the lucid moments spared him by his passions, if he dwells on his interior state, he suffers the reproach of a conscience troubled by the dreadful spectacles which his imagination presents to him. Thus it is that the murderer, during the night, even when awake, believes he sees the mourning ghosts of those whose throats he has cruelly cut; he sees the horrified state of the enraged crowd which cries aloud for vengeance.

Not surprisingly, such wretches give themselves up or commit suicide. Holbach here delivers a cautionary tale with some notably Gothic touches. The conclusion is that criminals succumb to despair because they cannot be reconciled to themselves. They have broken nature's law, and nature's law in turn breaks them. (pp. 80-3)

> *Seamus Deane, "Godwin, Helvétius, and Holbach: Crime and Punishment," in his* The French Revolution and Enlightenment in England: 1789-1832, *Cambridge, Mass.: Harvard University Press, 1988, pp. 72-94.*

FURTHER READING

Cushing, Max Pearson. *Baron D'Holbach: A Study of Eighteenth Century Radicalism in France.* New York: Columbia University Press, 1914, 108 p.
    Explores the baron's beliefs concerning politics and religion.

Hoagwood, Terence Allan. "Holbach and Blake's Philosophical Statement in 'The Voice of the Devil'." *English Language Notes* XV, No. 3 (March 1978): 181-86.
    Explores the possible influence of *The System of Nature* on Blake's *The Marriage of Heaven and Hell.*

Kors, Alan Charles. "The Myth of the Coterie Holbachique." *French Historical Studies* IX, No. 4 (Fall 1976): 573-95.
    Traces the development of the intellectual coterie surrounding d'Holbach, refuting the idea that this group was large in number and comprised completely of atheists.

Lough, J. "Helvetius and Holbach." *The Modern Language Review* XXXIII, No. 3 (July 1938): 360-84.
    Examines the relationship between d'Holbach and Helvétius, from social positions to philosophies.

Newland, T. C. "D'Holbach, Religion, and the 'Encyclopédie'." *The Modern Language Review* 69, No. 3 (July 1974): 523-33.
    Discusses d'Holbach's use of irony when treating religious topics in the *Encyclopédie.*

Richardson, Robert D., Jr. Introduction to *The System of Nature, Vol. 1,* by Paul Henri Thiery, Baron d'Holbach, pp. v-vii. New York: Garland Publishing, 1984.
    Discusses d'Holbach's antimythical beliefs while pointing out the important differences the baron distinguished between myth and theology.

Tallentyre, S. G. "D'Holbach: The Host." In his *The Friends of Voltaire,* pp. 118-49. London: Smith, Elder, and Co., 1906.
    Describes the atmosphere of the baron's house during the visits of fellow philosophes and other guests at Grandval.

Thomas, Ernest Chester. "The System of Nature." In *The History of Materialism and Criticism of Its Present Importance,* by Friedrich Albert Lange, translated by Ernest Chester Thomas, pp. 92-123. New York: Harcourt, Brace and Co., 1925.
    Examines thoroughly the ideas behind *Le Système de la Nature* while also pointing out criticism rendered by earlier readers such as Johann Wolfgang von Goethe.

Topazio, Virgil W. "D'Holbach's Conception of Nature." *Modern Language Notes* LXIX, No. 6 (June 1954): 412-16.
    Examines d'Holbach's philosophical belief that "a return to nature was nothing more than [a] desire to get man to act in conformance with his human nature."

―――. *D'Holbach's Moral Philosophy: Its Background and Development.* Geneva: Institut et Musee Voltaire les Delices, 1956, 180 p.
    Traces the development of d'Holbach's philosophy and discusses the rationalist-materialist background of eighteenth-century France. The influence of the English deists and Diderot are also considered.

Paracelsus

1493-1541

(Born Aureolus Philippus Theophrastus Bombast von Hohenheim) Swiss writer of alchemical and medical treatises.

Paracelsus was an alchemist and medical reformer who came to be known in his day as "the Luther of medicine." In an age when medical practice was closely intertwined with magic and astrology, and when treatments of purging and bleeding killed more patients than were cured, he departed from the medical orthodoxies of his time, rejecting the precepts and practices of Galen, Aulus Cornelius Celsus, Hippocrates, and Avicenna while introducing the primitive beginnings of homeopathic medicine. He and his followers thus helped remove medical practice from the exclusive domain of a handful of secretive quacks and elites to a science involving experimentation and holistic concern, much of it to some extent understandable by the layman.

Paracelsus was born in Einsiedeln, near Zurich, to Wilhelm and Els von Hohenheim. The boy's father was a doctor who groomed his son to join the same profession. At age nine, Hohenheim took Aureolus with him to live in Villach, Austria, where the boy studied metallurgy at a school operated at the nearby silver mines. In his teens, he attended the universities of Basel, Paris, Vienna, Cologne, and Ferrara, where he first styled himself Paracelsus ("peer of Celsus"). He received his doctorate in medicine from the University of Ferrara in 1515. During those years he also received instruction in occult knowledge from Johannes Trithemius, Abbot of Sponheim.

As he entered adulthood, Paracelsus began his career as a physician and his life became surrounded by controversy and legend. He had already rejected the precepts and remedies of medical tradition, later writing, "I considered with myself that if there were no teacher of medicine in the world, how would I set about to learn the art? Not otherwise than in the great open book of nature, written with the finger of God." For contrary to the received medical knowledge of his day, he believed that the supposed four elements of which all creation consists (earth, wind, fire, and water) are themselves composed of three primary principles, which he identified as sulphur, salt, and mercury. The human body, he believed, is itself a delicate balance of the three principles, and thus a microcosm of all nature. When the body's three principles go out of balance, the result is disease. He further believed that for every disease there is a cure somewhere in nature, and that for healing to occur it is necessary for the physician to find and administer the processed minerals and herbal elixirs necessary to arrest specific physical ailments and bring the principles back into their state of proper balance. His travels in search of curative knowledge took him from the mines of Cornwall, England to as far east as Moscow, and from Sweden to the Levant. He studied galenic medicine in Montpellier, France and served as an army surgeon in the Netherlands and Venice. While in Salzburg in 1526, Paracelsus was imprisoned for expressing open sympathy

with the peasants' revolt. Fleeing that city, he settled first in Strassburg, where he was appointed a practicing physician; then in Basel, where he was made city physician and given the right to lecture on medical science at the university.

In Basel, Paracelsus achieved wide fame by healing the ailments of the noted printer Johann Froben, publisher of Desiderius Erasmus's works. Erasmus himself became one of Paracelsus's patients. But Paracelsus disturbed the university medical faculty by refusing to teach from the works of the familiar authorities, such as Galen and Hippocrates. Instead he denounced these pillars of medieval medical knowledge as frauds and announced his intention to teach according to his own medical beliefs and experience. His ensuing lectures were less concerned with purging and bleeding, after the old remedies, than with chemically removing from wounds and ailments any imbalance or impurity which would prevent nature from healing them. Reprimanded for his departure from accepted practice, Paracelsus publicly attacked his fellow doctors as "a misbegotten crew of approved asses," and then further alienated himself from the faculty by lecturing in his own German dialect, not in the traditional Latin. Paracelsus thereby sought to transform medical study from the exclusive domain of an inner circle of adepts to a more widely comprehensible discipline. In one memorable act he thoroughly outraged his peers when, on St. John's Day (June 24), 1527, he threw one of the medical faculty's central texts, Avicenna's *Canon,* on the traditional bonfire while declaiming loudly against all his medical predecessors. Shortly afterward, having made enemies within the Church in Basel, Paracelsus was forced to flee the city.

For the next fourteen years Paracelsus wandered throughout Europe, attempting to study, teach, and heal where he could, but driven from each stopping place by the threat of arrest or mob violence sprung from the whispering campaigns that followed him everywhere. In each city and town in which he paused, he excited comment by his effective cures of dread ailments, his iconoclastic boastfulness, his Rabelaisian capacity for strong drink, and by his mysterious reputation. Some people, for example, claimed that Paracelsus was a necromancer and that he cured infirmities with the aid of a demonic familiar. Enemies noted with suspicion that he never removed his long sword "Azoth"; it was believed that he kept his familiar hidden in the weapon's hollowed handle, along with mysterious drugs possessing curative powers. (Indeed, early engraved portraits of Paracelsus depict him removing the pommel of his sword.) Often his patients were poor and unable to pay him, and he was himself often dressed in rags. Having wandered over much of central and southern Europe, Paracelsus at last settled in Salzburg in 1540. He died there a year later, several days after dictating his will. The circumstances of his death are uncertain, with admirers claiming he was poisoned and hurled to his death from a height and detractors claiming that he died of a fall suffered during a drunken brawl. According to Leslie Shepard, editor of the *Encyclopedia of Occultism and Parapsychology,* Paracelsus was most likely poisoned, at the instigation of the university medical faculty. Others have claimed that he died of a stroke, having been in poor health during the last few years of his life. He was buried in Salzburg, with his grave becoming from that time a place where the poor of the city have come to pray.

Although Paracelsus wrote many medical treatises during his lifetime, the manuscripts were squirreled away in private libraries and muniment rooms all over the Continent, and thus few of the works were published until after his death. Some works, like his treatise on the treatment of syphilis, were long suppressed for indecency. Other works—including discourses on mineral water, cosmology, and surgical practices—were scattered hither and yon. The first complete edition was published in 12 volumes between 1589 and 1591, thanks largely to the efforts of Paracelsus's disciples, physicians who followed their master's medical teachings and thus became known as "the Paracelsians." This group, which included Johannes Herbst (called "Operinus"), Adam von Bodenstein, Michael Schütz (called "Toxites"), and Gerard Dorn further advanced Paracelsus's teachings, basing the teaching and practice of medicine on natural philosophy and experimentation. Their efforts laid the groundwork for further advances in the medical field, and thus they played a key role in the development of modern medicine.

The medical theories of Paracelsus where closely bound up with his occult philosophy, which is expounded in his treatise *Archidoxa.* He never diagnosed his patients' ills without first consulting the horoscope, believing that diseases ultimately have their origin in the planets, with the seven macrocosmic planets corresponding to the seven microcosmic major organs of the human body. (Much of his cosmological theory is also expounded in his two best-known works, *Das Buch Paragranum* and *Opus Paramirum,* written in 1530 and 1534, respectively.) "Everything that astronomical theory has profoundly fathomed by studying the planetary objects and the stars . . ." he wrote, "can also be applied to the firmament of the body." This stated, Paracelsus anticipated one aspect of Cartesian philosophy by theorizing that by bringing the human microcosm into equilibrium with the macrocosm of nature, health may be restored and life sustained indefinitely. A believer in astral bodies, he further held that with the proper discipline, human will-power and imagination could be used to project one's astral body across great distances and that enemies could be wounded or killed by telekinetic force. He contended that the only obstacle preventing all people from exercising such abilities is lack of belief, a precept that places Paracelsus as one of the forerunners of the New Age movement. In this matter, he also believed astral bodies interact and communicate with each other and was the first person to use the word "magnetism" in this sense, laying the foundation upon which Franz Mesmer developed his theory of magnetic influence. As for the scientists of his day, Paracelsus scorned most alchemists as "gold-cooks" for their attempts to turn base metal into gold; he saw a higher use for alchemy, believing it useful for spiritual and medical purposes. Some of his findings in this field proved medically sound, and some proved fraudulent. (Among his more intriguing failures, he left formulae for creating a living homunculus, or artificial man, for distilling a life-perpetuating Elixir of Life, and for concocting the all-curative Philosopher's Stone.) Among his successes in the search for effective treatment of diseases, as Stephen Skinner has written, "Paracelsus discovered opium, introduced mineral baths, mercury, lead, sulphur, arsenic and copper sulphate, a large part of the then known pharmacopoeia, and popularised tinctures and alcoholic extracts. To what extent these new methods were original to him and to what extent accumulated during his wanderings in foreign lands, it is not possible to determine."

In the years since his death, Paracelsus has been the object of both bitter scorn and absurdly shrill applause. He has been described as everything from a dabbler in the black arts to a misunderstood orthodox Christian doctor. Not surprisingly (considering the stories of his conjuring a demonic familiar), his life story contributed greatly to the Faust legend and markedly influenced the poetry and belief system of Johan Wolfgang von Goethe. In one of his early poems, Robert Browning depicted Paracelsus as the consummate Romantic hero: a Promethean bringer of knowledge into an unworthy and ungrateful world. In the late nineteenth and early twentieth centuries, Paracelsus has been praised for his contribution to modern occult belief and to the development of the medical profession. Thanks to the attention given his works by occultist A. E. Waite, psychologist C. G. Jung, and novelist Robertson Davies, Paracelsus is recognized as one of the most intriguing and important figures in the history of medicine.

Paracelsus and his followers radically altered the direction of the medical profession, opening the door to modern homeopathic treatments of diseases and curative treatments of wounds. Further, adds Shepard, "Not only was he the founder of modern science of medicine, [but] the magnetic theory of Mesmer, the "astral" theory of modern spiritualism, [and] the philosophy of Descartes were all foreshadowed in the fantastic, yet not always illogical, teaching of Paracelsus."

PRINCIPAL WORKS

Opus paramirum   (treatise) 1531
  [*Volumen Medicinae Paramirum* published in journal *Bulletin of the History of Medicine,* 1949]
Chirurgia magna   (treatise) 1536
Das Buch Paragranum   (treatise) 1565
Medicorum de philsophorum facile principia . . . libri v. de vita longa (treatise) 1566
  [*The Secrets of Physick and Philosophy,* 1633]
Archidoxa   (treatises) 1570
  [*The Archidoxes of Magic,* 1975]
Chirurgia minor quam Bertheoneam intitulaut (treatises) 1570
Opera omnia. 12 vols. (treatises) 1589-91
The Hermetic and Alchemical Writings. 2 vols. (treatises) 1894
*Sämtliche Werke. 15 vols. (treatises) 1922-33
Selected Writings (prose) 1951

*This German edition, edited and annotated by Karl Sudhoff and Wilhelm Matthiessen, is considered definitive.

Paracelsus   (essay date 1541?)

[*In the following excerpt from a collage of Paracelsus's writings assembled by Jolande Jacobi, Paracelsus states his credo.*]

I am different, let this not upset you.

I am writing this to prevent you from being misled in any point; please read and reread it with diligence, not with envy, not with hatred, for you are students of medicine. Also study my books, and compare my opinions with the opinions of others; then you may be guided by your own judgment.

I have thus far used simple language, and I cannot boast of any rhetoric or subtleties; I speak in the language of my birth and my country, for I am from Einsiedeln, of Swiss nationality, and let no one find fault with me for my rough speech. My writings must not be judged by my language, but by my art and experience, which I offer the whole world, and which I hope will be useful to the whole world. (p. 77)

I am resolved to pursue the noblest and highest philosophy and to let nothing divert me from it. . . . I shall not be concerned with the mortal part of man, and I shall meditate only upon that within him which does not die; for that is what we hold to be the highest philosophy.

Ever since my childhood I have pursued these things and learned them from good teachers, who were thoroughly grounded in *adepta philosophia* and well versed in the arts. First, from Wilhelmus von Hohenheim, my father, who has never forsaken me, and later from a great number of others whom I shall not name here, also from many writings of ancients and moderns of diverse lands, who laboured mightily.

For many years I studied at the universities of Germany, Italy, and France, seeking to discover the foundations of medicine. However, I did not content myself with their teachings and writings and books, but continued my travels to Granada and Lisbon, through Spain and England, through Brandenburg, Prussia, Lithuania, Poland, Hungary, Wallachia, Transylvania, Croatia, the Wendian Mark, and yet other countries which there is no need to mention here, and wherever I went I eagerly and diligently investigated and sought after the tested and reliable arts of medicine. I went not only to the doctors, but also to barbers, bathkeepers, learned physicians, women, and magicians who pursue the art of healing; I went to alchemists, to monasteries, to nobles and common folk, to the experts and the simple. . . . I have oftentimes reflected that medicine is an uncertain and haphazard art scarcely honourable to practise, curing one, and killing ten. . . . Many times I abandoned medicine and followed other pursuits, but then again I was driven back to it. Then I remembered Christ's saying: The healthy need not a physician, but only the sick. And so I made a new resolve, interpreting Christ's words to mean that the art of medicine is true, just, certain, perfect, and whole, and there is nothing in it that should be attributed to the deception of spirits or chance, but that it is an art tested in need, useful to all the sick and beneficial in restoring their health.

This is my vow: To perfect my medical art and never to swerve from it so long as God grants me my office, and to oppose all false medicine and teachings. Then, to love the sick, each and all of them, more than if my own body were at stake. Not to judge anything superficially, but by symptoms, nor to administer any medicine without understanding, nor to collect any money without earning it. Not to trust any apothecary, nor to do violence to any child. Not to guess, but to know. . . .

To give to each nation its own type of medicine, the theoricam best suited to it, as it behooves. For I can well realize that my prescriptions may turn out to be ineffectual among the foreign nations, and that foreign recipes may turn out to be ineffectual in our nation. That is to say, I write for Europe, and I do not know whether Asia and Africa may profit by it.

There is nothing in me except the will to discover the best that medicine can do, the best there is in nature, the best that the nature of the earth truly intends for the sick. Thus I say, nothing comes from me; everything comes from nature of which I too am part.

I have been criticized for being a wayfarer as though this made me the less worthy; let no one hold it against me if I defend myself against such allegations. The journeys I have made up until now have been very useful to me, because no man's master grows in his own home, nor has anyone found his teacher behind his stove.

I am Theophrastus, and greater than those to whom you liken me; I am Theophrastus, and in addition I am *monarcha medicorum,* monarch of physicians, and I can prove to you what you cannot prove. I will let Luther defend his cause, and I will defend my cause, and I will defeat those of my colleagues who turn against me; this I shall do with the help of the arcana. . . . It was not the constellations that made me a physician: God made me. . . . I need not don a coat of mail or a buckler against you, for you are not learned or experienced enough to refute even one word of mine. I wish I could protect my bald head against the flies as effectively as I can defend my monarchy. . . . I will not defend my monarchy with empty talk but with arcana. And I do not take my medicines from the apothecaries; their shops are but foul sculleries, from which comes nothing but foul broths. As for you, you defend your kingdom with belly-crawling and flattery. How long do you think this will last? . . . Let me tell you this: every little hair on my neck knows more than you and all your scribes, and my shoebuckles are more learned than your Galen and Avicenna, and my beard has more experience than all your high colleges.

I cannot help being indignant at your simplicity, for you do not understand the origin of surgery. To believe you, I am a surgeon and not a physician; how can you think so when everyone knows that I administered medical treatment (I am not writing this to boast of it) to eighteen princes whom you had given up? And when I have also tended innumerable persons stricken with fever, and cured them of forty kinds of disease which I found in them, in the Netherlands, in the Romagna, in Naples, and in Venetian, Danish, and Dutch wars? Is there no physician to reveal the lies of the scribes, to denounce their errors and abuses, to bring them to an end? Will you turn to ridicule the experience that I have acquired with so much diligence?

If they hate me for writing otherwise than their own authors, that is the fault of their own ignorance, not of mine. . . . The art of medicine does not cry out against me, for it is imperishable and established upon foundations so imperishable that heaven and earth shall pass away before the art of medicine shall die. And since the art of medicine leaves me at peace, why should I be perturbed by the outcries of mortal physicians, who cry only because I overthrow and wound them? . . . They are more eager to obscure their own errors than to fight in behalf of what the patients need, that is to say, the art, erudition, experience, piety, in which I seek the foundations and sources of my own writing.

But since such useless rabble befoul the art of medicine with their bungling, and seek nothing but their own profit, what can it avail that I admonish them to love? I for my part am ashamed of medicine, considering what an utter fraud it has come to be. (pp. 78-81)

I am not an apostle or anything like an apostle, but a philosopher in the German manner.

Here I have no wish to philosophize or speak of the afterlife, except in so far as this can be done in the light of nature. I await the consummation of my hope; let me first achieve my own salvation through my faith in the Saviour, and then it will be time to impart it to others.

Although I have spoken here in a heathen way, as many might think, although I called man an animal, it is not concealed from me and I know full well that the difference between man and animal lies solely in the countenance and the spirit. To this I must bear witness before God.

Why should my Father's light be judged and looked upon as heathenish, and I as a heathen, and walk in the light of Christ, both old and new? . . . And since I love them both, and see the light of each, as God ordained everyone to do, how can I be a heathen? . . . I have written in the Christian spirit and I am not a heathen . . . and I would defend myself as a Christian by saying that . . . I will not be called a sorcerer, or a heathen, or a gypsy, but profess myself as a Christian in my writings, and let the false Christians sweat with their own sour dough.

Desiring to write like a Christian, I have omitted the four *entia*, i. e., the active principles of the stars, the poisons, nature, and the spirit, and I have not described them. For this is not Christian style but heathen style. But the last principle is Christian, and with it I shall conclude. And the heathen conception that we describe in the four *entia* ought not to harm our faith, but only to make our minds keener.

So I have deemed it good to describe not only the natural man . . . but also, and with more delight, to go further and describe the eternal man, the heavenly man in the new birth, so that the old man may see and observe what man is, and learn to guide himself accordingly and learn what this reborn man can do, here on earth, and after this life, in the eternal life.

The time for writing is ripe, for I must spare nothing of what I have spoiled. The field has not yet been plowed: . . . the time of geometry is ended, the time of artistry is ended, the time of philosophy is ended, the snow of my misery has gone; the time of growth is ended. The time of summer is here; whence it comes I know not, whither it goes, I know not: it is here! . . . And so also is come the time to write on the blessed life and the eternal. (pp. 82-3)

> *Paracelsus, in his* Selected Writings, *edited by Jolande Jacobi, translated by Norbert Guterman, Bollingen Series XXVIII, Pantheon Books, 1951, 347 p.*

Benedictus Figulus   (essay date 1608)

[*In the following excerpt from his prefatory statement in* A Golden Casket of Nature's Marvels (1608), *Figulus praises the writings of Paracelsus in all disciplines while heatedly attacking the pirating of his works by unscrupulous opportunists.*]

We have . . . to complain of those who mutilate and falsify the works of true seekers after Natural Wisdom and Art, for I have clearly discovered defects, alterations, and foreign matter in the "Triumphal Chariot" of Fr. Basilius, and also in the writings of A. von Suchten and Theophrastus. More especially, dear Friends, have we to complain of the devilish cunning way in which the works of Theophrastus have hitherto been suppressed, only a few of which (and those to be reckoned the very worst) having appeared in print. For although they have been collected together from all countries in which Theophrastus has lived and travelled—the books he has written in Astronomy, Philosophy, Chemistry, Cabala, and Theology, numbering some thousand volumes—yet the same has only been done from avarice to get riches. For, having been trafficked in and sold for great sums, they have become scattered among the courts of princes and nobles, while Christendom at large, for whose use and benefit Theophrastus wrote, has no part in them. Particularly his theological works (because they annihilate the godless, and do not suit children of this world—belly-servers, deceived by the devil), have hitherto been totally suppressed. For which devilish end Thurneyser, a true instrument of Satan, who with his lies and false Alchemy has cheated all the world, Electors and Princes, great and small, has (amongst others whom I will here spare) been made great use of.

But, at the Last Day, before the Judgment Seat of Christ, I, together with all true sons of the Doctrine, shall demand an account of them for having stolen, sold, divided, and shut Truth away in boxes, walls, and vaults, and behind locks and bolts. Now, these precious and revered writings were ordered by God in our latter times, through Theophrastus, for the use and weal of the whole of Christendom. As regards our dear, highly-favoured Monarch and Preceptor, Ph. Theophrastus, of blessed memory, we, for our part, will not suppress his Life, his well-merited praise, and his immortal fame, given him by God, the Angels, and the whole Firmament, but will heartily defend his honour and teaching to the very end our life. (pp. 26-8)

> *Benedictus Figulus, "Prolocutory Dedicatory Address," in his* A Golden and Blessed Casket of Nature's Marvels, *J. Elliot & Co., 1893, pp. 3-32.*

Robert Turner   (essay date 1655)

[*Turner was a seventeenth-century English editor who translated Paracelsus's* Archidoxa, *Cornelius Agrippa's* De Occulta Philosophia, *and other works into the English language. In the following excerpt from prefatory material completed a few months before publishing his translation of the* Archidoxa, *he commends that work to his readers, discoursing upon Paracelsus's (and his own) understanding of the relationship between Christianity and occult knowledge.*]

Courteous Reader,

In this last Iron age, ignorance hath so much prevailed, that many have, and yet do plead for it, and strive to uphold it, crying down all Arts, and endeavoring to hoodwink knowledge; so that nothing but the feces and dreggs of Art seems to remain: so that they seem but shadows, if compared with that pristine learning of the Ancients. What golden Legends formerly flourished among the Hebrews, and Ægyptians, and are now even almost all lost in Oblivion? (p. VII)

And therefore [with **Of the Supreme Mysteries of Nature**] I present the ingenious Reader with a part of the Workes of the renowned Paracelsus of the secrets of Alchymy, Occult Philosophy, and the wonderful operation of the Celestial bodyes, in curing diseases by sigils and characters, made and applyed in sit elected times and seasons, and under their proper constellations, as the Author hath directed, I must expect the sottish Malignant censures of

Zoylus and Momus, and such fools: but the Author himself in his Prologue in the ensuing discourse, sufficiently cleares all objections, and therefore I shall have that labour; onely I would have such men not be so wilfully ignorant, as altogether to forget, that the Heavens declare the glory of God, and the Firmament sheweth his handyworke. (p. VIII)

It is the General opinion of most ignorant people, to count all things that are above their Vulgar apprehensions, to be diabolicall, and meerly brought to pass by the works of the Devil: and under that notion they conclude all the secret and Magnetick operations of nature, and thereby rob God the creator of all things, of that glory that is due unto him onely, and attribute the same to the Devil, the enemy to God and all the world: I shall therefore here take occasion to tell such people (because their Priests, that should teach them knowledge, either cannot or else will not) what the Devil is. As in the Microcosmus or little world Man, the Soul is the best part, so is the Devil the excrement of that Universal Spirit, and the abject and *Caput mortuum* of the world; and the poorest and most wretched of all created beings: And that worketh a great Antipathy between him and us, and the blessed holy Angels, who are our Governors and Protectors, and continual guardians, and are continually employed about us, according to their orders

An early English edition of Paracelsus's medical-occult treatises.

and ministeries appointed them by the most High: although the Devil alwayes endeavoureth to imitate and counterfeit the good Angels, and thereby deceiveth many whose wickedness and malice suits with his nature, and at which the good Angel being grieved, leaves them; and many times for the wickedness of some Person or Family the good Angel curses such a person and family, or house; then the wicked Spirit haunts such houses, affrighting the people with many fearful apparitions; neither can that house be quiet, nor any such person; neither shall any of the Generation of any such family prosper untill that curse be expiated, and the angry Angel appeased; as this Author will tell you, and woful experience daily shews: how frequently, and familiarly did those blessed Angels visibly communicate with the holy men and Magicians of old! though now such is the wickedness of our age, that they have almost quite forsaken us: although they are alwayes present about us, though invisible, administring to us according to the orders given unto them from the second Hierarchy, who receive the same from the first Hierarchy, who always attend before the Throne of the divine Majesty, offering up the prayers of the Saints, &c. (p. IX-X)

> *Robert Turner, "To the Reader," in* Of the Supreme Mysteries of Nature *by Paracelsus, N. Brook and J. Harison, 1656, pp. VII-X.*

Bernard Le Bovier De Fontenelle   (dialogue date 1683)

[*A nephew of Pierre Corneille, Fontenelle was a French man of letters. He was the author of numerous works, the two most noted being* Entretiens sur la pluralité des mondes *(1686;* Conversations on the Plurality of Worlds) *and* L'histoire des oracles *(1686;* History of Oracles), *which reveal him as a champion of scientific research and refined reasoning in the tradition of the Enlightenment. One of his early works,* Nouveaux dialogues des morts *(1683;* Dialogues of the Dead), *consists of a series of imaginary conversations between the shades of famous European literary and cultural figures. In the following excerpt from an imagined dialogue between Paracelsus and the French playwright* Molière, *Fontenelle ridicules Paracelsus through Molière's sarcastic wit.*]

Molière. I should be delighted with you, if only because of your name, Paracelsus. One would have thought you some Greek or Roman, and never have suspected that Paracelsus was an Helvetian philosopher.

Paracelsus. I have made my name as illustrious as it is lovely. My works are a great aid to those who would pierce nature's secrets, and more especially to those who launch out into the knowledge of genii and elementals.

Molière. I can readily believe that such is the true realm of science. To know men, whom one sees every day, is nothing; but to know the invisible genii is quite another affair.

Paracelsus. Doubtless. I have given precise information as to their nature, employments, and inclinations, as to their different orders, and their potencies throughout the cosmos.

Molière. How happy you were to be possessed of this knowledge, for before this you must have known man so precisely, yet many men have not attained even this.

Paracelsus. Oh, there is no philosopher so inconsiderable as not to have done so.

Molière. I suppose so. And you yourself have no indecisions regarding the nature of the soul, or its functions, or the nature of its bonds with the body?

Paracelsus. Frankly, it's impossible that there should not always remain some uncertainties on these subjects, but we know as much of them as philosophy is able to learn.

Molière. And you yourself know no more?

Paracelsus. No. Isn't that quite enough?

Molière. Enough? It is nothing at all. You mean that you have leapt over men whom you do not understand, in order to come upon genii?

Paracelsus. Genii are much more stimulatory to our natural curiosity.

Molière. Yes, but it is unpardonable to speculate about them before one has completed one's knowledge of men. One would think the human mind wholly exhausted, when one sees men taking as objects of knowledge things which have perhaps no reality, and when one sees how gaily they do this. However, it is certain that there are enough very real objects to keep one wholly employed.

Paracelsus. The human mind naturally neglects the sciences which are too simple, and runs after those more mysterious. It is only upon these last that it can expend all its activity.

Molière. So much the worse for the mind; what you say is not at all to its credit. The truth presents itself, but being too simple it passes unrecognised, and ridiculous mysteries are received only because of their mystery. I believe that if most men saw the universe as it is, seeing there neither *virtues* nor numbers, nor properties of the planets, nor fatalities tied to certain times and revolutions, they could not help saying of its admirable arrangement: "What, is that all there is to it?"

Paracelsus. You call these mysteries ridiculous, because you have not been able to reach into them; they are truly reserved for the great.

Molière. I esteem those who do not understand these mysteries quite as much as those who do understand; unfortunately nature has not made every one incapable of such understanding. (p. 70)

> *Bernard le Bovier de Fontenelle, "Dialogues of Fontenelle," translated by Ezra Pound, in* The Egoist. *Vol. IV, No. 5, June, 1917, pp. 70-1.*

Robert Browning   (poem date 1849)

[*Browning was an English poet and playwright who is considered one of the outstanding poets of the nineteenth century. Much of his poetry expresses his metaphysical concerns with the nature of and relationship between love, knowledge, and faith. His work influenced such later poets as Ezra Pound and T. S. Eliot. Early in his career, in 1835, he published the lengthy poem* Paracelsus, *which consists of an imaginary dialogue between Paracelsus and three friends (created by Browning): Festus, Michal, and an Italian poet, Aprile. In the following excerpt from the final (1888) text of the poem, which is substantially the same as the text of the second (1849) edition, Browning's Paracelsus, in his dying speech, summarizes his life's goal as a bringer of the light of knowledge into the world.*]

POWER; I could not take my eyes from that:
That only, I thought, should be preserved, increased
At any risk, displayed, struck out at once—
The sign and note and character of man.
I saw no use in the past: only a scene
Of degradation, ugliness and tears,
The record of disgraces best forgotten,
A sullen page in human chronicles
Fit to erase. I saw no cause why man
Should not stand all-sufficient even now,
Or why his annals should be forced to tell
That once the tide of light, about to break
Upon the world, was sealed within its spring:
I would have had one day, one moment's space,
Change man's condition, push each slumbering claim
Of mastery o'er the elemental world
At once to full maturity, then roll
Oblivion o'er the work, and hide from man
What night had ushered morn. Not so, dear child
Of after-days, wilt thou reject the past
Big with deep warnings of the proper tenure
By which thou hast the earth: for thee the present
Shall have distinct and trembling beauty, seen
Beside that past's own shade whence, in relief,
Its brightness shall stand out: nor yet on thee
Shall burst the future, as successive zones
Of several wonder open on some spirit
Flying secure and glad from heaven to heaven:
But thou shalt painfully attain to joy,
While hope and fear and love shall keep thee man!
All this was hid from me: as one by one
My dreams grew dim, my wide aims circumscribed,
As actual good within my reach decreased,
While obstacles sprung up this way and that
To keep me from effecting half the sum,
Small as it proved; as objects, mean within
The primal aggregate, seemed, even the least,
Itself a match for my concentred strength—
What wonder if I saw no way to shun
Despair? The power I sought for man, seemed
   God's.
In this conjuncture, as I prayed to die,
A strange adventure made me know, one sin
Had spotted my career from its uprise;
I saw Aprile—my Aprile there!
And as the poor melodious wretch disburthened
His heart, and moaned his weakness in my ear,
I learned my own deep error; love's undoing
Taught me the worth of love in man's estate,
And what proportion love should hold with power
In his right constitution; love preceding
Power, and with much power, always much more love;
Love still too straitened in his present means,
And earnest for new power to set love free.
I learned this, and supposed the whole was learned:
And thus, when men received with stupid wonder
My first revealings, would have worshipped me,
And I despised and loathed their proffered praise—
When, with awakened eyes, they took revenge
For past credulity in casting shame
On my real knowledge, and I hated them—
It was not strange I saw no good in man,
To overbalance all the wear and waste

Of faculties, displayed in vain, but born
To prosper in some better sphere: and why?
In my own heart love had not been made wise
To trace love's faint beginnings in mankind,
To know even hate is but a mask of love's,
To see a good in evil, and a hope
In ill-success; to sympathize, be proud
Of their half-reasons, faint aspirings, dim
Struggles for truth, their poorest fallacies,
Their prejudice and fears and cares and doubts;
All with a touch of nobleness, despite
Their error, upward tending all though weak,
Like plants in mines which never saw the sun,
But dream of him, and guess where he may be,
And do their best to climb and get to him.
All this I knew not, and I failed. Let men
Regard me, and the poet dead long ago
Who loved too rashly; and shape forth a third
And better-tempered spirit, warned by both:
As from the over-radiant star too mad
To drink the light-springs, beamless thence itself—
And the dark orb which borders the abyss,
Ingulfed in icy night,—might have its course
A temperate and equidistant world.
Meanwhile, I have done well, though not all well.
As yet men cannot do without contempt;
'T is for their good, and therefore fit awhile
That they reject the weak, and scorn the false,
Rather than praise the strong and true, in me:
But after, they will know me. If I stoop
Into a dark tremendous sea of cloud,
It is but for a time; I press God's lamp
Close to my breast; its splendour, soon or late,
Will pierce the gloom: I shall emerge one day.

                                                    (pp. 493-99)

Robert Browning, "Paracelsus," in his The Poetical Works of Robert Browning, Vol. I, *edited by Ian Jack and Margaret Smith, Oxford at the Clarendon Press, 1983, pp. 129-499.*

Éliphas Lévi [pseudonym of Alphonse Louis Constant] (essay date 1860)

[*Lévi was a nineteenth-century French occultist. His works* Histoire de la magie (*1860; The History of Magic*), Dogme de la haute magie (*1854*), *and* Ritual de la haute magie (*1856, translated together with the 1854 volume as* Transcendental Magic) *played a prominent part in the revival of occult interest in the English-speaking world during the twentieth century. In the following excerpt from* The History of Magic, *Lévi offers a cautionary summary of the importance of Paracelsus: a man he elsewhere refers to as a "maniac."*]

[Paracelsus] was naturally aggressive and of the mountebank type; so did he affirm that his familiar spirit was hidden in the pommel of his great sword, and never left his side. His life was an unceasing struggle; he travelled, debated, wrote, taught. He was more eager about physical results than moral conquests, and while first among practical magicians he was last among adepts of wisdom. His philosophy was one of sagacity and, on his own part, he termed it *philosophia sagax*. He divined more than anyone without knowing anything completely. There is nothing to equal his intuitions, unless it be the rashness of his commentaries. He was a man of intrepid experiences, intoxicated with his own opinions, his own talk, intoxicated otherwise on occasion, if we may believe some of his biographers. The works which he has left are precious for science, but they must be read with caution. He may be called the divine Paracelsus, understood in the sense of diviner; he is an oracle, but not a true master. He is great above all as a physician, for he had found the Universal Medicine. This notwithstanding, he could not prolong his own life, and he died, while still young, worn out by work and by excesses. He left behind him a name shining with fantastic and ambiguous glory, due to discoveries by which his contemporaries failed to profit. He had not uttered his last word, and is one of those mysterious beings of whom it may be said, as of Enoch and St. John: He is not dead, and he will come again upon earth before the last day. (p. 259)

> *Éliphas Lévi [pseudonym of Alphonse Louis Constant], "On Certain Alchemists," in his* The History of Magic: Including a Clear and Precise Exposition of Its Procedure, Its Rites and Its Mysteries, *translated by Arthur Edward Waite, revised edition, 1969. Reprint by Rider & Company, 1982, pp. 250-59.*

Arthur Edward Waite   (essay date 1894)

[*Waite was an American-born British editor, translator, poet, and author of books on the occult. His translations of the key works of Éliphas Lévi helped spark a revival of interest in the occult in Britain and North America during the early twentieth century. In the following excerpt from his preface to Paracelsus's* Hermetic and Alchemical Writings *(1894), he introduces Paracelsus's reputation and esoteric wisdom to the modern reader.*]

There are many respects in which Paracelsus at the present day seems to be little more than a name. Even among professed mystics the knowledge concerning him, very meagre and very indefinite, is knowledge that has been obtained at second hand, in most cases from Eliphas Levi, who in his *Dogme et Rituel de la Haute Magie,* and again in his *Histoire de la Magie,* has delivered an intuitive judgment upon the German "Monarch of Arcana," expressed epigramatically, after the best manner of a Frenchman. But, whencesoever derived, the knowledge is thin and phantasmal. Paracelsus is indeed cited as an authority in occult science, as a great alchemist, a great magician, a great doctor; he is somehow supposed to be standing evidence of the "wisdom of a spoliated past," and to offer a peculiar instance of malignity on the part of the enemies of Hermetic philosophy, because such persons have presumed to pronounce him an impostor. Thus there is a very strong opinion concerning him, which occultists and mystics of all schools have derived from a species of mystical tradition, and this represents one side of modern thought concerning him. It is not altogether a satisfactory side, because it is not obtained at first hand. In this respect, however, it may compare, without suffering by comparison, with the alternative opinion which obtains among nonmystics, namely, that Paracelsus was a great charlatan, though at the same time it is true that he was a great physician, at least for the period in which he lived. This judgment as little, perhaps less than the other, is derived from any solid knowledge concerning the man or his writings. At the same time it is noticeable that even hearsay condemnations admit that Paracelsus performed notable

cures. How it comes about that the application of what would be termed a distracted theory both in medicine and physics enabled its inventor to astound his age by what seemed miracles of the healing art would be a crux for such criticism if the criticism knew anything about it. It is not a crux for the mystics, because by these it would be replied that Paracelsus was a veritable adept, that his Hermetic teachings require to be interpreted, and that the key to their meaning would lay open for those who possess it an abundant treasure of sapience to which the literal significance is only a *bizarre* veil. (pp. XVII-XVIII)

There can be no doubt that Paracelsus obtained a wide, though not altogether a happy, reputation during the brief period of his turbulent life, and there is also no doubt that this was immeasurably increased after death. It is in no sense inexact to affirm that he founded a new school both in medicine and in alchemy. The commentaries on his medical system became a literature which, in extent, at least, is formidable; out of the mystic physics of his alchemical teachings the Rosicrucian doctrines developed in the first part of the following century. The works of Benedictus Figulus are evidence that he was idolized by his disciples. He was termed the noble and beloved monarch, the German Hermes, the Philosopher Trismegistus, our dear preceptor and King of Arts, Theophrastus of blessed memory and immortal fame. The collection of his genuine writings was made with devout care, and as a consequence of his celebrity many fictitious treatises were in due course ascribed to him. Students attracted by his doctrines travelled far in search of like-minded persons to compare observations thereon, and to sift the mystery of his instruction. In the course of these inquiries it seems to have become evident, from the experience of his followers, that his prescriptions in many cases were not to be literally understood, even when they were apparently the ordinary formulæ and concerned with the known *materia* of medicine. It will scarcely be necessary to add that in things alchemical the letter of his teachings was found still more in need of interpretation. The very curious influence exercised by Paracelsus for something like two hundred years over certain sections of restless experiment and speculation is still unwritten, and it would be interesting to trace here, were it possible within the limits of a preface. A task so ambitious is, however, outside those limits, and will perhaps be more wisely surrendered to other hands, for it is, in the main, part of the history of medicine, and demands an expert in the medical literature and medical knowledge of the past. The translations which follow [in **The Hermetic and Alchemical Writings**] are concerned only with the Hermetic writings of Paracelsus, to the exclusion of many formidable treatises on surgical science, and on the causes and cure of disease. They comprise what Paracelsus would himself have comprised in a collection of his alchemical writings, and this in itself is much more than is ordinarily understood to be within the significance of the term. With Paracelsus the province of alchemy was not limited to the transmutation of metals. It was, broadly speaking, the development of hidden possibilities or virtues in any substance, whether by God, or man, or Nature. Thus it included the philosophy of creation, and dealt with the first matter as developed into the universe by Divine Power. It included also the natural evolution which takes place round us, whether in the formation of metals within the earth, or the formation of animals in the matrix. Finally, it included the development by man's skill and art of

An early tribute to Paracelsus, apparently published as a broadside of sorts.

whatsoever was capable of improvement in the products of Nature. Thus the Hermetic and Alchemical writings of Paracelsus have a wider scope than might at first be inferred from the title. (pp. XXI-XXIII)

> *Arthur Edward Waite, "Preface to the English Translation," in* The Hermetic and Alchemical Writings of Aureolus Philippus Theophrastus Bombast, of Hohenheim, called Paracelsus the Great: Hermetic Chemistry, Vol. I *by Paracelsus, edited by Arthur Edward Waite, 1894. Reprint by University Books Inc., 1967, pp. XVII-XXIV.*

Anna M. Stoddart   (essay date 1911)

[*Stoddart was an English journalist and biographer whose last completed work was a full-length critical biography of Paracelsus. In the following excerpt from that work, she attempts to strip away spurious myths that surround her subject's life, defending Paracelsus against common critical perceptions of being a Rosicrucian, a "gold-cook," and astrologer, and an occultist. She affirms, though, and discourses upon Paracelsus's Christian mysticism.*]

Paracelsus was no juggler, no vulgar trickster assuming the garb, ritual, and pose of the superman. He left such practices to the baser natures of his own and later days. To understand him as he was we must divest his memory of many legendary attributes. It was customary after his death to ascribe to him the occult manufacture of gold, the possession of the philosopher's stone, dominion over elemental and evil spirits, the powers of alchemic creation and astrological prediction. He was for centuries after his death claimed as the founder of Rosicrucianism, one of the first traces of which ascription is to be seen in the illustration mentioned in the last chapter as amongst the thirty-two symbolic wood-cuts in Huser's edition of the ***Prognostications,*** which was reproduced in the flying-sheet of 1606, and which shows his books inscribed with either the letter *R* or with the word *Rosa.*

One by one these legends can be discredited. (pp. 249-50)

Paracelsus died more than half a century before the foundation of the *Militia Crucifera Evangelica* [Rosicrucian Brotherhood] and the inventions of Johann Valentin Andreæ, a priest at Tübingen and later Abbot of Adelsberg in Stuttgart, did not begin to appear till 1614. This man compiled his fictitious pamphlets in the hope that they might effect a reformation amongst the clergy. On his deathbed he confessed that they were intended as satirical fables, but their title had gone forth into the German world, and Rosicrucian societies were formed at Nüremberg, Hamburg, Dantzic, and Erfurt. (p. 251)

The tradition that Paracelsus was a goldmaker lasted for centuries after his death: it was founded on the deathless faculty for chimerical conjecture which distinguishes the human from the animal mind. Paracelsus in speech and writing laughed the "gold-cooks" to scorn. For him chemistry meant the discovery by analysis and combination of medicines for healing. (p. 252)

We know already what was his attitude towards astrology, a study which fascinated men of his day and even men of the Renascence, as Girolamo Cardano in northern Italy and Melanecthon in Germany. (p. 254)

There is little doubt that Hohenheim gave it a thorough trial. Probably the mysterious visits to Esslingen fix periods of his investigation, and these may have been renewed at St. Gallen with Schobinger's assistance. It was shortly after these visits that his conclusions found expression in the ***Paramirum,*** where he declares his antipathy to astrological theories and to ascribing character, tendencies, and destinies to the influence of the heavenly bodies. He repudiates all such views and claims God as the giver of all human qualities and of their manifold combinations. In his two treatises upon comets, he expresses views directly opposed to those of the astrological writers of his time and seeks to define in exact terms the study of the heavenly bodies as an effort to know what they really are and how they are placed in relation to the earth, refusing to regard such a study as arrested in the hands of diviners and soothsayers, but instead as a true research beginning to yield fruits in discoveries as trustworthy as those made in the other provinces of nature. In fact, he was a keen student of positive astronomy.

Necromancy and sorcery he abhorred with all his might. He did not deny their claims to credence, but ascribed their effects to the invocation and exercise of powers at least evil, at worst infernal, and on both counts to be abjured. Nor did he give these the credit of all the malignant diseases popularly claimed for them. He argued forcibly against demoniacal possession and insisted that such maladies as St. Vitus' dance, St. Veltin's sickness, St. Anthony's fire and others, are not indications of saintly wrath inflicted, as penance, but proceed from some one or other of the natural origins of disease, and that each must be studied from the standpoint of true medical diagnosis. He taught that corrupted imagination had extraordinary power to bring about disease, but denied that the devil could create disease, although he was able to induce in men the evil spiritual and mental conditions which were favourable to disease. (pp. 255-56)

[In the writings of Paracelsus] we hear the voice of neither wizard nor charlatan, but of a devout believer in God, whose glory man's life must either set forth or be wrecked.

A mystic Paracelsus certainly was. From his early acquaintance with neo-platonism he developed his spiritual philosophy. It was union with God, a union whence the spirit of man derived all power to overcome the spirits of evil, to understand mysteries, to discover the hidden arcana of nature, to know good and discern evil, to live within the fortresses of the spirit, to see with illumined eyes through the mists and the dust-storms of sophistically devised and arbitrarily imposed theological and ethical systems to the throne of God, where wisdom, truth, and righteousness abide. He found the hand of God in all nature, in the recesses of the mountains where the metals await His will; in the vault of heaven where "He moves the sun and all the stars"; in the river sped with His bounty of food and drink for man; in the green fields and the forests where spring a pyriad ministering herbs and fruits; in the springs that pour His healing gifts into the laps of the valleys. He saw that the earth was God's handiwork and was precious in His sight.

Professor Strunz, writing of Hohenheim's personality,

presents him as charged with the dynamic force of the new age:

His was a mind of mighty features whose rare maturity converted the stating of scientific problems into warm human terms, and we owe to him the realisation of a cultured human community based upon Christian and humanitarian piety and faith, which things we may well regard as the bases of his teaching concerning both the actual and the spiritual. His restless life never robbed him of that witchery which ever and again flushed the immortal impulses of his soul like golden sunshine: that vision which belongs to the great nature-poet. And yet few men of his time recognised, as he did, the incalculable result to be attained by the empiric-inductive method. In the Natural Philosophy of Comenius, a deep and gifted soul who in many ways reminds us of Paracelsus, there quivers too that sense of the charm and joy of nature-research, which tells men of the becoming and of the passing away, of working and resting, and reveals the precious codex of nature in which we read concerning God and His Life Eternal. Not within himself shall man seek first the interpretation of the unity of all human consciousness, but in nature itself, where God guides, reason illumines, and the senses witness. Is there anything in our discernment which sense did not first apprehend? The nearer our reason to the apprehension of sense, the stronger in realisation, the mightier in grasp will our reason be: and the further our reason strays from the kernel-point of sense perception, the greater are its errors and vain fantasies. . . . Paracelsus felt like an artist and thought like a mathematician, just as he combined the laws of nature with the laws of the microcosm, that is of man with his consciousness, his feelings, and his desires. It was this delicate artistic sense which proved to be the daring bridge from the man Paracelsus to the keen-visioned observer of reality, a wondrous viaduct resting upon the traverses of the new humanity, the Renascence. For upon this viaduct moved forward that reconstruction of the universe of which Paracelsus was one of the greatest architects. It was the platform of a spiritual advance, completed later by Giordano Bruno, poet, philosopher, artist, and student of nature. . . . And with this Paracelsus found his religion in closest bond. Nature with all her unfathomable wealth and beauty, with her immortal types and her obedience to law, was for him the gate of medicine, just as love for all who laboured and were heavy laden, who rested within God's great hospital upon earth, meant for him that divine guide who unlocked the treasure-house of nature's arcana. The world of Francis of Assisi and of Henry Seuse expanded about him: again the summer sunlight lay upon the earth, again God within and deep love of nature became one with the intellectual inspiration of a man in earnest. Not only St. Francis in tender love and holy poverty, that saint who brought about a glorious springtime of Catholicism without violence—no, but that Francis too who sang the Canticle of the Sun, stands again before us. How should such a man as Paracelsus have escaped the touch of mysticism, when even a Luther felt its influence? . . . A feeling for nature like a wave issued from Paracelsus and reached to men of the future like Comenius and Van Helmont. And they too understood the consecration of research and the sweet, pure note of joy in discovering the laws of God. Paracelsus had just that piety which to-day we admire in the classic mystics. He stood against rationalism and all the fanciful religiosities. He saw God in nature just as he saw Him in the microcosm and was amazed at the reflection of the divine light. His conclusions form the ethics of a Christian humanism. The close brotherhood of God's children must spring from a well-ordered humanity, from human knowledge and from consciousness of the unspeakable value of the soul in each of its members. This world with its thousand forms and potentialities is in its unity and in its interdependence the revelation of the laws of God: nature is the true helper and friend of the sick and infirm, whether rich or poor. Nature with her miracles in the field, where the sower entrusts his seed to the dear earth without so much as guessing how what he hopes for will occur: above in the still mountains where the old trees die and the new come in their place; in the whispering grove and in the hedge, in the lake where the sun plays with the water as with precious pearls; wherever the fierce battle between tares and wheat goes on in the billowy glory—all, all is living nature. Paracelsus has enshrined it in pictures and similes, allegories and parables. The lapse of every year, its coming and its passing, springtime when the new rhythms sway to and fro, summer when young life reaches the harvest and the husk, and time hastens it to the fruiting, autumn when all is done and all is weary, and life languishes. How often he has likened his pilgrimage to autumn, his life to its full maturity, an abundance for the new world.

I have quoted at length from Dr. Strunz, because amongst the great German Paracelsian scholars he possesses perhaps the keenest insight into the character of Hohenheim, a character in which simplicity is combined with genius, with heroic veracity, with unclouded vision, with a spirit in touch with God.

As a Christian he listened to the teaching of Jesus Christ. Attempts were made by the Protestants of his time to claim him for their party, and are made by the Catholics of today to present him as a Catholic. To me it seems that while he abjured the fetters of the old historical ecclesiasticism, he dissented from the new limitations of Protestantism. He stood free from both and looked to Jesus Christ alone for guidance. (pp. 260-64)

He takes firm footing on the life and the teaching of our Lord, for *there* is the only foundation for our creed:

"It is there, in the Eternal Life described by the Evangel and in the Scriptures that we find all we need: no syllable is wanting in that." "In Christ only is salvation, and as we believe in Him so through Him we are saved. No worship of the saints is needed for that, no idol of our imagination. Faith in God and in His only begotten Son Jesus Christ is enough for us. Our fasts, our masses, our vigils, and the like effect nothing for us. What saves us is the mercy of God who forgives us our sins. Love and faith are one, for love comes through faith and true Christianity is revealed in love and in the works of love."

Much of this lucid reasoning is to be found in the theological and religious treatises discovered in 1899 and authenticated by Dr. Sudhoff. More particularly in his treatise on the Epistle of St. James does Paracelsus insist on the practical works of Christianity, for "faith without works is dead." He contends that the Lutherans have accentuated the importance of faith to the detriment of that of love.

What Hohenheim wanted was reformation of the human and acceptance of the divine conception of religion. He desired neither the domination of a human sacerdotal authority nor the domination of the Bible as interpreted textually by limited and varying human intelligence, but the domination of God revealed by the Holy Spirit in the person, teaching, and sacrifice of Jesus Christ. The Kingdom of God, which involved the brotherhood of men, was the pearl of great price, which Christ had shown to the world and had bidden men sell all that they had to secure. He believed that perfection in the spiritual life was God's design for all men, not for a few hermits, nor for a few monks and nuns, who had no warrant from God to assume the exclusive externalities of a holiness which but few of them attained. God had created men for His world, and in the world He claimed their faith and love both for Himself and for their fellows. If God were in very deed accepted as King of His own world, there would be an end of hypocrisy in the rays of righteousness. But the Kingdom of God contains in closest relationship with our life of faith and love a multitude of mysteries which the searching soul may discover one by one. They are the mysteries of God's providence which he who seeks shall find: the mysteries of union with God, the secret tabernacle at whose gate to him who knocks it shall be opened. And the men who seek and knock are the prophets and the healers of His Kingdom, for to them are delivered its keys, the keys which unlock the treasuries of earth and heaven. (pp. 267-69)

In touching upon the occultism ascribed to Paracelsus it is necessary to avoid many pitfalls into which the student of his doctrines may stumble by accepting too readily those mystical traditions which in the seventeenth and eighteenth centuries gathered round his memory. His name became a credential for the books of necromancers and hermetists, who appealed in those days of superstitious belief in wizardry and witchcraft to the terror which their squalid records inspired. He was accused of their own dark rites and malignant practices and his name was blackened by their own infamy. We may unhesitatingly refuse to accept their usurpation of his authority. All that was base, malignant, and diabolical he rejected in no obscure terms. His practice of telepathic and hypnotic powers, his exercise of healing magnetism, were sufficient to invest his name with magical reputation quite apart from any genuine evidence. But there was a residue of half-questioning faith in a number of unseen forces not all arcane and medicinal. There survived in him an admission of elemental beings, spirits of fire, which he called *acthnici;* of air, *nenufareni;* of water, *melosinœ;* and of earth, *pigmaci.* Besides these, imps, gnomes, and hobgoblins had a place in his inheritance from the teutonic realms of faerie. Dryads he knew as *durdales,* familiar spirits as *flagœ.* He believed in the astral body of man and called it *eventrum;* in the astral bodies of plants or *leffas;* in levitation, or *mangonaria;* in clairvoyance, or *nectromantia;* in wraiths, omens, and phantasms. It is, however, very possible that the book ascribed to him, on these uncanny relics of paganism, published in 1566 by Marcus Ambrosius Nissensis and dedicated to Constantine Farber at Dantzic, under the title of ***Ex Libro de Nymphis, Sylvanis, Pygmæs, Salamandris et Gigantibus,*** etc., may not have been his at all; it is given as an abstract of his writings on the subject, is

somewhat arbitrarily arranged, and is prefaced by a dedication which is not only full of errors, but suggests as well a very vague acquaintance with Hohenheim's books. (pp. 270-72)

> *Anna M. Stoddart, in her* The Life of Paracelsus, Theophrastus von Hohenheim, 1493-1541, *David McKay, 1911, 309 p.*

John Maxson Stillman　(essay date 1920)

[*Stillman was an American chemist and the author of two books:* The Story of Early Chemistry (*1924*) *and a critical biography of Paracelsus. In the following excerpt from the latter, he outlines Paracelsus's system of philosophy, tracing its origins and comparing it to that of Cornelius Agrippa von Nettesheim and others.*]

That we may be able to comprehend the nature of the conflict between the theories of Paracelsus and the traditional dogmatic philosophy which he opposed, it is essential that we attempt to understand something of the current thought in the domains in which Paracelsus endeavored to impress his reformatory ideas.

His great aim was to break the bonds of ancient authority and accepted dogma which had for centuries held medical science enchained, and to open the way for the foundation of that science upon a basis of open-minded experience, experiment and observation, or, as he expresses it, on the "Light of Nature."

But "nature" to the view of the school of philosophy which Paracelsus adopted comprehended much that to our modern view is occult or supernatural. It comprised the influence of the stars upon the life and health of men and many other mysterious phenomena then generally credited by all classes of people. The knowledge of nature was to be achieved not merely, therefore, by the eyes and the hands—by experiment and observation as we understand the study of nature—but also by a more mystical insight into the hidden properties of things.

For Paracelsus the phenomena of nature, seen or hidden, are the revelation of God's will to man in all those things relating to his physical and material welfare—just as the teachings of Christ are for him the revelation of God's will to man in things spiritual. Hence the physician as the highest human agent of God's will to man, must be thoroughly grounded in the complete knowledge of nature, and as thoroughly in obedience to the teachings of Christ. For the interpretation of the phenomena of nature as for the interpretation of the teachings of Christ, he claims the right for himself and for his individual judgment, and refuses to accept the authority of ancient Greek philosophers or physicians—or of Church-Fathers or other sources of dogmatic theology.

The study of nature and its phenomena was, it may be remembered, the latest field to feel the Renaissance impulse, and it was in the sixteenth century still largely dominated by the medieval point of view. (pp. 25-6)

Among the conventional scholars of the time the prevailing natural philosophy was a degenerate Aristotelianism, which had been transmitted, modified and obscured by Arabian interpreters and through Oriental influences corrupted by much more of mysticism than existed in the original Greek sources. During the Renaissance there had developed a revival of the neo-Platonic philosophy. The generally credited originator of this revival is Nicholas of Cusa (1401-1464), but its chief propagandists were in the Florentine Academy—notably Giovanni Pico della Mirandola (1463-94) and Marsilius Ficinus (1433-99). Through the latter this somewhat fantastic natural philosophy had spread to Germany, where Reuchlin (1455-1522), Trithemius (1462-1516), Cornelius Agrippa von Nettesheim (1486-1535) were prominent exponents, while in France Bovillus (1476-1553) was a prominent representative. (pp. 27-8)

As Paracelsus mentions both Ficinus and Agrippa, and acknowledges Trithemius as his teacher, we may well believe that he drew from all these sources in the construction of his own theories. Though the natural philosophy of Paracelsus was deeply rooted in the neo-Platonic philosophy of the Florentine Academy, yet Paracelsus was too original and venturesome a thinker to be a strict adherent of any particular form of philosophy. It probably especially appealed to him because it was in the nature of a revolt from the dry and lifeless Aristotelianism of the day, and because it opened the path to the recognition of the value of experiment and observation as the basis for the development of medicine.

Fantastic as the neo-Platonic philosophy of that time seems to our present views, there was much in it to appeal to the popular notions of the fifteenth and sixteenth centuries. The attempt to unite into a quasi natural philosophy the many mysterious phenomena of nature as they presented themselves to the belief of that time—the supernatural phenomena as well as many equally mysterious natural phenomena—was inspiring to the imagination. The "natural magic" of Agrippa and the philosophy of Paracelsus attempted to give rational explanations of many things which the orthodox philosophy of the period accounted for only in a purely mystical sense. (pp. 29-30)

[Alfred] Lehmann has given us [in *Aberglaube und Zauberei* (1908)] a synopsis of the natural magic of Agrippa, and the resemblance to much of Paracelsus's theories is striking. Agrippa attributes to all objects in the universe sympathies and antipathies, and believes that by influencing these sympathies and antipathies by appropriate methods extraordinary or supernatural results might be obtained. "This natural magic," says Lehmann, "first attained great importance when its fundamental ideas with certain changes were adopted as an essential element in the medical system of Paracelsus." Agrippa says, "The world is threefold, namely, elementary, sidereal, spiritual. Everything lower is ruled by the higher and receives thence its power. Thus the Architect and Prototype of the universe lets the powers of His omnipotence flow out through the angels, the heavens, the stars, the elements, the animals, plants, rocks, and thence into man." And thus, thinks Agrippa, it becomes possible for man through the powers of nature to reascend the ladder and to gain supernatural powers and knowledge. This natural magic is to him the greatest of the sciences. It comprises: *Physics,* or the knowledge of the nature of things which are in the universe—their causes, actions, times, places, appearances, as a whole and in its parts; *Mathematics,* which teaches us to know nature in three dimensions and to ob-

serve the paths of the heavenly bodies: *Theology,* which teaches us of God, the soul, intelligences, angels, devils and religion; it teaches us also the sacred observances, forms and mysteries; and finally it informs us concerning the faith and the miracles, the powers of words and symbols and the sacred operations and mysteries of the seals. These three sciences the natural magic brings together and perfects. He who does not know these three sciences cannot understand the rationality of magic.

Agrippa supposes all substances to be composed of the four Aristotelian elements, Fire, Earth, Water and Air. Everything is composed of these, not by a simple heaping together but by combination and metamorphosis, and everything falls back, when it perishes, into the elements. None of these elements occurs pure in nature, but they are more or less mixed and may be confused with one another. Each of the four elements has two special qualities of which one is the characteristic quality, the other forms the transition to another element. This is represented by a diagram illustrating the four qualities and the four elements in their relation to one another—in the Aristotelian fashion:

$$
\begin{array}{ccc}
\text{hot} & \text{---} Fire \text{---} & \text{dry} \\
Air \text{-------} & | & \text{-------} Earth \\
\text{moist} & \text{---} Water \text{---} & \text{cold}
\end{array}
$$

According to Agrippa also, all things of higher nature or sphere in the three divisions or worlds of the universe, influence the lower, but the lower also influence the higher, though in less degree. Also all things in the same sphere influence one another in that everything attracts and is attracted by its like.

The philosophy of Paracelsus presents distinct resemblances to that of Agrippa. The form of the neo-Platonic philosophy presented by Agrippa may well have served as his starting-point, but the differences are also important. Paracelsus was manifestly quite in agreement with Agrippa as to the three divisions of the universe and their mutual influences upon one another. The concepts of man as the microcosm, and the outer universe as the macrocosm, and that by the study of the macrocosm the knowledge of the microcosm must be reached, were with Paracelsus as with Agrippa and also with his contemporary Bovillus, dominant ideas.

Instead, however, of the three sciences of Agrippa, Physics (meaning natural philosophy), Mathematics (including magic numbers—the Cabbala) and Theology, upon which is founded the Science of Natural Magic, Paracelsus substitutes *Philosophy* (meaning also natural philosophy), *Astronomy, Alchemy* (meaning chemistry) and *Virtue* (or righteousness), which he constitutes the four pillars upon which the Science of Medicine must rest. "Virtue" as a separate science differs from the "Theology" of Agrippa mainly in the rejection by Paracelsus of the many forms, ceremonies and miracles upon which Agrippa places emphasis.

Paracelsus rejects the four Aristotelian elements as the determining constituent principles of all bodies and substitutes for them his three alchemical elements, *Mercury,* the principle of liquidity and volatility, *Sulphur,* the principle of combustibility, and *Salt,* that principle which is permanent and resists the action of fire.

Illustrated title page of Oswaldus Crollius's Basilic chymica *(1612?). Depicted on the border are six notable physicians and alchemists, including (clockwise, from lower left): Hermes Trismegistus, Morienus, Ramanus, Raimundus Lullus, Geber (Djabir), Robert Bacon, and Paracelsus.*

The philosophy of nature as presented by Paracelsus differed even more in the emphasis and the application of the fundamental ideas than in the formal philosophical notions. For Paracelsus was not a closet philosopher. His reasoning was often loose and careless. He was, it would seem, not so much interested in elaborating a natural philosophy for its own sake as in utilizing the neo-Platonic system in which he had been more or less schooled as a substitute for the Aristotelian and Galenic philosophy which to his mind stood in the way of the rational development of the science of medicine on the basis of the study of nature. His adaptation of the current neo-Platonic theories was not so much a carefully thought-out and consistent philosophy as it was an imaginative adaptation of such elements of it as could fit into the system of things as he saw them, and he introduced such modifications and extensions as harmonized with his medical, chemical and theological ideas—ideas which he had arrived at not only through the conventional channels of the schools, for which sources indeed he felt but little respect, but also through his contact with a wider school observation and experience among all classes of people and in many lands.

Thus his system of philosophy, less consistent and less logically developed than the philosophy presented by Ficinus, Bovillus, or even by Agrippa, nevertheless, because it had application to the practical profession of medicine and chemistry, was of more direct influence on the common thought of the time. (pp. 30-5)

While it is foreign to the purpose of this treatment to describe in great detail the natural philosophy of Paracelsus, a brief summary of some of the more characteristic features will serve to enable us better to understand the influence and significance they possessed for the time in which he wrote.

Paracelsus divides the external universe or macrocosm into three worlds, the *visible* and *tangible;* the *astral* (or sidereal), the world of the heavenly bodies; and the *celestial,* or the divine and spiritual. Similarly he sees in man, the microcosm, three corresponding spheres, the visible and tangible, that is, the fluids, organs, bones, etc.; the astral, the sensations, seeing, feeling, perception; the celestial, the soul (*Seele*). The sciences which treat of these three divisions of the macrocosm, are philosophy, the science of the phenomena of nature; astronomy (and astrology); and theology or virtue (*proprietas*). As, however, the microcosm is to be understood and interpreted through the macrocosm, he who would know what takes place in man, and what affects his life, health, and well-being must be thoroughly grounded in these three sciences. To these Paracelsus adds alchemy, which term, however, he uses in the sense of chemistry rather than in the mystical sense which at present we attribute to the word alchemy. He adds chemistry as the fourth pillar of medicine, as he considers that all substances, even the four Aristotelian elements, are made up of the three chemical principles Mercury, Sulphur and Salt, and the processes in nature which effect changes in the forms of matter are similar in character to the changes which may be produced in the laboratory of the chemist. Nature is herself an alchemist. So he says:

> Now further as to the third foundation on which medicine stands, which is alchemy. When the physician is not skilled and experienced to the highest and greatest degree in this foundation, all his art is in vain. For nature is so subtle and so keen in her matters that she will not be used without great art. For she yields nothing that is perfected, in its natural state, but man must perfect it. This perfecting is called alchemy. For the baker is an alchemist when he bakes bread, the vine-grower when he makes wine, the weaver when he makes cloth. Therefore whatever grows in nature useful to man—whoever brings it to the point to which it was ordered by nature, he is an alchemist.

When Paracelsus speaks of philosophy as the knowledge of nature—"As now the physician must develop from nature—what is nature other than philosophy?—what is philosophy other than invisible nature?"—it should be kept in mind that to his mind as to his contemporaries generally, the phenomena of nature included a great number of supposed facts which the knowledge of our day relegates to the domain of fable and superstition. The influences of the stars, of angels and devils, spirits of the air or the waters, gnomes and nymphs were generally credited in his time. The neo-Platonic view of the universe which Paracelsus represented encouraged the belief in such existences by its assumption of the influences exerted by all things upon one another and upon man through the sympathies and antipathies of their spirits (*Geister*). The belief in the influence of the stars was well-nigh universal, and "astronomy" comprehended "astrology." The customary interpretation of the nature of the influence of the heavenly bodies upon man's health was purely mystical. (pp. 36-8)

Even before Paracelsus there were symptoms of a tendency to discredit the mystical notions of the influence of the stars. Thus Giovanni Pico della Mirandola, who died the year following Paracelsus's birth, says:

> The stars can only indicate and predict what they themselves cause. Their real and natural signs belong to the material world and are subject to its laws. They are either the causes or the effects of the happenings which they indicate or predict. The heavenly bodies possess no occult qualities by whose power they are able to produce secret influences on earth. Not in the heavens but in himself must each read the foundations of his destiny. A great thinker such as Aristotle is indebted for his capacities and accomplishments not to the stars under which he was born, but to his own genius which he received from God.

So Paracelsus says:

> Adam and Eve received their bodies at the creation and through the principle of the seed up to the passing away of the world. And though no star or planet had existed nor yet were, children would be just so born, complexioned and natured as they now are—one melancholic, another choleric, one true, another untrue, one pious, another wicked. Such qualities are in the entity of their natures and do not come from the stars, for they have no part in the body, that is, they give no complexion, no colors, no form, no characteristic traits, no nature, no individuality.

(pp. 39-40)

But understand also the virtue of the stars. The stars have their nature and their manifold properties, just as on earth men have. The stars have also their changes, sometimes better, sometimes worse, sweeter or sourer, milder or bitterer. When they are good nothing evil comes from them, but when they are evil, evil comes from them. Take note that they surround the earth as the shell an egg: the air comes through the shell and passes first through them toward the center of the world. Therefore note now that those stars which are poisonous—they contaminate the air with their poison. Therefore when these poisons come to any place such diseases appear there as have the properties of those stars. It may not poison the whole earth but only that part where its influence is strongest. And so also it is with the good influences of the stars.

This is an illustration of a very characteristic habit of Paracelsus, of explaining generally accepted beliefs of his time by some plausibly rational theory. In his time when the Ptolemaic cosmology prevailed, the earth was the center—about which sun, moon and planets revolved, and the atmosphere was commonly supposed to extend to and to support them in their places. To the thought of our time strange and fantastic—yet to his own time there was nothing absurd in this imaginative hypothesis to account for such influences upon health and diseases as Paracelsus with others credited to the heavenly bodies. (pp. 41-2)

> *John Maxson Stillman, in his* Theophrastus Bombastus von Hohenheim Called Paracelsus: His Personality and Influence as Physician, Chemist and Reformer, *The Open Court Publishing Co., 1920, 184 p.*

Charles Williams   (essay date 1941)

[*Williams was a writer of supernatural fiction, a poet whose best works treat the legends of Logres (Arthurian Britain), and one of the central figures in the literary group known as the Oxford Christians or "Inklings." The religious, the magical, and the mythical are recurrent concerns in his works, reflecting his devout Anglicanism and lifelong interest in all aspects of the preternatural. Although his works are not today as well known as those of his fellow-Inklings C. S. Lewis and J. R. R. Tolkien, Williams was an important source of encouragement and influence in the group. In the following excerpt from an essay written to mark the four-hundredth anniversary of Paracelsus's death, he encapsulates Paracelsus's importance in the realms of medicine and metaphysics.*]

Paracelsus is perhaps the most generally famous of all the vagrant doctors of the 16th-17th centuries. (p. 820)

There were, he said, four columns of medicine. They are Philosophy, Astronomy, Alchemy, and Virtue. The first three correspond to the knowledge of the three worlds—the heavenly or spiritual, the astral, the material. The fourth is the proper union of the three in the physician himself. Philosophy therefore is of earth as of heaven, and alchemy is not limited to the search for the Stone at the Red, or the Tincture of Life. "Nature brings nothing to light that is at once perfect in itself, but leaves it to be perfected by man. This method of perfection is called Alchemy." Medicine must be produced by reference to the stars; heaven rules by means of the stars. The physician, therefore, must know the disease and know the star: "then you

clearly understand who is your guide and in what your power consists."

The three primary substances which went to the making of man were salt, sulphur and mercury, but these again were rather principles of physical existence than the bodies we mean by the names. It is these which produce disease. But the microcosmic body which they affect is but an image of the macrocosmic, and the visible of the invisible. It is by the interchange of the two that healing and vitality are achieved. Man's own operation is necessary to complete the body of man. For the body which is given to a man at birth is called "the body of justice", and while a child feeds from its mother it feeds only from the body of justice, but afterwards he lives by food and prayer and virtue and revives the "body of mercy" which is thus communicated to him. And it is our business in all ways, by studying principles, by learning the three worlds, celestial, sidereal, material, by experiment and by obedience, to perfect in ourselves the microcosmic body of man which is an image of all. "All Arts which flourish on this earth are divine."

His name was Theophrastus Bombast von Hohenheim; he

Engraving of Paracelsus rendered by Augustin Hirschvogel in 1540. Paracelsus is depicted clutching the pommel of his sword—wherein, some contemporaries charged, he kept his demonic familiar.

was called also Aureolus and Paracelsus; the first possibly because it was thought that a faint luminousness shone from him; the second either because he was greater than the Roman physician Celsus or because it was a latinized form of Hohenheim. Browning gave the name to a poem which, not very great in itself, contains two or three of his loveliest lyrics. The most famous saying attributed to him is: "He who eats a crust of bread communicates on all the starry heavens." He became a reputation, almost a myth, and he was for long enlarged into the grand master of all the occult schools. But perhaps he never gave us a greater imagination than that of "the body of justice" nourished always and everywhere by "the body of mercy". (p. 821)

Charles Williams, "Paracelsus," in Time & Tide, *Vol. 22, No. 39, September 27, 1941, pp. 820-21.*

C. G. Jung   (essay date 1942)

[*Jung was a Swiss psychologist and creator of analytical psychology. Disagreeing with Sigmund Freud's theory of the unconscious sexual origin of neurosis, Jung developed a school of psychology based on the hypothesis that the source of human psychic life resides both in the individual's personal history, the "individual unconscious," and in the collective history of humanity, the "collective unconscious." Evidence for this theory is supplied by recurring motifs, termed "archetypes," in the recorded traditions of diverse cultures throughout human history. Examples of such motifs are the hero, the wise old man, and the spiritual quest. In Jung's psychology, archetypal patterns from mythology and folklore replace the unconscious sexual conflicts of Freud's system as a source of illumination for common patterns in human behavior. Jung also discerned archetypal patterns in modern literature, a practice that has led to a modern school of literary criticism. In the following excerpt from a work originally published in 1942, Jung expounds upon the alchemical beliefs of Paracelsus, makeup relating them to his psychological makeup and the spirit of the age in which he lived.*]

Besides all the other things he was, Paracelsus was, perhaps most deeply of all, an alchemical "philosopher" whose religious views involved him in an unconscious conflict with the Christian beliefs of his age in a way that seems to us inextricably confused. Nevertheless, in this confusion are to be found the beginnings of philosophical, psychological, and religious problems which are taking clearer shape in our own epoch. (p. 110)

It is not easy to see this spiritual phenomenon in the round and to give a really comprehensive account of it. Paracelsus was too contradictory or too chaotically many-sided, for all his obvious one-sidedness in other ways. First and foremost, he was a physician with all the strength of his spirit and soul, and his foundation was a firm religious belief. Thus he says in his **Paragranum:** "You must be of an honest, sincere, strong, true faith in God, with all your soul, heart, mind, and thought, in all love and trust. On the foundation of such faith and love, God will not withdraw his truth from you, and will make his works manifest to you, believable, visible, and comforting. But if, not having such faith, you are against God, then you will go astray in your work and will have failures, and in consequence people will have no faith in you." (p. 111)

[To] Mater Ecclesia, he remained faithful all his life, despite the very free criticism he levelled at the ills of Christendom in that epoch. Nor did he succumb to the great temptation of that age, the Protestant schism, though he may well have had it in him to go over to the other camp. Conflict was deeply rooted in Paracelsus's nature; indeed, it had to be so, for without a tension of opposites there is no energy, and whenever a volcano, such as he was, erupts, we shall not go wrong in supposing that water and fire have clashed together.

But although the Church remained a mother for Paracelsus all his life, he nevertheless had two mothers: the other was Mater Natura. And if the former was an absolute authority, so too was the latter. Even though he endeavoured to conceal the conflict between the two maternal spheres of influence, he was honest enough to admit its existence; indeed, he seems to have had a very good idea of what such a dilemma meant. Thus he says: "I also confess that I write like a pagan and yet am a Christian." Accordingly he named the first five sections of his **Paramirum de quinque entibus morborum** "Pagoya." "Pagoyum" is one of his favourite neologisms, compounded of "paganum" and the Hebrew word "goyim." He held that knowledge of the nature of diseases was pagan, since this knowledge came from the "light of nature" and not from revelation. "Magic," he says, is "the preceptor and teacher of the physician," who derives his knowledge from the *lumen naturae*. There can be no doubt the "light of nature" was a second, independent source of knowledge for Paracelsus. . . . The light of nature is the *quinta essentia*, extracted by God himself from the four elements, and dwelling "in our hearts." It is enkindled by the Holy Spirit. The light of nature is an intuitive apprehension of the facts, a kind of illumination. It has two sources: a mortal and an immortal, which Paracelsus calls "angels." "Man," he says, "is also an angel and has all the latter's qualities." He has a natural light, but also a light outside the light of nature by which he can search out supernatural things. The relationship of this supernatural light to the light of revelation remains, however, obscure. Paracelsus seems to have held a peculiar trichotomous view in this respect.

The authenticity of one's own experience of nature against the authority of tradition is a basic theme of Paracelsan thinking. On this principle he based his attack on the medical schools, and his pupils carried the revolution even further by attacking Aristotelian philosophy. It was an attitude that opened the way for the scientific investigation of nature and helped to emancipate natural science from the authority of tradition. Though this liberating act had the most fruitful consequences, it also led to that conflict between knowledge and faith which poisoned the spiritual atmosphere of the nineteenth century in particular. Paracelsus naturally had no inkling of the possibility of these late repercussions. As a medieval Christian, he still lived in a unitary world and did not feel the two sources of knowledge, the divine and the natural, as the conflict it later turned out to be. As he says in his "Philosophia sagax": "There are, therefore, two kinds of knowledge in this world: an eternal and a temporal. The eternal springs directly from the light of the Holy Spirit, but the other directly from the Light of Nature." In his view the latter kind is ambivalent: both good and bad. This knowledge, he says, "is not from flesh and blood, but from the stars in the flesh and blood. That is the treasure, the natural *Summum Bonum*." Man is twofold, "one part temporal, the other part eternal, and each part takes its light from God, both the temporal and the eternal, and there is nothing that does not have its origin in God. Why, then, should the Father's light be considered pagan, and I be recognized and condemned as a pagan?" God the Father created man "from below upwards," but God the Son "from above downwards." Therefore Paracelsus asks: "If Father and Son are one, how then can I honour two lights? I would be condemned as an idolater: but the number one preserves me. And if I love two and accord to each its light, as God has ordained for everyone, how then can I be a pagan?"

It is clear enough from this what his attitude was to the problem of the two sources of knowledge: both lights derive from the unity of God. And yet—why did he give the name "Pagoyum" to what he wrote in the light of nature? Was he playing with words, or was it an involuntary avowal, a dim presentiment of a duality in the world and the soul? Was Paracelsus really unaffected by the schismatic spirit of the age, and was his attack on authority really confined only to Galen, Avicenna, Rhazes, and Arnaldus de Villanova?

Paracelsus's scepticism and rebelliousness stop short at the Church, but he also reined them in before alchemy, astrology, and magic, which he believed in as fervently as he did in divine revelation, since in his view they proceeded from the authority of the *lumen naturae*. And when he speaks of the divine office of the physician, he exclaims: "I under the Lord, the Lord under me, I under him outside my office, and he under me outside his office." (pp. 112-17)

One can easily object that Paracelsus said this, like so much else, only in passing and that it is not to be taken all that seriously. He himself would probably have been astonished and indignant if he had been taken at his word. The words that flowed into his pen came less from deep reflection than from the spirit of the age in which he lived. No one can claim to be immune to the spirit of his own epoch or to possess anything like a complete knowledge of it. Regardless of our conscious convictions, we are all without exception, in so far as we are particles in the mass, gnawed at and undermined by the spirit that runs through the masses. Our freedom extends only as far as our consciousness reaches. Beyond that, we succumb to the unconscious influences of our environment. Though we may not be clear in a logical sense about the deepest meanings of our words and actions, these meanings nevertheless exist and they have a psychological effect. Whether we know it or not, there remains in each of us the tremendous tension between the man who *serves* God and the man who *commands* God to do his bidding.

But the greater the tension, the greater the potential. Great energy springs from a correspondingly great tension of opposites. It was to the constellation of the most powerful opposites within him that Paracelsus owed his almost daemonic energy, which was not an unalloyed gift of God but went hand in hand with his impetuous and quarrelsome temperament, his hastiness, impatience, discontent-

edness, and his arrogance. Not for nothing was Paracelsus the prototype of Faust, whom Jacob Burckhardt once called "a great primordial image" in the soul of every German. From Faust the line leads direct to Nietzsche, who was a Faustian man if ever there was one. What still maintained the balance in the case of Paracelsus and Angelus Silesius—"I under God and God under me"—was lost in the twentieth century, and the scale sinks lower and lower under the weight of an ego that fancies itself more and more godlike. Paracelsus shared with Angelus Silesius his inner piety and the touching but dangerous simplicity of his relationship to God. But alongside this spirituality a countervailing chthonic spirit made itself felt to an almost frightening degree: there was no form of manticism and magic that Paracelsus did not practice himself or recommend to others. Dabbling in these arts—no matter how enlightened one thinks one is—is not without its psychological dangers. Magic always was and still is a source of fascination. At the time of Paracelsus, certainly, the world teemed with marvels: everyone was conscious of the immediate presence of the dark forces of nature. Astronomy and astrology were not yet separated. Kepler still cast horoscopes. Instead of chemistry there was only alchemy. Amulets, talismans, spells for healing wounds and diseases were taken as a matter of course. A man so avid for knowledge as Paracelsus could not avoid a thorough investigation of all these things, only to discover that strange and remarkable effects resulted from their use. But so far as I know he never uttered a clear warning about the psychic dangers of magic for the adept. He even scoffed at the doctors because they understood nothing of magic. (pp. 117-19)

For him magic and the wisdom of nature had their place within the divinely ordained order as a *mysterium et magnale Dei*, and so it was not difficult for him to bridge the gulf into which half the world had plunged. Instead of experiencing any conflict in himself, he found his archenemy outside in the great medical authorities of the past, as well as in the host of academic physicians against whom he let fly like the proper Swiss mercenary he was. He was infuriated beyond measure by the resistance of his opponents and he made enemies everywhere. His writings are as turbulent as his life and his wanderings. His style is violently rhetorical. He always seems to be speaking importunately into someone's ear—someone who listens unwillingly, or against whose thick skin even the best arguments rebound. His exposition of a subject is seldom systematic or even coherent; it is constantly interrupted by admonitions, addressed in a subtle or coarse vein to an invisible auditor afflicted with moral deafness. Paracelsus was a little too sure that he had his enemy in front of him, and did not notice that it was lodged in his own bosom. He consisted of two persons who never really confronted one another. He nowhere betrays the least suspicion that he might not be at one with himself. He felt himself to be undividedly one, and all the things that constantly thwarted him had of course to be his external enemies. He had to conquer them and prove to them that he was the "Monarcha," the sovereign ruler, which secretly and unknown to himself was the very thing he was not. He was so unconscious of the conflict within him that he never noticed there was a second ruler in his own house who worked against him and opposed everything he wanted. But every unconscious conflict works out like that: one obstructs and undermines oneself. Paracelsus did not see that the truth of the Church and the Christian standpoint could never get along with the thought implicit in all alchemy, "God under me." And when one unconsciously works against oneself, the result is impatience, irritability, and an impotent longing to get one's opponent down whatever the means. Generally certain symptoms appear, among them a peculiar use of language: one wants to speak forcefully in order to impress one's opponent, so one employs a special, "bombastic" style full of neologisms which might be described as "power-words." This symptom is observable not only in the psychiatric clinic but also among certain modern philosophers, and, above all, whenever anything unworthy of belief has to be insisted on in the teeth of inner resistance: the language swells up, overreaches itself, sprouts grotesque words distinguished only by their needless complexity. The word is charged with the task of achieving what cannot be done by honest means. It is the old word magic, and sometimes it can degenerate into a regular disease. Paracelsus was afflicted with this malady to such a degree that even his closest pupils were obliged to compile "onomastica" (word-lists) and to publish commentaries. The unwary reader continually stumbles over these neologisms and is completely baffled at first, for Paracelsus never bothered to give any explanations even when, as often happens, the word was a *hapax legomenon* (one that occurs only once). Often it is only by comparing a number of passages that one can approximately make out the sense. There are, however, mitigating circumstances: doctors have always loved using magically incomprehensible jargon for even the most ordinary things. It is part of the medical persona. But it is odd indeed that Paracelsus, who prided himself on teaching and writing in German, should have been the very one to concoct the most intricate neologisms out of Latin, Greek, Italian, Hebrew, and possibly even Arabic.

Magic is insidious, and therein lies its danger. At one point, where Paracelsus is discussing witchcraft, he actually falls into using a magical witch-language without giving the least explanation. For instance, instead of "Zwirnfaden" (twine) he says "Swindafnerz," instead of "Nadel" (needle) "Dallen," instead of "Leiche" (corpse) "Chely," instead of "Faden" (thread) "Daphne," and so on. In magical rites the inversion of letters serves the diabolical purpose of turning the divine order into an infernal disorder. It is remarkable how casually and unthinkingly Paracelsus takes over these magically distorted words and simply leaves the reader to make what he can of them. This shows that Paracelsus must have been thoroughly steeped in the lowest folk beliefs and popular superstitions, and one looks in vain for any trace of disgust at such squalid things, though in his case its absence was certainly not due to lack of feeling but rather to a kind of natural innocence and naïveté. Thus he himself recommends the magical use of wax manikins in cases of sickness, and seems to have designed and used amulets and seals. He was convinced that physicians should have an understanding of the magic arts and should not eschew sorcery if this might help their patients. But this kind of folk magic is not Christian, it is demonstrably pagan—in a word, a "Pagoyum."

Besides his manifold contacts with folk superstition there was another, more respectable source of "pagan" lore that had a great influence on Paracelsus. This was his knowledge of and intense preoccupation with alchemy, which he used not only in his pharmacology and pharmaceutics but also for "philosophical" purposes. (pp. 120-22)

Consciously, alchemy for him meant a knowledge of the *materia medica* and a chemical procedure for preparing medicaments, above all the well-loved arcana, the secret remedies. He also believed that one could make gold and engender homunculi. This aspect of it was so predominant that one is inclined to forget that alchemy meant very much more to him than that. We know this from a brief remark in the *Paragranum,* where he says that the physician himself is "ripened" by the art. This sounds as though the alchemical maturation should go hand in hand with the maturation of the physician. If we are not mistaken in this assumption, we must further conclude that Paracelsus not only was acquainted with the arcane teachings of alchemy but was convinced of their rightness. It is of course impossible to prove this without detailed investigation, for the esteem which he expressed for alchemy throughout his writings might in the end refer only to its chemical aspect. This special predilection of his made him a forerunner and inaugurator of modern chemical medicine. Even his belief in the transmutation of metals and in the *lapis philosophorum,* which he shared with many others, is no evidence of a deeper affinity with the mystic background of the *ars aurifera.* And yet such an affinity is very probable since his closest followers were found among the alchemical physicians. (pp. 123-24)

Paracelsus's preoccupation with alchemy exposed him to an influence that left its mark on his spiritual development. The inner driving-force behind the aspirations of alchemy was a presumption whose daemonic grandeur on the one hand and psychic danger on the other should not be underestimated. Much of the overbearing pride and arrogant self-esteem, which contrasts so strangely with the truly Christian humility of Paracelsus, comes from this source. What erupted like a volcano in Agrippa von Nettesheim's "himself demon, hero, God" remained, with Paracelsus, hidden under the threshold of a Christian consciousness and expressed itself only indirectly in exaggerated claims and in his irritable self-assertiveness, which made him enemies wherever he went. We know from experience that such a symptom is due to unadmitted feelings of inferiority, i.e., to a real failing of which one is usually unconscious. In each of us there is a pitiless judge who makes us feel guilty even if we are not conscious of having done anything wrong. Although we do not know what it is, it is as though it were known somewhere. Paracelsus's desire to help the sick at all costs was doubtless quite pure and genuine. But the magical means he used, and in particular the secret content of alchemy, were diametrically opposed to the spirit of Christianity. And that remained so whether Paracelsus was aware of it or not. Subjectively, he was without blame; but that pitiless judge condemned him to feelings of inferiority that clouded his life.

This crucial point, namely the arcane doctrine of the marvellous son of the philosophers, is the subject of unfriendly but perspicacious criticism by Conrad Gessner. Apropos the works of a pupil of Paracelsus, Alexander à Suchten, he writes to Crato: "But look who it is whom he reveals to us as the son of God, namely none other than the spirit of the world and of nature, and the same who dwells in our bodies (it is a wonder that he does not add the spirit of the ox and the ass!). This spirit can be separated from matter or from the body of the elements by the technical procedures of the Theophrastus school. If anyone were to take him at his word, he would say that he had merely voiced a principle of the philosophers, but not his own opinion. He repeats it, however, in order to express his agreement. And I know that other Theophrastians besmirch such things with their writings, from which it is easy to conclude that they deny the divinity of Christ. I myself am entirely convinced that Theophrastus has been an Arian. They endeavour to persuade us that Christ was a quite ordinary man, and that in him was no other spirit than in us."

Gessner's charge against the Theophrastus school and against the Master himself applies to alchemy in general. The extraction of the world soul from matter was not a peculiarity of Paracelsan alchemy. But the charge of Arianism is unjustified. It was obviously prompted by the well-known parallel between the *filius philosophorum* and Christ, though so far as I know this nowhere occurs in Paracelsus's own writings. On the other hand, in a treatise called "Apokalypsis Hermetis," ascribed by Huser to Paracelsus, there is a complete alchemical confession of faith which lends Gessner's charge a certain weight. There Paracelsus says of the "spirit of the fifth essence": "This is the spirit of truth, whom the world cannot comprehend without the inspiration of the Holy Ghost, or without the instruction of those who know him." "He is the soul of the world," moving all and preserving all. In his initial earthly form (that is, in his original Saturnine darkness) he is unclean, but he purifies himself progressively during the ascent through his watery, aerial, and fiery forms. Finally, in the fifth essence, he appears as the "clarified body." "This spirit is the secret that has been hidden since the beginning of things."

Paracelsus is speaking here as a true alchemist. Like his pupils, he draws the Cabala, which had been made accessible to the world at large through Pico della Mirandola and Agrippa, into the scope of his alchemical speculations. "All you who are led by your religion to prophesy future events and to interpret the past and the present to people, you who see abroad and read hidden letters and sealed books, who seek in the earth and in walls for what is buried, you who learn great wisdom and art—bear in mind if you wish to apply all these things, that you take to yourselves the religion of the Gabal and walk in its light, for the Gabal is well-founded. Ask and it will be granted to you, knock, you will be heard and it will be opened unto you. From this granting and opening there will flow what you desire: you will see into the lowest depths of the earth, into the depths of hell, into the third heaven. You will gain more wisdom than Solomon, you will have greater communion with God than Moses and Aaron."

Just as the wisdom of the Cabala coincided with the Sapientia of alchemy, so the figure of Adam Kadmon was identified with the *filius philosophorum*. Originally this figure may have been the $\alpha\nu\theta\rho\omega\pi o\delta\ \phi\omega\tau\epsilon\iota\nu o\delta$, the "man of light" who was imprisoned in Adam, and whom we encounter in Zosimos of Panopolis (third century). But the man of light is an echo of the pre-Christian doctrine of the Primordial Man. Under the influence of Marsilio Ficino and Pico della Mirandola, these and other Neoplatonic ideas had already become popularized in the fifteenth century and were known to nearly every educated person. In

alchemy they fell in with the remnants of classical tradition. Besides this there were the views of the Cabala, which had been philosophically assessed by Pico. He and Agrippa were probably the sources for Paracelsus's somewhat scanty knowledge of the Cabala. For Paracelsus the Primordial Man was identical with the "astral" man: "The true man is the star in us." "The star desires to drive man towards great wisdom." In his ***Paragranum*** he says: "For heaven is man and man is heaven, and all men are one heaven, and heaven is only one man." Man stands in the relationship of a son to the inner heaven, which is the Father, whom Paracelsus calls the *homo maximus* or Adech, an arcane name derived from Adam. Elsewhere he is called Archeus: "He is therefore similar to man and consists of the four elements and is an Archeus and is composed of four parts; say then, he is the great Cosmos." Undoubtedly this is the Primordial Man, for Paracelsus says: "In the whole Ides there is but One Man, the same is extracted by the Iliastrum and is the Protoplast." Ides or Ideus is "the gate through which all created things have proceeded," the "globule or materia" from which man was created. Other secret names for the Primordial Man are Idechtrum and Protothoma. The number of names alone shows how preoccupied Paracelsus was with this idea. The ancient teachings about the Anthropos or Primordial Man assert that God, or the world-creating principle, was made manifest in the form of a "first-created" (*protoplastus*) man, usually of cosmic size. In India he is Prajāpati or Purusha, who is also "the size of a thumb" and dwells in the heart of every man, like the Iliaster of Paracelsus. In Persia he is Gayomart (*Gayō-maretan*, 'mortal life'), a youth of dazzling whiteness, as is also said of the alchemical Mercurius. In the *Zohar* he is Metatron, who was created together with light. He is the celestial man whom we meet in the visions of Daniel, Ezra, Enoch, and also in Philo Judaeus. He is one of the principal figures in Gnosticism, where, as always, he is connected with the question of creation and redemption. This is the case with Paracelsus. (pp. 128-32)

I had long been aware that alchemy is not only the mother of chemistry, but is also the forerunner of our modern psychology of the unconscious. Thus Paracelsus appears as a pioneer not only of chemical medicine but of empirical psychology and psychotherapy.

It may seem that I have said too little about Paracelsus the self-sacrificing physician and Christian, and too much about his dark shadow, that other Paracelsus, whose soul was intermingled with a strange spiritual current which, issuing from immemorial sources, flowed beyond him into a distant future. But—*ex tenebris lux*—it was precisely because he was so fascinated by magic that he was able to open the door to the realities of nature for the benefit of succeeding centuries. The Christian and the primitive pagan lived together in him in a strange and marvellous way to form a conflicting whole, as in other great Renaissance figures. Although he had to endure the conflict, he was spared that agonizing split between knowledge and faith that has riven the later epochs. As a man he had one father, but as a spirit he had two mothers. His spirit was heroic, because creative, and as such was doomed to Promethean guilt. The secular conflict that broke out at the turn of the sixteenth century, and whose living image stands before our eyes in the figure of Paracelsus, is a prerequisite for higher consciousness; for analysis is always followed by synthesis, and what was divided on a lower level will reappear, united, on a higher one. (p. 189)

C. G. Jung, "Paracelsus as a Spiritual Phenomenon," in his Alchemical Studies, *translated by R. F. C. Hull, Bollingen Series XX, Princeton University Press, 1967, pp. 109-89.*

Jolande Jacobi   (essay date 1942)

[*Jacobi was a Hungarian psychologist, essayist, and editor. A student and associate of C. G. Jung, she published collections of Jung's shorter works and contributed original studies of her mentor, as well. With Jung she shared an interest in Paracelsus's works; she published an edition of Paracelsus's selected writings in 1942. In the following excerpt from her prefatory essay in* Paracelsus: Selected Writings, *Jacobi surveys Paracelsus's writings.*]

Paracelsus' written works treat of every domain of life and knowledge. To attempt even briefly to discuss them as they deserve would be to go far beyond the framework of this biographical note. Here we shall merely attempt to cast some light on a few points. The following attempt to arrange his work in articulated segments is undertaken for the sake of greater clarity; it also corresponds to the chronological order.

Until 1525, Paracelsus was chiefly preoccupied with medical and therapeutic problems. Before that year, he wrote his eleven treatises on various diseases, such as dropsy, consumption, colic, apoplexy, worms; a number of works devoted to gout and the tartaric, or stone, afflictions; as well as the *Herbarius* and other treatises on *materia medica* and mineral springs. To the same early period, however, belong **"On the birth of perceptible things in reason,"** *De generatione hominis* **("On the origin of man"),** and *De morbis amentium* **("On the diseases that deprive man of reason").** Though these works embody his first anthropological and philosophical insights, they still suggest the earthliness characteristic of his youthful mind.

In the following years, from 1526 to 1528, which include the period of Paracelsus' academic activities in Basel, the medical element is still predominant. The range of the medical subjects treated is astoundingly wide, comprising surgery, internal and external diseases of all kinds, and the preparation of the most complicated drugs, often involving the art of transforming metals and minerals. Within the same period falls his most important early work, the **Nine Books of Archidoxus,** a manual of the secret remedies, their virtues and forces. This work contains in germ all the mature knowledge of the most deeply hidden casualties of nature, which Paracelsus would later reveal. At about the same time he wrote *De renovatione et restauratione* and *De vita longa.* Both of these are "books of initiation" into the secret knowledge of death and rebirth and are already permeated with the symbolism of hermetic alchemy. With them, Paracelsus, then barely thirty years of age, enters the multiform realm of the Mothers. And in *De vita longa* he states the creed that gave substance to his life in the words: "The striving for wisdom is the second paradise of the world."

Feverish activity filled the next years, in which Paracelsus strove to effect a complete transformation of medical theory and practice. Disappointed by what he had seen of con-temporary medical knowledge, Paracelsus rejected all tradition lock, stock, and barrel; relentlessly he attacked the old "humoural medicine" and lashed out against his colleagues who clung to anatomy, "the dead carcass," instead of considering the living body as a whole. He now wrote his treatises on open wounds, on smallpox, paralysis, tumours, cavities, etc., the **Three Bertheonei Books ("The Little Surgery"),** and his basic contributions, written in Nuremberg, to the study of syphilis. But the "purified monarchy" of medicine, as he calls it, did not seem to welcome his drastic methods, for only a negligible part of these writings found a publisher. Through the intervention of the university authorities, the printing of his book *On the Origin and Derivation of "the French Disease,"* and of others of his works, was forbidden. The world refused to listen to new ideas; officials and dignitaries were just what they have always been. "Whoever stands up against you and tells the truth must die," Paracelsus observes in bitter disillusionment. But such bitterness is not his only or even his predominant attitude. The childlike enthusiasm and piety of his German romantic soul inspire yet another answer, which can be found in his preface to the **Book of Hospitals,** dating from 1528/29. "The supreme reason for medicine is love," he writes. And: "The main substance of the art lies in experience and also love, which is embodied in all the high arts. For we receive them from the love of God and we should give them with the same love."

From 1530 to 1534, Paracelsus was at the height of his creative activities. Although all of his previous writings have a philosophical and metaphysical substratum, the two great books dating from this period, the *Paragranum* and the *Paramirum,* display for the first time the full brilliance of his powerful philosophical vision. In their completeness, they are among the best and most characteristic Paracelsian writings; they are also his best known works. Following his disappointments in Basel and Nuremberg, he intended *Paragranum*—this is shown by its whole tenor—as a settlement of accounts and at the same time as a solemn statement of principles. After several sketchy attempts, Paracelsus in this book formulates "the principles of true medicine" in a grandiose and sharply articulated system. "But because I am alone," he pleads, "because I am new, because I am a German, do not scorn my writings, do not let yourself be drawn away from them." And driven by his anger, but also lifted by his self-assurance, he adds: "That you may henceforth understand me rightly, how I establish the foundations of medicine on which I rest and will rest, namely in philosophy, namely in astronomy, namely in alchemy, namely in virtue! But just as I myself take these pillars, so you must take them, and you must follow me, not I you!"

Thus the four main pillars upon which he founds his medicine are: philosophy, the science of the material and elemental aspect of creation; astronomy, the science of the sidereal aspect of creation (these two disciplines in their interrelations and their essence are the prerequisites for penetrating the structure of man, who is a microcosm exactly corresponding to the macrocosm, or the whole of creation); alchemy, the science of these natural phenomena and of their inner meaning; virtue (*proprietas*), the fourth pillar, which gives the physicians the support without which the other three could never be solid. In line with his earlier *Opus Paramirum,* in which he describes the five *entia,* i.e., disease-causing active principles—*ens veneni, ens naturale, ens astrale, ens spirituale,* and *ens deale*—Paracelsus now wrote **Volumen Paramirum,** giving a fundamental anthropological analysis of man's structure. Here he expands his thesis on the four basic elements of man and cosmos (water, earth, fire, air) and the three basic substances (sulphur, mercury, and salt); he unfolds all the aspects of his doctrine on the nature of the Matrix, the Womb (here he discusses all the problems of man and woman, sexuality, and related diseases); and he delves into a number of psychic phenomena and diseases.

He often approaches the most recent insights of the modern psychology of the unconscious, and just as his pharmaceutics makes him a precursor of modern chemotherapy, he may well be regarded also as a pioneer of modern psychotherapy. His faith in the "healing word," in the radiating efficacy of the physician's personality, is part of the modern psychologist's indispensable stock-in-trade. But since in Paracelsus each insight is ultimately rooted in ethics and religion, all these questions lead him back to God and the primordial problems of good and evil—he sees each disease as a conflict between good and evil. In his view the material-elemental body cannot sin, but only the sidereal body, i.e., the soul. Accordingly, only the soul, or its immortal spiritual part, is subject to the last "judgment" and thus has a hope of resurrection. Good and evil are powers created by God, realities, which man must take into account, and which therefore the physician must know thoroughly. Good fortune and good health reside in the just measure and in a harmony that accords with the law of creation: the destruction of this harmony and proportion brings degeneration and disease in its train. Thus Paracelsus' views lead back to the Platonic conception that harmony, beauty, the Good, and the True are identical. Besides these two important books, the writings of this period include treatises on hysteria (**Von den hinfallenden Siechtagen der Mutter**), on falling sickness (**Von den hinfallenden Siechtagen**), on the comets, on the plague, on the mineral springs of Pfäffers, and numerous other minor works. Though they contain many pearls, they seem little more than ornaments surrounding his crowning work.

Paragranum and **Paramirum** are a complete exposition of ideas that had matured for a long time; thus they conclude a period in Paracelsus' development. At the same time, they point ahead to his increasing concern with the problems of the absolute. To this field of knowledge Paracelsus devoted himself wholeheartedly, as is shown by the above-mentioned theological writings, numbering 123, which constitute more than half of all his works. These date from the years around 1533 and reflect a crucial turning-point in his life. Most of them have not yet been published; a small number were included in the first volume of the second part of the Sudhoff-Matthiessen edition, which, it is planned, will have approximately ten more volumes. Of these we shall mention the treatises *De religione perpetua, De summo bono et aeterno bono, De felici liberalitate,* and *De resurrectione et corporum glorificatione,* which all exist in German, and especially *Vita beata* ("**Book of the beatific life**"), which is among the most moving professions of a pure soul. In these works Paracelsus displays an extraordinary knowledge of the Scriptures and of Catholic liturgy. The preface to his *Libell über die Pest* ("**Pamphlet on the plague**") bears the proud signature "Theophrastus von Hohenheim, professor of Holy Writ, doctor of the two

medicines." The treatises on the Last Communion, on the Holy Mother of God, on the Gospel of St. Matthew, on the dogma of the Trinity, etc., demonstrate a truly fanatical preoccupation with the material. With typical Paracelsian self-wilfulness, they attack the official doctrine of the church, but in the depth of the sentiment that speaks from them, and the earnestness that inspires them, they are nevertheless documents of a marvelous religious ardour which will leave no reader indifferent. The spirit of the miracle of the Pentecost breathes in every line of them.

Having talked at length with his God and apparently recovered some peace of soul, he again turned to medical fields. The problems previously treated in his **Three Bertheonei Books** regained his attention, and the studies he now undertook resulted in the **Books of the Greater Surgery,** published in two successive editions in 1536 and 1537. Designed on a grandiose scale, the **Greater Surgery** covers this whole important field, and even today is a treasure trove for the surgeon. This was the only great publishing success of his life. His contemporaries, who otherwise showed so little understanding of his work, now listened with approval. Apart from this one, his only works to meet with no opposition were his numerous "prognostications." Such "forecasts" were in great vogue at that time, and presumably Paracelsus composed them to earn some money, but also in part no doubt because he found in them an appropriate vehicle for his admonitions and tirades, as we can see from his interpretation of the *Papstbilder* and the *Figuren des J. Lichtenberger.* In any event it would be erroneous to consider them as predictions of the future in the usual sense, even though Paracelsus, thanks to his mantic and intuitive gifts, might have been able to forecast or surmise some aspects of the future. These prognostications, as well as his so-called **Practica,** which were circulated with calendars, bear little relation to the main body of his works, although they include many profound thoughts.

But Paracelsus no longer sought security on earth or the approval of men. And even medicine was now for him only a stage on the path to the supernatural. Soon he left its tangible domains and returned to the realm of the incomprehensible. Words at best can give only a veiled notion of the adventure upon which he now embarked. He attempted to order and record what his inner eye had seen and experienced in the many years of his struggle against the world and the super-world. The accumulated material was elaborated in 1537 and 1539; today it forms a volume of more than five hundred closely printed pages. He called this work **Astronomia magna, or the Whole Sagacious Philosophy of the Great and Small World.** Any attempt to sum up the content of this unique book in a short sketch would expose it to incomprehension and misunderstanding. Only the deepest absorption in it can help one to understand it. It is a most mysterious work and presents the most mature and the ultimate of Paracelsus' cosmological and anthropological insights. Soaring on the wings of a magical and artistic spirit, it evokes and formulates the subtlest essential problems of being. The cosmosophic philosophy herein embodied is conceived as a guide to the supreme initiation into the mysteries of God and nature.

To give a glimpse of the immense range of this work, we shall briefly quote the titles and topics of some of its sections, in which, as he observes in his preface, he describes

Facsimile of Paracelsus's handwriting.

the "action of the internal heaven" with help "of the spirit that emanated from the Father." The "nine members" into which he divides his "sagacious philosophy" are: *Magica* (on will power); *Astrologia* (on the spiritual influences and their reactions); *Signatum* (on the knowledge of the inner essence as obtained through outward signs); *Nigromantia* (on apparitions); *Necromantia* (on second sight); *Artes incertae* (on the arts of the imagination and inspiration); *Medicina adepta* (on the occult science of supernatural cures); *Philosophia adepta* (on the wisdom of alchemistic skill and contemplation based on the science of the supernatural); *Mathematica adepta* (on the science of occult relations, geometry, cosmography, measures, weights, numbers). This is the first of the four books; the others encompass even more out-of-the-way domains under similar headings, and offer the ultimate, most occult knowledge of diabolical and divine things. He who possesses this knowledge has discarded the fetters of materiality while he is still here on earth.

With *Philosophia sagax,* Paracelsus reached the pinnacle of his work. His *Occulta philosophia* and *Archidoxis magica* attack the same themes and elaborate them in a still more sibylline manner; they are hermetic writings to which we have lost the key. After this final survey from the heights, which he made at the age of forty-five, and after which he began his descent into the valley of the beyond, he produced several minor but only two major works—the *Defensiones,* his passionate apologia, and the *Labyrinthus medicorum,* a last admonition and warning.

Then he lost himself in the pathless realm of mysteries which can no longer be expounded in writing.

It is impossible to draw an exact picture of the doctrines that inspired Paracelsus; without doubt he was to some extent influenced by the Neoplatonists and the early Gnostics. Numerous alchemists, philosophers, and physicians, among them Agrippa von Nettesheim and the famous Abbot of Sponheim, as well as the surgeons Hieronymus Brunschwig and Hans von Gersdorff, are often named as his teachers. Paracelsus himself deeply influenced the intellectual development of the following centuries. German mystics and romantics, from Gerhardus Dorn and Jacob Böhme to Novalis, were moved by his profoundly mystical writings. Separate works of Paracelsus were published shortly after his death by Adam von Bodenstein and Johannes Huser, but the first complete collection appeared only fifty years after his death. Since then they have on countless occasions been violently attacked and passionately defended, and subjected to arbitrary interpretations. But in the spiritual life of mankind, it has always been a small group that has held up the torch of the spirit. It is this group that carries it through centuries, from generation to generation. To this small group Paracelsus belongs. (pp. 64-72)

Jolande Jacobi, "Paracelsus: His Life and His Work," in Paracelsus: Selected Writings, *edited by Jolande Jacobi, translated by Norbert Guterman, Bollingen Series XXVIII, Pantheon Books, 1951, pp. 39-74.*

Henry M. Pachter   (essay date 1951)

[*Pachter was a German-born American historian and educator who wrote numerous books and essays on Nazi Germany, among other subjects. His biography* Paracelsus: Magic into Science (1951) *is something of an anomaly among such works as* The Axis Grand Strategy: Blueprints for the Total War (1942) *and* The Cuban Missile Crisis and Coexistence (1963). *In the following excerpt from his biography of Paracelsus, Pachter salutes his subject as one of the Promethean figures of human history.*]

Embracing the universe while he was seeking man, Paracelsus was a utopian. Like all great scientists, he overestimated the possibilities of his science. He strove to discover truths for which the science of his age had neither definitions nor methods of verification. He tried to grasp the whole before he knew the details. His genius was able to feel intuitively what he was unable to prove by reasoning or experiment, still less to express in words.

He tried to understand chemistry without having the notion of elements. He studied biology without ever having seen a cell. He sought to heal wounds when nobody knew how to stop a hemorrhage. He offered a theory of nature when there was no way to distinguish between organic and inorganic processes. He was a psychiatrist, when the very word "psychology" was not yet in the vocabulary. He could see no difference between a man's spirit and the spirit that steamed out of his alembic. He had to say "occult" when he was referring to the forces of nature which are known to the scientist but hidden from the layman. He tried to conceptualize laws of Nature, when only astrological terms were available.

He was fully aware of these shortcomings. It is all too true that Paracelsus not only is a difficult author, but often is obscure and enigmatic, not to say confused and inconsistent. His works are crowded with contradictions which he did not trouble to resolve. His concepts are not well-defined, his language is ill-adapted to handle the difficult problems he proposed to solve. He constantly struggled with words, shouting and yelling when he felt that otherwise he might only stammer. He remonstrated against logical deductions and ridiculed "school philosophy" because his ideas failed to fit any known system. Often they did not reach the phase of articulate thought, but came to him in the form of an aphoristic certitude, based on sympathetic understanding and compassionate intuition rather than on analysis and research.

Searching is not research. Theophrastus was unable either to separate or to integrate the two. Perhaps that was the cause of his failure; certainly it was the cause of his greatness. He sought metaphysical certitude in empirical studies, and formulas in his intuition of the Absolute. In all his studies of nature he never lost sight of the ultimate aim of science: to know the nature of Nature. And vice versa, he believed he held the key to all phenomena of nature because he believed he knew the secret of the whole.

The contributions of the great men who have advanced humanity are of various kinds. Some contributed a definite piece of knowledge to the stock of information on the structure of the universe, the body, the soul, or society. Others invented tools and techniques which facilitated mastery over natural forces. These are the great peaks in history which serve as beacons for the study of man's possibilities.

Paracelsus was not among those who created and stood in the light. He belonged to a third kind of great men—those who explored the darkness and held the torch while mankind traversed the valleys; those who struggled with the truth before knowledge had ripened to formulate it; those who tried to lift the veil before they knew the Goddess behind it.

These, too, are great. They want the full truth when it is easier to compromise with half-truths. They would rather err in their search for right than be right without ever having searched. They would rather be damned while seeking salvation by their own endeavor, than be saved without ever having tried to save themselves.

They are redeemed, asserts Goethe, because they strove. Their efforts, though frustrated, save humanity every day. (pp. 300-02)

> *Henry M. Pachter, in his* Magic into Science: The Story of Paracelsus, *Henry Schuman, 1951, 360 p.*

Walter Pagel   (essay date 1958)

[*Pagel was a German-born British pathologist, scientist, and medical historian. An author noted for placing the discoveries of important medical figures within their religious and philosophical contexts, he wrote many works about William Harvey, Paracelsus, and Jean Baptiste van Helmont. In the following excerpt from his monograph on Paracelsus, Pagel summarizes Paracelsus's importance as a figure of the Renaissance, his position in the humanist tradition, his relationship in spiritual matters to Martin Luther, and his role as a shaper of thought since his time.*]

The term "Renaissance" is applicable to too many divergent historical figures to convey more than a vague and in the last resort essentially chronological grouping of persons and ideas. Yet, in an overall appraisal of Paracelsus against the background of his period, it will not easily be dispensed with.

Understood as a literary, artistic and aesthetic revival of antiquity, the Renaissance has no place for Paracelsus. The man was no humanist who, like Paracelsus, publicly repudiated ancient tradition and felt called upon to create something entirely of his own, adapted to the new demands of a new age.

It is in Paracelsus that we witness a new clash of original Christian ideas with the classical heritage: the war which Paracelsus waged against "reason" in favour of parable and analogy, against the moderate attitude which is satisfied with the finite and visible form in favour of an unlimited search for an infinite number of forces. In all this, Paracelsus seems to challenge the highest ideals of the Renaissance.

If it is said, however, that the Renaissance stood for the revival of man as a whole and for the unfolding of unlimited activity, then Paracelsus is its true exponent. His view of the world is indeed "anthropocentric". The hierarchic principle of the Middle Ages—clerical as well as feudal—

had limited the freedom of man not only in the social and economic sphere, but above all in the realm of ideas—directing attention away from the reality of nature and of the individual towards that of universals. It had thus created a collective outlook in which the life of the individual was standardised by the central powers of Church and State. Among the individualists who were actuated by a desire to discuss rather than accept the scriptural sources of such uniformity, Paracelsus stood in the first rank.

Moreover, a "decentralising" tendency can be observed everywhere in his work. He seems to follow the alchemical principle of "separation" even where the issue is not concerned with matter and its nature. He "differentiates" and infinitely divides the world, which he sees peopled with demons, subhuman and superhuman beings and invisible principles which work under the surface of things visible. It is the emphasis on these as opposed to any synthesis or limitation by a few universal principles and entities, that is his leading idea. Even his anthropocentric view is thus open to qualification and is far from providing absolute standards.

Furthermore, in his search for the Invisible and in his vision of infinitely many higher and lower beings filling the universe and acting below the surface of visible objects, Paracelsus worked—however unconsciously—for the revival of Neoplatonism, Gnosticism and the Kabbala: in this respect, he appears as a true exponent of the Renaissance.

Perhaps the best illustration of this is provided by his general attitude towards the position of the celestial bodies with regard to Man and Nature. Aristotle had called them the "more divine among things visible". Possessed of "soul" and "life", he had regarded them as the driving forces responsible for all activity in the sublunar world. Nicolaus Cusanus, on the other hand, had deprived the stars of this divine superiority. In his universe they were just as remote from divine infinity and the unerring Ideas on High as was any other "finite" creature—with which they were perfectly comparable by measure and number. There was still a hierarchic principle—the subordination of things finite to divine infinity—but the dividing line was drawn differently than in Aristotelian cosmology. The celestial bodies were now considered on the same footing as earthly objects. In this Cusanus was followed by Pico della Mirandola.

Paracelsus' attitude is ambivalent. At all events it is not easy to grasp and has given rise to controversy, under the heading: Did Paracelsus adhere to astrology or not?

It would appear that this question is too narrowly formulated to lend itself to a simple answer.

Paracelsus does preserve the magisterial power of the "Astrum". This, however, is no longer a remote tyrant who subjects sublunary things in blind obedience to himself by "influxes" and "impressions".

Instead, Paracelsus emphasises "correspondences". But the idea of series of objects corresponding and bound to each other by sympathy had of course played a conspicuous part in gnostic and mediaeval, notably Arabic, speculation. Such series, however, still presented hierarchies, each crowned by a particular planet. It was from the sphere of this planet that spirits set out to penetrate other spheres, elements, minerals, plants and animals—taking possession at preordained times, conferring colour, smell, consistency, temperature, moisture or dryness, forming and guiding a particular organ, and so on.

There is still much of this in Paracelsus' work. But there is also a strong tendency to dissolve such hierarchies and to assign to the individual, power ("virtues") equal or even superior to that of the star. Each of these virtues, however, is still bound by sympathy to a group of others and to a particular star on High. Any action or change brought about by an astrum or virtue has inevitable repercussions on the members of the group and indeed on the world as a whole by disturbing the preordained order of things. For, as Leibniz formulated it, there is "Consensus" rather than "Commercium" between individual objects—each of them fulfilling its own schedule of action and life. Nevertheless, even to Paracelsus the stars spell the future—but merely by *indicating* the determined and concerted course of objects related to one another by sympathy. The stars are the inescapable signals, but do not influence objects and events by themselves.

"Astrum" finally becomes virtue in the widest sense—a virtue that is subject to the will and discretion of the individual, a virtue that can be used, cultivated and developed.

It is in this sense that Paracelsus saw "Astra" everywhere: on high as well as on the earth and in its "fruits". The Sun, the Moon, Saturn, Jupiter, Mars, Venus were to him intrinsic to man, animals, plants, metals and minerals, to earth, water, air and fire, since one of these stars corresponds to the invisible driving force in each particular object. Moreover, it was on the transference of astral correspondences to the body that Paracelsus based his original views of the harmonious action of the organs which makes an "organism" possible.

Paracelsus thus brought the "Astra" down to earth and implemented the ideal of "Magia Naturalis", which is to "marry Heaven and Earth". This redistribution of the "Astra" as common property of all objects in nature is indeed consonant with his general tendency to decentralise and with his distaste for hierarchy, dogmatism, rigidity and standardisation.

Paracelsus thus made bold strides to outgrow mediaeval astrology, but he did not accomplish this by any means. He remains "mediaeval" in recognising the limitations of human action and liberty by cosmic constellation in the traditional sense. In spite of his many progressive naturalistic observations in medicine and chemistry and an advanced insight into the working of nature, his thought as a whole cannot be called "scientific". Paracelsus is concerned not with measurable quantities and the mathematical laws underlying phenomena, but with individual objects determined by intrinsic divine virtues which defy scientific analysis.

Humanism at first sight seems incompatible with Paracelsus' attitude towards the ancients. Yet he is unthinkable without the Hellenistic blending of Jewish, Christian, Greek and Oriental ideas and symbolism ("syncretism") as expressed in Neo-Platonism, Gnosticism and Kabbala, Alchemy, Astrology and Magic. It was the humanists who revived these sources just before and at the time of Paracelsus. Contacts and parallels with such Platonists as Nicolaus Cusanus and Marsilius Ficinus followed by Picus,

Reuchlin, Jacobus Faber Stapulensis, Bovillus, Trithemius and Agrippa can easily be demonstrated in the work of Paracelsus.

Moreover, the humanistic reversion to classical models was associated with a quest for truth and reality as against the fictitious—"sophistic"—embellishments added by the Arabs. Hence the call for the restoration of the ancient texts in their original purity. This is well expressed, for example, in the title of the small plague treatise by Job. Ammonius Agricola which has an almost Paracelsean ring—promising that it is "based on good ground, without any sophistic or Arabic, additional and fictitious chatter unfounded in Medicine."

Finally, since Petrarch's days (1304-1374), humanism had taken a decisive stand against scholasticism and the exuberant claims of formal logic—an attitude that at Paracelsus' time was still fresh and went well with the revival of Platonism. However, little can be found in Paracelsus of the polished style and elegance in appearance and behaviour of the humanist of his days, although it was in humanist circles that he found resonance and support.

Yet, in contrast with the humanists pure and simple, Paracelsus was not interested in the preservation and revival of ancient sources for their own sake or for the sake of general culture and erudition, but moulded and re-formed them in his own way, conscious as he was of the demands of a new age with new needs and ideals. (pp. 35-9)

Paracelsus has often been compared with Luther—he himself mentioned and to a certain extent countenanced this comparison with a religious iconoclast of historic dimensions. There are the obvious common traits in their behaviour—the course and boisterous language, the use of the vernacular which had to be moulded and reformed in order to convey something un-traditional and unheard of, the crass rejection of learned predecessors and authorities, theatrical acts designed to appeal to students and the illiterate mob—such as the burning of books or the display of "theses" in public places.

Yet there was no love lost between Paracelsus and Luther. Paracelsus stood for religious and intellectual freedom. He believed in the free will of man which he supposed to enable him to act even upon the stars. He was a pacifist and advocate of the common people. Though in principle opposed to violence, his sympathy was with the insurgent peasants and in his early years at Salzburg he barely escaped persecution and death in the peasants' struggle against their feudal lords. His life and work was a permanent war against the privileged and mighty. His medicine was actuated by charitable motives. He sought eternal bliss in deeds of self-denial rather than in mere belief and divine grace, factors withdrawn from the sphere of human influence and understanding. Luther on the other hand forged a new religious dogmatism based on the rejection of human activity and free will in favour of mystical belief and the doctrine of election. He sides with the sovereigns and mighty burghers of Germany against the peasants and had his doctrine enforced against dissenters by fire, sword and torture. He notably hit the Baptists, the powerful appeal of whose "pure religion" made them a real focus of danger to the influence of Luther and his partisans.

A deep gulf thus divorces Paracelsus from Luther. He rather belongs to that group of men who, like Sebastian

Franck (1499-1543) and Hans Denck (died 1527) would have none of dogmatic religion in any form, but advocated progress and reform without violence. (pp. 40-1)

Among the most violent invectives hurled against Paracelsus by the "Prince" of his adversaries, Erastus, was the accusation of *gnostic* heresy. Indeed, the attitude of Paracelsus does seem to show something of the "Spiritual Man", the "Pneumatikos" of the Gnosis. Led by his superior insight the gnostic mystagogue found the way from the lower strata of the flesh and vegetative soul to the higher sphere of the spirit. He spanned in one vision all that happened from the beginning to the end. In Hellenistic times this had been the position of the Magus and Alchemist. In the Renaissance it was the ideal of the "Priest-Physician" as extolled by Ficino.

What makes Paracelsus unique in this tradition is his wide excursions into observable Nature. There are periods in his life and voluminous treatises among his works in which he appears to be nothing but a naturalist explorer and physician. Nor is it accidental that he boldly embraced nature as the object of study at a time that was eminently susceptible for this.

It would be wrong to forget, however, that even where the naturalist aspects are prevalent in Paracelsus it is the desire to probe and test Nature for the validity of his cosmological and religious philosophy that forms the driving motive for his research. It was at the end of his life, in a period of sad resignation, that he wrote his main metaphysical work—the ***Philosophia Sagax.*** Yet this puts forward nothing that is new over and above the general ideas which he imparted in his other and earlier works.

Paracelsus thus remains true to his device: "Alterius non sit qui suus esse potest": To contemporaries this marked him as a "brave" man rather than a "sound" man and one who was bent on "truth" (as he saw it) rather than on "good taste". To the modern mind he stands out not as a link in the chain of students of Nature to whom modern science owes its origin, not as a physician with modern and revolutionising ideas, not as one of a cohort of religious preachers, ethical thinkers or social reformers—but as a "Magus" who forged a new synthesis from personal experience. While this synthesis is in general not readily accessible to us, nevertheless certain parts and isolated aphorisms suggest by their brilliance to the modern mind the power of the whole and its impact at its own time. (p. 350)

> *Walter Pagel, in his* Paracelsus: An Introduction to Philosophical Medicine in the Era of the Renaissance, *S. Karger, 1958, 368 p.*

Diane Di Prima   (essay date 1965)

[*Di Prima is an American poet and essayist who has written on feminist and mystical themes. In the following excerpt from an essay written in 1965 which served to introduce a selection of Paracelsus's hermetic and alchemical writings, she presents Paracelsus as an unfairly maligned figure whose wisdom is much needed in the modern world.*]

Paracelsus—one of the greatest of western mystics and adepts, a man who brought to its highest point the science of alchemy, physician, philosopher, vagabond, who hurled invective at the doctors of his day, found himself sleeping by the wayside in the company of gypsies, bandits, and pilgrims, learning from them, poor, homeless, hunted, writing his best works only when his career was in ruins, when he had been expelled from the University of Basel for incensing the Medical Association of the time against himself. A name out of a myth, scholar, drinker, traveller—a man who some say gave rise to the Faust legend, beloved to this day, but rarely read, and almost never understood.

We have, perhaps, lost the key to the alchemical texts, as is so often stated, but they stand as one of the great documents of a great and high science. For alchemy was not, as we have been told in school, merely the "forerunner of modern chemistry," but a complete and highly developed discipline, a western equivalent of the great spiritual disciplines of the East.

Examine the tables of elements—how many are there now? Ninety-six? One hundred and eight? Well, for Paracelsus there were the four elements; fire, water, earth, and air; and the three substances: mercury, sulphur, and salt. What have we gained by the change? Aside from the inconveniences of nuclear fission, poisoned food, and fluoridated water, we are supporting the dead weight of a huge number of inane technicians, engaged day and night in inventing new entities to bolster their crumbling systems: fermions, bions, ergons, etc., *ad nauseam.*

Listen to this description of "ultimate matter": "I call the ultimate matter of anything that state in which the substance has reached its highest grade of exaltation and perfection." "Exaltation?" "Perfection?"—applied to matter? It is a kind of pantheism: spirit pervades even the densest substance. It has a *virtù,* gives forth a force. Gold "rejoices in its lucidity and transparency." There is a give and take going on between the substance and the mind of the observer, which we are today slowly coming to discover again. (p. v)

Europe in 1541, when Paracelsus died, bore little resemblance to the continent where he had been born, less than half a century earlier. The Reformation had effectively claimed England, Denmark, Sweden, and northern Germany. The nations of Europe had pretty much taken the form that they have to this day. The Hapsburgs were a rising family. Copernicus and Galileo were preparing to change the shape of the universe. "I see no end of it," Erasmus had written, "but the turning upside down of the whole world." The long, slow process of the dissolution of European society had begun.

But chaotic as the world was, it had not yet been fragmented as it is today. The unity of the microcosm and the macrocosm, the harmony between the courses of the stars, the cycles of the seasons, and the spiritual life of man, was not in question. "All things are concealed in all." It was possible, by looking into the heart of matter to study the matter of the heart. The alchemist's laboratory was the place where the secrets of man's essential nature surfaced, and were explored. And as the outer and the inner were one, there could be no basic antagonism between faith and reason, between experimental truth and the truth of intuition. Paracelsus was to this extent untouched by the Reformation. He is a bridge between the old order and the new. It may seem strange to us to find, in the midst of a highly

technical treatise, a reference to the subtle and glorious workings of God, but to him there was no strangeness in this, for how could there be one without the other? The human race was fortunately in a wholer state than it has been in since. To live one's life in harmony with the cosmos, to understand its laws and workings, was not only an ideal of philosophy, but practical commonsense. It was at once the root of the art of medicine, and a high expression of religion (reverence). (p. vii)

It is true that much of what Paracelsus writes is obscure to us. It is more obscure than it need be. For what is required to penetrate the secrets of these books is an attribute most difficult of accomplishment by the modern reader: faith. When Paracelsus declares that, having burned a flower, he can again raise its *eidolon,* or phantom, from the ashes, or that he has grown an homunculus out of human sperm incubated in horse dung, and educated it, he is not, as we would fain believe, speaking figuratively. He means exactly and literally what he says. The whole of modern criticism has as its aim the softening of the statements of poets, alchemists, philosophers, into something symbolical and therefore twice removed and digestible without effort and without faith. It is a conspiracy to render harmless the words of those who would not be silenced. Do you but bring the blind faith of a child to the works of Paracelsus or of any other great mystic, and you will find new universes opening before you. (p. ix)

Precise and lucid definitions are his forte. Embedded in an obscure paragraph, they leap out of it to delight mind and spirit. "To conjure is nothing else than to observe anything rightly, to know and to understand what it is." They often bring with them distinctions so fine as to anticipate Kant or Hume: " . . . death brings with it no disease, nor is it the cause of any. On the other hand, no disease causes death. And although the two coexist together, they are still no more to be compared one with the other than fire and water. They are no more akin one to another, nor do they agree better together. Natural sickness abhors death, and every member of the body avoids it. Death, then, is something distinct from disease."

Relying as he does on experience, it is not surprising to find somewhat unorthodox and highly delightful reinterpretations of the Scriptures (the vogue and new excitement of the age) scattered throughout his work. "He who created man also created science. What has man in any place without labor? When the mandate went forth: Thou shalt live by the sweat of thy brow, there was, as it were, a new creation. When God uttered his fiat the world was made. Art, however, was not then made, nor was the light of nature. But when Adam was expelled from Paradise, God created for him the light of Nature when he bade him live by the work of his hands."

You may read Paracelsus for his wonderful prose, as rich as the *Anatomy of Melancholy,* or for the marvelous universe he pictures, the images he calls up. I remember especially his description of the waters surrounding the earth, containing, like an eggshell, all that is needed within them, and the discussion of the generation of monsters through the imagination of a pregnant woman. Or, listen to this paragraph "Concerning the Death of the Elements, especially of water:"

"Elements die, as men die, on account of the corruption

in them. As water at its death, as it were, consumes and devours its own fruit, so does the earth its own fruits. Whatever is born from it returns to it again, is swallowed up and lost, just as time past is swallowed up by yesterday's days and nights, the light or darkness of which we shall never see again."

Or you may search out his prophecies, some of which may come to pass in our own day. "At present the palm is given to debauchery, until one third part of mankind or of the population of the world shall be killed, another shall be finished off by disease, and the remaining third only shall be saved and survive." It is a description of the inevitable, the events of the Kaliyuga. But he holds out a hope for the time that comes after: "By this arcanum the last age shall be illuminated clearly and compensated for all its losses by the gift of grace and the reward of the spirit of truth, so that since the beginning of the world no similar germination of the intelligence and of wisdom shall ever have been heard of."

No matter what your starting point, you will find yourself at last reading these volumes simply for the man that they reveal. He is surely one of the most fascinating figures of the Renaissance. Arrogant before his enemies, humble before his art, full of a childlike faith, investigating everything by the "light of nature," bombastic, despairing, hopeful, infinitely curious, a man who saw deeply into the secrets of matter, and into the souls of men, who at the end called a truce to anger, to restlessness and doubt and came to terms with the "uncreated," receiving the sacraments of the church and dividing his pittance among the poor. He stands neither in the medieval world, nor in the modern one, but bridges the two for us, making his era more accessible by his immediacy, his closeness to our own.

Today we stand again at the brink of a new age. Science has failed us, as the Church failed the man of Paracelsus' day. In five or ten years the "science bubble will burst," as a good friend of mine who specializes in the Philosophy of Science expressed it recently. To be born again, to make the world anew, will be no easy task. We shall have increasingly to have recourse to the wisdom of other times, to the philosophies of the East, to the mystics and masters of the "occult," to those adepts for whom there was no dualism, for whom spirit and matter, man and cosmos, were one. Paracelsus stands at the gateway of the old knowledge. He beckons to us, he leads us in by the hand. (pp. xi-xii)

> *Diane di Prima, in an originally unsigned essay titled "Paracelsus: An Appreciation," in* The Hermetic and Alchemical Writings of Aureolus Philippus Theophrastus Bombast, of Hohenheim, called Paracelsus the Great: Hermetic Chemistry, Vol. I *edited by Arthur Edward Waite, University Books Inc., 1967, pp. v-xii.*

Hugh Trevor-Roper   (essay date 1985)

[*Director of Times Newspapers Inc., historian, and educator, Trevor-Roper has written and edited numerous books on historical periods ranging from the age of imperial Rome to the era of the Third Reich. In the following excerpt, he summarizes the accomplishment of Paracel-*

sus, then outlines and expands upon three basic ingredients of his thought embraced by his successors, the Paracelsians.]

In the history of medicine in the period of the Renaissance there are several great names: Vesalius and Harvey, Fernel and Paré, Falloppio, Cesalpino, Fabricius . . . But if greatness is to be measured by public fame and the creation of a school of followers, no one can rival Paracelsus. For a century at least his very name was an explosive force. In the eyes of his numerous and vocal disciples, he was a prophet who had inaugurated a new age: thanks to a new vision of the universe, and of man's place in it, he had challenged the inveterate errors of a millennium and broken the monopoly of the rigid social caste which professed and perpetuated them. In the eyes of his enemies, he was an ignorant, self-opinionated heretic, an arrogant charlatan, the patron of revolutionary ideas which threatened the whole science of medicine and its honourable institutions: for he launched a frontal attack alike on the established medicine of Galen and on the medical faculties of the European universities. (p. 149)

Since he was so aggressively German, and so radical in his attacks on the establishment of his time, it is tempting to describe Paracelsus as a kind of medical Luther; and indeed this is how he has often been described, especially by his Catholic opponents in the later sixteenth century. . . . Protestantism and Paracelsianism had by then acquired certain common interests. . . . [However,] Paracelsus himself cannot be fitted into any sectarian category. He certainly hated the Catholic ecclesiastical establishment; but he equally hated Luther, whom he recognized, correctly enough after 1525, as the creature of the German princes. Although he made no public profession—he was never seen to pray—he was intensely religious and believed himself to be a devout Christian. Indeed, it was as such that he denounced the 'pagan' Aristotle; for it was through Aristotle, he believed, that the true philosophy—the mystical spiritual philosophy of those *prisci theologi*, Moses, Zoroaster, Plato, Hermes Trismegistus, the authentic precursors of Christ—had been fatally distorted and materialized, and through Aristotle's disciples, Galen and the medieval Schoolmen, that first medicine and then Christianity itself had been paganized. In fact he can be described, in religion, as a radical Christian in whom the new 'natural' philosophy of the Renaissance mingled with the Teutonic mysticism of the later Middle Ages: an individualist of the cast of his German contemporaries Caspar Schwenckfeld and Sebastian Franck and their successors Valentin Weigel and Jacob Boehme. His religious philosophy, like theirs, could no more easily be accommodated to that of Luther or to any established system of ideas, than its medical content to the teaching of the established schools.

What was that content? It was a content which was heavily masked by its deterrent form. Those who approached it from the established medical tradition were immediately repelled by its outward aspect. Paracelsus himself, and his disciples after him, not only declared frontal war on the established medical philosophy: they also used every means to shock their adversaries—aggressive dogmatism, wild claims, bombastic, arcane and insulting language. Into the stylized and conventional language of the medical world, they introduced challenging concepts and bizarre neoterisms: *archeus, magma, iliastrum, cagastrum, hylech, duelech;* for in order to destroy the old orthodoxy it was not enough to refute its central ideas: they needed to destroy its habits of thought, its very terminology. This in turn entailed a new vocabulary, new dictionaries. In the later sixteenth century there was a great industry of compiling such dictionaries. But if we can once get past this new and rebarbative language, and penetrate the system of Paracelsianism, we can see that, on three levels at least, it had an acceptable message for the time.

First, on the metaphysical level, it had an appeal which could be universal—i.e. which was not necessarily confined to Germans or Protestants. That appeal was to the Hermetic Platonism of the Renaissance. Galenism, the ruling orthodoxy of the medical schools, was essentially Aristotelean: it assumed an Aristotelean cosmology, Paracelsianism was essentially anti-Aristotelean. It was both Neoplatonic and Hermetic. Its theory depended, absolutely, on belief in the Neoplatonic cosmology, as elaborated by Marsilio Ficino (for whom Paracelsus expressed his admiration). In particular, it depended on the doctrine of the macrocosm and the microcosm: that is, on the idea that the body and soul of man are a miniature replica of the body and soul of the world, and that between these two worlds, the great and the little, there are correspondences, sympathies and antipathies, which the philosopher, the *magus,* could understand and control. Paracelsus not only accepted this theory as fundamental to his philosophy: he also gave it a new and exciting dimension; for, out of his study of the medieval alchemists and his own experience in the mines and furnaces of the Fugger family, he evolved the view that the universe, the macrocosm, was chemically controlled—was, in fact, itself a gigantic chemical crucible—and that its original creation had been a chemical operation, or rather 'separation' of the pure from the impure. From this it followed that the microcosm—the human body—was also a chemical system whose condition could be altered, adjusted, cured by could be altered, adjusted, chemical treatment. It was by reference to this general theory, from which he deduced some new and fertile ideas, but which he also encrusted with many bizarre and inconsequent details drawn from his own imagination and from German peasant folklore, that Paracelsus justified his particular medical innovations: his insistence that diseases were living parasites planted in the individual human body, not merely an accidental imbalance of 'humours'; his replacement of those four 'humours' of the Galenists by his three chemical 'principles', sulphur, mercury and salt; his search for a 'universal dissolvent'—the 'liquor Alkahest' as it would afterwards be called; his detoxication of poisons to convert them into cures; his homoeopathic remedies; his distillations and 'projections' which made this revolutionary innovator a continuator, in the age of the Renaissance, of the alchemical tradition of the Middle Ages.

Secondly, on the ideological level, this Neoplatonic philosophy easily acquired a prophetic, messianic, potentially revolutionary character. For if the world, as Christians held, was finite, with a beginning and an end, and if its beginning, the Creation, was a chemical operation, would not its end be chemical too? The Bible had promised that the Prophet Elijah would return 'before the coming of the great and dreadful day of the Lord', and this promise, often recalled by the contemporaries of Christ, had been taken up and put in a new context by the twelfth-century Calabrian abbot Joachim of Flora. Joachim had divided the history of the world into three ages and had placed the return of Elijah, and the coming of Antichrist, at the beginning of the third and last age, soon to come. Joachim's apocalyptic scenario was taken over by the radical friars of the later Middle Ages and would be their gift to their Protestant successors: Luther himself was seen by some as Elijah. Paracelsus too adopted it, but with a significant change. He not only adjusted the dates—Elijah, he said, would appear fifty-eight years after his own death: he also introduced him in a new guise, as 'Elias Arista,' Elijah the 'Artist'—that is, in the specialized language of the adepts, the Alchemist. As an alchemist, 'Elias' was to reveal all the secrets of chemistry, showing how iron could be transmuted into gold. He was also to begin the last transmutation of the world, which was to be not an operatic epiphany or a battle of Armageddon but, once again, a chemical act of separation. The millennium was to be a chemical millennium. Thus Paracelsianism offered, to those who took it whole, the prospect of a special kind of utopian revolution.

Finally, on a practical level, whether the theory was correct or not, its practitioners did in fact achieve certain results. These results were largely obtained by chemical or mineral remedies. Moreover, the Paracelsian remedies were often more agreeable to take or to endure than the time-honoured remedies of the Establishment. The Paracelsians respected the curative power of Nature: their treatment of wounds was, by modern standards, wonderfully enlightened. They used mild rather than strong doses, simple rather than elaborate drugs; they laid great emphasis on mineral waters and baths—the chemistry of Nature; and they devised narcotics and opiates to relieve pain. Paracelsus' most famous pain-killer was his 'laudanum'—another word invented by him. He also discovered how to make and use ether.

Thus, however heretical in theory, the Paracelsians could claim a growing number of supporters for the best of practical reasons: their patients were, or seemed to themselves to be, cured. . . . The claims of the physicians on both sides can perhaps be discounted. The claims of the patients cannot.

Neoplatonist 'theosophy', messianic prophecy, chemical medicine—these are the three chief ingredients of Paracelsus' philosophy, and the history of the movement is the history of their gradual separation, their periodic reunion. (pp. 155-58)

> *Hugh Trevor-Roper, "The Paracelsian Movement," in his* Renaissance Essays, *Secker & Warburg, 1985, pp. 149-99.*

P. M. Rattansi   (essay date 1985)

[*As editors John W. Shirley and F. David Hoeniger explain in their introduction to their* Science and the Arts in the Renaissance, *in the following excerpt Rattansi "gives a lucid account of some of the chief tenets of Paracelsus's Neoplatonic and highly peculiar medical philosophy" and then "shows how Paracelsus's vitalism and emphasis on the power of the imaginative faculty . . .*

exercised a strong attraction for such Romantic poets as Blake, Coleridge, and Wordsworth."]

"Paracelsus and Behmen appear'd to me," wrote William Blake in 1800, when recalling the influences that had shaped his poetical genius. Blake believed that Paracelsus had helped to free his imagination from the stifling authority of "the three great leaders of Atheism, or Satan's doctrine": Bacon, Locke, and Newton. Those founding fathers of Enlightenment rationalism belonged for Blake to Satan's party, because "everything is Atheism which assumes the reality of the natural and unspiritual world." Locke's entire system was "completely bodied out" of Cartesian doctrine, according to Coleridge, and it was Descartes who had been the first to conceive nature as "utterly lifeless and godless." It was scarcely surprising, then, that Locke had confounded human imagination with "Enthusiasm" or the false conceit of being divinely inspired, and that he had restricted human knowledge to the "primary properties" revealed in sensible knowledge, while dismissing as "secondary" all that revealed the splendor of the visible world. How could the poetic imagination take wing when oppressed by so narrow and misconceived a view of man and nature, of mind and imagination?

Blake and other romantics discovered in the works of Paracelsus a far more inspiring vision of man and nature. The material and sensible was for Paracelsus no more than a covering through which a fundamentally spiritual reality expressed itself. It was a spiritual kernel that gave everything that existed its properties and qualities. Nothing in the universe was truly lifeless. Descartes had been wrong to set up an unbridgeable gulf between material and spiritual. Since there was a life in all things, man could gain deeper insight into their nature by empathy than by mathematical analysis or the torturing of nature in experiments. "Correspondences" linked the macrocosm of the universe and the earth with the microcosm of man. (p. 50)

The liberating influence of Paracelsian ideas on the romantic generation can hardly be doubted. How authentic was their understanding of those ideas as they tried to select and fashion weapons for their own battles from complex and often seemingly contradictory doctrines scattered through the many tracts which the sixteenth-century iatrochemist had dictated in the course of a wandering existence?

Paracelsus, too, had struggled against what he believed to be a narrow and dogmatic rationalism. It was scholastic rationalism—the medieval "baptizing" of Aristotle, as it was often mockingly described in the Renaissance. It had split the universe into an immutable celestial region and a sublunary region which was the theater of ceaseless change. In the upper region revolved planetary spheres made of the most perfect of substances, the ether. All activity in the lower realm owed its beginnings to those superior motions. On the earth, the "complexion" of physical entities and changes in them were explained by the four elements and their associated qualities. So, too, were health and disease explained by the four humors whose particular balance determined the constitution of an individual. Man was the more or less passive receptor of heavenly and elemental powers and influences, and came closer to God when he engaged in the disinterested contemplation of nature. In understanding nature man focused his attention, above all, on the final causes or immanent purposes and ordered his knowledge through the use of syllogistic reasoning.

This essentially Aristotelian view of nature aroused the derision and contempt of Paracelsus. The principles and elements of the ancients, being general, were powerless to explain the irreducible specificity and individuality manifested by everything that existed. Their explanations dwelt only on the surfaces of things, never penetrating the visible and tangible, which was only the outward "signature," to reach the immanent soul-like power and force. The universe was basically divided between the spiritual and its material covering, rather than between a superior celestial region and an inferior terrestrial one. The macrocosm of the world and the microcosm of man were linked by concordances and coordination. Their relation could not be one of domination or dependence of one over the other. (p. 51)

Misled by their false conception of elements, the ancients had placed, as their counterparts, four humors in the human body. Just as the "complexion" of an object was determined by the predominance of one or more elements, so the balance of humors was thought to be responsible for the individual constitution or temperament. Health depended on the maintenance of that balance, while from the disequilibrium of the humors came disease. The physician was concerned with a single general condition, that of distemper. His task was essentially that of deciding how best to remove the humoral excess or to supply that which was deficient.

Paracelsus utterly rejected this conception of disease and of the role of the physician. The most striking characteristic of diseases was their diversity and specificity, which could never be explained by the humors. As in the greater universe, so in the human body, the three principles acted in the matrices of the four elements and generated a variety of species. The body could quite fittingly be compared to a mine, in which mineral constituents, which normally formed part of body substance and were invisible, rose to the surface in the form of a disease. Such an analogy implied that there were at least as many diseases as mineral species. Like minerals, they occurred in a particular site and were localized. Being specific entities, they could not be treated by a general therapy, which only affected the symptoms and not the underlying condition, only the smoke and not the fire. What caused diseases? Paracelsus traced them, on the whole, to the disturbance of the "firmamental" coordination normally existing between the inner "heaven" and the "outer" one. Consumption, for example, could be caused by the microcosmic sun distributing excessive heat. To correct that condition, additional dampness had to be fed to the microcosmic sun. The true physician could accomplish that by making "another heaven"—the *arcanum* that would feed it with rain and dew. The *arcanum* must be an extract in which the requisite virtue would be available in its most concentrated form, a chemical medicine in a volatile state, exercising a specific curative action. Efficacious medicines were made not by compounding, that is, putting together substances graded according to the "temperature" of their qualities, but by *separation* or isolation of the *arcanum* through distillation.

The theme of separation had a deep and poignant significance in Paracelsian thought. Creation itself, as described in the Genesis account, was a separation. But since it was a disruption of the primal unity, it implied a fall and degeneration. The fall of Lucifer and his host of rebellious angels had led God to create the world. Man, too, had separated himself from God by eating the forbidden fruit. In that *cagastrum* lay the roots of the inexhaustible diversity and the irreducible individuality and specificity of things, but equally of the seeds of conflict that resulted from each being egotistically seeking its own good at the expense of others. Separation and conflict was a transient state. All nature tended toward its own primitive state and would one day return to it. Christ's resurrection foreshadowed man's own repossession of his spiritual body.

Even in his fallen state, man retained his dignity as the creature made in God's image. He revealed the forces and powers God had sown in nature. He completed what God had left unfinished in nature. He had received a material body from the earth, an ethereal one from the stars, and a divine soul from God. Through his ethereal body, man was subject to the influence of the stars. They did not exercise it through stellar influx but by firmamental coordination. The earthly part was exempt from their influence and pursued its animal life by virtue of its own being. Stars did not determine the length of human life, nor was their power unilateral. The magical power of man's imagination could work on stars to benefit himself or, unwittingly and disastrously, produce plagues and epidemics.

All things in nature were first conceived in the divine imagination and were created as God exteriorized his will. The beginnings of all human actions and creations, too, were in the imagination. The faculty of imagination, which Paracelsus endowed with such great power and potency, was situated for him in man's astral body. Its force converted vital fluids from all parts of man's body into semen; it marked the unborn child with the thoughts of the mother. The imagination was a magical force. Since it was involved in all actions, human actions could be said to be essentially magical.

Paracelsus's conception of the imagination, as a supremely productive and creative power, helps to explain the attraction of his teachings for the romantics, as they attempted to rehabilitate the claims of the artistic imagination in an age dominated by science. Erastus had denounced the Paracelsian opinion in the late sixteenth century from an Aristotelian standpoint, pointing out that an idea could not act as the efficient cause of an object or event. Francis Bacon had attacked it in the early seventeenth century, condemning Paracelsus and his followers for having exalted the power of the imagination so much that they had made it almost the same as "the power of miracle-working faith . . . ," thereby sanctioning ceremonial magic. Imagination was according to Bacon no more than a messenger between the senses, the reason, and the will. In religion it served as an *instrument* of illumination. That was why faith always first insinuated itself through similitudes, parables, visions, and dreams. But imagination clearly possessed the dangerous power of overmastering reason and could make itself ungovernable. Such a power of mischief lurked in verbal eloquence and all poetry. (pp. 52-4)

Paracelsus took pains to deny that "acting, poetry, music" came from the devil. Nor were they human inventions. They were to be ranked as "high arts," just as much as astronomy, geometry, alchemy, medicine, philosophy, and theology. Like them, they came from God. Paracelsus compared the artistic work of the woodcutter, separating the wood "from that which does not belong to it" to the separation wrought by God in the work of creation. But such comparisons served for him generally to affirm the dignity of the craftsman's calling rather than to celebrate the artist. The woodcarver, whose work resembled God's, "discovered" in a piece of wood, indifferently, not only the forms of plants and animals, but also those of implements for human use. The first invention of the lyre was compared to that of the forge and of the alphabet as examples of the gifts bestowed by the divine spirit on fallen man.

Paracelsus prescribed severely practical ends to the arts. They existed, above all, to gratify needs "and help us to serve our fellow men." That applied to the art of music; it helped to cure melancholy and disordered fantasy, and to drive out the spirits of demons and witches. Knowing and doing must never be severed. All arts and crafts came into being only after the expulsion from Eden, when God in his mercy created the "light of nature" which enabled man to sustain himself—but only by toiling by the sweat of his brow to put his gifts to productive use. Paracelsus's ideal man, who combined knowing and doing in the highest measure, was the true physician. He was moved solely by compassion and the duty of charity to his neighbor: "Privilege and lineage pale to nothingness, only distress has meaning." God had planted a remedy for each disease, and the physician's insight into firmamental coordination enabled him to relieve suffering. The physician brought his vast knowledge of correspondences to the task of diagnosis; he read the condition of the urine in the macrocosm, related the pulse to the firmament, chiromancy to the minerals, breath to east and west winds, and fevers to earthquakes. He emulated the work of God, who in the greater world "himself practices medicine."

There were resemblances between the calling of the artist and that of the physician. The woodcarver and sculptor "separated" the essential from the dross as did the physician in collecting the *arcanum*. "Signatures" guided the physician to the hidden virtues lying within an object, and "physiognomy" and chiromancy to the mind and soul of a man. The artist and sculptor had to achieve equal mastery of the "art of signs" if he was to produce truly accomplished work. But while recognizing and praising the God-given talent of the artist, who used the visible appearance of men and women to lay bare their souls, the Paracelsian view was bound to confer preeminence on the physician-alchemist-philosopher as one who contributed most to fulfill God's plan in creation.

Moreover, a pervasive theme of Paracelsian thought was separation, the breaking up of the original unity, which brought conflict. Nothing could be said to be bad or evil in itself, only relative to something else. What was good for one was bad for another; fish inhabited the element of water, while men drowned in it. From such differences and divisions came disease, suffering, and death. The theme of harmony, and of beauty as the product of harmony, had given a peculiar importance to the artist in Renaissance thought. It is not a conspicuous feature of Paracelsian teachings. Paracelsus did not follow Galen in pointing continually to the aptness of structure to purpose in the animal body, nor in deriving from the correspondence between macrocosm and microcosm the strongest argument for the beauty and harmony of all creation. His work is replete with allusions to "anatomy," but it signified either chemical anatomy, which revealed the true nature of things, or the study of the concordance between the greater and lesser worlds.

Concordance served in Paracelsian thought as a continual reminder of the original unity from which the creation was a falling away. The term, *cagastrum,* was coined by Paracelsus to convey the loss and alienation resulting from a disjunction which gave rise to conflict, diseases, and death. Harmony could not have appeared to Paracelsus the leading characteristic of a world whose creation was a consequence of the rebellion of Lucifer, and where the acquisition by man of an astral body and the concordance between it and the stars followed man's disobedience in eating the forbidden fruit.

Indeed, the contrast between Paracelsus and Galen on beauty and harmony serves to illuminate the difficulties commonly experienced in placing Paracelsus within a convenient historical niche. Was he a Renaissance humanist or a medieval mystic, was he a great pioneer of modern science and medicine, or a purveyor of irrational and superstitious ideas in a confused, semiliterate form? Paracelsus pointed to the impotence of ancient concepts and categories when confronted with the inexhaustible diversity and irreducible individuality of the myriad beings in the world. That would seem to make him a spokesman for the Renaissance individualism. Paracelsus rejected the scientific and medical doctrines inherited from the ancients and affirmed that "the new time confronts us with new tasks." He wished to substitute "experiment" and experience for logical analysis in explaining natural phenomena. He offered a "chemical" conception of physiological as well as geological and meteorological processes. He developed an ontological conception of disease-entities to replace that of ancient medicine. He turned alchemy decisively from the search for metallic transmutation to the quest for chemical medicines. All these features of his teaching would appear to give Paracelsus an assured place as a great scientific and medical innovator.

However, these "progressive" aspects of Paracelsian thought were counter-balanced by others which are far less likely to evoke our commendation—but which emerged from the same general outlook. Paracelsus's

Signature and impression of the signet ring of Paracelsus.

novel interpretation of firmamental coordination justified the assumption that the sympathy between the *astrum* hidden in things and man's astral body offered the sole avenue to true insight into their virtues or working principles. Those virtues could be extracted by chemical distillation but could also be captured from the stars in amulets and talismans. Chiromancy and the science of physiognomy were essential to the physician since they disclosed the meaning of "signatures" carried by human beings no less than plants and minerals. While severely critical of the astrology and alchemy of his own time, Paracelsus conceived the ideal man as a *magus* who could capture the *astra* hidden in all things to work miracles in nature.

The mechanistic world view which the romantics sought to undermine attained its dominance only a century after the death of Paracelsus. But his work already embodied a protest at the increasing tendency of his contemporaries to materialize Peripatetic elements and physiological "spirits" by confusing them with tangible chemical substances. He insisted on the spiritual character of the working principles of all things, urging that beneath the tangible and perceptible lay the invisible and intangible kernel. (pp. 54-6)

Blended in Paracelsian doctrine were ideas from ancient Gnosticism and Neo-Platonism, medieval mystics, the alchemical tradition, and Renaissance humanism and the northern Reformation. All were stamped with that unique and individual vision which makes Paracelsus one of the most striking figures of a "transitional" century. (p. 57)

> *P. M. Rattansi, "Art and Science: The Paracelsian Vision," in* Science and the Arts in the Renaissance, *edited by John W. Shirley and F. David Hoeniger, The Folger Shakespeare Library, 1985, pp. 50-8.*

FURTHER READING

Boas, George. "Leibniz and His Predecessors." In his *Dominant Themes of Modern Philosophy: A History,* pp. 272-301. New York: Ronald Press Co., 1957.
   Attempts to identify the philosophical importance of Paracelsus.

Debus, Allen G. *The Chemical Philosophy: Paracelsian Science and Medicine in the Sixteenth and Seventeenth Centuries.* 2 vols. New York: Science History Publications, 1977.
   Attempts to describe the full breadth of the Paracelsians' approach to nature and medicine, noting as well the vicissitudes of this approach.

Downs, Robert B. "Complete Skeptic: Paracelsus (1493-1541)." In his *Landmarks in Science: Hippocrates to Carson,* pp. 78-81. Littleton, Colo.: Libraries Unlimited, 1982.
   Short biographical tribute, with commentary on Paracelsus's medical theories and developments.

Fairweather, William. "Spread of Christian Mysticism in the West: From the Fourteenth Century until the Reformation."

In his *Among the Mystics,* pp. 27-41. Edinburgh: T. & T. Clark, 1936.
  Briefly outlines the accomplishments of Paracelsus, noting the "vain conceit" of his "mystical pantheism which not seldom degenerated into superstition."

[Forster, John.] Review of *Paracelsus,* by Robert Browning. *The Examiner,* No. 1440 (6 September 1835): 563-65.
  Reviews Robert Browning's poem *Paracelsus* (see excerpt dated 1840). Forster briefly describes the historical Paracelsus as an unjustly maligned giant of thought.

————. "Evidences of a New Genius for Dramatic Poetry." *The New Monthly Magazine* XLVI, No. CLXXXIII (March 1836): 289-308.
  Another review of Browning's *Paracelsus.* Forster examines the historical Paracelsus as a Promethean figure in the history of human progress, comparing him, in his heroic "failure," with Jean-Jacques Rousseau.

[Fox, W. J.] "Paracelsus." *The Monthly Repository* n. s. IX, No. 107 (November 1835): 716-27.
  Reviews Browning's poem. In a biographical paragraph, Fox outlines the life of Paracelsus, describing his influence in medicine as "not unlike that of Aristotle among the schoolmen. . . ."

Hargrave, John. *The Life and Soul of Paracelsus.* London: Victor Gollancz, 1951, 253 p.
  Defensive biography, with artfully reconstructed scenes and recreated dialogues.

Jaffe, Bernard. "Paracelsus: A Chemical Luther Feeds a Bonfire." In his *Crucibles: The Story of Chemistry from Ancient Alchemy to Nuclear Fission,* pp. 18-33. New York: Simon and Schuster, 1951.
  Biographical essay. Jaffe praises Paracelsus throughout as "a real benefactor of mankind."

Jung, C. G. "Paracelsus the Physician." In his *The Spirit in Man, Art, and Literature,* pp. 13-30. The Collected Works of C. G. Jung, edited by Sir Herbert Read, Michael Fordham, Gerhard Adler, and William McGuire, translated by R. F. C. Hull, vol. 15. London: Routledge & Kegan Paul, 1966.
  Illustrates Paracelsus's beliefs as a practicing physician, primarily by drawing upon excerpts from the subject's own writings. This essay was originally delivered as a lecture in 1941.

Leonard, Jonathan Norton. "The Medical Luther." In his *Crusaders of Chemistry: Six Makers of the Modern World,* pp. 91-130. Garden City, N.Y.: Doubleday, Doran & Co., 1930.
  Popular biographical essay. Leonard hails Paracelsus as "the Luther of science" who promoted forward-looking innovation rather than doctrine and reverence to "the all-wise revelations of the past."

Lesser, J. "Paracelsus after Four Centuries." *The Contemporary Review* 160 (December 1941): 385-88.
  Summarizes the importance and achievement of Paracelsus on the four-hundredth anniversary of his death.

Llewellyn, Bernard. "Paracelsus." *The Contemporary Review* 184, No. 1055 (November 1953): 296-99.
  Adulatory biographical essay on Paracelsus.

Murray, W. A. "Erasmus and Paracelsus." *Bibliothèque d'humanisme et Renaissance* XX, No. 3 (1958): 560-64.
  Reprints and translates an exchange of letters written by Paracelsus and Desiderius Erasmus. Murray also attempts to piece together the sequence of events cryptically described in the letters.

Pagel, Walter. *Religion and Neoplatonism in Renaissance Medicine.* London: Variorum Reprints, 1985, 346 p.
  Reprints many of Pagel's key essays on the philosophical background of Renaissance medicine, with numerous references to Paracelsus and short studies devoted specifically to his accomplishment. Essays include "Paracelsus and Techellus the Jew," "Paracelsus and the Neoplatonic and Gnostic Tradition," and "The Prime Matter of Paracelsus," among others.

————. *From Paracelsus to Van Helmont: Studies in Renaissance Medicine and Science.* London: Variorum Reprints, 1986, 350 p.
  Reprints more of Pagel's key essays, with numerous brief references to Paracelsus. The collection also contains the essays "The Wild Spirit (Gas) of John Baptist Van Helmont (1579-1644) and Paracelsus" and "Vesalius and Paracelsus," the latter written in collaboration with P. M. Rattansi.

Perry, Whitall N. "The Alchemy in Homoeopathy." *Studies in Comparative Religion* 16, Nos. 1-2 (Winter-Spring 1984): 21-56.
  Short history of homeopathy's debt to alchemy, highlighting the contributions provided by Paracelsus and his most noteworthy predecessors, contemporaries, and successors.

Temkin, Owsei. "The Elusiveness of Paracelsus." In his *The Double Face of Janus, and Other Essays in the History of Medicine,* pp. 225-38. Baltimore and London: Johns Hopkins University Press, 1977.
  Balanced overview of Paracelsus's enigmatic life and medical theories, written "to facilitate the reading of Paracelsus' medical works."

Thorndike, Lynn. *A History of Magic and Experimental Science, Volumes VII and VIII: The Seventeenth Century.* 2 vols. New York: Columbia University Press, 1958.
  Many brief, scattered references to Paracelsus as his work relates to other scientists of the era that succeeded his own.

"The Father of Rational Therapy." *Today's Health* 41 (October 1963): 73.
  Biographical essay. The critic praises Paracelsus as "the savior of 16th century medicine" whose "ceaseless battle against the prevailing ignorance of his time opened the gate for modern medical scientists to enter."

Vickers, Brian. "Analogy versus Identity: The Rejection of Occult Symbolism, 1580-1680." In *Occult and Scientific Mentalities in the Renaissance,* pp. 95-163. Cambridge: Cambridge University Press, 1984.
  Places Paracelsus among a group of thinkers of the period 1580-1680 who together mark a transitional period in the way reality is understood, from a magical to a mechanistic approach.

Jean-Jacques Rousseau

1712-1778

Swiss-born French essayist, autobiographer, novelist, dramatist, and poet.

Rousseau was an eighteenth-century Swiss-born French philosopher, political theorist, and composer who is recognized as one of the greatest thinkers of the French Enlightenment. A prolific writer on many topics, he has been variously cited as intellectual father of the French Revolution, founder of the Romantic movement in literature, and engenderer of most modern pedagogical movements. The broad influence of his thought originates not only from his best-known political and philosophical treatises—*Du contrat social; ou principes du droit politique* (*The Social Contract*), *Discours sur les sciences et les arts* (*Discourse on the Sciences and the Arts*), and *Discours sur l'origine et les fondemens de l'inégalité parmi les hommes* (*Discourse upon the Origin and Foundation of the Inequality among Mankind*)—but also from his eloquent novels and autobiographical writings—*La Nouvelle Héloïse, Émile, ou de l'éducation* (*Emilius and Sophia: or, a new system of education*), and *Les Confessions de J. J. Rousseau* (*The Confessions of J. J. Rousseau*). However, Rousseau's life and works remain controversial despite their tremendous impact on Western thought. According to François Mauriac, "it is the artist in [Rousseau] that charms and that has poisoned the world."

Rousseau was born in 1712 to Isaac, a Genevese watchmaker, and Suzanne Bernard, daughter of an upper middle-class Genevese family. His mother died a few days after his birth, and until age ten he lived with his irresponsible father, who "educated" him by reading Calvinist sermons and seventeenth-century romance novels aloud to him. His father subsequently abandoned him to the tutelage of an uncle who apprenticed him at age thirteen to an abusive engraver. Young Rousseau endured three miserable years of apprenticeship before fleeing Geneva in 1728. A Roman Catholic priest directed him to the town of Annecy. There Rousseau met 29-year-old Mme. de Warens, who supported herself by taking in and encouraging Catholic converts. Under her protection he was sent to a hospice in Turin, where he converted to Catholicism, thereby effectively forfeiting his Genevese citizenship. He remained for several months, working variously as an engraver and a lackey. He returned to Annecy the following spring intending to enter the priesthood, but instead he taught music to girls of the wealthiest families in the area. In 1731, after an unsuccessful search for employment in Paris, he once again returned to Mme. de Warens, who by this time had moved to her small farm, Les Charmettes, near Chambéry, where Rousseau claimed he passed the happiest years of his life. Ultimately he became her lover, although he regarded himself more as her son than as her lover, affectionately calling her "Maman." Staying with her until 1740, he studied music, read philosophy, science, and literature, and began to compose and write.

Following his departure, Rousseau became a tutor in Lyons for a year, then returned once more to Paris in late

1742, when he presented a new system of musical notation to the Académie des Sciences, but without success. With the publication of his *Dissertation sur la musique moderne* in 1743, together with the composition of an opera and a comedy, *Les muses galantes* and *Les prisonniers de guerre,* he was appointed private secretary to the French ambassador in Venice. He lost the post the following year. In 1745, while in Paris, he initiated a lifelong intimacy with Thérèse Levasseur, a chambermaid by whom he reputedly had five children, all of whom were sent to a foundling home at birth. In Paris he came to know many prominent people, including Voltaire, Friedrich von Grimm, Georges Louis Buffon, Pierre Marivaux, Bernard Fontenelle, and Denis Diderot. The latter became his confidant and asked Rousseau to write articles on music and economics for the *Encyclopédie.* Thus began Rousseau's erratic association with the Encyclopedists and philosophes. In 1749, while walking to Vincennes to visit Diderot, who was imprisoned there, Rousseau read an announcement of a prize essay contest, sponsored by the Dijon Academy, on the question: Has the revival of the arts and sciences tended to purify morals? With Diderot's supposed encouragement, he responded in the negative, eloquently stating that culture had ruined morality. The *Discourse on the Sciences and the Arts,* while winning him the prize and immediate fame, provoked a three-year series of acrid literary disputes. During this time Rousseau also completed all the entries pertaining to music in the *Encyclopédie*. He later compiled and published these separately as the *Dictionnaire de musique* (*A Dictionary of Music*).

In 1752 Rousseau composed an Italianate operetta, *Le Devin du village* (*The Cunning Man*), which was first performed before the royal court at Fontainebleau. Its great success contributed to the growing popularity of Italian music, thereby setting Rousseau in opposition to Jean-Phillipe Rameau and advocates of French music. When the Dijon Academy announced another essay competition in 1754, Rousseau wrote a sequel to his first *Discourse* entitled *Discourse upon the Origin and Foundation of the Inequality among Mankind*. Essentially a diatribe against despotism and private property, he sought to expose and denounce artificially instituted social inequality by describing a hypothetical state of natural man. He believed that human beings are essentially good and potentially perfect. Human faults arise from the corrupting influences of conventional society—inequality, despotism, and privately owned property—which, he claimed, progressively restrict freedom and lessen moral virtue. In order to restore humanity to its natural goodness, Rousseau called for a return to nature so far as is practicable.

In 1756, following a sojourn in Geneva, where he re-embraced Calvinism and recovered his citizenship, Rousseau settled at Montmorency in the "Hermitage," a house offered to him by Mme. d'Épinay, a friend of the Encyclopedists. In the seclusion of the Hermitage, and later in that of "Montlouis," Rousseau began and completed the works that were to make him one of the most famous writers of his time. In *La Nouvelle Héloïse*, an epistolary novel, he demonstrated the triumph of a primitive family unit over the corruption of modern society. This work exhibited the author's interest in common people and championed the aggrandizement of nature—motifs later embraced by Romantic writers in France and elsewhere. In the *Lettre à d'Alembert sur les spectacles* (*Letter to d'Alembert on the Theater*) Rousseau declared the theater to be useless and harmful and called for its suppression—despite his own previous theatrical productions. *Émile* explicated his scheme for "natural" education in which man would preserve his fundamentally good instincts, while *The Social Contract*, initially stating that "Man is born free and is everywhere in chains," outlined the social order that would enable human beings to be natural and free—acknowledging no other bondage save that of natural necessity.

The Parlement of Paris condemned *Émile* and *The Social Contract* in 1762, compelling Rousseau to flee to Switzerland. There, too, his works were banned, and he was banished. He defended his writings in the *Lettre à Christophe de Beaumont,* an attack on the archbishop of Paris, who had condemned *Émile;* and, in response to a published defense of the Council of Geneva decree that had ordered the burning of *Émile* and *The Social Contract,* he wrote the *Lettres écrites de la montagne.* Upon its publication, opposition by the Protestant clergy in Switzerland grew even stronger, and in 1766 Rousseau fled the Continent. David Hume provided refuge in Derbyshire, England, but Rousseau, whose recent adversities had affected his reasoning abilities, began to suspect him of collusion with the Pari-

sian philosophes, whom he imagined were conspiring to ruin his reputation. Paranoid and panicked, he fled to France in 1767.

Rousseau assumed the name Renou and wandered throughout France, never remaining anywhere for long. During this period he married Thérèse in a civil ceremony and wrote his *Confessions*. In 1770 he returned to Paris and resumed his real identity unmolested. Determined to defend himself against the "conspirators," Rousseau read excerpts from his *Confessions* in the fashionable salons of Parisian society until Mme. d'Épinay requested police intervention to stop him from continuing. In 1771, when the Confederation of the Bar—noble Polish nationalists—requested his advice on institutional reform in Poland, he wrote *Considérations sur le gouvernement de Pologne et sur sa réformation projettée*. In the same year, as a means of further self-justification, he wrote *Rousseau juge Jean-Jacques: Dialogues*. (Four years later he tried to place this work on the altar of the Cathedral of Notre-Dame but was prevented by a locked gate from doing so—a rebuff that caused him to believe in despair that even God had joined the "conspiracy" against him.) Rousseau's madness lessened during the last two years of his life. He lived in seclusion with Thérèse and wrote *Les Rêveries du promeneur solitaire* (*The Reveries of the Solitary Walker*), which details the beauty of nature and man's feelings for nature. On 2 July 1778 he uttered his last words: "It is true so soon as it is felt." He was buried on the Île des Peupliers at Ermenonville. During the Revolution, his remains were re-interred in the Pantheon in Paris.

Critics have long considered much of Rousseau's work extremely controversial, if not decidedly revolutionary; Rousseau's comment on his *Confessions* as "an undertaking, hitherto without precedent" is representative of early critical opinion of his canon in general. In 1790 Edmund Burke criticized Rousseau for "giving rise to new and unlooked-for strokes in politics and morals" and declared that "the writings of Rousseau lead directly to shameful evil." Yet not all English critics shared this opinion. Sir James Mackintosh credited Rousseau as one "who unshackled and emancipated the human mind." Continental critics, during and following the Revolution, maintained a similar stance, with Burke writing of them: "Him [Rousseau] they study, him they meditate; him they turn over in all the time they can spare. . . . Rousseau is their canon of holy writ; in his life he is their canon of *Polyclitus;* he is their standard figure of perfection." Indeed, Rousseau's writings were widely read and critically acclaimed throughout Europe well into the early nineteenth century. Thomas Green claimed Britons generally esteemed Rousseau as "without exception, the greatest genius and finest writer that ever lived." Nevertheless, English enthusiasm for Rousseau began to wane by 1814—the watershed year for sympathetic English criticism. By the mid-1820s Rousseau's political writings drew serious objections and were labeled "dangerous moonshine." According to Edmund Gosse: "His influence was like a snow man in the sun; it melted and dripped from every limb, from all parts of its structure." By the end of the Georgian period Rousseau was regarded with contempt, as a detestable man whose works were not to be read—except in secret. Thus Rousseau generally remained neglected in the English-speaking world, only mentioned captiously and disparagingly through the turn of the century. One exception is noteworthy, however: John Morley's classic 1873 monograph, *Rousseau*.

In the early twentieth century, English critics of Rousseau acknowledged that they suffered, in the words of Gosse, from a "stigma which [had] lain on England for a hundred years of being dry with cynical neglect of Rousseau while all the rest of the threshing-floor of Europe was wet with the dews of vivifying criticism." As the bicentenary of Rousseau's birth approached, English commentary began to mirror Continental views as scholars reassessed the import of the writer's life and ideology. Critics became increasingly sentient of Rousseau's principles, especially toward the contradictory nature of much of his thought. J. Middleton Murry attributed Rousseau's penchant for paradox to an "unremitting endeavour to express an intuitive certainty in intellectual terms. . . . He seems to surge upwards on a passionate wave of revolutionary ideas, only to sink back into the calm of conservative or quietist conclusions." By mid-century, the anchoritic qualities of his life were more appreciated than denigrated. Jacques Maritain, though generally unsympathetic toward Rousseau's views, noted that the man "gives us in his very unsociability, his sickly isolation, a lyrical image, as dazzling as it is deceptive, of the secret needs of the spirit in us." In recent years, critical attention has shifted from a "paternity" approach—study of Rousseau's "formative influence" on modern society as the father of certain ideas, movements, and events—to attempts at lucid interpretation of the actual meaning of his thought. Yet most contemporary scholars concede that "it is unlikely that a completely satisfactory account of him and his works will ever be given . . . on account of the frightening immensity of the task."

Rousseau—the mournful lunatic, the noble savage, the irreverent revolutionary—has fixated generations of readers with his eloquently frank autobiographical writings, his illuminating observations on the nature and spirit of man, and his often disputatious, enigmatic sociopolitical theories. Exonerated or condemned, Rousseau and his thought continue to fascinate scholars and critics. In the words of R. A. Leigh, Rousseau "is not only the most original, the most profound and the most controversial of all the great eighteenth-century writers: he is also the most topical. . . . He will always remain both the prophet and the critic of modern times."

PRINCIPAL WORKS

Dissertation sur la musique moderne (essay) 1743
*Discours qui a remporté le prix à l'Academie de Dijon. En l'année 1750. Sur cette Question proposée par la même Académie: Si le rétablissement des Sciences et des Arts a contribué à épurer les moeurs (essay) 1750
[*A Discourse, to which the prize was adjudged by the Academy of Dijon on this question: whether the re-establishment of Arts and Sciences has contributed to purify our morals,* 1752]
Le Devin du village (operetta) 1752
[*The Cunning Man,* 1766]
Lettre sur la musique françoise (criticism) 1753
Discours sur l'origine et les fondemens de l'inégalité parmi les hommes (essay) 1755

[*A Discourse upon the Origin and Foundation of the Inequality among Mankind,* 1761]
Oeuvres diverses de M. J. J. Rousseau de Genêve. 2 vols. (essays and letters) 1756
[*The Miscellaneous Works of Mr. J. J. Rousseau.* 5 vols., 1767]
Discours sur l'oeconomie politique (essay) 1758
†*A M. D'Alembert, de l'Académie Françoise, de l'Académie Royale des Sciences de Paris, de celle de Prusse, de la Société Royale de Londres, de l'Académie Royale des Belles-Lettres de Suède, & de l'Institut de Bologne. Sur son Article Genève dans le VIIme Volume de l'Encyclopédie, et particulièrement, sur le projet d'établir un Théatre de Comédie en cette ville* (essay) 1758
[*A Letter from M. Rousseau to M. d'Alembert concerning the effects of theatrical entertainments on the manners of mankind,* 1759]
Lettre de J. J. Rousseau à Monsieur de Voltaire (letter) 1759
Jean Jacques Rousseau, citoyen de Geneve, à Christophe de Beaumont, Archevegue de Paris (letter) 1763
[*An Explanatory Letter from J. J. Rousseau to C. de Beaumont, Archbishop of Paris,* 1763]
‡*Lettres de deux amans, habitans d'une petite ville au pied des Alpes.* 6 vols. (novel) 1761; also published as *La Nouvelle Héloïse,* 1764
[*Eloisa: or, a series of original letters collected and published by J. J. Rousseau,* 1761]
Du contrat social; ou principes du droit politique (essay) 1762
[*A Treatise on the Social Compact; or the principles of politic law,* 1764; also published as *An Inquiry into the Nature of the Social Contract; or principles of political right,* 1791]
Émile, ou de l'éducation. 4 vols. (novel) 1762
[*Emilius and Sophia: or, a new system of education,* 1762-63]
Lettres écrites de la montagne (essays) 1764
Dictionnaire de musique (dictionary) 1768
[*A Dictionary of Music,* 1779]
Lettres Nouvelles de J. J. Rousseau, sur le motif de sa retraite à la campagne, adressées à M. de Malesherbes, et qui paroissent pour la première fois; suivies d'une relation des derniers momens de ce grand Homme (letters) 1780
Rousseau juge de Jean Jacques: Dialogues (autobiography) 1780
Considérations sur le gouvernement de Pologne et sur sa réformation projettée (essay) 1782
§*Les Rêveries du promeneur solitaire* (essays) 1782
[*The Reveries of the Solitary Walker* published in *The Confessions of J. J. Rousseau: with the Reveries of the Solitary Walker,* 1783-91; also published as *The Reveries of A Solitary,* 1927]
Les Confessions de J. J. Rousseau. 4 vols. (autobiography) 1782-89
[*The Confessions of J. J. Rousseau: with the Reveries of the Solitary Walker.* 4 vols., 1783-91]
Oeuvres complètes de J.J. Rousseau, classées par ordre des matières, avec des notes. 38 vols. (essays, poems, novels, and autobiographies) 1788-93
Nouvelles lettres de J. J. Rousseau (letters) 1789
[*Original Letters of J. J. Rousseau,* 1799]

Oeuvres complètes. 4 vols. (essays, novels, poems, and autobiographies) 1959-64
Correspondance complète. 45 vols. (letters) 1965-86

*This work is commonly known in French as *Discours sur les sciences et les arts* and in English as *Discourse on the Sciences and Arts.*

†This work is commonly referred to in French as *Lettre à d'Alembert sur les spectacles* and in English as *Letter to d'Alembert on the Theater.*

‡This work is sometimes known as *Julie: ou, La Nouvelle Héloïse.*

§This work first appeared with the publication of *Les Confessions* in 1782.

Jean-Jacques Rousseau (essay date 1750)

[*In the following excerpt from the preface to his* Discourse on the Sciences and Arts, *Rousseau defends his chosen position, claiming that it is "the side which becomes an honest man who knows nothing and esteems himself no less for it."*]

Here is one of the grand and finest questions ever raised. This **Discourse** is not concerned with those metaphysical subtleties that have spread to all departments of Literature, and of which the Programs of Academies are not always free: it is concerned, rather, with one of those truths that affect the happiness of mankind.

I expect that I shall not easily be forgiven for the side I have dared to choose. Clashing head on with all that is today admired by men, I can only expect universal blame: and to have been honored by the approbation of a few Wise men ought not to lead me to expect that of the Public. Hence my decision is made. I do not care whether I please Wits or the Fashionable. There will always be men destined to be subjugated by the opinions of their century, of their Country, of their Society: Some men today act the part of the Freethinker and the Philosopher who, for the same reason, would have been but fanatics at the time of the League. One ought not to write for such Readers when one wants to live beyond one's century.

One word more, and I have done. Little expecting the honor bestowed on me, I had, after sending off this **Discourse,** recast and expanded it to the point of making it, as it were, into another Work; I believed myself obliged to restore it today to the state in which it was awarded the prize. I have only thrown in some notes and let stand two additions easy to recognize and of which the Academy might perhaps not have approved. I thought that equity, respect, and gratitude required this notice of me. (p. 2)

• • • • •

Has the restoration of the Sciences and Arts contributed to the purification of Morals, or to their corruption? That is what has to be examined. Which side ought I to take in this question? The side, Gentlemen, which becomes an honest man who knows nothing and esteems himself no less for it.

I am sensible to the difficulty of conforming what I have to say to the Tribunal before which I appear. How shall I dare to blame the Sciences before one of the most learned Associations of Europe, praise ignorance in a celebrated Academy, and reconcile contempt for study with respect for the truly Learned? I have seen these contradictions, and they have not deterred me. It is not, so I have told myself, Science I abuse; it is Virtue I defend before virtuous men. Probity is even dearer to Good Men than erudition is to the Learned. What, then, have I to fear? The enlightenment of the Assembly listening to me? I acknowledge it; but only with regard to the composition of the discourse, not to the Speaker's sentiment. Equitable Sovereigns have never hesitated to pass judgment against themselves in debates of doubtful issue; and the most advantageous position in a just cause is to have to defend oneself against a Party of integrity and enlightenment judging in his own case.

To this motive which emboldens me, is joined another which decides me: namely that, having by my natural light upheld the side of truth, there is one Prize which cannot fail me whatever my success: I shall find it in the depths of my heart. (p. 3)

> *Jean-Jacques Rousseau, "First Discourse: Preface" and "First Discourse: Part: I," in his* The First and Second Discourses Together with the Replies to Critics and Essay on the Origin of Languages, *edited and translated by Victor Gourevitch, Perennial Library, 1986, pp. 1-2, 3-4.*

François Marie Arouet de Voltaire (letter date 1755)

[*A French philosopher and man of letters, Voltaire was a central figure of the Enlightenment. He was a vigorous proponent of the absolute primacy of personal liberty and an indefatigable opponent of religious traditions and political organizations that thwarted or curtailed individual freedom. Intensely interested in diverse subjects, he wrote prolifically in a variety of genres. Voltaire's most significant contribution to literature was his invention of the philosophical conte—a story that delineates an ethical or philosophical message—of which his most famous is the highly-regarded* Candide *(1759). In the following excerpt, he commends Rousseau's* Discours sur l'origine de l'inégalité, *remarking that it "makes one long to go on all fours."*]

I have received, sir, your new book [**Discours sur l'origine de l'inégalité**] against the human species, and I thank you for it. You will please people by your manner of telling them the truth about themselves, but you will not alter them. The horrors of that human society—from which in our feebleness and ignorance we expect so many consolations—have never been painted in more striking colors: no one has ever been so witty as you are in trying to turn us into brutes: to read your book makes one long to go on all fours. Since, however, it is now some sixty years since I gave up the practice, I feel that it is unfortunately impossible for me to resume it: I leave this natural habit to those more fit for it than are you and I. Nor can I set sail to discover the aborigines of Canada, in the first place because my ill-health ties me to the side of the greatest doctor in Europe, and I should not find the same professional assistance among the Missouris: and secondly because war is going on in that country, and the example of the civilized nations has made the barbarians almost as wicked as we are ourselves. I must confine myself to being a peaceful savage in the retreat I have chosen—close to your country, where you yourself should be.

I agree with you that science and literature have sometimes done a great deal of harm. Tasso's enemies made his life a long series of misfortunes: Galileo's enemies kept him languishing in prison, at seventy years of age, for the crime of understanding the revolution of the earth: and, what is still more shameful, obliged him to forswear his discovery. Since your friends began the Encyclopedia, their rivals attack them as deists, atheists—even Jansenists. (pp. 493-94)

Confess, sir, that all these things are, after all, but little personal pinpricks, which society scarcely notices. What matter to humankind that a few drones steal the honey of a few bees? Literary men make a great fuss of their petty quarrels: the rest of the world ignores them, or laughs at them.

They are, perhaps, the least serious of all the ills attendant on human life. The thorns inseparable from literature and a modest degree of fame are flowers in comparison with the other evils which from all time have flooded the world. (p. 495)

What makes, and will always make, this world a vale of tears is the insatiable greediness and the indomitable pride of men, from Thomas Koulikan, who did not know how to read, to a customhouse officer who can just count. Letters support, refine, and comfort the soul: they are serving you, sir, at the very moment you decry them: you are like Achilles declaiming against fame, and Father Malebranche using his brilliant imagination to belittle imagination.

If anyone has a right to complain of letters, I am that person, for in all times and in all places they have led to my being persecuted: still, we must needs love them in spite of the way they are abused—as we cling to society, though the wicked spoil its pleasantness: as we must love our country, though it treats us unjustly: and as we must love and serve the Supreme Being, despite the superstition and fanaticism which too often dishonor His service. (p. 496)

> *François Marie Arouet de Voltaire, in a letter to J. J. Rousseau on August 30, 1755, in his* The Portable Voltaire, *edited by Ben Ray Redman, The Viking Press, 1949, pp. 493-96.*

Jean-Jacques Rousseau   (essay date 1762)

[*In the following excerpt, Rousseau explains his motivation for composing* The Social Contract.]

This little treatise [**The Social Contract**] is part of a longer work which I began years ago without realising my limitations, and long since abandoned. Of the various fragments that might have been extracted from what I wrote, this is the most considerable, and, I think, the least unworthy of being offered to the public. The rest no longer exists.

• • • • •

I mean to inquire if, in the civil order, there can be any sure and legitimate rule of administration, men being taken as they are and laws as they might be. In this inquiry I shall endeavour always to unite what right sanctions with what is prescribed by interest, in order that justice and utility may in no case be divided.

I enter upon my task without proving the importance of the subject. I shall be asked if I am a prince or a legislator, to write on politics. I answer that I am neither, and that is why I do so. If I were a prince or a legislator, I should not waste time in saying what wants doing; I should do it, or hold my peace.

As I was born a citizen of a free State, and a member of the Sovereign, I feel that, however feeble the influence my voice can have on public affairs, the right of voting on them makes it my duty to study them: and I am happy, when I reflect upon governments, to find my inquiries always furnish me with new reasons for loving that of my own country. (p. 387)

> *Jean-Jacques Rousseau, "The Social Contract or Principles of Political Right," in* The Spirit of Laws *by Charles de Secondat, baron de Montesquieu, edited by J. V. Prichard, translated by Thomas Nugent.* On the Origin of Inequality. On Political Economy. The Social Contract *by Jean Jacques Rousseau, translated by G. D. H. Cole, Encyclopaedia Britannica, Inc., 1955, pp. 387-439.*

James Boswell   (letter date 1764)

[*A Scottish diarist, biographer, and man of letters, Boswell is one of the most colorful and widely read authors of the eighteenth century. He is esteemed for his conversational style and pictorial documentation of life among the London literati of his day. He has been labeled the greatest of English biographers on the basis of his* Life of Samuel Johnson *(1791). This immensely readable work firmly established biography as a leading literary form. In the following letter, originally written in French, he requests an interview with "eloquent and lovable" Rousseau, remarking on the effect of the latter's writings upon himself.*]

Sir,

I am a gentleman of an ancient Scotch family. You know my rank. I am twenty-four years old. You know my age. It is sixteen months since I left Great Britain, a good islander, knowing hardly a word of French. I have been in Holland and in Germany, but not yet in France. You will therefore make allowance for my language. I am on my travels, with a true desire to bring myself to perfection. I have come here in the hope of seeing you. (p. 74)

Do you ask me for letters of introduction? With you is there need of any? In worldly associations, a recommendation is required in order to protect people without insight against impostors. But you, Sir, who have made such a study of human nature, is it possible that you should be deceived with respect to character? This is the notion that I have regarding you. Apart from the incomprehensible nature of the soul, you are perfectly acquainted with all the principles of both body and spirit, with their actions and their sentiments, in short with all that they can accomplish which exerts a genuine influence upon the man himself. It is for this reason, Sir, that I venture to introduce myself to you. I dare to submit to the test. In cities and in courts where there is a numerous society, a man may disguise himself, and on occasion may dazzle the eyes of the greatest philosophers. But I submit myself to the most difficult test. It is in the silence and solitude of your holy retreat that you shall judge of me; and think you that in such circumstances I shall be capable of dissimulation?

Your writings, Sir, have softened my heart, exalted my soul, kindled my imagination. Believe me, you will be delighted to see me. You are acquainted with the pride of the Scotch.—Sir, I come to you to render myself worthy of the nation which has produced a Fletcher of Saltoun and a Lord Marischal. Pardon me, Sir, I am moved. I cannot restrain myself. O beloved St. Preux! inspired Mentor! eloquent and lovable Rousseau! I have a premonition that a truly noble friendship shall come into being this day.

I learn with great regret, Sir, that you are often indisposed. Possibly you may be so at this very time. But I beg you not to let this prevent you from receiving me. You will find in me a simplicity which will not disturb you, a cordiality which may contribute to make you forget your pains.

I have much to say to you. Although I am but a young man, I have had a varied life which will surprise you. I find myself in circumstances at once serious and delicate, regarding which I eagerly long for the advice of the author of the **Nouvelle Héloïse.** If you are the charitable man that I believe you to be, you will not hesitate to give it me. Open, therefore, your door, Sir, to a man who dares to assure you that he has a right to enter. Have faith in a singular foreigner. You will not regret it. But I beg of you, be alone. Despite all my enthusiasm, after having written to you in this way, I am not sure that I would not rather give up seeing you for ever than see you for the first time in company. I await your answer with impatience.

Boswell. (pp. 75-7)

> *James Boswell, in a letter to Jean-Jacques Rousseau on December 3, 1764, in* Essays— Yesterday and Today, *edited by Harold L. Tinker, The Macmillan Company, 1934, pp. 74-7.*

Jean-Jacques Rousseau   (essay date 1767-70)

[*In the following excerpt, Rousseau underscores the originality and sincerity of* The Confessions, *"an undertaking, hitherto without precedent."*]

I am commencing an undertaking, hitherto without precedent, and which will never find an imitator. I desire to set before my fellows the likeness of a man in all the truth of nature, and that man myself.

Myself alone! I know the feelings of my heart, and I know men. I am not made like any of those I have seen; I venture to believe that I am not made like any of those who are in existence. If I am not better, at least I am different. Whether Nature has acted rightly or wrongly in destroying the mould in which she cast me, can only be decided after I have been read.

Let the trumpet of the Day of Judgment sound when it will, I will present myself before the Sovereign Judge with

this book in my hand. I will say boldly: "This is what I have done, what I have thought, what I was. I have told the good and the bad with equal frankness. I have neither omitted anything bad, nor interpolated anything good. If I have occasionally made use of some immaterial embellishments, this has only been in order to fill a gap caused by lack of memory. I may have assumed the truth of that which I knew might have been true, never of that which I knew to be false. I have shown myself as I was: mean and contemptible, good, high-minded and sublime, according as I was one or the other. I have unveiled my inmost self even as Thou hast seen it, O Eternal Being. Gather round me the countless host of my fellow-men; let them hear my confessions, lament for my unworthiness, and blush for my imperfections. Then let each of them in turn reveal, with the same frankness, the secrets of his heart at the foot of the Throne, and say, if he dare, '*I was better than that man!*'" (p. 3)

> *Jean-Jacques Rousseau, in his* The Confessions of Jean Jacques Rousseau, *The Modern Library, 1945, 683 p.*

Edmund Burke   (essay date 1790)

[*Burke was an Irish-born English statesman, philosopher, and critic. Widely recognized as the founder of modern Anglo-American conservatism, he ranks among the most important and influential English statesmen and political writers of the eighteenth century. His writings are recognized today as having shaped and illuminated both conservative and liberal responses to major contemporary dilemmas. Among Burke's most renowned works is a condemnation of the French Revolution,* Reflections on the Revolution in France *(1790). In the following excerpt from that work, he argues against the practical application of literary paradoxes, particularly those of Rousseau.*]

[The] paradoxes of eloquent writers, brought forth purely as a sport of fancy to try their talents, to rouse attention and excite surprise, are taken up by [politicians and legislators], not in the spirit of the original authors, as means of cultivating their taste and improving their style. These paradoxes become with them serious grounds of action upon which they proceed in regulating the most important concerns of the state. Cicero ludicrously describes Cato as endeavoring to act, in the commonwealth, upon the school paradoxes which exercised the wits of the junior students in the Stoic philosophy. If this was true of Cato, these gentlemen copy after him in the manner of some persons who lived about his time—*pede nudo Catonem.* Mr. Hume told me that he had from Rousseau himself the secret of his principles of composition. That acute though eccentric observer had perceived that to strike and interest the public the marvelous must be produced; that the marvelous of the heathen mythology had long since lost its effect; that the giants, magicians, fairies, and heroes of romance which succeeded had exhausted the portion of credulity which belonged to their age; that now nothing was left to the writer but that species of the marvelous which might still be produced, and with as great an effect as ever, though in another way; that is, the marvelous in life, in manners, in characters, and in extraordinary situations, giving rise to new and unlooked-for strokes in politics and morals. I believe that were Rousseau alive and in one of his lucid intervals, he would be shocked at the practical frenzy of his scholars, who in their paradoxes are servile imitators, and even in their incredulity discover an implicit faith. (p. 150)

Edmund Burke, in his Reflections on the Revolution in France, *edited by J. G. A. Pocock, Hackett Publishing Company, 1987, 236 p.*

Francis Jeffrey   (essay date 1802)

[*Jeffrey was a founder and editor of the* Edinburgh Review. *A liberal Whig, he often allowed his political beliefs to color his critical opinions. In the following excerpt from a review of J. J. Mounier's* De L'Influence attribué aux Philosophes, aux Francs-Macons, et aux Illuminés, sur la Révolution de France (1801), *he refutes Mounier's contention that the French writers of the Enlightenment—including Rousseau—exerted no influence on public sentiment before the French Revolution, claiming instead that those writers' "presumptuous theories . . . had a necessary tendency to do harm."*]

[The] writings of those popular philosophers who have contended for political freedom, had some share in bringing about the revolution in France; how great, or how inconsiderable a share, we are not qualified to determine, and hold it indeed impossible to ascertain. There are no *data* from which we can estimate the relative force of such an influence; nor does language afford us any terms that are fitted to express its proportions. We must be satisfied with holding that it existed, and that those who deny its operation altogether, are almost as much mistaken as those who make it account for every thing.

But though we conceive that philosophy is thus, in some degree, responsible for the French revolution, we are far from charging her with the guilt that this name implies. The writers to whom we allude, may have produced effects very different from what they intended, and very different even from what their works might seem calculated to produce. An approved medicine may have occasioned convulsions and death; and the flame that was meant to enlighten, may have spread into conflagration and ruin. (pp. 9-10)

At the time when the writings we are speaking of were published, there was not a man in Europe who could discern in them the seeds of future danger. So far from denouncing them as the harbingers of regicide and confusion, the public received them as hostages and guides to security. It was long thought that their effects were inadequate to their merits: Nothing but the event could have instructed us that it was too powerful for our tranquillity. To such men, the reproach of improvidence can be made, only because their foresight was not prophetic; and those alone are entitled to call them imprudent, who could have predicted the tempest in the calm, and foretold those consequences by which the whole world has since been astonished.

If it be true, therefore, that writers of this description have facilitated and promoted the revolution, it is a truth which should detract but little, either from their merit or their reputation. Their designs were pure and honourable; and the natural tendency and promise of their labours was exalted and fair. They failed, by a fatality which they were not bound to foresee; and a concurrence of events, against which it was impossible for them to provide, turned that to mischief, which was planned out by wisdom for good. We do not tax the builder with imprudence, because the fortress which he erected for our protection is thrown down by an earthquake on our heads.

There is another set of writers, however, for whom it will not be so easy to find an apology, who, instead of sober reasoning, and practical observations, have intruded upon the public with every species of extravagance and absurdity. The presumptuous theories, and audacious maxims of Rousseau, Mably, Condorcet, &c. had a necessary tendency to do harm. They unsettled all the foundations of political duty, and taught the citizens of every established government, that they were enslaved, and had the power of being free. . . . [Instead] of promoting the revolution, it was the revolution that raised them into celebrity; that they rose into reputation, after it became necessary to quote them as apologists or authorities; but that before that time, their speculations were looked upon as brilliant absurdities, that no more deserved a serious confutation than the Polity of Plato, or the Utopia of Sir Thomas More. . . . Rousseau, in particular, was universally read and admired long before he was exalted into the Revolutionary Pantheon; and his political sagacity must have had some serious admirers, when he was himself invited to legislate for an existing community. Whatever influence he had, however, was unquestionably pernicious; and though some apology may be found for him in the enthusiasm of his disordered imagination, he is chargeable with the highest presumption, and the most blameable imprudence. Of some of the other writers, who have inculcated the same doctrines, we must speak rather in charity than in justice, if we say nothing more severe. (pp. 10-11)

Francis Jeffrey, "Mounier, 'De L'Influence attribuée aux Philosophes'," in The Edinburgh Review, *Vol. I, No. I, October, 1802, pp. 1-18.*

William Hazlitt   (essay date 1816)

[*An English essayist, Hazlitt was one of the most important critics of the Romantic age. He was a deft stylist and a master of the prose essay. He utilized the critical techniques of evocation, metaphor, and personal reference—three innovations that greatly influenced the development of literary criticism in the nineteenth and twentieth centuries. In the following excerpt, Hazlitt argues that Rousseau's own self-absorption is the chief characteristic and key to understanding of his works.*]

Neither imagination nor reason can properly be said to have been the original predominant faculties of [Rousseau's] mind. The strength both of imagination and reason, which he possessed, was borrowed from the excess of another faculty; and the weakness and poverty of reason and imagination, which are to be found in his works, may be traced to the same source, namely, that these faculties in him were artificial, secondary, and dependant, operating by a power not theirs, but lent to them. The only quality which he possessed in an eminent degree, which alone raised him above ordinary men, and which gave to his writings and opinions an influence greater, perhaps, than has been exerted by any individual in modern times, was extreme sensibility, or an acute and even morbid feeling of all that related to his own impressions, to the objects and events of his life. He had the most intense consciousness of his own existence. No object that had once made an impression on him was ever after effaced. Every feeling in his mind became a passion. His craving after excitement was an appetite and a disease. His interest in his own thoughts and feelings was always wound up to the highest pitch; and hence the enthusiasm which he excited in others. He owed the power which he exercised over the opinions of all Europe, by which he created numberless disciples, and overturned established systems, to the tyranny which his feelings, in the first instance, exercised over himself. The dazzling blaze of his reputation was kindled by the same fire that fed upon his vitals. His ideas differed from those of other men only in their force and intensity. His genius was the effect of his temperament. He created nothing, he demonstrated nothing, by a pure effort of the understanding. His fictitious characters are modifications of his own being, reflections and shadows of himself. His speculations are the obvious exaggerations of a mind, giving a loose to its habitual impulses, and moulding all nature to its own purposes. Hence his enthusiasm and his eloquence, bearing down all opposition. Hence the warmth and the luxuriance, as well as the sameness of his descriptions. Hence the frequent verboseness of his style; for passion lends force and reality to language, and makes words supply the place of imagination. Hence the tenaciousness of his logic, the acuteness of his observations, the refinement and the inconsistency of his reasoning. Hence his keen penetration, and his strange want of comprehension of mind: for the same intense feeling which enabled him to discern the first principles of things, and seize some one view of a subject in all its ramifications, prevented him from admitting the operation of other causes which interfered with his favourite purpose, and involved him in endless wilful contradictions. Hence his excessive egotism, which filled all objects with himself, and would have occupied the universe with his smallest interest. Hence his jealousy and suspicion of others; for no attention, no respect or sympathy, could come up to the extravagant claims of his self-love. Hence his dissatisfaction with himself and with all around him; for nothing could satisfy his ardent longings after good, his restless appetite of being. Hence his feelings, overstrained and exhausted, recoiled upon themselves, and produced his love of silence and repose, his feverish aspirations after the quiet and solitude of nature. Hence in part also his quarrel with the artificial institutions and distinctions of society, which opposed so many barriers to the unrestrained indulgence of his will, and allured his imagination to scenes of pastoral simplicity or of savage life, where the passions were either not excited or left to follow their own impulse,—where the petty vexations and irritating disappointments of common life had no place,—and where the tormenting pursuits of arts and sciences were lost in pure animal enjoyment, or indolent repose. Thus he describes the first savage wandering for ever under the shade of magnificent forests, or by the side of mighty rivers, smit with the unquenchable love of nature!

The best of all his works is the *Confessions,* though it is that which has been least read, because it contains the fewest set paradoxes or general opinions. It relates entirely to himself; and no one was ever so much at home on this subject as he was. From the strong hold which they had taken of his mind, he makes us enter into his feelings as if they had been our own, and we seem to remember every incident and circumstance of his life as if it had happened to ourselves. We are never tired of this work, for it everywhere presents us with pictures which we can fancy to be counterparts of our own existence. The passages of this sort are innumerable. There is the interesting account of his childhood, the constraints and thoughtless liberty . . . which are so well described; of his sitting up all night reading romances with his father, till they were forced to desist by hearing the swallows twittering in their nests; his crossing the Alps, described with all the feelings belonging to it, his pleasure in setting out, his satisfaction in coming to his journey's end, the delight of 'coming and going he knew not where'; his arriving at Turin; the figure of Madame Basile, drawn with such inimitable precision and elegance; the delightful adventure of the Chateau de Toune, where he passed the day with Mademoiselle G**** and Mademoiselle Galley; the story of his Zulietta, the proud, the charming Zulietta, whose last words, '*Va Zanetto, e studia la Matematica,*' were never to be forgotten; his sleeping near Lyons in a niche of the wall, after a fine summer's day, with a nightingale perched above his head; his first meeting with Madame Warens, the pomp of sound with which he has celebrated her name, beginning '*Louise Eleonore de Warens etoit une demoiselle de la Tour de Pil, noble et ancienne famille de Vevai, ville du pays de Vaud*' (sounds which we still tremble to repeat); his description of her person, her angelic smile, her mouth of the size of his own; his walking out one day while the bells were chiming to vespers, and anticipating in a sort of waking dream the life he afterwards led with her, in which months and years, and life itself passed away in undisturbed felicity; the sudden disappointment of his hopes; his transport thirty years after at seeing the same flower which they had brought home together from one of their rambles near Chambery; his thoughts in that long interval of time; his suppers with Grimm and Diderot after he came to Paris; the first idea of his prize dissertation on the savage state; his account of writing the *New Eloise,* and his attachment to Madame d'Houdetot; his literary projects, his fame, his misfortunes, his unhappy temper; his last solitary retirement in the lake and island of Bienne, with his dog and his boat; his reveries and delicious musings there; all these crowd into our minds with recollections which we do not chuse to express. There are no passages in the *New Eloise* of equal force and beauty with the best descriptions in the *Confessions,* if we except the excursion on the water, Julia's last letter to St. Preux, and his letter to her, recalling the days of their first loves. We spent two whole years in reading these two works; and (gentle reader, it was when we were young) in shedding tears over them

—As fast as the Arabian trees
Their medicinal gums.

They were the happiest years of our life. We may well say of them, sweet is the dew of their memory, and pleasant the balm of their recollection! There are, indeed, impressions which neither time nor circumstances can efface.

Rousseau, in all his writings, never once lost sight of himself. He was the same individual from first to last. The spring that moved his passions never went down, the pulse that agitated his heart never ceased to beat. It was this strong feeling of interest, accumulating in his mind, which overpowers and absorbs the feelings of his readers. He owed all his power to sentiment. The writer who most nearly resembles him in our own times is the author of the *Lyrical Ballads.* We see no other difference between them, than that the one wrote in prose and the other in poetry; and that prose is perhaps better adapted to express those local and personal feelings, which are inveterate creations. We conceive that Rousseau's exclamation, '*Ah, voila de la pervenche,*' comes more home to the mind than Mr. Wordsworth's discovery of the linnet's nest 'with five blue eggs,' or than his address to the cuckoo, beautiful as we think it is; and we will confidently match the Citizen of Geneva's adventures on the Lake of Bienne against the Cumberland Poet's floating dreams on the Lake of Grasmere. Both create an interest out of nothing, or rather out of their own feelings; both weave numberless recollections into one sentiment; both wind their own being round whatever object occurs to them. But Rousseau, as a prose-writer, gives only the habitual and personal impression. Mr. Wordsworth, as a poet, is forced to lend the colours of imagination to impressions which owe all their force to their identity with themselves, and tries to paint what is only to be felt. Rousseau, in a word, interests you in certain objects by interesting you in himself: Mr. Wordsworth would persuade you that the most insignificant objects are interesting in themselves, because he is interested in them. If he had met with Rousseau's favourite periwinkle, he would have *translated* it into the most beautiful of flowers. This is not imagination, but want of sense. If his jealousy of the sympathy of others makes him avoid what is beautiful and grand in nature, why does he undertake elaborately to describe other objects? *His* nature is a mere Dulcinea del Toboso, and he would make a Vashti of her. Rubens appears to have been as extravagantly attached to his three wives, as Raphael was to his Fornarina; but their faces were not so classical. The three greatest egotists that we know of, that is, the three writers who felt their own being most powerfully and exclusively, are Rousseau, Wordsworth, and Benvenuto Cellini. As Swift somewhere says, we defy the world to furnish out a fourth. (pp. 88-93)

> *William Hazlitt, "The Round Table: On the Character of Rousseau," in his* The Round Table and Characters of Shakespear's Plays, *J. M. Dent & Sons Ltd., 1936, pp. 88-93.*

George Gordon, Lord Byron   (poem date 1816)

[Byron was an early nineteenth-century English poet and dramatist who is now considered one of the most important writers of his day. Because of the satiric nature of much of his work, it is difficult to place him within the Romantic movement. His most notable contribution to Romanticism is the Byronic hero, a melancholy man, often with a dark past, who eschews societal and religious strictures to seek truth and happiness in an apparently meaningless universe. In the following excerpt from the poem "Childe Harold's Pilgrimage," Byron reminisces about "the self-torturing sophist, wild Rousseau."]

Are not the mountains, waves, and skies, a part
  Of me and of my soul, as I of them?
Is not the love of these deep in my heart
  With a pure passion? should I not contemn
  All objects, if compared with these? and stem

A tide of suffering, rather than forego
  Such feelings for the hard and worldly phlegm
Of those whose eyes are only turned below,
Gazing upon the ground, with thoughts which dare not glow?

But this is not my theme; and I return
  To that which is immediate, and require
Those who find contemplation in the urn,
  To look on One, whose dust was once all fire,
  A native of the land where I respire
The clear air for a while—a passing guest,
  Where he became a being—whose desire
Was to be glorious; 'twas a foolish quest,
The which to gain and keep, he sacrificed all rest.

Here the self-torturing sophist, wild Rousseau,
  The apostle of affliction, he who threw
Enchantment over passion, and from woe
  Wrung overwhelming eloquence, first drew
  The breath which made him wretched; yet he knew
How to make madness beautiful, and cast
  O'er erring deeds and thoughts a heavenly hue
Of words, like sunbeams, dazzling as they past
The eyes, which o'er them shed tears feelingly and fast.

His love was passion's essence—as a tree
  On fire by lightning; with ethereal flame
Kindled he was, and blasted; for to be
  Thus, and enamoured, were in him the same.
  But his was not the love of living dame,
Nor of the dead who rise upon our dreams,
  But of ideal beauty, which became
In him existence, and o'erflowing teems
Along his burning page, distempered though it seems.

This breathed itself to life in Julie, this
  Invested her with all that's wild and sweet;
This hallowed, too, the memorable kiss
  Which every morn his fevered lip would greet,
  From hers, who but with friendship his would meet;
But to that gentle touch, through brain and breast
  Flashed the thrilled spirit's love-devouring heat:
In that absorbing sigh perchance more blest
Than vulgar minds may be with all they seek possest.

His life was one long war with self-sought foes,
  Or friends by him self-banished; for his mind
Had grown Suspicion's sanctuary, and chose
  For its own cruel sacrifice the kind,
  'Gainst whom he raged with fury strange and blind,
But he was frenzied—wherefore, who may know?
  Since cause might be which skill could never find;
But he was frenzied by disease or woe
To that worst pitch of all, which wears a reasoning show.

For then he was inspired, and from him came
  As from the Pythian's mystic cave of yore,
Those oracles which set the world in flame,
  Nor ceased to burn till kingdoms were no more:
Did he not this for France? which lay before
Bowed to the inborn tyranny of years?
  Broken and trembling to the yoke she bore,
Till by the voice of him and his compeers,
Roused up to too much wrath, which follows o'ergrown fears?

(pp. 70-1)

> *George Gordon Byron, in an excerpt from a poem in his* Childe Harold and Other Poems, *D. Appleton and Company, 1899, pp. 70-1.*

C. A. Sainte-Beuve (essay date 1850)

[*Sainte-Beuve is considered the foremost French literary critic of the nineteenth century. He is especially noted for his literary and historical erudition. His "Causeries du lundi"—weekly newspaper articles that appeared every Monday morning for several decades—are the best-known of his extensive body of critical writings. He began his career as a champion of Romanticism, but eventually he formulated a psychological method of criticism that strongly stressed the importance of author biography in interpreting literary works. In the following excerpt from a "causerie" originally published on 29 April 1850, he offers a favorable overview of Rousseau's literary career.*]

Although the *Confessions* did not appear until after Rousseau's death, and when his influence was already in the plenitude of its power, it is in that work that it is most convenient for us to-day to study him, with all the merits, the prodigies, and the defects of his talent. We will try to do it, confining ourselves so far as we can to a consideration of the writer, but reserving the right to comment upon the ideas and the character of the man.

The present moment [1850] is not very favourable to Rousseau, who is charged with being the author, the promoter, of many of the ills that we are undergoing. "There is no writer," some one has judiciously said, "better fitted to make the poor man arrogant." In spite of all this, we will try not to be unduly influenced ourselves by this personal feeling, so to speak, which leads men of good judgment to blame him for the painful trials through which we are passing. Men who have such a range and such foresight should not be judged according to the emotions and reactions of a single day.

The idea of writing "Confessions" seems so natural in Rousseau, and so in harmony with his disposition and his talent alike, that one would hardly believe that it was necessary to suggest it to him. It came to him, however, in the first place, from his publisher, Rey of Amsterdam, and also from Duclos. After *La Nouvelle Héloïse,* after *Émile,* Rousseau began in 1764 to set down his *Confessions,* at the age of fifty-two, after his departure from Montmorency and during his sojourn at Motiers in Switzerland. There has just been published, in the last number of the *Revue Suisse* (October, 1850), an opening chapter of the *Confessions,* taken from a manuscript deposited in the library of Neuchâtel; it is Rousseau's first draft, which he afterward suppressed. This original exordium, which is much less emphatic and less ornate than that which we find in the *Confessions* as published, does not greet us with a blast from "the trumpet of the last judgment," nor does it end with the famous apostrophe to the "Eternal Being." Rousseau sets forth therein, at much greater length, but in philosophical language, his plan of painting himself, and making his confessions *à toute rigueur;* he makes it very clear in what the originality and singularity of his plan consists.

> No one can describe a man's life but the man himself. His inward being, his real life, is known to him alone; but when writing of it, he disguises it; under the name of his life, he writes his apology; he exhibits himself as he wishes himself to be seen, but not at all as he is. The most sincere of men are, at the best, truthful only in what they say; they lie by their reticences, and those things as to which they are silent put such a different face on what they pretend to confess, that by telling only a part of the truth they tell nothing. I put Montaigne at the head of those *sincere hypocrites,* who try to deceive by telling the truth. He exhibits himself with failings; but he ascribes to himself only those which are amiable; *there is no man living who has not some hateful ones.* Montaigne's portrait of himself is a good likeness, but taken in profile. Who can say that a scar on the cheek, or an eye gouged out on the side that he hides from us, would not have changed his aspect completely?

He proposes therefore to do what no one before him has ever planned or dared to do. As for style, it seems to him necessary to invent one as novel as his project, and proportioned to the diversity and dissimilarity of the things he has it in mind to describe. (pp. 147-49)

Rousseau's error was not the believing that, by confessing himself thus aloud before all men, in a frame of mind so different from Christian humility, he was doing a unique thing, or even a thing of the greatest interest for the study of the human heart; his error consisted in his belief that he was doing a *useful* thing. He did not see that he was acting like the physician who should undertake to describe in an intelligible, attractive way, for the behoof of worldly and ignorant people, some strongly characterised mental weakness or disease; such a physician would be in a measure blameworthy and responsible for all the maniacs and fools by imitation and contagion whom his book would make.

The first pages of the *Confessions* are over-emphasised and decidedly painful. I find at the outset "a hiatus occasioned by a failure of memory." Rousseau speaks of *the authors of his days;* he bore at his birth the germ of an *incommodity* which time has aggravated *(renforcée),* he says, and which now gives him occasional respites *(rélâches)* only to, etc., etc. All this is unpleasant; but beware! beside his harshness of accentuation and these native crudities, what words are these? what unwonted simplicity, intimate, and penetrating!

> I felt before I thought; that is the common lot of mankind. I experienced it more fully than others. I do not know what I did up to the time I was five or six years old. I do not know how I learned to read; I simply remember my first books and their effect on me.
>
> . . . My mother had left some novels; we began to read them after supper, my father and I. At first it was simply a question of giving me practice in reading by means of entertaining books; but soon the interest became so intense that we read by turns without intermission, and passed whole nights in that occupation. We could never put a book down until the end. Sometimes my father, hearing the swallows in the morning, would say shamefacedly: *"Let's go to bed, I am more of a child than you."*

Mark well this swallow; it is the first, and it announces a new springtime of the language; we begin to detect its appearance only in Rousseau. It is from him that the appreciation of nature dates, in the eighteenth century, in France. From him, too, dates, in our literature, the sentiment of domestic life, of that lowly, poor, reserved, intimate life, wherein so many treasures of virtue and amiability are amassed. Despite some details in execrable taste, where he talks about pilfering and victuals (*mangeaille*), how readily we forgive him in consideration of that old ballad of his childhood, of which he remembers only the tune and a few scattered words, but which he is for ever trying to recall, and never succeeds in recalling, old as he is, without a touching delight!

> It is a whim which I do not understand at all, but it is absolutely impossible for me to sing it through without being stopped by my tears. A hundred times I have thought of writing to Paris to have the rest of the words hunted up, that is, if there is still any one who knows them; but I am almost sure that the pleasure I take in remembering the song would disappear in great part, if I had proof that others besides my poor Aunt Suzon used to sing it.

That is the new thing in the author of the ***Confessions,*** that is what fascinates us by opening before us an unexpected fountain of private, domestic sensibility. And so, when we note with some regret that Rousseau did force and upturn and, as it were, run the plough through the language, we add instantly that at the same time he fertilised it and sowed it. (pp. 149-52)

Rousseau has in everything the sentiment of *reality*. He has it whenever he speaks of beauty, which, even when it is imaginary, as in his Julie, carries with it a body and shape that are quite visible, and is by no means an Iris, floating in the air and intangible. This sentiment of reality manifests itself in this, that he is careful that every scene that he remembers or invents shall be set, every character that he introduces shall act his part, in a definitely marked locality, the slightest details of which may be fixed in the mind and retained. One of his criticisms of the great novelist Richardson was that he did not connect the memory of his characters with some locality which it would be a pleasure to identify by his descriptions. Observe, for example, how perfectly he has naturalised his Julie and his Saint-Preux in the Pays-de-Vaud, on the shores of that lake about which his heart had never ceased to wander. His straightforward, steadfast mind at all times lent its graving tool to his imagination, so that nothing essential should be omitted in the design. Finally, this sentiment of reality appears even in the care with which, amid all the circumstances and adventures of his career, happy or unhappy, even amid the most romantic of them all, he never forgets to mention his repast and to give the details of a healthful, frugal régime, adapted to give joy to the heart as well as to the mind.

This last point, too, is an essential one; it is referable to those natural traits of the bourgeois, of the man of the people, which I have remarked upon in Rousseau. He has been hungry in his day; he notes in his ***Confessions,*** with a sense of gratitude to Providence, the last time that it was his fate literally to feel poverty and hunger. And so he will never forget, even in the ideal picture of his happiness which he draws on a later page, to introduce these incidents of real life and of the common lot, these things of the entrails. It is by all these veracious details, combined as they are in his eloquence, that he seizes us and holds us fast.

Nature, sincerely *felt* and loved for itself, forms the groundwork of Rousseau's inspiration, whenever that inspiration is sound and healthy and not diseased. When he

sees Madame de Warens again, on his return from Turin, he lives some time under her roof, and from the bedroom which is given him he sees gardens and has glimpses of the open country. "It was the first time," he says, "since Bossey [the place where he had been sent to boarding-school in his childhood], that I had had *green things before my windows.*" It had been been a matter of great indifference hitherto to French literature whether it had or had not *green things* before its eyes; it was Rousseau's part to call attention to that matter. From this point of view he may be defined in a word: he was the first who introduced *green things* into our literature. Living thus, at nineteen years of age, under the same roof with a woman whom he loved but to whom he dared not declare his passion, Rousseau gave way to a melancholy "in which, however, there was no touch of gloom, and which was tempered by a flattering hope." Having gone to walk alone outside of the town, on a great holiday, while the people were at vespers, he says:

> The ringing of the bells, which has always affected me strangely, the songs of the birds, the beauty of the day, the soft loveliness of the landscape, the scattered country houses wherein I fancied us two living together, all this made such a vivid, tender, melancholy, and moving impression upon me that I saw myself, as in a trance, transported to that blissful time and that blissful spot where my heart, in possession of all the felicity it could desire, would enjoy it in indescribable ecstasy, without even thinking of sensual pleasure.

Such were the feelings of this child of Geneva at Annecy in the year 1731, when people in Paris were reading the *Temple de Gnide.* On that day he discovered *reverie,* that new charm which had hitherto been abandoned to La Fontaine as a mere oddity, but which Rousseau was to introduce definitively into a literature until then either dissolute or materialistic. *Reverie*—that is his novelty, his discovery, his America. His dream of that day he realised some years later, in his sojourn at Les Charmettes, in that excursion on Saint-Louis' Day, which he has described as no similar thing had ever been described before:

> "Everything," he says, "seemed to conspire for the bliss of that day. It had recently rained; no dust, and the streams flowing abundantly; a light, cool wind fluttered the leaves, the air was pure, the horizon cloudless, serenity reigned in the sky as in our hearts. We dined at a peasant's cottage and shared with his family, who blessed us heartily. Those poor Savoyards are such kindly folk!"

And he goes on, in this strain of good-humour, of observation, and of artless sincerity, to develop a picture in which everything is perfect, everything enchants, and only the name *Maman,* applied to Madame de Warens, gives offence morally, and causes pain.

That brief moment at Les Charmettes, where it was given to that still novice heart to expand for the first time, is the most divine moment of the ***Confessions,*** and it will never be repeated, even when he has retired to the Hermitage. The description of the years at the Hermitage, and of the passion which sought him out there, has much that fascinates, it is true, and perhaps more salience than all that has gone before; he was justified, however, in exclaiming: *"This is not Les Charmettes."* The misanthropy and distrust by which he was already assailed followed him in

Madame de Warens's farm, Les Charmettes, near Chambéry, Switzerland, where Rousseau claimed he spent the happiest times of his life.

that period of solitude. He thought constantly of the society of Paris, of d'Holbach's little coterie; he enjoyed his retirement in spite of them, but such thoughts poisoned his purest enjoyment. His character became soured, and contracted during those years an incurable malady. Doubtless he did have blissful moments, then and afterward, until the end; he found in the island of Saint-Pierre, in the centre of the Lake of Bienne, an interval of calm and oblivion which inspired some of his finest pages,—the fifth "Promenade" of the *Reveries,* which, with the third letter to M. de Malesherbes, cannot well be distinguished from the divinest passages of the *Confessions.* But in lightness of touch, freshness, and gaiety nothing in them equals the description of the life at Les Charmettes. Rousseau's true happiness, of which no one, not even himself, could rob him, was the being able to evoke thus and to draw anew, with the accuracy and vividness which marked his memory of them, such pictures of youth, even in the midst of his most disturbed and anxious years.

The *pedestrian journey,* with its vivid impressions of each successive instant, was another of Rousseau's inventions, one of the novelties which he imported into literature; it has been much abused since. After enjoying the experience, it first occurred to him, but not until much later, to tell what he had felt. Only at such times, he assures us, when he was travelling on foot, in fine weather, through

a beautiful country, without haste, having for the goal of his journey an agreeable object which he was not in too great a hurry to reach,—only at such times was he absolutely himself, and only then did his ideas, which were cold and dead in the study, come to life and take their flight. (pp. 161-66)

Do not ask him to write down at such moments the thoughts, sublime, foolish, adorable, which pass through his mind: he much prefers to taste and relish them rather than put them in words. "Besides, did I carry paper and pens about me? If I had thought of all those matters, nothing would have come to me. I did not then foresee that I should have ideas; they come when it pleases them, not when it pleases me." And so, if we are to believe him, we have naught but far-off recollections and indistinct fragments of himself as he was at those moments. And yet, what could be more genuine, more exact, and more delightful at once! Let us recall the night that he passed in the open air on the bank of the Rhone or the Saone, in a sunken road near Lyons:

> I lay in voluptuous ease on the platform of a sort of recess or false gateway hollowed out of a terrace wall; the canopy of my bed was formed by the tops of the trees; a nightingale was directly over my head, and I fell asleep to his singing; my sleep was delicious, my awakening even more so. It was

broad daylight; my eyes, when they opened, saw the water, the verdure, a beautiful landscape. I rose and shook myself; hunger assailed me; I walked gaily toward the town, resolved to spend on a good breakfast two fifteen-sou pieces which I still had left.

There we have the natural Rousseau complete, with his reverie, his idealism, his reality; and that *fifteen-sou piece* itself, coming after the nightingale, is not misplaced to bring us back to earth, and to make us realise to the full the humble enjoyment which poverty carries hidden within itself, when it is combined with poesy and with youth.

The picturesque in Rousseau is composed, robust, and clearly outlined, even in the most delicate passages; the colours are always laid upon a fully perfected design; therein this Genevan is of the pure French breed. If he lacks now and then a warmer light and the brilliance of Italy or Greece; if, as sometimes happens about the lovely Lake of Geneva, the north wind cools the air and a cloud suddenly imparts a greyish tinge to the mountain sides, there are days and hours of a perfect, limpid serenity. Some later writers have improved upon this style, have thought to eclipse and surpass it; they have certainly succeeded with respect to some effects of colouring and of sound. However, Rousseau's style still remains the most unerring and robust that we can put forward as a pattern in the field of modern innovation. With him the centre of the language is not much displaced. His successors have gone farther; they have not only transferred the seat of the Empire to Byzantium, but have often carried it to Antioch and to the heart of Asia. In them the imagination in its splendour absorbs and dominates everything.

I have been able simply to point out, *currente calamo*, the leading features in the author of the **Confessions**, by virtue of which he remains a master; to salute the creator of *reverie*, who inoculated us with the appreciation of nature and the sense of reality, the father of intimate literature and of interior painting. What a pity that there should be an infusion of misanthropic conceit, and that cynical outbursts should make a smirch amid so many alluring and solid beauties! But these follies and vices of the man are powerless to prevail over his innate merits, or to conceal from us the great talents by favour of which he still proves himself superior to his successors.

Extraordinary man, powerful and bewitching writer, one must constantly play a double part in passing judgment upon him. If he was his own executioner, and if he tormented himself exceedingly, he tormented the world still more. Not only did he cast a spell upon passion—he succeeded, as Byron says, in giving to madness the aspect of beauty, and in cloaking mistaken acts or thoughts with the celestial colouring of words. He first imparted to our language a continuous force, a steadfastness of tone, a solidity of texture, which it had not before; and therein, it may be, lies his surest claim to glory. As for the substance of his ideas, everything in him is doubtful, everything may seem, fairly enough, equivocal and suspicious; sound ideas are constantly blended with false ones, and suffer from the contact. By encompassing half truths with a false glamour of evidence, he contributed more than any other writer to start the arrogant and the weak upon the pathway of error. One day, in an hour of unreserve, while talking about his works with Hume, and admitting that he was not ill-

content with them in respect to style and eloquence, he happened to add: "But I am always afraid of going astray in substance, and that all my theories are overloaded with extravagant conceits." That one of his works of which he thought most highly was **Le Contrat Social,** which is in fact the most sophistical of them all, and was destined to have the most revolutionary influence upon the future.

For us, whatever common sense may tell us, for all those who are, in whatever degree, of his posterity, poetically speaking, it will always be impossible not to love Jean-Jacques, not to forgive him much in favour of his pictures of youth, his impassioned appreciation of nature, for that *reverie,* of which he implanted the genius among us, and to which he was the first to give expression in our language. (pp. 166-70)

> *C. A. Sainte-Beuve, "Jean Jacques Rousseau (1712-1778)," in his* Portraits of the Eighteenth Century: Historic and Literary, *Vol. II, translated by Katharine P. Wormeley, Frederick Ungar Publishing Co., 1964, pp. 129-70.*

James Russell Lowell   (essay date 1867)

[*Lowell was an American poet and essayist who edited two leading journals, the* Atlantic Monthly *and the* North American Review. *Commentators generally agree that he displayed a judicious critical sense, and he is ranked with the major nineteenth-century American critics. In the following excerpt from an essay originally published in the* North American Review *in 1867, he focuses favorably on the type of sentimentalism evident throughout Rousseau's life and works.*]

Rousseau, no doubt, was weak, nay, more than that, was sometimes despicable, but yet is not fairly to be reckoned among the herd of sentimentalists. It is shocking that a man whose preaching made it fashionable for women of rank to nurse their own children should have sent his own, as soon as born, to the foundling hospital, still more shocking that, in a note to his **Discours sur l'Inégalité,** he should speak of this crime as one of the consequences of our social system. But for all that there was a faith and an ardour of conviction in him that distinguish him from most of the writers of his time. Nor were his practice and his preaching always inconsistent. He contrived to pay regularly, whatever his own circumstances were, a pension of one hundred *livres* a-year to a maternal aunt who had been kind to him in childhood. Nor was his asceticism a sham. He might have turned his gift into laced coats and châteaux as easily as Voltaire, had he not held it too sacred to be bartered away in any such losing exchange.

But what is worthy of especial remark is this—that in nearly all that he wrote his leading object was the good of his kind, and that through all the vicissitudes of a life which illness, sensibility of temperament, and the approaches of insanity rendered wretched—the associate of infidels, the foundling child, as it were, of an age without belief, least of all in itself—he professed and evidently felt deeply a faith in the goodness both of man and of God. There is no such thing as scoffing in his writings. On the other hand, there is no stereotyped morality. He does not ignore the existence of scepticism; he recognises its existence in his own nature, meets it frankly face to face, and makes it confess that there are things in the teaching of Christ that are deeper than its doubt. The influence of his early education at Geneva is apparent here. An intellect so acute as his, trained in the school of Calvin in a republic where theological discussion was as much the amusement of the people as the opera was at Paris, could not fail to be a good logician. He had the fortitude to follow his logic wherever it led him. If the very impressibility of character which quickened his perception of the beauties of nature, and made him alive to the charm of music and musical expression, prevented him from being in the highest sense an original writer, and if his ideas were mostly suggested to him by books, yet the clearness, consecutiveness, and eloquence with which he stated and enforced them made them his own. There was at least that original fire in him which could fuse them and run them in a novel mould. His power lay in this very ability of manipulating the thoughts of others. Fond of paradox he doubtless was, but he had a way of putting things that arrested attention and excited thought.

It was, perhaps, this very sensibility of the surrounding atmosphere of feeling and speculation, which made Rousseau more directly influential on contemporary thought (or perhaps we should say sentiment) than any writer of his time. And this is rarely consistent with enduring greatness in literature. It forces us to remember, against our will, the oratorical character of his works. They were all pleas, and he a great advocate, with Europe in the jury-box. Enthusiasm begets enthusiasm, eloquence produces conviction for the moment, but it is only by truth to nature and the everlasting intuitions of mankind that those abiding influences are won that enlarge from generation to generation. Rousseau was in many respects—as great pleaders always are—a man of the day, who must needs become a mere name to posterity, yet he could not but have had in him some not inconsiderable share of that principle by which man eternises himself. For it is only to such that the night cometh not in which no man shall work, and he is still operative both in politics and literature by the principles he formulated or the emotions to which he gave a voice so piercing and so sympathetic.

In judging Rousseau, it would be unfair not to take note of the malarious atmosphere in which he grew up. The constitution of his mind was thus early infected with a feverish taint that made him shiveringly sensitive to a temperature which hardier natures found bracing. To him this rough world was but too literally a rack. Good-humoured Mother Nature commonly imbeds the nerves of her children in a padding of self-conceit that serves as a buffer against the ordinary shocks to which even a life of routine is liable, and it would seem at first sight as if Rousseau had been better cared for than usual in this regard. But as his self-conceit was enormous, so was the reaction from it proportionate, and the fretting suspiciousness of temper, sure mark of an unsound mind, which rendered him incapable of intimate friendship, while passionately longing for it, became inevitably, when turned inward, a tormenting self-distrust. To dwell in unrealities is the doom of the sentimentalist; but it should not be forgotten that the same fitful intensity of emotion which makes them real as the means of elation, gives them substance also for torture. Too irritably jealous to endure the rude society of men, he steeped his senses in the enervating incense that women

are only too ready to burn. If their friendship be a safeguard to the other sex, their homage is fatal to all but the strongest, and Rousseau was weak both by inheritance and early training. His father was one of those feeble creatures for whom a fine phrase could always satisfactorily fill the void that non-performance leaves behind it. If he neglected duty, he made up for it by that cultivation of the finer sentiments of our common nature which waters flowers of speech with the brineless tears of a flabby remorse, without one fibre of resolve in it, and which impoverishes the character in proportion as it enriches the vocabulary. He was a very Apicius in that digestible kind of woe which makes no man leaner, and had a favourite receipt for cooking you up a sorrow *à la douleur inassouvie* that had just enough delicious sharpness in it to bring tears into the eyes by tickling the palate. "When he said to me, 'Jean Jacques, let us speak of thy mother,' I said to him, 'Well, father, we are going to weep, then,' and this word alone drew tears from him. 'Ah!' said he, groaning, 'give her back to me, console me for her, fill the void she has left in my soul!' " Alas! in such cases, the void she leaves is only that she found. The grief that seeks any other than its own society will ere long want an object. This admirable parent allowed his son to become an outcast at sixteen, without any attempt to reclaim him, in order to enjoy unmolested a petty inheritance to which the boy was entitled in right of his mother. "This conduct," Rousseau tells us, "of a father whose tenderness and virtue were so well known to me caused me to make reflections on myself which have not a little contributed to make my heart sound. I drew from it this great maxim of morals, the only one perhaps serviceable in practice, to avoid situations which put our duties in opposition to our interest, and which show us our own advantage in the wrong of another, sure that in such situations, *however sincere may be one's love of virtue,* it sooner or later grows weak without our perceiving it, *and that we become unjust and wicked in action without having ceased to be just and good in soul.*" (pp. 320-23)

Rousseau showed through life a singular proneness for being convinced by his own eloquence; he was always his own first convert; and this reconciles his power as a writer with his weakness as a man. He and all like him mistake emotion for conviction, velleity for resolve, the brief eddy of sentiment for the mid-current of ever-gathering faith in duty that draws to itself all the affluents of conscience and will, and gives continuity of purpose to life. They are like men who love the stimulus of being under conviction, as it is called, who, forever getting religion, never get capital enough to retire upon and spend for their own need and the common service.

The sentimentalist is the spiritual hypochondriac, with whom fancies become facts, while facts are a discomfort because they will not be evaporated into fancy. In his eyes, Theory is too fine a dame to confess even a country-cousinship with coarse-handed Practice, whose homely ways would disconcert her artificial world. The very susceptibility that makes him quick to feel, makes him also incapable of deep and durable feeling. He loves to think he suffers, and keeps a pet sorrow, a blue-devil familiar, that goes with him everywhere, like Paracelsus's black dog. He takes good care, however, that it shall not be the true sulphurous article that sometimes takes a fancy to fly away with his conjurer. (pp. 323-24)

George Sand speaking of Rousseau's ***Confessions,*** says that an autobiographer always makes himself the hero of his own novel, and cannot help idealising, even if he would. But the weak point of all sentimentalists is that they always have been, and always continue under every conceivable circumstance to be, their own ideals, whether they are writing their own lives or no. Rousseau opens his book with the statement: "I am not made like any of those I have seen; I venture to believe myself unlike any that exists. If I am not worth more, at least I am different." O exquisite cunning of self-flattery! It is this very imagined difference that makes us worth more in our own foolish sight. For while all men are apt to think, or to persuade themselves that they think, all other men their accomplices in vice or weakness, they are not difficult of belief that they are singular in any quality or talent on which they hug themselves. More than this; people who are truly original are the last to find it out, for the moment we become conscious of a virtue it has left us or is getting ready to go. Originality does not consist in a fidgety assertion of selfhood, but in the faculty of getting rid of it altogether, that the truer genius of the man, which commences with universal nature and with other souls through a common sympathy with that, may take all his powers wholly to itself—and the truly original man could no more be jealous of his peculiar gift, than the grass could take credit to itself for being green. What is the reason that all children are geniuses (though they contrive so soon to outgrow that dangerous quality), except that they never cross-examine themselves on the subject? The moment that process begins, their speech loses its gift of unexpectedness, and they become as tediously impertinent as the rest of us.

If there never was anyone like him, if he constituted a genius in himself, to what end write confessions in which no other human being could ever be in a condition to take the least possible interest? All men are interested in Montaigne in proportion as all men find more of themselves in him, and all men see but one image in the glass which the greatest of poets holds up to nature, an image which at once startles and charms them with its familiarity. Fabulists always endow their animals with the passions and desires of men. But if an ox could dictate his confessions, what glimmer of understanding should we find in those bovine confidences, unless on some theory of pre-existence, some blank misgiving of a creature moving about in worlds not realised? The truth is, that we recognise the common humanity of Rousseau in the very weakness that betrayed him into this conceit of himself; we find he is just like the rest of us in this very assumption of essential difference, for among all animals man is the only one who tries to pass for more than he is, and so involves himself in the condemnation of seeming less.

But it would be sheer waste of time to hunt Rousseau through all his doublings of inconsistency, and run him to earth in every new paradox. His first two books attacked, one of them literature, and the other society. But this did not prevent him from being diligent with his pen, nor from availing himself of his credit with persons who enjoyed all the advantages of that inequality whose evils he had so pointedly exposed. Indeed, it is curious to notice how little practical communism there has been, how few professors it has had who would not have gained by a general dividend. It is perhaps no frantic effort of generosity in a philosopher with ten crowns in his pocket when he offers to make common stock with a neighbour who has ten thousand of yearly income, nor is it an uncommon thing to see such theories knocked clean out of a man's head by the descent of a thumping legacy. But, consistent or not, Rousseau remains permanently interesting as the highest and most perfect type of the sentimentalist of genius. His was perhaps the acutest mind that was ever mated with an organisation so diseased, the brain most far-reaching in speculation that ever kept itself steady and worked out its problems amid such disordered tumult of the nerves. His letter to the Archbishop of Paris, admirable for its lucid power and soberness of tone, and his ***Rousseau juge de Jean Jacques,*** which no man can read and believe him to have been sane, show him to us in his strength and weakness, and give us a more charitable, let us hope therefore a truer, notion of him than his own apology for himself. That he was a man of genius appears unmistakably in his impressibility by the deeper meaning of the epoch in which he lived. Before an eruption, clouds steeped through and through with electric life gather over the crater, as if in sympathy and expectation. As the mountain heaves and cracks, these vapoury masses are seamed with fire, as if they felt and answered the dumb agony that is struggling for utterance below. Just such flashes of eager sympathetic fire break continually from the cloudy volumes of Rousseau, the result at once and the warning of that convulsion of which Paris was to be the crater and all Europe to feel the spasm. There are symptoms enough elsewhere of that want of faith in the existing order which made the Revolution inevitable—even so shallow an observer as Horace Walpole could forebode it so early as 1765—but Rousseau more than all others is the unconscious expression of the groping after something radically new, the instinct for a change that should be organic and pervade every fibre of the social and political body. Freedom of thought owes far more to the jester Voltaire, who also had his solid kernel of earnest, than to the sombre Genevese, whose earnestness is of the deadly kind. Yet, for good or evil, the latter was the father of modern democracy, and without him our Declaration of Independence would have wanted some of those sentences in which the immemorial longings of the poor and the dreams of solitary enthusiasts were at last affirmed as axioms in the manifesto of a nation, so that all the world might hear.

Though Rousseau, like many other fanatics, had a remarkable vein of common-sense in him (witness his remarks on duelling, on landscape-gardening, on French poetry, and much of his thought on education), we cannot trace many practical results to his teaching, least of all in politics. For the great difficulty with his system, if system it may be called, is, that, while it professes to follow nature, it not only assumes as a starting-point that the individual man may be made over again, but proceeds to the conclusion that man himself, that human nature, must be made over again, and governments remodelled on a purely theoretic basis. But when something like an experiment in this direction was made in 1789, not only did it fail as regarded man in general, but even as regards the particular variety of man that inhabited France. The Revolution accomplished many changes, and beneficent ones, yet it left France peopled, not by a new race without traditions, but by Frenchmen. Still, there could not but be a wonderful force in the words of a man who, above all others, had the secret of making abstractions glow with his own fervour; and his ideas—dispersed now in the atmosphere of thought—have influenced, perhaps still continue to influence, speculative minds, which prefer swift and sure generalisation to hesitating and doubtful experience.

Rousseau has, in one respect, been utterly misrepresented and misunderstood. Even Châteaubriand most unfilially classes him and Voltaire together. It appears to me that the inmost core of his being was religious. Had he remained in the Catholic Church he might have been a saint. Had he come earlier, he might have founded an order. His was precisely the nature on which religious enthusiasm takes the strongest hold—a temperament which finds a sensuous delight in spiritual things, and satisfies its craving for excitement with celestial debauch. He had not the iron temper of a great reformer and organiser like Knox, who, true Scotchman that he was, found a way to weld this world and the other together in a cast-iron creed; but he had as much as any man ever had that gift of a great preacher to make the oratorical fervour which persuades himself while it lasts into the abiding conviction of his hearers. That very persuasion of his, that the soul could remain pure while the life was corrupt, is not unexampled among men who have left holier names than he. His *Confessions,* also, would assign him to that class with whom the religious sentiment is strong, and the moral nature weak. They are apt to believe that they may, as special pleaders say, confess and avoid. Hawthorne has admirably illustrated this in the penance of Mr. Dimmesdale. With all the soil that is upon Rousseau, I cannot help looking on him as one capable beyond any in his generation of being divinely possessed; and if it happened otherwise, when we remember the much that hindered and the little that helped in a life and time like his, we shall be much readier to pity than to condemn. It was his very fitness for being something better that makes him able to shock us so with what in too many respects he unhappily was. Less gifted, he had been less hardly judged. More than any other of the sentimentalists, except possibly Sterne, he had in him a staple of sincerity. Compared with Châteaubriand, he is honesty, compared with Lamartine, he is manliness itself. His nearest congener in our own tongue is Cowper.

In the whole school there is a sickly taint. The strongest mark which Rousseau has left upon literature is a sensibility to the picturesque in Nature, not with Nature as a strengthener and consoler, a wholesome tonic for a mind ill at ease with itself, but with Nature as a kind of feminine echo to the mood, flattering it with sympathy rather than correcting it with rebuke or lifting it away from its unmanly depression, as in the wholesomer fellow-feeling of Wordsworth. They seek in her an accessory, and not a reproof. It is less a sympathy with Nature than a sympathy with ourselves as we compel her to reflect us. It is solitude, Nature for her estrangement from man, not for her companionship with him—it is desolation and ruin, Nature as she has triumphed over man—with which this order of mind seeks communion, and in which it finds solace. It is with the hostile and destructive power of matter, and not with the spirit of life and renewal that dwells in it, that they ally themselves. And in human character it is the same. St. Preux, René, Werther, Manfred, Quasimodo—they are all anomalies, distortions, ruins; so much easier is it to caricature life from our own sickly conception of it, than to paint it in its noble simplicity; so much cheaper is unreality than truth.

Every man is conscious that he leads two lives—the one trivial and ordinary, the other sacred and recluse; one which he carries to society and the dinner-table, the other in which his youth and aspiration survive for him, and which is a confidence between himself and God. Both may be equally sincere, and there need be no contradiction between them, any more than in a healthy man between soul and body. If the higher life be real and earnest, its result, whether in literature or affairs, will be real and earnest too. But no man can produce great things who is not thoroughly sincere in dealing with himself, who would not exchange the finest show for the poorest reality, who does not so love his work that he is not only glad to give himself for it, but finds rather a gain than a sacrifice in the surrender. The sentimentalist does not think of what he does so much as of what the world will think of what he does. He translates should into would, looks upon the spheres of duty and beauty as alien to each other, and can never learn how life rounds itself to a noble completeness between these two opposite but mutually sustaining poles of what we long for and what we must.

Did Rousseau, then, lead a life of this quality? Perhaps, when we consider the contrast which every man who looks backward must feel between the life he planned and the life which circumstance within him and without him has made for him, we should rather ask, Was this the life he meant to lead? Perhaps, when we take into account his faculty of self-deception—it may be no greater than our own—we should ask, Was this the life he believed he led? Have we any right to judge this man after our blunt English fashion, and condemn him, as we are wont to do, on the finding of a jury of average householders? Is French reality precisely our reality? Could we tolerate tragedy in rhymed alexandrines, instead of blank verse? The whole life of Rousseau is pitched on this heroic key, and for the most trivial occasion he must be ready with the sublime sentiments that are supposed to suit him rather than it. It is one of the most curious features of the sentimental ailment, that, while it shuns the contact of men, it courts publicity. In proportion as solitude and communion with self lead the sentimentalist to exaggerate the importance of his own personality, he comes to think that the least event connected with it is of consequence to his fellowmen. If he change his shirt, he would have mankind aware of it. Victor Hugo, the greatest living representative of the class, considers it necessary to let the world know by letter from time to time his opinions on every conceivable subject about which it is not asked nor is of the least value unless we concede to him an immediate inspiration. We men of colder blood, in whom self-consciousness takes the form of pride, and who have deified *mauvaise honte* as if our defect were our virtue, find it especially hard to understand that artistic impulse of more southern races to *pose* themselves properly on every occasion, and not even to die without some tribute of deference to the taste of the world they are leaving. Was not even mighty Cæsar's last thought of his drapery? Let us not condemn Rousseau for what seems to us the indecent exposure of himself in his *Confessions.*

Those who allow an oratorical and purely conventional side disconnected with our private understanding of the facts, and with life, in which everything has a wholly parliamentary sense where truth is made subservient to the momentary exigencies of eloquence, should be charitable to Rousseau. While we encourage a distinction which establishes two kinds of truth, one for the world, and another for the conscience, while we take pleasure in a kind of speech that has no relation to the real thought of speaker or hearer, but to the rostrum only, we must not be hasty to condemn a sentimentalism which we do our best to foster. We listen in public with the gravity of augurs to what we smile at when we meet a brother adept. France is the native land of eulogy, of truth padded out to the size and shape demanded by *comme-il-faut*. The French Academy has, perhaps, done more harm by the vogue it has given to this style, than it has done good by its literary purism; for the best purity of a language depends on the limpidity of its source in veracity of thought. Rousseau was in many respects a typical Frenchman, and it is not to be wondered at if he too often fell in with the fashion of saying what was expected of him, and what he thought due to the situation, rather than what would have been true to his inmost consciousness. Perhaps we should allow something also to the influence of a Calvinistic training, which certainly helps men who have the least natural tendency towards it to set faith above works, and to persuade themselves of the efficacy of an inward grace to offset an outward and visible defection from it.

As the sentimentalist always takes a fanciful, sometimes an unreal, life for an ideal one, it would be too much to say that Rousseau was a man of earnest convictions. But he was a man of fitfully intense ones, as suited so mobile a temperament, and his writings, more than those of any other of his tribe, carry with them that persuasion that was in him while he wrote. In them at least he is as consistent as a man who admits new ideas can ever be. The children of his brain he never abandoned, but clung to them with paternal fidelity. Intellectually he was true and fearless; constitutionally, timid, contradictory, and weak; but never, if we understand him rightly, false. He was a little too credulous of sonorous sentiment, but he was never, like Châteaubriand or Lamartine, the lackey of fine phrases. If, as some fanciful physiologists have assumed, there be a masculine and feminine lobe of the brain, it would seem that in men of sentimental turn the masculine half fell in love with and made an idol of the other, obeying and admiring all the pretty whims of this *folle du logis*. In Rousseau the mistress had some noble elements of character, and less taint of the *demi-monde* than is visible in more recent cases of the same illicit relation. (pp. 329-37)

> *James Russell Lowell, "Rousseau and the Sentimentalists," in his* The English Poets: Lessing, Rousseau, *1888. Reprint by Kennikat Press, 1970, pp. 311-37.*

T. H. Huxley　(essay date 1890)

[*Huxley was a prominent nineteenth-century English biologist. He was also the grandfather of Aldous Huxley, the noted twentieth-century novelist and critic. He is primarily recognized as the foremost English advocate of Darwin's theory of evolution. In the following excerpt, he criticizes the political and social speculations offered in the* Discours sur l'origine de l'inégalité *and* The Social Contract, *focusing on the issue of property ownership.*]

The political speculations set forth in Rousseau's ***Discours***

sur l'origine de l'inégalité parmi les hommes, and in the more noted essay, ***Du Contrat Social,*** which were published, the former in 1754 and the latter eight years later, are, for the most part, if not wholly, founded upon conceptions with the origination of which he had nothing to do. The political, like the religious, revolutionary movement of the eighteenth century in France came from England. Hobbes, primarily, and Locke, secondarily (Rousseau was acquainted with the writings of both), supplied every notion of fundamental importance which is to be found in the works which I have mentioned. But the skill of a master of the literary art and the fervour of a prophet combined to embellish and intensify the new presentation of old speculations; which had the further good fortune to address itself to a public as ripe and ready as Balak himself to accept the revelations of any seer whose prophecies were to its mind.

Missionaries, whether of philosophy or of religion, rarely make rapid way, unless their preachings fall in with the prepossessions of the multitude of shallow thinkers, or can be made to serve as a stalking-horse for the promotion of the practical aims of the still larger multitude, who do not profess to think much, but are quite certain they want a great deal. Rousseau's writings are so admirably adapted to touch both these classes that the effect they produced, especially in France, is easily intelligible. For, in the middle of the eighteenth century, French society (not perhaps so different as may be imagined from other societies before and since) presented two large groups of people who troubled themselves about politics—in any sense other than that of personal or party intrigue. There was an upper stratum of luxurious idlers, jealously excluded from political action and consequently ignorant of practical affairs, with no solid knowledge or firm principles of any sort; but, on the other hand, open-minded to every novelty which could be apprehended without too much trouble, and exquisitely appreciative of close deductive reasoning and clear exposition. Such a public naturally welcomed Rousseau's brilliant developments of plausible first principles by the help of that *à priori* method which saves so much troublesome investigation. It just suited the 'philosophes,' male and female, interchanging their airy epigrams in salons, which had about as much likeness to the Academy or to the Stoa, as the 'philosophes' had to the philosophers of antiquity.

I do not forget the existence of men of the type of Montesquieu or D'Argenson in the France of the eighteenth century, when I take this as a fair representation of the enlightened public of that day. The unenlightened public, on the other hand, the people who were morally and physically debased by sheer hunger; or those, not so far dulled or infuriated by absolute want, who yet were maddened by the wrongs of every description inflicted upon them by a political system, which so far as its proper object, the welfare of the people, was concerned was effete and powerless; the subjects of a government smitten with paralysis for everything but the working of iniquity and the generation of scandals; these naturally bailed with rapture the appearance of the teacher who clothed passion in the garb of philosophy; and preached the sweeping away of injustice by the perpetration of further injustice, as if it were nothing but the conversion of sound theory into practice.

It is true that anyone who has looked below the surface

will hardly be disposed to join in the cry which is so often raised against the 'philosophes' that their 'infidel and levelling' principles brought about the French Revolution. People, like the Marquis d'Argenson, with political eyes in their heads, saw that the Revolution was inevitable before Rousseau wrote a line. In truth, the Bull 'Unigenitus,' the interested restiveness of the Parliaments and the extravagancies and profligacy of the Court had a great deal more influence in generating the catastrophe than all the 'philosophes' that ever put pen to paper. But, undoubtedly, Rousseau's extremely attractive and widely read writings did a great deal to give a colour of rationality to those principles of '89 which, even after the lapse of a century, are considered by a good many people to be the Magna Charta of the human race. 'Liberty, Equality, and Fraternity,' is still the war-cry of those, and they are many, who think, with Rousseau, that human sufferings must needs be the consequence of the artificial arrangements of society and can all be alleviated or removed by political changes. (pp. 1-3)

[It] is needful to observe that the dicta of the author of the **Contrat Social,** published in 1762, are not unfrequently very hard—indeed I might say impossible—to reconcile with those of the author of the **Discours,** which appeared eight years earlier; and that, if any one should maintain that the older essay was not meant to be taken seriously, or that it has been, in some respects, more or less set aside by the later, he might find strong grounds for his opinion. It is enough for me that the same *à priori* method and the same fallacious assumptions pervade both.

The thesis of the earlier work is that man, in the 'state of nature,' was a very excellent creature indeed, strong, healthy, good and contented; and that all the evils which have befallen him, such as feebleness, sickness, wickedness, and misery, result from his having forsaken the 'state of nature' for the 'state of civilisation.' And the first step in this downward progress was the setting up of rights of several property. It might seem to a plain man that the argument here turns on a matter of fact: if it is not historically true that men were once in this 'state of nature'—what becomes of it all? However, Rousseau tells us, in the preface to the **Discours,** not only that the 'state of nature' is something which no longer exists, but that 'perhaps it never existed, and probably never will exist.' Yet it is something 'of which it is nevertheless necessary to have accurate notions in order to judge our present condition rightly.'. . . [The] amount of philosophy required to base an argument on that which does not exist, has not existed, and, perhaps, never will exist, may well seem unattainable—at any rate, at first sight. Yet, apart from analogies which might be drawn from the mathematical sciences— where, for example, a straight line is a thing which has not existed, does not exist, and probably never will exist, and yet forms a good ground for reasoning; and the value of which I need not stop to discuss—I take it that Rousseau has a very comprehensible idea at the bottom of this troublesome statement. What I conceive him to mean is that it is possible to form an ideal conception of what ought to be the condition of mankind; and that, having done so, we are bound to judge the existing state of things by that ideal. That assumption puts us on the 'high *priori* road' at once.

I do not suppose that any one is inclined to doubt the use-

fulness of a political ideal as a goal towards which social conduct should strive, whether it can ever be completely realised or not; any more than any one will doubt that it is useful to have a moral ideal towards which personal conduct should tend, even though one may never reach it. Certainly, I am the last person to question this, or to doubt that politics is as susceptible of treatment by scientific method as any other field of natural knowledge. But it will be admitted that, great as are the advantages of having a political ideal, fashioned by an absolute rule of political conduct, it is perhaps better to do without one, rather than to adopt the first phantasm, bred of fallacious reasonings and born of the unscientific imagination, which presents itself. The benighted traveller, lost on a moor, who refuses to follow a man with a lantern is surely not to be commended. But suppose his hesitation arises from a wellgrounded doubt as to whether the seeming luminary is anything but a will o' the wisp? And, unless I fail egregiously in attaining my purpose, those who read this paper to the end will, I think, have no doubt that the political lantern of Rousseauism is a mere corpse candle and will plunge those who follow it in the deepest of anarchic bogs.

There is another point which must be carefully borne in mind in any discussion of Rousseau's doctrines; and that is the meaning which he attaches to the word 'inequality.' A hundred and fifty years ago, as now, political and biological philosophers found they were natural allies. Rousseau is not intelligible without Buffon, with whose earlier works he was evidently acquainted, and whose influence in the following passage is obvious:—

> It is easy to see that we must seek the primary cause of the differences by which men are distinguished in these successive changes of the human constitution; since it is universally admitted that they are, naturally, as equal among themselves as were the animals of each species before various physical causes had produced, in some of them, the varieties which we observe. In fact, it is not conceivable that these first changes, by whatever means they were brought about, altered, at once and in the same way, all the individuals of a species; but some having become improved or deteriorated, and having acquired different qualities, good or bad, which were not inherent in their nature, the others remained longer in their original state; and such was the first source of inequality among men, which is more easy to prove thus, in a general way, than to assign exactly to its true causes.

In accordance with this conception of the origin of inequality among men, Rousseau distinguishes, at the outset of the **Discours,** two kinds of inequality:

> the one which I term *natural,* or *physical,* because it is established by nature, and which consists in the differences of age, health, bodily strength, and intellectual or spiritual qualities; the other, which may be called *moral,* or *political,* because it depends on a sort of convention, and is established, or at least authorised, by the consent of mankind. This last inequality consists in the different privileges which some enjoy, to the prejudice of others, as being richer, more honoured, more powerful than they, or by making themselves obeyed by others.

Of course the question readily suggests itself: Before drawing this sharp line of demarcation between natural and political inequality, might it not be as well to inquire whether they are not intimately connected, in such a manner that the latter is essentially a consequence of the former? This question is indeed put by Rousseau himself. And, as the only answer he has to give is a piece of silly and insincere rhetoric about its being a question fit only for slaves to discuss in presence of their masters, we may fairly conclude that he knew well enough he dare not grapple with it. The only safe course for him was to go by on the other side and as far as the breadth of the road would permit; and, in the rest of his writings, to play fast and loose with the two senses of inequality, as convenience might dictate.

With these preliminary remarks kept well in view, we may proceed to the discussion of those fundamental theses of the **Discourse** and of the **Social Contract** which Rousseau calls the 'principes du droit politique.' (pp. 5-7)

[Our] philosopher propounds 'sure,' that is 'absolute,' principles which are, at once ethically and politically, sufficient rules of conduct, and that I understand to be the precise object of all who have followed in his track. It was said of the Genevese theorist, 'Le genre humain avait perdu ses titres; Jean-jacques les a retrouvés;' just as his intellectual progeny declare that the nation ought to 're-sume' the landed property of which it has, unfortunately, lost the title-deeds.

We are now in a position to consider what the chief of these principles of the gospel according to Jean Jacques are:—

1. All men are born free, politically equal, and good, and in the 'state of nature' remain so; consequently it is their natural right to be free, equal, and (presumably, their duty to be) good.

2. All men being equal by natural right, none can have any right to encroach on another's equal right. Hence no man can appropriate any part of the common means of subsistence—that is to say, the land or anything which the land produces—without the unanimous consent of all other men. Under any other circumstances, property is usurpation, or, in plain terms, robbery.

3. Political rights, therefore, are based upon contract; the so-called right of conquest is no right, and property which has been acquired by force may rightly be taken away by force.

I am bound to confess, at the outset, that, while quite open to conviction, I incline to think that the obvious practical consequences of these propositions are not likely to conduce to the welfare of society, and that they are certain to prove as injurious to the poor as to the rich. Due allowance must be made for the possible influence of such prejudice as may flow from this opinion upon my further conviction that, regarded from a purely theoretical and scientific point of view, they are so plainly and demonstrably false that, except for the gravity of their practical consequences, they would be ridiculous.

What is the meaning of the famous phrase that 'all men are born free and equal,' which gallicised Americans, who were as much 'philosophes' as their inherited common sense and their practical acquaintance with men and with affairs would let them be, put forth as the foundation of the 'Declaration of Independence'? I have seen a considerable number of new-born infants. Without wishing to speak of them with the least disrespect—a thing no man can do, without, as the proverb says, 'fouling his own nest'—I fail to understand how they can be affirmed to have any political qualities at all. How can it be said that these poor little mortals who have not even the capacity to kick to any definite end, nor indeed to do anything but vaguely squirm and squall, are equal politically, except as all zeros may be said to be equal? How can little creatures be said to be 'free' of whom not one would live for four and twenty hours if it were not imprisoned by kindly hands and coerced into applying its foolish wandering mouth to the breast it could never find for itself? How is the being whose brain is still too pulpy to hold an idea of any description to be a moral agent either good or bad? Surely it must be a joke, and rather a cynical one too, to talk of the political status of a new-born child? But we may carry out questions a step further. If it is mere abracadabra to speak of men being born in a state of political freedom and equality, thus fallaciously confusing positive equality—that is to say, the equality of powers—with the equality of impotences; in what conceivable state of society is it possible that men should not merely be born, but pass through childhood and still remain free? Has a child of fourteen been free to choose its language and all the connotations with which words became burdened in their use by generation after generation? Has it been free to choose the habits enforced by precept and more surely driven home by example? Has it been free to invent its own standard of right and wrong? Or rather, has it not been as much held in bondage by its surroundings and driven hither and thither by the scourge of opinion, as a veritable slave, although the fetters and the whip may be invisible and intangible?

Surely, Aristotle was much nearer the truth in this matter than Hobbes or Rousseau. And if the predicate 'born slave' would more nearly agree with fact than 'born free,' what is to be said about 'born equal'? Rousseau, like the sentimental rhetorician that he was, and half, or more than half, sham, as all sentimental rhetoricians are, sagaciously fought shy, as we have seen, of the question of the influence of natural upon political equality. But those of us who do not care for sentiment and do care for truth may not evade the consideration of that which is really the key of the position. If Rousseau, instead of letting his children go to the *enfants trouvés,* had taken the trouble to discharge a father's duties towards them, he would hardly have talked so fast about men being born equal, even in a political sense. For, if that merely means that all newborn children are political zeros—it is, as we have seen, though true enough, nothing to the purpose; while, if it means that, in their potentiality of becoming factors in any social organisation—citizens in Rousseau's sense—all men are born equal, it is probably the most astounding falsity that ever was put forth by a political speculator; and that, as all students of political speculation will agree, is saying a good deal for it. In fact, nothing is more remarkable than the wide inequality which children, even of the same family, exhibit, as soon as the mental and moral qualities begin to manifest themselves; which is earlier than most people fancy. Every family spontaneously becomes a polity. Among the children, there are some who continue to be 'more honoured and more powerful than the rest, and to make themselves obeyed' (sometimes, indeed, by their elders) in virtue of nothing but their moral and mental qualities. Here, 'political inequality' visibly dogs the heels of 'natural' inequality. The group of children becomes a political body, a *civitas,* with its rights of property, and its practical distinctions of rank and power. And all this comes about neither by force nor by fraud, but as the necessary consequence of the innate inequalities of capability.

Thus men are certainly not born free and equal in natural qualities; when they are born, the predicates 'free' and 'equal' in the political sense are not applicable to them; and as they develop, year by year, the differences in the political potentialities with which they really are born, become more and more obviously converted into actual differences—the inequality of political faculty shows itself to be a necessary consequence of the inequality of natural faculty. It is probably true that the earliest men were nomads. But among a body of naked wandering savages, though there may be no verbally recognised distinctions of rank or office, superior strength and cunning confer authority of a more valid kind than that secured by Acts of Parliament; there may be no property in things, but the witless man will be poverty-stricken in ideas, the clever man will be a capitalist in that same commodity, which in the long run buys all other commodities; one will miss opportunities, the other will make them; and, proclaim human equality as loudly as you like, Witless will serve his brother. So long as men are men and society is society, human equality will be a dream; and the assumption that it does exist is as untrue in fact as it sets the mark of impracticability on every theory of what ought to be, which starts from it.

And that last remark suggests that there is another way of regarding Rousseau's speculations. It may be pointed out that, after all, whatever estimate we may form of him, the author of works which have made such a noise in the world could not have been a mere fool; and that, if, in their plain and obvious sense, the doctrines which he advanced are so easily upset, it is probable that he had in his mind something which is different from that sense.

I am a good deal disposed to think that this is the case. There is much to be said in favour of the view that Rousseau, having got hold of a plausible hypothesis, more or less unconsciously made up a clothing of imaginary facts to hide its real nakedness. He was not the first nor the last philosopher to perform this feat. (pp. 8-11)

[The] *à priori* arguments of the philosophers in the last century of the Republic, and the first of the Empire, stand examination no better than those of the philosophers in the centuries before and after the French Revolution. As is the fashion of speculators, they scorned to remain on the safe if humble ground of experience, and preferred to prophesy from the sublime cloudland of the *à priori;* so that, busied with deduction from their ideal 'ought to be' they overlooked the 'what has been,' the 'what is,' and the 'what can be.'

It is to them that we owe the idea of living 'according to nature'; which begot the idea of the 'state of nature'; which begot the notion that the 'state of nature' was a reality, and that, once upon a time, 'all men were free and equal'—which again begot the theory, that society ought to be reformed in such a manner as to bring back these halcyon days of freedom and equality; which begot *laissez faire* and universal suffrage; which begot the theory so dear to

young men of more ambition than industry, that, while every other trade, business, or profession requires theoretical training and practical skill, and would go to the dogs if those who carry them on were appointed by the majority of votes of people who know nothing about it and very little about them—the management of the affairs of society will be perfectly successful, if only the people who may be trusted to know nothing, will vote into office the people who may be trusted to do nothing. (pp. 11-12)

The conclusion of the whole matter, then, would seem to be that the doctrine that all men are, in any sense, or have been, at any time, free and equal, is an utterly baseless fiction. Nor does the proposition fare much better if we modify it, so as to say that all men ought to be free and equal, so long as the 'ought' poses as a command of immutable morality. For, assuredly, it is not intuitively certain 'that all men ought to be free and equal.' Therefore, if it is to be justified at all *à priori,* it must be deducible from some proposition which is intuitively certain; and unfortunately none is forthcoming. For the proposition that men ought to be free to do what they please, so long as they do not infringe on the equal rights of other men, assumes that men have equal rights and cannot be used to prove that assumption. And if, instead of appealing to philosophy we turn to revealed religion, I am not aware that either Judaism or Christianity affirms the political freedom or the political equality of men in Rousseau's sense. They affirm the equality of men before God—but that is an equality either of insignificance or of imperfection.

With the demonstration that men are not all equal under whatever aspect they are contemplated, and that the assumption that they ought to be considered equal has no sort of *à priori* foundation—however much it may, in reference to positive law, with due limitations, be justifiable by considerations of practical expediency—the bottom of Rousseau's argument, from *à priori* ethical assumptions to the denial of the right of an individual to hold private property, falls out. For Rousseau, with more logical consistency than some of those who have come after him, puts the land and its produce upon the same footing. (pp. 12-13)

From Rousseau's point of view, this is, in fact, the only rational conclusion from the premises. The attempt to draw a distinction between land, as a limited commodity, and other things as unlimited, is an obvious fallacy. For, according to him, the total habitable surface of the earth is the property of the whole human race in common. Undoubtedly, the habitable and cultivable land amounts to a definite number of square miles, which, by no effort of human ingenuity, at present known or suspected, can be sensibly increased beyond the area of that part of the globe which is not covered by water; and therefore its quantity is limited. But if the land is limited, so is the quantity of the trees that will grow on it; of the cattle that can be pastured on it; of the crops that can be raised from it; of the minerals that can be dug from it; of the wind; and of the water power, afforded by the limited streams which flow from the limited heights. And, if the human race were to go on increasing in number at its present rate, a time would come when there would not be standing ground for any more; if it were not that, long before that time, they would have eaten up the limited quantity of food-stuffs and died like the locusts that have consumed everything eatable in an oasis of the desert. The attempt to draw a distinction between land as limited in quantity, in the sense, I suppose, that it is something that cannot be imported—and other things as unlimited, because they can be imported—has arisen from the fact that Rousseau's modern followers entertain the delusion that, consistently with their principles, it is possible to suppose that a nation has right of ownership in the land it occupies. If the island of Great Britain is the property of the British nation, then, of course, it is true that they cannot have more than somewhere about 90,000 square miles of land, while the quantity of other things they can import is (for the present, at any rate), practically, if not strictly, unlimited. But how is the assumption that the Britons own Britain, to be reconciled with the great dictum of Rousseau, that a man cannot rightfully appropriate any part of this limited commodity, land, without the unanimous consent of all his fellow men? My strong impression is that if a parti-coloured plébiscite of Europeans, Chinese, Hindoos, Negroes, Red Indians, Maoris, and all the other inhabitants of the terrestrial globe were to decree us to be usurpers, not a soul would budge; and that, if it came to fighting, Mr. Morley's late 'hecklers' might be safely depended upon to hold their native soil against all intruders, and in the teeth of the most absolute of ethical politicians, even though he should prove from Rousseau,

> Exceedingly well
> That such conduct was quite atrocious.

Rousseau's first and second great doctrines having thus collapsed, what is to be said to the third?

Of course, if there are no rights of property but those based on contract, conquest, that is to say, taking possession by force, of itself can confer no right. But, as the doctrine that there are no rights of property but those based on the consent of the whole human race—that is, that A. B. cannot own anything unless the whole of mankind formally signify their assent to his ownership—turns out to be more than doubtful in theory and decidedly inconvenient in practice, we may inquire if there is any better reason for the assertion that force can confer no right of ownership. Suppose that, in the old seafaring days, a pirate attacked an East Indiaman—got soundly beaten and had to surrender. When the pirates had walked the plank or been hanged, had the captain and crew of the East Indiaman no right of property in the prize—I am not speaking of mere legal right, but ethically? But if they had, what is the difference when nations attack one another; when there is no way out of their quarrel but the appeal to force, and the one that gets the better seizes more or less of the other's territory and demands it as the price of peace? In the latter case, in fact, we have a contract, a price paid for an article—to wit peace—delivered, and certain lands taken in exchange; and there can be no question that the buyer's title is based on contract. Even in the former alternative, I see little difference. When they declared war, the parties knew very well that they referred their case to the arbitrament of force; and if contracts are eternally valid, they are fully bound to abide by the decision of the arbitrator whom they have elected to obey. Therefore, even on Hobbes's or Rousseau's principles, it is not by any means clear to my mind that force, or rather the state of express or tacit contract which follows upon force successfully applied, may not be plausibly considered to confer ownership.

But if the question is argued, as I think it ought to be, on empirical grounds—if the real question is not one of imagined *à priori* principle, but of practical expediency—of the conduct which conduces most to human welfare—then it appears to me that there is much to be said for the opinion that force effectually and thoroughly used, so as to render further opposition hopeless, establishes an ownership which should be recognised as soon as possible. I am greatly disposed to think, that when ownership established by force has endured for many generations, and all sorts of contracts have been entered into on the faith of such ownership, the attempt to disturb it is very much to be deprecated on all grounds. For the welfare of society, as for that of individual men, it is surely essential that there should be a statute of limitations in respect of the consequences of wrong-doing. As there is nothing more fatal to nobility of personal character than the nursing of the feeling of revenge—nothing that more clearly indicates a barbarous state of society than the carrying on of a *vendetta,* generation after generation, so I take it to be a plain maxim of that political ethic which does not profess to have any greater authority than agreeableness to good feeling and good sense can confer, that the evil deeds of former generations—especially if they were in accordance with the practices of a less advanced civilisation, and had the sanction of a less refined morality—should, as speedily as possible, be forgotten and buried under better things. (pp. 13-15)

However, the question whether the fact that property in land was originally acquired by force invalidates all subsequent dealings in that property so completely, that no lapse of time, no formal legalization, no passing from hand to hand by free contract through an endless series of owners, can extinguish the right of the nation to take it away by force from the latest proprietor, has rather an academic than a practical interest, so long as the evidence that landed ownership did so arise is wanting. Potent an organon as the *à priori* method may be, its employment in the region of history has rarely been found to yield satisfactory results; and, in this particular case, the confident assertions that land was originally held in common by the whole nation, and that it has been converted into severalty by force, as the outcome of the military spirit rather than by the consent, or contract, characteristic of industrialism, are singularly ill-founded.

Let us see what genuine history has to say to these assertions. Perhaps it might have been pardonable in Rousseau to propound such a statement as that the primitive landowner was either a robber or a cheat; but, in the course of the century and a half which has elapsed since he wrote, and especially in that of the last fifty years, an immense amount of information on the subject of ancient landtenure has come to light; so that it is no longer pardonable, in any one, to content himself with Rousseau's ignorance. Even a superficial glance over the results of modern investigations into anthropology, archæology, ancient law and ancient religion, suffices to show that there is not a particle of evidence that men ever existed in Rousseau's state of nature, and that there are very strong reasons for thinking that they never could have done so, and never will do so.

It is, at the least, highly probable that the nomadic preceded any other social state; and, as the needs of a wandering hunter's or pastor's life are far more simple than any other, it follows that the inequalities of condition must be less obvious among nomads than among settled people. Men who have no costume at all, for example, cannot be said to be unequally clothed; they are, doubtless, more equal than men some of whom are well clothed and others in rags, though the equality is of the negative sort. But it is a profound mistake to imagine that, in the nomadic condition, any more than in any other which has yet been observed, men are either 'free' or 'equal' in Rousseau's sense. I can call to mind no nomadic nation in which women are on an equality with men; nor any in which young men are on the same footing as old men; nor any in which family groups, bound together by blood ties, by their mutual responsibility for bloodshed and by common worship, do not constitute corporate political units, in the sense of the city of the Greeks and Romans. A 'state of nature' in which noble and peaceful, but nude and propertyless, savages sit in solitary meditation under trees, unless they are dining or amusing themselves in other ways, without cares or responsibilities of any sort, is simply another figment of the unscientific imagination. The only uncivilised men of whom anything is really known are hampered by superstitions and enslaved by conventions, as strange as those of the most artificial societies, to an almost incredible degree. Furthermore, I think it may be said with much confidence that the primitive 'landgrabber' did not either force or cheat his co-proprietors into letting him fence in a bit of the land which hitherto was the property of all.

The truth is we do not know, and, probably, never shall know completely, the nature of all the various processes by which the ownership of land was originally brought about. But there is excellent ground for sundry probable conclusions in the fact that almost all parts of the world, and almost all nations, have yielded evidence that, in the earliest settled condition we can get at, land was held as private or several property, and not as the property of the public, or general body of the nation. Now private or several property may be held in one of two ways. The ownership may be vested in a single individual person, in the ordinary sense of that word; or it may be vested in two or more individuals forming a corporation or legal person; that is to say, an entity which has all the duties and responsibilities of an individual person, but is composed of two or more individuals. It is obvious that all the arguments which Rousseau uses against individual landownership apply to corporate landownership. If the rights of A, B, and C are individually *nil*, you cannot make any more of your 0 by multiplying it by 3. (A B C)—the corporation—must be an usurper if A, B, and C taken each by himself is so. Moreover, I think I may take it for granted that those who desire to make the State universal landowner, would eject a corporation from its estates with even less hesitation than they would expel an individual.

The particular method of early landholding of which we have the most widespread traces is that in which each of a great number of moderate-sized portions of the whole territory occupied by a nation is held in complete and inalienable ownership by the males of a family, or of a small number of actual or supposed kindred families, mutually responsible in blood feuds, and worshipping the same God or Gods. No female had any share in the ownership of the land. If she married outside the community she might take

a share of the moveables; and, as a rule, she went to her husband's community. If, however, the community was short of hands, the husband might be taken into it, and then he acquired all the rights and responsibilities of the other members. Children born in the community became full members of it by domicile, so to speak, not by heredity from their parents. This primitive 'city' was lodged in one or more dwellings, each usually standing in a patch of inclosed ground; of arable land in the immediate neighbourhood of the dwellings; while pasture and uncleared forest land lay outside all. Each commune was as jealous of its rights of ownership as the touchiest of squires; but, so long as the population was as scanty in proportion to the occupied territory, as was usually the case in ancient times, the communities got along pretty peaceably with one another. Any notion that all the communities which made up the nation had a sort of corporate overlordship over any one, still more that all the rest of the world had any right to complain of their 'appropriation of the means of subsistence,' most assuredly never entered the heads of our forefathers. But, alongside this corporate several ownership, there is strong ground for the belief that individual ownership was recognised, to a certain extent, even in these early times. The inclosure around each dwelling was understood to belong to the family inhabiting the dwelling; and, for all practical purposes, must have been as much owned by the head of it as a modern entailed estate is owned by the possessor for the time being. Moreover, if any member of the community chose to go outside and clear and cultivate some of the waste, the reclaimed land was thenceforth recognised as his, that is to say, the right of ownership, in virtue of labour spent, was admitted.

Thus it is obvious that, though the early landholders were, to a great extent, collective owners, the imaginary rights of mankind to universal landownership, or even of that of the nation at large to the whole territory occupied, were utterly ignored; that, so far from several ownership being the result of force or fraud, it was the system established with universal assent; and that, from the first, in all probability, individual rights of property, under certain conditions, were fully recognised and respected. Rousseau was, therefore, correct in suspecting that his 'state of nature' had never existed—it never did, nor anything like it. But it may be said, supposing that all this is true, and supposing that the doctrine that Englishmen have no right to their appropriation of English soil is nonsense; it must, nevertheless, be admitted that, at one time, the great body of the nation, consisting of these numerous landowning corporations, composed of comparatively poor men, did own the land. And it must also be admitted that now they do not; but that the land is in the hands of a relatively small number of actually or comparatively rich proprietors, who constitute perhaps not one per cent of the population. What is this but the result of robbery and cheating? The descendants of the robbers and cut-throat soldiers who came over with William of Normandy, have been true to their military instincts, and have 'conveyed' the property of the primitive corporations into their own possession. No doubt, that is history made easy; but here, once more, fact and *à priori* speculations cannot be made to fit.

Let us look at the case dispassionately, and by the light of real history. No doubt, the early system of land tenure by collective several ownership was excellently adapted to the

Title page of Rousseau's Second Discourse, *published in 1755.*

by the opponents of individual ownership, that, by the extension of the private appropriation of the means of subsistence, the time would arrive when men would come into the world for whom there was no place, must needs make its appearance under any system, unless mankind are prevented from multiplying indefinitely. For, even if the habitable land is the property of the whole human race, the multiplication of that race must, as we have seen, sooner or later, bring its numbers up to the maximum which the produce can support; and then the interesting problem in casuistry, which even absolute political ethics may find puzzling, will arise: Are we, who can just exist, bound to admit the new-comers who will simply starve themselves and us? If the rule that any one may exercise his freedom only as far as he does not interfere with the freedom of others is all-sufficient, it is clear that the new-comers will have no rights to exist at all, inasmuch as they will interfere most seriously with the freedom of their predecessors. The population question is the real riddle of the sphinx, to which no political Œdipus has as yet found the answer. In view of the ravages of the terrible monster over-multiplication, all other riddles sink into insignificance.

But to return to the question of the manner in which individual several ownership has, in our own and some other countries, superseded communal several ownership. There is an exceedingly instructive chapter in M. de Laveleye's well-known work on 'Primitive Property,' entitled 'The Origin of Inequality in Landed Property.' And I select M. de Laveleye as a witness the more willingly, because he draws very different conclusions from the facts he so carefully adduces to those which they appear to me to support.

After enumerating various countries in which, as M. de Laveleye thinks, inequality and an aristocracy were the result of conquest, he asks very pertinently—

> But how were they developed in such countries as Germany, which know nothing of conquerors coming to create a privileged caste above a vanquished and enslaved population? Originally we see in Germany associations of free and independent peasants like the inhabitants of Uri, Schwyz, and Unterwalden at the present day. At the close of the middle ages we find, in the same country, a feudal aristocracy resting more heavily on the soil, and a rustic population more completely enslaved than in England, Italy, or France.

The author proceeds to answer the question which he propounds by showing, in the first place, that the admission of the right of individuals and their heirs to the land they had reclaimed, which was so general, if not universal, created hereditary individual property alongside the communal property, so that private estates arose in the waste between the sparse communal estates. Now, it was not every family or member of a community that was enterprising enough to go out and clear waste lands, or that had the courage to defend its possessions when once obtained. The originally small size of the domains thus acquired, and the strong stimulus of personal interest, led to the introduction of better methods of cultivation than those traditional in the communes. And, finally, as the private owner got little or no benefit from the community, he was exempted from the charges and *corvées* laid upon its members. The result, as may be imagined, was that the private proprietors, aided by serf-labour, prospered more than the com-

circumstances in which mankind found themselves. If it had not been so, it would not have endured so long, nor would it have been adopted by all sorts of different races—from the ancient Irish to the Hindoos, and from the Russians to the Kaffirs and Japanese. These circumstances were in the main as follows: that there was plenty of land unoccupied; that population was very scanty and increased slowly; that wants were simple; that people were content to go on living in the same way, generation after generation; that there was no commerce worth speaking of; that manufactures were really that which they are etymologically—things made by the hands; and that there was no need of capital in the shape of money. Moreover, with such methods of warfare as then existed, the system was good for defence, and not bad for offence.

Yet, even if left to itself, to develop undisturbedly, without the intrusion of force, fraud, or militarism in any shape, the communal system, like the individual-owner system or the State-owner system, or any other system that the wit of man has yet devised, would sooner or later have had to face the everlasting agrarian difficulty. And the more the communities enjoyed general health, peace, and plenty, the sooner would the pressure of population upon the means of support make itself felt. The difficulty paraded munities cultivated by their free members, seriously hampered them by occupying fresh waste lands, yielded more produce, and furnished wealth, which, with the help of the *majorat* system, remained concentrated in the hands of owners who, in virtue of their possessions, could maintain retainers; while, freed from the need to labour, they could occupy themselves with war and the chase, and, as nobles, attend the sovereign. On the other hand, their brethren, left behind in the communes, had little chance of growing individually rich or powerful, and had to give themselves up to agricultural toil. The Bishop of Oxford, in his well-known *Constitutional History of England,* puts the case, as his wont is, concisely and precisely: 'As the population increased, and agriculture itself improved, the mark system must have been superseded everywhere.' No doubt, when the nobles had once established themselves, they often added force and fraud to their other means of enlarging their borders. But, to begin with, the inequality was the result, not of militarism, but of industrialism. Clearing a piece of land for the purpose of cultivating it and reaping the crops for one's own advantage is surely an industrial operation, if ever there was one.

Secondly, M. de Laveleye points out that the Church was a great devourer of commune lands:—

> We know that a member of the commune could only dispose of his share with the consent of his associates, who had a right of resumption; but this right could not be exercised against the Church. Accordingly, in these days of religious fervour, the faithful frequently left to the Church all that they possessed, not only their house and its inclosure, but the undivided share in the *mark* attached to it.

Thus an abbot, or a bishop, became co-proprietor with the peasants of a commune; and, with such a cuckoo in the nest, one can conceive that the hedge-sparrows might have a bad time. 'Already by the end of the ninth century one third of the whole soil of Gaul belonged to the clergy'. But, if the men who left their property to the Church believed that they got their *quid pro quo* in the shape of masses for their souls, as they certainly did; and if the Churchmen believed as sincerely (and they certainly did) that they gave valuable consideration for the property left them, where does fraud come in? Is it not again a truly industrial operation? Indeed, a keen-witted and eminent Scotch judge once called a huge bequest to a Church 'fire insurance,' so emphatically commercial did the transaction appear to him.

Thirdly, personal several property was carved out of the corporate communal property in another fashion, to which no objection can be taken by industrialism. Plots of arable land were granted to members of the commune who were skilled artificers, as a salary for their services. The craft transmitting itself from father to son, the land went with it and grew into an hereditary benefice.

Fourthly, Sir Henry Maine has proved in a very striking manner, from the collection of the Brehon Laws of ancient Ireland, how the original communal landownership of the sept, with the allotment of an extra allowance of pasture to the chief, as the honorarium for his services of all kinds, became modified, in consequence of the power of keeping more cattle than the rest of the sept, thus conferred on the chief. He became a lender of cattle at a high rate of interest to his more needy sept-fellows, who when they borrowed

became bound to do him service in other ways and lost status by falling into the position of his debtors. Hence the chief gradually acquired the characteristics of what naturalists have called 'synthetic' and 'prophetic' types, combining the features of the modern gombeen-man with those of the modern rack-renting landlord, who is commonly supposed to be a purely imported Norman or Saxon product, saturated with the very spirit of industrialism—namely, the determination to get the highest price for an article which is to be had. As a fact, the condition of the native Irish, under their own chiefs, was as bad in Queen Elizabeth's time as it has ever been since. Again, the status of the original commoners of the sept was steadily altered for the worse by the privilege which the chief possessed, and of which he freely availed himself, of settling on the waste land of the commune such broken vagabonds of other tribes as sought his patronage and protection, and who became absolutely dependent upon him. Thus, without war and without any necessity for force or fraud (though doubtless there was an adventitious abundance of both), the communal system was bound to go to pieces, and to be replaced by individual ownership, in consequence of the operation of purely industrial causes. That is to say, in consequence of the many commercial advantages of individual ownership over communal ownership; which became more and more marked exactly in proportion as territory became more fully occupied, security of possession increased, and the chances of the success of individual enterprise and skill as against routine, in an industrial occupation, became greater and greater.

The notion that all individual ownership of land is the result of force and fraud appears to me to be on a level with the peculiarly short-sighted prejudice that all religions are the results of sacerdotal cunning and imposture. As religions are the inevitable products of the human mind, which generates the priest and the prophet as much as it generates the faithful; so the inequality of individual ownership has grown out of the relative equality of communal ownership in virtue of those natural inequalities of men, which, if unimpeded by circumstances, cannot fail to give rise quietly and peaceably to corresponding political inequalities.

The task I have set myself is completed, as far as it can be within reasonable limits. I trust that those who have taken the trouble to follow the argument, will agree with me that the gospel of Jean Jacques, in its relation to property, is a very sorry affair—that it is the product of an untrustworthy method, applied to assumptions which are devoid of foundation in fact; and that nothing can be more profoundly true than the saying of the great and truly philosophical English jurist, whose recent death we all deplore, that speculations of this sort are rooted in 'impatience of experience, and the preference of *à priori* to all other methods of reasoning.' (pp. 16-23)

> *T. H. Huxley, "On the Natural Inequality of Men," in* The Nineteenth Century, *Vol. XXVII, No. CLV, January, 1890, pp. 1-23.*

Leonora Blanche Lang (essay date 1891)

[*Wife of noted Scottish man of letters Andrew Lang, Leonora Blanche Lang was also a translator, novelist, and essayist. In the following excerpt, she analyzes the*

habits of the Wolmar household in La Nouvelle Héloïse.]

What did Rousseau think in after days, when the ***Nouvelle
Héloïse*** became the rage in Paris, and fine ladies stayed
away from a ball, and sent away their carriages at dawn,
unable to tear themselves away from the fascinating love-
story? Possibly it may have occurred to him that the state
of things described in the book was a vast improvement
on the actual condition of manners prevalent in Paris in
1757, when the ***Nouvelle Héloïse*** was published, or he
may have held the wide-spread theory that a married
woman can read with impunity literature that is fraught
with peril for a mere spinster.

However that might be, one thing is certain, that any one
who expects consistency in Rousseau is doomed to woful
disappointment. The well-meaning, ill-doing, ungrateful
atom of humanity, with *l'esprit et la vanité comme quatre,*
as Mlle. d'Ette truly says of him, had every opportunity
of knowing men and seeing life in all its modes. But he
mingled with his fellows possessed by a pre-conceived
idea, and only found what he looked for, which was the
bad side of the people that he met, and the unfortunate results of their mode of existence and of their education.

Still, in the intervals of heaping abuse on those who had
shown him nothing but kindness, he gave his attention to
improving the condition of the world generally, striking
at once at the root of the matter, in the bringing up of the
children. One of the most interesting and amusing aspects
of the whole question is the gigantic effort of Rousseau to
descend to practical details—Rousseau, who always cut
the knot of a difficulty by calmly running away. It is likewise quite in keeping with this extraordinary being that in
the midst of a whole host of transcendental notions, utterly incompatible with life in a community, he will lay down
some precepts which are not only useful, but absolutely
sensible and wise. (pp. 175-76)

[To] understand rightly Rousseau's views as to the conduct of a family, we must consider also the educational
principles laid down in ***Emile,*** published four years later.

Both books are ostensibly a crusade against the luxury and
artificiality of the age; yet in every page the self-
consciousness and want of simplicity characteristic of
their author are apparent. Apparent, too, is the inability
to realize the bearings of things which no experience of society could ever teach Rousseau. The man who had lived
with Genevese shopkeepers and Savoyard peasants, who
had mixed familiarly with Diderot, Grimm, and the aristocracy of finance, who was the secretary and friend of
some of the greatest ladies in France, the Comtesse
d'Egmont and Mme. de Brionne, was incapable, to the end
of his life, of learning the lessons of facts. His precepts are
totally unfitted for the give and take of society; they demand special beings amid special conditions in order to be
carried out. "Have you ever been so foolish as to believe
in Rousseau and his ***'Emile'?***" writes the Abbé Galiani to
Mme. d'Epinay in January, 1771. "Do you really think
that education, maxims, and lectures have any effect in
moulding our minds? If so, take a wolf, and turn him into
a dog."

This, of course, is an extreme way of putting the case; but
Rousseau's people only blossom in a state of isolation, and
are not fitted for contact with the world; and by his own

showing, in the instance of the ideal Emile's ideal wife Sophie, when they *do* come into collision with it, their principles are apt to give way. We could, most of us, be good
if we were not tempted, and if we lived under a perpetual
rule of thumb. In spite of all Rousseau's talk about freedom and happiness, this is what his characters really do.
To prove the truth of this statement, we have only to look
at the regulations laid down for the Wolmar household,
the neighboring village, and the education of children, all
of which may be gathered from the letters of St. Preux,
now an honored (though somewhat strange) guest of the
Wolmars, to his friend Lord Bomston.

First, as to the servants and dependents. The main thing
that strikes the reader (after the happy thought of choosing an English peer as the recipient of those details, imagine "old Q." in similar circumstances) is the artificiality
of all those personages. No one has any opportunity of developing an individuality of his own, or is allowed a spontaneous movement. Every hour is regulated and employed; the servants only exist for the glorification of *les
maîtres.* Sublime self-confidence is the foundation of the
Wolmar system, and a proportionately rooted mistrust of
the schemes of others. It is a fixed principle with them to
take their servants young and fresh from large families in
the villages round, and to train them themselves, *because*
it is a foregone conclusion that servants taken from another place will have learnt nothing but the vices of their em-
ployers, and so will ruin their masters (always meaning
the Wolmars), and corrupt their children. Modern mistresses need not exclaim at the amount of time and trouble
involved in educating a cook, for instance, in the manifold
tricks of her trade; it was quite worth Mme. Wolmar's
while to teach her, as no servant was ever known to give
warning in that fortunate house, and, once there, she was
certain to stay forever. One great inducement to the servants remaining lay in the fact that their wages were raised
1/20 for twenty years. It would be interesting to see the
sum that they started from; but Rousseau never commits
himself to that. Then, great care is taken to keep the sexes
properly apart, so that they never come across each other,
either in their work or in their pleasures, except at stated
times. The women usually walk out after dinner with
Mme. Wolmar and the children, like prisoners under the
eye of their gaoler, and on Sunday evenings they are permitted in turn to ask a friend to a light collation of cakes
and creams in the nursery. No "Sundays out" or "monthly holidays" for them! but then all that they desire is to
bask in the presence of *les maîtres.* While the female portion of the establishment is having its "constitutional," the
men are turned on to work out of doors, and on summer
Sundays have athletic sports in the meadow, with prizes,
for which strangers of good reputation are invited to compete. In the winter evenings they all dance, part of the time
in Julie's presence, and refresh themselves when tired with
cake and wine.

A good many of those customs are sensible enough, and
have their origin in the then perfectly unknown principle,
care for the comfort and well-being of servants and laborers. But all is spoilt by the perpetual *surveillance* of Julie.
It has an irritating effect on the reader, and must have
tended to hypocrisy in many of the persons so haunted and
watched. Even with all possible friendliness and consideration between servants and mistresses, the best servants in
the world would feel awkward and constrained in the con-

tinual and uncalled-for presence of their masters, and their self-respect would resent the inevitable inference. But Julie's dependents are made of different stuff. *They* become radiant whenever she appears, and fall into her innocent little schemes with gratitude. Happy and blessed as their existence is at all times, the crowning moment of bliss is during the vintaging. The whole household moves into the hills, and all day long the men work, singing over their toil like operatic peasants. In the evenings they gather in a large room built by the thoughtful Julie, and card hemp. When Julie thinks that enough has been carded, she says, "Let us send up our fireworks." Each gathers up his bundle of hemp, and goes into the court, where a bonfire is made and set alight. (pp. 176-77)

The relations of the Wolmars with the neighboring village are in every way as perfect and satisfactory as their relations with their household. They consider, with really good sense, that it is much wiser to try to make people content with "the state of life to which it has pleased God to call them" than to encourage them to push up the social ladder. They think, truly, that young men often mistake ambition (they might have added discontent) for genius, and that perhaps one in a hundred of those that leave their native place to seek their fortune ever finds it. So far we entirely agree with them; but they overstep their fair limits when they go on, characteristically, to observe that the one who succeeds probably does so by crooked means.

So Julie and her husband live on their own property, keeping their equals at a civil distance, and taking real pleasure only in the society of their inferiors. This state of things has always a debasing tendency, as it develops in the meekest breast self-complacency and a love of managing. Of course, Rousseau intends us to see in it only another proof of the superiority of his ideal couple; but a few healthy quarrels with their rich neighbors would have been infinitely more elevating to M. and Mme. Wolmar than the smiling condescension with which they played their self-allotted part in life. One instance of their dealings with their "poorer brethren" is related, in ecstasies of rapture, by St. Preux and Lord Bomston. We have not got the answer of that long-suffering peer; but it inspires the modern English reader with a violent desire to kick *les maîtres*. The whole thing is so despicably silly and unreal that it is hardly possible to narrate it with patience. This is, however, the outline of the story—one example among many of their daily customs.

Julie is in the habit of frequently inviting some aged villager to dinner. He is always given the seat of honor beside his hostess, who helps him herself, makes much of him (*le caresse*), and enters into conversation with him. The old man, enchanted by such behavior, bubbles over with delight, and talks freely of his own affairs. At least, that appears to be the English equivalent of "se livre à l'épanchement de son cœur." He brightens up while telling of the good old times, of his *amours* (*!*), and of his crops, and the dinner passes off gaily. When it is over the children are secretly instructed to give the old man a present with which their mother has furnished them, and, in order to produce reciprocity of feeling, the villager returns the compliment by another gift, from the same source. Then he takes his leave, and hurries back to his cottage, where, amidst tears of joy, he displays his gifts and relates to his family how he has been fêted, how attentive have

been the servants, and how *empressés* the hosts. Blessings are showered on *les maîtres,* and the whole village is raised to such a pinnacle of exaltation at the honor shown to one of their number that a fresh incentive is given to virtue in the knowledge that when they too enter the value of years they too shall be similarly rewarded.

And this is what Rousseau calls simplicity!

Before discussing Rousseau's views of education, we must glance for a moment at his theories of political economy as embodied in the all-wise M. de Wolmar. Even to a person not versed in the science, they appear a little unsound, and singularly lacking in common sense. They are mostly elicited by a conversation between Julie and St. Preux, who has been objecting that for people who are not rich the method of prizes, percentages, and gratifications, must be very costly. Julie denies it, explains the system by which her husband continues to have receipts in excess of his expenditure, which system merely consists in living for one year upon his capital, so as to allow his revenues to accumulate. In this manner he is always a year in advance, and he chooses that his capital should be diminished rather than that he should be continually anticipating his income. The proverb of "robbing Peter to pay Paul" was apparently unknown in the days of Rousseau.

M. de Wolmar desired above all things that his estate should be sufficient for the wants of those living on it; but his theories of agriculture seem little likely to produce this result. He holds that lands left fallow lose their fertility, and only bear in proportion to the number of hands employed on them.

Virgin soil had no charms for him, and he would have scouted the notion of rotation of crops as the dream of a madman. What a pity that he never made the acquaintance of Levine, the serious country gentleman in "Anna Karenine!" He could have considerably opened Wolmar's eyes on his favorite subject, "Agronomie."

It is soothing to the feelings to learn that even the beneficent influence of the Wolmars was not enough to preserve the district from professional beggars. They swarmed in such numbers on the roads as to call forth from St. Preux a question about the wisdom of encouraging them by giving them relief, as is Julie's invariable custom. Julie defends herself by observing that the relief given to each one is very small—merely a meal, and an insignificant coin, sufficient to carry him on to the next house along the route. It does not occur to her that if every one follows her plan beggars will be absolutely supported by the community, and will naturally never do anything to help themselves. St. Preux, however, is less satisfied than he is wont to be with Julie's reasoning, and, to crush him completely into the attitude of admiration he always prefers to occupy, she is reduced to quoting her husband.

Begging, says M. de Wolmar, using the same argument as that employed by Burns rather later, is a profession, like another. And there is no more discredit in being moved by the eloquence of a beggar than by the eloquence of an actor. It is necessary not that *we* believe it, but that *they* should do it well. Even in these days of indiscriminate philanthropy, the argument is somewhat startling; but Wolmar was right enough when he looked upon begging as a profession. In the days of my childhood a friend of my own was informed by a favorite housemaid that she wished to give warning, as she was going to be married.

"Indeed," said the lady, "and what is your future husband?"

"Please, 'm, he's an asker!"

"A what?"

"An asker."

"I don't understand. What does he *do?*"

"Well, 'm, he—he goes about the streets, and if he sees any one coming along that looks kind, he—well, he just stops 'em and asks 'em to give him a trifle, and he makes quite a comfortable living that way!"

"Do you mean a BEGGAR?"

"Well, 'm, some people do call it that; *we* call it asker."

It is to be regretted that *Autres temps, autres mœurs* is not true in this instance.

In sketching lightly some of Rousseau's theories of education, it will be needful to take **Emile** (published in 1762) with the **Nouvelle Héloïse,** which appeared about four years earlier. Julie's method of training her children contains the germ of what was developed later in **Emile;** but in the four years that elapsed between the two books Rousseau's views had made a great stride. In **Emile** he entirely ignores the influence of a mother during the opening years of infancy, and entrusts the boy from the moment he is able to speak to the care of what was called in those days a governor. He does, indeed, give regulations for the proper treatment of the baby by his nurse, from its earliest moments, and even bestows attention on the very limited number of toys proper to an infant six months old. Was his interest in other people's children, we wonder, a kind of expiation of his desertion of his own? or was it merely the iconoclasm so deeply rooted in Rousseau's nature that caused him to strike such vigorous blows at the thraldom in which helpless little creatures passed the first portion of their lives? Be that as it may, Rousseau, aided by the celebrated and fashionable Dr. Tronchin, of Geneva, certainly did manage to effect a revolution in this important matter, and children have cause to bless him unto this day. Of course, he is often absurd and unpractical, and as artificial as the people he abuses, or he would not be Rousseau; but then he is surprisingly often sensible and even wise. Again and again he insists that we are not to expect too much of children, for to demand that they should be capable of reasoning like grown-up people is only to cultivate superficiality and affectation. The aim of early education, says Julie, is to render a child capable of receiving instruction, and to this end his mind should never be pushed. No one should ever talk to him of what he cannot understand, or allow him to hear descriptions above his head. In his early years his body should be cultivated and his mind let alone, and, above all, he should be taught never to take things for granted. Let him put every assertion to the proof before he accepts it. Rousseau had clearly not been brought into contact with children whose senses are keenly alive to the conversation of their elders, or he would have found some practical difficulties in the way of this plan; but then his creations are docile infants, who never ask inconvenient questions. He perpetually informs us

that children should be free and happy; but it does not occur to him that companionship and friction are the most important of all elements in training for the work of life, and, as Emile happens to be an only child, he is kept in the absolute isolation which is always a necessary factor of Rousseau's projects. Unconscious development, instinct, the ideas that are blown about like the pollen of a flower, and germinate no one knows where, and no one knows why,—these things have no place in Rousseau's theories. His education is emphatically self-conscious; and the consequence is that the results, though often excellent, might be attained with much less trouble some other way.

The first essential condition of Rousseau's method is that the same person should have charge of the child from birth to bridal. "I would not have undertaken Emile at all if I had not been allowed to exercise my judgment in choosing his wife," he says more than once. It will be readily supposed that the competition for tutorships under the Rousseau system would not be excessive, especially as another condition of equal weight is insisted on. "The governor is to have no salary; he must be a family friend". A teacher who receives wages, like a person who receives gifts with gratitude, puts himself at once out of the reckoning, and draws upon himself Rousseau's everlasting contempt. Compare his views in **Emile** with the passage in the **Nouvelle Héloïse,** in which he treats of the same subject. "My father has returned," writes Julie to St. Preux, "and is well satisfied with my progress in music and drawing, and indeed with all my studies. But as soon as he discovered you were not of noble birth he inquired the amount of your monthly salary. My mother answered that it was impossible even to propose such an arrangement to you, and that you had even rejected any little presents she had tried to give you—presents such as any one might take. He then made up his mind that a certain payment should be offered, and that in the event of your refusal, you should, in spite of all your merits, be thanked for your instruction and politely dismissed". Of course, St. Preux is outraged by such a natural and sensible proposition. "What would my real position be if I consented to receive a salary in return for my lessons?" he writes in reply. "In selling him part of my time,—that is, of myself,—I should become a paid servant—a sort of valet—and my faith would be tacitly engaged for the preservation of all that belonged to him, as if I was the meanest of his retainers. If, after that, I gave reins to my feelings [*i.e.,* made love to Julie], I should be grossly in fault".

St. Preux is so far right that, if he voluntarily accepted a paid position of trust, the betrayal of confidence would be even greater than it was before. But how eminently characteristic the whole transaction is of Rousseau! The simplicity about which he talks so incessantly is an element absolutely foreign to his nature, or he would have seen nothing derogatory in receiving payment for services rendered. Then, as usual, he only looks at what concerns himself, and never once thinks of what the Baron d'Etange's feelings would be on discovering that his daughter was absorbing gratuitously the whole time and attention of a young and poor stranger. Lastly, he here manifests the impatience of obligation that led him to resent the bestowal of gifts by his dearest and most constant friends, and to insult the givers, though he by no means rejected what they gave. Rousseau understood that "a grateful heart, by owing, owes not, least of all men."

However, it is time we returned to the child, who by this time has ceased to be a mere "vegetable baby," and can talk and walk. Many children at this age will sit happily with a book before them, and, by comparing the pictures with the letterpress, will soon teach themselves to read without other help. But Rousseau is never in any hurry for his pupils to make acquaintance with books, and, indeed, perpetually changes the age at which they are able to read to themselves. Julie's little boy is only six when his curiosity is stimulated by his mother artfully leaving off the stories she is reading to him at exciting places, and forbidding the servants to finish them. (By the way, Swiss servants must have been much better educated than English ones of the same date, if there was any necessity for this prohibition.) The child finds that no one will attend to him, and is gradually pushed to spell out the end for himself. But Emile, though solitary, is by no means so precocious in this branch of study, in spite of his being more dependent on reading for amusement. Emile has spent his infancy in running about the fields, in learning to test objects by their weight, to measure distances, to swim (an accomplishment very rare in those days), in tennis, archery, and handball (*ballon*), to which, when he is grown up, will be added the chase. Who played tennis and handball with him is never told; it may have been the always obliging tutor. When not training his body by these athletic sports, he is prowling round the blacksmith's forge or "helping" the carpenter, preparatory to choosing a trade for himself, to guarantee him a livelihood in after life.

There is no denying that if a few companions had been added, and a few pedagogic sermons subtracted, Emile would have had an ideally happy boyhood. With all those occupations, reading would naturally go to the wall. Rousseau triumphantly boasts in one place that, at twelve, Emile will hardly know what a book is, which seems exceedingly probable; but a few pages farther on he observes that, having had his curiosity excited, the boy will be able to read and write perfectly before he is ten, though it is difficult to see what use reading and writing will be to him, as he has no one to write to, and is only to be allowed to read "Robinson Crusoe" till he grows up.

No history is to be taught him till he is nearly a man, and able to reason upon it; and all the geography he knows is to be gathered from his own experience. The classics and other languages are left out, as he will never have occasion to use them; but he may learn music (Rousseau's favorite pursuit), and a certain amount of practical geometry and mathematics. Rousseau would have the dancing master, instead of teaching dancing, lead the boy to the foot of rocks and teach him how to climb them; as if the dancing master were the man for such a task, and as if any active creature on two legs needed to be taught to climb! It reminds us of Miss Bingley, in "Pride and Prejudice," who said it would be much more rational to have conversation instead of dancing at a ball, while her brother agreed that it might be more rational, but felt that it would not be near so much like a ball.

Rousseau considers that children should be taught the truth, the whole truth, and nothing but the truth, ignoring that there are many things about which a child asks questions when he is quite incapable of comprehending the answers, and likewise that all through men's lives much must be taken for granted. It is impossible to prove for ourselves all the facts that we know to exist; faith must be placed in the tests brought by specialists, and this truth a child may as well learn early as late. But Rousseau assumes that a child's mind is an absolutely blank page till he chooses to write on it certain ideas, which he does with a cumbersome elaboration that would provoke suspicion and mirth in an idiot. One day, for instance, he desires to instil the notion of the rights of property into Emile's mind. Now it is hardly possible to find a baby so young that it has not some crude views on this subject; but Emile is a big boy before the question of *meum* and *tuum* occurs to him. So he is led artfully to take possession of a special plot of ground, which his cunning tutor knows to have been already "pegged down" (to use an Australian mining expression) by a working gardener, and Emile, greatly excited with his new acquisition, begins to hoe and dig, and finally to plant and water. All goes on merrily for some days, and his "ill weeds grow apace," when suddenly the real proprietor appears on the scene, scatters the thriving young vegetables to the winds, and upbraids Emile as an interloper, and the destroyer of some precious melon seeds which he had procured from Malta. Emile is aghast and bewildered; the tutor seizes the opportunity of pointing a moral; and the gardener plays up to him with vigor. He is promised more seeds, and Emile another plot, and the notion of real property is fixed indelibly in the boy's mind. Could anything be more ponderously silly? Yet the same machinery is put in motion to induce Emile to learn to run—though we are elsewhere given to understand he had done nothing else from babyhood—and to teach him to take observations of the sun, by the tutor losing himself and the boy (then about twelve), in a wood on the other side of their own garden hedge. Indeed the most subtle plot of all is concerned with Emile's introduction to Sophie, the wife who has been complacently and secretly educated for him in the depths of the country. After a long riding tour, Emile, always accompanied by his tutor, reaches the house of a peasant, and asks for food. While they are eating it, the peasant, garrulous and gushing, like all his kind in Rousseau's pages, begins to describe the neighborhood, and especially the blessings scattered abroad by a wealthy couple and their daughter, who live on the further side of the hills. Emile is naturally fired by the account of so much virtue, and burns to make their acquaintance, and the fact that the dwelling of these universal providers is some miles away only adds fuel to the flame. He goes; beholds Sophie, the essence of that mediocrity which, says Rousseau, "is to be desired in everything;" and is instantly conquered.

Except for the fact that she is to be Emile's wife, it is quite clear that Sophie has no independent attraction for Rousseau. He does not take much trouble in designing her, and in her description there is none of the loving skill he has bestowed on Julie. Julie is the perfect woman, whose brightness is thrown into relief by the shadows around her, beautiful, amiable, and accomplished, though her accomplishments seem almost useless, for after marriage she lays aside her studies, in order to devote herself to her household and her children. Sophie is merely intended to fill up the chinks in Emile's happiness. She is practical and sensible, a good housewife, has been taught by her parents to sing and dance in a very mild way, can dress herself neatly, and is "common-looking" but pleasant. After it is established in the family that the two young people are "keeping company" (for when they are regularly engaged

Emile is sent to travel for two years), he pleases himself with instructing her (after the eternal manner of priggish lovers), and is enchanted when he is allowed to give his lessons in mathematics and history on his knees!

The two years of probation, which to our thinking would more reasonably precede than follow an engagement, pass away; Emile and Sophie are married, have two children, and live in the country for ten years quite happily and successfully. At the end of that time Sophie loses her parents and one of her children, and, to divert her thoughts from her own troubles, Emile takes her with him to live in the town. But, alas! the principles which were excellently adapted to common every-day country wear will not stand the strain of town life. Sophie is gradually drawn into a whirl of dissipation, and is finally driven to confess to her husband *qu'elle a manqué à ses devoirs.* Emile leaves her, and after working for a short time at carpentering, resumes his travels; and we bid farewell to him a captive in Algiers.

The unregenerate reader will acknowledge that he feels some satisfaction in the downfall of the ideal wife. If principles are only a matter of locality, and if mediocrity so speedily succumbs to temptation, by all means let us aim at perfection!

In this brief sketch of the daily life which Rousseau conceived suitable in order to bring about the highest development of the duty owed by those in authority to any persons whom nature or circumstances have made dependent on them, all references to the love story which enchanted the ladies of Paris have been purposely avoided. The humorist who studies the *Nouvelle Héloïse* on its romantic side will find himself abundantly rewarded, provided, always, that his sense of humor is strong enough to overcome his disgust at the gross indecency of Wolmar's attitude to St. Preux on his return to Vaud, and his frequent allusions to that young man's love-passages with Julie. Of course the views of the eighteenth century on these subjects differed widely from those now prevalent; but, whatever the freedom of life and language considered permissible in fashionable society, M. de Wolmar's playful insinuations would probably have shocked the most hardened cynic of that time. Yet, however disagreeably certain things in the book may strike us, on the whole it is wonderfully free from coarseness, and in this respect compares favorably with "Pamela" and some contemporary English novels; and many of the descriptions are as graphic and beautiful as any in the French language. To any one acquainted with the memoirs and literature of the time, nothing is more curious than the contrast between the formal manners and the speech characteristic even of the highest classes in Paris and the amazing facility with which men as well as women kissed and cried and leaped upon each other's necks; while the letters of many of the wittiest men of the day—of Grimm, or Diderot, or Galiani—read like those of lovers in their assurances of undying affection. Rosalind would have been shaken in her belief that "men had died and worms had eaten them, but not for love," could she have seen the despair to which some of the most learned and cynical philosophers were reduced when the object of their adoration proved hardhearted. Even Grimm himself, the least emotional of men, was thrown into a sort of trance of misery on his rejection by Mlle. Fel, the actress, and lay for many days in this condition without receiving any other nourishment than a little cherry jam placed on his tongue. Strange people were they all, yet with an undying fascination about them—a fascination which in his day Rousseau exercised on most of those with whom he came into contact, and which it required an endless course of insult and ingratitude on his part to shake. After all, though his nature may have been baser and his manners worse, was he not essentially of the same clay as those with whom he lived and quarrelled, and never more so than when he wrote the *Nouvelle Héloïse,* with liberty, equality, and fraternity on his lips, and the sentiment of aristocracy deeply rooted in his heart? (pp. 177-82)

Leonora Blanche Lang, "Rousseau's Ideal Household," in Littell's Living Age, *Vol. CXCI, No. 2468, October 17, 1891, pp. 175-82.*

William A. Dunning   (essay date 1909)

[*Dunning was a prominent American historian, political scientist, educator, and editor of scholarly journals. He was the founder of the American Political Science Association and exerted a lasting influence on historical scholarship in the United States, especially on interpretations of the Reconstruction period following the American Civil War. In the following excerpt, he elucidates the primary principles of Rousseau's political philosophy.*]

Rousseau approached political theory by the well-worn pathway of the "state of nature." As to what precisely this term signified, he was not clear and consistent. He used it in practically all the various senses that had been attached to it in its long and notable career. Throughout the fluctuations of his usage, one idea alone appeared unmistakable, namely, that the natural state of man was vastly preferable to the social or civil state, and must furnish the norm by which to test and correct it.

In the *Discourse on Inequality* the natural man appears first as the solitary savage, living the happy, care-free life of the brute, without fixed abode, without articulate speech, with no needs or desires that cannot be satisfied through the merest instinct. Rousseau's handling of this conception compares favorably with that of the best among the long line of literary artists who have used it. More apparent than in most of them, however, are his admiration and sympathy for the savage. The steps by which men emerge from their primitive state are depicted with fascinating art, but the author's regret at their success pervades the picture. In the natural man are to be found the elements of perfect happiness. He is independent, contented, self-sufficing. For others of his own species he has no need, and he regards them with the same indifference that he feels toward other animals. Save for the casual and momentary union that perpetuates the race, nothing draws him to commerce with his kind. He is not, however, the timid, cowering creature that Montesquieu described, fearful of every force around him. Nor on the other hand is he the energetic, aggressive monster of Hobbes, ceaselessly driven by his passions to war upon his fellows. Only through society does man become unbalanced by either fear or ambition; the "simple, regular (*uniforme*) and solitary" life of nature involves none of the evils of either.

The natural state, as thus conceived, is a state of substantial equality. No baneful distinction is to be seen among the individuals who pursue in isolation the placid routine of satisfying their physical needs. But the deadly seeds of a different order are ready to germinate. With no necessary ground for it in his description of the savage state, Rousseau assumes that the human race becomes increasingly numerous; divergencies of soil, climate and season then cause differences in manner of life among men. On the shores of the seas and the rivers they catch fish and invent the hook and line. In the forests they become hunters and invent the bow and arrow. Fire is discovered by some accident, and the fortunate discoverers develop its utilities. Stone and then metal tools are made. Economic progress moves apace, and rude huts instead of casual caves become places of abode. With the appearance of fixed homes, family and property are at hand, and the knell of human equality is sounded. Social organization has begun. Intercourse of individuals and families becomes common and through it the ideas of competition and preference are developed. Evils follow in their train, but this primitive society is not, to Rousseau, an intolerable state. Looked upon as a mean between the indolence of the savage state and the too intense activity of the later phase, it appears to him the happiest period in the life of humanity—"the least subject to revolutions, the best for man."

It is quite characteristic of Rousseau that while he is describing the savage state he is disposed to consider it as the happiest and best, and when he has moved on to the tribal and early social state, this in turn appeals to him as preferable. We shall see that in time he has kind words for even fully developed society, which in the *Discourse* is the summation of evil.

Man's emergence from the primitive social condition must have been due, Rousseau says, to some fatal chance. His exposition of the process reveals a number of catastrophies that contributed to the sad result. The arts of agriculture and metallurgy were discovered; and in the application of them men had need of one another's aid. Coöperation revealed and emphasized the diversity of men's talents and prepared thus the inevitable result. The stronger man did the greater amount of work; the craftier got more of the product. Thus appeared the difference of rich and poor—the prolific source of all the other forms of inequality. Property was doing its disastrous work. The climax came with the diabolical device of property in land.

"The first man who, after enclosing a piece of ground, bethought himself to say 'this is mine,' and found people simple enough to believe him, was the real founder of civil society."

War, murder, wretchedness and horror without end followed this fatal proceeding. Rich and poor were ranged against each other in unrelenting hostility. Evils that had been unknown in the savage state, and but slightly manifested in primitive society, became now universal. To escape them, or at least to enable men to endure them, civil society was instituted. This was no recurrence to the natural order. It was, on the contrary, an enormous stride away from nature, and the introduction of still another mode of inequality among men. Its inevitable consequence was the final stage of inequality, the condition of master and slave.

Such was, in general outline, Rousseau's thought in the

Discourse on Inequality. With proper allowance for the incoherence and inconsistencies of the work, it may be said that his state of nature is on the whole a historical rather than a psychological concept. Yet Rousseau, like Locke, who is strongly suggested by many points in the *Discourse,* refrains from insisting on the objective reality of the conditions he describes. The state he is considering is one, he says, "which no longer exists, which perhaps has not existed and which probably never will exist, but which must be accurately understood in order to get just notions as to contemporary society." This view of his task would indicate that he, like Hobbes and Locke, was concerned merely with formulating the abstract qualities of human nature. But Rousseau's poetic faculty was too active and its pictures too vivid to leave room for the impression that his natural man was an abstraction or his state of nature a mere fancy. To one who does not read the warning of the preface, the *Discourse* can be nothing but an eloquent and moving narrative of the actual descent of man from natural peace and blessedness to social servitude and woe.

Psychological analysis is not wholly wanting in the *Discourse.* Rousseau employs it, *suo more,* with little pretence to consistency, but sometimes with rather striking effect. He takes pains to repudiate at the outset the idea that man's life in the state of nature is regulated by reason. The truly natural man, *i.e.,* the savage, acts on two principles that are anterior to reason, namely, the feeling of interest in his own welfare and preservation, and the feeling of repugnance toward the sight of death or suffering in any animate creature, especially a human being. These emotions rather than reason, determine the conduct of men throughout the various phases of the natural state and give way to reason only when degeneration has gone so far that civil society must be constituted. All the rules of natural right and natural law flow directly and exclusively from the operation of these primary sentiments—self-interest and pity.

This curious theory, whatever other sources it had, was an obvious generalization of certain conspicuous traits of Rousseau's own character. He was extremely selfish and extremely sensitive to suffering in others—qualities that are notoriously quite compatible with each other. One immediate application of his theory was in refuting the dogma of Hobbes that the state of nature was a state of war. The innate repugnance to suffering in his kind would necessarily operate to limit the brutality of man to man.

It is in the *Emile* that Rousseau most elaborately develops his conception of the state of nature and the natural man as a philosophic ideal rather than a historical reality. The general theme of the work is the rearing and training of a child, and the unceasing exhortation of the author is to abandon methods that have their origin or justification in the real or fancied needs of social life. "Back to nature" is his cry. This does not mean that society must be destroyed and the savage state resumed. It means merely that nature must be the rule for men in society. The incoherence of Rousseau's definitions and explanations and rhapsodies about this matter is in his most characteristic style; and seeking to comprehend clearly his conception of "nature" is like trying to visualize the fauna of the Apocalypse.

His purpose is in a general way intelligible; it is to strip the human mind of all the attributes that are in origin or manifestation ascribable to social life. The residue is the mental equipment of the natural man. At birth the human being is, through his senses, susceptible to impressions from without. Toward the objects that create the impressions he has a feeling of attraction or repulsion according as they are agreeable or disagreeable, and, as his mind develops, according to the rational judgment he forms about their effect upon his happiness. But meanwhile he develops and falls under the constraint of habits and opinions, and through these his dispositions toward things are modified. "Prior to that modification they constitute what I call nature in us."

Such is the nearest approach to precise definition that Rousseau gives his readers. Despite its doubtful psychology it might, if adhered to, serve a useful philosophic purpose. But he does not adhere to it. One clear feature of the natural man as defined above is the use of his reason in judging his surroundings. Elsewhere Rousseau declares it characteristic of the natural man "that he be * * * subject to no government save that of his own reason." With the rational faculty thus emphasized, it is discouraging to find pervading all Rousseau's philosophy, and often reïterated in set terms, the idea that reason and nature are antithetic and incompatible with each other. Reflection and its practical results he proclaims to be the pernicious product of society and its artificialities. "By nature man scarcely thinks." "The man who reflects is a corrupt creature." Our natural feelings (*passions*) alone give us peace and true liberty. So soon as we begin to reason and to project ourselves by induction and analogy into times and places and relations unknown to our original condition, oppression and misery crowd upon us. Thus, for example, man afflicts himself through unhappy foresight with the torture of anticipating death, while to unreflecting creatures it comes without distress.

In no small measure the vagaries and inconsistencies of Rousseau's views about nature and reason are due to the phrase-making instinct of the literary artist. He never thought of logic when the opportunity for a pretty turn of expression was at hand. "Forgive me my paradoxes," he wrote: "I like better to be a man of paradoxes than to be a man of prejudices." Nor did he suspect that he was a man of both. The fixed and ever-present, if not always conscious, motive of his thinking was to disparage those features of social life that were distasteful to himself. The violence of his protest was as excessive in dealing with the natural man in society as it had been in dealing with the natural man prior to society; the one, like the other, became an inhuman fantasy.

In stressing the emotions and minimizing the reason as the basis of the state of nature, Rousseau dissociated his doctrine from the whole philosophical tradition on this point. Reason had been always the characteristic ingredient of the pre-social or pre-civil order. Grotius, Hobbes, Pufendorf, Locke and all their predecessors, great and small, had found man in the state of nature endowed with reason, and enabled by means of it to rise into social and political organization. Rousseau, with whatever vacillation and inconsistency, strove in general to represent reason and all philosophy as a calamitous aberration, deluding men with visions that brought them to ruin.

The most pestilential reasoning and philosophy was, in Rousseau's opinion, that which sustained existing forms of political and social inequality. "Nothing can be farther from the law of nature, however we define it, than that a child give orders to an old man, an imbecile direct a sage, and a handful of people be gorged with luxuries while the starving multitude lacks the necessities of life." Yet society and government, though deplorable, were, he admitted, inevitable. It was necessary therefore to find some rational form through which their existence might be justified. In his *Social Contract,* Rousseau assumed the rôle of constructive philosopher and presented a theory of the state.

The precise problem that he undertakes in this work to solve is characteristically formulated in the famous phrases:

> Man is born free and everywhere he is in chains. One who believes himself the master of the rest is only more of a slave than they. How does that change come about? I do not know. What can render it legitimate (*légitime*)? That question I think I can answer.

That is to say, the liberty and equality that characterize the state of nature, in whatever sense the term is used, are in the civil state gone. He will justify their disappearance. And he does it, in his usual way, by proving that they are not gone at all, but subsist as fully after, as before, the institution of government. Nature and political society, liberty and authority, are absolute logical contradictories in the *Discourse* and the *Emile;* they become in the *Social Contract* inseparable and indistinguishable concepts. Such, at least, is the consequence of the theorizing in his earlier chapters. The author would not be Rousseau, however, if he did not later revert from time to time to the idea of a preëminent excellence in the non-political condition; and the typical climax of his method is to be seen in a rapturous glorification, at one point, of the political as compared with the natural state.

The device that he hit upon for solving the problem of his work was the social pact. Authority of man over man can have no rational basis, he holds, save agreement and consent. And there is but one species of agreement conceivable in which liberty is retained while authority is instituted. This single species is the pact through which a multitude of individuals become a collective unity—a society. Rousseau's thought here shows the very strong influence of both Hobbes and Locke. It is the latter, however, whom he follows to the end—and beyond. From the ingenious reasoning by which Hobbes made absolute monarchy a logical corollary of the social pact, Rousseau turns with strong denunciation. But the Hobbesian precision in defining the terms of the pact obviously appealed to him, and his own treatment of the subject is but the substance of Locke developed by the method of Hobbes.

The formula on which civil society rests is, according to Rousseau, this: "Each of us puts into a single mass (*met en common*) his person and all his power under the supreme direction of the general will; and we receive as a body each member as an indivisible part of the whole." Through the act of a group of individuals in pronouncing, tacitly or expressly, together or in succession, this formula a moral body is constituted, with an identity, a life and a will of its own distinct from those of any of its component members. It is a public person—a body politic. From various points of view it is known as state, sovereign, power;

and in the same way its members are known variously as the people, citizens, subjects.

Rousseau's exposition of the spirit and effects of his contract is an amazing medley of bad logic and utter puerility. Equality, he declares, is insured, because each individual makes complete alienation of himself and all his rights to the community. That is to say, the individuals, reducing themselves to zeros, are as such equal. By the same reasoning the union is, he explains, absolutely perfect, and no individual can claim anything. This would seem to mean as thorough submergence of the individual in the state as Plato ever conceived. But Rousseau finds the fullest liberty. For, he continues, "since each gives himself up to all, he gives himself up to no one; and as there is acquired over every associate the same right that is given up by himself, there is gained the equivalent of what is lost, with greater power to preserve what is left."

This demonstration of liberty contains as many fallacies as clauses, and finds a fitting climax in the reference to "what is left" to the individual after the pact, following repeated declarations that the individual by the pact gives up everything. It is hardly strange that controversy has continued active as to whether Rousseau stood for absolute sovereignty or for a sphere of inalienable rights in the citizen. He clearly stood for both, relying upon the simple device of maintaining each of two logical contradictories.

His analysis and exposition of the contract are of like fabric. By the terms of this formula the act of association is clearly conceived as merely the expression of an identical purpose by each of a group of individuals. The purpose is to recognize henceforth a social or general authority as a substitute for the varying and conflicting authorities of the individual wills. Locke and Sydney and others who set forth this same idea did not undertake to analyze it into the elements and categories of a contract in private law. Hobbes, more rigid and inexorable in his method, applied the conceptions of the jurists to the social pact, and showed who were the parties to it, what precise obligation they respectively took upon themselves, and what penalty was incurred when the obligation was repudiated. Rousseau seeks to imitate the method of Hobbes; but the result is ridiculous. The parties to the pact are declared to be on the one side of the individuals and on the other the community and this, though the community comes into existence only by virtue of the pact. The engagement made by the community appears at once, however, to be made in reality by the individuals. For, "each individual contracting, so to speak, with himself, finds himself engaged under a double relation, namely, as member of the sovereign toward the individuals, and as member of the state toward the sovereign." And Rousseau, after this sapient exposition, proceeds gravely to explain that there is no real opening here to apply the principle of the civil law according to which no one is bound by engagements made with himself; "for to be bound to one's self and to be bound to a whole of which one forms a part, are very different things."

If Rousseau could have remained certainly faithful through a whole section of his work to the truth embodied in this last sentence, his theory of the state would have been important. But his grasp on the distinction between the collective and the distributive aspect of an aggregate was very uncertain. Nothing better illustrates this fact

than his easy assumption, noted above, that a promise by a society is the same as a promise by each member of the society. The same confusion appears again and again in his treatise. He glimpses often the fruitful concept of a beneficent and all-determining force in the social organism; but he lacks the dialectic power to disentangle it from the mass of individualistic prejudice that obscures it. He is nearest success in the attempt in his detailed discussion of the notion of sovereignty.

Rousseau's doctrine on this subject combined elements that had previously been considered incompatible with each other. The definition and development of sovereignty, as a concept of political science, had been almost entirely the work of those who, like Bodin and Hobbes, were defending absolute monarchy. By the liberalizing school of Locke and Montesquieu the idea of sovereignty was evaded as unnecessary in theory and dangerous in practice—a mortal foe to liberty. Rousseau, with characteristic boldness, proceeded to reconcile the absolutist with the liberal doctrine. He defined sovereignty with the fulness and precision of Hobbes, and gave it an abode and an operation that satisfied the feeling of Locke.

The social contract, Rousseau maintains, furnishes the solution of all questions about sovereignty. The body politic that is created by this contract is itself the only conceivable possessor of supreme power. By the free act of those who enter into the pact all their rights and powers are resigned to the community, and their respective wills are merged into and superseded by the general will (*volonté générale*). By no possible process of reasoning or of fact, Rousseau holds, can sovereignty be traced to any other possessor than the body politic as a whole, or be identified in any other manifestation than that of the general will. He seizes with especial zest the idea of sovereignty as will, and uses it in many fantastic feats of pseudo-dialectic. His often absurd manipulation does not conceal, however, the real value of the idea. Hobbes had already exposed many of its possibilities as a clarifying agency in political speculation; but Rousseau gave the great impulse to that particular development which has centered about the idea of the social or group will.

The basis of will, Rousseau holds, is interest. The individual wills always what is for his interest. His interests conflict at many points with the interests of others; but at some point the interest of all is the same. This common interest is what makes the state possible. The general will is but the expression of what the common interest requires. The two ideas are inseparable in thought and in fact. If the interests of the individuals composing the state are at no point identical, a general will is inconceivable and society cannot exist. If an expression of will does not correspond to the common interest, it is not an expression of the general will and it lacks the quality of sovereignty. Only an act of the general will is properly called law (*loi*). Perfect generality is of the essence of it. Thus law can have no other source than the sovereign, that is, the community as a body politic. A rule or command prescribed by any other authority lacks the essential quality of law; and, conversely, a rule or command emanating formally from the sovereign body lacks the quality of law if its content or effect touches interests that are not general.

Sovereignty, conceived in such a way, is readily proved by Rousseau to be inalienable, indivisible and inerrant. It is inalienable, because the will cannot be bound by promises. "The sovereign can indeed say: I will now what such-and-such a man wills, or at least what he says he wills; but it cannot say: What that man shall will to-morrow, I shall still will." It can say: What that man shall will, I will do; but this is the formula of slavery, and pledges acts not conformed to the interest of the promisor. Since will in any true sense is inseparable from interest, the servile formula implies the dissolution *ipso facto* of the body politic that enacts it. "The instant there is a master, there is no longer a sovereign." Such is the argument by which Rousseau disposes of the ancient dogma that the people may transfer sovereignty to a prince.

That sovereignty is indivisible is equally clear to Rousseau.

> The will either is or is not general, is that of the whole people or that of part of the people. In the first case the expression of the will is a sovereign act and makes law; in the second case it is merely a particular will or an act of the magistrate—at most a decree.

All the distinctions so much debated by philosophers between the different kinds of public acts are unwarranted, Rousseau holds, so far as they imply a division of sovereignty. That there is legislative power and executive power; that taxation and judicature and the affairs of war and peace are variously administered—affects not at all the unity of the sovereign. An act of the whole people for the whole people is, regardless of any other feature of the act, a manifestation of sovereignty.

To prove that the sovereign cannot err is a task that evokes the best effort of Rousseau both as reasoner and as rhetorician. He is required to meet the familiar charge that a democracy is peculiarly apt to stray from expediency and justice. He meets it ingeniously if not conclusively thus:

> It follows from the foregoing that the general will is always right and tends always to the public advantage (*utilité publique*); but it does not follow that the judgments (*délibérations*) of the people always have the same rectitude. A man always wills his own good, but he does not always see it; the people is never corrupted, but it is often deceived, and only then does it appear to will what is wrong.

Thus the virtue of the sovereign people is saved at the expense of its intelligence; and the inerrancy of the general will is established by the simple process of ascribing all wrong-doing to some other source. It is indeed not hard to see that by its very definition Rousseau's sovereign always wills the public good. Sovereignty is only another name for a generalized collective volition of that content. Difficulty arises, however, when the question changes from the abstract conception of sovereignty to its concrete manifestation. Rousseau's doctrine implies that a resolution adopted unanimously by a community is not necessarily an expression of the sovereign will. He distinguishes the general will from the will of all (*volonté de tous*). This latter is but the sum of all the particular volitions of the individuals about their private interests. The general will is the aggregate of such of these volitions as are common to all the individuals—such as concern interests that are common to all. With this distinction in mind, it is easy to see that a resolution of the whole people lacks the quality

of sovereign law if it deals with any matter that does not involve the true interest of every citizen.

One important source of the mistakes often made by the people is to be found, Rousseau says, in the partial societies, or parties, that spring up in the state. When a party is constituted, a new corporate interest appears, coming between the individual interest and the general interest. There is no longer possible that comparison of individual wills through which alone the general will is determined. Party interest intervenes and misleads the people, with the result that the will of the party is mistaken for that of the sovereign. Rousseau's conclusion is, like that of many earlier thinkers, that if parties exist at all in a state, there should be many of them. Where two great parties divide the people, the will of one or the other of them habitually supersedes the general will, and the state ceases in fact to exist.

Rousseau is at some pains to exhibit the limits of sovereignty. They are manifest chiefly, we have just seen, as immediate inferences from the definition of the term: the sovereign cannot do what is not for the general welfare, and cannot intrude therefore into the field of purely individual interest. Is there, then, a sphere of individual rights secure against invasion by the state? In answering this crucial question Rousseau fairly bristles with paradox and contradiction. He declares that "as nature gives to every man an absolute power over all his members, the social pact gives to the body politic absolute power over all its members." This proposition is followed by reference to the distinction between the duties of the individual as a subject and his natural right as man. In pointblank contradiction of what was earlier said as to the terms of the social contract, Rousseau now observes: "It is agreed (*on convient*) that what each alienates by the social pact is only that part of his power, his property and his liberty which may be used with advantage by the community." This clearly points to a reserved sphere of individual rights. But the next sentence turns the tables decisively against the individual: "It must also be agreed that the sovereign alone is judge of that advantage."

Formally, thus, there are no limits to sovereign power. Substantially, however, there are, Rousseau insists, the very real limits inherent in the nature of sovereignty. The relation of the individual will to the general will insures at the least the equality of all citizens before the law, and the rule of justice and equity. The sovereign community is limited to prescriptions that are for general, not for any particular utility, and it can impose no burden that is not alike for all. Rousseau's rhetoric in sustaining these amiable ideals is admirable; but his reasoning, while often very specious, never wholly disguises the vitiating assumption that an aggregate cannot possess attributes distinct from those of its component parts.

The most clear and self-consistent feature of his speculation on this general subject is that which deals with the idea of law. Even on this point his predilection for contract leads him into some cloudy quibblings about law as essentially a convention, to which the parties are respectively the community and its individual members. But his central conception is made very distinct and suggestive. As has been stated above, a law is a resolution of the whole people for the whole people, touching a matter that concerns all.

The law regards the subjects as a whole and actions as abstract, never a man as an individual nor a concrete (*particulière*) act. Thus the law can determine that there shall be privileges, but it cannot give them to anybody by name; the law can establish a classification of the citizens and describe the qualifications for the various classes, but it cannot assign certain men to specify classes; it can establish a royal government and hereditary succession, but it cannot choose a king nor name a royal family . . .

From this conception of law Rousseau concludes that

it is no longer necessary to ask whose function it is to make laws, since they are acts of the general will; nor whether the prince is above the laws, since he is a member of the state; nor whether the law can be unjust, since no one is unjust to himself; nor how one is at the same time free and subject to the laws, since they are merely registers of our own wills.

No state is legitimate, according to Rousseau, unless it is ruled by laws, as thus defined; and every state so ruled, whatever the form of its government, is a republic. The lucid interval in which he sets forth these fresh and striking conceptions is followed at once by a lapse into dreaming and rhetoric. For the practical realization of the republican state, as he has defined it, he has no suggestion save recourse to a "legislator," a superhuman or divinely inspired being, to impose upon a people the institutional order that they are not qualified to discover for themselves—to enact that general will which they share but know not. In this recurrence to a useless and very much shop-worn device of political theory, Rousseau exposes the purely idealizing tendency of his whole speculation. His brave undertaking to show the rational conciliation of liberty and authority ends in a trite glorification of Numa, Lycurgus and John Calvin, with a few practical suggestions, drawn largely from Montesquieu, as to the course most desirable for the next "legislator" that may descend upon mankind.

The distinction between state or sovereign and government is developed by Rousseau with the utmost exactness and consistency. While "state" denotes the community as a whole, created by the social pact and manifesting itself in the supreme general will, "government" denotes merely the individual or group of individuals that is designated by the community to carry into effect the sovereign will. The government is created not by any contract but by a decree of the sovereign; and its function is in no sense to make, but only to administer law. Government, to Rousseau, means executive power. The individuals to whom this power is assigned are the officers or the agents of the sovereign. Collectively they may be called "prince" or "magistracy." Whatever their titles—kings, senators, governors—their function and their relation to the sovereign are the same. Their power is merely what is entrusted to them by their superior, and may be modified, curtailed or entirely withdrawn at the discretion of that superior.

This doctrine is substantially that of the whole anti-monarchic philosophy of the two centuries preceding Rousseau. His own contribution consists not in any new emphasis on the subordination of the prince to the people, but in the conclusions derivable from his definition of the people as sovereign. He indulges in a good deal of superfluous metaphysics over his conception of sovereignty as will, aiming apparently to clear up problems that would

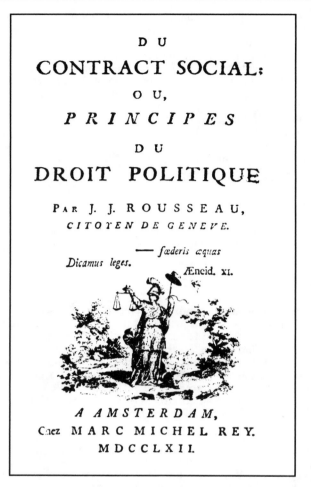

Title page of the first edition of Du contrat social *(1762).*

be as well solved without it. Thus he sets forth with great gravity the rather distressing condition of a citizen who is a member of the government. Such a one embodies three distinct wills: first, the will that rests upon his interest as a mere private individual; second, the will corresponding to the corporate interest of the magistracy; third, the will of the community as a whole—the sovereign general will. "In the order of nature" these wills are respectively the more active as they are the more concentrated: that is, the individual will prevails over the general. But the social order requires the domination of the general will. From this unfortunate contradiction Rousseau draws various inferences about the relative efficiency and desirability of different governmental arrangements—inferences that coincide with the commonplaces of earlier theory and observation.

His classification of governmental forms follows the ancient and familiar categories—monarchy, aristocracy, democracy and mixed. Democracy is that in which the sovereign assembly itself exercises the function of administrator. Such a union of functions does not appeal to Rousseau as a practicable system save possibly in a small and simple community. Sovereignty is necessarily democratic, in the most exclusive sense, in his theory, but democratic government is not suited to mankind. Rousseau expresses indeed no definite judgment as to what form of government is best. He follows on this question the thought of the most judicious of his predecessors, and finds that each form may be peculiarly adapted to some particular set of conditions. His discussion of the subject manifests a creditable knowledge and appreciation of the work of Montesquieu, in emphasizing the effect of varieties in economic and social conditions. But while the question as to what government is absolutely the best defies a categorical answer, Rousseau finds a single simple and conclusive test by which to determine whether a given nation is well or ill governed. This is the census.

> Other things being equal, that government is infallibly the better under which, without extraneous measures, without naturalization, without colonies, the citizens show the greater increase in numbers. That under which a people is decreasing and dying out is the worst. Statisticians, the matter is in your hands: count, measure, compare.

Both the establishment and the extinction of governments subject Rousseau's principles to rather severe tests; but his assurance carries him over the gaps that his reasoning fails to bridge. To set a government in operation would seem to be impossible under the conceptions of sovereignty and law that he so carefully defines; for while the sovereign may declare what the form of government shall be—a general act and hence appropriate to the sovereign—it cannot name the persons who are to man the offices, since that, Rousseau explicitly declares, is a particular act, wholly beyond the competence of the general will. Naming the magistrates is distinctively an act of government, not of sovereignty; and there is a difficulty, as Rousseau justly remarks, in understanding how there can be an act of government before the government comes into existence. To one who has achieved the delicate feat of creating a state by a contract to which the state itself is one of the parties, this later problem proves a matter, however, of no real concern. We perceive here, Rousseau says, "one of those astonishing properties of the body politic by which it reconciles operations that appear wholly contradictory." There takes place a sudden conversion of the sovereignty into government, so that with no perceptible change and merely by a new relation of all to all, the citizens, becoming magistrates, pass from general acts to particular acts, and from the law to its execution. That is to say, the sovereign people, assembled to institute a government, vote that a certain form shall be established, and vote that certain men shall fill the offices thus created. The first vote expresses the general will and is in the strictest sense law; the second vote is not an expression of the general will, and is not law, but a mere governmental decree. Between the two votes the assembly changes its character, just as a parliamentary body changes its character when it goes into committee of the whole. The people act in one instance as sovereign and in the other as a democratic government. Since the process here described is inevitable in the establishment of monarchy, aristocracy and all other forms, it follows that, in Rousseau's thought, every government must be considered as originating in democracy.

Such being the method by which the inception of government is reconciled with Rousseau's first principles, let us examine their bearing on its normal operation. Lawmaking, in the strict sense, is of course a function not of the government but of the sovereign. It can be performed only by an assembly of the whole people. Representation is wholly out of the question in this matter. The general will can no more be represented than it can be alienated. The vaunted modern device of representative assemblies Rousseau regards as but an evidence of political decay. "Because of indolence and wealth they at last have soldiers to enslave the country and representatives to sell it." Deputies may be chosen by the people for the despatch of certain duties; but they are merely agents, and have no final authority. "The English people thinks itself free; but it is greatly mistaken; it is free only during the elections for members of Parliament; so soon as they are elected the people is enslaved and becomes a zero." Whatever may be the inconvenience in large states, the whole people must be looked to as the sole legislator.

The question at once presents itself: shall the voice of the majority prevail as the general will? If so, how shall it appear that the minority, constrained by superior numbers, follows its own will and is free? Rousseau answers: only one political act requires unanimity, and that is the social pact. No one is a member of the community except in consequence of his own deliberate volition. Within the state once formed both sovereign and governmental acts are determined by the majority. That the minority seems no longer free, because subject to laws to which they have not given their consent, is an illusion, due to a wrong way of looking at the question. When a project of law is laid before the assembly of the people, they are asked, not whether they approve or reject it, but whether it is or is not conformed to the general will. The vote of each is merely his opinion on that question:

> When, therefore, the opinion contrary to mine prevails, it is merely proved that I was mistaken, and that the general will was not what I thought it was. If my opinion had prevailed, I should have done what I did not will; then indeed I should not have been free.

Such is the burlesque of reasoning by which Rousseau seems to think that he actually clears up one of the most troublesome difficulties in ultimate political theory. A deliberation of the sovereign people appears as a guessing match and the law by which men are free is fixed by a majority of guesses. The citizen who is in the minority is not a slave but only a poor guesser. Rousseau characteristically follows this word-juggling with a frank admission that he has begged the question at issue: "This assumes, it is true, that all the elements of the general will are in the majority; when they cease to be there, whichever side prevails, there is no longer any liberty."

The decline and death of the body politic are inevitable, Rousseau holds, and his analysis of the causes turns still on his doctrine of will. The government tends incessantly to invade the sphere of sovereignty; that is, to substitute the will of the magistrates for the general will. The greater intensity of volition in the smaller body accounts for this. At the same time there is a ceaseless tendency of government to contract itself from democracy to aristocracy and thence to monarchy—and thus to increase the intensity of its volitions, as compared with those of the growing community. Only in small nations, amid simple conditions, does the general will have any assured operation. As a society grows and conditions become complex, not only the government, but also the numerous rival groups of private citizens strive to advance their special interests instead of the public advantage, and to substitute a particular for the general will. Because civilization, however deplorable, is inevitable, this process is certain. "The body politic, as well as the human body, begins to die at its birth and carries within itself the causes of its destruction."

Something indeed may be done to retard decay and to preserve as long as possible liberty, equality and legitimate authority. Rousseau prides himself, and with some justification, on his suggestions in this respect. They concern only the usurpatory tendency of the government; the vices of human nature that bring the other evils are beyond correction by political devices. There must be, he says, periodical assemblies of the sovereign people, for the purpose of maintaining the social pact. The meetings must be spontaneous—wholly independent of the government in summons and action. To the people thus assembled, two questions must be submitted: "First, is it the pleasure of the sovereign to preserve the existing form of government; Second, is it the pleasure of the people to leave the administration to those who at present have it in charge." So long as a free expression of the people's will on these two points is obtainable at regular and not too long intervals, the usurpations of the government will be reduced to a minimum. As an additional guarantee of this result Rousseau lays down the principle that when the sovereign is assembled the functions of the government are *ipso facto* suspended.

The great political objection to Rousseau's scheme of legislation by a general assembly of the people was, of course, the apparent impossibility of its application to large states. Rousseau admitted that where population was great and the territory extensive, there would be grave inconvenience. Not for a moment on that account would he concede that representatives should be allowed to constitute the legislature. "Where right and liberty are everything inconveniences are nothing." In a large country the assemblies could be held at different places in turn, and thus distribute the inconvenience among all the citizens alike. But at all hazards the principle must be maintained that every citizen should be entitled to participate on equal terms in the supreme function of law-making.

Despite all the tiresome metaphysics with which Rousseau surrounds his device for maintaining the state, it is easy to see that he foreshadows two very familiar institutions of nineteenth-century democracy, namely, the periodical popular vote on the question of revising the constitution and the periodical election of officers. Whether Rousseau would approve the manner in which his device is applied in many states of the American Union may be doubtful; but there is no room to doubt that the spirit of our constitutional provisions is very closely akin to the spirit in which his propositions were conceived.

In the field of politics Rousseau's teaching was suggestive rather than conclusive; but the stimulating force of his suggestions long remained a cardinal fact of literature and history. His fancies, fallacies and quibbles often appealed more strongly than the sober observation and balanced reasoning of Montesquieu to the *Zeitgeist* of the later eighteenth century. Both the pure philosophy of politics and the practical statesmanship of the time clearly illustrate this. His spirit and his dogmas, however disguised and transformed, are seen everywhere both in the speculative

systems and in the governmental reorganizations of the stirring era that followed his death.

On the side of pure theory the most distinctive service of Rousseau was that due to his doctrine of sovereignty. The common interest and the general will assumed, through his manipulation, a greater definiteness and importance than philosophy had hitherto ascribed to them. They became the central features of almost every theory of the state. Through those concepts a way was opened by which the unity and solidarity of a population became the necessary presupposition of scientific politics. Rousseau thus contributed largely to promote the theory of the national state. His main purpose, however, was apart from this. Consciously he aimed only to devise a theory of sovereignty through which liberty and authority should be reconciled. His metaphysics and psychology, however ingenious, were not, as we have seen, equal to the task. He could offer no self-consistent reasoning by which it should appear that an individual's will was certain to be expressed in the general will, except in the same sense in which the individual's will was certain to be expressed in the will of a monarch to whom he had submitted himself. Rousseau failed, in short, to prove that the sovereignty of the community was any more compatible with individual liberty than the sovereignty of a monarch or an oligarchy. But his earnest and confident declamation about the virtues of the general will and the significance of the general interest brought those concepts into the foreground of political theory and evoked from more subtle reasoners than Rousseau more refined and self-consistent solutions of the problem he propounded. If their results were ultimately no more successful than his, that was due rather to the *a priori* conceptions of liberty and authority that were the common basis of this whole school of speculation than to any flaw in the logic by which the deductions from these conceptions were made. The assumption that true and perfect liberty could be predicted of only the non-social man, was fatal to any theory of political authority. Nothing could come out of this assumption save the empty paradoxes of Rousseau, the paralyzing transcendentalism of Kant, Fichte and Hegel, Rousseau's legitimate successors, or anarchy pure and simple. Making a state out of a group of perfectly free and independent individuals is like making a statue out of a heap of sand: some cohesive principle is necessary that it is beyond the art of the "legislator" or the sculptor to supply. Aristotle furnished such a principle in his dictum that the social and political element is as strong and fundamental as the individualistic in man—that dependence on his kind is to be presumed of the normal human being. But in the eighteenth century the Aristotelian way of approaching politics made small appeal to intellectual men, and least of all to Rousseau.

Where Rousseau's theorizing touched government in its more practical aspects, his ideas were in some cases singularly fruitful. His sharp distinction between the sovereign and the government was chiefly responsible for this. He has been criticised for his doctrine that only the sovereign can make law. But his theory here was perfectly self-consistent, and it moreover proved adaptable to the explanation of certain concrete institutions of a novel kind that soon after Rousseau's death became the subject of knowledge and interest to intellectual men in France. Law (*loi*) in Rousseau's thought, was a term that could designate properly only a rule of perfect generality both in content and in application. Such being the case, his sovereign community was logically the only law-maker. The enactments of any so-called legislature that formed a part of the government could have only the character of decrees for carrying into effect the superior mandates of the true legislature. Rousseau's requirements for law in the strict sense were, we have seen, very exacting. The assignment of a citizen to an office, or the assessment of a tax upon specific citizens could not be effected, he held, by law; for such acts were not general but particular in their application, and hence involved not the general, but some particular interest. It is hard to accept Rousseau's reasoning in this detail; for he holds that the filling of an office must be treated as a matter rather of private than of public concern, and this is scarcely a tenable proposition. But apart from this minor point it is easy to see that Rousseau's "law" is substantially what came to be called fundamental law or constitution. Thus conceived, his doctrine of law-making is merely that now familiar dogma of political science, that the constitution is made by the sovereign people, and the government must conform its acts to this supreme law.

During the decade succeeding the death of Rousseau the interest of Frenchmen became by the course of events deeply enlisted in the affairs and institutions of the American States just freed from Great Britain. The political systems of these states presented in concrete realization principles of sovereignty and law that strongly suggested the doctrine in the **Social Contract.** The formal written constitutions in which the organization and action of government were prescribed satisfied very well the requirements that Rousseau laid down for law in the strict sense. They were on their face the expression of the people's will; they dealt with only the fundamental questions of the political order; and they were clearly distinguished, both by their formal source and by their superior authority, from the mandates of the governments that they set up. Through these constitutions, thus, the sovereignty of the people and its relation to government were exemplified in actual institutions on lines that ran closely parallel to Rousseau's theory. This coïncidence, fortuitous though it was, did not fail of far-reaching influence on theory and on practice in the revolutionary movement that was impending. (pp. 382-407)

> *William A. Dunning, "The Political Theories of Jean Jacques Rousseau," in* Political Science Quarterly, *Vol. XXIV, No. 3, September, 1909, pp. 377-408.*

George Saintsbury   (essay date 1911)

[*Saintsbury was an English literary historian and critic. A prolific writer, he composed several histories of English and European literature as well as numerous critical works on individual authors, styles, and periods. In the following excerpt from an essay originally published in 1911, he offers an overview of and ruminative commentary upon Rousseau's literary career.*]

Rousseau's behaviour had frequently made him enemies, but his writings had for the most part made him friends. The quarrel with Madame d'Épinay, with Diderot, and through them with the philosophe party reversed this. In 1758 appeared his *Lettre à d'Alembert contre les spectacles,* written in the winter of the previous year at Mont-

louis. This was at once an attack on Voltaire, who was giving theatrical representations at Les Délices, on D'Alembert, who had condemned the prejudice against the stage in the *Encyclopédie,* and on one of the favourite amusements of the society of the day. Voltaire's strong point was not forgiveness, and, though Rousseau no doubt exaggerated the efforts of his "enemies," he was certainly henceforward as obnoxious to the philosophe coterie as to the orthodox party. He still, however, had no lack of patrons—he never had—though his perversity made him quarrel with all in turn. The amiable duke and duchess of Luxembourg, who were his neighbours at Montlouis, made his acquaintance, or rather forced theirs upon him, and he was industrious in his literary work—indeed, most of his best books were produced during his stay in the neighbourhood of Montmorency. A letter to Voltaire on his poem about the Lisbon earthquake embittered the dislike between the two, being surreptitiously published. *La Nouvelle Héloïse* appeared in the same year (1760), and it was immensely popular. In 1762 appeared the *Contrat social* at Amsterdam, and *Émile,* which was published both in the Low Countries and at Paris. For the latter the author received 6000 livres, for the *Contrat* 1000.

Julie, ou La Nouvelle Héloïse, is a novel written in letters describing the loves of a man of low position and a girl of rank, her subsequent marriage to a respectable freethinker of her own station, the mental agonies of her lover, and the partial appeasing of the distresses of the lovers by the influence of noble sentiment and the good offices of a philanthropic Englishman. It is too long, the sentiment is overstrained, and severe moralists have accused it of a certain complaisance in dealing with amatory errors; but it is full of pathos and knowledge of the human heart. The *Contrat social,* as its title implies, endeavours to base all government on the consent, direct or implied, of the governed, and indulges in much ingenious argument to get rid of the practical inconveniences of such a suggestion. *Émile,* the second title of which is *De l'Éducation,* is much more of a treatise than of a novel, though a certain amount of narrative interest is kept up throughout.

Rousseau's reputation was now higher than ever, but the term of the comparative prosperity which he had enjoyed for nearly ten years was at hand. The *Contrat social* was obviously anti-monarchic; the *Nouvelle Héloïse* was said to be immoral; the sentimental deism of the **"Profession du vicaire Savoyard"** in *Émile* irritated equally the philosophe party and the church. On June 11, 1762, *Émile* was condemned by the parlement of Paris. . . . The archbishop of Paris had published a pastoral against him, and Rousseau did not let the year pass without a *Lettre à M. de Beaumont.* The council of Geneva had joined in the condemnation of *Émile,* and Rousseau first solemnly renounced his citizenship, and then, in the *Lettres de la montagne* (1763), attacked the council and the Genevan constitution unsparingly. All this excited public opinion against him, and gradually he grew unpopular in his own neighbourhood. (pp. 124-26)

Many of the best-known stories of Rousseau's life date from [the summer of 1770,] when he was tolerably accessible to visitors, though clearly half-insane. He finished his *Confessions,* wrote his *Dialogues* (the interest of which is not quite equal to the promise of their curious sub-title, *Rousseau juge de Jean Jacques*), and began his *Rêveries du promeneur solitaire,* intended as a sequel and complement to the *Confessions,* and one of the best of all his books. It should be said that besides these, which complete the list of his principal works, he has left a very large number of minor works and a considerable correspondence. During this time he lived in the Rue Platière, which is now named after him. But his suspicions of secret enemies grew stronger rather than weaker, and at the beginning of 1778 he was glad to accept the offer of M. de Girardin, a rich financier, and occupy a cottage at Ermenonville. The country was beautiful; but his old terrors revived, and his woes were complicated by the alleged inclination of Thérèse for one of M. de Girardin's stable-boys. On July 2nd he died in a manner which has been much discussed, suspicions of suicide being circulated at the time by Grimm and others.

There is little doubt that for the last ten or fifteen years of his life, if not from the time of his quarrel with Diderot and Madame d'Épinay, Rousseau was not wholly sane—the combined influence of late and unexpected literary fame and of constant solitude and discomfort acting upon his excitable temperament so as to overthrow the balance, never very stable, of his fine and acute but unrobust intellect. He was by no means the only man of letters of his time who had to submit to something like persecution. Fréron on the orthodox side had his share of it, as well as Voltaire, Helvétius, Diderot and Montesquieu on that of the innovators. But Rousseau had not, like Montesquieu, a position which guaranteed him from serious danger; he was not wealthy like Helvétius; he had not the wonderful suppleness and trickiness which even without his wealth would probably have defended Voltaire himself; and he lacked entirely the "bottom" of Fréron and Diderot. When he was molested he could only shriek at his enemies and suspect his friends. His moral character was undoubtedly weak in other ways than this, but it is fair to remember that but for his astounding *Confessions* the more disgusting parts of it would not have been known, and that these *Confessions* were written, if not under hallucination, at any rate in circumstances entitling the self-condemned criminal to the benefit of considerable doubt. If Rousseau had held his tongue, he might have stood lower as a man of letters; he would pretty certainly have stood higher as a man. He was, moreover, really sinned against, if still more sinning. The conduct of Grimm to him was certainly bad; and, though Walpole was not his personal friend, a worse action than his famous letter, considering the well-known idiosyncrasy of the subject, would be difficult to find. It was his own fault that he saddled himself with the Le Vasseurs, but their conduct was probably, if not certainly, ungrateful in the extreme. Only excuses can be made for him; but the excuses for a man born, as Hume after the quarrel said of him, "without a skin" are numerous and strong.

His peculiar reputation increased after his death. During his life his personal peculiarities and the fact that his opinions were nearly as obnoxious to the one party as to the other worked against him, but it was not so after his death. The men of the Revolution regarded him with something like idolatry, and his literary merits conciliated many who were far from idolizing him as a revolutionist. His style was taken up by Bernardin de Saint Pierre and by Chateaubriand. It was employed for purposes quite different from those to which he had himself applied it, and the re-

action triumphed by the very arms which had been most powerful in the hands of the Revolution. Byron's fervid panegyric enlisted on his side all who admired Byron—that is to say, the majority of the younger men and women of Europe between 1820 and 1850—and thus different sides of his tradition were continued for a full century after the publication of his chief books. His religious unorthodoxy was condoned because he never scoffed; his political heresies, after their first effect was over, seemed harmless from the very want of logic and practical spirit in them, while part at least of his literary secret was the common property of almost every one who attempted literature.

In religion Rousseau was undoubtedly what he has been called above—a sentimental deist; but no one who reads him with the smallest attention can fail to see that sentimentalism was the essence, deism the accident of his creed. In his time orthodoxy at once generous and intelligent hardly existed in France. There were ignorant persons who were sincerely orthodox; there were intelligent persons who pretended to be so. But between the time of Massillon and D'Aguesseau and the time of Lamennais and Joseph de Maistre the class of men of whom in England Berkeley, Butler and Johnson were representatives did not exist in France. Little inclined by nature to any but the emotional side of religion, and utterly undisciplined in any other by education, course of life, or the general tendency of public opinion, Rousseau naturally took refuge in the nebulous kind of natural religion which was at once fashionable and convenient. If his practice fell far short even of his own arbitrary standard of morality, as much may be said of persons far more dogmatically orthodox.

In politics, on the other hand, Rousseau was a sincere and, as far as in him lay, a convinced republican. He had no great tincture of learning, he was by no means a profound logician, and he was impulsive and emotional in the extreme—characteristics which in political matters predispose the subject to the preference of equality above all political requisites. He saw that under the French monarchy the actual result was the greatest misery of the greatest number, and he did not look much further. The *Contrat social* is for the political student one of the most curious and interesting books existing. Historically it is null; logically it is full of gaping flaws; practically its manipulations of the *volonté de tous* and the *volonté générale* are clearly insufficient to obviate anarchy. But its mixture of real eloquence and apparent cogency is exactly such as always carries a multitude with it, if only for a time. Moreover, in some minor branches of politics and economics Rousseau was a real reformer. Visionary as his educational schemes (chiefly promulgated in *Émile*) are in parts, they are admirable in others, and his protest against mothers refusing to nurse their children hit a blot in French life which is not removed yet, and has always been a source of weakness to the nation.

But it is as a literary man pure and simple—that is to say, as an exponent rather than as an originator of ideas—that Rousseau is most noteworthy, and that he has exercised most influence. The first thing noticeable about him is that he defies all customary and mechanical classification. He is not a dramatist—his work as such is insignificant—nor a novelist, for, though his two chief works except the *Confessions* are called novels, *Émile* is one only in name, and *La Nouvelle Héloïse* is as a story diffuse, prosy and awkward to a degree. He was without command of poetic form, and he could only be called a philosopher in an age when the term was used with such meaningless laxity as was customary in the 18th century. If he must be classed, he was before all things a describer—a describer of the passions of the human heart and of the beauties of nature. In the first part of his vocation the novelists of his own youth, such as Marivaux, Richardson and Prévost, may be said to have shown him the way, though he improved greatly upon them; in the second he was almost a creator. In combining the two and expressing the effect of nature on the feelings and of the feelings on the aspect of nature he was absolutely without a forerunner or a model. And, as literature since his time has been chiefly differentiated from literature before it by the colour and tone resulting from this combination, Rousseau may be said to hold, as an influence, a place almost unrivalled in literary history. The defects of all sentimental writing are noticeable in him, but they are palliated by his wonderful feeling, and by the passionate sincerity even of his insincere passages. Some cavils have been made against his French, but none of much weight or importance. And in such passages as the famous "Voilà de la pervenche" of the *Confessions,* as the description of the isle of St Pierre in the *Rêveries,* as some of the letters in the *Nouvelle Héloïse* and others, he has achieved absolute perfection in doing what he intended to do. The reader, as it has been said, may think he might have done something else with advantage, but he can hardly think that he could have done this thing better. (pp. 127-31)

> *George Saintsbury, "Rousseau," in his* French Literature and Its Masters, *edited by Huntington Cairns, Alfred A. Knopf, 1946, pp. 119-31.*

Havelock Ellis   (essay date 1912)

[*Ellis was a pioneering sexual psychologist and a respected English man of letters. His most famous work is* The Psychology of Sex *(1897-1928), a seven-volume study containing frankly stated case histories of sex-related abnormalities. This work helped change British and American attitudes toward the hitherto almost forbidden subject of sexuality. In the following excerpt from an essay first published in the* Atlantic Monthly *in 1912 to commemorate the bicentennial of Rousseau's birth, Ellis discourses upon Rousseau's wide influence and philosophic roots, claiming that Rousseau "effected a spiritual revolution which no mere man of letters has ever effected, a revolution only comparable to that effected by Christianity."*]

Two centuries after his birth, Jean-Jacques Rousseau continues to exert a potent and disturbing influence; we still have among us his ardent advocates, his bitter enemies. For the most part, during the century that follows the death of any mere writer of books, he falls back into the historic background; the battles that may once have raged around him have subsided; and those persons who are still sufficiently interested to like or dislike his work combine to adjust him in the niche, large or small, which he is henceforth destined to occupy. It is so even with the greatest. Less than a century has passed since Goethe died; for some he is in the modern world 'the master of those who know'; for others he is 'a colossal sentimentalist'; but each

party recognises it has something big to deal with and there is no longer any inclination to fall into violent dispute. Not so with Rousseau. This man, who filled the second half of the eighteenth century, who inspired most of the literary and even social movements of the nineteenth century, remains a living and even distracting force in the twentieth century. At the present time there is probably more written about Rousseau than about any contemporary man of letters with the possible exception of Tolstoy, and Tolstoy, we may remember, was an avowed disciple of Rousseau. We have made up our minds about Voltaire, even about Diderot, but we have not made up our minds about Rousseau. According to the point of view, and the special group of alleged facts on which attention is concentrated, Rousseau figures as the meanest of mankind, as a degenerate pervert, as an unfortunate lunatic, as a suffering and struggling man of genius, as the noble pioneer of all the great humanitarian and progressive movements in the modern world, and as the seductive and empty rhetorician who is leading society astray from the orderly paths of civilisation into the abyss of anarchy. (pp. 95-6)

Since those who revile the name of Rousseau are at once with those who adore it in magnifying the extent of his influence, it becomes easier than it would otherwise be to estimate what our modern world presumably owes to Rousseau. It may be interesting to touch on two of these things: the Revolution and Romanticism.

The whole Revolution, say its friends and its enemies alike, was Rousseau; Berthelot, the great man of science, declared it in solemn admiration a quarter of a century ago. Lasserre, the acute critic, declares it in bitter indignation today. Rousseau was not, indeed, consciously working towards the Revolution, and he would have loathed its protagonists who acted in his name, just as Jesus would have loathed the scribes and Pharisees who have masqueraded in his Church. But, as we look back, it is easy to see how Rousseau's work, and Rousseau's alone among the men of his generation pointed to revolution. They appealed to intelligence, to good sense, to fine feeling, to elevated humanitarianism; but it is not these things of which revolutions are made. Rousseau appealed to fundamental instincts, to soaring aspirations, to blind passions, to the volcanic eruptive elements in human nature, and we are at once amid the forces of revolution. No wonder that all the men of the Revolution fed themselves on Rousseau's words. Not a single revolutionary, Mallet du Pan noted in 1789, but was carried away by Rousseau's doctrines, and burning to realise them. Marat was seen in public enthusiastically reading aloud the *Social Contract,* and Charlotte Corday, who slew him, was equally the fervent disciple of Rousseau. There was one other man beside Rousseau who had a supreme part in moulding the Revolution, at all events so far as concerns its final outcome. It is interesting to hear that this man, Napoleon, declared to Lord Holland that without 'that bad man' Rousseau there would have been no Revolution. Since the Christianisation of the Roman Empire there have been four great movements of the human spirit in Christendom—the Renaissance, the Reformation, the Counter-Reformation, and the Revolution. Three of these movements have been so diffused in time and space that we are scarcely justified in closely associating even one of them with the influence of a single man. But the Revolution, incalculably vast as its results have been, was narrowly circumscribed. It is comparatively easy to measure it, and when so measured its friends and its foes ascribe it—so far as any complex social-economic movement can be associated with one man—to Rousseau.

Mainly by virtue of his relation to the Revolution, Rousseau is claimed as the pioneer of Modern Democracy, alike in its direction towards Socialism and its direction towards Anarchism. For both these democratic movements—the collectivistic as well as the individualistic—rest on those natural instincts which it was Rousseau's mission to proclaim. The democracy which insists that the whole shall embody every unit, and the democracy which insists that each unit shall have its own rights against the whole, alike appeal to deep emotional reasons to which the humblest respond. 'There would have been no Republic without Rousseau,' says Lemaître. Republicanism, Socialism, Anarchism—these are the three democratic movements which have been slowly permeating and transforming the political societies of men since the Great Revolution of 1789, and we are asked to believe that the germs of all were scattered abroad by this one man, Rousseau.

The chorus of voices which acclaims or accuses Rousseau as the creator of Romanticism is even greater than that which finds in him the inventor of Revolutionary Democracy. The Revolutionary Movement and the Romantic Movement are one, we are told, and Rousseau was responsible for both. What, it may be asked, is Romanticism? There is not much agreement on this point. Lasserre, one of its ablest and most absolute opponents, tells us that it is 'a general revolution of the human soul' which may be described as 'a system of feeling and acting conformably to the supposed primitive nature of mankind,' and since we do not know what the primitive nature of mankind is, Romanticism becomes, in opposition to the classical spirit in general and the Gallic spirit in particular, 'absolute individualism in thought and feeling,' or in other words, 'a disorder of the feelings and ideas which overturns the whole economy of civilised human nature.' This definition is itself individualistic—and therefore on the theory Romantic—but it may, for the moment, serve. Fortunately, though there is no agreement as to what Romanticism is, there is less dispute as to the writers who may be termed Romantic.

It is a remarkable fact that though Rousseau so largely filled the second half of the eighteenth century he had little influence on its literature in France. He was the adored prophet, preacher, teacher, but not the inspired and inspiring artist with a new revelation of Nature peculiarly apt for literary uses. Beaumarchais, who here dominated that period, belongs to altogether another tradition. Only Bernardin de Saint-Pierre was the follower, as he was also the friend, of Rousseau, and *Paul and Virginia* opens the great literary tradition of Rousseau. The first notable names in French literature which we can at all associate with Rousseau are dubious names, more dubious perhaps than they deserve to be, but still distinctly dubious. It is highly probable that the **Confessions** moved Casanova to write his own immortal *Mémoires*. It is certain that they inspired that interesting picture of an unwholesome mind, the *Monsieur Nicolas* of Restif de la Bretonne, the 'Rousseau du ruisseau,' as he has been wittily and accurately termed. We must even recognise that Rousseau was the adored exemplar of the Marquis de Sade, who, in *Aline et Valcour,* makes Valcour, here speaking probably for his

author, assert that Rousseau encouraged him to devote himself to literature and philosophy. 'It was in the conversation of this deep philosopher, of this true friend of Nature and of Man, that I acquired my dominant passion for literature and the arts.'

In Germany, earlier than elsewhere, the influence of Rousseau was profoundly felt by men of an altogether different type of character. In France, Rousseau could only be potent by stimulating a revolutionary reaction against everything which had long been regarded as the classic norm from which no deviation was possible; that was why the morbid and unsound personalities in literature, rightly finding a real point of contact with Rousseau, felt his influence first. But an altogether different tradition, if we look beyond cosmopolitan aristocratic circles, prevailed in Germany. Here the subjective emotionalism of Rousseau, his constant appeal to the ultimate standard of Nature, were so congenial to the Teutonic spirit that they acted as an immediate liberating force. Rousseau was Kant's supreme master; only one portrait, Rousseau's, hung on the walls of the philosopher's simple study; all his doctrines in the three Critiques may be regarded (Thomas Davidson has ingeniously argued) as a formal crystallisation of Rousseau's fluid eloquence. Fichte also was largely moulded by Rousseau, as were Herder and Lessing. Goethe in the final stages of his long development aimed at serenely objective Neo-classic ideals which were far indeed from Rousseau, but at the outset he was as thorough a disciple as Kant. He went on pilgrimage to the beautiful island in the Lake of Bienne once hallowed by Rousseau's presence; his Werther is manifestly the younger brother of Saint-Preux, and it may be, as some have claimed, that without Rousseau there could have been no *Faust*.

It was not until the nineteenth century that the Romantic Movement finally burst into magnificent life in France. Chateaubriand appears as the quintessence of Romanticism, a more pure embodiment of its literary quality than even Rousseau himself. Senancour, especially as he shows himself in his *Obermann,* was an equally typical and much more genuine representative of the Movement. Madame de Staël, one of the first to write about Rousseau, was penetrated by his spirit, and became the revealer to France of Romantic Germany. Alfred de Musset was a Romantic through Byron, rather than directly from Rousseau. Victor Hugo, Lamartine, George Sand, even at times Balzac, all belonged to Romanticism. Michelet, writing history by the sole light of his own personal emotions, was peculiarly a Romantic. Flaubert, in a later generation, was Romantic on one side, altogether alien from Romanticism, as were his fundamental ideals. But during the first half of the nineteenth century in France, with the possible exception of Stendhal—for even he was really affected by the movement—it is not easy to name any notable figure in literature who was outside Romanticism. Rousseau's influence had become so all-pervading that, like the universal pressure of the air, it was sometimes unperceived by those who were experiencing it. Louis Dumur has pointed out that Alfred de Musset in his *Confession d'un Enfant du Siècle,* when trying to discover the sources of Romanticism, never so much as mentions Rousseau.

The attitude of England towards Romanticism and towards Rousseau was different from either that of Germany or of France. The Germans were made conscious by

Rousseau of their own unconscious impulses. The French were forced to undergo a violent conversion. But the English were Romanticists already from the outset and here the Romantic Movement could effect no revolution. All Rousseau's literary inspirations and aesthetic ideals had come, directly or indirectly, from England: Richardson's *Clarissa,* Kent's English garden, Locke's philosophy, English independence and English freedom, these were the things which had aroused the emulation or stirred the enthusiasm of Rousseau. English influence equally stimulated also the great apostle of Romanticism, and Chateaubriand composed *Atala* and *René* in Hyde Park. These splendid flowers were therefore easily acceptable in England for they were clearly raised from English seeds. Rousseau's influence recognised and unrecognised, reached English Romanticism, but Rousseau was here only giving back in a more highly developed form what he had himself received from England.

If we look beyond the Romantic Movement in its narrower literary sense, we still find that the influence of Rousseau remains just as plainly visible, in Russia, for instance. It is unnecessary to say that the greatest writer of modern times in Russia, the greatest writer in the world of his day, was from his earliest years a disciple of Rousseau; Tolstoy read and re-read the twenty volumes of Rousseau's works until some of the pages became so familiar that it seemed to him he had written them himself; he wore Rousseau's portrait next his skin as the devout Russian wears the cross; it was, he himself said, worship rather than admiration which he experienced for Rousseau; even shortly before his death he wrote that the two chief formative influences of his life had been Rousseau and the Gospels.

If we turn away from the apostles and the propagandists of avowed emotional revolution, we have not yet escaped Rousseau. The austere Emerson equally has his roots in Rousseau, if he was not actually, as Davidson termed him, 'the most loyal disciple Rousseau ever had.' The Transcendentalist was here at one with the Positivist. George Eliot, equally alien in temperament, was an equally ardent admirer of the **Confessions;** Rousseau, she said, 'quickened' her mind, not by imparting any new beliefs, but by 'the mighty rushing wind of his inspiration'; he 'made man and nature a fresh world of thought and feeling to me.' It was an accurate characterisation of the kind of power by which Rousseau has so often held the souls of men and women.

In the twentieth century the same potent force is still quickening ardent and aspiring souls who strive to create new ideals. Moreover, Rousseau is still the precursor even of those who are unconscious of his influence. He had long ago anticipated our latest philosophies. William James is counted the founder of Pragmatism, but the conception of 'truth' as 'practical truth' or 'cash value' rather than 'science,' was so clearly set forth in **Emile** and the second half of the **Nouvelle Héloïse,** that Schinz has been able to argue that 'the greatest of the Pragmatists is—and will probably remain—Jean-Jacques Rousseau.' So also with the fashionable Bergsonian philosophy of the day, with its depreciation of reason and its insistence on the vital force of instinct. That also is laid down, with a less subtle elaboration but not with less emphasis, by Rousseau.

Even those for whom Rousseau is nothing but a poison

have not escaped the operation of that seductive venom. Nietzsche, the most conspicuous and influential thinker of these latter days, was absolutely opposed to Rousseau. Rousseau's 'Nature,' his 'good man,' his sentiment, his weaknesses, especially his lack of aristocratic culture and his plebeianism—against all these things Nietzsche's hatred was implacable. Yet Rousseau was in his own blood. 'Nietzsche,' says Alois Riehl, 'is the antipodes of Rousseau, and yet his spiritual relation. He is the Rousseau of our time.'

In thus estimating the hold of Rousseau over the things which have been counted precious since the days in which he lived, we have the authority even of those who rebel against his influence. But there is always a fallacy involved in such attempts to fasten an unlimited responsibility upon any human figure, not excepting the greatest. Even the supreme man of genius, as Dumur truly says, is no aerolite from another sphere, no bolt from the blue. The most absolute innovator has found the terms of his fruitful ideas in ancient tradition. The most potent revolutionary owes his power to the fact that in his day certain conditions, especially economic and social conditions, combine to produce a vacuum his spirit is peculiarly fitted to fill. The name of Darwin is immortally associated with the idea of evolution, but the idea had been slowly germinating through thousands of years, sometimes in brains of as great a calibre as his own, until the moment arrived when at last fruition was possible, and the cautious, deliberate Darwin calmly completed the work of the ages. Even the great movement of Christianity, which sometimes seem to us so mighty as to be beyond the reach of reason to fathom, is seen to be necessary and inevitable when we realise the conditions under which it arose and see the figure of Jesus slowly hammered and annealed into the shape which best satisfied the deepest cravings of an epoch. Rousseau—again alike by friends and foes—has been counted, like Jesus, a prophet issuing with a new law from the desert into a decadent civilisation he was destined to dissolve and renew; he has been regarded as a great reformer of Christianity such as Luther was, the incarnation of a new wave of Christianity, adding to the renovation of its essential qualities—its abandonment to emotion, its magnification of the poor and humble, its insistence on charity—a new set of notes, a trend towards political realisation, a fresh ideal of natural beauty, a justification of passion, a refinement of voluptuous sentiment, which adjusted Christianity to the modern soul as it had never been adjusted before. Luther had de-Catholicised Christianity; Rousseau, who in his own person united the two traditions, while yet retaining the plebeian and individualistic basis which Luther established, re-Catholicised Christianity on a new plane, even though in the end he stood aloof from Christianity, and created a Church whose dogmas rested on the universal authority of instincts and emotions.

Yet, just as we can counterpart every Christian rite and dogma outside Christianity, so also it is easy to duplicate every tenet and tendency in Rousseau. Marivaux, within narrower limits and with a more restrained method, was a sympathetic and original moralist, a delicate artist, a subtle psychologist, to a degree that Rousseau never attained; in his earliest work Rousseau was frankly an imitator of Marivaux. The Abbé Prévost, again, more than any man had let the flood of early English romanticism into France, had translated *Clarissa,* and himself written novels of wild and sombre romantic passion; Rousseau knew Prévost, he was profoundly affected by his novels. Locke, in another sphere, had set forth epoch-making reflections on political government, and had written an enlightened treatise on education; the author of the **Social Contract** and **Emile** clearly reveals how much he owed to 'the wise Locke.' Before ever he began to write, Rousseau had soaked his mind in books and meditated on them in his perpetual long walks; he was brought up on romances, he had read everything he could find, English travel books especially, about savages in 'the state of Nature'; he had absorbed all that matters in the literature of the seventeenth century, though he knew comparatively little of the literature of his own century; without any guidance, by unerring instinct, he had seized on the things that fed his own mood, from Plutarch to Petrarch. Even without going outside the pale of Catholic Christianity, he could, had he known it, have found the authority for every intimate and daring impulse of his own heart.

The ideas and the emotions, therefore, which Rousseau manifested were by no means unique. The temperament he had inherited furnished the most exquisitely fertile of all conceivable soils for these seeds to flourish in. But the seeds were not new seeds and for the most part we can trace with precision the exact source from which each of them reached Rousseau. Moreover, when we come, calmly and critically, to measure and to weigh the ideas and the emotions we find in Rousseau's books, it happens, as often as not, that they fail to stand our tests. If we explore the **Social Contract,** we find that every page swarms with bold propositions for which no proof is, or can be, supplied. Rousseau had borrowed Hobbes's conception of sovereignty and Locke's conception of popular government and amalgamated them into the image of a Sovereign People which can do no wrong and governs by its own direct *fiat,* in such a way that the will of each finds its part in the will of all. No doubt it is a magnificent idea and it is still alive in the world moulding political institutions; it is responsible for the establishment of the Referendum which has had a certain vogue in new political constitutions and we are constantly endeavouring, however much in vain, to approach its realisation. But when we examine Rousseau's exposition of this idea, we find that verbal logic takes the place of inductive reasoning, that impassioned declamation is the agent of persuasion, and that the very lucidity of the statement only brings out more clearly the glaring inconsistencies and absurdities which the argument involves.

If we turn to a very different book, though not less famous and in its own way not less influential, we encounter the same experience. *La Nouvelle Héloïse,* in the effect it has had on the writing of novels, is second to none, except *Don Quixote.* Schopenhauer, himself a great literary artist, counted **La Nouvelle Héloïse** among the four great novels of the world. Shelley, who was a fine critic as well as a great poet, was enraptured by the 'sublime genius and more than human sensibility' displayed in this book, as well as by 'the divine beauty of Rousseau's imagination,' as he realised it on sailing across the famous lake which is the scene of the novel. A more modern French critic finds that 'Julie has the tongue of an apostle, she is our greatest orator after Bossuet.' That is a eulogy which may well serve to condemn any novel, but it is probably the most favourable judgment which from the modern stand-

point can be bestowed upon Rousseau's novel. This novel so unlike a novel yet re-created the novel; that is admitted. Today **La Nouvelle Héloïse,** for all the fine passages we may discover in it, is far less agreeable to read than the best of those novels by Marivaux, Prévost, and the younger Crébillon which it replaced in popular esteem. Its sentimental rhetoric is now tedious; as a story it fails to enchain us; of subtle characterisation or dramatic vigour we find nothing; as a work of art it is incomparably inferior to *Clarissa Harlowe* on which it was modelled.

If we look more broadly at Rousseau's work, the results of critical examination are similar. The world's great teachers are, for the most part, impressive by the substantial unity of the message they have proclaimed; we feel a convincing harmony between that message and the personality behind it. So it is with Marcus Aurelius and so with Thoreau. It is so, also, on what may seem a lower ethical plane, with Rousseau's chief contemporaries, with Voltaire and with Diderot. It is not clearly so with Rousseau. He often seems like an exquisite instrument, giving forth a music which responds to the varying emotions of the hand that strikes it. He is the supreme individualist, and yet his doctrines furnish the foundations for socialism, even in its oppressive forms. He is the champion of the rights of passion, and yet he was the leader in a movement of revolt against licentiousness, of return to domesticity and the felicities of family life and maternal devotion to children. He was opposed to the emancipation of women, even to the education of women side by side with men; he is denounced by the advocates of women's rights who see in the philosophers whom he opposed the pioneers of their own movement, and yet he was acclaimed as the liberator of womanhood; noble women, from Madame Roland onwards, were his enthusiastic disciples, the literary promulgators of his genius are headed by two distinguished women, Madame de Staël and Madame de Charrière.

Still more discordant seems to many the clash of Rousseau's doctrines with Rousseau's life. The uncompromising champion of virtue was nearly forty years old before he learnt how to earn his own living honestly. The regenerator of love was a solitary sensuous sentimentalist. The author of **Emile,** the gospel of childhood, put away his own children—if indeed he ever really had any—as foundlings.

When we thus critically survey Rousseau's books and personality, it is difficult to avoid the conclusion that, to a large extent, Rousseau has represented a backward movement in civilisation. His influence has tended to depreciate the value of the mighty instrument of reason by which civilisation is mainly wrought; it has consecrated prejudice under the sacred names of Nature and instinct; it has opened the way to the triumph of plebeianism and the sanctification of mob-rule; it has tended, by casting off the restraints on emotion, to an unwholesome divorce between the extravagancies of feeling and the limitations of life.

It is on this note, at all events, that so many discussions of Rousseau finally rest: Rousseau was a 'degenerate' from birth, and his teaching is the disorganisation of civilised society. Yet, even if we believe that there are elements of truth in such a view, we can scarcely choose this standpoint for our final survey of Rousseau. When we bear in mind that the most aspiring efforts of the noblest souls during more than a century have been directly or indirectly inspired by this man, it becomes clear that to attaint Rousseau is to stain our own human nature, to place ourselves in the ranks of the Yahoos. For, there can be no doubt, unreasonable as it may be to regard Rousseau or any other man as the primary cause of any great social movement, it is he, more than any man, who has moulded the form of our spiritual activities and shaped our ideals. His passions have become the atmosphere in which we move. Since the days of feverish activity which Rousseau spent in his little hermitage at Montmorency, not merely our aims in politics, but our feeling for religion, our feeling for love, our feeling for Nature, have been renovated. They would have been renovated even if Rousseau had never lived, though perhaps not so thoroughly, yet, as things are, the new forms they have assumed have been determined by this solitary dreamer. 'Religion,' said Butler in the orderly and reasonable eighteenth-century manner, 'is a useful piece of information concerning a distant region of which otherwise we should have had no explanation': the mystic enthusiasm of the Vicaire Savoyard would alone have sufficed to sweep away for ever so pedestrian a conception of religion. Before Rousseau, love was a highly refined form of social intercourse, a species of gallantry conducted with self-restraint and all the formalities of its special etiquette; any extravagance, whether in feeling, in speech, or in action, was banished. But when Saint-Preux, oppressed by his high-strung passions, came to the rock at Meillerie to pour forth in solitude the flood of his sentimental tears, all the witty refinements of eighteenth-century gallantry, for good or for evil, were finally swept away; extravagancy was free to lay down the law of love. It was Rousseau who enabled Mirabeau in his first letter to Julie Danvers (whom he had never seen) to declare: 'I, also, am a lover, have emptied the cup of sensibility to the dregs, and could give a thousand lives for what I love': it was Rousseau who laid down a new etiquette of love which every petty poet and novelist still adheres to. Finally, Rousseau renovated our feeling for Nature. The geometrically minded eighteenth century could see nothing beautiful in Nature until trimmed into symmetry by the hands of man; even for Madame de Staël the Alps were merely 'a magnificent horror.' But Rousseau, who told Bernardin de Saint-Pierre that he 'would rather be among the arrows of the Parthians than among the glances of men,' only breathed freely and thought freely in the solitude of mountains and forests and torrents, and here also he has inoculated mankind with the virus of his own passion. In all these ways (as indeed Höffding has pointed out in what is, so far as I know, the most profound statement of Rousseau's philosophic position), Rousseau stood, in opposition to our artificial and inharmonious civilisation, for the worth of life as a whole, the simple undivided rights of life, the rights of instinct, the rights of emotion. This was his assertion of Nature. This was the way in which he renovated life, and effected a spiritual revolution which no mere man of letters has ever effected, a revolution only comparable to that effected by Christianity, of which indeed it was but a modern renascence.

Yet the man who wielded, and continues to wield, this enormous power over the world cannot be called one of its great men. In intellect, one sometimes thinks, he was not conspicuously above the average; in what we conventionally call moral character, he was at the outset conspicuously below it. Ill-born and ill-bred, morbidly shy and

suspicious, defective in virility, he was inapt for all the social ends of life, mentally and physically a self-torturing invalid. No man more absolutely than Rousseau has ever illustrated the truth of Hinton's profound saying that the affinities of genius are not with strength but with weakness, that the supreme man of genius is the man who opposes no obstacle to the forces of Nature of which he is the channel. Or, as St. Paul had declared long previously in a passage which seems to bear the same sense, it is the despised and rejected things of the world, even the things which are not, that God has chosen to put to nought the things that are.

It may, indeed, be pointed out to those who insist on the ludicrous, mean, and contemptible incidents in Rousseau's early life—only known to us through his own narration of them—that, as Lemaître said in a book that is, for the most part, superficial as well as unsympathetic, Rousseau's life was a process of moral evolution, a continuous purification completed by 'insanity,' or, as Rousseau himself put it, 'a purification in the furnace of adversity.' It is this process which largely gives the clue alike to his intellect and to his moral contradictions. Rousseau's abandonment to emotion was always checked by his timidity, by the perpetual searching suspicion which he applied to himself as well as to others. That is how it comes to pass that we may find in his writings the warrant for the most contradictory doctrines. It was so in the political field. In 1754 in the ***Discours sur l'Inégalité,*** he proclaimed that revolt of the non-possessors against the possessors of property which has since fermented so mightily in the world. But towards the end of his life, in the Constitution for Poland which he prepared at the request of the Poles, he had become in these matters a timid opportunist: 'I do not say that we must leave things as they are; but I do say that we must only touch them with extreme circumspection.' The contrast between Rousseau's apparent abandonment of his children and the fervour which in ***Emile*** he expended over the parental training of children has often been set forth to his discredit. But, as he himself viewed the matter, that gospel of childhood was simply the atonement for his own neglect. He displayed throughout a very passion of expiation. Born defective, beset on every side, he was yet of those who, according to the ancient metaphor of Saint Augustine, make of their dead selves the rungs of a ladder to rise to higher things. To some he seems to have been a kind of moral imbecile. But Thérèse, the mistress-wife who had been at his side during the whole of the period of his literary life and knew his weaknesses as no other could know them, said after his death: 'If he was not a saint, who ever was?' To view Rousseau rightly, we must see him, on the one hand, as the essential instrument of genius, a reed stirred to magnificent music by all the mighty winds of the spirit, and on the other hand, as a much-suffering man, scourged more than most men by human frailties, and yet for ever struggling to aspire. In this double capacity, at once the type of genius and the type of humanity, we learn to understand something of the magic of Rousseau's influence; we learn to understand how it is that before this shrine the most unlike persons in the world—the Marquis de Sade as well as Emerson, Charlotte Corday as well as Kant—have alike bowed in reverence.

Rousseau was a creature of clay. He was also a devouring flame. But of such blended fire and clay, in the end, the most exquisite products of the divine potter's art are formed. Under that stress Rousseau's character was slowly purified to the highest issues. Under that same stress was finally woven the delicate and iridescent texture of the finest style which French speech has ever assumed. The great traditions of the literary art of France—through Montaigne, Pascal, La Bruyère—reached at last in the furnace of this man's tortured soul their ultimate perfection of sensitive and intimate beauty. This style, which is the man himself, the style of the **Confessions** and the **Rêveries,** alone serves to make these books immortal. Here in his art the consuming fire and the soft clay of Rousseau's temperament are burnt to shapes of a beauty that is miraculous and stirs the depths of the soul. What indeed can we say, in the end, of all the operation of this man's spirit on the world save that it is a miracle, with effects that immeasurably transcend their causes? The water, if not the very mud, is turned into wine, and a few small loaves and fishes suffice for the feeding of the nations. (pp. 97-112)

> Havelock Ellis, "The Bicentenary of Rousseau," in his From Rousseau to Proust, Houghton Mifflin Company, 1935, pp. 95-112.

J. Middleton Murry   (essay date 1918)

[*Murry is recognized as one of the most significant English critics and editors of the twentieth century. His critical works are noted for their impassioned tone and startling discoveries as well as their perspicuity, clarity, and supportive argumentation. In the following excerpt from an essay originally published in the* Times Literary Supplement *in 1918, he appraises the sincerity of Rousseau's works, claiming that they represent "the stammering honesty of a man of genius wandering in an age of talent."*]

[Rousseau] had no historical sense; and of a man who has no historical sense no real history can be written. Chronology was meaningless to him because he could recognise no sovereignty of time over himself. With him ends were beginnings. In the third **Dialogue** he tell us—and it is nothing less than the sober truth told by a man who knew himself well—that his works must be read backwards, beginning with the last, by those who would understand him. Indeed, his function was, in a deeper sense than is imagined by those who take the parable called the **Contrat Social** for a solemn treatise of political philosophy, to give the lie to history. In himself he pitted the eternal against the temporal and grew younger with years. He might be known as the man of the second childhood *par excellence.* To the eye of history the effort of his soul was an effort backwards, because the vision of history is focused only for a perspective of progress. On his after-dinner journey to Diderot at Vincennes, Jean-Jacques saw, with the suddenness of intuition, that that progress, amongst whose convinced and cogent prophets he had lived so long, was for him an unsubstantial word. He beheld the soul of man *sub specie æternitatis.* In his vision history and institutions dissolved away. His second childhood had begun. (pp. 16-17)

It is but common piety to seek to understand Jean-Jacques in the way in which he pleaded so hard to be understood. Yet it is now over forty years since a voice of authority told England how it was to regard him. Lord Morley was

magisterial and severe, and England obeyed. One feels almost that Jean-Jacques himself would have obeyed if he had been alive. He would have trembled at the stern sentence that his deism was 'a rag of metaphysics floating in a sunshine of sentimentalism,' and he would have whispered that he would try to be good; but, when he heard his **Dialogues** described as the outpourings of a man with persecution mania, he might have rebelled and muttered silently an *Eppur si muove.* We see now that it was a mistake to stand him in the social dock, and that precisely those **Dialogues** which the then Mr Morley so powerfully dismissed contain his plea that the tribunal has no jurisdiction. To his contention that he wrote his books to ease his own soul it might be replied that their publication was a social act which had vast social consequences. But Jean-Jacques might well retort that the fact that his contemporaries and the generation which followed read and judged him in the letter and not in the spirit is no reason why we, at nearly two centuries remove, should do the same.

A great man may justly claim our deference. If Jean-Jacques asks that his last work shall be read first, we are bound, even if we consider it only a quixotic humour, to indulge it. But to those who read the neglected **Dialogues** it will appear a humour no longer. Here is a man who at the end of his days is filled to overflowing with bitterness at the thought that he has been misread and misunderstood. He says to himself: Either he is at bottom of the same nature as other men or he is different. If he is of the same nature, then there must be a malignant plot at work. He has revealed his heart with labour and good faith; not to hear him his fellow-men must have stopped their ears. If he is of another kind than his fellows, then—but he cannot bear the thought. Indeed it is a thought that no man can bear. They are blind because they will not see. He has not asked them to believe that what he says is true; he asks only that they shall believe that he is sincere, sincere in what he says, sincere, above all, when he implores that they should listen to the undertone. He has been 'the painter of nature and the historian of the human heart.'

His critics might have paused to consider why Jean-Jacques, certainly not niggard of self-praise in the **Dialogues,** should have claimed no more for himself than this. He might have claimed, with what in their eyes at least must be good right, to have been pre-eminent in his century as a political philosopher, a novelist, and a theorist of education. Yet to himself he is no more than 'the painter of nature and the historian of the human heart.' Those who would make him more make him less, because they make him other than he declares himself to be. His whole life has been an attempt to be himself and nothing else besides; and all his works have been nothing more and nothing less than his attempt to make his own nature plain to men. Now at the end of his life he has to swallow the bitterness of failure. He has been acclaimed the genius of his age; kings have delighted to honour him, but they have honoured another man. They have not known the true Jean-Jacques. They have taken his parables for literal truth, and he knows why. . . . At the end of his days he felt that the great labour of his life, which had been to express an intuitive certainty in words which would carry intellectual conviction, had been in vain, and his last words are: 'It is true so soon as it is felt.'

Three pages would tell as much of the essential truth of

his 'religious formation' as three volumes. At Les Charmettes with Mme de Warens, as a boy and as a young man, he had known peace of soul. In Paris, amid the intellectual exaltation and enthusiasms of the Encyclopædists, the memory of his lost peace haunted him like an uneasy conscience. His boyish unquestioning faith disappeared beneath the destructive criticism of the great pioneers of enlightenment and progress. Yet when all had been destroyed the hunger in his heart was still unsatisfied. Underneath his passionate admiration for Diderot smouldered a spark of resentment that he was not understood. They had torn down the fabric of expression into which he had poured the emotion of his immediate certainty as a boy; sometimes with an uplifted, sometimes with a sinking heart he surveyed the ruins. But the certainty that he had once been certain, the memory and the desire of the past peace—this they could not destroy. They could hardly even weaken this element within him, for they did not know that it existed. They were unable to conceive that it could exist. Jean-Jacques himself could give them no clue to its existence; he had no words, and he was still under the spell of the intellectual dogma of his age that words must express definite things. In common with his age he had lost the secret of the infinite persuasion of poetry. So the consciousness that he was different from those who surrounded him, and from those he admired as his masters, took hold of him. He was afraid of his own otherness, as all men are afraid when the first knowledge of their own essential loneliness begins to trouble their depths. The pathos of his struggle to kill the seed of this devastating knowledge is apparent in his declared desire to become 'a polished gentleman.' In the note which he added to his memoir for M. Dupin in 1749 he confesses to this ideal. If only he could become 'one of them,' indistinguishable without and within, he might be delivered from that disquieting sense of tongue-tied queerness in a normal world.

If he cheated himself at all, the deception was brief. The poignant memory of Les Charmettes whispered to him that there was a state of grace in which the hard things were made clear. But he had not yet the courage of his destiny. His consciousness of his separation from his fellows had still to harden into a consciousness of superiority before that courage would come. On the road to Vincennes on an October evening in 1749—M. Masson has fixed the date for us—he read in a news-sheet the question of the Dijon Academy: 'Si le rétablissement des arts et des sciences a contribué à épurer les mœurs?' The scales dropped from his eyes and the weight was removed from his tongue. There is no mystery about this 'revelation.' For the first time the question had been put in terms which struck him squarely in the heart. Jean-Jacques made his reply with the stammering honesty of a man of genius wandering in age of talent.

The *First Discourse* seems to many rhetorical and extravagant. In after days it appeared so to Rousseau himself, and he claimed no more for it than that he had tried to tell the truth. Before he learned that he had won the Dijon prize and that his work had taken Paris by storm, he was surely a prey to terrors lest his Vincennes vision of the non-existence of progress should have been mere madness. The success reassured him. . . . He was, in fact, not 'queer,' but right; and he had seemed to be queer precisely because he was right. Now he had the courage. . . . [Yet

Rousseau in Armenian costume.

he] was still something of the child hallooing in the dark to give himself heart. He clutched hold of material symbols of the freedom he had won, round wig, black stockings, and a living gained by copying music at so much a line. But he did not break with his friends; the 'bear' suffered himself to be made a lion. He had still a foot in either camp, for though he had the conviction that he was right, he was still fumbling for his words. The memoirs of Madame d'Epinay tell us how in 1754, at dinner at Mlle Quinault's, impotent to reply to the polite atheistical persiflage of the company, he broke out: 'Et moi, messieurs, je crois en Dieu. Je sors si vous dites un mot de plus.' That was not what he meant; neither was the First Discourse what he meant. He had still to find his language, and to find his language he had to find his peace. He was like a twig whirled about in an eddy of a stream. Suddenly the stream bore him to Geneva, where he returned to the church which he had left at Confignon. That, too, was not what he meant. When he returned from Geneva, Madame d'Epinay had built him the Ermitage.

In the *Rêveries,* which are mellow with the golden calm of his discovered peace, he tells how, having reached the climacteric which he had set at forty years, he went apart into the solitude of the Ermitage to inquire into the configuration of his own soul, and to fix once for all his opinions and his principles. In the exquisite third *Rêverie* two phrases occur continually. His purpose was 'to find firm ground'—'prendre une assiette,'—and his means to this discovery was 'spiritual honesty'—'bonne foi.' Rousseau's deep concern was to elucidate the anatomy of his own soul, but, since he was sincere, he regarded it as a type of the soul of man. Looking into himself, he saw that, in spite of all his follies, his weaknesses, his faintings by the way, his blasphemies against the spirit, he was good. Therefore he declared: Man is born good. Looking into himself he saw that he was free to work out his own salvation, and to find that solid foundation of peace which he so fervently desired. Therefore he declared: Man is born free. To the whisper of les Charmettes that there was a condition of grace had been added the sterner voice of remorse for his abandoned children, telling him that he had fallen from his high estate. . . . He found in himself something more him than himself. Therefore he declared: There is a God. But he sought to work out a logical foundation for these pinnacles of truth. He must translate these luminous convictions of his soul into arguments and conclusions. He could not, even to himself, admit that they were only intuitions; and in the **Contrat Social** he turned the reason to the service of a certainty not her own.

This unremitting endeavour to express an intuitive certainty in intellectual terms lies at the root of the many superficial contradictions in his work, and of the deeper contradiction which forms, as it were, the inward rhythm of his three great books. He seems to surge upwards on a passionate wave of revolutionary ideas, only to sink back into the calm of conservative or quietist conclusions. . . . To the revolutionaries of his age he was a renegade and a reactionary; to the Conservatives, a subversive charlatan. Yet he was in truth only a man stricken by the demon of 'la bonne foi,' and, like many men devoured by the passion of spiritual honesty, in his secret heart he believed in his similitude to Christ. 'Je ne puis pas souffrir les tièdes,' he wrote to Madame Latour in 1762, 'quiconque ne se passionne pas pour moi n'est pas digne de moi.' There is no mistaking the accent, and it sounds more plainly still in the **Dialogues.** He, too, was persecuted for righteousness' sake, because he, too, proclaimed that the kingdom of heaven was within men.

And what, indeed, have material things to do with the purification and the peace of the soul? World-shattering arguments and world-preserving conclusions—this is the inevitable paradox which attends the attempt to record truth seen by the eye of the soul in the language of the market-place. The eloquence and the inspiration may descend upon the man so that he writes believing that all men will understand. He wakes in the morning and he is afraid, not of his own words whose deeper truth he does not doubt, but of the incapacity of mankind to understand him. They will read in the letter what was written in the spirit; their eyes will see the words, but their ears will be stopped to the music. The *mystique,* as Péguy would have said, will be degraded into *politique.* To guard himself against this unhallowed destiny, at the last Rousseau turns with decision and in the language of his day rewrites the hard saying, that the things which are Cæsar's shall be rendered unto Cæsar.

In the light of this necessary truth all the contradictions which have been discovered in Rousseau's work fade away. That famous confusion concerning 'the natural man,' whom he presents to us now as a historic fact, now as an ideal, took its rise, not in the mind of Jean-Jacques, but in the minds of his critics. The **Contrat Social** is a parable of the soul of man, like the *Republic* of Plato. The truth of the human soul is its implicit perfection; to that reality material history is irrelevant, because the anatomy

of the soul is eternal. And as for the nature of this truth, 'it is true so soon as it is felt.' When the Savoyard Vicar, after accepting all the destructive criticism of religious dogma, turned to the Gospel story with the immortal 'Ce n'est pas ainsi qu'on invente,' he was only anticipating what Jean-Jacques was to say of himself before his death, that there was a sign in his work which could not be imitated, and which acted only at the level of its source. We may call Jean-Jacques religious because we have no other word; but the word would be more truly applied to the reverence felt towards such a man than to his own emotion. He was driven to speak of God by the habit of his childhood and the deficiency of a language shaped by the intellect and not by the soul. But his deity was one whom neither the Catholic nor the Reformed Church could accept, for He was truly a God who does not dwell in temples made with hands. The respect he owed to God, said the Vicar, was such that he could affirm nothing of Him. And, again, still more profoundly, he said, 'He is to our souls what our soul is to our body.' That is the mystical utterance of a man who was no mystic, but of one who found his full communion in the beatific *dolce far niente* of the Lake of Bienne. Jean-Jacques was set apart from his generation, because, like Malvolio, he thought highly of the soul and in no wise approved the conclusions of his fellows; and he was fortunate to the last, in spite of what some are pleased to call his madness (which was indeed only his flaming and uncomprehending indignation at the persecution inevitably meted out by those who have only a half truth to one who has the whole), because he enjoyed the certainty that his high appraisement of the soul was justified. (pp. 18-28)

J. Middleton Murry, "The Religion of Rousseau," in his Aspects of Literature, *W. Collins Sons & Co. Ltd., 1920, pp. 15-28.*

Huntington Cairns, Allen Tate, and Mark Van Doren (conversation date 1941)

[*An American lawyer and literary critic, Cairns is the author of* Law and the Social Sciences *(1935) and* Legal Philosophy from Plato to Hegel *(1949). Tate, a prominent American man of letters, is associated with two critical movements: Agrarianism and New Criticism. Van Doren, perhaps best known as a poet, was also a respected critic. In the following conversation, they discuss Rousseau's* Confessions *in the light of his "dominating influence" on Western thought.*]

Cairns: More so than any other figure, Rousseau is the man who made our modern world. But hardly two people agree on what he stood for. He did not make his mark as a man of letters until middle age, with a famous essay attacking civilization and lauding the virtues of savages. What interested me on rereading the life story of this mentally, physically and morally weak man was to find some explanation of why he became and has remained a dominating influence for 150 years. If it is true that Western civilization is tottering, what has the life story of the man who—at least his enemies so assert—willed its destruction to tell us of the personality which so dominates our thoughts and actions? Mr. Van Doren, do you find in Rousseau's **Confessions** anything to account for his phenomenal influence?

Van Doren: Everything there, I think, accounts for this influence. The modern world, insofar as it has been made by Rousseau or insofar as it made him, is clearly a world which, if it knows a great deal about mental and moral weakness, to use your term, knows little about mental or moral strength. I take the chief fact about Rousseau, as he expresses himself here, to be that he knows little or nothing.

Tate: Mr. Van Doren, why do you think that? Why do you think that he lacked that kind of knowledge? Is it a personal deficiency in Rousseau or something about his time?

Van Doren: It is clear that he lacks the knowledge, but the fact of his reputation proves to me that his age lacked the knowledge—and our age too. Even as recently as the seventeenth century he would have been unable to get anywhere except as a curiosity.

Tate: I gather from something Mr. Cairns said that perhaps he thinks Rousseau created the modern age. I know we use that kind of expression in speaking historically, as a sort of shorthand.

Cairns: If I may answer for Mr. Van Doren, I will tell you exactly what I have in mind. He is regarded as the father of the French Revolution, romanticism, democracy, anarchism, republicanism, communism and fascism.

Van Doren: Well, the books we have been reading ourselves make it clear enough that he was not the inventor of democracy.

Cairns: But the men who work in those fields claim him as their ancestor. It is very unusual that a man should be the father of so many contradictory movements, but that is the claim made by his disciples in those fields.

Tate: Shouldn't we inquire a little further into the nature of this influence? In England the fashion for Rousseau, of course, was never so extreme as in France, but at the same time, a man like Byron took it up and developed it into a new phase.

Cairns: In the Romantic movement, and particularly in Byron and Shelley.

Tate: What do you think this Romantic movement consists of? Isn't it a glorification of sentiment and instinct, the expansion of the merely emotional aspect of life and a general neglect of objective truth?

Van Doren: Doesn't it seem clear to you, Mr. Tate, that only in an age which itself had lost wisdom such a man as Rousseau could become great?

Tate: Yes. It is not only a question of his writings. We know from the **Confessions** that Rousseau was a very popular person. He made a great many enemies, but he must have been exceedingly ingratiating because he found many supporters and patrons. That is a sad commentary on the age.

Cairns: What do you find in the **Confessions,** if anything, to account for this influence?

Tate: Over the Western world by the eighteenth century the decline of objective moral and religious standards had set in. The development of mere ego, reliance upon personality and a feeling for the natural rightness of one's ac-

tions—all that superseded the religious standards, and Rousseau appealed to everybody who wanted to let down the bars, so to speak.

Van Doren: Would you be willing to substitute the word "temperament" for "personality"?

Tate: Yes. Temperament.

Cairns: Schopenhauer said that on Rousseau alone has nature bestowed the gift to be a moralist without being a bore.

Van Doren: I am astonished in reading this book again to discover how ignorant Rousseau is in even the elementary matters of temperament. For instance, he is very proud of being unique and makes the claim in his first paragraph that he is telling the whole truth about himself as no man ever has done before, and he elsewhere says that he despises Montaigne because Montaigne who talked about himself seems to have talked only about those aspects of himself that would be attractive, whereas he will give us his vices. Now many of his vices, of which I am sure he is secretly proud, and many of the uniquenesses that he discovers in himself, I find in myself and believe to be in all persons. I am not referring to those things which might embarrass us, but to his claim, for instance, that it is difficult for him to write. He seems to think that there is something unique about that.

Cairns: I have a theory myself as to why the **Confessions** exerted such an influence. The most dangerous book in my library at home, I find, is a book entitled, *The Layman's Handbook of Medicine.* Every time I read that volume through I find that I have all the diseases enumerated in it, and I think that Rousseau occupied in the eighteenth century a similar position.

Tate: But don't you think that Rousseau made it possible for mediocrity to think itself distinguished? Anybody can practice this kind of muddled introspection and find in himself things, if he is ignorant, that he could consider unique.

Cairns: Rousseau was acclaimed as a great man and everyone who read this book said, just as Mr. Van Doren said: "My heavens, I have all these diseases. I must be a great man too."

Tate: Don't you think that we have a great many little Rousseaus in the modern world? The countless autobiographies that come out every year are all in the Rousseau tradition, or most of them, at any rate.

Van Doren: They are in the Rousseau tradition if they are strings of stories about how women have fallen in love with the author.

Tate: Yes, Rousseau certainly set the pattern for that.

Van Doren: Do you believe his stories of his love affairs, incidentally?

Tate: I don't know whether I do or not. I'm inclined not to believe them.

Cairns: Whether they are true or false, he did innovate intimate literature in France. I think that's a positive quality of the book.

Van Doren: I should deny that. I think that Montaigne is

much more intimate than Rousseau. Even Pascal is more intimate, although, curiously enough, Pascal is not writing about himself.

Tate: He is much more intimate and more impersonal.

Van Doren: But he tells us more about himself, paradoxically, than this man does. I do not believe this man.

Cairns: Rousseau, however, is intimate in a different sense. Whether you believe the man or not, he does, I think, have a point against Montaigne and Pascal, and that is they tell only the good things about themselves.

Van Doren: They didn't seem to think so. They were not calling them good or bad.

Tate: I don't believe that Pascal told only the good things. Don't you think that he says a great many things about his own limitations, even his own vices? He had a career as a man of the world.

Van Doren: For instance, Pascal at one point is afraid that he is proud. He says: "Perhaps the reason I am writing this paragraph is that I want someone to admire it." If he had been sure of that he would have erased the paragraph. He let it stand because he thought it was true, whoever had written it. But Rousseau is constantly proud.

Tate: There is a point about Rousseau's claim to self-knowledge that I'd like to make. He says somewhere in the **Confessions** that all his memories of the past are agreeable, but that all his anticipations of the future are fearful.

Cairns: He was a very timorous man.

Tate: He identified his memories with his temperament. He thinks of his temperament as something perfect and sacred. I mention this because I'd like to get at the fundamental thing Rousseau believed in. I think of the modern attacks on Rousseau, for example, the great attack by the late Irving Babbitt in a book called *Rousseau and Romanticism* [see Further Reading], in which Babbitt said that Rousseau's sentimental belief in the perfection of human nature had done incalculable damage to the modern world, and I am inclined to agree with Babbitt.

Van Doren: It's very interesting at this point to remember that although Rousseau says he loves mankind, he seems to hate or to feel maliciously toward every man whom he mentions in this book, every man, at any rate, of note. Some old tutor, about whom the world knows nothing, he may praise.

Tate: Some man who was not a literary rival.

Van Doren: Diderot, Grimm, Voltaire, Hume and, of course, among musicians (because he fancied himself a musician), Rameau, the great composer of his time, he endeavors clearly, I think, to put down.

Cairns: He did not feel that way toward women, although I was going to account for his attitude toward men on the ground that he had a persecution complex, which I think is evident as you read the **Confessions.** His attitude toward Mme. de Warens is one of the most interesting passages in the book. I feel that she herself was the person to whom he really owed his outlook on the world. It has seemed to me, as it has to others, that the golden age which Rousseau wished to bring back to earth was simply a generalization of the life he had lived at Les Charmettes with Mme. de Warens.

Van Doren: He owed a great deal to her, although you must remember that he tells us many things about her which she would not like him to have told. I mean, he criticizes her, often times in a way that one who loves someone else would certainly avoid.

Cairns: She was also a mystery to him. I do not believe he ever completely understood her, although it has been well stated that she herself in her temperament was Rousseau with the genius left out.

Van Doren: She was important to him, of course, because he could love her without having to be afraid of her. This great lover, if he is supposed to be that, was obviously a very incompetent one; he was afraid of most women. I read that in all the stories he tells. This woman he does not have to be afraid of because she is a mother to him. (pp. 99-104)

Cairns: [There] was another influence on Rousseau's life and that is Diderot. You will recall that . . .

Tate: That he quarreled with Diderot.

Cairns: He quarreled with Diderot and I think that is quite interesting. Rousseau went to see him at the time the competition was proposed on the subject whether or not the arts and sciences had contributed to the progress of civilization or had hurt it. He went to see Diderot and told him that he was going to compete with an essay on that subject, and that he was going to defend civilization. Diderot said: "Why do that? Everybody is going to defend civilization. Defend savages. Say that their culture is superior to civilization. Then you may stand a chance of winning the prize." That was not an original notion with Rousseau.

Tate: No. But that's a very damaging thing to say about Rousseau, isn't it?

Cairns: I think it is true, and Rousseau wrote the essay along those lines, won the prize and had to maintain that position the rest of his life, although he didn't really believe it.

Tate: Don't you think that he probably came to believe in it? That brings up one of the most interesting psychological facts about Rousseau, the capacity for self-deception that he seemed to have all his life. His literary fame depended upon a belief that he had expressed insincerely and then the fame convinced him that it was a sincere belief.

Cairns: You will notice that in his subsequent writings after this essay which gave him his great fame he slowly retreated. His first essay was really in praise of primitive life; his second essay qualified that view; the third essay represented a greater qualification. I think the remainder of his life he was returning to the position he had in mind before he called upon Diderot.

Tate: Mr. Cairns, won't you summarize for us Rousseau's fundamental belief?

Cairns: Recently I came across a summary by T. E. Hulme.

Tate: One of my favorite writers.

Cairns: T. S. Eliot admires him very much, and Eliot has

endorsed these views. Hulme summarized Rousseau's position in this way: "Man is by nature wonderful, of unlimited power, and if hitherto has not appeared so, it is because of external obstacles and fetters which it should be the main business of social politics to remove." Now Hulme and Eliot disagree violently with that position, and the position they take is that man is by nature bad or limited and can consequently only accomplish anything of value by discipline—ethical, heroic or political. In other words, they believe in original sin.

Tate: I wouldn't quite follow that summary. I would agree much more with Irving Babbitt, that man becomes bad—he is not inherently bad—but he becomes bad by refusing to acknowledge limitations. He is more limited than bad. The evil comes . . .

Cairns: Why do you think he is either bad or good? Why isn't he neutral?

Tate: I think we have a fundamental necessity to think in terms of moral good and evil.

Van Doren: I should say that the word "bad" is much more interesting than the word "neutral." Only those men can interest us in our virtue who begin by talking about our weaknesses and our vices.

Tate: We have no confidence in them if they don't.

Van Doren: We shall learn nothing from a man who begins by telling us we are good, because we know we are not; whereas we can be truly interested in a person who gives us credit for our faults and then tells us that we can still make something of ourselves.

Cairns: Is there any way of determining this question whether man is in his original nature either good or bad?

Tate: That is one of the fallacies Rousseau entertained: that he could tell what man was in his original nature.

Cairns: Isn't that the modern fallacy of Eliot and Hulme: that they can determine he is bad?

Tate: Oh, no, they don't determine that.

Cairns: It is their conviction that they can.

Van Doren: Our old friend Aristotle is on this point very simple and profound. He says man is a rational animal. He means by that that man is mostly an animal but that he has a little reason. The little reason is what makes all the difference. If you translate this into theological terms, man is bad, but he has a little capacity for good—which is what makes all the difference.

Cairns: I will go along on the word "limited," but I just can't swallow bad or good. I think he is neutral.

Tate: When we say man is wholly bad, we are talking about an essence or a substance. I prefer the word "limitation" too, but the evil is introduced in terms of experience by a refusal to recognize the limitation.

Van Doren: I think the reason we find Rousseau writing like an ignorant man, even though he writes extremely well—surely he is a good writer of some kind—is that he doesn't know this thing we have been talking about. That sounds vain, but is he capable of seeing man with any kind

of double vision—as actually limited but capable of virtue and strength?

Cairns: You quoted Aristotle a minute ago. I'd like to know if you disagree with him in his assertion in the *Poetics* that the author's personality should not intrude, because in the **Confessions** that is one of the principal things we have.

Van Doren: Certainly not.

Tate: It seems to me that Rousseau gives himself away in the most interesting fashion.

Cairns: That is what he intended to do.

Tate: Exactly, but in a way which he didn't intend. A common criticism of Rousseau is that he was very infirm in his perception of objective events. "I have but one faithful guide," says Rousseau, "on which I can depend. This is the chain of the sentiments by which the succession of my existence has been marked, and by these events which have either been the cause or the effect of the manner of it. I can easily forget my misfortunes, but I cannot forget my faults, and still less my virtuous sentiments. The remembrance of these is too dear to me ever to suffer them to be defaced from my mind. I may omit facts, transpose events and fall into some errors of dates, but I cannot be deceived in what I have felt nor in that which from sentiment I have done. And to relate this is the chief end of my present work. The real object of my **Confessions** is to communicate an exact knowledge of what I interiorly am and have been in every situation of my life. I have promised the history of my mind and to write it faithfully. I have no need of other memoirs. To enter into my own heart as I have hitherto done will alone be sufficient." (pp. 104-07)

Huntington Cairns, Allen Tate, and Mark Van Doren, "Jean Jacques Rousseau: Confessions," in their, Invitation to Learning, *Random House, 1941, pp. 97-107.*

Bertrand Russell   (essay date 1946)

[*Russell was an English philosopher and mathematician who gained recognition for his support of various social and political concerns. Two of his early works,* Principles of Mathematics *(1903) and* Principia Mathematica *(1910-13), written with Alfred North Whitehead, are considered classics of mathematical logic. His beliefs often led him to support unorthodox social issues, including free love, undisciplined education, and the eradication of nuclear weapons. For his work in a number of literary genres, Russell was awarded the Nobel Prize in literature in 1950. In the following excerpt, he provides an analysis of Rousseau's theology and political theory.*]

Jean Jacques Rousseau (1712-78), though a *philosophe* in the eighteenth-century French sense, was not what would now be called a 'philosopher'. Nevertheless he had a powerful influence on philosophy, as on literature and taste and manners and politics. Whatever may be our opinion of his merits as a thinker, we must recognize his immense importance as a social force. This importance came mainly from his appeal to the heart, and to what, in his day, was called 'sensibility'. He is the father of the romantic movement, the initiator of systems of thought which infer non-human facts from human emotions, and the inventor of the political philosophy of pseudo-democratic dictatorships as opposed to traditional absolute monarchies. Ever since his time, those who considered themselves reformers have been divided into two groups, those who followed him and those who followed Locke. Sometimes they cooperated, and many individuals saw no incompatibility. But gradually the incompatibility has become increasingly evident. At the present time, Hitler is an outcome of Rousseau; Roosevelt and Churchill, of Locke.

Rousseau's biography was related by himself in his **Confessions** in great detail, but without any slavish regard for truth. He enjoyed making himself out a great sinner, and sometimes exaggerated in this respect; but there is abundant external evidence that he was destitute of all the ordinary virtues. This did not trouble him, because he considered that he always had a warm heart, which, however, never hindered him from base actions towards his best friends. (p. 660)

There is much in Rousseau's work which, however important in other respects, does not concern the history of philosophical thought. There are only two parts of his thinking that I shall consider in any detail; these are, first, his theology, and second, his political theory.

In theology he made an innovation which has now been accepted by the great majority of Protestant theologians. Before him, every philosopher from Plato onwards, if he believed in God, offered intellectual arguments in favour of his belief. The arguments may not, to us, seem very convincing, and we may feel that they would not have seemed cogent to anyone who did not already feel sure of the truth of the conclusion. But the philosopher who advanced the arguments certainly believed them to be logically valid, and such as should cause certainty of God's existence in any unprejudiced person of sufficient philosophical capacity. Modern Protestants who urge us to believe in God, for the most part, despise the old 'proofs', and base their faith upon some aspect of human nature—emotions of awe or mystery, the sense of right and wrong, the feeling of aspiration, and so on. This way of defending religious belief was invented by Rousseau. It has become so familiar that his originality may easily not be appreciated by a modern reader, unless he will take the trouble to compare Rousseau with (say) Descartes or Leibniz.

'Ah, Madame!' Rousseau writes to an aristocratic lady, 'sometimes in the privacy of my study, with my hands pressed tight over my eyes or in the darkness of the night, I am of opinion that there is no God. But look yonder: the rising of the sun, as it scatters the mists that cover the earth, and lays bare the wondrous glittering scene of nature, disperses at the same moment all cloud from my soul. I find my faith again, and my God, and my belief in Him. I admire and adore Him, and I prostrate myself in His presence.'

On another occasion he says: 'I believe in God as strongly as I believe any other truth, because believing and not believing are the last things in the world that depend on me.' This form of argument has the drawback of being private; the fact that Rousseau cannot help believing something affords no ground for another person to believe the same thing.

He was very emphatic in his theism. On one occasion he threatened to leave a dinner party because Saint Lambert (one of the guests), expressed a doubt as to the existence of God. *'Moi Monsieur,'* Rousseau exclaimed angrily, *'je crois en Dieu!'* Robespierre, in all things his faithful disciple, followed him in this respect also. The 'Fête de l'Etre Suprême' would have had Rousseau's whole-hearted approval.

'The Confession of Faith of a Savoyard Vicar', which is an interlude in the fourth book of **Emile,** is the most explicit and formal statement of Rousseau's creed. Although it professes to be what the voice of nature has proclaimed to a virtuous priest, who suffers disgrace for the wholly 'natural' fault of seducing an unmarried woman, the reader finds with surprise that the voice of nature, when it begins to speak, is uttering a hotch-pot of arguments derived from Aristotle, St Augustine, Descartes, and so on. It is true that they are robbed of precision and logical form; this is supposed to excuse them, and to permit the worthy Vicar to say that he cares nothing for the wisdom of the philosophers.

The later parts of **'The Confession of Faith'** are less reminiscent of previous thinkers than the earlier parts. After satisfying himself that there is a God, the Vicar goes on to consider rules of conduct. 'I do not deduce these rules,' he says, 'from the principles of a high philosophy, but I find them in the depths of my heart, written by Nature in ineffaceable characters.' From this he goes on to develop the view that conscience is in all circumstances an infallible guide to right action. 'Thanks be to Heaven,' he concludes this part of his argument, 'we are thus freed from all this terrifying apparatus of philosophy; we can be men without being learned; dispensed from wasting our life in the study of morals, we have at less cost a more assured guide in this immense labyrinth of human opinions.' Our natural feelings, he contends, lead us to serve the common interest, while our reason urges selfishness. We have therefore only to follow feeling rather than reason in order to be virtuous.

Natural religion, as the Vicar calls his doctrine, has no need of a revelation; if men had listened to what God says to the heart, there would have been only one religion in the world. If God has revealed Himself specially to certain men, this can only be known by human testimony, which is fallible. Natural religion has the advantage of being revealed directly to each individual.

There is a curious passage about hell. The Vicar does not know whether the wicked go to eternal torment, and says, somewhat loftily, that the fate of the wicked does not greatly interest him; but on the whole he inclines to the view that the pains of hell are not everlasting. However this may be, he is sure that salvation is not confined to the members of any one Church.

It was presumably the rejection of revelation and of hell that so profoundly shocked the French government and the Council of Geneva.

The rejection of reason in favour of the heart was not, to my mind, an advance. In fact, no one thought of this device so long as reason appeared to be on the side of religious belief. In Rousseau's environment, reason, as represented by Voltaire, was opposed to religion, therefore away with reason! Moreover reason was abstruse and difficult; the savage, even when he has dined, cannot understand the ontological argument, and yet the savage is the repository of all necessary wisdom. Rousseau's savage—who was not the savage known to anthropologists—was a good husband and a kind father; he was destitute of greed, and had a religion of natural kindliness. He was a convenient person, but if he could follow the good Vicar's reasons for believing in God he must have had more philosophy than his innocent naïveté would lead one to expect.

Apart from the fictitious character of Rousseau's 'natural man', there are two objections to the practice of basing beliefs as to objective fact upon the emotions of the heart. One is that there is no reason whatever to suppose that such beliefs will be true; the other is, that the resulting beliefs will be private, since the heart says different things to different people. Some savages are persuaded by the 'natural light' that it is their duty to eat people, and even Voltaire's savages, who are led by the voice of reason to hold that one should only eat Jesuits, are not wholly satisfactory. To Buddhists, the light of nature does not reveal the existence of God, but does proclaim that it is wrong to eat the flesh of animals. But even if the heart said the same thing to all men, that could afford no evidence for the existence of anything outside our own emotions. However ardently I, or all mankind, may desire something, however necessary it may be to human happiness, that is no ground for supposing this something to exist. There is no law of nature guaranteeing that mankind should be happy. Everybody can see that this is true of our life here on earth, but by a curious twist our very sufferings in this life are made into an argument for a better life hereafter. We should not employ such an argument in any other connection. If you had bought ten dozen eggs from a man, and the first dozen were all rotten, you would not infer that the remaining nine dozen must be of surpassing excellence; yet that is the kind of reasoning that 'the heart' encourages as a consolation for our sufferings here below.

For my part, I prefer the ontological argument, the cosmological argument, and the rest of the old stock-in-trade, to the sentimental illogicality that has sprung from Rousseau. The old arguments at least were honest: if valid, they proved their point; if invalid, it was open to any critic to prove them so. But the new theology of the heart dispenses with argument; it cannot be refuted, because it does not profess to prove its points. At bottom, the only reason offered for its acceptance is that it allows us to indulge in pleasant dreams. This is an unworthy reason, and if I had to choose between Thomas Aquinas and Rousseau, I should unhesitatingly choose the Saint.

Rousseau's political theory is set forth in his *Social Contract*, published in 1762. This book is very different in character from most of his writing; it contains little sentimentality and much close intellectual reasoning. Its doctrines, though they pay lip-service to democracy, tend to the justification of the totalitarian State. But Geneva and antiquity combined to make him prefer the City State to large empires such as those of France and England. On the title-page he calls himself 'citizen of Geneva', and in his introductory sentences he says: 'As I was born a citizen of a free State, and a member of the Sovereign, I feel that, however feeble the influence of my voice may have been on public affairs, the right of voting on them makes it my duty to study them.' There are frequent laudatory references to Sparta, as it appears in Plutarch's Life of Lycurgus. He says that democracy is best in small States, aristocracy in middle-sized ones, and monarchy in large ones. But it is to be understood that, in his opinion, small States are preferable, in part because they make democracy more practicable. When he speaks of democracy, he means, as the Greeks meant, direct participation of every citizen; representative government he calls 'elective aristocracy'. Since the former is not possible in a large State, his praise of democracy always implies praise of the City State. This love of the City State is, in my opinion, not sufficiently emphasized in most accounts of Rousseau's political philosophy.

Although the book as a whole is much less rhetorical than most of Rousseau's writing, the first chapter opens with a very forceful piece of rhetoric: 'Man is born free, and everywhere he is in chains. One man thinks himself the master of others, but remains more of a slave than they are.' Liberty is the nominal goal of Rousseau's thought, but in fact it is equality that he values, and that he seeks to secure even at the expense of liberty.

His conception of the Social Contract seems, at first, analogous to Locke's, but soon shows itself more akin to that of Hobbes. In the development from the state of nature, there comes a time when individuals can no longer maintain themselves in primitive independence; it then becomes necessary to self-preservation that they should unite to form a society. But how can I pledge my liberty without harming my interests? 'The problem is to find a form of association which will defend and protect with the whole common force the person and goods of each associate, and in which each, while uniting himself with all, may still obey himself alone, and remain as free as before. This is the fundamental problem of which the Social Contract provides the solution.'

The Contract consists in 'the total alienation of each associate, together with all his rights, to the whole community; for, in the first place, as each gives himself absolutely, the conditions are the same for all; and this being so, no one has any interest in making them burdensome to others'. The alienation is to be without reserve. 'If individuals retained certain rights, as there would be no common superior to decide between them and the public, each, being on one point his own judge, would ask to be so on all; the state of nature would thus continue, and the association would necessarily become inoperative or tyrannical.'

This implies a complete abrogation of liberty and a complete rejection of the doctrine of the rights of man. It is true that, in a later chapter, there is some softening of this theory. It is there said that, although the social contract gives the body politic absolute power over all its members, nevertheless human beings have natural rights as men. 'The sovereign cannot impose upon its subjects any fetters that are useless to the community, nor can it even wish to do so.' But the sovereign is the sole judge of what is useful or useless to the community. It is clear that only a very feeble obstacle is thus opposed to collective tyranny.

It should be observed that the 'sovereign' means, in Rousseau, not the monarch or the government, but the community in its collective and legislative capacity.

The Social Contract can be stated in the following words.

'Each of us puts his person and all his power in common under the supreme direction of the general will, and, in our corporate capacity, we receive each member as an indivisible part of the whole.' This act of association creates a moral and collective body, which is called the 'State' when passive, the 'Sovereign' when active, and a 'Power' in relation to other bodies like itself.

The conception of the 'general will', which appears in the above wording of the Contract, plays a very important part in Rousseau's system. I shall have more to say about it shortly.

It is argued that the Sovereign need give no guarantees to its subjects, for, since it is formed of the individuals who compose it, it can have no interest contrary to theirs. 'The Sovereign, merely by virtue of what it is, is always what it should be.' This doctrine is misleading to the reader who does not note Rousseau's somewhat peculiar use of terms. The Sovereign is not the government, which, it is admitted, may be tyrannical; the Sovereign is a more or less metaphysical entity, not fully embodied in any of the visible organs of the State. Its impeccability, therefore, even if admitted, has not the practical consequences that it might be supposed to have.

The will of the Sovereign, which is always right, is the 'general will'. Each citizen, *quâ* citizen, shares in the general will, but he may also, as an individual, have a particular will running counter to the general will. The Social Contract involves that whoever refuses to obey the general will shall be forced to do so. 'This means nothing less than that he will be forced to be free.'

This conception of being 'forced to be free' is very metaphysical. The general will in the time of Galileo was certainly anti-Copernican; was Galileo 'forced to be free' when the Inquisition compelled him to recant? Is even a malefactor 'forced to be free' when he is put in prison? Think of Byron's Corsair:

> O'er the glad waters of the deep blue sea,
> Our thoughts as boundless and our hearts as free.

Would this man be more 'free' in a dungeon? The odd thing is that Byron's noble pirates are a direct outcome of Rousseau, and yet, in the above passage, Rousseau forgets his romanticism and speaks like a sophistical policeman. Hegel, who owed much to Rousseau, adopted his misuse of the word 'freedom', and defined it as the right to obey the police, or something not very different.

Rousseau has not that profound respect for private property that characterizes Locke and his disciples. 'The State, in relation to its members, is master of all their goods.' Nor does he believe in division of powers, as preached by Locke and Montesquieu. In this respect, however, as in some others, his later detailed discussions do not wholly agree with his earlier general principles. In Book III, chapter i, he says that the part of the Sovereign is limited to making laws, and that the executive, or government, is an intermediate body set up between the subjects and the Sovereign to secure their mutual correspondence. He goes on to say: 'If the Sovereign desires to govern, or the magistrate to give laws, or if the subjects refuse to obey, disorder takes the place of regularity, and . . . the State falls into despotism or anarchy.' In this sentence, allowing for the difference of vocabulary, he seems to agree with Montesquieu.

I come now to the doctrine of the general will, which is both important and obscure. The general will is not identical with the will of the majority, or even with the will of all the citizens. It seems to be conceived as belonging to the body politic as such. If we take Hobbes's view, that a civil society is a person, we must suppose it endowed with the attributes of personality, including will. But then we are faced with the difficulty of deciding what are the visible manifestations of this will, and here Rousseau leaves us in the dark. We are told that the general will is always right and always tends to the public advantage; but that it does not follow that the deliberations of the people are equally correct, for there is often a great deal of difference between the will of all and the general will. How, then, are we to know what is the general will? There is, in the same chapter, a sort of answer:

'If, when the people, being furnished with adequate information, held its deliberations, the citizens had no communication one with another, the grand total of the small differences would always give the general will, and the decision would always be good.'

The conception in Rousseau's mind seems to be this: every man's political opinion is governed by self-interest, but self-interest consists of two parts, one of which is peculiar to the individual, while the other is common to all the members of the community. If the citizens have no opportunity of striking logrolling bargains with each other, their individual interests, being divergent, will cancel out, and there will be left a resultant which will represent their common interest; this resultant is the general will. Perhaps Rousseau's conception might be illustrated by terrestrial gravitation. Every particle in the earth attracts every other particle in the universe towards itself; the air above us attracts us upward while the ground beneath us attracts us downward. But all these 'selfish' attractions cancel each other out insofar as they are divergent, and what remains is a resultant attraction towards the centre of the earth. This might be fancifully conceived as the act of the earth considered as a community, and as the expression of its general will.

To say that the general will is always right is only to say that, since it represents what is in common among the self-interests of the various citizens, it must represent the largest collective satisfaction of self-interest possible to the community. This interpretation of Rousseau's meaning seems to accord with his words better than any other that I have been able to think of.

In Rousseau's opinion, what interferes in practice with the expression of the general will is the existence of subordinate associations within the State. Each of these will have its own general will, which may conflict with that of the community as a whole. 'It may then be said that there are no longer as many votes as there are men, but only as many as there are associations.' This leads to an important consequence: 'It is therefore essential, if the general will is to be able to express itself, that there should be no partial society within the State, and that each citizen should think only his own thoughts: which was indeed the sublime and unique system established by the great Lycurgus.' In a footnote, Rousseau supports his opinion with the authority of Machiavelli.

Consider what such a system would involve in practice. The State would have to prohibit churches (except a State Church), political parties, trade-unions, and all other organizations of men with similar economic interests. The result is obviously the Corporate or Totalitarian State, in which the individual citizen is powerless. Rousseau seems to realize that it may be difficult to prohibit all associations, and adds, as an afterthought, that, if there *must* be subordinate associations, then the more there are the better, in order that they may neutralize each other.

When, in a later part of the book, he comes to consider government, he realizes that the executive is inevitably an association having an interest and a general will of its own, which may easily conflict with that of the community. He says that while the government of a large State needs to be stronger than that of a small one, there is also more need of restraining the government by means of the Sovereign. A member of the government has three wills: his personal will, the will of the government, and the general will. These three should form a *crescendo*, but usually in fact form a *diminuendo*. Again: 'Everything conspires to take away from a man who is set in authority over others the sense of justice and reason.'

Thus in spite of the infallibility of the general will, which is 'always constant, unalterable, and pure', all the old problems of eluding tyranny remain. What Rousseau has to say on these problems is either a surreptitious repetition of Montesquieu, or an insistence on the supremacy of the legislature, which, if democratic, is identical with what he calls the Sovereign. The broad general principles with which he starts, and which he presents as if they solved political problems, disappear when he condescends to detailed considerations, towards the solution of which they contribute nothing.

The condemnation of the book by contemporary reactionaries leads a modern reader to expect to find in it a much more sweeping revolutionary doctrine than it in fact contains. We may illustrate this by what is said about democracy. When Rousseau uses this word, he means, as we have already seen, the direct democracy of the ancient City State. This, he points out, can never be completely realized, because the people cannot be always assembled and always occupied with public affairs. 'Were there a people of gods, their government would be democratic. So perfect a government is not for men.'

What we call democracy he calls elective aristocracy; this, he says, is the best of all governments, but it is not suitable to all countries. The climate must be neither very hot nor very cold; the produce must not much exceed what is necessary, for, where it does, the evil of luxury is inevitable, and it is better that this evil should be confined to a monarch and his Court than diffused throughout the population. In virtue of these limitations, a large field is left for despotic government. Nevertheless his advocacy of democracy, in spite of its limitations, was no doubt one of the things that made the French Government implacably hostile to the book; the other presumably, was the rejection of the divine right of kings, which is implied in the doctrine of the Social Contract as the origin of government.

The Social Contract became the Bible of most of the leaders in the French Revolution, but no doubt, as is the fate of Bibles, it was not carefully read and was still less understood by many of its disciples. It reintroduced the habit of metaphysical abstractions among the theorists of democracy, and by its doctrine of the general will it made possible the mystic identification of a leader with his people, which has no need of confirmation by so mundane an apparatus as the ballot-box. Much of its philosophy could be appropriated by Hegel in his defence of the Prussian autocracy. Its first-fruits in practice were the reign of Robespierre; the dictatorships of Russia and Germany (especially the latter) are in part an outcome of Rousseau's teaching. What further triumphs the future has to offer to his ghost I do not venture to predict. (pp. 666-74)

> *Bertrand Russell, "Rousseau," in his* A History of Western Philosophy, and Its Connection with Political and Social Circumstances from the Earliest Times to the Present Day, *G. Allen and Unwin Ltd., 1946, pp. 660-74.*

François Mauriac　(essay date 1949)

[*Mauriac was a French novelist, essayist, and dramatist in the French-Catholic tradition. He was awarded the Nobel Prize in literature in 1952. In the following excerpt, he examines and objects to an attitude conveyed by Rousseau in his* Confessions, *namely, "a certain irritated satisfaction in being himself."*]

It is not enough to say that Jean-Jacques is close to us; he is one of us. His contemporaries and the generation that followed his have retained his redundancy and his eloquence. They have extracted from his general ideas all the absurd, and all the tragic, too. They have, in a manner of speaking, filtered Rousseau. And that part of his inheritance that comes down to us is his inner attitude—a certain irritated satisfaction in being himself. This master of falsehood and pride finds his true friends among us.

To-day whether Jean-Jacques arouses love or hatred, we love him as ourselves, and hate him as ourselves. The affection he awakens in us does not prevent us from seeing clearly. It is not what he confesses [in the *Confessions*] that makes us know him. We know him because we have one consciousness with him; we are his consciousness.

And in the same way, the dislike and aversion it is impossible not to feel for him is never unaccompanied by collusion. Even when he annoys us the most, we do not fail to discover in him that savor one finds only by oneself.

Nothing resembles us less than our own acts; that is what we learned from him in the first place. Rousseau treats his defects as he treated his children: he does not recognize them. And that is not all: he never doubted that he was the father of his poor children, and he does doubt being the author of certain frightful gestures. But if he is not their author, it must then be the rest of the world. This step is soon passed over.

Jean-Jacques is the best of men. Yet he accused the servant Marion of a petty theft he himself had committed. He has the most tender heart in a century that shed so many tears before cutting off so many heads. But the most tenderhearted of all men deserts his five children. He has the courage to accomplish this atrocious act five times. He confesses it, for he is sincere. Sincerity, the pleasure of public confession, we have found in his descendants. It is true he bequeathed us, at the same time, a method, so that confession should cost us very little,—a method in two points, which attain such a degree of perfection with him that his sons of to-day have been able to add nothing to it: it is first a question—and this is the first "period"—of establishing the fact that in so far as our acts deserve blame, society bears the burden of them.

Society, the scapegoat that assumes all Jean-Jacques' offences, is not, in his eyes, an abstract power. When he writes "society," he thinks "the others" and among the others, the Great,—those who took such care of him, spoiled him, fed his vanity, who entered with so much devotion into all his likes and dislikes. And yet how he hates them! If he had been a prophet, I doubt that the vision of the guillotine would have wrenched from him much more than hypocritical tears. "Why didn't I marry?" he wrote to Madame de Francueil, who questioned him on the desertion of his five children. "Inquire of your unjust laws, Madame . . . It is the estate of the rich, it is your estate that steals from mine my children's bread." It is the law's fault . . . But, in Jean-Jacques' eyes, these laws are Madame de Francueil's. He has incarnated them in that woman and it is that woman whom he hates. Neither the favors of Madame de Warens, nor those of Madame d'Epinay and Madame d'Houdetot, nor the patient kindness shown him by the Marshal of Luxembourg, Milord Maréchal and so many other great lords, prevailed against that hatred preserved and cooked over again. Envy, that base passion for equality which is the mark of our era, already exists full grown in Rousseau. That the prerogatives of the Great could offend him, he denies with a fury that proves conclusively that those who accuse him of it, have touched the spot: "Philosophers," they say, "would like to confuse all the states and pay respect to no one. No, Sirs, no. Philosophers don't wish to confuse anything; they are not jealous of the good fare which is killing you, nor of the carriage that prevents you from using your legs, nor of the impudent servants who steal from you and make you hateful so often; they do not even refuse to render you your due; just as they would have made no objections, in ancient Greece, to paying reverence to the idols that had no meaning."

A little jar of butter, sent to Thérèse Levasseur, was left by mistake at the home of the Count de Lastic who thought it was his, and at first refused to give it back to Thérèse's mother. It could be observed to what point Jean-Jacques' insolence mounted on this occasion! "I tried to console the good woman in her affliction, by explaining to her the rules of high society and well-bred people; I proved to her that it would not be worth while having a retinue if it were not used to send away the poor man when he comes to claim what belongs to him; and, by showing her that justice and humanity are vulgar words, I finally made her understand that she was highly honored to have a count eat her butter."

A vengeful note on "the man with the butter" is to appear in the *Nouvelle Héloïse.* Heaven and earth must be moved to allay the wrath of the great outraged citizen. Madame d'Epinay gets down on her knees; Madame de Chenonceaux entreats him: "A minute of misunderstanding,

whose import may have been very badly related to you, should not prevail against the apologies and civilities that I myself have been empowered to offer you in their behalf." Elsewhere the great lady writes humbly to his Philosophical Majesty! "Since I am engaged in asking your pardon . . . " How heavy with significance is that petty incident! We understand that gentlemen of the robe, who, moreover, washed their hands, and had experience and education, enjoined Sanson to pay society the civilities that they had showered upon their father Jean-Jacques. In Rousseau, resentment became creative, but of all his sons, it is perhaps Robespierre who is most like him.

Yet no massacre will divert the aristocracy from coddling the Jean-Jacques of all times. The "I hate you" that they pass from mouth to mouth, and that the head of French socialism was offering only yesterday, would not cost him a single invitation if he had a notion to dine in town. In the first place, because men of the world, in spite of all that is said, often have a sincere worship of the mind, respect for talent and a passion to serve it; and also because they are bored with each other,—and above all because the true anarchists, anarchists in their pure state, those whose revolt has its source neither in poverty nor hatred, nor in envy, are more commonly found in parlors than among the people. This strange liking of society people for the kind of man who works to have their heads cut off, may irritate, but it is not base, surely less base than the hatred Jean-Jacques aroused in French society, following those June days, and which forced Sainte-Beuve to handle the *Confessions* with gloves on under the pretext "that there is not a writer more fitting to render the poor man superb."

So society assumes the short-comings of Jean-Jacques. That is what makes confession easy. But he wants to make it still easier. It is not enough to avoid all blame, the most subtle (and this is the second "period") is to obtain an increased reputation and to push audacity to the point of offering to God the ridiculous prayer of the Pharisee that serves as a prelude to the *Confessions:* "Eternal Being, gather about me the great crowd of my fellow-men, so they may listen to my confessions, so they may groan for my indignities and blush for my misery. May each one, in his turn, uncover his heart at the foot of Thy throne with the same sincerity; and may a single one say to You, if he dare: 'I was better than that man.' "

Poor Jean-Jacques! No offense that he confesses can cause as much horror as such a word. It is enough to drag him down lower than the most infamous of men, who has taken measure of his baseness, who has beaten on his breast before infinite Purity and tremblingly repeated Saint-Peter's prayer: "Depart from me, Lord, for I am a sinner."

It remains for Jean-Jacques to persuade those who would hesitate to absolve him of his offenses in order to heap them on society, that his faults are not faults. This is the miracle of the new Messiah, the Wedding in Cana where evil is changed into good. Until the time of the Geneva citizen, murderers and libertines did not set themselves up as examples, nor sodomites teach morals, and courtesans answered abuse by the admirable words of some royal mistress or other to a man who was insulting her: "Since you know who I am, Sir, do me the favor of praying to God for me." Jean-Jacques can take up the word of the *Méde-*

cin malgré lui: "We have changed all that." The heart is on the right, the liver on the left. Rousseau committed an outrage much more serious than the simple reversal of the tribunal of the conscience which condemned all offenses,—yet an outrage for which, Bossuet assures us, there is almost no cure. Jean-Jacques did not destroy the conscience; he corrupted it. He adjusted it to lies and falsehood. And it is only after being assured it will henceforth render only oracles favorable to his passion that he installs this soiled conscience on the very throne of God, that he adores it, that he addresses prayers to it: "Conscience, divine instinct . . . "

Among a thousand examples, there is none more surprising than the famous letter to Madame de Francueil: "Yes, Madame, I put my children in a Foundling Asylum; I committed them to the charge of an institution made for that. If my poverty and misfortunes deprive me of the power of fulfilling so dear a duty, it is a misfortune for which I should be pitied and not a crime for which I should be blamed. I owe them a livelihood and I have procured a better and more sure one for them than I should have been able to give them myself (Could "tartuffery" be pushed further?) . . . To support my children and their mother with the blood of misery? (He meant: to support them with his literary work!) No, Madame, it is better for them to be orphans than to have a knave for a father!"

Jean-Jacques' whole work (especially his correspondence) would furnish us as many texts as we would want, like that one, in which it appears no man has, perhaps, carried the corruption of the inner senses so far. Virtue is now becoming the dummy for crime; now the conscience-divine-instinct is erected for the approval of mass murders whose time is approaching.

How far Rousseau is from Christianity, in spite of his professions of faith! I deny that, face to face with the atheism of the philosophers, he was even the soiled representative of Christianity. The presence of Grace in a man is measured by the clarity of the eye with which he judges. Salvation is not far away when we begin to see ourselves as we really are. Detestation of oneself increases with holiness, and the nearer a man draws to God, the more clearly the eternal light reveals his own blemishes. The complacency and satisfaction of a Rousseau in being oneself, is perhaps the feeling furthest away from the Christian. A few praises addressed to Christ can not balance it. When Jacques Maritain, in his admirable study on the *Three Reformers,* denounces in Rousseau a finished example of religious thought, anti-intellectual, pragmatist and immanentist, perhaps he pays him too high a compliment. For these various errors, especially the latter, are not always incompatible with a life of prayer, not even perhaps with a life of union, and all the self-denial such a life includes. There is not even enough Christianity in Rousseau to make a heretic of him.

It is not that some traces of Christian humility can not be found in him. Yes, indeed, when he writes to his friend Altuna: "I draw a favorable augury from the bitter trials that it has pleased God to send me. I have so greatly deserved punishment that I have no right to complain of them; and since He begins with justice, I hope He will finish with mercy . . . " You must know that this friend to whom he is writing is very pious and has reprimanded him . . . But

there we do not recognize Rousseau's accent. That is not his true thought.

For he was never a Catholic. At Turin, the young Rousseau is led on to conversion by the basest of sentiments. He himself does not conceal the shame that this self-interested conversion caused him. But his sincerity does not go far enough to recognize that he avenges himself for this shame on Catholicism. A guilty conscience soils everything it approaches. Because Rousseau does not give his heart's assent to the Church, he insists she requires only blind submission. He imputes to her the baseness of his own feelings. And that is what renders him unpardonable, in spite of his youth and circumstances fitting to extenuate his fault.

But Rousseau always lied; and the modern era rests altogether on Rousseau's falsehood—that essential falsehood: the transmutation of base lead into pure gold, of evil into good. This reversal appears in a text like Madame de Francueil's letter with an ingenuity that provokes laughter. As long as Jean-Jacques makes use only of his mind to convince us, everyone, according to his temperament, becomes angry or amused; but no one any longer takes him seriously. If he had only been what they called a philosopher in the eighteenth century, he would have been one of the lowest order—although at that time one was a philosopher without much trouble. It is the artist in him that charms and that has poisoned the world. We laugh when, in a letter, he boasts of having abandoned his children—but we weep with tenderness over the idyl of Charmettes. That is because in it he does not try to convince us; he listens to his heart, becomes intoxicated with his memories, is charmed with himself. In vain we are warned of the fraud: it spreads out all over, and never was the Infinite Being, Virtue, mingled with a more disturbing or uglier story. We know it and we know under what fine pretexts Madame de Warens covers up the favors she diverts—partly only—from the domestic, Claude Anet, and that she pours out on the pretty neophyte. It is a question of saving him from worse; it is a question of doing him good. All the Warenses of to-day have brought to perfection this method of "doing good": "I could not desert him," they say, "I'll raise him up; I'll educate him; I'll marry him off." (And so Madame de Warens makes the proposal herself when the young Wintzenreid, the boy who succeeded Rousseau in her favor, decides to marry.)

Is not this disturbing maternity her most secret pleasure? But what now:

> Calm sanctuaries! Calm years! Calm retreats!
> Rustling young alders sang among the beeches.
> One sometimes received the visit of a priest . . .

Those auxiliary love affairs, that sharing, all that should fill one with horror, and nothing shocks. We are accomplices in spite of ourselves. The magician invests the most corrupt customs with all the graces of purity.

It is to this hypochondriac, to this victim of persecution, that humanity perhaps owes the picture of the most enchanting happiness. This sick lover, whose sentimental life knew so few victories, leaves us this eternally fresh picture of his first love. At Charmettes, he seems to say to us, we were not guilty because we were ourselves. We took care not to be high-falutin'. We did not permit any touching up of God's work within us. And it is true that Madame

*1727 portrait of Madame de Warens, whom Rousseau affection-
ately called "Maman."*

de Warens never thought that her religion could interfere with her pleasures in any way. "One must be oneself," Rousseau repeated. "One must remain oneself." To-day that is the device of all his children. We tell ourselves in vain that what genius makes so attractive, is just the same, beastly. But there are the bowers, the terraced garden between the vine and the orchard, the little chestnut wood, the fountain . . . Unrestrained, the wind stirs the trees; the sun shines down on the roofs and makes the china on the set table glisten. Mythological shepherds and fabulous animals no longer stand between us and reality. Human history is rooted, framed and related in objects, odors and instants.

"Here begins the short happiness of my life . . . " Did he suspect that there was beginning, too, the intoxication of a world? But one had to wait a century and a half for the poison to accomplish its work: only to-day do we see its final effects. All of romanticism, literally faithful to Jean-Jacques, continued to believe in virtue. It cost it little more than it cost the Geneva citizen, to love it without practicing it, and to adore that outer divinity, inaccessible to the heart of poor men. But to-day, virtue after the pattern of Rousseau resides deep within our flesh; it has become our very flesh, its basest passion, its strangest and most unhappy inclination. That is still saying too much; it is interwoven with our own changing. In his day, Rousseau abstained from putting any order into his *Reveries,* because, said he, "order would divert me from my aim, which is to remark the modifications in my soul and their

succession . . . " There is a sentence that gives out a modern note, if I may say so.

And yet! Shall we join Rousseau's enemies to accuse him of every iniquity? Let us be afraid of giving in to the inclination to discover the source of our misery, cost what it may, and to give it a name. Rousseau's work, before being the cause of so many regrettable effects, is itself a result. Rousseau may be the father of the modern world, but first of all, it is the modern world that secreted Rousseau. A prolonged constraint has been set free in him. Like Luther, he is the outcropping, or the spurting up of accumulated subterranean forces. Deliverance, liberation which made him weak with joy on the road to Vincennes. He who maintained that the progress of the arts and sciences had corrupted customs, did not accuse artists and writers of that crime: "It was," he wrote to Voltaire, "neither Terence, nor Cicero, nor Virgil, nor Tacitus, it was not scholars or poets who caused the misfortunes of Rome or the crimes of the Romans; but without the slow, secret poison that, little by little, corrupted the most vigorous government history has ever mentioned, neither Cicero, nor Lucretius, nor Sallust would have existed or written." Here Rousseau presents his own defense, for he himself was the outlet through which all the pus of a decayed organism was escaping. But let us render him this justice. What comes out of him is not only all the disturbance of an era; he had the clearest vision of the problems of every order that were being presented at that time. Should we impute guilt to him for having proposed solutions with too much eloquence and the most dangerous passion?

We are sometimes inclined to see in him less a victim than a dangerous and irritating fool. It is true that if Rousseau charmed his century, he was, at the same time, unbearable to it. To-day there is no longer any society in the sense in which one then understood it. How would the salons of Paris have tolerated that insolent plebeian? High society indeed consented to opening the windows and looking at the green, but not to giving up the pleasure of being witty and of talking. Rousseau's greatest offence was his passion for solitude. By sensitive souls, which, in another connection, recognized themselves in him, he was reviled on account of that peculiarity. The most sagacious already foresaw that this embittered plebeian was a dangerous man, and the philosophers were irritated that sentiment should be given precedence over reason. They refused to go down on all fours and browse.

During his lifetime, he had enough enemies at his heels to have the right to cry out against persecution without anyone crying out: "Crazy man!" To tell the truth, his folly is not because he was convinced he was persecuted—which is true—but in thinking everyone was entirely taken up with Jean-Jacques. Such is the exaggeration of his ego: he does not doubt that a single combat exists between Jean-Jacques and the rest of the world. "He thinks," he writes of himself, in the second dialogue, "that all the disasters of his destiny, since his unfortunate fame, are the fruits of a far-reaching and secret plot, formed by a few persons who have found the way to make everyone whom they need for its execution join: the Great, the authors, the doctors, all the men of influence, all the women of the town, all accredited bodies," etc., etc.

What is true is that he had the misfortune to displease, at the same time, both the pious and the Encyclopedists: irreconcilable enemies who became reconciled on his back. And to-day still he has against him—in addition to the pious—philosophers and humanists. Just as the Encyclopedists despised him because instead of judging him by his desires, good will and the impulses of his heart, they judged him by his actions, so to-day he looks like a liar because *The Confessions, The Reveries* and *The Dialogues* show us a man who, not recognizing his acts, believes he is virtuous when he aspires to be so. Such is the eternal misunderstanding between Rousseau and the rest of the world.

His opponents, philosophers and humanists, have the right, in the name of logic, to reproach him with the contradiction between what he claims to be and what he is. But if he had claimed only to follow his passions, if he had not played the virtuous man, by what categorical moral could they have condemned him? Let us recognize it: Certain of Rousseau's faults, by any standard, cause horror. I am thinking especially of the ribbon theft of which he accused the servant Marion, and the desertion of his five children. For this last offence, one would be tempted to go further than Rousseau himself: that action resembles him so little that one yields to the desire to believe that he did not commit it. What is incredible is not that he took one new-born babe to the orphanage; what surpasses all belief is that he repeated the offence five times, that he had the perservering courage; and that he did not even feel sufficient aversion for it to keep himself from giving life in the future. Now this is striking: when he returned to Geneva in 1754, followed by Thérèse, and decided to go back to the Protestant Church, several members of the Consistory wanted to keep him from Communion because he was living with a woman out of wedlock, and because she slept in his room. Here is Rousseau's defense: "If my situation were known to those people, they would be convinced that I am absolutely incapable of carrying out their suspicions. For a long time, I have suffered terrible pains from an incurable retention of urine, caused by an excrescence in the urethra, that stops up that canal to such an extent that even Daran's bougies have never been able to enter."

This text makes clear that Rousseau's infirmity had deprived him for a long time of all sexual intercourse. Now there is no offense of which an impotent man would not accuse himself in order to hide his misfortune. In Stendhal's *Armance,* the impotent Octave goes to the point of pretending to his mistress that in his childhood he had a passion for stealing. He speaks to her continuously of fatal peculiarities; he sends her astray with a thousand clews, makes himself appear, in her eyes, as a debauched man. Let her think him capable of everything, but above all, let her not know he is incapable of possessing her!

That invention of Rousseau's seems to us similar. How fearful the mockery of a Diderot or a Grimm could appear to him! If he had had normal relations with Thérèse, would he, as he did, have taken the whole family Levasseur on his back? It seems as though this woman, almost an idiot, had the right to demand everything and that she expected compensations from him. Can't we imagine Rousseau letting himself go, by vanity and false shame, into this invention without understanding at first what a terrible load he was assuming before a world that did not yet know him? Some day, when he has become very famous, he will awaken prisoner of his lie—too late to deny

it, even to himself. Yes, all that would be credible, and even likely, if specialists did not insist they had found traces of the little abandoned children. Jules Lemaître who at first defended, with great ingenuity, the thesis of the invention and the lie, lays down his arms before proofs which, it seems to me, are not conclusive. The supposition remains that the children were not "his"; that Thérèse (who is suspected of not having waited for Jean-Jacques' death in order to take a pretty lowly lover) had yielded, as others have done, to the demands of a holy nature . . .

But let us leave that. After all the offences he confesses, that man remains, none the less, in Voltaire's century, God's wretched defender. At a time when the poverty-stricken thought of Voltaire passed for philosophy, it was fitting that the supernatural be defended by that maniac, that madman. If we look for Bossuet's descendant in the eighteenth century, we find no other than the solitary wanderer. There, indeed, was the age of the great Catholic humiliation! It is not sufficient to say that sometimes Jean-Jacques rediscovers Bossuet's eloquence; what is most astonishing is that he refound also his indomitable good sense and clear thinking. Especially in private letters in which he tries to appease the priests, a prey to doubt, or anxious young Catholics, one is amazed to find, under his pen, the expression of an almost earthly wisdom, advice practical and void of all pathos and lofty padding.

Lastly, let us do him this justice: however far he may be from true Christianity, he confessed Christ before men, and that too will be counted for him. Apart from the comparison between the death of Christ and that of Socrates, he said of Jesus' gentleness "that it was more angelic and divine than human"; and that the Gospels could not be read without weeping. The Vicar of Savoy does not blaspheme against the sacrifice of the Mass: "Whatever might be said of this inconceivable mystery, I do not think that, on the day of the Last Judgment, I shall be punished for ever having profaned it in my heart."

Doubtless, this profession of faith should have been enough to win him the right to attain the light, if he had not been to such a degree a prey to himself. When he fancies he is leaving the world, it is only that his immoderate personality does not distinguish the world any more; it scarcely distinguishes God. And that is why the apologists should use it only with prudence. To help us measure the poverty of Rousseau's Christianity, Jacques Maritain alludes to another solitary wanderer of the eighteenth century, Benoît-Joseph Labre, under his rags and vermin, whose feet bled on the roads of France and Italy at that time. Without a doubt, a certain Catholic revival in the nineteenth century had its source in Jean-Jacques, and text books have the right to teach us that Chateaubriand was born of him. But it is a question of knowing what the *Génie du Christianisme* is worth, *sub specie aeterni;* and if that apology conceived in Madame de Beaumont's bedroom is of a higher order than the effusions of the catechumen of Charmettes and his pious mamma, lifted up to the Author of nature. We owe the religious awakening of the nineteenth century in part to Rousseau, it is true, but the essence of Catholic life does not abide in the troubled stream of which he is the source—the mire.

The eye is struck by a shallow which runs from Madame Guyon to Madame de Warens, from Rousseau to Chateaubriand and to Lamennais. But the true current, the one with great depths, springs up under the hazel trees of Paray-le-Monial at the decline of a great century, flows unseen or scorned, under the feet of Benoît Labre (whose pilgrimage begins just at Paray); comes to light at Ars in the vicarage of a lost village. Alone, the most humble and ignorant dowsers uncover for the eyes of the world this water hidden deep down in the earth. The shepherds of La Salette pick up a secret; and between the rock and the mountain torrent, that calm little girl with a somewhat backward mind and an ordinary face, Bernadette Soubirous, forgets to pick up her wood and falls on her knees. Lastly, the demon of boredom and lucre unleashed against the little sister Thérèse does not succeed in darkening that martyred childish face.

Sometimes the deep inner river and the shallow current of Rousseau seem to draw near to each other and mingle their streams: in Lamennais and Lacordaire. But one stream always has to divert the other. Rousseau triumphs in Lamennais. By dint of humility and love, Lacordaire dominates the Geneva demon of eloquence without ever completely conquering him.

On the religious plane, Jean-Jacques Rousseau seems to us to have no other reason for existing than to offer the world a caricature of Catholicism. He is a kind of "skinned" Christian at the service of Nietzsche. Here is the privileged subject in whom break out all the defects of the slave. Here you have the weakest of the weak, the infirm, the madman interested in the great Christian treason, in the reversal of all values! How insignificant the services that Rousseau could render Christ, at the price of arms with which he enriches the opponents of the Cross, seem to us! Not that he wanted it that way; it is without knowing it that he deprives Christianity of its essence; to die in order to be born again; to die to oneself so as to be reborn in Christ, that is the secret that Jean-Jacques Rousseau either did not know or scorned. Only he finds it pleasing to think himself immortal. So he retains from religion a hope of survival. He can not give up the perspective of finding himself again after death. Why refuse oneself this consolation? It costs so little to pretend to believe it: "Illusion, perhaps," he dares to write; "but if I knew a more consoling one, I would adopt it . . . "

There you have the cowardly, fearful being whom Nietzsche denounces: "The one who thinks only of strict usefulness." Perhaps Nietzsche was not thinking of Rousseau when he wrote that; but when he added: "One scorns the suspicious being, with his restless glance, the one who abases himself, the man-dog who lets himself be ill-treated, the servile flatterer and above all the liar . . . " That involuntary portrait seems to us more shrieking of likeness than la Tour's pastel.

There is no denying that a work must be very alive still for us to keep on protesting against it after a century and a half—and with what heat! Our forefather Jean-Jacques is younger than his son Chateaubriand and his grandsons, the Romantics. They sleep, embalmed in their glory. He is one of us: I close with this word with which I began—his name is Romain Rolland, Marcel Proust, André Gide. Entire pages of the **Confessions** or the **Reveries** could be inserted into *Swann's Way* without it being easy to detect the fraud. May my shocked readers pardon me for thinking that such vehemence, in which love and hatred are

mingled, is exactly what every dead writer would most desire to inspire, if he were still alive. (pp. 30-46)

> *François Mauriac, "Jean-Jacques Rousseau,"
> in his* Men I Hold Great, *translated by Elsie
> Pell, Philosophical Library, 1951, pp. 30-60.*

Jacques Maritain   (essay date 1955)

[*A French philosopher and educator, Maritain was a prominent spokesman for the Catholic Literary Revival in France. His philosophical system, founded upon the teachings of Thomas Aquinas, emphasized the importance of rationality in theology, thereby opposing the intense mysticism of much nineteenth-century theology. In the following excerpt, Maritain outlines the mythical presuppositions of* The Social Contract, *concluding that "their 'mysticism,' which looks reasoned and rational, is just as mad as the mysticism of sentiment and passion" of* Émile *and* La Nouvelle Héloïse.]

"I have a deep affection for the 'lonely walker' in him; I hate the theorist." This saying of C.-F. Ramuz explains the attraction of Jean-Jacques for many noble souls, and the echo he will always find, even when they hate him, in those who, exempt from his psychopathy, are yet his brothers in lyricism, "sensitive workers" as he was. Why that sympathy? Because of the dreams, tears, transports, sentimental tinsel *à la Diderot?* Nonsense! I am speaking of true lyricists. Because of the wild genius of a true spirit of the woods? Because of the fresh unfolding of a song genuinely springing from the heart of the solitudes, the purity of rhythm, without artifice and attuned to the movements of the soul, which is the only part of himself where Rousseau is truly innocent? Even that is secondary. The true reason is, as Ramuz again said, that before being an anti-social theorist Rousseau was born *non-social,* and that he has told incomparably the condition of a soul so made.

Men naturally respect anchorites. They instinctively understand that the solitary life is of itself the most exempt from the diminution and the nearest to divine things. Does not the tragic flight of old Tolstoy on the eve of his death come primarily from that instinct? And so many goings forth, so many wanderings? *Quoties inter homines fui, minor homo redii.* In differing degrees, philosophers, poets, or contemplatives, those whose chief work is intellectual know too well that in man social life is not the heroic life of the spirit, but the realm of mediocrity, and most often of falsehood. It is the burden of the unnecessary and the sham, from which poets and artists, at least free from what is perceived by the senses, suffer most sensitively, but not perhaps most cruelly. Yet all need to live by the social life in so far as the very life of the spirit must come out of a human life, a *rational* life in the strict sense of the word.

The solitary life is not human; it is above or beneath man. "There is for man a double manner of living solitary. Either he so lives because he cannot endure human society, by reason of the brutality of his temperament, *propter animi saevitiam,* and that belongs to beasts. Or else it is because he cleaves wholly to divine things, and that is of the superhuman order. He who has no dealings with others, said Aristotle, is either a beast or a god." Extremes meet! Beast and god, the restless being who is but a fragment of the world, and the perfect being who makes up a universe in himself live an analogous life, whilst man is between the two, at once individual and person. As for Rousseau, paranoiac and genius, poet and madman, he leads at the same time and confuses voluptuously the life according to bestiality and the life according to intelligence. In this man, forced into solitary life by his physical blemishes, unfitted by his morbid shyness for the social régime, the unadaptability which rebels and complains, apes the unadaptability which dominates, that of the spirit, *set apart to govern,* as Anaxagoras said of the *nous.* He gives us in his very unsociability, his sickly isolation, a lyrical image, as dazzling as it is deceptive, of the secret needs of the spirit in us.

But let us not forget the theorist. Making his personal misfortune the rule of the species, he will consider the solitary life to be the life natural to the human being. "The breath of man is fatal to his fellow beings; that is no less true strictly than figuratively," he declares. Consequently the essential inclinations of human nature, and indeed the primordial conditions of moral health, require this blessed state of solitude which he pictures, projecting his own phantoms, as the perpetual flight through the woods of animals, dreamy, endowed with compassion, mating by chance meetings, and then going on with their innocent wandering. Such is the divine life in his eyes.

Thus the slip is immediate. The *supra hominem* has at once discharged into the bestial, not without giving it something of the sweetness of paradise. The conflict between the social life and the life of the spirit has become a conflict between the social life and savagery—and at the same time a conflict between the social life and human nature. By one stroke it has become an essential opposition, a harsh antinomy, absolutely insoluble.

What, however, does Christian wisdom say? It knows well that life according to the intellect leads to solitude, and that the more highly spiritual it is, the more apart is its solitude. But it knows also that this life is a superhuman life—relatively, with respect to the ways of rational speculation; purely and simply, with respect to the ways of contemplation in charity. That is the supreme end to be reached, the ultimate perfection, the last degree of the soul's growth. And for man to arrive at it, his progress must be inhuman environment. How should he go to the superhuman without going through the human? "We must consider that the state of a solitary is that of a being who should be self-sufficient; in other words, one who lacks nothing; and that pertains to the definition of what is perfect. Solitude, therefore, only befits the contemplative who has already come to perfection, either by the divine bounty alone, like John the Baptist, or by the exercise of the virtues. And man should not be exercised in the virtues without the help of the society of his fellow beings—with respect to the intelligence, to be taught; with respect to the heart, that harmful affections be repressed by the example and correction of others. Whence it follows that social life is necessary to the exercise of perfection, and that solitude befits souls already perfect." That is doubtless why, in very early times people ran to the desert to drag out hermits in order to make them their bishops. . . . Finally St. Thomas concludes "the life of solitaries, if it be adopted rightly, is higher than social life; but if it be adopted without previous exercise of that life,

it is most perilous unless, as with the blessed Antony and Benedict, divine grace supply what in others is acquired by exercise."

Thus solitude is the flower of the city. Thus social life remains the life natural to man, required by his deepest specific needs. Its conventions and meannesses, the difficulties and lessening of the intellectual life which it occasions, all the "pleasantry" which so struck Pascal, remain accidental defects, which only betray the radical weakness of human nature—the price, sometimes terrible to pay, of an essential advantage. It is social life which leads to the life of the spirit: but by that very ordination, just as the activity of the reason is ordered to the simple act of contemplation, so the social life is ordered to the solitary life, to the imperfect solitude of the intellectual, to the solitude, perfect, at least interior, of the saint.

Hence harmony instead of an irreducible antinomy. The conflict is not suppressed (for that you would need to suppress man): it is surmounted. Theoretically it is overcome perfectly; actually it is more or less overcome, according to our own state. The suffering remains, the opposition vanishes. Where is that seen better than where the harmony of social and spiritual is most purely realized, in that state of life specially established for the human conquest of perfection?

In the religious state, the very defects of social life work together for the good of the spirit. How is that? By the virtue of obedience, of a limitless sacrifice. Mistakes of government in superiors, mediocrity in environment, everything that man is capable of, and that a calced Carmelite can make a discalced Carmelite suffer, what do these accidents do but hasten the mystical death of a heart vowed to immolation? They cast it further into the divine life. So true is it that man has made peace with himself only on the Cross of Jesus.

Not in this way did Jean-Jacques undertake to resolve (for he fears nothing) the opposition which he himself made absolute and insoluble.

It is a flagrant absurdity, and at the same time an act of cowardly deceit, to treat men as if they were perfect, and the perfection which has to be acquired, from which most of them will always be far removed, as a constituent of nature itself. Yet such is Rousseau's principle, his perpetual postulate. This method of his is an astonishing system of vacuum cleaning, quite typical of his debility, and consists in passing at a leap to the conditions of absolute perfection or of the pure act. The geometrician refines the idea of stick or disc to define the straight line or circle. But Rousseau refines the human being of all potentiality, so that he may contemplate the ideal world, alone worthy of his thought, which will allow him to condemn in holiness the injustice of the existing world. He begins by placing himself in the unrealizable so that he may breathe and utter himself as God utters Himself in creation. He dreams, and he tells his dream; and if reality in no way corresponds with it, he cannot help it; it is reality that is wrong. "Only what is not, is beautiful," he delighted to repeat, in a formula which is metaphysically hateful. In 1765 at Strasbourg, a M. Angar procured an introduction to him in order to say to him: "You see, sir, a man who brings up his son on the principles which he had the happiness to learn from your *Émile.*" "So much the worse, sir," he replied, "so much the worse for you and your son!" No, no, he knows better than we—it was his distinct intention—that all his ideology is only a romantic piece of mechanism, and idle dream.

Rousseau begins, then, by assuming men to be in the pure exercise of their human activity. Then solutions come of themselves. And sublime ideas flow. Are you at a loss for the best form of government? It is that designed for the perfect: *"regimen perfectorum, ergo regimen perfectum,"* holy Democracy. Do you want a sound method of education? It is the one which requires: 1, princely conditions of wealth and isolation; 2, a single tutor for a single pupil; 3, an ideal tutor and an essentially good pupil—the hypocritical negative Education in which Nature (conveniently faked at a pinch) does all the work; all is perfect in it.

As to the social state, it must be built of self-sufficing individuals—who have not, so far, succeeded in coming together without sinking. "The wicked man lives alone," Diderot might well hurl this treacherous bolt at him. Jean-Jacques will suffer as an innocent victim, but will hold fast to his axiom: man would be good if he were alone. But if our nature, corrupted by the discovery of civilized life, has to be mended by the help of some more sublime discovery, he, Jean-Jacques, has the secret of the perfect city, built in his head with the perfect, that will restore man in a new way to the privileges of the state of solitude in the very midst of social life.

And behold, there rises before us the rich ideological forest of the *Contrat Social.* We will here enumerate, and try to express in a short formula which will give an idea of their essential spirit, the chief myths which the modern world owes to that famous work.

NATURE.—In his limpid and subtle Treatise on Law, St. Thomas explains that the term "natural law" can be taken in two quite different senses. A thing can be said to be "of natural law" either because nature inclines towards it (as that one should not harm others), or only because nature does not at once assert the contrary arrangement. "In this latter sense it might be said that to be naked is *de jure naturali* for man, because it is art, not nature, which provides him with clothes. It is in this sense that we should understand Isidore when he says that the state of common possession and of one and the same liberty for all is *of natural law;* in fact, the distinction of property and submission to a master are not things provided by nature, but introduced by man's reason as useful to human life."

In other words, the word nature can be taken in the metaphysical sense of *essence* involving a certain finality. Then what is natural is that which answers the requirements and propensities of the essence, that to which things are ordered, by reason of their specific type and finally, by the Author of Being. And it can be taken in the material sense of an actual primitive state. Then what is natural is that which actually existed before all developments due to the intelligence.

The weakening of the metaphysical spirit was bound gradually to obscure the first sense of the word nature. In the radically nominalist and empiricist theory of Hobbes, followed in that by Spinoza, the second sense alone remains and, badly stated, leads the philosopher to logical errors. According to Hobbes, the absolute isolation of individuals is "natural"; so is the battle of every man against his neighbour which he takes to be the primitive state of humanity. And with the rational mystic's peculiar pessimism, Spinoza declares: "The natural right of each stretches as far as his power. Whoever is deemed to live under the sway of nature alone has absolute right to covet whatever he considers useful, whether he be led to this desire by sound reason or by the violence of the passions. He has the right to seize it in any way, whether by force, by cunning, by entreaty, by whatever means he considers easiest, and consequently to regard as an enemy anyone who would hinder the satisfaction of his desires." Nothing could be clearer.

What does Jean-Jacques do? Because he is of a religious disposition, and because withal what good sense he has is solidly traditionalist, he returns to the notion of nature in the first sense of the word, to the notion of a nature ordered to an end by the wisdom of a good God. But because he is powerless to realize that notion intellectually, and restore to it its metaphysical value and range, he insinuates it into the picture of a certain primitive and, so to say, antecultural state, which exactly corresponds to the second sense of the word nature. He muddles up these two different senses, he locks into a single equivocal pseudoconcept the "nature" of the metaphysicians and the "nature" of the empiricists. Hence comes the Rousseauist myth of Nature, which needs only to be clearly expressed for its absurdity to be seen: *Nature is the primitive condition of things, at which they should stop, or which they should restore, to comply with their essence.* Or again: *Nature is the essential need, divinely placed in things, of a certain primitive condition or ante-culture which things are made to realize.*

From this myth of Nature will come logically the dogma of Natural Goodness. All that is necessary is the discovery that nature in the sense of the metaphysician, the immutable essence of things, and particularly the human essence with its faculties and specific propensities, is good. The conclusion will follow that the primitive state and the primitive conditions of human life, the state before culture and before the institutions of reason (whether it be pictured as formerly realized in history, or be conceived only as an abstraction), was necessarily good, innocent, happy, and that a state of goodness, a fixed condition of innocence and happiness, is due to humanity. . . .

Rousseau's discovery of the dogma of natural goodness dates from the writing of his *Discours,* after the revelation of the Bois de Vincennes and the coat wet with tears. In the *Contrat Social* which he wrote later, but from his old Venetian note-books, this dogma is not formulated, it is even sometimes contradicted. Yet the myth of Nature, which has the seeds of it, is certainly there. We realize that, when we remark that it is the myth of Nature that engenders the myth of Liberty, absolutely essential to the *Contrat Social.*

LIBERTY.—"Man is born free." (A savage in a wood.) In other words, *the state of liberty or sovereign independence is the primitive state, whose maintenance or restoration is required by man's essence and the divine order.*

Henceforward no kind of submission to a master or lording over a subject is allowable. The condition which, according to theologians, prevailed in the earthly paradise, in which all were of free estate (that is, where none worked in the service of another and for the private good of another, because in the state of innocence there was no servile work), becomes the state required by human nature. Nay more, according to St. Thomas, the state of innocence must have involved that kind of domination over free men which consists in guiding them towards the *common good*,—"because man is naturally social, and because social life is impossible unless someone be pre-eminent to aim at the common good—*"multi enim per se intendunt ad multa unus vero ad unum"*—and because, on the other hand, if a man is eminent injustice and knowledge he naturally serves the utility of others, that is to say, he governs. But Jean-Jacques, on the contrary, would have us say that that very kind of sway is precluded by nature. Man is born free, Liberty is an absolute requirement of Nature, all subjection of any kind to the authority of any manner of man is contrary to Nature.

EQUALITY.—An equal condition for all is likewise required by Nature. All of us are born equally men, and so equally "free," equal as to specific *essence* and consequently (and this is the tremendous confusion of thought peculiar to egalitarianism) equal in regard to the State, whose realization for each individual is required by our essence and the divine order. There are, doubtless, so-called "natural" inequalities between individuals more or less hardy, more or less intelligent. But they are against Nature's desires, and who knows if they do not go back to some remote malformation?

Nature requires that the strictest equality should be realized amongst men, so that, in every political state which is not directly against Nature and her Author, an absolute social equality should exactly balance natural inequalities.

This myth of Equality is supported by two oddly clumsy sophisms:

1. The confusion of *equality* with *justice*—which destroys justice. Justice indeed implies a certain equality, but a *geometrical* or *proportional* equality (which treats both sides in proportion to their deserts), and not *arithmetical* equality or that of *absolute size* (which treats both sides the same, whatever be their deserts); so that to confound justice with that second species of equality, with equality pure and simple, is just precisely to destroy justice.

2. The confusion—which would render the constitution of any social body impossible—of what concerns *recompense* to parts with what concerns the *constitution* of the whole. St. Thomas explained this vigorously against Origen, the metaphysical patriarch of egalitarianism, who claimed that God must have created all things equal (for before being created they were all equally nothing), and that the diversity of things and the arrangement of the world came from the sin of the creature. He says that in the order of *retribution* justice should be exercised, and it demands that equal things should be rendered to equals, because in that order you must necessarily presuppose deserts. But in the order of the *constitution* of things, or of their *first institution,* these requirements of justice have not to be exercised, because in that order merits are not necessarily to be presupposed, but only a work to bring into existence, a whole to be produced. "The artist places in different parts of the building stones which are by hypothesis all alike, and this without wronging justice: not that he assumes in them some pre-existent diversity, but because he

is aiming at the perfection of the whole thing to be built, which could not be if the stones were not placed in the building differently and unequally. Likewise, it is without injustice, and yet without presupposing any diversity of merits, that God from the beginning established in His wisdom different and unequal creatures, that there might be perfection in the universe." And in the same way, assuming by hypothesis that all men are equal in worth, it is no injustice that in order to establish the body politic—and otherwise that body could not be—they should be set in different parts of it and consequently have unequal rights, functions, and conditions.

THE POLITICAL PROBLEM.—The myth of Liberty and the myth of Equality led Rousseau to formulate the political problem in a way which is wholly and absurdly Utopian. How make a society with individuals all perfectly "free" and "equal"? How, to use Rousseau's own expressions, harmonize *men* (such as nature would have them) and *laws* (such as a social body requires)? *How "find a form of association by which each being united with all should yet obey only himself, and still be as free as before"?*

It simply amounts to establishing an organic whole without its parts being subordinate to one another. That is absurd; but Jean-Jacques is happy. The more difficult the problem, the more merit he will have for devising the solution. His prophetic mission consists in condemning and anathematizing the existent unjust city, and showing men the only conceivable type of just city. Is it impossible that this just city should exist? Let the unhappy beings who are condemned to existence get out of the business as best they can; they can always "throw themselves on the ground and lament that they are men," as Jean-Jacques himself does when he despairs of democracy and remembers Caligula.

THE SOCIAL CONTRACT.—It is the social contract which "gives the solution" of the "fundamental problem" which has just been stated. *The social contract is a pact concluded by the deliberate will of sovereignly free individuals whom the state of nature formerly held in isolation and who agree to pass into the social state.*

Although it derives from it by a long progress of degradation which goes from Althusius and Grotius to Rousseau, this myth of the Contract is quite different from the *consensus* which the ancients allowed to have been at the beginning of human societies, and which was the expression of a natural aspiration. The Rousseauist contract has its first cause in the deliberate will of man, not in nature, and it gives birth to a product of human art, not to a work proceeding from nature; it presupposes that "the individual alone is the work of nature."

Hence it follows that the first author of society is not God, the Author of the natural order, but the will of man, and that the birth of civil law is the destruction of natural law. The ancients taught that human law derives from natural law as making specific what was left indeterminate by the latter. Rousseau teaches that after the pact there are no more natural rights, and it will be granted henceforth that in the social state there could be no right but from the agreement of free wills. . . .

But the notion of the Rousseauist contract is not yet complete. It is, indeed, not an indefinite covenant; it has a fixed nature, it implies essentially certain terms without which it is nothing and from which Jean-Jacques will deduce his whole system. *These terms can really all be reduced to a single one; that is the complete transfer of each associate, with all his rights to the whole community.* Where, then, is liberty? And how is the "fundamental" problem solved? Ah! That is just the wonder. "As each gives himself to all, he gives himself to no one"; he is subject to all, but he is subject to no man, and that is the essential thing, there is no man above him. Nay more, as soon as the covenant begets the social body, each is in such wise absorbed in that common self which he has willed, that by obeying the still obeys himself. Then the more we obey, not a man—God forbid!—but the general will, the more free we are. A happy solution! In the state of nature we only existed as persons, in no way as parts; in the state of society we no longer exist except as parts. Thus does pure individualism, precisely by misconceiving the reality which belongs to the social bonds added to individuals by natural need, end inevitably in pure bureaucracy as soon as it undertakes to construct a society.

THE GENERAL WILL.—This is the finest myth of Jean-Jacques, the most religiously manufactured. We might call it the myth of political pantheism. The *General Will* (which must not be confused with the sum of the individual wills) *is the Common Self's own will, born of the sacrifice each has made of himself and all his rights on the altar of the city.*

Truth to tell, here there is a question of a kind of immanent God mysteriously evoked by the operation of the pact, of whose decrees the majority of votes is only a sign, a sacred sign which is only valid under certain conditions—particularly, Rousseau teaches, under the condition that no partial society exist in the whole.

Immanent social God, common self which is more I than myself, in whom I lose myself and find myself again and whom I serve to be free—that is a curious specimen of fraudulent mysticism. Note how Jean-Jacques explains that the citizen subject to a law against which he voted remains free, and continues to obey only himself: men do not vote, he says, to give their opinion; they vote that, by the counting of votes, the general will may be ascertained, which each wills supremely, since it is what makes him a citizen and a freeman. "When then the opposite opinion to my own carries the day, that proves nothing but that I was wrong, and that what I thought to be the general will was not so. If my private opinion had carried the day, I should have done differently from what I willed; and then I should not have been free." What does he hold out to us here but a preposterous transposition of the case of the believer who, when he prays for what he thinks expedient yet asks and wills chiefly that God's Will may be done? The vote is conceived by him as a species of ritual petition and evocation addressed to the General Will.

LAW.—The myth of the General Will is central and dominant in Rousseau's political theory, like the notion of the common good in Aristotle's. The common good, as the end sought, essentially implies the guidance of an intelligence, and the ancients defined law as an arrangement of the reason tending to the common good and promulgated by him who has the care of the community. The General Will, which animates and moves the social body, imposes itself on all by its mere existence; it is enough for it to be, and it is shown by Numbers. *Law will then be defined as*

the expression of the General Will, and it will no longer proceed from reason but from numbers.

It was essential to law as the ancients understood it that it should be just. Modern law has no need to be just, and it demands obedience all the same. Law as the ancients understood it was promulgated by some ruler; modern law is in sole command. As Malebranche's God reserved to Himself alone the power of acting, so that mythical sign enthroned in the heaven of abstractions reserves authority. Below it on earth men are, from the point of view of the relations between authority and submission, mere dust, alike and absolutely shapeless.

THE SOVEREIGN PEOPLE.—The law only exists in so far as it expresses the General Will. But the General Will is the will of the people. "The people who are subject to the laws, should be author of the laws," for so they obey only themselves, and we are at the same time "free and subject to the laws, since they are only records of our wills."

Sovereignty, then, resides essentially and absolutely in the people, in the shapeless mass of all individuals taken together, and since the state of society is not natural but artificial, it has its origin not in God but in the free will of the people itself. Every state which is not built on this foundation is not a *State governed by laws,* a legitimate State; it is a product of tyranny, a monster violating the rights of human nature.

There we have the true myth of modern Democracy, its spiritual source, absolutely opposite to Christian law which will have sovereignty derive from God as its first origin and only go through the people to dwell in the man or men charged with the care of the common good.

Notice that the question here raised is quite distinct from that of forms of government. Although in themselves of unequal merit, the three classical forms of government have their place in the Christian system, for in democratic régime sovereignty will reside in those chosen by the multitude. And in the same way they all three have their place at least theoretically in Rousseau's system—and are all three equally vitiated in it. "I call any State that is governed by laws a republic (that is, any State where the laws are the expression of the General Will and where therefore the people is sovereign), *"under whatever form of administration it may be. . . .* Every lawful government is" consequently "republican. . . . To be lawful, the government must not be identified with the sovereign, but the *minister* of the sovereign; then monarchy itself is republican." The prince does not perform acts of sovereignty but of "magistracy"; he is not the author, but the minister of the Law, not a scrap of authority resides in him, and authority is all in the General Will; there is no man responsible for looking after the common good, the General Will is adequate for that. In the Rousseauist system, that holds good for the aristocratic or monarchial régime, as for the democratic.

Yet, in fact, with Rousseau himself and in the world which he fathered, there is inextricable confusion between Democracy as myth and universal doctrine of sovereignty, and democracy as a particular form of government. There may be discussion as to whether the democratic form of government is good or bad for a certain people in certain conditions; but it is beyond dispute that the myth of Democracy as the sole legitimate sovereign, the spiritual principle of modern egalitarianism, is a gross absurdity.

THE LAWGIVER.—The people always wills the good, but it is not always sufficiently informed, it is even often deceived, "and then only does it seem to will what is bad." The General Will needs enlightenment. The immanent God of the republic is a child God who wants helping, like the God of the pragmatists. *The lawgiver is the superman who guides the General Will.*

Neither magistrate (for the magistrate administers the law already made), nor sovereign (for the sovereign who proposes the law, is the people) he is, for formulating and propounding the law, outside and above every human order, in the void. "The lawgiver is a man in every respect extraordinary in the State. If he should be extraordinary by genius, he is not less so by his work. That work founds the republic; it does not enter into its constitution; it is a peculiar and higher function which has nothing in common with human rule."

This amazingly hackneyed myth is not without its dangers. Let us listen to Rousseau and understand that his utterances are a perfectly logical consequence of his principles and of the doctrine which will not allow that man is *by nature a political animal.* "He who dares to undertake to found a nation should feel that he is in *a position to change human nature, so to say;* to *transform* each individual, who by himself is a perfect and solitary *whole, into a* part of a greater whole, from which that individual should in some measure receive his life and being; *to change man's constitution* in order to make it stronger. . . . He must, in a word, deprive man of his own powers, to give him powers foreign to him, powers which he cannot exercise without the help of others. *The more dead and ruined these natural powers are,* the greater and more lasting are those acquired, *the more solid and perfect* [sic] *too is the foundation;* so that if each citizen is nothing and can do nothing except with all the others, and the power acquired by the whole be equal to or greater than the sum of the natural powers of all the individuals, you can say that the legislation is as perfect as it could possibly be."

Everything in this valuable passage should be remembered and pondered. But what then is this extraordinary and extra-cosmic lawgiver? We have not far to seek. It is Jean-Jacques himself—Jean-Jacques who, quite meaning to be the perfect Adam who completes his paternal work by education and political guidance, finds comfort for bringing children into the world for the Foundling Hospital in becoming Émile's tutor and the lawgiver of the Republic. But it is also the Deputy (*Constituant*), and in general every city-builder on the revolutionary plan, and it is most precisely Lenin.

Such, very briefly outlined, are some of the fables of the **Contrat Social.** Their "mysticism," which looks reasoned and rational, is just as mad as the mysticism of sentiment and passion which we find in **Émile** and the **Nouvelle Héloïse.** It is noteworthy that the former had its chief success in France, where we have tried it to our cost; whilst the second met with extraordinary success in Germany, and in another sphere did amazing damage. (pp. 119-40)

> *Jacques Maritain, "Rousseau," in his* Three Reformers: Luther—Descartes—Rousseau, *Charles Scribner's Sons, 1955, pp. 93-166.*

J. B. Priestley (essay date 1960)

[*A highly prolific English man of letters, Priestley was the author of numerous popular novels that depict the world of everyday, middle-class England. His best-known critical work is* Literature and Western Man (1960), *a survey of Western literature from the invention of movable type through the mid-twentieth century. In the following excerpt, he considers Rousseau's influence upon the development of romantic literature.*]

It was inevitable that Jean-Jacques Rousseau should have quarrelled bitterly with Voltaire and the Encyclopædists. As Lytton Strachey has pointed out: " . . . he possessed one quality which cut him off from his contemporaries, which set an immense gulf betwixt him and them: he was modern . . . he belonged to another world." We are still living in the world that owes much, for good or evil, to Rousseau; but the age that flourished just after his death in 1778, the Romantic Age, owed a great deal more to him: its most characteristic attitudes of mind either were imitated from him or were exaggerations of various attitudes of his. It is not a matter of vague influences but of direct inspiration: the Romantics, first in Germany, then in England, later in France and elsewhere, discovered in him their prophet. No doubt the Age of Reason, decaying to make room for its opposite, would sooner or later have been succeeded by an Age of Romance, even if there had been no Rousseau, but he hurried on the process of transformation; he was the catalyst. So large was Rousseau's legacy to romantic literature that, before estimating it, we had first better dispose of those elements in later eighteenth-century life that contributed to the Romantic Age without the intervention of Rousseau.

These elements belong to the natural reaction against the Age of Reason, against the over-valuation of consciousness, against what was rational, general, abstract, public, existing only in daylight, not in the dark. A one-sided attitude, if persisted in, inevitably produces its opposite, equally one-sided. Too much dependence upon reason sooner or later inspires the glorification of unreason. So the later eighteenth-century ushers in a new and widespread interest in the occult; it was a time when pseudo-mystical secret societies flourished all over Europe, when charlatans like Cagliostro found their way into the highest society, when alchemy and astrology, love-philtres and elixirs of youth, became fashionable and profitable again, as in the Renaissance. These new or revived tastes owned nothing directly to Rousseau but ultimately contributed something to romantic literature. (pp. 113-14)

All those critics who have tried to explain the difference between the Classical and the Romantic would have saved much time, temper and paper if they had been acquainted with the discoveries of depth psychology. For the Classical depends upon conscious mind, the Romantic upon the unconscious. So each misjudges the other: the Classical considers the Romantic unbalanced, childish, mad; the Romantic sees the Classical as drearily formal, tedious, lifeless. When either is hopelessly one-sided, it moves towards death; the Classical, deprived of zestful energy, dying of anaemia and boredom; the Romantic, losing all contact with reality, destroying itself in madness. When Rousseau was dying, after suffering for years from persecution mania, he thought himself "alone on the earth" and condemned to be alone for eternity. The fantasies of the unconscious had invaded his consciousness; he was living in a dream, or indeed a nightmare, out of which he could not wake himself. Not only his outlook and opinions but the major events of his life, the very shape of it, had been dominated by his unconscious. He lived the romanticism he was to bequeath to the age that followed him. His life and work, as Romain Rolland observes, "offer in literary history the case, perhaps unique, of a man of genius, upon whom genius descended not only unsolicited, but against his will". Will belongs to the conscious mind; the genius of Rousseau exploded from the unconscious. He describes the very moment of this explosion, on a hot summer day on the road to Vincennes, where he was going to visit Diderot, who was imprisoned there. He was thirty-seven, and had spent years wandering and idling and brooding, making little use of his quite able conscious mind, but storing energy, stoking up the boilers, so to speak, in his unconscious. Then in an instant, as he tells us, he lived in another world, he became another man. 'Great truths' descended upon him in a torrent; he saw in a flash his life's work. A prophet was born. The shy Swiss idler became an impassioned orator, an author of great force and originality, whose influence was so strong and far-reaching that a massive genius like Tolstoy, a century later, could declare himself to be inspired by Rousseau's teaching and example. The immediate effect of his political and social discourses, and his didactic fiction and confessions, was electrical. It was as if, by-passing the wary and dubious conscious mind, unconscious called to unconscious. But then of course the time was ready: the solution had been prepared, and here was the catalyst.

There are elements in Rousseau, reaching from Kant to Marx, that must be ignored here, but sufficient is left to show how much the Romantic Age owed to Rousseau's unconscious bursting like a dam. It is not that all the romantic poets and story-tellers wished to imitate him; we are not considering here an ordinary literary influence; but what was released in him soon came, with of course many individual differences and developments, to be released in them. So the age represents first the reaction and then the triumph of the unconscious, challenging and then defeating the rational conscious mind. The medal was not refashioned but merely reversed. What had been formerly admired was now despised; what had been distrusted and feared was now exalted. Created in this way, Romantic Western Man is as unbalanced and one-sided as Rational Western Man had been. There is, however, one important difference. In the previous age, the authors were expressing the society of their time; Molière and Louis XIV, as we have seen, had more or less the same outlook; Pope the poet and John Churchill, Duke of Marlborough, knew they were living in the same world. But when we come to the Romantic Age, we are no longer concerned with the character of a whole society but only with one small, though deeply significant, part of it; so that, for example, Chateaubriand the Romantic and Napoleon have not at all the same outlook; and Byron the poet and Arthur Wellesley, Duke of Wellington, seem to be living in two very different worlds. Literature has begun to move away from the general society of its time; and this oblique movement, as we shall see, now continues down to our own day.

Everything released by the explosion of Rousseau's unconscious, creating romanticism, must necessarily be intensely private, never general and public. So the romantic writer, like Rousseau, is not at home in society. He must discover himself in solitude, far from salons and cities, musing in the forest, lost in reverie among the mountains or on the seashore. He is not trying to express what men in general are thinking and feeling, not seeking any common denominator. It is what arises from the depths of his own being—really whatever comes from the unconscious—that deserves expression, which means that, when all is well with his genius, he will in fact discover for us original and profound truths, states of mind never described before, hidden treasures of the soul, but that, when he is below his best, he will tend to be merely affected, egoistic, even touched with megalomania. Exploring himself, he will give us what is either far richer and more valuable than common-sense or considerably worse, just nonsense. This is the risk the romantic writer and his readers run. But it is worth running because the romantic writer in his moments of genius illuminates, with an effect that is magical, the reader's own depths. For that balance of thought and feeling understood by the conscious mind and the classical writer, the Romantic, who sees nothing in this balance but tedium and lifelessness, substitutes the sense of infinity, the sudden ecstasy justifying all the mere mechanics of living, the supreme magical moment.

So the Romantic, following both Rousseau's practice and precept, seeks solitude and reverie. He is a wanderer, like the remote ancestors stirring in his unconscious; to become a settled member of a society is to frustrate his genius. Though longing for the most intensely sympathetic relationship with another soul, in undying love, eternal friendship, he is for ever being misunderstood, the world of men being the wretched thing it is, and almost welcomes the persecution that for poor Rousseau became a nightmare mania. Now the young child is only struggling into full consciousness and still enjoys a profoundly satisfying relation, through the unconscious, with Nature, like the *participation mystique* of primitive men; so to the Romantics, again following Rousseau, the child is no longer a half-grown man or woman, the young of our species, but the archetypal holy innocent, whose joy and unthinking wisdom we should try to recapture if only for a moment, whose happiness irradiates a lost world. So the cult of childhood begins. A companion figure to the holy child is the unspoilt savage, the dusky Arcadian, flower-crowned in some Eden of the South Seas or the Amazonian jungle, whose very existence proves how hollow and false our boasted civilisation is. It is true that the literary members of this cult did not take leave of civilisation to share the lives of these glorious creatures—for they could hardly expect to find them on walking tours or visits to Italy—but they lived with them in imagination and various editions of their works. And again, Rousseau, whose political theory is haunted by this dream, began it.

The magical images of the unconscious are projected by the Romantic on Nature and Woman. What seemed 'a horrid wilderness' to the Age of Reason, which hurried through it in search of roast chicken and clean linen, is now welcomed as a reflection, beautiful or terrible, of the beauty or storm in the Romantic's soul. Nature, especially when remote from traffic and agriculture, responds like a devoted mistress to his every mood. Oceans and mountains, forest and health, provide the enchanted scenery for his unending drama of the defiant lonely spirit. But somewhere across the ocean or beyond the mountains is the

Woman for whom the Romantic is searching, the Woman who will lead him out of his dream of love, those erotic reveries that Rousseau describes, into a real but endlessly ecstatic relationship. The love is there, as it is in the mind of a dreamy adolescent, before the Woman. And as there arise from the unconscious certain strange symbolical images of the other sex, images that may be vague but are still illuminated by the green and gold of the depths, the Romantic turns away from ordinary sensible women who cannot help thinking about children, houses and a steady income. So there flit through the literature of this age feminine creatures who are anything but ordinary sensible women, a host of faerie beings, nymphs, water sprites, savage queens, Oriental princesses, mysterious gipsy girls, anybody in fact who is sufficiently strange and cannot be domesticated. For love here is a pursuit, a torment, an unquenchable thirst, a fleeting ecstasy, a bitter aftermath, disillusion, unending regret, anything but the foundation of an enduring and fruitful relationship between a man and a woman. The Romantic, following Rousseau, is not turning outward, to look at and enjoy women as they are, but continues to turn inward, lost in erotic dreams and reveries, entangled in the uncriticised, unchecked fantasies of the unconscious.

Unless the end, however, is to be madness—as it so often was—a sense of reality must break in, the conscious mind must make its comparisons, and then unless some sort of balance can be arrived at, the result is the famous romantic melancholy, the canker and the worm, the inexplicable sadness, the gnawing homesickness that never knew a home. It was said of one romantic poet: "He wanted better bread than could be made of wheat", and that is true of them all. So they go in search of the blue flower, the lost kingdom of childhood, the happy valley of Arcadia, the forests of fairyland, the tower where they will find at last the strange woman who will enchant them for ever, forgetting if they are foolish, remembering if they grow wiser, that these things do not exist in the outward world, as revealed to consciousness, but belong, with much else, to the hidden realm of the unconscious, to the dreamer in his dream, to the solitary drama of the soul. To ignore the romantic as an aspect of life is to be blind to the rainbow; to accept the romantic as a way of life is to try and pack a rainbow in a crate. Rousseau cannot be considered among the poets, but he was a creator of poets, just because his example helped to release the dark energy, the zest that consciousness can control but cannot produce, the magical symbols that transform verse into unforgettable poetry, all from the depths of the unconscious. The conscious mind can accept and refine, but cannot create those phrases and lines that seem pregnant with many meanings and haunt us like music. The best of the authors of the Romantic Age opened themselves to the fire and sorcery of the unconscious without abandoning themselves to it, without leaving the conscious mind helpless, its will and judgment shattered, its sense of reality lost for ever. The less fortunate of them drifted rudderless into the dark, beyond communication, into madness. Rousseau, the prophet of Romance, the prototype of the romantic writer, ran the whole course. He ended by seeing the world as a conspiracy against him. Drifting into madness, he cried: "Here I am, alone on the earth, no brother, neighbour, friend, society, save myself . . ." He had turned his gaze inward too long, stared too hard into the dark depths of the unconscious. He should have looked the other way,

for it is our consciousness that shows us brothers, neighbours, friends, society.

"Man is born free; and everywhere he is in chains." It is the most famous of all Rousseau's pronouncements, and it still reverberates. So far as it merely means that men in our civilisation have allowed a reasonable personal liberty to be dangerously reduced by power organisations, it was true when he wrote it, and it is true today, when we cannot even move about the world without state permission. But in its larger sense, it is untrue and perilously misleading. However man may be regarded, he is not born free. A baby is not free but severely conditioned by its helplessness. Primitive men, moving fearfully and warily in their own elaborate world of menacing spirits, taboos and tribal customs, have less freedom than we have. With the famous *Social Contract* and the arguments that Rousseau based upon it, we have nothing to do here. But what does concern us, because it is something he bequeathed to the Romantic Age and we have not done with it even yet, is his idea that freedom has nothing to do with any appreciation of necessity, any accommodation to the real world, the right balance between the conscious mind, looking outward, and the unconscious; but that, in practice if not in theory, man comes nearest to freedom by breaking that balance, by interpreting the objective world entirely in terms of the subjective inner world of dream and desire, by running away from any challenge to that inner world, escaping from, instead of facing and mastering, reality. A man who prefers erotic reveries to living in love with a real woman will certainly have more liberty, but all that it offers him is an unrewarding erotic relationship with himself. He will be freer if, like Rousseau, he deposits the children he has by his mistress in foundling hospitals, but only at the price of forfeiting parenthood and self-respect. He has more freedom as something; but not as a father, good lover or husband, decent citizen. The complete Romantic, for ever looking inward, swelling his ego into vast proportions, may tell us that he demands freedom to be completely himself—and undoubtedly there are times in an artist's life when he must have such freedom at all costs—but if he keeps running away, refusing to be bound by any obligation, then he cuts down this self by not allowing it new functions, responsibilities, relationships, diminishing instead of enriching his real life, until at last, when the final and narrowing path of escape turns into a *cul-de-sac*, he cries out in terrible despair that he is alone. Thus there is all of romanticism, exploding from the unconscious, in Rousseau: its sudden release of creative energy, its triumph as an aspect of life to be celebrated in literature, its ultimate danger, hurrying to despair and madness, when it is taken unchecked as a way of life. (pp. 116-21)

> *J. B. Priestley, "Rousseau and the Romantic Age," in his* Literature and Western Man, *Harper & Brothers, 1960, pp. 113-21.*

Lionel Gossman   (essay date 1961)

[*Gossman is a Scottish essayist and educator. In the following excerpt, he discusses the implications and contradictions of Rousseau's idealism in* The Social Contract.]

When we speak of ideals in ordinary, everyday language, we usually refer to goals that are to be realized; even if it is very difficult to realize them, we commonly assume that they are in principle realizable. To the plain man an unrealizable ideal is comic, "crying for the moon." It is true that the *Contrat social* is about questions of right and not primarily about questions of fact, but it is not a geometry of politics. Political and moral relations are not formal relations; they are not like mathematical or logical ones and they cannot be evaluated independently of the existential situations they purport to deal with. They emerge from our experience of and reflection about real situations involving ourselves and others and they seek a way back to reality. One might well wonder what would be the point of an ideal of justice or equity that did not demand to be realized in the world. Rousseau, at any rate, did not see the *Contrat social* as a pure construction of his mind. If he had, he would not have written the seventh chapter of the second Book, in which he raises and discusses the question: how is the society of the *Contrat social* to be brought into being? As he raises this question, however, Rousseau finds he is faced with a logical problem. In order to be realized, his society requires that the very conditions it is intended to create be already in existence.

To be good, the State must be the creation of the moral will, but moral will can be transferred from the conceptual to the existential realm only in the conditions created by the State. Rousseau himself recognized this contradiction in his work. . . . While it is true that the education envisaged in the *Emile* was intended to produce moral men and citizens capable of appreciating "sound political maxims," this work is beset by the same difficulties we find in the *Contrat.* The ideal world of Emile cannot be translated into historical terms; there is the difficulty of finding the right tutor and there is the difficulty of educating Emile outside of time and place. Only Emile could be tutor to Emile. If we consider the two works as complementary, and there is every reason why we should, we find that the new society needs Emiles to bring it into being, while the Emiles need the new society in order to come into being.

The introduction of the Legislator does not resolve the problem. In his edition of the *Contrat* Maurice Halbwachs observed that, though it is possible to find in the *Discours sur l'inégalité* the suggestion that religion might be necessary in order to give power and prestige, if not actual bindingness, to the law, the whole point of the *Contrat social* was rather the creation of a just society by a collective act of will on the part of its members, without any recourse to religion. . . . The chapter on the Legislator, the individual who stands above the group, introduces a principle which, according to Halbwachs, is not in harmony with the rest of the work. Rousseau seems to have known that this criticism could be levelled against him and in the Geneva manuscript he tried to forestall it. . . . The import of the observation in the Geneva manuscript is that the rights of the Legislator rest only on his relation to the general will, on his knowing the general will better, in fact, that the people knows it itself. The general will wills the general good, but it does not know what the general good is; the Legislator's job is to guide the general will towards what he recognizes is the general good. While Rousseau thus makes it clear that he does not want his Legislator to be thought of as above society or distinct from it, but rather as the very mind and eye of society, he still does not explain how the general will comes into being in the first case, even as ignorant and requiring guidance. The only explanation would appear to be that the general will being

what each individual *would will* if he hearkened to the voice of conscience, the legislator can act upon it even before the members of society recognize it as their own. Unfortunately, on this argument the relation between the ideal and the existentially or historically real becomes once again an open question. Is there no difference at all, one wonders, between rational postulate and empirical existence, between the general will that the Legislator tries to interpret and act upon, what each individual *ought to will* and *would will* as a moral creature, and that which each individual *will in fact will* when he does will as a moral creature, between the realm of values out of time and the realm of moral acts in time? Again, Rousseau's condition that the people be the sole judge of whether the Legislator's will is truly the general will cannot be fulfilled. It is precisely because the people does not in fact judge according to the general good that the Legislator is necessary in the first place; how then can it judge whether the Legislator's will is really the general will or not? Furthermore, since the general will is not a mere totality of individual wills, but what people would will "dans le silence des passions"—and can indeed be *forced* to will—only the judgment of those who are willing morally can count. There is thus no empirical way of determining the identity of the Legislator's will and the general will. The general will itself is the only measure both of the Legislator's will and of that of his critics; but the general will is nothing, a concept without content, until it becomes actual in individual wills. On what grounds it is to be decided in which individual wills the general will has become actual, since it is not known as anything other than a cipher until it does become individual will? . . . [It] is the Legislator's task to create the conditions in which the general will becomes actualized in individual wills. It cannot consequently be known whether his own will is identical with the general will until he has *in fact* created the moral society. The Legislator's integrity will then be determined not by the people, as the Geneva manuscript maintained, but by his success in creating the moral society. Rousseau appears to acknowledge this at the end of II, vii, and this acknowledgment is tantamount to a confession that he does not know how the good society is to be created. He admits, further, that the existence of the Legislator would be "un vrai miracle" and that to create the good society it would be necessary to employ means of persuasion which, as outlined in the same chapter, are not only of uncertain efficacity but disturbingly dishonest.

Rousseau's moral idealism thus turns out to be completely ineffectual. He himself argued powerfully in the two *Discours* and in the *Emile,* as well as in the *Contrat* that the values and behaviour of men are governed by the nature of their real relations in society: to transform man, to make him truly *homme* and *citoyen,* he claimed, we have to change these relations. For Rousseau, however, the means by which they are to be changed is not a material, historical one, it is an act of the moral will. Only by such a leap can man free himself from the physical (i.e. historical) realm and reach the moral realm of timeless values. But how is a community whose will is "corrupt" to make such an act of the moral will, by what miracle can it escape from the historical and physical world by which it is totally informed? Invoking the Legislator does not answer this question. In the first place, the Legislator may never be found; in the second, there is no way of judging whether he is the true one; in the third, in order to translate the ideal society into an historically real one (in order to place the timeless in time!) he must employ dubious devices of persuasion, which might or might not work, and which, in any case, could only have the effect of making the people's will passively accept laws instead of actively creating them. The general will would thus never be or become the will of the people: the content of both would perhaps be the same, but they would not be two aspects, the essential and the existential, of the same reality.

Furthermore, Rousseau never really describes the material basis of his new society, a surprising omission in view of the method of analysis used in the Discourses. It is only through isolating himself from the social group that a man recognizes, according to Rousseau, the moral law, which, as a human being, he must obey. The true community of men is thus experienced, paradoxically enough, only through abstraction from all real relations, through contemplation of man's ideal nature. But the society that will embody the ideal relation of man to man—a relation of total equality—must have some material basis of existence if it is to be realized in the historical world of time and place, and this means that alongside the ideal relations of men there will be real ones. The only way Rousseau envisages of ensuring the harmony and community of the members of society, the fusion of man and citizen, is a radical primitivism. To be sure, he is not a primitivist in the sense that many people still imagine. He denied that man should or can return to the "natural"—pre-social and premoral—state ("la nature humaine ne rétrograde pas," he wrote in the *Emile*), and his aim was to lead humanity beyond the Hobbesian world of men-wolves to a higher society of free and equal, moral and rational beings. One has a right to ask, however, what sort of basis in reality he foresaw for such a higher society. Rousseau gives no direct answer to this question, but he does imply that the economic structure of his society would be extremely simple, since he rules out any material inequalities that might give some men significantly greater power than others and thus threaten their ideal equality as moral persons. In practical terms this involves a negative attitude to trade and commerce, in fact to all entrepreneurial activity whatsoever, and it accounts in large measure for Rousseau's hatred of those material advances which were so highly prized by Voltaire and most other eighteenth-century writers. The good society, for Rousseau, precluded all wealth, all material satisfaction, all self-indulgence, even in their most refined emotional and artistic forms.

Rousseau's cultural primitivism raises a second difficulty, to my mind, in his doctrine of the State. Not only is his just society hard to realize on his own terms, it seems unlikely that it could be realized even if force or well-intentioned deceit were successfully used. Progress on the moral and political level from a society of beast-men to a society of human beings is found to involve, paradoxically, regression on the material and cultural level. The paradox is more than curious. Rousseau acknowledged that human nature cannot move backwards and he argued that there was an indestructible unity of man's moral, social and economic being; yet his plan for the political regeneration of man involves a regressive movement of his economic and material being, which *in fact* seems as impossible as a return to the pre-social, pre-moral state of nature. Furthermore, even if it were possible to go forward morally while

going back culturally, this would involve renunciation of an entire aspect of man's aspirations for himself.

Two deeply tragic contradictions emerge from the *Contrat social* in my view, and both of them are important not only for Rousseau, but for much that came after him. One lies in the positing of ideals that are unrealizable in the human world of time, the other in the implied incompatibility of two of the cardinal demands of the human being—social justice and individual self-realization.

The problem of realizing justice justly in the world was not new in the eighteenth-century. Rousseau's strange involvement in the character of Alceste recalls but one earlier and particularly savory treatment of the theme. As the individual's private and public personalities move further and further apart in the eighteenth century, however, as his own yearnings and the demands that society makes upon him enter more and more into conflict, the problem of justice becomes increasingly acute. Literature is full of virtuous heroes and heroines bravely suffering the blows of an often incomprehensible fate. Virtue is rarely active; from Zaïre to Miss Sarah Sampson and Madame de Tourvel it is passive and suffering, for virtue cannot fight evil without becoming stained by it. The only recourse lies in suffering: refusal to compromise, renunciation of the world rather than acceptance of evil is itself the pathetic affirmation of the "triumph" of virtue. In the *Contrat social* this theme is vastly enlarged and expressed in the widest political terms, as I have tried to suggest. The world is to be transformed so that it will conform to ideal standards of justice, but it turns out that our ideals are in themselves powerless; there is no way of translating them into action except by means that contradict them. The full contradictoriness of this situation was brilliantly exploited by Diderot in his comedy *Est-il bon? est-il méchant?* and it is one of the main themes of *Le Neveu de Rameau*. Diderot also saw, with astonishing insight, that unrealizable idealism and smug hypocrisy are frequent bedfellows, and that it is dangerously easy, given certain conditions, to slip from tragic anguish into cosy acceptance. Rousseau never believed, as many of his contemporaries did, that all the conflicts and injustices of social life could be made to "cancel out" naturally in a glorious harmony; but if to some of us in the twentieth century they cut rather odd figures as they point so confidently to an immanent harmony that we can no longer discern, Rousseau's own trumpet-call to the virtuous is at best tragic. The failure of the *Incorruptible* and of the entire Jacobin movement provides a concrete illustration of the contradictions embedded in Rousseau's idealism. With ghastly realism it demonstrates on the one hand that virtue cannot operate as pure will in the real world but requires to be implemented by material means, and on the other that society has its own inner dynamic against which the absolute moral will pits itself in vain. Man cannot escape his historical nature, and the idealist denial of historical process is itself no more than a part of the historical process.

In his play *Fiesko, oder die Verschwörung zu Genua*, Schiller developed another tragic contradiction implicit in Rousseau's idealism. The quarrel between Rousseau and the *philosophes*, between the paranoiac prophet of virtue and the brilliant and talented circle of epicurean reformers was followed as closely in Germany as elsewhere in Europe. Schiller's play seems to offer a concrete representa-

The Hermitage at Montmorency, where Rousseau began composition of some of his most celebrated works.

tion of the principal issues involved in this quarrel. Fiesko is a hearty young patrician who revolts against the despotism of the Dorias, but he has in himself the makings of a despot and he is skilled by one of the conspirators, the severe republican Verrina. The depth Schiller gives to this material is astonishing. It is Fiesko, with his epicureanism, his lusts, his joy in life, who is related to the people, who is their idol and who organizes the revolt, for he is close to the people not through an abstract moral will, but through his generous and passionate nature. Verrina, on the other hand, is a lonely, harsh old man, with few friends and scarcely any relation to the society he seeks to transform. Fiesko's revolt is inspired by an intense longing for self-realization, for freedom to exercise all his capacities in a world ruled not by violence and oppression, but by love and trust, Verrina's by a harsh, unyielding dedication to honor and virtue. Together these two destinies enclose the tragedy of eighteenth-century republicanism: the one too easy-going, too frivolous and adventurous, and inevitably encountering the very conflict between passion and purity it set out to resolve, the other too puritanical, idealistic and remote from the lives and aspirations of ordinary men. Rousseau himself experienced this contradiction within his own being. . . . It also runs through *La Nouvelle Héloïse.* The tensions in this work between a passionate demand for self-fulfilment on the one hand and a moralistic doctrine of renunciation on the other are too

well known to need re-examination. Conscience, the moral will, triumphs in the end, but the price of victory is high, too high. The same theme recurs again and again in the work of Goethe, in *Werther,* in *Wilhelm Meister,* in *Götz,* in *Clavigo,* in *Stella* and in *Faust.* Only Goethe, unlike Rousseau, refuses to sacrifice the human being to the moral law.

In the society of the ***Contrat Social*** order and justice are bought at the same cost as in ***La Nouvelle Héloïse.*** It is a society without joy. The rich world of Thélème has shrunk to the homely simplicity of a Quaker meetinghouse.

I have by no means intended to belittle Rousseau's achievement in the ***Contrat.*** No writer in the eighteenth century, with the exception of Diderot, offers as profound an analysis of the nature and goals of political society as Rousseau, none suffered more intensely than he from the injustice of the world and the degradation of man. He spoke for the little people, however, and the world he demanded was the highest they could aspire to: a world of uncomplicated virtues—often, significantly, identified with chastity and abstinence—of simple duties and frugal equality. Yet Rousseau was a passionate, sensuous and talented man. It is his personal tragedy and the tragedy of his time that the only alternative he could see to the easygoing and sanguine epicureanism of his contemporaries was a harsh, idealistic moralism, in which the Renaissance goal of a concrete harmony within the human personality of man as independent individual and man as member of the human community was given up in favor of the total subservience of all his faculties, his emotions, his intellect and his creative genius, to an abstract principle of morality, an ideal system of right and wrong. The petit-bourgeois nature of Rousseau's solution, its inadequacy to deal with the rich texture and the challenges of real life was early appreciated by Goethe. Again and again Goethe portrays the painful contradiction in modern life between individual desire and "moral obligation," but he no longer envisages the problem as Rousseau did. Individual desire is not to be baldly identified with anarchistic passion, nor is commitment to the community identifiable with obedience to some abstract moral law. The community is not, for Goethe, a unity of true moral wills, but a complex and organic whole, embracing all concrete individuals in their concrete relations with each other. In many cases the community is served only by failing to fulfill obligations to individual members of it; and by a strange paradox it is served not by the fastidious formalist but by the man of passion, for he alone has the imagination to envisage and desire great goals for the entire community and the strength to inflict and bear the particular evils without which these great goals cannot be carried out. In the idealist terms of Rousseau there must never be any contradiction within the good itself; the community is therefore conceived of as an ideal association of moral beings who realize their communal existence only by renouncing or being made to renounce all that makes them the particular individuals they are. For Goethe individuals cannot be transformed into moral abstractions and their relations with each other cannot be emptied of all concrete historical and psychological content. What Rousseau saw as a conflict between passionate wilfulness and moral will becomes for Goethe a dilemma within the individual consciousness of the good man: realizing one concrete good involves sacrificing another, involves doing evil, and this reflects an objective contradiction in the good itself, a contradiction that no act of the mind can resolve. The rationalist-utopian solution to the problems of human conduct thus remains a pure *jeu d'esprit;* in the real conditions of human existence moral problems remain a source of anguish, a challenge that the man of moral imagination must meet in his concrete activity and overcome by an historical act. The decision he makes is his own affair; the act of moral decision, however, completely escapes the neat formal categories of the idealist. It is not obedience to a clearly defined, given moral law; it is a creative act that is closer to a wager on his own destiny and on human destiny than to an equation of individual action with any universal law, whether the universality of the law be conceived of as objectively given or postulated by reason. (pp. 173-82)

Lionel Gossman, "Rousseau's Idealism," in The Romanic Review, *Vol. LII, No. 3, October, 1961, pp. 173-82.*

Leslie F. Claydon   (essay date 1969)

[*Claydon is an Australian educator and author. In the following excerpt, he probes the underlying principles of* Émile, ou de l'éducation, *arguing that "it is not an au-*

tonomous disquisition upon the educational proprieties, . . . [but] part of a much larger project."]

Émile is not an autonomous disquisition upon the educational proprieties, a brilliant rag-bag of methodological hints and tips, nor yet only a new attack upon an old problem. It is part of a much larger project; a component of a root and branch reappraisal of the condition of civilised man which concludes with a radical proposal to reshape everything according to a totally new ground plan. Unless this is realised, one obtains a very restricted view of the book; one narrowly confined to the undoubted insights of a psychological character which it contains. Rousseau's consideration of what is to be learned and what not is disastrously ignored or misinterpreted. The central purpose of the book is missed. (p. 2)

The purpose informing the [*Émile ou de l'education*] is to be discovered at its very outset. Rousseau states a basic premiss. Man is a meddler who manipulates and distorts the design of the 'author of nature' out of all recognition, pursuing this folly to the ultimate by following the same course in respect of man himself.

Example after example is provided, all purporting to embody Rousseau's own observation of this disastrous course of action. One sees immediately that they are strictly confined to that section of French society possessed of power, wealth and leisure. . . . A contrast is continually being drawn by Rousseau between this social group or class and that of the humble folk of France, who, it is suggested, are freer of social distortions and manipulations than their 'betters'. However, Rousseau is careful not to grant them complete clearance; he frequently makes a second contrast between France of his day and the far-off societies of, say, the Caribbean Islands (distance) or the ancient civilisations (time).

The basic premiss yields two important propositions, which guide the direction of the whole work.

(*a*) What is thought of as wisdom is merely slavish subscription to received opinion.

(*b*) The granting of this subscription chains us to the interests and influences which find these opinions conservative of their power and influence.

The direction of the attack is clearly indicated; it is against the artifices of society. In *Émile* it takes the form of pointing out the enormity of educating with the intention of fostering subscription to them in the receptive and helpless child, so robbing him of innocence and denying him the possibility of achieving real wisdom. Plainly only the already corrupted could perpetrate such a thing. Rousseau now sets out to exemplify this. All the talk about right posture and the protection of the helpless babe, which is supposed to justify such practices as swaddling, becomes, by Rousseau's account, no more than an elaborate and baseless system of excuses for the abandonment of the most fundamental of duties, the most natural of functions; the care and sustenance of a baby by its own mother.

The main point of the first part of *Émile* is the substantiation of the charge. From the very outset, it is maintained, we have moved away from the 'path of nature'. Every step we take drags the child farther away from his true nature and into the ways of the corrupted things we are.

A caution is necessary here, however. We should not think that Rousseau requires a return to nature in the sense of some sort of retreat into primitivism, although his frequent references to the Caribs does nothing to help us avoid the mistake. It is rather the case that he urges that we follow the dictates of nature without jettisoning our potentialities for advance in wisdom and power.

But the recommendations stemming from the policy of proceeding 'according to nature' still possess a certain starkness, and Rousseau was nervously well aware of the fact. He goes to some pains to show that the endurance of hardship is as inevitable and beneficial to the growing child as is growth itself. He makes a number of interesting moves to persuade the reader to his view. For example, we are asked to defer not to '*the* natural' but to the guidance of a 'she', rather as the Greeks referred to this or that Goddess, to the author of a design which it is beyond the capacity of mere man to improve upon, even when hardship *is* involved.

Then, to strengthen his case further, Rousseau cites two alleged and commonly accepted facts. In the France of his time a high rate of mortality persisted among children below the age of eight years. Secondly, children who were 'delicately reared' were more likely to die than those not so carefully protected.

Now it is relatively easy to find particular examples in this way, and to neglect the fact, or blind others to it, that one can just as easily produce examples which support an opposite point of view. This is particularly true with the example just mentioned. We can turn Rousseau's own claim that many children in France died before becoming eight years of age against his argument. Were all these children medically attended? This is doubtful enough, but it is still more doubtful whether they were attended by the sort of 'fashionable' doctor who receives so much criticism from Rousseau; the part charlatan whose medical advice is tailored to what it will please the patient to hear and so bring in a large fee. It seems possible to point to many infant deaths not caused or assisted by such deadly ministrations. Rousseau's example by no means establishes the invariable beneficience of nature.

On the other hand, we can readily agree that a certain amount of hardening is important for the healthy development of the child. He must stand at risk to some extent if he is to exercise his growing powers of locomotion and so forth. That this is so does not entail acceptance of Rousseau's contentions, however. It does not follow that it is the suffering of pain as such that is beneficial. It is not shown that we must accept some pain and cruelty to escape something worse. Before this last proposition is accepted it must be demonstrated that suffering some pain does prevent later and greater cruelty and pain.

Rousseau does not show this. It is true that he does state later on and in a quite different context (a discussion of the distinction between man as himself and man as a citizen: i.e. Frenchman or Englishman) that where we are 'pulled this way by nature and that way by man' the resulting inner conflict—which constitutes the more cruel and painful—does occur, but one cannot make a direct transposition from this to the present discussion. It is not obvious that inner conflicts and emotional upheavals, caused in adult life, or even sooner for that matter, are prevented by

any sort of upbringing in infancy. Suppose a mother to heed Rousseau's strictures. She neither swaddles the infant, puts him to a nurse nor does she coddle him herself. Consequently he falls from time to time, bumps himself against objects and contracts minor ailments while building up immunity against more deadly diseases. To begin with it is somewhat fanciful to say that he suffers in the way implied by the statement, 'Suffering is the lot of man', which implies a constant background of pain. Ignoring this, however, it remains the case that it is no logical contradiction to say that such a child could grow to experience the unhappiness and anguish of acute inner conflict. Indeed, Rousseau himself says later that a great deal more than has so far been ensured is necessary if such a possibility is to be obviated.

Finally, in defence of nature, even when uncharitable or seeming to be so, Rousseau argues for a somewhat ruthless approach to the child. There is little in what he says which caters for the weak or sickly, even though he is bound to acknowledge the inconvenient truth that such children do exist. He seeks to show that no good can come of attempts to preserve that which nature has decreed shall cease. He sophisticates this argument to protect it against a charge of callousness by purporting to explain the sickly child as none of nature's doing at all. It is only because there have been generations of departure from the natural that there has been a progressive deterioration—man meddling with man has produced the sorry result. Thus the biblical saw is turned upside down to become that the transgressions against the parents shall be visited upon the children unto the third and fourth generation.

It is important to keep in view this implication of application over generations of human beings. The whole of **Émile** is written as an antidote to what has gone wrong with the human being as a species. It cannot therefore be taken in isolation, . . . the task is to correct centuries of degeneration by a radical change of direction. In this sense Rousseau is a true revolutionary; few things must remain as they are.

Having taken these steps to save his contention that experience of adversity is no argument against the recommendation to rear and educate according to nature, Rousseau later extends the claim to have relevance even to the beginnings of language in the child. The infant feels a need, perhaps to possess or handle an object some distance from him. He indicates his need by making sounds of distress that the object is not within reach. Rousseau sees this situation as involving the first stages in the acquisition of language. This is to the good, but it must be understood that the situation demands something *of* the child much more than that something be done *for* him. Once the child has been carried to distant objects which he has attempted to reach and distressed himself upon finding he cannot just stretch out a hand for them, once he has gained the ability to distinguish between the near to hand and the distant, one must be careful about continuing this practice or, alternatively, of carrying the object to the child. The child must set himself to gain the ability to reach what he desires or he must learn to tolerate his weaknesses until he can overcome them. By Rousseau's account the child cries mainly because it experiences strong feelings in respect of its own lack of power. Nothing is gained when things are done for the child to cancel out this weakness, which nature will remedy providing that man does not distort the process. In a simple society there are no servants to fetch and carry and too many things to be done for either parent to act as lackey.

Moving now to a discussion of what would today be termed the 'roles' of the mother and father, one discovers that Rousseau is not always so able to assist his case by making reference to what occurs in the simple or primitive group. We have seen that his first concern is to point to what happens now and to condemn it because it is in no way demanded by nature, and in respect of maternal duties the case is bolstered by comparison with Caribs, etc. When it comes to fathers a comparison is made here also, but we notice a change in that the Caribs or the Peruvians cannot serve. Rousseau has a footnote which refers to Plutarch's report that Cato, the Roman Censor, a man with many administrative and political cares, still contrived to bring up his sons and grandsons from their cradles.

This is a curious stratagem. It seems somewhat doubtful as to the extent to which the Roman civilisation could escape the criticisms Rousseau levels at his own. No doubt this is partly explained by Rousseau's somewhat idealistic picture of both Ancient Rome and Greece, gained at his father's knee, but one may also entertain a suspicion that any stick will do to beat the dog of his own contemporary society.

A second difference where fathers are concerned is that the hireling tutor, engaged to relieve the father of the duties Cato apparently did not shirk, is not said to usurp the father's place. It appears that the child loses a father and teacher and gains no more than a flunkey who teaches. This is not quite the same result as is supposed by Rousseau in respect of the mother substitute. The nurse may oust the mother from her place in the child's affections as well as perform the functions properly hers alone.

Combing the consideration of the roles of both parents Rousseau produces a hypothesis of considerable interest. To begin with the fate of the family structure is seen as determined by the attitudes and behaviour of the mother. Secondly, there is a modern sociological flavour to the whole discussion. A 'culture pattern' is presented to us here: the subject of the discussion is the social unit of the family as it is caught up in the larger patterns of the society. The individual mother or father is once more shown to be trapped and snared by the customs and fashions of this larger group. The underlying intent of *Émile* is constantly in view. Man is trapped by his society. He can do nothing.

At this point Rousseau lands himself in something of a dilemma. From his lonely vantage point he points still to the prevailing condition of society and declares again his contempt for it and for those who have permitted themselves to become enmeshed in it. He will have no part of it, for then he would be as they are, unable to do what should be done and incapable of rectifying the state of affairs which has brought them to their plight.

But if it is the case that there is a certain inevitability about the pattern of family life within the section of society which is the main target of his attack, as seems to be suggested by the sketching out of what we would now call a culture pattern, then there is also something odd about the indictment of the individual who is victim of it. It is strange to condemn the individual for the fault which is not of his making and which is not to be avoided. Yet this seems to be what is happening. We can recall the account of infancy and the way in which the tiny child is inducted into wilfulness and obstinacy before he is capable of resisting the pressures which so corrupt his nature.

Let us concede this but remember that Rousseau, throughout his life and work, found himself in the position of seeking to persuade to his way of thought those very people whom his thesis principally condemned. Now whether the prosecutor is in the right or in the wrong, it is rarely the case that anything approaching universal acclaim is accorded from those who find themselves so assailed. The modern sociologist will tell us that the group is a conservative agency, and he may provide us with techniques of persuasion and personnel management which is often the blow when the point is put, techniques which leave the recipient grateful for help rather than aware of blameworthiness. Rousseau, it could be said, chose his own weapons rather than selecting palliatives offered by others. His task was consequently the more difficult.

Chief among his weapons was rhetoric. Now it is frequently and properly pointed out that Rousseau is guilty of inconsistency time and again, but it must be borne in mind that sometimes what is identified is really a tactical manoeuvre. The individual man, Rousseau knew as well as does the modern sociologist, tends to dismiss unpalatable comment when there is a chance to see what is said as being merely general comment. He finds this considerably more difficult, if even less palatable, when, as is often the case in *Émile,* the reference is to *a* man, to any one man who, as say a father, finds himself in the situation described. There may indeed be a certain injustice in Rousseau's indictment of the trapped individual, but there is greater impact.

Of course, the situation presented to the individual remains a bleak one, full of anxieties. Man in general can be piloted out of his dilemma only when the particular individual has swallowed the bitter pill of his degeneration and joined Rousseau in the resolve that things be changed. The test of Rousseau as a revolutionary thinker is the degree to which he achieved this *general* effect rather than any particular effect.

'Yet another problem which Rousseau must face is the obvious query as to why, in view of all that has so far been said, propose that there be a tutor to *Émile.* A first step to answering this is that the nature of the work is not that of a manual of procedure. A rescue operation is required if mankind is not to fall further into degeneration. Someone must map out the programme for it, but Rousseau's task is to put out guide lines as to its character rather than to detail its form.

Is a programme possible at all? The affirmative answer given by Rousseau rests upon the claim that man has only to look for guidance to nature to discover the sort of thing that can and must be done. Secondly, the possibility of the project is evidenced by the fact that some men at least (or *a* man at least) can recognise the necessity and venture upon the prior, if easier, task of alerting others to it.

He is not yet out of the wood, however. Whatever element of analogy there is in the idea of a tutor, Rousseau still has to deal with his own argument that it is only when the father fails to fulfil his role in its entirety that the provision of a tutor must be made. But then one laments the lack. One does not turn it into a positive and generalised proposal.

Rousseau retreats still further into the hypothetical at this point. To point out the nature of the revolutionary plan one must pluck a pupil from the air as it were, one without flaws either in himself or ones which had been foisted upon him. Any child of flesh and blood not receiving a totality of care from his own mother and father could not be such, and any actual child receiving this care in society as it is, must, of necessity, be corrupted. A child not spoiled in either of these ways will thrive as the tutor follows the principles proposed: it is up to someone to devise the necessary programme from them to suit the actual child.

The expedient of creating an imaginary pupil is only a first step of course. It allows Rousseau to legislate that there be no flaws in him as he comes to the tutor. This done, the second consideration is that no flaws are inflicted upon him after birth and before the tutor receives him. Bearing in mind the proposition that the nurse is the real mother (which is why the mother should nurse), and the further one that the only proper tutor is the father, there can be only one expedient. Rousseau makes the apparently paradoxical statement that 'Émile is an orphan whether he has a mother or father or not'. This must be read as meaning that, whether the mother and father of the child are alive or not, if there is a tutor for Émile who is not his father, then Émile is to be regarded *as if* an orphan and from the very outset at that. The tutor assumes the role of father but for the duty of providing for the material well-being of the child.

Immediately one sees that the *relationship* involved is a special one and of supreme importance. Rousseau is not talking of a sort of male governess or caretaker, nor yet of an instructor or preceptor, a flunkey who teaches. For him the term 'tutor' carries very different implications. It must do if one is to be at all satisfied that he has overcome his problem.

If the child has a tutor of the calibre indicated as necessary the latter will be the source of all authority. He will oversee the nurse so that none of the malpractices which have been discussed are allowed to occur. Rousseau proposes that he will oversee her in her diet, her living conditions and in the assessment of her temperamental suitability.

The tutor is in no way a professional with a limited sphere of activity and jurisdiction bounded by details of a particular service given for payment. This would be utterly inappropriate to the comprehensive nature of Rousseau's notion of what education is. The tutor occupies a position in Rousseau's thinking similar to other figures in his political works such as 'the man of genius', the lawgiver and, in some instances, the king or ruler. All of these are men of vision, unaffected by the corrupting influences of society. They are therefore able to realise and work for the elimination of the factors possessed of this influence, hence they are granted the legislative supremacy each is invested with in the various works.

But it might be thought to be very justifiable to inquire why Rousseau has it *this* way round. We are to educate according to nature. What more natural a thing is there,

by Rousseau's own account, than the care of a mother for her own child? Why should she not direct and control the tutor?

One explanation could be that Rousseau just did not see this alternative at all, and so did not deal with it. A second could be that a nurse could not have the freedom from corruption which the tutor possesses. A third possibility is that, for Rousseau, education extends from infancy to adulthood and through all the vicissitudes of living which this time will contain, during which the tutor never leaves his charge for any other nor does he fail to oversee every aspect of the progress. The tutor is therefore a most versatile and wise person in a great many directions; more so than one could reasonably expect any mother to be, or want her to be either, because this would be unnatural for a woman. Whichever stands, it is made still plainer now that 'tutor' must not be given a narrow interpretation if Rousseau is to be understood aright.

This last point leads Rousseau to make a number of interesting distinctions. He contrasts his 'tutor' with the terms 'master' and 'teacher' and/or 'preceptor'. It seems plain that by 'master' Rousseau refers to one equipped with the understanding and knowledge of the 'science of human duty'. For any sort of intimation of the content of this science one must go beyond *Émile,* although, since Rousseau has already stated that a 'judicious though ignorant (unschooled) father' may better educate his son than the cleverest teacher in the world, we can suppose that the mastery involved here is not to do with the areas of knowledge which, when unattained in a man, yield the term 'ignorant'. We may also suppose from this that Rousseau would wish us to gather that a clever teacher is not, of necessity, a judicious man. Plainly also, the tutor *must* be judicious, and this will involve being master of the rather nebulous science of human duty. We may gather from the comment about the fitness of an unschooled father to educate that what is involved is sound judgment and conduct in life rather than concern with some particular form of thought or combination of forms of thought.

Rousseau's account correctly implies that, to be a teacher, is to engage in some activity with the intention that a pupil shall learn as a consequence. However, some things are learned but better not taught. Sound judgment and moral actions are better arrived at through the efforts, mistakes, experiments and reflections of the simple individual himself than through receiving and following the dictates of another, the teacher. What happens when this latter procedure is adopted is no more than the acquisition of conventional patterns of behaviour. One knows 'the one thing' and no more. We are thus already well on the way to enslavement by custom. Judgment is diminished to prejudice, thought is tramlined, action becomes stereotyped. All behaviour is routinised performance.

Now this is all right up to a point, but only up to a point. The mistake in the account is a serious one. The variety of activities which can fall under the category of teaching is quite illegitimately restricted to those which might make Rousseau's argument incontestable. What a teacher does is not confined to, and need not even include, 'the giving of precepts' if by this we are to mean the issuing of solemn injunctions upon the back of a deal of even more solemn sermonizing.

Explaining, examining, demonstrating, questioning and answering may all be included under the activity described as teaching, and so, too, may 'guiding' unless one legislates that the meaning to be attached to that word will exclude the other activities just given. This would be extremely difficult to uphold, of course, and Rousseau most certainly does not do so, with the result that, as one reads on in *Émile,* one finds that the tutor does teach.

There is a second confusion in the account. The tutor, it is maintained, must be a master of the 'science of human duty'. This may or may not be so. What is certainly not the case is that one who is a master of something is, of necessity, a good instructor, teacher or guide (tutor) of that something. Similarly, the teacher who is not a judicious man cannot be automatically discounted as a possible master of something. To have mastery of something is not logically tied to instructing, teaching or guiding. For example, we may call a man a master baker even when he downright refuses to have anything to do with assisting others to bake. The sole criterion is whether or not he attains to certain standards of baking in his own work. It could even be allowed that he never baked anything in the presence of another person or ever watched any other person bake. Although the 'science of human duty' is obviously different from bakery, the conceptual point still holds.

If, therefore, Rousseau is seeking to deny the possibility of mastery to the teacher, even when he *is* a giver of precepts, his argument quite fails to achieve its end. It would seem that the distinction between tutor and teacher rests upon something quite apart from considerations of mastery or of the giving or withholding of precepts. It rests upon the sort of relationship supposed between tutor and pupil in comparison with that supposed between teacher and pupil. Even then the distinction must surely concern tutor and *professional* teacher. The nearest one can get to clearing up the muddle is to say that the tutor incorporates the concept of teacher and, at the same time, modifies and governs the scope of the latter concept to all but exclude that kind of teaching which is sometimes referred to today by the somewhat enigmatic term 'direct teaching'.

Now it would be true to say that the professional teacher could not and would not want to establish precisely the sort of relationship which Rousseau's tutor has with *Émile.* He is not then bound by the restriction of manner of teaching which applies to the tutor. Once we have this clear we need not take Rousseau to be saying that the tutor may not teach but only that he may not teach in certain ways. For the present day we may take from Rousseau the valuable insight that the 'role of the teacher' is inclusive of more things than the activity of teaching and that these things may exercise a considerable influence upon the manner of teaching.

This may shed some light upon the mysterious term, 'science of human duty' as it is used by Rousseau. It seems that what is meant by it has its modern equivalent in such phrases as 'understanding of human nature', 'right attitudes towards people', and 'respect for persons'. These are not without their own problems when they are used with the same lack of explication Rousseau allows for 'science of human duty'. Alternatively, it might be argued with some justice that Rousseau was anticipating the emergence of the social sciences as we know them, the contemporary concern to make disciplined study of human behaviour and to use the results to solve problems of intolerance and maladjustment, both between individuals and between groups of people. To the extent that this can be maintained, Rousseau emerges as a subscriber to the notion of education as a process of socialisation—a somewhat strange possibility for the champion of man as and for himself. Yet another alternative is to argue that what is supposed in the human individual is an innate or natural morality from which he is deviated by social pressures. Education now appears as that which should equip man to resist these pressures. It is impossible to settle the problem with any conclusiveness. All the alternatives are plausible, in that all find some support within the work, a fact that indicates the contradictions to be found in Rousseau's thesis. All that is plain is that, in Rousseau's view, the science of human duty is neither to be equated with nor attained through study of the traditional areas of knowledge as he knew them and the manner of their teaching.

Rousseau points out the folly of separating the function of the teacher from the relationship supposed between child and tutor by asking the rhetorical question whether one would wish to make a parallel distinction between 'pupil' and 'scholar' (disciple). This stratagem tells us something about what Rousseau sees as the activity and cast of mind necessary in the individual being educated. It reinforces the exclusion of precept-giving from the activity of teaching as the latter activity is practised by the tutor. In the notion of either scholar or disciple there are implications of the giving of a voluntary submission to what is requisite and of active subscription to the task in hand as possessed of intrinsic worthwhileness. The scholar addresses himself to the business of learning, of informing himself, of seeking information and knowledge for himself, rather than sitting back and waiting to be taught. The disciple is not merely or even essentially a follower, but rather he is one who upholds in himself understood principles, and of choice refers his actions to them. He is not one who is constantly told what it is proper to do and is happy to be so ruled. Nevertheless of course, both scholar and disciple may *seek* to be taught at times.

What Rousseau is asking here is whether it is possible to consider it to be sufficient to have a pupil who, being neither scholar nor disciple, lacks all this. He would not ask the question were it not that an affirmative answer is difficult to imagine. The tactic may blind us to the possibility that one is not always able to secure these attributes in an individual without having to pilot him through a condition and attitude of mind which Rousseau ascribes to 'pupil'. Rousseau, of course, counters this by contending that this should never happen; that rather than adopt this course one should do nothing and await the signs of interest, etc., which will avoid it. This is where the term 'negative education', which is applied to Rousseau's scheme, has its application. More importantly, the counter indicates the predomination of psychological criteria in Rousseau's argument which will become increasingly evident as one progresses through the book. Much of the second book of *Émile* evidences all of this. (pp. 14-25)

Once again Rousseau anticipates what is to come at a later time. The doctrine of interest and the importance of sense experience are central to the educational recommendations of John Dewey. Before Dewey, Pestalozzi and Froebel advanced methodologies which owed much to the thinking of Rousseau.

Now fully concerned with a discussion of *Émile* himself, the new man in the making, Rousseau has a number of things to say in the first section of the work about the fit subject for education. Who stands most in need of education, where 'education' means what Rousseau contends it should mean? The answer must be that it is the child most subject to the distortions of fashion and custom. In France one will find him in the family of the convention-ridden people of the town and the world of business and fashion.

Notice here that the basis for this selection is in no way grounded in any contention that there is an innate superiority in the child of favoured parents. Quite the opposite in fact. Unless they are rescued they are doomed. By removing them from their situation at birth they are snatched from prejudice. Once more one sees the truly revolutionary nature of Rousseau's work.

Rousseau talks of a 'natural education' in connection with all this. Once more we run into difficulties about this word 'natural'. The concept of education appears to require that something be supplied which would otherwise not be gained. 'Natural', on the other hand, would seem to deny the necessity for supplying anything and hence to make a strange companion for 'education'. Would not the best of educations consist in allowing things to take their own course? Indeed, Rousseau does use many negatives with respect to what is educative for the young child, and this presents us with the idea of 'negative education' which is quite as puzzling a term as 'natural education'. The problem is not completely unravelled in *Émile* (if it is ever completely unravelled). One must follow Rousseau's intention and move on to *The Social Contract* to tackle these paradoxes.

Having obtained his pupil and scholar, Rousseau now begins to use his acute observation to outline the characteristics of childhood. Long before the age of 'scientific' psychology this man was able to make generalisations of a kind which will still stand examination today. The psychological dominates everything in the account, and not always to the benefit of the consistency of some of the arguments which underpin the work. For example, with reference to the account of how to eliminate fear of, say, loud noises, there is some ground for accusing Rousseau of contradicting himself by recommending that one works from the contrived to the natural. Children are brought to a condition where they can experience thunder without alarm by arranging for a series of prior experiences of lesser noises of progressively greater impact. This is surely strange. If children are allowed to regard thunder as a sort of sporadic meteorological accompaniment to living one wonders why they should come to fear it if it is natural not to do so. And why they should not fear it if it is natural to do so?

This underlines again the fact that 'natural' is a concept that one can use as one chooses. The emotion of fear does not, it seems, fall within the concept in this instance at least. The ruling is that all fear is disadvantageous. Rousseau makes no distinction between fear and caution as a consequence. Of course, the latter involves a degree of rational appraisal which should not be expected of the very young, but Rousseau appears to require the elimination of

caution at any stage. One could object to this by contending that caution does not involve fear but merely refers to a degree of care. One could go further than this, however. If one talks of caution in respect of such unpredictable phenomena as violent thunderstorms, or the traffic of a busy street, it could be argued that a degree of fear is very justifiable. No degree of care can guarantee one's safety.

The value of Rousseau's work in drawing attention to the importance of the senses in the business of learning has been pointed out, but the above indicates that this emphasis can also be misleading. One can demonstrate this by referring to Rousseau's discussion of the sense of smell. It becomes obvious that he fails to notice that the connection between smell as a sense and the source of the smell is by no means as easily grasped as, say, the connection between an object and the sight or touch of that object. This leads him to the dubious proposition that the *sense* of smell develops later than the other senses.

Secondly, and leading on from this, ruled by the notion of unfolding patterns of nature within us, Rousseau gives the impression that there are smells which are noxious of themselves. This is another dubious proposition. Our reaction to a smell is largely determined by the sort of associations which adhere to the source of the smell. What 'develops' later therefore is not the *sense* of smell but the degree of *learning* required before a smell is classified as pleasant or unpleasant. A certain gain in concept-formation is requisite to this. Indeed, Rousseau makes just this point in the second book when he explicitly states that training the senses is 'not solely a matter of use' for the reason that 'we neither touch nor see nor hear with any understanding but that we have been taught to do so'.

The importance of concept formation and the result of the conflation of what is involved in it with what is involved in merely sighting, hearing, smelling, etc., continues to cause tangles in the argument. This is particularly true when Rousseau comes to a discussion of language. The vital point is that concepts are essentially public and rule governed: sensation is not. A child, a dog and a bird may all sight the same object, but they do not see it as the same thing. The child may see it as a ball. It is unlikely that the dog will and improbable that the bird could. The point increases in pertinence once one considers the relatively small part of language which merely functions to name material objects. Concepts such as 'same' or 'and' can be employed only after we have learned the conventions for their use, and these are much more complex than labelling or naming by using words like 'dog'. They are not acquired through the senses in any way that might be suggestive of the way in which one could come to acquire the convention of calling a particular object a dog. One cannot see, or smell, 'and', nor in a strict sense can one even hear an 'and'.

These are considerations which create difficulties for the acceptance of Rousseau's claim that there is a 'natural language' (which is a quite different claim from asserting that language is natural to man of course), for it is clear that Rousseau supposes this language to be essentially affective, to do with the communication of feeling.

We can be sorrowful or enraged and be known to be so without the use of language: we can be soothed or mollified by vocalisations of one sort and another which either do not include the use of words at all or do not rely upon words *as* words. (Think of 'There there then—never mind—ah'.) But we can admit this and still question the validity of Rousseau's analysis. It does not follow from the above that, when a child feels a need—say for food—and cries as a consequence, that, in so doing, he *asks* for help as Rousseau would have us think. It is one thing to identify a casual connection between the discomfort of muscular action in the stomach walls and crying; it is quite another thing to build into the crying implications of intention and purpose which are essential to the business of asking, begging or imploring. The casual connection is likely enough, but we should be very careful before according to a newborn infant an understanding of what it is to ask, beg or implore. The prerequisite to such an ability is surely experience and learning.

One clue to the muddle might well be the fact that Rousseau does not attribute differentiations of kinds of distress to the infant. 'All misfortunes bring to him but a single feeling of sorrow.' This observation is, in fact, irrelevant to the point at issue; indeed, if anything, it merely points up the error. It is the nurse then who must interpret. This cry of the young infant is an indication of hunger; that an indication of distress of some other sort. If there is this utter lack of differentiation in the infant, how can one assert any purpose in the cry unless one will go so far as to assume that the purpose is to provide the nurse with a task of interpretation! If one cannot, then it is difficult to see how one can subsume the cry under the category of language at all.

Since the muddles in Rousseau's position are by no means fully exhausted at this point and must be further examined, it is timely to point out the value of his work in case one loses sight of the fact that deficiencies are worth noting only in that which has a value. The entirely valueless can be dismissed without examination.

Rousseau attacks the idea that infants cry for 'the devil of it'. His use of the phrase *des vices naturels* when coupled with this carries the attack farther to counter the notion of original sin. Children cry because they lack an essential or are in pain; the cry is therefore to be heeded and not to be ignored as a first manifestation of the sinfulness of man. In a state of total dependence the child lacks all ability to remedy its own distress. We should take all steps to facilitate his progress towards strength and independence, but, at the same time, recognise his needs and meet them until and unless we know him to be capable of doing so himself. To adopt any other course is to corrupt his innocence and to turn his prayers into commands and threats. There would seem to be much good sense in this.

Returning now to the problems arising in connection with a natural language, perhaps the most serious of these is that it leads Rousseau to put a restriction upon the extent to which an adult engages in conversation with a very young child. Now a great deal of recent work serves to show that one cannot overestimate the gain that results when children are talked to freely. Rousseau is consistently guilty of underestimating this, probably because what he really, and justifiably, wishes to attack is the treatment of young children on a basis which assumes that they should understand all that is said to them. (pp. 25-9)

In many commentaries on Rousseau's book about educat-ing a child much is made of his identification of stages of growth and the distinctness of each stage from the next. Much has been said about his insistence that the child is not an adult in miniature. No doubt this is all to the good. It is also a modern truism.

It is the contention of this writer that the essential arguments which Rousseau wishes to further are somewhat different from these particular and important insights and that they are all contained in the first of the five sections of the work. This commentary has therefore been founded on that section. For the rest, and the value to be found in the rest, the reader could not do better than to read *Émile* for himself.

Has the work of an eighteenth-century writer any relevance for the present time? Could one find an urging in favour of education according to nature in the day of space travel? It is proposed to allow the reader his own conclusions to these questions, but it is of interest to read the words of a North American Professor.

> The planet itself is now a little school. It's like being back to primitive times again. Then nature was education. You learned from nature around you. In this audio-tactile world it's happening again—only this time it won't be haphazard.
>
> (pp. 29-30)

> *Leslie F. Claydon, "Introduction: The Man and His Work," in* Rousseau on Education, *edited by Leslie F. Claydon, Collier-Macmillan Limited, 1969, pp. 1-30.*

Maurice Cranston   (lecture date 1983)

[*An English economist, political scientist, and editor, Cranston has written several books on liberal politics, including* What Are Human Rights? *(1963) and* The Mask of Politics *(1974). In the following essay, he contrasts the "smiling face of romanticism," presented in Rousseau's writings on music, with the "stern face of romanticism," revealed in Rousseau's political treatises.*]

Rousseau has returned in recent years to public esteem. Between the two wars, he was condemned by right and left alike, seen as the forerunner at once of fascism and of communism, an enemy of science and of reason, responsible both for the excesses of romanticism and the French revolution, a mountebank and a freak, sick in the mind. Fashions, however, change in philosophy as in clothes, and events have conspired to make many of the main themes of Rousseau's writings disturbingly topical. The invention of nuclear weapons has undermined faith in the benevolence of science; the pollution of nature by industry has made people question the virtues of technology; the enlargement of bureaucracy has thwarted men's hopes of participatory democracy, and the freedom which the victory of 1945 promised seems to have brought with it new constraints and burdens almost everywhere. We are acutely aware today of problems which Rousseau in the eighteenth century was almost alone in discerning.

This renewed popularity has, however, its negative aspect; there is a danger of Rousseau being transformed from a philosopher into an ideologue, the prophet of the alienated, the inspiration of revolutionary yearnings, nourishing imaginative minds with visions of an ideal state. Paradoxically, this is just the impact which Rousseau wished not to have. He sought not to propel men forward to revolution, but to urge them to retrace their steps, and recover the moral virtues which had been valued in the ancient world.

The eighteenth century was a progressive age. The great *Encyclopédie* which Rousseau's best friend Diderot edited, and for which he himself wrote many articles, was fully and enthusiastically committed to the doctrine of development in technology, art, commerce and industry. 'Science will save us' was the motto not only of Diderot, but of all the *philosophes* who dominated the Enlightenment. However, at the age of 37, Rousseau had what he called an 'illumination' on the road to Vincennes while walking to visit Diderot who had been imprisoned there on charges of injuring religion in the interests of science. Rousseau says it came to him in a terrible flash that the arts and sciences had corrupted instead of improving men's morals; and he promptly lost all his faith in progress. He went on to write his first important publication, his **Discourse on the Arts and Sciences,** in which he argued that the history of culture had been a history of decay. This **Discourse** is by no means Rousseau's best work, but its central theme was to inform almost everything else he wrote throughout his life; he kept coming back to the idea that man is good by nature and has been corrupted by society and civilisation. Rousseau did not say that society and civilisation were inherently bad, but rather that both had taken a wrong direction and become harmful as they had become more advanced and more sophisticated.

This idea in itself was not unfamiliar when Rousseau published his **Discourses on the Arts and Sciences** in 1749. Many Christians, especially Catholics, deplored the direction that European culture had taken since the middle ages. Disapproving of the Renaissance, the Reformation, and the rise of science and industry, such readers shared the hostility towards progress that Rousseau expressed, even if they did not share his belief that man is naturally good. But it was just his belief in natural goodness that Rousseau regarded as the most important part of his argument and this idea, as he developed it, set him even further apart both from the progressives and the reactionaries. Even so, he remained for several years after the publication of his first **Discourse** a close collaborator with Diderot, and one of the most active contributors to successive volumes of the *Encyclopédie.*

Rousseau's speciality on the *Encyclopédie* was music, and it was in this sphere that he first established his influence as a reformer. His early writings on music are not well known; they have not been translated into English, and the world seems to have forgotten the importance they had at the time they were published. Rousseau's **Confessions** contains a paragraph which has puzzled many readers: 'In 1753, the *parlement* of Paris had just been exiled by the King; unrest at its height; all the signs pointed to an early uprising. My **Letter on French Music** was published, and all other quarrels were immediately forgotten. No one thought of anything but the danger to French music, and the only uprising that took place was against me. The conflict was so fierce that the nation was never to recover from it . . . If I say that my writings may have

averted a political revolution in France, people will think me mad; nevertheless, it is a very real truth'.

It is ironical that the philosopher most often named as being responsible for the French revolution should have seen himself as a man who prevented a revolution taking place in France, but there is no reason to think him mad for making the claim. The attempt of Louis XV in 1753 to dissolve the great chamber of the Paris *parlement* and replace it with a Royal Chamber met with such furious resistance that the capital appeared to responsible observers to be on the brink of a rebellion. It was not a rebellion to command the sympathy of Rousseau or Diderot or anyone else connected with the *Encyclopédie.* The Paris *parlements* were judiciary bodies, not to be confused with parliaments on the English model, where representatives of the people sit to legislate: the *parlements* were composed of lawyers, often more eager than the royal government at Versailles to defend the Church and suppress books of the kind that the *Encyclopédistes* wrote. As between the King and the *parlements,* the typical free-thinking French intellectual or *philosophe* was disposed to prefer the former.

But is it conceivable that a dispute about music could have diverted aggression that would otherwise have gone into a political rebellion? Others besides Rousseau believed it. Mercier in his *Tableau de Paris* wrote 'The operatic factions made all other factions disappear'. And Melchior Grimm, in his *Correspondence Littéraire,* reported that the French public was 'much more interested in the quarrel provoked by Rousseau's **Letter** than by the affair of the Royal Chamber'. Culture was taken seriously in eighteenth-century Paris, and a quarrel about music had already been brewing when Rousseau burst into print on the subject. This dispute, known at the time as the *querelle des Bouffons* or war of the opera companies, dated from the arrival in Paris in the summer of 1752 of an Italian opera company to perform works of *opera buffa* (hence the name 'Bouffon') by Pergolesi, Scarlatti, Vinci, Leo and other such composers new to France. This event promptly divided the French music-loving public into two excited camps, supporters of the new Italian opera against supporters of the familiar French opera. The *Encyclopédistes* entered the fray as champions of Italian music, and Rousseau, who knew more about Italian music than the others after the months he spent haunting the opera houses of Venice when he was attached to the French Embassy there in 1743 and 1744, and who was the leading expert on musical subjects for the *Encyclopédie,* emerged as the most forceful and effective combatant, a leader of a little army of pamphleteers. He was the only one to direct his fire squarely at the leading living exponent of French music, Rameau, and he kept up the controversy with Rameau long after the Italian opera company had packed their bags and departed from Paris.

Rousseau was quick to realise that the *querelle des Bouffons* was as much an ideological as a musical one. This is what gave him the advantage over Rameau. For Rameau, already in his seventieth year in 1752, was not only the leading composer of French opera, he was, as the author of a *Treatise on Harmony* and other technical treatises, Europe's leading musicologist. His prestige as a theorist of music matched his popularity as a creative musician. Rousseau, by contrast, was a newcomer to music, with no professional training, no standing, and no authority. In the end, none of these factors hindered his triumph. Rousseau entered the dispute as a reformer against a conservative; and it was a reformer of musical taste that he made his first real mark in the world.

The French opera that Rameau defended was not simply national, it was traditional, authoritarian, academic. Its intellectual complexity had much in common with Descartes' philosophy of mathematical elaboration and rational order; its pomp expressed the self-esteem of the French kings. Moreover, the *libretti* of French operas proclaimed the same Cartesian principles of order and the same Bourbon myth of *gloire,* the splendour of earthly princes being represented on the stage in the image of Gods. Superior beings were impersonated by the actors, and celebrated with the kind of music which appealed, with its intricate harmonies, to superior minds, or which evoked martial feelings by the sound of trumpets and drums. French opera spoke to the ear in the same manner in which the architecture of Versailles appealed to the eye.

In all these respects, the Italian *opera buffa* was different from the French. It was not imposing; it was pleasing. In place of *déclamation,* it introduced arias or songs. And whereas French operatic music was both pompous and highbrow, the Italian was tuneful and simple. Almost anyone could sing the arias of an Italian opera, and in Naples and Venice almost everyone did. The themes of *opera buffa* were domestic and familiar; instead of Gods and Kings, ordinary people occupied the stage. Pergolesi's *La Serva padrona,* with which the Italian company opened their season in Paris and which Rousseau himself edited for publication in France, is about bourgeois bachelor being driven by jealousy into marrying his maid. One can well imagine that even the plot of this opera might alarm conservatives in Paris, if such people took seriously the moral of the tale, that a maid is as good as her mistress.

Rousseau built up his case for the superiority of Italian music over French on one central principle: that melody must have priority over harmony. Rameau took the opposite position—asserting that harmony must have priority over melody. Now this is not a mere technical point, as both disputants realised. Rousseau, pleading for melody, was asserting what came to be recognised as a central belief of romanticism: namely that the free expression of the creative spirit in art is more important than strict adhesion to formal rules and technical precision. Rameau, pleading for harmony, was reaffirming the first principle of French classicism—that conformity to rationally intelligible principles is a necessary condition of true art.

In music Rousseau was a liberator. He not only argued for freedom in music in his pamphlets, he proved the possibility of adapting the Italian style of music to the French theatre in a little opera he composed himself: *Le Devin du village.* This work not only had an immense success before the royal family at Fontainebleau and with the public in Paris, it proved an inspiration for later composers. Gluck, who succeeded Rameau as the most important operatic composer in France, acknowledged his debt to Rousseau's teaching and example. Mozart based his *Bastien and Bastienne* on Rousseau's *Devin du village.* Rousseau had propelled European music into new channels: he put an end to the age of classicism, and initiated an age of romanticism.

But having composed *Le Devin du village* Rousseau decided to turn aside from composing music. He would go on writing articles about musical subjects, and copying other people's music as a means of earning a living, but his creative talents he decided to devote henceforth entirely to literature and philosophy. It was all part of his 'reform' or improvement of his own character; a process which took him back to some of the austere principles that had been instilled in him as a child in the Calvinist republic of Geneva.

The political structure of Geneva was unique in Europe, and no one can understand what Rousseau felt and said about politics without paying attention to the peculiar circumstances of the political education he received. In the middle of the sixteenth century, the townsfolk of Geneva, who had been ruled for generations by a dual principate of Counts and Bishops, were given so many powers by the Bishop in his efforts to overcome the Count, that they contrived to turn those powers against the giver, outwit the Bishop as he had outwitted the Count, and proclaim themselves sovereigns over their own city. However, the people quarrelled so much among themselves, that their democratic constitution soon ceased to function democratically, and the upper-class families took possession of all public offices. The population was increasingly composed of French Protestant refugees, and Calvin himself appeared among them at a critical moment almost as a Law-giver, providing Geneva with a constitution in which democracy and aristocracy and theocracy were curiously balanced, and with institutions to ensure that government was honest and private morality upheld. Calvin's Protestantism was so fanatical, however, that the Catholic cantons refused to admit Geneva to the Swiss Confederation, so that the city had to remain an independent state despite its having a population of less than 25,000 people.

The Genevans consoled themselves with the thought that their little city was a free republic, like the cities of antiquity, as noble and splendid as Rome. Rousseau heard a great deal of this sort of talk when he was a boy. His father was a fervent patriot, and he encouraged him to read Plutarch and other classical authors who proclaimed the value of 'republican virtues': courage, heroism, endurance, devotion, honour. 'I believed myself to be a Greek or a Roman'. Rousseau wrote in *Emile,* looking back on his childhood. On another occasion he wrote: 'At twelve I was a Roman'.

What Rousseau seems to have been unaware of when he was young was that there were profound political dissensions beneath all these appearances of 'Roman' freedom and splendour in the Genevan city state. Every adult male citizen—and there were about 1,500 of them when Rousseau was boy—had, in principle, a share in the sovereignty of the republic and a right to participate and vote at meetings of the General Assembly. In effect, despite Calvin's constitution, the old patriciate prevailed; all decisions were taken by the Small Council which recruited its members exclusively from a few rich families—all living in elegant houses on the top of the hill. This Small Council, which was supposed to be the administrative body, had in effect become also the sovereign body of Geneva. The constitution was a facade; although there were some citizens—including, it seems, Rousseau's father—who chose not to see it as a facade. There were others, liberals or champions of citizens rights, who at different periods were openly or convertly trying to recover the lost rights of the ordinary citizens; but in the years immediately before Rousseau's birth this liberal movement had been suppressed by the execution of its leaders, and Rousseau grew up at a time of tranquillity, when the conservative propaganda of the patrician regime went unchallenged.

Rousseau remained in most respects conservative in his politics. He kept his idealised vision of the character of the Genevan state until his fifties; and then, dismayed at being persecuted by the regime as a result of the publication of *Emile* and *The Social Contract*—books condemned in Geneva as irreligious—he attacked the government while continuing to plead for national unity. Even in his strongest attack on the regime, his *Letters from the Mountains,* a pamphlet written at the prompting of his friends in the liberal and radical factions, Rousseau condemns all factions, and urges his readers in Geneva to think and act together as patriots.

Rousseau's most 'revolutionary' publication his *Discourse on the Origins of Inequality* is dedicated to Geneva; and he always claimed that his *Social Contract* was inspired by the constitution of Geneva. Geneva lies at the heart of all his thinking about politics. Empires, kingdoms and principalities—constitutions of the kind which were standard form in almost all parts of the world when Rousseau was born in 1712—were alien to him. As a result of this he had many ideas about politics which to others seemed strange or unintelligible or were simply misunderstood.

One of the most important of these ideas was Rousseau's conception of freedom. He was passionately devoted to freedom, but freedom meant something different to him from what it meant to almost everyone else. People who talked about liberty in France, or England or America meant the right of the individual to do what he wanted to do, provided it was lawful; freedom was freedom from the constraints of the state. For Rousseau freedom was the freedom the people of Geneva had obtained when they expelled the ruling Bishop in the sixteenth century, the right to participate in the making of the laws, the right to rule themselves.

This distinction between Rousseau's concept of freedom and that of other people was very clearly detected by Benjamin Constant, a fellow Swiss, but a Swiss from the canton of Vaud, accustomed only to being ruled by the Dukes of Savoy or the equally alien magistrates of Berne. Benjamin Constant said Rousseau did not understand 'modern freedom', but always thought in terms of 'ancient freedom'—freedom as it was known in Greek city-states or the Roman republic, when freedom meant not 'being allowed to do what you want to do', but 'participating actively in the legislation of the city'. Constant suggested that Rousseau was ruinously misguided in trying to revive in the modern world this ancient concept of freedom. Why ruinously? Because if the state were thought of something that expressed my will then I would have no motive for writing to diminish the activity of the state, and might well want to enlarge it. Constant feared that the cause of freedom, which was seen by those who thought of 'modern freedom', as requiring curbs and checks being placed on the powers of the state for the protection of the individual was a cause that would be abandoned by people who thought of freedom on the model 'ancient freedom', and whose purpose was simply to make the state their own.

This is a fair criticism. For Rousseau the political independence of Geneva was a good thing, despite the tiny size of Geneva in the eighteenth-century—which many Genevans in the seventeenth-century regretted because they feared themselves too vulnerable in being left outside the Swiss confederation, and which their successors in the nineteenth-century ended by securing admission to that Confederation—that 'weakness' of Geneva Rousseau saw as its merit. For only in a small community, in a 'face-to-face society' can all the citizens meet to make the laws they live under; and hence, if we follow Rousseau's conception of freedom, it is only in a small community that men can experience freedom. The theory of freedom which he develops in depth in his *Social Contract* is simply not applicable to the large scale empires, kingdoms and principalities within which most Westerners lived. It could not even apply to Venice, which had grown from a city to the size of a small empire. It made no sense at all in France, where the population was 25 million.

And yet the French and other foreigners feasted on Rousseau's ideas. Or should we rather say, that they feasted on his eloquence? Few of them saw what Constant saw, that when Rousseau wrote of *'liberté'*, he meant something sharply opposed to what their own philosophers meant by *'liberté'*. It seems equally improbable that Rousseau's readers really grasped what he meant by 'equality', another word which he propelled into the forefront of ideological language.

His *Discourse on the Origins of Inequality* is a masterpiece of speculative anthropology. It follows up the argument of his first *Discourse,* which stresses the theme that

Rousseau's friend Madame d'Épinay, by Jean Étienne Liotard.

modern civilisation is bad, by developing the proposition that natural man is good, and by tracing the successive stages by which man has descended from primitive innocence to sophisticated corruption. The ***Discourse on Inequality*** is remarkable achievement. In less than a hundred pages, Rousseau outlined a theory of evolution which prefigured the discoveries of Darwin, opened new channels for the study of linguistics, and made a seminal contribution to political and economic thought.

He begins his enquiry by noting that there are two kinds of inequality among men: the first are natural inequalities, arising from differences in strength, intelligence and so forth; the second are artificial inequalities deriving from the conventions which govern society. It is the inequalities of the latter sort that he proposes to investigate, and ask if they are ethically justifiable. Adopting what he considered the properly 'scientific' method of studying a phenomenon by research into its origins in time, he tries to reconstruct the first phases, or pre-history, of human societies. He suggests that original man was not social but solitary; and to this extent Rousseau agrees with Hobbes's account of the state of nature, but against Hobbes's view that the life of man in such a state must be 'poor, nasty, brutish and short', Rousseau claims that original man, though admittedly solitary, is healthy, happy, good and free. The vices of men, Rousseau claims, date from the time when each entered into society and began to compare himself with his neighbours, to compete and covet and desire to dominate.

Thus Rousseau blames society, and exonerates nature from responsibility for men's vices. Passions, which hardly exist in the state of nature, develop in society. It is 'the calm of their own passions and their ignorance of vice' which preserve savages from evil. Society began when man started to build huts, which facilitated co-habitation; and, later, from co-habitation there arose the habit of living as a family and associating with neighbours. 'Nascent society', as Rousseau calls it, was good: it was the golden age of man. But it did not last. Neighbours started to compare their achievements one with another: and this 'marked the first step towards inequality, and at the same time, towards vice'.

Men started to demand consideration and respect: their innocent self-love became a culpable pride as everyone wanted to be better than everyone else. The institution of property marked another decisive step towards modern inequality. In the primitive state, according to Rousseau, the earth belonged to everybody or to nobody; but when agriculture was invented, an inevitable consequence was a claim being made for the rightful ownership of the piece of land which a particular farmer had cultivated, and this introduced the 'fatal' concept of property. Property, in turn, entailed institutions of law and government: 'the first man who enclosed a piece of land and took it upon himself to say "This is mine", and found people simple enough to believe him, was the true founder of civil society. What crimes, what wars, what murders, what miseries, what horrors the human race might have been spared if someone had pulled up the stakes and filled in the ditch crying out to his fellow men "Beware of this imposter: you are lost if you forget that the fruits belong to all, and the earth to no one".'

This is inflammatory language: and one can readily imagine that such passages from Rousseau excited revolutionaries like Robespierre and Lenin. But Rousseau is not in fact recommending anyone to 'cry out' today the appeal he would like to have been uttered at an earlier period. He does not suggest this appeal would have any relevance whatever at any other time, than at that moment which marked the passage from 'nascent society' to 'civil society'.

'Civil society' comes into being to serve two purposes: to provide peace for everyone and ensure the right to property for anyone lucky enough to have possessions. In effect it enables the rich to enjoy their riches at the expense of the poor in the context of civil tranquillity. Unfortunately it does not ensure happiness for either rich or poor. The savage, according to Rousseau, has only to eat and he is at peace with nature 'and the friend of all his fellow men'. Man in civil society is never happy because he is never satisfied: 'first it is a question of providing the necessities, then the extras, afterwards come the luxuries, then riches, then subjects, then slaves—there is no letting up'. Society leads men to hate one another in proportion to the conflict between their interests; and 'the universal desire for preference for oneself makes all men enemies'.

It will be noticed that Rousseau treats the inequality between men as one of the characteristics of society, but he does not treat it in isolation. He sees it as one feature of a longer process, the progressive alienation of man from nature and innocence. He is certainly not pleading for equality to be introduced into modern society, since he makes it plain enough that inequality lies at the very roots of society as such.

Nevertheless in the 'Dedication' which he wrote for the ***Discourse on Inequality*** in order to offer it to the 'Republic of Geneva', Rousseau makes it clear what sorts of equality—and inequality—are desirable in a well-ordered state in the modern world. The arrangement he praises in Geneva is similar to that which Plato demanded for his ideal republic: namely one whereby the best men are in the highest places. Again he makes several references to ancient Rome—'that model for all free Peoples'; and then goes on to congratulate Geneva for having its wise men as its magistrates, its virtuous men as its clergy and begs that 'precious half' of the republic, the women folk, to rule the rest, but 'always as chaste wives, on the model of the women of Sparta'. There are no 'egalitarian' sentiments in Rousseau in the sense in which egalitarianism features in later ideologies. He does not even hold with Jefferson, who often responded to Rousseau's influence, that 'all men are born equal'. He holds that they *were* born equal just as they *were* born free. But that was a long time ago. As to the measures of equality and liberty that men might be able to recover in modern civilisation, Rousseau is nowhere very encouraging. Having rejected the doctrine of progress, he could hardly believe that time alone would bring improvement. He left that optimistic thought to the more superficial *Encyclopédistes,* to philosophers like Voltaire. Rousseau had no desire to tell people what they wanted to hear. He wanted only to tell the truth. He believed that *civil* liberty, as distinct from a general liberty, and civil equality, as distinct from social equality, could be obtained in a genuinely republican state: but that such a state can only exist on the strength of the moral virtues of its citizens. Man has lost his natural goodness by entering into society; and to overcome the distinctive passions that society breeds, men must acquire virtues, every man must teach himself to be as disciplined, brave, upright, honest, and patriotic as the ancient Romans.

In his writings on music, Rousseau unveiled the smiling face of romanticism, its promise of freedom from all external constraints that bind the voice of the heart; in his writings on politics he shows us the stern face of romanticism, its demand that a man who is not subservient to others must fiercely govern himself. (pp. 34-45)

> *Maurice Cranston, "J. J. Rousseau and the Birth of Romanticism," in* Essays by Divers Hands, *n.s. Vol. XLIII, 1984, pp. 34-45.*

David Marshall   (essay date 1986)

[*In the following excerpt from an essay first published in* Representations *in 1986, Marshall considers the social implications of Rousseau's* Lettre à d'Alembert sur les spectacles.]

The book that we refer to today as Rousseau's *Lettre à d'Alembert sur les spectacles* usually is situated in the antitheatrical tradition, even if defenders of the stage from d'Alembert to Jonas Barish have considered it a belated and almost anachronistic contribution to that tradition. [Here] I would like (at least temporarily) to dislocate the *Lettre* from both the tradition of attacks on the stage and the immediate occasion that prompted Rousseau to publish the book: d'Alembert's proposal in the seventh volume of the *Encyclopédie* that a theater be established in Geneva. I will argue that although Rousseau genuinely was concerned about the effects of a theater in Geneva, and although much of his argument against the stage reiterates the charges of Plato and later antitheatrical polemicists, we blind ourselves to the full scope of Rousseau's indictment if we regard the *Lettre* only as a particularly eloquent antitheatrical tract.

The original title of the book refers to d'Alembert's proposal to establish a "théâtre de comédie" in Geneva, but the title that Rousseau later used to refer to his text is the *Lettre à d'Alembert sur les spectacles*—which I would insist on translating as the *Letter to d'Alembert on Spectacles.* The title is *not,* as Rousseau's modern American translator would suggest, the *Letter to M. d'Alembert on the Theatre.* The question of whether a "théâtre de comédie" should be established in Geneva provides an occasion for Rousseau to reflect on the character of *spectacles*—which include but by no means are limited to dramatic representations performed by actors on a stage. Rousseau is concerned not just with how Geneva should govern its spectacles but with how spectacles govern our lives: how we are affected by the theatrical relations enacted outside as well as inside the playhouse by people who face each other as actors and spectators. I will suggest that the issue for Rousseau finally is not whether *a* theater should be established but whether theater (in its many manifestations) can be avoided at all.

The possibility that theatrical acts and relations are inescapable in Rousseau's view sets the stage for a consideration of Rousseau's own role in the *Lettre,* his own predicament in indicting actors and spectators. The original title page not only names Rousseau as author; it includes Rous-

seau's name in the title, which begins: "J. J. ROUSSEAU / CITOYEN DE GENEVE, / A M. D'ALEMBERT . . . " In announcing the completion of his book, Rousseau wrote to his publisher, "Non seulement vous pourrez me nommer, mais mon nom y sera et en fera même le titre" ("Not only may you name me, but my name will be in the title and indeed will be the title"). The subject of the book is identified with the subject of Rousseau from the very first line of the text. I do not mean to suggest that the text is strictly autobiographical; my point is that identity and identification are themselves key issues in the text. Not only does Rousseau's own involvement with the theatrical situations he is depicting come into play; Rousseau himself discusses theater in terms of an interplay between subjects. As a book about theater, the *Lettre* examines the conditions of projection, identification, and sympathy; it asks what it means to take the part of someone, to put oneself in someone else's place, to imagine that a story is about oneself. . . . [Rousseau writes,] "Let us dare to say it directly: who among us is sure enough of himself to bear the performance of such a comedy without halfway taking part in the turns that are played out? . . . . For is being interested in someone anything other than putting oneself in his place?" This chapter will consider Rousseau's interest in both actors and spectators. It will trace the risks and possibilities Rousseau sees in spectacles, in theatrical relations, and in writing about spectacles and theatrical relations.

The *Lettre à d'Alembert sur les spectacles* has been seen as a continuation of the reactionary crusade against civilization Rousseau began in his early discourses. One could reverse this perspective, however, and see Rousseau's earlier writing—particularly the *Discours sur l'origine et les fondements de l'inégalité parmi les hommes*—as the beginning of a critique of theatricality: a critical investigation into the role of spectacles and theatrical relations in European culture. In the second *Discours,* for example, when Rousseau asserts, "dans le véritable état de nature, l'Amour propre n'existe pas" ("in the true state of nature, vanity does not exist"), he goes on to describe . . . "each man regarding himself as the only spectator who observes him, as the only being in the universe who takes an interest in him". The state of nature seems untheatrical; it is in part defined by the absence of any consciousness of beholders.

As society develops, according to Rousseau, people become aware of the regard of others. They become conscious of others as both spectacles and spectators: . . . "They become accustomed to assembling in front of the huts or around a large tree; song and dance . . . became the amusement, or rather the occupation, of idle men and women gathered together in groups. Each one started to look at the others and to want to be looked at himself, and public esteem acquired a value" The invention of these performers, audiences, and displays of beauty and talent constitutes the first step toward inequality, according to Rousseau, and is soon followed by vanity, shame, contempt, and envy. Such an elevation of talents and personal qualities (over power and property, for example) is also seen to turn people into actors: . . . "these qualities being the only ones which could attract consideration, it soon became necessary either to possess them or to affect them; it was necessary, for one's own advantage, to show oneself to be other than one in fact was. To be and to seem to be become two completely different things".

Rousseau's illustrations are carefully chosen to serve as both specific examples and more general emblems. Consequently, it is not so much the assembly of people singing and dancing for each other that is theatrical, although this is a literal instance of theater; what Rousseau is focusing on here is the exchange of regards, the awareness of others as beholders, that creates a theatrical consciousness. Rousseau's indictment of the acting and posing that develop in society is not limited to a denunciation of deception, hypocrisy, or false representation. People become actors—and this acting is problematic—from the moment they are aware that they must represent themselves for others. The "representative signs [signes représentatifs] of wealth", for example, are not necessarily false; people become actors the moment they imagine what eighteenth-century English writers referred to as the eyes of the world. For Rousseau, there is as much danger in *se montrer* (showing oneself) as there is in *se montrer autre que ce qu'on est* (showing oneself to be other than one is). Those for whom "the gaze of the rest of the universe [les regards du reste de l'univers] counts for something, who are happy and content with themselves according to the testimony of others [le témoignage d'autrui] rather than their own", seem to depend on those they imagine as eyewitnesses for their very being. Anticipating his own indictment of stage actors, as well as Sartre's critique of theatrical self-consciousness, Rousseau writes: . . . "the savage lives within himself; social man, always outside of himself, knows how to live only in the opinion of others; and it is, so to speak, only from their judgment that he derives the sentiment of his own existence". He concludes that a universal desire for reputation and distinction is responsible for what is best and worst in society. For better or for worse, however, the development of *amour-propre* and of the social relations that accompany it is seen as a theatrical problem.

Theater, then, in Rousseau's descriptions, represents the fall from the state of nature. The story of this fall and the rise of a society governed by *amour-propre* is told in part as if it were a story about the invention or establishment of theater. The rise of a theatrical perspective turns people into actors and encourages them to make spectacles of themselves; it also weakens the natural bonds between people by turning them into spectators. Rousseau describes in the second *Discours* how philosophy and reason isolate people and replace sympathy and commiseration with *amour-propre*: man is taught to say "at the sight of a suffering man: 'Perish if you wish; I am safe.' No longer do any dangers (except those that threaten all of society) trouble the tranquil sleep of the philosopher or pull him from his bed. One may cut the throat of his fellow man [son semblable] beneath his very window with impunity; he has only to cover his ears with his hands and argue with himself a little, to prevent nature, which revolts within him, from identifying with the man being murdered".

This description of the ability to view someone suffering from a distance, through a frame, is throughout eighteenth-century aesthetics and moral philosophy a major figure for a theatrical perspective. Writers such as Hume, Smith, Du Bos, and Rousseau himself (in the *Lettre à d'Alembert*) tried to explain the paradox that audiences received pleasure from viewing representations of suffering in paintings or on the stage. As I have argued, Lucretius's description in *De Rerum Natura* of the pleasure of watching a shipwreck from a position of safety becomes a paradigm in the eighteenth century for the aesthetic experience of watching someone suffering from a position of distance and nonidentification. Thus, in condemning the lesson of difference and indifference supposedly taught by philosophy, Rousseau is condemning a point of view that allows people to look at others from the position of an audience, through a distancing frame that is associated with the theater. Theater in its literal manifestation represents or figures the theatrical relations formed between self and others that Rousseau denounces in society. In Rousseau's view, society is theater and what goes on in the playhouse between actors and audience mirrors the more dangerous theater that society has become.

These are the terms in which Rousseau casts his critique of both theater and "social man" in the *Lettre à d'Alembert sur les spectacles.* If Geneva bears some resemblance to the more pleasant aspects of the state of nature in Rousseau's nostalgic and pastoral descriptions, this is partly because Rousseau highlights Geneva's untheatrical characteristics. Unlike the social and cosmopolitan citydwellers who seek reputation and the regard of others, the "true genius" Rousseau associates with Geneva and small towns "is unaware of the path of honors and fortune, and does not even think of looking for it; he compares himself to no one [il ne se compare à personne]". The Genevan seems to escape having the "relative self" Rousseau associates with *amour-propre*. "Imagine that as soon as vanity [amour-propre] is developed," writes Rousseau in the *Émile*, "le moi relatif se met en jeu sans cesse, et que jamais le jeune homme n'observe les autres sans revenir sur lui-même et se comparer avec eux" ("the relative self comes constantly into play, and the young man never observes others without coming back to himself and comparing himself to them". Like the *homme sauvage*, the Genevan in Rousseau's portrait does not seem to depend on the regard of others for a sense of his own existence. His economic autonomy is analogous to the autonomy of his self: "all his resources are in himself alone".

Like the inhabitants of the state of nature, the inhabitants of Geneva seem to live in themselves more than in others. . . . "If our habits in a retired life arise from our own sentiments, in society they arise from the opinion of others. When one does not live within oneself, but in others, their judgments rule everything." In large cities, according to Rousseau, this concern for the eyes of the world turns people into actors. "L'homme du monde est tout entier dans son masque" ("The man of the world is completely in his mask"), he writes in the *Émile;* . . . "Almost never in himself, he is always a stranger to himself. . . . What he is, is nothing; that which he seems is everything for him". This dislocation and loss of self occurs in both men and women in Rousseau's view. In large cities, he writes in *La Nouvelle Héloïse,* "men become other than they are, and . . . society gives them so to speak a being that is different from their own." Women in particular, he continues, "derive the only existence they care for from the regard of others [des regards d'autrui]. When approaching a lady at a gathering [assemblée], instead of the Parisian woman you think you see, you see only a simulacrum of the current fashion [un simulacre de la mode]".

Theater, in Rousseau's view, does more than mirror the theatrical representations and relations of cosmopolitan life. It reproduces these representations and relations outside as well as inside the playhouse. Theater is especially dangerous for women, according to Rousseau, because it plays on their already theatricalized character. Despite his condemnation of Parisian women who, he says, "derive the only existence they care for from the regard of others [des regards d'autrui]", Rousseau insists in the *Émile* that "woman is specially made to please men" and that "a woman's conduct is subjugated to public opinion". In addition to using her arts to disguise her thoughts and desires, a woman (in Rousseau's terms) seems condemned to living outside of herself, in the regards and judgments of others. Like the actor who becomes "le jouet des spectateurs" ("the plaything of the spectators"), the little girl who plays with her doll "attend le moment d'être sa poupée elle-même" ("awaits the moment when she herself will be her doll"). Once on the stage, then, women seem unbearably theatrical as they double what Rousseau sees as their inherent dissimulation, *amour-propre,* and exhibitionism.

Actresses are signed out in the *Lettre à d'Alembert sur les spectacles* for an especially vitriolic attack; Rousseau condemns . . . "a state in which the sole object is to show oneself in public, and what is worse, to show oneself for money". Yet this condemnation also extends to the women who expose themselves as spectators in the . . . "exhibition of married ladies and young girls dressed in their best and arranged in their boxes as in a shop window, waiting for purchasers". According to Rousseau, women who enter the theater must enter theater; spectators become spectacles who are caught up in the "traffic de soi-même" ("traffic of the self ") that characterizes the actor's profession.

This kind of theatricalization, Rousseau argues, would be the fate of women in Geneva if a theater were established. "Les femmes des Montagnons," he writes, "allant d'abord pour voir, et ensuite pour être vues, voudront être parées" ("The women [wives] of the Montagnons, going first to see, and then to be seen, would want to be elegantly dressed"); they would want to distinguish themselves and "se montrer au spectacle", which is to say, they would want to show themselves *en spectacle,* as spectacles. At this point, it seems, a woman already would be lost: . . . "to seek men's looks is already to let oneself be corrupted by them. . . . every woman who shows herself dishonors herself ". To show oneself is to dishonor oneself. This seems to apply to men as well as women. Rousseau notes that . . . "a working man does not go to a gathering to show himself in his work clothes; he must wear his Sunday best". Rousseau is concerned about the economic and moral consequences in a Geneva suddenly preoccupied with clothing, ornament, display, appearance, distinction. What would be most dangerous, however, would be the mere desire of the relatively untheatrical Genevans to show themselves; making them spectators would threaten to transform them into spectacles and actors.

What is at stake in the *Lettre à d'Alembert sur les spectacles* is less the presence of a theater in Geneva than the possibility of Geneva as theater. Rousseau argues that d'Alembert's proposal to establish a "théâtre de comédie en Genève" would make a theater of Geneva. Theater would threaten to transform Geneva into Paris, to change it from a modern-day state of nature to a theatrical society in which not just the actors and actresses but all citizens would be condemned to exist in the regard of others. Theater would reproduce itself off the stage by drawing spectators into theatrical positions and by promoting the internalization in individual consciousness of the theatrical relations that in Rousseau's view characterize social life.

We saw that Rousseau condemned philosophy and reason for teaching a theatrical perspective that (in effect) promoted distance, indifference, and isolation. Theater is especially dangerous, according to Rousseau, because its business is to present and represent this theatrical perspective. It teaches people how to become spectators, how to act like spectators. "L'on croit s'assembler au spectacle, et c'est là que chacun s'isole" ("We think that we come together in the theater, but it is there that we isolate ourselves") asserts Rousseau in a declaration that might stand for much of the argument of the *Lettre* in the way that the aphoristic "Man is born free, and everywhere he is in chains" has come to stand for the *Contrat social.* Both the *Contrat social* and the *Essai sur l'origine des langues* emphasize the importance of assemblies in social and political life. Theater represents a perversion of the gatherings that brought people together in antiquity. Unlike those "assemblés en plein air" ("open air assemblies"), the spectacles of the playhouse "renferment tristement un petit nombre de gens dans un antre obscur" ("sadly close up a small number of people in a dark cavern"); there, the spectators are kept "craintifs et immobiles dans le silence et l'inaction" ("fearful and immobile in silence and inaction").

The problem is not merely that spectators are powerless to act or that they are not called upon to act. Rousseau claims that theater teaches them how not to act. He asks how audiences are able to tolerate the tableaux of Greek tragedy, insisting that . . . "the massacres of the gladiators were not as barbarous as these frightful spectacles. One saw blood flow, it is true, but one did not soil one's imagination with crimes at which nature shudders". One of the answers Rousseau suggests to this question is that . . . "everything that is represented at the theater is not brought closer to us but rather placed at a distance". Other eighteenth-century theoreticians of sympathy (such as Du Bos and Adam Smith) imagine a weak or secondary sympathy occurring in the minds and hearts of audiences. Rousseau claims that we are taught to respond in the theater with a kind of false sympathy, "a sterile pity" that is "transitory and vain" and somehow too pure and abstract to mean very much to us. Arguing against the defenders of the stage who evoke catharsis and speak of the moral and sentimental education of audiences, Rousseau insists that the theater teaches us how to replace real sympathy with a painless representation or imitation of sympathy. This occurs not so much through an aestheticization of other people's suffering as through a false sense that one has fulfilled one's responsibilities toward others by responding in the playhouse: . . .

> In shedding our tears for these fictions, we have satisfied all the claims of humanity, without having to give any more of ourselves. . . . Finally, when a man has gone to admire fine actions in fables, and to weep over imaginary misfortunes, what more can one demand of him? . . . Has he not acquitted

himself of all he owes to virtue by the homage he has just rendered it? What more would one have him do? . . . he has no role to play: he is not an actor.

Passages such as this one should make us aware of the inadequacy of merely assigning the *Lettre à d'Alembert* to a tradition of conservative antitheatrical polemics. In presenting a critique of theatricality (a critical investigation of what it means to face others as a spectator or a spectacle) Rousseau goes beyond the standard warnings about how plays arouse passions and incite their audiences to commit moral crimes. He offers a more radical analysis of the pathos, subjectivity, and sympathy that take place in the playhouse—an analysis that anticipates the critique Brecht would direct against the liberal, bourgeois theater he inherited from the eighteenth-century. Brecht, of course, thought there was too much identification and empathy in modern audiences, not too little. Yet he shared with Rousseau the conviction that the emotions exchanged and experienced in the playhouse served to release people from a responsibility for action and analysis. Both Brecht and Rousseau objected to the self-congratulatory sympathy that turns people into passive spectators both inside and outside of the theater. Action inside the playhouse seems to substitute for action in social and political life. Rousseau complains that the great sentiments celebrated in plays are relegated forever to the stage; virtue becomes "un jeu de théâtre" which is . . . "a game of the theater . . . good for amusing the public, but which it would be madness to wish to see seriously transported into society".

Furthermore, as if anticipating the Kantian tradition of disinterested and purposeless art (against which Brecht would oppose his didactic and political epic theater), Rousseau raises the question of utility: . . . "these productions of the mind . . . have no other aim but applause. . . . and one looks for no other utility in them". Unlike Brecht, however, Rousseau is not interested in reforming or radicalizing the theater. The only theater Rousseau can imagine stands condemned for the failure of sympathy it institutionalizes. All it can teach (aside from the dissimulation and self-display exhibited by those who show themselves to the eyes of the world) is the false sympathy that allows people to think they have no role to play in the scenes and dramas around them. Paradoxically, this also turns the world to theater.

The *Lettre à d'Alembert sur les spectacles* indicts spectators for their ultimate failure of sympathy; it condemns the theatrical perspective that turns others into spectacles by substituting distance and isolation for the identification between *semblables* that is supposed to take place in the state of nature. In his analysis of these situations, Rousseau insists that the spectator has a role to play. But what would it mean to play a role, inside or outside the playhouse, and how would this role differ from the exhibitionism, imitation, posing, and living in others that Rousseau condemns in both actors and spectators? To answer these questions, we need to return to Rousseau's characterization of the actor. Following the standard accusations of the antitheatrical tradition, Rousseau charges the actor with counterfeiting, with appearing to be different than he really is, and deception (although he admits that while encouraging deception, the actor himself is not exactly "un trompeur" ["a deceiver"]). He calls attention to the shame

of having to . . . "take on a role different from your own before the eyes of the public", contrasting the actor with the orator who shows himself only . . . "to speak, and not to make a spectacle of himself".

Rousseau also follows tradition in comparing the actor to a prostitute. However, the *traffic de soi-même* that disconcerts Rousseau the most is metaphysical rather than physical and commercial. The usual moral issues such as the deception or corruption of actors seem to concern Rousseau less than the loss of self that appears to take place in the actors themselves. The orator, claims Rousseau, . . . "represents only himself, he acts his own role only . . . the man and the character being the same, he is in his place". The actor, in contrast, must "oublier enfin sa propre place à force de prendre celle d'autrui" ("finally forget his own place after having taken the place of someone else"); "représentant souvent un être chimérique," the actor "s'anéantit, pour ainsi dire, s'annule avec son héros" ("often representing a chimerical being," the actor "annihilates himself, so to speak, annuls himself in his hero"). For Rousseau, the actor's art amounts to an "oubli de l'homme" ("a forgetting of the man").

What is at stake, then, is nothing less than the self-annihilation of the actor. Indeed, as we have seen, Rousseau's fears about the theater are not limited to professional actors. Rousseau also worries about self-forgetting and self-alienation in his characterizations of the theatrical aspects of women, social man, cosmopolitan life, and *amour-propre*. In the *Lettre*, he speaks of the "oubli d'eux-mêmes" ("forgetting of themselves") that makes lovers vulnerable and he warns that if the Genevan attended the theater he would begin to "s'oublier soi-même et s'occuper d'objets étrangers" ("forget himself and occupy himself with foreign objects"). According to Rousseau, self-forgetting follows self-estrangement, trying to be other than one really is: . . . "he who begins to be estranged from himself soon forgets himself completely"; and this self-estrangement is associated with leaving the self. The man of the world, for example, is reduced to nothing ("rien") because he leaves the self for a foreign state: . . . "Almost never existing within himself, he is always a stranger there, and ill at ease when forced to return".

In all of these descriptions, Rousseau is preoccupied with the transport outside of the self that accompanies (or constitutes) self-forgetting. These characterizations go beyond Rousseau's descriptions of those who live in and for the opinion of others. Writing of those who practice imitation to "trick others [imposer aux autres] or to get applause for their talent," Rousseau asserts: "Imitation among us is based on the desire always to transport ourselves outside ourselves [se transporter toujours hors de soi]". His critique of *amour-propre* is based on the claim that social man is "always outside of himself [toujours hors de lui]"; the search for a reputation, according to Rousseau, "takes us almost always outside of ourselves [hors de nous-mêmes]". In fact, following the *renvoi* of an endnote to the discussion of self-knowledge that begins the preface to the second *Discours*, one could argue that the hidden epigraph to the *Discours* is a passage from *L'Histoire naturelle de l'homme* in which Buffon asks why we "seek only to extend beyond ourselves, and exist outside ourselves [exister hors de nous]". A theatrical consciousness, whether on the stage or in society, seems to threaten the integrity of the self by taking people outside of themselves. The transport outside of the self that occurs in these acts of imitation, *amour-propre,* self-display, and representation seems to cause the actor to forget his own place and person, to leave himself behind.

Rousseau's characterizations of the state and state of mind of the actor—in particular, his account of the self-annihilation caused by a transport outside of the self—present us with a paradox in Rousseau's conception of the roles of actor and spectator. Although spectators are condemned for lacking genuine sympathy, it appears that the actor is condemned precisely because he is sympathetic. The problem with the actor is that he exhibits and performs acts of sympathy; he almost embodies sympathy. According to Rousseau's characterizations, the actor forgets his own place and takes the place of someone else; he forgets his own identity in an act of identification that carries him outside of himself. These terms are precisely the terms with which Rousseau and his contemporaries defined sympathy. For moral philosophers, aestheticians, novelists, and protopsychologists in the eighteenth century, sympathy was an act of identification in which one left one's own place, part, and person and took the place and part of someone else; while representing to oneself the other's feelings, one was transported outside of the self: placed beyond or beside the self in a moment of self-forgetting.

Rousseau agrees that this is what happens to spectators who accept that they have a role to play when faced with a scene that demands their sympathy. In the second **Discours,** for example, he writes that commiseration is "a sentiment which puts us in the place of the one who suffers"; it depends on an act of identification, even in animals: "the commiseration will be that much more energetic as the observing animal [l'animal Spectateur] identifies itself with the suffering animal". In the **Essai sur l'origine des langues,** Rousseau asks: "Comment nous laissons-nous émouvoir à la pitié?" ("How do we let ourselves be moved to pity?"), and he answers: . . . "by transporting ourselves outside of ourselves, by identifying ourselves with the being who suffers".

A similar description of pity occurs in the **Émile:** . . . "how do we let ourselves be moved to pity, if not by transporting ourselves out of ourselves, by identifying with the suffering animal, by leaving our own being, so to speak, to take on its being?" He continues: . . . "Thus one achieves sensibility only when his imagination is animated and starts to transport him outside of himself". When we feel pity, writes Rousseau, we experience "cet état de force qui nous étend au délà de nous" ("that state of strength that extends us beyond ourselves"). Rousseau joined other theoreticians of sympathy in countering Hobbes's claim that sympathy was selfish rather than altruistic (since we imagine ourselves suffering, for example, not someone else) by insisting that we leave ourselves behind, so to speak, and become the other person. In both the **Essai sur l'origine des langues** and the **Émile,** Rousseau writes: . . . "It's not in ourselves but in him that we suffer". Thus, according to Rousseau's depictions of these parts, persons, and positions, while the orator might remain "in his place," the actor *and* the sympathetic spectator each must . . . "finally forget his own place after taking that

of others". Actors must act with sympathy and spectators should act like actors.

Rousseau's identification of acting and sympathy takes place within a long tradition of portraying the actor (and the author) as the epitome of sympathetic imagination. Indeed, Rousseau's basic premise about the actor's art of sympathetic identification would not have been disputed by most actors or advocates of the stage in the first half of the eighteenth century. Diderot's argument in his *Paradoxe sur le comédien* that the best actor would not feel or become his part but rather coolly exhibit the exterior signs and symptoms of feelings was directed against prevalent theories of acting and poetic imagination that date back at least as far as the *Ion.* Jonas Barish situates Rousseau in this context and remarks that Rousseau, in not rejecting the "sensibilist" or "emotionalist" view of acting as Diderot did, "is guilty of perpetuating an old confusion which others in his day were beginning finally to disentangle." What interests me here, however, is that having accepted and elaborated contemporary beliefs about the experiences of sympathy and acting, Rousseau is in the position of condemning actors for possessing what he condemns spectators for lacking.

Theater is dangerous for Rousseau because it teaches people how to avoid sympathy: it completes the lesson of philosophy and reason by creating a theatrical perspective that inhibits acts of identification and fellow feeling, by substituting a simulacrum of sympathy for actual human interaction, and by promoting *amour-propre* among both actors and audiences. Theater is also dangerous for actors because in transporting them outside of themselves from their own place to the place of someone else, in making them forget themselves and take on the point of view of someone else, it threatens them with self-annihilation. However, as we have seen, this self-annihilation and transport out of the self feels remarkably similar to sympathy; indeed, the actor's role is to sympathize. This suggests that sympathy, too, may be dangerous; it too may threaten to annihilate the self. Rousseau's paradoxical portrayal of the actor should lead us to revise our understanding of Rousseau's indictment of theater and theatrical relations. To do this, we need to consider two questions: one concerns the opposition between sympathy and *amour-propre;* the other concerns Rousseau's sympathy with the actor.

We have seen that Rousseau's depictions of the state of nature suggest that the performances and self-displays of *amour-propre* and the theatrical perspective of philosophy and reason are partly responsible for the decline of sympathy and the fall from that primitive state into society. We are now in a position to see that Rousseau's representations of the primitive relations between self and other suggests that sympathy and *amour-propre* have disturbing similarities for him. According to Rousseau's analysis in the **Discours sur l'origine et les fondements de l'inégalité parmi les hommes,** the savage man is not afflicted with *amour-propre* since *amour-propre* has its source in "comparisons that he is not inclined to make." Regarding himself as his only spectator, and regarding his "semblables" or fellow beings as if they were "animals of another species," he can neither "appraise himself" nor "compare himself". He cannot wish to distinguish himself in the eyes of other people because he imagines that he is alone. The *moi relatif* of *amour-propre* is set in play when he observes other people in order to "compare himself to them". Like the true genius that ignores reputation because it "compares itself to no one", savage man is untheatrical because he has no one with whom he can compare himself. Other people strike him as giants, not humans, suggests Rousseau in the *Essai sur l'origine des langues:* . . . "They had the idea of a father, a son, a brother, but not of a man. Their hut contained all their fellow beings; a stranger, a beast, a monster, were for them the same thing".

At the same time, however, Rousseau argues that pity cannot take place in this primitive condition. Sympathy or fellow feeling also depends on an act of comparison: a moment of identification in which one compares oneself to another and recognizes a *semblable* rather than a giant, a monster, or an animal of another species. After stating that pity depends on a transport out of the self in an act of identification, Rousseau adds, "How could I suffer when seeing another suffer, if I did not even know that he suffers, if I were unaware of what he and I have in common?" Sympathy is impossible without some kind of identification. In order to pity someone, we must see the person as our *semblable,* imagine the person as a reflection of ourselves rather than an other. "To become capable of sensibility and pity [devenir sensible et pitoyable]," writes Rousseau in the *Émile,* "the child must know that there are beings like himself [êtres semblables à lui] who suffer what he has suffered". What happens in the moment of comparison of self with other that teaches one that one is not alone?

In his dramatizations of the passage from the state of nature to society, Rousseau implies a sketchy chronology. At first, it seems, primitive people do not recognize each other as *semblables;* but then, with an act of comparison which identifies the other as someone with whom one shares something in common, comes a moment of imagination in which one transports oneself outside of oneself and identifies with the other. This moment of simultaneous imagination, comparison, recognition, transport, and identification does not so much allow sympathy as constitute it. However, this act of comparison in which one leaves oneself and enters into the sentiments of someone else, this moment of recognition that one is not alone in the world and thus not one's only spectator, is also the moment when *amour-propre* is made possible and inevitable. *Amour-propre* seems to follow sympathy in Rousseau's scheme since its theatrical relations threaten the apparently natural bonds of fellow feeling. Yet sympathy and *amour-propre* both are born in the moment the self compares itself with others. Each is structured by an act of identification through which one transports oneself to someone else's place, a comparison of the self with an other turned *semblable* in which one forgets oneself and imagines the point of view of the other. In this sense, both sympathy and *amour-propre* are inherently theatrical relations, structured by an exchange between a spectator and a spectacle, dependent on acts of acting. Rousseau's own terms suggest that the state of nature is always already theatrical.

It is not surprising, then, that it is sometimes difficult to tell the difference between sympathy and *amour-propre.* In an early version of the beginning of his *Confessions,* Rousseau speculates on the need to compare oneself with others

in order to know both others and oneself; he worries, however, that such comparisons must be based on an imperfect knowledge of oneself. "On se fait la règle de tout" ("One makes oneself the measure of all things"), writes Rousseau, defining this dilemma as . . . "the double illusion of self-love: either in falsely ascribing to those we judge the motives which would have made us act like them in their place, or, in this very assumption, deceiving ourselves about our own motives, not knowing how to transport ourselves sufficiently into a situation different from our own". At the moment when one is supposed to be entering into someone else's sentiments, one might be guilty of *amour-propre,* which here amounts to a double failure of sympathy: as Hobbes and Mandeville warned, one might only imagine oneself, not the other; and furthermore, one might even lack the sympathy and imagination to imagine oneself in a different situation. In an act of comparison one sees the other as a *semblable;* but what does it mean to look at the other and see a reflection of oneself? How does one know whether one sees oneself or the other in the mirror of comparison?

The breakdown of Rousseau's distinctions between sympathy and *amour-propre,* along with the breakdown of the temporal scheme in his dramatization of these relations, helps to account for (if not explain) the apparent contradiction in Rousseau's claims about the role of reflection: his assertion in the *Essai sur l'origine des langues* that pity depends on reflection ("He who has never reflected [réfléchi] can be neither merciful nor just, nor capable of pity" and his insistence in the *Discours* that pity precedes "the use of all reflection," that it operates "without reflection," that reflection contributes to *amour-propre.* What is at issue in both of Rousseau's claims about reflection is the moment of comparison that appears to constitute both pity and *amour-propre.* "La réflexion naît des idées comparées" ("Reflection comes from the comparison of ideas"), writes Rousseau in the *Essai,* insisting that we must compare ourselves with others to recognize them as our *semblables.* Yet "la réflexion," which strengthens *amour-propre,* "turns man back on himself; it is what separates him from everything that disturbs and afflicts him".

Comparison teaches one about one's difference from others; it also allows one to turn one's back on others because it turns one back on oneself. The double illusion of *amour-propre* turns one into a spectacle for others and a spectacle to oneself. The moment of comparison creates the double reflection through which one becomes both a spectator to one's *semblable* and a spectacle for one's *semblables* and oneself—although part of the vertigo of these double illusions is that one might be looking in the mirror of *amour-propre* precisely at the moment one thought one was looking in the mirror of sympathy. The theatrical structure of these relations creates mirror images of reflection: the act of comparison of the self with an other who appears as a *semblable* (that is, pity) and the act of comparison of the self with a *semblable* who appears as an other (that is, *amour-propre*). The reflection of sympathy is always in danger of being or becoming the reflection of *amour-propre* since sympathy and *amour-propre* appear as mirror images of each other. (pp. 135-51)

David Marshall, "Rousseau and the State of Theater," in his The Surprising Effects of Sympathy: Marivaux, Diderot, Rousseau, and Mary Shelley, *The University of Chicago Press,* 1988, pp. 135-77.

Allan Bloom   (essay date 1986)

[*Bloom is an American philosopher, educator, editor, and author. He is perhaps best known for his controversial best-seller* The Closing of the American Mind: How Higher Education Has Failed Democracy and Impoverished the Souls of Today's Students *(1987). In the following excerpt from another work, he discusses the natural and social functions of men and women and addresses the question of sexual equality during the eighteenth century, focusing on Rousseau's comprehensive treatment of these themes in* Émile.]

Prior to Rousseau, it might be said with some exaggeration, the teachers of equality paid little attention to men and women and the family. They concentrated on the political order and seemed to suppose that the subpolitical units would remain largely unaffected. But there are two different understandings of nature present here, one in which nature has nothing to say about relationships and rank order and another in which nature is prescriptive. Are the relations between men and women and parents and children determined by natural impulse or are they the products of choice and consent? The former view is part and parcel of ancient political philosophy, as one easily sees in Aristotle's *Politics* I, whereas the latter view is at least implicit in Hobbes's and Locke's state of nature. The common teaching of the political philosophers has always been that the political regime will inform its parts. Hence democratic politics will produce democratic sexual and family relations. But what are they?

In *Emile* Rousseau addressed this question more comprehensively than anyone had done before or has done since, and it is to a few reflections on this enormously influential but now largely forgotten book that I shall limit myself, in the belief that Rousseau, because of his privileged position at the beginnings of modern democracy, saw the problems with special clarity and intransigence, and that, however unpalatable his views have since become, he both played an important and unsuspected part in forming our views and is especially helpful if one wishes to get a perspective on our peculiar form of wishful thinking.

To begin where we are at, the moral and perhaps even the political scene has been dominated for two decades by two movements, sexual liberation and feminism. Both have somehow to do with the status of sexual differentiation or "roles," and both are explicitly connected with the extension and radicalization of egalitarianism. The two are not necessarily harmonious—witness the squabbles over pornography—but each probably presupposes the other, and they represent aspects of the struggle to adjust free individuality to the demands of our sexual nature. Rousseau foresaw both as necessary consequences of liberal theory and practice and was strongly against them. His reasons for this stance are of little concern to his contemporary critics who are committed to liberation and feminism, and he is now probably the archvillain of sexual politics. He is qualified as a guilt-ridden puritan by one camp and as a sexist by the other, and is subjected to the indignities of psychological interpretation. His continuing good reputation in other quarters is attributable to his powerful advocacy of community, which is all the rage. But that his treatment of sex can be explained only by his concern for the conditions of community—conditions that were, according to him, rapidly disappearing—is hardly mentioned. Rousseau's dedication to the cause of close communitarian ties between free and equal men and women forced him to pay the closest attention to that most powerful motive, sex, which joins and separates men and women.

Puritan he surely was not. He was one of the most powerful critics of the notion of original sin, and instead on the natural goodness of man, especially of his sexual desire. It is a common error to treat opponents of sexual liberation as though their only ground were theological, whereas it is possible to limit sexual gratification for economic, social, and political reasons and even in the name of good sex or love. Rousseau wished to liberate sex from its theological yoke in order to consider its delicate relationship to all the powers of the soul. If sexism means insistence on essential differentiation of function between man and woman both naturally and socially, then Rousseau was indeed a sexist. If, on the other hand, it means treating women as objects and subordinating them, he certainly was not a sexist. Rather he was concerned with enhancing the power of women over men. Beginning from the community of man and woman in the act of procreation, he attempts to extend it throughout the whole of life. Procreation is not incidental to life but, properly elaborated, is the end, that for the sake of which all things are done. It is the relatedness, the harmonious relatedness of man and woman, which he takes as the model and foundation of all human relatedness.

Because modern political theory and practice begin from the rights of individuals "to life, liberty, and the pursuit of property," the dangers of egoism (read "narcissism" today), of a constricting of the soul within the limits of the individual and material I, and hence of a diminution of man, are, according to Rousseau, great. Liberal democracy, unless its characteristic springs of action are complemented or sublimated, would not then be a simply choiceworthy regime, even though it were founded on just principles. Rousseau discerned in man's historical experience three great loves that could draw him out of his selfish concerns and solicit his soul on the highest level—love of God, love of country, love of woman. Each is an enthusiasm, even a fanaticism, the objects of which are made unique and beyond purchase by the activity of imagination. The operations of the first two have been rendered nugatory, or at least have been radically attenuated, by modern philosophy itself, which had as one of its primary goals the destruction of fanaticism. Tocqueville summarizes Rousseau's observations about patriotism and religion in an egalitarian age: Attachment to country is a calculated judgment, not a passion, and religion is largely a moral teaching intended to put a damper on materialism. Neither has the character of an end in itself or a consummation, the proper domain of the noble or the heroic. Religious authority is undermined by reason, and government becomes the protector of private rights, not the school of public virtue. Fanaticism is, Rousseau and Tocqueville agree, a cruel and sanguinary disposition, an enemy of reason and of peace. But it is also frequently the cause of a self-forgetting and dedication absent in preservative and economic motives. It displays generosity and splendor. It is possessed of a poetic charm not present in dreary commercialism. The immediate consequence seen by Rousseau is that the love between man and woman must be preserved and encouraged, for it is the politically undangerous fanaticism that ennobles human beings and can, by way of the family, even strengthen the political order. It can be thought to be natural and healthy in a fuller sense than the other two, because it has a bodily base and a bodily fulfillment in sex. The further consequence is that sexual liberation, as opposed to religious and political liberation, must be combated in order to avoid the demystification of love, as God and country have been demystified. As faith had become superstition and fatherland the state, so love would become sex, and there would be nothing left to oppose the atomizing tendencies of egalitarianism. Love means the directedness of the two sexes to one another and their complementarity, so that a true unity can be achieved instead of the contractual and conditional connection of two like and selfish individuals.

As a consequence of such reflections, Rousseau put eroticism at the center of his thought, and these reflections provide the answer to the question of the unity of his writings, which appear to be divided between public and private, political and romantic works. The defectiveness of politics requires the supplement of love, and eros as the proper realm of imagination, idealism, and beauty reveals itself only by the demystification of the theological and political realms. What at first glance seems to be a disaster—the coming into being of that which Rousseau was the first to call "bourgeois" society—turns out to provide the opportunity to gain clarity on the human situation and to separate out its elements so that they may be harmoniously reordered. Thus the new political science, which was intended to be self-sufficient, was father to a new science of morals and a new aesthetics—noble interpretations of equality and freedom—providing for the full development of the human faculties. The sentimentality, romanticism, and idealism of Rousseau, which so infuriate latter-day Enlightenment rationalists and seem so far from the coolness and sobriety of Locke, are merely the result of thinking Locke through, especially the latter's comparative neglect or downplaying of sex and imagination. They must be given their due for the sake of preserving the political order and avoiding the impoverishment of man.

Hence Rousseau's novelistic works, **Emile, La Nouvelle Héloïse,** and **Confessions**—each of which is much longer than his primary political treatises, the two **Discourses** and the **Social Contract,** put together—constitute an attempt to establish what was missing in earlier democratic thinkers, a democratic art. He does for democracy what Socrates did for aristocracy in the *Republic.* The artistic need—which Rousseau understood to be related to the religious need—was unsatisfied in liberalism, with the attendant risk of either philistinism or the persistence of the influence of artistic forms and models drawn from the old tradition—biblical or Plutarchian—inappropriate to democratic life. Democracy requires democratic taste, for taste, much more than abstract principle, determines way of life and choice of pleasures and pains. There is the closest of links between taste and morals. In his **Letter to M. d'Alembert on the Theater** Rousseau criticizes the aristocratic and urban character of the theater as well as its bloated heroes, whose example has nothing to do with the lives democratic men lead. The novel, in the establishment

of which as *the* literary form in an egalitarian age Rousseau played a leading part, is better suited to democratic men. It is cheap and accessible everywhere, does not presuppose extensive and fixed periods of leisure, does not require participation in a public ritual where wealth and rank are on display, and is therefore not as necessarily allied with vanity and snobbism. Its personages can be people more like ourselves. The tedium of the daily life of democratic man, with its lack of splendid actions, can more appropriately find its place in a novel, and the cultivation of the private life and private sentiments are more satisfactorily depicted in it than on the stage. The joys of rusticity, the presence of nature, and the attachments of family belong especially to the novel. Good novels can be the constant, life-interpreting companions of men and women in regimes where communal sharing in the sublime has all but disappeared.

And the central theme of Rousseau's novels is the relations between men and women—love, marriage, children. *La Nouvelle Héloïse* is the archetype of the romantic novel; and **Emile,** the prototype of the *Bildungsroman,* is nothing but the education of a husband. One does not often imagine that the thoughts of Hobbes, Spinoza, Locke, and Hume were primarily occupied with sexual relations. Rousseau was the first of the modern philosophers to return to Plato's concern with eros. And the connection between this concern and art is evident. The love of the beautiful unites them. The early modern thinkers put their emphasis on fear of death as the fundamental motivation, and it is an individuating passion as well as one that looks to the ugliness of man's situation. The coupling passion become secondary if the passion that isolates the self is more powerful. The world that is devoted to avoiding death or providing comfortable preservation is prosaic. Rousseau was attempting to restore the Platonic eros for the beautiful on new grounds and, if not to render the world poetic again, at least to embellish its prose. The sexual fantasy and the perfect partner that it envisages is the natural base from which he begins. (pp. 69-74)

Men and women have to adapt themselves to one another because they must get sexual satisfaction and civilized human beings want willing partners. Traditionally, since it was women who put up the resistance and had to approve those who were attracted to them, men had to do and be what was necessary to gain a woman's consent. If women were promiscuous and lived in the atmosphere of a court, a man had to be of a different kind to succeed with them from the one who would appeal to chaste women desirous of a rustic and domestic life. The inner difference here can be measured by the distance between seduction and courtship. Whatever a man's public responsibilities or work, a large part of his most intimate private life, taste, and fantasy is involved with his sexual relations (unless sex is trivialized and made meaningless) and the demands his partners make on his character. If the two sides of his life do not cohere, both public and private suffer and regimes change. The private pleasures win out in the long run. Plato suggested that the austere, public-spirited Spartans secretly longed for voluptuous sexual satisfactions to which their lascivious women tempted them. Therefore Spartan virtue was forced and founded on repression rather than on love of virtue. The almost impossible task of harmonizing the public demands on the male warriors with what their attractions to women inclined them toward led Plato, or rather his Socrates in the *Republic,* to innovate and give women the same education and the same work as men. All the elements of liberation with which we are so familiar are found there—day-care centers, birth control, abortion, equal access to athletic facilities, along with less familiar items such as infanticide and nudity in common exercises. Sexual differentiation disappears and has no more significance than does the difference between the bald and the hairy. But this is done not in the name of women's rights but of what is needful for the community. (pp. 75-6)

Rousseau's analysis begins from Plato. He does not dispute the desirability of total dedication to and involvement with the community. Morality means self-overcoming in favor of the common good. His disagreement with Plato is about the natural desirability of the political order. Men care naturally about themselves in the first place, and Spartan civic virtue requires a "denaturing" of man both difficult to achieve and harsh on individuals. National attachment is both fanatic and abstract; there is no natural impulse toward the large community, which requires myths—that is, lies—to be believable and the rewards of which are honor and glory, imaginary and dangerous will-o'-the-wisps. Such a city is achieved at the cost of the sweetest natural pleasures—erotic satisfactions—and their associated natural sentiments, love of men and women for one another and love of children. The differences between the two kinds of relatedness is measured by the contrast between the overwhelming and also questionable passions of Plutarch's heroes, which make them capable of their political sacrifices, and the gentler, more common, and more effective motives for sacrifices on the part of men and women in love, and parents, the persons depicted in Tolstoy's novels, for example. Rousseau puts family where Plato put city, as the end for which other things are done and as the ground of relationships, partly because he lowered standards and expectations, partly because he saw in the former greater humanity. (pp. 76-7)

The family, in Rousseau's view, can be defended only if both men and women believe that it is the highest enterprise, more complete and more fulfilling than any career. The belief that being in love is very high and very important is not too difficult to encourage (although easy sex can deflate it). Against the background of love, the vocations tend to pale and appear as at best necessities. In love men and women do care for another, perhaps as much as they care for themselves. This care comes from within; it has a powerful bodily root and is clearly not a product of others' opinions. The difficulty is to extend this passion throughout a lifetime, to keep it singular as it necessarily is at its inception, and to make it culminate in the care of children. This requires education, morality, literature, and reasoning. Persuasion, which is not as powerful as love but in which certain human passions do cooperate—such as love of one's own and longing for immortality—can sometimes convince men and women that raising and educating children is a nobler activity than being a lawyer or a banker, so that those whose family responsibilities exclude them from such professions will not feel that they are maimed by the drudgery of domestic life. These two prerequisites—love of a sexual partner and involvement with children—together can contribute a substantial common good that solicits the individual members of the partnership. This is the only common good of which, according

to Rousseau, we know by nature and which is available to us modern men. All other collectivities are the result of force or the contingent private interests of individuals. To put it otherwise, earlier contract teachings provided only a negative motive for abandoning natural individual freedom to enter society—fear of death. Love provides a private motive, and one that does not treat other human beings as means but as ends in themselves. Sex is the only social, or sociable, impulse in man. All other natural impulses leave him isolated, even in the midst of his fellows.

Given the primacy of the family, finally to come to the point, the division of labor between man and woman, their different functions with respect to, and different contributions to, the common good become manifest again. The bodily difference is decisive here. The woman bears the children and nurses them. All the other differences are but corollaries of this first, bodily difference. All that is intolerable to contemporary sensibilities about Rousseau is connected with this point. He asserts that the difference between men and women is natural and that liberation from natural destiny, although surely possible, takes away all gravity from the beings thus liberated. And it is not his fault, Rousseau insists, that nature imposes very special responsibilities on a woman.

In sexual union a woman has two considerations—pleasure and the possibility of pregnancy—whereas a man has only one. Like it or not, the sexual act has far-reaching consequences for her which it does not have for a man. Naturally, without the mediation of law or education, she must make do for herself and for her child. Whatever help she gets comes from the free choice of others, whereas she is constrained by natural necessity. Very simply, it is up to her to constitute the family and hold it together. She must be the one who keeps the man and makes him into a father. Law, once constituted and enforced, can help her, but law will be effective only when it is supported by the inclinations. When men no longer wish to remain with women, they will abandon them and their children. This is still the case even today, when, with the burgeoning divorce rate and enlightenment about men's responsibilities, 90 percent of children remain with their mothers when the parents separate. And this is no accident, as Rousseau sees it, for women have a natural tie to children. They bear them, they nurse them, they are certain they are theirs, and they seem to have an instinctive attachment to children, even to the point of risking their lives for their sake. This is the only natural social bond Rousseau is able to discern. Men will die for their countries or for the women they love, but this sacrifice is not natural or instinctive. It is the product of education and imagination. Naturally men do not have a country and women are not loved in any way other than as means of bodily gratification. At the real foundations, the sole impulse of sociality is that of mother toward child, and all the other seminatural and healthy kinds of sociality cluster around this one. The unit composed of mother and child is the building block out of which society can be constructed. Otherwise only individual self-interest—which means, practically, fear or gain—remains to motivate human beings. The mother's sentiments are the only example we have of unambiguously selfless ones, and these sentiments must be made use of if society is to have an admixture of real concern for others as ends in themselves. In short, women are the link between fathers and children. They are involved with both, and by way of the father's involvement with and faith in the mother, he can become attached to the children, because he loves the mother and because he believes the children are his. Thus the women are the principle of sociality, and it is their responsibility to bring the elements together. Love and motherhood are their domain. (pp. 78-80)

Rousseau argues that it is precisely owing to sentiments of social respect for and duty toward women and men become gentle, humane, civil, and responsible to others. The fact that women need protection and men feel they owe it to them is a powerful form of relatedness. Take such sentiments away, by persuading men that they should not feel them or by making women independent, and what takes their place in human relatedness? If the gentlemen on the *Titanic* do not believe that ladies, deserving special consideration, should be the first to leave the ship, then it is every person for him- or herself. The untrustworthiness of protectiveness, or of men in general, does not constitute a refutation of Rousseau. If men sometimes do behave like gentlemen, it is morally good for them to do so and beneficial to women, particularly if nothing else adequately protects them. It is the mutual dependence of men and women that ties them together. If women do not need men, and men are emotionally and legally able to avoid responsibilities that are always painful and are now made utterly unattractive, men and women will always be psychologically ready for separation and will separate at the first difficulty. A man betrayed and a woman abandoned have always been particularly pitiable, but a world in which neither can happen because neither party really needs or cares for the other would be an abomination of isolation and separateness.

Rousseau's romantic prescriptions may appear to modern eyes to be merely a reaffirmation of age-old sex "roles," but he actually is engaged in a revolutionary reconstitution of the relation between the sexes in the light of the new science of man. Against the background of the abstractness of individual rights, he tries to introduce a sentiment of—not a reasoning about—naturalness which provides real guidance in life. The goodness of nature and its permanence, as opposed to the artificiality of the life created by the conquest of nature with its quest for power after power without being able to generate goals for the attainment of which that power is to be used, is Rousseau's theme, and it has enjoyed an enduring success in back-to-nature and environmentalist movements. It is only the highest expression of that theme, back to the nature of man and woman, which has evoked a negative response in recent times. Rousseau introduced feeling as the counterpoise to calculating reason, which discards such considerations if they do not contribute to economic benefit. In his thought, love of the country tempers conquest of nature, compassion tempers exploitation of men, and eros tempers selfishness or individualism. Recognition and rediscovery of feeling, letting it act as the first principle of action, reconstitutes the world of meaning which modern science and philosophy has dissolved. Thus Rousseau's treatment of love and marriage concentrates not on the rational ordering of the household and the appropriateness of the partners for their common business but on the inclination of the man and woman for one another. . . . [Rousseau] holds that duty can be derived only from prior inclination; the ends of marriage flow from the beginnings in passion. Without such beginnings, there is no sub-

stance, no inner vitality in the institution. Love is the root that provides the life to the plant. Without nourishment from it, the plant cannot flourish and grow. The delicate structure of Rousseau's erotic teaching is meant to found the family in all its ramifications without the imposition of alien and alienating law. As the modern state was intended to derive all its force and functions from the primary, natural passion of fear, so Rousseau attempted to found a new kind of family corresponding to and corrective of that state, deriving its force and functions from the sexual passion. Natural freedom comes first; duty is derivative and is assented to in order to exercise the freedom effectively. And just as Rousseau's predecessors, Hobbes and Locke, had to remind their readers that, with conventions stripped away, fear and the quest for well-being are natural and powerful, so Rousseau had to remind his readers that sex is natural, attractive, and good. Hobbes and Locke adopted a powerful rhetoric about the unattractive character of the state of nature to reconcile men to the civil state. Rousseau founds a rhetoric about eros to attract men and women to the married state. He is the first philosopher to collaborate with the illusions of love, because they produce a more sublime sense of duty than do the realities of the modern state. This is another perspective on why Rousseau had to write novels. The game of love takes on social and political significance, and men and women must recover their capacity to feel. Nature recaptured gives witness to the sexual attraction of men and women to each other and their mutual differences in possible unity. Sex, far from being sinful, is one of the tiny number of truly natural rights. Actually Rousseau's concentration on the right of following sexual feeling has been adopted by almost everyone, even though his elaboration on its concomitant duties has been rejected.

Rousseau's central reform in the relation between the sexes is an attempt to conciliate nature and freedom by giving women the absolute right to choose their husbands, emancipating them from the authority of their parents. . . . A woman who has chosen her lot is not just a plaything of authority. She finds dignity in her moral self-esteem even when events disappoint her hopes. All of this applies to a man, too, but to a lesser degree. Woman's morality is the legislative principle of the family and the society of families. There is more possible suffering in her lot but also more nobility. Thus Rousseau makes freedom the continuing foundation of the family, and equality in free choice does not require the homogenization of unlike beings. (pp. 81-5)

The issue is not merely marriage but human freedom and morality itself. Sexual conduct is for Rousseau the crucial case proving whether or not human beings can convert natural freedom into moral freedom. Natural freedom means the absence of external impediments, particularly those provided by other human beings, to fulfilling one's desires. But these desires are not freely chosen. They happen to one. And in that sense one is as much a slave to natural lust as are brutes. Only if one can control those desires, not simply by other, more powerful desires but in the name of the good or the ideal, can one make the claim to specifically human dignity, which means autonomy or self-legislation, emancipated from God, nature, or the human law made by others, from heteronomy or alienation. In other words, is man capable of will and hence does he possess human dignity? Rousseau's definition of human freedom is obedience to a law one sets for oneself. With sex he tries to indicate how this is possible or to illustrate the formation of the will. (p. 85)

The promise made in marriage, which both parties presumably second with their sexual desire, must be able to survive the change in that desire. Otherwise the promise is nothing but animal sexual desire masquerading as morality in order to fulfill its end. Rousseau finds that sex is the only one of the natural desires that might possibly produce this conversion—truly pointed toward another, powerful, and capable of producing sublime objects. Experience of the heroism of lovers distinguishes sex from hunger as an ideal force. This is the natural way to love another as oneself.

Love is Rousseau's solution to the problem of establishing a non-mercenary morality within the context of rational liberalism. From this first obligation flow all the others—to children, to the civil society that protects the family. Modern regimes understand themselves to be founded by a contract. The contract as presented by its teachers is purely negative, joined in because, without the state's power, the life of natural freedom is too precarious. This is an unsociable sociability and one not sufficient to make the social contract sacred or to justify the sacrifice of life to it. No other contract carries with it the requirement that one die in fulfilling it. Naturally only the marriage contract is positive, made not only for the individual benefit of those who enter into it, and is felt to demand, in case of need, the supreme sacrifice. Rousseau makes the sexual contract into the essence of the social contract in order to provide society with a positive impulse. Marriage is the

contract of contracts, and, if this one can be fulfilled in good faith, so can the others that can be made to be derivative from it. A family man can be said to be moral for good reason as an individual cannot, and marriage is something almost all men and women must face. It does not have the abstract character of modern politics, where moral obligation has no real contact with everyday life and concerns people one has never met. The pleasures and duties of marriage are truly lived. (p. 86)

Rousseau saw something miraculous in sex. Body can become spirit. Seminal effervescence becomes creativity in animating the imagination. He was among the earliest thinkers, if he was not himself the earliest, to see in this creativity, as opposed to reason, the specific difference of man. The beautiful object that solicits desire and leads it upward is the creation of man the artist. This beautiful ideal forms in turn a model of behavior with respect to itself which is the final cause of noble behavior. The work of art both imitates and encourages such behavior. The beautiful and the moral are inseparable. Rousseauan morals, aesthetics, and psychology are the grandest description of the sublime and sublimation in an egalitarian society that needs both while threatening both. We need him, if only for fear that we forget the very question. (pp. 87-8)

Allan Bloom, "Rousseau on the Equality of the Sexes," in Justice and Equality Here and Now, *edited by Frank S. Lucash, Cornell University Press, 1986, pp. 68-88.*

Peter Gay   (essay date 1987)

[*A German-born American, Gay is a social historian who has written numerous essays and books on the Enlightenment, nineteenth-century middle-class culture, and the arts and politics of Imperial and Weimar Germany. In the following excerpt, he examines the complexities of* The Social Contract, *noting that it is "at once a most abstruse and a most personal exploration of the question of authority."*]

[Rousseau,] the proud "citizen of Geneva," dedicated his second discourse to his native city-state. And a few years later, as he meditated on the political treatise that was to become the *Social Contract,* it was Genevan society, Genevan scenes, Genevan political controversies, as he recalled and reshaped them in the urgency of intellectual creation, that dominated his mind. His celebrated assault on representation in the *Social Contract* is a striking instance of how much Geneva was on his mind as he laid down principles he proclaimed to be universally valid. It was with the pride of a Genevan that he loaded the English political system with contumely: "The English people believes itself to be free. It is greatly mistaken; it is free only during the election of the members of Parliament. Once they are elected, the populace is enslaved; it is nothing." Then a parting shot: "the use the English people makes of that freedom in the brief moments of its liberty certainly warrants its losing it." Certainly its first readers had no difficulty tracing the arguments, the whole tenor of the *Social Contract,* to its Genevan roots. Voltaire, then resident there and passionately meddling in local politics, took it to be a blatant intervention in the domestic constitutional struggles then at a feverish pitch. And when the Genevan Council of Twenty-Five condemned the *Social*

Thérèse Levasseur, Rousseau's wife, in 1791.

Contract in June 1762, its principal reason was the same: in his plaidoyer, Geneva's attorney-general, Jean-Robert Tronchin, cited numerous passages as proof that Rousseau was retailing rebellious notions that had been circulating in his republic since the beginning of the eighteenth century. Tronchin greatly underrated both the originality of the *Social Contract* and Rousseau's gift for synthesis. But in *placing* the governing fantasies of the work he was perceptive and largely right.

"Geneva," of course, meant more to Rousseau than a political style by which other political styles could be measured. It was, for him, a place of cherished recollections, the city where he had first encountered the Greek and Roman classics and had encountered them—note well—among his father's books. Plutarch, he was to say years later, "was the first reading of my childhood; it will be the last reading of my old age." His highly selective and tendentious classicism, as the *Confessions* leave no doubt, was indeed mingled with his first memories. To him, the best of good societies would always be a republic unfettered by a hereditary aristocracy. "Ceaselessly occupied with Rome and Athens; living, so to speak, with their great men, myself born Citizen of a Republic, and son of a father whose patriotism was his strongest passion, I took fire from his example; I thought myself Greek or Roman; I became the personage whose life I was reading." As passages in the *Social Contract* testify, he was enough of a relativist—the disciple of Montesquieu in this matter as in others—to see the possibility of freedom in moderate aristocracies or elective monarchies. But his ultimate preference was for a Geneva purified, the Geneva in his fertile mind.

And "Geneva" also implied a powerful incentive toward a certain religious style. Rousseau's native city was, of course, a Calvinist stronghold—the very home of Calvinism. And while secular doctrines of the Enlightenment had invaded cultivated circles in Geneva, the Calvinist atmosphere remained a palpable legacy even among Voltaire's sophisticated Genevan friends. And this is the atmosphere that pervades Rousseau's thinking. He was never an orthodox believer; never a good Calvinist, never a good Catholic. As a mature thinker, he adopted the deism current among the *philosophes* of his time: the doctrine that a beneficient god had created the world with its laws and then withdrawn from it to leave virtuous men to discover its moral rules and live according to its dictates. It is not an accident that Voltaire, the arch-deist who had little use for Rousseau, should applaud Rousseau's deistic **"Profession of Faith of the Savoyard Vicar,"** that long set-piece he placed into his *Emile.* Rousseau therefore responded not to the Christian theology associated with Calvin's name, but to what I would call its moral energy, its gospel of usefulness and simplicity, its call for self-discipline and virtue, and its austerity. That classical philosophical doctrines—especially Stoicism, which had some significant affinities with this Calvinist posture—also appealed to Rousseau, only wove Calvinist earnestness all the more inextricably into the texture of his thought. This—shall I call it Stoical Calvinism—probably emerges most aggressively in Rousseau's *Lettre à d'Alembert sur les spectacles* of 1758, in which he vehemently rejected d'Alembert's playful proposal that the Genevan republic admit a theatre within its borders. The suggestion, as his heated prose shows, hit Rousseau at a sensitive spot: it struck him as a perilous invitation to immorality, an offensive defiance of prized Genevan virtue.

In the diatribe he addressed to d'Alembert, Rousseau's virtuous austerity descends into plain philistinism: in the *Social Contract,* it serves the ideal of education: and that is why the *Social Contract* and *Emile* belong together. Yet a third work of this period, the epistolary novel *La nouvelle Héloïse,* published in 1761, is intimately related to his political masterpiece, and helps to clarify his political theory further.

The relevance of *La nouvelle Héloïse* to the *Social Contract* is not immediately apparent. Its hero, Saint-Preux, a striving, intelligent bourgeois, finds that the beautiful aristocratic Julie, whose tutor he is, has fallen in love with him; this bold though eminently virtuous girl first seduces and then dismisses him, and eventually chooses to marry an elderly, unemotional but highly eligible atheist, Wolmar. Even though her marriage is happy, blessed with children, money, local good works, and endless opportunities for self-examination and self-expression, Julie never forgets her first lover. But, though Saint-Preux returns and reawakens old temptations, she does not succumb to his charm but dies, in her accustomed self-sacrificing way, after saving one of her children from drowning. This allows her survivors to worship her as a secular saint. In portraying the idyllic little community that Julie and Wolmar govern with a light hand, superintending honest toil and decent festivals, and in permitting Julie to probe her moral and erotic condition in interminable exchanges with an understanding correspondent, Rousseau celebrates the virtues of candor, maturity, simplicity, self-restraint, good health, reason warmed by love and love ennobled by reason. The ethical religion which the leading characters explore with considerable gusto in *La nouvelle Héloïse* reads like the application of the **"Profession of Faith of the Savoyard Vicar,"** while the social, cultural, economic, and implicitly political Utopia as well as the pedagogic practice in the novel, foreshadow the rest of *Emile.* The implicit, sometimes explicit message of *La nouvelle Héloïse* is that men and women must make themselves over if they are to be worthy of true self-government.

Emile gives this ideal its theoretical underpinning. It is only fitting that contemporaries should have thought the book a novel; its time of publication just a year after *La nouvelle Héloïse,* its free use of dialogue and interpolated stories, and the artificial environment in which Emile grows up, made *Emile* seem a work of the imagination. So it is, but its severely chronological structure, its coherent argument, and its polemical drive, make it the most radical educational treatise possible—radical in the original sense of the term: a treatise reaching down to the roots of man. Modern society, as Rousseau had already insisted at length in his discourses, is so corrupt and so unnatural that only a fundamental upheaval in the formation of human beings can make man truly human.

While *Emile* is substantial, its governing idea is simple. It is not just kindness to the young: that was not an invention of Rousseau's but can be found in earlier pedagogic treatises including John Locke's *Some Thoughts Concerning Education,* of which Rousseau thought highly. It is kindness with a purpose. Rousseau, the amateur of ancient philosophy, wanted children educated in obedience to the Stoical doctrine that man must live in accord with nature.

The consequences of applying this maxim to the training of the young are far-reaching: the child may be father to the man, but he is a child first. Others, to be sure, had claimed to know this; Locke had said as much in his book on education. But nobody had seriously pursued the implications of this saying. Rousseau now spelled out in detail precisely what it meant in practice. The educator must closely consult the child's capacities and use them to help him grow. Rote learning and forced reading are nonsensical: they make the child into a parrot, not a man. Even reasoning with the young, though superficially kind, is at best futile and in effect cruel. For reason is the last capacity of the human animal to awaken; it should therefore be the last to be brought into action. It is absurd to make the child learn geography from books or maps; make him ramble across rivers and meadows, teach him to keep his eyes open as he walks; set him adrift on purpose to teach him how to find his way: *that* is the only road to geography. And other disciplines must be acquired in the same practical and memorable way. Young Emile, Rousseau says emphatically, needs not "words, more words, still more words," but "things, things!" Rousseau was the Bacon of education. Only the educator who enters emphatically into the nature of the growing child's development and the range of his experience can lastingly enrich him.

While young Emile comes to reading late, this is not anti-intellectualism on Rousseau's part, though in the hands of Rousseau's belated followers, modern Progressive educators, it was often to become just that. It is, rather, a perfectly logical inference from his developmental scheme. Emile will begin to read when he is ready for it, at fifteen, and his first book will be the bible of the self-reliant, *Robinson Crusoe.* But practicality is not all there is to learning, even for Emile; in adolescence, Emile will discover, and love, history and biography and, by the time he is twenty, the Latin classics. A surprising agenda, but not a reading list for philistines.

This timetable is more than a pedagogic procedure designed to have Emile remember what he has learned. It embodies a cultural criticism and a cultural ideal. Since Emile's tutor discountenances pretty ways, conventional lies, impressive displays of erudition, his charge will grow up not with a false "civilized" facade, but with all the marks of authenticity. He will be confident but not conceited, discriminating but not snobbish, rational but not cold, self-reliant but not self-centered; he will be sound in mind and body alike, honest, affectionate, and disinterested. And to be disinterested means to be public-spirited. Emile will be the one kind of adult, in short, who can make the good community of Rousseau's *Social Contract* work. The immoral society of his day was making immoral men, incapable of reforming a culture in whose corruption they could not help but connive. Hence they were compelled to perpetuate that which they should destroy. The one way to break this impasse was to create a new man who could, in turn, create a new society. It is an essential precondition for this work that the young must be rapidly removed from corrupting influences: that is why Rousseau has his tutor live in isolation with his little charge.

The link between Rousseau's *Emile* and *Social Contract* should be obvious. Each requires the other. The makers and beneficiaries of the general will, which, Rousseau insists, is always right, are a gathering of Emiles. If man is born free yet is everywhere in chains, who but an Emile can do the work of liberation?

Once the community of Emiles has been formed, it will govern itself calmly, wisely, and generously. The key element in the citizen's activity is his participation in decision-making, and as a sound citizen he will cast his vote by listening not to his own selfish interests, but to his perception of the public weal. Of course, with the best of intentions, he may confound the two. But then the decision of the majority—not just any majority, but the intelligent, sensible, uncorrupted majority that Rousseau envisions—will recall the straying minority to its duty, to its true, larger interest. The closer private wills, as Rousseau puts it, approximate the general will, the more likely can that will realize itself in action. In a word, Rousseau seeks the virtuous citizen, who will, as he puts it in the *Social Contract,* "make virtue reign."

Rousseau's *Social Contract,* then, is a complex personal document drawing on all his experience and obliquely addressing his deepest problems, but it also forms a link in the great chain of treatises in political theory that began with Plato's *Republic.* Such treatises are about many things—the best form of government, the origins of the state, the place of religion in the polity, the relation of morals to laws, the interaction between legislature and executive. And Rousseau's *Social Contract* is about all these matters. But above all it is about the fundamental question agitating all political thinkers: that of authority. The question for the individual has always been: Why, and whom, should I obey? It is not simply a political question or, rather, the political question is a familial question writ large. It is a question the child may never consciously ask, but it is lodged somewhere in his mind. It is a question that the slave, or the subject wholly habituated to unconditional obedience, may never seriously canvass, but it will occur to him in rebellious moments. Rousseau raises the question again, and answers it in a wholly original way.

The liberals of Rousseau's time, and those both before and after him, had sought to delimit the respective boundaries of freedom and constraint, giving freedom as much scope as seemed reasonable. And Rousseau, like them, attempts to establish the respective rights of the sovereign and the citizen. But he goes further. He sees this tension not as a relation to be mapped, but as a paradox to be resolved. In Rousseau's version of the *Social Contract,* man surrenders all his rights without becoming a slave. This is how he formulates the problem: "To find a form of association which defends and protects with the whole common power the person and property of each associate, and in which each, uniting himself to all, yet obeys himself alone, and remains as free as before." As one reflects on Rousseau's earlier writings, notably the discourses, one recognizes that the "one principle" which he professed had always guided him, is at work once again, on a larger stage. Man is good. And he can afford to exchange his natural for his civic freedom, to translate his original goodness into social action. Rousseau, we must remember, was not a primitivist; he did not condemn all organized society, and he believed that there was one society, one yet to be constructed, that was infinitely preferable to prepolitical conditions. Man can surrender his natural freedom because, while he becomes a subject, he remains a master. In the good community he essentially obeys himself.

This position, which Rousseau works out in considerable detail in the *Social Contract,* is certainly not without its difficulties. But one difficulty, imported by critics into Rousseau's text, is not there, and we may therefore dismiss it quickly: the state, in Rousseau's system, is never the master, always the servant. For the body to which the individual yields his natural rights is not the government but society—a community of beings like himself. Just as Rousseau insisted that force does not create rights, so he insists that government, though it holds the monopoly of force, is always an agent of the citizens it protects.

Another difficulty, though, that surrounding Rousseau's civil religion, is a real stumbling block for the modern reader. Rousseau was, as a true *philosophe,* anticlerical. And he had particular reasons, implicit in his political philosophy, for inveighing against clerical establishments: he vehemently opposed any associations, lay or clerical, that might impose obligations on individuals and thus divide their loyalties. Rousseau's good society needed all of the citizen. At the same time, Rousseau, again with the *philosophes* on this point, thought that men require the prod and the curb of religion to assure their moral conduct. This notion was a commonplace among the men of the Enlightenment, though just what kind of frightening superstitions enlightened rulers should inculcate in their subjects to keep them docile was a matter of earnest debate and real uncertainty. Voltaire, for one, believed that thoughtful men did not need any superstition whatever; even if they should fall into the error of atheism they would not surrender to a life of self-indulgence or crime. It was different with illiterate laborers or peasants: freed from the spectre of eternal divine punishment, they might well take to stealing and murdering. Yet some *philosophes,* at least, were so implacably hostile to the superstitions which, in their view, all organized religions professed, that they were willing to take their chances with the truth, and leave the securing of society to the police.

Rousseau took part in this debate, and, as his chapter on the civil religion, added to the *Social Contract* late, reveals, was torn by it. On the one hand, he wanted no part of intolerance, of persecutions, of lying. On the other hand, he was convinced, as I have said, that men—all men—must have some religious beliefs that would make, and keep, them moral beings. This meant that the sovereign of the good society must devise "a purely civil profession of faith, the articles of which it belongs to the sovereign to establish, not exactly as dogmas of religion, but as sentiments of sociability, without which it is impossible to be a good citizen or a faithful subject." The dogmas should be simple and few in number, including belief in the existence of a powerful, intelligent, beneficent deity, a life to come, the good fortune of the just and the punishment of the wicked, the sacredness of the social contract and of the laws. Whoever does not believe these dogmas can be banished from the state, and whoever has officially subscribed to them and then acts as if he does not believe in them should be put to death.

This harsh set of propositions is not a casual or accidental addition to Rousseau's political thinking; it lies squarely at the heart of his earnest Calvinist commitment to virtue. And as the reader of his *Social Contract,* with all its imaginativeness, all its rich panoply of ideas, must recognize, the dictatorship of virtue is a strenuous and in many ways a dangerous ideal. (pp. xi-xvii)

> *Peter Gay, in an introduction to* Basic Political Writings, *edited and translated by Donald A. Cress, Hackett Publishing Company, 1987, pp. vii-xvii.*

Christopher Kelly   (essay date 1987)

[*In the following excerpt, Kelly examines Rousseau's objectives in writing his* Confessions.]

The success of Rousseau's *Confessions* must be judged in relation to each of his objects in writing the work. Rousseau's treatment of the genre of lives and his explicit statements about the *Confessions* reveal three different goals. First, Rousseau presents a moral fable. This image of human experience is meant to form certain feelings in readers in order to change the way they experience their lives. Second, Rousseau gives a philosophic account of human nature by showing its modifications in a uniquely revealing example. Third, Rousseau reveals the epistemological underpinnings for his "system" by showing how it is possible for a civilized human to acquire knowledge of human nature. To these goals of Rousseau, the author of the *Confessions,* can be added the goal of Jean-Jacques, the protagonist of the *Confessions*—to cure his civilized corruption and to return to a quasi-natural condition of wholeness.

Jean-Jacques's project shows the way to evaluate Rousseau's goals. One can address the epistemological issue by considering how Jean-Jacques acquires his knowledge of nature and how this knowledge affects him. One can arrive at the account of human nature by seeing how naturalness is lost in an individual and whether some approximation of naturalness can be recovered by an extraordinary individual in unusual circumstances. One can identify the substance of Rousseau's moral fable by reflecting on the general image of human experience given in the account of Jean-Jacques's life.

Before appraising the *Confessions* on these issues, we should consider Rousseau's own testimony. . . . [The] enigmatic conclusion of the work does not, in itself, prove that Rousseau considered the *Confessions* a failure. To that argument, based largely on evidence within the text, can be added the evidence of Rousseau's efforts to preserve the work by depositing copies with several guardians. In addition, Rousseau writes his last work, the *Reveries,* as if the reader is familiar with the contents of the *Confessions.* It is indisputable that Rousseau regarded the *Confessions* as worthy of preservation, if not as a complete success.

It must be admitted, however, that the existence of the subsequent autobiographical works and the absence of the promised Part Three of the *Confessions* testify to reservations on Rousseau's part. In both the *Dialogues* and *Reveries* he discusses the reasons for these new excursions in autobiography and for his use of very different formats. In his preface to the *Dialogues,* "On the Subject and Form of This Writing," Rousseau distinguishes between his new work and the *Confessions:* "As for those who wish only an agreeable and rapid reading, those who have sought, who have found only that in my *Confessions,* who cannot suffer a little fatigue, or sustain a coherent attention for the interest of justice and truth, they will do well to spare themselves the boredom of this reading. Far from seeking to please them, I will avoid at least this final indignity that the tableau of the miseries of my life might be an object of amusement for anyone". This statement is more a criticism of some readers of the *Confessions* than it is of the work itself. Rousseau argues that those who read the *Confessions* only as an agreeable work have missed its point. To the extent that this is a criticism of the *Confessions* itself, it implies that Rousseau made it too easy for the reader to read for pleasure rather than understanding. The very title of the *Dialogues, Rousseau Judges Jean-Jacques,* shows his disappointment in the audience of the *Confessions.* The title implies that rather than playing the role of subservient confessor to an audience of judges, Rousseau now undertakes to educate his audience about how they should act as his judges. Thus the *Dialogues* can be regarded as a manual for the readers of the *Confessions.* Once they have learned from Rousseau how to judge Jean-Jacques, readers can read the *Confessions* properly. Whatever defects the *Confessions* may have from being too agreeable can be overcome by the more fatiguing *Dialogues.*

The criticism of the *Confessions* found in the *Reveries* is more damaging. The first reference to the *Confessions* occurs in the First Walk. After describing his hopes for the *Dialogues* and the shattering of these hopes, Rousseau describes his new position: "Nothing remains for me to hope or to fear any longer in this world, and here I am tranquil at the bottom of the abyss, a poor unfortunate mortal, but impassive like God himself". This description represents the attainment of the condition Jean-Jacques strives for in the *Confessions.* Thus it is fitting that Rousseau continues, "It is in this state that I again take up the continuation of the severe and sincere examination that I previously called my *Confessions.*" This statement shows the continuity between the *Confessions* and the *Reveries.* The latter work is the continuation or sequel (*suite*) of the former. This statement, however, also reveals an important change. Although there is a continuity between the two works in that each is a "severe and sincere" self-examination, the continuation is no longer called a confession. It is not a confession because it is not directed at a divine or human judge. Rousseau's assessment of the failure of the *Dialogues* entails the judgment that it is impossible to educate the public about how to judge him. Thus the position of the audience moves from judge (or confessor) in the *Confessions,* to pupil in the *Dialogues,* and then to nothing in the *Reveries.* Rousseau says that he will converse with his soul rather than with any particular audience of other people. This is the necessary result of the abandonment of hope and fear. He ceases to have any relations with others. The *Confessions* begins by asking God to assemble an audience for Rousseau. The *Reveries* begins by declaring quasi-divine independence from his audience.

From the perspective of this argument, the *Confessions* is simultaneously necessary and dispensable for the *Reveries.* It is necessary in that Rousseau could not achieve the position of divine impassivity without having gone through the experiences of the *Confessions.* The *Confessions* is dispensable because once these experiences have been undergone and transcended they need not be repeat-

ed or remembered. Among the dispensable aspects of the *Confessions* is its author's desire to write for, or confess to, an audience. To the extent that the *Reveries* is the goal toward which the *Confessions* moves, it is a continuation of the earlier work, but as a goal that has been attained, it transcends that work altogether. Thus, after explaining the difference between the two books, Rousseau loosens the connection between them. Instead of calling the *Reveries* a continuation of the *Confessions,* he finally decides, "These pages can be regarded then as an appendix of my *Confessions*". An appendix both is and is not a part of the book it accompanies.

Thus, in the *Reveries,* although he expresses certain reservations about the *Confessions,* Rousseau does not precisely reject the earlier work. From the perspective of his new state of impassivity, the *Confessions* has lost much of its importance for him. The earlier work retains, however, its importance for the reader of the *Reveries* who wishes to understand Rousseau's progress toward that state. The same point can be put somewhat differently in terms of structure. The *Confessions* proceeds chronologically, the *Reveries* does not. In the *Confessions* Rousseau wishes to reveal an ordered chain of sentiments. In the *Reveries* he wishes to "apply the barometer" to his soul at different distinct moments. These projects can be approached in their own terms without the second constituting a rejection of the first.

Rousseau turns his attention to the *Confessions* at one other place in the *Reveries*—the discussion of truthfulness, lying, and moral fables in the Fourth Walk. In Chapter 1, I argue that Rousseau both qualifies his claim that the *Confessions* is a simply factual report and substitutes the standards of general and moral truth for factual truth. In the Fourth Walk Rousseau refers to three sorts of lies he might be accused of committing in the *Confessions:* lies in interpreting the significance of facts, lies in adding to the facts, and lies of omission. His ultimate evaluation of the *Confessions* is found in his analysis of these possible accusations.

With regard to the first sort of lie, Rousseau admits a degree of guilt. He says that at times he may have accused himself "with too much severity." After making this admission, he dismisses its significance because it compromises his openness very little. With regard to the second sort of lie, Rousseau admits that he has practiced it but denies that it constitutes a crime. None of his embellishments or additions have violated the truth; they have merely given it charm. Of this sort of departure from the truth he concludes, "I am wrong to call it a lie." These two types of lie have no effect whatsoever on the success of the *Confessions.*

The third sort of lie is more serious. Rousseau says that he omitted from the *Confessions* stories that would have shown his "happy qualities." To illustrate and correct this omission, he tells two stories about incidents in his childhood in which he lied to protect friends from punishment that they would have incurred for injuring him. The focus of these stories is Rousseau's compassion, which is remarkable in that these are cases in which he himself has been injured. He feels compassion for the pain that the sight of his suffering inflicts on the people who cause it. These stories about Rousseau's failure to accuse when he could have done so with justice balance to a degree his story about the false accusation of Marion. Accordingly, they remedy a slight but real defect in the *Confessions.*

A second aspect of these stories is that they show Rousseau as a liar as well as a compassionate boy. In relating the incidents, Rousseau drops his normal motto, *"Vitam impendere vero"* (To stake one's life on the truth), and adopts the new motto, *"Magnanima menzogna! or quando e il vero / Si bello che si possa a te preporre?"* (Magnanimous lie! what truth could be so beautiful as to be preferred to you). Thus, while accusing himself of lying in the *Confessions,* Rousseau corrects the lie by adding two true stories and disposes of the accusation by using these stories to defend magnanimous lies. In the end he appears to excuse the *Confessions* as much as he accuses it.

These last words of Rousseau's on the *Confessions* are a dazzling display of the complex relations among factual truth, moral truth, and philosophic truth. They reopen the question of whether the *Confessions* succeeded in combining these forms, but they do not answer it. They are a powerful warning to Rousseau's readers not to dismiss or accept his claims unreflectively, an invitation to a cautious attempt to appraise Rousseau's success in each of his goals for the *Confessions.*

Rousseau's system is based on the assertion that man is naturally good and has been corrupted by society. This assertion entails a claim that the scientific progress on which humans pride themselves moves them further and further from the experience of their own nature. Thus Rousseau asserts a more or less radical split between civilized self-consciousness and knowledge of the natural condition. If this split were complete, Rousseau's system might be true but he could not know it. For him, or anyone else, to become aware of this split, he must have overcome it at least in his own consciousness. The *Confessions* is in part the story of how someone learns about the split between nature and convention.

The decisive moments in the account of Jean-Jacques's rediscovery of nature occur in Books VII and VIII. Prior to this point Rousseau has shown his education leading him away from nature. This is true, not only in the general sense that his imagination is becoming more active, but also in the specific way his vanity takes on a desire for public distinction. His absorption in the opinion of others turns him toward the conventions of society and away from the question of their foundation in nature. The period at les Charmettes narrated in Book VI is only an apparent and temporary exception to this rule of departure from nature. For the brief period of his illness, Jean-Jacques is cured of his vanity and other artificial sentiments. He lives like a natural man, however, both in lacking these sentiments and in failing to understand the significance of this lack. He lives in a quasi-natural condition but has no awareness of its naturalness. One could say that only the Rousseau at the end of the *Confessions* is capable of describing the happiness of Jean-Jacques at this period. Jean-Jacques feels it, but he does not understand it.

Only in his encounter with Zulietta in Book VII is Jean-Jacques confronted with the question of the relations among social institutions, his imagination, and nature. Zulietta's social condition is in marked contrast to her natural beauty and to Jean-Jacques's image of her. For the first time, Rousseau presents himself as being struck by a

disproportion among the three factors of nature, convention, and imagination. The case of Zulietta is too personal to resolve this issue, but it leaves Jean-Jacques in a condition of troublesome doubt which makes him receptive to the discovery of its general resolution.

This discovery comes in Book VIII with the famous "illumination," or inspiration, on the road to Vincennes. This experience, which gives birth to Rousseau's system, has both rational and arbitrary aspects. Jean-Jacques's rediscovery of nature is rational and conscious in that it is the result of reflection on the specific question posed by the Academy of Dijon, "Has the restoration of the sciences and arts tended to purify morals?" Because of the rational form of the question, it is logically possible that someone other than Rousseau might answer it correctly. It is equally possible that Jean-Jacques himself might develop his system on presentation of a different question, such as "What is the origin of inequality among men; and is it authorized by natural law?" According to this view, the circumstances of Jean-Jacques's reading of a particular question are merely occasional causes that could be replaced by any number of others. As Diderot explained years later when asked about his role in the composition of the *First Discourse,* "If the impertinent question of Dijon had not been proposed, would Rousseau have been less capable of writing his discourse?" Thus, to be rationally intelligible, Rousseau's system must be independent of the circumstances of its discovery.

At the same time, Rousseau consistently emphasizes the accidental character of the discovery, as if it could have been avoided altogether. There is the accident of reading the proposed question. There is the accident of Jean-Jacques's encounter with Zulietta, which puts him in a condition of openness to the discovery of his system. There is the accident of his unique character and education, which makes him react to Zulietta in a singular way. Rousseau presents the discovery of his system as contingent on a whole series of accidents. Although certain purely rational factors such as regular discussions with Condillac and Diderot contribute to his discovery, they do not sufficiently explain it according to Rousseau's own account.

To emphasize the arbitrary, accidental character of Jean-Jacques's discovery may seem to undermine its validity, but Rousseau argues the opposite. If his system is correct in asserting that civilized humans are radically removed from naturalness, the rediscovery of nature must depend on a fortunate or fateful accident rather than systematic thought alone. Some of Rousseau's writings can be understood as attempts to precipitate such fateful accidents in his readers. To be sure, not all readers can be convinced. Each reader who is convinced must have been predisposed to the discovery by one Zulietta or another. Again, while this might be regarded as reducing Rousseau's system to psychological factors alone, it can also be viewed as a declaration of the truth of his argument.

In the terms in which the *Confessions* presents it, the epistemological foundation of the discovery of nature must retain this ambiguity. The nature of Rousseau's system does not allow him to present it as the necessary outcome of every course of reflection. Accordingly, he presents it as both true and of an arbitrary, fortunate origin. The consequent uneasiness is not overcome either by the external evidence available to test the system or by the narrative of the *Confessions.* Everything depends on the uniqueness of Jean-Jacques's nature and his education. At most, Rousseau can claim to have shown that his system may be solidly grounded.

Rousseau's second philosophic project in the *Confessions* is to provide an account of human nature, or at least to give an important "piece for comparison" that can contribute to such an account. This topic can be considered independently of the epistemological grounding of the system because it concerns only its comprehensiveness and intelligibility. The *Confessions* contributes to Rousseau's account of human nature in two major ways: It shows the formation and development of artificial characteristics, and it reveals the extent to which these artificial characteristics can be overcome. Both aspects are connected with Rousseau's presentation of himself as an extraordinary human. His unusual natural characteristics and almost universal experience make him a particularly good test case for examining some of the extreme directions that denaturing can take. The same attributes also allow him to claim that he represents a virtually unique case of the overcoming of denaturing. He is both an exemplary unnatural man and an exemplary natural man.

Accidents play a decisive role in Jean-Jacques's departure from nature and in his return. In Book I the first experiences of imaginary activity, sexuality, indignation, and vanity are each presented as the result of mistakes made by his father or teachers. Each is presented as an irreversible departure from nature. At the same time, the development of the artificial sentiments set in motion by these experiences is presented as subject to alteration. For example, Jean-Jacques's first sexual experience predisposes him toward masochism, but his later experiences turn him to his imagination for satisfaction. At least part of the reason for this change is his accidental failure to meet more than one Mlle Goton. A similar variability is seen in his indignation and vanity. As a rule, when one of these sentiments is strong, the other is proportionately weak. This is true in two ways. First, indignation at affronts to him, such as his experience with M. de Montaigu at Venice, leads him to reject the pursuit of public recognition. Second, compassionate indignation against injustice to others turns him into something like a citizen who feels a fierce pride rather than vanity. In the end, these two feelings seem to unite in his project for posthumous glory as a benefactor of humanity, but even this merger is effected only by the accidental inspiration on the road to Vincennes.

Among the artificial sentiments or faculties, it is imagination that pursues the most constant path. Throughout Part One, Rousseau shows this first faculty changing from a reflective power to a creative one through the intermediate stages of productivity and generation. Even though the imagination can be checked at a particular stage, such as a period of illness, it increasingly dominates Jean-Jacques's existence. Finally, the imagination could be said to point in the direction of a cure for itself, when Jean-Jacques constructs his belief in a universal conspiracy which puts an end (tentatively in the *Confessions*) to his imaginary hopes and fears and restricts him to the tranquil imaginary pleasure of botany and recollection. The imagination can in certain circumstances end by destroying the tormenting hopes and fears that it began by creating. In other words, the effects of the imagination can be overcome by means of the imagination.

Jean-Jacques's return to quasi-natural wholeness are also conditioned by accidents. The clearest example is the period at les Charmettes, in which a physical "revolution" with an accidental origin temporarily cures him of artificial hopes and fears. His final return to nature on St. Peter's Island is brought about by the accident of the conspiracy against him. Even if one regards the conspiracy as largely a figment of his imagination, his banishment from country after country is real. Thus Rousseau's teaching about the possibility of a return to nature is ambiguous. First, the strength and charm of the artificial passions make it impossible for civilized humans even to desire a return to a natural condition. While the prospect of wealth, satisfaction of vanity, love, and the multitude of other objects of civilized hopes remains, the abandonment of these desires has no immediate attraction. Rousseau shows, however, that there are certain accidents that can end these hopes and restore humans to a quasi-natural happiness, against their wills, as it were. In a few extraordinary people, perhaps only in one extraordinary person, the imagination can develop to such an extent and in such a direction that these salutary accidents are more likely to occur. It should be kept in mind, however, that Rousseau begins his description of his ultimate happiness and self-sufficiency in the *Reveries* by saying, "The most sociable and the most loving of humans has been proscribed [from society] by a unanimous accord". He does not seek a return to nature; it is forced on him. Furthermore, as the *Confessions* shows, if the opportunity for a new project, such as legislation for Corsica, arises, the natural self-sufficiency may disappear. The longing for wholeness which Rousseau stimulates so well in his audience is likely to remain unfulfilled for all but the most extreme cases.

This picture of the departure from and return to nature corresponds to and adds to the pictures in *Emile* and the *Second Discourse.* Rousseau's case study of himself illustrates the growth of artificial sentiments in a civilized human and then throws into relief the important features of the healthy development recommended in *Emile.* It also illustrates the possibilities of domestic life, citizenship, and independence on the fringes of society which are available to humans who find themselves in the corrupt social position described at the end of the *Second Discourse.* Thus, although the *Confessions* may not lay the most solid foundation for Rousseau's system, it complements and adorns the edifice of the system as it is revealed in the other theoretical writings.

The picture of Jean-Jacques's departure from and return to nature is a part of the moral fable of the *Confessions* as well as a complementary part of Rousseau's system. With the account of his own life, Rousseau gives a persuasive image of human experience. Jean-Jacques may be too idiosyncratic and at times too unattractive to be an exemplary figure. Nevertheless, the description of his experiences does transform the readers of the *Confessions* by exposing them to a new way of looking at a life. . . . [The] success of Rousseau's description is indicated by the enduring popularity of autobiographies. To the extent that this new way of looking at a life is now taken for granted, Rousseau's *Confessions* has caused or signaled a "revolution in the universe."

Intrinsic to Rousseau's autobiographical enterprise is an emphasis on feelings, the interior life, and a corresponding depreciation of external actions including speeches. It cannot be denied that Christian confessional literature brought to the fore some aspects of interior life long before Rousseau, but Rousseau's "human" autobiography stresses the richness of internal life rather than the struggle between sinfulness and grace. What Rousseau means by "confession" is different from what Augustine means because of this new understanding of internal life. It is this new understanding that makes Rousseau "the Columbus of a new internal world."

Rousseau's new understanding of the internal life leads to a new judgment about the purpose of its revelation. For Augustine, confession is evidence of repentance and acknowledgment of God; for Rousseau it is a token of sincerity and acknowledgment of oneself. Rousseau offers sincerity, frankness, and openness as the standards for judging a life, and the *Confessions* as the standard for judging sincerity, frankness, and openness. Those who attack Rousseau for not being open enough, for being insincere, are precisely the ones who have been most persuaded to accept Rousseau's standard of judgment. Their enthusiasm for beating Rousseau at his own game betrays their lack of reflection about whose game they are playing and why they are playing it.

Rousseau's revolution extends beyond the praise of sincerity. The terrain of the internal world he reveals has its own distinctive features. Its specific contours are given by the imagination, which Rousseau presents as the source of the charms and afflictions of human life. The imagination's primary products are the feelings of sexuality, vanity, and indignation. Rousseau's philosophic teaching about these artificial sentiments is neither widely accepted nor widely understood. Nevertheless, his view that feelings and faculties like these are the most important aspects of life is widely shared. Rousseau's moral fable encourages readers to dwell on their feelings, to seek parallels with his presentation in their own lives, and to cultivate parallels where they did not exist before. Rousseau may not have settled the debate about the precise nature of these feelings, but he has in large part succeeded in setting the terms of the debate. His account of the origin of faculties and feelings invites one to pay special attention to the early experiences that elicit them and gives them their form. The open-endedness of the potential development of these characteristics entails the understanding of human life as an ongoing process subject to change. By teaching the importance of the particular experiences that give feelings their shape, it also encourages a view of life as radically individual. Rousseau's insistence on his own uniqueness may well make his readers wonder whether nature did not break the mold after making each of them.

Thus the decisive elements in the orientation toward human life given by the *Confessions* are new perspectives about sincerity, the imagination, feelings, and individuality. The novelty in Rousseau's presentation of the importance in these elements can be seen with reference to the exemplary figures Rousseau sought to replace. Jesus does not speak of the charms of an embellishing imagination. Cato spends little time dwelling on his feelings. The ironic Socrates may praise wisdom, but not sincerity. It is Jean-Jacques who is the champion and exemplar of these char-

acteristics. By focusing on them, he turns attention away from other qualities such as Christian charity, Roman courage, and philosophic wisdom. The significance of Rousseau's attempt to focus attention in new directions is also revealed in his opposition to these three exemplary figures. Rousseau's revision of the Sermon on the Mount reveals his attempt to turn people's attention to this world. His presentation of the richness of the inner life, the capacity of the imagination, and the possibilities for wholeness or completeness are meant to show that a turn away from Heaven need not be an abandonment of high aspirations in a quest for mere preservation or power. Rousseau attempts the daunting task of showing that a life that takes its bearing by nothing higher than itself need not be a base one. Perhaps the greatest merit of this attempt is Rousseau's awareness of the gravity of the issues at stake and his insistence on exposing false solutions to the problems he poses.

Rousseau's treatment of Cato shows the magnitude of his project as well as its limitations. It is clear that he regarded his reattainment of natural wholeness as superior to Cato's virtue when judged according to the natural standard. Cato nonetheless remains the greatest of humans when judged from the standard of social utility. The moral fable of the *Confessions* has a limited value from this standpoint. Rousseau's presentation of himself as a lover of solitude who enjoys innocent pleasures and occasionally rises above himself to champion justice is an attainable object of emulation for corrupt civilized humans who cannot be citizens. It is on this point that Rousseau's project appears to be most moderate, but it is also on this point that serious questions can be raised. It is not clear whether the moderation Rousseau wishes to encourage can resist the powerful longings for individual and social wholeness he stimulates. His presentation of these longings can give birth to demands for their fulfillment which cannot be satisfied.

To judge the final success of the *Confessions,* it is necessary to consider the significance of the longing for natural wholeness which Rousseau presents as the deepest human desire. This is the point at which the moral fable joins the philosophic teaching, because the life of natural wholeness is the standard Rousseau uses to judge everything else. . . . [It is] this standard that justifies the judgment of Socrates as superior to Cato yet ultimately calls Socrates' life into question. In the end it is the adequacy of this standard by which Rousseau's philosophic system and moral fable both stand and fall.

The judgment of Socrates is somewhat ambiguous. On one hand, Rousseau's attack on the natural basis of human reason leads him to interpret the philosophic life as a manifestation of artificial pride. On the other, in at least one context Rousseau admits that he is not sure he has disposed of Socrates' submission to public opinion properly. Perhaps one of the reasons for Rousseau's hesitation in dismissing Socrates is his own desire to give a rational account of a justification for the lives of natural humans and citizens which are not based on reason. Someone who wishes to be philosophic will find it hard to dismiss the exemplar of philosophy. Rousseau insists on the separation between reason and nature, or reason and happiness, but he also tries to combine the things he has split asunder.

By attempting to be both a philosopher and a poet, Rousseau attempts to serve the causes of both reason and happiness as he understands them. His desire to combine philosophy and practical effectiveness without subordinating one completely to the other can be contrasted with the understanding of philosophy given by Nietzsche. In *Schopenhauer as Educator* Nietzsche says: "I profit from a philosopher *only* insofar as he can be an example. That he is capable of drawing whole nations after him through his example is beyond doubt; the history of India, which is almost the history of Indian philosophy, proves it. But this example must be supplied by his outward life and not merely in his books—in the way that is, in which the philosophers of Greece taught, through their bearing, what they were and ate, and their morals, rather than by what they said, let alone by what they wrote." The extent to which Rousseau shares this view of philosophers as examples rather than as thinkers is indicated by his enterprise in writing an autobiography that presents his feelings more than his thoughts. His attempt to be both an example and a thinker who tries to understand the system of nature shows that he did not completely abandon the standard set by Socrates.

The **Confessions** shows the most far-reaching elements of Rousseau's thought in relation to the most personal incidents of his life. The work forges a link between the reflective concerns of a philosopher and the practical cares of all people. Rousseau's ability to capture his readers' feelings was appreciated by Stendhal, who declared, "I must try to undo the prejudices that J. J. Rousseau has given me and he has given me plenty." Rousseau's appeal to feelings is indeed the source of many prejudices, but his efforts to reason as well as to form prejudices make his books among the best antidotes to prejudice. His accomplishment in the **Confessions** confirms his claim to have written "a precious book for philosophers." (pp. 239-52)

> *Christopher Kelly, in his* Rousseau's Exemplary Life: The "Confessions" as Political Philosophy, *Cornell University Press, 1987, 262 p.*

Paul Johnson   (essay date 1988)

[*Johnson is an English editor, historian, and publisher. He is the author of* A History of Christianity *(1976),* Modern Times: The World from the Twenties to the Eighties *(1983),* A History of the Jews *(1987), and* Intellectuals *(1988). In the following excerpt from the last-named book, he presents a psychological analysis of Rousseau's character (as it is revealed in his writings) and considers his influence on intellectual matters, noting that Rousseau's "ideas are so wide-ranging as to constitute, almost by themselves, an encyclopedia of modern thought."*]

[Rousseau] was the first of the modern intellectuals, their archetype and in many ways the most influential of them all. Older men like Voltaire had started the work of demolishing the altars and enthroning reason. But Rousseau was the first to combine all the salient characteristics of the modern Promethean: the assertion of his right to reject the existing order in its entirety; confidence in his capacity to refashion it from the bottom in accordance with principles of his own devising; belief that this could be achieved by the political process; and, not least, recognition of the huge part instinct, intuition and impulse play in human

conduct. He believed he had a unique love for humanity and had been endowed with unprecedented gifts and insights to increase its felicity. An astonishing number of people, in his own day and since, have taken him at his own valuation.

In both the long and the short term his influence was enormous. In the generation after his death, it attained the status of a myth. He died a decade before the French Revolution of 1789 but many contemporaries held him responsible for it, and so for the demolition of the *ancien régime* in Europe. This view was shared by both Louis XVI and Napoleon. Edmund Burke said of the revolutionary elites: 'There is a great dispute among their leaders which of them is the best resemblance of Rousseau . . . He is their standard figure of perfection.' As Robespierre himself put it: 'Rousseau is the one man who, through the loftiness of his soul and the grandeur of his character, showed himself worthy of the role of teacher of mankind.' During the Revolution the National Convention voted to have his ashes transferred to the Panthéon. At the ceremony its president declared: 'It is to Rousseau that is due the health-giving improvement that has transformed our morals, customs, laws, feelings and habits.'

At a much deeper level, however, and over a far longer span of time, Rousseau altered some of the basic assumptions of civilized man and shifted around the furniture of the human mind. The span of his influence is dramatically wide but it can be grouped under five main headings. First, all our modern ideas of education are affected to some degree by Rousseau's doctrine, especially by his treatise *Émile.* He popularized and to some extent invented the cult of nature, the taste for the open air, the quest for freshness, spontaneity, the invigorating and the natural. He introduced the critique of urban sophistication. He identified and branded the artificialities of civilization. He is the father of the cold bath, systematic exercise, sport as character-forming, the weekend cottage.

Second, and linked to his revaluation of nature, Rousseau taught distrust of the progressive, gradual improvements brought about by the slow march of materialist culture; in this sense he rejected the Enlightenment, of which he was part, and looked for a far more radical solution. He insisted that reason itself had severe limitations as the means to cure society. That did not mean, however, that the human mind was inadequate to bring about the necessary changes, because it has hidden, untapped resources of poetic insight and intuition which must be used to overrule the sterilizing dictates of reason. In pursuit of this line of thought, Rousseau wrote his **Confessions,** finished in 1770, though not published until after his death. This third process was the beginning both of the Romantic movement and of modern introspective literature, for in it he took the discovery of the individual, the prime achievement of the Renaissance, a giant stage further, delving into the inner self and producing it for public inspection. For the first time readers were shown the inside of a heart, though—and this too was to be a characteristic of modern literature—the vision was deceptive, the heart thus exhibited misleading, outwardly frank, inwardly full of guile.

The fourth concept Rousseau popularized was in some ways the most pervasive of all. When society evolves from its primitive state of nature to urban sophistication, he argued, man is corrupted: his natural selfishness, which he calls *amour de soi,* is transformed into a far more pernicious instinct, *amour-propre,* which combines vanity and self-esteem, each man rating himself by what others think of him and thus seeking to impress them by his money, strength, brains and moral superiority. His natural selfishness becomes competitive and acquisitive, and so he becomes alienated not only from other men, whom he sees as competitors and not brothers, but from himself. Alienation induces a psychological sickness in man, characterized by a tragic divergence between appearance and reality.

The evil of competition, as he saw it, which destroys man's inborn communal sense and encourages all his most evil traits, including his desire to exploit others, led Rousseau to distrust private property, as the source of social crime. His fifth innovation, then, on the very eve of the Industrial Revolution, was to develop the elements of a critique of capitalism, both in the preface to his play *Narcisse* and in his *Discours sur l'inégalité,* by identifying property and the competition to acquire it as the primary cause of alienation. This was a thought-deposit Marx and others were to mine ruthlessly, together with Rousseau's related idea of cultural evolution. To him, 'natural' meant 'original' or pre-cultural. All culture brings problems since it is man's association with others which brings out his evil propensities: as he puts it in *Émile,* 'Man's breath is fatal to his fellow men.' Thus the culture in which man lived, itself an evolving, artificial construct, dictated man's behaviour, and you could improve, indeed totally transform, his behaviour by changing the culture and the competitive forces which produced it—that is, by social engineering.

These ideas are so wide-ranging as to constitute, almost by themselves, an encyclopaedia of modern thought. It is true that not all of them were original to him. His reading was wide: Descartes, Rabelais, Pascal, Leibnitz, Bayle, Fontenelle, Corneille, Petrarch, Tasso, and in particular he drew on Locke and Montaigne. Germaine de Staël, who believed he possessed 'the most sublime faculties ever bestowed on a man' declared: 'He has invented nothing.' But, she added, 'he has infused all with fire.' It was the simple, direct, powerful, indeed passionate, manner in which Rousseau wrote which made his notions seem so vivid and fresh, so that they came to men and women with the shock of a revelation. (pp. 2-4)

The power of the French intellectuals was just beginning [in the mid 1700s] and was to increase steadily in the second half of the century. But in the 1740s and 1750s their position as critics of society was still precarious. The State, when it felt itself threatened, was still liable to turn on them with sudden ferocity. Rousseau later loudly complained of the persecution he suffered, but in fact he had less to put up with than most of his contemporaries. Voltaire was publicly caned by the servants of an aristocrat he had offended, and served nearly a year in the Bastille. Those who sold forbidden books might get ten years in the galleys. In July 1749 Diderot was arrested and put in solitary confinement in the Vincennes fortress for publishing a book defending atheism. He was there three months. Rousseau visited him there, and while walking on the road to Vincennes he saw in the paper a notice from the Dijon Academy of Letters inviting entries for an essay competition on the theme 'Whether the rebirth of the sciences and the arts has contributed to the improvement of morals.'

This episode, which occurred in 1750, was the turning point in Rousseau's life. He saw in a flash of inspiration what he must do. Other entrants would naturally plead the cause of the arts and sciences. He would argue the superiority of nature. Suddenly, as he says in his *Confessions,* he conceived an overwhelming enthusiasm for 'truth, liberty and virtue'. He says he declared to himself: 'Virtue, truth! I will cry increasingly, truth, virtue!' He added that his waistcoat was 'soaked with tears I had shed without noticing it'. The soaking tears may well be true: tears came easily to him. What is certain is that Rousseau decided there and then to write the essay on lines which became the essence of his creed, won the prize by this paradoxical approach, and became famous almost overnight. Here was a case of a man of thirty-nine, hitherto unsuccessful and embittered, longing for notice and fame, at last hitting the right note. The essay is feeble and today almost unreadable. As always, when one looks back on such a literary event, it seems inexplicable that so paltry a work could have produced such an explosion of celebrity; indeed the famous critic Jules Lemaître called this instant apotheosis of Rousseau 'one of the strongest proofs ever provided of human stupidity'.

Publication of the *Discours* on the arts and sciences did not make Rousseau rich, for though it circulated widely, and evoked nearly three hundred printed replies, the number of copies actually sold was small and it was the booksellers who made money from such works. On the other hand it gave him the run of many aristocratic houses and estates, which were open to fashionable intellectuals. Rousseau could, and sometimes did, support himself by music-copying (he had a beautiful writing-hand) but after 1750 he was always in a position to live off the hospitality of the aristocracy, except (as often happened) when he chose to stage ferocious quarrels with those who dispensed it. For occupation, he became a professional writer. He was always fertile in ideas and, when he got down to it, wrote easily and well. But the impact of his books, at any rate in his own lifetime and for long after, varied greatly. His *Social Contract,* generally supposed to encapsulate his mature political philosophy, which he began in 1752 and finally published ten years later, was scarcely read at all in his lifetime and had only been reprinted once by 1791. Examination of five hundred contemporary libraries showed that only one possessed a copy. The scholar Joan Macdonald, who looked at 1114 political pamphlets published in 1789-91, found only twelve references to it. As she observed: 'It is necessary to distinguish between the cult of Rousseau and the influence of his political thought.' The cult, which began with the prize essay but continued to grow in force, centred around two books. The first was his novel *La Nouvelle Héloïse,* subtitled *Letters of Two Lovers* and modelled on Richardson's *Clarissa.* The story of the pursuit, seduction, repentance and punishment of a young woman, it is written with extraordinary skill to appeal both to the prurient interest of readers, especially women—and especially the burgeoning market of middle-class women—and to their sense of morality. The material is often very outspoken for the time, but the final message is highly proper. The Archbishop of Paris accused it of 'insinuating the poison of lust while seeming to proscribe it', but this merely served to increase its sales, as did Rousseau's own cunningly-worded preface, in which he asserts that a girl who reads a single page of it is a lost soul, adding however that 'chaste girls do not read love stories.' In fact both chaste girls and respectable matrons read it and defended themselves by citing its highly moral conclusions. In short it was a natural bestseller, and became one, though most of the copies bought were pirated.

The Rousseau cult was intensified in 1762 with the publication of *Émile,* in which he launched the myriad of ideas, on nature and man's response to it, which were to become the staple fare of the Romantic Age but were then pristine. This book too was brilliantly engineered to secure the maximum number of readers. But in one respect Rousseau was too clever for his own good. It was part of his growing appeal, as the prophet of truth and virtue, to point out the limits of reason and allow for the place of religion in the hearts of men. He thus included in *Émile* a chapter entitled **'Profession of Faith'** in which he accused his fellow intellectuals of the Enlightenment, especially the atheists or mere deists, of being arrogant and dogmatic, 'professing even in their so-called scepticism to know everything' and heedless of the damage they do to decent men and women by undermining faith: 'They destroy and trample underfoot all that men revere, steal from the suffering the consolation they derive from religion and take away the only force that restrains the passions of the rich and the powerful.' It was highly effective stuff, but to balance it Rousseau felt it necessary to criticize the established Church too, especially its cult of miracles and encouragement of superstition. This was highly imprudent, especially since Rousseau, to frustrate the book-pirates, took the risk of signing the work. He was already suspect in French ecclesiastical eyes as a double-renegade: having converted to Catholicism, he later returned to Calvinism in order to regain his Genevan citizenship. So now the Paris *Parlement,* dominated by Jansenists, took the strongest objection to the anti-Catholic sentiments in *Émile,* had the book burnt in front of the Palais de Justice and issued a warrant for Rousseau's arrest. He was saved by a timely warning from high-placed friends. Thereafter he was for some years a fugitive. For the Calvinists objected to *Émile* too and even outside Catholic territory he was forced to move on from one town to another. But he was never without powerful protectors, in Britain (where he spent fifteen months in 1766-67) and in France too, where he lived from 1767 onwards. During his last decade the State lost interest in him, and his chief enemies were fellow intellectuals, notably Voltaire. To answer them Rousseau wrote his *Confessions,* completed in Paris where he finally settled in 1770. He did not venture to publish them but they were widely known from the readings he gave at fashionable houses. By the time of his death in 1778 his reputation was on the eve of a fresh upsurge, consummated when the revolutionaries took over.

Rousseau, then, enjoyed considerable success even in his lifetime. To the unprejudiced modern eye he does not seem to have had much to grumble about. Yet Rousseau was one of the greatest grumblers in the history of literature. He insisted that his life had been one of misery and persecution. He reiterates the complaint so often and in such harrowing terms, that one feels obliged to believe him. On one point he was adamant: he suffered from chronic ill-health. He was 'an unfortunate wretch worn out by illness . . . struggling every day of my life between pain and death'. He had 'not been able to sleep for thirty years'. 'Nature,' he added, 'which has shaped me for suffering, has given me a constitution proof against pain in order that, unable to exhaust my forces, it may always make itself felt with the same intensity.' It is true that he always had trouble with his penis. In a letter to his friend Dr Tronchin, written in 1755, he refers to 'the malformation of an organ, with which I was born'. His biographer Lester Crocker, after a careful diagnosis, writes: 'I am convinced that Jean-Jacques was born a victim of hypospadias, a deformity of the penis in which the urethra opens somewhere on the ventral surface.' In adult life this became a stricture, necessitating painful use of a catheter, which aggravated the problem both psychologically and physically.' (pp. 6-9)

Incessant concern about his health, justified or not, was the original dynamic of the self-pity which came to envelop him and feed on every episode in his life. (p. 10)

Behind the self-pity lay an overpowering egoism, a feeling that he was quite unlike other men, both in his sufferings and his qualities. He wrote: 'What could your miseries have in common with mine? My situation is unique, unheard of since the beginning of time . . . ' Equally, 'The person who can love me as I can love is still to be born.' 'No one ever had more talent for loving.' 'I was born to be the best friend that ever existed.' 'I would leave this life with apprehension if I knew a better man than me.' 'Show me a better man than me, a heart more loving, more tender, more sensitive . . . "Posterity will honour me . . . because it is my due.' 'I rejoice in myself.' ' . . . my consolation lies in my self-esteem.' ' . . . if there were a single enlightened government in Europe, it would have erected statues to me.' No wonder Burke declared: 'Vanity was the vice he possessed to a degree little short of madness.'

It was part of Rousseau's vanity that he believed himself incapable of base emotions. 'I feel too superior to hate.' 'I love myself too much to hate anybody.' 'Never have I known the hateful passions, never did jealousy, wickedness, vengeance enter my heart . . . anger occasionally but I am never crafty and never bear a grudge.' In fact he frequently bore grudges and was crafty in pursuing them. Men noticed this. Rousseau was the first intellectual to proclaim himself, repeatedly, the friend of all mankind. But loving as he did humanity in general, he developed a strong propensity for quarrelling with human beings in particular. One of his victims, his former friend Dr Tronchin of Geneva, protested: 'How is it possible that the friend of mankind is no longer the friend of men, or scarcely so?' Replying, Rousseau defended his right to administer rebukes to those who deserved it: 'I am the friend of mankind, and men are everywhere. The friend of truth also finds malevolent men everywhere—and I do not need to go very far.' Being an egoist, Rousseau tended to equate hostility to himself with hostility to truth and virtue as such. Hence nothing was too bad for his enemies; their very existence made sense of the doctrine of eternal punishment: 'I am not ferocious by nature,' he told Madame d'Épinay, 'but when I see there is no justice in this world for these monsters, I like to think there is a hell waiting for them.'

Since Rousseau was vain, egotistical and quarrelsome, how was it that so many people were prepared to befriend him? The answer to this question brings us to the heart of his character and historical significance. Partly by accident, partly by instinct, partly by deliberate contrivance, he was the first intellectual systematically to exploit the guilt of the privileged. And he did it, moreover, in an entirely new way, by the systematic cult of rudeness. He was the prototype of that characteristic figure of the modern age, the Angry Young Man. (pp. 10-11)

He deliberately stressed sentiment as opposed to convention, the impulse of the heart rather than manners. 'My sentiments,' he said, 'are such that they must not be disguised. They dispense me from being polite.' He admitted he was 'uncouth, unpleasant and rude on principle. I do not care twopence for your courtiers. I am a barbarian.' Or again: 'I have things in my heart which absolve me from being good-mannered.'

This approach fitted in very well with his prose, which was far more simple than the polished periods of most contemporary writers. His directness admirably suited his outspoken treatment of sex (*La Nouvelle Héloïse* was one of the first novels to mention such articles as ladies' corsets). Rousseau highlighted his ostentatious rejection of social norms by a studied simplicity and looseness of dress, which in time became the hallmark of all the young Romantics. He later recorded: 'I began my reformation with my dress. I gave up gold lace and white stockings and wore a round wig. I gave up my sword and sold my watch.' Next followed longer hair, what he called 'my usual careless style with a rough beard.' He was the first of the hirsute highbrows. Over the years he developed a variety of sartorial ways of drawing public attention to himself. At Neufchâtel he was painted by Allan Ramsay wearing an Armenian robe, a sort of kaftan. He even wore it to church. The locals objected at first but soon got used to it and in time it became a Rousseau hallmark. During his celebrated visit to England he wore it at the Drury Lane Theatre, and was so anxious to respond to the plaudits of the crowd that Mrs Garrick had to hang onto the robe to prevent him falling out of the box.

Consciously or not, he was a superb self-publicist: his eccentricities, his social brutalities, his personal extremism, even his quarrels, attracted a vast amount of attention and were undoubtedly part of his appeal both to his aristocratic patrons and to his readers and cultists. It is a significant fact, as we shall see, that personal public relations, not least through quirks of dress and appearance, was to become an important element in the success of numerous intellectual leaders. Rousseau led the way in this as in so many other respects. Who can say he was wrong? Most people are resistant to ideas, especially new ones. But they are fascinated by character. Extravagance of personality is one way in which the pill can be sugared and the public induced to look at works dealing with ideas.

As part of his technique for securing publicity, attention and favour, Rousseau, who was no mean psychologist, made a positive virtue of that most repellent of vices, ingratitude. To him it seemed no fault. While professing spontaneity, he was in fact a calculating man; and since he persuaded himself that he was, quite literally, the best of moral human beings, it followed logically that others were even more calculating, and from worse motives, than he was. Hence in any dealings with him, they would seek to take advantage, and he must outwit them. The basis on which he negotiated with others, therefore, was quite simple: they gave, he took. He bolstered this by an audacious argument: because of his uniqueness, anyone who helped him was in fact doing a favour to himself. He set the pattern in his response to the letter of the Dijon Academy awarding him the prize. His essay, he wrote, had taken the unpopular line of truth, 'and by your generosity in honouring my courage, you have honoured yourselves still more. Yes, gentlemen, what you have done for my glory, is a crown of laurels added to your own.' (pp. 11-13)

As one of Rousseau's biographers has pointed out, he was always setting little traps for people. He would emphasize his difficulties and poverty, then when they offered help affect hurt surprise, even indignation. Thus: 'Your proposal froze my heart. How you misunderstand your own interests when you try to make a valet out of a friend.' He adds: 'I am not unwilling to listen to what you have to propose, provided you appreciate that I am not for sale.' The would-be host, thus wrong-footed, was then induced to reformulate his invitation on Rousseau's terms. It was one of Rousseau's psychological skills to persuade people, not least his social superiors, that common-or-garden words of thanks were not in his vocabulary. Thus he wrote to the Duc de Montmorency-Luxembourg, who lent him a château: 'I neither praise you nor thank you. But I live in your house. Everyone has his own language—I have said everything in mine.' The ploy worked beautifully, the Duchess replying apologetically: 'It is not for you to thank us—it is the Marshal and I who are in *your* debt.'

But Rousseau was not prepared just to lead an agreeable, Harold Skimpole-like existence. He was too complicated and interesting for that. Alongside his streak of cool, hard-headed calculation there was a genuine element of paranoia, which did not permit him to settle for an easy life of self-centered parasitism. He quarrelled, ferociously and usually permanently, with virtually everyone with whom he had close dealings, and especially those who befriended him; and it is impossible to study the painful and repetitive tale of these rows without reaching the conclusion that he was a mentally sick man. This sickness cohabited with a great and original genius of mind, and the combination was very dangerous both for Rousseau and for others. The conviction of total rectitude was, of course, a primary symptom of his illness, and if Rousseau had possessed no talent it might have cured itself or, at worse, remained a small personal tragedy. But his wonderful gifts as a writer brought him acceptance, celebrity, even popularity. This was proof to him that his conviction that he was always right was not a subjective judgment but that of the world—apart, of course, from his enemies.

These enemies were, in every case, former friends or benefactors, who (Rousseau reasoned after he broke with them) had sought, under the guise of amity, to exploit and destroy him. The notion of disinterested friendship was alien to him; and since he was better than other men, and since he was incapable of feeling such an urge, then *a fortiori* it could not be felt by others. Hence the actions of all his 'friends' were carefully analysed by him from the start, and the moment they made a false move he was onto them. He quarrelled with Diderot, to whom he owed most of all. He quarrelled with Grimm. He had a particularly savage and hurtful break with Madame d'Épinay, his warmest benefactress. He quarrelled with Voltaire—that was not so difficult. He quarrelled with David Hume, who took him at his own valuation as a literary martyr, brought him to England and a hero's welcome and did everything in his power to make the visit a success, and Rousseau happy. There were dozens of minor rows, with his Genevan friend Dr Tronchin, for instance. Rousseau marked most of his major quarrels by composing a gigantic letter of remonstrance. These documents are among his most brilliant works, miracles of forensic skill in which evidence is cunningly fabricated, history rewritten and chronology confused with superb ingenuity in order to prove that the recipient is a monster. The letter he wrote to Hume, 10 July 1766, is eighteen folio pages (twenty-five of printed text) and has been described by Hume's biographer as 'consistent with the complete logical consistency of dementia. It remains one of the most brilliant and fascinating documents ever produced by a disordered mentality.'

Rousseau gradually came to believe that these individual acts of enmity by men and women who had pretended to love him were not isolated but part of a connected pattern. They were all agents in a ramifying, long-term plot to frustrate, annoy and even destroy him and to damage his work. (pp. 13-15)

His last works, the *Dialogues avec moi-même* (begun in

Title page of Les Rêveries du promeneur solitaire, *published posthumously in 1782.*

1772) and his *Rêvéries du promeneur solitaire* (1776) reflect this persecution-mania. When he finished the *Dialogues* he became convinced that 'they' intended to destroy them, and on 24 February 1776 he went to Notre Dame Cathedral with the intention of claiming sanctuary for his manuscript and placing it on the High Altar. But the gate to the choir was mysteriously locked. Sinister! So he made six copies and deposited them superstitiously in different hands: one went to Dr Johnson's bluestocking friend, Miss Brooke Boothby of Lichfield, and it was she who first published it in 1780. By that time, of course, Rousseau had gone to his grave, still sure that thousands of agents were after him.

The agonies of mind caused by this form of dementia are real enough to the sufferer and it is impossible, from time to time, not to feel pity for Rousseau. Unhappily, he cannot be thus dismissed. He was one of the most influential writers who ever lived. He presented himself as the friend of humanity and, in particular, as the champion of the principles of truth and virtue. He was, and indeed still is, widely accepted as such. It is necessary, therefore, to look more closely at his own conduct as a teller of truth and a man of virtue. What do we find? The issue of truth is particularly significant because Rousseau became, after his death, best known by his *Confessions.* These were a self-proclaimed effort to tell the whole inner truth about a man's life, in a way never before attempted. The book was a new kind of ultra-truthful autobiography, just as James Boswell's life of Dr Johnson, published ten years later (1791), was a new kind of ultra-accurate biography.

Rousseau made absolute claims for the veracity of this book. In the winter of 1770-71 he held readings of it, in packed salons, lasting fifteen to seventeen hours, with breaks for meals. His attacks on his victims were so unsupportable that one of them, Madame d'Épinay, asked the authorities to have them stopped. Rousseau agreed to desist, but at the last reading he added these words: 'I have said the truth. If anyone knows facts contrary to what I have just said, even if they were proved a thousand times, they are lies and impostures . . . [whoever] examines with his own eyes my nature, my character, my morals, inclinations, pleasures, habits, and can believe me to be a dishonest man, is himself a man who deserves to be strangled.' This produced an impressive silence.

Rousseau bolstered his title to be a truth-teller by claiming a superb memory. More important, he convinced readers he was sincere by being the first man to disclose details of his sex life, not in a spirit of macho boasting but, on the contrary, with shame and reluctance. As he rightly says, referring to 'the dark and dirty labyrinth' of his sexual experiences, 'It is not what is criminal which is hardest to tell, but what makes us feel ridiculous and ashamed.' But how genuine was the reluctance? In Turin, as a young man, he roamed the dark back streets and exposed his bare bottom to women: 'The foolish pleasure I took in displaying it before their eyes cannot be described.' Rousseau was a natural exhibitionist, in sexual as in other respects, and there is a certain relish in the way he narrates his sex life. He describes his masochism, how he enjoyed being spanked on his bare bottom by the strict pastor's sister, Mademoiselle Lambercier, being deliberately naughty to provoke punishment, and how he encouraged an older girl, Mademoiselle Groton, to spank him too: 'To lie at the feet of an imperious mistress, to obey her commands, to ask her forgiveness—this was for me a sweet enjoyment.' He tells how, as a boy, he took up masturbation. He defends it because it prevents the young from catching venereal disease and because, 'This vice which shame and timidity find so convenient has more than one attraction for live imaginations: it enables them to subject all women to their whims and to make beauty serve the pleasure which tempts them without obtaining its consent.' He gave an account of an attempt to seduce him by a homosexual at the hospice in Turin. He admitted he had shared the favours of Madame de Warens with her gardener. He described how he was unable to make love to one girl when he discovered she had no nipple on one breast, and records her furious dismissal of him: 'Leave women alone and study mathematics.' He confesses to resuming masturbation in later life as more convenient than pursuing an active love life. He gives the impression, part intentionally, part unconsciously, that his attitude to sex remained essentially infantile: his mistress, Madame de Warens, is always 'Maman'.

These damaging admissions build up confidence in Rousseau's regard for truth, and he reinforces it by relating other shameful, non-sexual episodes, involving theft, lies, cowardice and desertion. But there was an element of cunning in this. His accusations against himself make his subsequent accusations against his enemies far more convincing. As Diderot furiously observed, 'he describes himself in odious colours to give his unjust and cruel imputations the semblance of truth.' Moreover, the self-accusations are deceptive since in every critical one he follows up the bare admission by a skilfully presented exculpation so that the reader ends by sympathizing with him and giving him credit for his forthright honesty. Then again, the truths Rousseau presents often turn out to be half-truths: his selective honesty is in some ways the most dishonest aspect both of his *Confessions* and his letters. The 'facts' he so frankly admits often emerge, in the light of modern scholarship, to be inaccurate, distorted or non-existent. This is sometimes clear even from internal evidence. Thus he gives two quite different accounts of the homosexual advance, in *Émile* and in the *Confessions.* His total-recall memory was a myth. He gives the wrong year for his father's death and describes him as 'about sixty', when he was in fact seventy-five. He lies about virtually all the details of his stay at the hospice in Turin, one of the most critical episodes of his early life. It gradually emerges that no statement in the *Confessions* can be trusted if unsupported by external evidence. Indeed it is hard not to agree with one of Rousseau's most comprehensive modern critics, J. H. Huizinga, that the insistent claims of the *Confessions* to truth and honesty make its distortions and falsehoods peculiarly disgraceful: 'The more attentively one reads and re-reads, the deeper one delves into this work, the more layers of ignominy become apparent.' What makes Rousseau's dishonesty so dangerous—what made his inventions so rightly feared by his ex-friends—was the diabolical skill and brilliance with which they were presented. As his fair-minded biographer, Professor Crocker, puts it: 'All his accounts of his quarrels (as in the Venetian episode) have an irresistible persuasiveness, eloquence and air of sincerity; then the facts come as a shock.'

So much for Rousseau's devotion to truth. What of his virtue? Very few of us lead lives which will bear close scruti-

ny, and there is something mean in subjecting Rousseau's, laid horribly bare by the activities of thousands of scholars, to moral judgment. But granted his claims, and still more his influence on ethics and behaviour, there is no alternative. He was a man, he said, born to love, and he taught the doctrine of love more persistently than most ecclesiastics. (pp. 16-18)

Was Rousseau capable of loving a woman without strong selfish reservations? According to his own account, 'the first and only love of all my life' was Sophie, Comtesse d'Houdetot, sister-in-law of his benefactress Madame d'Épinay. He may have loved her, but he says he 'took the precaution' of writing his love-letters to her in such a way as to make their publication as damaging to her as to him. Of Thérèse Levasseur, the twenty-three-year-old laundress whom he made his mistress in 1745 and who remained with him thirty-three years until his death, he said he 'never felt the least glimmering of love for her . . . the sensual needs I satisfied with her were purely sexual and were nothing to do with her as an individual.' 'I told her,' he wrote, 'I would never leave her and never marry her.' A quarter of a century later he went through a pseudo-wedding with her in front of a few friends but used the occasion to make a vainglorious speech, declaring that posterity would erect statues to him and 'It will then be no empty honour to have been a friend of Jean-Jacques Rousseau.' (p. 19)

The truth seems to be that she was devoted to Rousseau, in most respects, but had been taught, by his own behaviour, to use him, as he used her. Rousseau's warmest affection went to animals. Boswell records a delightful scene of him playing with his cat and his dog Sultan. He gave Sultan (and his predecessor, Turc) a love he could not find for humans, and the howling of this dog, whom he brought with him to London, almost prevented him from attending the special benefit performance Garrick had set up for him at Drury Lane.

Rousseau kept and even cherished Thérèse because she could do for him things animals could not: operate the catheter to relieve his stricture, for instance. He would not tolerate third parties interfering in his relations with her: he became furious, for instance, when a publisher sent her a dress; he promptly vetoed a plan to provide her with a pension, which might have made her independent of him. Most of all, he would not allow children to usurp his claims on her, and this led him to his greatest crime. Since a large part of Rousseau's reputation rests on his theories about the upbringing of children—more education is the main, underlying theme of his *Discours, Émile,* the *Social Contract* and even *La Nouvelle Héloïse*—it is curious that, in real life as opposed to writing, he took so little interest in children. There is no evidence whatever that he studied children to verify his theories. He claimed that no one enjoyed playing with children more than himself, but the one anecdote we have of him in this capacity is not reassuring. The painter Delacroix relates in his *Journal* (31 May 1824) that a man told him he had seen Rousseau in the gardens of the Tuileries: 'A child's ball struck the philosopher's leg. He flew into a rage and pursued the child with his cane.' From what we know of his character, it is unlikely that Rousseau could ever have made a good father. Even so, it comes as a sickening shock to discover what Rousseau did to his own children.

The first was born to Thérèse in the winter of 1746-47. We do not know its sex. It was never named. With (he says) 'the greatest difficulty in the world', he persuaded Thérèse that the baby must be abandoned 'to save her honour'. She 'obeyed with a sigh'. He placed a cypher-card in the infant's clothing and told the midwife to drop off the bundle at the Hôpital des Enfants-trouvés. Four other babies he had by Thérèse were disposed of in exactly the same manner, except that he did not trouble to insert a cypher-card after the first. None had names. It is unlikely that any of them survived long. (pp. 20-1)

Twice in [his *Confessions*] he defends himself about the babies, and he returns to the subject in his *Reveries* and in various letters. In all, his efforts to justify himself, publicly and privately, spread over twenty-five years and vary considerably. They merely make matters worse, since they compound cruelty and selfishness with hypocrisy. First, he blamed the wicked circle of godless intellectuals among whom he then moved for putting the idea of the orphanage into his innocent head. Then, to have children was 'an inconvenience'. He could not afford it. 'How could I achieve the tranquility of mind necessary for my work, my garret filled with domestic cares and the noise of children?' He would have been forced to stoop to degrading work, 'to all those infamous acts which fill me with such justified horror'. 'I know full well no father is more tender than I would have been' but he did not want his children to have any contact with Thérèse's mother: 'I trembled at the thought of entrusting mine to that ill-bred family.' As for cruelty, how could anyone of his outstanding moral character be guilty of such a thing? '. . . my ardent love of the great, the true, the beautiful and the just; my horror of evil of every kind, my utter inability to hate or injure or even to think of it; the sweet and lively emotion which I feel at the sight of all that is virtuous, generous and amiable; is it possible, I ask, that all these can ever agree in the same heart with the depravity which, without the least scruple, tramples underfoot the sweetest of obligations? No! I feel, and loudly assert—it is impossible! Never, for a single moment in his life, could Jean-Jacques have been a man without feeling, without compassion, or an unnatural father.' (p. 22)

Rousseau asserts that brooding on his conduct towards his children led him eventually to formulate the theory of education he put forward in *Émile.* It also clearly helped to shape his *Social Contract,* published the same year. What began as a process of personal self-justification in a particular case—a series of hasty, ill thought-out excuses for behaviour he must have known, initially, was unnatural— gradually evolved, as repetition and growing self-esteem hardened them into genuine convictions, into the proposition that education was the key to social and moral improvement and, this being so, it was the concern of the State. The State must form the minds of all, not only as children (as it had done to Rousseau's in the orphanage) but as adult citizens. By a curious chain of infamous moral logic, Rousseau's iniquity as a parent was linked to his ideological offspring, the future totalitarian state. (p. 23)

Rousseau's reputation during his lifetime, and his influence after his death, raise disturbing questions about human gullibility, and indeed about the human propensity to reject evidence it does not wish to admit. The acceptability of what Rousseau wrote depended in great part on

his strident claim to be not merely virtuous but the most virtuous man of his time. Why did not this claim collapse in ridicule and ignominy when his weaknesses and vices became not merely public knowledge but the subject of international debate? After all the people who assailed him were not strangers or political opponents but former friends and associates who had gone out of their way to assist him. Their charges were serious and the collective indictment devastating. Hume, who had once thought him 'gentle, modest, affectionate, disinterested and exquisitely sensitive', decided, from more extensive experience, that he was 'a monster who saw himself as the only important being in the universe'. Diderot, after long acquaintance, summed him up as 'deceitful, vain as Satan, ungrateful, cruel, hypocritical and full of malice'. To Grimm he was 'odious, monstrous'. To Voltaire, 'a monster of vanity and vileness'. Saddest of all are the judgments passed on him by kind-hearted women who helped him, like Madame d'Épinay, and her harmless husband, whose last words to Rousseau were 'I have nothing left for you but pity.' These judgments were based not on the man's words but on his deeds, and since that time, over two hundred years, the mass of material unearthed by scholars has tended relentlessly to substantiate them. One modern academic lists Rousseau's shortcomings as follows: he was a 'masochist, exhibitionist, neurasthenic, hypochondriac, onanist, latent homosexual afflicted by the typical urge for repeated displacements, incapable of normal or parental affection, incipient paranoiac, narcissistic introvert rendered unsocial by his illness, filled with guilt feelings, pathologically timid, a kleptomaniac, infantilist, irritable and miserly'.

Such accusations, and extensive display of the evidence on which they are based, made very little difference to the regard in which Rousseau and his works were, and are, held by those for whom he has an intellectual and emotional attraction. During his life, no matter how many friendships he destroyed, he never found any difficulty in forming new ones and recruiting fresh admirers, disciples and grandees to provide him with houses, dinners and the incense he craved. When he died he was buried on the Île des Peupliers on the lake at Ermononville and this rapidly became a place of secular pilgrimage for men and women from all over Europe, like the shrine of a saint in the Middle Ages. Descriptions of the antics of these *dévotés* make hilarious reading: 'I dropped to my knees . . . pressed my lips to the cold stone of the monument . . . and kissed it repeatedly.' Relics, such as his tobacco pouch and jar, were carefully preserved at 'the Sanctuary', as it was known. One recalls Erasmus and John Colet visiting the great shrine of St Thomas à Becket at Canterbury in c. 1512 and sneering at the excesses of the pilgrims. What would they have found to say of 'Saint Rousseau' (as George Sand was reverently to call him), three hundred years after the Reformation had supposedly ended that sort of thing? The plaudits continued long after the ashes were transferred to the Panthéon. To Kant he had 'a sensibility of soul of unequalled perfection'. To Shelley he was 'a sublime genius'. For Schiller he was 'a Christlike soul for whom only Heaven's angels are fit company'. John Stuart Mill and George Eliot, Hugo and Flaubert, paid deep homage. Tolstoy said that Rousseau and the Gospel had been 'the two great and healthy influences of my life'. One of the most influential intellectuals of our own times, Claude Lévi-Strauss, in his principal work, *Tristes Tropiques,* hails him as 'our master and our brother . . .

every page of this book could have been dedicated to him, had it not been unworthy of his great memory'.

It is all very baffling and suggests that intellectuals are as unreasonable, illogical and superstitious as anyone else. The truth seems to be that Rousseau was a writer of genius but fatally unbalanced both in his life and in his views. He is best summed up by the woman who, he said, was his only love, Sophie d'Houdetot. She lived on until 1813 and, in extreme old age, delivered this verdict: 'He was ugly enough to frighten me and love did not make him more attractive. But he was a pathetic figure and I treated him with gentleness and kindness. He was an interesting madman.' (pp. 26-7)

> *Paul Johnson, "Jean-Jacques Rousseau: 'An Interesting Madman'," in his* Intellectuals, *1988. Reprint by Harper & Row, Publishers, 1989, pp. 1-27.*

FURTHER READING

Babbitt, Irving. *Rousseau and Romanticism.* Cleveland: World Publishing Co., 1955, 324 p.
  Seminal study of Rousseau's impact on the development and character of the Romantic movement. Babbitt contends that Rousseau provides "the most significant illustrations of it."

Bernstein, John Andrew. "Rousseau." In his *Shaftesbury, Rousseau, and Kant: An Introduction to the Conflict Between Aesthetic and Moral Values in Modern Thought,* pp. 61-112. Toronto: Associated University Press, 1980.
  Monograph on the relationship between Rousseau's moral and aesthetic values.

Blanchard, William H. *Rousseau and the Spirit of Revolt.* Ann Arbor: University of Michigan Press, 1967, 300 p.
  Presents a psychological study of Rousseau's life and political ideas.

Bloom, Allan. Introduction to *Emile, or On Education,* by Jean-Jacques Rousseau, pp. 3-29. New York: Basic Books, 1979.
  Describes the general intention of *Émile,* a work "whose study is so imperative for an understanding of the human possibility."

Blum, Carol. *Rousseau and the Republic of Virtue: The Language of Politics in the French Revolution.* Ithaca, N.Y.: Cornell University Press, 1986, 302 p.
  Analyzes the popular appeal of Rousseau's literary canon "to explore what expression 'Rousseauvian virtue' found in revolutionary discourse."

Buchner, Margaret Louise. *A Contribution to the Study of the Descriptive Technique of Jean-Jacques Rousseau.* New York: Johnson Reprint Corp., 1973, 184 p.
  Centers on Rousseau's interpretation and application of the Enlightenment theory of sensationalism.

Caird, Edward. "Rousseau." *The Contemporary Review* XXX (September 1877): 625-41.
  Study of the ideas of Rousseau, "the short abstract and chronicle of his time."

Cameron, David. *The Social Thought of Rousseau and Burke: A Comparative Study.* Toronto: University of Toronto Press, 1973, 242 p.
  Demonstrates Burke and Rousseau "are similar in their negations, and similar in their efforts to elaborate . . . a more satisfactory account of political life."

Cassirer, Ernst. *The Question of Jean-Jacques Rousseau,* edited by Peter Gay. New York: Columbia University Press, 1954, 129 p.
  Attempts to reveal the meaning of Rousseau's thought "by providing an understanding of his work as a whole."

Champlin, Carroll D. "Jean Jacques Rousseau: Human Derelict and Educational Pathfinder." *Education* XLIV, No. 3 (November 1923): 133-43.
  Recognizes Rousseau's "incomparable services to education and democracy."

Chapman, John W. *Rousseau—Totalitarian or Liberal?* New York: Columbia University Press, 1956, 154 p.
  Approaches Rousseau's political theory "with a view of explaining the sense in which it deserves to be called liberal."

Cranston, Maurice. *Jean-Jacques: The Early Life and Work of Jean-Jacques Rousseau, 1712-1754.* London: Penguin Books, 1983, 382 p.
  A " 'Lockean' biography" of Rousseau's first forty-two years.

"Rousseau for Our Time." *Daedalus, Proceedings of the American Academy of Arts and Sciences* 107, No. 3 (Summer, 1978).
  Special issue includes studies of Rousseau's influence on utopian theory, politics, the drama, education, anthropology, and autobiography, among others.

De Man, Paul. "Part II: Rousseau." In his *Allegories of Reading: Figural Language in Rousseau, Nietzsche, Rilke, and Proust,* pp. 135-301. New Haven: Yale University Press, 1979.
  Deconstructionist readings of the *Discourse upon Inequality, La Nouvelle Héloïse, Profession de foi, The Social Contract,* and *The Confessions.*

Dent, N. J. H. *Rousseau: An Introduction to his Psychological, Social and Political Theory.* New York: Basil Blackwell, 1988, 258 p.
  Close study of the ideas and arguments of the *Discourses, The Social Contract,* and *Émile.*

Derrida, Jacques. " . . . That Dangerous Supplement . . ." In his *Of Grammatology,* translated by Gayatri Chakravorty Spivak, pp. 141-64. Baltimore: Johns Hopkins University Press, 1976.
  Claims that Rousseau, "straining toward reconstruction of presence [in his writings], . . . valorizes and disqualifies writing at the same time."

Eckstein, Walter. "Rousseau and Spinoza: Their Political Theories and Their Conception of Ethical Freedom." *Journal of the History of Ideas* V, No. 3 (June 1944): 259-91.
  Uncovers affinities in the political and social theories of Benedictus de Spinoza and Rousseau.

France, Peter. *Rousseau: Confessions.* Landmarks of World

Literature, edited by J. P. Stern. New York: Cambridge University Press, 1987, 113 p.

Outlines the context, composition, and aim of *The Confessions,* with analysis of its form and meaning.

Gildin, Hilail. *Rousseau's Social Contract: The Design of the Argument.* Chicago: University of Chicago Press, 1983, 206 p.

Delineates the major components of *The Social Contract.*

Gosse, Edmund. "Rousseau in England in the Nineteenth Century." In his *Aspects and Impressions,* pp. 169-92. London: Cassell and Company, 1922.

Provides retrospective of nineteenth-century English criticism of Rousseau's works and philosophy.

Graves, Frank Pierrepont. "Rousseau and Naturalism in Education." In his *Great Educators of Three Centuries: Their Work and Its Influence on Modern Education,* pp. 77-111. New York: Macmillan Co., 1912.

Utilizes biographical analysis to explain Rousseau's paradoxes, focusing on *Émile.*

Green, F.C. *Jean-Jacques Rousseau: A Critical Study of his Life and Writings.* New York: Cambridge University Press, 1955, 376 p.

Twentieth-century biography of Rousseau in the manner of John Morley's nineteenth-century *Rousseau.*

Grimsley, Ronald. *Rousseau and the Religious Quest.* London: Clarendon Press, 1968, 148 p.

Examines Rousseau's religious experience, thought, and imagination, focusing on their main values and guiding principles.

Hamilton, James F. *Rousseau's Theory of Literature: The Poetics of Art and Nature.* York, S.C.: French Literature Publications Co., 1979, 219 p.

Attempts to bridge the gap between nature and art in Rousseau's works on aesthetics, through examination of his theory of literature.

Harvey, Simon; Hobson, Marian; Kelley, David; and Taylor, Samuel S. B. *Reappraisals of Rousseau.* Totowa, N.J.: Barnes & Noble Books, 1980, 312 p.

Selection of contemporary critical essays in English and French, concentrating on Rousseau's psychological experience, his politics, his writing, and his intellectual relationships.

Havens, George R. *Jean-Jacques Rousseau.* Boston: Twayne Publishers, 1978, 140 p.

Biography treating Rousseau the man and Rousseau the writer.

Heartz, Daniel. "The Beginnings of the Operatic Romance: Rousseau, Sedaine, and Monsigny." *Eighteenth-Century Studies* 15, No. 2 (Winter 1981-82): 149-78.

Contains discussion of the musical importance of Rousseau's operetta, *The Cunning Man.*

Horowitz, Asher. *Rousseau, Nature, and History.* Toronto: University of Toronto Press, 1987, 273 p.

Reveals the theoretical foundations of Rousseau's historical anthropology and clarifies its relation to *La Nouvelle Héloïse, The Social Contract,* and *Émile.*

Josephson, Matthew. *Jean-Jacques Rousseau.* New York: Harcourt, Brace and Co., 1931, 546 p.

Comprehensive biography, with selected bibliography.

Kavanagh, Thomas M. *Writing the Truth: Authority and Desire in Rousseau.* Berkeley and Los Angeles: University of California Press, 1987, 227 p.

Emphasizes "the impossibility in Rousseau's [life] of separating textuality from existence."

Kirk, Russell. "Rousseau on Education." *National Catholic Register* (9 September 1979): 7.

Reviews Allen Bloom's translation of *Émile.* Kirk, one of the key figures in modern conservative thought, praises Bloom's translation and introduction while dissecting *Émile* as an educational manual "in form only. Actually this book is an endeavor to undo the Christian account of the human condition."

Landor, Walter Savage. "Rousseau and Malesherbes." In his *Imaginary Conversations, third series,* pp. 288-302. London: J. C. Nimmo and Bain, 1883.

Literary dialogue between Rousseau and Chrétien de Malesherbes, touching on society, government, and philosophy.

Laski, Harold J. "A Portrait of Jean Jacques Rousseau." In his *The Dangers of Obedience and Other Essays,* pp. 178-206. New York: Harper & Brothers, 1930.

Historical study of Rousseau's life and influence.

Leigh, R. A., ed. *Rousseau After Two Hundred Years: Proceedings of the Cambridge Colloquium.* Cambridge: Cambridge University Press, 1982, 299 p.

Collection of scholarly essays, including "From Orangutan to the Vampire: Towards an Anthropology of Rousseau," by Christopher Frayling and Robert Wokler, among others.

Macdonald, Frederika. *Jean Jacques Rousseau: A New Criticism.* New York: G. P. Putnam's Sons, 1906, 2 vols.

Seeks to demonstrate that Rousseau was indeed the victim of a conspiracy to defame him, documenting the activities of reputed primary instigators such as Grimm, Diderot, and Mme. d'Epinay.

Masters, Roger D. *The Political Philosophy of Rousseau.* Princeton, N.J.: Princeton University Press, 1968, 464 p.

Extensively annotated exegesis of Rousseau's major works of political philosophy.

Misenheimer, Helen Evans. *Rousseau on the Education of Women.* Washington, D.C.: University Press of America, 1981, 95 p.

Discusses Rousseau's "reactionary concepts" of female education, focusing on Chapter V of *Émile.*

More, Paul Elmer. "Rousseau." In his *Shelburne Essays, Sixth Series: Studies of Religious Dualism,* pp. 214-41. Boston and New York: Houghton Mifflin Co., 1909.

Comments on Rousseau's "formative influence" upon educational theory.

Morley, John. *Rousseau.* London: Chapman and Hall, 1873, 2 vols.

Seminal biography, including interpretation of Rousseau's major works.

Muggeridge, Malcolm. "Rousseau Re-read." *Punch* CCXXV, No. 5886 (22 July 1953): 128-29.

Surmises that the enduring fascination of Rousseau's *Confessions* "lies in peeling off . . . successive layers of deception to see what, if anything, lies beneath them."

Neill, Thomas P. "Rousseau—Mother Nature's Bad Boy."

The Catholic World CLXIV, No. 981 (December 1946): 240-47.

> Accentuates Rousseau's insistence on the "natural" in man and society.

Noone, John B., Jr. *Rousseau's Social Contract: A Conceptual Analysis.* Athens: University of Georgia Press, 1980, 222 p.

> Attempts to "find a single complete, systematic presentation of Rousseau's argument" in *The Social Contract* and "lay it out in all its logical splendor."

O'Neal, John C. "Along the Byways to the Self." In his *Seeing and Observing: Rousseau's Rhetoric of Perception,* pp. 115-38. Saratoga, Calif.: ANMA Libri & Co., 1985.

> Treats solitude, botanizing, and promenades as central issues of Rousseau's *Les Rêveries.*

Rice, Richard Ashley. *Rousseau and the Poetry of Nature in Eighteenth Century France.* Smith College Studies in Modern Languages, edited by Caroline B. Bourland, et al., Vol. VI, Nos. 3 & 4. Northampton, Mass.: Departments of Modern Languages of Smith College, 1925, 96 p.

> Studies Rousseau's relation to traditional pastoral modes, particularly his variations and innovations.

Shklar, Judith N. *Men and Citizens: A Study of Rousseau's Social Theory.* London: Cambridge University Press, 1969, 245 p.

> Investigates the relevance of Rousseau's political philosophy to mid-twentieth-century society.

Starobinski, Jean. *Jean-Jacques Rousseau: Transparency and Obstruction.* Translated by Arthur Goldhammer. Chicago: University of Chicago Press, 1988, 421 p.

> Chronological analysis of Rousseau's writings "as if [they] represent a kind of imaginary action" and his life "as if it constituted a lived fiction."

Stephen, Leslie. "Cowper and Rousseau." In his *Hours In a Library,* Vol. II, pp. 193-222. London: Smith, Elder & Co., 1909.

> Remarks upon the contrast and likeness of the two authors.

Strachey, Lytton. "The Rousseau Affair." In his *Books &*

Characters: French & English, pp. 165-78. London: Chatto and Windus, 1922.

> Examines the possibility of a conspiracy among Rousseau's acquaintances to defame his character.

Temmer, Mark J. *Time in Rousseau and Kant: An Essay on French Pre-Romanticism.* Paris: Librairie Minard, 1958, 79 p.

> Parallels Rousseau's "emotional transfiguration of neo-classical realities" to Kant's "intellectual transfiguration and transcendence" of the same.

Vance, Christie McDonald. *The Extravagant Shepherd: A Study of the Pastoral Vision in Rousseau's Nouvelle Heloise.* Studies on Voltaire and the Eighteenth Century, edited by Theodore Besterman, Vol. CV. Banbury, England: The Voltaire Foundation, 1973, 184 p.

> Examines the underlying literary and political ideologies of *La Nouvelle Héloïse.*

Vulliamy, C. E. *Rousseau.* Port Washington, N.Y.: Kennikat Press, 1972, 294 p.

> Detailed literary-biography, including short analyses of the *Discourses,* the *Letter to d'Alembert, La Nouvelle Héloïse, The Social Contract,* and *Émile.*

Wexler, Victor G. " 'Made for Man's Delight': Rousseau as Antifeminist." *American Historical Review* 81, No. 2 (April 1976): 266-91.

> Explores Rousseau's representation of woman in his theory, fiction, and autobiographies.

Whibley, Charles. "Jean Jacques Rousseau." In his *Political Portraits, Second Series.* 1923. Reprint. Freeport, N.Y.: Books for Libraries Press, 1970, 293 p.

> Appraises Rousseau as "the apotheosis of the half-baked."

Williams, Huntington. *Rousseau and Romantic Autobiography.* New York: Oxford University Press, 1983, 252 p.

> Deconstructionist reading of Rousseau's autobiographical writings—*The Confessions, Dialogues,* and *The Rêveries.*

Voltaire

1694-1778

(Born François Marie Arouet) French essayist, dramatist, poet, historian, critic, conte writer, and autobiographer.

Voltaire was a principal figure of the French Enlightenment. He wrote dramas, poetry, history, occasional essays, literary criticism, political and social treatises, an autobiography, and contes—short tales of adventure. Among the latter, *Zadig; ou, La destinée* (*Zadig; or, The Book of Fate. An Oriental History*) and *Candide; ou, L'optimisme* (*Candide*) are highly esteemed. He also composed analytical and philosophical works, notably *Letters concerning the English Nation* (*Lettres philosophiques*) and *Dictionnaire philosophique portatif* (*Philosophical Dictionary*), and was an astonishingly versatile and prolific letter-writer. Throughout his long life, Voltaire was both lauded and despised. To the European literary world, he embodied the highest ideal of the Age of Reason: faith in humankind's ability to perfect itself. Yet he was feared and denigrated by victims of his biting wit. Today, Voltaire is recognized as a leading world philosopher and as a master essayist and storyteller.

Voltaire's life is extremely well documented. He was born François Marie Arouet in 1694, in or near Paris, the son of a prosperous solicitor. His mother, Marie Daumart, was from an upper middle-class family; she died when the boy was seven. Voltaire studied with the Jesuits at the Collège Louis-le-Grand from 1704 to 1711. He was, by all accounts, a brilliant and devoted student. Soon after leaving Louis-le-Grand, he set out to make a name for himself as a professional writer. His father, however, eager to crush his son's rising literary ambitions, sent him out of the country with the French ambassador. In Holland, Voltaire fell madly in love with Olympe de Noyer—nicknamed "Pimpette"—but the affair turned into a scandal and Voltaire was sent home. Back in Paris and miserable at the prospect of practicing law for the rest of his life, he wrote and circulated vitriolic verse attacks on the regent, Phillipe d'Orléans. These works deeply offended Phillipe and brought upon their author state-mandated internal exile at the château of the duc de Sully. In 1717, having again incurred royal wrath, Voltaire was imprisoned for eleven months in the Bastille. Upon his release, his first drama, *Oedipe,* enjoyed tremendous success. He next completed an epic about Henri IV, *La henriade,* infusing it with indictments of fanaticism and praise for religious toleration. Two more dramas followed, then an ugly incident. Having quarreled publicly with the chevalier de Rohan, a member of one of the most powerful families of France, Voltaire was seized by lackeys of the chevalier and caned before a crowd of aristocrats. In the wake of this beating, none of the onlookers supported Voltaire; all saw justice in the action of the chevalier. Recognizing at once that he could not overcome aristocratic prejudices against a common-born poet like himself—ability and achievement, he learned, count for nothing where birth takes precedence—Voltaire fumed. He proposed a duel, was arrested, and spent fifteen days in prison. A sentence of exile was

handed down. In 1726 he left France for England: a crucial and decisive moment.

In England Voltaire found relative freedom in matters of conscience and religion. He met Jonathan Swift and Alexander Pope; studied the works of Shakespeare, Isaac Newton, and John Locke; found backing for a luxurious edition of *La henriade;* and began work on a highly sympathetic portrait of the English, *Letters concerning the English Nation.* Back in France by 1730, he wrote drama upon drama, including the hugely successful *Zaïre.* In 1731 he issued his first historical work, *Histoire de Charles XII, Roi de Suède* (*History of Charles XII, King of Sweden*). This was followed by *Le temple du goust* (*The Temple of Taste*), an essay on literary themes. When *Lettres philosophiques,* the French-language edition of *Letters concerning the English nation,* appeared in 1734, it was greeted with outrage and was ordered burned by censors who denounced the author's implied criticism of French institutions. Alarmed by this incident, Voltaire exercised extreme caution in the voicing of his opinions for years thereafter.

Voltaire was a tremendously rich man by the mid-1730s, having invested heavily in a series of highly successful ventures. Financially independent, he embraced life and literature ever more completely. He began a love affair with the married Gabrielle Emile Le Tonnelier de Breteuil, Marquise du Châtelet. Together they studied chemistry and physics—two of the marquise's abiding interests—at Château de Cirey in Lorraine. All the while, Voltaire continued to write successful dramas, notably the tragedies *Alzire; ou, Les Américains* (*Alzire*), *Mahomet* (*Mahomet the Impostor*), and *La mérope française* (*Merope*). He also began a lively and intimate philosophical correspondence with the crown prince of Prussia. After the crown prince became Frederick II, King of Prussia, in 1740, he attempted repeatedly to entice Voltaire to come live in Potsdam, but Madame du Châtelet strictly opposed such a move. Voltaire and madame were also briefly welcomed by Louis XV at Versailles, where the former was appointed king's historiographer and gentleman of the king's bedchamber. The welcome quickly wore out, however, when Voltaire and the marquise unleashed a series of highly critical remarks about court society.

In 1747 Voltaire completed his first major conte, *Zadig*. He and Madame du Châtelet returned to Lorraine, this time to the court of Stanislas, ex-king of Poland. Their romantic attachment abruptly dissolved, however, when madame took a young officer as her lover. Madame du Châtelet died just after giving birth to the officer's child in 1749. The following year, Voltaire accepted Frederick's invitation to live in Potsdam. The state of affairs between king and commoner was initially highly satisfactory for both, but in time they grew appart philosophically. Among the works of the Potsdam period is a sympathetic history of the reign of Louis XIV, *Le siècle de Louis XIV* (*The Age of Lewis XIV*). Frederick and Voltaire had a stormy falling-out in 1752. The latter, claiming poor health, began his return to France, only to be arrested in Frankfurt in 1753 and forced to surrender a volume of Frederick's poetry, earlier presented to him by the king himself. This indignity deeply distressed Voltaire.

Voltaire now found himself unwelcome in Paris and shunned at the great courts. Moreover, a stolen manuscript of his world history was published in a distorted and ludicrously adulterated version, causing the author much embarrassment. This incident prompted publication of an authorized text under the title *Essai sur l'histoire générale, et sur les moeurs et l'esprit des nations* (*An Essay on Universal History, the Manners and Spirit of Nations*). With his new mistress, his niece Marie Louise Mignot Denis, Voltaire settled near Geneva on an estate he named "Les Délices." This move is considered a milestone in Voltaire's career. Henceforth, financially secure and relieved of the need to satisfy the whims of powerful acquaintances, he devoted himself to writing history and criticism. Above all, he championed the chief social issues of the age, religious and political toleration. In 1756 he wrote his celebrated *Poème sur le désastre de Lisbonne*, a strongly philosophical meditation upon the devastating 1755 Lisbon earthquake. Therein he attempted to reconcile the disaster with the Leibnizian doctrine of Optimism, which held that this world is the best possible world, and with the idea of the existence of a benevolent providence. Three years later, in *Candide,* he again attacked Optimism. Meanwhile, to avoid possible interference with his work from the Protestant authorities of Geneva, he purchased two estates in France near the Swiss border, settling at Ferney. By about 1760 he had begun to attack organized religion

mercilessly, adopting the expression "Écrasez l'infâme"— "Crush the infamous"—as his personal motto. In numerous short, sarcastic works published anonymously or pseudonymously but unmistakably bearing his touch, he defended the Encyclopedists against charges of impiety, targeting conservative laymen and ecclesiastics alike. He also decried judicial malpractice and sought redress for victims of wrongful conviction. One such case, known as the Calas Affair, remains one of the most celebrated incidents of its kind. Jean Calas, a Protestant merchant in fiercely Roman Catholic Toulouse, was convicted, against very strong evidence to the contrary, of murdering his own son in order to prevent the young man from becoming a Catholic. Calas was ruthlessly tortured and brutally executed by order of the Parlement of Toulouse. Voltaire was shocked by what he saw as a terrible and willful miscarriage of justice, and he set out against enormous odds to have the verdict reversed. In his 1763 *Traité sur la tolérance* (*A Treatise on Religious Tolerance, Occasioned by the Execution of the Unfortunate Jean Calas, Unjustly Condemned and Broken on the Wheel at Toulouse, for the Supposed Murder of His Own Son*), he marshaled evidence that young Calas was not murdered by his family. He also enlisted the aid of his most powerful allies in swaying public opinion in this matter. Ultimately, he succeeded in having the name of Jean Calas rehabilitated, although the authorities of Toulouse never accepted the new verdict. Scholars agree that Voltaire put himself at real personal risk in this campaign.

The years following the Calas Affair were spent chiefly at Ferney. Voltaire continued to write tirelessly: dramas, criticism, eulogies, treatises, histories, contes, essays, an autobiography, and ream upon ream of letters—all bearing the imprint of the man who now often signed his writings with motto alone, "Écrasez l'infâme." His best-known work of this period is his 1764 *Philosophical Dictionary,* which underwent extensive revisions and several title changes during the next decade or so. In 1778, at the age of eighty-four, Voltaire returned to Paris, where he was thunderously acclaimed at a performance of *Irène*. He died soon after and was buried at the Abbey of Scellières. In 1791, his ashes were transferred to the Panthéon in Paris.

Voltaire was an extremely prolific author who wrote several acknowledged world masterpieces. Among them, *Candide, Letters concerning the English Nation,* and the *Philosophical Dictionary* are very widely known. Nevertheless, Voltaire is known more for the general tenets of his thought than for any particular text or group of works. Most commentators agree that this is because his motto, "Écrasez l'infâme," is mirrored to some degree in nearly everything he wrote, early or late, and helps to unify his literary canon under a general theme. Voltaire constantly fought prejudice and injustice. He embraced progress and liberty while denouncing what he perceived as wanton excesses of church and state. He tirelessly promoted freedom of speech and thought. He decried fanaticism and intolerance. In a way, critics have argued, he presaged in his writings a later fascination with the "common man." Sometimes militantly anticlerical, he was just as often determinedly eager to maintain at least the appearance of objectivity in his analyses of contemporary events. This is especially apparent in his historical works.

Critics concur that as a propagandist Voltaire was practically unrivaled in his day. In *Candide,* for example, he castigated Optimism with irony, tricking his readers into thinking about two of the most pressing intellectual issues of the age: God's role in world events and the apparent errors of metaphysics. By his own admission, he aimed thereby to improve the human lot. In religious matters, Voltaire was for most of his life a deist. He believed in God but abhorred false, "priestly" traditions. Above all, he faulted cultish closed-mindedness. These views are apparent in the contes, in the philosophical and topical works—even in the dramas. Critics are divided about the nature of Voltaire's most deeply held convictions, however. While it is clear that organized religion held no appeal for him, he nevertheless maintained a lifelong admiration of his Jesuit teachers. Equally, though he denounced Optimism as a doctrine, he apparently viewed the alleged "necessity" of despair with no less horror. In the end, scholars have noted, he probably saw life as a kind of insoluble mystery, fascinating to observe and quick to reward those who embrace it without prejudice.

Perhaps because of the enormity of his literary output and its tremendous variety, Voltaire has long defied capsule critical assessment. Most commentators, however, have freely acknowledged his unique place in eighteenth-century French literature. Wrote Gustave Lanson in his 1906 critical study of Voltaire: "We may consider Montesquieu, Rousseau, Buffon, and Diderot as greater geniuses, but Voltaire was, in the broadest sense, the most representative mind of his age, the one in whom the brilliance of eighteenth century French society was summed up most completely and brought to its most exquisite perfection. He embodied its good and bad features, its graces and blemishes, its breadth of view and its limitations, its impulses and enthusiasms as well as its hesitations and timidities." From earliest times, Voltaire was recognized as a genius who had something important to say. His topical essays were viewed as seminal analyses of pressing issues; his poems and plays were considered masterful examples of their respective genres; his epic *La henriade* was acclaimed as the French counterpart of *The Aeneid;* and his contes were enjoyed by casual reader and serious thinker alike. According to Nikolai Mikhailovich Karamzin, who visited Ferney shortly after the author's death, Voltaire was "the most illustrious writer of our age. . . . It must be acknowledged that no other writer of the eighteenth century had such an impact upon his contemporaries as Voltaire. . . . [He] wrote for every kind of reader, for the unlearned as well as the learned."

Karamzin's view is echoed again and again in writings of the late eighteenth century. During the first third of the nineteenth century, however, Voltaire's reputation as the supreme dramatist and poet of his age was eclipsed somewhat, overshadowed by his elevation as one of the greatest thinkers of all time. Since then, critics have focused more on Voltaire's thought than on his technical skills as a writer. George Saintsbury, writing in 1911, assessed earlier criticism of Voltaire as decidedly partisan. "Most judgments of Voltaire," he claimed, "have been unduly coloured by sympathy with or dislike of what may be briefly called his polemical side. When sympathy and dislike are both discarded or allowed for, he remains one of the most astonishing, if not exactly one of the most admirable, figures of letters." Twentieth-century critics have studied Voltaire from a variety of angles. The tone and tempo of his contes have been explored; the form and purpose of his philosophical writings have been scrutinized; his moral and religious thought have been examined; and, very recently, his depictions of women have been closely studied. Equally, the generic elements of his best-known poems and dramas have been reassessed, often favorably.

Today, Voltaire remains one of the chief figures of the French Enlightenment and an author of world importance. He played a major part in spreading the gospel of rational skepticism to the world, and he infused his message with pleas for religious and political toleration. His faith in humankind's ability to perfect itself was deep and abiding. A statement in his introduction to the seventh edition of the *Philosophical Dictionary* sums up much of his thinking: "Persons of every estate will find here something that will instruct, while it amuses, them. The book does not demand a continuous reading; but at whatever place you open it, you will find something to think about. Those books are most useful in which the readers do half the work themselves; they develop the thought whose germ has been presented to them; they correct what seems defective, and with their own reflections strengthen what appears weak."

PRINCIPAL WORKS

Oedipe (drama) 1719
La ligue; ou, Henry le Grand (poetry) 1723; also published as *La henriade,* 1728
    [*Henriade: An Epick Poem,* 1732]
Hérode et Mariamne (drama) 1725
L'indiscret (drama) 1725
An Essay upon the Civil Wars of France and upon Epick Poetry, 1727; also published as *Essai sur la poésie épique* [partial translation], 1728
Le Brutus de Monsieur de Voltaire, avec un discours sur la tragédie (drama and criticism) 1731
Histoire de Charles XII, Roi de Suède (history) 1731
    [*History of Charles XII, King of Sweden,* 1732]
Zayre (drama) 1732; also published as *Zaïre,* 1736
    [*Tragedy of Zara,* 1736]
Letters concerning the English Nation (prose) 1733; also published as *Lettres écrites de Londres sur les Anglois et autres sujets,* 1734; also published as *Lettres philosophiques,* 1734
Le temple du goust (essay) 1733
    [*The Temple of Taste,* 1734]
La mort de César (drama) 1735
Alzire; ou, Les Américains (drama) 1736
    [*Alzire,* 1736]
Elémens de la philosophie de Neuton, mis à la portée de tout le monde (treatise) 1738
    [*The Elements of Sir Isaac Newton's Philosophy,* 1738]
L'enfant prodigue (drama) 1738
    [*The Prodigal,* 1750]
Oeuvres de M. de Voltaire. 12 vols. (essays, dramas, philosophy, poetry, prose, history, and criticism) 1738-60
    [*The Works of Voltaire,* 35 vols., 1761-69]
Vie de Molière, avec des jugements sur ses ouvrages (biography and criticism) 1739
Anti-Machiavel; ou, Essai de critique sur le Prince de Machiavel [with Frederick the Great] (criticism)

1740; also published as *Examen du Prince de Machia-vel, avec des notes historiques & politiques* [revised edition], 1741

Mahomet (drama) 1742
    [*Mahomet the Impostor,* 1744]

Lettre à Mr. Norberg, chapelain du roy de Suède, Charles XII (essay) 1744

La mérope française, avec quelques petites pièces de littérature (drama and criticism) 1744
    [*Merope,* 1744]

La Princesse de Navarre (drama) 1745

Memnon: Histoire orientale (prose) 1747; also published as *Zadig; ou, La destinée,* 1749
    [*Zadig; or, The Book of Fate. An Oriental History,* 1749]

Le monde comme il va (prose) 1748; published in *Oeuvres de M. de Voltaire*
    [*Babouc; or, The World As It Goes,* 1754]

Nanine (drama) 1749

La tragédie de Semiramis, et quelques autres pièces de littérature (drama and criticism) 1749
    [*Semiramis* (partial translation), 1760]

Oreste (drama) 1750

Remercîment sincère à un homme charitable (essay) 1750

Samson (drama) 1750

Le siècle de Louis XIV. 2 vols. (history) 1751
    [*The Age of Lewis XIV,* 2 vols., 1752]

Le duc de Foix (drama) 1752
    [*Matilda,* 1811]

Le Micromégas de Mr. de Voltaire, avec une histoire des croisades & un nouveau plan de l'histoire de l'esprit humain (prose) 1752
    [*Micromegas: A Comic Romance,* 1753]

Rome sauvée (drama) 1752
    [*Rome Preserv'd,* 1760]

Abrégé de l'histoire universelle, depuis Charlemagne, jusques à Charlequint (history) 1753

Annales de l'empire depuis Charlemagne. 2 vols. (history) 1753
    [*Annals of the Empire from the Reign of Charlemagne,* 1781]

L'histoire de la guerre de mil sept cent quarante & un. 2 vols. (history) 1755
    [*History of the War of Seventeen Hundred and Forty One,* 1756]

L'orphelin de la Chine (drama) 1755
    [*The Orphans of China,* 1756]

La pucelle d'Orléans (poetry) 1755; also published as *La pucelle d'Orléans; ou, Jeanne d'Arc* [complete edition], 1756
    [*La Pucelle,* 1789]

Saul (drama) 1755
    [*Saul,* 1820]

Essay sur l'histoire générale, et sur les moeurs et l'esprit des nations, depuis Charlemagne jusqu'à nos jours. 7 vols. (prose) 1756
    [*An Essay on Universal History, the Manners and Spirit of Nations, from the Reign of Charlemaign to the Age of Lewis XIV,* 4 vols., 1759]

Poèmes sur le désastre de Lisbonne et sur la loi naturelle (poetry) 1756

La religion naturelle (poetry) 1756

Le porte-feuille trouvé; ou, Tablettes d'un curieux (poetry and prose) 1757

La femme qui a raison (drama) 1758

Candide; ou, L'optimisme, traduit de l'Allemand, de Mr. le Docteur Ralph (prose) 1759
    [*Candide; or, All for the Best,* 1759]

Précis de l'Écclesiaste, et du Cantique des Cantiques (prose) 1759

Histoire de l'empire de Russie sous Pierre le Grand. 2 vols. (history) 1759-63
    [*History of the Russian Empire under Peter the Great,* 2 vols., 1763]

Le Caffé; ou, L'Écossaise (drama) 1760
    [*The Coffee House; or, Fair Fugitive,* 1760]

Lettre de M. de Voltaire au Roi Stanislas (letter) 1760

Lettres de Monsieur de Voltaire, à M. Palissot, avec les réponses, à l'occasion de la comédie des Philosophes (prose) 1760

Ma confession (essay) 1760

Ode sur la mort de Son Altesse Royale Madame la Markgrave de Bareith (poetry) 1760

Tancrède (drama) 1760
    [*Almida,* 1771]

Épître de M. de Voltaire à Madame Denis sur l'agriculture (prose) 1761

Épître de Monsieur de Voltaire à Mademoiselle Clairon (prose) 1761

Lettres de M. de Voltaire à l'Electeur Palatin, et au Roi de Prusse (prose) 1761

Lettres sur La nouvelle Héloïse; ou, Aloisa de Jean Jacques Rousseau (criticism) 1761

Réponse de Monsieur de Voltaire, à Monsieur le Duc de Bouillon (letter) 1761

Le droit du seigneur (drama) 1762

Éloge de M. de Crébillon (eulogy) 1762

Histoire d'Elisabeth Canning et de Jean Calas (essay) 1762

Pièces originales concernant la mort cruelle du Sieur Calas, qui fut condamné par le Parlement de Toulouse, a être roué tout vif, sur une accusation fausse, d'avoir fait mourir son fils aîné, pour l'empêcher de se déclarer Catholique Romain (essay) 1762

Le théâtre de M. de Voltaire. 5 vols. (dramas) 1762-63

Lettre de M. de Voltaire à M. Dalembert (prose) 1763

Traité sur la tolérance (essay) 1763
    [*A Treatise on Religious Tolerance, Occasioned by the Execution of the Unfortunate Jean Calas, Unjustly Condemned and Broken on the Wheel at Toulouse, for the Supposed Murder of His Own Son,* 1764]

Zulime (drama) 1763

Aux plaisirs, 27 janvier 1764 (letter) 1764

Contes de Guillaume Vadé (criticism and prose) 1764; revised edition, 1765

Dictionnaire philosophique portatif (prose) 1764; revised editions, 1765, 1767; also published as *La raison par alphabet* [revised edition], 1769
    [*Philosophical Dictionary for the Pocket,* 1765]

Macare et Thélème (poetry) 1764

Doutes nouveaux sur le testament attribué au Cardinal de Richelieu (essay) 1765

Lettre de M. de Vol. . . . . à M. D'Am. . . . . . premier mars 1765, au Château de Ferney (essay) 1765

Lettres secrettes de Mr. de Voltaire, publiées par Mr. L. B. (letters) 1765

La philosophie de l'histoire, par feu l'Abbé Bazin (prose) 1765

[*The Philosophy of History*, 1766]
Avis au public sur les parricides imputés aux Calas et aux Sirven (prose) 1766
Commentaire sur le livre des Délits et des Peines, par un avocat de province (criticism) 1766
Lettre de Monsieur de Voltaire à Monsieur Hume (essay) 1766
Lettres de M. de Voltaire à ses amis du Parnasse, avec des notes historiques et critiques (letters) 1766
Le philosophe ignorant (prose) 1766
[*The Ignorant Philosopher*, 1767]
Le Président de Thou justifié contre les accusations de M. de Buri, auteur d'une Vie de Henri IV (essay) 1766
Charlot (drama) 1767
La défense de mon oncle (essay) 1767
[*A Defence of My Uncle*, 1768]
L'ingénu: Histoire véritable, tirée des manuscrits de Père Quesnel (prose) 1767
[*The Pupil of Nature*, 1771; also published as *The Sincere Huron*, 1786]
Les scythes (drama) 1767
Les droits de l'homme, et les usurpations des autres (essay) 1768
L'épître aux romains, par Le Comte Passeran, traduite de l'Italien (prose) 1768
La guerre civile de Génève; ou, Les amours de Robert Covelle (poetry) 1768
[*The Civil War of Geneva; or, The Amours of Robert Covelle*, 1769]
L'homme aux quarante écus (prose) 1768
[*The Man of Forty Crowns*, 1768]
La Princesse de Babilone (prose) 1768
[*The Princess of Babylon*, 1927]
Les singularités de la nature, par un académicien de Londres, de Boulogne, de Petersbourg, de Berlin, &c. (prose) 1768
Les guèbres; ou, La Tolérance (drama) 1769
Histoire du Parlement de Paris, par Mr. l'Abbé de Big. . . . . 2 vols. (prose) 1769
L'évangile du jour. 10 vols. [with other authors] (essays) 1769-75
Questions sur l'Encyclopédie. 5 vols. (prose) 1770-71
La méprise d'Arras (essay) 1771
Le depositaire (drama) 1772
Les lois de Minos; ou, Astérie (drama) 1772
Fragments sur l'Inde. 2 vols. (prose) 1773
[*Fragments on India*, 1937]
Lettre de Monsieur de Voltaire, à Messieurs de la Noblesse de Bevaudan, qui ont écrit en faveur de Monsieur le Comte de Morangies (letter) 1773
Le taureau blanc (prose) 1774
[*The White Bull: An Oriental History*, 2 vols., 1774]
Le cri du sang innocent (prose) 1775
Don Pèdre, Roi de Castille (drama) 1775
La Bible enfin expliquée par plusieurs aumoniers de S. M. L. R. D. P. 2 vols. (criticism) 1776
Lettres chinoises, indiennes et tartares, à Monsieur Paw, par un bénédictin, avec plusieurs autres pièces intéressantes (prose) 1776
Un chrétien contre six juifs (essay) 1777
Irène (drama) 1778
Ériphile (drama) 1779
Mémoires de M. de Voltaire écrits par lui-même (autobiography) 1784

[*Memoirs of M. de Voltaire Written by Himself*, 1784]
Correspondance de Voltaire et du Cardinal de Bernis, depuis 1761 jusqu'à 1777 (letters) 1799
Lettres inédites de Voltaire, a Frédéric-le-grand, Roi de Prusse (letters) 1802
[*Letters of Voltaire and Frederick the Great*, 1927]
Correspondance. 107 vols. (letters) 1953-65

The Gentleman's Magazine and Historical Quarterly (essay date 1759)

[*In the following excerpt from a 1759* Gentleman's Magazine *review, the anonymous critic challenges Voltaire's understanding of the very philosophy he criticized in* Candide—*"the notion that 'all things are for the best'."*]

[*Candide*] is an attempt to ridicule the notion that 'all things are for the best,' by representing the calamities of life, artfully aggravated, in a strong light. This notion has been maintained by many philosophers antient and modern, and has been adopted by Mr *Pope* in his celebrated epistles, called, *An Essay on Man.* It is indeed true, that there are earthquakes, wars, vices, and diseases, which are perpetually productive of very extensive and complicated misery among mankind; and, it is equally true, that if another system was possible, in which there would have been more good upon the whole, we cannot conceive how infinite goodness could produce this: It still follows, therefore, for all that human beings can know to the contrary, that if the author of nature is infinitely good, this is the best possible system; and that if this is not the best possible system, the author of nature is not infinitely good.

To prove that the author of nature is not infinitely good, by proving that this is not the best possible system, it is necessary to know this and every other possible system perfectly in all their extent, relations, connections, and dependencies, which is impossible to man; but there are many arguments to prove that the author of nature is good, which lie within the compass of human knowledge, and as the only argument for the contrary lies confessedly beyond our knowledge, it may still be inferred, notwithstanding the mal-apert smartness of such witling-metaphysicians as M. *de Voltaire*, that whatever is, is right.

Voltaire seems indeed to have understood the opinion, which he has endeavoured to ridicule, and the arguments by which it is supported, in a very imperfect and confused manner; he has, in several places, confounded the scheme of the best with the scheme of *fitness,* & of *eternal relations of things;* & he has, like other ignorant persons, considered the appointments of providence as implying an absurd necessity, which, supposing poison to be offered a man to drink, would afford him this argument: It is now certain either that I shall die to night, or I shall not; if that I shall, I shall die, tho' I do not drink the poison; if that I shall not, I shall live, tho' I do drink it; so that my drinking, or not drinking the poison, is a matter of mere indifference, and can have no influence upon my life. Not considering, that the means and the end are inseparable, and that if it is certain that a man shall die by poison, it is also certain that he shall drink it. (pp. 233-34)

A review of "Candide," in The Gentleman's Magazine and Historical Chronicle, *Vol. XXIX, May, 1759, pp. 233-35.*

Gotthold Ephraim Lessing   (essay date 1767)

[*Lessing is considered the greatest aesthetic theorist of the German Enlightenment. Through his critical and dramatic works he helped free German literature from the conventional strictures of the then-dominant French classical school. In his highly influential aesthetic study* Laokoon; oder, Über die Grenzen der Mahlerey und Poesie *(1766;* Laocoon; or, The Limits of Poetry and Painting, *1836) he defined and differentiated the provinces of the plastic arts and literature, arguing in lucid, pithy, and ironic prose against imposing the characteristics proper to one artistic medium upon the other. His* Die Hamburgische Dramaturgie *(2 vols., 1767-68;* Hamburg Dramaturgy, *1962) is a revolutionary plea for a drama based on imaginative inspiration and observation rather than on arbitrary rules. In the following excerpt from this work, he compares Voltaire's* Zaire *to dramas by Shakespeare.*]

The sixteenth evening *Zaire* by Voltaire was performed. "To those who care for literary history," says M. de Voltaire, "it will not be displeasing to know how this play originated. Various ladies had reproached the author because his tragedies did not contain enough about love. He replied that in his opinion, tragedy was not the most fitting place for love; still if they would insist on having enamoured heroes he also could create them. The play was written in eighteen days and received with applause. In Paris it is named a Christian tragedy and has often been played in place of 'Polyeucte.'"

To the ladies therefore we are indebted for this tragedy and it will long remain the favourite play of the ladies. A young ardent monarch, only subjugated by love; a proud conqueror only conquered by love; a Sultan without polygamy; a seraglio converted into the free and accessible abode of an absolute mistress; a forsaken maiden raised to the highest pinnacle of fortune, thanks solely to her lovely eyes; a heart for which religion and tenderness contest, that is divided between its god and its idol, that would like to be pious if only it need not cease loving; a jealous man who recognises his error and avenges it on himself: if these flattering ideas do not bribe the suffrages of the fair sex, then what indeed could bribe them?

Love itself dictated *Zaire* to Voltaire! said a polite art critic. He would have been nearer the truth had he said gallantry; I know but one tragedy at which love itself has laboured and that is 'Romeo and Juliet' by Shakespeare. It is incontestable, that Voltaire makes his enamoured Zaire express her feelings with much nicety and decorum. But what is this expression compared with that living picture of all the smallest, most secret, artifices whereby love steals into our souls, all the imperceptible advantages it gains thereby, all the subterfuges with which it manages to supersede every other passion until it succeeds in holding the post of sole tyrant of our desires and aversions? Voltaire perfectly understands the—so to speak—official

language of love; that is to say the language and the tone love employs when it desires to express itself with caution and dignity, when it would say nothing but what the prudish female sophist and the cold critic can justify. Still even the most efficient government clerk does not always know the most about the secrets of his government; or else if Voltaire had the same deep insight as Shakespeare into the essence of love, he would not exhibit it here, and therefore the poem has remained beneath the capacities of the poet.

Almost the same might be said of jealousy. His jealous Orosman plays a sorry figure beside the jealous Othello of Shakespeare. And yet Othello has unquestionably furnished the prototype of Orosman. Cibber says Voltaire avails himself of the brand that lighted the tragic pile of Shakespeare. I should have said: a brand from out of this flaming pile and moreover one that smoked more than it glowed or warmed. In Orosman we hear a jealous man speak and we see him commit a rash deed of jealousy, but of jealousy itself we learn neither more nor less than what we knew before. Othello on the contrary is a complete manual of this deplorable madness; there we can learn all that refers to it and awakens it and how we may avoid it.

But is it always Shakespeare, always and eternally Shakespeare who understood everything better than the French, I hear my readers ask? That annoys us, because we cannot read him. I seize this opportunity to remind the public of what it seems purposely to have forgotten. We have a translation of Shakespeare. It is scarcely finished and yet seems already forgotten. Critics have spoken ill of it. I have a mind to speak very well of it. Not in order to contradict these learned men, nor to defend the faults they have discovered, but because I believe there is no need to make so much ado about these faults. The undertaking was a difficult one, and any other person than Herr Wieland would have made other slips in their haste, or have passed over more passages from ignorance or laziness and what parts he has done well few will do better. Any way his rendering of Shakespeare is a book that cannot be enough commended among us. We have much to learn yet from the beauties he has given to us, before the blemishes wherewith he has marred them offend us so greatly that we require a new translation.

To return to *Zaire.* It was brought out on the Parisian stage in 1733 by the author; and three years after it was translated into English and played in London at Drury Lane. The translator was Aaron Hill, himself no mean dramatic poet. This greatly flattered Voltaire, and what he said of it in his dedication to the Englishman Falkener deserves to be read, for it is in his peculiar strain of proud humility. Only we must not think everything is as true as he asserts.

Woe to him who does not always read Voltaire's writings in the sceptical spirit wherein he has written a portion of them.

For instance, he says to his English friend "Your poets had a custom to which even Addison himself submitted; for custom is as mighty as reason or law. This unreasonable custom was that every act must be concluded by verses in a style quite different from that of the rest of the play, and also these verses must of necessity contain a comparison. Phædra before her exit, compares herself poetically to a stag, Cato to a rock, and Cleopatra to children who weep themselves to sleep. The translator of *Zaire* is the first who has ventured to maintain the laws of nature against such an abnormal taste. He has abolished this custom, for he felt that passion must speak its own language and that the poet must everywhere conceal himself in order that we may recognise the hero."

There are only three untruths in this passage; that is not much for M. de Voltaire. It is true that the English since Shakespeare or perhaps even before him, had the habit of ending their blank verse acts with a few rhyming lines. But that these rhyming lines consisted only of comparisons, that they necessarily contained such comparisons, is entirely false; and I cannot imagine how M. de Voltaire could say such things to the face of an Englishman who might also be presumed to have read the tragic poets of his nation. Secondly it is not true that Hill departed from this custom in his translation of *Zaire.* It is indeed almost incredible that M. de Voltaire should not have looked more closely at a translation of his own play than I or some one else. And yet so it must be. For as certainly as it is in blank verse, so certainly does every act close with two or four rhymed lines. Comparisons, it is true, they do not contain, but as I said, among all the rhymed lines with which Shakespeare and Jonson and Dryden and Lee and Otway and Rowe and all the rest conclude their acts, there are certainly a hundred against five that likewise do not contain them. Therefore where is Hill's speciality? But even had he had the speciality that Voltaire confers on him, it is not true, in the third place, that his example has had the influence that Voltaire accords it. Of the tragedies that even now appear in England, half, if not more, have their acts ending with rhymes, rather than without them. Hill himself has never entirely abandoned the old custom even in those plays he has written since the translation of *Zaire.* And what does it matter whether we hear rhymes at the end or no? If they are there, they may perhaps be useful to the orchestra to warn them to take up their instruments; a sign which in this way would be more prettily given out of the play itself than by means of a whistle or other signal. (pp. 40-3)

> *Gotthold Ephraim Lessing, in an excerpt from his* Hamburg Dramaturgy, *Dover, 1962, pp. 40-3.*

Nikolai Mikhailovich Karamzin   (letter date 1789)

[*Karamzin was the most important Russian writer of his generation and the leader of the Russian Sentimentalist movement in literature. He was also influential in linguistic reform. He introduced French syntax and cultural terms to his native tongue, eliminated many Slavonic words, and based his writing on the spoken language of the gentry. In 1789, at age twenty-two, Karamzin left Moscow and traveled through Germany, Switzerland, France, and England. Eighteen months later he returned to Russia and founded the literary journal* Moskovsky zhurnal *in which he began the serial publication of his* Pis'ma Russkogo puteshestvennika *(Travels from Moscow through Prussia, Germany, Switzerland, France, and England, 1803); he called this work the "mirror of my soul." Influenced by Laurence Sterne's* Sentimental Journey *and characterized by an intense subjectivity, these letters brought Karamzin im-*

mediate recognition and established him as a leading literary figure in Russia. In the following excerpt from one such "sentimental letter," written in Geneva and dated 2 October 1789, Karamzin recounts a visit to Voltaire's château at Ferney, favorably noting the universal appeal of the literary works of "the most illustrious writer of our age."]

Who, being in the republic of Geneva, would not consider it a pleasant duty to visit Ferney, where the most illustrious writer of our age lived?

I walked there with a young German. The late Voltaire's home is situated on an elevation a short distance from the village of Ferney. There is a beautiful *allée* leading to it. In front of the house, on the left, we saw a small church bearing the inscription, "From Voltaire to God."

"Voltaire was one of the ardent worshipers of the deity," said La Harpe in his eulogy on the famous sage of Ferney. " 'Si Dieu n'existait pas, il faudrait l'inventer' (If God did not exist, he would have to be invented)—this wonderful line was written in his old age, and it indicates his philosophy."

A man, who came out to meet us, refused us admission, saying that his master, to whom Voltaire's famous heiress had sold this mansion, had given orders that no one be permitted to enter. However, as soon as we assured him of our generosity, he opened the door to the sanctuary, the rooms where Voltaire had lived and where everything has been left just as it was. The furnishings in the room are fine and rather sumptuous. Voltaire's heart was kept in the chamber where his bed stands, until Madame Denis took it to Paris with her. Now there remains only a black monument with the inscription, "Son esprit est partout et son coeur est ici" (His spirit is everywhere, his heart is here). And over this, "Mes manes sont consolés, puisque mon coeur est au milieu de vous" (My shades are comforted, for my heart is amongst you).

On the walls hang several portraits: first, our empress (embroidered on silk, with the inscription, "Présenté à M. Voltaire par l'auteur." This one I contemplated with greater attention and greater pleasure than the others); second, the late king of Prussia; third, LeKain, the noted Parisian actor; fourth, Voltaire himself; and fifth, the Marquise du Châtelet, who was his friend and more than a friend. Among the engravings I noticed portraits of Newton, Boileau, Marmontel, d'Alembert, Franklin, Helvétius, Clement XIV, Diderot, and Delisle. The other prints and paintings are not particularly interesting.

Voltaire's bedroom served him also as a study from which he taught, stirred, and amused Europe. Yes, my friends! It must be acknowledged that no other writer of the eighteenth century had such an impact upon his contemporaries as Voltaire. To his honor let it be said that he spread that tolerance in religious matters which characterizes our time, and covered with shame the infamous superstition which, even in the beginning of the eighteenth century, created bloody victims in our Europe.

Voltaire wrote for every kind of reader, for the unlearned as well as the learned. All understood him and all were captivated by him. No one else could expose so skillfully the ridiculous in all things, and no philosophy has been able to withstand his irony. The public was always on his side, for he gave them the pleasure of laughing! We do not find in Voltaire's works, generally, those lofty ideas with which the Genius of Nature, so to speak, inspires its chosen mortals. But these ideas are given to but a few people, and therefore their influence is very limited. Everyone likes to watch the skylark soar, but whose eye will dare to follow the eagle to the sun? Who does not feel the beauties of **Zaïre**? But do many admire *Othello?*

The location of Ferney is so beautiful that I envied Voltaire. From his windows he could see Mont Blanc, the loftiest peak in Europe, and other snowy piles, together with verdant fields, gardens, and further pleasing sights. The Ferney garden Voltaire himself planned, and it reflects his taste. I liked most of all a long path, which seems to join the mountains. A large, clear pond serves as a mirror for the tall trees which shade its bank.

Voltaire's name is on the lips of all the inhabitants of Ferney. Sitting there beneath the boughs of a chestnut tree, I read with feeling this passage of La Harpe's eulogy:

> His subjects, robbed of their father and master, and their children, heirs of his bounty, will say to the wanderer who leaves his path to see Ferney, 'Here are the houses he built, the sanctuary he gave to the useful arts, the fields he enriched with fruit. This populous and thriving village was born under his eye, was born in the midst of a wilderness. Here are the roads, the paths, the groves where we so often saw him. Here the grief-stricken Calas family gathered round their defender. Here these wretched ones embraced his knees. This tree was dedicated with gratitude, and no axe will ever sever it from its root. He sat beneath its shade when the ruined villagers came to ask his help. Here he shed tears of compassion and turned the grief of the poor into joy. In this place they saw him for the last time!'— and the attentive wanderer, who could not restrain his tears while reading *Zaïre,* will weep anew, perhaps, in memory of the friend of mankind.

I took dinner at the inn in Ferney with two young Englishmen, and drank some very excellent French wine to the eternal blessedness of Voltaire's soul. (pp. 147-49)

> *Nikolai Mikhailovich Karamzin, in a letter on October 2, 1789, in his* Letters of a Russian Traveler, 1789-1790: An Account of a Young Russian Gentleman's Tour through Germany, Switzerland, France, and England, *edited and translated by Florence Jonas, Columbia University Press, 1957, pp. 144-50.*

James Boswell   (essay date 1791)

[*One of the most colorful and widely read figures in eighteenth-century English literature, Boswell is esteemed for his inimitable conversational style and pictorial documentation of life in such nonfiction works as* Journal of a Tour to the Hebrides with Samuel Johnson, LL.D. *(1785), his posthumously published* London Journal, *and the masterpiece for which he has been labeled the greatest of English biographers,* The Life of Samuel Johnson, LL.D. *(1791). In this immensely readable and memorable work, Boswell firmly established biography as a leading literary form through a conscious, pioneering attempt to recreate his subject by*

combining life history with anecdote, observation, dialogue, theme, and plot. In the following excerpt from The Life of Johnson, *Boswell, recounting events that took place in 1759, briefly compares* Candide *with Johnson's* Rasselas, Prince of Abyssinia.]

Considering the large sums which have been received for compilations, and works requiring not much more genius than compilations, we cannot but wonder at the very low price which [Johnson] was content to receive for this admirable performance [*Rasselas, Prince of Abyssinia*]; which, though he had written nothing else, would have rendered his name immortal in the world of literature. None of his writings has been so extensively diffused over Europe; for it has been translated into most, if not all, of the modern languages. This Tale, with all the charms of oriental imagery, and all the force and beauty of which the English language is capable, leads us through the most important scenes of human life, and shews us that this stage of our being is full of "vanity and vexation of spirit." To those who look no further than the present life, or who maintain that human nature has not fallen from the state in which it was created, the instruction of this sublime story will be of no avail. But they who think justly, and feel with strong sensibility, will listen with eagerness and admiration to its truth and wisdom. Voltaire's **Candide,** written to refute the system of Optimism, which it has accomplished with brilliant success, is wonderfully similar in its plan and conduct to Johnson's *Rasselas;* insomuch, that I have heard Johnson say, that if they had not been published so closely one after the other that there was not time for imitation, it would have been in vain to deny that the scheme of that which came latest was taken from the other. Though the proposition illustrated by both these works was the same, namely, that in our present state there is more evil than good, the intention of the writers was very different. Voltaire I am afraid, meant only by wanton profaneness to obtain a sportive victory over religion, and to discredit the belief of a superintending Providence: Johnson meant, by shewing the unsatisfactory nature of things temporal, to direct the hopes of man to things eternal. Rasselas, as was observed to me by a very accomplished lady, may be considered as a more enlarged and more deeply philosophical discourse in prose, upon the interesting truth, which in his "Vanity of Human Wishes" he had so successfully enforced in verse. (p. 210)

> *James Boswell, in an excerpt from his* The Life of Samuel Johnson, *1960. Reprint by J. M. Dent & Sons, Ltd., 1978, pp. 210-11.*

George Gordon, Lord Byron   (poem date 1816)

[*An English poet and dramatist, Byron was a major exponent of certain aspects of English Romanticism. Yet because of the satiric nature of much of his work, he is difficult to place within the Romantic movement itself. His most notable contribution to Romanticism is the Byronic hero, a melancholy man, often with a dark past, who eschews social and religious strictures, seeking truth and happiness in an apparently meaningless universe. Byron had a pronounced distaste for poetic theory, however, and ridiculed the critical work of Romanticists William Wordsworth and Samuel Taylor Coleridge. In the following excerpt from the third canto (1816) of*

Childe Harold's Pilgrimage—*a poem describing the travels, experiences, and reflections of its pilgrim-hero, Childe Harold—he pays tribute to Voltaire and Jean-Jacques Rousseau.*]

Lausanne! and Ferney! ye have been the abodes
Of names which unto you bequeathed a name;
Mortals, who sought and found, by dangerous roads
A path to perpetuity of fame:
They were gigantic minds, and their steep aim
Was, Titan-like, on daring doubts to pile
Thoughts which should call down thunder, and the flame
Of Heaven, again assail'd, if Heaven the while
On man and man's research could deign do more than
    smile.

The one was fire and fickleness, a child,
Most mutable in wishes, but in mind,
A wit as various,—gay, grave, sage, or wild,—
Historian, bard, philosopher, combined;
He multiplied himself among mankind,
The Proteus of their talents: But his own
Breathed most in ridicule,—which, as the wind,
Blew where it listed, laying all things prone,—
Now to o'erthrow a fool, and now to shake a throne.

The other, deep and slow, exhausting thought,
And hiving wisdom with each studious year,
In meditation dwelt, with learning wrought,
And shaped his weapon with an edge severe,
Sapping a solemn creed with solemn sneer;
The lord of irony,—that master-spell,
Which stung his foes to wrath, which grew from fear,
And doom'd him to the zealot's ready Hell,
Which answers to all doubts so eloquently well.

Yet, peace be with their ashes,—for by them,
If merited, the penalty is paid;
It is not ours to judge,—far less condemn;
The hour must come when such things shall be made
Known unto all,—or hope and dread allay'd
By slumber, on one pillow,—in the dust,
Which, thus much we are sure, must lie decay'd;
And when it shall revive, as is our trust,
'Twill be to be forgiven, or suffer what is just.

                                        (pp. 89-90)

George Gordon, Lord Byron, in a poem from his Child Harold's Pilgrimage and Other Romantic Poems, *edited by John D. Jump, J. M. Dent & Sons Limited, 1975, pp. 62-92.*

John Morley   (essay date 1872)

[*An English author and critic, Morley is perhaps best remembered for his biographies:* Edmund Burke: An Historical Study *(1867),* Voltaire *(1872),* Rousseau *(1873),* Burke *(1879),* The Life of Richard Cobden *(1881),* Oliver Cromwell *(1900), and* Life of Gladstone *(1903). He also edited the English Men of Letters series. In the following excerpt from* Voltaire—*a work that is credited with greatly expanding understanding of Voltaire among English-speaking audiences—he discusses Voltaire as a literary stylist.*]

To us, who can be wise after the event, it is clear that if ever man was called not to science, nor to poetry, nor to theology, nor to metaphysics, but to literature, the art, so hard to define, of showing the ideas of all subjects in the double light of the practical and the spiritual reason, that

man was Voltaire. He has himself dwelt on the vagueness of this much-abused term, without contributing anything more satisfactory towards a better account of it than a crude hint that literature, not being a special art, may be considered a kind of larger grammar of knowledge. Although, however, it is true that literature is not a particular art, it is not the less true that there is a mental constitution particularly fitted for its successful practice. Literature is essentially an art of form, as distinguished from those exercises of intellectual energy which bring new stores of matter to the stock of acquired knowledge, and give new forces to emotion and original and definite articulation to passion. It is a misleading classification to call the work of Shakespeare and Molière, Shelley and Hugo, literary, just as it would be an equally inaccurate, though more glaring piece of classification, to count the work of Newton or Locke literature. To take another case from Voltaire, it would not be enough to describe Bayle's Dictionary as a literary compilation; it would not even be enough to describe it as a work of immense learning, because the distinguishing and superior mark of this book is a profound dialectic. It forms men of letters and is above them.

What is it then that literature brings to us, that earns its title to high place, though far from a highest place, among the great humanizing arts? Is it not that this is the master organon for giving men the two precious qualities of breadth of interest and balance of judgment; multiplicity of sympathies and steadiness of sight? Unhappily, literature has too often been identified with the smirks and affectations of mere elegant dispersiveness, with the hollow niceties of the virtuoso, a thing of madrigals. It is not in any sense of this sort that we can think of Voltaire as specially the born minister of literature. What we mean is that while he had not the loftier endowments of the highest poetic conception, subtle speculative penetration, or triumphant scientific power, he possessed a superb combination of wide and sincere curiosity, an intelligence of vigorous and exact receptivity, a native inclination to candour and justice, and a pre-eminent mastery over a wide range in the art of expression. Literature being concerned to impose form, to diffuse the light by which common men are able to see the great host of ideas and facts that do not shine in the brightness of their own atmosphere, it is clear what striking gifts Voltaire had in this way. He had a great deal of knowledge, and he was ever on the alert both to increase and broaden his stock, and, what was still better, to impart of it to everybody else. He did not think it beneath him to write on Hemistichs for the Encyclopædia. 'Tis not a very brilliant task, he said, but perhaps the article will be useful to men of letters and amateurs; 'one should disdain nothing, and I will do the word Comma, if you choose.' He was very catholic in taste, being able to love Racine without ignoring the lofty stature of Shakespeare. And he was free from the weakness which so often attends on catholicity, when it is not supported by true strength and independence of understanding; he did not shut his eyes to the shortcomings of the great. While loving Molière, he was aware of the incompleteness of his dramatic construction, as well as of the egregious farce to which that famous writer too often descends. His respect for the sublimity and pathos of Corneille did not hinder him from noting both his violence and his frigid argumentation. Does the reader remember that admirable saying of his to Vauvenargues; '*It is the part of a man like you to have preferences, but no ex-*

clusions?' To this fine principle Voltaire was usually thoroughly true, as every great mind, if only endowed with adequate culture, must necessarily be.

> Nul auteur avec lui n'a tort,
> Quand il a trouvé l'art de plaire;
> Il le critique sans colère,
> Il l'applaudit avec transport.

Thirdly, that circumfusion of bright light which is the highest aim of speech, was easy to Voltaire, in whatever order of subject he happened to treat. His style is like a translucent stream of purest mountain water, moving with swift and animated flow under flashing sunbeams. 'Voltaire,' said an enemy, 'is the very first man in the world at writing down what other people have thought.' What was meant for a spiteful censure, was in fact a truly honourable distinction.

The secret is incommunicable. No spectrum analysis can decompose for us that enchanting ray. It is rather, after all, the piercing metallic light of electricity than a glowing beam of the sun. We can detect some of the external qualities of this striking style. We seize its dazzling simplicity, its almost primitive closeness to the letter, its sharpness and precision, above all, its admirable brevity. We see that no writer ever used so few words to produce such pregnant effects. Those whom brevity only makes thin and slight, may look with despair on pages where the nimbleness of the sentence is in proportion to the firmness of the thought. We find no bastard attempts to reproduce in words deep and complex effects, which can only be adequately presented in colour or in the combinations of musical sound. Nobody has ever known better the true limitations of the material in which he worked, or the scope and possibilities of his art. Voltaire's alexandrines, his witty stories, his mock-heroic, his exposition of Newton, his histories, his dialectic, all bear the same mark, the same natural, precise, and condensed mode of expression, the same absolutely faultless knowledge of what is proper and permitted in every given kind of written work. At first there seems something paradoxical in dwelling on the brevity of an author whose works are to be counted by scores of volumes. But this is no real objection. A writer may be insufferably prolix in the limits of a single volume, and Voltaire was quite right in saying that there are four times too many words in the one volume of D'Holbach's System of Nature. He maintains too that Rabelais might advantageously be reduced to one-eighth, and Bayle to a quarter, and there is hardly a book that is not curtailed in the perfecting hands of the divine muses. So conversely an author may not waste a word in a hundred volumes. Style is independent of quantity, and the world suffers so grievously from the mass of books that have been written, not because they are many, but because such vast proportion of their pages say nothing while they purport to say so much.

No study, however, of this outward ease and swift compendiousness of speech will teach us the secret that was beneath it in Voltaire, an eye and a hand that never erred in hitting the exact mark of appropriateness in every order of prose and verse. Perhaps no such vision for the befitting in expression has ever existed. He is the most trenchant writer in the world, yet there is not a sentence of strained emphasis or overwrought antithesis; he is the wittiest, yet there is not a line of bad buffoonery. And this intense sense of the appropriate was by nature and cultivation become

so entirely a fixed condition of Voltaire's mind that it shows spontaneous and without an effort in his work. Nobody is more free from the ostentatious correctness of the literary precisian, and nobody preserves so much purity and so much dignity of language with so little formality of demeanour. It is interesting to notice the absence from his writings of that intensely elaborated kind of simplicity in which some of the best authors of a later time express the final outcome of many thoughts. The strain that society has undergone since Voltaire's day has taught men to qualify their propositions. It has forced them to follow truth slowly along paths steep and devious. New notes have been struck in human feeling, and all thought has now been touched by complexities that were then unseen. Hence, as all good writers aim at simplicity and directness, we have seen the growth of a new style, in which the rays of many side-lights are concentrated in some single phrase. That Voltaire does not use these focalising words and turns of composition only means that to him thought was less complex than it is to a more subjective generation. Though the literature which possesses Milton and Burke need not fear comparison with the graver masters of French speech, we have no one to place exactly by the side of Voltaire. But, then, no more has France. There are many pages of Swift which are more like one side of Voltaire than anything else that we have, and Voltaire probably drew the idea of his famous stories from the creator of Gulliver, just as Swift got the idea of the Tale of a Tub from Fontenelle's History of Mero and Enegu (that is, of Rome and Geneva). Swift has correctness, invention, irony, and a trick of being effectively literal and serious in absurd situations, just as Voltaire has; but then Swift is often truculent and often brutally gross, both in thought and in phrase. Voltaire is never either brutal or truculent. Even amid the licence of the Pucelle and of his romances, he never forgets what is due to the French tongue. What always charmed him in Racine and Boileau, he tells us, was that they said what they intended to say, and that their thoughts have never cost anything to the harmony or the purity of the language. Voltaire ranged over far wider ground than the two poets ever attempted to do, and trod in many slippery places, yet he is entitled to the same praise as that which he gave to them.

Unhappily, one of the many evil effects which have alloyed the revolution that Voltaire did so much to set in motion, has been both in his country and ours that purity and harmony of language, in spite of the examples of the great masters who have lived since, have on the whole declined. In both countries familiarity and slang have actually asserted a place in literature on some pretence that they are real; an assumed vulgarity tries to pass for native homeliness, and, as though a giant were more impressive for having a humped back, some men of true genius seem only to make sure of fame by straining themselves into grotesques. In a word, the reaction against a spurious dignity of style has carried men too far, because the reaction against the dignified elements in the old order went too far. Style, after all, as one has always to remember, can never be anything but the reflex of ideas and habits of mind, and when respect for one's own personal dignity as a ruling and unique element in character gave way to sentimental love of the human race, often real, and often a pretence, old self-respecting modes of expression went out of fashion. And all this has been defended by a sort of argument that might just as appropriately have been used by

Diogenes, vindicating the filthiness of his tub against a doctrine of clean linen. (pp. 117-25)

John Morley, in his Voltaire, *Macmillan and Co., 1872, 365 p.*

Lytton Strachey   (essay date 1905)

[*Strachey was an English biographer, critic, essayist, and short story writer. He is best known for such biographies as* Eminent Victorians *(1918),* Queen Victoria *(1921), and* Elizabeth and Essex: A Tragic History *(1928). Critics agree that these iconoclastic reexaminations of historical figures revolutionized the course of modern biographical writing. In the following essay, originally published in the* Independent Review *in 1905, he studies Voltaire as a tragedian, focusing on the 1736 drama* Alzire; ou, Les Américains.]

The historian of Literature is little more than a historian of exploded reputations. What has he to do with Shakespeare, with Dante, with Sophocles? Has he entered into the springs of the sea? Or has he walked in the search of the depth? The great fixed luminaries of the firmament of Letters dazzle his optic glass; and he can hardly hope to do more than record their presence, and admire their splendours with the eyes of an ordinary mortal. His business is with the succeeding ages of men, not with all time; but *Hyperion* might have been written on the morrow of Salamis, and the Odes of Pindar dedicated to George the Fourth. The literary historian must rove in other hunting grounds. He is the geologist of literature, whose study lies among the buried strata of forgotten generations, among the fossil remnants of the past. The great men with whom he must deal are the great men who are no longer great—mammoths and ichthyosauri kindly preserved to us, among the siftings of so many epochs, by the impartial benignity of Time. It is for him to unravel the jokes of Erasmus, and to be at home among the platitudes of Cicero. It is for him to sit up all night with the spectral heroes of Byron; it is for him to exchange innumerable alexandrines with the faded heroines of Voltaire.

The great potentate of the eighteenth century has suffered cruelly indeed at the hands of posterity. Everyone, it is true, has heard of him; but who has read him? It is by his name that ye shall know him, and not by his works. With the exception of his letters, of **Candide,** of **Akakia,** and of a few other of his shorter pieces, the vast mass of his productions has been already consigned to oblivion. How many persons now living have travelled through **La Henriade** or **La Pucelle?** How many have so much as glanced at the imposing volumes of **L'Esprit des Mœurs? Zadig** and **Zaïre, Mérope** and **Charles XII.** still linger, perhaps, in the schoolroom; but what has become of **Oreste,** and of **Mahomet,** and of **Alzire?** *Où sont les neiges d'antan?*

Though Voltaire's reputation now rests mainly on his achievements as a precursor of the Revolution, to the eighteenth century he was as much a poet as a reformer. The whole of Europe beheld at Ferney the oracle, not only of philosophy, but of good taste; for thirty years every scribbler, every rising genius, and every crowned head, submitted his verses to the censure of Voltaire; Voltaire's plays were performed before crowded houses; his epic was pronounced superior to Homer's, Virgil's, and Milton's; his

epigrams were transcribed by every letter-writer, and got by heart by every wit. Nothing, perhaps, shows more clearly the gulf which divides us from our ancestors of the eighteenth century, than a comparison between our thoughts and their thoughts, between our feelings and their feelings, with regard to one and the same thing—a tragedy by Voltaire. For us, as we take down the dustiest volume in our bookshelf, as we open it vaguely at some intolerable tirade, as we make an effort to labour through the procession of pompous commonplaces which meets our eyes, as we abandon the task in despair, and hastily return the book to its forgotten corner—to us it is well-nigh impossible to imagine the scene of charming brilliance which, five generations since, the same words must have conjured up. The splendid gaiety, the refined excitement, the pathos, the wit, the passion—all these things have vanished as completely from our perceptions as the candles, the powder, the looking-glasses, and the brocades, among which they moved and had their being. It may be instructive, or at least entertaining, to examine one of these forgotten masterpieces a little more closely; and we may do so with the less hesitation, since we shall only be following in the footsteps of Voltaire himself. His examination of *Hamlet* affords a precedent which is particularly applicable, owing to the fact that the same interval of time divided him from Shakespeare as that which divides ourselves from him. One point of difference, indeed, does exist between the relative positions of the two authors. Voltaire, in his study of Shakespeare, was dealing with a living, and a growing force; our interest in the dramas of Voltaire is solely an antiquarian interest. At the present moment, a literal translation of *King Lear* is drawing full houses at the Théâtre Antoine. As a rule it is rash to prophesy; but, if that rule has any exceptions, this is certainly one of them—a hundred years hence a literal translation of **Zaïre** will not be holding the English boards.

It is not our purpose to appreciate the best, or to expose the worst, of Voltaire's tragedies. Our object is to review some specimen of what would have been recognised by his contemporaries as representative of the average flight of his genius. Such a specimen is to be found in **Alzire, ou Les Américains,** first produced with great success in 1736, when Voltaire was forty-two years of age and his fame as a dramatist already well established.

Act I.—The scene is laid in Lima, the capital of Peru, some years after the Spanish conquest of America. When the play opens, Don Gusman, a Spanish grandee, has just succeeded his father, Don Alvarez, in the Governorship of Peru. The rule of Don Alvarez had been beneficent and just; he had spent his life in endeavouring to soften the cruelty of his countrymen; and his only remaining wish was to see his son carry on the work which he had begun. Unfortunately, however, Don Gusman's temperament was the very opposite of his father's; he was tyrannical, harsh, headstrong, and bigoted.

> L'Américain farouche est un monstre sauvage
> Qui mord en frémissant le frein de l'esclavage . . .
> Tout pouvoir, en un mot, périt par l'indulgence,
> Et la sévérité produit l'obéissance.

Such were the cruel maxims of his government—maxims which he was only too ready to put into practice. It was in vain that Don Alvarez reminded his son that the true Christian returns good for evil, and that, as he epigrammatically put it, 'Le vrai Dieu, mon fils, est un Dieu qui pardonne.' To enforce his argument, the good old man told the story of how his own life had been spared by a virtuous American, who, as he said, 'au lieu de me frapper, embrassa mes genoux.' But Don Gusman remained unmoved by such narratives, though he admitted that there was one consideration which impelled him to adopt a more lenient policy. He was in love with Alzire, Alzire the young and beautiful daughter of Montèze, who had ruled in Lima before the coming of the Spaniards. 'Je l'aime, je l'avoue,' said Gusman to his father, 'et plus que je ne veux.' With these words, the dominating situation of the play becomes plain to the spectator. The wicked Spanish Governor is in love with the virtuous American princess. From such a state of affairs, what interesting and romantic developments may not follow? Alzire, we are not surprised to learn, still fondly cherished the memory of a Peruvian prince, who had been slain in an attempt to rescue his country from the tyranny of Don Gusman. Yet, for the sake of Montèze, her ambitious and scheming father, she consented to give her hand to the Governor. She consented; but, even as she did so, she was still faithful to Zamore. 'Sa foi me fut promise,' she declared to Don Gusman, 'il eut pour moi des charmes.'

> Il m'aima: son trépas me coûte encore des larmes:
> Vous, loin d'oser ici condamner ma douleur,
> Jugez de ma constance, et connaissez mon cœur.

The ruthless Don did not allow these pathetic considerations to stand in the way of his wishes, and gave orders that the wedding ceremony should be immediately performed. But, at the very moment of his apparent triumph, the way was being prepared for the overthrow of all his hopes.

Act II.—It was only natural to expect that a heroine affianced to a villain should turn out to be in love with a hero. The hero adored by Alzire had, it is true, perished; but then what could be more natural than his resurrection? The noble Zamore was not dead; he had escaped with his life from the torture-chamber of Don Gusman, had returned to avenge himself, had been immediately apprehended, and was lying imprisoned in the lowest dungeon of the castle, while his beloved princess was celebrating her nuptials with his deadly foe.

In this distressing situation, he was visited by the venerable Alvarez, who had persuaded his son to grant him an order for the prisoner's release. In the gloom of the dungeon, it was at first difficult to distinguish the features of Zamore; but the old man at last discovered that he was addressing the very American who, so many years ago, instead of hitting him, had embraced his knees. He was overwhelmed by this extraordinary coincidence. 'Approach. O heaven! O Providence! It is he, behold the object of my gratitude. . . . My benefactor! My son!' But let us not pry further into so affecting a passage; it is sufficient to state that Don Alvarez, after promising his protection to Zamore, hurried off to relate this remarkable occurrence to his son, the Governor.

Act III.—Meanwhile, Alzire had been married. But she still could not forget her Peruvian lover. While she was lamenting her fate, and imploring the forgiveness of the shade of Zamore, she was informed that a released prisoner begged a private interview. 'Admit him.' He was admit-

ted. 'Heaven! Such were his features, his gait, his voice: Zamore!' She falls into the arms of her confidante. 'Je succombe; à peine je respire.'

> ZAMORE: Reconnais ton amant.
> ALZIRE: Zamore aux pieds d'Alzire!
>   Est-ce une illusion?

It was no illusion; and the unfortunate princess was obliged to confess to her lover that she was already married to Don Gusman. Zamore was at first unable to grasp the horrible truth, and, while he was still struggling with his conflicting emotions, the door was flung open, and Don Gusman, accompanied by his father, entered the room.

A double recognition followed. Zamore was no less horrified to behold in Don Gusman the son of the venerable Alvarez, than Don Gusman was infuriated at discovering that the prisoner to whose release he had consented was no other than Zamore. When the first shock of surprise was over, the Peruvian hero violently insulted his enemy, and upbraided him with the tortures he had inflicted. The Governor replied by ordering the instant execution of the prince. It was in vain that Don Alvarez reminded his son of Zamore's magnanimity; it was in vain that Alzire herself offered to sacrifice her life for that of her lover. Zamore was dragged from the apartment; and Alzire and Don Alvarez were left alone to bewail the fate of the Peruvian hero. Yet some faint hopes still lingered in the old man's breast. 'Gusman fut inhumain,' he admitted, 'je le sais, j'en frémis;

> Mais il est ton époux, il t'aime, il est mon fils:
> Son âme à la pitié se peut ouvrir encore.'

'Hélas!' (replied Alzire), 'que n'êtes-vous le père de Zamore!'

Act IV.—Even Don Gusman's heart was, in fact, unable to steel itself entirely against the prayers and tears of his father and his wife; and he consented to allow a brief respite to Zamore's execution. Alzire was not slow to seize this opportunity of doing her lover a good turn; for she immediately obtained his release by the ingenious stratagem of bribing the warder of the dungeon. Zamore was free. But alas! Alzire was not; was she not wedded to the wicked Gusman? Her lover's expostulations fell on unheeding ears. What mattered it that her marriage vow had been sworn before an alien God? 'J'ai promis; il suffit; il n'importe à quel dieu!'

> ZAMORE: Ta promesse est un crime; elle est ma perte; adieu. Périssent tes serments et ton Dieu que j'abhorre!
> ALZIRE: Arrête; quels adieux! arrête, cher Zamore!

But the prince tore himself away, with no further farewell upon his lips than an oath to be revenged upon the Governor. Alzire, perplexed, deserted, terrified, tortured by remorse, agitated by passion, turned for comfort to that God, who, she could not but believe, was, in some mysterious way, the Father of All.

> Great God, lead Zamore in safety through the desert places. . . . Ah! can it be true that thou art but

the Deity of another universe? Have the Europeans alone the right to please thee? Art thou after all the tyrant of one world and the father of another? . . . No! The conquerors and the conquered, miserable mortals as they are, all are equally the work of thy hands. . . .

Her reverie was interrupted by an appalling sound. She heard shrieks; she heard a cry of 'Zamore!' And her confidante, rushing in, confusedly informed her that her lover was in peril of his life.

> Ah, chère Emire [she exclaimed], allons
> le secourir!
> EMIRE: Que pouvez-vous, Madame? O Ciel!
> ALZIRE: Je puis mourir.

Hardly was the epigram out of her mouth when the door opened, and an emissary of Don Gusman announced to her that she must consider herself under arrest. She demanded an explanation in vain, and was immediately removed to the lowest dungeon.

Act V.—It was not long before the unfortunate princess learnt the reason of her arrest. Zamore, she was informed, had rushed straight from her apartment into the presence of Don Gusman, and had plunged a dagger into his enemy's breast. The hero had then turned to Don Alvarez and, with perfect tranquillity, had offered him the blood-stained poniard.

> J'ai fait ce que j'ai dû, j'ai vengé mon injure;
> Fais ton devoir, dit-il, et venge la nature.

Before Don Alvarez could reply to this appeal, Zamore had been haled off by the enraged soldiery before the Council of Grandees. Don Gusman had been mortally wounded; and the Council proceeded at once to condemn to death, not only Zamore, but also Alzire, who, they found, had been guilty of complicity in the murder. It was the unpleasant duty of Don Alvarez to announce to the prisoners the Council's sentence. He did so in the following manner:

> Good God, what a mixture of tenderness and horror! My own liberator is the assassin of my son. Zamore! . . . Yes, it is to thee that I owe this life which I detest; how dearly didst thou sell me that fatal gift. . . . I am a father, but I am also a man; and, in spite of thy fury, in spite of the voice of that blood which demands vengeance from my agitated soul, I can still hear the voice of thy benefactions. And thou, who wast my daughter, thou whom in our misery I yet call by a name which makes our tears to flow, ah! how far is it from thy father's wishes to add to the agony which he already feels the horrible pleasure of vengeance. I must lose, by an unheard-of catastrophe, at once my liberator, my daughter, and my son. The Council has sentenced you to death.

Upon one condition, however, and upon one alone, the lives of the culprits were to be spared—that of Zamore's conversion to Christianity. What need is there to say that the noble Peruvians did not hesitate for a moment? 'Death, rather than dishonour!' exclaimed Zamore, while Alzire added some elegant couplets upon the moral degradation entailed by hypocritical conversion. Don Alvarez was in complete despair, and was just beginning to make another speech, when Don Gusman, with the pallor of death upon his features, was carried into the room. The

implacable Governor was about to utter his last words. Alzire was resigned; Alvarez was plunged in misery; Zamore was indomitable to the last. But lo! when the Governor spoke, it was seen at once that an extraordinary change had come over his mind. He was no longer proud, he was no longer cruel, he was no longer unforgiving; he was kind, humble, and polite; in short, he had repented. Everybody was pardoned, and everybody recognised the truth of Christianity. And their faith was particularly strengthened when Don Gusman, invoking a final blessing upon Alzire and Zamore, expired in the arms of Don Alvarez. For thus were the guilty punished, and the virtuous rewarded. The noble Zamore, who had murdered his enemy in cold blood, and the gentle Alzire who, after bribing a sentry, had allowed her lover to do away with her husband, lived happily ever afterwards. That they were able to do so was owing entirely to the efforts of the wicked Don Gusman; and the wicked Don Gusman very properly descended to the grave.

Such is the tragedy of *Alzire,* which, it may be well to repeat, was in its day one of the most applauded of its author's productions. It was upon the strength of works of this kind that his contemporaries recognised Voltaire's right to be ranked in a sort of dramatic triumvirate, side by side with his great predecessors, Corneille and Racine. With Racine, especially, Voltaire was constantly coupled; and it is clear that he himself firmly believed that the author of *Alzire* was a worthy successor of the author of *Athalie.* At first sight, indeed, the resemblance between the two dramatists is obvious enough; but a closer inspection reveals an ocean of differences too vast to be spanned by any superficial likeness.

A careless reader is apt to dismiss the tragedies of Racine as mere *tours de force;* and, in one sense, the careless reader is right. For, as mere displays of technical skill, those works are certainly unsurpassed in the whole range of literature. But the notion of 'a mere *tour de force*' carries with it something more than the idea of technical perfection; for it denotes, not simply a work which is technically perfect, but a work which is technically perfect and nothing more. The problem before a writer of a Chant Royal is to overcome certain technical difficulties of rhyme and rhythm; he performs his *tour de force,* the difficulties are overcome, and his task is accomplished. But Racine's problem was very different. The technical restrictions he laboured under were incredibly great; his vocabulary was cribbed, his versification was cabined, his whole power of dramatic movement was scrupulously confined; conventional rules of every conceivable denomination hurried out to restrain his genius, with the alacrity of Lilliputians pegging down a Gulliver; wherever he turned he was met by a hiatus or a pitfall, a blind-alley or a *mot bas.* But his triumph was not simply the conquest of these refractory creatures; it was something much more astonishing. It was the creation, in spite of them, nay, by their very aid, of a glowing, living, soaring, and enchanting work of art. To have brought about this amazing combination, to have erected, upon a structure of Alexandrines, of Unities, of Noble Personages, of stilted diction, of the whole intolerable paraphernalia of the Classical stage, an edifice of subtle psychology, of exquisite poetry, of overwhelming passion—that is a *tour de force* whose achievement entitles Jean Racine to a place among the very few consummate artists of the world.

The château de Ferney, from the engraving by F.M.I. Queverdo after L. Signy.

Voltaire, unfortunately, was neither a poet nor a psychologist; and, when he took up the mantle of Racine, he put it, not upon a human being, but upon a tailor's block. To change the metaphor, Racine's work resembled one of those elaborate paper transparencies which delighted our grandmothers, illuminated from within so as to present a charming tinted picture with varying degrees of shadow and of light. Voltaire was able to make the transparency, but he never could light the candle; and the only result of his efforts was some sticky pieces of paper, cut into curious shapes, and roughly daubed with colour. To take only one instance, his diction is the very echo of Racine's. There are the same pompous phrases, the same inversions, the same stereotyped list of similes, the same poor bedraggled company of words. It is amusing to note the exclamations which rise to the lips of Voltaire's characters in moments of extreme excitement—*Qu'entends-je? Que vois-je? Où suis-je? Grands Dieux! Ah, c'en est trop, Seigneur! Juste Ciel! Sauve-toi de ces lieux! Madame, quelle horreur . . .* &c. And it is amazing to discover that these are the very phrases with which Racine has managed to express all the violence of human terror, and rage, and love. Voltaire at his best never rises above the standard of a sixth-form boy writing hexameters in the style of Virgil; and, at his worst, he certainly falls within measurable distance of a flogging.

He is capable, for instance, of writing lines as bad as the second of this couplet—

> C'est ce même guerrier dont la main tutélaire,
> De Gusman, votre époux, sauva, dit-on, le père,

or as

> Qui les font pour un temps rentrer tous en eux-mêmes,

or

> Vous comprenez, seigneur, que je ne comprends pas.

Voltaire's most striking expressions are too often borrowed from his predecessors. Alzire's 'Je puis mourir,' for instance, is an obvious reminiscence of the 'Qu'il mourût!' of le vieil Horace; and the cloven hoof is shown clearly enough by the 'O ciel!' with which Alzire's confidante manages to fill out the rest of the line. Many of these blemishes are, doubtless, the outcome of simple carelessness; for Voltaire was too busy a man to give over-much time to his plays. 'This tragedy was the work of six days,' he wrote to d'Alembert, enclosing **Olympie.** 'You should not have rested on the seventh,' was d'Alembert's reply. But, on the whole, Voltaire's verses succeed in keeping up to a high level of mediocrity; they are the verses, in fact, of a very clever man. It is when his cleverness is out of its depth, that he most palpably fails. A human being by Voltaire bears the same relation to a real human being that stage scenery bears to a real landscape; it can only be looked at from in front. The curtain rises, and his villains and his heroes, his good old men and his exquisite princesses, display for a moment their one thin surface to the spectator; the curtain falls, and they are all put back into their box. The glance which the reader has taken into the little case labelled *Alzire* has perhaps given him a sufficient notion of these queer discarded marionettes.

Voltaire's dramatic efforts were hampered by one further unfortunate incapacity; he was almost completely devoid of the dramatic sense. It is only possible to write good plays without the power of character-drawing, upon one condition—that of possessing the power of creating dramatic situations. The *Oedipus Tyrannus* of Sophocles, for instance, is not a tragedy of character; and its vast crescendo of horror is produced by a dramatic treatment of situation, not of persons. One of the principal elements in this stupendous example of the manipulation of a great dramatic theme has been pointed out by Voltaire himself. The guilt of Oedipus, he says, becomes known to the audience very early in the play; and, when the *dénouement* at last arrives, it comes as a shock, not to the audience, but to the King. There can be no doubt that Voltaire has put his finger upon the very centre of those underlying causes which make the *Oedipus* perhaps the most awful of tragedies. To know the hideous truth, to watch its gradual dawn upon one after another of the characters, to see Oedipus at last alone in ignorance, to recognise clearly that he too must know, to witness his struggles, his distraction, his growing terror, and, at the inevitable moment, the appalling revelation—few things can be more terrible than this. But Voltaire's comment upon the master-stroke by which such an effect has been obtained illustrates, in a remarkable way, his own sense of the dramatic. 'Nouvelle preuve,' he remarks, 'que Sophocle n'avait pas perfectionné son art.'

More detailed evidence of Voltaire's utter lack of dramatic insight is to be found, of course, in his criticisms of Shakespeare. Throughout these, what is particularly striking is the manner in which Voltaire seems able to get into such intimate contact with his great predecessor, and yet to remain as absolutely unaffected by him as Shakespeare himself was by Voltaire. It is unnecessary to dwell further upon so hackneyed a subject; but one instance may be given of the lengths to which this dramatic insensibility of Voltaire's was able to go—his adaptation of *Julius Caesar* for the French stage. A comparison of the two pieces should be made by anyone who wishes to realise fully, not only the degradation of the copy, but the excellence of the original. Particular attention should be paid to the transmutation of Antony's funeral oration into French alexandrines. In Voltaire's version, the climax of the speech is reached in the following passage; it is an excellent sample of the fatuity of the whole of his concocted rigmarole:—

ANTOINE:	Brutus . . . où suis-je? O ciel! O crime! O barbarie!
	Chers amis, je succombe; et mes sens interdits . . .
	Brutus, son assassin! . . . ce monstre était son fils!
ROMAINS:	Ah dieux!

If Voltaire's demerits are obvious enough to our eyes, his merits were equally clear to his contemporaries, whose vision of them was not perplexed and retarded by the conventions of another age. The weight of a reigning convention is like the weight of the atmosphere—it is so universal that no one feels it; and an eighteenth-century audience came to a performance of *Alzire* unconscious of the burden of the Classical rules. They found instead an animated procession of events, of scenes just long enough to be amusing and not too long to be dull, of startling incidents, of happy *mots.* They were dazzled by an easy display of cheap brilliance, and cheap philosophy, and cheap sentiment, which it was very difficult to distinguish from the real thing, at such a distance, and under artificial light When, in *Mérope,* one saw La Dumesnil; 'lorsque,' to quote Voltaire himself, 'les yeux égarés, la voix entrecoupée, levant une main tremblante, elle allait immoler son propre fils; quand Narbas l'arrêta; quand, laissant tomber son poignard, on la vit s'évanouir entre les bras de ses femmes, et qu'elle sortit de cet état de mort avec les transports d'une mère; lorsque, ensuite, s'élançant aux yeux de Polyphonte, traversant en un clin d'œil tout le théâtre, les larmes dans les yeux, la pâleur sur le front, les sanglots à la bouche, les bras étendus, elle s'écria: "Barbare, il est mon fils!" '—how, face to face with splendours such as these, could one question for a moment the purity of the gem from which they sparkled? Alas! to us, who know not La Dumesnil, to us whose *Mérope* is nothing more than a little sediment of print, the precious stone of our forefathers has turned out to be a simple piece of paste. Its glittering was the outcome of no inward fire, but of a certain adroitness in the manufacture; to use our modern phraseology, Voltaire was able to make up for his lack of genius by a thorough knowledge of 'technique,' and a great deal of 'go.'

And to such titles of praise let us not dispute his right. His vivacity, indeed, actually went so far as to make him something of an innovator. He introduced new and imposing spectacular effects; he ventured to write tragedies in which no persons of royal blood made their appearance; he was so bold as to rhyme 'père' with 'terre.' The wild diversity of his incidents shows a trend towards the romantic, which, doubtless, under happier influences, would have led him much further along the primrose path which ended in the bonfire of 1830.

But it was his misfortune to be for ever clogged by a tradition of decorous restraint; so that the effect of his plays is as anomalous as would be—let us say—that of a shilling shocker written by Miss Yonge. His heroines go mad in epigrams, while his villains commit murder in inversions. Amid the hurly-burly of artificiality, it was all his cleverness could do to keep its head to the wind; and he was only able to remain afloat at all by throwing overboard his humour. The Classical tradition has to answer for many sins; perhaps its most infamous achievement was that it prevented Molière from being a great tragedian. But there can be no doubt that its most astonishing one was to have taken—if only for some scattered moments—the sense of the ridiculous from Voltaire. (pp. 121-34)

Lytton Strachey, "Voltaire's Tragedies," in his Books and Characters: French and English, *1922. Reprint by Chatto and Windus, 1924, pp. 121-34.*

Gustave Lanson   (essay date 1906)

[Lanson was a distinguished French literary historian, critic, and bibliographer. He is perhaps best known for his seminal 1906 critical biography of Voltaire. Writing in 1951, George R. Havens appraised this work in glowing terms: "Probably the best brief survey of Voltaire's life and work in any language—accurate, intelligent, succinct, written with a verve worthy of Voltaire himself. No doubt the best book for the general reader or student to begin his acquaintance with Voltaire." In the following excerpt from Voltaire, *Lanson considers Voltaire's influence and reputation during the century following his death.]*

That Voltaire influenced his own century as well as the nineteenth century is an indisputable fact, but it is impossible at the present time to ascertain with any degree of accuracy the precise extent of his influence. I am not sure that it will ever be possible to do so. Voltaire very definitely received from his own age, and from the intellectual currents of his time, the majority of the ideas and suggestions that he reflected and re-echoed. His influence in many instances was that of a transmitter, a relay-station, as it were, adding the enormous energy of his contagious passions and seductive power to an output of ideas that had originated elsewhere but would never have reached so vast an audience without the tremendous boost Voltaire provided. It is difficult to distinguish and dissociate his personal role and influence from the collective tendencies and individual efforts of others moving in the same direction.

Perhaps he served his age primarily as a kind of executive officer, drawing up the "Order of the Day" for public opinion. By the bells he rang and the fireworks he set off, he rallied the minds of the century and made all available forces converge on a single target. He disciplined his troops and coordinated their common objectives. It is not easy to decide whether he was always the general in command of the army of progress or simply its drum major. The difficulty is compounded by Voltaire's aversion to any systematic organization of his ideas. The presence of a Montesquieu or a Rousseau in any given plan of action is quickly discernible from the traces of doctrinal views held by these philosophers. Voltaire often did little more than whip up certain sentiments without imposing any dogmatic preference of his own.

Perhaps these difficulties will some day be resolved. For the present, at any rate, it would be vain to pretend to have done so. The history of ideas, their formation, and their modes of propagation in the eighteenth and nineteenth centuries have not as yet been sufficiently studied and analyzed. We have not yet accurately determined the relationship of social and political facts to moral and literary facts. It would be necessary to take a close look at the intellectual training and development of many individuals, distinguished or mediocre, illustrious or obscure. But as of now, we have not collected an adequate number of such observations to permit formulating any general conclusions. And it will be only after this work is completed that the question of Voltaire's influence can be answered with some degree of accuracy.

Therefore, without laying claim to any precision or certainty on a subject that is still illusory, I shall offer a few observations on what seem to me the most plausible facts of the matter. In the first place, while we cannot establish with accuracy the detail or extent of Voltaire's influence, we can scarcely question its reality. Voltaire was the intellectual nourishment of many minds for several generations, and consequently he affected to some degree the thoughts of multitudes. Almost no one escaped his influence among the last generation of the eighteenth century. And Christians, like Joseph de Maistre and Chateaubriand, often did no more than oppose Voltaire with the very facts and opinions they had acquired from him.

It would be interesting to know how widely Voltaire was read at various moments of history. Bibliography can give us some help on this point. From 1740 to 1778 there were nineteen collections of his complete works, not counting the separate editions of his principal writings, which were very numerous. From 1778 to 1815 Quérard indicates six editions of his complete works, not including two that were incomplete but still sizable. Finally, for the twenty-year period from 1815 to 1835, Bengesco has found 28 editions of Voltaire's complete works. Then nothing from 1835 to 1852. From 1852 to 1870 there were five editions, including the propagandistic one sponsored by the daily newspaper *Le Siècle* ("The Century"). After 1870 there were two or three editions, only one of which, that of Louis Moland, is important. The Moland edition [1877-85] is of a purely literary and historical nature, entirely free of any intent to preserve or spread Voltairian ideas.

Generally speaking, there was great interest in his writings down to the outbreak of the Revolution, then a falling off and lull until 1815. A prodigious renewal of interest during the Restoration [1815-1830] was followed by another decline and then an appreciable upturn during the Second Empire [1852-1870]. This curve corresponds rather closely to the waves of liberalism in France. Voltaire was printed or reprinted particularly during those periods when liberal movements encountered their greatest opposition and consequently became more militant. Yet we must recognize the fact that, with so many editions of Voltaire's works already available—the special edition of 1775 (with each page framed in decorative lines), the two Kehl editions prior to the Revolution, and the 28 consecutive editions prior to the reign of Louis-Philippe [1830-1848]—there could very well have been a glut in the Voltaire market. The public needed time to absorb the publishers' output. Moreover, the extensive offerings by the publishers indicated a considerable demand from readers of liberal persuasion.

We need to know the number of copies of each edition. The Restoration government tried to compute the number of "bad books" that were distributed. From an official report, analyzed by the newspapers of the day, it was estimated that between 1817 and 1824 there were twelve published editions of Voltaire's works, comprising a total of 31,000 sets and 1,598,000 volumes. At the same time thirteen editions of Rousseau totaled 24,500 sets and 480,500 volumes. Separate editions of the writings of one or the other put 35,000 sets and 81,000 volumes on the market. In all, there were 2,159,500 volumes of philosophical writings launched against the royalist and clerical reaction over a seven-year period, and of this frightening number of projectiles, Voltaire accounted for more than 75 percent.

Let us try to discover some of the ways in which this powerful force was utilized. Voltaire acted as both artist and philosopher, the one usually supporting the other. Yet there were times he could be the one without the other. Hence, the two roles must be studied separately. He influenced literature mainly by his discriminating taste and choice of language: first as a propagandist and initiator, but very soon, and down to the time of his death, as the guardian and defender of classical precepts. The intellects he trained had limited and refined principles of taste coupled with a clear, colorless style of writing. They were meticulous about linguistic purity and accuracy. They were frightened by any novelties or bold, unfamiliar imagery. They were quick to heap ridicule on expressive or stylistic details if the inherent thought or idea startled or shocked them. Voltairians shuddered at Chateaubriand, and they detested Romanticism. His devotees, in matters of taste, flourished throughout the nineteenth century, particularly in the University and the magistracy. Thiers exemplified this spirit quite well.

As for tragedy, Voltaire was ranked by his contemporaries alongside Racine and Corneille. A whole generation of writers of tragedy, mediocre, alas, were to follow in his footsteps: Marmontel, La Harpe, Lemierre, etc. His best disciples were foreigners, and we may legitimately include among them the *misogallo* Alfieri who appropriated the Voltairian concept of tragedy. But his influence was to be checked, on the one hand, by the partisans of English drama and the bourgeois *drame*, which went beyond Voltaire's experiments, and on the other hand, by the pure classicists of the Revolutionary and Imperial era who, in the name of Racine and the Greeks, reacted against Voltairian innovations. Meanwhile, the moderate experimentation which occurred during the Restoration, incorporating certain Romantic elements into the writing of tragedy, as with Casimir Delavigne, continued the Voltairian tradition.

Voltaire was the undisputed master of light verse, but Delille replaced him as the authority for didactic poetry, and Jean-Baptiste Rousseau remained, with Malherbe, the arbiter of the ode. The influence of Voltaire's clear and ironic genius was offset, above all, by the vogue for melancholy literature and Ossianism which struck a dominant elegiac note in poetry between 1770 and 1820. Yet despite the effects of Delille and Roucher, Voltaire's fluid, even, monotonous verses retained all their seductive charm to find renewed expression even in the poetry of Lamartine.

In the writing of history, Voltaire's influence radiated outside France. He created a school of philosophical historians who were accused of having sacrificed facts for opinions and critical research for dogmatic philosophical premises. There is truth in these accusations, and neither Mably nor Raynal can satisfy us today as competent historians. But here we must make an exception for Montesquieu and his *Considérations*. Voltaire, for all his flippancies and hasty judgments, for all his passions and prejudices, nonetheless advocated a serious examination and a truthful exposition of historical facts. He had given the world models of composition and simplification and had written narrative masterpieces. We find his precepts and techniques emulated by the English historians Robertson and Gibbon. And the same is true for the best works of French historians who preceded the Romantic Movement

or were uninfluenced by it. Many tried to copy his clear methods of exposition and expression while eschewing his philosophy or surpassing him in erudition. If Ruhlière is completely Voltairian, he communicated something of Voltaire to Anquetil, Daunou, Daru, and Thiers. Even Michelet, who had read Voltaire carefully, remembered him in his youth when he wanted to make a clear, concise *précis* of modern history. He even incorporated in his work an entire chapter, intact, from Voltaire's **Essai sur les moeurs,** certain he could not improve on it.

Voltaire's philosophical tales were imitated in the eighteenth-century novel. But *La Nouvelle Héloïse* [Rousseau] and *Werther* [Goethe], and the torrent of sensibility heralding the Romantic Movement, arrested Voltaire's influence on the development of this literary genre. Even in the short story, people wanted something more than sarcasm. It was necessary to write for sensitive souls. Marmontel himself forsook Voltaire.

In the nineteenth century, Chateaubriand, George Sand, and Balzac led the novel into paths ever more remote from **Candide** and **L'Ingénu.** Stendhal, who had an unmistakable affinity for the eighteenth century, is closer to Laclos and Duclos than to Voltaire. And perhaps Mérimée's artistic sobriety owes nothing to Voltaire. However, traces of Voltaire persisted in the short story writers of a lively, piquant style, like Mme de Girardin or Tillier, the Nivernais author of *Mon Oncle Benjamin,* who is not yet sufficiently well known in France, or again, like Edmond About and his friend Sarcey. Toward the close of the nineteenth century the Voltairian novel had an unexpected revival in the work of a great artist, Anatole France, and in a certain number of younger writers who, between the movements of Naturalism, Lyricism, and Symbolism, tried to preserve Voltaire's qualities of light, witty, trenchant writing, a bit dry and colorless, but always perfectly clear. Among these I would mention Veber, Hermant, and Beaunier.

But where Voltaire's influence was immense, obvious, and still persistent is in the field of journalism, pamphleteering, and all forms of polemical writing. He was the master of militant irony and murderous ridicule. He taught the art of cunning devices, ingenious inventions of plot and incident, and ludicrous or saucy transpositions that tantalized the bored or inattentive reader. He demonstrated how a ponderous question could be deflated, simplified, and reduced to a few truths of common sense. He showed how an opponent's arguments may be transformed into propositions so absurd as to require no refutation whatever. He taught the art of repetition in such a way as to implant an idea in the reader's mind without wearying him, always restating the idea in an unending variety of clever situations and amusing symbols. He was a great artist in forms of writing not usually noted for their artistic merit. He was the forerunner of nineteenth-century polemicists who dramatized current events with imaginative artistry. Among his disciples were Paul-Louis Courier during the Restoration and Tillier under Louis-Philippe. Prévost-Paradol studied him and so, no doubt, did Henri Rochefort. Edmond About and Francisque Sarcey were as Voltairian in style as in wit in their periodical *Le XIXe Siècle* ("The Nineteenth Century"), written during the Third Republic. And when Anatole France, in his latter years, moved away from the pure novel into social and political satire, he again accentuated the Voltairian spirit of his work in his exquisite dialogues *L'Orme du Mail* ("The Elm Tree on the Mall") and *L'Anneau d'améthyste* ("The Amethyst Ring"), in which dramatic action is relegated to the background by philosophical criticism.

Setting aside his controversial writings, we may say that in the nineteenth century Voltaire was the principal arbiter of style for literate Frenchmen whose temperament was disinclined to assimilate the Romantic or Parnassian schools, who avoided lyrical effervescence, pictorial intensity, or the sculptured, plastic effect in poetry. Wherever the style was primarily intellectual without being oratorical and dialectic (I make this reservation for Brunetière, who surely borrowed nothing from Voltaire), we can easily discern Voltairian elements in the style of these cultivated Frenchmen. Cherbuliez, Boissier, Lemaître, Faguet, and many university people furnish ample proof. Voltaire confirmed, without creating it, the French need for ease, lightness, clarity, finesse, and a bright "gaiety" of expression. His prose became the symbol for qualities we consider typically French, and it imposed on others the obligation to emulate these qualities. One may add to them whatever one pleases, but they remain the indispensable prerequisites. Flaubert did not disavow Voltaire while admiring Chateaubriand and Hugo, and although he achieved in his own style a beauty that was hardly Voltairian, he took care to avoid the faults Voltaire deemed unpardonable. There is also a bit of Voltaire (of Voltaire's taste, that is) to be found in Ernest Renan. It is reflected in his vibrant and colorful prose amid the bold interplay of subtle metaphysics and mystical imagery, revealing that luminous smile of an alert common sense, ever wary of dangerous extremes and ever anxious to avoid the heavy-handed or the obscure. More than one Voltairian has been converted to the Christian faith while remaining a disciple of Voltaire in matters of style and intelligence. And more than one Catholic has found an affinity of taste with Voltaire.

But for a long time, and oftener than not, Voltaire's seductive literary charms were the vehicle for his ideas and opinions. It is especially difficult to analyze this question insofar as the eighteenth century is concerned. To a very large degree, Voltaire's strength resided in his talent for bestowing the beguiling form of his inimitable wit upon the opinions and aspirations of his contemporaries. The duchesse de Choiseul has clearly explained what it is that makes his precise influence as difficult of analysis as it was undoubtedly significant and widespread. On September 21, 1779, she wrote:

> Whatever faults may be attributed to Voltaire, he will always be for me the writer whom I shall read and reread with the greatest pleasure because of his taste and his universality. What does it matter that he tells me nothing new if he articulates and develops my own thoughts, and if he tells me better than anyone else what others have already told me? I have no need for him to teach me more than what everyone knows, and what other author can tell me, as he does, what everyone knows?

There is a bit of self-deception in this observation, and it was part of Voltaire's art to be able to make his reader believe that everyone, including the reader himself, already knew and thought precisely those things Voltaire wanted him to know and to think. Nevertheless, there is a great

deal of truth in Mme de Choiseul's remark. We may consider Montesquieu, Rousseau, Buffon, and Diderot as greater geniuses, but Voltaire was, in the broadest sense, the most representative mind of his age, the one in whom the brilliance of eighteenth century French society was summed up most completely and brought to its most exquisite perfection. He embodied its good and bad features, its graces and blemishes, its breadth of view and its limitations, its impulses and enthusiasms as well as its hesitations and timidities.

The memoirs of Bachaumont show clearly the extent of this harmony between Voltaire and the age in which he lived, and they indicate the strong hold that Voltaire had on eighteenth-century society. Cultivated and sophisticated people paid little attention to Voltaire's violent anti-Christian tirades. They were too indifferent to the truth, too unconcerned about articles of faith to become excited over questions of dogma. As good Frenchmen, it cost them nothing to go to mass, to be married by the parish priest, and to have their children baptized: ceremonial acts of little importance but socially respectable.

Voltaire de-Christianized many minds without inoculating them with the virulence of his hatred. In the eighteenth and early nineteenth centuries there were even Voltairian women, quietly, serenely agnostic, who managed quite well to do without religious faith or fervor: the duchesse de Choiseul, the vicomtesse d'Houdetot, Mme Quinet, Mme Dumesnil (Michelet's friend), etc. I do not know if the species was ever very numerous. Doubtless Rousseau made more converts among women than Voltaire. But all France, or almost all, applauded and followed Voltaire when he championed deism and rejected atheism, when he fought ecclesiastical abuses and the financial privileges and tyranny of Rome, when he sought to subject the clergy to taxation, to reduce the number of monks or even eliminate them, and when he became indignant over fanaticism and religious persecution. In these matters Voltaire found support even among many of the clergy, as well as among the less serious-minded elements of society.

The people were still marching behind his banner when he accepted the principle of an absolute monarchy, provided it used its power and authority in the nation's true interests. They were behind him when he denounced all the abuses of the judiciary and came to the aid of its victims, when he fought governmental abuses and called for practical reforms, when he voiced his contempt for war, and when he advocated a peaceful monarchy that would create public prosperity through wise legislation in favor of commerce and agriculture.

Generally speaking, Voltaire acted upon his age by developing its critical faculties, by creating a public with an *esprit critique*. He brought to the court of public opinion every question concerning government and administration, as well as religious, political, judicial, and economic questions. He accustomed public common sense to regard itself as competent in all matters, and he turned public opinion into one of the controlling forces in public affairs. To be sure, this movement did not begin with Voltaire and was not confined to him and his influence. In the affairs of the Constitution *Unigenitus* and in parliamentary and ministerial conflicts, since the time of the Regency, one had heard the same appeals to the public, the same voices of opinion. Every *philosophe* used as his main weapon in the battle for men's minds this same technique for manipulating and arousing the nation's collective thoughts and feelings. However, it is here that Voltaire seems to have played the most active and conspicuous role. It was he who . . . served *par excellence* the function of a newspaper and of an entire press. With his innumerable writings he formed a spirit and attitude designated in his day as *patriotique* or *républicain*. It could be defined as the interest that the ordinary citizen, the private individual, took in all matters concerning the public welfare and in all the means of achieving general prosperity. It involved the individual's participation in the affairs of state, even under an absolute monarchy, by engaging in constant criticism of social abuses and by endeavoring at all times to bring about practical reforms and improvements.

It was in large measure Voltairianism that disarmed the nobility in 1789 and handed it over to the Revolution, an accessory, in its thinking, to its own dispossession. Montesquieu favored a social élite. Rousseau was too paradoxical and extreme. Voltaire gave the privileged classes what they wanted, both of good and evil, and thus he indoctrinated and molded them so well that he furnished them with a rationale that was allied, from the outset, to the intentions of their enemies. They would be forced to emigrate in order to recreate a nobility with a conservative, Catholic outlook, suspicious of criticism or new ideas.

Obviously, Voltaire's influence was halted by the Revolution. Events moved at such a pace that all his ideas were quickly outdated. The abuses he had denounced were uprooted along with the institutions Voltaire would have retained. The reforms he thought realizable around 1760 or 1775 were either rapidly enacted or found to be no longer applicable to the new France. Perhaps he helped in defining the new relationship between Church and State, the establishment of civil marriages, the standardization of weights and measures, and the unifying of the legislative processes. The Declaration of the Rights of Man was no more his handiwork than anyone else's. It was a product of the entire movement of the eighteenth century. We can only observe that if Montesquieu appears prominently in article 16, articles 7, 9, 10, and 11 correspond to the objectives most strongly advocated by Voltaire. But once again, the various credits cannot be accurately allocated.

During the Revolution itself, the Voltairian mind was no longer fashionable. It was a time when the public demanded enthusiasm, passion, oratory, and emotional excesses. Rousseau, better than Voltaire, spoke in tones that suited the occasion and touched men's souls. But the Consulate and the Empire recalled Voltaire to active duty. A substantial portion of Voltaire's ideas were unquestionably ignored under Bonaparte, particularly his views on the control and criticism of public authority and his hatred of war. But in the man who had served as "the journalist of the opposition," as Voltaire had done under Louis XV, there were the makings of a Prefect of the Empire: an enlightened skepticism, a hatred of metaphysical ideologies and political systems, a conception of benevolent and active despotism which develops a nation's resources, a materialistic philosophy of government administration dedicated to practical improvements and an increase in social well being, and unequivocal views on the subordination of the Church to civil authority. The Concordat, with its several amendments, was not at variance with Voltaire's aspirations.

But it was from 1815 to 1830, during the Restoration, that Voltairianism triumphed. It led the struggle against legitimist and Catholic reaction. It furnished arms, a strategy, arguments, and an arsenal of facts, views, and witticisms for liberal journalists and pamphleteers. It was the favorite reading matter for the liberal bourgeoisie which found Voltairian ideas within its grasp and a spirit pleasing to its taste. As the Church had made herself the protectress and directress of the monarchy, so liberalism tended to identify itself with Voltairianism. And from the Voltairian spirit emerged a portion that eventually came to be considered Voltairianism in its entirety; namely, a hatred for the Church and a contempt for religion. Moreover, after the Revolution almost all of Voltaire's politics was useless except his pleas for freedom of the press. The new France of the Restoration reduced Voltaire to little more than his anticlericalism. That was to be his function throughout the rest of the nineteenth century, a supply depot, as it were, for anticlerical ammunition. Consequently, Voltaire's popularity would reflect those moments in which clericalism appeared to pose the greatest threat to liberal forces. Voltairianism governed after 1830 and educated the youth of the nation in the university. Mme Ackermann, born in 1828, was imbued with Voltaire under her father's influence. The great revolution of 1848 rejected Voltaire, who was no longer sufficient for the situation. But during the Second Empire and the Third Republic we discovered him again in the polemical writings of such newspapers as *Le Siècle* ("The Century") and *Le XIXe Siècle* ("The 19th Century").

From 1850 on, however, Voltairian influence continued to decline, losing itself in the mass of eighteenth-century traditions which likewise thinned out and exhausted themselves. The Revolution had lost Voltaire his following among the nobility. In the nineteenth century the Falloux education law and a rising fear of socialism rallied the bourgeoisie to the cause of religion, thereby depriving Voltaire of those very readers who appreciated him most and for whom he was the writer *par excellence*. The more anticlericalism filtered down among the masses, the less readily it could draw sustenance from Voltaire or arm itself with Voltairian wit and irony. Common people demanded simpler reading matter and cruder weapons.

Among the literate class which the Church had failed to win back Voltaire lost ground. The rich and powerful literature of the nineteenth century gave us new requirements in taste and an artistic ideal that Voltaire no longer satisfied. His influence on us decreased with every new position taken by the Romantic Movement, the Parnassian school, the Symbolists, and contemporary writers. But more especially, an educated man in our day and age, knowing the requirements for scholarly research, will no longer draw his information from Voltaire. Apart from material errors and inadvertencies which rigorous modern standards no longer condone, the progress made in philosophical and historical sciences, psychology, and Biblical exegesis has brought to light aspects of problems that Voltaire had never suspected. If Renan, who replaced him, had already made him obsolete, all the more reason for our not adopting at face value Voltaire's views of religious phenomena and religious history. We can no longer discuss these matters in Voltaire's terms. Accordingly, while aware that we are continuing in our time the work he undertook in his day, we now find in all Voltaire's anti-Christian polemics, whether in their argumentation or form of presentation, nothing more than an historical museum. It was serviceable in combating the Church in 1770. It has scarcely any relevance to the twentieth century.

The Church, moreover, is no longer what it was. It has, to a certain extent, revised its apologetics, abandoned certain theses, and reformed its scholarship. Even against conservative theologians, those, for example, who still defend the authenticity of the Pentateuch, we need other arguments than those of Voltairian polemic. The result of all this is that Voltaire is read less frequently today, or else he is read for different reasons. Outside the circle of cultivated readers there are a certain number who, in reading Voltaire, make no distinction between form and substance and are not in the least troubled by a concern for historical perspective. They apply everything Voltaire wrote to the world we now live in. There are such. But how many are there? What role do these Voltairians play in the intellectual movement of our time?

It seems to me beyond question that if Voltaire still has an influence to wield in the France of today, it should be, above all, a literary and intellectual influence of pure form. His definitions of good taste, and his enslavement to those definitions, will never again be taken as infallible authority. But as Romanticism fades into the distance, it is possible that there will be a rebirth of the desire for clear, carefully winnowed thoughts and ideas, and a renewed love of the simple, refined expression. It is possible that there will be a demand for lessons in literary style and analysis such as are found in those parts of Voltaire's work least bound by rules and classical ornamentation, in such writings as his **Mélanges** ("Miscellanies"), **Romans** ("novels"), and **Correspondance.** It would appear that, since the passing of Naturalism and the crisis in Symbolism, the evolution of prose writing has been in the direction of clarity and simplicity, which is to say, toward the Voltairian qualities of the eighteenth century.

Shall I say a word about Voltaire in countries outside France? Here again, it would be easier to write a history of his reputation than of his influence. We need to know the precise extent to which French civilization influenced the rest of Europe in the eighteenth and nineteenth centuries in order to claim credit for clearly distinguishing the part that Voltaire played. If I venture to suggest what seems to me probable as of the present moment, I would judge Voltaire's influence very weak in England, except in the area of historical writing. Philosophical thought in England was well ahead of Voltaire and had little, if anything, to gain from him. Also Voltaire shocked the English conscience and English notions of decency. And finally, the age in which France's classical forms made their imprint on English literature was drawing to a close while Voltaire was just on the threshold of his career and England was taking cognizance of her own genius. It is not that Voltaire was unappreciated in that country. Indeed, he was perhaps better appreciated there than in France. But England studied and judged him more than she followed him.

On the other hand, in every continental country, even in Spain and Portugal, there were a considerable number of

Voltairian minds in the second half of the eighteenth century. They included princes, noblemen, and members of the bourgeoisie, all imbued with Voltairian skepticism, fond of trenchant mockery, and alien to feelings of respect or reverence, who delighted in a style of writing that was deft and clear in expression and elegantly casual in tone. Frederick II was the most illustrious representative of this category of men in whose intellectual development Voltaire played what seems to have been the preponderant role. The same intellectual type can be discovered among men of all backgrounds: Germans, Hungarians, Russians, Italians, etc.

The birth and development of a national literature in Germany barred the road to Voltairian influence in that country and, by its extension, prevented the spread of Voltairianism in other parts of eastern Europe. It was Voltaire whom "the bards" of Goettingen despised in Wieland. Then came Romanticism to add new obstacles. As in France, liberalism and the need to counteract ecclesiastical power prolonged Voltaire's influence in certain countries. It was strong in Italy where aspirations for social reform, for liberty and unity, and a hatred for monks and priests found nourishment in Voltaire. In varying degrees and in different ways, and despite all sorts of divergent views, such men as Gorani, Beccaria, Pietro Verri, and later on in the nineteenth century, Foscolo, Monti, and a number of writers and journalists received and transmitted Voltairian thoughts and ideas. We find in Spain, among the liberal *afrancesados,* controversialists molded in the school of Ferney, writers who cultivated the neatly turned phrase and the pithy, caustic comment. I mention only Mariano de Larra.

In general, in countries outside France, to the extent that historical circumstances moved further away from the conditions that obtained in France when Voltaire's work first appeared, his influence is not easily discernible except among certain clear-thinking minds at odds with their social group or in revolt against its demands and prejudices. In Germany it was the skeptic Wieland and later on the ironist Heinrich Heine, who called himself "a German nightingale nesting in Voltaire's wig." And is there not also a bit of Voltairian humor in the sarcasm of Lord Byron? He would allow no one to criticize Voltaire, "the greatest genius of France, the universal Voltaire." He dedicated to him a stanza of his *Childe Harold* in which he drew a sympathetic portrait that attests to a precise and first-hand knowledge of the man as well as his work [see excerpt dated 1816].

> The one was fire and fickleness, a child,
> Most mutable in wishes, but in mind
> A wit as various,—gay, grave, sage, or wild,—
> Historian, bard, philosopher combined;
> He multiplied himself among mankind,
> The Proteus of their talents: but his own
> Breathed most in ridicule,—which, as the wind,
> Blew where it listed, laying all things prone,
> Now to o'erthrow a fool, and now to shake a throne.
>
> (pp. 169-83)

Gustave Lanson, in his Voltaire, *translated by Robert A. Wagoner, John Wiley & Sons, Inc., 1966, 258 p.*

George Saintsbury   (essay date 1911)

[Saintsbury was an English literary historian and critic. Hugely prolific, he composed histories of English and European literature as well as numerous critical works on individual authors, styles, and periods. In the following excerpt from a work first published in 1911, he considers the variety and intent of Voltaire's major writings.]

Vast and various as the work of Voltaire is, its vastness and variety are of the essence of its writer's peculiar quality. The divisions of it have long been recognized, and may be treated regularly.

The first of these divisions in order, not the least in bulk, and, though not the first in merit, inferior to none in the amount of congenial labour spent on it, is the *theatre.* Between fifty and sixty different pieces (including a few which exist only in fragments or sketches) are included in his writings, and they cover his literary life. It is at first sight remarkable that Voltaire, whose comic power was undoubtedly far in excess of his tragic, should have written many tragedies of no small excellence in their way, but only one fair second-class comedy, **Nanine.** His other efforts in this latter direction are either slight and almost insignificant in scope, or, as in the case of the somewhat famous **Écossaise,** deriving all their interest from being personal libels. His tragedies, on the other hand, are works of extraordinary merit in their own way. Although Voltaire had neither the perfect versification of Racine nor the noble poetry of Corneille, he surpassed the latter certainly, and the former in the opinion of some not incompetent judges, in playing the difficult and artificial game of the French tragedy. **Zaïre,** among those where love is admitted as a principal motive, and **Mérope,** among those where this motive is excluded and kept in subordination, yield to no plays of their class in such interest as is possible on the model, in stage effect and in uniform literary merit. Voltaire knew that the public opinion of his time reserved its highest prizes for a capable and successful dramatist, and he was determined to win those prizes. He therefore set all his wonderful cleverness to the task, going so far as to adopt a little even of that Romantic disobedience to the strict classical theory which he condemned, and no doubt sincerely, in Shakespeare.

As regards his *poems* proper, of which there are two long ones, the **Henriade** and the **Pucelle,** besides smaller pieces, of which a bare catalogue fills fourteen royal octavo columns, their value is very unequal. The **Henriade** has by universal consent been relegated to the position of a school reading book. Constructed and written in almost slavish imitation of Virgil, employing for medium a very unsuitable vehicle—the Alexandrine couplet (as reformed and rendered monotonous for dramatic purposes)—and animated neither by enthusiasm for the subject nor by real understanding thereof, it could not but be an unsatisfactory performance. The **Pucelle,** if morally inferior, is from a literary point of view of far more value. It is desultory to a degree; it is a base libel on religion and history; it differs from its model *Ariosto* in being, not, as *Ariosto* is, a mixture of romance and burlesque, but a sometimes tedious tissue of burlesque pure and simple; and it is exposed to the objection—often and justly urged—that much of its fun depends simply on the fact that there were and are many people who believe enough in Christianity to make its jokes give pain to them and to make their disgust at such jokes piquant to others. Nevertheless, with all the **Pucelle**'s faults, it is amusing. The minor poems are as much above the **Pucelle** as the **Pucelle** is above the **Henriade.** It is true that there is nothing, or hardly anything, that properly deserves the name of poetry in them—no passion, no sense of the beauty of nature, only a narrow "criticism of life," only a conventional and restricted choice of language, a cramped and monotonous prosody, and none of that indefinite suggestion which has been rightly said to be of the poetic essence. But there is immense wit, a wonderful command of such metre and language as the taste of the time allowed to the poet, occasionally a singular if somewhat artificial grace, and a curious felicity of diction and manner.

The third division of Voltaire's works in a rational order consists of his *prose romances* or *tales.* These productions—incomparably the most remarkable and most absolutely good fruit of his genius—were usually composed as pamphlets, with a purpose of polemic in religion, politics, or what not. Thus **Candide** attacks religious and philosophical optimism, **L'Homme aux quarante écus** certain social and political ways of the time, **Zadig** and others the received forms of moral and metaphysical orthodoxy, while some are mere lampoons on the Bible, the unfailing source of Voltaire's wit. But (as always happens in the case of literary work where the form exactly suits the author's genius) the purpose in all the best of them disappears almost entirely. It is in these works more than in any others that the peculiar quality of Voltaire—ironic style without exaggeration—appears. That he learned it partly from Saint-Évremond, still more from Anthony Hamilton, partly even from his own enemy Le Sage, is perfectly true, but he gave it perfection and completion. If one especial peculiarity can be singled out, it is the extreme restraint and simplicity of the verbal treatment. Voltaire never dwells too long on his point, stays to laugh at what he has said, elucidates or comments on his own jokes, guffaws over them or exaggerates their form. The famous "pour encourager les autres" (that the shooting of Byng did "encourage the others" very much is not to the point) is a typical example, and indeed the whole of **Candide** shows the style at its perfection.

The fourth division of Voltaire's work, the *historical,* is the bulkiest of all except his correspondence, and some parts of it are or have been among the most read, but it is far from being even among the best. The small treatises on Charles XII. and Peter the Great are indeed models of clear narrative and ingenious if somewhat superficial grasp and arrangement. The so-called **Siècle de Louis XIV.** and **Siècle de Louis XV.** (the latter inferior to the former but still valuable) contain a great miscellany of interesting matter, treated by a man of great acuteness and unsurpassed power of writing, who had also had access to much important private information. But even in these books defects are present, which appear much more strongly in the singular olla podrida entitled **Essai sur les mœurs,** in the **Annales de l'empire** and in the minor historical works. These defects are an almost total absence of any comprehension of what has since been called the philosophy of history, the constant presence of gross prejudice, frequent inaccuracy of detail, and, above all, a complete incapacity to look at anything except from the narrow standpoint of a half pessimist and half self-satisfied *philosophe* of the 18th century.

His work in *physics* concerns us less than any other here; it is, however, not inconsiderable in bulk, and is said by experts to give proof of aptitude.

To his own age Voltaire was pre-eminently a poet and a philosopher; the unkindness of succeeding ages has sometimes questioned whether he had any title to either name, and especially to the latter. His largest *philosophical* work, at least so called, is the curious medley entitled **Dictionnaire philosophique,** which is compounded of the articles contributed by him to the great *Encyclopédie* and of several minor pieces. No one of Voltaire's works shows his antireligious or at least anti-ecclesiastical animus more strongly. The various title-words of the several articles are often the merest stalking-horses, under cover of which to shoot at the Bible or the church, the target being now and then shifted to the political institutions of the writer's country, his personal foes, &c., and the whole being largely seasoned with that acute, rather superficial, commonsense, but also commonplace, ethical and social criticism which the 18th century called philosophy. The book ranks perhaps second only to the novels as showing the character, literary and personal, of Voltaire; and despite its form it is nearly as readable. The minor philosophical works are of no very different character. In the brief **Traité de métaphysique** the author makes his grand effort, but scarcely succeeds in doing more than show that he had no real conception of what metaphysic is.

In general *criticism* and *miscellaneous* writing Voltaire is not inferior to himself in any of his other functions. Almost all his more substantive works, whether in verse or prose, are preceded by prefaces of one sort or another, which are models of his own light pungent *causerie;* and in a vast variety of nondescript pamphlets and writings he shows himself a perfect journalist. In literary criticism pure and simple his principal work is the **Commentaire sur Corneille,** though he wrote a good deal more of the same kind—sometimes (as in his **Life** and notices of Molière) independently sometimes as part of his **Siècles.** Nowhere, perhaps, except when he is dealing with religion, are Voltaire's defects felt more than here. He was quite unacquainted with the history of his own language and literature, and more here than anywhere else he showed the extraordinarily limited and conventional spirit which accompanied the revolt of the French 18th century against limits and conventions in theological, ethical and political matters.

There remains only the huge division of his *correspondence,* which is constantly being augmented by fresh discoveries, and which, according to Georges Bengesco, has never been fully or correctly printed, even in some of the parts longest known. In this great mass Voltaire's personality is of course best shown, and perhaps his literary qualities not worst. His immense energy and versatility, his adroit and unhesitating flattery when he chose to flatter, his ruthless sarcasm when he chose to be sarcastic, his rather unscrupulous business faculty, his more than rather unscrupulous resolve to double and twist in any fashion so as to escape his enemies,—all these things appear throughout the whole mass of letters.

Most judgments of Voltaire have been unduly coloured by sympathy with or dislike of what may be briefly called his polemical side. When sympathy and dislike are both discarded or allowed for, he remains one of the most astonishing, if not exactly one of the most admirable, figures of letters. That he never, as Carlyle complains, gave utterance to one great thought is strictly true. That his characteristic is for the most part an almost superhuman cleverness rather than positive genius is also true. But that he was merely a mocker, which Carlyle and others have also said, is not strictly true or fair. In politics proper he seems indeed to have had few or no constructive ideas, and to have been entirely ignorant or quite reckless of the fact that his attacks were destroying a state of things for which as a whole he neither had nor apparently wished to have any substitute. In religion he protested stoutly, and no doubt sincerely, that his own attitude was not purely negative; but here also he seems to have failed altogether to distinguish between pruning and cutting down. Both here and elsewhere his great fault was an inveterate superficiality. But this superficiality was accompanied by such wonderful acuteness within a certain range, by such an absolutely unsurpassed literary aptitude and sense of style in all the lighter and some of the graver modes of literature, by such untiring energy and versatility in enterprise, that he has no parallel among ready writers anywhere. Not the most elaborate work of Voltaire is of much value for matter; but not the very slightest work of Voltaire is devoid of value in form. In literary craftsmanship, at once versatile and accomplished, he has no superior and scarcely a rival. (pp. 112-17)

George Saintsbury, in his French Literature and Its Masters, *edited by Huntington Cairns, Alfred A. Knopf, 1946, pp. 94-118.*

Georg Brandes (essay date 1917)

[*Brandes was a distinguished Danish literary historian. He is best known for his* Main Currents in Nineteenth-Century Literature (1872-90), *a pioneering study valued for its insight and lucidity. In the following excerpt from a work originally published as* François de Voltaire (2 vols., 1916-17), *he studies Voltaire as a satirist.*]

During the reaction of Romanticism against Classicism and during the transformation of the language, which took place through the efforts of Victor Hugo and Theophile Gautier, Voltaire as a poet was forgotten. He lost standing in his country, as he had been shamefully overlooked in Germany because of the attacks of Lessing and the disparagement of the German Romanticists. But from the very first there was one among the French Romanticists, the only great critical talent, Sainte-Beuve, who gave Voltaire his due as a lyric poet.

After showing that the odes of Jean Baptist Rousseau, though perfect, were cold and that he had exerted no influence, Sainte-Beuve said:

> The contrary is the case with Voltaire, the only true, the only great lyric poet of the eighteenth century. His imagination is always awake. One can find the poet in every fragment that came from his pen: trifles, satires, introductions to poetic works, impromptu lines which circle the globe. In his conversation he is a poet, by the brilliant flashes of his

wit, the continuous lightning of his words, the lively and charming twist he gives each of his remarks.

In any period there are only a few who are able to raise themselves above their contemporaries' narrow conceptions of poetry, and who appreciate the fact that people's ideas of poetry change. These will rely upon their own judgment, and without any consideration of fashion will approve that which they feel to be good. The critic who amounts to more than a weather vane of literary fashion will esteem Voltaire as a lyric poet.

His prose is today far better appreciated than his poetry. . . . (pp. 136-37)

His prose is read and appreciated in his short novels only. Unfortunately considerable knowledge of history is essential to the understanding of these productions one and a half centuries old.

For a proper appreciation of this prose, one should read one or two of the *Facéties.* Here his art is still better, his mental superiority still more striking, even for one who comes to them without any preliminary study. (p. 137)

Voltaire, who had been educated by the Jesuits, tried to show his gratitude. In 1748 he wrote to Père Vionnet: "I have fought for a long time under the banner of your society. You scarcely have a more insignificant soldier, but not one more devoted"—strong words. In spite of his fundamental difference of outlook he showed the Jesuits an almost childish respect, and had they responded with equal consideration everything would have gone smoothly. But there were belligerent Jesuits. Their chief publication attacked him again and again, until the editor, Father Berthier, incited Voltaire to a reply which in spite of its sting has charming gaiety and irresistible wit.

The title is: **Report of the Jesuit Berthier's Illness, Confession, Death and Revelation Including the Report on the Journey of Brother Garassie, and everything that Followed and Will Follow.**

This joke was perpetrated in November, 1759, and the man whose death is described so vividly lived twenty-three years longer. Father Berthier had just returned to Bourges and had been granted a pension. His journal was a Church paper and its purpose was to attack freethinking and freethinkers, Voltaire in particular.

The story runs thus:

> On October 12, 1759, Brother Berthier set out on this unhappy journey from Paris to Versailles, with Brother Coutu who usually accompanied him. Berthier had put several numbers of *Le Journal de Trevoux* in the coach, which he wished to give to his protectors and protectresses, the chambermaid of Madame Nourrice, a royal cook, one of the pharmacy boys of the King, and several other gentlemen in high positions, who could appreciate real talent. Several times on the way Berthier felt ill; his head grew heavy; he had to yawn.—'I don't know what is wrong with me,' he said to Coutu; 'In all my life I never yawned so much.'—'Reverend Father,' said Coutu, 'that will pass away.'—'What? What do you mean by your "pass away"?'—'I mean,' said Brother Coutu, 'that I too am yawning, and I don't know why, for, I have read nothing all day nor have you spoken to me since we set out.'— While Brother Coutu spoke these words he yawned

more than before. Berthier answered that this yawning apparently would never end.—The coachman turned around, and when he saw the two clerical gentlemen yawning, he yawned with them. The malady affected the people passing by. Everybody in the houses nearby was yawning. Such a great influence has a scholar sometimes by mere proximity.

After several chills both travelers fall asleep, in a deep, deathlike sleep from which they have not yet waked when the coach stops at the gate of Versailles. The coachman tries to wake them and get them out of the coach, but in vain. He calls for aid. Coutu, who is more robust, shows some signs of life, but Berthier remains cold. Several royal physicians coming from lunch, either pass by without looking at the patients or else give absurd explanations of their condition. Finally, a famous physician, who had studied under Boerhave, opens the patient's mouth, notices his bad breath, and decides that he is poisoned, and this with one of the most virulent poisons. The coachman is asked if by chance he has a package of drugs for the pharmacist in Versailles.—"No," he answers, "the only package I have for the Reverend Father is this."—He looks in the basket of the coach and brings out two dozen numbers of *Le Journal de Trevoux.*—"There you are, gentlemen, was I wrong?" asks the great physician, and all those present admire his astonishing penetration.

Now everybody understands the cause of the illness. On the spot, the dangerous package is burned, and this brings Berthier around a little; but his head is affected and the danger is not yet over. The physician gets an inspiration to make him drink a page of the *Encyclopedia* dissolved in white wine, whereupon a great amount of gall is got rid of. But as his condition grows worse, it is necessary to call a father confessor. The first priest who is approached for this purpose refuses to take the responsibility for a Jesuit soul, the second agrees with the first. The dying man is asked if he has loved God and his neighbor.—"I love God," he answers, "and my neighbor as far as I can."

"Have you not read bad books?" asks the father-confessor. "I don't mean just boring books, like so and so," here follow the names of a dozen books by authors whom Voltaire wants to hit, "but I mean so and so," a number of theological writings are enumerated, among which are books of the old Jesuit Sanchez whom Pascal had attacked some time previously.

Berthier states that his position allows him to read everything; he is the editor of *Le Journal de Trevoux.* "What, you publish this paper which judges and rends all good writers? Don't you know that whoso calls his brother a fool is in danger of Hell fire? Yet you tempt honest people who happen to read your writings to call you a fool! You who so complacently criticize everything you do not understand. Two vices have you in their grip, haughtiness and greed. I cannot absolve you from your sins unless you swear not to work any more for *Le Journal de Trevoux.*"

When Berthier refuses, the priest declines to absolve him from his sins. Just then Brother Coutu comes running and calls, perspiring and stinking: "For God's sake, don't take the Sacrament from his hand! Do you know who he is? The editor of *Les Nouvelles Ecclésiastiques* (the rival Church paper). You are lost if you confess to him."

Astonishment, shame and anger bring back life to the

dying man for a moment. "Scoundrel," he exclaims, "opponent of God, of Kings, of the Jesuits! So you fancy you are less of a fanatic than I! Granted that I have written against enlightened men who have not lowered themselves to answer and to destroy me! Haven't you been just as arrogant? Don't we have to admit that in this century, the sewer of all centuries, we are the two most miserable of all insects that buzz around the dung-heap?"

The power of truth forced Father Berthier to speak thus in his hour of death. He spoke as one inspired. But soon the moment of death came; he pressed the hand of Brother Coutu, who said, "O Reverend Father, you are a saint, you are the first writer in the world to confess that he was boring. May you die in peace!"

The next chapter, *Brother Berthier's Ghost Reveals Itself to Brother Garassise,* begins thus:

> When I, Brother Ignaz Garassise, woke October 14th, at two o'clock in the morning, a ghost was there. It was Brother Berthier. I was seized by the longest and most terrible fit of yawning I ever knew.—'You are dead, Reverend Father?' I said.—Yawning, he made a sign to me which meant; yes!—'All the better,' I said, 'for, doubtless Your Reverence is accepted among the Saints. You must have one of the first places. Speak, Reverend Father, yawn no more but tell me.'

The deceased now informs him that he is mistaken; Paradise is closed to him. And Garassise must refrain from slander in his future contributions to the *Journal de Trevoux,* for that is not forgiven in Heaven. Above all he must take care not to be boring, as Berthier was, for tedium is regarded as the unpardonable sin. Berthier, it seems, did not go to Hell but to Purgatory. There he is to remain for 333 333 years, three months, three weeks, three days; and he is not to be discharged until a Brother is found who is devoted, peaceful, and unworldly, and who slanders nobody to reigning princes.

The last chapter treats of Brother Garassise's arrival in Paris from Lisbon in the year 1760; he gets into the convention of the Brothers who have gathered in order to determine who is to take over the *Journal de Trevoux* after Berthier. Among others Fréron gives himself the highest recommendation: "My Reverend Fathers," he says, "I have been a Jesuit; you expelled me; but I belong to you; for, as Horace says: The barrel retains for a long time the smell of that which was in it. I am fit for the task. I am more ignorant, more impudent, and more of a liar than any other. Give me a lease of the *Journal de Trevoux* and I shall pay you as I can."

There is, however, no inclination to take the bread away from the children of the house and give it to the dogs, as the Bible says, and Brother Garassise claims his rights:

> I was chosen by Berthier himself, who, yawning, consecrated me as a journalist. I worked with the *Journal de Trevoux* until at your order I had to embark for Paraguay. I possess the pen of Berthier, the tedium of Catrou, the cantankerousness of Porée and the dryness of Daniel. I therefore ask for the prize that is due my merits.

And the Journal was given to him unanimously.

A striking passage in **Micromégas** pictures the inhabitants of Sirius and Saturn observing a battle on the Earth. The way in which the inhabitant of Sirius criticizes war, the anger and pity of the Giant over its stupidity, make a deep impression:

> "Can one understand such madness? I feel like taking three steps and crushing this ridiculous, murderous heap of ants under my feet." "It's not worth the trouble," answers the inhabitant of Saturn; "they are working hard enough at their own destruction. Ten years from now not one per cent of these poor wretches will be left. If they do not slay each other, then hunger, or debauchery will finish all of them. Besides, these are not the ones who should be punished, but those barbarians who sit calmly in their warm rooms, comfortably digesting, and order a million people to wholesale murder, and then go ceremoniously to thank God in the churches."

Voltaire's hatred of war never abated, not even in his obligatory odes in honor of war heroes. He told Frederick the Great just what he thought of the conquest of Silesia: "I wish you would be so kind as to tell me the truth: Are you any happier now than when you were in Rheinsberg?" (March 25, 1741). And in almost the same words (April, 1742): "I do not know if you are now, in all this noise of fame, any happier than you were in Rheinsberg in quiet seclusion." He speaks very freely in his letter of May 26, 1742, in which he says: "I think of the human race, Sire, before I think of you; I shed tears, like Abbé Saint-Pierre, for the human race, whose terror you are becoming, and only thereafter can I rejoice in your glory." In the same letter he expresses the same thought in verse. . . . (pp. 137-42)

Seventeen years later in a letter to Frederick he says: "Believe me, Sire, I was made for you, and I am ashamed of being happier than you; for I live with philosophers, while you have only first class murderers in uniform around you. Move to Sans-Souci, Sire, to Sans-Souci!" (p. 142)

In **Candide** Voltaire treats a broad question: Is our world really, as Leibnitz believes and Pope stated, the best of all possible worlds?

The distaste for metaphysical debate which Voltaire expresses in **Candide** is his reply to Pope's "everything is well" and Leibnitz' "everything is for the best." He answers, not with suppositions, but with facts: Slavery and syphilis, thirty thousand dead in the Lisbon earthquake, ten times as many dead and countless injured in the Seven Years War, the smoke and flames of the stake.

Candide meets a negro who has been horribly disfigured by a barbarous master and he says: "O Pangloss, you did not foresee this horror. It's all I need to see. I must renounce your optimism."—"What is optimism," asks Cacambo.—O, said Candide, "that is the insanity which insists that all is well when everything is going wrong."

Had one, after the earthquake of Lisbon, called to the unfortunate survivors that lay mangled beneath the ruins: "Everything is all right, the necessary effect of inevitable causes; your misfortune means nothing, it is all for the greatest good of the greatest number."—it would have sounded like a cruel attempt to be witty. Everything is all right? For whom? Obviously not for us. For some God? It is clear that this God does not suffer from our misfortune. What consolation do these phrases bring? What use is it to tell the slandered, to tell the persecuted, to tell those who stand bound to the stake waiting for the flames to reach them, that everything is well, that nothing better can be expected from a fate that embraces the whole universe in its love?

Voltaire was naturally inclined to enjoy life. Everything gave him pleasure from a good meal, a good bed, a merry conversation, up to the sight of a lovely woman or the effect of a fine poem. He enjoyed being a poet, historian, physicist, architect, upholsterer, gardener, wine-grower, combatter of errors, fighter against folly and superstition. Comparing his epoch with the past, he felt with satisfaction that progress had been made.

But about the middle of the century his joy in life decreased. Too many horrible events occurred in the world at large and in his own private life. Lisbon's catastrophe gave the signal for every sort of public calamity. The fires of religious persecution again flamed up. The Seven Years War drowned in blood all hope of peaceful progress.

Fresh news nearly always means fresh misfortunes. After one has lived for some time, all illusions are gone. Fate hurls us along, toying with us. Let us try, let us try . . . what a word! Nothing depends upon us, we cannot decide anything, we are puppets, ruled forces.

From this mood came *Candide,* and as the book had been so thoroughly prepared, its elaboration required but a few weeks. Toward the end he became so keen to finish that he locked himself in for three days and refused to open the door, except to have his meals and his coffee brought.

On the fourth day his worried niece forced him to let her enter. He tossed her the completed manuscript and said: "Here, curious Madame, is something you may read."

Even though *Candide* mocks at optimism on every page, is it fair to say that it preaches pessimism? Not at all. One system is as much detested by Voltaire as the other. He knows there are good people and beneficent people, and he does not try to hide it. With his restless inclination to work, his insuperable belief in human progress, he is by no means inclined to see everything black. He himself is well off; but he gets no pleasure, as Lucretius expressed it, from watching the fierce storm from a safe harbor. His *joie de vivre* is depressed by sympathy and fellow-feeling for the suffering of others.

Read carefully the end of the story: outside of Constantinople Candide and his companions meet a good old man who is enjoying the fresh air in front of his door under an arbor of orange trees. They ask him the name of a Mufti who had recently been murdered in the city. He knows nothing about the case, but invites the travelers into his house and prepares a choice meal for them. His hospitality is lordly. He possesses a few acres of land which he cultivates with the help of his children. The work keeps them free of three great evils: ennui, sin, and poverty.

This makes a deep impression on Candide. Pangloss says that man is not made for rest, and Martin admits that there is one way to make life bearable: to work without brooding too much. The entire little company is converted to this view. And everyone turns out to be good for something. Even Brother Giroflée becomes a good worker, still

more, a good fellow. And when Pangloss wishes to resume his long discourse about how man was perfect before the fall, and that all events are for the best in the best of all possible worlds, Candide interrupts him with the words: "Well said, but we must attend to our garden."

This which cannot be called an expression of cynicism, or of despair, or of pessimism, or of surrender, is Voltaire's own final motto. It is the consolation he holds out to the human race.

Feeling independent and safe through his ownership of several estates, Voltaire did not hesitate, this time, to publish his work. His friends recognized his style, but as usual he promptly disclaimed authorship of the book whose title page read: *Translated from the German by Dr. Ralph.* He wrote to his acquaintance, the Genevese pastor Jacob Vernes: "I have finally got around to reading *Candide,* and, as with *Jeanne d'Arc,* I tell you that anyone must be out of his senses to ascribe such stuff to me." Even to his own publishers, the Brothers Cramer, he wrote carefully: "What sort of work is this *Candide,* of which it is said that it is scandal to sell it, and which is supposed to have originated in Lyons? I might like to have it. Couldn't you, gentlemen, get me a bound copy? It is said that some people are brazen enough to claim that I am the author of this work, which I have never laid eyes on."

In spite of this little farce, agreed upon in advance with the publishers, they succeeded in smuggling a considerable number of copies into Geneva.

In March, 1759, *Candide* was denounced to the Council, who ordered that it should be burned by the hangman at once. This was done, to Voltaire's anger. He took revenge shortly by flooding Geneva with brief anti-Church and anti-Christian pamphlets. The authorities of Paris as well as of Geneva were furious. The encyclopedists had almost got the best of them. The clergy urged that some decisive action should be taken. Helvetius's book *De l'Esprit,* which had caused a considerable sensation, was condemned by the Parliament and burned by the hangman on February 10, 1759. (pp. 143-46)

> *Georg Brandes, in his* Voltaire, Vol. 2, *translated by Otto Kruger and Pierre Butler, 1930. Reprint by Frederick Ungar Publishing Co., 1964, 385 p.*

Richard Aldington   (essay date 1925)

[*Aldington was an English essayist, novelist, literary critic, and biographer. He is perhaps best known for his controversial biographies, including* Lawrence of Arabia: A Biographical Enquiry *(1955), in which he attacked Lawrence as an "impudent mythomaniac." In the following excerpt from his 1925 biography* Voltaire, *he surveys Voltaire's contes and philosophical pamphlets.*]

Voltaire would have been astonished and grieved to learn that most of his readers in the twentieth century prefer *Candide* to *La Henriade* and *Jeannot et Colin* to *Zaïre.* One can imagine the restless shade of Voltaire eagerly conferring with new literary arrivals in the Elysian Fields and wringing shadowy hands in anguish at the decline of "bon goût" in Europe. (Indeed, there would be some reason for this, but not in the way he would mean). The Voltaire we most admire is not the epic poet, the dramatist, the historian, but the charming poet of light verse, the witty correspondent and, above all, the brilliant satirist and prose stylist of the Romans and Mélanges. In the forty volume edition of Voltaire, the Romans and Mélanges fill eight volumes; and this is exactly four volumes too many. In spite of Voltaire's wit and artistry, his gift of variety in treating the same ideas and topics, many of these pamphlets are redundant and abound in vain repetitions. The explanation is that they were in most cases intended as nothing but journalism, as light skirmishes in the Philosopher's War, "philosophical" propaganda against l'infâme and the abuses of the French political system, a popularization of the *Encyclopédie* for the lower ranks of readers. And since Voltaire knew that truth for such people is that which they hear most often repeated, he indulged in repetition of his main points to an extent which is now tedious.

A reader who knows the Romans and other pamphlets only from modern selections, will no doubt feel inclined to protest against this view; let him read perseveringly through the whole eight volumes, and it will be surprising indeed if he does not agree. After the fourth volume (and, by the way, the four volumes of the **Dictionnaire Philosophique** might be added to the eight mentioned above) a reader becomes more and more aware of the presence of certain Voltairean clichés. Finally, he gets to know what is coming in the pamphlet from reading only its opening paragraph. He grows weary of raillery at the absurdities, contradictions, and indecencies of the Bible—information chiefly derived from Bolingbroke, by the way. Directly this topic is broached, an experienced Voltairean reader knows that he will get the impostures of Moses, the immoral practices of the Patriarchs, the genealogy of the House of David with remarks on the private morals of this family, the indecent passages in Exodus, Genesis, and Ezechiel (particularly "Oohla and Oohlibah"), the singular commands of the Lord to Hosea. The Jesuits cannot be mentioned without a reference to Sanchez and his grotesque discussion of the relations between the Virgin Mary and the Holy Ghost. For the rest, the romans and pamphlets run upon the topics of the Inquisition, Jesuits, Jansenists and monks, bonzes, fakirs, mages, gymnosophists, the Sorbonne, the Papacy; Frederick, Catherine, Locke, Newton, the Encyclopédie, la saine philosophie, Deism, advantages of luxury, virtue of Chinese mandarins and North American Indians, fearful calamities, rapes, wars, shipwrecks, autos-da-fe, famines, earthquakes, mutilations, ghastly judicial executions, small-pox, venereal disease, petrified oysters on mountains, the Donation of Constantine, the constitution of England, the magnificence and brilliance of Paris, the trivial causes of wars, the example of Peter the Great, facile and faithless mistresses, imbecility and obstinacy of lawyers, indecency and peculation of monks, corruption of judges, superior antiquity and morality of the Far East, relative smallness of the Earth, insignificance of man, improbability of man's being immortal, rarity of human happiness, characteristics (usually arbitrary and inaccurate) of the nations of Europe; the frequency of human vanity, perfidy, cruelty, stupidity, persecution, sensuality, idleness, levity, inconsequence, drunkenness, heartlessness, calumny; and rare examples of "saine philosophie", hospitality, wisdom, tolerance, vegetarianism, contentment, righteousness, nobility of soul (usually among Turks, Chinese, brahmins, Indians, philosophers and agricultural small-holders).

This chaplet of clichés might be increased by a methodical compiler; however, the above list should be adequate for its purpose, which is to show that the romans and pamphlets repeat in popular form the notions and prejudices of the philosophe. But this repetition and a certain superficiality of thought do not destroy the art of Voltaire. He is usually praised as a satirist, and satire is indeed a true description of these innumerable pamphlets; but it is not a vituperative or gross satire. Sarcasm, raillery, irony, wit are the Voltairean weapons; he rarely breaks into serious denunciation and reproof, and still more rarely loses his temper, though when he does either, his satire loses its force and skill. The mood of Voltairean satire is complex, and is expressed metaphorically in the traditional Voltairean smile of Houdon's statue. That smile is malicious but humorous, sarcastic but not unkindly; it is that of a tolerant and witty man whose intelligence is prodigiously alert. And these are the qualities of Voltaire's prose satire. Human beings alternately aroused his pity and his mirth; their crimes and follies exasperated him, but he thought men could more easily be laughed and mocked than reproved and denounced out of them. At times the imbecilities of human conduct and of human systems left him aghast; but he took pity on us—poor ignorant creatures seduced by priests, crowned fools, stupid ideals, and mad prejudices—and laboured ceaselessly to enlighten us with the truths of "la saine philosophie", though with no great hope of permanently reforming us:

> Fools will be fools, say what we will,
> And rascals will be rascals still.

"In the name of common sense, act a little reasonably and learn to face facts" is the burden of these numberless diatribes. The personal attacks on his enemies are an invitation *urbi et orbi* not to take seriously the notions of people so unreasonable and foolish. But, on the whole, the Voltairean satire is an encouragement not to look at things and life too solemnly and lugubriously. Let us be reasonable, but let us make life endurable; we may not be immortal, the world may be and probably is a mass of ills, sufferings, and stupidities, but for God's sake let us crack a jest when we may. Let us, in fact, model ourselves upon the sage of Ferney; let us be active, industrious, sober, witty, ironic, philanthropic, Deistic, well-informed, and cheerful Rationalists; the deuce take the Pope and Rousseau, the Jesuits and the Jansenists, Leibnitz and Calvin, all the fanatics and the excessive, gloomy misanthropy and absurd optimism; let us mind our own business and cultivate our own gardens. Ituriel, the guardian genius of the earth, having received Babouc's report, "resolved to allow the world to go its way; for, said he, if all is not well, it is all tolerable." This is the "lesson" of many of these brilliant little pieces; it is madness to hope for the earthly paradise, fantastic to assert that all is well with the world, idiotic to be gloomy about it; make the best of what you have.

This Rationalist acceptation of the tolerability of life was quite common in the eighteenth century, at least among the upper classes. It is well put by Lord Chesterfield who in many respects was a living illustration of Voltaire's views and was in perfect sympathy with the Frenchman's philosophie.

> A wise man, without being a stoic, considers, in all misfortunes that befall him, their best as well as their worst side; and everything has a better and a

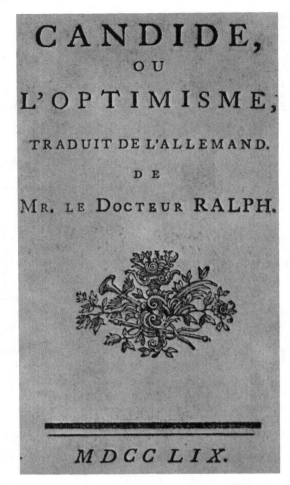

Title page of the first edition of Candide *(1759).*

worse side. . . . It is the rational philosophy taught me by experience and knowledge of the world, and which I have practised above thirty years. I always made the best of the best, and never made the bad worse by fretting; this enabled me to go through the various scenes of life, in which I have been an actor, with more pleasure and less pain than most people.

And again, in a letter to the Bishop of Waterfield, Chester-field expresses an idea which is the very essence of Voltaire's rationalism:

In the general course of things, there seems to be upon the whole a pretty equal distribution of physical good and evil, some extraordinary cases except-ed; and even moral good and evil seem mixed to a certain degree, for one never sees anybody so per-fectly good or so perfectly bad, as they might be.

Many instances of praise for these short pieces might be cited. One alone must suffice. Voltaire's "frère ennemi", the King of Prussia, who knew him so well, writes to him many years after the Frankfort episode: "You know I have always admired your writing and particularly those collec-tions of short prose pieces called Mélanges." The wit, the gaiety, the diablerie, the clear sparkle, the absence of any-thing heavy or pedantic in these pamphlets, have kept

them alive when Voltaire's more serious and ambitious works have fallen into disrepute. The romans especially are still regularly reprinted, and especially *Candide.* It is not unjust to say that thousands of readers know Voltaire only by that jeu d'esprit with which he amused himself in Switzerland. But others among the romans are equally brilliant and the wit of that brief satire on the nouveaux riches—*Jeannot et Colin*—is even more concentrated and amusingly malicious. The consummate art of these pieces has kept them young and fresh for a century and a half. It is not wholly a matter of wit and style, which are indeed almost imperishable when perfect, as with Voltaire they often were; but he possessed the art of telling a story—l'art de conter—in such a way that whatever he related became interesting and held the attention. We have testimony in abundance to Voltaire's charm of conversation and won-derful ability to retail anecdotes. The romans are simply wonderful examples of that charm and ability transferred to paper. The style is that of "polite conversation", chas-tened and polished without losing any of its familiarity and ease and without acquiring the least tinge of "literary" affectation and pedantry. The stories of his romans are told as lightly and without effort as he told a fable to young Florian. And just as Voltaire interested a child with the talking animals of a fable, so he interested the larger children of Europe with fanciful and fabulous tales in order to make them absorb his "lessons" while they scarcely knew they had done so. He smeared the rim of the cup with honey, as Tasso says, so that the reader, "de-ceived, drinks in the bitter juices and from his deceit gains life"—

Succhi amari ingannato intanto ei beve,
E dall' inganno suo vita riceve.

He drew on his extensive reading as well as on his experi-ence of life for the machinery and setting of these tales; the old medieval French romances he pretended to despise were levied upon, as well as many books of travel and imaginative literature, from Cyrano de Bergerac to the Arabian Nights, from Gulliver's Travels to Boccaccio. But Heaven forbid that anyone should laboriously seek for the "sources" of Voltaire's tales! The pure gold of the Ro-mans is all Voltaire's own. . . . (pp. 213-20)

Candide appeared in 1759, under the pseudonym of *le Docteur Ralph;* but since the style and wit of every para-graph signed it "Voltaire", the precaution was wasted. All the world who read knew that only Voltaire could have written it. The object of attack was the optimistic philoso-phy of Leibnitz and the no less optimistic statement of Rousseau that "tout est bien." An ingenious modern critic has tried to show that some of the passages of Candide's adventures refer to the career of Baron Trenck, who was arbitrarily imprisoned by Frederick the Great; it is sup-posed that Voltaire knew of Trenck's sufferings and used *Candide* as a method of informing Frederick. However this may be, *Candide* is certainly one of the most entertain-ing prose satires ever penned. Its likeness to *Rasselas* is su-perficial; both Johnson and Voltaire show the misfortunes of man, but Johnson leads the reader to religion, Voltaire to rational acquiescence and a small garden. The manner of the two authors again is dissimilar; a squirrel and an ele-phant can both pick nuts, but the one does it nimbly and petulantly, the other with solemnity and ponderosity. *Candide* might by an extension of meaning be called "philosophical", because under its gay fiction and satire it combats two philosophical ideas; it attacks the theory of optimism formulated by Leibnitz, that God is the perfect monad, that He created a world to show His perfection, that He chose this out of the infinite number of worlds, that He was guided by the "principium melioris", and that therefore the universe is the "best possible"; and it attacks the optimism of Rousseau, who denied the doctrine of original sin and affirmed that man in a state of nature is wholly good, from which follows the abandonment of rational self-discipline and the paradoxical assertion of the aristocracy of the plebs. Both doctrines are obviously heavy with dangers to human society and both are repugnant and absurd to rational common-sense; their truth, if they be truths, is obviously mystic, and to Voltaire all mysticism was disgusting and barbarous. Vulnerable as Voltaire's Rationalism must be to a concerted metaphysical attack, it was good enough for most people, and he had the wit to bring the laughers over to his side. Nevertheless, the Rousseau paradox of the "domination of the proletariat" has survived Voltaire's "government by the enlightened" as a popular idea; no doubt because it flatters more people and is irrational—an additional proof of Voltaire's pessimistic attitude towards human nature.

The machinery of **Candide** is simple. An ingenuous youth called Candide grows up in the Westphalian home of the Baron Thunder-ten-Troncke, instructed in philosophy by Dr. Pangloss, who taught "metaphysico-theologo-cosmolonigologie", and proved that all is for the best in this best of all possible worlds. The adventures of Candide, which range from China to Peru, are one long and humorous contradiction of this assumption; they are also a contradiction of the natural goodness of man. Obviously, the art of the narrator lies in the fecundity of invention with which he devises new episodes, his skill in making each arise naturally from those before, and the indefinable gift of the raconteur which makes the incredible acceptable and compels interest. Voltaire's novels and tales are lively parables, not novels in our meaning of the word, and his characters . . . are allegorical, well-masked types or embodied opinions. But these parables of philosophie have many of the essential qualities of good fiction, and these types are so shrewdly observed and so skillfully portrayed that for all their abstraction and generalization they seem to live. What is true of **Candide** in this respect is true of most of them, though in the less successful romans (the **Lettres d'Amabed,** for instance) the device is too artificial.

In reading steadily through these romans, one is most delighted and entertained by the flashes of wit and satire; the stories themselves are often slight, but the satiric wit of situation and comment is incomparable. Candide thinks Pangloss "the greatest philosopher of the province and consequently of all mankind." He meets an eloquent anabaptist and ingenuously confesses that he had not heard the Pope was Antichrist: "The orator's wife put her head out of the window and, perceiving a man who doubted that the Pope was Antichrist poured on his head a full . . . O Heavens! to what excess are ladies carried by religious zeal!" "A lady of honour", says Cunegonde, "may be raped once, but her virtue is fortified by it." When Candide and Martin approach the coast of France, Candide asks what the country is like: "In some provinces half the inhabitants are mad, in others they are over cunning, elsewhere they think they are witty, and in all the principal occupation is making love, the second scandal, and the third talking nonsense." As a more extended example of Voltaire's "admirable fooling" in **Candide,** take this fragment of dialogue:

> 'Apropos,' said Candide, 'do you think the earth was originally a sea, as we are assured by that large book belonging to the captain?'
>
> 'I don't believe it in the least,' said Martin, 'any more than all the other whimsies we have been pestered with recently!'
>
> 'But to what end was this world formed?' said Candide.
>
> 'To infuriate us,' replied Martin.
>
> 'Are you not very surprised,' continued Candide, 'by the love those two girls of the country of the Oreillons had for those two monkeys, whose adventure I told you?'
>
> 'Not in the least,' said Martin, 'I see nothing strange in their passion; I have seen so many extraordinary things that nothing seems extraordinary to me.'
>
> 'Do you think,' said Candide, 'that men have always massacred each other as they do to-day? Have they always been liars, cheats, traitors, brigands, weak, flighty, cowardly, envious, gluttonous, drunken, grasping, ambitious, bloody, backbiting, debauched, fanatical, hypocritical, and silly?'
>
> 'Do you think,' said Martin, 'that sparrow-hawks have always eaten the pigeons they came across?'
>
> 'Yes, of course,' said Candide.
>
> 'Well,' said Martin, 'if sparrow-hawks have always possessed the same nature, why should you expect men to change theirs?'
>
> 'Oh!' said Candide, 'there is a great difference; free will . . . '
>
> Arguing thus, they arrived at Bordeaux."

Amusing traits of this kind are scattered through all the romans. The **Vision de Babouc** is a fable to show the alternate good and evil of mankind and the world; Babouc is sent by the djinnee, Ituriel, to render an account of Persepolis, which needless to say is Paris. One day Barbouc is for destruction, the next for preservation, and so on alternately; finally he decides that there are "de très bonnes choses dans les abus" and, from his report, Ituriel decides to "let the world go on as it is, for if everything is not right, everything is tolerable." **Cosi-Sancta** is not a tale for puritans; it relates the misfortunes which occurred owing to the peevish chastity of a woman, and the good which resulted when her scruples dissolved. **Zadig** shows in a series of witty episodes the disadvantage of numerous estates of life and the misfortunes an honest man has to endure from the world; in short, the rarity and fragility of happiness. **Zadig** contains the famous verse which was sung every day to the conceited courtier by order of the king who wished to cure him of that vice:

> Que son mérite est extrême!
> Que de grâces! que de grandeur!
> Ah! combine monseigneur
> Doit être content de lui-même.

Memnon is a short but extremely clever satire on human prudence. Memnon one day "conceived the absurd project of being parfaitement sage". His fate in Voltaire's hands was assured; for apparently he was a disciple of Jean Jacques. *Bababec* is still shorter but even wittier; it is a satire on "fakirs" and hence upon those whom Voltaire chose to assimilate to fakirs:

> Some walked on their hands; others swung on a loose cord; others always hobbled. Some wore chains; others a pack-saddle; some hid their heads under a bushel; *au demeurant les meilleurs gens du monde.*

Micromégas is a "philosophique" tale, inspired partly by Swift's Brobdingnagians and partly by Voltaire's astronomical studies. An inhabitant from Sirius and another from Saturn are dispatched to the world by Voltaire, in order to persuade us of our insignificance and the pettiness of our planet compared with the hugeness of inter-stellar space and the great suns of the universe.

To linger over these romans is to expose oneself to a "damnable iteration" of praise. Yet several others must be at least mentioned. There is *L'Ingénu,* a kind of pendant to *Candide,* where a virtuous Huron is promenaded ruthlessly through the follies and ills of Europe; for a time the reader is anxiously asking himself whether Voltaire is not exposing for admiration one more specimen of the noble savage; but such is not the case, the Huron is an "honnête homme" and does not exhort us to return to caves and reindeer. *L'Ingénu* is filled with amusing traits, like the famous: "l'abbé de Saint-Yves supposait qu'un homme qui n'était pas né en France n'avait pas le sens commun." *L'Homme aux Quarante Ecus* is more nearly related to the political pamphlets and is one of the least interesting to us because it runs upon topics which have mostly lost all actuality. *La Princesse de Babylon* forms another excuse for a vertiginously swift ramble through divers states of the world; the *Lettres d'Amabed* are a virulent satire on the Catholic missionaries in the East; *L'Histoire de Jenni, Le Taureau Blanc, Aventure Indienne, Les Oreilles du Comte de Chesterfield* are all amusing for their wit and malice.

Turning from these gems of Voltairean art with their glitter and polish to the huge miscellany of pamphlets, one feels a sense of weariness, almost disgust, before the profuse repetitions of this abounding but limited mind. Take a few of them and the result is wholly pleasing; the Voltairean charm and wit achieve their effect, but after a time the mind is surfeited with raillery, disgusted with the diffusion and the repetition which are the inevitable mark of journalism. They are the relics of the campaigns of our Philosopher's War, and like all such relics look a little rusty and rather harmless when the war is over. They are ranged together helter-skelter like an unclassified museum of weapons, over-crowded and furnished with too many specimens of the same sort; any one taken separately will interest, in their disorderly bulk they weary and confuse the mind. In one of his pamphlets Voltaire described himself as a man who has spent his life "à sentir, à raisonner, et à plaisanter." The "sentir" might be disputed, but there can be no doubt about the "raisonner" and the "plaisanter"; the question is whether these functions may not eventually be abused. There is a quality in Voltairean raillery which is "agacant"—piquant but exasperating—as if

he said, "Come, let us make fools of all who do not think as we think." The raillery of Voltaire must be intolerable to earnest-minded persons. Even to those who hope they take life more lightly this perpetual tittering becomes an irritation.

No doubt, the reason for this is that we weary of the same mood when it is prolonged beyond our appetite. It is amusing to spend an evening with an irrepressibly humorous man, but what a penance to be forced to live with him. Pass a few evenings over Voltaire's pamphlets, and you will be charmed and entertained; but read them solidly for a month, and you will be cloyed with raillery and you will turn for relief, as the age after Voltaire's turned, to poetry and sentiment and romance; you will understand then the immense vogue of Chateaubriand. In order to persuade men to live rationally, to abandon the dreams of mysticism, the "amour de l'impossible" which prevents us from being content with carnal and reasonable felicity; Voltaire concentrated the clear light of his intelligence upon the pettiness, the inconsistencies, the lamentable failures, the ignominies of mankind. His brilliant shafts flashed through the air and pierced unerringly all aspiring souls in their flight. He brings us back to the hard facts as pitilessly as the family solicitor, though with more wit. There is something almost gross in his utilitarianism, which sensitive minds feel instinctively as an affront. Not so Chateaubriand. Superbly disregarding the useful and the practical, he soars away into an empyrean of poetic sentiment. His works are a kind of Bible of Romanticism, devoted to the extirpation of the Voltairean spirit. Chateaubriand rehabilitated the picturesque, the mysterious, solitude and melancholy, the poetry of wild lonely places, of ruins and fallen grandeur, of fine sentiment and loyalty—all the ideas and ideals and sentiments which Voltaire had laughed away for half a century. The whole Romantic movement in France was in open hostility to Voltaire: the battle of Hernani was fought between the rear-guard of Voltaireans and the main body of Chateaubriand's pretorian legion. It was a Pyrrhic victory for the Romantics. Our world to-day is far more the world of Voltaire than of Chateaubriand. Vicisti, Ferniense!

The reaction of which Chateaubriand was the creator (or the mouthpiece) was a failure; as he lay dying, that dramatic genius which controlled his life wafted into his bedroom the clamour of the Revolution of 1848. Probably Chateaubriand joined battle with Voltaireanism on a false issue; at any rate, he failed. To us the important reflection is that the modern world of "Democracy and Progress" is to a large extent an awkward alliance of the ideology of Rousseau with the Rationalism and Utilitarianism of Voltaire and the Encyclopædists. One must insist upon this, because few democratic politicians appear to be aware of their origins; and the political strife between left and right in commercial countries is often only the struggle between Rousseau's ideology and Voltaire's realism. The Church, which sits at the extreme right, is really hostile to both parties, but is fully aware of what she is contending with; moreover, the Church is more hostile to Rousseau then to Voltaire. I copy from to-day's *Times* a declaration of the Cardinal-Archbishop of Bordeaux: [8 October 1924]

> This programme [of the Government's] is none other than that of the "Social Contract" of Jean Jacques Rousseau, that well-known writer, who was born vicious and died insane, whose apoph-

thegms on the independence of man, individual or collective, who is subject neither to God nor morals, nor any principle whatsoever, have done more harm to France than the blasphemies of Voltaire and all the Encyclopædists together.

I shall not pursue farther the polemics of the matter, but the Cardinal's heated words touch upon a problem which interests a student of Voltaire. To what extent do writers create public opinion and how far are they responsible for great mutations of the State? Was the French Revolution and all its tremendous consequences, which every one of us still undergoes, "created" by Rousseau, Voltaire, and the Encyclopædists; or were they simply the mouthpieces which made audible and coherent a vast inchoate movement which would have been equally effective without them? Men "of the robe", whether authors or clergy, are inclined to overestimate the power of the spiritual leader; as the rest of mankind are apt to rate it too low. There is no possibility of estimating the extent of Voltaire's influence without an exhaustive examination of all kinds of documents by a body of scholars; and even then the results would be doubtful. Voltaire and Rousseau were only megaphones, if you like, but the advice they shouted gave direction to vast bodies of men wandering in perplexity or sunk in apathy. The rebellion against the Monarchy was an armed protest against misgovernment and despotism, such as the Fronde had been. The rebellion against the Church was the logical outcome of the Renaissance—the revival of pre-Christian Rationalism. The Reformation failed in France when Henri IV became a Catholic and ended the wars of the Ligue; the Fronde failed because it was merely a negative disturbance. But between 1789 and the flight to Varennes the French monarchy was faced with a Fronde backed by principles and a Ligue where the antagonists were not Huguenots and Catholics, but Rationalists and Christians. The combined attack was too powerful to be resisted; Monarchy and Church went down together. It seems to me that Voltaire and Rousseau, mutatis mutandis, stand in much the same relation to the French Revolution that Luther and Calvin do to the Reformation; some such movement was perhaps inevitable, given the circumstances, but these great minds set the mass in motion and gave it direction. (pp. 220-30)

[The] philosophie of Voltaire . . . was not philosophic speculation or a metaphysical system, but a practical Rationalism, addressing itself to ordinary common sense and proposing in truth only material objects as an aim in life. This Rationalist Materialism, with certain modifications, is the basis of the actions of most people in modern commercial democracies; it is the "philosophy" of the plain tired business man. The immense and indefatigable propaganda of the Ferney pamphlets undoubtedly contributed towards establishing that "philosophy" in France. Such a bombardment of the intelligence is probably unique in history. Think for a moment of the energy, the will-power, the perpetual mental tension, implied by that unremitting discharge of philosophical pamphlets. I have called them journalism and that is what they are—diluted and repetitive thought in a popular form; but Voltaire put something of his genius as well as his energy into every one of them. They are not the mechanical and conventional productions of a leader-writer; each had to contain a statement of a principle or principles of philosophie and each had to be entertaining. The eighteenth century public was piti-

less, even to the Patriarch of Ferney; if he fell below his own standard they let him know it. All the resources of his wit and invention were drawn upon to the utmost to meet the situation, to continue the flow of propaganda in fresh and attractive ways. Hence the extraordinary variety of forms—sermons, dialogues, speeches, tales, allegories, letters, and a score of others—designed to pique the curiosity and satisfy the taste of innumerable readers. But the correctness and beauty of the prose, the eternal raillery are always there; necessarily, because they were Voltaire's manner and they were what principally charmed his readers.

The greater number of these pamphlets were directed against Christianity, the Roman Catholic Church, and the priests. They may be called blasphemies, if the reader chooses, but Voltaire was not the man to waste his time on mere senseless insults to a religion. Neither was he attacking only a corrupt clergy; for the Church possessed many worthy and good servants in the eighteenth century. For one libertin abbé there were fifty village priests of good morals. No, Voltaire was not merely blaspheming, not merely attacking the clergy; he wished to destroy belief in the divinity of Jesus Christ, the authority of the Old as well as of the New Testament, Protestantism as well as Catholicism. The attacks on the religious orders and the Church were political and a matter of economics; Voltaire wished to remove from the State the financial burden of a considerable non-productive population which controlled an immense income and paid taxes only as a "voluntary contribution". That end might have been attained without attacking Christianity. But why this perpetual disparagement of miracles, of the authenticity of the gospels? And why the attack on the Old Testament, which is not fundamental to the Church of Rome? Because, as a Deist and a Rationalist, Voltaire desired to overthrow all sects of Christianity, all revealed religion, especially the persecuting religions, Christianity and Mahommedanism. The purer Deism of Mahommedanism seemed to him preferable to the doctrine of the Trinity. He preferred Confucianism and the thought of a Marcus Aurelius to both. But, above all, the ideas of the incarnation of God in man profoundly repelled him and, whenever he dared touch upon it, he asserted that the belief was blasphemous. In the last analysis his view comes down to this: God exists, but remotely, intangibly, unknowably; the duty of men is to think and to act rationally. That is the substance of Voltaire's anti-religious pamphlets. (pp. 230-32)

Richard Aldington, in his Voltaire, *George Routledge & Sons, Ltd., 1925, 278 p.*

G. K. Chesterton   (essay date 1933)

[*Regarded as one of England's premier men of letters during the first half of the twentieth century, Chesterton is best known today as a colorful* bon vivant, *a witty essayist, and as the creator of the Father Brown mysteries and the fantasy* The Man Who Was Thursday *(1908). Much of Chesterton's work reveals his childlike enjoyment of life and reflects his pronounced Anglican and, later, Roman Catholic beliefs. His essays are characterized by humor, frequent use of paradox, and a chatty, rambling style. In the following excerpt from an essay originally published in the* Illustrated London News *in*

1933, he compares Voltaire and Frederick the Great as authors and personalities.]

All Christian history began with that great social occasion when Pilate and Herod shook hands. Hitherto, as everybody knew in Society circles, they had hardly been on speaking terms. Something led them to seek each other's support, a vague sense of social crisis, though very little was happening except the execution of an ordinary batch of criminals. The two rulers were reconciled on the very day when one of these convicts was crucified. That is what many people mean by Peace, and the substitution of a reign of Love for one of Hatred. Whether or not there is honour among thieves, there is always a certain social interdependence and solidarity among murderers; and those sixteenth-century ruffians who conspired to assassinate Rizzio or Darnley were always very careful to put their names, and especially each other's names, to what they called a 'band', so that at the worst they might all hang together. Many political friendships—nay, even broad democratic comradeships, are of this nature; and their representatives are really distressed when we decline to identify this form of Love with the original mystical idea of Charity.

It sometimes seems to me that history is dominated and determined by these evil friendships. As all Christian history begins with the happy reconciliation of Herod and Pilate, so all modern history, in the recent revolutionary sense, begins with that strange friendship which ended in a quarrel, as the first quarrel had ended in a friendship. I mean that the two elements of destruction, which make the modern world more and more incalculable, were loosened with the light of that forgotten day when a lean French gentleman in a large wig, by name M. Arouet, travelled north with much annoyance to find the palace of a Prussian King far away in the freezing Baltic plain. The strict title of the King in dynastic chronicles is Frederick the Second, but he is better known as Frederick the Great. The actual name of the Frenchman was Arouet, but he is better known as Voltaire. The meeting of these two men, in the mid-winter of eighteenth-century scepticism and secularism, is a sort of spiritual marriage which brought forth the modern world; *monstrum horrendum, informe, ingens, cui lumen ademptum.* But because that birth was monstrous and evil, and because true friendship and love are not evil, it did not come into the world to create one united thing, but two conflicting things, which, between them, were to shake the world to pieces. From Voltaire the Latins were to learn a raging scepticism. From Frederick the Teutons were to learn a raging pride.

We may note at the start that neither of them cared very much about his own country or traditions. Frederick was a German who refused even to learn German. Voltaire was a Frenchman who wrote a foul lampoon about Joan of Arc. They were cosmopolitans; they were not in any sense patriots. But there is this difference; that the patriot does, however stupidly, like the country: whereas the cosmopolitan does not in the least like the cosmos. They neither of them pretended to like anything very much. Voltaire was the more really humane of the two; but Frederick also could talk on occasion the cold humanitarianism that was the cant of his age. But Voltaire, even at his best, really began that modern mood that has blighted all the humanitarianism he honestly supported. He started the horrible habit of helping human beings only through pitying them, and never through respecting them. Through him the oppression of the poor became a sort of cruelty to animals, and the loss of all that mystical sense that to wrong the image of God is to insult the ambassador of a King.

Nevertheless, I believe that Voltaire had a heart; I think that Frederick was most heartless when he was most humane. Anyhow, these two great sceptics met on the level, on the dead solid plain, as dull as the Baltic Plain; on the basis that there is no God, or no God who is concerned with men any more than with mites in cheese. On this basis they agreed; on this basis they disagreed; their quarrel was personal and trivial, but it ended by launching two European forces against each other, both rooted in the same unbelief. Voltaire said in effect: 'I will show you that the sneers of a sceptic can produce a Revolution and a Republic and everywhere the overthrowing of thrones.' And Frederick answered: 'And I will show you that this same sneering scepticism can be used as easily to resist Reform, let alone Revolution; that scepticism can be the basis of support for the most tyrannical of thrones, for the bare brute domination of a master over his slaves.' So they said farewell, and have since been sundered by two centuries of war; they said farewell, but presumably did not say 'adieu'.

Of every such evil seed it may be noted that the seed is different from the flower, and the flower from the fruit. A demon of distortion always twists it even out of its own unnatural nature. It may turn into almost anything, except anything really good. It is, to use the playful term of affection which Professor Freud applies to his baby, 'a polymorphous pervert'. These things not only do not produce the special good they promise; they do not produce even the special evil they threaten. The Voltairean revolt promised to produce, and even began to produce, the rise of mobs and overthrow of thrones; but it was not the final form of scepticism. The actual effect of what we call democracy has been the disappearance of the mob. We might say there were mobs at the beginning of the Revolution and no mobs at the end of it. That Voltairean influence has not ended in the rule of mobs, but in the rule of secret societies. It has falsified politics throughout the Latin world, till the recent Italian Counter-Revolution. Voltaire has produced hypocritical and pompous professional politicians, at whom he would have been the first to jeer. But on his side, as I have said, there does linger a certain humane and civilized sentiment which is not unreal. Only it is right to remember what has really gone wrong on his side of the Continental quarrel when we are recording the much wilder and wickeder wrong on the other side of it.

For the evil spirit of Frederick the Great has produced, not only all other evils, but what might seem the very opposite evil. He who worshipped nothing has become a god who is quite blindly worshipped. He who cared nothing for Germany has become the battle-cry of madmen who care for nothing except Germany. He who was a cold cosmopolitan has heated seven times a hell of narrow national and tribal fury which at this moment menaces mankind with a war that may be the end of the world. But the root of both perversions is in the common ground of atheist irresponsibility; there was nothing to stop the sceptic from turning democracy into secrecy; there was nothing to stop him interpreting liberty as the infinite licence of tyranny. The spiritual zero of Christendom was at that freezing instant when those two dry, thin, hatchet-faced men looked in each other's hollow eyes and saw the sneer that was as eternal as the smile of a skull. Between them, they have nearly killed the thing by which we live.

These two points of peril or centres of unrest, the intellectual unrest of the Latins and the very unintellectual unrest of the Teutons, do doubtless both contribute to the instability of international relations, and threaten us all the more because they threaten each other. But when we have made every allowance for there being, in that sense, dangers on both sides, the main modern fact emerges that the danger is mostly on one side, and that we have long been taught to look for it only on the other side. Much of Western opinion, especially English and American, has been trained to have a vague horror of Voltaire, often combined with a still vaguer respect for Frederick. No Wesleyans are likely to confuse Wesley with Voltaire. No Primitive Methodist is under the impression that Voltaire was a Primitive Methodist. But many such Protestant ministers really were under the impression that Frederick the Great was a Protestant Hero. None of them realized that Frederick was the greater atheist of the two. None of them certainly foresaw that Frederick, in the long run, would turn out to be the greater anarchist of the two. In short, nobody foresaw what everybody afterwards saw: the French Republic becoming a conservative force, and the Prussian Kingdom a purely destructive and lawless force. Victorians like Carlyle actually talked about pious Prussia, as if Blücher had been a saint or Moltke a mystic. General Göring may be trusted to teach us better, till we learn at last that nothing is so anarchical as discipline divorced from authority; that is, from right. (pp. 55-61)

> *G. K. Chesterton, "About Voltaire," in his* As I Was Saying: A Book of Essays, *Methuen & Co. Ltd., 1936, pp. 55-61.*

René Wellek   (essay date 1955)

[*Wellek's* A History of Modern Criticism (1955-65), *from which the following excerpt is drawn, treats literary criticism during the last three centuries. Wellek's critical method involves describing, analyzing, and evaluating a work according to the problems it poses for itself and how they are solved by the author. For Wellek, biographical, historical, and psychological information about writers and works is incidental. Although many of his critical methods are reflected in the work of the New Critics, Wellek was not a member of that group, and he rejected their more formalistic tendencies. Below, he discusses Voltaire's place in the history of literary criticism.*]

Voltaire (1694-1778) is the best representative of late French classicism. There are, it is true, other writers who summarize the position of neoclassical orthodoxy more systematically than the volatile Voltaire. But he is such a key figure in French literature, thought, and life of the 18th century, he is a lively writer of such wide range and scope, and, of course, he is so much more widely known and discussed than any of the critics who were his contemporaries that it seems best to start with him. He is, besides,

of particular interest to the English-speaking world because of the considerable attention he paid to English literature and his many pronouncements on Shakespeare which are worth knowing, discussing, and understanding.

Voltaire cannot be described as a rigid neoclassicist who merely echoed the views of the 17th century. He is strongly opposed to the growing geometrical spirit, the excessive rationalism of the end of the 17th and the beginnings of the 18th century. He shares, however, some views of the party of the Moderns against the Ancients, and he found it surprising that Boileau and Sir William Temple were obstinate enough not to recognize the superiority of their own age over classical antiquity. He endorsed the attacks of La Motte on Homer and generally preferred Virgil, yet he was skeptical of rigid prescriptive poetics as expounded by D'Aubignac and Le Bossu. Voltaire is also never weary of defending poetry and verse against the rationalists, such as La Motte, who actually wrote odes and tragedies in prose and saw the end of the age of poetry as inevitable and even desirable. Voltaire, whom we think of as the foremost representative of the Enlightenment, who certainly was proud of the achievements of his time in promoting tolerance and science and thought highly of his share in such progress, nevertheless did not believe in continuous uniform progress in civilization or, of course, in literature. He rather shared the view which can be described as cyclical progress. He believed that humanity had passed through four great ages of flowering: the Athens of Pericles, the Rome of Augustus, the Rome of Leo X, and the Paris of Louis XIV. But in between there were troughs of utter decay or ages of utter darkness, and in literature ages of bad taste and barbarism. Voltaire was well aware how precarious the hold of civilization is on mankind. The violence of some of his late opinions must be interpreted as the aroused feelings of an old man who sees a new flood of barbarism advancing.

Voltaire's taste was, no doubt, already substantially formed when he arrived in England in 1726. Still, the English years (1726-28) proved of very great importance for the widening of his literary horizon and the actual writing of criticism. Voltaire certainly learned to read English very well, though it may be doubted that he ever spoke or wrote well. He met many of the literary figures then famous in England—Pope, Swift, Edward Young, Congreve, etc.—and he frequented the theater in London, partly to learn English and partly to learn something about the English drama. He saw Shakespeare's *Julius Caesar* and *Hamlet*, not to speak of Addison's *Cato* and any number of comedies. In England he wrote **Essai sur la poésie épique,** which was published as an English original as **Essay upon the Epic Poetry of the European Nations from Homer down to Milton** in 1727. It was not, of course, a history of the epic, but mainly served an immediate purpose: it was a defense of Voltaire's own epic, the **Henriade,** which he was then preparing and for which he was anxious to get English subscriptions. The **Henriade** needed defense against the strict neoclassical prescriptions such as those laid down by Le Bossu, since it chose a historical and not a mythical hero (Henry IV) and since it did not use pagan machinery. Voltaire argues against the classicists that a modern epic must be different from an ancient. He also wanted to anticipate any unfavorable comparison of the **Henriade** and *Paradise Lost* by pleading that a French epic must be different from an English epic.

His defense is based on a distinction which he could have found in Perrault and St. Évremond: there are essential beauties and conventional beauties, rules which are based on common sense and universal reason and rules which are merely customary and local. Machinery is local, based on national taste. Voltaire then gives a short sketch of the history of epic poetry which is quite superficial as history but argues both for the independence of modern literatures from the classical, by pointing to a deep gulf of social and technological changes between the two civilizations, and for the differences between the main modern national traditions. No attention is paid to Dante or Ariosto (Voltaire admired the latter but excluded him from the epic), and only Trissino, Tasso, Camoẽs, Ercilla, and Milton are taken up in some detail. Though the information on Camoẽs and Ercilla is secondhand, the range of observation is remarkable for the time, and the discussion of Milton (cautious as it is in order not to offend his hosts) is certainly novel for France for its recognition of different taste. "If the difference of genius between nation and nation ever appeared in its full light, it is in Milton's *Paradise Lost,*" begins the discussion, and Voltaire concedes that "he is very far from thinking that one nation ought to judge its productions by the standard of another." In the later French version, published in 1733, Voltaire again pleads for the importance of knowing other literatures than one's own and for the divergencies of national taste which must be accepted as a matter of fact. "It is impossible that a whole nation could err in matters of feeling and be wrong in being pleased." Some scholars have hailed the **Essay on Epic Poetry** as the beginning of comparative literature and of true critical relativism and toleration. But in the light of Voltaire's later writings it seems rather doubtful that it can claim such a position, for he never gave up the idea of one universal taste. It also seems questionable whether total relativism is such a great advance on the neoclassical point of view, and there is, of course, hardly anything like true comparative literature in Voltaire's remarks on different epics, often discussed before, or on the differences of national taste, a topic broached by St. Évremond and many others before him.

Still, Voltaire in England did become more open minded and interested in English literature. The **Letters concerning the English Nation** were also published first in English in 1733, while the French original, rechristened **Lettres philosophiques,** came out a year later. There is no need to discuss the importance of the book in the history of French thought, but the discussions of English literature belong to our province. The key is established in the characterization of Shakespeare. "Shakespeare boasted of a strong, fruitful genius: he was natural and sublime, but had not so much as a single spark of good Taste, or knew one Rule of the Drama." Shakespeare's influence was the ruin of the English stage, though there are "beautiful, noble and dreadful scenes in this writer's monstrous farces, to which the name of tragedy is given." Voltaire then gives a list of Shakespeare's most obvious "absurdities": Desdemona speaking after being strangled, the gravediggers in *Hamlet,* the jokes of the Roman cobblers in the same scene with Brutus and Cassius. But Voltaire wants also to present some of the beauties of Shakespeare and produces a translation of "To be or not to be":

Demeure, il faut choisir et passer à l'instant
De la vie à la mort, ou de l'être au néant . . .

He then quotes, in his translation, a speech of Dryden's, and comments: "It is in these detached passages that the English have hitherto excelled. Their dramatic pieces, most of which are barbarous and without decorum, order or verisimilitude, dart such resplendent flashes through this gloom as amaze and astonish." Addison was the first writer to write a regular tragedy, *Cato,* but Voltaire objects to the love intrigue and its general frigidity. "One would think," he concludes, "that the English had been hitherto formed to produce irregular beauties only. The shining monsters of Shakespeare give infinitely more delight than the judicious images of the moderns. Hitherto the poetical genius of the English resembles a tufted tree planted by the hand of nature, that throws out a thousand branches at random, and spreads unequally, but with great vigor. It dies if you attempt to force its nature, and to lop and dress it in the same manner as the trees of the garden of Marly." The same comparison was soon to be reversed in favor of the untamed forest.

The discussion of English comedy is of far less interest. Voltaire seems to admire Wycherley, though his summary of the *Plain Dealer* stresses the absurdity of the intrigue, and his account of the *Country Wife* the grossness of the situation. Rochester is then praised as "the man of genius," "the great poet," and as an illustration of his "shining imagination" Voltaire translates a part of the *Satyr against Mankind.* The same chapter gives a lukewarm account of Waller, and the next some enthusiastic praise of Butler, Swift, and Pope. Voltaire deplores only Butler's local wit, but Swift is preferred to Rabelais and is called, rather oddly, a "Rabelais in his senses, and frequenting the politest company." "The poetical numbers of Dean Swift are of a singular and almost inimitable taste"—a judgment which will surprise those who remember only the "Lady's Dressing-Room" or the "Progress of Love." The highest praise goes to Pope. "He is in my opinion the most elegant, the most correct poet, and at the same time the most harmonious that England ever gave birth to. He has mellowed the harsh sounds of the English trumpet to the soft accents of the flute." Voltaire then translates a passage from the *Rape of the Lock* and concludes with some envious reflections on the regard shown to men of letters in England.

But with the years Voltaire's opinion of Shakespeare grew more unfavorable. One could not say that he actually changed it. The basic assumptions stayed the same, but the tone becomes much more sharp and even bitter and the acknowledgment of beauties much less frequent and generous. One must have in mind the circumstances: in the **Lettres philosophiques** Voltaire felt himself to be a discoverer; in 1776, when his attacks were most violent, he felt that bad taste had triumphed in France and that his own countrymen were now preferring Shakespeare to Corneille and Racine, not to speak of the tragedies of Voltaire himself. A letter explains it quite honestly thus:

> What is frightful is that the monster has a party in France: and to fill up the measure of calamity and horror, it is I who long ago was the first to speak of this Shakespeare. It is I who was the first to show the French some pearls which I had found in his enormous dunghill. I did not then expect that one day I should help to trample under foot the crowns of Corneille and Racine in order to adorn the brow of a barbarous stage player.

The most extravagant condemnation of Shakespeare is the

famous letter to the French Academy which was read by D'Alembert at the Festival of St. Louis on August 25, 1776. Voltaire's wrath was then overflowing because of the new translation of Shakespeare by Le Tourneur and the very high praise of Shakespeare in a prefatory epistle addressed to Louis XVI, who, together with Catherine the Great and the King of England, figured among the list of subscribers. Voltaire's method of attack is twofold. Partly it consists in more or less literal translations of what he considered crude and obscene passages in Shakespeare: the first scene of *Othello,* with Iago waking the father of Desdemona and telling him, in coarse terms, that she had run away with a blackamoor; the porter in *Macbeth;* the wooing of Catherine by Henry V; the punning of the servants at the beginning of *Romeo and Juliet;* the first scene in *King Lear,* when the Duke of Gloucester introduces Edmund as his illegitimate son and jokes about the manner of his procreation. Even details are recounted when to the taste of Voltaire they seemed undeniably "low," such as the talk of the soldiers at the beginning of *Hamlet.* To Bernardo's question: "Have you had a quiet guard?" Francisco answers, "Not a mouse stirring." The shocked Voltaire translates it "Je n'ai pas entendu une souris trotter." He is particularly angry since Lord Kames had preferred these words to those of an officer of Agamemnon in Racine's *Iphigénie:* "Mais tout dort, et l'armée, et les vents, et Neptune." "Yes, sir," Voltaire comments, "a soldier may answer thus in a guard-house; but not on the stage before the first persons of a nation who express themselves with nobleness and before whom he must express himself in the same manner."

The other method is one in which Voltaire excelled: the burlesque recounting of the contents of Shakespeare's plays, especially of *Hamlet,* which appears in his summary as an absurd murder story without rhyme or reason. This conclusion thus seems obvious: Shakespeare is nothing but a "village clown" (*gille de village*), a "monster," a "drunken savage," a "water-carrier." But it would be a mistake to think that Voltaire has completely forgotten his praise. He constantly held to the view that Shakespeare was a "beautiful, though very savage nature," who knew no regularity, no decorum, no art, who mixed baseness and grandeur, buffoonery and the terrible: "It is a chaotic tragedy with hundreds of rays of light." Shakespeare always represented to him the crude genius of nature in the beginnings of art. When Voltaire wrote his final comparison between Corneille and Racine he had in mind Scaliger's comparison of Homer and Virgil. But he also alludes to Shakespeare: "Corneille was unequal like Shakespeare, and full of genius like him: but Corneille's genius was greater than Shakespeare's as that of a nobleman is greater than that of a man of the people who was born with the same mind as he." The final argument, which must have seemed to Voltaire quite unanswerable, is the view that Shakespeare is admired only locally.

> He was a savage who had some imagination. He has written many happy lines: but his pieces can only please at London and in Canada. It is not a good sign for the taste of a nation when that which it admires meets with favor only at home. On no foreign stage has any piece of Shakespeare ever been performed. The French tragedies are acted in every capital of Europe from Lisbon to St. Petersburg. They are played from the borders of the Arctic sea to the sea that separates Europe from Africa. Let

the same honor be done to a single piece of Shakespeare, and then we shall be able to enter into an argument.

It requires a considerable effort of sympathy not to dismiss much of this criticism as totally absurd. The last argument certainly would refute Voltaire completely today; we refuse to be worried about lowness and even obscenity; we easily make allowance for improbabilities of plot and situation. Least of all can we think why Voltaire should be so annoyed by the "stirring mouse." After all, the soldiers are speaking among themselves and not to the king who may be in the audience.

We must try to describe Voltaire's taste, his different opinions and judgments, in order to arrive at something like an understanding of his view of Shakespeare. Voltaire was not a systematic thinker or even a systematic critic. He prided himself on his mobility, his distaste for mere metaphysical speculations, his refusal to become pedantic and stuffy. He has no theory of beauty, and the little he said on questions of general aesthetics would point to a radical individualism. There is the famous beginning of the article "Beau" in the ***Dictionnaire philosophique:*** "Ask a toad what is beauty . . . and he will answer his she-toad." But actually he was far from being a mere relativist. He stressed taste and disliked judging by mere rules. To Pascal's well-known view that "a man who judges by rules is like a man who tells time by a watch compared to a man who has none," Voltaire answered dryly: "In matters of taste, in music and poetry and painting, taste takes the place of a watch: and those who judge only by rules, judge badly." Taste, again, seems at first sight something purely individual. There are passages in Voltaire which suggest such conclusions. "Every man according to his taste," he would say, "I cannot convince a man that he is wrong if he feels bored." But actually Voltaire believes only in one universal taste, that which found its models in Roman antiquity and in the French 17th century. "Fine taste consists in a prompt feeling for beauty among faults and faults among beauties." The man of taste must not judge "in the lump"; he is a born anthologist, a culler of passages. That is why Voltaire detested complete works (and would have detested the fifty-two volumes of Moland). "The mania of editors to collect everything," he says, "resembles that of sacristans who collect rags they want to have worshiped; but still just as one judges true saints by their good actions, so one should judge talents by their good works."

Most of Voltaire's principles can thus be studied only in his concrete pronouncements, but these are fortunately so numerous and cover so many authors that a general view emerges with astonishing consistency. Voltaire adheres to the classical tradition of *decorum, bienséance, convenance.* "Perfection consists in knowing how to adjust one's style to the matter one treats." Style, form, way of expression are always decisive for critical judgment. "As far as making the passions speak, all men have almost the same ideas; but the way of expressing them distinguishes the man of wit from the man who has none." Voltaire restates the ancient doctrine of the three levels of style: each subject has its level, "natural," "tempered," or "elevated." The natural style is not, of course, the style of the barbarian, the savage, or even the natural man. Simplicity is precisely the result of civilization. Clarity, purity, ease are associated with it. Barbarous people emerge from rudeness by flying into preciosity, bombast, comparable to the drunkenness of the newcomer to Paris or the squandering of the newly rich. Voltaire is thus an enemy of anything "baroque," or what he calls "oriental." He attacks Ossian and the grandiloquence of the Old Testament, and obviously the style of Shakespeare's speeches seemed to him mere bombast. Voltaire frequently translates verse into prose to "test" it and to achieve comic effects. Simplicity of style means also homogeneity of style, unity of tone: a view which is implicit in the whole insistence on purity of genre and the disapproval of mixtures of style. He is extremely pedantic and also subtle in his linguistic criticisms: only contemporary good usage is his standard. Even Molière, La Fontaine, and Corneille must be read with caution. The standard of clarity applies also to poetry: "Poetry must have the clarity, the purity of the most correct prose." He praises some lines of verse by saying: "All the ideas are closely linked, the words are the right words, and it would be beautiful in prose."

But it would be a misunderstanding of Voltaire to think of him as a disparager of poetry. Poetry is not superfluous or obsolete. "Verse which does not say more, better and more quickly than prose would say it, is simply bad verse." In his elaborate commentary on Corneille's plays Voltaire subjects them to a minute linguistic criticism which points out all instances of preciosity as a vice. Clarity is thus a prime requirement of both prose and verse. "Any verse or any sentence which requires explanation does not deserve to be explained" is his surprising statement which makes short work of one-half of the world's literature, the half which we seem to love most today and which our poets are augmenting in every issue of the little magazines. Also poetry should impress itself on the memory and thus must be easily understood.

Still, Voltaire recognizes higher styles: above the natural style rises the elegant, which is always based on selection, a result of justness and agreement. Virgil and Racine are the masters of elegance and the greatest poets. Poetry is not mere rhymed prose. Voltaire thus disapproves of the prose poem advocated by La Motte, and resents Fénelon's calling his prose epic *Télémaque* a poem. Rhyme is not a shackle: it rather forces the poet to think more justly and to express himself more correctly. Poetry, he says frequently, is the "music of the soul," and in practice he stressed the qualities of euphony in verse. Translation of poetry is thus, he knew, all but impossible. "Don't believe," he wrote, "you know the poets from translations; that's like wanting to see the colors of a picture in an engraving." It would be a mistake to think that Voltaire ranked the mere reasoners in rhyme highest. He did not admire Boileau or Pope excessively and he realized that he was living in an age of decay in French poetry. His admiration was for Virgil and Racine, their harmonious poetry, their "language of the soul." In French literature he recognized at the most, besides Racine, some passages in Corneille, in La Fontaine, and in Quinault, and possibly some stanzas in Malherbe and Racan, as perfect poetry.

Beyond the poetic style there was the elevated, the dramatic, tragic style. Voltaire loved and admired the French theater above any other institution or tradition. Corneille, he said, "established a school of the greatness of soul: Molière founded one of social life." The drama is to him the supreme result of civilization, especially, of course, of French civilization. "There was no good comedy until

Molière, just as there was no art of expressing true and delicate sentiments before Racine, because society had not yet arrived at the perfection it reached in their times." Drama, to him, must first of all have an emotional effect; it must move us, interest us. This interest is damaged by improbability, by unnecessary complications of plot or intricate reasonings. The three unities which Voltaire defends in the early preface to *Oedipe* (1729) are merely guards against improbability. The unity of action is there "because the human mind cannot embrace several objects at the same time"; the unity of place "because a single action cannot occur in several places at the same time"; and the unity of time because only the moment of decision can be interesting. The stage must never be empty, and no character must appear on it without sufficient part in the action. Tragedy, according to Voltaire, should and must be lofty, even pathetic, theatrical. He thus had no patience with the new bourgeois tragedy, which seemed to him a debasement of the true kind, though he was rather tolerant of the *comédie larmoyante* and wrote several himself. Still, to a certain extent he was discontented with some of the traditions of French 17th-century tragedy. He objected especially to love intrigues if they were not the center of the play and were only dragged in as obligatory diversion, and also to the rigid exclusion of scenes of violence and death, at least in his early period. He wanted to bring the death of Mariamne on the stage, and he was obviously at first favorably impressed with the amount of action in a play like Shakespeare's *Julius Caesar* or Otway's *Venice Preserved*. His own plays, *La Mort de César,* which violates the unity of time, and *Semiramis,* which introduced a ghost in broad daylight, are certainly examples of Voltaire's own desire and willingness to experiment. But later he became more and more hostile to stage business, to elaborate actions and costumes, and thought that the theater was sinking back into barbarism.

This short description alone should show how well defined Voltaire's taste was, how firmly rooted in the French 17th century to which he looked back with nostalgia, with a clear feeling of the inferiority of his own time in poetic genius but with pride in the advance of freedom of thought and civil liberties. There is nothing merely capricious about Voltaire's taste: he feels it definitely to be an expression of a society and a standard which has the moral and social sanction of that society. He is neither an impressionist nor a mere dogmatist: he is a man of taste, the voice of a civilization which may have irrevocably passed away but has left its deep impress on French literature and criticism. Clarity, measure, design, taste are still words to conjure with in France, and French neo-classical taste represents in its purity a permanent contribution to civilization.

Voltaire cannot be placed with the pioneers of historical criticism. No doubt he knew a great deal of history; he has been described, not unjustly, as the founder of the history of civilization, of economic and world history. But even as a historian he was primarily interested in the present and the future. As a critic he was not concerned with literary antiquarianism, though he wrote some sweeping surveys which could be called literary history: the sketch of the epic in *Essai sur la poésie épique,* the survey of literature in *Siècle de Louis XIV,* or the slight sketch of the history of dramatic art in the *Dictionnaire.* Occasionally Voltaire would use historical arguments: in order either to apologize for faults or to stress historical merit, the introduction or origination of something. Thus the bombast in Corneille's *Le Cid* would be excused as Spanish taste which then was "the spirit of the time." The Church Fathers would be called great in spite of their bad taste for allegories and metaphors. Voltaire would recommend indulgence in order to understand Nausicaa or the Song of Songs, which he translated, toning down the erotic passages. Voltaire was struck by the similarities of all primitive literature, and by primitive he meant any writing which was not derived from the tradition of Roman antiquity. Thus he compared the *Iliad* with the Book of Job, the ancient Greek theater with the operas of Metastasio. The *Prometheus Bound* of Aeschylus strikes him as similar to a Spanish *auto sacramental.* Homer, the Bible, and Ossian he sometimes classed together as representing a kind of literature which is considered to be inferior to true taste. Still, he shows some awareness of the existence of different standards of taste in different ages and nations. On the whole, however, Voltaire recognizes only one kind of literature: classical Latin and French, or anything which, in nations other than France, seems to approach it. He is sometimes described as a pioneer of cosmopolitanism in literature; but surely his hopes for a future republic of letters, for a grand society of spirits, could be rather described as French cultural imperialism, since the "French language would be its essential idiom" and certainly French taste would be its central point of reference.

In his early years Voltaire thought of the role of the English as one of contributing to a liberalizing of French taste. He recognized the existence of local beauties and the different geniuses of the main European nations. Occasionally he would give social explanations for differences of taste. In speaking of Oriental poetry, he refers to the different status of women: "Poetry will be different with a people that locks up its women in harems and with a people that gives them unlimited freedom." But basically he always appeals to universal taste, and that universal taste is the classical taste which is founded on the principles of general human nature. One of his attacks on Shakespeare is called *Appel à toutes les nations de l'Europe* (1761), and he recurs again and again to the argument that an author who pleases only locally (such as Shakespeare or Lope de Vega) cannot be really great and correct. French taste he thinks of as the nucleus of European taste to which all other nations can only contribute, a view which will seem less absurd if we consider the tremendous spread of French language, taste, and customs during the 18th century. Six years after Voltaire's death Rivarol could win a prize of the Prussian Academy with his *Discours sur l'universalité de la langue française* (1784). Voltaire himself was feted at the court of Frederick the Great, whose great ambition was to be considered a French poet. In Russia French had become the language of the court and of the nobility, a state of affairs which lasted far into the 19th century, as any reader of Tolstoy must know. French was certainly the second language of Italy. The dominance of neoclassicism in Spain, Italy, Germany, and even England began to be challenged only in the years immediately preceding Voltaire's death. No wonder that he saw other literatures through the spectacles of French taste. In England, of course, he would have to be classed among the most conservative. His attitude toward Shakespeare is proof enough; there is no doubt that he read and knew Rymer and even learned from his method. He certainly was, after some general professions of admiration and puz-

zlement, hostile also to Milton. One suspects that the views of Pococurante, the Venetian nobleman in *Candide,* are not too far removed from Voltaire's own.

> "Milton?" said Pococurante; "that barbarian who made a tedious commentary on the first chapter of Genesis in ten books of rugged verse? That clumsy imitator of the Greeks, who disfigures the creation and, instead of representing the Eternal Being, as Moses does, creating the universe at a word, makes the Messiah take a large pair of compasses from one of the cupboards of Heaven to draw a plan of his intended work? Do you expect me to appreciate the man who has spoiled Tasso's conception of Hell and the Devil, who disguises Lucifer first as a toad and then as a pigmy, who makes him repeat the same speeches a hundred times, and even argue about theology? Why, the man has so little humor as to imitate in all seriousness Ariosto's comic invention of firearms and make the devils fire cannon in Heaven! Neither I nor anyone else in Italy can take pleasure in these sorry extravagances. The marriage of Sin and Death and the snakes to which Sin gives birth sicken every man with any delicacy of taste, and his long description of a hospital will only please a gravedigger. This obscure, bizarre, and disagreeable poem was despised on publication. I judge it today as it was first judged by the author's fellow-countrymen. I say what I think, and care little whether others agree with me."

Though Pococurante's memory of Milton is curiously inaccurate (he even changes hellhounds into snakes), and though he does not know of the biblical authority for the compasses, the view expressed fits so well with Voltaire's taste that his ridicule of Pococurante does not affect the criticism of Milton.

Again, as with Shakespeare, Voltaire admired individual beauties and flights of imagination. He translated the monologue of Satan after his fall, but the episode of Death and Sin is called "disgusting and abominable." On the whole, he concludes that *Paradise Lost* is a "work rather singular than natural, more full of imagination than of graces, of boldness than of selection, whose subject is all ideal and seems not to have been made for man."

The same attitude is behind the rather scarce pronouncements on Dante, who is praised for being frequently naive and sometimes sublime. But usually he is charged with "bizarre taste," and Voltaire even wrote two burlesque imitations in the *Essai sur les mœurs* and the *Dictionnaire.* Among foreign poets the one who receives the highest praise is Ariosto, who to Voltaire combines the invention of Homer with the elegance and taste of Virgil. He adds the imagination of the *Arabian Nights* to the sensibility of Tibullus and the pleasantry of Plautus. He is superior to La Fontaine as a story teller and is at times equal to Racine in pathos. Tasso is also admired by Voltaire, though less fervently. Ariosto and Tasso surpass Homer: *Orlando Furioso* is better than the *Odyssey, Gerusalemme Liberata* than the *Iliad.* He censures them only for too many marvels in an epic poem and admits occasional *clinquant* with which Boileau had charged Tasso.

Among the French writers Voltaire singles out Racine for the highest praise. Voltaire's tone becomes positively lyrical when he speaks of Racine, and in tones of deep emotion he describes *Iphigénie* and *Athalie* as masterpieces of the human mind. Molière is to him undoubtedly the greatest of all writers of comedy, while he showers generous praise on Pascal and Bossuet, though he disagreed with their views profoundly and argued against Pascal much of his life. Among the contemporaries Voltaire naturally disapproved of Rousseau, for personal and later ideological reasons. His method of ridiculous summaries of plot certainly shines at its wittiest when he retells *La Nouvelle Héloïse* or picks holes in the grammar, the images, and the morals of Rousseau's novel. But privately Voltaire was not totally unappreciated of his eloquence and genius. "He is a Diogenes, who sometimes speaks like Plato."

One could go on giving examples of Voltaire's innumerable literary judgments. But the more one reads him, the more one is impressed with the coherence and consistency of his taste: the uniformity of his outlook, in spite of occasional contradictions or shifts of emphasis. His literary opinions are an almost instinctive assertion of this taste. The main criteria are always standards of style, composition, harmony, and eloquence, and the central concept is that of decorum, understood in terms of the French gentleman. Socially Voltaire was certainly the French aristocrat, in spite of his religious skepticism and his hatred of despotism and intolerance. His literary judgments are never or very rarely colored by his religious and political opinions. *Athalie,* a pernicious example of fanaticism, is still the "chef-d'œuvre de l'esprit humain."

I thus cannot agree with Saintsbury's discussion of Voltaire as a critic. The view that Voltaire's "treasure" and heart were nowhere in literature, "that for literature he had very little genuine love," seems to me completely mistaken. He was a man of letters, first of all, and it seems surprising that anyone could doubt his fervent love and interest in literature and his lifelong ambition to be a poet. One must have narrowly romantic taste not to appreciate the very real artistic success of some of Voltaire's tales such as *l'Ingénu* and **Candide.** And within limits even his tragedies, his burlesque poems such as **La Pucelle,** and many fugitive pieces show genuine power. He himself knew that he was merely a follower of the great men of the 17th century and that he could not measure up to them. That is why he held to their standards so strongly: he thought of himself as a defender of the poetic faith in an age of prose, as a representative of aristocratic civilization in the age of the rising bourgeoisie with its low "foreign" taste for the violent and the commonplace. There may be a paradox in the fact that Voltaire can be considered a forerunner of the French Revolution as well as the last outpost of the age of Louis le Grand. But it can be resolved in the unity of personality of a man who hated injustice, intolerance, obscurantism, irrationality, just as he despised what he considered the gross, the low and the violent, the absurd in taste and poetry. Religious skepticism and even political radicalism are not incompatible with literary conservatism and have never been so in history. (pp. 31-45)

> *René Wellek, "Voltaire," in his* A History of Modern Criticism, 1750-1950: The Later Eighteenth Century, *Yale University Press, 1955, pp. 31-45.*

René Pomeau　(essay date 1956)

[*Pomeau is a leading French authority on the life and works of Voltaire. In the following excerpt from a 1968 translation of the conclusion of his 1956 study* La religion de Voltaire, *he considers the origin and impact of Voltairean deism.*]

Voltaire's religion reflects the concurrence of a character and an age. It is impossible to impute his deism or theism to frivolity. It was not a huckster's doctrine, borrowed from Chaulieu and the English, and propagated out of mischievousness to flout the priesthood. In such a view Voltaire's passion—that relentless thrust of a lifetime which turns into a mania—becomes incomprehensible. In so immense a production, almost every page of which is occasional, one can ignore what is said once, in passing. What counts is what Voltaire repeated throughout his entire life. What counts is the ideas to which he clung tenaciously, his obsessions. Now, from one end of his long life to the other, Voltaire was ardently and aggressively a deist. For some sixty years he kept seeking historical and philosophical justifications. A Fontenelle, an Anatole France were perhaps characterized by frivolity—surface and, as it were, inadvertent rationalists. As for him, he never stopped fighting for and against, for so-called natural religion and against Christianity.

We must search for Voltaire's secret in depth, in that soul of his which was so out of the ordinary and difficult to plumb. Few writers have expressed themselves so copiously. There is perhaps no other figure whose biography is so richly detailed. Yet, for all that, Voltaire eludes us. We have at our disposal vast inventories on the man, but we do not know him. Extroverted, obstreperous, blabbermouthed though he was, his unceasing agitation conceals his true self. His notebooks contain not a single word about his intimate feelings. He who wrote about everything wrote almost nothing about himself. Can it be that he is invincibly averse to looking into the depths of his soul? He did, nevertheless, give himself away somewhat on the day when he let slip the words: "Où fuir loin de moimême?" ["Where can I flee far away from myself?"] But what does this brilliant, light veneer cover over? Some secret inhibition? We have seen him experience and express mystical emotions, not just once or during a temporary crisis. But when he is seventeen, the rumor spreads, among those who know him, that he is going to become a Jesuit. Ten years later he cries out to God: "Je ne suis pas chrétien, mais c'est pour t'aimer mieux!" ["I am not a Christian, but it is so that I may love Thee better!"] In the **Henriade** of 1730 he adds a hymn to the glory of the Eternal Geometer. On a bitter-cold night he is enraptured by the divine spectacle of the starry universe. At Ferney he worships the sun, image of the Supreme Being; he repeatedly hymns the cosmos; he dies "adoring God." These facts and these texts testify to Voltaire's religious propensity; but they add up to very little in so long and so busy a life and in an immense output, compared with countless negations. Did he deliberately stifle mystical tendencies which he feared beneath fiercely negative sarcasms? This hypothesis would make it possible to explain Voltaire's irreligious religion: very critical, yet still retaining a few positive elements, his deism may have rendered innocuous an inhibited mysticism, barely allowing it an occasional vent. In such a light the development of his life takes on a meaning.

In his youth Voltaire begins by combatting the double obsession of the terror-inspiring God and the cruel priest. As far back as one can go, the Voltairean complex is already fully developed: a rather morbid picture of men's sufferings would have it that those responsible for them are the priests serving a blood-thirsty God. What traumatic experience had torn little Arouet apart, for him to employ his talents at the very outset in composing an *Œdipe*, an *Henriade*? All we know is that he did not find in the Jesuits' engaging religion a refuge against the cruel God, perhaps because, under Father Le Tellier's administration, the champions of Molinism had abandoned their erstwhile insinuative approach and become persecutors. The godson of Abbé de Châteauneuf preferred to give himself over to free-thinking frivolity; he exorcised the tyrant God by means of Chaulieu's facile deism. But Voltaire remained aggressive in his writings and in his speech. He was already an anti-Christian soldier; already he saw in the Christian religion only his two enemies, a sanguinary God and priest. It is true to say that, from the very beginning, Voltaire "grounds his peace of mind (or that which he would like to have) in his denial of the faith," provided we specify that the object of this denial is the terror-inspiring God he identifies with the God of the Christians.

Suddenly the revelation of English philosophy lends substance to the Divinity who represents the antithesis of the Christian God, that clement and until then rather vague God of the merry abbés of the Temple. Henceforth Voltaire knows that his God is the God of Locke, of Clarke, and of Newton, the God attested and demonstrated by the order of the cosmos, who partakes of the cold majesty of

Opening page of the La Vallière manuscript of Candide.

outer space. The metaphysical, scientific, and historical labors of Cirey consolidate this acquired knowledge. The obsession of a pettily vindictive God is shunted aside; God is rendered remote by his very sublimity, and life is gay, whatever Pascal may say about it. All that remains is to concentrate on the fraudulent and persecuting priests: they are told off in *Mahomet*. But the end of the Cirey period reveals the permanence of Voltaire's obsessions. He doubts free will; he feels dominated by a superior power; he feels futile and frail; his imagination sees crawling on the surface of our little pile of mud a denigrated humanity composed of insect men. He discovers the style of the philosophic tale at the same time that he is arguing the problem of evil, and again the image of the terror-inspiring God appears in clear outline.

The pessimistic crisis, aggravated by the death of Madame du Châtelet, prolonged by the Prussian tribulations, quickened anew by the Lisbon disaster, divides Voltaire's life into two parts. But he reacts against pessimism, as he had fought the tyrant God, without being able completely to liquidate this haunting idea either. Up to the moment of his death Voltaire is tormented by the insoluble problem of evil. His recourse is to escape pessimism through action. It is at the height of the crisis that he attempts to launch the campaign against *l'infâme*. He expects Frederick II to destroy Christianity and to impose on Europe a "pure" religion, that deism which Voltaire has framed for his personal use. The King of Prussia has not the slightest interest in these fine schemes. So Voltaire turns to the "enlightened" pastors of Geneva, but these "faint-hearted Socinians" slip away. A moderate and reasonable temperament would have given up. Prudence dictated that the old man enjoy his glory in peace and quiet, *by cultivating his garden*. But once again the obscure forces which possess him plunge him into battle. The wear and tear of age have weakened the other inclinations of his soul, but the irreligious passion has gathered strength with the passing of the years. Since the King of Prussia and the Genevan clergy have failed him, the Patriarch will himself be the apostle of modern times, the successor of Luther and Calvin. Solidly entrenched in his ambush at Ferney, he leads the attack, armed with his pen. He pounces upon the enemy with all his might: he is going to *crush* it beneath arguments, sarcasms, insults, lies. This paradoxical champion of tolerance abandons himself to the fanaticism of a savage hatred. Passionate but practical, he foresees the replacement of the old-time religion. He has railed so profusely against the imposture of the founders of religions that he imitates it. We must, he says, preach to the masses that the Eternal Geometer "rewards and punishes." Voltaire is not at all certain that the Being of beings concerns Himself with punishing and rewarding creatures as insignificant as man. No matter, the interests of society and morality demand this pretense: *"fingo, fingo."* But Voltaire is at least sure that the Supreme Being exists. He adores Him in His handiwork, the world: "I believe, I believe in Thee"; and when the free-thinkers of the younger generation seek to bring him into their atheistic fold, he balks. Fully half of his last quiverful of arrows is aimed at the "fourth impostor." The mystical need which remains buried in the inmost recesses of his being holds fast to the naked affirmation that God exists.

It is therefore unfair to accuse Voltaire of substituting mind for soul. The arguments and behavior of this vehement polemicist are motivated by deep-lying forces which he embellishes with his consummate intellectual charm. He made it his calling to crush the Christian religion; he found, not his peace of mind, but his well-being in the religious struggle; he rode to his salvation on the back of *l'infâme.*

This negation, required by his most intimate being, was in harmony with the option of a society which actively preferred earth to heaven. All those who, in Paris, London, Amsterdam, even Geneva, want to live for enjoyment, pursue wealth. In all those localities business prosperity is bound up with the appetites of flesh and spirit. Voltaire's irreligious propaganda is not the only one which provides assurance of a good conscience for those who neglect to merit heaven by denying themselves earthly pleasures. But by reason of its bulk and its expressive force it is the most persuasive. To be sure, its brutalities are not always approved. Madame du Deffand and the Choiseul coterie censure excesses that are shocking to good form. But all these well-bred persons live, and when the opportunity offers, the Duke governs, as if Voltaire were right. Voltaire is the natural ally of enlightened despotism practised by princes and ministers who have chosen, or at least maintain they have chosen, to ensure the temporal happiness of their people, and no longer their eternal felicity. The attempts at an "enlightened" policy sketchily initiated in France by Madame de Pompadour and Choiseul, the philosophical and military régime of Frederick II, the enlightenment propaganda disseminated by Catherine of Russia, find in Voltaire a guarantee and a support.

On the level of ideas, those which the *philosophe*'s temperament appropriated were the key ideas of the century. His first negations took the form of the free thought in vogue under the Regency. Then he came up against the philosophies of Leibniz, Locke, and Clarke, which issued from a classical rationalism that was Christian only by compromise. Even Malebranche and Fénelon yield to the trend which is drawing the thought of the great century toward deism: by a dialectical necessity the mechanistic representation of the cosmos eliminates the supernatural, and the existing religion therefore seems encumbered with superstitions. When Voltaire appears on the scene, the war against the supernatural has already been declared. Before him the century has begun to lose the feeling of God's immediate presence. Voltaire, who means to substitute for the Christian Divinity a God too pure to have anything human about Him, moves to the forefront of this current of thought. He has sworn to destroy faith in the God of the Incarnation. So it is not accurate to assert that he attacks only the vulnerable positions on the periphery of Christianity after isolating them from the whole. He doubtless does practise this tactic when he dins into our ears the harlotries of Oholah and Oholibah, and the incestuous affairs of Alexander VI. But when he denies that the Supreme Being kept providential watch over the destinies of the Jews and the Church, when he would have it that Jesus was a man and only a man, he attacks the very citadel of Christianity. Details aside, it is his denial of the Incarnation which sets him against the Christian religion. All his hatred of Christianity is centered upon this negation, in which he persists on his death-bed, when to the question posed by the curate of Saint-Sulpice on the divinity of Christ he replies: "Let me die in peace." But all around him the religious crisis of the eighteenth century

was a crisis focused on the Incarnation. In Protestant Europe the Socinians and Neo-Arians, in France the clerics who had more or less secretly shifted to deism, denied with all possible respect that Jesus had possessed a divine nature. The former welcomed Voltaire; and do what he might, there are some, as we know, whom he never succeeded in scandalizing.

However, despite his general agreement with his time, and despite the insinuative pliancy with which he accommodates himself to ideas very different from his own, certain trends of the century proved alien or repugnant to him. He paid the penalty of great men who outlive their generation. Those who resisted his influence became more and more numerous after 1770. His coquettish stratagems failed to relieve the conflict which opposed him to the atheistic group. As is well known, the *Système de la nature* created a following; that following has still not forgiven the Patriarch his deism. Whether one deplores it or not, Voltaire originated no form of modern atheism, neither the indifferent nor the vehement variety. Voltaire felt an even greater aversion to Rousseau's sentimentalism. When, after 1730, he realized that the public was asking for sentiment, he had perfected in *Zaïre* the formula for tearful tragedy. But when he saw that that Rousseau fellow, after riddling Christianity with Voltairean gibes, confessed his love for this religion of his childhood, Voltaire lost patience: Jean-Jacques must be a "malicious madman." Voltaire is alien to the sentimental logic of all those who will say, after Rousseau, that one must be a Christian because Christianity stirs the emotions.

When he dies, his gospel, which he called "today's Gospel," has become yesterday's while Diderot and Rousseau are preparing the future. Vistas are opening up in the direction of atheism or of a religion of the heart, not of Voltairean deism. Is Voltaire, then, as a man of his century, for that very reason a prisoner of the past? It is a fact that the deistic attempt of the theophilanthropists failed, for reasons that are obvious enough. Not only was Voltaire, the apostle of the new faith, too fond of buffoonery for his most determined admirers to take him quite seriously, but his inhibitions had reduced this "pure" religion to less than a bare sufficiency. Granted that God exists and that one must practise virtue; what then? The ceremonies of the artless theophilanthropists are a crashing bore, or a farce. Being purely allegorical, this cult cannot be saved even by the mystical efficacy of its rites. Finally, Voltaire, like the audacious reformers of the Revolution, did not know how durable religions are. The god outlives the city. After the furious assaults of an entire century, after the tidal wave which swept away a throne and a social order, the Church is still standing at the dawn of the new century. The failure of Voltairean deism is a definitively established fact of history, confirmed by the later failures of an Isambart who, in 1829, invited the theists to reorganize themselves into a Church (a police investigation put an end to that undertaking); of an Henri Carle, who during the Second Empire founded the periodical *Alliance religieuse universelle* and polemicized for a few years against Dupanloup and the materialists; of a Décembre, whose "Philanthropic Commission" and journal managed a meager existence from 1882 to 1888; of a Camerlynck, who contented himself with publishing a bulky theistic treatise in 1900. The lay spiritualism of Jules Simon, author of a noble and frigid work on *La Religion naturelle,* likewise failed of its effect. It is not in these otiose repetitions that the spirit of Voltaire lives on.

It does, nonetheless, live on. The wounds inflicted by Voltaire are still bleeding. He continues to be detested by some to an extent that is rare for so old a writer. The smile of the dilettante Renan allows for compromises, but not Voltaire's grin. His enemies will not forgive him for having known God and for having so fiercely vilified the Christian religion. Poor Father Adam, Reverend Gal-Pomaret, estimable Abbé Gaultier, and bizarre Abbé Marthe had judged correctly. There is something about Voltaire that tempts proselyters. It is not surprising that even today there are critics who try their luck at it. But the old man resists; his case is hopeless. So others prefer to get rid of him by disqualifying him: he has no sense of mystery, they say, he does not understand religion at all. But this is not true either. The old fox had made arrangements to have his tomb at Ferney half inside and half outside the church. It is no longer possible either to admit him completely into the sanctuary or to eject him from it altogether. This Voltaire fellow remains a very awkward corpse for the guardians of the temple.

An anti-Christian, but not without a sense of the divine, Voltaire ushered in a form of religiousness which does not adhere to established faiths, even when it does not combat them. After him the religion of some persons became a marginal one, and individual state of mind, manifested, not by the practice of a cult, but through literary expression. That is how it was with Rousseau, and Lamartine, and Vigny, and Hugo, and Lamennais, who sought his way outside the communion of the faithful, and even Péguy, who died before he could put himself right with those whom his popular anticlericalism continued to call "the curates."

No indeed, all is not dead in what Voltaire wrote. Over the ashes of yesterday's gospel plays the flame of the eternal gospel. Voltaire has not finished inciting readers to thought and action. The life which sparkles in the slightest phrase of his production is infectious. He has no equal in bestirring the sluggish. He is the best tonic one can find in our tradition to remedy a decline of French vitality. He is as eternal as his enemies, the fools and the tyrants.

> Nous savons qu'il naîtra, dans le lointain des âges,
> Des dominateurs durs, escortés de faux sages . . .

> ["We know that in the far-off future harsh rulers will
> arise, escorted by false sages . . ."]

announced Vigny, that reader of Voltaire. The rulers, who have come with their escort of theologians and inquisitors, continue to find in Voltaire a formidable adversary. It was not the fashion of a day that he was initiating when he said that "freedom [i.e., free will—Transl.] in man is spiritual health" and that freedom of thought and expression is the law of civilized societies. Has the lesson lost its vital pertinence in the twentieth century?

Even in the churches Voltaire has not ceased to exert an influence. Father Lacordaire has been credited with the following astonishing statement: "God, by a diabolical (sic!) ruse, sent Voltaire to combat His Church for the purpose of regenerating it." This spokesman for liberal Catholicism doubtless meant that the Church, once it had abandoned its untenable outposts, had established itself solidly in its main positions. Without attempting here to weigh precisely the importance of this influence by reaction, one may admit, with Albert Monod, that the crisis of the eighteenth century profoundly transformed religious life. In order to reply to the attacks of Voltaire and the *philosophes,* it would seem that the defenders of the Church sought their inspiration chiefly in the Christian humanistic tradition. This accounts for the strengthening of the old party of those who refuse to oppose heaven to earth; and it may be that there are not many individuals left today who would support that conception of religion which led Bossuet to affirm: "A Christian is never alive on earth, because he is always practising mortification here, and mortification is a trial, an apprenticeship, a beginning of death." In the disputes over China, did not the Society of Jesus win on appeal the trial which opposed it to Monsieur de Meaux? But it won with the support of Voltaire. It is the *philosophe*'s propaganda which spread abroad the idea that every religion contains something valid. To cite but one or two instances, Durkheim was in the tradition of the ***Philosophie de l'histoire*** when he revealed that there was a sort of eternal truth running through the various faiths; the noblest elements of the spirit of Voltaire also permeate certain of Alain's *Propos sur la religion.* It is Voltaire who dissuaded men from believing that any one sect had a monopoly on truth. Today the sense of the universal and the mockery of all that is petty and limited remain living values in his works: "All of you who are listening to me, remember that you are men before being citizens of a certain city, members of a certain society, believers in a certain religion. The time has come to enlarge the sphere of our ideas, and to be citizens of the world. . . . We are all of the same religion without realizing it" (***Sermon de J. Rossette***). That Voltaire still has something to say to us Jean Guéhenno, who knew it, was able to confirm when he dropped in on a class of young Africans engaged in reading the *Prière à Dieu:* "May all men remember that they are brothers . . . "

Voltaire, old friend, if we may address you after writing so many pages about you, we must begin by apologizing: how can one be laconic in speaking of you who were so interminably brief? What was it that you had to say at such great length? You were malicious, jealous, mendacious; but when you had before you a man, your fellow-human, you felt him to be your brother. "Quiconque avec [toi s'entretenait semblait] disposer de [ton] âme." ["Whoever conversed with you seemed to have your soul at his disposal."] You dreamed of a fraternal humanity, and you were right to do so. For after all . . . But Pangloss has held forth long enough. If the Being of beings has somewhere preserved the flame of your spirit, you are murmuring: "That is well said, but may all men who crawl about on this globe or globule where I once stirred things up a bit remember that they are brothers." (pp. 140-49)

René Pomeau, "Voltaire's Religion," in Voltaire: A Collection of Critical Essays, *edited by William F. Bottiglia, Prentice-Hall, Inc., 1968, pp. 140-49.*

André Maurois   (essay date 1957)

[*Maurois—born Emile Salomon Wilhelm Herzog—was a distinguished French biographer and literary critic. He is perhaps best known for his lives of Percy Bysshe Shelley (1923), Benjamin Disraeli (1927), George Gordon, Lord Byron (1930), Voltaire (1932), Charles Dickens (1934), and Marcel Proust (1949). In the following essay, originally published in* Lecture mon doux plaisir *(1957), he explores the tone and tempo of Voltaire's philosophic fictions.]*

Philosophical fiction is a difficult, because a hybrid, literary form. Since the author uses it for the purpose of espousing or attacking certain accepted ideas, it belongs to the class of essays or pamphlets. But because it narrates a sequence of imaginary events, it can also claim the title of fiction. It cannot, however, have either the seriousness of the essay or the credibility of the novel. Not that it even pretends to be credible. On the contrary, it deliberately stresses the fact that it is an exercise in intellectual ingenuity. Not Voltaire when he created **Candide,** nor Anatole France when he wrote *L'Île des Pingouins,* nor Wells when he invented *The Island of Dr Moreau* believed for a moment that the reader would mistake these fictions for reality. On the contrary, it was their considered intention to present these stories with a philosophical content as fantastic tales.

But why, it may be asked, should an author have recourse to this whimsical and indirect method of philosophizing? In order to enjoy greater freedom in expressing ideas which, in an essay, might seem to be subversive, shocking and unacceptable to the reader. The more he can be made to feel that he has been transported into a world where nonsense reigns supreme, the more reassured will he feel, and the readier to digest many surprising truths. Swift was able to say a number of disturbing things about human nature and the England of his own day, merely by pretending to describe a nation of midgets, a kingdom of giants, or a country in which horses ruled over human beings. Montesquieu was able, through the mouth of an imaginary Persian, to mock at customs for which his birth and position compelled him to make a show of respect.

The philosophical tale, or novel, will, therefore, be peculiarly well suited to a period in which ideas are changing more quickly than institutions and manners. Writers, tormented by the need they feel to say what they think, but hampered by the severity of police regulations, censorship or an Inquisition, will be tempted to take refuge in the absurd, and to make themselves invulnerable by making their books incredible. Such was the position in the France of the eighteenth century. To all appearances the monarchy was still powerful. It was the protector of religious and philosophic orthodoxy. Its judges administered the Law with a heavy hand. But, in fact, the writers and the members of the privileged classes had been won over to the new ideas, and were eager to air them. It was not altogether impossible for them to do so openly, as is proved by the publication of the **Dictionnaire Philosophique,** the **Essai sur les Moeurs** and the *Encyclopédie.* But there still remained a number of themes on which it was difficult to touch. There was, however, a good chance that, if treated as elements in a fictitious narrative, they could be brought to the notice of a more timorous and, therefore, a wider public, the more so since this type of reading matter was very much in the fashion. Ever since the publication of *The Arabian Nights* in Galland's translation (1704-1717) and of the *Lettres Persanes* (1721), the oriental mode had become the favoured and transparent mask of those who, in this way, could temper their audacities with prudence. Voltaire, more than anybody else, had recourse to it.

It is a matter for no little surprise that he should have adopted this lively and, in both senses of the word, free form at a comparatively advanced age. Apart from the **Adventures du Baron de Gangan** which never found its way into print, though its existence is proved by a series of letters exchanged between the author and the Crown-Prince of Prussia, Voltaire's first philosophic tale was **Le Monde Comme il Va,** written in 1747. It was at this time that, as the result of an unfortunate episode, he, together with Mme du Châtelet, took refuge with the Duchesse du Maine at Sceaux. It was under her roof that **Babouc, Memnon, Scarmentado** and **Zadig** were composed. Voltaire wrote a chapter every day, which he showed to the Duchess in the evening. "Sometimes, after supper, he would read a tale or a short novel which he had written during the day for the express purpose of entertaining her. . . ."

These philosophic fictions, always contrived so as to illustrate some moral truth, were written in a gay and charming style, and the Duchesse du Maine took so great a delight in them that others soon expressed a wish to share her pleasure, with the result that Voltaire was compelled to read them aloud to a wider circle. This he did with the skill of a trained actor. The tales enjoyed a great success with his listeners, who begged that he would have them printed. For a long time he refused to do so, saying that such trivial works, designed for the amusement of a small and intimate circle, did not deserve to be perpetuated. Writers are bad judges of their own productions. At the age of eighteen Voltaire had believed that he would go down in literary history as a great tragic dramatist: at thirty, that he was destined to be a famous historian: at forty, an epic poet. He could not have foreseen, when he wrote **Zadig** in 1748, that it would still be regarded as entertaining reading, together with his other short tales, in 1958, whereas **La Henriade, Zaïre, Mérope** and **Tancrède** would be condemned to an eternal sleep on library shelves.

In this matter Voltaire's contemporaries were no less wrong than he was. They attached but little importance to frivolous stories in which what struck them most forcibly were numerous allusions to the author's personal enemies. "It is easy to recognize Voltaire under the disguise of the sagacious Zadig. The calumnies and spite of courtiers . . . the disgrace of the hero are so many allegories to be interpreted easily enough. It is thus that he takes revenge upon his enemies . . . " The abbé Boyer, who was the Dauphin's tutor and a powerful ecclesiastic, took in very bad part the attacks on one whose identity was but thinly concealed behind the anagram *Reyob.* "It would please me mightily if all this to-do about **Zadig** could be ended," wrote Mme du Châtelet, and it was not long before Voltaire disowned a book "which some there are who accuse of containing audacious attacks upon our holy religion". In point of fact the audacities of **Zadig** were pretty mild, and were limited to showing that men, at different times and in different places, have had different beliefs, though the solid basis of all religions is the same. Such a thesis was the most obvious common sense, but common sense was, at that time, most certainly not in general circulation.

Those who dared not attack Voltaire's theology accused him of plagiarism. That has always been an easy method of belittling a great writer. Everything has been said before—not excepting the statement that everything has been said before—and nothing is easier than to establish a connexion between passages in two different authors. Molière imitated Plautus who, in his turn, had imitated Menander who, no doubt, had imitated some earlier model unknown to us. Fréron (some twenty years later) charged Voltaire with having borrowed the best chapters of *Zadig* from sources "which that prize copyist took great pains to conceal". For instance, the brilliant *L'Ermite* chapter was borrowed from a poem by Parnell, and that entitled *Le Chien et le Cheval* (an anticipation of Sherlock Holmes) was lifted from *Le Voyage et les Adventures des Trois Princes de Serendip.* "Monsieur de Voltaire", wrote the treacherous Fréron, "reads often with intention, and much to his advantage, more especially in such books as he thinks have now been long forgotten. . . . From these obscure mines he brings a great many precious jewels to the surface."

Is that so terrible a crime? Must an author refuse to touch seams which have not been completely worked out? What honest critic has ever maintained that a writer can create *ex nihilo?* Neither Parnell's *The Hermit* nor *Le Voyage de Serendip* were original productions. "All these brief tales", says Gaston Paris, "were told long ago in many languages before being recast in that flexible and lively French which, today, gives them a seeming novelty . . . " The unique and brilliant character of Voltaire's *tales* lies not in originality of invention, but in that combination of diverse and seemingly contradictory qualities which are their author's own and unequalled contribution.

He had been educated by the Jesuits, and from them had learned intellectual discipline and elegance of style. During a temporary period of exile in England he had read Swift and studied his technique. "He is the English Rabelais," he had said of the author of Gulliver, "but without Rabelais' bombast." Under the influence of Swift he had developed a liking for strange fancies (whence *Micromégas* and *Babouc*), for travellers' tales which were no more than an excuse for satiric writing, and a literary variant of what we, today, should call a "poker face" which enabled him to give expression to the most monstrous propositions as though they were obvious and natural truths. Onto this living tree had been grafted the Galland of the *Arabian Nights.* "The combination of the classic French mind, with its love of proved statements, its lucid deduction of conclusions from strict logical premises, and the completely illogical view of life common in the fatalistic East, might have been expected to produce a new dimension: and this it did." The subject matter was provided by stories as old as the human race: the technique contained elements drawn from Swift, from Eastern story-telling and from Jesuit teaching: but it was the inimitable synthesis of all these influences that produced the tales which Voltaire continued to concoct over a long period of time.

It has already been pointed out that he began his experiments in this, for him, new literary form, in 1747, that is to say, when he was fifty-three. He wrote his masterpiece in that kind, *Candide,* when he was sixty-five; *L'Ingénu,* which is another of his most successful products, when he was seventy-four, in the same year that saw the publica-

tion of *La Princesse de Babylone;* and he was over eighty when he brought out such minor works as *L'Histore de Fenni, Le Crocheteur Borgne* and *Les Oreilles du Comte de Chesterfield.* Hence, Paul Morand's generalization to the effect that French writers are never younger, never more free from constraint, than when they have passed their sixtieth birthday. By that time they have broken free from the romantic agonies of youth and turned their backs on that pursuit of honours which, in a country where literature plays a social rôle, absorbs too much of their energies during the years of maturity. Chateaubriand was never more "modern" than in his *Vie de Rancé,* and in the concluding sections of the *Mémoires d'Outre-Tombe.* Voltaire wrote his best book at sixty-five, and Anatole France his, *Les Dieux ont Soif,* at sixty-eight. The old writer, like the old actor, is a master of his craft. Youthfulness of style is no more than a matter of technique.

It has become customary to bring together under the blanket title of "Romans et Contes de Voltaire" a number of works greatly differing in kind and in value. Among them are such masterpieces as *Zadig, Candide* and *L'Ingénu:* there are the relatively unimportant *Princesse de Babylone* and *Le Taureau blanc;* there are *Cosi-Sancta* and *Le Crocheteur Borgne* which are no more than short stories of ten pages or so, and genuine novels of a hundred; there are rough sketches of the general type of *Les Voyages de Scarmentado,* which is really only a foretaste of *Candide; Les Lettres d'Amabel* which belongs to the tradition of *Lettres Persanes,* and dialogues like *L'Homme aux Quarante Ecus,* in which there is no fictional element at all, but only a discussion about political economy reminiscent of *Dialogues sur le Commerce des Blés,* by the abbé Galiani, or Voltaire's own *Oreilles due Comte de Chesterfield* in which theology is argued instead of economics.

What have all these odds and ends of writing in common? First and foremost, the *tone* which, in Voltaire, is always mocking, mercurial and, at least apparently, superficial. There is not, in all these fictions, a single character who is treated with genuine seriousness. All are either embodiments of an idea or a doctrine (Pangloss stands for optimism, Martin for pessimism), or fairy-tale heroes from a lacquer screen or a piece of Chinese embroidery. They can be tortured or burned to death without the author or the reader feeling any real concern for them. Even the beautiful Saint-Yves, when dying of despair because she has sacrificed what she calls her honour in order to save her lover, can weep without bringing the slightest hint of moisture to the eyes of anybody else. The stories, catastrophic though they may be, are always dominated by the author's wit, and so rapid is their *tempo* that the reader is given no time in which to be deeply distressed. A *prestissimo* has no place in a Funeral March or a Requiem Mass, and the *prestissimo* or the *allegretto* are Voltaire's favourite "movements".

Puppets, variously labelled, jig to this devil's tattoo. Voltaire delighted in bringing on to his stage priests, to whom he gave the name of *magi;* judges, whom he called *mufti;* financiers, inquisitors, Jews, innocents and philosophers. Certain routine enemies reappear in all the tales, variously disguised. Of women he has no very high opinion. To judge from his treatment of them, their minds are exclusively occupied by the prospect of making love to handsome young men with good figures, though, being both venal and timid, they are prepared to hire their bodies to old inquisitors or soldiers if, by so doing, they can save their own lives or amass riches. They are inconstant, and will gladly cut off the nose of a husband fondly mourned in order to cure a new lover. For such conduct he does not blame them. "I have", says Scarmentado, "seen all that the world can offer of the beautiful, the good and the admirable, and am determined for the future to confine my attention to my household gods. I took me a wife in my own country: I was cuckolded, and concluded that my state was the pleasantest that life can give."

It is from the author's philosophy that these writings truly derive a unity. It has been described as "a chaos of lucid ideas", in short, incoherent. Faguet accused Voltaire of having considered everything, examined everything, and never gone deeply into anything. "Is he an optimist? Is he a pessimist? Does he believe in free-will or predestination? Does he believe in the immortality of the soul? Does he believe in God? Does he deny the validity of metaphysics? Is there something in him of the agnostic spirit, but only up to a certain point, in other words, is he really a metaphysician at heart? . . . I defy anybody to answer any of these questions with an unqualified yes or no."

All that is perfectly true. There is something of everything to be found in Voltaire, and also the opposite of everything. But the chaos is reduced to order as soon as one sees the apparent contradictions against the background of his times. In this case, as in that of most men, a personal philosophy was in a continuing state of evolution throughout his life. *La Vision de Babouc* and *Zadig* were written when Fortune was smiling on him. He was enjoying the favour and protection of Mme de Pompadour, and, consequently, of a considerable section of the Court. All the kings of Europe were inviting him to visit them. Mme du Châtelet was attending to his sensual needs, giving him affection and assuring his independence. He had every reason, therefore, for finding life tolerable. That is why the conclusions reached in *Babouc* are, relatively speaking, lenient.

"Would you have me chastise Persepolis or destroy it?" the djinn Ituriel asks him. Babouc has an observant and impartial eye. He is present at a bloody battle, in which, on neither side, do the soldiers know why they are killing and getting killed, but that same battle is the occasion for innumerable acts of bravery and humanity. He enters Persepolis and finds there a dirty and ill-favoured people, temples where the dead are buried to an accompaniment of harsh, discordant voices, and women of the town on whose activities the magistrates turn an indulgent eye. But, as he continues his tour, he comes upon finer temples, a wise and polished people who are deeply attached to their king, an honest merchant. It is not long before he comes to like the city which is, at once, frivolous, scandalmongering, pleasant, beautiful and intelligent. When he reports his findings to Ituriel, the latter decides not even to try to correct its shortcomings, but "to let the world go its way, since though everything is far from well, everything is not too bad".

Zadig sounds a somewhat deeper note. In it Voltaire shows, by a series of ingenious parables, that it would be a rash man indeed who would maintain that the world is bad because it contains a certain number of evils. The future is hidden from us, and we cannot be sure that from these seeming errors of the Creator salvation may not come. "There is no evil", says the Angel to Zadig, "of which some goodness is not born." "But", asks Zadig, "what if everything were good and nothing evil?" "Then", says the angel Jesrad, "this world would be a different place: the interconnexion of events would belong to a different order of wisdom, and this different order, which would be perfect, could exist only in the eternal dwelling-place of the Supreme Being . . . "—a form of reasoning which is far from being irrefutable, since, if God is good, why did He not confine the world within the bounds of that eternal dwelling-place? If He is all-powerful, why did He not, in creating the world, keep it free from suffering?

Voltaire was far too intelligent not to have asked himself these questions, and, in *Micromégas,* he gives them a disillusioned answer. Micromégas is an inhabitant of Sirius who travels from planet to planet in the company of a dweller in Saturn. One day, the giant discovers the Earth and the almost invisible animalculae who live upon it. He is amazed to find that these tiny creatures can talk, and is outraged by their presumption. One of these midgets, wearing a doctor's cap, tells him that he knows the whole secret of existence, which, he says, is to be found in the *Summa* of St Thomas. "He looked the two celestial beings up and down, and informed them that their persons, their worlds, their suns and their stars had been created for the sole purpose of serving Man." Hearing this, Micromégas gives vent to Homeric laughter.

This laughter is Voltaire's own. So, human beings complain that the world is ill-made, do they? But ill-made for whom? For Man, who, in the immense design of the Universe is no more than an unimportant mould! The probability is that everything in this world which we think is botched or erroneous has its reasons at a totally different level of existence. The mould endures, no doubt, a small amount of suffering, but somewhere there are giants who, huge in stature as in mind, live in a state of semi-divinity. This is Voltaire's answer to the problem of evil. It is not very satisfactory because the mould need never have been created, and, in the eyes of God, it may well be that mere size is of no importance.

But *Micromégas* is still comparatively optimistic. Ridiculous though these human insects may be when they presume to speak of philosophy, they astonish the celestial visitors when they apply the principles of their science, and measure with accuracy the exact size of Micromégas, and the distance of Sirius from the Earth. That these all but invisible mites should have penetrated so deeply into the mysteries of the Universe in which they are themselves, perhaps, no more than accidents, was already causing no little wonder in Voltaire's time, and would still more surprise a Micromégas who should make a similar voyage of discovery in our own day. Pascal had already said as much, and so had Bacon. Men may be no more than mites, but mites who dominate the Universe by obeying its laws. Their absurdities are counter-balanced by their intelligence.

In *Micromégas* we have the second Voltaire of the "tales". The third is a far sadder figure, for he has come to understand that Man is not only absurd but also extremely wicked. By that time he had had his own personal misfortunes. Mme du Châtelet had deceived him with his best friend, and, got with child by Saint-Lambert, had died in labour. The Kings, whether of France or Prussia, had treated him badly, and he found himself condemned to live in exile. True, it was a very comfortable exile. Neither Les Délices nor Ferney could be called unpleasing residences. But such happiness as he enjoyed there he owned to his own prudence, and not at all to his fellow men among whom he had met with such bitter persecution. But his worst sufferings resulted from public disasters. Too many wars, too much intolerance. Then, in 1755, to the cruelty of men was added the enmity of Nature. It was the year of the Lisbon earthquake which destroyed one of the finest cities in Europe. It had a profound effect upon him. No longer was it possible to maintain that everything is tolerable. The present, for him, was hideous.

> *One day, all will be well.* That is our hope.
> *All is well now,* that is an illusion.

One day all would be well, but only on condition that men set to work to transform society. In this poem we see the first sketch of a doctrine of progress and of the philosophy of *Candide.*

Candide was the outcome of Voltaire's own experiences and of the exasperation bred in him by the works of certain philosophers, such as Rousseau who had written:"If the Eternal Being has not done better, the reason is that he could not," or Leibnitz who laid it down that all was for the best in the best of all possible worlds. This generalization Voltaire put into the mouth of Pangloss, the teacher of optimism, and, to show how false it was, sent wandering about the world a simple-minded disciple of that same Pangloss, the young Candide, who saw at first hand armies, the Inquisition, murders, thievings and rapes, the Jesuits of Paraguay and conditions in France, England and Turkey. As a result of what he found in all these places, he came to the conclusion that everywhere and always Man is a very vicious animal. All the same, the last words of the book are: *Il faut cultiver notre jardin*—we must cultivate our garden—in other words, the world is mad and cruel: the earth trembles and the skies shoot lightning: kings engage in wars, and the churches tear one another to pieces. Let us limit our activities and try to do such humble work as many come our way, as best we can. That "scientific and bourgeois" conclusion was Voltaire's last world, as it was to be Goethe's. Everything is bad, but everything can be bettered. It sounds the prelude to our modern world, to the wisdom of the engineer, which may be far from complete, but is useful all the same. Voltaire, as Bainville said of him, "cleared the world of many illusions". On the ground thus swept and tidied it is possible to build anew.

Certain writers of our own day have discovered that the world is absurd. But in *Candide* Voltaire said all that can be said on that subject, and he said it with wit and intelligence, which is a good deal better than merely growing irritable, and leaves to us that legacy of courage which we need for action.

Candide was the high-point of Voltaire's art. Of the tales that followed it, *L'Ingénu* is the best. It still has the swiftness of the true Voltaire *tempo* and all his charm, but the themes round which it is constructed are of less importance than those of *Candide. L'Histoire de Fenni* is a defence of Deism, "the sole brake on men who are so shrewd in the committing of secret crimes. . . . Yes, my friends, atheism and fanaticism are the two poles in a Universe of

confusion and horror." *Les Oreilles du Comte de Chesterfield* is a story which sets out to prove that fatality governs all things in this world. So, why reason and why worry? "Swallow hot drinks when you freeze, and cool drinks in the dog-days. Steer a middle course between the too much and the too little in all things. Digest, sleep and take your pleasure, all else is mockery." That is the conclusion of *Candide,* minus the poetry.

For the dominant quality of Voltaire's prose in his days of happiness is poetry. "There is", said Alain, "a prayer in every great work, even in Voltaire's tales." The poetry in all great writing is born, to a very large extent, of the fact that the madness of the universe is expressed by the disorder of ideas, but dominated by rhythm. In this, Shakespeare was a master with his witches' chants and his fairies' songs, so incoherent and so perfect. Voltaire's best work has the same two characteristics. Unforeseeable cascades of factual absurdities splash every page, yet the rapidity of the movement, the return at regular intervals of Martin's lamentations, of Candide's simplicities, of the misfortunes of Pangloss and of the Old Woman's stories, bring assurance to the mind of that tragic repose which only great poetry can give.

And so it is that Voltaire, who wanted to be a great poet in verse, and worked so hard at his tragedies and his epic, ended, though he did not know it, by finding pure poetry in his prose tales which he wrote for fun, and without, for a moment, thinking that they were important. Which proves, as he would have said, once again, that bad is good, good bad, and that fatality rules the world. (pp. 35-50)

> *André Maurois, "Voltaire: Novels and Tales,"*
> *in his* The Art of Writing, *translated by Gerard Hopkins, The Bodley Head, 1960, pp. 35-50.*

Roland Barthes   (essay date 1958)

[*A French critic, essayist, and autobiographer, Barthes was a leading exponent of the French "new criticism," "la nouvelle critique." His critical works, including* S/Z *(1970), helped usher structuralism to the forefront of French intellectual thought in the 1960s.* Le degré zéro de l'écriture *(1953;* Writing Degree Zero, *1967), considered to be Barthes's most seminal work, outraged many prominent French academicians. In it Barthes presented his concept of* écriture, *the idea that a literary text has a meaning independent of, and possibly different from, the author's intentions. In the following 1958 essay, he appraises Voltaire as "a happy writer, but doubtless the last."*]

What have we in common, today, with Voltaire? From a modern point of view, his philosophy is outmoded. It is possible to believe in the fixity of essences and in the chaos of history, but no longer in the same way as Voltaire. In any case, atheists no longer throw themselves at the feet of deists, who moreover no longer exist. Dialectics has killed off Manicheanism, and we rarely discuss the ways of Providence. As for Voltaire's enemies, they have disappeared, or been transformed: there are no more Jansenists, no Socinians, no Leibnizians; the Jesuits are no longer named Nonotte or Patouillet.

I was about to say: there is no longer an Inquisition. This is wrong, of course. What has disappeared is the theater of persecution, not persecution itself: the *auto-da-fé* has been subtilized into a police operation, the stake has become the concentration camp, discreetly ignored by its neighbors. In return for which, the figures have changed: in 1721 nine men and eleven women were burned at Grenada in the four ovens of the scaffold, and in 1723 nine men were burned at Madrid to celebrate the arrival of the French princess: they had doubtless married their cousins or eaten meat on Friday. A horrible repression, whose absurdity sustains Voltaire's entire *oeuvre.* But between 1939 and 1945, six million human beings were killed, among others, because they were Jews—they, or their fathers, or their grandfathers.

We have not had a single pamphlet against that. But perhaps it is precisely because the figures have changed. Simplistic as it may appear, there is a proportion between the lightness of the Voltairean artillery and the sporadic artillery of religious crime in the eighteenth century: quantitatively limited, the stake became a principle, i.e., a target: a tremendous advantage for its opponent: such is the stuff of which triumphant writers are made. For the very enormity of racist crimes, their organization by the State, the ideological justifications with which they are masked—all this involves today's writer in much more than a pamphlet, demands a philosophy rather than an irony, an explanation rather than an astonishment. Since Voltaire, history has been imprisoned in a difficulty which lacerates any committed literature and which Voltaire never knew: *no freedom for the enemies of freedom:* no one can any longer give lessons in tolerance to anyone.

In short, what separates us from Voltaire is that he was a happy writer. Better than anyone else, he gave reason's combat a festive style. Everything is spectacle in his battles: the adversary's name—always ridiculous; the disputed doctrine—reduced to a proposition (Voltairean irony is invariably the exposure of a disproportion); the points scored, exploding in every direction until they seem to be a game, dispensing the onlooker from all respect and all pity; the very mobility of the combatant, here disguised under a thousand transparent pseudonyms, there making his European journeys a kind of feinting farce, a perpetual Scapinade. For the skirmishes between Voltaire and the world are not only a spectacle but a superlative spectacle, proclaiming themselves such in the fashion of those Punchinello shows Voltaire loved so much—he had a puppet theater of his own at Cirey.

Voltaire's first happiness was doubtless that of his times. Let there be no mistake: the times were very harsh, and Voltaire has everywhere described their horrors. Yet no period has helped a writer more, given him more assurance that he was fighting for a just and natural cause. The bourgeoisie, the class from which Voltaire came, already held most of its economic positions; a power in commerce and industry, in the ministries, in culture and the sciences, it knew that its triumph coincided with the nation's prosperity and the happiness of each citizen. On its side, potential power, certainty of method, and the still-pure heritage of taste; against it, all a dying world could display of corruption, stupidity, and ferocity. It was indeed a great happiness, a great peace to combat an enemy so uniformly condemnable. The tragic spirit is severe because it ac-

knowledges, by obligation of nature, its adversary's greatness: Voltaire had no tragic spirit: he had to measure himself against no living force, against no idea or individual that could induce him to reflect (except the past: Pascal, and the future: Rousseau; but he conjured them both away): Jesuits, Jansenists, or parliaments, these were great frozen bodies, drained of all intelligence and filled with no more than a ferocity intolerable to the heart and the mind. Authority, even in its bloodiest manifestations, was no more than a decor; merely subject such machinery to human eyes, and it would collapse. Voltaire had that sly and tender gaze (*Zaïre's very heart,* Mme de Genlis tells us, *was in his eyes*), whose destructive power lay in simply bearing life among those great blind masks which still ruled society.

It was, then, a singular happiness to have to do battle in a world where force and stupidity were continually on the same tack: a privileged situation for the mind. The writer was on history's side, all the happier in that he perceived history as a consummation, not as a transcendence which risked sweeping him along with it.

Voltaire's second happiness was precisely to forget history, at the very moment it was supporting him. In order to be happy, Voltaire suspended time; if he has a philosophy, it is that of immobility. We know what he thought: God created the world as a geometer, not as a father. Which means that He does not bother to accompany His creation and that, once regulated, the world no longer sustains relations with God. An original intelligence established a certain type of causality once and for all: there are no objects without ends, no effects without causes, and the relation between one and the other is immutable. Voltairean metaphysics is therefore never anything but an introduction to physics, and Providence a mechanics. For once God has left the world He created (like the clockmaker his clock), neither God nor man ever moves again. Of course good and evil exist; but we are to translate them as happiness and misery, not sin or innocence; for they are merely the elements of a universal causality; they have a necessity, but this necessity is mechanical, not moral: evil does not punish, good does not reward: they do not signify that God is, that He surveys all, but that He has been, that He has created.

If man should take it upon himself to turn from evil to good by a moral impulse, it is the universal order of causes and effects which he injures; he can produce, by this movement, only a farcical chaos (as Memnon does, the day he decides to be wise). Then what can man do with regard to good and evil? Not much: in this machinery which is the Creation, there is room only for a *game,* that is, the very slight amplitude the constructor allows his pieces in which to move. This game is reason. It is capricious—i.e., it attests to no direction of history: reason appears, disappears, with no other law than the very personal effort of certain minds: among the benefits of history (useful inventions, great works) there is a relation of contiguity, never of function. Voltaire's opposition to any intelligence of time is very intense. For Voltaire, there is no history in the modern sense of the word, nothing but chronologies. Voltaire wrote historical works expressly to say that he did not believe in history: the age of Louis XIV is not an organism, it is a cluster of chance meetings, here the dragonnades, there Racine. Nature itself, of course, is never historical: being essentially art, i.e., God's artifice, it cannot move or have moved: the mountains were not wrought by the earth and the waters, God created them once and for all for the use of His creatures, and the fossil fishes—whose discovery so excited the age—are only the prosaic leavings of picnicking pilgrims: there is no evolution.

The philosophy of time will be the contribution of the nineteenth century (and singularly of Germany). We might assume that the relativist lesson of the past is at least replaced in Voltaire, as in his entire age, by that of space. At first glance, this is what occurs: the eighteenth century is not only a great age of travel, the age in which modern capitalism, then preponderantly British, definitively organizes its world market from China to South America; it is above all the age when travel accedes to literature and engages a philosophy. We know the role of the Jesuits, by their *Edifying and Curious Letters,* in the birth of exoticism. From early in the century, these materials were transformed and soon produced a veritable typology of exotic man: we have the Egyptian Sage, the Mohammedan Arab, the Turk, the Chinese, the Siamese, and most prestigious of all, the Persian. All these Orientals are philosophy teachers; but before saying which philosophy, we must note that just when Voltaire begins writing his Tales, which owe a great deal to Oriental folklore, the century has already elaborated a veritable rhetoric of exoticism, a kind of digest whose figures are so well formed and so well known that they can henceforth be utilized without troubling further over descriptions and astonishments; Voltaire will not fail to utilize them in this fashion, for he never troubled to be "original" (an entirely modern notion, moreover); for him, as indeed for any of his contemporaries, the Oriental is not the object, the term of a genuine consideration, but simply a cipher, a convenient sign of communication.

The result of this conceptualization is that the Voltairean journey has no density; the space Voltaire covers so obsessively (we do nothing but travel in his Tales) is not an explorer's space, it is a surveyor's space, and what Voltaire borrows from the allogeneous humanity of the Chinese and the Persian is a new limit, not a new substance; new habitations are attributed to the human essence, it flourishes from the Seine to the Ganges, and Voltaire's novels are less investigations than inspections of an owner whom we "orient" in no particular order because his estate never varies, and whom we interrupt by incessant stops during which we discuss not what we have seen but what we are. This explains why the Voltairean journey is neither realistic nor baroque (the picaresque vein of the century's first narratives has completely dried up); it is not even an operation of knowledge, but merely of affirmation; it is the element of a logic, the figure of an equation; these Oriental countries, which today have so heavy a weight, so pronounced an individuation in world politics, are for Voltaire so many forms, mobile signs without actual content, humanity at zero degrees (Centigrade), which one nimbly grasps in order to signify . . . oneself.

For such is the paradox of Voltairean travel: to manifest an immobility. There are of course other manners, other laws, other moralities than ours, and this is what the journey teaches; but this diversity belongs to the human essence and consequently finds its point of equilibrium very rapidly; it is enough to acknowledge it in order to be done

with it: let man (that is, Occidental man) multiply himself a little, let the European philosopher be doubled by the Chinese Sage, the ingenious Huron, and universal man will be created. To aggrandize oneself in order to confirm, not in order to transform oneself—such is the meaning of the Voltairean voyage.

It was doubtless Voltaire's second happiness to be able to depend upon the world's immobility. The bourgeoisie was so close to power that it could already begin not to believe in history. It could also begin to reject any system, to suspect any organized philosophy, that is, to posit its own thinking, its own good sense as a Nature which any doctrine, any intellectual system would offend. This is what Voltaire did so brilliantly, and it was his third happiness: he ceaselessly dissociated intelligence and intellectuality, asserting that the world is an order if we do not try too much to order it, that it is a system if only we renounce systematizing it: this conduct of mind has had a great career subsequently: today we call it anti-intellectualism.

Notable is the fact that all of Voltaire's enemies could be named, that is, their being derived from their certainty: Jesuits, Jansenists, Socinians, Protestants, atheists, all enemies among themselves, but united under Voltaire's attack by their capacity to be defined by a word. Conversely, on the level of denominative systems, Voltaire escapes. Doctrinally, was he a deist? a Leibnizian? a rationalist? Each time, yes and no. He has no system except the hatred of system (and we know that there is nothing grimmer than this very system); today his enemies would be the doctrinaires of history, of science (*vide* his mockery of pure science in **The Man with Forty Ecus**), or of existence; Marxists, existentialists, leftist intellectuals—Voltaire would have hated them, covered them with incessant *lazzi,* as he did the Jesuits in his own day. By continuously setting intelligence against intellectuality, by using one to undermine the other, by reducing the conflicts of ideas to a kind of Manichean struggle between stupidity and intelligence, by identifying all system with stupidity and all freedom of mind with intelligence, Voltaire grounded liberalism on a contradiction. As system of the nonsystem, anti-intellectualism eludes and gains on both counts, perpetually ricocheting between bad faith and good conscience, between a pessimism of substance and a jig of form, between a proclaimed skepticism and a terrorist doubt.

The Voltairean festivity is constituted by this incessant alibi. Voltaire cudgels and dodges at the same time. The world is simple for a man who ends all his letters with the cordial salutation *Ecrasons l'infâme* (i.e., dogmatism). We know that this simplicity and this happiness were bought at the price of an ablation of history and of an immobilization of the world. Further, it is a happiness which excluded many, despite its dazzling victory over obscurantism. Thus, in accord with the legend, the anti-Voltaire is indeed Rousseau. By forcefully positing the idea of man's corruption by society, Rousseau set history moving again, established the principle of a permanent transcendence of history. But by doing so he bequeathed to literature a poisoned legacy. Henceforth, ceaselessly athirst and wounded by a responsibility he can never again completely honor nor completely elude, the intellectual will be defined by his bad conscience: Voltaire was a happy writer, but doubtless the last. (pp. 83-9)

Roland Barthes, "The Last Happy Writer," in

his Critical Essays, *translated by Richard Howard, Northwestern University Press, 1972, pp. 83-9.*

Ira O. Wade   (essay date 1959)

[*Wade was a leading American writer on Voltaire. In the following essay, he surveys Voltaire's views concerning science and scientific method.*]

It is customary to present *Candide* as the result of Voltaire's reaction to Leibniz and Pope, or to the Lisbon earthquake, the Seven Years War, his unfortunate experience at Potzdam, the philosophy of optimism, or to his growing pessimism as he delved further into the horrors of history. It is indeed not unusual to present these incidents as "causes," sometimes stressing one of the events over another, sometimes accumulating one upon the other to produce the effect of total exasperation. Thus Voltaire's reactions would seem more important than his actions, his incentives more important than his creative power, and his despair a greater source of creation than his intellect. With these explanations I have no quarrel; indeed, I myself have given them upon many an occasion as "causes" of the work. However, to assert that he was led to compose his conte because of his dissatisfaction with Leibniz and Pope, his distrust of optimism, his personal fright at the earthquake, his anger at Frederick, or because of any other emotional imbalance does not explain in any relevant way either the origin and genesis of the work or its worth and meaning.

None of these so-called "causes" can be formulated in a clear-cut statement. If one asserts, for instance, that *Candide* is the result of Voltaire's rejection of Leibniz, or Pope, or optimism, the statement insofar as it affects the meaning of the conte is practically meaningless. Besides, it is not true. Until Voltaire wrote *Candide,* he accepted as much of Leibniz as he rejected. After *Candide,* he appears to have the same attitude. As a matter of fact, his reaction to Leibniz is at first mildly enthusiastic. From there he passes to modified imitation, to cautious discussion of points, to rejection of this and acceptance of that, to violent and witty onslaught, to more reasonable reactions. His attitudes toward Pope, toward the philosophy of optimism follow very much the same lines: moderate enthusiasm, modified acceptance, more critical examination, violent rejection, more reasonable acceptance. In this shifting critical attitude (which is none other than the normal rationalist approach) we have difficulty in clearly defining the cause, being reduced to explaining the "why" and the "how."

This difficulty of definition and the resultant quandary are probably most obvious in Voltaire's optimist-pessimist fluctuations. It is very difficult (or should I say all too easy?) to assign him either of these attitudes. If we wish to prove him a pessimist, we may find in his works an abundance of material to do so and to establish forever his place among the pessimists: the *Mémoires,* for instance, or his *Poème sur le désastre de Lisbonne,* or his correspondence, which overflows with pessimistic observations. But the opposite is equally true. If we wish to prove his fundamental optimism, there is no lack of material to do so and to establish him forever among the naïve optimists: the 25th *Lettre philosophique,* the *Mondain,* the *Discours*

en vers, and especially his correspondence overflowing with optimistic observations.

It is notorious, for instance, that Voltaire in the contes is optimistic and pessimistic in turn. *Le Monde comme il va* sets the tone, but the same mixture of optimism-pessimism exists in all of them. What surprises at first is that his histories also disclose both tones: the facts seem to drive towards pessimism, sometimes even to cynicism, but the conclusions he draws from horrible events are rather optimistic. This is particularly manifest in the final chapters of either his *Siècle de Louis XIV* or his *Essai sur les mœurs.* This observation is especially disturbing, because the pessimistic trend of Voltaire's historical studies has always been considered one of the "causes" of *Candide.* Obviously, if the trend is not there, *Candide* loses a "cause."

In some respects, these historical statements might actually impair our understanding of the work, either because of their irrelevance, their generality, or the exaggerated importance we give them. It is conceivable that all these incidents played some part in releasing *Candide* without being in the least important in its inception. Taken together, they could have been episodes in the confection of the work, or even mere examples justifying Voltaire's "position." Though they are certainly parts of a "situation" which offered a frame of reference for his *"plaisanterie,"* their "pre-established harmony" is by no means evident. Further, it is questionable that they would have operated so effectively had there not been some inherent weakness in Voltaire's structural foundations. I shall attempt to analyze this "situation" and seek out this weakness.

The situation comprises two fundamental factors. Leibniz, Pope, and the philosophy of optimism are only a part of a much greater complex which involves the rise of modern science on the one hand and the doctrine of Progress on the other. The latter indeed took its origin in the elation of man over his scientific advance. Fired by his new discoveries, eighteenth-century man came to believe in the unity of knowledge, the utility of truth, the eudaemonic value of science; he was easily persuaded that human institutions are modifiable for man's comfort and enjoyment and that human nature is molded by institutions; he was convinced that knowledge is a source of power and he therefore assumed more and more responsibility for his human lot. Progress, equated as happiness, was possible, but possible only through knowledge, that is to say science.

This conviction, which even in the twentieth century we have not renounced, was perhaps best expressed by D'Alembert in the Preliminary Discourse of the *Encyclopédie:* "It suffices that we should find," wrote D'Alembert, "real advantage in certain knowledge, where at first we had not suspected any, to feel justified in regarding all research springing from pure curiosity, as being useful to us some day. That is the origin and the cause of the progress in the study of that vast science, called in general 'La Physique,' or study of nature which comprises so many different branches."

However, the mere statement that knowledge can be useful and that its constant increase assures progress was not sufficient to the man of the Enlightenment. He had, just like ourselves today, to devise ways of making it useful. This was not an easy task, seeing that there might be much divergence of opinion regarding the concept of utility. There had always been a confusion among the true, the beautiful, and the useful. The difficulty was apparent in one simple question: Is virtue useful? Thus a problem of natural science became at once a problem of morality.

But the science of morality presented also its difficulties. D'Alembert pointed out in the same article that science cannot achieve its end unless we more fully understand ourselves. He concludes, though, that what we call "nous" is a being formed of two principles different in nature, really united; that there is between the movements of the one and the affections of the other a correspondence which we can neither suppress nor change, and which keeps both principles in subjection. This very subjection is proof of the existence of a Higher Power. His existence is proved by our *"sentiment intérieur"* as well as by the *"consentement général,"* as well as by the "évidence de la nature." Thus the problem of morality leads straight to the problem of metaphysics. As D'Alembert concluded: "It is clear that the purely intellectual notions of vice and virtue, the principle and the necessity of laws, the spirituality of the soul, the existence of God and our duties toward Him, in a word the truths which are most readily needed and most indispensable are the fruit of the first ideas occasioned by our sensations." Science, morality, metaphysics, and religion have an inner relationship; or, rather, all are but parts of that all-embracing science we call knowledge.

This, however, was only one side of the picture. The new scientific discoveries produced a "condition" which called into question former beliefs and reactivated former troublesome problems. Scientists showed no intention of wanting to upset religious convictions. There nonetheless arose occasions when the metaphysical assumptions of Christianity were contradicted by the physical facts. It became only too apparent that a readjustment was imperative. But readjustments of this sort are not easily made, since any change in the structure of thought inevitably involves a large number of complementary problems. Comparable to the conflict between the new science and the accepted religious beliefs there was a conflict between the new science and the old metaphysical foundations.

It would perhaps be wise to examine these complementary problems. Two of them—the relationship between natural science and metaphysics and the relationship between natural science and moral science—have already been mentioned, but further amplification is necessary. The basic problem of morality was the problem of psychology. If, as many in the century believed, sensations led to the discovery of facts which in turn led to the formation of complex ideas which subsequently led to the establishment of theories, how could one assure himself that the fact led to the correct idea or the right theory? If our actions are derived from our knowledge, how can we be certain that our knowledge is leading to right action? How can we know, in short, the way a fact may be converted into action? It was this problem that led to the rise of psychology as a science. This psychology was naturally preoccupied with how we think and why we act; thus the relationship between thought and action became paramount.

Various views were expressed concerning this relationship. In 1749 the Academy at Dijon proposed the current and appropriate subject for its competitive essay: "Whether the reestablishment of sciences and the arts have con-

tributed to purifying morals." Although it is quite evident that the Academy expected its candidates to take for granted the accepted relationship among science, thought, and action and was undoubtedly surprised by Rousseau's paradox, the resultant discussion demonstrated how necessary it was to clear up the notion of this relationship. Rousseau's position that the sciences and arts actually might lead and did in fact lead to the corruption of morality was only one way of interpreting this relationship. It was opposed by Formey in a little essay entitled *Examen philosophique de la liaison qu'il y a entre les sciences et les mœurs* (Avignon, 1755), in which he said, "One will find the solution to the dispute of J. J. Rousseau with his adversaries on the question proposed by the Academy of Dijon concerning the good or ill which the sciences have done to morals."

Formey takes the initial position that the sciences have neither helped nor injured morals; in fact, their influence is so slight that it is hardly worth discussing. He insists that the principle of right action is in the heart, which will convert to good or evil all this increase in knowledge. He insists, further, that every man has his "penchant," his "tempérament," his "caractère inné." Science only serves to bring out and to fortify these individual penchants and these personal temperaments. He takes the final position that a science has the same effect upon the state: it serves in confirming national traits just as it confirms personal traits of the individual. "The English, the Italians, the French and the people of the north are tigers, foxes, monkeys, and bears who have received humanizing lessons, so to speak."

Formey nonetheless admits that science penetrates civilization, though slowly, that it may pass from one nation to another, and that a wise ruler, like Peter the Great, may impose it upon a nation and thereby change its civilization. "Sciences, and especially the arts which come after them, undoubtedly change the face of a state . . . but it is not so much by creating new manners and customs as by developing those which already existed in germ, and which only awaited an opportunity to manifest themselves." And he concedes that only in so far as sciences furnish rules of conduct and reasons for observing these rules will they have any direct influence upon morals. Although he maintains that ordinary man will live as he has always lived, despite scientific discoveries, and that scientists despite their discoveries do not improve their character but use their knowledge rather to forge evil weapons, he argues that each science has a moral side which could be utilized for the common good. Since they all lead to God, they should also lead to the formation of those rules which control our actions in a way comformable with our ideas of God. In short, all sciences should lead to morality.

It is thus clear that in Voltaire's time there was a strong tendency to express faith in the power of science and at the same time some doubts as to the workings of that power. A D'Alembert might express a deep confidence in man's knowledge to shape man's world, and the *Encyclopédie* might have as its goal the accumulation of that knowledge for the shaping of that world. An Ange Goudar might actually assert that only in scientific development could a state become powerful. The general public might express a very positive belief in progress through knowledge. There remained nonetheless hesitations and doubts. No one seemed to know how the facts of science could be turned to man's advantage nor how knowledge could be turned to power. There were even those, like Montesquieu, Diderot, and Rousseau, who thought that science—knowledge and civilization—devitalized man, especially his moral qualities; those, like Formey, who felt that knowledge had but little effect upon moral man, although it should have much. Everybody seemed to agree that an intimate relationship existed between science and metaphysics, science and religion, science and morality, and even science and aesthetics, but no one seemed able to define these relationships.

All had the uneasy feeling that the sciences might be leading man astray or that they themselves were declining. Regarding this latter view, Jaucourt's article "Science" in the *Encyclopédie,* though short, is most enlightening. After defining science as "clear and certain knowledge of things, founded either on evident principles or demonstrations"; after dividing science into four branches—intelligence, wisdom, prudence, and art; after noting that the immensity of nature is revealed to us through the sciences and that they have taught humanity its duties, Jaucourt adds rather significantly that they have become so extensive that only a man of letters can really profit from them. And he laments that they are already declining. "Sciences offer to us a beautiful avenue, but it is very short and ends in an arid desert. Among us their high noon is close to their rise, and their setting is not far removed from their high noon."

It is against this background that Voltaire's reaction should be read. It is not my purpose to retrace Voltaire's interests in science. That has already been admirably presented in Miss Libby's *Voltaire's Attitude to Magic and the Sciences* (New York, 1935), where she has sketched in great detail his preoccupations with natural science, particularly in the Cirey period, when he was most active in that field. Indeed, in a summary paragraph (p. 72), she has noted that after 1744

> . . . he abandoned all work of this kind. He even ceased to keep regularly in touch with scientific writings during the last forty years of his life. His scientific comments in this period are written only when some author sends him a complimentary copy of his work, or when he is inspired to attack scientists whose hypotheses conflict with his notion of the way God made the universe. This last indicates another important influence which we have noted as affecting Voltaire's attitude toward science of his time—his religion, that odd combination of skepticism and deism which he preached so ardently from the time of his first acquaintance with Bolingbroke in 1723 until his death. His skepticism made him ever ready to reject *a priori* reasoning and *philosophical systems* and to insist that science could not explain the universe; his deism made him emphasize the elaborate laws which govern the universe as a proof of the existence of a supreme intelligence, Plato's eternal geometer, and to belittle any purely mechanistic theory of the universe.

This composite judgment, though superficially correct, is not an accurate statement of affairs, as I have attempted to show in *Search for a New Voltaire* (Philadelphia, 1958) and *Voltaire's Micromégas* (Princeton, 1950). Voltaire's interests merely expanded; from natural science he turned toward the other sciences: history, morality, metaphysics, even anthropology and ethnography. This was of course

in keeping with his time, since he was inclined to hold with Jaucourt that the fields of science had become so varied that only a man of letters could profit from them. His initial interest, as we have shown, was awakened because he saw them as a source of literary creation; his interest continued because he saw himself as the eighteenth-century humanist, the *Polygraphe,* that is to say the *Philosophe* of his time. And as he expanded his interests, he came to regard science, that is, knowledge, as the power of creation and the source of progress.

The problems attendant upon this attitude, as far as Voltaire and his time are concerned, can be seen in the relationship between his *Traité de métaphysique* and the *Eléments de la philosophie de Newton.* It is important that Voltaire worked on these two books simultaneously and that he ultimately decided to merge the problems discussed in the *Traité* (the existence of God, the immortality of the soul, the nature of matter, free will, and the problem of good and evil) in the first part of the *Eléments,* under the heading "De la métaphysique." He believed that physics has no validity if it is not based on metaphysics and, to judge by the matter discussed in the *Traité,* he entertained the further belief that there could be no sound metaphysics which was not based squarely on the existence of a friendly Providence, room for the operation of a "natural" law, the immutability or at least the perfect equilibrium of nature's laws, and a "reasonable" ethical standard. Everything indicates that Voltaire held in 1734-1741 an organic view of the world of knowledge where God is in His Heaven and all is right with the world.

Then, in 1758, precisely while he was busy with *Candide,* he wrote a letter to the Comte de Tressan in which science is violently demoted:

> February 13, 1758.
>
> You continue then in your liking for physics. It is an amusement for all the stages of life. Have you set up a natural-history collection? If you have begun, you will never end. As for myself, I have given it all up; and here is the reason for it: one day while stirring my fire I began to think why wood made flame; nobody has been able to tell me; and I have found that there is not an experiment in physics comparable to that one. I have planted trees, and I hope to die if I know how they grow. You have been good enough to have children, and you do not know how. A word to the wise is sufficient. I give up being an observer. Besides I do not see much more than charlatanism in it; and except for the discoveries of Newton and two or three others, everything is an absurd system. The story of Gargantua is much better.

Voltaire's letter is a swan song to a movement which had begun under such enthusiastic auspices around 1729, reached a climax with *Micromégas,* and all but disappeared between 1744 and 1758. His objections to science are now both vocal and persistent: it fails to answer the questions about the universe. It leads to the making of systems and not to something useful like the making of a pin. Its discoveries resemble romances rather than scientific truths. Even its outstanding devotees are more concerned with fiction than with truth. It has a tendency to overmechanize the universe, and it refuses steadfastly to recognize its limitations. True it can weigh, measure, calculate, but it cannot penetrate the nature of things. Voltaire condemns it for leading to hypotheses and to the making of a priori systems. As it has been developed, science is in conflict with the notion of a static universe, as well as with the notion of order, wisdom, and the goodness of God.

These opinions, repeated over and over, lead to the suspicion that Voltaire is prepared to reject science for reasons having nothing to do with science. When, for instance, he maintains that science conflicts with the idea of a static universe, he prejudges the case in a way no scientist would permit. When he complains that it does not conform to deism, he is also making an assumption no scientist would consider in his province. Once he wrote that "a false science creates Atheists, while a true science forces man to kneel before Divinity." Such a statement, though laudable, is profoundly unscientific.

He still has very curious ideas concerning the relationships of science and metaphysics, science and religion, science and morality, natural science and history, which give the impression that he is not rejecting science at all, but only deploring that it is not doing its job. He insists still, for instance, that no science is valid if it is not solidly grounded in metaphysics, and by metaphysics, he understands such problems as the existence of God, immortality of the soul, thinking matter, free will, and good and evil. Most essential to any principle of science is the existence of a God who guarantees the static universe. He believes that the discoveries of science will serve to purify religion. In a passage which has a ring almost prophetic, Voltaire writes: "We must absolutely purify religion; all Europe cries forth its need. We began this great task nearly two hundred and fifty years ago; but humanity is enlightened only by slow degrees. Who would ever have suspected then that we would analyze a beam of light, that we would electrify with lightning, and that we would discover universal gravitation, the law which presides over the universe?" In other words, science has the means of purifying religion, of giving what Voltaire calls "the real system"—"the one of a supreme Being who has done everything, and who has given to each element, to each species, to each gender, its form, its place, and the eternal functions." He believes also that science should serve to improve man's lot and laments that the discoveries in physics and the inventions of genius have aided in drenching the earth in blood rather than in cultivating it. He maintains that the errors of physics are as nothing compared to the errors of the social sciences: "If so many errors in physics have blinded whole nations, if we have failed to know for so many centuries the direction of the loadstone, the circulation of the blood, the weight of air, what extraordinary errors have men not committed in government? When it is a question of a law in physics, we examine it today at least with some objectivity. . . . But when it is an affair of government, we have allowed ourselves to be swayed by passions, prejudices, and the need of the moment. They are the three causes for the bad administration which has brought about the misfortune of so many peoples."

This interrelationship of science with the other categories of living is for Voltaire vital. He insists upon keeping a foundation of metaphysics, a foundation of religion, a foundation of politics and morality, a foundation of aesthetics. Science must build upon these firm foundations, since they too are realms of knowledge. It is in this way that man preserves the unity of knowledge, the central no-

tion of the doctrine of progress, just as happiness, intellectual happiness, is its goal. But in each of these categories of living there is also a central point which is, so to speak, the foundation of the category: central to all metaphysical problems is the existence of a good, wise, benevolent God—just as "natural law" is central to the category of morality and "bienfaisance" central to the social. For physics, static laws in a changing universe are quite as essential. Thus a God, and a small body of eternal laws (both natural and moral) are all that man needs to be able to create his happiness. Voltaire's system of intellectual relationships is as complete as Newton's universe; unfortunately, the slightest slip and the whole universe will come toppling over his ears.

That the slip actually took place in 1758 needs no elaboration. After the evidence of the Lisbon earthquake, the horrors of the Seven Years War, and the personal experiences of the author at Potzdam and Frankfort, it did not require an extremely fertile imagination or a very unbalanced intellect or even an overly sensitive personality to see that something must be wrong with nature's laws, something must be awry in natural law and that justice and freedom—human justice and human freedom—which each of us craves for himself even if he does but little to grant them to others, are mere utopian dreams.

It is no wonder that Voltaire thought that science has its limitations, that scientists are charlatans, that scientific theories are *"romans,"* that scientific systems are absurd, that poets like Virgil and Lucretius, although terrible scientists are sublime poets "because of their beautiful descriptions, their healthy morality, their admirable pictures of human life." Voltaire revolted against a science which was not performing its function, against a philosophy which had lost its organic quality, against two philosophers who were responsible for its delusions, against everything which stood in the way of personal creation, even including a false conception of Providence, if not Providence Itself. Was he thinking scientifically, or aesthetically, or morally? But can one make distinctions such as these in life? Probably merely as a man, certainly as an eighteenth-century humanist, most certainly as an artist. Once again, the man of letters asserted his "rights."

It would be interesting to know just how well after the revolt of **Candide** Voltaire succeeded in remedying the weakness in his intellectual armor. Did he find the proper place for science among the categories of living? Did he understand more clearly the relationships among science, morality, metaphysics, religion, and aesthetics? Did he still believe that knowledge is an organic thing and a source of power and creation? Was there an explicit relationship between knowing and doing? The answer to all these troublesome questions is certainly affirmative. It is significant that Voltaire does not renounce science after all, in spite of his letter to Tressan. If one reads carefully the **Dictionnaire philosophique** and the subsequent amplifications like the **Questions sur l'Encyclopédie** or the innumerable so-called **Mélanges,** he will be aware of a greater modesty, a greater prudence, but no less firmness in the beliefs expressed in the **Traité de métaphysique** and the **Eléments de la philosophie de Newton.** Voltaire is less naïve in his claims, less ambitious in his desires, less swayed by details. Perhaps he insists more upon action, any kind of action, whether moral, political, or aesthetic. But he shows no inclination to reject science. He had treated it in the same way he treated Leibnitz, Pope and Optimism, the way he treated everything: with moderate enthusiasm, modified imitation, cautious discussion of points, violent assault, more reasonable acceptance. That is the only way the Human Mind can cultivate its garden. (pp. 287-98)

> *Ira O. Wade, "Voltaire's Quarrel with Science," in* Bucknell Review, *Vol. VIII, No. 4, December, 1959, pp. 287-98.*

Peter Gay (essay date 1959)

[*Gay, a German-born American historian, is recognized as a world authority on the European Enlightenment. Among his writings on this subject are Voltaire's Politics:* The Poet as Realist *(1959),* The Party of Humanity: Essays in the French Enlightenment *(1964),* The Enlightenment: An Interpretation *(2 vols., 1966-69), and* Eighteenth-Century Studies *(1972). He has also written about nineteenth-century European middle-class culture and the art and politics of Imperial and Weimar Germany. In the following excerpt from the first-named work, he discusses the significance of the expression "écraser l'infâme" to Voltaire.*]

Voltaire had many faithful friends, from Genevan Natives to French noblemen, but he was such a witty and tenacious controversialist that he is known less for his friends than for his enemies. As he matured into the Old Invalid of Ferney, a new enemy—or an old enemy with a new name—appeared in his letters: *l'infâme*. Untiringly he urged the brethren to *écraser l'infâme;* he was so intoxicated with the slogan that he repeated it endlessly, sometimes spelling it out, sometimes abbreviating it, sometimes using it as a signature: "Ecr. linf." One of the censors who opened his letters was impressed with the style of that Swiss gentleman, monsieur Ecrlinf: "That M. Ecrlinf doesn't write badly."

Authentic or invented, the anecdote symbolizes the confusion over the meaning of *l'infâme*. After two centuries of debate there remain four distinct interpretations: fanaticism, Catholicism, Christianity, and religion. The writers who restrict *l'infâme* to fanaticism point out that Voltaire never openly left the faith into which he was born and that he occasionally practiced it, that other educated Catholics objected to fanatical and superstitious displays as violations rather than manifestations of true Roman Catholicism, that he treated his Jesuit teachers with respect and affection, and that his violent diatribes against Christianity may be dismissed as the hyperbole of propaganda. Those who enlarge the term to mean Catholicism call attention to his membership in a masonic order which was Christian but anti-Catholic, his statements that Protestantism is greatly preferable to Catholicism, his friendships with Genevan pastors whose philosophical Protestantism resembled his own religious convictions, his obvious admiration for the freedom and toleration of Protestant countries, his contention that deism had grown naturally from the Protestant Reformation. Those who interpret *écrasez l'infâme* as an attack on supernatural religions in general and Christianity in particular cite the vehemence of Voltaire's assault on doctrines shared by Catholics and Protestants, his conviction that all forms of Christianity are the source of fatal infection, his disappointment

in the Genevan clergy, and the famous line in his *Henriade:*

> Je ne décide point entre Genève et Rome,

which they take as a rejection of both. Finally, those who expand *écrasez l'infâme,* into a war against all religion stress his Aesopianism, his need to mask his dangerous opinions, his skepticism which they think is ill-disguised behind a polite deism.

All these interpretations have some plausibility, but I regard the last as too extreme, and the first two as not extreme enough. Voltaire had genuine, deep religious convictions; he was an emotional, even a mystical deist. "A miracle, according to the origin of the word," he wrote without irony, "is an admirable thing. In that case everything is a miracle." And as a young man, he wrote in his notebook in somewhat uncertain English: "We are commonly unconcerned and careless of all things which deserve our search, and our admiration, but for to make amends we admire the most common objects, and the less whorthy of attention of a wise man. How very few are wise enough to admire the daily birth of light and the new creation of all things wich born every day with light; the everlasting regulation of stars, the perpetual miracle of generation, effects of loadstone, of lime burned with water. . . . "

Voltaire's enthusiasm for the Divine Watchmaker, the creator of these miracles of nature, grew more intense with the years. Early one morning in 1774, he asked a Ferney visitor to join him in watching the sun rise. After a strenuous climb the men rested on a hill to survey the magnificent panorama. Voltaire took off his hat, prostrated himself and exclaimed, "I believe, I believe in you!" and again, "Powerful God, I believe!" Then he rose and told his guest drily: "As for monsieur the Son, and madame His Mother, that's a different story."

The implacable enemy of enthusiasts himself an enthusiast—it is an arresting sight. Such demonstrations were rare, but the feelings that inspired them were vivid and lasting. A sense of awe, of man's littleness before the divine greatness, pervades the philosophical works of the 1730's composed under the impact of Newtonianism, the short tales of the 1740's and 1750's, and the polemics of his old age. In Voltaire's universe there must be a supreme being, despite evil, irrationality, and Lisbon earthquakes.

This poetic deism was not a Voltairian invention: it had been preached by French and English freethinkers since the late seventeenth century. When they thought of religion at all, the worldly and debauched associates of Voltaire's youth were deists, and even Christians like Fénelon and skeptics like Fontenelle employed the deist watchmaker argument to prove the existence of God.

Their watchmaker was also Voltaire's, a God of order and love, infinitely removed from the little insects that crawl on this pile of slime, the earth. He was the God who consoled Stendhal's Julien Sorel in prison: "Not the God of the Bible, a petty despot, cruel and filled with a thirst for vengeance . . . but the God of Voltaire, just, good, infinite. . . . " Voltaire often spoke of this God as "commanding" men to love each other, but that was picturesque, anthropomorphic language designed for purposes of propaganda. The real God was beyond ordinary words.

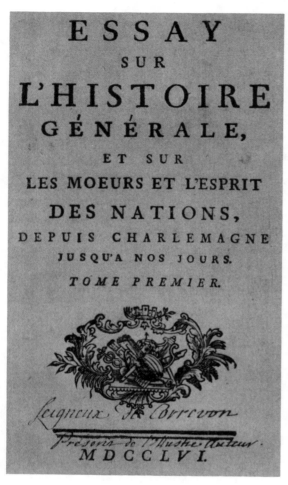

Title page of the first authorized edition of Voltaire's world history.

And yet, the inexactitude of Voltaire's language also betrays a need of his own. Voltaire yearned for a mild rather than a severe father; his opposition to the stern theology of Jansenism and the strict Protestant sects was more than rational opposition, it was hatred. Voltaire's God was like Voltaire's ideal king, kind rather than cruel. In his political as in his religious thought we can sense his longing for the loving rather than the repressive authority.

But whatever the reasons for Voltaire's metaphorical language, its significance for morals is unmistakable: the existence of God imposes upon all men an obligation to recognize their littleness, their impermanence, their brotherhood. This recognition, in turn, imposes the obligation of mutual toleration and mutual love. For Voltaire, toleration is thus as much a religious duty as a political goal; it is an affirmation of what is most human in human nature: "It is clear that every individual who persecutes a man, his brother, because he does not share his opinion, is a monster. . . . We must tolerate each other, for we are all feeble, inconsistent, subject to change and error." This tolerance is the fruit of man's rational insight into his condition, the most sublime teaching of natural religion.

A God who imposes such obligations on mankind and only such obligations is not a metaphysical construct emptied of all content. He is real enough, but he is not a Christian God. Precisely when Voltaire gave up that Christian God, precisely when his anticlericalism became anti-Christianity is impossible to determine: there is no sharp line between these two positions. In the elegant world in which Voltaire moved as a young poet, anticlericalism was fashionable. After the death of Louis XIV, high society celebrated its new freedom with adolescent abandon, and its favorite victims were Christians and Christianity. Aristocrats circulated scandalous irreligious poems and tracts in manuscript. They were afraid to publish them, but equally afraid to be thought pious; piety was for peasants and the bourgeoisie. By 1720, wrote the Cardinal de Bernis in his *Mémoires,* "it was no longer considered well-bred to believe in the gospels."

Voltaire was nothing if not well-bred; his anticlerical sallies of the Regency were acts of conformity rather than of defiance. Still, for many years he disguised his real views—a duc de Richelieu could profess deism more safely than a François-Marie Arouet—and modestly claimed to criticize only those political and emotional excrescences that any rational Catholic had to view with abhorrence. It was not until he was securely established at Ferney that the fashionable anticlerical worldling openly became the implacable anti-Christian crusader.

Privately, Voltaire had ceased to be a Christian many years before. French freethinkers had been the first to plant doubt in his mind. His godfather, the abbé de Châteauneuf, taught him the *Moïsade,* a rationalist poem so daring that it could not even be printed clandestinely; the Jesuits (religious men, no matter what their reputation) further prepared him for apostasy by training him in the pagan classics; the society of the Temple professed a natural religion. The notorious ***Epitre à Uranie,*** probably written late in September 1722, shows how far Voltaire had departed from the faith of his fathers. In this poem he declares war on the "sacred lies that fill the world," and defies a hateful God who created men to be miserable. The true God is the very antithesis of the God that the Christians worship:

> On te fait un tyran, en toi je cherche un Père.
> Je ne suis pas Chrétien, mais c'est pour t'aimer mieux.

Before he was thirty, then, he could confess that he was not a Christian that he might love God better. His visit to England and his years at Cirey provided him with new ammunition against Christianity: he read the critical deists Tindal and Woolston, and with madame du Châtelet he studied the Bible verse by verse and steeped himself in Biblical exegesis. At Potsdam he worked out the tactics for the inevitable conflict: he drafted the first articles of the ***Dictionnaire philosophique*** and discussed them with the King of Prussia. But only after he was old, rich, famous, and safe was he ready to *écraser l'infâme.* He conducted petty skirmishes against the clergy of the neighborhood, major battles against Catholic fanaticism in the cases of Calas and de La Barre, and an unceasing war against Christianity in general in a torrent of anti-Christian pamphlets.

His declaration of war was the ***Sermon des cinquante,*** published in 1762 but written ten years before at Potsdam. it is a scandalous work—it reads as if it had been written to *épater le roi,* to surpass in vehemence the royal cynic of Prussia. It is also a revealing work—in a few pages it sums up Voltaire's campaign against *l'infâme:* the Bible is the most improbable and contradictory of books; the Pentateuch, ostensibly the work of Moses, reports Moses' death; the miracles reported in it are oriental folk tales; transubstantiation is nonsense. But the Bible is reliable in one respect: it accurately records the moral ideals and practices of the Jews, and those ideals and practices are both horrible. The God of the Jews is vain and selfish, his chosen people is cruel, mendacious, and debauched. Away with such a God, away with such "infamous mysteries!" The true God is not the God of the Christians, he is the loving father of all men. "May this great God who is listening to me, this God who can surely neither be born of a virgin, nor die on the gallows, nor be eaten in a piece of dough, nor have inspired these books filled with contradictions, madness, and horror—may this God, creator of all the worlds, have pity on this sect of Christians who blaspheme him!" No wonder Voltaire attributed this pamphlet to La Mettrie! No wonder he was appalled when Rousseau pointed the finger at him, the innocent invalid of Ferney!

This was the message of *écrasez l'infâme;* it never changed. But since it challenged convictions that men held most tenaciously, Voltaire reiterated his message innumerable times. He understood, better than most writers, that men cannot be persuaded when they are bored, so he reiterated it with different jokes, different dialogues, different demonstrations. The lesson, however, never varied: "Every sensible man, every honorable man, must hold the Christian sect in horror."

To help men hold the Christian sect in horror, he adopted many stratagems. After the **Sermon des cinquante,** which presumably had been written by a materialist, he published the powerful **Extrait des sentiments de Jean Meslier** (1762), which summarized the last will of a parish priest who had died in 1729 and had repented of his Christian vocation on his deathbed. After the **Extrait,** he appeared as a good Catholic in **Traité sur la tolérance** (1763), movingly and moderately pleading for Christian toleration. After the **Traité,** he brought out the **Dictionnaire philosophique** (1764), ostensibly written by many hands. He never tired: in 1767 there appeared the **Examen important de Milord Bolingbroke,** which used Voltaire's work on the Bible of the Cirey years in denouncing Jesus as a Jewish fanatic. A few years later came the **Questions sur l'Encyclopédie** (1770-1772), a larger and even more virulent Philosophic Dictionary. And finally, in Voltaire's eighty-second year, he published **La Bible enfin expliquée** (1776), a long and tendentious exegesis, summarizing decades of research and spleen, and rounding out, with its nice title, the fight against *l'infâme.*

In his eulogy, Frederick the Great said that Voltaire was worth a whole academy. But in his fight against *l'infâme,* Voltaire's versatility appeared in his wit rather than his arguments, which never departed far from the **Sermon des cinquante,** his opening salvo: the theology of the Bible is a nonsensical, indeed a diabolical, invention; the morality preached by the Bible is abhorrent.

Modern Biblical criticism makes Voltaire's arguments appear quaint and largely of historical interest. But the wit remains as fresh and as impudent as ever. Consider **Relation du bannissement des Jésuites de la Chine,** in which

a Jesuit tries to explain the Christian mysteries to the Emperor of China:

> Frère Rigolet: 'Our God was born in a stable, seventeen hundred and twenty-three years ago, between an ox and an ass. . . . [his mother] was not a woman, she was a girl. It is true that she was married, and that she had two other children, named James as the old gospels say, but she was a virgin none the less.'
>
> The Emperor: 'What! She was a virgin, and she had children!'
>
> Frère Rigolet: 'To be sure. That is the nub of the story: it was God who gave this girl a child.'
>
> The Emperor: 'I don't understand you. You have just told me that she was the mother of God. So God slept with his mother in order to be born of her?'
>
> Frère Rigolet: 'You've got it, Your Sacred Majesty; grace was already in operation. You've got it, I say; God changed himself into a pigeon to give a child to a carpenter's wife, and that child was God himself.'
>
> The Emperor: 'But then we have two Gods to take into account: a carpenter and a pigeon.'
>
> Frère Rigolet: 'Without doubt, Sire; but there is also a third, who is the father of these two, and whom we always paint with a majestic beard: it was this God who ordered the pigeon to give a child to the carpenter's wife, from whom the God-carpenter was born; but at bottom these three make only one. The father had engendered the son before he was in the world, the son was then engendered by the pigeon, and the pigeon proceeds from the father and the son. Now you see that the pigeon who proceeds, the carpenter who is born of the pigeon, and the father who has engendered the son of the pigeon, can only be a single God; and that a man who doesn't believe this story should be burned in this world and in the other.'
>
> The Emperor: 'That is as clear as day.'

That was the blasphemous and playful Voltaire. When he came to the morality of God's Chosen People, his playfulness acquired a different edge: "If the style of the Books of the Kings and of Chronicles is divine, it may yet be that the actions reported in these histories are not divine. David assassinates Uriah; Ishbosheth and Mephibosheth are assassinated; Absalom assassinates Amnon; Joab assassinates Absalom; Solomon assassinates Adonijah, his brother; Baasha assassinates Nadab; Zimri assassinates Elah; Omri assassinates Zimri; Ahab assassinates Naboth, Jehu assassinates Ahab and Joram; the inhabitants of Jerusalem assassinate Amaziah, son of Joash; Shallum, son of Jabesh, assassinates Zachariah, son of Jeroboam; Menahem assassinates Shallum, son of Jabesh; Pekah, son of Remaliah, assassinates Pekahiah, son of Menahem; Hoshea, son of Elah, assassinates Pekah, son of Remaliah. One passes over in silence many other minor assassinations. I must admit that if the Holy Ghost wrote this history, he did not choose a very edifying subject."

These two quotations from Voltaire's most active and most optimistic period, the mid-1760's, indicate the strength and the limitations of *écrasez l'infâme.* It was a brilliant and a witty campaign; it was erudite, drawing on a close reading of the Bible and Christian exegesis; it used all of Voltaire's formidable stylistic resources. But it was also cruel and unfair. For all the truth embodied in the slogan, it was a propagandist's half-truth, silent on the civilizing labors of the Christian tradition, silent on the benign behavior of ecclesiastics through the ages, silent on the advancement of learning under the auspices of Christian schools and universities. But that did not matter to Voltaire. *Ecrasez l'infâme* was a good battle cry, and a good cry, says the Statue in Shaw's *Man and Superman,* is half the battle.

Voltaire knew that it was a good cry, and in the 1760's he uttered it again and again in his correspondence with the most reliable of the philosophes: "I finish all my letters by saying *Ecr. l'inf . . .*" he wrote to Damilaville on 26 July 1762, "as Cato always said, 'It is my opinion that Carthage must be destroyed.'" There were times, especially in his last years, when he had doubts that Carthage could in fact be destroyed. As he wrote desparingly on 12 May 1776, "that which is founded on a great deal of money and a great deal of preferment is founded on a rock." But whether he was optimistic or pessimistic, he knew, and his friends knew, what he meant when he urged them to help him *écraser l'infâme:* extirpate Christianity.

But why extirpate Christianity? Why this brutal ridicule of what was most holy to most Europeans? Much of Voltaire's vehemence was an expression of rage—rage against a religion that preached a cruel God and against its lieutenants, "priests, whom I have hated, hate, and I shall hate till doomsday," executioners in the service of their divine tyrant. Rational debate, Voltaire intimated, was impossible with the Christian: "What shall we put in its place, you ask. What! a ferocious animal has sucked the blood of my kindred; I tell you to get rid of that beast, and you ask me what shall we put in its place!" His rage against fanaticism was fanatic in its intensity: on 24 August of every year, the anniversary of Saint Bartholomew's Day, he ran a fever.

That fever and these words are not the language of detached analysis; they speak of frustration, of fury against harsh authority. Voltaire's intense concern with that authority can be gauged by his preoccupation with Pascal. All his life he tried to discredit the "sublime misanthrope," to teach mankind that Pascal's teachings about the terrible God and hateful humanity were wrong. But he would not have pursued this feverish debate with Pascal if he had not harbored the fear that Pascal might, after all, be right. "Pascal," J.-R. Carré tells us, "is in Voltaire"; he represented a part of Voltaire that Voltaire sought to escape and to repudiate. To win a victory over Pascal's theology was, for Voltaire, to win a victory over his own anxieties and depressions.

But this explains only part of Voltaire's vehemence against *l'infâme.* Voltaire belonged to an intellectual and polemical movement that thought it necessary to deride Christianity in the harshest terms. As a constructive deist, Voltaire preached a natural religion "as old as creation," uniform in all ages and for all men, in language that was rational, moderate, and sometimes lyrical. As a critical deist, adapting the audacious blasphemies of English deists to French conditions, Voltaire treated Christianity as the enemy of true religion.

For Voltaire, Christianity was dangerous because it was the source of a malignant disorder. Even at its most reasonable, Christianity inculcates superstitions, and superstitions are the germs that cause the religious disease. In its mild form, this disease is enthusiasm; in its virulent form, it is fanaticism, "the rage of the soul," which almost inevitably leads to murder. Voltaire warned that while some superstitions appeared merely picturesque and hence harmless, all were sources of infection. He conceded that the naturalistic pagan cults of antiquity had preached sound morality and rarely indulged in persecution; he conceded, too, that Protestantism had claimed far fewer victims than Catholicism. But even a little superstition is a dangerous thing, and Voltaire's definition of superstition included all existing organized religions: "Almost everything that goes beyond the adoration of a supreme being and of submitting one's heart to his eternal orders is superstition." Crosses, relics, rosaries vulgarize true religion and substitute superstitious sickness for religious health: "The emblems of the divinity were one of the first sources of superstition. Once we made God in our image, the divine cult was perverted."

The most striking symptom of the religious malady is a sense of certainty, doctrinaire yet uneasy. Voltaire did not make the mistake of dismissing fanatics as hypocrites: their danger lay precisely in their sincerity. The fanatic is sure that he knows what in fact he does not know, cannot know, and does not need to know. But his certainty—and this is what makes it so vicious—masks a disturbing sense of uncertainty. The more men are torn with doubts, the more assertive they become; the more ignorant men are, the more reluctant they are to confess their ignorance: "If you were fully persuaded you would not be intolerant. You are intolerant only because deep in your heart you feel that you are being deceived." Anticipating Nietzsche by over a century, Voltaire saw that cruelty is a symptom of weakness rather than strength: "Only the weak commit crimes. The strong and happy man has no need to be evil." The fanatic hides sickness behind assumed toughness; he seethes with resentment.

Since superstition is the direct cause of fanaticism, the only way to blunt the force of the latter is to reduce the influence of the former: "The fewer superstitions, the less fanaticism; and the less fanaticism, the fewer calamities." Voltaire had little expectation that the endemic disease of superstition could be eradicated, but he hoped that it could be gradually brought under control. Superstition is the antiphilosophic disease, and "the philosophic spirit, which is nothing but reason, has become the only antidote against these epidemics." He emphasized that it was the *only* antidote: religion does not soothe the fanatic, since in his diseased condition he transforms its pacific teachings into fuel for further cruelties; the laws are equally helpless, since the fanatic's insane fantasies are his only law. Hence, the statesman who is dedicated to rooting out fanaticism must first root out superstition, and the only way to do this is to spread the message of the philosophes, a message that is not another dogma but the negation of all dogma. In a phrase, *écrasez l'infâme.*

When Voltaire shifts from psychological analysis to political polemics his tone also shifts, and his diagnosis turns into an indictment. History, he tells his readers, is one long demonstration of the crimes caused by superstition.

It was Christian fanaticism that guided the hand of Damiens, the would-be assassin of Louis XV, of Ravaillac, the assassin of Henri IV, and of countless other regicides. It was Christian fanaticism that directly inspired the horrors of Saint Bartholomew's Day, the murder of Servetus by Calvin, the judicial assassination of untold thousands of innocents labeled heretics, witches, and blasphemers. The humane teachings of Jesus have been redefined, perverted, ignored by the infamous church that claims to speak in his name. The pacific truths of the New Testament have been buried under a mountain of subtle distinctions, absurd tales of miracles, indecent grasping for wealth, power, and comfort, and murder upon murder committed for the sake of the victim's soul: "When the Mohammedans kill a sheep, they say, 'I kill you in the name of God.' True motto of religious wars." In a savage article on "Massacres," Voltaire drew up a balance sheet purporting to show the total number of victims of Christianity. His estimate—a conservative estimate, he said—was 9,718,800.

It was ironic, Voltaire suggested, that these victims had lost their lives over theological conundrums which neither they nor their butchers understood. Take the Trinity:

> Here is an incomprehensible question which for over sixteen hundred years has exercised curiosity, sophistical subtlety, bitterness, the spirit of cabal, the rage to dominate, the rage to persecute, blind and bloodthirsty fanaticism, barbaric credulity, and which has produced more horrors than the ambition of princes, which indeed has produced enough. Is Jesus Word? If he is Word, did he emanate from God, is he coeternal and consubstantial with him, or is he of a similar substance? Is he distinct from him, or not? Is he created or engendered? Can he engender in turn? Has he paternity, or productive virtue without paternity? Is the holy ghost created or engendered, or produced? Does he proceed from the father, or from the son, or from both? Can he engender, can he produce? Is his hypostasis consubstantial with the hypostasis of the Father and the son? and why, having precisely the same nature, the same essence as the father and the son, can he not do the same things as these two persons who are himself? I certainly do not understand any of this; nobody has ever understood any of this, and this is the reason for which people have slaughtered one another.

For all its psychological and historical penetration, this indictment is better propaganda than psychology or history. In eighteenth-century Europe, *l'infâme* was far from infamous, and, as Voltaire himself acknowledged, its history did not lack grandeur. He knew, even if he was not willing to concede, that enthusiasm had fostered charitable as well as cruel actions, that supernatural theology had fostered scholarship as well as war. But while Voltaire could introduce some objectivity in his histories, he was not objective in his polemics. Evidently he believed that propaganda cannot be effective without oversimplification, without distortion.

There has been much debate over whether Voltaire's attack on *l'infâme* was "good" or "bad," a debate that is unsolvable and irrelevant. The attack was inevitable. The struggle between the philosophes and the orthodox was not a simple struggle between light and darkness, as the liberals tell us, or between impiety and true religion, as the conservatives tell us. The philosophes had no monopoly on wisdom or impudence; the orthodox had no monopoly on charity or ignorance. The two parties represented two world views. Educated clergymen could make concessions to new ideas; they could express urbane reservations about the foundations of their faith; they could support scientific inquiry. But the philosophes were in no mood, and indeed in no position, to compromise with Christianity. They could infiltrate the bureaucracy, the administration, the parlements, the aristocracy, the bourgeoisie, and even the clergy itself, but by definition Christians could not be expected to espouse the secular ideals of naturalistic morality. Jesuits could attenuate the Christian view of man's fall from grace, they could substitute attrition for contrition, but they could never admit that man was without sin. "The church could forgive much," writes R.R. Palmer [in *Catholics and Unbelievers in Eighteenth-Century France*], "it could absolve from sin and countenance much latitude in thinking; but it could not forgive those who denied its ability to remove sin, or its right to propound the dogmas by which thinking should be governed. It could not tolerate those who questioned its authority." And to question its authority was precisely what the philosophes did and had to do; accommodation was impossible and war was inevitable.

Voltaire, after all, was not the only soldier in the army of modernity. He was merely the wittiest. His diagnosis of enthusiasm as a mental disease was familiar to most educated men in eighteenth-century Europe. "Above all, monsieur," wrote Lord Chesterfield to him after reading the *Siècle de Louis XIV* four times, "I am grateful to you for the light in which you place the lunacy and frenzy of the sects! You employ the proper weapons against these madmen or impostors; to employ others against them would be to imitate them: it is with ridicule that they must be attacked, it is with contempt that they must be punished."

Ridicule and contempt were not new weapons in the eighteenth century. A hundred years before Voltaire, Robert Burton advanced a remarkably modern diagnosis of religious emotionalism. In his *Anatomy of Melancholy*, first published in 1621, he both mocks and pities Puritan enthusiasm: the emotional displays of the sectaries are symptoms of a desire for notoriety or of "lamentable and tragical" illness. Politicians and priests ruthlessly exploit this "religious melancholy" by playing upon fear, pride, stupidity, jealousy, frustration, despair, and guilt: "What else can superstition, heresy produce, but wars, tumults, uproars, torture of souls, and despair . . . ?" The cure is partly medical, partly philosophical: "To purge the world of idolatry and superstition will require some monster-taming Hercules, a divine Aesculapius. . . . " And to purge individuals of melancholy will require self-control and creative activity: "Be not solitary, be not idle." The resemblance of Burton's teachings to Voltaire's is startling: did not Voltaire dream of being a Hercules-Aesculapius? Did he not flee despair through society and good works?

Burton's sane humanism was echoed by other English writers. Sir Thomas Browne, in the midst of the civil war, pilloried religious excesses in his *Pseudodoxia Epidemica;* in 1655, while the Puritans were at the height of their power, Meric Casaubon published a searching *Treatise*

Concerning Enthusiasm which suggested that religious excitement was "an effect of nature . . . mistaken by many for either Divine Inspiration, or Diabolicall Possession." The Cambridge Platonists, in search of a piety that rational men could accept, carefully distinguished true religion from enthusiasm. "I oppose not rational to spiritual," wrote Benjamin Whichcote, "for spiritual is most rational: But I contradistinguish rational to conceited, impotent, affected CANTING."

The decline of the Puritans after the Restoration made this condescending diagnosis more popular. In *Hudibras,* which Voltaire read, Samuel Butler crudely satirized Puritan worship; Dryden derided the "true old enthusiastic breed" in *Absalom and Achitophel;* Sir William Temple, Swift's friend and protector, lamented that Casaubon had died before he could finish his investigations into "the hidden or mistaken sources of that delusion," enthusiasm; Swift himself traced the hidden or mistaken sources of that delusion to physical and psychological disorders, especially sexual frustration. These literary and scientific studies of the religious disease were easily absorbed into the urbane theology of eighteenth-century Anglicanism, and into the empiricist epistemology of the philosophers. Bishop Hoadly ridiculed religious fervor; John Locke devoted a chapter to it in his *Essay Concerning Human Understanding.* Enthusiasm, he wrote, "takes away both Reason and Revelation, and substitutes in the room of it the ungrounded Fancies of a Man's own Brain. . . ."

Sophisticated students of ungrounded fancies, from Burton to Locke, had all England as their laboratory, the sectaries as their most rewarding specimens. French scholars had to be content with somewhat rarer outbreaks of religious hysteria: in the early seventeenth century, the celebrated case of the curé of Loudun, Urbain Grandier, who was burned in 1634 for introducing diabolical possession among a convent of Ursuline nuns; in the late seventeenth century, the Quietist movement led by Madame Guyon; in the early eighteenth century, the Jansenist convulsionaries at the cemetery of Saint-Médard. With increasing boldness, skeptics like François de La Mothe le Vayer and epicureans like Pierre Gassendi questioned miracles, and physicians like Gabriel Naudé ridiculed widely accepted tales of possession: Naudé called the nuns of Loudun victims of "Hysteromanie or rather Erotomanie." Half a century later, freethinkers like Fontenelle and Bayle treated religious frenzy as a species of madness, and dramatists like Molière savagely satirized the *dévots* not so much for their hypocrisy as for their genuine ardor. Chaulieu, Voltaire's mentor in the Temple, attributed belief in the God of Christianity to fears inculcated in childhood, while Formont, Voltaire's urbane friend, warned that the convulsionaries must be treated as sincere.

Hence, in treating most expressions of religious conviction as examples of psychopathology, Voltaire was not an innovator; he was working in a well-developed and widely accepted tradition. Indeed, he stands in the middle of the tradition rather than at its beginning. Many of his predecessors, like Locke and Swift, had written against enthusiasm because they sought to purify Christianity of the flaws of excess; Voltaire wrote against enthusiasm because he sought to purify religion of Christianity. He told Boswell that he was a man rather than a Christian. Despite their great divergences of opinion, therefore, Voltaire's

closest ally was not Locke but Hume. In words that Voltaire could have written, Hume argued that enthusiasm sprang from "hope, pride, presumption, a warm imagination"; and in a significant metaphor that is echoed in Voltaire's writings, Hume concluded: "Examine the religious principles, which have, in fact, prevailed in the world. You will scarcely be persuaded, that they are any thing but sick men's dreams. . . . "

David Hume detested these dreams with the intensity of an ex-Presbyterian who was made to suffer through interminable sermons every Sunday of his early life. But his intensity is mild compared to Voltaire's crusading ardor. "When all Christians will have cut each others' throats; when they will have devoured the entrails of their brothers assassinated for arguments; when only a single Christian remains on the earth, he will look at the sun and recognize and adore the Eternal Being; he will be able to say in his suffering: 'My fathers and my brothers were monsters, but God is God.' " And this was the God for whose sake Voltaire wanted to *écraser l'infâme,* the God in whose defense he insisted on the extirpation of Christianity. (pp. 239-58)

Peter Gay, in his Voltaire's Politics: The Poet as Realist, *1959. Reprint by Yale University Press, 1988, 417 p.*

William F. Bottiglia (essay date 1968)

[*Bottiglia is an American academic who has written extensively on Voltaire and his times. In the following 1968 abridgment of a chapter in his* Voltaire's "Candide": Analysis of a Classic *(2d ed., 1964), he explores* Candide *as "a literary masterpiece risen out of time to timelessness."*]

Internal Analysis

A close analysis of the Conclusion of *Candide* will yield internal evidence which historians of ideas are prone to dismiss as beneath serious attention; but literary critics will accept it as objectively valid and will recognize in it the voice of Voltaire addressing his readers with authoritative immediacy. Once this analysis has been made, its results will be checked against, and correlated with, external considerations; and those results will be seen to shed light on the author's life and on his other writings. If the background of *Candide* helps illuminate its meaning, *Candide,* in turn, helps elucidate its historical context. This reciprocal relationship between art and history is a reality that needs to be constantly re-emphasized. *Candide* is not a mere passive product of "heredity, environment, and momentum." As a great literary statement, it has an agency of its own: it contributes to the making of history. More than this, as a work of art instinct with enduring values, it reflects and reveals the essential Voltaire in ways impossible to his humbler media of expression, such as his correspondence.

Since the Conclusion *is* a conclusion, and since the point at issue is one of meaning, it seems wise to begin by showing how the progression of ideas in the tale as a whole leads inevitably to the final climax. *Candide ou l'Optimisme* contains more—much more—than the promise of its subtitle. Voltaire is not on exhibition here as a systematic philosopher. He does not dialectically anatomize a doctrine and throw it piecemeal to the dogs as lacking in logical coherence or in correspondence to reality. He displays himself as a theatrically self-aware artist, skillfully co-ordinating an atmosphere of clear ideas into a philosophic attitude charged with social dynamism. His central problem is that of human conduct in relation to the somber mystery of physical and social evil. His drive toward a solution of that problem develops as an assault on the vulnerable aspects of senescent classicism—its intellectual and its sentimental infirmities. But the assault alone, although it pervades the work from beginning to end, does not solve the problem. By routing the enemy and clearing the ground, it implies and prepares a positive solution. Meanwhile many hints are dropped along the way, prefiguring such a solution. Thus the great melioristic finale effectively concludes the tale by converging everything which has gone before into an epigrammatic statement of Voltaire's answer to the basic problem.

The intellectual presentation of physical evil in *Candide* includes natural disasters utterly beyond human control (e.g., tempest, earthquake), social calamities which outrun human responsibility (e.g., syphilis, plague), and misfortunes visited indiscriminately upon the good and the wicked (e.g., death of Jacques, naval battle)—all correlated with the view that the individual is helpless because completely predetermined by general laws. Throughout the tale there are repeated assertions that these workings of a "diabolical" principle mock the pursuit of happiness with miseries so numerous and so universal as to appear the normal lot of mankind, and so afflictive as to make one wonder at the tenacity of the will to live. Identical assertions are made with even greater frequency in the intellectual presentation of social evil, which occupies most of *Candide* with its grim catalogue of human ills rendered all the more execrable by their origin in human ignorance, weakness, and malice. A complete enumeration of these would rival the tale itself in length, and would show that Voltaire ranges with astonishing comprehensiveness through time and space as he satirizes man-made evils in their manifold appearances—metaphysical, theological, ecclesiastical, political, social, economic, and cultural.

Brilliantly interwoven with the intellectual presentation of physical and social evil is the complementary assault on the sentimental foibles of the age—an aspect of *Candide* either ignored or understressed by most critics. This takes the form of fictional parody, which saturates the work with ironic imitations of heroic, pastoral, picaresque, and utopian adventure-romances; also, by natural extension, of idealized travel-accounts. Numerous narrative devices, most of the character-types, many of the settings, and frequent turns of phrase are combined in this deliberate mimicry, which the author makes all the more amusing with occasional sly comments uttered through his personages. In mocking the sentimental ideals of his period, Voltaire powerfully rounds out his treatment of physical and social evil, for he is thereby enabled not only to enlarge the area of his illustrations but also to re-emphasize ironically the helplessness of the individual, driven as if fortuitously by the necessary specific effects of the general, immutable, unhuman laws of nature.

The bulk of *Candide* is an attack, in accordance with Voltaire's conception of "true *philosophes*" as "decent persons who have no fixed principles on the nature of things, who do not know what is, but who know very well what

isn't. . . . " Yet the affirmation at the end is not thrust upon the reader suddenly, without preparation. To repeat, the attack itself is a preparation, in that it routs the enemy and clears the ground, thus implying a positive solution by elimination of its opposite. In addition, there are affirmative hints pointing in the same direction: two invincible biological drives, the will to live and the desire for food; the value of experience as a corrective for naïveté and as a means to practical wisdom; instinctive goodness, "conscience," and its normal civilized product, social goodness or "beneficence"; the benefits of culture, such as freedom of expression, good theater, good literature, good taste. And above and beyond all this, far-distant and half-lost in a luminous haze, the dream of Eldorado.

The final chapter of *Candide* funnels these many elements into an epigrammatic conclusion which summarizes and unifies the tale by answering the central problem. This answer, in keeping with the entire presentation, is not the scheme of a systematic philosopher, but the terse melioristic affirmation of a profound practical moralist doubled by a great literary artist.

Physical evil disturbs Voltaire for two reasons: (1) it calls into question the nature and purposes of a Creator whose general laws cause so much specific wretchedness for His predetermined creatures; (2) it gives rise to speculation which romances about the unknown as though it were the known, with disastrous effects on the moral motivation of mankind. The answer given by Voltaire through the dervish is no attempt to solve the insoluble. It is the resort of a pragmatist concerned with preserving the moral initiative. Physical evil is declared to be ultimately unknowable, and men are exhorted to resign themselves to that which they can never know, hence never control.

Social evil, on the other hand, is knowable and to some extent controllable. Much of what men have constructed in ignorance, weakness, and malice can be torn down and replaced by those who are willing to work for the betterment of the human family. To the entrenched ruthlessness of man-made evil the champions of social goodness must oppose disingenuous tactics which spring from the will to live combined with a sense of practical necessities. Thus, like the old Turk and Candide, they will turn their backs on public abominations in a gesture of philosophic disdain. They will assemble in small, like-minded groups safely removed from the centers of corruption. As members of model societies, they will work concretely, each at his appointed task, and with a minimum of windy theorizing, toward the diminution of social evil and the spread of social virtue. Already, in this way, men can enjoy the pleasures of good dinners seasoned with good conversation, as well as the precious benefits of culture. They can also legitimately envision an ideal State which, though beyond complete realization, may at least be more or less approached through co-operative work, through practical action—through the weeding and the cultivation of the garden and the sale of its produce in the market of the world.

The progression of ideas just outlined is significantly punctuated by a series of symbolic gardens, or ways of life, culminating in the three which rapidly succeed one another at the very end:

1   the Westphalian "terrestrial Paradise,"

2   the kingdom of the Bulgares,
3   Protestant Holland,
4   Catholic Lisbon,
5   the Jesuit "vineyard" of Paraguay,
6   the primitive society of the Oreillons,
7   the model society of Eldorado,
8   Paris, the social and cultural hub of civiliza-
     tion,
9   Pococurante's ornamental garden,
10   Cacambo's accursed, backbreaking garden,
11   the modest garden of the old Turk,
12   Candide's garden, cultivated by a small model
     society.

Most of these are, of course, false Edens. Westphalia is the center of optimistic fatalism, sentimental quixotism, and petty aristocratic tyranny. The kingdom of the Bulgares is a naked military despotism, while Paraguay is a military despotism masquerading as a kingdom of God on earth. Holland is a mercantile utopia where "all are rich" and Christian charity is practised—with discrimination. Lisbon is the home of Inquisitorial fanaticism, with its attendant superstition and corruption. The country of the Oreillons is the habitat of state-of-nature savagery. The eighth garden symbolizes the tedium and the moral depravity of rootless and fruitless urban sophistication; the ninth, the sterile artificiality of blasé indolence; the tenth, the depression which accompanies work unillumined by a social purpose. Of the remaining three, Eldorado is negative in the sense that it is a myth, perfect and unreal; but it is also positive in the sense that it offers a philosophic ideal for human aspiration. Eldorado is the standard of perfection toward which the eleventh and twelfth gardens are dynamically directed. The old Turk's garden is a concrete example, however modest, of mankind advancing along the lines indicated above. Already less modest because involving a larger group than a family circle, and big with promise, is Candide's garden—a co-operative model society working ever so gradually, but with practical assurance, for the betterment of civilization.

The first and last gardens are specially related to each other by a common Biblical reference. The opening episode to some extent parodies the story of the Fall, with Candide, originally in a state of innocence, succumbing to temptation at the hands of a woman, and being expelled from the "terrestrial Paradise" by a very Teutonic Jehovah. In the final chapter the reader is reminded of the same story of Pangloss's quotation from the Vulgate. Before the Fall man was placed in the garden to dress it and to keep it. After the Fall he was condemned to work as a punishment. But the conclusion of *Candide* looks upon work as man's most wholesome activity . . . ; hence the ironical aptness of Pangloss's quotation, which seems to ignore the malediction of God following "man's first disobedience."

Before we look more closely at other key details of the finale, a few general observations are in order. In *Candide* the letter alone kills. Undeniably, the genre of the philosophic tale by its very nature invites interpretation that goes far beyond the naïve and unimaginative oversimplifications of Fundamentalist criticism. It is not quite true, however, to say that the literal invariably serves as nothing more than a pretext for the symbolical. If the symbolical rightly understood is always true in *Candide,* the literal may also contain a measure of truth; but due allowance must be made for overstatement, duplicity, inversion, etc. Another, and related, point involves the negative empha-

sis which pervades the tale, and concerning which [George R. Havens correctly says in the introduction to his 1934 edition of *Candide, ou l'Optimisme*]: "Of course **Candide** is intentionally one-sided. No carefully balanced account of good and evil could shock mankind into revolt." In other words, the tale is a deliberately exaggerated polemic, which sets an example by protesting vigorously against current evils, so that its negations imply corresponding affirmations. A third point, related to the second, is that there are a number of direct affirmations strewn through **Candide,** and that these are not swept away by the Conclusion, but gathered up into it. The tale does not recklessly destroy the good along with the bad. It is an exemplary exercise in creative, or constructive, criticism. A final point, connected with the third, is that **Candide,** as [Jean Sareil correctly stresses in his 1961 *Romanic Review* essay "De *Zadig* à *Candide*"], is a *comic* work with a *happy* ending.

Now for those other key details of the finale. That the message conveyed by the dervish contains a certain degree of overstatement should be obvious. It is necessary to distinguish between what he literally says and what the author soberly means. Thus "be silent" appears to enjoin silence about ultimates, but actually would prohibit speculation on final problems only when it becomes a waste of time or is taken seriously enough to be exploited by power-hungry opportunists, to threaten moral initiative, to warp or obstruct social productivity. Earlier in the tale it was established that such discussion is permissible for purposes of intellectual stimulation and mutual consolation: "Candide continued his conversations with Martin. They argued unceasingly for two weeks, and at the end of two weeks they were as far advanced as on the first day. But after all they were expressing themselves, they were communicating ideas to one another, they were consoling one another" (Chapter XX). The dervish also prescribes resignation to physical evil on the ground that it can be neither known nor controlled. "His Highness" has instituted a certain general order and given men a certain basic equipment. The rest, it is implied, is strictly up to them. Let them carve out for themselves whatever destiny remains possible within these limits. Those critics who insist that there is an effect of contraction or shrinkage at the end of **Candide** are obviously right, since Voltaire makes it clear through the dervish that all ultimates, including physical evil, are fated to remain forever beyond human reach. The author is so utterly convinced of this that he presents his dervish accordingly, self-assured to a point of being impatient and even curt with those who think otherwise.

The role of Martin has often been misconstrued because of a critical failure to catch some of Voltaire's finer distinctions. The Manichaean's arrival on the scene is strategically timed to symbolize Candide's drift toward pessimism in Chapter XIX. He serves as a devil's advocate, arguing consistently that all is for the worst and that man is powerless to change the situation. Now, the fact that Voltaire is attacking optimism does not mean that he is embracing its opposite. If he rejects optimism, he does so not only on the ground of its metaphysical bluff but also on account of its "devitalizing agency," its discouraging fatalism. It is true that he treats Martin much more sympathetically than Pangloss, partly for polemical reasons, partly because the former's philosophy does less violence to the facts of life. But his handling of Martin in Chapter XXX shows plainly that pessimism does not triumph at the end. The author himself refers to Martin's principles as "detestable"—a valuation completely ignored by all critics who favor a pessimistic interpretation of the Conclusion. What is more, when Martin states that man was born to live "in the convulsions of anxiety, or in the lethargy of boredom," Candide *disagrees,* although he is not yet ready to voice a positive opinion of his own. Later, in the ripeness of time, it is Candide who makes the great affirmation, while Martin, like Pangloss, merely falls into line with an echoing judgment. Thus the pessimist and the optimist lose their respective identities to merge with their former disciple, now suddenly matured into the meliorist. In sum, Voltaire carefully shuns *both* extremes. Indeed, if, after his sustained assault on optimistic fatalism, he had concluded by adopting *pessimistic* fatalism, he would have perpetrated a glaring non sequitur, he would have killed the point of his tale, destroyed his case, lost the battle he had set out to win—the battle to preserve the moral initiative for his deistic humanism. In connection with Martin's echoing judgment, some scholars have understood the "let us work without arguing" to exclude from Candide's garden all forms of intellectual activity, philosophic or other. Actually, "without arguing" is the exact equivalent of the dervish's "be silent," which has already been explicated.

The first of the three gardens in Chapter XXX is Cacambo's. *Physically, it is the same garden as Candide's.* On this point [René Pomeau comments in *La Religion de Voltaire* (1956)]: "The survivors of the tale had been settled there for some time without knowing it. A profound lesson: all men are already in the only possible paradise. It is quite simply up to them to realize it." Voltaire's full meaning is richer than Pomeau suggests. Cacambo's garden and Candide's are physically identical, but the one precedes and the other follows the dawning of wisdom through consultation of the dervish and the old Turk. Before that dawning Cacambo works alone and curses his fate; after it the entire group finds happiness in co-operative labor. The example had been set for both him and Candide by the Eldoradans. Neither, however, was then mature enough to appreciate the contentment that comes from socially purposeful collaboration. [In *The Spirit of Voltaire* (1938), Norman L. Torrey] says of Candide's garden that it reveals a Voltaire at "the bottom of his emotional curve." More accurately, it is Cacambo's garden which represents such a depression of spirits, along with the attitudes of Martin, of Pococurante, and of Candide at Surinam.

The second of the three gardens in Chapter XXX is the old Turk's. Here the author has blended *overstatement* with *duplicity,* hammering home the former—"I know nothing about it," "I have never known," "I know absolutely nothing," "I never make inquiries"—in order to prepare the reader for the latter—"I content myself with sending the fruits of the garden I cultivate to market there." The old Turk is no rude, untutored peasant. He is head of a well-bred, hard-working family, and he is a master of literary utterance, climaxing his series of incisive, elegantly turned observations with the magnificent aphorism: "work keeps away from us three great evils: boredom, vice, and want." If such a person insists that it is best to remain rigidly indifferent, even ignorant, respecting the world, Voltaire is soberly implying: 1) that men of good will should turn their backs on public abominations in a

gesture of philosophic disdain; 2) that they should seek positions wherein they can maximize their personal safety and provide the fullest possible scope for their self-determination; 3) that they should work to banish the basic evils of boredom, vice, and want by producing for the market of the world. Once again there is an effect of shrinkage. The *philosophe* must dissociate himself from all corrupt governments, since they would embrace him only to stifle him; and he must withdraw to where he is secure from their abuses of power. But there is also countermovement, with potentially explosive overtones. After so much ironic emphasis on the helplessness of the individual, Voltaire now seriously suggests that men have a certain freedom of action. He further suggests that they can exert an influence for the better on the world at large, not by overt participation in its political affairs, but by supplying it with nutriment, as well as by setting a good example. Considering the heavy exaggeration of the old Turk's opening remarks, his traits of character, the many values directly or indirectly affirmed throughout the tale as worth salvaging, and its calculated symbolism, what critic would be so rash as to propose that the nutriment being supplied is restricted to food? The fruits of the old Turk's garden include more than legumes; they include intellectual pabulum.

A comparison of Candide's garden with those of Cacambo and the old Turk reveals *a deliberate progression from lone individual to family circle to small model group;* also, in all three (explicitly in the first two, implicitly in the third), the practical enterprise of selling their produce in the metropolitan market. The progression is objectively there, and it has profound implications. It proves that the effect of shrinkage is accompanied and balanced by an effect of expansion. The former, however, fulfills its function within the limits of the tale. The latter projects beyond those limits. The Conclusion of **Candide** is an ending with a vista. The vista is neither infinite nor insipidly roseate, but it does hold promise of solid humanistic advancement, of augmentative and ameliorative evolution in the direction of Eldoradan values. The pattern of the final chapter, no less eloquent than its language, informs the alert and sensitive reader that Candide's garden is not a terminus, but a commencement. Animated by an inherent dynamism, it will outgrow itself—*provided* its inhabitants continue to work together and are spared a natural catastrophe. This vista suffices by itself to destroy the Fundamentalist interpretation, for the future of the garden must entail something more than the growing of bigger and better vegetables.

As for interpretations which dwell on "selfish indifference" and "the doctrine of minding one's own business," they are refuted by Voltaire's own words. Candide's garden is co-operatively cultivated by "the entire little community." Pomeau contends that Pangloss constitutes an exception: "He alone escapes the final reformation of the little community. Still addicted to metaphysico-nigology, still 'arguing without working,' he remains imperturbably Pangloss, the man who is nothing but talk." The text of the tale, however, makes Pangloss a member of "the *entire* little community," and therefore one of its active workers. Moreover, it represents him as relapsing only "sometimes" into otiose speculation. Like his companions, then, he becomes socially useful in accordance with deistic doctrine. But social utility is not confined to the "little community." The garden is not "an Iland, intire of it selfe." The sale of produce establishes a connection with the big city—a connection wherein it is the small model group which influences the world, and not the other way around. But if the garden is to be understood symbolically as well as literally, then its yield must be such as to affect not only the bodies but also the minds of men.

In this regard it is a point of key importance that *Candide's garden involves more than gardening.* Each member of the group puts his particular talents to use. Cunégonde becomes a pastry cook, Paquette embroiders, the old woman takes care of the linen, Friar Giroflée does the carpentry. Cacambo presumably continues to grow vegetables and to market them in the metropolis. What of the remaining three members? Voltaire uses the others to illustrate very concretely the beginnings of specialized labor in a civilized society. Why does he say nothing specific about the work of Candide, Pangloss, and Martin? Several times in the course of the final chapter he focuses attention on them as *the intellectual subgroup* of the "little community." They undoubtedly help in the physical garden, but they, too, must have a specialty. Both Martin and Candide, applying the lesson taught by the dervish, discourage Pangloss from speculating about ultimates. That does not, however, preclude the composition and dissemination of socially useful literature. The activities of this civilization-in-miniature not only go beyond literal gardening to the extent of including carpentry, laundering, embroidery, and baking; they also include the life of the mind concentrated on the spreading of utilitarian knowledge. To argue the opposite would, of course, be absurd. Does Candide achieve mature wisdom by repudiating the life of the mind and degenerating into a brute fellah? Voltaire's silence respecting the intellectual activity of Candide's model group is not a denial of its existence. Once again, his patterns powerfully convey his full meaning. I have just mentioned the pattern of the intellectual subgroup. There is, in addition, the pattern of *the disingenuous stance.* The duplicity of the old Turk's family circle prepares that of Candide's little band. Pomeau nonetheless flatly denies that there is any suggestion of "pamphletary activity" in the Conclusion of the tale. He does find in the garden an "engineering philosophy" whose goal is to "develop natural resources." This is in itself a large admission. A society devoted to applied science is a society that believes in socially useful knowledge and in the indispensability of book-learning, hence fosters the life of the mind. Pomeau is certainly right to find this in the garden. In my judgment, if he had closely examined the *form* of Chapter XXX, as well as *the language in relation to the form,* he would have found more. In fact, he would have found enough to prove that the wisdom of the Conclusion is not narrow and disappointing . . . , but excitingly dynamic, expansive, and challenging at every level of the civilized adventure.

There is still another pattern which contributes in an important way to the elucidation of Voltaire's closing message. *Voltaire has Candide state his conclusion, not once, but twice, the second time with dilated meaning.* In good music the restatement of a theme after an intervening development constitutes something more than a mechanical repetition. It enables the listener to hear the theme with a new understanding of its meaning, to appreciate it in a richer perspective. And so with Candide's conclusion. The first time he makes his affirmation, it is already charged with considerable significance. It chokes off Pangloss's pedantic prolixity, opposing the Deed to the Word. It dramatically underlines the antithesis between those who bloody the earth and those who cultivate it. It proclaims the immeasurable superiority of productivity to power politics. It invites to reflection on the values preached and practised by the old Turk and his family. And it casts a fitful light over the long, fantastic road traveled by Candide and his companions. But all this is not yet fully clear. The author has said too much and moved too swiftly for the reader to be able to absorb the final wisdom in one abrupt, climactic judgment. With great tactical skill he goes on to the elaboration of his theme. First he varies it. The variation sounded by Pangloss harks back to the beginning of the tale and, with consummate irony, to the beginning of the Scriptural Revelation. That voiced by Martin picks up the dervish's message and beautifully fuses the effect of shrinkage with that of expansion. The effect of expansion, however, still remains to be clarified. Having stated and varied his theme, Voltaire now proceeds to develop it. He shows us the little band purposefully hustling and bustling about its business, achieving co-operative contentment, serving as a miniature model for the world, and seeking to help make the world's business more like its own. The picture is much clearer now, provided the reader has been alert to the stylistic and structural devices which the master-storyteller is dynamically interweaving as he approaches the end of his story. The end takes the form of a summation in two contrasting speeches. That of Pangloss, a parody of periodic eloquence and a caricature of optimistic dialectic, nevertheless manages to provide a rapid review of several major motifs and episodes: namely, both the intellectual and the sentimental aspects of optimism, the inhumanity of man to man, religious fanaticism, the aimlessness of the South-American adventure, the visit by special dispensation to Eldorado, and the worthlessness of unearned wealth. This review rings a number of changes on social unproductiveness, while reminding us of its ideal opposite. Candide's response, quietly tolerant of his comrade's occasional aberrations, pointed, terse, lapidary, reaffirms the theme of productivity, which this time, because of the intervening development, renews, enriches, deepens, and broadens the meaning of the garden. The restatement flashes both back and forward. It is a wondrous epitome of the tale's wisdom, coined neither for mere show nor for mere contemplation, but for *use.*

Among other things, after mercilessly caricaturing love and woman throughout his narrative, Voltaire redresses the balance at the very end, but with subtlety, so as to preserve congruity of tone. If Candide reluctantly agrees to marry an ugly and shrewish Cunégonde whom he no longer loves, but who later develops into an excellent pastry cook, the author is soberly suggesting: 1) that sentimental quixotism warps or obstructs social productivity; 2) that the dignity and the moral value of the individual's life depend strictly on such productivity; 3) that a sound marriage demands mutual respect, and mutual respect becomes possible only through such productivity; 4) that a sound marriage further involves the procreation and proper upbringing of children who may eventually, *like the sons and daughters of the old Turk,* themselves become useful citizens.

Thus one of the Conclusion's many functions is to blunt the cutting edge of the satirical sword wielded up to the final moments of the battle with a bravura relish which might otherwise be mistaken for sadistic abandon. But in addition, from the very beginning Voltaire has taken care to sow his recital with salutary affirmatives, with examples of moral sanity and true civilized refinement; and this seed will bear fruit in Candide's garden. One reason why the message of Chapter XXX has been so often misread is that readers fail to appreciate the constructive character of Voltaire's criticism. He razes in order to rebuild more solidly, but he does not raze indiscriminately. While demolishing he picks out what is worth saving and makes ready to re-use it. The cultivation of the garden must therefore be understood to include immediately a humanitarian feeling for the wretched and the oppressed, and sooner or later the various cultural pursuits. This salvaging operation effectively illustrates Voltaire's belief in *the conservation and exploitation of all truly human resources*.

Pomeau raises the interesting and very important question of how the garden is socially and administratively organized. "Good humor," he states, "prevents the problem of social relationships from being posed. No leadership, no subordination in 'the little community.' Voltaire, easy-to-get-along-with fellow that he is, assumes that work organizes itself. . . ." Since it is Candide who makes the big decision while the others simply accept it, and since it is he who has the last word, I think it plain enough that he has now become the leader of the group. Moreover, Voltaire is under no obligation to do more than start the group on its way at the end. The rest is a matter of time, effort, intelligence, and good will. Nor must it be forgotten that the general direction of possible development may be inferred from the ideal society in the Eldorado episode. Voltaire definitely knows that it is men who organize work, and that in due course, if things go reasonably well, equality before the law will be preserved, but a social and economic hierarchy will take shape.

The nature of Candide's garden makes it dependent on those who work in it, to be sure, but also, as already noted, on the lucky avoidance of physical disasters, and, finally, on its security against destruction by hostile governments. There is nothing automatic or certain about it, then. Its existence is precarious. It is a beautiful but fragile thing. Yet it represents man's best hope—indeed, his only hope *as* man; and it is therefore the only thing with which he has a human right to occupy himself.

One more point: Voltaire's conception of the garden is plural. Wherever a few persons gather in the name of social productivity, a garden comes into existence. Given enough of these developing, setting an example, and influencing the world, a global metagarden is conceivable. Conceivable, that is, as Eldorado is conceivable; but Voltaire is too much the realist to regard a global metagarden as fully realizable on this "globule." It is sufficient for him that men should move toward it, no matter how modestly, in attestation of their higher humanity.

The great mass of internal evidence proves that the meaning of the Conclusion is complex but not obscure, and that Voltaire does not end by abandoning the world to the wicked after flaying them with his verbal lash. He ends by affirming that social productivity of any kind at any level constitutes the good life, that there are limits within which man must be satisfied to lead the good life, but that within

these he has a very real chance of achieving both private contentment and public progress.

External Considerations

Nothing outside *Candide* can be legitimately used to refute or to alter or to question what is actually expressed and communicated inside it by its author composing at a superconscious pitch of creative intensity. It is common sense to check the results of internal analysis against the available external evidence, to correlate the text of *Candide* with its historical context, to show how the work reflects the background and vice versa. But at no point should the work be treated as a mere result of mechanical forces functioning in time and space, hence susceptible of definitive measurement from without. The container theory of causation cannot be successfully applied to art, because the artist is a "sovereign Alchemist" who transmutes "Life's leaden metal into Gold," who creates new values. Investigations of origins and influences are therefore limited. Carefully conducted, they may prove highly suggestive. They should never be substituted for direct literary analysis of the work, and they should respect the great qualitative gap that separates the raw material from the finished product. This is why I have begun with a presentation of the internal evidence. What follows will serve to corroborate that evidence, both in general and in particular.

"Voltaire's tales," according to Torrey, "have a way . . . of summing up certain periods of his existence and certain problems with which he was then faced." In the case of *Candide* the period was the decade of the fifties; the central problem, as already stated, that of human conduct in relation to the somber mystery of physical and social evil. And viewed as a whole, *Candide* pursues a course of argument which parallels the evolution of its author's philosophic attitude during that decade—a decade wherein he irrevocably abandoned the relative complacency of his earlier years, inclined toward pessimism, and finally won through to a melioristic affirmation.

The pessimistic trend of the fifties is clearly perceptible in several important branches of Voltaire's production: in the correspondence; in the tales, from *Zadig* (1747-48) to *Scarmentado* (1753); in poetry, from the *Poème sur la loi naturelle* (1752) to the *Poème sur le désastre de Lisbonne* (1756). Surveyed in broad perspective, this gradual, cumulative movement assumes dominant proportions between 1752 and 1756. A mere enumeration of the major contributing factors will suffice to prove that this effect had its proper causes: the onset of old age coupled with poor health; the death of Mme. du Châtelet; the cynicism of Frederick's entourage; the rupture with His Majesty; the consequent sense of homelessness or exile; various literary and philosophic quarrels (Maupertuis, Rousseau, etc.); the Seven Years' War; the Lisbon disaster; the study of history, leading to disgust and skepticism; a painful awareness of the unresolvable conflict between the clocklike order of a rational, mechanical universe and the mad confusion of an illogical, capricious actuality. This last factor underlies the others. Metaphysics had become the unknowable. The purposes of God were inscrutable. Physical evil was a matter for stoical submission. Free will had been reluctantly abandoned in favor of determinism; yet optimistic fatalism was dispiriting and repugnant to one who could confront social evil only with programs of reform based on faith in man's progressive possibilities.

In the latter part of the decade, as the correspondence and the contributions to the *Encyclopédie* and **Candide** itself reveal, the pessimistic trend was checked and turned back upon itself by a melioristic countercurrent, which, gathering volume and momentum, swelled at last into an irresistible flood at Ferney. . . . Here again, sufficient reasons can be adduced to account for this fateful reversal of direction. The effect of Mme. du Châtelet's death wore off with time. Failing health and old age became conventional complaints, as Voltaire absorbed himself in active interests. He created for himself a secure haven, whence he was able to resume relations with Frederick at a safe distance. He attained genuine happiness through gardening and humanitarian projects. Confirmation of his genius all over the civilized world gave him renewed strength. Collaboration with the Encyclopaedists revived his confidence in at least a partial triumph of his ideas. And so his instinctive pugnacity spurred him on with increasing boldness against personal enemies, optimistic fatalism, "l'infâme," and social evil in general.

Thus the period of Voltaire's life which extends from the death of his mistress to the composition and publication of **Candide** can be summed up as a progression from relative complacency through pessimistic drift to meliorism. When due allowances have been made for literary license and accentuation, the movement of ideas in the tale is seen to follow pretty much the same line of development. Shortly after the beginning of the story Candide is ejected from his "terrestrial Paradise," the seat of optimism. The ensuing series of fantastically cumulated misadventures first disenchants, then disheartens him; until finally, in Chapter XIX, he renounces optimism as "the mania of maintaining that all is well when one is miserable," and is plunged into "a black melancholy," such that "the wickedness of men presented itself to his mind in all its ugliness, he harbored only gloomy thoughts." From this point on, symbolically accompanied by a devil's advocate in the person of Martin, he is drawn for a time toward pessimism; but concludes on a note which avoids both extremes by sounding the call to positive, practical action unobstructed by windy theorizing. This broad similarity between the evolution of Voltaire's philosophic attitude during the fifties and the movement of ideas in **Candide** lends no small degree of autobiographical distinctiveness and realism to its content.

There are certain principles of Voltaire's thought which, despite hesitations and vacillations, remain essentially consistent through the years. To see that this is so one need only look beneath the mercurial surface. As [Emmanuel Berl expresses it in the introduction to an edition of Voltaire's **Traité sur la tolérance**], "one needs but a minimum of intellectual discrimination to distinguish his caprices from his serious ideas and his petulant outbursts from his permanent views. So it is pointless to say: 'He is a chaos of clear ideas'; the chaos is made up of ideas solid enough to have endured intact through a meditation carried on for seventy years with undiminished energy." His attitude may evolve, as just shown, and it may even appear to shift from one pole to the other; yet invariably, in his serious moods, in his key works, it finds a way to avoid extremes. Thus he moves from free will to determinism,

but interprets the latter as self-determination for purposes of human conduct, and so stays clear of fatalism. He attacks Jansenism from one direction and atheism from the opposite, again with the Golden Mean as his goal. What, then, of **Candide**? Is it a spectacular exception? "His entire intellect was an engine of war," says Flaubert . . . of the satirist who never wrote but to act, who recognized that "he who takes pen in hand has a war on his hands," and who fought with a pen mightier than the sword for concrete social reforms. Did this same satirist, to indulge a fleeting mood of discouragement, compose his masterpiece on the problem of evil and pour into it all of his consummate artistry and ripened wisdom, only to arrive at a bucolic conclusion—the result of a paltry choice between cabbages and kings? Common sense tells us what the internal evidence and the evolution of Voltaire's attitude have already told us: that the Conclusion of **Candide** rejects pessimism no less than optimism, embracing instead a healthy, equilibrating meliorism.

Another permanent principle of Voltaire's thought is his social conception of morality. In his seventh **Discours en vers sur lhomme** (1737) he had censured the piety of the hermit:

> Mais quel en est le fruit? quel bien fait-il au monde?
> Malgré la sainteté de son auguste emploi,
> C'est n'être bon à rien de n'être bon qu'à soi

> [But what fruit does it yield? What good does he
> do the world? / Despite the holiness of his August
> occupation, / To be good only to oneself is to be
> good for nothing.]

In his **Traité de métaphysique** (1734) he had defined virtue as *what is useful . . . to society.* On this point he remains perfectly consistent from start to finish of his long career. Once more, what shall we say of **Candide**? Does his greatest work end in selfish withdrawal, indifference, escape, as some have maintained? The evidence inside the tale eloquently witnesses Voltaire's unbroken fidelity to his deistic ethic. Candide affirms that "we must cultivate *our* garden." Accordingly, the garden is co-operatively cultivated by the *entire* group. And what the group produces is fed to the *world*. Love of neighbor is thereby pursued in large as well as in small, and the meaning of "our garden" is expanded.

There are critics who defend a purely literal interpretation of that "garden" by reference to the author's gardening activities of 1758. Now, a Voltairean inclination toward allegorical and/or symbolical invention is clearly perceptible in as early a work as the **Henriade,** and has its roots deep in his psychology, his literary training, and his philosophic orientation. Long before 1758 this propensity had found apt raw materials for imaginative exploitation in the garden and the cultivation of the soil. In 1736 Voltaire had already utilized the Biblical garden of Eden in **Le Mondain,** contrasting its crudity with the "terrestrial paradise" of Cirey, and bantering Adam in these terms:

> Mon cher Adam, mon gourmand, mon bon père,
> Que faisais-tu dans les jardins d'Eden?
> Travaillais-tu pour ce sot genre humain?

> [My dear Adam, my glutton, my good father, /
> What were you doing in the garden of Eden? /
> Were you working for our foolish human race?]

The Leningrad notebooks include the following entry: "The soil of Florence seemed made to produce Petrarchs, Galileos. We must cultivate ours, fertilize it, etc. Geniuses, like fruit, have come to France from Greece" (*Notebooks*, II, 277-78). Part IV of the *Poème sur la loi naturelle* (1752) contains a prolonged metaphor representing France as a garden, the king as the gardener, and his subjects as plants of various kinds and sizes, which he "cares for and prunes in the interests of a better garden." During the same year Voltaire writes to Argental, concerning his *Rome sauvée:* "It is by emendations that one must turn one's victory to account. This Roman soil was so unproductive that we must recultivate it after getting it, by dint of art, to bear fruit which was relished." A letter to Thieriot, dated 26 March 1757, affirms: "I have done everything I could throughout my life to help spread the spirit of philosophy and tolerance which seems today to characterize our century. That spirit, which inspires all decent Europeans, has successfully taken root in [this] country [Switzerland]. . . . " In a letter of 3 March 1758 to Cideville, he says of his theater at Lausanne: "The actors trained themselves in one year. They are fruits which the Alps and Mount Jura had not previously borne." In another, also to Cideville, dated 1 September 1758, he writes: "You are content to pick the flowers of Anacreon in your gardens."

The remarkable early pamphlet, *Ce qu'on ne fait pas et ce qu'on pourrait faire* (1742), reproduces a Roman citizen's imaginary memorandum containing a program of reform which definitely prefigures the conclusion of *Candide,* and closes with the words: "The obscure citizen's memorial turned out to be a seed which gradually germinated in the minds of great men." Also prefigurative is the following passage from the philosophic tale, *Lettre d'un Turc* (1750), with Omri saying to Bababec: "I value a man who sows vegetables or plants trees a hundred times more highly than all your comrades who stare at the tip of their nose or carry a pack out of excessive nobility of soul."

But the most astonishing anticipation of all is Voltaire's ode on *La Félicité des temps, ou l'Eloge de la France,* read before the French Academy on 25 August 1746. Stanzas VII, VIII, IX, and XI of this poem develop the following line of thought: in olden times a wilderness infested with intestine wars, France is today a peaceful commonwealth overlaid with splendid cities and ennobled by cultural pursuits; this immense progress was made possible by industrious tillage of the soil; work increased fertility, fertility produced wealth, wealth gave rise to all the benefits of higher civilization; such is the history and the promise of our nation, as indeed of all mankind.

> Loin ce discours lâche et vulgaire,
> Que toujours l'homme dégénère,
> Que tout s'épuise et tout finit:
> La nature est inépuisable,
> Et le Travail infatigable
> Est un dieu qui la rajeunit.

> [Away with the craven and vulgar opinion / That man is constantly degenerating, / That everything is giving out and coming to an end: / Nature is inexhaustible, / And tireless Work / Is a god who rejuvenates it.]

Here is one more fixed principle of Voltaire's thought, found from the *Lettres philosophiques* through the *Essai*

sur les mœurs to the *Questions sur l'Encyclopédie.* Given time and good will, and unimpeded by earthquakes or invasions, human societies will advance by natural stages, beginning with agriculture and rising to culture in an ever more elaborate fusion of "pleasure" with "need." Agriculture is necessary for survival—which is why it has its indispensable place in the garden; but culture is necessary for higher civilization—which is why public works, the arts, and the general cultivation of the mind will sooner or later follow from the cultivation of the soil. In this connection I have already shown how the garden salvages the good seed from the experiences of the group in order to sow it for the future. Furthermore, in keeping with the values of the *Essai sur les mœurs,* the garden stands for every form of activity which helps produce civilization, as opposed to the criminally irresponsible and infertile practices of "the higher powers."

In addition to these inventions on the part of Voltaire, there is the striking passage from *Gulliver,* with which he had long been familiar, wherein the King of Brobdingnag expresses the opinion "that whoever could make two ears of corn or two blades of grass to grow upon a spot of ground where only one grew before, would deserve better of mankind, and do more essential service to his country than the whole race of politicians put together." There is the even more striking passage from a letter addressed to him by Bolingbroke as early as 27 June 1724. Writing from his "hermitage" at La Source, Bolingbroke develops at some length a comparison between the cultivation of the literal garden and that of "the mind," "the heart," and "the talents." Shortly before the composition of *Candide,* Voltaire, writing to Alembert from *his* "hermitage" at Les Délices, preaches a crusade of ideas against "l'infâme" and in favor of tolerance, speaks of the advances already made, and states that the vineyard of truth is being admirably cultivated by such *philosophes* as his correspondent, Diderot, Bolingbroke, Hume, etc. Bolingbroke had been dead for several years, yet Voltaire links him here with three other exemplary thinkers who are still alive and active. These associations, considered in the light of Voltaire's remarkable memory, fully justify, it seems to me, Besterman's suggestion that the Bolingbroke letter should be regarded as "one of the sources of Candide's final conclusion."

Since a majority of these inventions and readings—the above list is by no means exhaustive—antedate Les Délices by a number of years, and since they prove that the metaphorical use of the garden is a literary habit with Voltaire, there is no compelling biographical reason for arguing a one-to-one relationship between the author's literal garden and Candide's.

There is a much closer relationship between the author's philosophic activities of 1758 and the old Turk's garden. The latter's attitude toward news of public affairs is an absolute contradiction of Voltaire's irrepressible curiosity. In fact, as already pointed out, the Turk professes ignorance and indifference with an overemphasis which broadly hints at, and prepares the reader for, an effect of duplicity. It happens that "a certain form of duplicity was the necessary condition of Voltaire's life and works." . . . Now, the deceptions practised by Voltaire in his war against social evil, although the proved very effective in circumventing the established authorities, are never diffi-

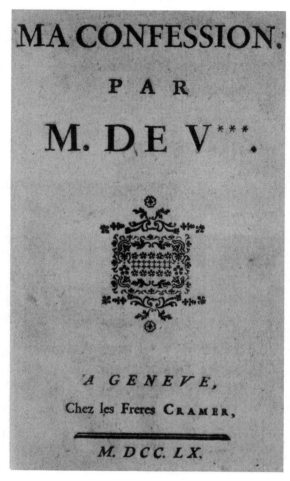

Title page of the first edition of Voltaire's Ma confession *(1760).*

cult to fathom. Like the author, the Turk and Candide do not withdraw completely from the world; they merely affect to do so. Actually, they turn their backs on public abominations in a gesture of philosophic disdain, and they retire to safe positions, where they will work concretely toward the spread of social virtue, and whence they will fight social evil with disingenuous tactics.

What was the justification for disingenuousness in 1758? Exile and homelessness were recent experiences and still-painful memories. The **Poème sur le désastre de Lisbonne,** issued in 1756, had had to be cautiously worded in order to avoid dangerous opposition. A royal decree of 1757 had restored the death penalty for writers and publishers convicted of attacking religion. In the very year 1758 the philosophic quarrel reached an acute stage, with the Encyclopaedic party deeply involved. Shortly before the publication of **Candide** a censorship of the mails was instituted. Voltaire was an eminently practical fighter. He believed that false heroics leading to martyrdom would only play into the hands of the enemy; hence his elaboration of the adroit stratagems usually associated with his Ferney period, but already being practised in connection with the composition and the publication of **Candide.**

As a disciple of Bayle, a contributor to the *Encyclopédie,* and a master-tactician in his own right, he established his "four paws." He wrote **Candide** in great secrecy. . . . He published it anonymously and denied his authorship. Shortly before its publication he feigned in his letters a loss of interest in the reading and the writing of books. He included in the tale only a few anti-Biblical thrusts, and these mostly indirect. He scattered through his letters repeated affections of complete withdrawal from the world, and gave literary expression to this ruse in the final chapter of **Candide.** Finally, he may in part have chosen the metaphor of the garden because he could thereby screen an aggressive social intention behind a literal occupation. The old Turk's meaning, veiled yet strangely clear, shines through the following characteristic excerpts from the correspondence:

> (28 February [1757], to Diderot) "It is with pleasure that I forget in my retreat all those who are working to make men unhappy or to brutify them; and the more I forget those enemies of the human race, the more I remember you. I exhort you to diffuse as widely as possible through the *Encyclopédie* the noble freedom of your spirit";
>
> (26 March [1757], to Thieriot [the Damiens affair]) "We avert our eyes from those abominations in our little Romanic country. . . . We are doing here what one should be doing in Paris; we are living in tranquillity, we are cultivating literature without any cabals";
>
> (12 December [1757], to Alembert [the article *Genève*]) "there are some who accuse me of an impious conspiracy with you. You know I am innocent";
>
> (24 December [1757], to Vernes [same subject]) "I haven't yet received the new volume of the *Encyclopédie* and I know absolutely nothing of what it's about. . . . Let's be neither Calvinists nor papists, but brothers, adorers of a merciful and just God";
>
> (15 May [1758], to Argental) "Do you have any news about the *Encyclopédie?* I prefer it to news of public affairs, which is almost always distressing";
>
> (3 September 1758, to Mme. Du Bocage [the Encyclopaedic party]) "The few sages, Madame, must not expose themselves to the wickedness of those who are mad. They must live together and shun the general public."

As most of these excerpts plainly show, Voltaire was vitally interested in the victory of the Encyclopaedic party. He declared himself the "admirer and . . . partisan to his dying day" of those who were compiling "the greatest work in the world," and contributed not a few articles of his own to the great enterprise. In 1757, and especially in 1758, when the opposition was making progress on the work increasingly difficult, Voltaire repeatedly exhorted his colleagues to strengthen themselves by forming a closely-knit philosophic group: "Gather the little flock. Courage.—Unite all the *philosophes* as best you can against the fanatics.—Form a group, gentlemen; a group always commands respect. . . . Get together, and you will be masters of the situation.—This is the moment when all the *philosophes* should join together.—All the *kakouaks* should form a pack, but they separate and the wolf devours them." Finally, recognizing the seriousness of their plight, he suggested that they flee from public life to where they could live together as free men, not in defeat, not in escapist retirement, but for the purpose of completing their task. To that end he even invited them to share his own retreat, just as in 1766 he was to recommend withdrawal to one of Frederick's southern provinces: (7 March [1758], to Alembert) "if we could reach an agreement, if we had courage, if we dared make a resolution, we could very well complete the *Encyclopédie* here. . . . If we were sufficiently detached from our age and our country to make this decision, I should contribute half of what I own to its execution. I should have the wherewithal to house you all, and very comfortably at that. I should like to see this project through and die happy."

The topical connection of the *Encyclopédie* with the conclusion of *Candide* is implicit in this epistolary evidence that Voltaire thought of the Encyclopaedists as a "little community," a model group of *philosophes,* who, like the old Turk and Candide—and Voltaire—should shelter themselves from exposure to public abominations, and work together toward the reduction of social evil and the spread of social virtue, by setting a concrete example and by enlightening the world. But the correspondence of the period immediately preceding *Candide* does more than imply such a connection; it explicitly links the Encyclopaedists with the metaphor of the garden:

> (30 January [1755], to Gauffecourt) "Speaking of philosophy, do you still get to see my lords of the *Encyclopédie?* They are the proprietors of the greatest domain in the world. I hope they will always cultivate it with complete freedom; they are made to enlighten the world boldly, and to crush their enemies";

> (6 December [1757], to Alembert) "I do as Cato did, I always end my harangue with the words: *Deleatur Carthago.* . . . It takes only five or six *philosophes* leagued together to overturn the colossus. It is not a question of preventing our lackeys from going to mass or attending Protestant services; it is a question of rescuing heads of families from the tyranny of impostors, and of inspiring a spirit of tolerance. This great mission is already enjoying success. The vineyard of truth is being well cultivated by Alemberts, Diderots, Bolingbrokes, Humes, etc.";

> (7 March [1758], to Alembert) "If you again take up the ill-harnessed plow of the *Encyclopédie* and want some of those articles, I shall send them back proofread."

Torrey makes much of the fact that in his correspondence Voltaire differentiates the metaphor of the garden from that of the vineyard. Actually, before the publication of *Candide* there is no such pattern, for the figure of the vineyard appears but once in the letters that have survived. After the publication of *Candide* the "garden-vineyard" distinction does develop, and it is maintained with consistency, but it proves quite the opposite of what Torrey would have it prove. The "vineyard" metaphor becomes the ironic battle-cry of the philosophic party in its attack on "l'infâme": e.g., (13 February 1764, to Alembert) "so labor in the vineyard, crush 'l'infâme'." The "garden" figure, which tends to recur especially at times when "l'infâme" seems to be gaining the advantage over the philosophic party, becomes the symbol for an affectation

of retreat accompanied by vigorous clandestine activity, so that, in the correspondence as in the Conclusion of *Candide, the garden includes the vineyard.* An excellent example of this fusion by absorption is found in Voltaire's letter of 2 April 1764 to Damilaville: "So we shall have to end like Candide by cultivating our garden. Good-bye, dear brother. Crush 'l'infâme' "; another, in his letter of 14 July 1773 to Alembert: "We must cultivate literature or our garden. . . . Please do not fail to remember me to Monsieur de Condorcet and your other friends who are very quietly supporting the good cause."

In fine, the correspondence posterior to *Candide* corroborates the message of its Conclusion as expressed and communicated in the text itself. The note of duplicity which is sounded in the letters echoes that of the old Turk's garden and Candide's, and so is necessarily present to Voltaire's mind. After the tale even more than before he is aware that the inherent dynamism of the garden inescapably compels its figurative extension. I have taken pains to describe the limitations which circumscribe and the dangers which attend that extension; but limitations and dangers notwithstanding, the basic, concrete example of gardening and/or farming has in it the stuff of expansion, so that it cannot be confined within a purely literal conception.

Concluding Remarks

It is difficult for historians of ideas to accept the principle that in a genuine work of art material and efficient causes are transcended by formal and final causes; but art critics know that to enter a work of art is to enter a sanctuary where the raw material of experience becomes aesthetically significant form-fused-with-content, and where quantitative measurement must accordingly be replaced by qualitative insight. I have been careful here to consider every kind of external evidence which has relevance either as raw material for *Candide* or as a subsequent reflection of *Candide,* and to consider it with a proper respect for its real importance—and a sensible appreciation of its limitations. My approach, in sum, has steered clear of both the Scylla of *in-vacuo* analysis and the Charybdis of unimaginative historicism in order to do full justice to a literary masterpiece risen out of time to timelessness. (pp. 87-111)

William F. Bottiglia, "Candide's Garden," in Voltaire: A Collection of Critical Essays, *edited by William F. Bottiglia, Prentice-Hall, Inc., 1968, pp. 87-111.*

Haydon Mason   (essay date 1975)

[*An English scholar and critic, Mason has written widely on Voltaire and the French Enlightenment. In the following excerpt, he studies the philosophy and literary art of Voltaire's* Essai sur les moeurs.]

The study of history preoccupied Voltaire the whole of his literary life; it is quite characteristic that his epic poem *La Henriade* (first published in 1723), should be based not on a classical or Biblical theme but upon the recent age of Henri IV. By 1727 he is producing his first historical work proper, the *Essay upon the Civil Wars of France,* which relates to the same period. Indeed, Voltaire's first interest was in modern history; the *Histoire de Charles XII* (1731), for instance, dealt with the life of its eponymous hero as king of Sweden in the early years of the eighteenth century. A year later, Voltaire had begun *Le Siècle de Louis XIV,* though its origins may date back even to 1729; this study was to occupy the next twenty years of his life, the full work not appearing till 1751 and undergoing important revisions in subsequent editions. Voltaire was also to write other historical works including an *Histoire de l'empire de Russie sous Pierre le Grand* (1759-63), a *Prècis du Siècle de Louis XV* (1768), and an *Histoire de la guerre de 1741;* an authentic version of the last work (completed in 1752) has only recently been published in full for the first time.

With the *Essai sur les mœurs,* however, Voltaire took a wider canvas, and extended his range backwards in time as well as in space. This historical enterprise appears to have begun as a sketch for his mistress and fellow-*philosophe* at Cirey, Mme Du Châtelet, and is first referred to by Voltaire in a letter to Frederick of Prussia of 1 June 1741. The work, like the *Siècle,* grows apace over the years. A pirated edition appeared in 1753, the first complete text officially authorized by the author was published in 1756, and he went on making substantial additions and changes until the very end of his life. In 1765 appeared *La Philosophie de l'histoire,* a work devoted wholly to ancient history which thereafter became attached as an introduction to the *Essai.* The breadth of subject in the *Essai sur les mœurs* is even greater than for the *Siècle,* and it is not an exaggeration to claim, as does Theodore Besterman [in *Voltaire* (1969)], that this is 'the work in which Voltaire concentrated the essence of his thought, on which he laboured the longest, and which he wrote with the highest seriousness'.

To start with, [the *Essai sur les mœurs*] is of colossal length, running to well over 1600 pages in the excellent modern edition established by René Pomeau: more than a half-million words. In the main body of the work (excluding *La Philosophie de l'histoire*) Voltaire undertakes what had scarcely ever before been attempted: a history of the world, such a project as no single writer would not attempt. Here we see the glory of the Enlightenment ideal of scholarship, handed on from the Renaissance but with more pragmatic intent: to encompass in encyclopedic fashion all that is proper for a gentleman of learning to know, so that reason and *philosophie,* developing their resources in the light of this new information, can increase the hopes of peace, prosperity and happiness, as old superstitions and prejudice are destroyed. As Voltaire put it in 1763, looking back on the *Essai:* 'C'est dans l'histoire de nos propres folies qu'on apprend à être sage, et non dans les discussions ténébreuses d'une vaine antiquité.' (It is in the history of our own follies that one learns wisdom, not in the obscure discussions of a futile antiquity.)

But Voltaire was not the first to conceive of a universal history. The idea of a global 'histoire de l'esprit humain' with its consequences for 'les lois, et . . . les usages des nations' had been recommended by Pierre Bayle in his *Dictionnaire historique et critique* (1967). A general world history had indeed been completed some years earlier by Bossuet in his *Discours sur l'histoire universelle* (1681), the author providing a broad survey of events from the beginning of the world to Charlemagne and the foundation of the French monarchy. Bossuet's vast study is however limited by its being a frank apologetic for Christian doctrine. The successive orders of history demonstrate, in Bossuet's view, God's plan for mankind working out His great scheme through the Judaic tradition, the Bible (His revealed word) and the establishment of the Christian Church. The nature of this aim dictates also the spatial limits of Bossuet's work. Islam, India and China, regarded as peripheral to the essential meaning of human history, receive little or no mention.

This providentialist and parochial account could not appeal to Voltaire. He refers slightingly in *Le Pyrrhonisme de l'histoire* (1769) to Bossuet's

> prétendue *Histoire universelle,* qui n'est que celle de quatre à cinq peuples, et surtout de la petite nation juive, ou ignorée, ou justement méprisée du reste de la terre.

> (so-called *World history,* which deals with only four or five peoples, and especially the tiny Jewish nation, that is either unknown to the rest of the earth or rightly scorned by it.)

In the *Essai* itself he will explicitly establish the different tenor of his work in dramatic fashion by beginning his narrative precisely where Bossuet left off, at Charlemagne's accession. For Voltaire, there is no chosen race or creed. While he comes to regard European civilization as having unique qualities, he rebels against the Christian viewpoint that relegates all events outside Europe to manifestations of a secondary order. Human nature is the same the world over, so all history is basically alike: 'La terre est un vaste théâtre où la même tragédie se joue sous des noms différents.' (The earth is a vast theatre where the same tragedy is played under different names.)

It is with this conviction that Voltaire sets out to write his great history. The title sufficiently indicates what he has in mind; he will expatiate primarily on 'les mœurs et l'espirit des nations'. This Essay is to give a strong emphasis to intellectual and social history. As in the *Lettres philosophiques,* the reader is wooed by flattery, being appealed to directly as an intelligent person weary of what passes for history and interested to know only 'ce qui mérite d'être connu de vous: l'esprit, les mœurs, les usages des nations principales, appuyés des faits qu'il n'est pas permis d'ignorer' (what deserves to be known by you: the spirit, manners, customs of the leading nations, supported by the facts of which one may not remain ignorant). He will not want a mere chronology of all the dynasties, or exclusive concentration on battles, or a compilation of petty details like disputes over marriage contracts, genealogies and titles. This is to be a history of peoples; kings will be of interest to the extent that they have improved the living conditions of their subjects. In short, Voltaire is writing a history of civilization.

But the term 'civilization' raises perplexing difficulties. What does Voltaire have in mind? Not the least problem is that he does not use the term itself; its first known appearance in French as a substantive dates from 1757, after the first editions of the *Essai.* Voltaire tends to use 'police' in the modern sense of 'civilization', but even this word makes a relatively rare appearance. In general, he prefers to describe the salient characteristics of 'un peuple policé', often enough for us to distinguish them in the end with some measure of clarity. The essential elements appear to be humane government and tolerant religion, permitting the development of trade, affluence and consequently lei-sure, which give the necessary conditions for enlightened living in which the arts and sciences can flourish. From all this emerges a way of life that respects personal rights and individual freedom, accompanied by the equality of all before the law, such that every man's life and property are legally protected against arbitrary tyranny. The main theme of the *Essai* is that, amid a background of horrors and follies of every kind, mankind gradually makes prog-ress. This is particularly true of Europe, which began late but has overtaken the civilizations of such as China and India. Starting in the twelfth century and spreading from Italy, culture makes an advance through all of western Eu-rope. As true *philosophie* gains the ascendancy, belief in myth decays, and man's innate reason, encouraged to de-velop in the new climate, prefers to seek the truth instead of being seduced by the instinctive impulse to believe the extraordinary and marvellous.

This historical survey, then, ends on an optimistic note that may seem a little surprising after all the bloodshed that has gone before:

> Quand une nation connaît les arts, quand elle n'est point subjuguée et transportée par les étrangers, elle sort aisément de ses ruines, et se rétablit tou-jours.

> (When a nation is acquainted with the arts, when it is not subjugated and bodily removed by foreign-ers, it emerges with ease from its ruins and is invari-ably restored.)

But the correct balance has been struck a little earlier in this final chapter:

> I faut donc, encore une fois, avouer qu'en général toute cette histoire est un ramas de crimes, de folies, et de malheurs, parmi lesquels nous avons vu quelques vertus, quelques temps heureux, comme on découvre des habitations répandues, çà et là dans des déserts sauvages.

> (We must therefore acknowledge once again that in general the whole of this history is a heap of crimes, follies and misfortunes, among which we have no-ticed a few virtues, a few happy times, just as one finds scattered dwellings here and there in wild de-serts.)

The implication seems to be that 'vertus', once thrown up, stand a good chance of attracting others, until they form a general climate much as the 'habitations répandues' may increase until they eventually form a town.

But how do such favourable circumstances come about in the first place? Here Voltaire's answer seems less clear. What he opposes is easier to discern than what he pro-poses. The hand of God which Bossuet had found to be ordering all things has no place in this resolutely secularist work. Civilization emerges fitfully, in response to certain needs and circumstances, without any finalist pattern be-coming apparent. As for Christianity's contribution to civ-ilization, the *Essai* is throughout at pains to show the baneful effect of the Church upon the whole of this period. Christian fanaticism has been more effective than wars in depopulating the earth. In particular, the last five hundred years ever since the Albigensian massacres have been an uninterrupted history of bloodshed. From time to time Voltaire may have words of commendation for certain

Christian institutions: some of the monastic orders have an excellent record, while the Church in Rome merits praise for the way it has based advancement on talent rather than on birth. This does not prevent the *Essai* from being, as one critic puts it, 'un long réquisitoire contre le christianisme' (a lengthy indictment of Christianity).

If then the history of the world reveals no external plan, how far do men make their own destiny? Voltaire seems to incline to the view that moral causes—human institu-tions and motives—are more powerful than physical. In the final summing-up, he discerns three constant influ-ences on the human mind: climate, government and reli-gion. However, he is less keen elsewhere to give climate an important role in the development of European civili-zation. The *Avant-Propos,* indeed, makes a clear-cut dis-tinction between East and West: 'Les climats orientaux, voisins du Midi, tiennent tout de la nature; et nous, dans notre Occident septentrional, nous devons tout au temps, au commerce, à une industrie tardive.' (Eastern climes, akin to southern Europe, derive everything from nature; and we, living in the northern part of the Western world, owe everything to time, trade, a late-developing industry.) The accent is placed upon European freedom of action; and the impression one gains as the *Essai* advances is that certain great men can seize upon favourable circum-stances and exploit them for the good of all.

To the 'great man' theory we shall return presently; for the moment let us consider what constitutes favourable cir-cumstances. It rapidly becomes clear, as civilization be-gins to emerge in Europe, that it rests upon a bedrock of economic prosperity. It has survived in Constantinople be-cause of that city's suitable geographical situation for commerce. The only happy result of the Crusades is that certain towns achieve freedom and begin to build up trade and culture. By contrast, medieval England was too poor to establish the middle class that will later on be seen as the backbone of English liberty; it is not so in the 'belles villes commercantes' of Italy, where prosperity encour-ages freedom and culture. The number of such examples could be multiplied indefinitely. Throughout the *Essai* Voltaire is attentive to the state of finances and commerce, delineating with care the particular amount of affluence in given countries at a particular time. He does not, like his admired contemporary Turgot, try to establish a theory of economic progress; but the underlying assumptions are the same. Man's needs urge him on to make discoveries. Knowledge, once obtained, is a basis for further accre-tions. Trade, urbanization, a leisured class spring up, all of them increasing the place of culture.

So it emerges that although the word 'esprit' appears with such prominence in the title and introductory chapter as to suggest an idealist view of history, in practice there is a strong material stress in the work. Voltaire's discussion of economic history lacks profundity, but at least he re-members to include it explicitly in his surveys of particular stages in a country's social development. Almost apologet-ically, he defends this emphasis: 'J'insiste souvent sur ce prix des monnaies; c'est, ce me semble, le pouls d'un Etat, et une manière assez sûre de reconnaître ses forces.' (I often insist on this matter of the currency's value; it is, I feel, the pulse of a State and a fairly reliable way of telling its strength.)

But when it comes to determining who are the creators of

civilization, then we find the tradesmen generally absent. Pride of place goes to those few great men who combine wisdom, enlightenment and strength of conviction. 'Il n'est point de véritablement grand homme qui n'ait un bon esprit.' (No truly great man is lacking a good mind.) Military leaders like Genghis Khan are ineligible for this distinction, for they have left nothing constructive behind them that will improve society; indeed, Voltaire throughout rejects any *mystique* based on military prowess, making it clear that courage is not a virtue but merely a fortunate quality to possess. The outstanding heroes of the *Essai* are few: Alfred the Great, Pope Alexander III, perhaps Henry I of England, but above all Henri IV. For Henri IV was a giant among his contemporaries: not only a man of learning, as was the Emperor Rudolph, but a brave and bold warrior as well (unlike Philip II of Spain, who was merely a prudent tyrant); whereas Elizabeth of England had had fewer obstacles to overcome and had sullied her glory by the execution of Mary, Queen of Scots, while Pope Sixtus V, though a patron of the arts, was both treacherous and cruel. In brief, Henri IV surpasses even Louis XIV in stature, though he had the disadvantage of living in a lesser age.

It becomes clear from this summary that Voltaire is not merely awarding honours to those who promote the arts and sciences. The outstanding sovereigns are those with all-round ability, no less in the moral and political fields than in the cultural. Significantly, the first measure which Voltaire mentions as undertaken by Henri IV once war has been concluded is an economic one: he restores the financial situation. Thereafter, he undertakes judicial reforms and establishes religious toleration. 'Le commerce, les arts sont en honneur'; luxury objects reappear. A programme of public works develops Paris, making it more beautiful. Nor is this a matter of delegating authority to his minister Sully who, though capable and loyal, lacks the imagination of genius.

This isolation of the great man exemplifies Voltaire's conviction about how progress is achieved: 'Il ne s'est presque jamais rien fait de grand dans le monde que par le génie et la fermeté d'un seul homme qui lutte contre les préjugés de la multitude . . .' (Almost nothing of greatness has ever been achieved in the world except through the genius and firmness of a single man at odds with the prejudices of the crowd . . .) Strong government is the remedy to political disorders, as Elizabeth I demonstrated; by this Voltaire means a certain firm integrity, not the ceaseless intriguing and steely vengeance such as kept Richelieu in power. Given this strong affection for centralized power, it is not surprising to find the author antipathetic to feudal institutions, which in his view are both repressive and ineffective at the same time, permitting no room for free protest or trade or the arts, promoting lawless anarchy and consequent revolutions, in short destroying the conditions essential to the establishment of a civilized society. By contrast, great men are treated by Voltaire with a respect which reminds one that he is also a classical tragedian; for they do not suffer as does the ordinary man with his 'petites prétentions' and 'vains plaisirs', but much more terribly.

The enlightened king, as we saw above, 'lutte contre les préjugés de la multitude'. In the *Essai* the source of all the horrors is firmly identified as popular fanaticism; a king who sows the wind of superstition reaps the whirlwind of rebellion, as the populace, inflamed by blind prejudice, enslaves its masters. Intellectual servitude gives not peace but war because it panders to man's blood-lust; therefore it is stupid as well as wicked to deny men the chance of enlightenment.

So we find a certain number of unresolved paradoxes in the *Essai.* Despite the repeated emphasis on economic aspects, Voltaire does not include them when he sums up the main motivating forces affecting mankind, and professes a more idealist line than he follows in practice. In the political realm, enlightened sovereigns are the saviours of mankind, firmly hauling their benighted subjects after them along the path of progress; yet one of the essential conditions of the civilized society is an insistence upon personal freedom and universal rights before the law. On the one side, Voltaire believes that men have a basic love of order and can achieve progress, and he offers prescriptions for liberal rule which combine justice with enlightened self-interest; on the other, he has to admit that historical happenings are largely meaningless, that men have often plumbed the depths of savagery, that utter tyrants like Aurengzeb live to a peaceful old age, that 'le maître le plus dur est le plus suivi' (the harshest master is the most popular). It is the problem of the Enlightenment liberal, seeking to inaugurate a more civilized way of life but dealing with very imperfect institutions for accomplishing it, and wishing to believe that man's rationality is more truly human than his instincts. In fairness to Voltaire's 'great man' theory, he himself is the first to point out the dangers of such a simplistic view, which attributes all great things to a single man when he has performed only some of them; most of the time leaders merely profit from the conjuncture of events. Few impose a positive imprint upon history, and few emerge as heroes in the *Essai.* Furthermore, as Peter Gay notes [in *Voltaire's Politics: The Poet as Realist* (2d ed., 1965), in an age that antedated universal literacy, universal suffrage and organized political parties, dynastic politics counted for much more than now. The nation still appeared to be a political creation, infinitely malleable by a strong leader, rather than a natural reality evolving organically, as the nineteenth century would come to see it. Meanwhile, despite the discouraging world in which he lives, Voltaire sees his task as to help improve the chances for civility, peace and happiness by affecting public opinion. The *Essai,* in pleading for greater enlightenment, is itself an emblem of that enlightenment.

For Voltaire history was quite as much a literary art as it was a science, and his comments place it close to tragedy. As he said in a famous letter to Shuvalov in 1758: 'J'ai toujours pensé que l'histoire demande le même art que la tragédie, une exposition, un nœud, un dénouement . . .' (I have always thought that history requires the same artistic approach as tragedy, an exposition, a knot, a denouement . . .) In the last months of his life he goes so far as to assert that the only merit history can have is in the style. Nor are these isolated opinions. As one might expect from someone who considered language an index of civilization, formal presentation would enter strongly into any writings by Voltaire.

Even so, the analogies with theatre are disconcerting. How far if at all can a reliable historian treat personalities of the past as dramatis personae and life itself as a vast stage *décor*? The most forceful statement of Voltaire's short-comings in this respect has come in a brilliant article by Lionel Gossman ["Voltaire's *Charles XII:* History into Art" (*Studies on Voltaire and the Eighteenth Century* XXV, 1963)]. Professor Gossman bases his case on the *philosophe*'s most 'theatrical' history, **Charles XII,** but his argument is of general import since he asserts that Voltaire's **Charles XII** 'is not . . . *fundamentally* different from his more mature works of history'. In this paper he argues that Voltaire reduces history to a formal object, something that is only seen, never penetrated intellectually, so that 'the inner substance . . . remains enigmatic, like Watteau's *Gilles* . . . '

It is certainly true that Voltaire very often uses the metaphor of the world as a theatre; one such was quoted above. Furthermore, the verb 'voir' or its equivalent plays a large part in the narration. But whether this reduces the **Essai** to a purely aesthetic display is not so simply resolved. For one thing, Voltaire's linking of history to tragedy does not imply an ironic distancing, as Gossman suggests. Quite the contrary, in fact; his plays suffer from the opposite defect of undue commitment to their subject. It is surely the same in the **Essai.** The ultimate weakness is not that it is too detached but that Voltaire can never forget he must write history 'en *philosophe*' (as he had put it long before in a letter to his friend Thieriot) and cannot resist the urge to proselytize.

Considering first the ironic qualities, one would be surprised, with such a subject and such an author, not to find countless examples. Voltaire's skilful use of the antithetical paradox allows many a well-turned phrase. The complex quarrel over status and power between the medieval popes and emperors is well summed up when Frederick I goes to Rome in 1152:

> Il fallut aller prendre à Rome cette couronne impériale, que les papes donnaient à la fois avec fierté et avec regret, voulant couronner un vassal, et affligés d'avoir un maître.

> (It proved necessary to go to Rome in order to take this imperial crown, which the popes bestowed with mingled pride and regret, since they wanted to crown a vassal but were distressed at having a master.)

The death of Charles VII of France is tragic bathos:

> Le malheureux Charles VII mourut, comme on sait, par la crainte que son fils ne le fît mourir; il choisit la faim pour éviter le poison qu'il redoutait.

> (The unfortunate Charles VII died, as we know, from the fear that his son might kill him; he chose hunger to avoid the poison that he dreaded.)

Voltaire is master of the ridiculous detail that deflates all human dignity. One such is the papal ceremony at which the new emperor is to kiss the pope's feet, then hold his stirrup and lead his palfrey by the bridle for nine Roman paces. The nonsense is increased when the emperor agrees to the kissing of feet but not to the other more dignified obligations—the first was acceptable because customary, the second was revolting because new. Voltaire rings a further change on this later when Durazzo, king of Naples takes the pope's bridle, but only to lead him into prison. On occasion Voltaire strings together a concatenation of senseless horrors, entirely devoid of casual conjunctions, in a way that is reminiscent of **Candide.** One of the best such examples is an enumeration a page long of murders and mutilations in eighth-century Constantinople. The details are horrifying—eyes put out, tongue and nose cut off, a murdered man's skull used as a cup by his killer—but the senseless succession, heightened by the meaningless list of names, downgrades the protagonists to absurd puppets in a grotesque Punch and Judy show.

If this were all, then Voltaire would merely be writing an historical **Candide.** But the atmosphere is not the same. Mordant irony is the exception, not the norm; the more constant tone is one of sadness tinged with horror at such madnesses. Typically, the enumeration of horrors in Constantinople mentioned above does not end with some devastating pirouette of black humour but in a direct appeal to the reader's judgement: 'Quelle histoire de brigands obscurs, punis en place publique pour leurs crimes, est plus horrible et plus dégoûtante?' (What story of obscure brigands, punished in the public square for their crimes, is more horrible and more disgusting?) Flaubert commented on one eloquent passage that here 'éclate d'une façon presque lyrique la tristesse de Voltaire en songeant à la barbarie des siècles qui suivirent la splendeur de l'empire romain' (bursts forth in almost lyrical fashion Voltaire's sadness when he thinks about the barbarism of the centuries which followed the splendour of the Roman Empire).

This statement could be widened to take in the whole work. Sometimes the author explicitly avoids facile wit, as when talking about the Catholic accusation that Luther was in the Devil's employ:

> Il ne faut point plaisanter sur les sujets tristes. C'était une matière très sérieuse, rendue funeste par le malheur de tant de familles et le supplice de tant d'infortunés . . .

> (One must not jest about sad subjects. This was a very serious matter, turned into catastrophe through the unhappiness of so many families and the torment of so many unfortunates . . .)

History is not futile nor to be mocked at, though many of its participants and happenings are foolish to a degree. The picture should rather evoke our compassion and sense of justice which, says Voltaire, are the two feelings on which society is founded; for this dual attitude will save us from useless scorn and urge us instead to work for a better society.

Comparison of the way the same material is treated here and in the *contes* helps to show that the style of the **Essai sur les mœurs** is not basically caustic. The most suitable for our purposes is the **Histoire des voyages de Scarmentado** (written probably 1753-4), partly because some of the episodes are also found in the **Essai,** partly because this *conte* is one of Voltaire's most brilliant demonstrations of irony and the only one to rival **Candide** in this respect. In **Scarmentado,** the Mogul Emperor Aurengzeb makes an appearance as a pious figure who receives a present of the broom which had swept out the temple: 'Ce balai est le symbole qui balaye toutes les ordures de l'âme.' (This broom is the symbol which sweeps away all the filth of the soul.) Being such a devout man, Aurengzeb did not seem to be in need of such a gift. But Voltaire adds, almost as though it were an afterthought:

Il est vrai qu'il avait égorgé un de ses frères et empoisonné son père. Vingt rayas et autant d'omras
étaient morts dans les supplices; mais cela n'était
rien, et on ne parlait que de sa dévotion.

(It is true that he had slit a brother's throat and poisoned his father. Twenty rayas [non-Moslem sub-
jects] and as many omras [Mohammedan lords]
were executed; but that was nothing, and people
spoke only of his devoutness.)

The treatment of Aurengzeb in the *Essai* displays none of
this ferocious humour:

Aurengzeb, dans le Mogol, se révoltait contre son
père; il le fit languir en prison, et jouit paisiblement
du fruit de ses crimes.

(Aurengzeb, during the Mogul period, rebelled
against his father; he let him languish in prison and
peacefully enjoyed the fruits of his crimes.)

The other comments on this figure are similar. Once again,
it is a matter for melancholy wonder that such a villain
should enjoy success: 'Nul homme n'a mieux montré que
le bonheur n'est pas le prix de la vertu.' (No man has demonstrated better that happiness is not the reward of virtue.)

It would therefore seem unfair to apply to the *Essai* Gossman's conclusion about *Charles XII:* 'The princes and po-
tentates of the world are revealed in the last analysis as the
playthings of destiny and the victims of their own roles.
The true heroes and conquerors are the intellectuals, the
spectators of the great comedy. Few though they are, the
true heroes of the *Essai sur les mœurs* are kings like Henri
IV who embrace the intellectual world as but one of their
many domains of action; and they move in a tragic, not
a comic, universe.

The defects of the history as an art form are therefore similar to those of Voltaire's tragedies. In a work where the
writer pays so much attention to individual leaders, the
psychological analysis is too flat for the reader to gain any
clear insight into their make-up. While the few heroes are
idealized beyond belief, the villainous majority are equally
unbelievable, being stupid or malicious or both. If these
characters have any vitality, it is not so much in isolation
as in the dramatic oppositions which Voltaire contrives
between some of them: Pope Gregory VII and the Emper-
or Henry IV; François I and Henry VIII; Elizabeth I and
Mary, Queen of Scots. To some extent the faults stem from
Voltaire's peruasion that all men are alike under the skin;
but there is an aesthetic weakness too. As one critic has
put it, he lacked the historical imagination to enter into
the feelings or cares of a medieval cathedral builder.

Fortunately this is not the whole story. Voltaire has
strengths well suited to a historian of civilization. The
structure of the *Essai* is not built upon pure narration, for
every so often Voltaire interrupts the chronological account to give us a panoramic view, comprising tableaux
of the different countries at a particular point in time.
After the meaningless succession of wars and disputes,
these portraits come as a welcome relief; and they fit in
well with Voltaire's tendency, evident in so many of his
works, to break down a continuous flow into sharply-
defined episodes. Furthermore, they allow Voltaire to
bring into play his extraordinary ability to sum up a complex situation in a brief space, as when he unravels the

complexities of the Crusades or the Reformation. Here his
lucid mind removes all ambiguity and paints the picture
plain (albeit with the danger of superficiality). As . . .
with **Candide,** there is a price to be paid for such clarity;
but the virtues should not be minimized. Voltaire is mas-
terly at picking the representative detail which sums up a
whole situation or period in striking fashion: details about
affluence . . . ; the primitive climate of fifteenth-century
Paris captured in the religious tableau played at Charles
VII's entry into the city in 1437; the crudity of morals in
Sweden a hundred years later, seen in the way King John
gets rid of his brother in prison by publicly sending him
poison. The *Essai,* like many of Voltaire's other writings,
is a remarkable piece of popularization.

Capitalizing upon the growth of historical scholarship in
the seventeenth century. Enlightenment historiography
displayed as strong a scepticism in this field as Descartes
had shown for metaphysics when he wrote his seminal
Discours de la méthode (1637); indeed, the emphasis upon
'methodical doubt' as a means for constructing new ave-
nues of approach to knowledge may be placed squarely in
the Cartesian tradition. But Descartes's edifice of doubt
had removed history from the field of knowledge and it
was left to others to make this particular link. Inheriting
the legacy of erudite sceptics like Pierre Bayle, Voltaire
applies Cartesian principles to the historical domain. As
he had put it in his 1748 Preface to **Charles XII,** 'L'in-
crédulité . . . est le fondement de toute sagesse . . .'
(Incredulity . . . is the basis of all wisdom . . .) Scepticism will help one to seek out falsity, to separate the dross
of myth and fable from the gold ore of true fact. The historian must avoid partisan views; in particular, Voltaire objects in the *Essai* to sycophantic professional writers who
praise leaders like Charlemagne or Alfonso III of Spain,
or spread false stories such as the ridiculous rumour that
Henry V of England died of haemorrhoids as divine punishment for sitting on the French throne. The weaknesses
of Voltaire's position are all too clear to modern scholars,
who will take his scepticism one stage further in asking
what he means by a true historical fact. At the same time,
in his laudable desire to avoid repeating the unverified details of sectarian historians, Voltaire does not fall into the
opposite error of those nineteenth-century writers who believed that a godlike perspective on the past was possible,
all prejudice removed. By deciding that one must take a
philosophe's point of view, he commits himself to a consistent historical perspective that does not pretend to the aspirations of pure positivism.

For Voltaire it is above all written sources that count. He
explicitly rejects the faked speeches and harangues of oral
traditions and only rarely falls into the trap of supplying
a patently contrived anecdote. Extra-literary sources are
scarcely considered, and scepticism is shown towards such
evidence as contemporary medals. In consequence of such
views, the farther back one goes into the past the more difficult it becomes for Voltaire to discover truth. Nonetheless, although so much of his research must be based on
second-hand compilation (much of it faulty, as for instance on ancient Indian history), Voltaire reads widely,
though in haste. [In the 1969 *Complete Works* edition of
La Philosophie de l'histoire, J. H. Brumfitt] shows that he
is thoroughly documented on the history of religion as
background to **La Philosophie de l'histoire.** Furthermore,
his standard of accuracy in using sources is high, as

Pomeau has shown in an illuminating check on various sections of the *Essai.* (A similar conclusion had emerged from a careful study by Lanson of certain chapters in *Le Siècle de Louis XIV.*) And as Lanson points out elsewhere [*Voltaire* (2d ed., 1910)], Voltaire had the rare merit for his time of appreciating that no history can be written without a critical examination of evidence and documents.

The criteria for this examination, however, are unreliable, since they are based on a rationalist view of what is likely to have happened. The dangers are manifest; Voltaire can so easily conclude that what is accurate is what supports his own outlook. He rejects the idea that temple prostitution could have existed in Babylon and elsewhere, on the *a priori* grounds that no man would do such a thing in the presence of those he respected. For similar reasons Voltaire denies that any religion has ever been set up which encourages men to vice; he would doubtless have found voodoo and black magic difficult to fit in with this optimistic outlook. Even the rule, inherited from Bayle and others, that when a historian admits a fact contrary to his interests it must be right does not take account of the possibility that unknown to him it could still turn out later to be false.

Nor does this approach protect the writer from sharing the fashionable view of his time. The Enlightenment's scant regard for the Middle Ages is notorious and it constitutes one of the greatest weaknesses of Voltaire's *Essai.* The price to be paid for his admirably secularist approach is a refusal to see any cultural hopes in the medieval Church, with the rare exceptions of isolated monasteries or a quite exceptional pope like Alexander III. It is this tendentiousness which most deforms the work as history; examples are the disturbingly ferocious onslaught on Jewish civilization because above all 'ce sont nos pères!', the reduction of the Reformation to simplistic causes and the exaltation of non-Christian civilizations above their merits. In respects like these Voltaire is most the prisoner of his age.

But let us conclude on a more positive note. The *Essai* 's claim to count among Voltaire's most important writings rests on firmer foundations than these. What most distinguishes this history is the ability to see how a civilization can become an object of study. Escaping from servitude to a plethora of inconsequential details, Voltaire demonstrates that here is a topic rich for future exploration as the most complex and sophisticated of human enterprises, to the charting of whose fragile and gradual beginnings he has devoted such formidable energy. (pp. 32-47)

Haydn Mason, in his Voltaire, *Hutchinson & Co. Ltd., 1975, 204 p.*

A. Owen Aldridge   (essay date 1975)

[*Aldridge is an American academic and scholar who has written widely on eighteenth-century French and American culture. In the following excerpt, he discusses style and characterization in* Candide.]

No single event—either the Seven Years' War, which represented man-made evil, or the Lisbon earthquake, which represented that caused by nature—can be considered the major impetus for the writing of *Candide,* even though both events figure prominently in the narrative. Voltaire

had already expressed his feelings about the earthquake in his *Poem* of 1755, and he was not passionately committed against war as an instrument of national grandeur. He quite accurately remarked that his purpose in *Candide* was "to bring amusement to a small number of men of wit." With equal appropriateness, he rendered an almost opposite judgment, that it was "Job brought up to date." *Candide* is literally "a mixture of ridicule and horror," an unflinching scrutiny of the miseries of life carried on with comic detachment.

Voltaire's major philosophical themes are not as apparent in his title, *Candide or Optimism, Translated from the German of Doctor Ralph,* as they are in the title of the metaphysical treatise by Leibniz, which he is attacking, *Essay of Theodicy on the Goodness of God, the Liberty of Man and the Origin of Evil.* In both works, the questions of the goodness of god and the origin of evil are interrelated, as are those of free will and determinism. Modern criticism of *Candide* has emphasized the problem of evil, which Voltaire does not resolve or even seek to resolve. His contemporaries, however, properly recognized his parallel concern with free will and his burlesque of "the appointments of providence as implying an absurd necessity" [see excerpt dated 1759].

In his *Poem on the Disaster of Lisbon,* Voltaire had presented Pope as the chief exponent of optimism and had attacked his axiom "whatever is, is right." In *Candide,* he does not even allude to Pope, but instead pillories Leibniz as the apostle of optimism and endlessly ridicules his axiom, "the best of all possible worlds." We may ask why Leibniz was substituted for Pope, particularly since Pope was the more contemporary author, his *Essay on Man* following Leibniz's *Théodicée* by almost a quarter of a century. The answer is that the Lisbon poem consists of sincere philosophical argument, whereas *Candide* is unmitigated satire. Voltaire admired Pope and the English deists and had no desire to subject them to ridicule; whereas he was still smarting from his discomfiture at the German court and relished the opportunity to bring anything German into disrespect.

The action of *Candide* begins, therefore, in Germany, offering Voltaire at the outset the opportunity to poke fun at the deficiencies in aristocratic refinements and excess of pretensions in that nation. The Baron of Thunder-ten-tronckh—a name with more German sound than authenticity—has a wife weighing 350 pounds and lives in a castle, magnificent by reason of being graced with a door, windows, and even a tapestry in the great hall. He despises his sister's suitor because the latter can prove only seventy-one quarterings in his escutcheon. Voltaire's target is not aristocratic pretentiousness in general, but that of the Prussian court, for he elsewhere points out that the genealogy of German barons goes no further back than to Witikind.

From Germany, Voltaire may also have acquired the inspiration for the personality of his protagonist Candide. The trait of extreme credulousness or sentimental simplicity was associated at that time with the German national character. Frederick said of himself, for example, that he was "only a good German" and that he did not "blush to reveal the character of candor attached to that nation." In 1669, Johann Jakob Christoffel von Grimmelshausen had published a picaresque novel *Simplicius Simplicissimus,* the adventures of an exceedingly simple or naïve young man, who in one episode descends to the bottom of the sea, a parallel to the Eldorado chapter in **Candide.** Since Voltaire admitted familiarity with fifteenth-century German authors who used a "bold and buffoonish" style, it is quite possible that he knew *Simplicissimus* as well. Like Grimmelshausen's creation, Voltaire's protagonist has "the most unaffected simplicity," and his physiognomy is "the index of his mind." Candide believes everything and everyone and wears his heart on his sleeve.

Unlike **Zadig** and Voltaire's other philosophical tales that have a protagonist but no other characters, **Candide** has a roster of personae. In this sense it is closer to a conventional novel than is *Gulliver's Travels,* the literary work which it resembles most and which served as a partial model. It can even be considered as a parody of the seventeenth-century *Bildungsroman,* in which moral education is carried on by means of extensive travel in the company of an all-knowing tutor. Of this genre, Fénelon's *Télémaque* was the prototype. Candide's mentor is the perennially cheerful Pangloss, who taught not that all is right, as did Pope and many other optimists, but that all is for the best in the best of all possible worlds, an exaggeration of ordinary deism, and a verbal echo of Leibniz. Sex interest is provided by Cunégonde, the daughter of the castle, whose fatal kiss causes Candide's first misfortune. Cunégonde is later repeatedly raped or seduced by a series of masters, but Candide himself is never introduced to sexual pleasure. As a refrain to the empty declamations of Pangloss, Candide repeats with naïve confidence after every scene of horror his conviction that this is the best of all possible worlds. The completely opposite point of view is expressed by two characters who serve as foils to Candide and his mentor: Jacques, a charitable Anabaptist, expounds the doctrine of the moral degeneration of man; and Martin, a Manichean, teaches the supremacy of evil rather than a balance of evil and good. Both are more often than not spokesmen for Voltaire. A Venetian nobleman, Pococurante, with many exterior resemblances to Algarotti, expresses literary and dramatic theories exactly parallel to those in Voltaire's previously published works, even though he cannot be taken as a *porteparole* of all of Voltaire's esthetic notions. Even Frederick appears briefly as the king of the Bulgares, a military conqueror spreading bloodshed and destruction. The band is completed by a picaresque valet, Cacambo, from South America; an old woman (daughter of a pope); a priest, and a prostitute, the latter two living together in apparent bliss but actual torment. These assorted philosophical symbols and character types have uncanny resemblances to flesh and blood creatures.

In *Gulliver's Travels* Swift used many methods of satire to convey his message of gloom, but Voltaire concentrates on one only—contrast or ludicrous juxtaposition—developed in many forms. The basic structure of **Candide** consists of a naïve, idealistic mind coming into constant contact with opposing realities. Doctrines are refuted by events, not arguments. Candide, among other misadventures, is turned out of his home; is forcibly impressed into the Bulgarian army; is brought to the verge of death by being forced to run the gauntlet; witnesses a bloody battle in which thirty thousand men are slaughtered; survives a tempest, a shipwreck, and the famous Lisbon earthquake; and is whipped to insensibility by the Inquisition. During these and scores of other horrible episodes, he repeats the phrases of Pangloss, that everything is for the best in the physical and moral realms, and that nothing could be any otherwise than it is. He persists, as he himself admits, in "the mania of saying all is well when all is evil." Early in the narrative, a recruiting officer promises Candide, "Your fortune is made, your glory assured." Immediately he is clapped into irons. At the hands of the Inquisition, Candide is "preached at, beaten, absolved, and blessed."

Only once in his narrative does Voltaire abandon the technique of exposing the evils of life and of nature by stark realistic portrayal—in a visit to Eldorado. This mythical realm in South America represents the reverse of the world of actuality in both physical and intellectual characteristics. It belongs to the universe of fantasy or science fiction because of its location and natural resources. Hidden in the midst of inaccessible mountains, Eldorado is paved with gold and precious stones, which the inhabitants treat as baubles. From the perspective of society and ideas, Eldorado is a pure Utopia. Its people are completely rational; they can conceive of only one possible religion, deism; they have no priestly class, no prisons, and no law courts, but in their place, they have a palace of science filled with instruments of mathematics and physics. Voltaire, in employing this reversal of perspective—that is, in passing from the exposing of reality to portrayal of the ideal—is following the example of *Gulliver's Travels,* in which we find an identical duality of perspective. Unlike Swift, however, Voltaire reveals that even Utopia is not satisfying to mankind. It is human nature, he affirms, "to enjoy running around, to make oneself to be esteemed by one's peers, and to make a show of what one has seen on one's travels." Voltaire subtly reveals that the perfection in Eldorado is pure exaggeration by pointing out that all of the jokes told by its king are funny. Of all the astonishing features of the land, this is not the least astonishing.

Throughout his narrative, Voltaire brings into review many scientific, social, and philosophical notions of paramount interest to him and to the age. He glances at Rousseau's doctrine of equality in the state of nature in a chapter on the land of the *oreillons* or ape men, deriving the name of the race from Garcilaso de la Vega's description of *Orejones,* or Indians with big ears. When Candide sees two ape men beating two females of their kind, who respond amorously, Candide is bewildered and curious over why they should take pleasure in the pain inflicted upon them. Later the whole tribe of ape men prepare to eat Candide for dinner, and they are kept from doing so only when they discover that he is not a Jesuit. The existence of cannibalism represented throughout Voltaire's intellectual career one of the major arguments against the doctrine of a universal natural law. The artless Candide concludes that since he has been saved from being devoured merely by the circumstance of not being a Jesuit, the state of pure nature is good.

The evils of institutionalized religion are symbolized by the Jesuits in Paraguay. In their missionary settlement, *los Padres* have everything, the people nothing; the Jesuits consume a delicious luncheon in the shade, the Indians nibble their corn in the heat of the noonday sun.

The common attitude toward suicide, which Voltaire had previously considered in print and in his personal correspondence, he treats in **Candide** as an example of the perversity of human nature. The ridiculous weakness of clinging to one's life is one of the most baneful inclinations, "for there is nothing more stupid than to desire to carry continually a burden which one always wishes to throw to the ground."

Candide takes from Eldorado to Europe a sheep bearing red wool, and the Academy of Bordeaux offers a prize for the best explanation of the causes of this phenomenon. This is a parody of an actual prize offered by this academy in 1741 for the best essay on why the skin of the Negro race is black. True to his prejudices against biological science, Voltaire satirized this inquiry, but he treated with respect a geological query which had previously intrigued him personally, whether the earth was at one time completely covered with water. Candide merely asks Martin his opinion, and the latter says that he has none.

In commenting on the European political scene, Voltaire described six dethroned kings eating together at a cabaret in Venice, each of the kings representing an actual monarch in history who had lost his reigning power. This episode serves to reduce the grandeur associated with royalty and to provide Voltaire with a small measure of revenge for the indignities he had suffered at the hands of Louis XV and Frederick.

In one passage, Voltaire repeats the arguments he had previously used to vindicate his *Poem on the Disaster of Lisbon,* particularly the theory that both man and nature have degenerated and that the Christian myth of the fall of man in Eden is closer to the truth than the system of optimism. Through the person of the charitable anabaptist Jacques, Voltaire affirms that men have tended to corrupt nature: they were not born wolves, but have become wolves; god gave them neither canon nor bayonets, but they forged their weapons in order to destroy. If Jacques is a spokesman for Voltaire himself, and there is good reason for believing that he is, Voltaire almost seems to be vindicating Rousseau's doctrine that society vitiates mankind. He is certainly repudiating the doctrine of the unchanging nature of the universe, which he had previously expounded in his *Discourse on the Changes which Have Occurred on Our Globe.* In a sense, Rousseau was correct in insisting that *Candide* was an answer to his letter in which he had affirmed that "providence is always right, according to the pious, and always wrong, according to the philosopher." In *Candide,* Pangloss and Martin, the Manichean, think exactly alike concerning the presence of suffering in the world; they disagree only in the interpretation of the evidence. Pangloss recognizes only good; the other, only evil. From this prospect, Pangloss represents Rousseau and Martin, Voltaire. At the end of the story, Voltaire succeeds in bringing their opposing perspectives toward a common plane: the question then to be resolved is no longer whether all is right, but whether the other people whom Candide meets on his travels are more to be pitied than he. It is significant to note with Jean Sareil that there is no philosophical discussion in the story which is not abruptly cut short and left hanging in the air. In his conclusion Voltaire also refuses "to accept an abstract, philosophical answer to the long debate over Optimism."

In his final chapter, Voltaire completely abandons the metaphysical speculation he had shared with other poets and philosophers in order to present notions typical of himself alone. Much of the universal popularity of *Can-*

dide, therefore, is due to this final chapter. Here all the characters are brought together in the same locale—a house in the country. This circumstance, together with the constant disappearances and mysterious reappearances of the main characters throughout the narrative, suggests that *Candide* is a parody of the structure of romantic fiction of the time as well as an intellectual satire. Voltaire elsewhere ridiculed Calprenède's seventeenth-century method of constructing a novel upon a heap of improbable adventures brought into the semblance of order by the interrogation of an old man or a nurse. He may also have had in mind the more modern "roman polisson," or even novels such as *Manon Lescaut* of the abbé Prévost.

In the concluding section the old woman, after summarizing the worst mishaps and physical agonies suffered by the entire band, wants to know which is worse, "to experience all the miseries which all of us have experienced, or to stay here and do nothing." "It is a great question," says Candide. The doctrine of boredom, one of Voltaire's most characteristic, is expressed several times in his works. "Our greatest enemy is boredom," he affirmed in a poem dedicated to Mme Denis in 1748; "one cannot live with company, or without it" [*A Mme Denis nièce de l'auteur, La Vie de Paris et de Versailles*]. In his early *Philosophical Letters,* however, he had considered resentment at the tedium of life to be one of the salutary characteristics of man. Contrary to Pascal, who had described the state of mankind as wretched because man can be discontented without any external cause for his dissatisfaction, Voltaire insisted that "on the contrary man is fortunate on this point, and we have an obligation to the author of nature to the degree that he has attached ennui to inaction in order thus to compel us to be useful to our neighbor and to our selves." In his *Philosophical Letters* Voltaire looks at boredom in the optimistic spirit of Pangloss; in *Candide* Voltaire does not consider ennui a blessing, but he offers a means of escape—his famous conclusion, "we must cultivate our garden."

This conclusion—apparently clear and simple—has puzzled critics and ordinary readers ever since the publication of *Candide.* What exactly does it mean? One might assume that Voltaire is suggesting husbandry as a remedy for boredom. This is borne out by a letter from Voltaire to Mme Denis in 1753 in which he described gardening as "an occupation which destroys boredom." In the same month, while deploring "the idleness of the country," he remarked, "it is better to dig in the ground than to suffer boredom." In a letter to Cideville written during the composition of *Candide,* however, he seemed to give a contrary interpretation, affirming that "retirement is good only with good company" and that the secret of happiness is found neither in the fields, the court, nor the city.

Whether or not the cultivation of one's garden is necessarily linked to the dispelling of boredom, we still need to interpret the meaning of Voltaire's famous conclusion. It might refer simply to hedonism, as in the phrase "The Gardens of Epicurus," which he had used in an ode describing his arrival at Les Délices. The injunction to horticulture might be alluding to the antiquity and respectability in the humanistic tradition of the concept of orderly cultivation. As Bacon had previously said in reference to Eden, "God almightly first planted a garden." In this sense, Voltaire's prescription of cultivation seems to rebuke Rousseau's emphasis on wild nature. Or Voltaire might simply have wished to suggest abandoning activities of the world in favor of personal ease—activities of either an egocentric or a philanthropic nature, both of which occasionally obtruded on his personal composure. The eighteenth-century Russian novelist Karamzin [see excerpt dated 1789] believed that Voltaire had in mind respite from the weariness of metaphysical speculation. One could add to Candide's phrase, according to Karamzin, "Let us love our family, relations, and friends, and leave the rest to the will of destiny." Voltaire may even have been thinking of himself as a writer and social critic, and conceived of his garden as a retreat from the attacks of his enemies. In a fragment of unknown date published in his *Notebooks,* he denounced the secret rage with which envy pursues all real talents, and concluded that minds kindred to his should follow the example "of the author of *La Henriade* and cultivate his talents in a desert." Some critics have assumed that Candide's final words reflect a faith in the future, and some have even maintained that they foreshadow the political doctrine of anarchism, each man going his own way. One might even see a foreshadowing of Sartrean existentialism.

The obvious meaning of Candide's words is, of course, the literal one, not only that gardening dispels boredom, but that it produces positive good. There are many passages in Voltaire's correspondence to confirm this interpretation, beginning with Bolingbroke's letter in 1724 setting forth a parallel between cultivating one's character and one's garden. Soon after taking up residence at Les Délices, Voltaire wrote to Robert Tronchin, to whom the estate would revert after Voltaire's death, "I am concerned only with cultivating your garden in peace." Somewhat later he wrote to Diderot, the "labors of the country seem to belong to philosophy. The good experiments of physics are those of the cultivation of the land." In the year following the publication of *Candide,* Frederick commended Voltaire on his wisdom in following the counsel to cultivate his garden. Frederick seemed to suggest that Voltaire was reflecting his own experience and contentment at Les Délices. Soon after taking up his residence there, Voltaire exulted: "Happy is he who lives in his own property with his nieces, his books, his garden, his vines, his horses, his cows, his eagle, his fox and his rabbits, which rub their noses with their paws. I have all of that and the Alps to boot which create an admirable effect. I much prefer to lecture my gardeners than to play courtier to kings." In similar mood he observed to Mme Du Deffand that there is only one pleasure to be preferred to literary ones, and that is "seeing vast prairies turn green and beautiful crops grow." If Candide's words are to be taken literally, they foreshadow the tribute of Thomas Jefferson, "Those who labour in the earth are the chosen people of God, whose breasts he has made his peculiar deposit for substantial and genuine virtue" [*Notes on Virginia,* 1785, Query XIX]. This is as close to primitivism as Voltaire ever came.

Thanks to the development of computerized methods of research, we are able to discover that the word used most frequently in *Candide* is the particle *de* (1299 times). Apart from Candide's own name (373 times), the most common substantive is *vieille* (53 times), followed by *monde* (52 times). *Vieux* is not used at all as a noun, but *vieillard* appears twelve times and *vieillards* once. There is no warrant for assuming from these statistics, however, that old age in women made a greater impression on Voltaire than old age in men, or that he agreed with those Renaissance theologians who maintained that the world itself was growing old.

Structural analysis does very little to explain the universal appeal of *Candide.* It ranks as one of the masterpieces of European literature, not primarily because of style but because of its realistic portrayal of the human condition. The character of the protagonist arouses our sympathy. We commiserate with his misfortunes at the same time that we derive amusement from his naïveté. Apart from certain elements of the ludicrous and grotesque and humorous exaggeration incumbent upon the techniques of satire, *Candide* presents an essentially true picture of life. It addresses itself, moreover, to the basic philosophical questions of concern to all men: are we free to make our own choices or are we the puppets of destiny? and is the evil that we all perceive and experience the most pervasive force in the universe or can it be made subservient to a contrary force of beneficence? (pp. 251-60)

> *A. Owen Aldridge, in his* Voltaire and the Century of Light, *Princeton University Press, 1975, 443 p.*

Theodore Besterman   (essay date 1976)

[*Besterman was a renowned English parapsychologist, editor, bibliographer, and author. He worked as a joint editor of the Oxford Books on Bibliography, as general editor of the Association of Special Libraries and Information Bureaux, and as editor and executive officer of the British Union Catalogue of Periodicals. In 1952, he founded the Institut et Musée Voltaire in Geneva and served as its director until 1973. In the following excerpt from a 1976 revision of his 1969 biography* Voltaire, *he considers the method and intent of Voltaire's* Philosophical Dictionary.]

First planned in Berlin in 1752 during the last months of Voltaire's bitter-sweet stay with Frederick of Prussia, the *Dictionnaire philosophique* became one of his most cherished writings. Held up by the exile's long search for a home (the evil star that led him to Geneva caused also long prudential delays) and a thousand other activities, the first edition finally came off the press in 1764. Published a few weeks before Voltaire's seventieth birthday, it is in many ways a young man's book, angry, hard-hitting, uncompromising. Its impact was prompt, powerful and lasting. However, the most immediately perceptible though least important result was its condemnation by all the establishments, religious and governmental, drawing from Voltaire the usual flood of protestations and disavowals. However, also as usual, these disavowals were accompanied by new editions of the 'alphabetic abomination', containing additions which, like the inevitably anonymous original *Dictionnaire,* could obviously have come from no other pen than his. . . . Voltaire was always happy to play the formal game of denial, as required by the unwritten laws of governmental and even ecclesiastic censorship, according to which a protestation of not guilty was accepted as evidence of innocence unless some police spy like Fréron could produce positive evidence of guilt. But though Voltaire went through the motions, and gleefully played this charade of 'as if ', he never unwillingly withdrew a word he had written or an opinion he had advanced.

In short, the book was condemned by the authorities, but read by 'all', that is, by the few who could read and the still fewer who had access to books. 'Few', 'fewer', these are relative terms, and it would be a mistake to imagine that the French reading public in the second half of the eighteenth century comprised only a tiny élite. By no means, for the **Dictionnaire** went into numerous editions, rivalling **Candide** (published five years earlier) which sold 6000 copies in a few weeks.

The **Dictionnaire philosophique** is not what we now understand by a dictionary, least of all a dictionary of philosophy, for its alphabetic arrangement is little more than a literary *trompe l'œil*. This epoch-making little book is in fact a series of essays on a wide variety of subjects, sometimes arranged under convenient headings in alphabetic sequence, but sometimes placed under deliberately misleading or even provocative catchwords. Thus, under 'Catéchisme chinois', the reader will find nothing whatever about any kind of Chinese catechism, but instead he will be able to enjoy a far-reaching demonstration of the superiority of ethics over religion.

To say further that the **Dictionnaire** is even less a treatise on philosophy than a dictionary is not a paradox but, in our time, a necessary explanation. This gloss was not needed in the eighteenth century: the contemporary reader of a new work which, though anonymous, showed on every page the unmistakable hallmark of the sage of Ferney, and the titlepage of which bore the words **Dictionnaire philosophique,** knew exactly what to expect. For in the language of Voltaire and his fellow *philosophes,* a language by then quite widely understood and even accepted, the term philosophy was used in such a context in the sense of what we now call freethought or rationalism—either one a better and more accurate term than the now fashionable humanism, a word as vague as it is ambiguous. In other words, philosophy in the language of the Enlightenment was a state of mind, not a discipline of the schools. But of course the eighteenth-century use of *philosophe* in French can be as misleading as the humanism of twentieth-century English. Every time it occurs the reader has to determine whether it is being used in the general or its special sense, and the translator has to decide whether to render it as philosopher or as freethinker; and as Voltaire was rightly convinced that the only true philosopher was a *philosophe* in the special sense, the difficulty is much compounded. Generally speaking, what we today understand by philosophy was usually referred to by Voltaire as metaphysics. As for our metaphysics, he stigmatised it as nonsense. Pangloss, it will be remembered, taught Candide metaphysico-theologo-cosmolo-nigology.

What is certain is that the **Dictionnaire philosophique** is a world away from the academic or even the systematic. Voltaire wrote what his preoccupied genius impelled him to write, and the result could turn out to be a play or an epigram, a letter or a poem, a controversial dissertation or a treatise in several volumes. If it was a fairly short piece of 'non-fiction' in prose, he would sometimes print it as a pamphlet or even a leaflet, but more often he would file it in a series of folders marked *Mélanges* (miscellanies). From the contents of these folders Voltaire built up his innumerable volumes of essays, published both separately

Voltaire at the age of 24, by Nicolas Largillière.

and as parts of his various, ever more voluminous sets of collected works. When, however, Voltaire's writings were of this kind but of a still more precise type, consciously hortatory or propagandist, they found their way, beginning with essays composed in 1752 and added to thereafter without interruption until the end of his life, into volumes eventually destined to be entitled **Dictionnaire philosophique portatif** (from 1764), **Opinion par alphabet** (this title never appeared in print), **La Raison par alphabet** (from 1769), **Dictionnaire philosophique** (from 1770), **Questions sur l'encyclopédie** (from 1770).

Voltaire's wider object in publishing these works is evident, and he made his specific purpose clear beyond a peradventure in a lapidary remark on the great *Encyclopédie:* 'Twenty folio volumes will never make a revolution. It is the little portable volumes of thirty *sous* that are to be feared. Had the gospel cost twelve hundred sesterces the Christian religion would never have been established'.

Voltaire acted on this conviction. His alphabetic essays, dialogues, skits and other papers, and even more the mixed volumes containing them, vary in tone and emphasis, but all quickly became enormously popular in their collected forms, and were frequently revised and reprinted. Some of these editions were prepared under Voltaire's supervision, but most often they were pirated by the booksellers. They are interrelated in so complicated a pattern that it would be a considerable critical and bibliographical enterprise to disentangle the various states of many of the texts. So one cannot but sympathise with Condorcet and Beaumarchais. When, after the great man's death, they were preparing the so-called Kehl edition of his works they were confronted with a vast mass of miscellaneous material, most of it in print, but some left by Voltaire only in manuscript. Unwilling or unable to cope with it logically, or even, it must be said, intelligently, and finding that a good deal of it could be forced into an alphabetic semblance, they poured as much as they could into a vast cornucopia for which they purloined the label *Dictionnaire philosophique* which had been used by Voltaire for a very different kind of work, short and cheap.

It is true that in adopting this desperate procedure they imitated up to a point Voltaire's own example, for he was decidedly casual in such matters, like most of his contemporaries. Yet Beaumarchais and his collaborators went far beyond anything authorised by Voltaire's practices. Indeed, the title they used was even less justified since they included a great deal of not even ostensibly alphabetic material, and even a complete book (the **Lettres philosophiques** or **English letters**) that has nothing remotely alphabetic about it, to say nothing of many long essays, and contributions published or intended for Diderot's *Encyclopédie*. For good measure they also went so far as to throw in a number of lexicographic notes written for the *Dictionnaire de l'Académie*. All this makes up the wretched and unnaturally distended rag-bag which is nowadays accepted as Voltaire's **Dictionnaire philosophique.**

As I have said, the original **Dictionnaire philosophique** was repeatedly condemned by the civil and religious authorities in several countries, but nowhere with more congenial venom than in Geneva, whose unco guid still hate Voltaire. Thus, when the *procureur général* (public prosecutor) of that little town, Jean Robert Tronchin, was asked by the city council in 1764 to state his opinion of Voltaire's book, with a view to a prosecution, his very long report described it as a 'deplorable monument of the extent to which intelligence and erudition can be abused'. Among the terms the *procureur* used to describe the **Dictionnaire** are 'baneful paradoxes', 'indiscreet researches', 'audacious criticism', 'errors, malignity and indecency', 'contagious poison', 'temerarious, impious, scandalous, destructive of revelation', and so on and on. The book was to the end included in the unlamented official Roman index of forbidden books. This fate was only to be expected, and indeed it can almost be said to have been invited, for Voltaire deliberately planned the **Dictionnaire** as a revolutionary book, in which the most liberal ideas were to be expressed openly and lucidly, and made available to all who could read. Most decidedly Voltaire did not regard himself as a 'harmless drudge': his intention was to be as harmful as possible to superstition and all forms of conventional thought. Dangerous undertaking! Did not the presence of the **Dictionnaire** among the books of the chevalier de La Barre contribute to his frightful execution for blasphemy?

The **Dictionnaire philosophique** also provoked widespread condemnation by the Jesuits and other religious polemists. The abbé Louis Maïeul Chaudon's *Dictionnaire antiphilosophique* (re-named even more explicitly *Anti-dictionnaire philosophique*), first published in 1767, went into several editions. Three years later appeared *Observations sur la Philosophie de l'histoire et sur le Dictionnaire portatif* and a *Dictionnaire philosophico-théologique portatif,* respectively by the abbés Laurent François and Aimé Paulian. The egregious Nonotte contributed his mite in four vol-

umes entitled *Dictionnaire philosophique de la religion* (1772).

Voltaire's general purpose being to undermine credulity, all these attacks and many more of the same kind can be ignored. It is more interesting to see whether Voltaire's more precise intentions in launching the **Portatif** can be determined from the contents of the little book. Here is a list of the articles contained in the first edition of 1764 (in French these are of course in alphabetical sequence): Abraham; Soul; Friendship; Love; Socratic love; Self-love; Angel; Anthropophagi; Apis; Apocalypse; Atheist; Atheism; Baptism; Beautiful; Beauty; Beasts; Good, sovereign good; All is good; Limits of human understanding; Character; Certain, certainty; Chain of events; Chain of created beings; the Heaven of the ancients; Circumcision; Body; China; Chinese catechism; Japanese catechism; Catechism of the clergy; Historical researches on Christianity; Convulsions; Criticism; Destiny; God; Equality; Hell; State, government (which is the best?); Ezekiel; Fables; Fanaticism; Falsity of human virtues; End, final causes; Folly; Fraud; Glory; War; Grace; History of the Jewish kings and paralipomena; Idol, idolator, idolatry; Flood; Jephte, or sacrifices of human blood; Joseph; Freewill; Laws; Civil and ecclesiastic laws; Luxury; Matter; Wicked; Messiah; Metamorphosis; Metempsychosis; Miracles; Moses; Fatherland; Peter; Prejudices; Religion; Resurrection; Solomon; Feeling; Dreams; Superstition; Tyranny; Tolerance; Virtue.

It is clear that Voltaire's preoccupations in the first **Dictionnaire philosophique** were overwhelmingly theological and philosophical. Indeed, although . . . it is not a systematic treatise, the **Portatif** does contain preponderantly philosophical writing in the widest sense. This is evident in the articles themselves even more than in their titles, which, I repeat, do not always define very exactly the texts that follow them. Even such essays as 'Friendship' and 'Beautiful' have religious or ethical overtones. And this tendency is strongly confirmed by the second edition of 1765, in which Voltaire added articles entitled Abbé; Confession; Dogmas; False intelligence; Faith; War; Idea; Letters, men of letters; Martyr; Paul; Priest; Sect; Superstition II; Theist; Theologian.

Voltaire's treatment of the religious subjects, indeed of all subjects, is above all scientific: that is, he was concerned to establish the truth. Here and elsewhere his first question is always: did an alleged event really occur? He never fell into the universal theological error of examining a thing before knowing whether it exists. This fact explains what so many people find disconcerting: the destructiveness of Voltaire's writings on religion. This negative kind of approach is no longer necessary, thanks very largely to Voltaire himself. Besides, in the twentieth century mere facts have become almost irrelevant: theologians have learned the subtle art of selective symbology. Educated laymen, of course, learned it even more quickly.

One of the bitterest complaints made by the *procureur général* of Geneva was that Voltaire quoted from the *Bible* passages which 'taken literally would be unworthy of Divine Majesty'. Tronchin, mercifully for him, was not conscious of the fact that he had himself swallowed a large dose of the 'contagious poison' of Voltaire's thought, and had been affected by it to an extent amply revealed by the innocent confession I have just quoted. It must be remembered that it was then quite exceptional even to envisage the mere possibility that there could be things in holy writ considered unworthy of 'Divine Majesty', or that these things could be taken in any other way than literally. Indeed, when the **Dictionnaire** was first published men were still simple and logical enough to believe that scriptures proclaimed to be sacred and inspired must be taken to mean what they say. They could not but hold it to be blasphemous to select for belief what was convenient to believe, and to ignore or 'interpret' the rest. Voltaire often satirises this tendency, as when he inquires in 'Pierre' whether, if a reference to Babylon is interpreted to mean Rome, we must assume, when Rome is really named, that Babylon is in fact intended. At the end of 'Prophètes' Voltaire makes a sustained attack on this kind of selective pseudo-symbolism. He sums up in 'Résurrection': 'To give clear passages arbitrary meanings is the surest way to prevent people from understanding each other, or rather to be regarded by honest people as people of bad faith.'

The fundamental task of the freethinker was therefore to throw the light of reason into this murky backwater of belief, an undertaking well within Voltaire's capacity and knowledge, to say nothing of his courage.

In most cases it was of course impossible for Voltaire to determine positively whether or not a given Biblical narrative was historically true, and often this is still impossible. But he always tried to establish the truth in the light of the available facts. Whether or not he succeeded, he never wavered in the scientific certainty that the effort should be made. And if he felt unable to arrive at any conclusion he did not hesitate to admit his ignorance.

Having pushed the factual investigation as far as he could, Voltaire proceeded to a second inquiry: even if the Biblical story is true, were the events depicted good? In other words, Voltaire added an ethical judgement to a primary scientific evaluation. The whole of his work, in the **Dictionnaire philosophique** as in all his writings, is indeed an illustration of his notion of reason: the search for the true and the good. This general idea can be even more briefly subsumed: Voltaire's master idea, one can almost speak of an obsession, was the notion of justice, for to him that which is just is that which is true and good. It is not too much to say that Voltaire was also obsessed by man's ignorance of himself, his world and his universe.

These being Voltaire's guiding principles, and his interests being universal, it was inevitable that the range of subjects treated in the **Dictionnaire philosophique** should steadily widen, until it finally took in nearly everything of 'philosophical' interest in the widest possible sense. Thus it was that Voltaire's little 'portable' finally came to have profound influence on men's thinking in all fields of reflection and public policy.

The very first words of the first edition of the **Dictionnaire philosophique** characterise the whole: 'Abraham is one of the names famous in Asia Minor and in Arabia, like Thoth among the Egyptians, the first Zoroaster in Persia, Hercules in Greece, Orpheus in Thrace, Odin among the northern nations, and so many others whose fame is greater than the authenticity of their history'. This opening paragraph appears to us simple, direct, innocuous: but this is only because we have completely absorbed the Voltairean idiom and mode of thought. In the middle of the eigh-

teenth century all readers were staggered, and most of them horrified, to find so distinguished and respectable a Biblical personage as Abraham quietly classed, without fuss or apology, with pagan and even mythological figures who are described as more famous than authentic. Voltaire then added that he of course, though perhaps not quite consistently, excluded from this category the Jews, about whose history he felt as he must, since it had manifestly been written by the holy ghost in person. This double irony emphasised what was being denied, and it served also to underline the revolutionary nature of his comparative and critical method of religious investigation.

Voltaire goes on to explain that he is concerned only with the Arabs (he means the Mohammedans—for he hardly distinguished between them), who boast of their descent from Abraham. Yet, as he shows all that is doubtful about this claim, he cannot but demonstrate also the doubtful historicity of the Jewish patriarch, and the mistakes and contradictions of the references to him in the *Bible*. Of course Voltaire does not expect the reader to follow him blindly; he concludes his original article on Abraham by referring the reader to the many volumes published to resolve the difficulties: 'They are all written by delicate wits and discerning minds, excellent philosophers, unprejudiced, no pedants'.

Such was always, in a literary sense, Voltaire's method: he tried to ascertain the facts, then drew ethical conclusions from them, and finally presented these conclusions with the lucidity and elegant irony which were the secrets of his unique style. In the **Dictionnaire philosophique** Voltaire did indeed follow his own precepts: 'I think the best way to fall on the infamous is to seem to have no wish to attack it; to disentangle a little chaos of antiquity; to try to make these things rather interesting; to make ancient history as agreeable as possible; to show how much we have been misled in all things; to demonstrate how much is modern in things thought to be ancient, and how ridiculous are many things alleged to be respectable; to let the reader draw his own conclusions'. What was the 'infamous'? Here Voltaire clearly means Christianity. Was this always what he intended? That is another story.

No wonder Alembert begged for another copy of the 'dictionary of Satan' which had issued from the 'printing press of Beelzebub'; and that Grimm widely distributed this 'precious *vade mecum* which all the elect should carry in their pockets'. Voltaire, I repeat, was of course obliged to disavow the book, which he did frequently and energetically. His view was always that the infamous should be crushed but that the hand which did the crushing should remain unknown. His friends agreed, and anyway it appeared to them obvious from internal evidence that the **Dictionnaire** had at least four authors: Beelzebub, Astaroth, Lucifer and Asmodeus, whom the angelic doctor (saint Thomas Aquinas) had so ably demonstrated not to be consubstantial one with the other. Voltaire himself from the very beginning accepted the title of 'theologian of Beelzebub', but the article 'Théologien' is a rather more faithful self-portrait of the author of the **Dictionnaire philosophique.**

One is struck by Voltaire's high standards of accuracy in his search for historical truth. To be sure, modern notions of textual fidelity were unknown in the eighteenth century. The words Voltaire places within quotation marks are not always accurate or even direct quotations. True, they are seldom so inaccurate as those quoted by, say, Montesquieu or Diderot, but still every quotation has to be checked, especially as Voltaire often relied on his wonderful memory, as can be seen in his *Notebooks.* On the other hand, an intrinsically interesting point has to be made before one condemns Voltaire: it will be found that often, when Voltaire has been criticised by the devout for misquoting the *Bible,* he has in fact faithfully translated the Latin Vulgate, which he regarded (wrongly, as we now know) as the best available text.

However, when it comes to objective facts, Voltaire can seldom be faulted. Even his references to sources are usually accurate, a rare thing in the eighteenth century. In his Introduction (p. xxiii) to his edition of Voltaire's *Essai sur les mœurs* (1963) René Pomeau has analysed the references to authorities in sample sections of that wonderful book. The results are remarkable: 351 substantially accurate references, 32 wrong or unverifiable ones have been counted. This compares very favourably indeed with his contemporaries, and not unfavourably with a great many more recent scholars.

Moreover, Voltaire's knowledge of these sources can justly be described as exceptional, both in the *Essai* and the *Dictionnaire.* Specialists had of course read more widely in their own fields. Those who knew the Biblical languages enjoyed an evident advantage, but they were very few. On the other hand Voltaire read English and Italian fluently, and Latin of course, and above all, if his reading was deep only in limited fields, it was amazingly wide. This is reflected, for instance, in his vocabulary, possibly unsurpassed by any other French writer, other, of course, than those who were specialists.

It is not too difficult to know what Voltaire had read. His own works, his library, his letters provide ample evidence. What is more difficult is to evaluate all this information in eighteenth century terms. A few generalisations can be ventured. The English reader will take Voltaire's Biblical quotations and references as matters of course. But the position on the other side of the Channel was different. Indeed, Voltaire probably knew the *Bible* better than any other layman in France, and better even than most ecclesiastics. It must be remembered that Rome discouraged, and still discourages, the reading of the *Bible.*

As for the secondary sources, such as the church fathers. Voltaire read some of them at first-hand, others in such works as Louise Ellies Du Pin's *Bibliothèque des auteurs ecclésiastiques* and Augustin Calmet's *Commentaire littéral sur tous les livres de l'Ancien et du Nouveau testament.* And he also obtained much information from experts and even, in non-theological fields, from eye-witnesses, for he knew everybody. Many of his more than 1800 known correspondents were exposed to his insatiable curiosity and passion for authenticity.

Voltaire's scrupulous exactitude is amusingly illustrated by his account of the miracles of Saint Francis Xavier. In 'Convulsions' he says that this Jesuit missionary 'exhausted the society's grace by resuscitating nine dead men by exact count'. Now Voltaire's library catalogue shows that he possessed a copy of *La Vie de saint François Xavier* (1754) by the Jesuit Dominique Bouhours. He described this book on the titlepage of his copy as 'a masterpiece of

fanatical folly', for he was a passionate annotator, and his library contains many hundreds of his marginalia, very few of which have yet been published. It was in Bouhours that Voltaire found the story of the nine miracles attributed to the future saint. In 'Miracles' the number was reduced to eight, no doubt an error of memory—yet not, as might have been expected from a man holding his views, an error of exaggeration. However, when he was writing 'Christianisme' Voltaire extended his researches, as can be seen from a passage towards the end of that essay: 'Saint Francis Xavier, who carried the holy gospel to India and Japan when the Portuguese went there to search for merchandise, performed a very large number of miracles, all attested by the reverend Jesuit fathers. Some say that he resuscitated nine dead men, but the reverend father Ribadeneyra limits himself to saying in his *Flower of the saints* that he resuscitated four: which is quite enough'. The reference is perfectly correct. What minute computation of non-events!

And when it comes to things verifiable and to contemporary history it is enough to say that Voltaire is a reliable guide. Thus, all the books and events mentioned in 'Etats, gouvernements' were intimately known to him. However, though it is so obvious it must still be repeated that the words 'verifiable' and 'contemporary' are used in the context of more than two hundred years ago: Voltaire must not be blamed because he had no access to the authentic Pali and Chinese classics, which were then for the most part known only in the original languages, and often as mere titles.

The literary methods used by Voltaire to sweeten the bitter pill of reason or to shock the reader into swallowing it, are varied, complex, and often very subtle. Everybody knows that admiral Byng was executed to encourage others. Why has this witticism become so famous? Because it is a firmly rooted superstition that society punishes offenders to discourage the others. Hence every time a reader encounters Voltaire's 'encourage' he is startled, stops, reads again, and perhaps begins to think and wonder.

These little shocks are felt on every page of the *Dictionnaire.* Each paragraph of 'Concile', for instance, administers one. Thus, Voltaire tells us that 600 bishops 'after four months of quarrels, unanimously deprived Jesus of his consubstantiality'. Every word is a dart. 'Deprived'? The contemporary reader at once reflected that these men were bishops *because* Jesus is the son of god. If he is divine is it for his servants to take away or to award him his essential nature? Besides, if they quarrelled for four months the bishops must have disagreed pretty deeply. How then could their unkind deprivation have been unanimous? They must have compromised. A compromise about an eternal verity? If Voltaire had said all this, his essay would have been merely another contribution to Christian polemics. But by stating the implications in this particular way, in these particular words, he made the inevitable conclusion as it were melt into the reader's consciousness by means of the reasoning that follows empathy—what is vulgarly called intuition.

A still more subtle procedure can be seen in the immediately preceding paragraph of 'Concile': 'It is reported in the supplement of the council of Nicaea that the fathers, being very perplexed to know which were the cryphal or apocryphal books of the Old and New Testaments, put them all pell-mell on an altar, and the books to be rejected fell to the ground. It is a pity that this elegant procedure has not survived.' The attention of the reader is at once pulled up by the amusing invention 'cryphal', and he is thus made even more receptive by this pregnant pause to the shocking character of the grotesque anecdote that follows, and Voltaire's ironic comment on it.

This kind of treatment often goes beyond the mere surface of the words. Our thinking, as mirrored by the words we use, is too often painfully banal. Clichés become polished to invisibility by incessant use. It is so commonplace to say that man makes god in his own image, that the implications of the words are no longer felt. Voltaire knew exactly how to remedy this: by defining man in a particular way the contrast becomes shocking, and arrests the attention, and so we get: 'Two-legged, featherless animals, how long will you make god in your image?'

This oblique way of obliging the reader to make his own case is occasionally replaced by a direct exhortation. So in 'Prêtre' Voltaire exclaims: 'What things could be said about all this! Reader, it is for you to say them to yourself' or when he ends 'Sensation' with the injunction: 'What are we to conclude from all this? You who read and think, conclude'. Sometimes this kind of approach is overwhelmed by a thunderclap, all the more devastating by being so rare and so, as it were, out of character. Every so often Voltaire's indignation does indeed become uncontrollable, leaving no room for literary and rhetorical devices. He begins by guffawing at 'the humbug we are told about the martyrs', but as he goes on he becomes more and more indignant, and finally bursts out: 'Do you want good, well-attested barbarities? good well-authenticated massacres? rivers of blood that really ran? fathers, mothers, husbands, women, children at the breast really butchered and piled upon each other? Persecuting monsters [Christians], seek these truths only in your annals: you will find them in the crusades against the Albigensians, in the massacres of Mérindol and Cabrières, in the appalling day of Saint Bartholomew, in the Irish massacres, in the valley of the Waldenses. . . . '. Note the 'good' barbarities, the 'good' massacres. This passage is immediately preceded by yet another example of the 'shocking' word: a little boy was condemned to have his tongue cut out because he stuttered; the emperor's chief physician, adds Voltaire, 'had the decency to perform the operation himself '.

The first of these nerve-tingling blows is struck without a moment's delay, for proper receptivity is produced by the very first amusingly satirical sentence of the book, that on Abraham, quoted above.

Let there be no doubt about it, all these techniques were deliberate, self-conscious, meditated. Voltaire did not write his masterpieces by accident, as some have maintained. A thousand passages could be quoted in proof. In a letter of 1764, the year that saw the first publication of the ***Dictionnaire philosophique,*** he wrote to his disciple, the marquis d'Argence: 'I implore you, my dear sir, not to argue with obstinate people. Opposition always irritates them instead of enlightening them; they jib, they get to hate those whose opinions are cited against them: argument has never convinced anyone. They can be made to change their minds only by being made to think for themselves, by appearing to share their doubts, by leading them

as it were by the hand without their being aware of it'. And Voltaire even printed the same sentiments in the preface of an early edition of the ***Dictionnaire,*** though of course in a less outspoken form: 'The most useful books are those to which the readers contribute half; they develop the ideas presented to them in seed; they correct what appears to them to be defective, and strengthen by their reflections what seems to them to be weak'.

Another aspect of Voltaire's mind and style, for the two things are inseparable, must strike the reader: his acute sense of humour, very nearly unique in the French Enlightenment. Examples can be found on nearly every page. If I single out this one it is because its secondary implications may escape the modern reader. In 'Prophètes' Voltaire writes: 'It is thought that king Amaziah had the prophet Amos's teeth drawn to prevent him from talking. In fact it is not absolutely impossible to speak without teeth. Very talkative old and toothless ladies have been known. But a prophecy must be pronounced distinctly, and a toothless prophet is not listened to with the respect that is his due'. Here Voltaire's fun did not spare himself: by this time he had lost all his teeth, and he could safely assume that this fact was known to 'everybody'.

It was Voltaire who taught the world the lesson beyond price, that high seriousness is not merely compatible with a sense of humour, but runs with it in tandem with elegance and speed. Bernard Shaw and Bertrand Russell were among those who acknowledged that they had learned that lesson at his knee. Voltaire is indeed one of the most *enjoyable* of all great writers. 'Unless you have signed a pact with the infamous, I defy you to not to admire, not to love Voltaire.' (pp. 473-87)

> *Theodore Besterman, in his* Voltaire, *revised edition, Basil Blackwell, 1976, 718 p.*

Gloria M. Russo   (essay date 1984)

> [*Russo is an American academic and scholar. In the following essay, she discusses Voltaire's portrayal of women in his literary works.*]

From Ninon de Lenclos, who encouraged the young boy, to Marie-Louise Denis, who cheered the old man, women were vital to the happy existence of Voltaire. As a young man, he traveled in the aristocratic and intellectual circles dominated by the women of eighteenth-century Parisian society. Charmed by his wit, elegance, brilliant conversation, and verve, they invited him to adorn their gatherings of the politically and intellectually powerful.

Disappointed in his first youthful love affair, Voltaire slipped easily from one romantic involvement to the next until finally he met the "divine Emilie," Mme du Châtelet. Mutually fascinated by their intellectual pursuits, the self-taught scientist and the well-known *philosophe* formed a liaison that endured until her death, a period of over sixteen years. In the company of his unfailingly stimulating intellectual companion, Voltaire's literary production was prodigious; plays, poems, intensive work on the histories, short stories, philosophical and scientific treatises, as well as the semisecret work on ***La Pucelle,*** all flowed from his pen while at Cirey.

The next woman in his life, his niece Marie-Louise Denis,

offered him much less in the way of mental stimulation, but she did reawaken his sexual appetite. Long before Mme du Châtelet's death, uncle and niece had become lovers. Voltaire spent the remaining twenty years of his life with "mia carissima" at Ferney. Stimulated by her flesh but not her mind, he continually sought to educate her and to encourage her to write plays. The contrast between his two mistresses of such long duration, revealed in his and his acquaintances' correspondence, is striking.

His interest in women who are both intellectually and sexually stimulating, with heavy emphasis on the former, is equally evident in his literature. In this brief essay, we shall examine his theater and short stories in order to demonstrate his predilection for strong, almost virile women, but especially those women in whom this quality is tempered or offset by a sensual, loving nature. We shall also consider the women who figure in *La Pucelle,* the single work that allows us to glimpse our author and, hence, his viewpoints directly without the barriers of literary convention.

Voltaire's dramatic outpouring includes some twenty tragedies, as well as several comedies and operas. The tragedies, being of superior quality, merit our attention. These works give clear evidence of Voltaire's often stated preference for and adherence to the classical structure of a play: verse rather than prose, observance of the *bienséances,* respect of the Aristotelian rules of time, place, and action. In imitation of his acknowledged model, Racine, Voltaire's heroes, male or female, pursue with vigor *la gloire,* relegating all other considerations to an inferior level of desire and intensity of need. Hence, many of these characters exhibit a drive or relentlessness that brooks no obstacle and that may thus earn them a qualification as cruel, egomaniacal, faithless. However, these descriptions apply equally or more aptly to the male figures in the tragedies. Although frequently torn between love and duty—the classic dilemma—the women demonstrate a gentler nature, one in which their grandeur, a natural correlative of *la gloire,* is tempered by their love, whether maternal or passionate.

The vocabulary of Voltaire's tragic heroines is heavy with references to *la gloire, l'honneur, le devoir, la vertu.* Jocaste (*Oedipe,* 1718), even in the face of the horror of her personal situation, is able to state: "I have lived virtuously." Mariamne (*Mariamne,* 1725) declares to her husband that she possesses a heart which will preserve its virtue to the tomb." Even Eriphyle (*Eriphyle,* 1732), whose murder of her husband would seem to exclude her from those who can claim pure lives, purifies herself to the point where her subjects proclaim "our grateful hearts bear witness to her virtue."

Le devoir is another leitmotif of these heroines, one that begins with Voltaire's earliest tragedies and persists throughout the entire series. Artemire, heroine of the play bearing her name (1720), which exists only in fragments, remains faithful to a hated husband, thus preserving *la gloire* and enabling her to state with equanimity "My duty is enough for me." Eriphyle, in the presence of her long-absent son and touched by a reawakening maternal love, calls upon her innate sense of *la gloire* to reestablish her values: " . . . love of my duty, resume your absolute power over my soul." Zulime (*Zulime,* 1739) also speaks frequently of *la gloire* in association with *le devoir* in trying

to explain or justify her forbidden love of Ramire. At the moment of her death she too can state: " . . . I have fulfilled my duty." Alzire (*Alzire,* 1734) is always pushed to act by *le devoir,* although she seems more susceptible to love than the other heroines.

Another facet of *la gloire* is *l'honneur,* a mobile that directs the actions of such heroines as Zaïre (*Zaïre,* 1733), Adélaïde (*Adélaïde du Guesclin,* 1734), Alzire, Zulime, Palmire (*Mahomet,* 1741), and Mérope (*Mérope,* 1743). Accused by Orosmane, the sultan and master of the harem, of loving another, Zaïre insists upon her innocence by replying "honor . . . is engraved in my heart." Guided by her unfailing sense of *l'honneur,* Adélaïde agrees to marry one brother in order to save the life of the other, whom she deeply loves. Alzire seeks to free her lover from imprisonment by her husband after a war battle, and Zulime ceases to persecute two lovers on the basis of each character's sense of *l'honneur.* The same is true of Palmire and Mérope. *L'honneur* saves Palmire from the extremes of anguish when she discovers the ugly side of her idolized Mahomet's fanaticism. Mérope also speaks the language of *la gloire* and *l'honneur* while, at the same time, exhibiting maternal love and protection toward her rediscovered son.

And how many of these tragic heroines die, in the classic tradition, to preserve their *gloire?* To mention only a few, Jocaste, Tullie (*Brutus,* 1730), Zulime, and Palmire all commit suicide as a purificatory act that assures them of the restoration or retention of *la gloire,* whether this be in the guise of *l'honneur, la vertu,* or *le devoir.* Sémiramis (*Sémiramis,* 1732) and Eriphyle, both guilty of their husband's deaths, die by accident at the hands of their sons, thus purified and once again fully clothed in *la gloire.*

And so the procession of grandiose heroines winds its way across the tapestry of Voltaire's tragedies. The common thread of *la gloire,* variously disguised as *l'honneur, le devoir, la vertu,* weaves them all together with an occasional thread of an entirely different hue, maternal love, a heart that responds on the basis of love alone. Strong-willed, single-minded, indomitably dedicated to the pursuit of a given goal, Jocaste and the many other women who follow her parade before us creating the image of a strong, almost inflexible female, yet one whose heart responds readily to the voice of the beloved but never at the expense of *la gloire.* In the tragedies, the women do not so much inspire love as respect. If they are loved—and they are—there are no great outpourings of passionate desire from their men. Their sensuality is not so much hidden as simply ignored. The opposite holds true in the short stories. The women who people these tales exude an aura of desirability, of personal attraction, that bears no relation to their other traits of characters. Vicious or meek, intelligent or foolish, conniving or forthright, these women inspire a passion capable of driving their lovers to any lengths.

Astarté (*Zadig,* 1748), strong, honorable, virtuous, moves Zadig so strongly that he "left her presence bewildered and wild with joy, his heart weighted by a burden he could no longer bear." The strength of this love impels an eager but certainly not faithful Zadig through the rest of the tale in search of his beloved from whom he is suddenly separated. His infidelities during his quest as well as his previous amorous attachments to Sémire and Azora, his wife, bear witness not only to his weakness but also to the sensuous nature of each of these women.

In the same story, Zadig is not alone in his enchantment. Moabdar, Astarté's jealous husband, falls under the spell of Missouf, a woman who attracts men without effort and who delights in their attentions. Preoccupied with her and her pleasure, Moabdar "seemed to have drowned his sense of virtue in his prodigious love for the beautiful wench." Consumed by their passion, Moabdar loses his kingdom and his sanity. Missouf certainly will have little difficulty in finding a new lover.

Le Monde comme il va (1748) presents women with the same sensuality, the same ability to inflame men. Early in the story, the women of Persepolis are found in the temple pretending to stare directly ahead, but they are in reality watching the men out of the corner of their eyes. Immediately on the heels of this scene follows another one in which two women give ample evidence of their desire and desirability. The first is a young widow whose sensuality leaps from the page. She luxuriates in contact with not one but two men: "[she] had one hand around the magistrate's neck while holding out the other to a handsome and modest young citizen of the city." Meanwhile, this same magistrate's wife slips away with her "advisor" and returns from their rendezvous with "her eyes moist, her cheeks flaming, her step ill-assured, her voice trembling."

One woman stands out in contrast to the female cast of characters in *Le Monde comme il va:* Téone. She, indeed, has a lover, totally devoted to her, whose actions are dictated by the desire to merit Téone's "esteem." She herself wins Voltaire's highest recognition; he awards her the worth of an "honnête homme" (gentleman). Thus, this heroine resembles more closely those of Voltaire's tragedies than her sister characters in *Le Monde comme il va.*

Cosi-Sancta (*Cosi-Sancta,* written in 1746-1747, published in 1784) combines qualities from both Astarté (*Zadig*) and Téone (*Le Monde comme il va*). Cosi-Sancta attracts men with the same ease as her two predecessors, inspires them with passionate devotion, and saves them from death. However, unlike the other two, Cosi-Sancta is forced to surrender herself physically in order to prevent her husband's execution. Unwilling at first, she concedes at her husband's direction: "Impelled by charity, she saved his life; this was the first of three times." She saves her brother and son in the same manner and is canonized after her death "for having done so much good for her family by humbling herself. . . ."

Woman's seductive nature is again vigorously underscored in *Memnon ou la sagesse humaine* (1749). Memnon, who has vowed never to love a woman, immediately falls under the spell of a young woman seen from his window: "young, pretty . . . she was sighing and weeping which only added to her charm." Completely taken in both by her beauty and her false story of persecution, Memnon becomes more and more captivated until "they no longer knew where they were." The young Ninivien succeeds not only in captivating the wise Memnon but also in relieving him of a considerable sum of money.

In *Les Deux Consolés* (1756), an historic parade of women passes before the reader's eyes: Henriette-Marie de France, Marie Stuart et Elisabeth I d'Angleterre, Jeanne de Naples, Hécube, Niobé. The historic trials and tribulations of these women are not the topic but rather their love affairs and their suffering at the loss of the beloved, thus underscoring their sensuality as being of fundamental importance.

This desire for pleasure is transformed into the principal mobile of the existence of Cunégonde (*Candide,* 1759). This one-dimensional character sets out on the road of bodily pleasure at the age of seventeen and follows it vigorously to the story's final line. In the opening pages, the naïve girl watches the lovemaking of Pangloss, her philosophy teacher, and Paquette, her maid; she returns home "yearning for knowledge and dreaming that she might be the sufficient reason of young Candide—who might also be hers." The leitmotif is set, and Cunégonde begins her weary journey from rapist to lover after lover (on two continents and in countless countries) to finally end her days with Candide. Throughout her odyssey, Cunégonde seems to delight in physical sensation and accepts as a matter of course her ability to attract men. That she delights in physical pleasure becomes amply evident in her descriptions of her lovers' bodies: "I won't deny that he [the Bulgarian captain] was a handsome fellow, with a smooth white skin." Her description of Candide is equally sensual: "I saw you stripped for the lash . . . I may tell you, by the way, that your skin is even whiter and more delicate than that of my Bulgarian captain. Seeing you, then redoubled the torments which were already overwhelming me."

Her desire for Candide remains steadfast throughout the entire tale. Unaware at the end that her ravishing beauty has vanished," she reminded Candide of his promises in so firm a tone that the good Candide did not dare to refuse her." Once married, however, Cunégonde "growing every day more ugly, became sour-tempered and insupportable." Clearly her bad temper and ugliness are linked; her physical unattractiveness has become a barrier to her sensual pleasure. Candide married her but offers little satisfaction to Cunégonde's sensual nature.

Mlle de St. Yves (*L'Ingénu,* 1767) presents a sharp contrast to Cunégonde. This young woman is the warmest, most touching heroine of Voltaire's short stories. Like Cunégonde, her sensuality awakens early in the story but is always surrounded by an aura of simplicity, charm, and naïveté far removed from the sometimes lascivious interest of the characters in other short stories. Without innuendo, she asks "how people made love in the land of the Hurons." To the Ingénu's reply, "They do fine deeds so as to give pleasure to people who look like you," la St. Yves blushes with delight. The combination of blushing and taking pleasure in his appreciation of her person underscores both native modesty and her already nascent desire. The latter is made clearer still by her observation through the keyhole of l'Ingénu under the pretext of wanting to know "how a Huron slept;" she finds him sleeping, to her evident pleasure, "in the most graceful attitude in the world." There is no doubt of the pleasure she derives, several scenes later, from watching him "in midstream a tall pale figure." Her first instinct is to turn away but her senses triumph and draw her back to hide in the bushes in order to see "what it was all about." When, finally, l'Ingénu bursts into her room intending to "marry" her, la St. Yves' sense of probity forces her to refuse him and

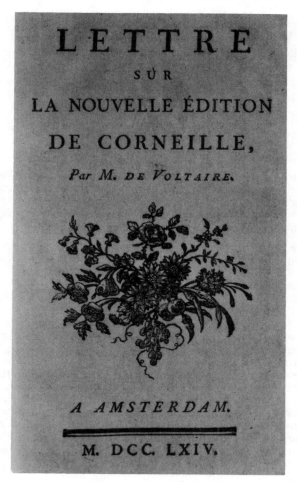

Title page of the first edition of Voltaire's Lettre sur la nouvelle édition de Corneille *(1764).*

to force him to leave. Significantly, however, his departure leaves her deeply troubled.

Unlike Cunégonde, or even Cosi-Sancta, she is unable to reconcile her love of l'Ingénu and any infidelity to him. Faced with the choice of either leaving her beloved in prison or freeing him "at the price of her most precious possession, which should belong only to the unfortunate lover," she prefers death. Dissuaded by her companion, who explains that most men owe their positions and fortunes to their wives ("it is a sacred duty which you are bound to carry out", la belle St. Yves finally allows herself to be led to the rendezvous with l'Ingénu's liberator and pays the price of his freedom.

In a moving and almost lyrical passage, Voltaire describes her flight to the prison, armed with the order to free l'Ingénu:

> It is difficult to describe what she felt during the journey. Imagine a noble and virtuous woman, humiliated by her disgrace, yet intoxicated with tenderness, torn with remorse at having betrayed her lover, yet radiant with pleasure at the prospect of rescuing the man she adored. Her bitter experiences, her struggles, her success, all these were mingled in her reflections. She was no longer the simple

girl with her ideas restricted by her provincial up-bringing. Love and misfortune had formed her character.

Her contradictory emotions, her pain and confusion, all render her eminently human and believable. No longer simple and naïve but still clinging to her innate nobility and sense of *la gloire,* la belle St. Yves, at once "elated and heartbroken," falls ill from shame and distress, "her soul . . . destroying her body." Her death follows quickly upon her recital of her painful adventure, her memory purified by the nobility and depth of her love of l'Ingénu.

Mlle de St. Yves perhaps comes closest to approximating a flesh-and-blood creature in both the tragedies and the short stories of Voltaire. She incarnates strength and weakness, wisdom and folly, self-control and sensuality on a human scale. She is a sympathetic character who lives and dies, figuratively and literally, for her beloved. The reader senses a certain affection for her from Voltaire that is lacking in the other female characters created by his prolific pen in the two genres thus far examined.

Affection for a character, or group of characters, women all, is, however, apparent in one of his lesser read works, **La Pucelle** (1730-1761). This burlesque mock epic, originally intended only for private consumption and not publication, was written and rewritten over a lengthy period that corresponds to a very fertile era in Voltaire's production of the tragedies and short stories. Voltaire lavishes great attention upon four female characters, Jeanne (**La Pucelle**), Judith, Agnès, and Dorothée. These women form two distinct couples, Judith and Dorothée serving as the alter egos of their counterparts, Jeanne and Agnès; each one exhibits characteristics common to the female cast of characters of the tragedies and short stories.

In order to situate this tale, based very loosely on the story of Jeanne d'Arc, suffice it to say that the preservation of France depends entirely on the preservation of Jeanne's virginity:

> The greatest of her rare exploits
> was to preserve her virginity for a year
>
> . . . she bore beneath her short skirt
> the entire destiny of England and France

War with England is only secondary and symbolic. The main story line involves the sexual adventures of all the characters, the four women obviously in the forefront.

Their sensuality is, therefore, heavily underscored. Examples abound throughout the epic, especially in reference to Agnès. The two lovers, Agnès and Charles VII, mutually share the fire of their passion:

> Our two lovers filled with trouble and joy,
> drunk with love, exchanged bewitching glances,
> the fiery forerunners of their pleasure

A single verse most fully captures the full extent of her inebriation from and dedication to the pursuit of physical pleasure: "I am Agnès; long live France and love."

For her, love and sensual gratification are the mobiles of existence; little else matters, even fidelity to Charles. Thrown from her mount, while seeking Charles, she is helped by the young English page Monrose:

> The beautiful Agnès blushing without anger did not

find his hand too daring and looked at him invitingly without
knowing precisely why, swearing meanwhile to be faithful
to the king.

Needless to say, her fidelity is extremely short-lived. She continues her search but now in the company of her young lover.

Dorothée, her mirror-image, possesses an equally sensuous nature. She describes the "delectable moment" of her first encounter with La Trémouille:

Ah! overcome I could neither speak nor see. My
blood burned with an unknown fire; I was unaware
of the dangers of tender love and from sheer
pleasure I could not eat.

Unlike Agnès, however, she does remain faithful to her lover and almost pays with her life for this fidelity.

Her brush with death does not strengthen Dorothée; she remains weak and frightened even in the company of the extraordinary Judith de Rosamore. The boastings of Judith's lover give ample proof of her sensual nature, but she is more notable for her spirit and unflinching sense of *la gloire*. Forced to protect not only herself but also the hapless Dorothée from the unveiled demands of their captor, she states unequivocally:

I intend to give him something quite other. . . .
we shall see what I dare to do. I know how to
avenge my honor and my charms. I am
faithful to the knight I love.

And, like her biblical namesake, she beheads her captor and saves herself and her companion. "Speaking little, but beautiful and shapely, tender by night, insolent by day, capricious at table and in bed," Judith de Rosamore is, indeed, the opposite in everything to Dorothée.

Yet, Dorothée does find the strength to save La Trémouille's life in a duel by placing herself between the combatants. The unhappy result of this attempt to be more than passive is her own death at the hand of her beloved, who then kills himself in grief. Judith, on the other hand, fights side-by-side on the battlefield with her lover. At the sight of his body transpierced with a spear—"Not a single sigh, she shouted revenge"—she grievously wounds one attacker before she is killed by another. Judith dies in full possession of *la gloire*, clothed as a warrior, at the side of her lover:

One would think to see the superb Pallas
abandoning her needle in order to plunge
into battle, or Bradamant, or even Jeanne herself.

The characteristics that Jeanne and Judith share include a combination of sensuality and strength of character—as well as physical strength—unknown to the other two women in *La Pucelle.* These two aspects of Jeanne's personality are well-reflected in her reaction to the impending deaths of herself and Dunois, her lover, by impalement:

Jeanne, impervious as always to danger, languidly
gazed upon the handsome bastard, and for him alone
her heart groaned. Their nakedness, their
beauty, their youth, in spite of them awakened
their tenderness.

Even in the midst of the most extreme danger, she, un-

afraid, derives pleasure from the sight of Dunois' naked body.

Voltaire, himself, best summarizes these dual qualities in the opening lines of the first poem:

Jeanne demonstrated the vigorous courage
of a true Roland hidden behind a woman's
face, behind a corset and a petticoat.
I should prefer for my own use in the evening
a beauty gentle as a sheep; but Jeanne d'Arc
had a lion's heart; you will see this if
you read this work.

It would seem, then, that the author prefers Agnès or Dorothée, who, during the course of the epic, are referred to as a "lamb" or "sheep." Yet he describes Judith de Rosamore with such obvious affection and in such glowing terms that it hardly seems possible.

The key, of course, lies in his allusion to Judith as "tender by night" and in the closing lines of the final poem.

The king, ranked among the conquerors, dined
with Agnès in Orléans. That same night
the proud and tender Jeanne . . . kept
her word to her friend Dunois.

Judith's counterpart and the burlesque epic's principal character, Jeanne, also possesses the same traits. She is "proud" and "tender" but forced by her own naïveté and the necessity of preserving her virginity not to develop the latter to its full potential. Judith is the promise of Jeanne's continuing metamorphosis into a woman capable of balancing both aspects of her personality. Significantly, Agnès is dismissed by the author without a backward glance, but Jeanne is led into the future of shared passion, shared pursuit of *la gloire* with her beloved.

Thus, within the context of the twenty-one poems of *La Pucelle,* Voltaire does not radically change his portrait or preference of his ideal woman. He simply adds to his choice of "a beauty as gentle as a sheep" a desire for an intelligent, sympathetic companion conscious of her personal *gloire*. Humorously epitomized in Judith and Jeanne, particularly the wiser Jeanne of the future, are the qualities of the heroines of Voltaire's tragedies: *la gloire, l'honneur, la vertu, le devoir*. They also reflect the characteristics of the sensually alive and aware women who people the short stories. They most closely resemble Mlle de St. Yves, or perhaps it would be more exact to say that she resembles them, since *L'Ingénu* followed publication of *La Pucelle.* Agnès and Dorothée certainly show no similarity to the women of the tragedies but a great affinity to those of the short stories.

There can be no doubt that in *La Pucelle* Voltaire presents the composite of his perception of the ideal female, aspects of which appear in the two other genres examined. Realization of the importance of the role this mock epic plays in the free expression of Voltaire's thought erases the confusion concerning his position on women. He is not ambivalent in his other works; he simply presents one aspect only in each, either constrained by literary conventions, or, possibly, length or philosophical intent.

It is equally clear that the "divine Emilie" and the "mia carissima" of Voltaire's personal life appear in various guises in both his plays and short stories. In *La Pucelle,* his cherished mock epic written for the most part at Cirey and completed at Ferney, these two women who dominated his life reappear. Mercilessly but ever so lovingly burlesqued, the force and energy of Mme du Châtelet echo in the virile but vulnerable Jeanne (Voltaire refers to each of them as "a man"); hapless Agnès and Dorothée, the objects of every man's sexual desire, strongly resemble Mme Denis, who knew how to awaken passion but showed little other aptitude. In Judith de Rosamore, Jeanne's exciting counterpart, the characteristics of the two women merge, and Voltaire's ideal woman is revealed: she equals her lover on all planes—intellectual, moral, physical, sexual—and her strength and intelligence are enhanced by a sensual, loving nature. She is the woman who was Mme du Châtelet during the happiest period of their liaison and the one he continually tried to make of Mme Denis. (pp. 285-94)

> Gloria M. Russo, "Voltaire and Women," in French Women and the Age of Enlightenment, *edited by Samia I. Spencer, Indiana University Press, 1984, pp. 285-95.*

Maurice Cranston   (essay date 1986)

[*Cranston is an English social philosopher and political scientist who has written on human rights, John Locke's works, and political theories of the Enlightenment. In the following excerpt, he scrutinizes Voltaire's moral philosophy.*]

Like other philosophers of the French Enlightenment, Voltaire is commonly said to have favoured 'enlightened despotism', but this is not true; what he favoured was enlightened royalism, and he separated the idea of absolute from despotic sovereignty as sharply as Montesquieu himself distinguished monarchy from despotism. Although Voltaire wrote—late in life—a work entitled **Idées républicaines,** he was never enthusiastic about the republican ideal. He rejected Montesquieu's idea that the central principle of a republic was virtue. 'A republic', he wrote in his **Pensées sur le gouvernement,**

> is not founded on virtue; it is founded on the ambition of every citizen, the pride which subdues pride, the desire to dominate which will not put up with another's domination. Out of this come laws which preserve equality as much as possible. A republic is a society where the diners, with equal appetite, eat at the same table until there appears a vigorous and voracious man who takes the lot for himself and leaves the crumbs to the others.

Voltaire was ready to admit that a republican system might work well in small states, and he disagreed with Bayle's assertion that Macedonian monarchy was preferable to Athenian democracy: 'le gouvernement populaire est donc par lui-même moins inique, moins abominable que le gouvernement tyrannique'.

For Voltaire, all government entailed limitations on freedom, and since he wanted as much freedom as possible, he argued that government should be limited to the necessary and the useful. This was another reason why he admired England so much; there was religious toleration.

'In England, everyone is allowed to go to heaven in his own way . . . If there were one religion in England, they would have to fear its despotism; if there were two, men

would be at each other's throats; but there are thirty, so they live happily and peaceably together.'

The religious toleration which prevailed in England never ceased to command Voltaire's admiring attention, if only because it was such a marked contrast to the situation in France. Here he was entirely in agreement with Montesquieu, holding that religious toleration was not only good in itself but beneficial, useful to the economic life of the nation. 'If you enter the London Stock Exchange', he wrote, ' . . . you will see the representatives of different nations gathered there for the service of mankind. There the Jew, the Muhammadan and the Christian do business together as if they were of the same religion, and they give the name of "infidel" only to those who go bankrupt.'

Voltaire also remarked on the extent to which England had gained economically as a result of offering refuge to the Huguenot industrialists banished from France by Louis XIV. He argued that toleration was the fruit of liberty, the origin of happiness and of abundance; where there was no freedom of thought there was no freedom of trade, because the same tyranny encroached on commerce and religion alike. 'In England, commerce, by enriching the people, has extended their freedom, and this freedom has in turn extended their commerce and furthered the greatness of the state.'

Voltaire was no less impressed by the English fiscal system, which seemed to him to impose its burdens fairly, and not to grant privileges, like the French, to the clergy and nobility at the expense of everyone else. In England justice and prosperity went hand in hand; taxation was not a restraint on enterprise as it was in France.

Writing in English to a French friend from London, he declared: 'I think, I write like a free Englishman.' He had reached England at an opportune moment. Philosophers and men of letters were held in high esteem in the reigns of Queen Anne or George I. Voltaire had some inkling of this before he crossed the Channel, for in 1718 at the age of 25 he had sent from Paris a copy of his **Oedipe** to George I with a fulsome dedicatory epistle, and received in return a medallion and a gold watch—a marked contrast to his experience at Versailles, where he 'had to hang ignobly about in the crowd at the marriage of Louis XV to gain a paltry pittance from the Queen's privy purse'. In England men of letters were being liberally patronized, Prior and Gay having embassies, Addison holding the office of secretary of state, and Rowe, Philips, and Congreve all enjoying well-paid sinecures. With the accession to power of Walpole, this golden age for authors came to an abrupt—and permanent—end in England; and by 1776, when David Hume arrived in Paris, the situation had been reversed, for it was in France, Hume noted, that literary men were honoured and fêted, while in England they were held in contempt.

During his stay in England, Voltaire developed a fervent admiration for English literature which matched his enthusiasm for English government. Afterwards he would boast that he alone had introduced Milton, Pope, Swift, and Dryden to France and that he was the first to explain Shakespeare to French readers. What is more he saw himself as a champion of the empiricist philosophy of Newton and Locke and Bacon against the rationalist metaphysics of Descartes and Malebranche, and thus the champion, in a sense, of science against religion. On the other hand, it must be remembered that there was a fair amount of both rationalism and religion in Locke and Newton, and this Voltaire very willingly assimilated. He was never a materialist or an atheist, as were many of the younger philosophers of the Enlightenment. Like Newton, Voltaire invoked the 'argument from design' for God's existence—the wonderfully engineered 'watch' of the universe proclaimed the existence of a watchmaker. Besides these rational grounds for his own genuine belief in God, Voltaire also thought there were practical grounds for wishing that belief to be generally held:

> I want my lawyer, my tailor, my servants, even my wife to believe in God, because it means that I shall be cheated and robbed and cuckolded less often . . . God is needed to provide a divine sanction for morality. It is absolutely necessary not only for ordinary people, but also for princes and rulers to have an idea of the Supreme Being, Creator, governor, rewarder and avenger profoundly engraven on their minds . . . if God did not exist, it would be necessary to invent him.

Privately Voltaire did not believe that God really intervened in the workings of the universe to secure the enforcement of morality, but he thought it important for ordinary people to imagine that he did. For himself, his faith was limited to belief in the existence of a single Creator or Supreme Being; in a word, Voltaire was a deist.

> There is only one God . . . Lift your eyes to the celestial globes, turn them to the earth and the seas, everything corresponds, each is made for the other; each being is intimately related to other beings; everything forms part of the same design: therefore there is only one architect, one sole master, one sole preserver.

Voltaire could not go beyond his deism to accept the latitudinarian Christianity of Newton and Locke, undemanding as that version of Christianity might be considered; all the Christian Churches, with the exception of the Quakers, had too black a record of persecution in Voltaire's eyes. Indeed his own deism became attenuated with the passage of time; his Deity was originally conceived as being benevolent as well as omnipotent; but the longer Voltaire lived, the less reason could he find for ascribing goodness to the Creator. The earthquake of 1755 in Lisbon, where thousands of innocent lives were lost, convinced him that his God must have gone to sleep and allowed some fallen angel to take over the direction of the universe. The Lisbon disaster prompted what is perhaps Voltaire's best book, and certainly the one which is still most widely read, *Candide ou l'optimisme,* which makes such brilliant mockery of the idea that ours is 'the best of all possible worlds' and all 'partial evil, good misunderstood'.

And yet Voltaire was an optimist himself—more of an optimist in a sense than the optimists he attacked, Leibniz and Alexander Pope, for they at least subscribed to the Christian doctrine of the Fall of Man, whereas Voltaire believed in progress. In his *Essai sur les mœurs* he argued that human history was a continuous movement of human betterment through the progressive enlargement of useful knowledge. This was the optimism which characterized most men of the Enlightenment; an optimism which went together with a curious sort of cosmic pessimism.

The English philosopher whom Voltaire praised most frequently was Locke. Late in life, he declared how he always returned to the philosophy of Locke: 'like a prodigal son returning to his father, I threw myself into the arms of that modest man, who never pretends to know what he does not know'. Voltaire considered himself an adherent both of Locke's epistemological and of his political teaching. Of his debt to Locke's writings there can be no question; Voltaire's own *Traité sur la tolérance* adds little to the arguments of Locke's *Letter for Toleration.* But it is by no means evident that Voltaire subscribed to the political theory expounded in Locke's *Two Treatises of Government.* For example, Voltaire did not accept the theory of the contractual origins of society, any more than Montesquieu accepted it. Voltaire suggests that men are naturally social and that governments come into existence through conquest, not contract. His argument is that with the passage of time, the force which had originally established the dominion of one man over another came to be transformed by custom and habit and the development of civilization into a regulated government. The modern kingdom is a product of progress for which men have every reason to be grateful.

Voltaire admired the attack on metaphysics which Locke had undertaken in his *Essay Concerning Human Understanding,* and he carried that attack into the areas where Locke had stopped short—the areas of politics and law. Voltaire chose to assert the natural rights of man without invoking either the concept of a state of nature or the doctrine of natural law which had traditionally been assumed to provide the logical foundation for any theory of natural right. What Voltaire saw, and admired, in Locke was a practical philosopher. Locke had produced a doctrine of natural rights which stood up to the test of experience; in other words, what had happened in England since 1689 had shown that the 'natural rights to life, liberty and property' as Locke had defined them could be translated into positive rights which the English people were able to enjoy. In his *Dictionnaire philosophique* Voltaire restated those rights for the benefit of his French readers. They were: 'the right to liberty for a person and his property; the right to speak to the nation with voice or pen; the right to be tried in any criminal cause by a jury of independent persons; the right to be judged only according to precise and known terms of law; and to profess any religion a man pleases'.

Voltaire separated the Lockian theory of natural rights both from traditional natural law and from Locke's Whiggish doctrine of parliamentary sovereignty. The Whiggish doctrine was good for England, he thought, but it was not necessarily suitable for export to other countries, and certainly not to France. The theory of the natural rights of man, however, was of universal application; natural rights were, by definition, the rights of all men everywhere; they were the rights of man as man, and the French authorities had the same duty to respect them as had the English.

It was Voltaire's sense of history which prompted him to think that the English system of government could not be copied by the French. Whereas Montesquieu, the political sociologist, said that the social circumstances and climate of France precluded any full-scale reproduction of the English model, Voltaire said it was the history of the two kingdoms which made that impossible. As Voltaire understood it, the history of England had for several centuries moved in a different direction from that of France. In medieval times, both countries had lived under much the same kind of feudal regime, with power divided between Crown, Church, and nobility; but by the sixteenth-century the Tudor monarchs had succeeded in making themselves masters in England; having nationalized the Church and used the Church's wealth to buy up the nobility, they were able to use their monopoly of power to give their kingdom the blessings of peace at a time when France was tearing itself apart in atrocious civil wars—civil wars provoked in part by religious fanaticism and in part by the belligerence of noblemen. In the seventeenth century, the situation, as Voltaire perceived it, had been reversed; the Bourbon kings, by subduing the nobility and conspiring with cardinals, had given France a century of internal peace while the English, tormented by parliamentary factions and religious sects, had relapsed into civil war. By the end of the seventeenth century, the two kingdoms had been shaped by different histories, inherited different problems and acquired a different set of institutions; so that the same remedies could not be expected to be effective in both kingdoms. In so far as Locke's political theory was appropriate in every detail for the English, it was unlikely to be suited in every detail to the French.

There was, however, another English philosopher whose message seemed to speak precisely to the condition of France, and that was Francis Bacon. Bacon had died in 1626, but that did not mean that his message was out of date. On the contrary, it had a kind of actuality for eighteenth-century France which made him, to a greater extent even than Locke or Newton, a prophetic figure for Voltaire and indeed for the whole French Enlightenment. For Bacon was the first philosopher of science. It was not that Bacon had made any scientific discoveries of his own; he simply proclaimed the doctrine that science could save us. In a way, he was typically English in his stress on utility. Science, he suggested, was not just an intellectual exercise to give us knowledge, but a practical enterprise to give us mastery over our world. Once men knew how nature worked, they could exploit nature to their advantage, overcome scarcity by scientific innovations in agriculture, overcome disease by scientific research in medicine, and generally improve the life of man by all sorts of developments in technology and industry.

Voltaire thrilled to this vision of progress, and he was no less excited by the programme Bacon sketched out as a means of achieving it: first, the abolition of traditional metaphysics and of idle theological disputes on which scholarship was wasted; and second, the repudiation of old-fashioned legal and political impediments to the efficient organization of a progressive state. Bacon was frankly in favour of an enlarged royal prerogative at the expense of the rights of Parliament and the courts. Voltaire approved. Bacon had, in his time, the scheme of fostering the desire of James I to become an absolute monarch so that he himself might enact the role of philosopher at the elbow of a mighty king; if Bacon failed, that did not mean his method could not be tried elsewhere.

Besides, the Baconian plan had a better chance of success in France, because France had had, in Voltaire's opinion, an altogether happy experience of absolute monarchy under the Bourbon kings of the seventeenth century. One

can readily understand Voltaire's admiration for Henri IV; it is less easy to understand his veneration for Louis XIV, the persecutor of Protestants, the oppressor of dissent, and the protector of the pious. It has been suggested that Louis XIV appealed to the aesthetic side of Voltaire's imagination, which saw the King as an artist imposing unity on the chaos of society. In any case, Voltaire saw no necessary threat to freedom in the centralization of royal government. On the contrary, he considered that in French experience the great enemies of liberty were the Church and the institutions controlled by the nobility, including the *parlements*. By suppressing or emasculating such institutions, a strong central government could enlarge the citizen's liberty; it had done so in the past in France and could do so in the future. It is interesting to compare this argument with Montesquieu's doctrine of power checking power to produce freedom through equilibrium. For Voltaire, one single power that can be trusted is needed not to counterbalance, but rather to subdue those other powers which menace freedom.

When Voltaire's **Lettres philosophiques** was published in Paris in 1734 it was burned by the public executioner, a sign from the Paris *parlement* of what he might expect from them in reply to his criticisms. It would not be beyond their powers, after all, to burn the author with the book. On the other side, the King's government at Versailles did very little to reward his royalism; he was simply warned by Comte d'Argenson to go to ground to avoid arrest. Even though he was appointed Royal Historian in 1745, and gentleman of the King's Chamber in 1746, Voltaire alienated other courtiers with his indiscretions, and had to leave Versailles.

In the dispute between the government and the Church which followed the edict of 1749 imposing income tax on the clergy as well as other people, Voltaire produced a brilliant pamphlet entitled **La Voix du sage et du peuple** supporting the royal government and refuting the claims of the clergy to fiscal privileges. Priests, he argued, were teachers, and like all teachers they should be told by the state what to teach; not only should they be taxed like every other subject of the king, they should be disciplined like every other civil servant. Such arguments proved all too radical for a pusillanimous king, and Voltaire received no thanks from Versailles. And then in 1771, when the royal government summarily dismissed the *parlements* and replaced them with appointed magistrates, Voltaire, almost alone among the *philosophes*, gave public support to the King's action; again there were no signs of gratitude in Versailles. It is hardly surprising that Voltaire chose to live so much of his life beyond the French King's jurisdiction.

And yet he was never willing to support the French *parlements* in any of their conflicts with the King. Diderot, Holbach, and other *philosophes* came in time to see the *parlements* as some sort of guarantee of legality, a brake on the despotic tendencies of the royal government. Voltaire never changed his mind. To him the *parlements* were bigoted—often Jansenist—agents of oppression, burning books, torturing prisoners, arresting the innocent, and generally impeding any progressive legislation that the King might devise.

It is not difficult to understand Voltaire's implacable hostility to the *parlements* if we look at the famous cases he emerged from his study to publicize. The victims of perse-cution he defended were always victims of judicial, not royal, persecution. The *parlementaires* were the enemies of freedom, together with their allies in the Church. These were the people Voltaire had in mind when he uttered re-peatedly his battle-cry *'Écrasez l'infâme!'*

The Calas case will always be remembered for Voltaire's triumphant intervention in the shameful actions of the French judiciary. On this occasion it was a court at Tou-louse which accepted a far-fetched allegation that Calas, a Protestant, had murdered his son because that son was on the point of converting to Catholicism. Calas was duly tried, tortured, and condemned to be strangled by the exe-cutioner and burned on the scaffold.

The case attracted very little attention at the time, but one interested individual, a tradesman from Marseilles named Audibert, made the journey to Geneva where Voltaire was then living, and brought the fate of Calas to his notice. Audibert realized that while Voltaire might proclaim that everyone should be content to cultivate his own garden, Voltaire himself was the last person to obey that injunc-tion.

'Was Calas innocent or guilty?', Voltaire asked. 'In either case his story is evidence of the most horrible fanaticism in this supposedly enlightened century . . . One must do what one can to render execrable the fanaticism which has either led a father to hang his son or led eight magistrates to break an innocent man on the wheel.'

Voltaire decided to intervene. He paid lawyers and investi-gators to collect the facts, and once he was convinced that Calas was innocent, he started to publicize the case, writ-ing innumerable letters to individuals and articles for pub-lication. His purpose was not only to clear the name of the unfortunate Calas, but to turn public opinion against the kind of religious intolerance which had prompted the in-justice and against the use of torture as a method of en-forcing the law. In one of his pamphlets he noted that it was not only the English—'those hard-headed people who have robbed us of Canada'—who had renounced the use of torture; even the Russians—'who not so long ago were considered barbarians'—had abolished it; and only the French 'cling to their ancient atrocious practices'.

In his campaign against torture Voltaire had the support of Versailles. The government was ready to revoke the edict of 1670 which authorized torture, but the *parlements* insisted on retaining it. Malesherbes, the minister respon-sible for the censorship, encouraged Voltaire's friend the Abbé Morellet to publish in 1762 *A Manual for Inquisi-tors,* drawn from the most sadistic parts of the *Directorium* of the Holy Office of the fourteenth century. This brought the cruellest practices of the Inquisition into the light of the eighteenth century, and startled readers by the resusci-tation of horrors supposed to be dead. Malesherbes told Morellet that he might imagine he was publishing a collec-tion of unheard-of facts and forgotten practices of the Church, but the truth was that the procedures described were 'as nearly as possible identical with the criminal ju-risprudence of France at that very moment'.

Voltaire devoted much of his time for three years to clear-ing Calas's name. Finally, on the third anniversary of his death, Calas was exonerated of all guilt by the *maîtres des requêtes,* a royal court sitting at Versailles. In the words

of his most recent biographer, 'It was to prove the greatest of all Voltaire's individual triumphs.'

But if the Calas case was the most famous in Voltaire's ca-reer as a champion of *les droits de l'homme,* it was certain-ly not the only one. There was the case of a Protestant cou-ple named Sirven, a father and mother accused of murder-ing their daughter because she wanted to become a nun, and sentenced to death *in absentia* by the *parlement* of Toulouse. Then there was the case of the Comte de Lally, a general beheaded in the Place de Grève on the orders of the Paris *parlement* as a scapegoat for a military defeat in India. There was also the case of a girl of eighteen being hanged for stealing eighteen napkins from a mistress who had failed to pay her wages. The case which caused Vol-taire the most distress and provoked his undying hostility to the *parlements* of France was that of the Chevalier de la Barre, another eighteen-year-old, who had sung songs thought blasphemous near a crucifix at Abbeville, and was thereupon arrested, tried, tortured, and condemned by the local magistrates to have his hand cut off and his body burned by a slow fire. When the appeal came before the *parlement* of Paris, fifteen of the twenty-five noble judges confirmed the verdict and only reduced the sentence to de-capitation: the Chevalier de la Barre, like the Comte de Lally, was allowed an upper-class death by the axe, but that was the extent of the *parlement*'s humanity. A copy of Voltaire's **Lettres philosophiques** was thrown on the scaffold where the victim died.

La Barre's companion in the escapade of singing the blas-phemous songs, a youth named Étallonde, escaped from France to be promptly, and pointedly, invited by Freder-ick II to Potsdam and offered a commission in the Prus-sian army. Frederick had played a key role in the drama of Voltaire's life, and at one time raised hopes that he might become the kind of 'philosopher-king' who would realize Voltaire's dream of enlightened absolute monar-chy. Louis XV, unenlightened in his philosophy and unap-preciative of Voltaire's genius, was a disappointment. King Stanislas of Poland, while both an intellectual and an admirer of Voltaire, had the marked disadvantage of being no longer on his throne; but Frederick of Prussia was every inch a monarch. He invited Voltaire in the most flattering terms to join his court in Germany, and Voltaire went, full of the highest expectations. It was a doomed en-terprise. Like Plato in Syracuse, or Francis Bacon at the court of James I, and Denis Diderot, some years later, at the court of the Empress Catherine, Voltaire was destined to find himself unable to control the mind of a monarch who considered himself a philosopher already. Voltaire soon learned that Frederick had no desire to receive advice on how to rule, but only to receive the critical guidance— or rather the praise—of a literary man on his literary en-deavours.

Voltaire did not like living in Prussia in a cold climate, surrounded by handsome soldiers but denied the company of beautiful women, and expected to flatter a vain, despot-ic king. Frederick's hostility to religion was hardly an ade-quate basis for enduring friendship with Voltaire. Besides, Voltaire could not dissimulate his disapproval of Freder-ick's policy of building up a powerful army and then going to war. Voltaire was by way of being a pacifist, and war was an evil which he felt had to be ascribed, for the most part, to kings. 'War', he wrote, is something invented by men, by those three or four hundred persons scattered over the globe who are known as kings or princes and who are said— perhaps because of the harm they do—to be the image of divinity on earth . . . War is undoubtedly a fine art, which destroys the countryside, and which kills forty thousand or a hundred thousand men a year . . . And what is most marvellous about the infernal enterprise is that every Chief of murderers has his colours blessed and invokes God's name solemnly before he sets forth to kill his fellow men.

Disappointment at the court of Frederick of Prussia made a dent in Voltaire's royalism. Some commentators claim that he became a democrat in his later years, and even publicly proclaimed himself to be one. The evidence for this is the dialogue written in 1768 entitled **L'A.B.C.,** where Voltaire has one of the speakers say:

> I'll admit to you that I could easily put up with a democratic government . . . I enjoy seeing free men making the *laws* under which they live, as they have made their *houses*. It pleases me that my mason, my carpenter, my blacksmith who helped me build my dwelling, my neighbour the farmer, and my friend the manufacturer, all rise above their craft and know the public interest better than the most insolent Turkish governor. In a democracy, no day labourer, no artisan, need fear anyone or contempt . . . To be free, to have none but equals, that's the true life, the natural life of man.

Leaving aside the patronizing tone of Voltaire's reference to the democratic classes, we must remember that this dialogue dates from the period of his connection with Geneva. There is nothing inconsistent in Voltaire's favouring democracy in Geneva or the cantons of Switzerland and royal absolutism in France, since he had always said that a political system must suit the character of the country concerned. Geneva was small enough, and had experience enough of republican government, for democracy to be a sensible system for its people.

Voltaire's **Idées républicaines,** often cited as evidence of his having been converted in old age from royalism to republicanism, dates from this same period. In fact **Idées républicaines** is a tract for the Genevans, as the journalist Friedrich Melchior Grimm explained in his *Correspondence littéraire* in January 1766, when the work first appeared:

> The genius who lives at Ferney finds this a good moment to say his word about the quarrels that are dividing the republic of Geneva. He has published, continuing to hide himself from us, a little work of forty-five pages large octavo *Idées républicaines*, *'par un membre d'un corps'* [sic]. This is not a humorous work. It contains very sensible ideas, and without entering into the Genevan bickering, it proposes very wise solutions.

Voltaire's attitude to the politics of Geneva changed as he came to know that city better. On the surface Geneva was an almost ideal republic. Underneath it was a city of intolerance and strife. The people were divided into three classes; a patriciate of rich families, a hundred or two; a middle class of citizens, 1,500 adult males; and a lower class of *natifs* and *habitants* composing the majority of the population of 25,000 souls.

Originally Voltaire's friends in Geneva were members of the patriciate. When he first settled in the city in 1755 it was the patrician Tronchin who acquired his house, Les Délices, in his name, since Catholics were not allowed to own property in Geneva. Voltaire could then see nothing wrong with an arrangement whereby the richest and most cultured inhabitants directed the republic; the government seemed thoroughly enlightened, and even the Calvinism of the established Church appeared to have mellowed with time into a harmless unitarianism.

Gradually certain aspects of the regime began to trouble Voltaire. There was the incident of one Robert Covelle, condemned to genuflect before the consistory of Geneva as a sign of repentance for fathering an illegitimate child. Covelle refused to kneel, and Voltaire, who greeted him with mock ceremoniousness as *'Monsieur le Fornicateur'*, proclaimed the right of a free man to stand upright before his accusers. When Rousseau's *Émile* and *Social Contract* were burned in Geneva in 1762, and an order issued for the author's arrest, Voltaire was horrified. He detested Rousseau and Rousseau's opinions, but he believed in every author's right to freedom of expression, and he sprang to Rousseau's defence.

By this time Voltaire had given up the house in Geneva, and installed himself in the Château of Ferney just beyond the frontier. But he continued to intervene in the affairs of the republic. When Rousseau in his *Lettres écrites de la montagne* described the patrician council of Geneva as 'twenty-five despots' Voltaire was forced to agree. So Voltaire deserted his patrician friends to support the middle-class citizens in their endeavour to restore the authentic republican constitution of their state. Voltaire's **Idées républicaines** puts the case of republicans in a republic—and in so far as it is anti-aristocratic, it is in no way at odds with the anti-aristocratic elements in those writings where Voltaire advocates royalism for a kingdom. Both are pleas for undivided sovereignty; where the *nation* is sovereign *its* sovereignty should be absolute: where the *king* is sovereign *his* sovereignty should be absolute.

Voltaire's basic political philosophy had not changed. He did not advocate the introduction of republican ideas into kingdoms: he only proposed that a republic should be governed according to republican principles. Besides, he drew from history the lesson that republican constitutions were only suited to small states, and frankly he did not think much of tiny states; apart from Geneva, he sometimes spoke, with ill-concealed contempt, of 'the republic of San Marino and the canton of Zug'.

Even the republicans of Geneva disappointed Voltaire in the end. He found that the middle-class citizens were no better democrats than the patricians. For once these citizens had achieved satisfaction, the lower classes of the city—the *natifs* and *habitants*—asked in turn for rights and liberties to be extended to them, as they had been promised when the citizens needed their help against the patricians; to this plea the citizens replied with the same violence with which the patricians had formerly reacted to their claims. Fearing lower-class rebellion in 1770, the middle classes took up arms, killed three *natifs*, wounded more, and put a hundred or so in prison.

Voltaire, disgusted by the hypocrisy of the Genevan citizens, became the champion of the plebeian cause, and tried to persuade the French government to establish at Versoix, near the frontier, a place where persecuted workers from Geneva could find refuge on French soil. It was an ironical situation, since Geneva had itself grown up as a city of refuge from French persecution. In the event the Versoix project came to nothing, but Voltaire, all on his own as chatelain of Ferney, found homes and jobs for dozens of exiled *natifs*. It was a characteristic act of Voltaire as practical reformer and benevolent *seigneur*.

Read in the light of these circumstances, Voltaire's **Idées républicaines** cannot be taken as evidence of any sort of conversion of the author to a republican ideology; on the other hand, it does indicate a diminution of his earlier contempt for the popular classes, and a greater belief in the capacity of the ordinary man, if only he were decently educated, to enact the role of citizen.

Voltaire once described himself as an 'Epicurean'. 'Stoicism', he wrote,

> is undoubtedly better than Christian moral teaching. It breeds a better character. A Stoic must earn salvation by living well, whereas a Christian needs only a last-minute repentance after thirty years of crime to be assured of eternal bliss. But I am not a Stoic. I am rather an Epicurean. I do not think life is to be endured: I think it is to be enjoyed.

In his later years Voltaire moved closer to Stoicism, but it would perhaps be better to describe him with a modern word as a utilitarian. He did not seek happiness for himself alone; he wanted it for everyone. The famous formula of Cesare Beccaria, 'la massima felicità del massimo numero', was one which well expressed Voltaire's own measure of the good, and Jeremy Bentham, who corresponded with Voltaire, acknowledged him as his 'master'. Even so, Voltaire did not carry his utilitarianism to the lengths of those theorists who believed that the elimination of poverty should be a matter of public policy and that the state should tax the rich in order to redistribute wealth among the poor. Voltaire retained a more typically bourgeois outlook. One of the reasons why he admired Locke so much was that Locke took such care to justify a natural right to property, and put that right together with the rights to life and liberty. When Voltaire read Rousseau's *Discourse on the Origin of Inequality* one of the things which enraged him most was Rousseau's suggestion that the right to property was somehow fraudulent: "What!' Voltaire wrote in the margin of his text, 'has a man no right to the fruit of his labour?'

Voltaire was very much a man of property. In the course of a long life he made a great deal of money—some of it by shrewd organization of the publication of his books, some by inheritance from his father, much more by shrewd investment, and some by luck in a lottery—if 'luck' is the word for finding a loophole in the rules which enabled him to sweep in the prize.

Towards the end of his life he said that he had once thought nothing of money, but had then seen so many men of letters poor and despised that he resolved not to augment their number: 'I turned myself into a hammer to avoid being used as an anvil. The first efforts to make money are painful, but it soon becomes very satisfying to watch one's wealth accumulate; and in old age, when money is most necessary, it is almost a duty to be rich'.

The wealth he acquired enabled Voltaire to live in luxury—especially at his château at Ferney, where he had his private theatre and his private chapel (the only one dedicated, he explained, to God alone). He was delighted to find in the writings of the economists of his time reasons to believe that luxury was socially advantageous. Among his favourite economists was J. F. Melon, author of *Essai politique sur le commerce,* published in 1734. Melon argues in these pages that commerce consists in the exchange of what is superfluous for what is necessary. The more prosperous a country, the more advantage it will gain from trading with other nations. Commerce elevates a country from savage customs to the benefits of civilization. The wealth acquired by one section of a society will have useful effects for all the other sections; the high consumption of some will provide a profitable market for the production of others. The desire of each to increase his well-being will lead to the enjoyment of luxury, which Melon defines as 'extraordinary sumptuosity produced by wealth and secure government'. With the passage of time, yesterday's luxuries become today's necessities; and thus the innocent pursuit and enjoyment of luxury become motives of general progress.

Voltaire not only read Melon; he also read Bernard Mandeville, and was at the same time attracted and repelled. If Voltaire's poem in defence of luxury, **Le Mondain,** reproduces the arguments of Melon, its sequel, **La Defense du mondain,** is closer to Mandeville, but Mandeville without his naked cynicism.

Mandeville, as Voltaire understood him, maintained that it was vice that kept the economic system moving. The vanity of women made them demand more and more clothing, indeed more elaborate and original styles of clothing every season; and this is what kept the textile industry active together with the wholesalers and retailers of clothes. The greed of men made them demand ever greater refinement in their food and drink, and this generated business for farmers and vintners and purveyors of every sort. The avarice of merchants prompted them to risk their capital in the hope of gain, and this made industry and commerce possible. Even the dishonesty of thieves made work for locksmiths and policemen.

Voltaire, with his special reverence for property, was particularly scandalized by this last of Mandeville's suggestions. After all, he protested, there was poison in many medicines, but that did not mean that poison could be praised as what cured patients. However, under the influence of Madam du Châtelet, his blue-stocking mistress, who admired Mandeville to the point of translating his work into French, Voltaire came to see more merit in *The Fable of the Bees.*

Mandeville's argument was that men could not have both the comforts of life and virtue and innocence. The comforts of life—luxury, wealth, power—were the products of vice. A virtuous people according to Mandeville would not do much or change much (and here one is reminded of Montesquieu's Troglodytes); a virtuous people would be frugal, public-spirited, and weak; they would have no dynamic, and nothing would motivate their economy. On the other hand, a vicious people, greedy for more and more private satisfaction, would be active, industrious, and adventurous, and their economy would therefore become prosperous and powerful.

It pleased Voltaire that Mandeville should cut short the cackle and the cant about virtue; but Voltaire, for all his scepticism, was not a cynic. He took an altogether more kindly view of man's sociability than did Mandeville. He believed that men acquired altruistic habits as a result of living in families, and that nature had instilled in everyone both compassion for others and a *bienveillance générale*. He could not accept Mandeville's suggestion that morality was bred entirely from the so-called vice of pride, society exacting good behaviour from its members only by making them ashamed of being ill regarded by their neighbours. Indeed, Voltaire refused to treat as vices what Mandeville considered vices, or as virtues what Mandeville called virtues, nor could he accept the suggestion that Sparta was morally better than Athens. He agreed with Mandeville that Sparta was the city of austerity but he could see no evidence of greater virtue among the Spartans; on the contrary, he regarded Sparta, with its militarism and regimentation and its massacres, as morally repugnant. In the end he came to see Mandeville—a Dutchman who wrote in English—as an inverted Calvinist, taking Calvin's conception of what virtue was and then mocking virtue. Voltaire had an altogether different conception of virtue: right or good actions were those which either diminished the amount of suffering in the world or which increased the amount of happiness.

In other words, Voltaire's moral philosophy was that of Beccaria. When Beccaria's famous book *Dei delitti e delle pene* (*On Crimes and Punishments*) came out in 1765 Voltaire read it in Italian, pronounced it 'philosophical'—his highest word of praise, and added: 'The author is a brother.' He then produced a short commentary on the book which shows us Voltaire drawing out the policy implications for France of Beccaria's penal theories. Voltaire insists on the importance of keeping the province of law separate from that of morality. Prisons and penalties should not be used as forms of retribution, but as a means of deterrence and reform. Society must protect itself, but no man should assume the office of God and inflict punishment on sinners. Penalties could be justified only in terms of utility. The death penalty was rarely, if ever justified: and torture was as useless as it was odious. 'True jurisprudence is to prevent crime, not to put to death the unfortunate.'

Just procedures were needed in the administration of laws—fair and open trials, strict rules of evidence, and so forth—and in the making and codification of laws. It was very necessary for laws to be both uniform and intelligible; the only test should be that of social advantage and the public interest.

It was in his thoughts about law that Voltaire came closest to Montesquieu, which is not altogether surprising in view of the fact that Beccaria, who inspired him, had been inspired in his turn by Montesquieu. But Voltaire was close to Montesquieu in many other ways as well. Despite the differences between them, they shared an intense belief in freedom. For both Voltaire and Montesquieu the central problem of politics is how to contrive government so that men may be at the same time free and ruled. Montesquieu proposes a solution on Aristotelian lines: men can be both free and ruled if they are ruled by law rather than by men, and he argues that this can be accomplished if sovereignty is so divided that one power can balance and correct the

others. Voltaire's solution is to entrust the protection of freedom to an enlightened sovereign whose power is undivided and entirely committed to the promotion of his people's rights and happiness.

The weakness of Voltaire's formula is that it allows for no institutional corps to ensure that the sovereign adheres to such policies. There is no appeal to the law, since Voltaire's sovereign would be the ultimate arbiter of the law. There is no appeal to God, since Voltaire's God had been shown by the Lisbon earthquake to be asleep. There is just one way by which Voltaire might be thought to be able to solve his problem: by proposing that the sovereign should be answerable to and, if need be, controlled by the people.

Indeed as he grew older and became less confident of finding an enlightened monarch among the actual princes of the world, it seems that Voltaire moved towards adopting this solution, advocating not democracy (except perhaps for the Swiss), but something which resembles democracy—that is, a populistic absolutism—a conception of the undivided sovereignty of a monarch being derived from the authorization of the people constantly renewed—'le plébiscite de tous les jours', in the phrase of Ernest Renan. It is not as appealing to the Anglo-Saxon mind as is Montesquieu's solution, but it gives an intimation of, and suggests an intellectual justification of, something which actually emerged in French political experience after Voltaire's time—the centralized rule of a Napoleon I, a Napoleon III or a Charles de Gaulle, drawing its authority not from intermediate institutions in the state but from a direct appeal to the electorate.

Voltaire never faced squarely, with Locke, the question of the people's right to decide whether their sovereign had abused his office, and their corresponding right to dismiss him. Voltaire, who had no wish to be an apologist of revolution, shrank from pressing his argument to such disturbing conclusions. But those revolutionary implications were there, and one can well understand why, apart from such extraordinary rulers as Frederick and Catherine, the monarchs of Europe regarded Voltaire with a certain dread. He was their friend, their champion and advocate. The trouble was that he swept away, one by one, all the things that made a king feel safe on his throne: religion, tradition, habit, customs, and the established order of society. He gave people new reasons for obedience, but he took away their old motives for obedience. And thus, paradoxically, Voltaire proved to be even more subversive of absolute government in defending it than Montesquieu in attacking it. (pp. 42-61)

Maurice Cranston, "Voltaire," in his Philosophers and Pamphleteers: Political Theorists of the Enlightenment, *Oxford University Press, Oxford, 1986, pp. 36-61.*

A. J. Ayer   (essay date 1986)

[*Ayer is recognized as a leading twentieth-century philosopher and logician. His* Language, Truth, and Logic (*1936; 2d revised edition, 1967*), *published when he was 25 years old, is considered by many critics to be a seminal work in the field of logical positivist philosophy. In the following excerpt from his 1986 critical study of Voltaire, he elucidates Voltaire's conception of history.*]

It is not generally known that Voltaire was a voluminous historian. One of his earliest publications was a history of Charles XII of Sweden [*Histoire de Charles XII*] who lived from 1682 to 1718 and came to the throne in 1697. His reign was remarkable for the fact that it was almost entirely devoted to the pursuit of war for which Charles had an insatiable passion and an extraordinary aptitude. In nine years of campaigning, almost always with forces inferior in number to those of his opponents, he extended the influence of Sweden over Denmark, all the Baltic states, Poland, and the north of Germany. I speak of the influence rather than the empire of Sweden, because Charles's habit was not so much to annex territory as to install rulers who were subservient to himself. Like other military adventurers, he came to grief in Russia. Having penetrated deep into the Ukraine he was defeated in 1709 at the battle of Poltava by Peter the Great, and forced to take refuge in Turkey, where he vainly attempted to persuade the Sultan to supply him with an army to lead against Russia. In 1714 he reappeared at Stralsund, then still a Swedish outpost on the Baltic, after riding through Hungary, Austria and a large part of Germany in sixteen days, with an escort of only two officers. He spent the next four years in a mainly unsuccessful attempt to restore the fortunes of his country, which had suffered military reverses during his absence, and was killed by a stray cannon-ball while directing the siege of a Norwegian fortress. Charles XII left Sweden the poorer both in influence and territory than when he embarked, at the age of eighteen, upon his career of conquest.

Voltaire told this story well, though it is a little surprising, in view of the number of his other interests, that he should have chosen to tell it at all. What is even more surprising is that the book was considered subversive by the authorities, so that it had to be printed surreptitiously in Rouen. [In his *Voltaire* (1969; rev. ed., 1976)] Mr. Besterman quotes as evidence a paragraph in the preface to the effect that the only events worth recording are those that have produced great changes, or those that stand out from the mass through being described by some very good writer, like the portraits of obscure men painted by great masters, but this hardly seems sufficient to have alarmed the youthful Louis XV or his ministers, even on Besterman's careless reading of the passage which led him to substitute 'kings' for 'events'. Perhaps it was just assumed, unwarrantably, that anything that Voltaire wrote about a monarch was likely to be irreverent.

In this connection, it is worth quoting Voltaire's summary of Charles's career, if only as a good example of his style of writing history:

> So perished, at the age of thirty-six and a half, Charles XII, King of Sweden, having experienced the heights of prosperity and the utmost bitterness of adversity, without being softened by the one or cast down for a moment by the other. Nearly all his actions, consistently with his private life, went far beyond the bounds of probability. He is perhaps the only man, and so far the only king, to have lived without any weakness; he carried all the heroic virtues to a pitch where they became as dangerous as their opposite vices. His strength of will, developed into obstinacy, caused his misfortunes in the Ukraine and kept him for five years in Turkey: his generosity, degenerating into extravagance, ruined Sweden; his courage, swollen into rashness, caused

his death: his justice developed sometimes into cruelty; and in the last years of his life the maintenance of his authority came near to being tyrannical. His great qualities, of which any single one could have immortalized another prince, were injurious to his country. He never attacked anyone; but he cast aside prudence in his implacable pursuit of revenge. He was the first man to be ambitious for conquest, without desiring to increase his possessions; he wanted to win empires in order to give them away. His passion for glory, for war, and for revenge, prevented him from being a good politician, a quality which no conqueror has ever been seen to lack. Before battle and after victory he was never anything but modest; unfailingly resolute after defeat; hard on others as he was on himself, heedless of the suffering and lives of his subjects as he was of his own; an exceptional rather than a great man, and one to admire rather than to imitate. His life should teach kings how far a peaceful and happy government is superior to such an abundance of glory.

Voltaire's history of Charles XII inevitably overlapped at several points with his subsequent *History of the Russian Empire under Peter the Great* in two volumes, of which the first appeared in 1759 and the second in 1763. The very great enthusiasm which they display for Peter's character and achievements cannot be wholly attributed to Voltaire's friendship with the Empress Catherine II, since . . . their correspondence started only in 1762, but this friendship may have been partly responsible for Voltaire's gingerly treatment in the second volume of the blackest episode in Peter the Great's career, his execution in 1718 of his eldest son Alexis on a charge of treason based on very slender evidence. It is to Voltaire's credit that he does put his readers in a position to draw the inference that Peter's actions were not only inhumane but unjust. At the same time Voltaire does not disguise his sympathy for what he conceives to have been Peter's strongest motive: the fear that Alexis, who had succumbed to the influence of Russian priests and had indeed offered to renounce his title to the succession if he were permitted to retire into a monastery, would go back upon his word and having ascended to the throne would allow power to pass into the hands of the patriarchs of the Orthodox Church. Not that Peter the Great believed that the doctrines of the Orthodox Church were less acceptable than those of other forms of Christianity. He took as little interest as Voltaire in the question whether the Holy Ghost proceeds from both the Father and the Son or only from the Father via the Son. His opposition to the Church was political. His primary purpose during the thirty-six years of his effective rule from the time he acquired entire authority in 1689 at the age of seventeen, having reigned for five years under his half-sister Sophia's tutelage, was to turn Russia into a European power, and he feared that unless his successors kept the Church in subordination, its leaders would undo the social reforms by which this purpose had been achieved.

When I speak in this context of social reforms, I do not intend to imply that the condition of the peasantry, which constituted the bulk of the Russian people, was significantly altered in the reign of Peter the Great. He did not alleviate their state of serfdom, diminish the extent of their illiteracy, or relieve them of their superstitious beliefs. Internally, the changes which he effected were those that in earlier centuries had brought such countries as England

and France out of the era of feudalism. He divested both the clergy and the nobility of their independent power and subjected them to the control of the central government, which in the case of Russia was, and in theory remained, an absolute monarchy for nearly two hundred years and longer still in practice. Externally, he made Russia a force in Europe, not only by the influence over Poland and the northern states of Germany which he owed to his defeat of Charles XII, but still more by his development of a navy which secured Russia the control of the Baltic. To prepare himself for this he went abroad in 1697 and spent over a year first at Sadom in Holland and then at Deptford in England learning the trade of a shipwright. The account which Voltaire gives of his seriousness in this undertaking and of his supposedly simple standard of living shows him in an attractive light which, unfortunately, is not sustained. The absence of the Tsar from Russia encouraged a section of the Russian militia to march on Moscow, induce his half-sister Sophia to leave the monastery in which she had resided since his accession, and resume the throne. According to Voltaire, the opposition of the clergy to the sale of tobacco in Russia, which Peter had been the first Tsar to permit, was one of the principal stimuli to the revolt. The rebels had been defeated by troops loyal to Peter, before his return to Moscow, but the reprisals which he then exacted attained a severity and in some instances a refinement of cruelty for which Voltaire admits that reasons of state did not supply a sufficient excuse. In the light of recent Russian history it does, however, give one a certain chill to find him saying that instead of Peter's executing so many of his enemies it would have been more in the country's interest to put them to forced labour.

In Voltaire's eyes, and I should imagine in those of the majority of his readers, Peter's greatest achievement was the construction of St Petersburg on what was previously a marshy waste. The operation was begun in 1703 and something which Voltaire describes as a city was built in five months. It took rather longer for the Scottish and Italian architects whom Peter imported to complete the erection of one of the most beautiful cities in Europe. From the start Peter intended it to look towards Europe, in contra-distinction to Moscow, and it is an interesting fact that not only has it been restored to its former beauty, after its devastation in the last war, but its difference from Moscow has persisted. Its transformation into Leningrad has not wholly deprived it of its western orientation.

How far did Peter the Great exemplify Lord Acton's saying that absolute power corrupts absolutely? I think that he did to a very large extent. He had an unbridled temper and pursued his ends without much regard to the suffering that was caused. It is suggested by Voltaire that his second wife, who succeeded him as Catherine I, was a softening influence, to the point even where she tried to persuade him to show mercy to her stepson Alexis, in opposition to her own interests, but whatever attempt she made we have seen that it failed. Peter's attachment to her, and his belief that she would continue his policies, may rather have strengthened his resolve. The criterion by which Voltaire judged the worth of a society was the extent to which it flourished in commerce, science and the arts: a negative aspect of its advance in science was its tolerance in matters of religion. Judged in this way, the Russia of Peter the Great comes out fairly well. There is no doubt that he developed its commerce; if he did not weaken the hold of the

Orthodox Church upon the people at large, he curtailed its political power; St Petersburg became, as I have said, a most beautiful city; and while Peter's own court was hardly an ornament to the arts or sciences, it can be said to have been an indispensable precursor of the civilized court of Catherine the Great. The question, which defies an answer, like most of the unfulfilled conditionals in history, is whether the same results could not have been achieved more slowly perhaps but at a smaller human cost. The value of these results can also be put in question. The trend which Peter the Great initiated was continued by the four empresses who succeeded him, Catherine I, Anna, Elizabeth and Catherine the Great. . . . Voltaire was beguiled by Catherine the Great and she did indeed invite mathematicians and writers of great distinction to her court, though noticeably not Voltaire. It can, however, hardly be said that the Russia over which she ruled had yet become a civilized country.

That Voltaire would not have agreed with Acton's view of absolute power is confirmed not only by his predominantly sympathetic attitude towards Peter the Great, but by his almost unqualified enthusiasm for Louis XIV. The history of the century of Louis XIV [*Le Siècle de Louis Quatorze*] was a book on which Voltaire worked for many years. He wrote a preface, dedicated to Lord Hervey, as early as 1740; . . . the book was first published in Berlin in 1752; notes were added, chiefly in reply to criticisms; and what may be regarded as the definitive edition appeared in Geneva in 1768. The reason why it was not published in France seems to have been the fear that it would elicit invidious comparisons with the current reign. Consequently, there were many pirated editions. Like all Voltaire's historical work, it is written with verve but risks being overburdened with narrative detail.

In the very first paragraph of the book Voltaire announces that it has a wider purpose than that of merely relating the life of Louis XIV. He will try to portray for posterity not just the actions of a single man, but the spirit of men in the most enlightened century that there had ever been. If it is known as the century of Louis XIV, it is because the apogee of civilization was reached in France at Louis XIV's court.

All history is much alike, he continues, for those who are interested only in committing facts to memory. But for any thinking person, or what is even rarer, any person of taste, there are only four centuries that count in the history of the world. The first, which was confined to Greece, was the century of Philip of Macedon and his son Alexander the Great, that is to say the first three quarters of the fourth century BC, though Voltaire takes it well back into the fifth century by including Pericles and Phidias among its ornaments as well as Plato, Aristotle, Demosthenes, Apelles and Praxiteles. The second was the century of Caesar and Augustus, that is the greater part of the first century BC running over into the second decade of the first century AD. Its luminaries in Voltaire's reckoning were all Roman, his list comprising Lucretius, Livy, Cicero, Virgil, Horace, Ovid, Varro and Vitruvius. The third golden age is said to be the century following the capture of Constantinople by Mahomet II in 1453. This was the period in which the arts and sciences flourished above all in Italy, especially under the patronage of the Medicis in Florence. The only names which Voltaire cites apart from the Medicis, are those of Michelangelo, Palladio and Galileo. He admits that some progress towards civilization was made during this period also in France, England, Germany and Spain but mentions only Rabelais. It is noteworthy that he allows Shakespeare to fall outside it.

Of the fourth age, the century of Louis XIV, Voltaire writes that perhaps it came closest to perfection. He takes as its starting-point the founding of the French Academy in 1635, three years before Louis XIV's birth, so that it covers two regencies, the one following his elevation to the throne in 1643, and the one following his death and the accession of his great-grandson in 1715. Voltaire writes of it that in certain respects more was accomplished in this century than in all of his other three golden ages put together.

> In truth [he continues] the arts as a whole were not carried further forward than under the Medicis, Augustus and Alexander: the improvement was to be found in the development of human reason. It was the starting-point of a sound knowledge of philosophy, and one can truly say that [in the period in question] a revolution was accomplished in our arts, our minds, our manners and in our government, which should serve for ever as a sign of the true glory of our country. This happy influence was not confined to France: it extended to England and wakened the necessary spirit of rivalry in that bold and gifted nation; it brought taste to Germany and science to Russia; it reanimated Italy which had fallen into decline, and Europe owed its culture and its social sense to the court of Louis XIV.

Voltaire was not especially noted for his patriotism, but here it seems to have led him astray. If the superiority of his fourth golden age over the previous three consists above all in the progress achieved in science and philosophy, then the palm should surely go to England rather than France. Locke, Berkeley, Newton and Boyle are more than a match for Descartes, Pascal, Bayle and Montesquieu. Again, when it comes to poetry Milton, Marvell, Dryden and Pope collectively do not fall short of Racine, Corneille, Boileau and Jean-Baptiste Rousseau. Let it be granted that Molière excelled in comedy; he has no Frenchman of his own standing to back him against Congreve and the other playwrights of the English restoration. Voltaire does not mention the spread of civilization to Holland, but if Poussin and Claude were great painters, so also were Rembrandt and Vermeer. Under the heading of music in his catalogue we find only the name of Lulli. Yet the period covers the first fifty years of the life of Johann Sebastian Bach.

How then did it come about that Voltaire awarded the prize to France? It might be suggested that the reason lay partly in his self-esteem. The period which has become known in history as the Age of Enlightenment is the second half of the eighteenth century; France was its centre and it was presided over by Voltaire. Diderot and d'Holbach may have thought that he made too great a concession to deism; d'Alembert excelled him in his knowledge of mathematics and the physical sciences, but they all deferred to him. Part of the bitterness of Jean-Jacques Rousseau lay in his fury that Voltaire had been given pride of place. The theory then would be that Voltaire saw in what he called the century of Louis XIV the indispensable precursor of the Age of Enlightenment.

The main objection to this theory is one of dating. Even though Voltaire did not publish *Le Siècle de Louis Quatorze* until 1752, the letter to Lord Hervey in 1740 shows that he had already decided on its central theme: and Diderot's and d'Alembert's revised prospectus for their *Encyclopédie,* the standard-bearer of the Enlightenment, did not appear until 1750. It could be argued that Voltaire foresaw the growth of an intellectual movement with himself as its leader, and it is true that by 1740 he already saw himself as making an outstanding contribution to what Peacock was to call 'the march of mind'. Nevertheless, it is unlikely that he foresaw his own longevity or the full extent of his fame. Moreover, the Age of Enlightenment culminated in the French Revolution of which it is far from clear that Voltaire would have approved.

A simpler and more plausible hypothesis is that Voltaire was dazzled by the magnificence of Louis XIV. Indeed, he confesses as much in his letter to Lord Hervey. He admits that Louis XIV cannot claim any credit for the emergence of Newton and other great Englishmen of the period, but then he goes on to argue that Pope Leo X did not accomplish everything in the time of the Medicis. If that century is named after him, it is because he then did more for the arts than any other prince. So 'what king has rendered a greater service to humanity in this respect than Louis

LETTERS

CONCERNING THE

ENGLISH
NATION.

BY

Mr. DE VOLTAIRE.

LONDON,
Printed for C. Davis in *Pater-Noster-Row,*
and A. Lyon in *Ruffel-Street, Covent-Garden.*
MDCCXXXIII.

Title page of the first edition of Voltaire's Letters concerning the English Nation *(1733).*

XIV? What king has distributed more benefactions, shown more taste and lived in such a splendid style?' He had his faults, like other men, but he was a great man with a greater reputation than any of his contemporaries. 'In spite of his depriving France of a million men, all of whom have had reason to decry him, all Europe admires him and ranks him with the greatest and the best of monarchs.'

The admission that Louis XIV cost France a million men is an allusion not, as it might superficially seem, to the civil and foreign warfare in which the country was almost constantly engaged throughout his reign, but to his revocation of the Edict of Nantes in 1685 rather less than a century after Henri IV had promulgated it. The Edict of Nantes secured toleration for the Huguenots, France's Protestant community, and its revocation sent them into exile. Many of them came to England and Voltaire goes so far as to give Louis XIV the credit for the growth of the English manufacture of silk and glass to which the Huguenots contributed. Thus Voltaire is disposed to forgive Louis even his religious bigotry which was indeed fostered in him by the most tenacious of his many mistresses, Madame de Maintenon, who not only ousted Madame de Montespan, who had borne him seven children, but after he was widowed, secretly became his wife.

It is noteworthy that all Voltaire's golden ages were periods of political turmoil. Was it because this attracted him that his first historical study was devoted to Charles XII of Sweden? At first sight, Charles XII and Louis XIV have very little in common. Even if Charles XII had not been personally engaged in warfare to the extent that we have seen, his tastes would not have led him to assemble a brilliant court. He had none of the *politesse,* the ceremonious manners, for which Voltaire so greatly admired Louis XIV. Yet the total effect of their reigns upon the fortunes of their respective countries was very similar. Louis XIV was not himself a warrior, but had able ministers in Fouquet and Colbert, a master of fortifications in Vauban, outstanding generals in Turenne, Condé and Villars. At one time France was the strongest military power in Europe. Yet the War of the Spanish Succession was disastrous for her. Had the Duchess of Marlborough not quarrelled with Queen Anne, so that Marlborough was prevented from pursuing the war, France might have ended with a smaller territory than she commanded on Louis XIV's accession. The country paid a high price for the splendours of Versailles.

At one time *Le Siècle de Louis Quatorze* formed part of a larger work in seven volumes which was published in Geneva in 1756 under the title of *Essai sur l'histoire générale et sur les moeurs et l'esprit des nations.* This universal history was the book on which . . . Voltaire started work in the 1730s for the edification of Madame du Châtelet. In 1769 he wrote an introduction to it for the benefit of Catherine the Great, removed the story of the century of Louis XIV, and gave it the full title, which it has since retained, of *Essai sur les moeurs et l' esprit des nations et sur les principaux faits de l'histoire depuis Charlemagne jusqu'à Louis XIII.* With the addition of Voltaire's *Annales de L'empire,* written in 1753—a work of little interest beyond its justifying Voltaire's saying 'This agglomeration which was called, and which still calls itself the Holy Roman Empire is in no respect either holy, Roman or an empire'—the whole work occupies three vast volumes, av-

eraging just under six hundred pages each, of the 1878 Paris edition of the complete works of Voltaire.

Voltaire's introduction is a gallop through the customs and beliefs of ancient societies. He speaks of the Chaldeans, the Indians and the Chinese as the earliest nations to be civilized. Some account is given of the progress of the Chaldeans in astronomy; the Indians are said to have been the beneficiaries of a favourable climate; their belief in reincarnation is held responsible for their pacific nature; the Chinese are said to have written reasonably as soon as they wrote at all; they were governed like a family and believed in a benevolent first principle. The earliest belief in the combination of God, the Devil, resurrection, paradise and hell is attributed to the Persians. All primitive people were subject to their priests. It was only in Greece that philosophy flourished and even there, in Voltaire's opinion, it did not amount to much.

> From Thales [he writes] until the time of Plato and Aristotle, the schools resounded with philosophical disputes, all of which revealed the wisdom and folly of the human mind, its greatness and its weakness. They nearly always argued without understanding one another, as we have done since the thirteenth century, when we began to reason. The reputation which Plato enjoyed does not surprise me; all the philosophers were unintelligible: he was as unintelligible as the rest, but he expressed himself more eloquently.

Nearly a quarter of the introduction is given over to an attack on the Old Testament. A quotation from the section on the Jews in Egypt typifies the tone of the assault:

> It is to no purpose that a host of learned men find it surprising that the King of Egypt should have ordered two midwives to put to death all the male children of the Hebrews; or that the King's daughter who lived at Memphis, should have gone to bathe far from Memphis, in a branch of the Nile, where no one ever bathes because of the crocodiles. It is to no purpose that they cavil at the age of eighty which Moses had already attained before undertaking to lead a whole people out of slavery . . . They wonder how Pharoah could have pursued the Jews with a large body of cavalry, when all his horses had died in the fifth, sixth, seventh and tenth plagues. They wonder why six hundred thousand warriors took to flight with God in the lead, and having the advantage that all the first-born of the Egyptians had been struck dead. They again wonder why God did not give the fertile land of Egypt to his chosen people, instead of making them wander for forty years in a horrible desert.

> There is only one answer to these and other countless objections, and that is: God willed it, the Church believes it and we ought to believe it.

One can sympathize with Voltaire's irony, but it is regrettable that he has allowed his resentment at the fidelity of the Christian churches to ancient Jewish myths to fester into a violent hostility towards the Jewish people. This comes out shockingly in a passage of the main volume where he contrasts the Jews with the Mahometan Arabs, to whom he attributes the same religious ferocity but much more courage and magnanimity.

In this passage Voltaire writes as if the barbarous treatment of unfriendly tribes, attributed to the Jews in the Old

Testament, were still characteristic of the Jews of his own time. He upbraids them for their addiction to usury, a reproach which he was not the person to make, and one that takes no account of the fact that their exclusion from the liberal professions and the ban on their ownership of land directed their talents into the management of money. Voltaire goes so far as to call them the enemies of the human race, adding that at no time has 'that atrocious nation' been responsible for any improvement in culture, science or art. On the other hand, there was a period when the Arabs were the teachers of Europe in the sciences and the arts, even though their Koran seems inimical to the arts. What Voltaire says of the Arabs is true, but he might have given a thought to Spinoza and Maimonides.

Voltaire does not give the Jews any credit for the ten commandments, since he strongly objects to the pretence that what he calls the natural laws which are common and useful to all societies were dictated by God. These laws in Voltaire's version are: 'Thou shalt not rob or kill thy neighbour; thou shalt have a respectful care for those who gave thee life and brought thee up as a child; thou shalt not ravish thy brother's wife; thou shalt not tell lies in order to do him injury; thou shalt minister to his needs, so as to deserve to be helped in thy turn.' These 'truths' are said to be engraved on all hearts from Japan to the shores of the West. Voltaire is not so foolish as to suggest that they are universally observed. One would have to construe 'neighbour' and 'brother' very narrowly to be able to claim that they were universally acknowledged.

Apart from his effort to discredit the Old Testament, Voltaire is not concerned in his introduction with the details of ancient history. In his passing references to the Greeks and the Romans, he overlooks their polytheism, singling out Zeus and Jupiter in support of his dubious thesis that every society has believed in the existence of one supreme being. He praises both peoples for their intellectual and religious tolerance. The fate of Socrates might appear to constitute a counter-example, but Voltaire argues, I think rightly, that it had more of a political than a doctrinal ground, and anyhow that it was a crime of which the Athenians repented.

The explanation for the fall of the Roman Empire is given in a single paragraph:

> The weakness of the emperors, the fractious divisions of their ministers and their eunuchs, the blood-stained quarrels nurtured in Christianity, the theological disputes displacing the exercise of arms, and lethargy displacing valour; a multitude of monks replacing farmers and soldiers; all this attracted the very barbarians who had been unable to conquer the warlike republic, but crushed a Rome languishing under emperors who were cruel, effeminate and devout.

Voltaire is consistently hostile to the fruits of the Christian religion, though he resorts to irony when attacking the religion itself.

> The amount of fraud, the errors, the disgusting stupidity in which we have been drenched for seventeen hundred years have not discredited our religion. It must be divine, since seventeen centuries of mischief and idiocy have not managed to destroy it; and we revere truth all the more for our contempt for lying.

After making easy fun of the theological absurdities of the Bishop Eusebius, an ally of Constantine's who imposed Christianity upon the Roman Empire, Voltaire amuses himself by giving a list of Constantine's major crimes, which weakened his hold upon the Romans who had never wanted him as their emperor in the first place. Voltaire suggests that it may have been for this reason, rather than the message from God which Constantine claimed to have received, that he transferred the seat of the Empire to Byzantium.

Voltaire takes less than twenty pages to cover the five centuries separating Constantine from Charlemagne who became King of the Franks in 768 AD and Holy Roman Emperor in 800. His court has been described by at least one authority as a centre of learning, though if Voltaire is to be believed, he could not sign his name. After giving a brisk account of the chief events of Charlemagne's reign, Voltaire dwells at rather greater length upon the laws and customs of the time and upon its religious beliefs. One point of interest which emerges is that a number of pious persons still believed that they would live to see the end of the world with the reappearance of Christ. I doubt, indeed, if this belief has ever been wholly extinguished, even in the twentieth century.

After leaving Charlemagne, we are taken at a fair pace through the division of his empire, the descent of the Normans into Europe and their acquisition of Naples and Sicily, the state of England before and after the Norman conquest, with a word of praise for Alfred the Great, the troubles of the papacy brought to a happy issue at the beginning of the eleventh century, with three popes dividing the revenues of the Church and each living peacefully with his mistress, the quarrels of the empire and the papacy, with the emperor Henry IV submitting to Pope Gregory VII at Canossa in 1077, the degradation of the Eastern empire, the incursion of the Moors into Spain, the exploits of Genghis Khan, the melancholy story of the Crusades, the horrible massacre of the Albigenses at the beginning of the thirteenth century. Towards the end of the first volume Voltaire delivers his verdict on the papacy:

> You will have already observed that since the death of Charlemagne we have not come across a single Roman pontiff who has not been engaged in thorny or violent disputes with emperors and kings; you will see that these quarrels continue into the century of Louis XIV, and that they are the necessary consequence of the most absurd form of government to which men have ever submitted. This absurdity consisted in letting a foreigner be master in one's own kingdom; in effect allowing him to dispense feudal rights in it, being unable to receive payment from the holders of these fiefs without his permission, and without giving him his share, being constantly liable to witness the closure at his command of temples that you have built and endowed, allowing a number of your subjects to bring lawsuits three hundred leagues away from your dominions; that is a small fraction of the chains with which the Sovereigns of Europe loaded themselves insensibly, and almost without knowing it. It is clear that if the original suggestion were made today to the council of a Sovereign, that he should submit to such practices, the person who dared to put it forward would be regarded as an utter madman. The burden, which was light at first, became gradually heavier; it was felt that it ought to be di-

minished, but the wisdom, knowledge and resolution were lacking to get rid of it entirely.

After touching on the relatively successful attempt of John Wycliffe in England at the end of the fourteenth century to anticipate the Reformation, and relating how John Huss, his counterpart in Bohemia, was lured to his martyrdom, Voltaire proceeds to give a succinct review of the Hundred Years War. He gives Joan of Arc due credit for restoring the fortunes of France, reserving his sarcasms for his poem **La Pucelle.** There follows a chapter of ten pages on the state of the sciences and arts in the thirteenth and fourteenth centuries. Italy and especially Florence was then the centre of European culture and Voltaire mentions the painters Cimabue and Giotto, the architect Brunelleschi, and the poets Dante, Petrarch and Boccaccio. Consistently with his view that literature progresses, he remarks that these writers have been surpassed by Ariosto and Tasso in the fifteenth and sixteenth centuries. It is characteristic of him also that he devotes several paragraphs to the popular belief that the ass on which Jesus rode into Jerusalem walked over the waters to Verona, and its exploitation by Pope Boniface VIII who drew the profitable inference that if the ass was capable of such mobility the Virgin Mary's house could have made its way to Loreto, where the house was transformed into a handsome church. Nor could Voltaire refrain from a gibe at scholasticism.

> If [he writes] the light shone only on Tuscany, it wasn't as if there was no talent anywhere else. St Bernard and Abélard in France, in the twelfth century, can be regarded as men of superior intellect; but their tongue was a barbarous jargon, and they paid tribute in Latin to the bad taste of their time. The rhyme to which those Latin hymns of the twelfth and thirteenth centuries was subjected set the seal on barbarity. That was not how Horace wrote his secular songs. Scholastic theology, the bastard daughter of Aristotle's philosophy, badly translated and misunderstood, did more harm to reason and scholarship than the Huns and the Vandals had done.

Proceeding on his rapid way, noting the conquests of Tamerlane, the fall of Constantinople, the wickedness of King Louis XI of France, the Wars of the Roses in England and the decline of feudalism, Voltaire congratulates Ferdinand and Isabella of Spain not only on their success in defeating the Moors at the end of the fifteenth century but also on their expulsion of the Jews, against whom he delivers yet another virulent tirade, despite his surprising aside that 'at bottom we are no more than Jews with a foreskin'. After giving a passing salute to Galileo and his predecessor Copernicus, who first caused the light of 'true philosophy' to shine upon men in the sixteenth century, in spite of the efforts of the Church to put it out, Voltaire concentrates upon the chequered career of the Holy Roman Emperor Charles V, who abdicated in 1556 having had to defend his possessions both against Suleiman II the Magnificent, Sultan of the Ottoman Empire, and against Francis I, one of the more powerful of the Kings of France. Another of Charles's serious problems lay in the political consequences of the Reformation to which Voltaire devotes ten chapters, followed by one on the state of religion in France under Francis I and his successors, one on the religious orders, and one on the Inquisition. In those first ten chapters, Luther is given pride of place, with

Calvin a close second, and mention is also made of the violent Anabaptists, of Zwingli, a Swiss who denied the Eucharistic presence, of Servetus, a Spanish theologian who went too far and was condemned by Calvin to be burned at the stake for denying the Trinity and the divinity of Christ, of the establishment of the Anglican Church under Henry VIII, and of the triumph of Calvinism in Scotland. Voltaire sums up the religious issue in a couple of sentences: 'So, while those who were called Papists ate God but not bread, the Lutherans ate both bread and God. Soon after there came the Calvinists who ate bread and did not eat God.' Not one to overlook the state of corruption into which the Roman Catholic Church had fallen, he also makes the obvious point that the questions at issue were not merely theological.

Going back a little in time, Voltaire turns his attention to the exploits of the Spaniards and the Portuguese at the end of the fourteenth and the beginning of the fifteenth centuries, notably the discovery of Japan and Abyssinia, the circumnavigation of the globe, the discovery of America, the conquest of Mexico and Peru. Voltaire finds it problematic whether Europe has profited by its incursion into America.

> It is certain that at the outset the Spaniards drew great riches from it; but Spain was depopulated and the fact that the treasures were shared at the end by so many other nations restored the equality which they had at first upset. The price of commodities has everywhere increased. So no one has really gained. It remains to be seen whether cochineal and quinine are sufficiently valuable to make up for the loss of so many men.

The French retained relatively few possessions in the New World: Martinique, Guadeloupe, some small islands in the Antilles and half the island of San Domingo, for which they were indebted to their pirates. Voltaire reckoned that in the French part of San Domingo in 1757 there was a free population of 30,000 living off the labour of 100,000 black and mulatto slaves, and this gave him the opportunity for an eloquent denunciation of slavery.

> We tell them that they are men like ourselves, that they are redeemed by the blood of a God who died for their sake, and then they are made to work like beasts of burden; they are worse fed; if they try to escape they have a leg cut off; they are given a wooden leg and put to the manual labour of turning the shaft of a sugar mill. And then we have the effrontery to talk about human rights.

After giving an account of the revenues which France derived from the colonies, Voltaire concludes 'This commerce does not enrich a country; quite the contrary, it destroys men, it causes shipwrecks; it is questionable whether it is a real good; but since men have created new needs, it saves France from having to buy dearly abroad a luxury which has become a necessity.' In appraising Voltaire, we should remember that the very first onslaught on the institution of slavery in the New World, the British abolition of the slave trade, did not take place until nearly thirty years after his death.

The sixteenth century to which Voltaire's narrative returns saw the rise of England and Holland at the expense of Spain and the death of Francis. He expresses some admiration for Queen Elizabeth while deploring her treatment of Mary Queen of Scots. His account of the misfortunes of France overlaps with his poem *La Henriade.* He duly denounces the massacre of Saint Bartholemew's day on 24 August 1572, on which several thousand Huguenots were murdered, linking it with the Counter-Reformation, endorsed in 1563 by the Council of Trent, which had taken twenty-one years to agree on the anathemas that it finally pronounced. The Council helped to foment the religious wars of the following century.

Since Voltaire is purporting to write a history of the world he intersperses his European narrative with chapters, usually short, on India, Persia, the Ottoman Empire, the African coast, Morocco, and the Far East. A whole chapter is devoted to the battle of Lepanto in 1571 when a Christian fleet gathered together by Pope Pius V, Philip II King of Spain and the rulers of Venice and commanded by Don Juan of Austria, bastard son of Charles V, defeated the Turks. This battle earned Don Juan a place in history but as Voltaire does not fail to point out, its consequences were nugatory. Venice gained no territory by it and the Turks retook Tunis in 1574.

In writing about Asians, Africans, and Orientals, Voltaire tends to exaggerate the differences between them and Europeans. The following passage is typical:

> The difference between Eastern customs and our own, as great as the difference between our languages, is a subject fit for the attention of a philosopher. The most civilized peoples of these vast countries have nothing in common with our civilization; their arts are not ours. Food, clothing, houses, gardens, laws, worship, manners, all are different. Is there anything more contrary to our customs than the way in which merchants bargain in Hindustan? The most important deals are concluded, without speech or writing; everything is done by signs. How could there not be such numerous differences between oriental customs and our own? Nature is fundamentally the same everywhere, but the differences between their climate and ours are enormous. In southern India puberty is reached at the age of seven or eight. Marriages are often contracted there at that age. Those children, who become fathers, enjoy a measure of reason which nature grants them at an age when our reason is scarcely developed.
>
> All these peoples resemble us only in their passions, and in the universal reason which offsets the passions, and imprints on human hearts the law. 'Do not do to others what you would not want to have done to you.' These are the two characteristics which nature stamps on so many different human races, and the two external bonds by which she unites them, in spite of everything that divides them. All the rest is the fruit of the sun, the earth and custom.

In general Voltaire likes to find a salient characteristic or set of characteristics in the people whom he describes, such as the morality of the Chinese, the military skill of the Tartars, the addiction of the Persians to astrology and their excellence in poetry. He finds next to nothing to admire in the character of the American Indians, saying of the Peruvians, who worshipped the sun, that they alone of all the American people had a religion which was not obviously irrational. He then goes on to condemn the Mexican indulgence in human sacrifice. It is to Voltaire's

credit that he devotes a chapter to the extraordinary achievements of the Jesuit missionaries in Paraguay who gradually gained control of the country at the beginning of the seventeenth century and ruled it until the middle of the eighteenth, when, at the instigation of the papacy, they were ousted by the Portuguese, operating from Brazil. So far from exploiting the Indians, they brought them prosperity, instructed them in agriculture, industry, architecture and military self-defence. They governed them justly and gave them the benefits of communism, without its perversions, employing gold and silver to embellish their churches but not to enrich themselves. It is perhaps the only place and time where the introduction of Christianity has been wholly beneficial, barring the fact that the Paraguayan Indians were not entrusted with self-government.

After a long chapter on the achievements of Cardinal Richelieu, a brief review of the state of Spain in the seventeenth century, where Voltaire, without mentioning Velasquez, is able to discover only a few painters of the second rank, and a slightly longer account of the misfortunes of the Empire and the suffering of Germany in the Thirty Years War, Voltaire devotes four chapters to the history of England. Conventionally, he condemns the Gunpowder Plot, pities Charles I, respects Cromwell and applauds the 'theism' of the court of Charles II and the foundation of the Royal Society. There follows a review of the state of Italy, with some praise for Pope Gregory XII and his introduction of the Gregorian calendar, and for his successor Pope Sixtus V, who reformed the papal administration, enriched the Vatican library and carried out Michelangelo's design for the dome of St Peter's. We are then treated to a series of chapters in which the fortunes of Holland, Sweden, Denmark, Poland and Russia are swiftly recalled. The principal events, in the record, are the revolt against Spain of the seven provinces of Holland, under the Princes of Orange, and the exploits of the Dutch Navy, the substitution in Denmark in 1660 of an absolute for an elective monarchy, the conquests of Gustavus Adolphus of Sweden, the defeat of the Turks outside Vienna in 1683 by an army commanded by John Sobieski, King of Poland, and the usurpation of the throne of Russia by Boris Godunov, who reigned from 1598 to 1605. A parade of the rulers of the Ottoman Empire, beginning with Mahomet III, who is said to have inaugurated his reign by causing nineteen of his brothers to be strangled and twelve of his father's pregnant widows to be drowned, is followed in rapid order by an account of civil strife in Persia exacerbated by religious differences, a résumé of the career of the Mogul emperor Aurangzeb, the story of the establishment of the Manchu dynasty in China, and that of the expulsion of all foreigners, including Christian missionaries, from Japan.

Voltaire concludes his work with a short retrospective commentary. Towards the end he deplores the cost to European civilization of the entombment in monasteries of an astonishing number of useless men and women. He also considers it regrettable that Europe should have been in such a constant state of warfare, often for very slender reasons. A contemporary reader may find it ironical that Voltaire feels entitled to remark that the conduct of war has grown more humane and that the cities which are fought over change their ownership without much disturbance to the civilians who inhabit them. I quote his final paragraphs:

There were long periods when Germany, France and England were afflicted by civil wars; but the damage was soon repaired and the flourishing state of these countries shows that human industry has by far prevailed over human fury. Things are not the same in Persia, for instance, which has been a prey to devastation for forty years; but if it is united under a wise prince, it will recover its solidity in less time than it lost it.

When a nation is mistress of the arts, when it is not subjugated and deformed by foreigners, it rises easily from its ruins, and always regains its health.

Lytton Strachey in the chapter on Hume included in the section 'Six English Historians' of his *Portraits in Miniature* writes of Voltaire, who outlived Hume by nearly two years though he was born over sixteen years earlier, that he 'was indeed a master of narrative, but was usually too much occupied with discrediting Christianity to be a satisfactory historian.' If sufficient emphasis is laid on Voltaire's mastery of narrative, I think that this verdict is just. (pp. 86-107)

A. J. Ayer, in his Voltaire, *Weidenfeld and Nicolson, 1986, 182 p.*

Walter E. Rex (essay date 1987)

[*An American academic and critic, Rex has written widely on eighteenth-century French life and culture. In the following excerpt, he offers a close reading of Voltaire's 1743 tragedy,* Mérope.]

In contrast to playwrights of our own era, Voltaire preferred to start his tragedies with the loftiest affairs of state: with royal marriages that have taken, or are just about to take place, with political power that has been consolidated or is changing hands, with peace being restored, or war being declared, in short, with matters imperial. As a result, the human drama that follows has the grandest possible setting, and the psychological entanglements of the characters—the hatreds, jealousies, loves and loyalties—are seen not merely as personal involvements, but as part of a national situation as well. This insistence on the unbroken continuity between the psychological and the political is a classical trait, of course, Corneille and Racine having brought it to perfection. It is also clear that the phenomenon was a natural outgrowth of the aristocratic traditions of tragedy: if the principal characters are all royal, their affairs are, by definition, affairs of state, as any courtly audience would have understood. This point of view implicitly denies the cleavage which Rousseau and others in the eighteenth century were exploring, and which seems indispensable to us in the modern age, between the private individual and the public one: in classical tragedy, privacy is literally unthinkable, since everything, ultimately, belongs to the public weal; it is all onstage, just as the tragedy itself is. There are no corners in which to hide.

Voltaire's *Mérope* (1743) looks like an exception to the rule. Though at the beginning the traditional confidante relays the usual, rather heavy dosage of affairs of state (peace has been restored, but Queen Mérope will have her hands full if she wants to keep her rightful place on the throne, for the tyrant Polyphonte is threatening to take over), yet, strange to relate in a classical tragedy, Mérope

appears to be turning her back on the whole business. She doesn't care a bit about the urgent situation that so clearly calls for energetic action if she is to preserve her right to rule. Mérope's concerns are of another nature entirely (or so it seems); it is not her status as Queen that matters, but solely and uniquely her role as MOTHER:

> Je suis mère . . .   (I, i, 36)

she declares in solemn, passionate tones, and instantly everything else—thrones, wars, governments, successions, politics—dwindles to inconsequentiality by comparison.

It hardly needs to be pointed out that Voltaire was exploiting here a new trend in the eighteenth century as he so dramatically brought to the fore the sentiment of maternity. In fact the passions and lofty politics of traditional tragedy seem to be giving way, in Voltaire's play, to new and very intense sentiments *of a family nature,* and their appearance here in 1743 is particularly interesting because it precedes the great tide of middle-class sentimentality that would later flood into so many forms of literature and art. In other words, the excitement surrounding the idea of motherhood at the opening of *Mérope* belongs to a general shift in social attitudes.

On the other hand, Mérope's maternal role here is rather peculiar in that, at the beginning, it seems to be playing itself out in a void. During the late civil wars Mérope's only surviving child, her son Egisthe, disappeared, having been taken off into hiding by the faithful Narbas. That was fifteen years ago (numerous characters remind us of these "quinze ans" during the course of the play). Since then, scarcely a word has been heard about him; just one letter from Narbas, received over four years ago, attested to the fact that the son was even alive. How can it be that this child, who vanished while a mere babe, whom Mérope scarcely knew, could still preoccupy her so much that she is willing to let an empire slip through her fingers rather than break out of her fixation about him? Mérope's own answer is that although Egisthe disappeared literally from sight, her heart has never ceased to see him, in remembrance:

> Mon coeur a vu toujours ce fils que je regrette;
> Ses périls nourissaient ma tendresse inquiète:
> Un si juste intérêt s'accrut avec le temps.   (I, i, 41-3)

[My heart never ceased to see the son I longed for;
Dismay at his peril gave life to my tender feelings for him:
My righteous concern grew stronger as time passed.]

While normally we think of time dimming people's memories, here obviously an opposite effect occurs, and there is a special reason for the increase where one would expect diminution. The famous "quinze ans" have endowed Egisthe with one quality beyond price to Mérope: manhood, and, being a man, he is now old enough to *reign.* This is the key to all Mérope's behavior, so that, contrary to our earlier impression, there is no opposition between politics and maternity for this Queen. She is vitally concerned for the fate of the empire, but she wants it for her son, who is now of age to ascend the throne. Nothing else matters. Why does he not appear?

How instructive, in this connection, to compare Voltaire's play with the two main "sources" he himself admitted were standing in the background of his tragedy. One of them was a popular Italian tragedy, *Merope* by Scipione

Maffei (1713), and Voltaire openly declared that his play was simply an adaptation of the Italian version, to make it conform to French tastes. Maffei had written a number of maternal scenes similar to those that would characterize the *Mérope francaise.* Yet Maffei's play does not begin by putting Mérope's maternal instincts in the forefront of the action. In fact, Queen Merope is battling on a number of psychological fronts as she faces the tyrant Polyphonte in Maffei's opening scene (the Italian play begins with this confrontation). Her emotions are not simple, but diverse, and one of the main ones is the utter loathing she feels for the man she faces because she knows him to be the murderer of two of her sons, defenseless children, slaughtered in the most brutal fashion. In contrast, Voltaire's heroine does not yet know the identity of the slayer of one (sic) of her sons, and she is freer to give herself entirely to her positive motherly feelings as she converses with her confidante. This concentration on maternity would have had a modish appeal to Parisian audiences, as was suggested earlier. Such a simplification of psychological motives was also very much part of the French tragic tradition, allegedly deriving from Racine. By comparison, the texture of the Italian play seems slightly richer, and less uniform.

The other main "source" of Voltaire's tragedy was Racine's biblical play, *Athalie* (1691), which featured a lost "son," too, Joas, who had been hidden out of sight in the temple of the Israelites for eight long years, but was destined to overcome all the strategies of the enemies seeking to destroy him, and reign, just as Mérope's son would. According to Racine, God's Grace was the miracle that kept his hero alive amid so many perils, for it was the divine plan that this boy should survive and lead God's chosen people.

Voltaire professed high regard for Racine's play; however, he was not so certain that religion was one of its merits. He even hinted that the play was a masterpiece despite all the piety. Naturally, when he came to compose *Mérope,* it never occurred to him to put in anything that would suggest Catholicism. On the other hand, his "son," Egisthe, though lost from sight in the desert, survives, almost miraculously, too, and from the opening scenes we sense that his quasi-supernatural survival emanates somehow from his mother.

> L'empire est à mon fils . . .   (I, i, 53)
>
> [The empire belongs to my son . . .]

she declares, even though she has almost nothing but his absence and his silence to go on. Pronouncements such as these are really acts of faith, themselves almost supernatural, and they convey to us the conviction that, somehow, what kept Egisthe alive was simply the power of Mérope's determination that he should live (even as his memory had sustained her). It was her will that, so to speak, grew him to manhood (even as she had grown him in her womb), and that, like a magnet, draws him to the throne where he will reign (even as Joas had done, for Racine). His appearance onstage will be, in effect, her creation, even as originally she created him at birth. Perhaps this also implies that in composing *Mérope* Voltaire did not so much omit the role of Grace, as convert it into something else: the irresistible power of mother love. Needless to say, this in turn relates to a third source of power, which is the author's own creative act: Mérope's long-sustained determi-

nation forms the substance of Voltaire's play; his creation *is* her creation of a son—king.

Mérope's resolve that her son will reign goes back (fifteen years) to a specific event that set the course of her destiny forever. She recalls it (I, i), speaking with her confidante, in a very accomplished description (Voltaire was a master of this kind of *récit*—which had innumerable classical precedents, of course). In her mind's eye, Mérope sees again the nightmare: the palace is filled with the sound of voices crying out to save the king, his wife, his sons. There is blood on the walls, the portals are in flames, women are being crushed under the weight of the smoking panels, the slaves are fleeing, and all around her, she says, are tumult, fear, torches and death. Amid this general disarray, the figure of her husband, King Cresphonte, appears, bathed in his own blood, filthy with dust. And now the moment that will determine the rest of her life: he turns his dying eye upon her—but English can never do what the French does:

> Tournant encor vers moi sa mourante paupière,
>
> [Turning again towards me in his dying eye,]

and he expires even as he embraces her:

> Cresphonte en expirant me serra dans ses bras.   (I, i, 70-1)
>
> [Cresphont pressed me in his arms as he expired.]

The instant Cresphonte dies, our attention turns to the children, two sons, mere babes, and apparently twins. They too are bloody as they lean, propped against their father, and they try to lift their arms as if in supplication to be saved from the assassins. Only one of them, Egisthe, will escape alive, thanks to the protection of Hercules, and to the faithful Narbas who spirits him away. But meanwhile, Cresphonte's last look, the dying eyelid, has bequeathed to the Queen a sacred trust, and the almost miraculous saving of the infant, baptized in his father's blood, makes clear which way her duty lies.

We are still in the opening scene of Voltaire's tragedy, but already casting a shadow over the action is the villain of the piece, Polyphonte, whose name was pronounced for the first time shortly before the lines we have been considering. We know, too, that he is Mérope's rival for control of the empire; in fact elections are about to be held and Polyphonte's chances of winning look excellent. According to Voltaire's version of the play, we have not yet learned—nor does Mérope know—that Polyphonte is also guilty of the assassination of Mérope's husband; for in fact Polyphonte did murder Cresphonte, though he managed to keep the deed secret. (Was that what Cresphonte's dying lid was trying to tell her?) Nor was it mere chance that tradition made the names of the two men—Polyphonte, Cresphonte—so rhymingly similar: Polyphonte will attempt to replace Cresphonte not only by winning the election, but by persuading the widow to become his queen in marriage. The plot of the whole play will begin to turn around his efforts to replace his murdered victim both as king and as husband.

During much of the action Polyphonte behaves as if he had the upper hand, and he will make a blustery show of strength that at moments intimidates Mérope (though it never affects Egisthe who, like Racine's Joas, never wavers). Yet clearly the tyrant is unacceptable as a replacement for Cresphonte, and neither Voltaire, nor Mérope, nor Egisthe, nor the audience will have any part of him. Even if one could believe his lying words about how much service in combat he has performed, and how proud he is to have earned the throne by his own deeds, he would not be an acceptable mate for Mérope, if only because, as she harshly reminds him again and again, he does not have Cresphonte's royal blood in his veins—only Egisthe has that.

It is no doubt the "call" of this blood that brings Mérope so close to recognizing Egisthe when he at last appears, even though he has been given another name for his protection, by the faithful Narbas. Nevertheless, the instant she meets him (II, ii) she comes within an inch of finding his true identity, simply because her (maternal) feelings are so stirred and she is so strongly drawn to him by instinct. Paradoxically, this aroused mother also comes within an inch of killing her son (III, iv) when she gullibly believes the story spread by the false tyrant, that this young man, far from being Egisthe, is Egisthe's murderer. Of course this was traditionally considered one of the two most exciting scenes in the play: the moment when Mérope, who has been longing for her son for so many

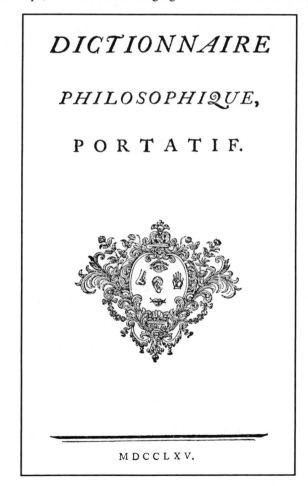

Title page of an early edition of Voltaire's Dictionnaire philosophique portatif. *The design in the center represents the five senses.*

years, rushes toward him with dagger raised, bent on murder. . . . Such drama! Such irony! To think that she is only acting out of love for the son she is about to kill! Unfortunately for us, Freud has ruined most of the fun of such moments, since mistakes such as this one by Mérope are just the sort he has revealed to be secret desires, usually unmentionable, heavily disguised. We will not enter into the tangle of complicated motives opened up by such a psychiatric reading. For present purposes it will suffice to infer from what actually transpires in this scene that Mérope's mother love, for all its intensity, has a dangerous, even lethal side to it, and that for just an instant, as she raised her dagger against Egisthe, Mérope was acting on behalf of the tyrant and in effect doing away with his rival. We are supposed to believe that the unthinkable almost happened: if it hadn't been for the faithful Narbas' miraculous appearance out of nowhere at the last second to stay her hand, the plot might have gone off the rails entirely, or, worse, gone into reverse, so that the tyrant came out on top.

This uncomfortably close call makes us doubly grateful for the other most famous scene (IV, ii): Mérope had been trying to keep Egisthe's identity a secret, fearing quite rightly for his life if ever the tyrant spotted his rival. But by one of those quirks of fate Voltaire invented as often as he could for his tragedies, it turns out that Polyphonte, claiming he believed the young man in question was Egisthe's murderer, but also sensing something rather suspicious in Mérope's flustered behaviour, orders the guards to kill him. Concerned, and with no other recourse, Mérope now goes into action. What a gaudy moment it must have made in Mlle Dumesnil's original performance. Voltaire describes how she flung herself, actually running across the whole length of the stage under Polyphonte's gaze, tears in her eyes, brow grown pale, sobbing, arms outstretched, and how at last, as Mérope interposed her own maternal body between her son and the weapons of the guards, she gave the unforgettable cry—

> Barbare! Il est mon fils.   (IV, ii, 960)

> [Barbarian! He is my son.]

—one of the only lines in eighteenth-century tragedy that everyone agreed was destined for immortality. This is a recognition scene, of course, and a double one: Egisthe recognizes the woman who just moments before had tried to stab him as his mother, and their reunion carries with it all the bliss and pathos sentimental eighteenth-century audiences could wish for. But the identification of the lost son has revealed him to the enemy and placed him at the tyrant's mercy, just as anguished Mérope had been dreading. Polyphonte, with his usual bluster, promptly announces that he will have Egisthe put to death unless he agrees to be legally adopted as Polyphonte's son, to subject himself to Polyphonte's governance, and to see Polyphonte marry Mérope and rule with her on the throne. In other words, the price of existence for Egisthe is the agreement that Polyphonte shall do everything his late father once did.

Of course Polyphonte's demands are extravagant and his scheme won't work. Egisthe will never submit; we have already seen enough of his manly pride to know that. And so, in act V, when the "wedding party" straggles off to the temple where Polyphonte thinks he will marry Mérope and receive Egisthe's submission in pomp and splendor before the whole populace, we in the audience are left waiting with the kind of dread and expectation we feel in Corneille's *Polyeucte,* just before the hero, receiving an extra large dose of heavenly Grace, bursts out into violence and starts smashing all the pagan idols—offstage, of course. The blood and violence in **Mérope** are offstage, also, and for us it happens only in the mind's eye, as we listen to Isménie's breathless *récit* (V, vi). But what an extraordinary drama she paints, what a grandiose, horrific spectacle is evoked in Voltaire's slightly cramped Alexandrines, with their all-too-familiar rhymes. Just as in Mérope's earlier description of the death of Cresphonte, the scene will be full of crowds crying out in dismay (the thunder of their voices can even be heard by the audience). But as Isménie tells the story, we see, first, sad Mérope, her head crowned with flowers for the ceremony, advancing toward the altar glittering in the light of torches. Suddenly there is a movement, someone is darting forward—Egisthe, of course, and before anyone can stop him, he seizes not a dagger, not a sword, not even a spear, but the axe (*la hache*) kept at hand for religious ceremonies, and strikes Polyphonte to the ground. Treacherous Erox, too, is laid low, when he tries to take vengeance. But now, Polyphonte revives enough to wound Egisthe, and, bizarre touch, their flowing blood mingles in a single stream. Polyphonte's guard, loyal to the tyrant, springs into action and would have killed Egisthe were it not for Mérope who again shields her son from their weapons and bravely reveals herself to be his mother and their Queen. Her loyal friends rush to her aid, and suddenly all is confusion, in fact the scene simply dissolves into a great blur (again reminiscent of Cresphonte's death) of running crowds, of altars overthrown and their débris scattered in the streams of blood, of children crushed in their mothers' arms, of soldiers, priests, and friends dying on top of each other. There is trampling on the bodies of the fallen, while great surging masses of people are hurtled from one end of the temple to the other, back and forth, again and again. Finally, the vast throng swallows Mérope and her son from sight, so that at the end of the *récit* their fate remains uncertain. (They have survived, of course.)

What a pity that the music and verse forms of decadent romanticism were so far off in the future, and that Voltaire insisted on snipping his lines so primly into Alexandrine lengths. The forceful qualities of the scene barely have a chance amid so many traditional constraints. Nevertheless, despite these confines, Voltaire is going as far as he ever would go to achieve an effect that cannot be accounted for by the precepts of classicism such as he understood and preached them: the deliberate blurring of outlines, the wild movement of the hysterical crowds, the mindless massacres, the streams of blood, all this takes us into an insane world closer to the surrealists than to the Age of Reason. Above all, Egisthe's bloody axe—it will actually be brought onstage for the final scene—strikes a lurid note and gives a nightmarish tone to everything that follows. How one longs for Richard Strauss' indecent harmonies and shrieking crescendos! They would have done so much to bring out the unnatural horror of this scene, and Strauss would have relished, too, all the "sordid" Oedipal implications that are quite visible if one takes the trouble to peer behind the clipped hedges of Voltaire's Alexandrines. For of course with that bloody axe Egisthe has murdered the man who was trying to marry his mother and become his

father. As he killed him, Egisthe was baptized in the false father's blood, even as he had been in that of his real father, and this rite has prepared him to assume all the King's roles. To make things perfect, the tyrant's corpse, covered with a bloody robe, will be brought onstage for the final scene, so that Egisthe claims his mother for himself and prepares to mount the throne with her, in full view of the man he is replacing:

> Allons monter au trône, en y plaçant ma mère . . .
> (line 1401)

> [Come let us go mount the throne, where I will place my mother]

This is the climax: Egisthe now rises with his mother, his Queen, in a kind of apotheosis of their relationship, while, for those of a Freudian persuasion, the moment reveals implications that would seem undeniably Oedipal, at least on a symbolic level. No doubt we must assume that Voltaire was not actually conscious of all these implications, yet he must have felt especially pleased with himself as he boasted everywhere that he had succeeded in writing a tragedy in which there was no love interest at all, from which love was totally absent. To make doubly certain no one missed the point, he got the Reverend Father Tournemine to back him up in a prefatory epistle.

All the pieces of this accomplished tragedy fit into place, except two. The first is easily explained: Voltaire confuses his own French version with the Italian version when he occasionally has a character refer to *two* sons of Mérope who were killed (a third having escaped). Actually he had reduced the number to *one* son killed, a second having escaped—another instance of simplifying for French audiences what could be more complex for Italians. But the second mistake is truly incomprehensible: we all know that Egisthe and faithful Narbas have been gone for exactly fifteen years. There can be no question about this number. Isménie, Mérope, Polyphonte, Narbas, and Voltaire himself (in his preface) have all confirmed it. Even Maffei wrote of the *quindici anni.* How then are we to explain that faithful Narbas, who never lies, and who elsewhere refers to the *quinze ans,* also declares, concerning Egisthe—

> Je l'ai conduit, seize ans, de retraite en retraite . . . ? (III, v, 801)

> [I guided him, for sixteen years, from one safe refuge to another.]

Sixteen years! The word *seize* is not a rhyme position, which might justify the alteration; nor does it have either more or less syllables than *quinze* to make the Alexandrine correct; the use of the right number would not have created a cacophony with the surrounding syllables, nor is Narbas given to stretching the facts. Nothing in the immediate context accounts for the error. But then, the rules of *vraisemblance,* for conscientious authors, *are* a sort of slavery: to compose five acts (1402 lines in this case) in which every single word belongs perfectly with every other word is a discipline without mercy. Perhaps one should expect that a few syllables will go astray. Such is human nature. And yet for this reader the inexplicable, inconceivable *seize* also suggests the one small slip which according to legend even the smartest criminals make, and that gives their strategies away. Evidence has come to light implying that the *seize* may be an unconscious borrowing from a famous tragedy by Corneille, a tragedy for which Voltaire had composed elaborate commentaries, criticizing it on various counts, one of them being the unlikelihood that so many years, *seize ans,* should have elapsed between the hero's murder of his own father and his reappearance in Thebes, where he married his mother. In other words, *seize ans* had been one of the disapproved features of Corneille's *Oedipe.* In the most literal sense, Voltaire's slip was Oedipal. To my mind this curious flaw is a tip pointing to the fact that nothing in this so-called tragedy-without-love is quite what it seems, and that Voltaire's determined efforts to make his play conform to aristocratic propriety—the relentless high style, the exclusive concern with royal destinies, the refusal to admit anything that might be extraneous to the main action—actually bears a contrapuntal relationship to the daring underside of his dramatic enterprise.

Indeed, the "forme" acts as a cover-up for the "fond"; but more than this, the constantly implied denial of any indecency (a denial we find implied in both the style and the structure of the work) is probably what made the "indecency" possible in the first place. Rather like Abbé Prévost before him, the author could never have allowed himself to create such a sensational plot unless he accompanied it with endless testimonials (both stylistic and formal, and directed as much to himself as to the audience) guaranteeing that all such thoughts could not be further from his mind. Thus, through a rather perverse operation of opposite motivations, the denial permits the existence of its contrary—just as in eighteenth-century music, the exquisite purity of the melody on top may actually depend for its life, and even for its character, on the coarse rumblings, the raucous rattles of the bass line, down below.

In *Mérope* all the disparate elements, the decencies and the indecencies, still fit together, and yet, seen from a historical vantage point, Voltaire's play appears to be pointing towards an inevitable fracture between moral values and formal ones in the theatre. Actually, I don't think subsequent playwrights chose to exploit this division very much. On the contrary, the aim of the new bourgeois theatre was to lower the high level of style associated with traditional tragedy, and at the same time, to "elevate" the moral tone. As a result, Voltaire's ambiguities (duplicities?) simply ceased to exist. (pp. 83-93)

> *Walter E. Rex, "On Voltaire's 'Mérope'," in his* The Attraction of the Contrary: Essays on the Literature of the French Enlightenment, *Cambridge University Press, 1987, pp. 83-93.*

FURTHER READING

Andrews, Wayne. *Voltaire.* New York: New Directions, 1981, 165 p.
   Brief biography and character study of Voltaire by a critic best known for his works on the history of architecture.

Auden, W. H. "A Great Democrat." *The Nation* 148, No. 13 (25 March 1939): 352-53.
   Determines that Voltaire "was not only one of the greatest Europeans of all time but, though he might be surprised to hear it, one of the greatest fighters for democracy, and one who should be as much a hero to us as Socrates or Jefferson."

Barr, Mary-Margaret H. *A Century of Voltaire Study: A Bibliography of Writings on Voltaire, 1825-1925.* New York: Publications of the Institute of French Studies, Inc., 1929, 123 p.
   Secondary Voltaire bibliography, citing works written about the author between 1825 and 1925.

———. *Voltaire in America, 1744-1800.* The Johns Hopkins Studies in Romance Literatures and Languages, Vol. XXXIX. Baltimore: Johns Hopkins Press, 1941, 150 p.
   Attempts to determine how widely Voltaire was known in the United States during the second half of the eighteenth century.

Berlin, Isaiah. "The Divorce between the Sciences and the Humanities." In his *Against the Current: Essays in the History of Ideas,* edited by Henry Hardy, pp. 80-110. London: Hogarth Press, 1979.
   Includes a brief discussion of Voltaire as "the central figure of the Enlightenment." Berlin notes: "[Voltaire] accepted its basic principles and used all his incomparable wit and energy and literary skill and brilliant malice to propagate these principles and spread havoc in the enemy's camp. Ridicule kills more surely than savage indignation: and Voltaire probably did more for the triumph of civilised values than any writer who ever lived."

Besterman, Theodore. *Voltaire Essays, and Another.* London: Oxford University Press, 1962, 181 p.
   Contains ten essays and lectures on Voltaire, including "Voltaire Judged by Flaubert," "Voltaire and the Lisbon Earthquake: or, The Death of Optimism," "Voltaire's Love Letters," and "The Terra-Cotta Statue of Voltaire Made by Houdon for Beaumarchais."

Bottiglia, William F., ed. *Voltaire: A Collection of Critical Essays.* Englewood Cliffs, N. J.: Prentice-Hall, Inc., 1968, 177 p.
   Collects essays on a variety of issues concerning Voltaire's life and writings. Of particular interest is Theodore Besterman's "The Real Voltaire through His Letters," a fourteen-part study of Voltaire's correspondence that focuses on the private side of Voltaire's life, "the real Voltaire."

Coleman, Patrick. "Reading Voltaire's *Contes.*" *The Eighteenth Century: Theory and Interpretation* 28, No. 2 (Spring 1987): 171-80.
   Reviews Carol Sherman's *Reading Voltaire's Contes: A Semiotic of Philosophical Narration* (1984), contending that, contrary to Sherman's claims, Voltaire does not evade serious philosophical discussion in his contes.

Crist, Clifford M. "Some Judgments of Voltaire by Contemporaries." *Modern Language Notes* L, No. 7 (November 1935): 139-40.
   Summarily treats five late eighteenth-century works—four dramas and one essay—that appraise Voltaire's achievements in philosophy and literature. Crist singles out the anonymously published *Dialogue entre Voltaire*

et Rousseau, après leur passage du Styx (1778) for "the accuracy of its judgment."

Durant, Will, and Durant, Ariel. *The Age of Voltaire: A History of Civilization in Western Europe from 1715 to 1756, with Special Emphasis on the Conflict between Religion and Philosophy.* The Story of Civilization, Part IX. New York: Simon and Schuster, 1965, 898 p.

Documentary history of intellectual life in Western Europe during the mid-eighteenth century, focusing on Voltaire's place in the "continuing conflict between religion and science-plus-philosophy."

Gay, Peter. "The *Philosophe* in His Dictionary." In his *The Party of Humanity: Essays in the French Enlightenment,* pp. 97-108. New York: Alfred A. Knopf, 1964.

Approaches Voltaire's *Philosophical Dictionary* as "a polemical tract, in turn sober and witty, sensible and outrageous, sincere and disingenuous. . . . [It] is Voltaire's most characteristic work—as characteristic as its more famous companion piece *Candide.*"

Henry, Patrick. "Voltaire as Moralist."*Journal of the History of Ideas* XXXVIII, No. 1 (January-March 1977): 141-46.

Concludes that "[in] the final analysis, Voltaire is primarily a moralist because he did not construct any philosophical system, had little or no interest in speculation *per se,* was interested in thought only to the extent that it could be applied to concrete reality, and because his major concern consisted of a desperate search for a moral basis in a century where belief in traditional Christianity was toppling, where the absolute value of reason was being questioned, and where atheism was on the rise."

Howells, R. J.; Mason, A.; Mason, H. T.; and Williams, D., eds. *Voltaire and His World: Studies Presented to W. H. Barber.* Oxford: Voltaire Foundation, 1985, 425 p.

Contains twenty-six specially commissioned essays on the life, works, and times of Voltaire. Articles include: R. J. Howells, "The Burlesque as a Philosophical Principle in Voltaire's *contes*"; Adrienne Mason, "Voltaire's Portrait of Augustus"; and E. D. James, "Voltaire's Dialogue with the Materialists."

James, E. D. "Voltaire on Free Will." *Studies on Voltaire and the Eighteenth Century* 249 (1987): 1-18.

Probes, through a study of sources and influences, Voltaire's numerous statements concerning free will.

Lévy-Bruhl, L. "Voltaire (1694-1778)." *The Open Court* XIII, No. 2 (February 1899): 65-71.

Considers the impact of science on Voltaire's religious views, concluding that "the real name of Voltaire's God is: Justice."

Lounsbury, Thomas R. *Shakespeare and Voltaire.* New York: Charles Scribner's Sons, 1902, 463 p.

Contends that Voltaire was grossly unfair in his negative criticisms of Shakespeare's works, owing in part to the Frenchman's immature critical faculties and "outraged vanity."

Meyer, Paul H. "Voltaire and Hume as Historians: A Comparative Study of the *Essai sur les moeurs* and the *History of England.*" *PMLA* LXXIII, No. 1 (March 1958): 51-68.

Compares David Hume's *History of England* to Voltaire's *Essai sur les moeurs,* addressing historical methodology, levels of discernment, and possible reciprocal influences.

Mudrick, Marvin. "Truth, Justice, and Other Spice for the Immature." *The Hudson Review* XXXIV, No. 4 (Winter 1981-82): 525-48.

Detailed review of Wayne Andrew's *Voltaire,* with commentary on Voltaire's principal literary works. Of the *contes* Mudrick claims: "[They] are like Catholic jokes about the Pope: electric-buzzer tickles for friends of the family, in-jokes for the already mesmerized; painting by the numbers."

Nablow, Ralph Arthur. *A Study of Voltaire's Lighter Verse.* Studies on Voltaire and the Eighteenth Century, edited by Theodore Besterman, Vol. CXXVI. Banbury, England: Voltaire Foundation, 1974, 320 p.

Examines Voltaire's lighter poems—"the *contes en vers,* the *satires,* the *épîtres,* and the *pièces fugitives*"—from historical, analytical, and critical points of view.

Noyes, Alfred. *Voltaire.* New York: Sheed & Ward, 1936, 643 p.

Comprehensive biography of Voltaire based on the author's extensive reading of primary and secondary sources.

[Oliphant, Margaret]. "Voltaire." *Blackwood's Edinburgh Magazine* CXI, No. DCLXXVII (March 1872): 270-90.

Evaluates Voltaire's religious views in the light of emerging eighteenth-century philosophies.

Redman, Ben Ray. Introduction to *The Portable Voltaire,* by Voltaire, edited by Ben Ray Redman, pp. 1-47. New York: Viking Press, 1963.

Surveys Voltaire's life and works, concentrating on the evolution of his literary interests and writing style.

Russell, Trusten Wheeler. *Voltaire, Dryden & Heroic Tragedy.* New York: Columbia University Press, 1946, 178 p.

Discusses the effect of epic theory upon Voltaire's critical writings.

Sainte-Beuve, C. A. "Voltaire." In his *Portraits of the Eighteenth Century, Historic and Literary,* translated by Katharine P. Wormeley, Part I, pp. 185-236. New York: G. P. Putnam's Sons, 1905.

Early biographical sketch of Voltaire by a leading nineteenth-century French man of letters, with scattered brief commentary on Voltaire's dramas and correspondence.

Saintsbury, George. "Voltaire and Rousseau." In his *A Last Vintage: Essays and Papers,* edited by John W. Oliver, Arthur Melville Clark, and Augustus Muir, pp. 140-55. London: Methuen & Co., 1950.

Compares Voltaire's literary achievements with those of Jean-Jacques Rousseau.

[Stephen, J. F.]. "Voltaire as a Theologian, Moralist, and Metaphysician." *Fraser's Magazine* LXXVI, No. CCCCLV (November 1867): 541-68.

Surveys Voltaire's major works, commenting on their meaning, purpose, and literary style.

Strachey, Lytton. "Voltaire and Frederick the Great." In his *Biographical Essays,* pp. 80-105. London: Chatto and Windus, 1948.

Historical essay, originally published in 1915, treating the "intersection of . . . two momentous lives"—those of Voltaire and Frederick the Great—as "one of the most curious and one of the most celebrated incidents in history."

Temmer, Mark J. "*Candide* and *Rasselas* Revisited." In his *Samuel Johnson and Three Infidels,* pp. 77-123. Athens: University of Georgia Press, 1988.
    Compares the method and purpose of *Candide* with that of Samuel Johnson's *Rasselas.*

Trapnell, William H. *Christ and His "Associates" in Voltairian Polemic: An Assault on the Trinity and the Two Natures.* Stanford French and Italian Studies, edited by Ralph Hester, Vol. XXVI. Saratoga, Calif.: Anma Libri, 1982, 268 p.
    Explores Voltaire's "fundamental antagonism to the Trinity," focusing on *Lettres philosophiques, Examen important de milord Bolingbroke, Sermon des cinquante, Essai sur les moeurs, Pot-Pourri, Questions sur les miracles, Dictionnaire philosophique, Dieu et les hommes,* and *Questions sur l'Encyclopédie.*

Trevor-Roper, Hugh. "Voltaire at Les Délices." *New Statesman* LXIV, No. 1658 (21 December 1962): 901-02.
    Briefly explores Voltaire's attitude toward progress.

Voegelin, Eric. "The Emergence of Secularized History: Bossuet and Voltaire." In his *From Enlightenment to Revolution,* edited by John H. Hallowell, pp. 3-34. Durham, N. C.: Duke University Press, 1975.
    Views Voltaire as an early proponent of secularized history, one who "could dream of a paradise of compassion and humanity because he experienced these qualities as active in his person."

ISBN 0-8103-6113-2